P9-BZC-171

2018 EDITION
Best
COLLEGES

HOW TO ORDER: Additional copies of U.S. News & World Report's Best Colleges 2018
guidebook are available for purchase at usnews.com/collegeguide or by calling (800) 836-6397.
To order custom reprints, please call (877) 652-5295 or email usnews@wrightsmedia.com.
For permission to republish articles, data or other content from this book, email permissions@usnews.com.

College of Wooster in Ohio
MATT SLABY-LUCEO FOR USN&WR

CONTENTS

46

WHY I PICKED...

WE ARE
THE ULTRA-CURRICULAR

WE ARE THE GO-GETTERS. ACHIEVERS OF FEATS,

SOLVERS OF PROBLEMS AND MAKERS OF WONDER.

WE SEEK A PLACE THAT NURTURES OUR CURIOSITY

AND DRIVES US TO CHASE OUR DREAMS.

Furman is that place—where every student is promised a four-year pathway of high-impact engaged learning through research, internships and study away, guided by a team of mentors. The advantage—a meaningful life and career. *This* is **THE FURMAN ADVANTAGE.**

HAVE THE METTLE TO BECOME A FURMAN PALADIN.

Learn more **FURMAN.EDU**

FURMAN

GREENVILLE, SC

PRINCETON
UNIVERSITY

Chapter Three

The U.S. News Rankings

Build your future at Queens College.

Distinguished Professor of English Kimiko Hahn (second from right) mixes art and poetry lessons with her students in Queens College's Godwin-Ternbach Museum.

Academic rigor. Amazing affordability. Award-winning faculty.

- Among top 1% of colleges that move students from poverty to prosperity*
- More than 170 undergraduate & graduate programs
- Over 100 clubs & organizations, including NCAA Division II athletics
- Beautiful, tree-lined 80-acre campus
- On-campus housing in our Summit Apartments

To learn more about Queens College, visit **qc.cuny.edu/futurestudents.**

*As reported in the *New York Times.*

146

134
Emmanuel Betancourth and Dayna Cardalena

SUDDENLY
THE WORLD
OPENS

At Seton Hall, we foster those defining moments when passion becomes a profession — when a new idea leads to a deep personal discovery. With rigorous academics that elevate expectations and faculty mentorship that leads to career-shaping discoveries, we help our students live these moments every day. Then they show the world the greatness they can accomplish.

 SETON HALL UNIVERSITY 1856

What great minds can do.
www.shu.edu/greatminds

@USNEWS.COM

GETTING IN

COLLEGE ADMISSIONS PLAYBOOK

Get tips from Varsity Tutors, an academic tutoring and test-prep provider. This blog offers advice on mastering the SAT and ACT as well as the college application process.
usnews.com/collegeplaybook

STUDENTS ON HOW THEY MADE IT IN

Seniors from high schools across the country talk about their admissions experiences and offer advice to students getting ready to apply to college.
usnews.com/studentprofiles

COLLEGE VISITS

TAKE A ROAD TRIP

We've gone on numerous trips to visit campuses in case you can't. Check out our compendium of 30 different trips to 100-plus schools.
usnews.com/roadtrips

RANKINGS INSIGHT

MORSE CODE BLOG

Get the inside scoop on the rankings – and the commentary and controversy surrounding them – from U.S. News' Bob Morse, the mastermind behind our education rankings projects.
usnews.com/morsecode

IN-DEPTH DATA

COLLEGE COMPASS

Gain access to the U.S. News College Compass, which offers comprehensive searchable data and tools for high school students starting down the path to campus. To get a 25 percent discount, subscribe at
usnews.com/compassoffer

PAYING FOR COLLEGE

RESEARCHING AID

Visit our guide to all your possible sources of college funds. Learn about your savings options and which schools meet students' full need.
usnews.com/payforcollege

SCHOLARSHIP SEARCH INSIDER

There's free money out there to help you finance a college education. Expert bloggers offer tips on how to search, apply for and win scholarships.
usnews.com/scholarshipinsider

THE STUDENT LOAN RANGER

Don't fall into the trap of taking on too much debt. Bloggers from American Student Assistance provide guidance if you must turn to loans to pay for college.
usnews.com/studentloanranger

DISTANCE LEARNING

ONLINE EDUCATION

Do you need to balance school with work or other obligations? Consult our rankings of the best online degree programs for leads on how to get your diploma without leaving home.
usnews.com/online

FOR SCHOOLS ONLY

ACADEMIC INSIGHTS

U.S. News Academic Insights is an analytics dashboard intended for use by institutions that comprises all of the undergraduate and graduate historical rankings data we've collected. The dashboard allows for peer group comparisons and includes easy-to-understand visualizations.
ai.usnews.com

One life powered by ASU can change millions

"To see those kids drink clean water for the first time, it's the most rewarding feeling you can ever have. I went to ASU because I wanted to change the world. The thing I never would have expected was how the world would have changed me." —Mark Huerta, ASU student and CEO of 33 Buckets

Arizona State University

Top 10 for graduate employability

Ahead of MIT, Columbia and UCLA
— Global University Employability Survey 2016

asu.edu ✖@ASU 🅵🄾 @Arizona State University #1 innovation

Paying for college is one of the biggest risks families face – AXA Achievement℠ can help.

TAB STICKERS

AXA Achievement℠ can help you take the next step toward college.

Use these stickers to tab your college choices inside this issue.

Next steps toward college

Taking the right small steps today can help eliminate the risk of not being able to afford a college education

Filling out the FAFSA helps you minimize borrowing. It's a misconception that filling out the Free Application for Federal Student Aid (FAFSA) is the fast track to student loan debt. You risk losing need-based grants and scholarships from the university. The reason? The universities you selected on the FAFSA to receive your information use it to evaluate your financial aid eligibility.

To avoid losing need-based aid you might qualify for:

1. Fill out the FAFSA as early as possible. Some need-based aid is limited in numbers and available on a first-come first-served basis for those who qualify. Universities have a limited amount of grant aid. Applying late could mean you miss out.

2. Select schools. Always select schools that are being considered on the form. Otherwise, the information won't arrive at the colleges that need it. Amend the FAFSA form online if school choices change.

3. Fill out the special circumstances forms when needed. Whether you're applying for next year or are already in college, you need to fill out a special circumstances form if your income changes due to a number of reasons, such as a medical situation, a layoff, or a salary reduction.

4. Practice filling out the FAFSA on the FAFSA4caster site from the Department of Education as early as middle school. It's designed to roughly estimate financial aid years in advance.

5. Follow up with schools to make sure information is received and to check on financial aid availability. Bonus: you may find out about a scholarship you previously didn't know about during the phone call.

Choosing universities with the lowest listed tuition prices can sometimes cost you more money. A private school with "sticker price" that is four times more than that of a state school may offer scholarships and grants that make it the cheaper alternative. Find out which schools offer the best financial aid packages before applying. Net price calculators available on most college websites are one way to estimate what you would pay based on individual circumstances.

To better understand the relative costs of higher education:

1. Narrow college choices down to ten using factors such as majors, campus size and internship placement. Talk with your high school counselor early to start the process of college selection and career exploration.

2. Request information from each school on what's important to you. For instance, call the career center to ask about graduate employment rates.

3. Visit the websites of your top ten college choices. Find the net price calculator on their website by entering "net price calculator" into the search box on the school's home page. Enter information such as family income and number of children in college.

4. Call financial aid offices at your top five choices to see if there are any changes in grant awards for the year you will be attending. Available funds change, so you want to make sure you factor in the most recent information into your family's application decisions.

5. Use the net price calculator as a baseline. You may also qualify for merit-based aid.

To learn more and apply, visit www.axa.com/achievers

From the Editor's Desk

by Brian Kelly

This college search thing can be a little intimidating, especially if you're going through it for the first time. This is our 33rd go-round at U.S. News, so we feel like we've got some experience worth sharing.

Over the years, we've improved our information and sharpened our focus, with our primary objective being to help students and their parents make one of life's most important - and costliest - decisions. Prospective students and their parents need objective measures that allow them to evaluate and compare schools. The U.S. News rankings are one tool to help them make choices,

along with all the other insights and guidance contained in these pages. This sort of assistance is more relevant than ever, with some private colleges now costing around $250,000 for a bachelor's degree. At the same time, many public high schools have greatly reduced their college counseling resources, leaving students and parents to educate themselves about the search and admission process.

Of course, we have adjusted our ranking methodology over the years to reflect changes in the world of higher education, and we make it clear that we are not doing peer-reviewed social science research, although we do maintain very high survey and data standards. We have always been open and transparent. We have always said that the rankings are not perfect. The first were based solely on schools' academic reputation among leaders at peer institutions; we later developed a formula in which reputation accounts for 22.5 percent of a school's score and important quantitative measures such as graduation and retention rates, average class size and student-faculty ratios account for the rest. Over time, we have shifted weight from inputs (indicators of the quality of students and resources) to outputs (success in graduating students). We operate under this guiding principle: The methodology is altered only if a change will better aid our readers and web audience in comparing schools as they're deciding where to apply and enroll.

A starting point. It has helped us a great deal to have these principles to focus on as we have faced the inevitable criticisms from academia about our rankings' growing influence. One main critique remains: that it is impossible to reduce the complexities of a college's offerings and attributes to a single number. It's important to keep in mind that our information is a starting point. The next steps in a college search should include detailed research on a smaller list of choices, campus visits and conversations with students, faculty and alumni wherever you can find them. Feedback from academia has helped improve the

rankings over time. We meet with our critics, listen to their points of view, debate them on the merits of what we do, and make appropriate changes.

U.S. News is keenly aware that the higher education community is also a major audience for our rankings. We understand how seriously academics, college presidents, trustees and governing boards take our data. They study, analyze and use them in various ways, including benchmarking against peers, alumni fundraising, and advertising to attract students.

What does all of this mean in today's global information marketplace? U.S. News has become a respected, unbiased resource that higher education administrators and policymakers and the college-bound public worldwide turn to for reliable guidance. In fact, the Best Colleges rankings have become a key part of the evolving higher education accountability movement. Universities are increasingly being held responsible for their policies, how their funds are spent, the level of student engagement, and how much graduates have learned. The U.S. News rankings have become the annual public benchmark to measure the academic performance of the country's colleges and universities.

We know our role has limits. The rankings should only be used as one factor in the college search – we've long said that there is no single "best college." There is only the best college for you or, more likely, a handful of good options, one of which will turn out to be a great fit. Besides the rankings, we can help college-bound high school students and their parents by providing a wealth of information on all aspects of the application process, from getting in to getting financial aid. Our website, usnews.com, features thousands of pages of rankings, research, sortable data, photos, videos and a personalized tool called College Compass.

We've been doing this for over three decades, so we know the process is not simple. But our experience tells us the hard work is worth it in the end. ●

Dedicated to the noble pursuit of unmaking the world a better place.

There are two types of people. Those who accept the world for what it is, and those who refuse to see it for anything less than what it could become.  Here at the University of California San Diego, we tend to attract the latter. The ever-curious ones. The defiant. These are the mischievous minds who will someday change our world simply because it demands change. We call them Breakers. Why? Because they are convinced that the only way to truly solve a problem is to first break it apart and examine every angle to discover what makes it tick. So when the pieces are reassembled, they will work better than before. Now, if tackling the world's ugliest issues with truckloads of creative problem solving  piques your interest, read on. We've got much to cover.

Like the most recent global financial crisis. And how our very own writing professor Rae Armantrout wielded her poetry like a spiked club to crack Wall Street's greed wide open.

Dictatorial injustice? Well, literature professor Luis Martín-Cabrera is fighting to protect Latin America's political, economic and cultural future by diving headfirst into people's memories of its oppressive past. And now that we have a stage to highlight what a few curious minds here on the clifftops have been up to, perhaps Professor Robert Brill can erect us a more elaborate one. After all, he already made Broadway do a double-take with sets that incorporate audiences directly into classic stage productions, like *Cabaret*. Of course, unconventional thinking like this is what each bright-eyed student should expect. That, and a grueling academic boot camp that thoroughly whips their impressionable minds into peak Breaker condition. So, before we send our army of motivated,  well-equipped grads off to conquer the world's biggest problems by applying solutions no one ever thought up before, first we'll cue the victory music. Perhaps a recording from Professor Roger Reynolds. He's famous for mashing together music and technology to create unique experiences that engage on multidimensional levels — smack dab in our collective "Breaker" comfort zone.

ucsd.edu/breakthingsbetter

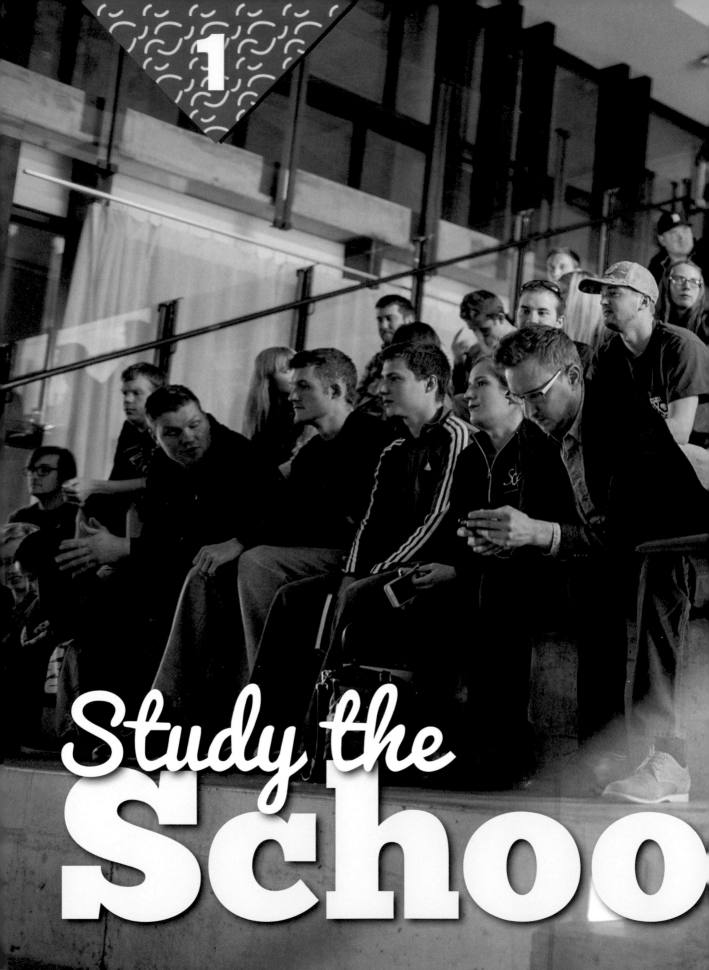

1

Study the
Schoo

**IN CLASS AT
OHIO STATE**

Should You Get a
LIBERAL ARTS

Employers value the training in critical thinking, communication and teamwork, educators say

by Margaret Loftus

WHEN EMORY UNIVERSITY freshman Carl Lejuez told his mother he planned to major in psychology, she broke down in tears. "I thought you were going to make something of yourself!" he recalls her saying. That was in 1989, but a generation later, liberal arts continues to be a hard sell for many parents, who worry that a broad and often costly education – a year at many liberal arts colleges can top $65,000 – won't prepare their children to compete in today's job market.

Lejuez did make something of himself: He's the dean of the College of Liberal Arts and Sciences at the University of Kansas. And he's still making the case for liberal arts to families and students. "I help them to understand that they don't have to choose between the thing that inspires them and the thing that they think will help them get a job," he says. "It's our job to help them do both."

In fact, many schools, both large universities and small colleges, are newly intent upon helping liberal arts grads translate their skills into successful careers, by emphasizing experiential learning, funding internships and turbocharging career services. They argue that the skills grads acquire – critical thinking and the ability to communicate effectively, for starters – are highly prized by employers and will only get more so. A 2013 survey of employers by Hart Research Associates revealed that 93 percent agreed that candidates' ability to think critically, communicate clearly, and solve complex problems is more important than their undergraduate major.

"In a world where rapidly changing technology means rapid obsolescence," the liberal arts can offer preparation to be adaptable

A DICKINSON ARCHEOLOGY METHODS CLASS GETS EXPERIENCE IN THE FIELD.

and flexible, says Lynn Pasquerella, president of the Association of American Colleges & Universities. Students these days "understand they may be moving into professions that don't exist yet," adds Neil Weissman, provost and dean at Dickinson College in Pennsylvania.

Some research suggests that they should hold their own financially, too. It's true that engineering grads earn the highest median salaries among people who have degrees. But during their peak earning years between ages 56 and 60, those who majored in the humanities or social sciences made an average of about $2,000 more than those who had a major in professional fields, according to a 2014 study by the AAC&U and the National Center for Higher Education Management Systems.

Nonetheless, the value of a liberal arts degree continues to be called into question; "the humanities, especially, are seen as a luxury reserved for those in the ivory tower," says Pasquerella. And it's clearly true that a vast number of good-paying jobs now being created require technical skills that can be achieved without any kind of four-year degree at all (box, Page 21).

But educators point out that a liberal arts education can offer a host of marketable skills to students who may want to work in many types of organizations and rise into leadership roles. Many schools are implementing "high-impact" practices that develop critical thinking, writing, leadership and teamwork skills even as they do a better job of bonding freshmen to each other and faculty. Seminar-style instruction, original research and study abroad, for example, are eminently practical.

The job market demands "nuanced communication, the ability to collaborate, the ability to travel comfortably across borders, the capacity for nimbleness and creative thinking, and the ability to connect ideas in novel ways," Connecticut College President Katherine Bergeron says. "If you put all that together, and ask what prepares you for those kinds of skills, the answer is liberal arts."

Case in point: While Tai Ragan had some electrical engineering courses under his belt when he decided to switch gears and attend St. John's College in New Mexico, he mainly credits his experience there with his confidence on the job now. The St. John's curriculum is based entirely on reading and discussing the great books, from Plato's "The Republic" to Adam Smith's "The Wealth of Nations," and the school is

DEGREE?

unique in that there are no majors. "It gave me so many tools. I handle systems on a daily basis, and St. John's turned out to be an incredible education for that," says Ragan, 29, who works for a NASA contractor in Washington, D.C., fine-tuning the camera on a weather satellite. "Whether it's math as a system or poetry as a system, [the program] taught me to ask, 'What are the components that make this up, and how do I work with and manipulate them?'"

That's music to employers' ears, says Jonathan Lash, president of Hampshire College in Massachusetts, where students customize their studies by formulating and investigating questions that drive them, guided by a faculty committee. The first year entails courses in required fields such as science, culture and social justice, in which students explore connections between subject areas. They spend the second and third years investigating their concentration – Peace and World Security Studies, for instance, or Dance or Entrepreneurship – through classes, internships, research, study abroad and apprenticeships. The final year involves work on an advanced project; examples range from writing a software program or novel to building a robot. "One of the things I hear from alumni and industry leaders," Lash says, is that they "want people who can invent and innovate. We're desperately in need of people who can think for themselves."

In similar fashion, Connecticut College has re-tooled its curriculum to focus on problem-solving and training students to make connections between very disparate subjects. Sophomores choose a pathway based on a question or a problem that matters to them. Someone interested in how climate change affects indigenous communities, say, would choose applicable courses, which might range from Environmental Studies to Cases and History of Equality. The third year might find her studying abroad and doing an internship in South America. A senior capstone project pulls the experiences and insights together.

Dickinson offers a more traditional curriculum, but has added opportunities for students to apply what they're learning to contemporary problems. For instance, students might take a sustainability class in which they might learn about the economics of energy systems and work on solutions to reduce campus energy use. Students in the sciences begin conducting research with faculty as early as freshman year.

Makensie Jones, an archeology and anthropology dou-

ble-major at Dickinson from Edmonds, Washington, says the chance to get her hands dirty in the field was a big draw. In a course on archeological methods, she worked on a dig at the site of a former camp that housed German and Japanese POWs. The excavation simulated the procedure for weighing the importance of cultural resources such as the site and its artifacts as part of an environmental impact study for a new road.

Liberal arts programs within universities can deliver similar experiences, often at considerably lower cost, albeit with much less hand-holding and generally bigger classes. And university students can benefit from a wider array of interdisciplinary course choices and expansive research facili-

IN ART CLASS AT MILLSAPS, A LIBERAL ARTS COLLEGE IN JACKSON, MISSISSIPPI

ties. They "are working in labs with professors who are at the top of their field," says Donald Hall, the dean of the College of Arts and Sciences at Lehigh University. Choosing between a college and a university may come down to personal preference. Jones considered both, but the more intimate size of Dickinson won out. "I don't do well in larger settings," she says.

Recognizing the importance to employers of critical thinking and an expansive worldview, many schools are even broadening professional tracks like business and engineering by making room for humanities and social science classes. KU adopted a new curriculum in 2013 called the KU Core that expanded flexibility for students wishing to pursue dual degrees – to combine, say, a business degree with a foreign language major – and still graduate in four years. St. Lawrence University in New York has introduced a Business in the Liberal Arts program that requires students to complete a second major. It also offers a combined liberal arts and engineering program in which students spend three years on campus and two years at a participating engineering school, such as Columbia or Dartmouth.

Another trend: Many schools are doubling down on their efforts to thread career preparation through all four years of the program. Real-world learning through internships, study abroad and courses that integrate community service, for example, are increasingly common – and worth looking for in a college search. At Bennington College in Vermont, students are required to take on internships or "field work" for seven weeks each winter. Mount Holyoke in Massachusetts is among a growing group offering students stipends so they can accept an unpaid internship. St. John's, too, funds summer internships. Ragan was thus able to accept an unpaid position at the U.S. Naval Observatory in Washington, D.C., a connection that led to his current job.

Career counseling, too, is becoming much more intentional. Last year, for example, Dickinson launched the Dickinson Four, a roadmap of programs intended to foster better planning from the beginning. Freshmen, for example, are urged to forge connections with peers, mentors and faculty; sophomores, to focus on their priorities by attending a dinner series on "what matters most" and doing January externships. Juniors typically participate in internships and/or study abroad. Seniors reflect on what they've accomplished through career and leadership seminars.

Alex Emmanuele, a 2016 Hampshire graduate who specialized in the science of learning, says the exploratory nature of his experience has had much to do with his career success. That process of discovery led him to dream up and pitch an internship to the education consulting firm where he now works as director of innovation and eventually to even design his job. "In most liberal arts settings, not everything is prescribed for you, so you have to figure out how to get it done," he explains. "If you need more support, you ask for it. If you need funding, you ask for it."

More than 90 percent of Hampshire graduates get job offers within the first year, says Lash. Lehigh boasts that 93 percent of its graduates land opportunities "within their plans," and liberal arts grads have been matching almost exactly the success rates of business and engineering grads in finding jobs or grad-school placements. He points to an alumna he recently saw who spun her liberal arts degree into a sales job and climbed the hierarchy faster than colleagues with business degrees. How'd she do it? he asked. "I learned how to be interesting,' she said. And that's what liberal arts students are." ●

> **'Many liberal arts schools are now threading career prep through all four years of the program.**

Four-year degree not needed

FOR MANY HIGH SCHOOL graduates, a bachelor's degree is not the only – or even best – track to a rewarding career. Some of the occupations with the strongest prospects these days are "middle-skill" jobs, requiring more than a high school diploma but less than a four-year degree. They include such traditional choices as veterinary and medical technicians, electricians and realtors as well as many of the hottest in tech: web developers, IT systems administrators and advanced manufacturing employees. They make up more than half of all jobs today and will account for 48 percent of openings between 2014 and 2024, according to the National Skills Coalition, a research and advocacy group focused on workforce development. NSC research shows that only 43 percent of workers are trained at a middle-skill level, so employers struggle to fill positions.

The ticket into these fields is an associate degree, a vocational certificate or another professional credential. An aircraft mechanic, for instance, requires certification from a technical school and can expect to earn about $60,000. A certificate from a six- to 28-week coding boot camp, which could run $9,000 to $21,000, could land you a web developer job at around $66,000. Many middle-skill jobs rely on partnerships between employers and educators. A number of small and large companies – General Electric, Toyota and CVS Health among them – offer apprenticeships, employing students full time as they apply concepts they are learning in class (typically at a community college) while earning a salary and benefits. Students who sign on for Newport News Shipbuilding's Apprentice School in Virginia, which works with the Tidewater Community College Apprenticeship Institute, are earning around $55,000 by the end of the program, for example, says the institute's director, Todd Estes.

On average, those with a bachelor's earn more than those with an associate degree. But nearly 30 percent of workers with the two-year credential out-earn people with a bachelor's. Avoiding the debt load of the typical four-year grad – more than $30,000 – and starting to work earlier is a consideration, too. In an "earn while you learn" apprenticeship, you could even graduate with money in the bank.

And remember, you can always build on your training. Katie Spiker, senior federal policy analyst at the NSC, says that a two-year degree or other credential can be "a good way to test the waters in an industry" before you commit to more study. –*Mariya Greeley*

A Focus on Student Success

Some colleges and universities are much more determined than others to provide freshmen and all undergrads with the best possible educational experience, recognizing that certain enriched offerings, from learning communities and internships to study abroad and senior capstone projects, are linked to student success. Here, U.S. News highlights schools with outstanding examples of eight programs that education experts, including staff members of the Association of American Colleges and Universities, agree are key.

College presidents, chief academic officers and deans of admissions were invited in the spring of 2017 to nominate up to 10 institutions with stellar examples of each, from a list of all bachelor's-granting regionally accredited colleges. Schools that were named the most times in each area are listed in alphabetical order.

(*Public)

First-Year Experience

Orientation can go only so far in making freshmen feel connected. Many schools now build into the curriculum first-year seminars or other academic programs that bring small groups of students together with faculty or staff on a regular basis.

Agnes Scott College (GA)
Appalachian State University (NC)*
Butler University (IN)
College of Charleston (SC)*
College of William & Mary (VA)*
Dartmouth College (NH)
Drake University (IA)
Elon University (NC)
Evergreen State College (WA)*
Franklin and Marshall College (PA)
Georgia State Universityardt*
Indiana U.-Purdue U.-Indianapolis蒂*
Indiana University-Bloomington*
James Madison University (VA)*
Northeastern University (MA)
Oberlin College (OH)
Ohio State University-Columbus*
Princeton University (NJ)
Purdue Univ.-West Lafayette (IN)*
Stanford University (CA)
U. of North Carolina-Chapel Hill*
Univ. of South Carolina*
Univ. of Wisconsin-Madison*
University of Michigan-Ann Arbor*
University of Notre Dame (IN)
University of Texas-Austin*
Vanderbilt University (TN)
Williams College (MA)
Yale University (CT)

Internships

Schools nominated in this category require or encourage students to apply what they're learning in the classroom to work in the real world through closely supervised internships or practicums, or through cooperative education, in which one period of study typically alternates with one of work.

Belmont University (TN)
Bentley University (MA)
Berea College (KY)
Butler University (IN)
Claremont McKenna College (CA)
Cornell University (NY)
Creighton University (NE)
Drexel University (PA)
Elon University (NC)
Embry-Riddle Aeronautical U. (FL)
Endicott College (MA)
Georgia Institute of Technology*
Kettering University (MI)
Massachusetts Inst. of Technology
Messiah College (PA)
Northeastern University (MA)
Purdue Univ.-West Lafayette (IN)*
Rochester Inst. of Technology (NY)
University of Cincinnati*
Worcester Polytechnic Inst. (MA)

Learning Communities

In these communities, students typically take two or more linked courses as a group and get to know one another and their professors well. Some learning communities are also residential.

Belmont University (TN)
Brown University (RI)

Bucknell University (PA)
Dartmouth College (NH)
Elon University (NC)
Evergreen State College (WA)*
Indiana U.-Purdue U.-Indianapolis*
Indiana University-Bloomington*
Iowa State University*
Michigan State University*
Ohio State University-Columbus*
Univ. of Maryland-College Park*
Univ. of South Carolina*
Univ. of Wisconsin-Madison*
University of Michigan-Ann Arbor*
University of Washington*
Vanderbilt University (TN)
Yale University (CT)

Senior Capstone

Whether they're called a senior capstone or go by some other name, these culminating experiences ask students nearing the end of their college years to create a project that integrates and synthesizes what they've learned. The project might be a thesis, a performance or an exhibit of artwork.

Alverno College (WI)
Brown University (RI)
Carleton College (MN)
Carnegie Mellon University (PA)
College of Wooster (OH)
Duke University (NC)
Elon University (NC)
Harvey Mudd College (CA)
Northeastern University (MA)
Occidental College (CA)
Princeton University (NJ)
Stanford University (CA)
Swarthmore College (PA)

YOU'RE GOING TO COLLEGE, WE CAN HELP YOU GET THE MOST OUT OF IT.

ARMY ROTC

Enhance your college experience through Army ROTC. Gain professional experience, while reducing your financial burden. Army ROTC is an elective course available at almost 1,000 college campuses nationwide that focuses on equipping you with leadership and management skills for life-long success. Army ROTC also offers full tuition merit-based scholarships with a monthly stipend and allowances for books and fees.

Explore options through ROTC visit goarmy.com/rotcinfo or text ROTCINFO to 462769

U.S.ARMY

University of California-Berkeley*
University of Michigan-Ann Arbor*
Yale University (CT)

Service Learning

Required (or for-credit) volunteer work in the community is an instructional strategy in these programs. What's learned in the field bolsters what happens in class, and vice versa.

Augsburg College (MN)
Bates College (ME)
Belmont University (TN)
Berea College (KY)
Brown University (RI)
College of the Ozarks (MO)
Cornell University (NY)
Duke University (NC)
Elon University (NC)
Fairfield University (CT)
Georgetown University (DC)
Indiana U.-Purdue U.-Indianapolis*
Michigan State University*
Northeastern University (MA)
Portland State University (OR)*
Stanford University (CA)
Tulane University (LA)
U. of North Carolina-Chapel Hill*
University of Michigan-Ann Arbor*
University of Notre Dame (IN)
Vanderbilt University (TN)
Wagner College (NY)
Xavier University (OH)

Study Abroad

Programs at these schools involve substantial academic work abroad for credit - a year, a semester or an intensive experience equal to a course - and considerable interaction with the local culture.

Agnes Scott College (GA)
American University (DC)
Arcadia University (PA)
Austin College (TX)
Belmont University (TN)
Brown University (RI)
Butler University (IN)
Carleton College (MN)
Centre College (KY)
Colby College (ME)
College of St. Benedict (MN)
Dartmouth College (NH)
Dickinson College (PA)
Duke University (NC)

Elon University (NC)
Georgetown University (DC)
Goshen College (IN)
Goucher College (MD)
High Point University (NC)
Indiana University-Bloomington*
Kalamazoo College (MI)
Lewis & Clark College (OR)
Macalester College (MN)
Messiah College (PA)
Michigan State University*
Middlebury College (VT)
New York University
Northeastern University (MA)
Pepperdine University (CA)
Rollins College (FL)
St. John's University (MN)
St. Olaf College (MN)
Stanford University (CA)
Syracuse University (NY)
U. of Illinois-Urbana-Champaign*
Univ. of Minnesota-Twin Cities*
Univ. of Wisconsin-Madison*
University of Evansville (IN)
University of Michigan-Ann Arbor*
University of Richmond (VA)
University of Texas-Austin*
Wake Forest University (NC)
Webster University (MO)
Yale University (CT)

Undergraduate Research/ Creative Projects

Independently or in small teams, and mentored by a faculty member, students do intensive and self-directed research or creative work that results in an original scholarly paper or product that can be formally presented on or off campus.

Allegheny College (PA)
Amherst College (MA)
Brown University (RI)
Butler University (IN)
California Institute of Technology
Calvin College (MI)
Carleton College (MN)
Carnegie Mellon University (PA)
Clemson University (SC)*
College of Wooster (OH)
Creighton University (NE)
Dartmouth College (NH)
Davidson College (NC)
Duke University (NC)
Elon University (NC)

Emory University (GA)
Furman University (SC)
Georgia Institute of Technology*
Grinnell College (IA)
Harvard University (MA)
Harvey Mudd College (CA)
Hope College (MI)
Massachusetts Inst. of Technology
Northwestern University (IL)
Pomona College (CA)
Princeton University (NJ)
Rice University (TX)
Stanford University (CA)
Stevens Institute of Technology (NJ)
SUNY-Geneseo*
U. of North Carolina-Asheville*
U. of North Carolina-Chapel Hill*
Univ. of Wisconsin-Madison*
University of California-Berkeley*
University of Michigan-Ann Arbor*
University of Texas-Austin*
University of Virginia*
University of Washington*
Vanderbilt University (TN)
Williams College (MA)
Worcester Polytechnic Inst. (MA)
Yale University (CT)

Writing in the Disciplines

These colleges typically make writing a priority at all levels of instruction and across the curriculum. Students are encouraged to produce and refine various forms of writing for a range of audiences in different disciplines.

Brown University (RI)
Carleton College (MN)
Colorado State University*
Cornell University (NY)
Duke University (NC)
Elon University (NC)
George Mason University (VA)*
Grinnell College (IA)
Hamilton College (NY)
Harvard University (MA)
Middlebury College (VT)
North Carolina State U.-Raleigh*
Princeton University (NJ)
Stanford University (CA)
Swarthmore College (PA)
University of California-Davis*
Washington State University*
Williams College (MA)
Yale University (CT)

DEGREES *for*

DREAMERS, DOERS, *and* LEADERS

Whether you want to travel the world or make a difference in your hometown, Indiana University has the degree program that will help you achieve your goals. Choose from more than 200 majors that give you the tools to succeed, no matter where life takes you.

Learn more at go.iu.edu/indiana.

 INDIANA UNIVERSITY
FULFILLING *the* PROMISE

HANDLING A
DIVERSITY
OF IDEAS

How safe spaces and trigger warnings might impact you

by Beth Howard

THIS PAST SPRING, after students at Lewis and Clark College in Oregon invited Jessica Vaughan of the Center for Immigration Studies to debate immigration policy on campus, they learned that the Southern Poverty Law Center designated the center as a hate group. The student committee in charge struggled with whether to let the event go on as planned, but ultimately decided to proceed. As protesters from the community shouted and played sirens to disrupt the debate, students and faculty listened to Vaughan's views and asked tough questions. Samuel Stites, a senior majoring in international affairs and music, doesn't believe the group's research methods "stand up to academic rigor." But he helped plan the event.

No matter one's views on immigration, the Lewis and Clark event stands in stark contrast to happenings on many college campuses these days. In March, when conservative writer Charles Murray was invited to speak at Middlebury College in Vermont, student protesters shouted over his remarks, forcing the event to be moved to a video studio. Afterwards, Murray and the Middlebury faculty member who had moderated a discussion with him were swarmed by protesters, and the professor was hurt in the melee. In February, the University of California at Berkeley canceled an appearance by Milo Yiannopoulos, a former editor at the far-right website Breitbart, after violent protests broke out.

Challenging the expression of unpopular ideas is just one of several related trends recently roiling college campuses. Schools are struggling with such perceived threats to intellectual debate as calls for "trigger warnings" to protect students

from material that might offend or traumatize them and the rise of the "safe space," which can mean a campuswide culture that discourages disturbing discussions or simply a place where students who are in a minority can congregate and let their guard down. The controversy gives prospective students new dimensions of college life to consider as they choose a school. How much do you value the free exchange of ideas? Can you tolerate living and studying with people whose religious beliefs or political views are diametrically opposed to your own?

"A university really is supposed to be a marketplace of ideas, and those ideas can and should be divergent at times," argues Shaun R. Harper, a professor of education and executive director of the Race and Equity Center at the University of Southern California. "Universities should be places where ideas are contested and debated. You can't do

that if you're not engaging with people who disagree with you." Adds Geoffrey R. Stone, a law professor at the University of Chicago and a noted First Amendment scholar: "We want to educate our students about not only the value of free expression and debate and courage, but also civility and mutual respect."

Instead, at some schools, "many students say they walk on eggshells and are afraid to speak up," says Jonathan Haidt, a social psychologist at New York University who has studied the issue. "In seminar classes, no one disagrees anymore. Students are pressuring the university to take sides on the issues of the day. But when the university takes sides, that shuts down discussion and debate."

In response, Haidt co-founded Heterodox Academy, a nationwide group of about 1,100 professors of all political stripes who call for greater "viewpoint diversity" on

UNIVERSITY OF WISCONSIN STUDENTS TALK TO VICE PROVOST LORI BERQUAM ABOUT HOLDING A RACISM AWARENESS MEETING.

campus. "We believe that the vast majority of high school seniors and their parents, whether they are on the left or the right, believe in free speech and believe that people should be able to challenge each other's ideas," he says. The group's Guide to Colleges (heterodoxacademy.org/resources/guide-to-colleges) evaluates schools based on an institution's regulations, ratings by outside groups, and news stories about events on campuses. For instance, Johns Hopkins University this summer received an upgraded rating when it announced a $150 million initiative to "facilitate the restoration of open and inclusive discourse" by conducting research and holding events examining divisive policy issues, among other plans.

While visiting speakers may set off alarms only occasionally, more day-to-day concerns have arisen around the concept of trigger warnings, which let students know when potentially upsetting material is on the syllabus. The idea is that they could excuse themselves from discussions or class assignments that they believe might harm their mental health, such as content related to sexual violence or combat.

Opponents of such policies argue that they encroach on academic freedom and deny students critical knowledge and the opportunity to face uncomfortable ideas and grow from pondering them. The University of Chicago made waves last year when its dean of students told incoming freshmen in a welcome letter not to expect trigger warnings or intellectual safe spaces. (The university does not mandate a formal policy for faculty, allowing them "broad freedom in how they accommodate concerns that students may express, including advising students about difficult material," according to a university spokesperson.)

Indeed, many students and teachers say it's possible to give

students a heads-up without omitting upsetting facts or causing them to walk out. "It's just a precursor, like when you go to a movie, and you're about to see a really violent trailer," says Samantha Brinkley, a junior at SUNY-Purchase majoring in photography and gender studies. "Before they show it, they have a rating, like rated R, because you want to get ready for what you're about to see."

"I believe that they are warranted in certain situations," says Lauren Griffith, a cultural anthropologist at Texas Tech University, "but should not be used as a way of sheltering students from encountering and wrestling with uncomfortable ideas." Before Griffith shows films on Afro-Caribbean or Siberian religions, for instance, she lets students know

Try to get a sense of a school's culture from current students.

that they will depict animal sacrifice. "No one has actually left the room," she says, "but several averted their gaze during the films." Griffith says she doesn't know whether the warnings have influenced class discussions but students do want to talk about what they've seen. "It's possible my calling attention to it prior to the film made them pay attention to its significance," she says.

Hasan Jeffries, who teaches African-American history at Ohio State University, takes a similar approach, giving an overview of topics that will be covered during the semester on the first day and offering context. "I will say that there is no way to teach this history without talking about violence that was done to people of color," he says. "Today, people may call that a trigger warning. I see it as more of 'Look, this is American history, not Disney history. We're going to encounter the hard truths of it.' It's how you create a learning environment in which everyone is comfortable so they can learn."

So far, few institutions appear to mandate trigger warnings or prohibit them, leaving such decisions to the discretion of individual faculty members. Prospective students may want to explore their own values and ask about the policies at a school.

The notion of a college campus as a safe space, and the more prevalent creation of places where students can retreat from the stresses of being in the minority and spend time among like-minded peers, are also the subject of considerable controversy. Such spaces, often at a university's multicultural center or a dedicated area within a student union, have evolved from the black cultural and women's centers that are common on campuses.

Some administrators and academics worry that when the safe space idea is carried too far, it might stifle the diversity of viewpoints in conversations and could leave graduates unprepared for situations in the real world where such "bubbles" won't be available. Celebrating diversity is a good thing, they might argue, but it's not helpful in the long run for students to become too insular or to avoid dissenting opinions entirely.

Proponents say that having a sense of security can actually encourage minority students who elsewhere feel silenced to engage in debate. "They're places where students can decompress and access some cultural familiarity and support," says Harper, who has conducted campus climate surveys of almost 50 colleges and universities. "At every campus we've studied, we heard black and Latino students especially talk with us about how they are often, and sometimes always, the only nonwhite person in class." Ricardo de la Cruz II, a senior English major at the University of

Over 100 tracks to success

With over 100 undergraduate degree programs, the University of New Haven is the ride of a lifetime to any career destination you can imagine.

Success starts here

 University *of* New Haven

www.newhaven.edu/usnews

Wisconsin–Madison, says he "sometimes feels like an alien" on campus as one of just about 2 percent of undergrads who are black, and that the Multicultural Student Center has become an important support system.

On the whole, colleges are making myriad efforts to support a diverse range of students. At the University of Tampa, an initiative called Diversity Fellowship hosts events to raise awareness of groups who are often marginalized based on their sexual orientation, gender, religion, race and socio-economic status, among other factors. "We try to make sure the university is educated and at the same time foster a sense of inclusivity," says student coordinator Caroline Stadler, a senior majoring in public health. Numerous schools – Armstrong State University in Georgia, Concordia College in Minnesota, Kent State University in Ohio, the University of South Carolina, and James Madison University in Virginia, among them – have Safe Zone and Safe Space programs in place that train students, faculty members and administrators to be special allies to LGBTQ and other groups and to provide support to any student who may turn to them.

For prospective students of color and those seeking a diverse and inclusive learning environment, it's important to try to get a genuine sense of a school's culture during a visit or by connecting with current or former undergrads.

HANGING OUT AT A MULTICULTURAL CENTER AT DAVIDSON COLLEGE

You "have to be willing to talk to alumni of color about the realities of race on the campus and to students of color who are juniors and seniors," Harper advises.

Harper also suggests asking about the racial composition of the faculty and the student body as well as where in the curriculum students will learn about other people's cultural histories. Starting in 2018, the USC Race and Equity Center will set about providing a new data tool called the National Assessment of Collegiate Campus Climates, a survey of students of color, women, LGBT students, people with disabilities, and religious minorities about their experiences. "We will be able to benchmark institutions against each other and highlight those that have exemplary inclusive campus climates," says Harper.

Prospective students should consider what is most important to them when it comes to finding the right fit and how much shelter and support they think they'll want. If you're looking for a pretty conservative or religious environment, say, then you might feel out of place at a large university known for its party atmosphere or at a college where a vast majority of students lean the other way. If trigger warnings and having a safe space are essential to you, consider a place with some sort of track record you can check out. A little reflection and research will go a long way in helping you find a place where you can thrive. ●

THIS IS A SMART CHOICE.

THIS IS AUBURN.

 AUBURN
UNIVERSITY

Ranked among the Top 50 public universities in the nation by *U.S. News & World Report*, Auburn is charming, engaging, and impressive. It's a place where spirit and traditions are intertwined with success, a place with a roster of 233,000 alumni that includes the CEO of Apple, the founders of Habitat for Humanity and Wikipedia, and an Oscar-winning actress. For students seeking an environment both academically challenging and socially supportive, Auburn is a wise investment in a future that's anything but ordinary. **auburn.edu**

ALYSSA RUFFA
WILL SERVE IN THE
ARMY RESERVES.

5 WAYS TO TRIM THE TAB

As you put together your list of possible colleges, consider a few pathways that could save you money

by Courtney Rubin

ALYSSA RUFFA WAS HALFWAY through college when she realized she'd need money, and lots of it. Her parents were no longer able to contribute as much, and she wanted to continue on to vet school. She considered borrowing and working, but then found an option that would pay for school, give her a career boost, and satisfy her strong sense of patriotism: The Reserve Officers Training Corps. In exchange for her commitment to serve one weekend a month for eight years in the Army Reserves, Ruffa, now a senior majoring in biological sciences at the University of Georgia, receives tuition plus books and a living stipend through ROTC, for a total of some $14,000 per semester.

"It's been great for me not to be stressed out by loans or trying to hold down a part-time job," Ruffa says. "I can just focus on school." For her grad degree, she hopes to qualify for a separate Army scholarship available to commissioned officers that pays full tuition plus a monthly stipend.

According to two 2016 reports from the College Board, college tuition and fees are rising at a faster rate than financial aid and family income – by about 3 percent yearly, compared to virtually no inflation in the rest of the economy. Including room and board, the average total cost of a year of college at a public university is now some $20,000

for in-state students and $35,000 for out-of-staters, and more than $45,000 at a private school.

That means there's a greater need than ever for ways to lessen the pain. Here are some ways to do it.

1 Public Honors College

One way to gain the small liberal arts college experience at a discount is to choose an honors college at a public university. These schools within schools are a more formal and comprehensive version of the university honors program, often with extra resources such as dedicated counselors and scholarship coordinators, specially designated residences, and activities aimed at fostering a scholarly community – meetings with distinguished alumni, say, and discounted or free trips to the theater.

According to the National Collegiate Honors Council, which has identified 12 basic characteristics of an honors college, the curriculum should account for at least 20 percent of a student's degree program, and an honors thesis or project should be required. Many colleges offer funding opportunities for the thesis, and students present their work at national conferences. Public honors colleges offer small classes (South Carolina Honors College at USC boasts an average class size of 16, for example) and research opportunities with faculty that otherwise might be tough to get at a university.

Admission to these colleges is highly selective, and often comes with scholarship aid. For example, City University of New York's Macaulay Honors College offers students a four-year tuition scholarship plus a laptop. Pennsylvania State University's Schreyer Honors College admits just 300 students a year, and they receive a $5,000 scholarship (in-state tuition and fees are roughly $17,500) and access to grants for travel, research and internships.

And there are other perks. At the University of Oregon's Clark Honors College, among others, students are given priority registration so they get their pick of professors and time slots and don't risk getting shut out of a class required for graduation. At the University of Nevada–Las Vegas, honors college students get prep for grad school admission – and pizza and bagels during exams.

2 Community College

According to the College Board, average tuition and fees at a public two-year college are just $3,520 – a little over a third that of public universities. So attending a community college for the first year or two – or knocking out some credits during summers – can be a smart move. Many high schools offer dual enrollment with a local community college, so students can

'ROTC scholarships amount to about $1 billion a year.

earn college credit for courses that also count toward their high school diploma. As a recruiting tool, two-year schools often offer a free taste: one free class per semester junior and senior year, say, or free STEM (science, technology, engineering and mathematics) courses. According to a 2013 report on dual enrollment from the National Center for Education Statistics, 77 percent of colleges said that they picked up the tab for high school students.

There are other incentives, too: Massachusetts, for example, offers residents who keep their grades up a 10 percent tuition rebate if they start at a community college and transfer to a public state university. Community college is free to all qualified Tennessee and Oregon high school grads, and other states are considering similar moves.

For some students, community college offers a second chance to attend a dream school. Robert Bardwell, a school counselor at Monson High School in Massachusetts, cites a student who wanted to attend the University of Massachusetts–Amherst, but didn't get in. She chose to attend community college rather than either of her other four-year choices, and then transferred. "I'm sure there were people who thought, 'What did she do wrong?' But when she graduates, her degree will say UMass–Amherst," he says.

Many two-year schools have articulation agreements with public universities that govern the smooth transfer of credits and often guarantee a spot at the university for qualified transfer students. But there can be hiccups. Consider: CUNY LaGuardia offers a major in real estate marketing. But if your goal is to transfer to a liberal arts college without that major, not all your credits will come with you.

To avoid any headaches, Lisa Sohmer, director of college counseling for the Garden School in Queens, New York, advises introducing yourself the first week of school to the community college's transfer office. The staff will have relationships with four-year schools and will know what you need to do. "Nobody in a transfer office wants to deny a student because he took the wrong classes," she says.

3 AP Courses

There are two potential advantages of Advanced Placement courses over dual enrollment in community college (though many students take both paths). AP courses are vetted and consistently taught, says Jayne Fonash, director of school counseling at the Loudoun Academy of Science, a Virginia magnet school. Schools may be more apt to accept AP credit, assuming you score high enough on the test, since community college courses can differ significantly from one another. Second, AP courses offer a college-level challenge "while you're still in the comforting nest of high school teachers you know and trust," says Fonash. Dual enrollment, on the other hand, may offer access to electives not available in high school.

Still, every college has its own rules about what they accept, and it can change from year to year. Some schools will grant you full credit; others, typically the most selective schools, won't grant you any credit at all. Many won't grant credit but will allow you to place into a higher level class. Generally, you're going to get "more bang for your AP score the less selective the school is," Sohmer says. (Whether or not you get credit for AP or college courses, your star is apt to shine brighter in the admissions process for having taken them.)

If you are interested in taking a test for a course your school doesn't offer (for example, AP economics), some students opt to take a class at a local community college to prepare and simply pay to take the AP exam ($93 in 2017).

The credits earned can add up to big savings. "We'll have kids that basically go into college as sophomores," says Nancy Beane, associate director of college counseling at the private Westminster Schools in Atlanta.

4 ROTC

The military's ROTC scholarships are the country's single largest source of scholarship money

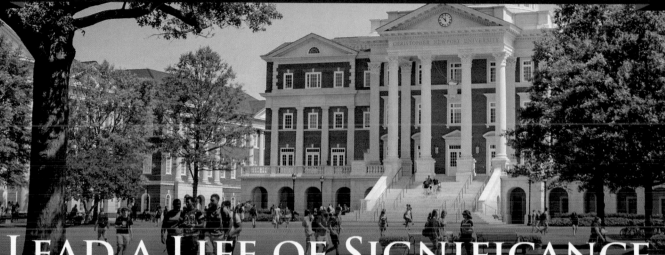

CHRISTOPHER NEWPORT
U N I V E R S I T Y

LEADERSHIP /// SERVICE /// HONOR /// SCHOLARSHIP

LEAD A LIFE OF SIGNIFICANCE

At Christopher Newport we care about minds *and* hearts. We believe real success is a life well lived. We want our students to choose to live lives of meaning, consequence and purpose. We call that a life of significance.

Because we care about minds and hearts and lives of significance, our curriculum is based on the liberal arts and sciences. We emphasize the study of leadership and created a nationally respected President's Leadership Program. Our core curriculum is rigorous, cited by the American Council of Trustees and Alumni as the most rigorous core curriculum of any public college or university in America. Because we care about hearts and minds and creating good citizens and leaders, our students perform thousands of hours of community service, we built a chapel, and we celebrate our speaking tradition and honor code.

We want our students to lead, serve, engage and set the world on fire. That's what makes Christopher Newport special and that's what makes Christopher Newport an irresistible force.

1 AVENUE OF THE ARTS, NEWPORT NEWS, VA 23606 • (757) 594-7015 • CNU.EDU

not based on need – about $1 billion each year. Unlike attending one of the service academies, where the education is free but cadets have highly-regimented schedules, joining ROTC is a bit like having a part-time job or an extracurricular activity.

Cadets attend classes and pursue their major just like anyone else on campus does, but they also take one ROTC academic class per semester for which they earn elective credit. In these courses, they might learn about the principles of war and military operations and tactics, for example. Cadets also may attend a basic training camp, and typically have physical training during the semester, often three days a week at 6 a.m. There are also occasional weekend commitments, such as trips to a gun range or 12-mile hikes at a 15-minute-mile pace – while carrying a 45-pound backpack.

"It doesn't really impact my social life, because I'd be spending time at the gym anyway," says Ruffa, who estimates her obligations consume 15 hours per week.

After graduation, the terms of service vary. The reserves are certainly a popular choice, though some cadets opt to fulfill their commitment with active service in their chosen branch of the military. (Commitments are shorter with active service – often four years as opposed to an eight-year commitment in the reserves.)

5 Other Options

Keep in mind that it (quite literally) pays to do your research; opportunities to save are always cropping up. Florida State University offers a "First Year Abroad" program through which out-of-staters study abroad freshman year and pay in-state tuition rates for the next three years (for more on getting in-state rates when you're out-of-state, see box). Under the CyberCorps Scholarship for Service, the National Science Foundation and the Department of Homeland Security will pay for two or three years of college (up to $22,500 per year) for students who are interested in programs relating to cybersecurity. If you're accepted, you have a service commitment upon graduation – but you also have a guaranteed job. New York lawmakers recently approved a free tuition program for state residents who qualify.

Among the rules: The program, dubbed the Excelsior Scholarship, pays tuition costs for public institutions in New York State after other sources of financial aid have been applied. It covers families with incomes of up to $100,000 (ultimately this will be $125,000). Recipients must live and work in New York for the same number of years they receive the award. Finally, the College Board points out one money-saving no-brainer: Finish college in four years. About a third of students take longer. ●

THE IN-STATE EDGE

PART OF THE college experience is getting away from home – and outside of your comfort zone. For many students, an appealing way to do this is to choose an out-of-state university.

More than a few states and schools are clamoring for out-of-staters, and they're prepared to offer you a deal. A number of tuition reciprocity programs dangle in-state or discounted tuition as an incentive for students to cross state lines.

Students who live in one of the 15 member states of the Western Interstate Commission for Higher Education, for instance, can attend public colleges in another member state for a maximum of 150 percent of in-state tuition. Member states are Washington, Oregon, Nevada, California, Hawaii, Idaho, Utah, Arizona, Montana, Wyoming, Colorado, New Mexico, Alaska, North Dakota and South Dakota. Though universities are not obliged to be involved in the program, there are more than 150 participating institutions.

"I had always wanted to go out-of-state," says Jolie Cornell, of West Hills, California, who was able to do so without taking out loans through the program. Paying the same price as an Arizona resident, Cornell graduated from Northern Arizona University in 2016 with a major in psychology.

The markets. The Southern Regional Education Board hosts the Academic Common Market, a similar collaboration of states ranging from Texas and Oklahoma to Virginia and Maryland (North Carolina is not in the program). The Midwest Student Exchange Program grants tuition reductions from $500 to $5,000 per year for students from Illinois, Indiana, Kansas, Michigan, Minnesota, Missouri, Nebraska, North Dakota and Wisconsin. This past year, the New England Regional Student Program offered an average $8,000 break to students from one of its six members: Maine, New Hampshire, Vermont, Massachusetts, Connecticut and Rhode Island. The DC Tuition Assistance Grant offers up to $10,000 a year to District of Columbia residents to help cover the difference between out-of-state and in-state tuition at universities across the country. In total, 44 states participate in some form of tuition reciprocity program.

– Peter Rathmell

Kelsey, B.Arch., Class of 2020

Told to play house.
Now designs skyscrapers.

93.4% of NYIT's grads are employed
or in grad school within 6 months
of graduation.

Learn more at **nyit.edu**

 **New York Institute
of Technology**

THE FUTURE IS OURS™

Want to be a doctor or lawyer? Some colleges let high schoolers apply for the track to an advanced degree, too

by Elizabeth Gardner

MADELINE PESEC knew by eighth grade that she wanted to work in medicine. But she also loved the humanities and didn't want to spend her undergraduate years slaving over pre-med classes and worrying about the Medical College Admission Test. So she applied to Brown University's eight-year Program in Liberal Medical Education, which fulfilled her dream criteria: Once admitted as freshmen, PLME students have a guaranteed spot at Brown's Alpert Medical School and can study whatever they want until then, aside from making sure they have a grounding in the sciences so that med school won't be too much of a shock. Pesec double majored in public health and in Latin American and Caribbean studies.

"It's impossible to do the medical school application process and have a fulfilling undergraduate career unless you have 26 hours in your day," Pesec says. She took two biology classes at Brown and a chemistry class one summer at Cleveland State, near her home, and fulfilled a couple of other requirements with high school courses.

For ambitious high school students who know early that they're headed toward medicine, dentistry, pharmacy, law or other fields requiring a professional degree, programs similar to Brown's now offered by many schools can provide a chance to pursue their undergraduate degrees without the specter of professional school admission looming so large over junior and senior year. Though Pesec's path and many other undergrad/medical school programs take the usual eight years total, sometimes students may also save a year, cutting their tuition and potential indebtedness.

Applicants to George Washington University and Rutgers University, for example, can aim for admittance to dual degree programs that lead to an M.D. degree in seven years. Drexel University, Rutgers, and the University of Denver offer programs leading to a bachelor's and a law degree in six. "Legal educators know how expensive higher education is, and shortening it is a good option for some students," says Judy Areen, executive director of the Association of American Law Schools. The association doesn't track

Get Into
College & Gra

these bachelor's/J.D. programs formally, but Areen says their numbers are growing.

Some of these programs allow (or require) you to enter them once you're in college. Colin Sheehan was attracted to Rutgers by the bachelor's and law program, for example, but waited to apply until sophomore year. He then made sure to complete his political science major by the end of junior year, enrolling in summer classes to fit everything in. Besides keeping his GPA at or above 3.5, he had to take

MADELINE PESEC WITH MED SCHOOL CLASSMATES AT BROWN

the LSAT and complete a separate application to the law school in his junior year. "At some points, it was very challenging," allows Sheehan, who is now both a senior and a first-year law student. Meharry Medical College in Nashville works with seven historically black colleges and universities, including Fisk University, Tennessee

d School, Too

State University, and Hampton University, to offer conditional admission to science students with strong high school records and test scores who maintain their performance after entering college. Based on their freshman GPA and personal recommendations from their schools, they are invited into the B.S./M.D. program and spend their undergraduate summers at an enrichment program at Meharry that helps prepare them for med school.

These programs not surprisingly target high achievers, since the coursework is often compressed, and typically require students to keep up the good work to hold their place. The Brown program is competitive even compared with the

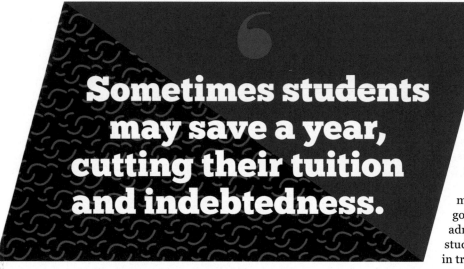

Sometimes students may save a year, cutting their tuition and indebtedness.

university's already minuscule 8.3 percent acceptance rate: It gets almost 2,500 applications every year and admits 80 to 90 students, for an acceptance rate of under 4 percent. The upside? Once you're in, you're in, and Brown does not require PLME students to take the MCAT. Julianne Ip, associate dean of medicine, says 90 percent of PLME students complete the program. The Pre-Professional Scholars Program at Case Western Reserve University extends conditional acceptance to medical or dental school to "outstanding" high school applicants who must then maintain a 3.5 GPA and get no grade lower than a B as undergrads.

The Association of American Medical Colleges

keeps a list of joint undergraduate/M.D. programs at aamc.org, by state and length of program. The American Association of Colleges of Pharmacy (aacp.org) lists more than 50 pharmacy programs offering "early assurance" or guaranteeing a spot in a Pharm.D. program to high school students, contingent on their successful completion of anywhere from two years of pre-professional study to a bachelor's degree. A few "early assurance" schools: University of Missouri-Kansas City, Oregon State University, and University at Buffalo.

Some professional schools, like the University of Iowa

law school and the Illinois Institute of Technology's Chicago-Kent College of Law, work with multiple colleges. In addition to its own undergraduate college, Iowa has set up programs with 13 schools in the state, including Cornell College, Coe College, and Iowa Wesleyan. Chicago-Kent has joint programs with IIT, Shimer College, Lake Forest College, and the University of Illinois at Chicago. Pesec, who has completed her first year at Alpert Medical School, observes that being absolved from the standard pre-med track has its downside.

"I knew that for the first three months of med school I wasn't going to know up from down," she admits. "You have to learn how to study as an undergrad or you'll be in trouble."

For Zoie Sheets, 22, having a spot reserved in medical school "created more freedom to explore," she says. Sheets immediately accepted her offer of a place in the University of Illinois at Chicago's Guaranteed Professional Program Admissions track in medicine, one of a number of UIC pathways that also include options in the health sciences, law, engineering, business, education and urban planning. Most of the programs, which typically entail a four-year bachelor's and full-length professional program, require admission to UIC's Honors College plus an additional selection process. About 250 to 300 Honors College students are in a GPPA program, says Honors College Dean Ralph Keen.

Sheets, who has completed her bachelor's in biology with minors in chemistry and Spanish, has appreciated being able to study a mix of arts and sciences. She also was able to get a feel for the med school campus and to shadow physicians, which confirmed her career choice. She'll now take a year to get a master's in public health before heading to medical school next fall. ●

Tricks of the Tour

Don't be shy about asking your guide to go beyond the script

by Mariya Greeley

SEVERAL UNDERGRADUATE tour guides at Dartmouth College told admissions that they felt the need to conceal some of their real opinions – about safety and Greek life, for example – during a recent revamp of the script they follow when showing visitors around campus. "We're always looking for new ways to present Dartmouth that are up-to-date with the current students, that are offering a genuine and fresh perspective," says Paul Sunde, director of admissions. But having a script, as many schools do, left certain students feeling like there were things they were "supposed" to say, notes Matthew Goff, a tour guide and senior admissions fellow who has been helping with the edits. "I don't think that's how it was ever meant, but I think that's how it's perceived." The school is moving toward a more open-ended format, he says, to emphasize sharing personal experiences and to make clear that guides have "complete autonomy to say what they feel is important to say."

Dartmouth's move is a reminder, as you make your college visits, that getting a sense of a school's culture – of whether it's a good fit – may require digging. Try these tour-guide-approved tactics to steer your guide off script:

Probe for specifics. This is key if you want to get the details that matter to you. "There's only so much you can say in an hour and a half," says Allie Cohen, a recent graduate of (and former tour guide at) Chapman University in California. Guides there touch briefly on diversity, for example, as they pass certain buildings, such as the Cross-Cultural Center and Fish Interfaith Center, and describe them as spaces where students can embrace different cultures and identities. But they generally only expand on the subject – adding detail about the popular and inclusive black student union, for example – if someone shows an interest. As you walk through cutting-edge science facilities, say, you might ask: Is under-graduate research with a faculty member possible? What types of research projects do students in all disciplines get to do? Whatever it may be, "If there's an interest definitely, definitely ask us to elaborate," says Audrey Schlimm, a sophomore and tour guide at Dickinson College in Pennsylvania.

Ask about your guide's experiences. This will help you put context around the facts and figures. You might hear that one-third of students join a fraternity or sorority, for example. Is that a little or a lot? The social scene can become "Greek-dominated" at that ratio, says Scott Friedhoff, vice president for enrollment and college relations at The College of Wooster in Ohio. And even at lower percentages, Greek life may feel like an outsize presence at a rural school, where there are fewer attractions.

Meanwhile, a large number of students living off campus could be a sign of a disconnected community – or of an exciting rite of passage for upperclassmen. Try asking: What do you and your friends do on weekends? What's the social scene like for people who live off campus?

Ask to meet with other students. This is a good way to round out your perspective. If you're interested in horseback riding or helping the homeless, for instance, ask your guide for a referral to someone on the equestrian team or who volunteers at a local shelter.

And as you plan your trips, find out about ways to go beyond a standard tour. Milyon Trulove, vice president and dean of admissions and financial aid at Reed College in Oregon, considers overnight visits the "gold standard" for diving into a school's "culture and ethos." The "Day in the Life" visit at Bucknell University in Pennsylvania includes a casual one-on-one hour with a guide. And at Wooster you can sign up for the "Lunch Buddy" program and eat at the dining hall with a student who is expressly not a tour guide. ●

WHY I PICKED...

SANTA CLARA UNIVERSIT

...Santa Clara University

Santa Clara, California

➤ **I SAW SCU** as a school that would allow me to get hands-on experience in engineering (my major) while also letting me develop other interests. The engineering program is strong. You learn concepts in the classroom and then can apply them, working on things like SCU's Tiny House Project (a compact solar-powered home built by a student team) and in the Robotics Systems Laboratory, where students can collaborate on underwater robots, say, or prototypes for CubeSats, miniaturized satellites that can scan disaster sites and send back images to help target relief efforts.

Nathan Metzger, '17

❝ The engineering school's motto is "Engineering with a Mission."

My senior design project, building a man-powered concrete mixer to aid the recovery efforts in Nepal after an earthquake, speaks to the engineering school's motto of "Engineering with a Mission." SCU as a whole follows the Jesuit traditions of advancing social justice and educating the whole person. For me, the latter meant picking up a music minor and joining the Chamber Singers, a campus choir. I also spent a summer in Nicaragua working with a nonprofit on community development projects such as water systems, just another of SCU's many enriching experiences. ●

IN TH MISSIO GARDEN AT SC

> There's an enthusiasm about the school that extends beyond the classroom.

Corina Fitzgerald, '17

...Lehigh University
Bethlehem, Pennsylvania

➤ **I WAS REALLY IMPRESSED** when I first visited Lehigh. It's a midsized private university with the huge range of programs that you tend to see only at big state schools. The extensive study abroad program and availability of fully funded internships is a particular strength. Last year the Iacocca International Internship Program, for example, set up 100 students in internships in 29 different countries. I was an Asian studies and Chinese double major, so the Iacocca program sent me to work for a nongovernmental organization in Cambodia, developing a third-grade English curriculum for local students. The entire experience was completely funded, including airfare, housing and a living stipend.

Roughly 50 percent of each year's incoming class are early-decision applicants,

ACADEMIC IMAGE – LEHIGH UNIVERSITY

so there's an enthusiasm about the school that extends beyond the classroom and athletic fields and into the city of Bethlehem where students participate in service and community engagement projects. Alumni stay very engaged and are always looking to give back, like through Lehigh's online career network, where they help students looking for internship and job opportunities. Throughout my four years, I have found that the richness of Lehigh's academic experience extends campuswide, reaching all academic colleges. ●

...Amherst College
Amherst, Massachusetts

➤ **DURING MY FIRST VISIT** to Amherst, I marveled at both the intellectual curiosity of the students and the passionate dedication of the professors. On this visit, my campus conversations ranged from deconstructing Kanye West's album "Yeezus" to investigating the effects of data structures on code runtimes. The open curriculum, which provides true academic freedom, assists students in concurrently pursuing their varied academic interests. Though I study philosophy, I've taken classes in mathematics, environmental studies, religion, chemistry and computer science.

Amherst also encourages growth outside the classroom. As a musician, I have found the school resources plentiful. A friend and I partnered to record an album – using the campus recording studio – and released it on Spotify. I also joined other classmates on a school-sponsored trip to Chicago, where we learned from and played with professional jazz musicians.

Emmanuel Osunlana, '18

The alumni network is another tremendous asset. In my case, it helped me secure a summer internship at Google. Amherst has expanded my horizons in so many ways – I even studied Buddhism with Tibetan monks in India! My time here has taught me how to innovate, lead and constantly grow, making me confident I can succeed on whatever path I take after graduation. ●

> The alumni network helped me secure an internship at Google.

MARIA STENZEL – AMHERST COLLEGE

2

Take a Road Trip

WASHINGTON

University of Washington
Seattle

Gonzaga University
Spokane

University of Puget Sound
Tacoma

Whitman College
Walla Walla

A laid-back vibe complements spectacular views in the Evergreen State. Starting in eastern Washington, U.S. News stopped at Gonzaga University in Spokane and Whitman College in Walla Walla, then drove to the coast for visits to the University of Puget Sound in Tacoma and the University of Washington in Seattle.

by Lindsay Cates

GONZAGA UNIVERSITY

SPOKANE

››› Gonzaga attracts students who want to make a difference in the world (and enjoy a hefty dose of the Bulldogs' March Madness basketball). The mindset at this school overlooking the Spokane River in eastern Washington is centered around the Jesuit philosophy of educating the mind, body and spirit. Although students from all religions attend, about half of Gonzaga's 5,100 undergrads are Catholic.

Zags are "social justice-centered" and want to get out into the world and solve problems, says Dean of Admission Julie McCulloh. The vast array of service opportunities available through the Center for Community and Service Learning run the gamut from spring break service trips to pairing off with senior citizens in the community. The school is routinely recognized as a top feeder for Teach for America and the Peace Corps.

Spirituality pervades the liberal arts core

Spokane Falls Skyride

curriculum, which requires all students to take classes in writing, global studies, philosophy and religion. First-year seminars teach new students about Gonzaga's Jesuit mission and prep them to meet the school's academic standards; choices have included an English class on Freaks, Geeks and Outsiders and a religion seminar titled Psalms and the Human Condition. The school's 16 Jesuit priests teach classes and act as spiritual mentors, and some also live in residence halls. "They

know a little bit about everything," says Analuz Torres, a junior from El Paso, Texas, who took a Latin class with a Jesuit professor. Students say it's a bucket-list item to befriend at least one Jesuit before graduation. Popular academic paths include accounting, science programs focused on undergraduate research, and degrees in business, special education, psychology, nursing and engineering.

With a 12-1 student-faculty ratio and average class size of 22, professors take time to get to know their students, students say. "They really care about our success," says Alexis Brown, a junior nursing major from Rocklin, California.

UNDERGRADUATES
Full-time: 5,160

TOTAL COST*
$52,880

U.S. NEWS RANKING
Regional Universities
(West): #4

*Tuition, fees and room & board for 2017-18

Gonzaga competes in Division I athletics and boasts an intramural program with one of the highest participation rates in the U.S. Teams in Ultimate Frisbee, soccer and badminton, among other sports, hold regular practices while on the quest for a coveted championship T-shirt. "Everybody wants a shirt," says sophomore Julian Moreno, a broadcast journalism major from San Francisco who participated in the Freshman Games intramural competition last year in soccer, flag football, volleyball and inner tube basketball.

But sports enthusiasm reaches its peak during basketball season, also known as "tenting season." To secure one of the 1,200 student seats in the Mc-Carthey Athletic Center for a Bulldogs game, students routinely camp out overnight. Torres, who grew up watching the team's March Madness games on TV, says tenting is a "must-do," even in freezing weather. Gonzaga's student section is often listed as one of the most enthusiastic in the country for men's basketball, rivaling those of universities three times its size.

A VIEWING PARTY FOR THE '17 NCAA BASKETBALL CHAMPIONSHIP GAME. GONZAGA LOST.

Freshmen and sophomores live on campus in housing ranging from four- and six-person suites and traditional doubles to apartments. About 60 percent of juniors and most seniors live off campus. A new student center houses dining options, a technology bar (with the latest gadgets from Microsoft, Apple, Google and Amazon), and a rooftop greenhouse. The 152-acre campus also boasts the Jundt Art Museum, which holds glass pieces by Dale Chihuly, along with other rotating exhibits. A new performing arts center should be completed next winter.

Some 50 study abroad programs are available, and Gonzaga has a campus in Florence where students can study for a year, a semester, or during the summer. Closer to home, there's easy access to hiking, biking, fishing, skiing and rock climbing, and students need only walk down the scenic Centennial Trail to get to theaters, museums, restaurants and shopping in downtown Spokane. ●

WHITMAN COLLEGE

WALLA WALLA

>>> Whitman's 117-acre campus doubles as an outdoor art museum and arboretum, a landscape that helps create the "peaceful balance" students say they've found at the small liberal arts school. A few minutes is all it takes to get from one end of campus to the other, and with only about 1,500 undergrads and a 9-1 student-faculty ratio, students develop close ties with professors.

Academics are rigorous, students say. First-years must take a yearlong seminar that explores texts by Shakespeare, Darwin and Plato, among other greats. Thirty professors across all disciplines teach sections of the class in the same time slot, which creates a shared but varied experience. While one student is studying with a chemistry professor, say, her roommate will be reading the same texts with a psych professor. "It fosters a community," says Dana Burgess, a classics professor. Every senior wraps up with a thesis and a presentation to faculty and peers.

Environmental Studies is a popular major among the 46 that Whitman offers. Most students pair it with another hard science or social science, and those looking for a hands-on experience can opt for the Semester in the West program, during which selected students camp out for 90 days to immerse themselves in the rural life and public land manage-ment issues impacting a dozen western states. Students hear from conservationists, energy experts, ranchers, ecologists and community activists to gain perspective.

Further off campus, 40 percent of students take advantage of 88 study abroad programs in 40 countries. Access to a planetarium and an ob-

IN SCULPTURE CLASS AT WHITMAN COLLEGE

servatory on campus, and typically clear night skies, make astronomy another popular choice.

Madison Wray, a junior from Portland, Oregon, says being environmentally conscious is "ingrained into the mindset" of the Whitman community, and so is community service; 70 percent of the student body participates in service annually. A fellows program funds part-time jobs for 12 students at nearby nonprofit organizations.

Fully 80 percent of stu-dents take part in an intramural sport – one of the highest percentages in the nation – and 20 percent play for one of Whitman's 14 Division III varsity athletic teams. Club sports include climbing, cycling, alpine skiing, rugby and Ultimate Frisbee. Forty percent of students participate in Greek life, and the more than 70 other clubs include the Glean Team, which collects crops left behind after local farm harvests to donate to food banks, and the Story Time Project, which arranges for students to travel to schools and daycare centers to read to children.

Sean Terada, a recent grad from Honolulu, liked the college's laid-back vibe, and the sense he got that he would be able to do it all – compete on the swim team, join clubs, and pursue a major in biochemistry, biophysics and molecular biology (or BBMB) in preparation for medical school. The faculty is "really invested in making sure you succeed," says Chloe Weinstock, a recent grad in marine biology from Davis, California.

Students acknowledge that they are off the beaten path (three hours from Spokane, four from Portland), but say they enjoy the local charm. People "come here very intentionally," says Wray. Walla Walla, located at the foot of the Blue Mountains, is known for miles of wheat fields, sweet onions and wine tourism, and quaint coffee shops, art galleries and restaurants are just a block off campus.

An award-winning outdoor program facilitates trips to nearby rafting, kayaking, biking and hiking locations and provides leadership training. (Students joke that Whitman is the best campus to get injured on, because so many complete first responder training.) A highlight of the program is a 7,000-square-foot climbing wall in the athletic center, site of the annual Sweet Onion Crank intercollegiate climbing competition. ●

Walla Walla Balloon Stampede

UNDERGRADUATES
Full-time: 1,493

TOTAL COST*
$62,304

U.S. NEWS RANKING
National Liberal Arts: #41

*Tuition, fees and room & board for 2017-18

UNIVERSITY OF PUGET SOUND

Mount Rainier
Tacoma, Washington

TACOMA

>>> Experiential, interdisciplinary learning is a big part of the mission here. A class about the Mississippi River teaches history, science and leadership and culminates with an adventure rowing the length of the Mississippi River. Education students are required to work in local classrooms, and students interested in health can take a bioethics practicum and work at nearby Tacoma General Hospital. Hands-on practice also weaves into residential life: Students help run The Cellar, a popular pizza place, and many upperclass students choose to live in one of 20 Greek or theme houses, where service projects and activities are built around shared interests from baseball to green living. Unlike most small liberal arts schools, Puget Sound offers a program in business and leadership and has a conservatory-style school of music. Interdisciplinary majors such as science, technology and society and international political economy are popular.

Located in Tacoma's residential North End, Puget Sound's scenic campus boasts towering Douglas fir trees and Tudor Gothic-style buildings. On clear days Mount Rainier is visible from the center of campus. Location is a big draw Tacoma is only 35 miles south of Seattle, with all that the city has to offer (including high-tech companies such as Google, Microsoft, Snapchat, Boeing, Starbucks and Amazon offering coveted internships and jobs). Megan Schowalter, a 2017 grad from Yakima, Washington, who chose the science, tech and society major, says Puget Sound is often referred to as the Pacific Northwest's "best-kept secret."

The school attracts students from 46 states and eight countries, with only 20 percent of its 2,600 or so undergraduates coming from in-state. Starting last year, submitting test scores was optional.

An 11-1 student-faculty ratio and small class sizes were part of Puget Sound's appeal for Keao Rivera-Leong, a senior from Hilo, Hawaii, with an interest in conservation biology. "You can go into a professor's office, and they know you by name," she says. First-years are introduced to the school's interdisciplinary approach early on by taking a two-semester seminar such as Rhetoric, Film and National Identity or The Third Wave: Rock After the Beatles to hone their research, speaking and writing skills. A strong

---

UNDERGRADUATES
Full-time: 2,508

TOTAL COST*
$60,210

U.S. NEWS RANKING
National Liberal Arts: #68

*Tuition, fees and room & board for 2017-18

BETWEEN CLASSES ON A RAINY DAY IN TACOMA

interdisciplinary Asian studies program prepares about 25 students for an every-three-year intensive academic year traveling and studying in eight Asian countries. "It's the epitome of a liberal arts education," says Kumar Flower Kay, a junior politics and government major going on the 2017-18 trip.

About 15 percent of students take advantage of the music offerings. Anyone can perform in groups and audition for scholarships. Senior English major Sophie Myers auditioned with a few piano pieces and got $24,000 towards her tuition each year. To retain her scholarship she takes weekly piano lessons, accompanies vocalists, and keeps her GPA up.

Puget Sound fields 23 varsity teams that compete in the Division III Northwest Conference, and the newly renovated Athletics and Aquatics Center now has tennis courts, a climbing wall and a smoothie bar. Many students note that the campus can feel small, but also that that can be easily remedied by taking advantage of nearby attractions. The student-run Expeditionary rents outdoor equipment and organizes trips every weekend with Puget Sound Outdoors, a campus group. Nearby Point Defiance Park offers hiking trails, kayaking, beach access, a zoo and an aquarium. The campus is also a short walk from Tacoma's vibrant arts scene, waterfront and downtown. A bus gets students to Seattle for only a few dollars. ●

UNIVERSITY OF WASHINGTON

SEATTLE

>>> One of the oldest public universities on the West Coast, U-Dub (as it's informally known) attracts its roughly 31,000 undergrads with a strong commitment to undergraduate research, rich diversity (about 41 percent of students are white; 14 percent come from abroad) and proximity to some of the nation's leading tech companies. Starla Sampaco, a senior from nearby Bellevue, was drawn to the school because of its diversity and vast array – more than 180 – of majors. She chose journalism with the ultimate goal of covering immigrant communities. UW had "an inclusive learning environment that could support what was really important to me," she says.

The university ranks No. 1 in the nation for federal research funding among public schools, and undergrads can start working in the lab as early as freshman year. Roughly 25 percent of the student body undertakes a serious research project, in fields from history to bioengineering, and students can present their findings to their peers at the annual Undergraduate Research Symposium. The calendar divides into three 10-week quarters plus an optional summer term.

One drawback of the school's size,

UNDERGRADUATES
Full-time: 30,933

TOTAL COST*
In-State: $23,091
Out-of-State: $47,655

U.S. NEWS RANKING
National Universities: #56

*Tuition, fees and room & board for 2017-18

students say, is that you may have to work to establish close relationships with your professors, and getting acquainted with all the activities and resources available can be overwhelming. "No one is holding your hand," says John Dahl, a 2017 grad from Bellingham, Washington. He was on track to be a biochemistry major before he realized business was his passion after starting an online marketing and sales business with some fraternity brothers. The academic resources available at UW made the transition easy, he says.

The average class size is about 50 students, although upper-level

classes are smaller. The largest lecture hall seats 750. On the other hand, there are all those opportunities: the richly varied academics, some 800 student clubs, and over 50 sororities and fraternities, not to mention unparalleled access to internship and job opportunities at the nearby headquarters of big-name companies like Google and Microsoft.

THE U-DUB CAMPUS IN FULL BLOOM, LEFT, AND A STUDY SESSION AT THE UNIVERSITY'S ICONIC SUZZALLO LIBRARY

About 75 percent of students live off campus, and the school has a sizeable commuter population. However, two-thirds of freshmen do live in the residence halls and three new dorms will be completed in 2018.

On nice days, a central gathering place is Red Square, where student groups set up tables and tents to promote their organizations. The square is surrounded by Gothic-style buildings (Suzzallo Library's Reading Room is widely considered a masterpiece of college Gothic architecture), and on a rare sunny day, a walk down Rainier Vista, just off the square, provides a stunning view of the snow-topped mountain. Japanese cherry trees bloom in the quad every spring making up at least in part for the usual gray weather.

Athletics are a big draw.

The Huskies field 20 Division I teams. The rowing team is among the best in the nation, and UW holds the prestigious Windermere Cup event at Montlake Cut every spring. UW's PAC-12 football games are also popular. A new light rail station near Husky Stadium makes it easier for fans to get to sporting events, and also puts downtown Seattle just six minutes away. Construction is underway for more light rail stops to reach the U District neighborhood, where many students live. Popular off-campus excursions include Pike Place Market on the waterfront, nightlife in the Capitol Hill neighborhood, and Puget Sound for beach bonfires.

UW now uses only the Coalition for Access, Affordability and Success application – no official transcript or recommendation letters required. ●

OHIO

U.S. News visited four schools in the Buckeye State, tracing a path from the bustling urban campus of Ohio State in Columbus to Case Western Reserve in Cleveland, with stops at the College of Wooster and Oberlin amid the farmland along the way.

by Michael Morella

OHIO STATE UNIVERSITY

COLUMBUS

》》 At 59,500 students, Ohio State University is the biggest school in the Big Ten Conference, and it has the fourth largest undergraduate enrollment (45,800) in the country. That community is especially evident on Saturdays in the fall, when more than 100,000 students and spectators come out to Ohio Stadium – better known as the Shoe, for its horseshoe shape – to cheer on the Buckeye football team. With more than 200 undergraduate majors and 1,300-plus student clubs and organizations, OSU's size and scope are a big draw for many.

Located in Columbus, a city of about 860,100,

Ohio State's campus creates a college town feel inside an urban environment. At the heart of the university's 1,664-acre campus is the Ohio Union, a hub for student activities that features meeting and event spaces, the university's Multicultural Center and several dining spots (including Sloopy's

Diner, a student favorite). Between the Union and Thompson Library is the Oval, a tree-ringed lawn that is a popular spot for studying, sunbathing and casual sports.

Most first- and second-year students live on campus in one of about three dozen residence halls. Students can apply to join one of about 20 learning communities, where those with a common interest in the arts, say, or women in engineering can live together and share some academic experiences. Nearly 80 percent of freshman classes have 50 or

fewer students, and the overall student-faculty ratio is 19-to-1. Students say that even larger lecture classes break down into smaller lab sections or recitations of about 20 to 25 students, led by a teaching assistant. For those who take the initiative to get to know faculty, "they're willing to put that time into you as well," says senior LeRoy Ricksy Jr., a criminology major from New York City.

From academic to career advising, OSU offers undergrads considerable support. In fact, "we have so many resources here, you can get lost looking," says DaVonti' Haynes, a 2016 public affairs grad from Cleveland who is pursuing a master's degree in social work at OSU. For instance,

UNDERGRADUATES
Full-time: 45,831

TOTAL COST*
In-State: $22,843
Out-of-State: $41,911

U.S. NEWS RANKING
National Universities: #54

*Tuition, fees and room & board for 2017–18

READY TO TAKE THE
FIELD FOR A MARCHING
BAND PRACTICE
ON HALLOWEEN

the Office of International Affairs offers services for international students and those who are interested in studying abroad, while the Office of Undergraduate Research and Creative Inquiry helps students connect with research and artistic projects. Students can also apply for the university honors program, which gives those who qualify access to select smaller classes, learning communities, and the chance to pursue one-on-one research with faculty. Once you find your niche, "then the breadth and depth of Ohio State becomes more of an opportunity and less of a burden," says Aaron

READY TO TAKE THE FIELD FOR A MARCHING BAND PRACTICE ON HALLOWEEN

Kimson, a 2017 finance grad from Aurora, Ohio.

The university is closely intertwined with Columbus and has active partnerships with Nationwide Children's Hospital, Columbus City Schools, and other local organizations. "I'm extremely thankful for how much connectivity there is between the city and institution," says Gerard Basalla, a 2017 political science and strategic communications grad from Parma, Ohio, who interned downtown for U.S. Sen.

Rob Portman and Ohio Attorney General Mike DeWine during his time at OSU and nabbed a postgrad job at the Columbus Partnership, an economic development organization.

Another 2017 grad, social work major Maggie Griffin of Madeira, Ohio, developed a project with local organizations around Columbus to establish community refrigerators for people living in food deserts or facing food insecurity.

For fun, many students enjoy exploring the Short North Arts District, watching local professional soccer and hockey teams, and visiting the restaurants, stores and bars along High

Street, on the east edge of campus. Roughly 12 percent of students join a fraternity or sorority.

Just over half of those who applied to join OSU's class of 2020 were admitted, and roughly 4 in 5 domestic undergrads hail from the Buckeye State. School pride tends to run deep. The university boasts an alumni network of more than half a million people across the world. In a nod to the school's call-and-response tradition, "wherever you are," says 2017 grad Anthony Stranges, an information systems major from Blacklick, Ohio, "if you yell O-H, someone will probably respond I-O." ●

COLLEGE OF WOOSTER

WOOSTER

>>> Before they graduate, all 2,000 or so students at the College of Wooster complete an independent study, a substantial research or creative project that they work on for at least a year. The I.S., as it's known, might take the form of a studio art exhibit, a music or theatrical performance, or a long research paper, supervised by a faculty mentor.

"I.S. really defined my experience here," says 2017 chemistry grad Rachel Molé, of Jamestown, New York, who examined disinfection systems at wastewater treatment plants in Chicago. She presented her research at a number of academic conferences and is now pursuing a Ph.D. in environmental science at Baylor University.

When seniors turn in their projects after spring break, they earn modest but highly coveted prizes: a Tootsie Roll and a black-and-yellow pin that reads, "I did it." At five o'clock, the college bagpipe band leads a parade across campus to celebrate this "rite of passage," says Jared Berg, a 2017 history grad from Cleveland, who like other students here values the college's emphasis on undergraduate research and the close-knit community it fosters among classmates and with professors.

Set on 240 acres in the city of Wooster (population 27,000), the private liberal arts college is roughly halfway between Columbus and Cleveland. About two-thirds of undergrads come from outside Ohio, including about 12 percent from abroad. With an 11-1 student-faculty ratio, professors and advisers generally get to know their students inside and outside the classroom. "These are people that really, really care about me," says Chadwick Smith, a 2017 grad in history and Africana studies from Decatur, Georgia. He says it's common for faculty members to invite students to lunch or dinner. He even once housesat for a professor during spring break.

Nearly all students live on campus, so "you get to be like just a very large family," says Spencer Gilbert, a 2017 grad from Shaker Heights, Ohio, who majored in political science.

Many upperclassmen reside in college-owned program houses, each affiliated with a particular community organization. Residents perform eight hours of volunteer service a month at places like the Boys & Girls Club of Wooster or 4 Paws for Wooster, a service dog group. During snowstorms, hundreds of

Wooster Jazz Festival

UNDERGRADUATES
Full-time: 2,003

TOTAL COST*
$60,000

U.S. NEWS RANKING
National Liberal Arts: #63

*Tuition, fees and room & board for 2017-18

students come together to haul snow and fill the arch at the center of the castlelike Kauke Hall, which according to campus legend is supposed to cancel classes the next day. Though most students appreciate the size, the college "can become too insular if you let it," says Gilbert.

Students can choose from more than 40 majors, and everyone must complete a diverse mix of courses in writing, global and cultural perspectives, religious perspectives and quantitative reasoning. All freshmen begin with a 15-person first-year seminar, led by a professor who becomes a student's initial academic adviser until he or she declares a major.

To help them navigate all of the college's opportunities, many students visit Wooster's center for Advising, Planning, and Experiential Learning, also known as APEX, a one-stop shop where undergrads can meet with advisers and find resources related to landing an internship, career planning, exploring an off-campus program and more.

There are over 120 student organizations, such as the Black Student Association, the Wooster Activities Crew, the Yoga Club, and WOO 91, the student-run radio station. At Wooster, there is "no certain thing that dominates," says sophomore Nashmia Khan, a neuroscience major from Pakistan.

On any given weekend, undergrads might hear a poetry reading or play board games at the student-run Common Grounds coffee shop, go to a dance party at the College Underground club/bar, or cheer on the Fighting Scots Division III sports teams. Says recent graduate Gina Williamson, a psychology and Spanish major from Twinsburg, Ohio: "I didn't feel like I was going to have to change myself at all to fit in here." ●

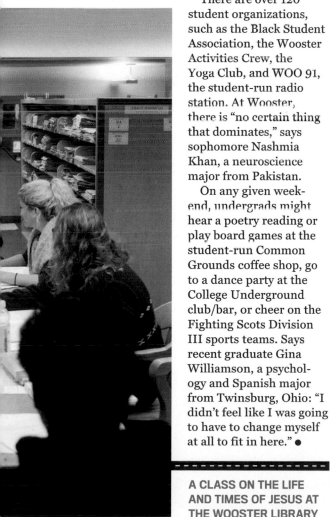

A CLASS ON THE LIFE AND TIMES OF JESUS AT THE WOOSTER LIBRARY

OBERLIN COLLEGE

OBERLIN

>>> Walk around Oberlin College's campus and you might hear a classical piano concerto, a steel drum band, a rock group in the student union bar and venue Dionysus Disco, an impromptu a cappella show outside the library, and an eclectic midnight "organ pump" performance on the towering, 4,014-pipe organ in Finney Chapel — all on the same day. Oberlin hosts more than 500 concerts and performances each year, in part thanks to its 152-year-old Conservatory of Music, a rarity at a liberal arts college and the oldest such continuously operating facility in the country.

At Oberlin, home to roughly 2,900 undergraduates, "creativity is in the air," says Rebecca Whelan, chair and associate professor of chemistry and biochemistry. After all, this is a place where students camp out for the popular art rental program, through which they can borrow real artwork for $5 per piece per semester from the Allen Memorial Art Museum on campus, which has more than 14,000 pieces of art.

Founded in 1833, Oberlin opened its doors to women and African-American students very early in its history. Today, underrepresented minority students make up about a fifth of those enrolled, while 94 percent come from outside Ohio, including about 9 percent from abroad. Many students say that their peers share a progressive attitude about politics, the environment and social issues. "So many people care about social justice," says senior Thobeka Mnisi, a politics major from South Africa.

UNDERGRADUATES
Full-time: 2,895

TOTAL COST*
$68,672

U.S. NEWS RANKING
National Liberal Arts: #26

*Tuition, fees and room & board
for 2017-18

"People are really good at questioning everything here," says junior Andrea Wang, a neuroscience and linguistics major from Valley Forge, Pennsylvania.

Located in the small northern Ohio city of Oberlin, about 35 miles southwest of Cleveland, the college adjoins a quaint downtown of shops and restaurants. In an effort to break out of the campus bubble, more than half of students participate in some sort of community service project annually; the Bonner Center for Service and Learning helps facilitate programs with more than 200 community organizations. Sustainability is also a shared interest on campus, and each spring students participate in

OBERLIN'S ALLEN MEMORIAL ART MUSEUM

Ecolympics, a water and electricity conservation competition.

About 2,300 students enroll in the College of Arts and Sciences, where the liberal arts curriculum offers more than four dozen majors. The 600 or so conservatory students can choose from 10 divisions – jazz studies, say, or musicology – and private study in 42 areas. (About 180 students pursue a double degree from both the college and conservatory in five years.) All students enjoy generally small classes – about three-fourths have fewer than 20 students. For many, a sense of community is

established during the first-year seminar, an interdisciplinary course capped at 16 students; Whelan, for instance, teaches a class on Marie Curie that blends history, chemistry and art. Students can even create and teach their own for-credit courses through the Experimental College on topics like "Seinfeld" and basic Korean.

Each January, Obies can participate in winter term, a four-week minisemester where they pursue

a project, internship or study abroad experience. At least three are required for graduation. Sarah Minion, a 2017 grad in politics and comparative American studies from Cherry Hill, New Jersey, helped a health care advocacy group in Alabama, interned on Capitol Hill in Washington, D.C., and

studied political street art in Berlin, Amsterdam, Tel Aviv and Jerusalem.

Nearly all undergrads live on campus, and roughly 1 in 4 are members of the Oberlin Student Cooperative Association, which manages eight student-run co-ops. These close-knit communities, each with its own vibe, give students of like interests the space to come together to cook, eat, listen to music, debate and more. Obies also can participate in more than 175 student groups and 21 Division III sports teams. ●

CASE WESTERN RESERVE UNIVERSITY

Rock & Roll Hall of Fame

CLEVELAND

»» Located in the midst of several major Cleveland cultural institutions, Case Western Reserve University embraces Ohio's second largest city as a sort of living laboratory. Many students pursue internships, research and academic opportunities at the Cleveland Museum of Art, Cleveland Clinic, the Cleveland Botanical Garden and the Cleveland Museum of Natural History, all within walking distance of campus. "It's really nice to be actually able to do these things so hands-on as an undergrad," says junior Emily Szabo, a biomedical engineering major from the Cleveland area. Szabo is doing research to restore natural human sensation to amputees with prosthetics at the nearby Louis Stokes Cleveland VA Medical Center. "You really see science come to life."

Formed in 1967 when the Case School of Applied Science merged with Western Reserve University, Case Western Reserve is steeped in science. Engineering students can complete paid co-ops at employers such as General Electric Co., NASA and Tesla. A 156-foot wind turbine towers over the Veale Convocation, Recreation and Athletic Center, providing power and research opportunities. Today, the school has a reputation as a hotbed for health and STEM fields, but students say the arts, humanities and social sciences should not be underestimated.

True, biology, biomedical engineering, mechanical engineering and psychology made up the most popular majors in 2015-16, but "people are not one-

STUDENTS IN THE LIBRARY AT CASE WESTERN RESERVE

UNDERGRADUATES
Full-time: 5,152

TOTAL COST*
$62,284

U.S. NEWS RANKING
National Universities: #37

*Tuition, fees and room & board for 2017-18

dimensional," says 2017 grad Brian Ward, an English and political science major from Eugene, Oregon. "I have very rarely met a student that is just majoring in STEM and does not have a minor in something like political science, history or business management."

Many students channel their passions for engineering and artistry at the Larry Sears and Sally Zlotnick Sears think[box], a 50,000-square-foot facility that is part makerspace (complete with 3-D print-

ers, laser cutters and other tools) and part innovation and entrepreneurship hub.

About 5,100 undergraduates and 6,500 graduate and professional students attend Case Western Reserve. Undergrads come from all 50 states and some 80 countries. Just over a third are minority students. The university offers about 95 undergraduate majors, minors and concentrations across the schools of nursing, engineering, management, and arts and sciences. As part of the university's Seminar Approach to

General Education and Scholarship (or SAGES) curriculum, students must complete a series of 17-person writing-intensive, discussion-based seminars that cover three broad thematic areas: the natural or technological world, the social world and the symbolic world. They also take a seminar related to their major(s) and complete a senior capstone.

While intro courses can be large, class sizes tend to thin out as students advance in their majors. Overall, the university boasts an 11-1 student-faculty ratio, and undergraduates can enjoy the advantages of a medium-sized urban research university. "I feel very connected to the community," says 2017 grad Temi Omilabu, from Katy, Texas, who studied English and bioethics. Students describe their peers as driven. "Case students like having a lot on their plate, but also being able to balance," says senior Keagan Lipak, a chemistry and psychology major from Columbus, Ohio.

About a third of students join fraternities and sororities, and Spartans stay busy in the more than 160 student clubs and activities as well as 19 Division III varsity sports. Downtown Cleveland, home to several professional sports venues, the Rock & Roll Hall of Fame, the Playhouse Square theater district, and more, is only about 5 miles away. Many also enjoy the food, nightlife and entertainment options in the school's immediate University Circle neighborhood. ●

NORTH CAROLINA

North Carolina's central region is a hub for innovation driven by the 7,000-acre Research Triangle Park, home to a wide range of science and tech companies and closely connected to UNC–Chapel Hill, Duke, and NC State. U.S. News visited those three schools along with Elon University to the west for a rich taste of the Tar Heel State.

by Alexandra Pannoni

Elon University — Elon
Duke University — Durham
UNC-Chapel Hill — Chapel Hill
North Carolina State University — Raleigh

UNC–CHAPEL HILL

CHAPEL HILL

>>> Like many of her peers growing up in the Tar Heel State, Hannah Macie always dreamed of attending the University of North Carolina in Chapel Hill, about 20 miles from her hometown of Cary. Now a senior studying strategic communication, Macie cherishes the wide variety of options and resources available at the university. "There's a class for everything here," she says.

UNC enrolls some 18,500 undergraduates from all 50 states and more than 90 countries,

Chapel Hill

and many students proudly wear Carolina blue to celebrate the school's top-notch academics and athletics. If the Division I Tar Heels basketball team wins a matchup against archrival (and neighbor) Duke or takes home the NCAA national championship as it did in 2017 (beating Gonzaga, Page 46), tradition calls for students to "rush" Franklin Street, the lively gathering place just off campus that is home to many shops, restaurants and bars. The tradition "really makes you feel like a part of the UNC community," says junior media and journalism major Alexis Allston of Wendell, North Carolina.

There's a lot to do on campus, too, with more than 600 student organizations. About 19 percent of undergrads join fraternities and sororities.

Students at Carolina like to have fun, but they take academics very seriously, says junior Carina McDermed, a media and journalism and political science major from Chapel Hill. UNC is highly selective, with just about 26.2 percent of all first-year applicants gaining admission. (The admit rate is about 48.8 percent in-state compared to 15.2 percent for non-Carolina natives.)

More than 77 undergraduate majors are available. Admission to certain programs, such as business administration, media and journalism, and public health, is competitive. Incoming students can get used to college academics by

UNC STUDENTS PRACTICE THEIR JOURNALISM SKILLS IN A CAMPUS BROADCAST STUDIO.

UNDERGRADUATES
Full-time: 18,523

TOTAL COST*
In-State: $20,561
Out-of-State: $46,144

U.S. NEWS RANKING
National Universities: #30

*Tuition, fees and room & board for 2017-18

taking a small first-year seminar on topics such as Change in the Coastal Ocean or Philosophy on Bamboo. But throughout their academic career at UNC, students will find a mix of large lecture-style and smaller discussion-based courses. The student-faculty ratio is 13-to-1, and only about 15 percent of classes have more than 50 students. A relatively new program with nearby North Carolina State offers undergraduates a degree in biomedical and health sciences engineering.

All students must fulfill an experiential learning requirement, which could include a study abroad stint, an internship, a performing arts project, mentored research, or a service-learning experience. Participating in community service is "definitely a huge part" of campus life at UNC, says 2017 grad Jenn Morrison, a strategic communication major from Brookeville, Maryland. Morrison participated in a spring break service experience in the eastern part of the state and took a course on social and economic justice.

Undergraduate research opportunities are also abundant. Junior Wanyi Chen, from Shenzhen, China, says the university does a good job with helping undergraduates find research opportunities, especially with about 10,900 graduate and professional students also enrolled. Chen, an information science and cultural studies double major, completed an independent study research project last year on computer science education. Students can take advantage of the resources available through the Office for Undergraduate Research to help land opportunities.

Minority students make up roughly one-third of UNC's latest first-year class. Senior economics major Eric Smith, of Warsaw, North Carolina, says finding a social group at UNC as an African-American male was somewhat challenging at first, but that the school is actively trying to help students from diverse backgrounds through multicultural events, mentoring opportunities and other support services. ●

ELON UNIVERSITY

ELON

>>> Every Tuesday morning at 9:40, members of the Elon University community gather on campus for College Coffee, a 40-minute celebration and school tradition dating back to 1984. No classes are scheduled during that time, so students can catch up with professors and peers while they enjoy beverages, food and conversation. Community spirit is woven into the fabric of life at the private university about 20 miles east of Greensboro, students say.

In addition to a traditional liberal arts and sciences core curriculum, the school's 6,000 undergraduates are required to complete at least two experiential learning opportunities, which can include service learning, study abroad,

internships, research or a leadership experience before they graduate.

Before she completed her degree in marketing in May, Caralea Prentice, of Vienna, Virginia, studied abroad in Cuba, France and Ireland and did service learning on behalf of the Elon town government. So many students here want to "save the world" in their own way, she says, and Elon works to help

them build that into their academic experience. Many undergrads participate in community service projects, and overall, about 79 percent study abroad at least once.

In another nod to building global awareness, students need to complete a foreign language requirement, and all freshmen take a seminar on the global experience, for which professors choose their own topics; recent examples include human

migration and immigration and the worldwide reach of soccer. With a student-faculty ratio of 12-to-1, students can expect generally small classes and close contact with professors. At the end of one of his first-year courses, notes Tommy Hamzik, a 2017 journalism grad from Cleveland, the prof invited students home for dinner.

There are more than 60 undergraduate majors offered in the College of Arts and Sciences and the schools of business, communications and education. (About 700 graduate students also attend Elon.) Along with the liberal arts foundation, all students can benefit from a range of pre-professional skills programs. Most of those majoring in the business and communications schools

UNDERGRADUATES
Full-time: 6,008

TOTAL COST*
$46,142

U.S. NEWS RANKING
Regional Universities
(South): #1

*Tuition, fees and room & board
for 2017-18

ELON'S 12-1 STUDENT-FACULTY RATIO GIVES IT A CLOSE-KNIT VIBE.

ALAMANCE BATTLEGROUND STATE HISTORIC SITE

are required to complete an internship, and these schools have dedicated offices to help students find opportunities.

All undergrads have access to career services at the Student Professional Development Center, through which they are encouraged to complete a four-year career action plan that gets them thinking early about their path. After taking advantage of these opportunities, "I felt 100 times more confident going into an interview," says Prentice, who interned with a strategic communications firm in Washington, D.C., and the Coca-Cola Co. in Atlanta.

When they are not thinking about their future, Elon students can get involved with more than 250 campus organizations and programs. Elon fields 17 NCAA Division I sports teams that play in the Colonial Athletic Association. About 31 percent of undergraduates participate in Greek life, which drives a big part of the social scene but is not the only way for people to build connections or have fun, students say.

First- and second-year students are required to live on campus, while many upperclassmen choose to live in the quaint community of Elon, home to about 10,000 residents. The downtown area has a number of shops, restaurants and bars, including the Oak House, a popular coffeehouse and bar co-founded by an Elon grad. Some professors even host office hours there, says Hamzik. ●

DUKE UNIVERSITY

DURHAM

››› Tiana Horn graduated from Duke University this year with a degree in public policy and a job that she created for herself. Horn, from Deltona, Florida, co-founded a hair-care product business during her time at Duke, where she embraced the university's entrepreneurship program; it provides students everything from access to alumni mentors in the professional world to funding to develop their own products or services. One Duke alumna who mentored Horn taught her important business foundations like how to purchase bar codes and the best ways to approach retail buyers to get into stores.

Like many of the 6,600 undergraduates who attend the private university in Durham, Horn has high academic and professional ambitions and

UNDERGRADUATES
Full-time: 6,609

TOTAL COST*
$69,244

U.S. NEWS RANKING
National Universities: #9

*Tuition, fees and room & board for 2017-18

has taken advantage of some of the wide range of opportunities available to Duke students. "Everyone has big dreams here," and that can be "really inspiring," says Jennifer Alspach, a 2017 earth and ocean sciences graduate from Yuma, Arizona. Alspach, who is going on to pursue a Ph.D. in

---

UNDERGRADS IN A MOLECULAR BIOLOGY LAB AT DUKE

atmospheric science at the University of Alaska–Fairbanks, spent a summer volunteering on a wetland conservation project along the Colorado River and completed an independent study about Arctic sea ice and cloud interactions.

Duke is one of the most selective universities in the country, with only about 11 percent of freshman applicants earning a spot for the class of 2020. The university offers some 49 majors as well as several dozen minors and certificate programs. Most undergraduates study in the Trinity College of Arts and Sciences, which has a traditional liberal arts curriculum. Students can also enroll in the Pratt School of Engineering, which has bachelor's degree programs in biomedical, civil, environmental, mechanical, and electri-

cal and computer engineering. Undergrads enjoy generally small classes thanks to the 6-1 student-faculty ratio.

Duke's 8,470-acre campus is filled with Gothic-style buildings, including the prominent Duke Chapel and stately Perkins Library. Academics are rigorous and the atmosphere can be intense, students say, but the university has a number of resources and support systems to help. For instance, a new wellness center on campus offers a one-stop shop for student health needs, including mental health counseling, sexual health education and meditation, among other services.

Durham Bulls Athletic Park

About 85 percent of undergrads come from outside North Carolina, and about 10 percent are international students. Roughly half of Duke's class of 2020 are minority students, and nearly 1 in 10 are the first in their families to go to college.

Horn, last year's president of the Black Student Alliance, says that Duke does a pretty good job of enrolling a diverse population by working with minority- and advocacy-focused student organizations to recruit and support undergrads through campus events and cultural centers.

Students must live on campus for at least three years. About a third of undergrads participate in Greek life. When they aren't hanging out together on campus, many students explore the lively Durham community. They can check out theater performances at the Durham Performing Arts Center or seek an internship at one of the many businesses located in nearby Research

HANGING OUT IN THE PLAZA AMIDST DUKE'S GOTHIC ARCHITECTURE

Triangle Park, a hub for science, health and tech.

Duke's undergrads turn out in droves to support their Division I teams. That support reaches a fever pitch for men's basketball when the five-time NCAA champion Blue Devils make their annual run at the Final Four. During a visit last winter, hundreds of students had been camping outside for several weeks in front of Cameron Indoor Stadium, the school's basketball venue in Krzyzewskiville – named after famed men's basketball coach Mike Krzyzewski – for a chance at prime tickets to an upcoming game against Duke's perennial nearby rival, the University of North Carolina in Chapel Hill. ●

NORTH CAROLINA STATE

RALEIGH

>>> North Carolina State University is situated in the heart of the swing state's political action, adjacent to the headquarters of both North Carolina's Republican and Democratic parties and just a couple miles from the state capitol building in downtown Raleigh. Both Hillary Clinton and Donald Trump held campaign events on campus and nearby just before last year's election.

The culture at the school, which draws about 87 percent of its roughly 23,800 undergrads from within the state, reflects both the political divide and a willingness to listen to diverse viewpoints, students say. "There are some people who think this way, and there are some people who think that way," says 2017 grad Bianca Pearson, a history major from Fuquay-Varina, North Carolina. But for the most part, students are generally "very open" to hearing new perspectives, she says.

About 127 bachelor's programs are available to undergraduates. (The university also enrolls approximately 10,000 grad students.) Incoming students select a first- and second-choice program of study, since admission to certain majors, such as those in engineering and design, is competitive. Undecided freshmen can choose exploratory studies to start. No one is locked in, since you can apply to other programs once on campus, says senior Madi-

son Hoell, of Bozeman, Montana. She switched her major from animal science to communications in an "incredibly easy" process last year, and she still expects to graduate on time. Because colleges have different requirements, the ease of the process will vary.

Adjacent to the main undergraduate campus is Centennial Campus, a center of technology and research that is home to most of the College of Engineering's facilities and the College of Textiles, where students can study medical fabrics such as scrubs and artificial skin and technical textiles like seat belts and firefighter uniforms. The campus houses offices for more than 70 businesses, nonprofits and government agencies, including LexisNexis, the North Carolina Military Foundation and the National Weather Service, giving students a range of places to look for research opportunities, jobs and internships. Between obligations, undergrads can study at Centennial's state-of-the-art library, where a robotic system retrieves books from the collection.

Shraddha Rathod, now a senior, really likes the university's "think-and-do" mentality. "We don't just talk about it, we actually do things and make things," says Rathod, an electrical and computer engineering major from Charlotte. For example, during her junior year, she took an Introduction to Embedded Systems class in which students created working toy cars. It was probably her most difficult and time-consuming class during college, she says, but she learned "so much" by actually building a system and not just listening to a professor talk about it.

Outside of academics, there's plenty to do both on and off campus. The 900-plus student organizations include everything from Genetics Club and Disney Film Club to a chapter of the American Meteorological Society. About 15 percent of students participate in Greek life. Twenty-three NCAA Division I sports teams, known as the Wolfpack, draw plenty of fans.

Off campus, students frequent Raleigh restaurants, nightlife and cultural institutions, including the North Carolina Museum of Art and the North Carolina Museum of Natural Sciences.

Starting this fall, most first-year students will be required to live on the university's 2,099-acre campus. While student housing is available to all full-timers, many upperclassmen choose to live in the surrounding area, a diverse community that also draws professionals from around the world to multinational employers such as Cisco Systems and IBM. ●

WORKING TOGETHER IN A TEXTILE CLASS AT NC STATE

UNDERGRADUATES
Full-time: 23,847

TOTAL COST*
In-State: $19,912
Out-of-State: $38,260

U.S. NEWS RANKING
National Universities: #81

*Tuition, fees and room & board for 2017-18

3

The U.S. NEWS Rankings

How We Rank
Colleges

College-bound students can make good use of our statistics

by Robert J. Morse And Eric M. Brooks

THE HOST OF INTANGIBLES that make up the college experience cannot be measured by a series of data points. But for families concerned with finding the best academic value for their money, the U.S. News Best Colleges rankings, now in their 33rd year, provide an excellent starting point for the search. They help you compare at a glance the relative quality of institutions based on such widely accepted indicators of excellence as first-year retention rates, graduation rates and the strength of the faculty. As you check out the data for colleges already on your shortlist, you may discover unfamiliar schools with similar attributes and thus broaden your options.

Yes, many factors other than those spotlighted here will figure in your decision, including location and the feel of campus life; the range of academic offerings, activities and sports; and the cost plus the availability of financial aid. But if you combine the information in this book with campus visits, interviews and your own intuition, our rankings can be a powerful tool in your quest for the best fit.

How does the methodology work? The U.S. News rank-

XAVIER UNIVERSITY
OF LOUISIANA

ing system rests on two pillars. The formula uses quantitative and qualitative statistical measures that education experts have proposed as reliable indicators of academic quality, and is based on our researched view of what matters in education.

First, we categorize regionally accredited institutions by their mission to establish valid comparisons: National Universities, National Liberal Arts Colleges, Regional Universities and Regional Colleges. The national universities offer a full range of undergraduate majors plus master's and Ph.D. programs and emphasize faculty research (Page 70). The national liberal arts colleges focus almost exclusively on undergraduate education (Page 80). They award at least 50 percent of their degrees in the arts and sciences.

The regional universities (Page 88) offer a broad scope of undergraduate degrees and some master's degree programs but few, if any, doctoral programs. The regional colleges (Page 106) focus on undergraduate education but grant fewer than 50 percent of their degrees in liberal arts disciplines; this category also includes schools that have small bachelor's degree programs but primarily grant two-year associate degrees. The regional universities and regional colleges are further divided and ranked in four geographical groups: North, South, Midwest and West.

The framework used to group schools is derived from the 2015 Update of the Carnegie Classification of Institutions of Higher Education's Basic Classification. Now the responsibility of the Indiana University Center for Postsecondary Research, the Carnegie classification has always been the basis of the Best Colleges ranking categories because it is used extensively by higher education researchers. The U.S. Department of Education and many higher education associations use the system to organize their data and to determine colleges' eligibility for grant money, for example.

Next, we gather data from each college on up to 15 indicators of academic excellence. Each factor is assigned a weight that reflects our research about how much a measure matters. Finally, the colleges and universities in each category are ranked against their peers using their overall scores, which are calculated from the sum of their indicators.

Some schools are not ranked and thus do not appear in the tables. The most common reason is that the school does not use ACT or SAT test scores in admissions decisions for first-time, first-year, degree-seeking applicants. (Schools with test-optional and test-flexible admission policies are included because they do consider ACT or SAT scores when provided.) In fewer cases, colleges are not ranked because they received too few ratings in the peer assessment survey, had a total enrollment of fewer than 200 students, had a large proportion of nontraditional students, or had no first-year students (as is the situation at upper-division schools). As a result of these standards, many for-profit institutions are not ranked. We also did not rank highly specialized schools in the arts, business and engineering, although eligible specialized schools are included in our separate rankings of business and engineering programs.

Colleges report most of the data themselves, via the annual U.S. News statistical survey. This year, 92 percent of the 1,389 ranked colleges and universities returned their statistical information during our spring and summer 2017 data collection period. To ensure the highest possible quality of data, U.S. News compared schools' survey responses to their earlier cohorts' statistics, third-party data, and data reported by other schools. Schools were instructed to review, revise and verify the accuracy of their data, particularly any flagged by U.S. News as requiring a second look.

For eligible colleges that declined to complete our survey, we made extensive use of data they reported to the U.S. Department of Education's National Center for Education Statistics and other organizations. We obtained missing data on alumni giving from the Council for Aid to Education. The NCES provided data on ACT and SAT scores, acceptance rates, freshman retention and six-year graduation rates, faculty counts, student-faculty ratios, and information on financial resources.

Data that schools did not report in this year's U.S. News survey are footnoted. Schools that did not submit their surveys altogether are identified as nonresponders. Estimates were used in the calculations when schools failed to report data not available from other sources, but these estimates are not displayed in this guidebook. Missing data are reported as N/A. The small number of national universities and liberal arts colleges receiving fewer than 10 ratings from high school counselors also have N/A instead of a counselor score.

The indicators we use to capture academic quality fall into a number of groupings: assessment by administrators at peer institutions (and, for national universities and liberal arts colleges, also by high school guidance counselors), how well schools retain and graduate students, the quality of and investment in their faculty, admissions selectivity, financial resources, and alumni giving. The indicators include input

Weighing What's Important

The U.S. News rankings are based on several key measures of quality, listed below. Scores for each measure are weighted as shown to arrive at a final overall score. In the case of the national universities and national liberal arts colleges, the assessment figure represents input from both academic peers (15 percent) and high school guidance counselors (7.5 percent); for regional universities and colleges, it reflects peer opinion only.

The Scoring Breakdown

Graduation and retention rates	22.5%
Assessment of excellence	22.5%
Faculty resources	20%
Student selectivity	12.5%
Financial resources	10%
Graduation rate performance*	7.5%
Alumni giving	5%

*The difference between actual and predicted graduation rates.

measures that reflect schools' student bodies, faculties and resources. They also include outcome measures that signal how well institutions are engaging and educating their students. Outcome measures account for 30 percent of the rankings and are the most heavily weighted indicators.

An explanation of the measures and their weightings in the ranking formula follows; more detail on the methodology can be found at usnews.com/collegemeth.

Retention (22.5 percent). The higher the proportion of first-year students who return to campus for sophomore year and eventually graduate, the better a school most likely is at offering the classes and services that students need to succeed. This measure has two components: six-year graduation rate (80 percent of the retention score) and first-year retention rate (20 percent).

The graduation rate indicates the average proportion of a

DUKE UNIVERSITY

class earning a degree in six years or less. We consider freshman classes that started from fall 2007 through fall 2010. First-year student retention indicates the average proportion of freshmen who entered the school in the fall of 2012 through fall 2015 and returned the following fall.

A related measure, **graduation rate performance** (7.5 percent), shows the effect of programs and policies on the graduation rate when controlling for other factors that might influence the rate. These are spending per student, admissions selectivity, the proportion of undergraduates receiving Pell grants, and – new this year for national universities only – the proportion of undergrad degrees awarded in science, technology, engineering and mathematics disciplines. We compare a school's six-year graduation rate for the class that entered in 2010 to the graduation rate we predicted for that class. If the actual graduation rate is higher than the predicted rate, then the college is enhancing achievement.

Assessment by peers and counselors (22.5 percent). These assessments allow presidents, provosts and deans of admission to account for qualitative attributes of peer institutions, such as faculty dedication to teaching. The average academic peer scores are derived from a weighted average of the two most recent sets of survey results, collected in spring 2016 and spring 2017. For their views on the national universities and the national liberal arts colleges, we also surveyed 2,200 counselors sampled from a geographically and ethnically diverse group of public high schools that appeared in a recent U.S. News ranking of Best High Schools.

Each person surveyed was asked to rate schools' academic programs on a 5-point scale from 1 (marginal) to 5 (distinguished). Those who did not know enough about a school to evaluate it fairly were instructed to mark "don't know." The score used in the rankings is the weighted average of these scores; "don't knows" are not counted.

In the case of the national universities and national liberal arts colleges, the academic peer assessment accounts for 15 percentage points of the weighting, and 7.5 percentage points go to the counselors' ratings. The three most recent years' results were combined to compute the average high school counselor score. For the full results of the high school counselors' ratings of the colleges, visit usnews.com/counselors. In terms of reputation, the regional universities and the regional colleges are judged by peers only.

To reduce the possible impact of strategic voting by respondents, we eliminated the two highest and two lowest scores each school received before calculating the average score. Ipsos Public Affairs collected the most recent year's data in the spring of 2017; of the 4,608 academics who were sent questionnaires, 40.4 percent responded. The counselors' response rate for just this past spring was 7 percent.

Faculty resources (20 percent). Research shows that the more satisfied students are about their contact with professors, the more they will learn and the more likely they are to graduate. We use five factors from the 2016-17 academic year to assess a school's commitment to instruction.

Class size (40 percent of this measure) is expressed by a single index taking account of all the data schools reported on fall 2016 class size. Schools receive the most credit in this index for their proportion of undergraduate classes with fewer than 20 students. Classes with 20-29 students score second highest; those with 30-39 students, third highest; and those with 40-49 students, fourth highest. Classes that have 50 or more students receive no credit. Faculty salary (35 percent) is the average faculty pay, plus benefits, during the 2015-16 and 2016-17 academic years, adjusted for regional differences in the cost of living using indexes from the consulting firm Runzheimer International.

We also weigh the proportion of professors with the highest degree in their field (15 percent), the student-faculty ratio (5 percent), and the proportion of faculty who are full time (5 percent).

Student selectivity (12.5 percent). A school's academic atmosphere is determined in part by the abilities and ambitions of the students. We factor in the admissions test scores for all enrollees who took the critical reading and math portions of the SAT and the composite ACT score (65 percent of the selectivity score); the proportion of enrolled freshmen at national universities and national liberal arts colleges who graduated in the top 10 percent of their classes or in the top quarter at regional universities and regional colleges (25 percent); and the acceptance rate, or the ratio of students admitted to applicants (10 percent). The data are all for the fall 2016 entering class.

While the ranking calculation takes account of both SAT and ACT scores of all entering students, the table displays the score range for whichever test was taken by the larger share. Footnotes indicate schools that did not report fall 2016 test scores for all new students for whom they had scores (including athletes, international students, minority students, legacies, those admitted by special arrangement, and those who started in summer 2016) or schools that declined to tell us whether all students with scores were represented. We discounted the value of these schools' reported scores by 15 percent, since the effect could be that lower scores are omitted. If under 75 percent of the 2016 entering class submitted test scores, those scores were discounted by 15 percent. The SAT scores used in the rankings and published in this guidebook are for the SAT exam administered prior to March 2016.

Financial resources (10 percent). Generous per-student spending indicates that a college can offer a wide variety of programs and services. U.S. News measures financial resources by using the average spending per student on instruction, research, student services and related educational expenditures in the 2015 and 2016 fiscal years. Spending on sports, dorms and hospitals does not count.

Alumni giving rate (5 percent). This reflects the average percentage of living alumni with bachelor's degrees who gave to their school during 2014-15 and 2015-16 – an indirect measure of student satisfaction.

To arrive at a school's rank, we calculated the weighted sum of its standardized scores. The scores were rescaled so the top college or university in each category received a value of 100 and the other schools' weighted scores were calculated as a proportion of the top score. Final scores were rounded to the nearest whole number and ranked in descending order. Tied schools appear in alphabetical order.

Be sure to check out usnews.com regularly over the coming year, because we may add content to the Best Colleges pages as we obtain additional information. And as you mine the tables that follow for insights (a sense of which schools might be impressed enough by your ACT or SAT scores to offer some merit aid, for example, or where you will be apt to get the most attention from professors), keep in mind that the rankings provide a launching pad for more research, not an easy answer. ●

Best National Univer

Rank School (State) (*Public)	Overall score	Peer assessment score (5.0=highest)	High school counselor assessment score	Graduation and retention rank	Average first-year student retention rate	2016 graduation rate		Over-performance (+) Under-performance (-)	Fac reso ra
						Predicted	Actual		
1. Princeton University (NJ)	100	4.9	4.9	2	98%	96%	97%	+1	
2. Harvard University (MA)	98	4.9	5.0	2	97%	95%	97%	+2	
3. University of Chicago	96	4.6	4.8	11	99%	95%	94%	-1	
3. Yale University (CT)	96	4.8	5.0	1	99%	96%	98%	+2	
5. Columbia University (NY)	95	4.7	4.9	4	99%	95%	96%	+1	
5. Massachusetts Inst. of Technology	95	4.9	5.0	14	98%	95%	93%	-2	1
5. Stanford University (CA)	95	4.9	5.0	9	98%	94%	94%	None	1
8. University of Pennsylvania	93	4.5	4.8	4	98%	95%	95%	None	
9. Duke University (NC)	92	4.4	4.8	9	97%	95%	95%	None	
10. California Institute of Technology	91	4.6	4.6	14	97%	95%	94%	-1	
11. Dartmouth College (NH)	90	4.3	4.9	4	98%	95%	97%	+2	1
11. Johns Hopkins University (MD)	90	4.6	4.9	14	97%	95%	94%	-1	1
11. Northwestern University (IL)	90	4.4	4.6	11	98%	95%	94%	-1	
14. Brown University (RI)	86	4.4	4.9	4	98%	95%	96%	+1	1
14. Cornell University (NY)	86	4.6	4.9	14	97%	94%	94%	None	2
14. Rice University (TX)	86	4.1	4.7	21	97%	93%	93%	None	
14. Vanderbilt University (TN)	86	4.2	4.7	14	97%	94%	92%	-2	1
18. University of Notre Dame (IN)	85	4.1	4.7	4	98%	94%	95%	+1	1
18. Washington University in St. Louis	85	4.1	4.5	11	96%	96%	94%	-2	1
20. Georgetown University (DC)	80	4.1	4.8	14	96%	95%	94%	-1	3
21. Emory University (GA)	78	4.0	4.4	30	94%	93%	91%	-2	1
21. University of California–Berkeley*	78	4.7	4.7	21	97%	91%	92%	+1	4
21. Univ. of California–Los Angeles*	78	4.3	4.4	24	97%	90%	91%	+1	2
21. Univ. of Southern California	78	4.0	4.5	24	96%	93%	92%	-1	4
25. Carnegie Mellon University (PA)	76	4.3	4.6	32	96%	89%	90%	+1	2
25. University of Virginia*	76	4.2	4.5	14	97%	94%	94%	None	3
27. Wake Forest University (NC)	75	3.6	4.2	36	94%	92%	88%	-4	2
28. University of Michigan–Ann Arbor*	74	4.4	4.5	24	97%	94%	91%	-3	5
29. Tufts University (MA)	72	3.7	4.5	21	96%	94%	92%	-2	3
30. New York University	71	3.9	4.5	49	93%	85%	85%	None	2
30. U. of North Carolina–Chapel Hill*	71	4.0	4.5	28	97%	89%	91%	+2	9
32. Boston College	70	3.6	4.4	24	95%	92%	93%	+1	5
32. College of William & Mary (VA)*	70	3.8	4.3	28	96%	91%	91%	None	4
34. Brandeis University (MA)	68	3.6	4.2	32	93%	91%	90%	-1	4
34. Georgia Institute of Technology*	68	4.2	4.5	41	97%	90%	86%	-4	17
34. University of Rochester (NY)	68	3.4	3.9	38	96%	90%	85%	-5	2
37. Boston University	67	3.6	4.3	41	93%	83%	87%	+4	3
37. Case Western Reserve Univ. (OH)	67	3.7	4.2	60	93%	85%	82%	-3	5
37. Univ. of California–Santa Barbara*	67	3.5	3.9	56	93%	87%	88%	+1	1
40. Northeastern University (MA)	66	3.3	4.2	41	97%	80%	86%	+6	2
40. Tulane University (LA)	66	3.5	4.2	66	92%	85%	83%	-2	2
42. Rensselaer Polytechnic Inst. (NY)	65	3.5	4.4	56	93%	84%	83%	-1	4
42. University of California–Irvine*	65	3.6	4.1	38	92%	85%	87%	+2	2
42. Univ. of California–San Diego*	65	3.8	4.2	36	95%	87%	87%	None	15
42. University of Florida*	65	3.7	3.9	34	96%	83%	87%	+4	8
46. Lehigh University (PA)	64	3.2	4.0	34	95%	93%	89%	-4	4
46. Pepperdine University (CA)	64	3.3	4.3	49	92%	76%	87%	+11	3
46. University of California–Davis*	64	3.9	4.2	49	93%	86%	85%	-1	10
46. University of Miami (FL)	64	3.4	3.9	60	92%	86%	82%	-4	3
46. Univ. of Wisconsin–Madison*	64	4.0	4.0	41	95%	83%	85%	+2	12
46. Villanova University (PA)	64	3.2	4.1	30	95%	84%	90%	+6	10

More @ usnews.com/bestcolleges

Note: Key to footnotes, Page 78.

% of classes under 20 ('16)	% of classes of 50 or more ('16)	Student/ faculty ratio ('16)	Selectivity rank	SAT/ACT 25th-75th percentile** ('16)	Freshmen in top 10% of HS class ('16)	Acceptance rate ('16)	Financial resources rank	Alumni giving rank	Average alumni giving rate
73%	11%	5/1	6	1400-1590	94%[5]	7%	10	1	61%
74%	10%	7/1	3	1430-1600	95%[5]	5%	8	9	35%
77%	6%	5/1	1	1450-1600	98%	8%	4	3	41%
75%	8%	6/1	6	1420-1600	94%[5]	6%	1	17	30%
83%	9%	6/1	3	1430-1600	95%[5]	6%	12	14	32%
70%	13%	3/1	3	1460-1590	97%[5]	8%	3	8	36%
70%	12%	4/1	6	1380-1580	95%[5]	5%	4	11	34%
70%	10%	6/1	6	1380-1570	95%[5]	9%	12	7	36%
71%	7%	6/1	15	1380-1570	91%[5]	11%	15	9	34%
67%	9%	3/1	1	1510-1600	97%[5]	8%	2	22	25%
52%	8%	7/1	11	1350-1560	93%[5]	11%	15	2	45%
74%	10%	7/1	6	1420-1570	94%[5]	12%	6	6	37%
77%	6%	7/1	11	32-34	91%[5]	11%	9	18	28%
58%	11%	7/1	11	1370-1570	92%[5]	9%	22	13	32%
58%	18%	9/1	19	1330-1530	90%[5]	14%	17	20	27%
71%	8%	6/1	15	1410-1570	88%[5]	15%	20	11	34%
56%	9%	8/1	11	32-35	87%[5]	11%	12	22	25%
50%	10%	10/1	15	32-35	91%[5]	19%	27	3	41%
55%	11%	8/1	15	32-34	86%[5]	17%	6	26	24%
51%	7%	11/1	21	1320-1520	91%[5]	17%	37	15	31%
51%	13%	9/1	23	1290-1500	83%[5]	25%	18	33	21%
52%	17%	18/1	19	1300-1530	98%	16%	37	79	12%
57%	18%	17/1	26	1160-1460	97%	18%	19	140	8%
59%	12%	8/1	29	1280-1500	88%[5]	17%	22	3	41%
57%	12%	13/1	23	1380-1550	75%[5]	22%	37	56	15%
56%	15%	15/1	23	1240-1460	89%[5]	30%	55	33	21%
59%	1%	10/1	33	28-32[2]	78%[5]	30%	11	25	24%
50%	17%	15/1	37	29-33	74%[5]	29%	42	47	18%
58%	7%	8/1	57	31-34	N/A	14%	32	36	20%
50%	9%	10/1	39	1250-1480[2]	61%[5]	32%	32	110	10%
39%	14%	13/1	39	27-32	73%	27%	27	51	16%
49%	7%	12/1	28	1260-1460	80%[5]	31%	66	22	25%
49%	7%	12/1	33	1250-1470	78%[5]	37%	111	18	28%
52%	10%	10/1	32	1270-1480[2]	72%[5]	33%	49	33	21%
38%	26%	20/1	22	1320-1500	87%[5]	26%	55	26	24%
71%	12%	10/1	47	1250-1460[2]	68%[5]	38%	20	32	21%
51%	13%	10/1	45	1220-1420	63%[5]	29%	52	110	10%
59%	13%	11/1	29	30-34	71%[5]	35%	41	41	19%
49%	20%	17/1	33	1140-1390	100%	36%	69	54	16%
57%	6%	14/1	26	31-34	76%[5]	29%	81	92	11%
52%	6%	8/1	37	29-33	61%[5]	26%	46	51	17%
53%	13%	13/1	39	1280-1480	66%[5]	44%	65	92	11%
57%	21%	18/1	60	1060-1330	98%	41%	55	198	5%
36%	36%	19/1	29	1140-1420	100%	36%	22	198	5%
48%	15%	20/1	47	1180-1370	73%	46%	49	86	12%
50%	11%	9/1	43	1230-1420	64%[5]	26%	55	36	20%
59%	2%	14/1	79	1110-1330	49%[5]	37%	66	152	8%
38%	27%	20/1	57	1050-1330	100%	42%	32	162	7%
54%	7%	12/1	47	28-32	60%[5]	38%	26	67	14%
44%	21%	18/1	52	27-31	54%[5]	53%	61	67	13%
42%	3%	12/1	45	30-32	62%[5]	44%	103	21	26%

What Is a National University?

• • • •

To assess more than 1,600 of the country's four-year colleges and universities, U.S. News first assigns each to a group of its peers, based on the categories of higher education institutions developed by the Carnegie Foundation for the Advancement of Teaching and recently revised. The National Universities category consists of 311 institutions (190 public, 114 private and seven for-profit) that offer a wide range of undergraduate majors as well as master's and doctoral degrees; some emphasize research. A list of the top 30 public national universities appears on Page 78.

Data on up to 15 indicators of academic quality are gathered from each institution and tabulated. Schools are ranked by total weighted score; those tied at the same rank are listed alphabetically. For a description of the methodology, see Page 66. For more on a college, turn to the directory at the back of the book.

Rank School (State) (*Public)	Overall score	Peer assessment score (5.0=highest)	High school counselor assessment score	Average first-year student retention rate	2016 graduation rate Predicted	2016 graduation rate Actual	% of classes under 20 ('16)	% of classes of 50 or more ('16)	SAT/ACT 25th-75th percentile** ('16)	Freshmen in top 10% of HS class ('16)	Acceptance rate ('16)	Average alumni giving rate
52. Pennsylvania State U.–Univ. Park*	63	3.7	3.9	93%	65%	86%	28%	19%	1090-1300	36%[5]	56%	14%
52. U. of Illinois–Urbana-Champaign*	63	3.9	3.9	94%	82%	85%	40%	21%	26-32	49%[5]	60%	8%
54. Ohio State University–Columbus*	62	3.8	4.1	94%	78%	84%	30%	22%	27-31	63%[5]	54%	14%
54. University of Georgia*	62	3.5	4.1	95%	79%	85%	46%	11%	1140-1340	55%	54%	13%
56. George Washington University (DC)	61	3.6	4.4	92%	90%	84%	51%	10%	1180-1390[2]	55%[5]	40%	9%
56. Purdue Univ.–West Lafayette (IN)*	61	3.8	4.2	92%	70%	77%	38%	18%	1080-1330	43%[5]	56%	19%
56. University of Connecticut*	61	3.3	3.9	93%	74%	82%	51%	15%	1130-1340	51%[5]	49%	11%
56. University of Texas–Austin*	61	4.0	4.2	95%	84%	81%	35%	26%	1140-1410	70%	40%	12%
56. University of Washington*	61	3.9	3.9	94%	84%	84%	32%	24%	1120-1370	62%[5]	45%	12%
61. Brigham Young Univ.–Provo (UT)	60	3.1	3.8	88%	76%	83%	55%	14%	27-31	55%	51%	13%
61. Fordham University (NY)	60	3.2	4.1	91%	76%	80%	50%	1%	1170-1370	46%[5]	45%	15%
61. Southern Methodist University (TX)	60	3.1	3.8	90%	79%	79%	59%	9%	28-32	49%[5]	49%	24%
61. Syracuse University (NY)	60	3.3	3.9	92%	68%	82%	59%	10%	1090-1290	36%[5]	52%	15%
61. Univ. of Maryland–College Park*	60	3.6	4.0	95%	84%	87%	45%	17%	1210-1420	71%[5]	48%	8%
61. Worcester Polytechnic Inst. (MA)	60	3.0	3.8	96%	81%	86%	65%	10%	1200-1400[2]	65%[5]	48%	11%
67. Clemson University (SC)*	59	3.3	4.0	93%	77%	81%	51%	15%	26-31	57%	51%	23%
68. University of Pittsburgh*	58	3.5	3.7	92%	76%	81%	41%	20%	1190-1380	52%[5]	55%	10%
69. American University (DC)	57	3.2	4.0	89%	81%	81%	52%	1%	1150-1340[2]	35%[5]	26%	6%
69. Rutgers University–New Brunswick (NJ)*	57	3.4	4.0	92%	71%	80%	38%	22%	1110-1350	41%[5]	57%	8%
69. Stevens Institute of Technology (NJ)	57	2.8	3.8	94%	77%	83%	36%	9%	1260-1440[2]	65%[5]	39%	17%
69. Texas A&M Univ.–College Station*	57	3.6	4.1	91%	76%	80%	22%	26%	1070-1310	66%	66%	17%
69. Univ. of Minnesota–Twin Cities*	57	3.7	3.8	92%	77%	78%	36%	21%	26-31	48%	44%	9%
69. Virginia Tech*	57	3.5	4.1	93%	74%	84%	29%	21%	1100-1320	40%	71%	11%
75. Baylor University (TX)	56	3.1	3.9	89%	72%	74%	52%	9%	26-30	41%	40%	17%
75. Colorado School of Mines*	56	3.3	4.3	93%	79%	77%	35%	21%	29-32	56%[5]	40%	13%
75. Univ. of Massachusetts–Amherst*	56	3.4	3.8	90%	65%	76%	49%	17%	1130-1330	34%[5]	60%	9%
78. Miami University–Oxford (OH)*	55	3.2	3.8	91%	67%	78%	36%	10%	26-31	39%[5]	65%	20%
78. Texas Christian University	55	2.9	3.6	90%	71%	77%	43%	5%	25-30	44%[5]	38%	19%
78. University of Iowa*	55	3.6	3.6	86%	69%	72%	52%	12%	23-28	28%	84%	10%
81. Clark University (MA)	54	2.9	3.5	88%	70%	75%	59%	5%	1110-1325[2]	36%[5]	55%	18%
81. Florida State University*	54	3.2	3.6	93%	71%	80%	33%	17%	25-29	41%	58%	20%
81. Michigan State University*	54	3.6	3.8	92%	68%	78%	27%	23%	24-29	30%[5]	66%	8%
81. North Carolina State U.–Raleigh*	54	3.2	3.5	94%	72%	78%	38%	15%	27-31	50%	46%	11%
81. Univ. of California–Santa Cruz*	54	3.1	3.8	90%	81%	79%	49%	24%	1060-1300	96%	59%	4%
81. University of Delaware*	54	3.2	3.7	92%	75%	83%	33%	16%	1090-1300	31%[5]	65%	8%
87. Binghamton University–SUNY*	53	3.0	3.5	91%	73%	83%	46%	13%	1230-1400	N/A	41%	6%
87. University of Denver	53	2.9	3.6	86%	77%	79%	53%	5%	26-31	42%[5]	53%	9%
87. University of Tulsa (OK)	53	2.7	3.5	90%	87%	73%	62%	3%	26-33	76%[5]	37%	20%
90. Indiana University–Bloomington*	52	3.6	3.8	90%	72%	76%	35%	18%	1060-1290	35%[5]	79%	11%
90. Marquette University (WI)	52	3.1	3.9	90%	75%	81%	40%	14%	24-29	31%[5]	74%[4]	14%
90. University of Colorado–Boulder*	52	3.6	3.7	86%	70%	70%	46%	16%	25-30	29%[5]	77%	6%
90. University of San Diego	52	2.9	3.7	89%	76%	78%	41%	0%	26-30	39%[5]	51%	12%
94. Drexel University (PA)	51	3.1	3.8	86%	70%	70%	57%	9%	1080-1300	40%[5]	75%	7%
94. Saint Louis University	51	2.9	3.7	89%	76%	77%	51%	7%	24-30	41%[5]	65%	11%
94. Yeshiva University (NY)	51	2.8	N/A	90%	80%	82%	55%	1%	1090-1360	N/A	51%	12%
97. Rochester Inst. of Technology (NY)	50	3.3	4.2	87%	68%	68%	49%	5%	1140-1330	39%	55%	6%
97. Stony Brook–SUNY*	50	3.2	3.5	90%	69%	72%	38%	24%	1150-1370	48%[5]	41%	10%
97. SUNY Col. of Envir. Sci. and Forestry*	50	2.7	3.4	84%	65%	74%	50%	10%	1070-1260	36%	54%	18%
97. University at Buffalo–SUNY*	50	3.1	3.4	88%	66%	74%	31%	23%	1070-1270	27%[5]	59%	9%
97. University of Oklahoma*	50	3.1	3.6	86%	72%	67%	47%	11%	23-29	36%	71%	17%
97. University of Vermont*	50	3.0	3.5	86%	69%	74%	48%	14%	1100-1300	33%[5]	69%	10%
103. Auburn University (AL)*	49	3.3	3.8	90%	78%	75%	32%	16%	24-30	30%	81%	13%
103. Illinois Institute of Technology	49	2.8	3.6	92%	74%	71%	53%	9%	26-31	60%[5]	57%	7%
103. Loyola University Chicago	49	3.0	3.8	85%	71%	75%	42%	6%	24-29	34%[5]	73%	6%
103. University of New Hampshire*	49	2.9	3.5	86%	61%	78%	42%	17%	990-1200	19%	76%	7%
103. University of Oregon*	49	3.3	3.7	87%	63%	72%	40%	21%	980-1220	25%[5]	78%	9%
103. Univ. of South Carolina*	49	3.1	3.7	88%	68%	73%	36%	17%	25-30	28%	68%	15%
103. University of Tennessee*	49	3.2	3.6	86%	71%	69%	30%	13%	24-30	54%[4]	77%	10%

Note: Key to footnotes, Page 78.

FARAI SIMOYI, Fashion, Dress and Merchandising, '05
President and Creative Director, Farai Inc.
GC4W: Top 100 Women in the World | Featured by **Forbes**

DESIGN YOUR FUTURE.

With resources like faculty mentors, industry coaches and hands-on experience, West Virginia University students land dream jobs and internships at Fortune 500 companies. Think Facebook, Amazon, Marathon Petroleum, GE and Disney. Or they become entrepreneurs like fashion designer Farai Simoyi, who designed for Beyoncé and Nicki Minaj with her unique creations.

MOUNTAINEERS GO FIRST.

WestVirginiaUniversity. | wvu.edu

Rank	School (State) (*Public)	Overall score	Peer assessment score (5.0=highest)	High school counselor assessment score	Average first-year student retention rate	2016 graduation rate Predicted	2016 graduation rate Actual	% of classes under 20 ('16)	% of classes of 50 or more ('16)	SAT/ACT 25th-75th percentile** ('16)	Freshmen in top 10% of HS class ('16)	Acceptance rate ('16)	Average alumni giving rate
110.	Howard University (DC)	48	3.0	3.9	86%	54%	61%	55%	5%	1040-1240[3]	28%[5]	30%	10%
110.	University of Alabama*	48	3.2	3.7	87%	73%	69%	36%	22%	23-31	37%	53%	30%
110.	University of San Francisco	48	2.9	3.7	86%	62%	72%	52%	1%	1030-1250	25%[5]	71%	6%
110.	University of the Pacific (CA)	48	2.6	3.5	85%	66%	68%	58%	4%	1030-1300	37%[5]	66%	7%
110.	University of Utah*	48	3.1	3.4	89%	65%	65%	40%	18%	21-27	35%[5]	76%	10%
115.	Arizona State University–Tempe*	47	3.4	3.6	86%	60%	67%	41%	18%	22-28[2]	30%	83%	11%
115.	Iowa State University*	47	3.3	3.5	87%	68%	74%	29%	25%	22-28	22%	87%	12%
115.	Temple University (PA)*	47	3.0	3.7	90%	59%	70%	38%	9%	1050-1280[2]	24%[5]	52%	6%
115.	University of Kansas*	47	3.3	3.6	80%	70%	63%	52%	11%	23-29	26%	93%	13%
115.	University of St. Thomas (MN)	47	2.5	3.4	88%	70%	76%	41%	2%	24-29	25%[5]	83%	15%
120.	Catholic University of America (DC)	46	2.8	3.6	84%	67%	70%	63%	3%	1040-1250[2]	N/A	80%	9%
120.	DePaul University (IL)	46	2.9	3.7	85%	64%	73%	41%	1%	22-28[2]	23%[5]	70%	6%
120.	Duquesne University (PA)	46	2.7	3.6	88%	65%	77%	42%	8%	1055-1230[2]	25%	74%	7%
120.	Univ. of Missouri*	46	3.2	3.6	86%	70%	68%	40%	18%	23-29	30%	75%	14%
124.	Clarkson University (NY)	45	2.6	3.3	90%	65%	72%	41%	24%	1080-1283	38%	68%	15%
124.	Colorado State University*	45	3.0	3.5	87%	63%	67%	35%	19%	22-28	21%	78%	11%
124.	Michigan Technological University*	45	2.7	3.8	84%	68%	67%	46%	16%	25-30	29%	76%	10%
124.	Seton Hall University (NJ)	45	2.8	3.7	85%	60%	64%	49%	2%	1070-1250	34%[5]	67%	9%
124.	University of Arizona*	45	3.6	3.7	81%	63%	60%	39%	16%	21-27[2]	28%[5]	79%	7%
124.	Univ. of California–Riverside*	45	3.0	3.5	90%	72%	73%	20%	31%	940-1190	94%	66%	3%
124.	University of Dayton (OH)	45	2.6	3.4	90%	71%	75%	40%	4%	24-29[3]	27%[5]	60%	13%[4]
124.	Univ. of Nebraska–Lincoln*	45	3.2	3.4	83%	68%	67%	37%	18%	22-28	24%	75%	18%
132.	Hofstra University (NY)	44	2.8	3.6	80%	68%	64%	49%	3%	1070-1260[2]	27%[5]	62%	11%
133.	Louisiana State Univ.–Baton Rouge*	43	2.9	3.6	84%	70%	68%	36%	22%	23-28	25%	76%	11%
133.	Mercer University (GA)	43	2.4	3.7	84%	67%	66%	64%	4%	25-29	39%	69%	10%
133.	The New School (NY)	43	2.8	3.6	82%	61%	68%	91%	1%	1030-1280[2]	18%[5]	60%	2%
133.	Rutgers University–Newark (NJ)*	43	2.8	3.9	85%	58%	66%	31%	15%	910-1100	20%	65%	5%
133.	University of Arkansas*	43	2.9	3.4	82%	70%	64%	48%	18%	23-29	25%	63%	22%
133.	University of Cincinnati*	43	2.8	3.2	87%	60%	67%	39%	16%	23-28	19%	76%	12%
133.	University of Kentucky*	43	3.1	3.6	83%	70%	64%	31%	16%	22-28	30%[5]	91%	14%
140.	George Mason University (VA)*	42	3.1	3.8	88%	62%	70%	30%	14%	1060-1250[2]	21%[5]	81%	3%
140.	New Jersey Inst. of Technology*	42	2.6	3.5	87%	58%	61%	37%	5%	1110-1310[3]	31%[5]	59%	8%
140.	San Diego State University*	42	2.9	3.6	89%	55%	74%	27%	25%	1000-1220	31%[5]	35%	5%
140.	University of South Florida*	42	2.7	3.4	89%	60%	67%	31%	14%	1070-1250	35%	47%	10%
140.	Washington State University*	42	3.0	3.6	79%	63%	67%	34%	20%	930-1165	36%[5]	72%	13%
145.	Kansas State University*	41	3.0	3.4	83%	64%	63%	41%	14%	22-28[2]	24%	94%	22%
145.	Oregon State University*	41	3.0	3.5	84%	60%	63%	29%	21%	990-1240	28%	77%	10%
145.	St. John Fisher College (NY)	41	2.3	3.3	86%	60%	73%	45%	1%	970-1150	25%	65%	9%
145.	University of Illinois–Chicago*	41	3.0	3.5	80%	61%	58%	38%	20%	21-27	27%	74%	3%
145.	University of Mississippi*	41	2.9	3.5	86%	63%	60%	41%	17%	22-29[2]	25%	78%	16%
145.	University of Texas–Dallas*	41	2.8	3.7	87%	71%	68%	24%	24%	1140-1380	32%	68%	3%
151.	Adelphi University (NY)	40	2.3	3.1	83%	60%	68%	46%	3%	1010-1210[9]	31%[5]	70%	10%
151.	Florida Institute of Technology	40	2.4	3.5	80%	50%	58%	45%	5%	1060-1260	33%[5]	61%	5%
151.	Ohio University*	40	3.0	3.5	80%	55%	64%	30%	18%	21-26	15%	75%	5%
151.	Seattle Pacific University	40	2.4	3.5	85%	59%	71%	56%	3%	990-1230	1%[4]	87%	6%
151.	University at Albany–SUNY*	40	2.9	3.3	83%	60%	66%	36%	16%	1010-1170[3]	16%[5]	54%	7%
156.	Oklahoma State University*	39	2.8	3.5	81%	65%	63%	32%	16%	21-27	25%	75%	11%
156.	Univ. of Massachusetts–Lowell*	39	2.5	3.3	85%	55%	56%	53%	5%	1070-1260[2]	25%[5]	60%	12%
156.	University of Rhode Island*	39	2.8	3.5	83%	56%	63%	42%	10%	990-1190[3]	18%	71%	6%
159.	Biola University (CA)	38	2.0	3.5	85%	63%	72%	48%	6%	950-1220	30%[5]	65%	7%
159.	Illinois State University*	38	2.5	3.3	82%	62%	72%	32%	10%	21-26	N/A	89%	7%
159.	University of Alabama–Birmingham*	38	2.8	3.4	81%	65%	53%	37%	18%	21-28	28%	89%	9%
159.	University of Hawaii–Manoa*	38	2.7	3.3	78%	61%	58%	52%	12%	970-1190	26%	80%	6%
159.	University of La Verne (CA)	38	2.0	3.2	87%	53%	66%	68%	0.4%	930-1130	18%[5]	48%	6%
159.	Univ. of Maryland–Baltimore County*	38	2.8	3.4	87%	67%	64%	36%	14%	1120-1320	24%	57%	4%
165.	Immaculata University (PA)	37	2.0	3.2	81%	47%	68%	86%	0%	860-1080[2]	15%	82%	8%
165.	Maryville Univ. of St. Louis	37	1.9	3.4	87%	68%	75%	69%	0.4%	22-27[2]	28%	93%	9%
165.	Missouri Univ. of Science & Tech.*	37	2.7	3.5	84%[8]	71%	64%	25%	27%	25-31	33%	79%	14%

Note: Key to footnotes, Page 78.

Rank	School (State) (*Public)	Overall score	Peer assessment score (5.0=highest)	High school counselor assessment score	Average first-year student retention rate	2016 graduation rate Predicted	Actual	% of classes under 20 ('16)	% of classes of 50 or more ('16)	SAT/ACT 25th-75th percentile** ('16)	Freshmen in top 10% of HS class ('16)	Acceptance rate ('16)	Average alumni giving rate
165.	St. John's University (NY)	37	2.8	3.6	81%	57%	58%	32%	5%	970-1180[2]	18%[5]	63%	5%
165.	University of California–Merced*	37	2.7	3.6	85%[8]	55%	66%	26%	29%	860-1070[3]	N/A	74%	10%
165.	University of Louisville (KY)*	37	2.8	3.5	80%	65%	53%	36%	8%	22-29[3]	29%[5]	73%	13%[4]
171.	Mississippi State University*	36	2.6	3.3	80%	61%	60%	35%	15%	21-28	28%	71%	16%
171.	Rowan University (NJ)*†	36	2.3	N/A	87%	57%	71%	38%	1%	990-1210	N/A	58%	3%
171.	University of Central Florida*	36	2.7	3.2	88%	67%	69%	27%	24%	1080-1270	33%	50%	8%
171.	University of Idaho*	36	2.7	3.3	78%	57%	56%	53%	9%	930-1170	19%	76%	10%
171.	Virginia Commonwealth University*	36	2.8	3.5	87%	59%	62%	31%	18%	980-1200[2]	19%	75%	5%
176.	Kent State University (OH)*	35	2.6	3.3	81%	43%	54%	52%	8%	21-25	15%	85%	4%
176.	Robert Morris University (PA)	35	2.2	2.9	82%	50%	61%	55%	4%	940-1140	14%	80%	6%
176.	Texas Tech University*	35	2.8	3.5	83%	61%	60%	28%	21%	1020-1200	21%	63%	11%
176.	Union University (TN)	35	1.9	N/A	89%	70%	68%	74%	0%	23-30[3]	32%[5]	63%	5%
176.	University of Hartford (CT)	35	2.4	3.3	75%	53%	60%	72%	1%	920-1160	N/A	72%	4%
181.	Edgewood College (WI)	34	1.8	N/A	81%	53%	63%	83%	0%	21-25	15%	78%	8%
181.	Lesley University (MA)	34	2.1	3.3	78%	51%	55%	69%	0%	960-1170	15%[4]	64%	4%
181.	Lipscomb University (TN)	34	2.0	3.3	81%	66%	58%	59%	5%	22-28	30%[5]	61%	13%
181.	Suffolk University (MA)	34	2.3	3.2	75%	53%	59%	48%	0.2%	910-1120	19%[6]	84%	5%
181.	University of Maine*	34	2.7	3.3	78%	57%	59%	39%	16%	950-1190	18%	90%	7%
181.	University of Wyoming*	34	2.7	3.3	75%	64%	55%	39%	11%	21-27	22%	95%	9%[7]
187.	Azusa Pacific University (CA)	33	2.1	3.3	85%	63%	70%	58%	2%	930-1160	N/A	84%	N/A
187.	Ball State University (IN)*	33	2.6	3.2	81%	57%	62%	42%	6%	990-1170[9]	17%	62%	9%
187.	Montclair State University (NJ)*	33	2.2	2.8	83%	50%	65%	39%	2%	870-1070[2]	11%	66%	4%
187.	Pace University (NY)	33	2.5	3.2	77%	55%	58%	49%	2%	940-1160[2]	15%[5]	84%	4%
187.	West Virginia University*	33	2.8	3.2	78%	58%	57%	38%	18%	21-26	20%	76%	10%
192.	Andrews University (MI)	32	1.8	N/A	81%	58%	63%	70%	4%	21-29	20%	40%	5%
192.	Indiana U.–Purdue U.–Indianapolis^	32	2.9	3.7	73%	51%	47%	34%	11%	890-1130	16%	74%	7%
192.	University of Houston^	32	2.7	3.4	86%	58%	51%	27%	24%	1040-1250	32%	59%	13%
192.	University of New Mexico*	32	2.8	3.3	79%	52%	44%	55%	11%	19-25	N/A	47%	4%[4]
192.	University of North Dakota*	32	2.6	3.4	79%	61%	55%	38%	9%	21-26[3]	18%	84%	7%
192.	Widener University (PA)	32	2.2	3.0	78%	52%	57%	54%	2%	930-1130	9%[5]	70%	3%
198.	New Mexico State University*	31	2.5	3.2	74%	38%	45%	47%	10%	18-24	22%	60%	6%
198.	North Dakota State University*	31	2.5	3.3	79%	58%	55%	32%	22%	21-26	16%	93%	7%
198.	Nova Southeastern University (FL)	31	2.0	3.0	75%	54%	50%	82%	1%	1000-1220	30%[5]	53%	2%
198.	U. of North Carolina–Charlotte*	31	2.7	3.6	82%	53%	57%	29%	24%	22-26	22%	62%	3%
202.	Bowling Green State University (OH)*	30	2.5	3.3	75%	51%	53%	42%	9%	20-25	12%	75%	6%
202.	California State U.–Fullerton*	30	2.5	3.3	89%	50%	62%	23%	9%	920-1120	20%[5]	48%	2%[7]
202.	Dallas Baptist University	30	1.9	2.9	73%	55%	59%	66%	2%	19-25	19%	43%	1%
202.	Univ. of Massachusetts–Boston*	30	2.6	3.5	79%	50%	45%	41%	6%	960-1180[9]	15%[5]	69%	5%
202.	University of Nevada–Reno*	30	2.5	2.9	81%	61%	54%	40%	21%	21-26	23%	83%	9%
207.	Central Michigan University*	29	2.3	3.1	77%	55%	57%	33%	7%	20-25	14%[5]	72%	5%
207.	East Carolina University (NC)*	29	2.4	3.2	81%	53%	60%	30%	18%	970-1130	14%	70%	3%
207.	Florida A&M University*	29	2.2	3.3	83%	36%	41%	36%	12%	19-24	16%[5]	31%	6%
207.	Montana State University*	29	2.5	3.2	76%	60%	53%	42%	15%	21-28	20%	83%	9%
207.	University of Alaska–Fairbanks*	29	2.4	3.1	76%	55%	40%	69%	5%	19-26	19%	73%	4%
207.	University of Colorado–Denver*	29	2.8	3.4	72%	61%	48%	35%	9%	21-26	14%[5]	61%	3%
207.	Univ. of Massachusetts–Dartmouth*	29	2.6	3.6	76%	52%	49%	41%	10%	910-1130	13%[4]	76%	3%
207.	University of Montana*	29	2.7	3.3	72%	54%	48%	49%	9%	20-26	17%	92%	8%
207.	Western Michigan University*	29	2.4	3.0	78%	57%	53%	40%	11%	19-25	12%	82%	4%
216.	Florida International University*	28	2.4	3.1	86%	58%	56%	21%	22%	1030-1210	18%[5]	49%	4%
216.	Louisiana Tech University*	28	2.4	3.2	80%	63%	53%	48%	9%	21-27	25%	63%	10%
216.	South Dakota State University*	28	2.5	3.4	77%	59%	54%	29%	18%	20-26	14%	91%	8%
216.	Southern Illinois U.–Carbondale*	28	2.3	3.0	66%	55%	45%	60%	6%	19-25	11%	77%	5%
216.	University of Alabama–Huntsville*	28	2.4	3.2	80%	66%	49%	31%	17%	25-31	29%[5]	76%	3%
216.	Univ. of Missouri–Kansas City*	28	2.5	3.2	74%	64%	49%	56%	10%	21-28	31%	62%	6%
216.	Utah State University*	28	2.6	3.2	70%	58%	46%	46%	13%	20-27	19%	90%	6%
223.	Ashland University (OH)	27	1.8	3.1	77%	57%	62%	50%	0.2%	20-25	15%	72%	5%
223.	Benedictine University (IL)	27	2.0	2.9	70%	52%	51%	64%	0.3%	20-26	13%[5]	73%	N/A
223.	California State Univ.–Fresno*	27	2.5	3.3	82%	42%	56%	19%	10%	800-1010	15%	54%	3%

Rank School (State) (*Public)	Overall score	Peer assessment score (5.0=highest)	High school counselor assessment score	Average first-year student retention rate	2016 graduation rate Predicted	2016 graduation rate Actual	% of classes under 20 ('16)	% of classes of 50 or more ('16)	SAT/ACT 25th-75th percentile** ('16)	Freshmen in top 10% of HS class ('16)	Acceptance rate ('16)	Average alumni giving rate
223. Gardner-Webb University (NC)	27	1.9	3.1	73%	47%	45%	72%	0%	870-1110	16%	52%	8%
223. Georgia State University*	27	2.7	3.4	82%	55%	53%	21%	17%	950-1180[3]	17%[5]	53%	5%
223. Shenandoah University (VA)	27	1.9	2.9	78%	54%	57%	57%	1%	880-1120	15%[4]	88%	5%
223. University of South Dakota*	27	2.6	3.3	76%	58%	55%	47%	8%	19-25[2]	1%	88%	6%[7]
223. Wayne State University (MI)*	27	2.5	3.1	78%	51%	39%	53%	8%	20-27	24%[5]	68%	5%

School (State) (*Public)	Peer assessment score (5.0=highest)	High school counselor assessment score	Average first-year student retention rate	2016 graduation rate Predicted	2016 graduation rate Actual	% of classes under 20 ('16)	% of classes of 50 or more ('16)	SAT/ACT 25th-75th percentile** ('16)	Freshmen in top 10% of HS class ('16)	Acceptance rate ('16)	Average alumni giving rate
SCHOOLS RANKED 231 THROUGH 300 ARE LISTED HERE ALPHABETICALLY											
American International College (MA)	1.7	2.7	68%[8]	41%	40%[8]	51%[4]	4%[4]	790-980[4]	N/A	64%[4]	8%[4]
Augusta University (GA)*	2.1	3.2	73%[8]	60%	26%	N/A	N/A	N/A	N/A	74%[4]	2%
Barry University (FL)	1.9	3.1	63%[8]	39%	31%	78%	0%	850-1010	N/A	62%	2%
Boise State University (ID)*	2.6	3.3	75%	51%	39%	34%	11%	910-1150[2]	13%	82%	7%
Cardinal Stritch University (WI)	1.8	N/A	71%[8]	45%	52%	74%	0%	18-22[2]	20%[4]	82%	3%
Clark Atlanta University	2.2	3.0	65%	30%	38%	33%	7%	18-21	9%	72%	N/A
Cleveland State University*	2.2	2.9	70%	46%	41%	35%	11%	19-25	14%	88%	4%
Eastern Michigan University*	2.3	2.8	74%	49%	41%	38%	4%	19-25	13%	73%	2%
East Tennessee State University*	2.0	2.8	69%	54%	40%	47%	8%	20-26	20%	80%	3%
Florida Atlantic University*	2.3	3.1	76%	53%	50%	30%	17%	950-1150	15%	60%	3%
Georgia Southern University*	2.3	3.3	81%	56%	51%	25%	11%	22-26	18%	65%	6%
Grand Canyon University[1] (AZ)	1.7	2.8	63%[8]	32%	31%[6]	N/A	N/A	N/A[2]	N/A	43%[4]	N/A
Indiana State University*	2.5	3.3	64%	41%	38%	29%	10%	790-1020	9%	86%	4%
Indiana Univ. of Pennsylvania*	2.2	2.7	75%	44%	54%	31%	14%	840-1050[3]	8%	92%	5%
Jackson State University (MS)*	1.9	2.7	75%[8]	32%	38%	40%	10%	16-24	N/A	69%	N/A
Kennesaw State University (GA)*	2.2	3.0	78%	55%	42%	33%	12%	21-26	21%[5]	59%	3%
Lamar University (TX)*	1.9	2.7	59%	42%	33%	34%	9%	860-1050	14%	76%	2%
Liberty University (VA)	1.7	2.9	80%	48%	54%	32%	4%	950-1190[3]	26%[5]	28%	1%
Lindenwood University (MO)	1.7	N/A	69%	55%	49%	68%	0.1%	20-25[2]	15%	55%	5%
Middle Tennessee State Univ.*	2.1	2.9	72%	51%	43%	46%	7%	19-25	N/A	69%	4%
Morgan State University (MD)*	2.1	2.8	75%	37%	33%	42%	2%	800-990	N/A	60%	11%
National Louis University[1] (IL)	1.8	N/A	72%[8]	38%	34%[6]	N/A	N/A	N/A[2]	N/A	81%[4]	N/A
North Carolina A&T State Univ.*	2.0	3.0	77%	31%	43%	26%	10%	850-1010	11%	54%	8%
Northern Arizona University*	2.5	3.3	74%	55%	53%	28%	17%	940-1160[2]	21%	78%	3%
Northern Illinois University*	2.4	3.1	71%	53%	47%	48%	9%	19-25	12%	52%	4%
Oakland University (MI)*	2.1	3.1	77%	56%	47%	37%	14%	20-27	18%	86%	4%
Old Dominion University (VA)*	2.5	3.3	80%	52%	51%	36%	10%	890-1140[2]	9%	85%	5%
Portland State University (OR)*	2.7	3.3	72%[8]	50%	46%	31%	16%	19-25[2]	11%	89%	3%[4]
Prairie View A&M University (TX)*	1.8	2.6	67%	27%	31%	21%	10%	750-940	5%	85%	N/A
Regent University (VA)	1.8	3.1	78%	50%	46%	57%	0%	920-1140	10%[5]	83%	3%
Sam Houston State University (TX)*	2.2	2.9	78%	50%	51%	27%	13%	870-1070	14%	72%	8%
San Francisco State University*	2.6	3.3	82%	48%	53%	27%	13%	860-1090	N/A	68%	2%
Spalding University[1] (KY)	1.7	N/A	75%[8]	38%	40%[6]	N/A	N/A	18-23[4]	N/A	50%[4]	N/A
Tennessee State University*	2.0	3.0	47%[8]	33%	27%	78%	2%	16-20	N/A	53%	N/A
Tennessee Technological Univ.*	2.2	N/A	76%	59%	51%	43%	10%	21-27	32%	67%	7%
Texas A&M University–Commerce*	2.2	3.4	68%	43%	43%	32%	5%	850-1060	15%	45%	3%
Texas A&M Univ.–Corpus Christi*	2.2	3.5	57%	44%	37%	18%	22%	850-1060	8%	86%	2%
Texas A&M Univ.–Kingsville*	2.1	3.3	67%	28%	29%	36%	6%	17-23[2]	16%	82%	1%
Texas Southern University*	2.0	2.9	51%	24%	17%	37%	14%	715-900	6%	51%	2%[4]
Texas State University*	2.2	3.1	77%	54%	54%	26%	16%	930-1120	14%	71%	4%
Texas Woman's University*	2.2	3.1	71%	44%	38%	47%	8%	820-1050[2]	14%	86%	1%
Trevecca Nazarene University (TN)	1.6	N/A	78%	50%	48%	71%	4%	19-25[3]	N/A	72%	N/A
Trinity International Univ. (IL)	1.8	N/A	70%	54%	40%	47%	0.4%	19-26	15%[4]	88%	N/A
University of Akron (OH)*	2.2	2.9	72%	48%	43%	42%	9%	19-26	16%	96%	10%
Univ. of Arkansas–Little Rock*	2.3	2.9	74%	48%	28%	59%	2%	19-25[3]	14%	77%	3%[4]
University of Louisiana–Lafayette*	2.2	3.2	75%	53%	45%	35%	9%	21-26	21%	52%	7%
University of Louisiana–Monroe*	2.1	3.1	72%	53%	43%	36%	13%	19-25	25%	86%	4%

Note: Key to footnotes, Page 78.

School (State) (*Public)	Peer assessment score (5.0=highest)	High school counselor assessment score	Average first-year student retention rate	2016 graduation rate		% of classes under 20 ('16)	% of classes of 50 or more ('16)	SAT/ACT 25th-75th percentile** ('16)	Freshmen in top 10% of HS class ('16)	Accept- ance rate ('16)	Average alumni giving rate
				Predicted	Actual						
SCHOOLS RANKED 231 THROUGH 300 ARE LISTED HERE ALPHABETICALLY											
Univ. of Maryland–Eastern Shore*	2.1	2.9	67%	35%	36%	56%	3%	790-950	N/A	38%	3%
University of Memphis*	2.5	3.1	75%	49%	43%	45%	11%	19-25	13%	94%	6%
Univ. of Missouri–St. Louis*	2.4	3.2	77%	61%	53%	53%	7%	21-27	26%	71%	5%
University of Nebraska–Omaha*	2.5	3.4	77%	58%	45%	38%	10%	19-26	15%	86%	5%
University of Nevada–Las Vegas*	2.5	3.0	76%	55%	41%	26%	16%	19-24	20%	83%	4%
University of New Orleans*	2.1	2.9	66%	55%	36%	42%	10%	20-24	12%	60%	3%
U. of North Carolina–Greensboro*	2.6	3.5	76%	50%	54%	21%	25%	910-1100[3]	14%	74%	6%
University of Northern Colorado*	2.3	3.2	69%	53%	48%	37%	11%	19-25	13%	90%	3%
University of North Texas*	2.5	3.1	78%	60%	53%	25%	23%	980-1200[3]	20%	72%	4%
University of South Alabama*	2.0	3.0	71%	53%	38%	44%	9%	20-26[2]	N/A	80%	N/A
Univ. of Southern Mississippi*	2.2	3.0	73%	52%	45%	42%	9%	20-26	N/A	60%	8%
University of Texas–Arlington*	2.6	3.4	71%	57%	48%	31%	27%	950-1190	31%	70%	2%
University of Texas–El Paso*	2.4	3.1	71%[8]	37%	39%	32%	14%	810-1030	17%	100%	4%
University of Texas–Rio Grande Valley*	2.2	N/A	N/A	47%	41%[6]	N/A	N/A	18-22	24%	63%	N/A
University of Texas–San Antonio*	2.5	3.3	67%	49%	35%	19%	30%	920-1130	18%	76%	6%
University of the Cumberlands (KY)	1.7	N/A	62%	54%	43%	59%	1%	19-25	14%	71%	3%
University of Toledo (OH)*	2.3	3.0	71%	53%	43%	36%	15%	20-26	18%	94%	5%
University of West Florida*	2.0	3.1	72%	56%	49%	37%	9%	21-26	12%	41%	4%
University of West Georgia*	2.0	2.7	73%	42%	41%	30%	10%	870-1020	N/A	59%	3%
Univ. of Wisconsin–Milwaukee*	2.7	3.4	71%	53%	39%	41%	11%	20-25[2]	9%	72%	3%
Valdosta State University (GA)*	1.9	3.0	70%	45%	36%	52%	5%	890-1060	N/A	65%	2%
Wichita State University (KS)*	2.4	3.1	72%	57%	46%	48%	11%	21-27[2]	19%	92%	7%
Wright State University (OH)*	2.3	2.9	65%	48%	36%	27%	29%	18-25	18%	95%	4%

STANFORD
UNIVERSITY

THE UNIVERSITY OF
PENNSYLVANIA

▶The Top 30 Public National Universities

Rank School (State)

1. University of California–Berkeley
1. Univ. of California–Los Angeles
3. University of Virginia
4. University of Michigan–Ann Arbor
5. U. of North Carolina–Chapel Hill
6. College of William & Mary (VA)
7. Georgia Institute of Technology
8. Univ. of California–Santa Barbara

Rank School (State)

9. University of California–Irvine
9. Univ. of California–San Diego
9. University of Florida
12. University of California–Davis
12. Univ. of Wisconsin–Madison
14. Pennsylvania State U.–Univ. Park
14. University of Illinois–Urbana-
    Champaign

Rank School (State)

16. Ohio State University–Columbus
16. University of Georgia
18. Purdue Univ.–West Lafayette (IN)
18. University of Connecticut
18. University of Texas–Austin
18. University of Washington
22. Univ. of Maryland–College Park
23. Clemson University (SC)

Rank School (State)

24. University of Pittsburgh
25. Rutgers University–New Brunswick
    (NJ)
25. Texas A&M Univ.–College Station
25. Univ. of Minnesota–Twin Cities
25. Virginia Tech
29. Colorado School of Mines
29. Univ. of Massachusetts–Amherst

Footnotes:
1. School refused to fill out U.S. News statistical survey. Data that appear are from school in previous years or from another source such as the National Center for Education Statistics.
2. SAT and/or ACT not required by school for some or all applicants.
3. In reporting SAT/ACT scores, the school did not include all students for whom it had scores or refused to tell U.S. News whether all students with scores had been included.
4. Data reported to U.S. News in previous years
5. Data based on fewer than 51 percent of enrolled freshmen.
6. Some or all data reported to the National Center for Education Statistics.
7. Data reported to the Council for Aid to Education.

8. This rate, normally based on four years of data, is given here for fewer than four years because school didn't report rate for the most recent year or years to U.S. News.
9. SAT and/or ACT may not be required by school for some or all applicants, and in reporting SAT/ACT scores, the school did not include all students for whom it had scores or refused to tell U.S. News whether all students with scores had been included.
**The SAT scores used in the rankings and published in this guidebook are for the "old" SAT test taken prior to March 2016.
† School's Carnegie classification has changed. It appeared in a different U.S. News ranking category last year.
N/A means not available.

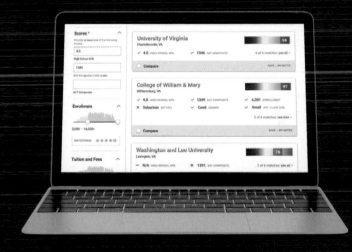

Best National Liberal

Rank School (State) (*Public)	Overall score	Peer assessment score (5.0=highest)	High school counselor assessment score	Graduation and retention rank	Average first-year student retention rate	2016 graduation rate Predicted	Actual	Over-performance (+) Under-performance (-)	Fac resou ra
1. Williams College (MA)	100	4.7	4.7	1	98%	94%	94%	None	
2. Amherst College (MA)	95	4.7	4.5	1	98%	93%	93%	None	3
3. Bowdoin College (ME)	93	4.4	4.6	5	97%	93%	94%	+1	2
3. Swarthmore College (PA)	93	4.6	4.5	4	97%	94%	94%	None	1
3. Wellesley College (MA)	93	4.5	4.6	12	95%	92%	91%	-1	2
6. Middlebury College (VT)	92	4.3	4.4	5	96%	95%	93%	-2	2
6. Pomona College (CA)	92	4.4	4.4	1	98%	95%	97%	+2	2
8. Carleton College (MN)	90	4.3	4.4	5	96%	92%	92%	None	1
8. Claremont McKenna College (CA)	90	4.2	4.5	12	95%	92%	93%	+1	
10. Davidson College (NC)	89	4.2	4.3	8	95%	92%	93%	+1	
10. Washington and Lee University (VA)	89	3.8	4.2	17	96%	94%	92%	-2	
12. Colby College (ME)	87	4.0	4.4	17	93%	92%	89%	-3	1
12. Colgate University (NY)	87	4.1	4.4	17	94%	89%	90%	+1	1
12. Harvey Mudd College (CA)	87	4.4	4.6	8	98%	94%	93%	-1	8
12. Smith College (MA)	87	4.3	4.6	31	93%	84%	89%	+5	2
12. United States Military Academy (NY)*	87	4.2	4.7	43	94%	84%	86%	+2	1
12. Vassar College (NY)	87	4.2	4.6	12	95%	88%	91%	+3	2
18. Grinnell College (IA)	86	4.3	4.1	31	94%	85%	86%	+1	1
18. Hamilton College (NY)	86	3.9	4.2	12	94%	91%	92%	+1	1
18. Haverford College (PA)	86	4.1	4.2	8	97%	95%	91%	-4	4
21. United States Naval Academy (MD)*	85	4.3	4.8	23	98%	88%	86%	-2	5
21. Wesleyan University (CT)	85	4.2	4.4	8	95%	88%	91%	+3	4
23. Bates College (ME)	82	4.1	4.3	21	94%	89%	88%	-1	4
23. Colorado College	82	3.9	4.1	28	96%	88%	87%	-1	8
23. University of Richmond (VA)	82	3.9	4.1	31	94%	84%	88%	+4	8
26. Barnard College (NY)	81	4.0	4.4	17	96%	88%	91%	+3	68
26. Kenyon College (OH)	81	3.9	4.2	23	95%	89%	90%	+1	4
26. Macalester College (MN)	81	4.0	4.4	23	94%	88%	88%	None	5
26. Oberlin College (OH)	81	4.1	4.3	31	92%	90%	85%	-5	2
26. Scripps College (CA)	81	3.8	4.3	31	93%	83%	84%	+1	2
26. United States Air Force Acad. (CO)*	81	4.1	4.7	49	93%	91%	83%	-8	9
32. Bryn Mawr College (PA)	80	4.0	4.2	43	93%	87%	83%	-4	4
33. Bucknell University (PA)	77	3.8	4.2	23	93%	89%	88%	-1	8
33. College of the Holy Cross (MA)	77	3.6	4.1	12	95%	86%	92%	+6	6
33. Pitzer College (CA)	77	3.7	4.2	39	93%	85%	88%	+3	3
36. Lafayette College (PA)	76	3.6	3.9	23	93%	87%	89%	+2	4
36. Mount Holyoke College (MA)	76	3.9	4.1	54	90%	83%	84%	+1	7
36. Union College (NY)	76	3.4	3.9	31	92%	85%	87%	+2	2
39. Franklin and Marshall College (PA)	75	3.6	3.9	31	92%	87%	87%	None	4
39. Soka University of America (CA)	75	2.5	3.3	39	95%	82%	90%	+8	
41. Sewanee–University of the South (TN)	74	3.6	4.1	67	89%	83%	82%	-1	1
41. Skidmore College (NY)	74	3.5	4.1	31	93%	79%	89%	+10	4
41. Whitman College (WA)	74	3.5	3.9	28	94%	86%	88%	+2	5
44. Occidental College (CA)	73	3.8	4.1	39	93%	82%	81%	-1	8
44. Trinity College (CT)	73	3.7	4.1	43	90%	82%	85%	+3	7
46. Bard College (NY)	71	3.5	4.1	84	87%	89%	78%	-11	1
46. Centre College (KY)	71	3.5	4.0	43	91%	84%	86%	+2	10
46. Connecticut College	71	3.5	4.1	49	90%	87%	84%	-3	4
46. Denison University (OH)	71	3.5	4.0	64	89%	81%	81%	None	3
46. Gettysburg College (PA)	71	3.5	3.9	43	90%	87%	87%	None	6

▶ More @ usnews.com/bestcolleges

Note: Key to footnotes, Page 86.

Arts Colleges

% of classes under 20 ('16)	% of classes of 50 or more ('16)	Student/ faculty ratio ('16)	Selectivity rank	SAT/ACT 25th-75th percentile** ('16)	Freshmen in top 10% of HS class ('16)	Acceptance rate ('16)	Financial resources rank	Alumni giving rank	Average alumni giving rate
3%	2%	7/1	4	1330-1540	91%[5]	18%	5	3	54%
9%	2%	8/1	4	1360-1560	87%[5]	14%	9	9	47%
8%	2%	9/1	9	1290-1510[2]	80%[5]	15%	11	2	55%
4%	3%	8/1	4	1305-1530	91%[5]	13%	10	25	36%
9%	0.2%	7/1	10	1310-1500	81%[5]	29%	6	5	49%
8%	2%	8/1	7	30-33	85%[5]	16%	4	10	46%
0%	0.2%	8/1	1	1340-1540	92%[5]	9%	6	54	28%
0%	1%	9/1	12	30-33	75%[5]	23%	32	5	49%
5%	1%	9/1	21	31-33	68%[5]	9%	16	25	36%
5%	0.2%	10/1	14	28-33	77%[5]	20%	27	7	48%
6%	0%	8/1	7	30-33	83%[5]	24%	25	7	47%
4%	2%	10/1	13	1260-1460[2]	76%[5]	19%	21	12	43%
2%	1%	9/1	14	30-33	72%[5]	29%	32	14	42%
1%	5%	8/1	1	1420-1580	88%[5]	13%	12	51	28%
9%	4%	9/1	23	1230-1480[2]	71%[5]	37%	12	32	33%
7%	0%	7/1	36	1180-1390	48%	10%	8	40	32%
6%	1%	8/1	14	1330-1500	68%	27%	18	57	27%
7%	0%	9/1	14	30-33	66%[5]	20%	21	18	39%
5%	0.2%	9/1	20	1300-1480	65%[5]	26%	21	18	38%
2%	2%	9/1	1	1320-1520	94%[5]	21%	16	15	41%
0%	0.1%	8/1	50	1170-1390	59%	8%	2	128	17%
3%	3%	8/1	18	1250-1480[2]	69%[5]	18%	45	20	37%
7%	2%	10/1	34	1150-1390[2]	61%[6]	23%	45	15	41%
0%	0.2%	10/1	18	28-32[2]	69%[5]	16%	25	85	23%
7%	0.2%	8/1	28	1220-1420	61%[5]	32%	27	70	24%
0%	8%	10/1	10	1270-1470	81%[5]	17%	54	67	25%
9%	1%	9/1	23	1230-1440	63%[5]	27%	41	20	37%
9%	1%	10/1	21	29-33	69%[5]	37%	54	24	36%
6%	1%	9/1	23	1250-1450	61%[5]	28%	35	53	28%
2%	1%	11/1	31	1290-1440	67%[5]	30%	27	46	29%
7%	0.1%	9/1	28	27-33	52%	15%	2	153	14%
3%	3%	8/1	27	1220-1450[2]	66%[5]	40%	18	25	36%
7%	2%	9/1	31	1200-1380	59%[5]	30%	41	46	29%
3%	2%	10/1	58	1220-1370[2]	61%[5]	38%	53	10	46%
1%	0%	11/1	46	1300-1450[2]	54%[5]	14%	32	46	29%
3%	1%	10/1	33	1200-1390	60%[5]	28%	37	44	30%
8%	2%	10/1	40	1220-1460[2]	49%[5]	52%	37	32	33%
8%	1%	10/1	26	1200-1390[2]	67%[5]	37%	49	32	33%
4%	1%	9/1	28	1200-1410[2]	67%[5]	36%	37	62	26%
6%	0%	8/1	73	1070-1370	22%[5]	38%	1	54	27%
6%	0%	10/1	50	27-31[2]	33%[5]	44%	54	32	33%
3%	1%	8/1	52	1120-1330[2]	32%[5]	29%	49	99	21%
7%	0%	8/1	36	1200-1420[2]	55%[5]	51%	54	43	31%
3%	0%	10/1	36	1200-1420	52%[5]	46%	60	117	19%
8%	1%	9/1	73	1210-1370[2]	50%[5]	34%	27	46	29%
1%	0%	10/1	91	1140-1370[2]	43%[5]	56%	15	39	32%
1%	0%	10/1	40	26-31	62%[5]	74%	78	12	43%
5%	1%	9/1	63	1230-1398[2]	45%[5]	35%	45	64	25%
9%	0.2%	9/1	34	28-32[2]	56%[5]	44%	65	99	21%
9%	0.2%	9/1	36	1210-1360[2]	64%[5]	43%	54	70	24%

What Is a National Liberal Arts College?

• • • •

The country's 233 liberal arts colleges emphasize undergraduate education and award at least half of their degrees in the arts and sciences, which include such disciplines as English, the biological and physical sciences, history, foreign languages, and the visual and performing arts but exclude professional disciplines such as business, education and nursing. There are 213 private and 20 public liberal arts colleges; none are for-profit. The top public colleges appear below.

The Top Public Colleges

Rank School (State)

1. United States Military Academy (NY)
2. United States Naval Academy (MD)
3. United States Air Force Acad. (CO)
4. Virginia Military Institute
5. St. Mary's College of Maryland
6. New College of Florida
7. University of Minnesota–Morris
7. U. of North Carolina–Asheville

Rank	School (State) (*Public)	Overall score	Peer assessment score (5.0=highest)	High school counselor assessment score	Average first-year student retention rate	2016 graduation rate Predicted	2016 graduation rate Actual	% of classes under 20 ('16)	% of classes of 50 or more ('16)	SAT/ACT 25th-75th percentile** ('16)	Freshmen in top 10% of HS class ('16)	Acceptance rate ('16)	Average alumni giving rate
51.	Dickinson College (PA)	70	3.5	3.9	91%	85%	84%	78%	0%	1200-1385[2]	48%[5]	43%	26%
51.	Rhodes College (TN)	70	3.5	4.1	91%	81%	80%	71%	0%	27-31	48%[5]	54%	34%
53.	DePauw University (IN)	69	3.4	3.8	93%	80%	85%	73%	0%	24-29	45%[5]	65%	24%
53.	Furman University (SC)	69	3.5	4.0	89%	85%	84%	54%	0%	1120-1320[2]	45%	68%	22%
53.	Sarah Lawrence College (NY)	69	3.4	4.2	85%	81%	82%	93%	2%	1170-1400[2]	40%[5]	50%	20%
53.	St. John's College (MD)	69	3.5	4.1	83%	78%	76%	97%	1%	1180-1440[2]	33%[5]	53%	22%
57.	St. Olaf College (MN)	68	3.6	4.0	93%	82%	88%	56%	3%	26-31	44%[5]	45%	23%
58.	Lawrence University (WI)	67	3.3	3.8	90%	77%	79%	79%	2%	26-31[2]	43%[5]	63%	33%
58.	St. Lawrence University (NY)	67	3.3	3.7	90%	78%	84%	64%	1%	1110-1300[2]	45%[5]	43%	25%
58.	Thomas Aquinas College (CA)	67	2.7	3.4	93%	72%	83%	100%	0%	1140-1360	25%[5]	75%	57%
61.	Agnes Scott College (GA)	66	3.3	3.8	84%	68%	70%	73%	0%	24-30[2]	43%	65%	37%
61.	Spelman College (GA)	66	3.6	4.0	90%	60%	77%	62%	1%	980-1170	38%[5]	36%	35%
63.	College of Wooster (OH)	65	3.4	3.9	88%	77%	76%	72%	1%	24-30	45%	58%	21%
63.	Wheaton College (IL)	65	3.0	3.9	95%	82%	91%	63%	4%	27-32	48%[5]	79%	21%
65.	Hobart & William Smith Colleges (NY)	64	3.2	3.9	87%	77%	77%	68%	0%	1160-1350[2]	32%[5]	60%	29%
65.	Virginia Military Institute*	64	3.1	4.0	87%	68%	78%	69%	0.1%	1060-1240	16%	51%	30%
65.	Wabash College (IN)	64	3.4	3.7	88%	76%	71%	75%	1%	1020-1230	29%	63%	40%
68.	Berea College (KY)	63	3.4	3.8	84%	52%	63%	79%	0.4%	22-27	23%	33%	16%
68.	Earlham College (IN)	63	3.3	3.9	84%	72%	71%	77%	2%	1130-1380[2]	36%[5]	58%	24%
68.	University of Puget Sound (WA)	63	3.3	3.7	87%	74%	80%	61%	1%	1100-1330[2]	34%[5]	79%	15%
71.	Hillsdale College (MI)	62	2.6	3.6	95%	82%	83%	75%	1%	28-32	N/A	45%	14%
71.	Illinois Wesleyan University	62	3.0	3.7	92%	78%	81%	68%	1%	25-29	34%[5]	58%	23%
71.	Knox College (IL)	62	3.2	3.6	87%	74%	77%	75%	1%	24-30[2]	46%[5]	65%	33%
71.	Muhlenberg College (PA)	62	2.9	3.6	91%	78%	84%	66%	1%	1130-1320[2]	36%[5]	48%	19%
71.	Wofford College (SC)	62	3.2	3.9	89%	79%	81%	60%	0%	24-29	43%	70%	24%
76.	Beloit College (WI)	61	3.3	3.7	88%	76%	73%	69%	0%	24-30[2]	31%[5]	70%	21%
76.	Hendrix College (AR)	61	3.4	3.9	85%	80%	69%	68%	1%	26-32	49%	77%	26%
76.	Kalamazoo College (MI)	61	3.3	3.8	91%	79%	81%	59%	1%	26-30[2]	52%[5]	66%	26%
76.	Lewis & Clark College (OR)	61	3.3	3.9	85%	77%	79%	66%	2%	27-31[2]	51%[5]	55%	18%
76.	St. John's College (NM)	61	3.2	4.0	83%	70%	49%	98%	0%	1210-1490[2]	52%[5]	63%	20%
76.	Wheaton College (MA)	61	3.3	4.0	85%	77%	79%	68%	2%	1050-1270[2]	27%[5]	62%	19%
82.	Allegheny College (PA)	60	3.2	3.6	84%	74%	76%	71%	0.2%	1070-1290[2]	37%[5]	68%	23%
82.	Reed College[1] (OR)	60	3.8	4.2	91%[8]	73%	81%[6]	N/A	N/A	1290-1480[4]	N/A	35%[4]	N/A
82.	Willamette University (OR)	60	3.2	3.8	86%	76%	78%	51%	0%	1100-1330	41%[5]	78%	13%
85.	Gustavus Adolphus College (MN)	59	3.2	3.7	90%	72%	80%	65%	0.2%	24-29[2]	29%	65%	19%
85.	St. John's University (MN)	59	3.2	3.8	87%	73%	79%	58%	1%	22-28	19%[5]	77%	24%
87.	Bennington College (VT)	58	3.0	3.7	82%	75%	70%	91%	1%	1190-1378[2]	N/A	60%	23%
87.	College of St. Benedict (MN)	58	3.1	3.5	88%	72%	84%	58%	1%	22-28	36%	80%	18%
87.	Cornell College (IA)	58	3.1	3.8	82%	68%	68%	83%	0%	23-29[2]	19%[5]	71%	19%
87.	Luther College (IA)	58	3.1	3.5	85%	73%	79%	64%	1%	23-28	23%	68%	25%
87.	Millsaps College (MS)	58	3.0	3.7	79%	76%	72%	75%	0%	23-28	30%	59%	22%
87.	Transylvania University (KY)	58	2.9	3.5	85%	75%	75%	70%	0%	25-30[2]	36%	95%	34%
93.	Austin College (TX)	57	3.1	3.9	84%	73%	73%	62%	1%	23-29	37%[5]	53%	19%
93.	College of the Atlantic (ME)	57	2.6	3.4	82%	71%	64%	94%	0%	1110-1290[2]	27%[5]	65%	35%
93.	Ursinus College (PA)	57	2.8	3.4	88%	75%	78%	77%	0.2%	1033-1290[2]	24%[5]	82%	20%
96.	Hampden-Sydney College (VA)	56	2.9	3.6	82%	68%	66%	75%	0%	1010-1230	10%	56%	31%
96.	Southwestern University (TX)	56	3.0	3.8	85%	76%	72%	63%	1%	1050-1280	36%	45%	24%
96.	St. Mary's College of Maryland*	56	2.9	3.7	87%	74%	73%	72%	0%	1000-1250	N/A	80%	12%
96.	Washington College (MD)	56	2.9	3.4	84%	76%	73%	77%	0%	1050-1260	40%[5]	49%	19%
96.	Westmont College (CA)	56	2.8	3.5	84%	76%	78%	68%	1%	1040-1280	36%[5]	83%	17%
101.	Augustana College (IL)	55	3.1	3.5	86%	71%	77%	66%	1%	23-28[2]	29%	52%	14%
101.	Lake Forest College (IL)	55	3.0	3.7	85%	68%	70%	61%	0%	24-29[2]	33%[5]	57%	24%
101.	New College of Florida*	55	3.0	4.0	82%	76%	63%	70%	2%	1140-1350	35%	71%	17%
101.	Ohio Wesleyan University	55	3.0	3.9	80%	73%	67%	69%	0%	22-28[2]	22%	72%	23%
101.	St. Mary's College (IN)	55	2.9	3.7	88%	70%	77%	54%	2%	22-28	18%[5]	82%	31%
106.	Hope College (MI)	54	3.0	3.5	89%	72%	80%	60%	2%	23-29	26%	84%	21%
106.	Juniata College (PA)	54	2.8	3.5	87%	72%	75%	71%	2%	1040-1240[9]	39%[5]	75%	26%
106.	St. Anselm College (NH)	54	2.8	3.5	88%	66%	72%	66%	2%	1050-1220[2]	20%[5]	76%	17%
106.	St. Michael's College (VT)	54	2.8	3.5	89%	72%	79%	60%	2%	1100-1270[2]	26%	77%	18%
106.	Washington and Jefferson Col. (PA)	54	2.9	3.6	81%	73%	76%	69%	0%	1070-1250[2]	24%	46%	14%
111.	Stonehill College (MA)	53	2.8	3.6	90%	75%	80%	50%	0.3%	1000-1210[2]	20%	73%	16%

Rank	School (State) (*Public)	Overall score	Peer assessment score (5.0=highest)	High school counselor assessment score	Average first-year student retention rate	Predicted	Actual	% of classes under 20 ('16)	% of classes of 50 or more ('16)	SAT/ACT 25th-75th percentile** ('16)	Freshmen in top 10% of HS class ('16)	Acceptance rate ('16)	Average alumni giving rate
						2016 graduation rate							
112.	Drew University (NJ)	52	2.8	3.4	83%	71%	61%	73%	1%	1030-1250[2]	27%[5]	57%	24%
112.	Goucher College (MD)	52	3.0	3.8	81%	71%	68%	69%	1%	1000-1240[2]	13%[5]	79%	20%
112.	Hanover College (IN)	52	2.7	3.6	82%	65%	71%	72%	0.3%	22-27	25%	57%	14%
112.	Hollins University (VA)	52	2.8	3.5	74%	63%	53%	89%	1%	1020-1233	23%	60%	21%
112.	Principia College (IL)	52	2.3	3.1	87%	68%	68%	92%	0%	970-1240	11%[5]	91%	N/A
117.	Concordia College–Moorhead (MN)	51	2.7	3.5	84%	68%	74%	59%	1%	22-28	27%	65%	17%
117.	Elizabethtown College (PA)	51	2.6	3.3	83%	69%	74%	67%	0%	990-1160	30%	73%	17%
117.	Linfield College (OR)	51	2.6	3.7	84%	60%	70%	72%	1%	920-1150	27%	81%	14%
117.	Marlboro College (VT)	51	2.3	3.4	74%	59%	64%	100%	0%	24-30[9]	17%[4]	96%	23%
117.	Ripon College (WI)	51	2.7	3.2	84%	64%	68%	72%	1%	21-26	21%	65%	27%
117.	Salem College (NC)	51	2.3	3.5	80%	44%	57%	87%	0%	21-27	40%	57%	24%
123.	Birmingham-Southern Col. (AL)	50	2.8	3.7	83%	71%	68%	63%	1%	23-29[2]	30%	48%	17%
123.	Coe College (IA)	50	2.9	3.5	77%	66%	67%	72%	1%	22-28	30%	50%	18%
123.	Presbyterian College (SC)	50	2.8	3.6	81%	69%	63%	68%	0.3%	20-27[2]	31%	60%	15%
126.	Grove City College (PA)	49	2.5	3.4	91%	73%	81%	52%	4%	1060-1325	39%	82%	20%
126.	Randolph-Macon College (VA)	49	2.9	3.3	79%	63%	59%	65%	0%	975-1190	24%	61%	37%
128.	Albion College (MI)	48	2.8	3.4	82%	74%	70%	62%	0%	20-26	N/A	72%	16%
128.	Central College (IA)	48	2.7	3.4	80%	64%	65%	70%	1%	21-26	23%	73%	13%
128.	Eckerd College (FL)	48	2.8	3.7	82%	67%	66%	53%	1%	22-28	N/A	72%	N/A
128.	Wartburg College (IA)	48	2.7	3.4	79%	65%	69%	59%	1%	21-26	24%	68%	21%
128.	Westminster College (PA)	48	2.6	3.4	82%	62%	71%	66%	1%	920-1140	22%	74%	14%
128.	Whittier College (CA)	48	3.1	3.4	81%	63%	64%	57%	1%	920-1130[2]	24%	69%	20%
134.	McDaniel College (MD)	47	2.7	3.5	80%	63%	67%	69%	0%	980-1210	22%	78%	16%
134.	Siena College (NY)	47	2.7	3.6	88%	68%	75%	41%	0%	980-1200[2]	25%	60%	13%
134.	St. Norbert College (WI)	47	2.7	3.3	83%	68%	73%	50%	0%	22-27	24%	81%	16%
134.	Sweet Briar College (VA)	47	2.0	3.4	57%	72%	61%	97%	0%	880-1180	15%	93%	28%
138.	Illinois College	46	2.6	3.4	79%	63%	68%	54%	0%	19-24[2]	17%	54%	22%
138.	Randolph College (VA)	46	2.6	3.2	75%	68%	60%	85%	0.4%	900-1150	16%	83%	21%
138.	Roanoke College (VA)	46	2.9	3.3	81%	66%	63%	57%	0%	970-1200	21%	73%	22%
141.	Alma College (MI)	45	2.5	3.4	81%	67%	67%	69%	1%	21-26	18%	68%	19%
141.	Hiram College (OH)	45	2.5	3.4	70%	55%	61%	84%	0%	19-25[2]	16%	54%	12%
141.	Susquehanna University (PA)	45	2.8	3.1	84%	69%	74%	55%	0.4%	1010-1210[2]	23%	68%	11%
141.	University of Minnesota–Morris*	45	2.7	3.5	80%	63%	64%	69%	4%	22-28	20%	58%	11%
141.	U. of North Carolina–Asheville*	45	3.0	3.8	79%	61%	62%	51%	1%	23-28	20%	78%	9%
141.	Wesleyan College (GA)	45	2.5	3.8	75%	59%	58%	81%	0%	930-1118	22%	38%	28%
147.	Bard College at Simon's Rock[1] (MA)	44	2.9	3.7	75%[8]	75%	39%[8]	97%[4]	0%[4]	1250-1400[4]	60%[4]	89%[4]	N/A
147.	Centenary College of Louisiana	44	2.4	3.4	76%	63%	47%	86%	0%	22-28	25%	64%	13%
147.	Franklin College (IN)	44	2.5	3.5	77%	58%	66%	70%	0%	850-1080[3]	26%	78%	19%
147.	Georgetown College (KY)	44	2.5	3.6	72%	65%	57%	100%	0%	20-26	17%[4]	56%	11%
147.	Houghton College (NY)	44	2.4	3.4	86%	65%	71%	58%	1%	963-1240	26%	95%	16%
147.	Lycoming College (PA)	44	2.4	3.2	80%	59%	72%	63%	2%	940-1120[2]	18%	70%	19%
147.	Monmouth College (IL)	44	2.7	3.6	75%	55%	56%	75%	0%	19-26	15%	52%	19%
147.	Saint Vincent College (PA)	44	2.3	3.3	84%	63%	73%	51%	0%	940-1160	20%	66%	21%
147.	Simpson College (IA)	44	2.6	3.3	80%	63%	63%	76%	1%	21-27	26%	85%	14%
147.	Westminster College (MO)	44	2.6	3.5	79%	63%	64%	74%	0%	21-26	21%[4]	65%	12%
147.	William Jewell College (MO)	44	2.6	3.4	79%	68%	63%	72%	1%	22-28[2]	25%	51%	10%
158.	Doane University (NE)	43	2.3	3.4	73%	43%	59%	73%	2%	21-26[3]	11%	76%	15%
158.	Wittenberg University (OH)	43	2.7	3.6	77%	67%	68%	47%	1%	22-28[2]	16%	78%	14%
160.	Guilford College (NC)	42	2.9	3.7	72%	52%	61%	56%	0%	870-1160[2]	10%	61%	14%
160.	Morehouse College (GA)	42	3.3	3.8	81%	55%	50%	50%	1%	19-24	15%[5]	66%	11%
160.	Warren Wilson College (NC)	42	2.6	3.5	65%	66%	51%	90%	0%	23-28[2]	14%[5]	82%	13%
163.	Carthage College (WI)	41	2.6	3.2	79%	62%	63%	55%	0.2%	21-27[2]	26%[5]	70%	14%
163.	Meredith College (NC)	41	2.3	3.6	77%	59%	61%	63%	0.2%	920-1123	23%	61%	21%
165.	Elmira College (NY)	40	2.4	3.2	77%	64%	60%	78%	0.3%	960-1150[2]	20%	82%	16%
165.	Hartwick College (NY)	40	2.6	3.3	75%	60%	61%	65%	1%	900-1090[2]	9%	94%	13%
165.	Moravian College (PA)	40	2.5	3.2	79%	65%	69%	61%	1%	900-1120[3]	20%	80%	17%
168.	College of Idaho	39	2.6	3.2	81%	65%	58%	60%	1%	21-27[9]	23%	85%	33%
168.	Covenant College (GA)	39	2.2	N/A	85%	62%	67%	60%	2%	24-29	26%[5]	96%	11%
168.	Emory and Henry College (VA)	39	2.6	3.4	72%	55%	51%	76%	1%	890-1120	14%	70%	23%
168.	Gordon College (MA)	39	2.3	3.1	84%	68%	71%	60%	4%	890-1210[3]	27%[5]	92%	9%
168.	Wells College[1] (NY)	39	2.5	3.6	73%[8]	56%	54%[8]	80%[4]	1%[4]	900-1090[4]	N/A	N/A	N/A

evolving

demands

demand
evolving

We are always a step ahead of an ever-changing world. By combining Philadelphia University and Thomas Jefferson University, two world-class models of professional education, we are reimagining how students learn and establishing the new standard for 21st century discovery and scholarship.

Introducing the new Jefferson. Our approach to thinking and doing creates unexpected collaborations that deepen your expertise and broaden your understanding across disciplines. We deliver an academic experience that brings together entrepreneurs and researchers, fashion designers and architects, or engineers and health professionals with industry partners; bringing an unmatched level of innovation to learning. We build your communication and analytical skills, as well as the global awareness needed to excel in your career. The result? Graduates equipped with the leadership skills that make employers eager to hire them.

Together we are transforming what it means to educate. Together we are redefining what is humanly possible.

⊠ *Visit Jefferson.edu to learn more.*

Jefferson
**Philadelphia University +
Thomas Jefferson University**

HOME OF SIDNEY KIMMEL MEDICAL COLLEGE

School (State) (*Public)	Peer assessment score (5.0=highest)	High school counselor assessment score	Average first-year student retention rate	2016 graduation rate Predicted	2016 graduation rate Actual	% of classes under 20 ('16)	% of classes of 50 or more ('16)	SAT/ACT 25th-75th percentile** ('16)	Freshmen in top 10% of HS class ('16)	Acceptance rate ('16)	Average alumni giving rate
SCHOOLS RANKED 173 THROUGH 229 ARE LISTED HERE ALPHABETICALLY											
Albright College (PA)	2.5	3.2	74%	56%	54%	53%	1%	950-1143[2]	19%	51%	10%
Allen University[1] (SC)	1.8	N/A	52%[8]	27%	23%[6]	N/A	N/A	N/A[2]	N/A	N/A	N/A
American Jewish University[1] (CA)	2.4	3.0	68%[8]	56%	68%[6]	N/A	N/A	N/A[2]	N/A	80%[4]	N/A
Ave Maria University[1] (FL)	1.9	2.8	72%[8]	53%	50%[6]	N/A	N/A	21-27[4]	N/A	43%[4]	N/A
Bethany College (WV)	2.3	3.2	62%	48%	41%	84%	1%	17-23	7%	65%	16%
Bethany Lutheran College (MN)	2.1	3.1	75%	57%	55%	71%	1%	20-27	9%	80%	15%
Bethel College (KS)	2.3	3.2	65%	60%	53%	76%	1%	20-26	14%	56%	17%
Bethune-Cookman University (FL)	2.1	3.4	64%	27%	38%	47%	2%	15-18	13%	44%	7%
Bloomfield College (NJ)	2.0	2.6	68%	33%	31%	76%	0%	760-940[2]	7%	62%	7%
Bridgewater College (VA)	2.4	3.2	77%	58%	66%	56%	0%	910-1110	15%	53%	14%
Bryn Athyn Col. of New Church (PA)	1.9	3.2	58%[8]	68%	54%	72%	0%	785-1105[4]	N/A	82%	N/A
Cheyney U. of Pennsylvania*	1.7	2.8	54%[8]	32%	16%	N/A	N/A	650-860	N/A	46%	N/A
Claflin University (SC)	2.0	3.3	74%	36%	56%	64%	2%	830-950	17%	42%	50%
Davis and Elkins College[1] (WV)	2.3	3.2	62%[8]	37%	41%[6]	N/A	N/A	17-22[4]	N/A	59%[4]	N/A
Dillard University (LA)	2.3	3.4	70%	38%	39%	57%	1%	18-22	14%[5]	38%	15%
East-West University[1] (IL)	1.7	N/A	33%[8]	35%	10%[6]	N/A	N/A	N/A	N/A	N/A	N/A
Emmanuel College (MA)	2.4	3.2	79%	61%	67%	35%	0%	1030-1200[2]	N/A	71%	12%
Erskine College (SC)	2.3	3.5	67%	64%	63%	79%	0%	890-1115	18%	68%	17%
Fisk University (TN)	2.8	3.6	78%	46%	32%	70%	0.4%	17-22	16%[5]	78%	21%
Fort Lewis College (CO)*	2.5	3.2	64%	51%	45%	45%	2%	19-24	9%	92%	3%
Holy Cross College[1] (IN)	2.6	3.7	59%[8]	51%	33%[6]	59%[4]	0%[4]	890-1170[4]	16%[4]	91%[4]	N/A
Johnson C. Smith University (NC)	2.1	3.1	64%	34%	51%	77%	0.2%	740-915	5%	45%	16%
Judson College[1] (AL)	2.0	3.0	62%[8]	51%	42%[6]	N/A	N/A	19-25[4]	N/A	63%[4]	N/A
The King's College (NY)	2.3	3.1	65%[8]	67%	54%	N/A	N/A	24-28	N/A	41%	N/A
LaGrange College (GA)	2.2	N/A	64%	56%	47%	75%	0.4%	20-24	15%	58%	15%
Louisiana State University–Alexandria*	2.0	3.3	59%	46%	25%	52%	3%	18-23	11%	31%	4%
Lyon College (AR)	2.5	3.2	69%	63%	39%	56%	0%	22-26	23%	59%	11%
Marymount Manhattan College (NY)	2.3	3.4	72%	58%	45%	78%	0%	930-1170	N/A	78%	11%[4]
Maryville College (TN)	2.5	3.5	73%	56%	55%	58%	2%	21-27	20%[5]	58%	19%
Massachusetts Col. of Liberal Arts*	2.4	3.2	78%	51%	54%	63%	0.2%	890-1130	17%[5]	77%	8%
Northland College (WI)	2.3	3.1	70%	58%	50%	73%	0%	21-26[2]	17%	54%	13%
Oglethorpe University[1] (GA)	2.7	3.6	74%[8]	59%	55%[6]	N/A	N/A	22-28[4]	N/A	78%[4]	N/A
Ouachita Baptist University (AR)	2.3	N/A	78%	69%	70%	62%	0.4%	21-28	34%	67%	16%
Pacific Union College (CA)	2.5	3.5	79%	53%	48%	62%	4%	860-1110	N/A	47%	8%
Paine College[1] (GA)	1.9	3.1	52%[8]	27%	20%[6]	N/A	N/A	14-17[4]	N/A	31%[4]	N/A
Philander Smith College (AR)	1.9	N/A	66%	35%	40%	64%	3%	14-19	8%	52%	5%
Pine Manor College (MA)	1.9	2.4	56%	42%	28%	80%	0%	N/A	N/A	74%	N/A
Providence Christian College[1] (CA)	2.1	N/A	77%[8]	57%	63%[6]	83%[4]	0%[4]	1400-1400[4]	N/A	N/A	N/A
Purchase College–SUNY*	2.5	3.5	81%	59%	63%	65%	3%	970-1180	N/A	44%	4%
Schreiner University (TX)	2.4	N/A	69%[8]	50%	45%	67%	0%	900-1080	20%	91%	5%
Shepherd University (WV)*	2.2	3.5	66%	48%	46%	63%	1%	19-24	N/A	92%	8%
Southern Virginia University[1]	1.9	3.5	73%[8]	43%	31%[6]	N/A	N/A	19-26[4]	N/A	38%[4]	N/A
Spring Hill College (AL)	2.4	3.5	77%	61%	53%	58%	1%	22-27	27%[5]	44%	18%
Stillman College[1] (AL)	2.4	3.3	63%[8]	31%	23%[6]	N/A	N/A	14-21[4]	N/A	57%[4]	N/A
Thiel College (PA)	2.1	3.1	67%	49%	42%	64%[4]	1%[4]	800-1050	8%	61%[4]	14%
Thomas More Col. of Lib. Arts[1] (NH)	2.3	3.2	86%[8]	56%	50%[6]	N/A	N/A	N/A[2]	N/A	97%[4]	N/A
Tougaloo College (MS)	2.1	2.5	74%	31%	54%	66%	1%	16-24	22%	52%	22%
University of Maine–Machias[1]*	2.1	3.0	68%[8]	42%	30%[8]	78%[4]	0%[4]	770-1010[4]	N/A	87%[4]	0.2%[4]
University of Pikeville (KY)	1.9	3.3	55%	42%	27%	58%	2%	17-22	10%	100%	5%
Univ. of Science and Arts of Okla.*	2.3	3.3	77%	52%	40%	73%	4%	20-24	19%	50%	N/A
University of Virginia–Wise*	2.5	3.5	68%	47%	39%	75%	1%	850-1070	15%	78%	9%
Univ. of Wisconsin–Parkside*	2.1	3.3	73%	47%	24%	41%	8%	18-23[2]	10%	82%	1%
Virginia Union University	2.2	3.2	57%	28%	33%	53%	0.2%	700-890[2]	9%	41%	8%
Virginia Wesleyan University	2.4	3.3	65%	54%	44%	79%	0%	850-1060	9%	90%	6%
West Virginia State University*	2.1	3.3	57%	43%	29%	56%	1%	17-22	N/A	96%	4%
William Peace University[1] (NC)	2.0	3.1	62%[8]	44%	41%[6]	N/A	N/A	760-980[4]	N/A	50%[4]	N/A
Young Harris College (GA)	2.2	N/A	66%	58%	44%	71%	0%	880-1120	14%	55%	11%

Footnotes:

1. School refused to fill out U.S. News statistical survey. Data that appear are from school in previous years or from another source such as the National Center for Education Statistics.
2. SAT and/or ACT not required by school for some or all applicants.
3. In reporting SAT/ACT scores, the school did not include all students for whom it had scores or refused to tell U.S. News whether all students with scores had been included.
4. Data reported to U.S. News in previous years.
5. Data based on fewer than 51 percent of enrolled freshmen.
6. Some or all data reported to the National Center for Education Statistics.
7. Data reported to the Council for Aid to Education.

8. This rate, normally based on four years of data, is given here for fewer than four years because school didn't report rate for the most recent year or years to U.S. News.
9. SAT and/or ACT may not be required by school for some or all applicants, and in reporting SAT/ACT scores, the school did not include all students for whom it had scores or refused to tell U.S. News whether all students with scores had been included.

****The SAT scores used in the rankings and published in this guidebook are for the "old" SAT test taken prior to March 2016.
N/A means not available.

Best Regional Universities

What Is a Regional University?

Like the national universities, the institutions that appear here provide a full range of undergraduate majors and master's programs; the difference is that they offer few, if any, doctoral programs. The 659 universities in this category are not ranked nationally but rather against their peer group in one of four regions – North, South, Midwest and West – because in general they tend to draw students most heavily from surrounding states.

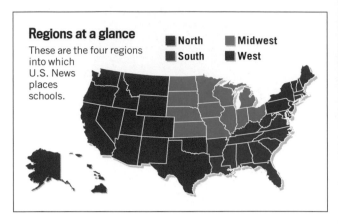

Regions at a glance
These are the four regions into which U.S. News places schools.
■ North ■ Midwest ■ South ■ West

NORTH ▶

Rank School (State) (*Public)	Overall score	Peer assessment score (5.0=highest)	Average first-year student retention rate	2016 graduation rate Predicted	2016 graduation rate Actual	% of classes under 20 ('16)	% of classes of 50 or more ('16)	Student/faculty ratio ('16)	SAT/ACT 25th-75th percentile** ('16)	Freshmen in top 25% of HS class ('16)	Acceptance rate ('16)	Average alumni giving rate
1. Providence College (RI)	100	3.7	92%	74%	83%	54%	3%	12/1	1030-1240[2]	69%[5]	55%	18%
2. Bentley University (MA)	96	3.5	94%	78%	89%	22%	5%	12/1	1150-1320	72%[5]	46%	6%
3. Fairfield University (CT)	95	3.5	89%	82%	82%	46%	1%	12/1	1110-1270[2]	67%[5]	61%	15%
4. College of New Jersey*	92	3.3	94%	82%	87%	47%	0.2%	13/1	1100-1300	76%[5]	49%	7%
4. Loyola University Maryland	92	3.6	88%	78%	81%	41%	1%	12/1	1100-1280[2]	68%[5]	66%	12%
6. University of Scranton (PA)	90	3.3	89%	69%	79%	54%	0.1%	12/1	1030-1220	62%[5]	75%	11%
7. Emerson College (MA)	88	3.4	88%	79%	80%	67%	1%	13/1	1120-1330	70%[5]	48%	6%
8. Ithaca College (NY)	87	3.5	86%	73%	75%	61%	3%	11/1	1090-1280[2]	57%[5]	70%	9%
9. Marist College (NY)	85	3.2	91%	74%	83%	43%	0%	16/1	1070-1270[2]	58%[5]	41%	12%
10. Bryant University (RI)	84	3.1	89%	72%	77%	24%	0%	13/1	1085-1255[2]	49%[5]	69%	9%
11. St. Joseph's University (PA)	82	3.2	90%	72%	80%	34%	1%	12/1	1050-1230[2]	50%[5]	78%	11%
11. SUNY–Geneseo*	82	3.5	89%	77%	81%	32%	10%	19/1	1090-1300	74%[5]	67%	11%
13. Quinnipiac University (CT)	81	3.4	88%	76%	77%	41%	3%	16/1	980-1190	62%	76%	4%
14. Simmons College (MA)	80	3.0	85%	71%	74%	66%	4%	10/1	1080-1260	71%[5]	64%	19%
15. Manhattan College (NY)	74	2.9	86%	68%	71%	44%	0%	13/1	1000-1210[3]	60%[5]	71%	16%
15. SUNY Polytechnic Institute*	74	2.6	78%	58%	45%	72%	1%	13/1	990-1230[3]	63%	66%	5%
17. Le Moyne College (NY)	73	2.9	87%	61%	67%	50%	2%	13/1	1000-1210[2]	54%	65%	16%
18. Massachusetts Maritime Academy*	72	3.1	89%	65%	76%	38%	2%	17/1	950-1150	N/A	80%	14%
18. St. Francis University (PA)	72	2.6	86%	61%	75%	73%	2%	13/1	950-1170	50%	67%	21%
20. CUNY–Baruch College*	71	3.1	90%	60%	66%	20%	16%	17/1	1090-1310	76%	31%	4%
21. St. Bonaventure University (NY)	70	2.9	83%	57%	64%	62%	0%	11/1	930-1165	46%[5]	66%	18%
22. Canisius College (NY)	69	2.7	83%	64%	71%	55%	1%	11/1	970-1190	53%	78%	11%
22. Gallaudet University (DC)	69	3.2	71%	60%	43%	95%	0%	7/1	14-20	N/A	66%	N/A
24. Lebanon Valley College (PA)	68	2.5	84%	69%	76%	61%	2%	11/1	970-1220[2]	59%	76%	14%
25. Mount St. Mary's University (MD)	67	2.7	77%	63%	71%	52%	0%	12/1	940-1160	38%	62%	19%
25. Rutgers University–Camden (NJ)*	67	3.1	84%	59%	59%	46%	7%	10/1	890-1120	44%	57%	3%
25. Springfield College (MA)	67	2.7	85%	50%	70%	51%	2%	12/1	900-1120	41%	66%	9%
28. Assumption College (MA)	66	2.7	83%	63%	74%	44%	0.2%	11/1	1010-1200[2]	38%	78%	12%
28. CUNY–Hunter College*	66	3.2	85%	59%	53%	38%	7%	14/1	1060-1250	57%[4]	38%	11%
28. Hood College (MD)	66	2.8	78%	62%	65%	76%	0%	10/1	900-1100[2]	46%	71%	17%
28. Monmouth University (NJ)	66	2.9	81%	64%	70%	41%	0.1%	13/1	930-1120	41%[5]	77%	4%
28. Nazareth College (NY)	66	2.6	83%	65%	69%	58%	0%	9/1	980-1190[2]	58%	72%	10%
28. SUNY–New Paltz*	66	2.9	88%	62%	72%	30%	3%	15/1	1010-1200	58%[5]	43%	3%
34. Endicott College (MA)	65	2.6	84%	62%	79%	59%	0%	13/1	1000-1150[2]	42%[5]	79%	13%
34. La Salle University (PA)	65	2.9	79%	56%	65%	45%	1%	11/1	870-1080	36%	77%	11%
34. Rider University (NJ)	65	2.7	80%	66%	66%	49%	1%	11/1	916-1110	40%[5]	69%	9%
37. Ramapo College of New Jersey*	64	2.7	87%	66%	73%	35%	0%	18/1	970-1190	26%[5]	53%	5%
37. Roger Williams University (RI)	64	2.9	82%	66%	64%	47%	0.4%	14/1	990-1180[2]	N/A	79%	4%
37. Salve Regina University (RI)	64	2.7	83%	66%	68%	45%	0%	13/1	1020-1180[2]	45%	68%	17%

Note: Key to footnotes Page 101.

SMALL CAMPUS & BIG CITY

 **MANHATTAN COLLEGE**

When everything New York City holds lies just outside a quintessential college campus, the opportunities are endless.

EXPERIENCE THE UNCOMMON
MANHATTAN.EDU

BEST REGIONAL UNIVERSITIES

NORTH ▶

Rank School (State) (*Public)	Overall score	Peer assessment score (5.0=highest)	Average first-year student retention rate	2016 graduation rate Predicted	Actual	% of classes under 20 ('16)	% of classes of 50 or more ('16)	Student/faculty ratio ('16)	SAT/ACT 25th-75th percentile** ('16)	Freshmen in top 25% of HS class ('16)	Acceptance rate ('16)	Average alumni giving rate
37. Wagner College (NY)	64	2.8	86%	76%	67%	62%	4%	13/1	1030-1230[2]	61%[5]	70%	8%
41. CUNY–Queens College*	63	2.8	85%	57%	60%	35%	8%	14/1	1000-1180	66%[4]	41%	20%
41. Misericordia University (PA)	63	2.5	82%	59%	74%	46%	0%	11/1	950-1140[3]	40%	74%	16%
41. Molloy College (NY)	63	2.2	88%	64%	75%	61%	2%	10/1	980-1170	56%[5]	77%	11%
41. Sacred Heart University (CT)	63	3.0	82%	65%	60%	41%	1%	15/1	1040-1200[2]	31%	57%	7%
41. Stockton University (NJ)*	63	2.7	87%	59%	70%	24%	2%	17/1	960-1160	52%	77%	2%
41. Towson University (MD)*	63	3.1	86%	60%	71%	30%	3%	17/1	980-1160	42%[5]	74%	4%
47. New York Inst. of Technology	62	2.8	75%	67%	44%	66%	1%	13/1	950-1180	52%[5]	73%	14%
48. Alfred University (NY)†	61	2.7	75%	62%	61%	70%	3%	13/1	910-1140	41%	63%	10%
48. Arcadia University (PA)	61	2.5	81%	64%	61%	75%	3%	10/1	1000-1210	59%	63%	11%
48. Gannon University (PA)	61	2.7	81%	59%	64%	54%	0.1%	12/1	920-1130	49%	78%	9%
48. Mercyhurst University (PA)	61	2.5	80%	46%	67%	48%	0.3%	15/1	920-1160[2]	29%	75%	12%
48. Niagara University (NY)	61	2.7	84%	57%	67%	56%	1%	12/1	930-1130	42%[5]	83%	9%
48. SUNY College–Cortland*	61	2.7	80%	56%	75%	30%	6%	16/1	990-1140[9]	39%	52%	8%
48. SUNY College–Oneonta*	61	2.7	86%	61%	72%	39%	5%	18/1	980-1160[3]	N/A	53%	8%[4]
48. SUNY–Oswego*	61	2.8	80%	56%	66%	55%	5%	17/1	1010-1180[3]	50%	54%	7%
56. CUNY–City College*	60	2.9	87%	48%	45%	44%	0.4%	15/1	1035-1220[3]	N/A	38%	18%
56. Marywood University (PA)	60	2.4	82%	57%	66%	60%	0.2%	12/1	940-1120	40%	69%	13%
56. Merrimack College (MA)	60	2.7	82%	62%	73%	39%	1%	14/1	900-1090[2]	24%	82%	9%
56. Notre Dame of Maryland University	60	2.7	76%	62%	50%	88%	4%	7/1	960-1140[2]	69%	61%	8%
56. Seton Hill University (PA)	60	2.8	80%	56%	57%	57%	1%	12/1	930-1170[2]	56%	73%	N/A
56. SUNY–Fredonia*	60	2.7	79%	56%	62%	59%	4%	14/1	900-1120	38%	62%	4%
62. King's College (PA)	59	2.4	75%	57%	65%	54%	0%	13/1	940-1160[2]	43%	71%	14%
62. SUNY Maritime College*	59	3.0	84%	57%	57%	36%	2%	16/1	1030-1210	50%[5]	58%	5%
64. College at Brockport–SUNY*	58	2.6	82%	55%	68%	39%	5%	17/1	920-1120	40%	55%	4%
64. DeSales University (PA)	58	2.4	82%	59%	68%	56%	3%	13/1	940-1180	45%[5]	76%	8%
64. Fairleigh Dickinson Univ. (NJ)	58	3.0	77%	58%	55%	70%	1%	13/1	920-1120	38%[5]	78%	4%
64. Johnson & Wales University (RI)	58	2.9	79%	43%	58%	50%	0%	21/1	860-1080[2]	N/A	88%	N/A
64. Philadelphia University	58	2.6	80%	60%	58%	71%	0.1%	13/1	960-1130	39%	61%	5%
64. West Chester Univ. of Pennsylvania*	58	2.8	87%	57%	70%	24%	6%	19/1	970-1150	34%	64%	5%
64. Western New England Univ. (MA)	58	2.6	76%	61%	57%	57%	0%	12/1	990-1190[2]	39%[5]	80%	4%
71. Keene State College (NH)*	57	2.7	75%	52%	63%	51%	1%	15/1	880-1070	28%[5]	83%	5%
71. St. Joseph's College New York	57	2.4	85%	57%	72%	63%	0%	14/1	900-1110	N/A	67%	5%
71. SUNY–Plattsburgh*	57	2.5	83%	54%	64%	41%	4%	15/1	990-1210[3]	52%[5]	51%	7%
71. Wentworth Inst. of Technology (MA)	57	2.8	83%	61%	65%	35%	1%	17/1	1010-1220	N/A	71%	6%
75. Chatham University (PA)	56	2.4	78%	59%	52%	74%	1%	10/1	950-1170[2]	55%	53%	12%
75. Geneva College (PA)	56	2.3	81%	49%	65%	65%	3%	11/1	950-1190	48%	71%	9%
75. Iona College (NY)	56	2.7	80%	64%	68%	34%	0.1%	15/1	890-1100	28%[5]	91%	8%
78. Eastern University (PA)	55	2.3	78%	55%	65%	85%	0.3%	10/1	930-1140	44%[4]	61%	12%
78. Roberts Wesleyan College (NY)	55	2.4	80%	52%	59%	68%	2%	11/1	960-1140	54%	65%	10%
78. Salisbury University (MD)*	55	2.7	82%	63%	68%	33%	5%	16/1	1080-1230[9]	55%[5]	66%	6%
78. Slippery Rock U. of Pennsylvania*	55	2.8	83%	54%	68%	16%	11%	22/1	910-1090	37%	69%	6%
78. University of New England (ME)	55	2.7	78%	59%	59%	49%	6%	13/1	940-1150	N/A	83%	8%
78. University of St. Joseph (CT)	55	2.4	75%	58%	63%	75%	1%	10/1	830-1100[2]	53%	87%	14%
78. Wilkes University (PA)	55	2.4	78%	60%	62%	53%	5%	13/1	895-1130	51%	76%	14%
78. York College of Pennsylvania	55	2.4	78%	56%	60%	52%	0%	15/1	940-1140	38%	62%	8%
86. CUNY–Brooklyn College*	54	2.8	83%	53%	51%	30%	5%	17/1	970-1180	50%[4]	37%	6%
86. Eastern Connecticut State Univ.*	54	2.6	76%	54%	54%	35%	0.2%	16/1	950-1120[9]	37%	58%	9%
86. Norwich University (VT)	54	2.7	75%	61%	58%	55%	2%	17/1	930-1140[9]	28%[5]	70%	12%
86. Southern New Hampshire University	54	2.8	74%	40%	56%	64%	0%	13/1	880-1100[2]	23%[5]	93%	2%
86. Stevenson University (MD)	54	2.7	77%	56%	53%	62%	0%	14/1	910-1130	43%	61%	5%
91. Champlain College (VT)	53	2.6	80%	59%	62%	58%	0%	14/1	1020-1240[3]	40%[5]	70%	4%
91. College of Saint Rose (NY)	53	2.3	77%	56%	60%	61%	0.3%	14/1	935-1140[9]	30%	84%	15%
91. SUNY College–Potsdam*	53	2.5	76%	49%	52%	71%	2%	11/1	990-1210[2]	14%[5]	72%	8%
94. Central Connecticut State Univ.*	52	2.5	78%	51%	54%	42%	3%	15/1	900-1100	32%	60%	4%
94. Millersville U. of Pennsylvania*	52	2.6	78%	56%	61%	28%	6%	19/1	930-1120	30%	69%	4%
94. University of New Haven (CT)	52	2.5	79%	57%	56%	45%	3%	16/1	930-1140	41%[5]	81%	8%
97. The Sage Colleges (NY)	51	2.5	79%	55%	58%	62%	0%	11/1	830-1060[2]	52%	58%	10%
97. Saint Peter's University (NJ)	51	2.5	80%	46%	54%	55%	0%	13/1	830-1030[2]	46%	74%	10%
97. Waynesburg University (PA)	51	2.3	80%	55%	60%	74%	1%	12/1	860-1070	37%	94%	7%
97. Wheelock College (MA)	51	2.4	70%	56%	61%	60%	0%	9/1	800-1015	10%[5]	84%	12%
101. Shippensburg U. of Pennsylvania*	50	2.7	72%	50%	56%	29%	6%	20/1	870-1070	25%	88%	11%

Note: Key to footnotes Page 101.

Rank	School (State) (*Public)	Overall score	Peer assessment score (5.0=highest)	Average first-year student retention rate	2016 graduation rate Predicted	2016 graduation rate Actual	% of classes under 20 ('16)	% of classes of 50 or more ('16)	Student/faculty ratio ('16)	SAT/ACT 25th-75th percentile** ('16)	Freshmen in top 25% of HS class ('16)	Accept-ance rate ('16)	Average alumni giving rate
102.	Bay Path University (MA)	49	2.2	75%	44%	61%	86%	0%	11/1	845-1065[2]	44%	60%	6%
102.	Bloomsburg U. of Pennsylvania*	49	2.6	78%	51%	62%	25%	7%	20/1	870-1070	27%	78%	6%
102.	Bridgewater State University (MA)*	49	2.5	80%	48%	59%	44%	1%	19/1	890-1090[2]	N/A	81%	6%
102.	Caldwell University (NJ)	49	2.2	77%	48%	58%	62%	1%	12/1	850-1070[3]	32%[5]	85%	13%
102.	College of Our Lady of the Elms (MA)	49	2.0	82%	46%	64%	76%	0.3%	10/1	840-1055[3]	N/A	76%	13%
102.	LIU Post (NY)	49	2.3	73%	47%	46%	74%	1%	14/1	920-1120	33%[5]	81%	3%
102.	Manhattanville College (NY)†	49	2.5	78%	57%	48%	60%	0.2%	12/1	950-1150[2]	32%[5]	77%	11%
102.	Point Park University (PA)	49	2.3	76%	50%	58%	75%	0.3%	13/1	890-1110	36%	71%	3%
102.	William Paterson Univ. of N.J.*	49	2.5	76%	49%	50%	53%	0.4%	14/1	890-1080	N/A	76%	4%
111.	Alvernia University (PA)	48	2.4	77%	45%	53%	64%	2%	12/1	880-1090	32%	74%	9%
111.	Carlow University (PA)	48	2.2	75%	46%	57%	75%	1%	12/1	870-1070	40%	86%	8%
111.	CUNY–John Jay Col. of Crim. Justice*	48	3.0	78%	40%	44%	27%	1%	16/1	860-1060	N/A	34%	2%[7]
111.	St. Thomas Aquinas College (NY)	48	2.4	77%	51%	60%	63%	0%	13/1	832-1057	18%[5]	79%	12%
115.	Plymouth State University (NH)*	47	2.5	73%	46%	54%	53%	1%	17/1	880-1090[2]	20%	79%	6%
116.	Albertus Magnus College (CT)	46	2.3	79%	42%	56%	90%	0%	14/1	820-950	N/A	63%	N/A
116.	Mansfield Univ. of Pennsylvania*	46	2.3	74%	45%	55%	45%	5%	16/1	860-1060[2]	31%	66%	8%[4]
116.	Westfield State University (MA)*	46	2.3	78%	49%	66%	32%	1%	17/1	890-1090	27%[5]	78%	3%
116.	Worcester State University (MA)*	46	2.4	80%	53%	56%	64%	0.2%	18/1	890-1100	N/A	71%	7%[4]
120.	Cabrini University (PA)	45	2.2	74%	52%	60%	78%	0.4%	13/1	N/A[2]	N/A	94%	8%
120.	College of Mount St. Vincent (NY)	45	2.2	73%	40%	55%	53%	0%	13/1	780-980	28%[5]	93%	14%
120.	Frostburg State University (MD)*	45	2.5	77%	48%	49%	50%	2%	16/1	860-1060	31%	63%	5%
120.	Keuka College (NY)	45	2.2	72%	45%	60%	59%	3%	11/1	840-1050[2]	33%	94%	12%
120.	SUNY Buffalo State*	45	2.7	72%	47%	50%	38%	12%	16/1	770-980[3]	30%	64%	3%
120.	Western Connecticut State Univ.*	45	2.3	76%	52%	46%	49%	1%	12/1	880-1090[2]	25%	67%	3%
126.	Delaware Valley University (PA)	44	2.3	69%	60%	57%	59%	2%	14/1	870-1090	27%	68%	7%
126.	Framingham State University (MA)*	44	2.5	74%	51%	55%	44%	1%	14/1	890-1090	26%[5]	65%	5%
126.	Kutztown Univ. of Pennsylvania*	44	2.5	73%	48%	55%	29%	8%	18/1	880-1070	22%	80%	5%
126.	Mount St. Mary College (NY)	44	2.2	75%	51%	54%	51%	1%	13/1	890-1070	34%	90%	7%
130.	Daemen College (NY)	43	2.2	78%	56%	55%	61%	2%	12/1	920-1160[2]	58%	52%	4%
130.	Delaware State University*	43	2.5	70%	43%	43%	44%	3%	16/1	820-970	30%	41%	10%
130.	Lasell College (MA)	43	2.3	76%	53%	51%	68%	0%	13/1	870-1060[2]	N/A	76%	10%
130.	Southern Connecticut State Univ.*	43	2.4	76%	50%	51%	43%	1%	14/1	830-1030	8%	64%	4%
130.	Utica College (NY)	43	2.5	72%	46%	45%	61%	0.3%	12/1	910-1120[2]	31%	82%	7%
135.	Centenary University (NJ)	42	2.1	78%	51%	58%	88%[4]	0%[4]	10/1	850-1050	N/A	88%	N/A
136.	St. Joseph's College[1] (ME)	41	2.4	78%[8]	45%	57%[6]	N/A	N/A	12/1[4]	890-1080[4]	N/A	78%[4]	N/A
137.	Chestnut Hill College (PA)	40	2.1	74%	45%	48%	85%	0%	10/1	840-1070	26%	94%	14%
137.	Clarion U. of Pennsylvania*	40	2.2	75%	47%	50%	33%	4%	19/1	840-1040	26%	97%	7%
137.	College of St. Elizabeth (NJ)	40	2.1	66%	54%	50%	83%	0%	10/1	716-928	N/A	66%	11%[4]
137.	CUNY–Lehman College*	40	2.7	84%	43%	44%	39%	1%	16/1	860-1040[3]	N/A	32%	1%
137.	Fitchburg State University (MA)*	40	2.4	76%	53%	54%	39%	1%	14/1	890-1090	N/A	75%	4%
137.	Georgian Court University (NJ)	40	2.1	76%	53%	42%	79%	0%	12/1	850-1040	24%	74%	9%
137.	Kean University (NJ)*	40	2.4	74%	45%	50%	37%	0.1%	16/1	830-1010	28%[4]	78%	3%
137.	Lock Haven U. of Pennsylvania*	40	2.3	70%	43%	48%	39%	8%	18/1	850-1040	29%	88%	5%
137.	Salem State University (MA)*	40	2.4	80%	50%	52%	45%	0.3%	15/1	890-1090[2]	N/A	74%	5%

School (State) (*Public)	Peer assessment score (5.0=highest)	Average first-year student retention rate	2016 graduation rate Predicted	2016 graduation rate Actual	% of classes under 20 ('16)	% of classes of 50 or more ('16)	Student/faculty ratio ('16)	SAT/ACT 25th-75th percentile** ('16)	Freshmen in top 25% of HS class ('16)	Accept-ance rate ('16)	Average alumni giving rate
SCHOOLS RANKED 146 THROUGH 187 ARE LISTED HERE ALPHABETICALLY											
Anna Maria College (MA)	1.9	67%	45%	40%	N/A	N/A	N/A	N/A[2]	N/A	83%	N/A
Bowie State University (MD)*	2.3	74%	41%	36%[6]	46%	1%	16/1	810-960	N/A	41%	6%
Cairn University[1] (PA)	1.9	73%[8]	53%	64%[6]	N/A	N/A	N/A	850-1095[4]	27%[4]	99%[4]	N/A
California U. of Pennsylvania*	2.2	76%	46%	54%	33%	11%	19/1	810-1030[3]	23%	94%	4%
College of New Rochelle (NY)	2.0	73%	43%	28%[6]	71%	1%	14/1	840-1020	53%[5]	43%	16%
Coppin State University[1] (MD)*	2.1	69%[8]	34%	17%[6]	52%[4]	2%[4]	13/1[4]	810-970[4]	N/A	37%[4]	N/A
CUNY–College of Staten Island*	2.6	81%	45%	46%	23%	6%	18/1	900-1100	N/A	100%	1%
Curry College (MA)	2.1	70%	51%	47%	63%	0%	11/1	840-1040[2]	16%[5]	89%	6%
Dominican College (NY)	2.1	70%	46%	43%	66%	0%	15/1	800-970	N/A	75%	N/A
D'Youville College (NY)	2.0	79%	53%	45%	67%	2%	10/1	900-1090	36%	83%	13%
Eastern Nazarene College (MA)	2.0	71%	45%	45%	N/A	N/A	8/1	820-1110	34%[5]	66%	N/A
East Stroudsburg Univ. of Pa.*	2.5	72%	51%	56%[8]	37%	9%	19/1	840-1040[2]	12%	73%	3%

NORTH ▶

School (State) (*Public)	Peer assessment score (5.0=highest)	Average first-year student retention rate	2016 graduation rate Predicted	Actual	% of classes under 20 ('16)	% of classes of 50 or more ('16)	Student/faculty ratio ('16)	SAT/ACT 25th-75th percentile** ('16)	Freshmen in top 25% of HS class ('16)	Acceptance rate ('16)	Average alumni giving rate
CONTINUED (SCHOOLS RANKED 146 THROUGH 187 ARE LISTED HERE ALPHABETICALLY)											
Edinboro Univ. of Pennsylvania[1]*	2.3	71%[8]	43%	48%[6]	N/A	N/A	19/1[4]	850-1050[4]	N/A	96%[4]	N/A
Felician University (NJ)	2.1	80%	45%	41%	72%	0%	13/1	790-1010	31%	79%	3%
Franklin Pierce University (NH)	2.3	66%	53%	43%	62%	1%	14/1	870-1070[2]	30%	81%	5%
Green Mountain College (VT)	2.1	63%[8]	54%	49%	71%	0%	N/A	900-1170[2]	N/A	79%	10%
Gwynedd Mercy University (PA)	2.3	80%	46%	50%	63%	4%	11/1	840-1032	20%	91%	5%
Harrisburg Univ. of Science and Tech. (PA)	2.1	54%	67%	29%	N/A	N/A	32/1	N/A[2]	N/A	N/A	N/A
Holy Family University (PA)	2.1	76%	55%	60%	68%	0%	13/1	830-1040	30%	68%	4%
Husson University (ME)	2.2	74%	46%	53%	48%	0%	14/1	860-1070	39%	80%	5%
Johnson State College[1] (VT)*	2.1	N/A	41%	35%[6]	N/A	N/A	19/1[4]	N/A[2]	N/A	N/A	N/A
Lincoln University (PA)*	2.0	74%	38%	43%	22%	0%	12/1	750-925	25%	87%	7%
Medaille College[1] (NY)	1.9	N/A	44%	43%[6]	N/A	N/A	N/A	N/A	N/A	29%[4]	N/A
Metropolitan College of New York	1.8	44%[8]	27%	31%	96%	0%	9/1	N/A[2]	N/A	39%	N/A
Monroe College (NY)†	1.9	77%	52%	71%	44%	0%	18/1	718-1018[2]	N/A	53%	3%
Neumann University (PA)	2.1	70%	52%	53%	62%	3%	14/1	800-980	N/A	94%	8%
New England College (NH)	2.3	60%	40%	38%	77%	0%	16/1	790-1060[2]	11%[5]	99%	5%
New Jersey City University*	2.2	74%	44%	31%	43%	0%	13/1	760-990	32%[5]	85%	2%
Nyack College (NY)	2.1	69%	36%	38%	72%	3%	12/1	770-1026[2]	28%[5]	100%	6%
Post University (CT)	2.1	41%	31%	39%	74%	0%	21/1	770-1000[9]	N/A	41%	N/A
Rhode Island College*	2.5	77%	48%	47%	48%	1%	14/1	790-1020[3]	36%	75%	4%
Rivier University[1] (NH)	2.1	76%[8]	50%	50%[6]	N/A	N/A	18/1[4]	N/A[2]	N/A	57%[4]	N/A
Rosemont College (PA)	2.2	70%	45%	48%	68%	0%	12/1	810-1010	46%[4]	69%	12%
SUNY College–Old Westbury*	2.3	80%	44%	43%	32%	1%	18/1	880-1060[3]	N/A	69%	N/A
Thomas College[1] (ME)	2.1	68%[8]	39%	45%[6]	57%[4]	0%[4]	19/1[4]	N/A[2]	N/A	N/A	N/A
Touro College (NY)	1.9	62%	58%	42%	87%	1%	17/1	960-1250[2]	N/A	52%	1%[4]
Trinity Washington University[1] (DC)	2.7	61%[8]	33%	41%[6]	N/A	N/A	12/1[4]	N/A[2]	N/A	94%[4]	N/A
University of Baltimore*	2.6	72%	45%	36%	34%	0%	15/1	810-1030	N/A	83%	5%
University of Bridgeport (CT)	2.1	63%	42%	29%	66%	1%	17/1	840-1010	44%[5]	58%	3%
University of Southern Maine*	2.6	65%	51%	34%	55%	3%	14/1	870-1090	37%	80%	2%
Univ. of the District of Columbia*	1.9	59%	53%	33%	65%	0%	N/A	700-910[3]	N/A	54%	1%
Washington Adventist University (MD)	1.9	69%	44%	38%	85%	0%	9/1	720-1000[2]	N/A	34%	1%

SOUTH ▶

Rank School (State) (*Public)	Overall score	Peer assessment score (5.0=highest)	Average first-year student retention rate	2016 graduation rate Predicted	Actual	% of classes under 20 ('16)	% of classes of 50 or more ('16)	Student/faculty ratio ('16)	SAT/ACT 25th-75th percentile** ('16)	Freshmen in top 25% of HS class ('16)	Acceptance rate ('16)	Average alumni giving rate
1. Elon University (NC)	100	4.0	91%	79%	82%	50%	0%	12/1	1100-1280	62%[5]	60%	22%
2. Rollins College (FL)	98	3.8	85%	71%	72%	69%	0.2%	10/1	1120-1290[2]	67%[5]	61%	12%
3. Samford University (AL)	89	3.8	88%	76%	73%	61%	2%	12/1	23-29	57%[5]	91%	10%
4. The Citadel (SC)*	88	3.8	86%	60%	69%	38%	2%	12/1	20-25	30%	82%	25%
5. Belmont University (TN)	86	3.8	83%	73%	70%	41%	1%	13/1	24-29	60%[5]	81%	16%
6. Stetson University (FL)	85	3.5	78%	64%	64%	60%	0%	13/1	1040-1250[2]	59%	66%	9%
7. James Madison University (VA)*	84	4.0	88%	72%	82%	35%	12%	16/1	1030-1220	38%	72%	6%
8. Berry College (GA)	81	3.3	82%	75%	66%	53%	0%	12/1	24-29[3]	69%	62%	15%
9. Appalachian State University (NC)*	79	3.6	87%	61%	72%	35%	7%	16/1	23-27	57%	68%	7%
10. Loyola University New Orleans	78	3.4	79%	71%	55%	56%	1%	10/1	23-29	55%[5]	68%	7%
11. Christopher Newport Univ. (VA)*	77	3.1	86%	67%	75%	59%	3%	15/1	1060-1250[2]	54%	62%	19%
12. College of Charleston (SC)*	75	3.6	80%	68%	69%	38%	5%	15/1	22-27	52%	84%	5%
12. Embry-Riddle Aeronautical U. (FL)	75	3.6	79%	53%	54%	27%	3%	16/1	1000-1240[2]	50%	71%	2%
14. Univ. of North Carolina–Wilmington*	73	3.4	85%	64%	72%	31%	9%	18/1	22-26	61%	65%	5%
15. Asbury University (KY)	72	3.0	81%	63%	64%	71%	1%	12/1	21-28	59%	70%	18%
15. Bellarmine University (KY)	72	3.1	80%	66%	64%	56%	1%	12/1	22-27	52%[5]	82%	13%
17. John Brown University (AR)	71	3.0	83%	63%	65%	61%	1%	13/1	23-29[2]	62%[5]	77%	12%
17. Univ. of Mary Washington (VA)*	71	3.2	81%	67%	72%	49%	4%	14/1	1010-1210[2]	46%	74%	12%
19. Florida Southern College	69	2.9	80%	58%	60%	60%	0%	15/1	24-29	60%[5]	46%	9%
20. Queens University of Charlotte (NC)	68	2.9	74%	60%	53%	72%	0%	9/1	940-1140	43%	83%	22%
21. Hampton University (VA)	67	2.9	77%	53%	66%	51%	6%	9/1	860-1040[2]	51%	65%	16%
21. University of Tampa (FL)	67	3.2	74%	60%	58%	37%	2%	17/1	990-1160	46%[5]	48%	20%
23. Harding University (AR)	66	3.0	83%	63%	64%	50%	6%	15/1	22-28	42%	76%	10%
23. Milligan College (TN)	66	2.7	81%	61%	63%	79%	1%	10/1	22-27	65%	72%	19%
25. Winthrop University (SC)*	65	3.3	75%	57%	58%	47%	3%	14/1	20-25	51%	69%	7%

Note: Key to footnotes Page 101.

FLORIDA SOUTHERN COLLEGE

flsouthern.edu/guarantee

Zoe Trout '17
Fulbright Scholar

"When you're studying abroad, the whole world has a kind of rosy hue to it. You're living this dream world ... and you get to experience the wonders of new people and places and cultures every single day. It truly feels almost magical."

THE **FLORIDA SOUTHERN COLLEGE**

GUARANTEES

Florida Southern College goes beyond the conventional college experience, guaranteeing each student an internship, a travel-study experience, and graduation in four years. These signature opportunities, combined with our devoted faculty and stunning historic campus, create a college experience unlike any other.

INTERNSHIPS | JUNIOR JOURNEY | 4-YEAR GRADUATION

SOUTH ▶

Rank School (State) (*Public)	Overall score	Peer assessment score (5.0=highest)	Average first-year student retention rate	2016 graduation rate Predicted	Actual	% of classes under 20 ('16)	% of classes of 50 or more ('16)	Student/faculty ratio ('16)	SAT/ACT 25th-75th percentile** ('16)	Freshmen in top 25% of HS class ('16)	Acceptance rate ('16)	Average alumni giving rate
25. Xavier University of Louisiana	65	3.2	72%	51%	41%	54%	4%	14/1	20-26	58%	62%	19%
27. Campbell University (NC)	62	3.0	75%	57%	55%	59%	8%	17/1	920-1130	53%	81%	9%
27. Converse College (SC)	62	2.7	71%	58%	55%	83%	0%	13/1	20-26	50%	60%	12%
27. Longwood University (VA)*	62	2.9	79%	56%	67%	49%	1%	16/1	870-1070	31%	74%	11%
27. Tuskegee University[1] (AL)	62	3.1	72%[8]	53%	45%[6]	57%[4]	9%[4]	14/1[4]	18-23[4]	60%[4]	53%[4]	10%[4]
31. Georgia College & State Univ.*	61	3.1	86%	63%	59%	37%	6%	17/1	22-26	N/A	85%	3%
32. Christian Brothers University (TN)	60	2.7	80%	61%	51%	67%	0%	12/1	22-27	63%	52%	16%
32. Columbia International Univ. (SC)	60	2.4	77%	49%	74%	72%	10%	15/1	930-1190	34%	36%	9%
32. Mississippi College	60	3.0	75%	58%	59%	49%	3%	15/1	21-28[3]	66%	49%	6%
32. Murray State University (KY)*	60	3.0	73%	54%	49%	58%	3%	15/1	21-27	48%	85%	6%
32. Western Kentucky University*	60	3.1	73%	49%	52%	48%	5%	18/1	19-26	44%[5]	94%	8%
32. Wingate University (NC)	60	2.9	74%	52%	54%	46%	1%	14/1	940-1130	53%	70%	10%
38. Lynchburg College (VA)	59	2.6	76%	55%	56%	61%	1%	10/1	920-1120	N/A	64%	15%
38. University of Montevallo (AL)*	59	3.0	76%	56%	50%	48%	1%	14/1	20-26	N/A	65%	10%
38. Western Carolina University (NC)*	59	3.1	79%	49%	56%	26%	5%	17/1	20-25	38%	41%	6%
41. Eastern Mennonite University (VA)	58	2.4	75%	62%	62%	69%	1%	10/1	890-1170	N/A	61%	18%[4]
41. Wheeling Jesuit University (WV)	58	2.6	71%	62%	58%	68%	1%	10/1	18-23	36%	93%	12%
43. Marshall University (WV)*	56	3.4	73%	52%	45%	43%	5%	19/1	19-24	N/A	89%	5%
43. Mary Baldwin University (VA)	56	2.9	62%	43%	46%	65%	2%	10/1	860-1080	27%	99%	17%
43. Radford University (VA)*	56	3.1	76%	49%	58%	35%	9%	16/1	860-1050[2]	22%	81%	4%
46. Freed-Hardeman University (TN)	55	2.4	76%	60%	57%	53%	3%	13/1	21-27	59%[5]	96%	10%
46. University of Tennessee–Martin*	55	2.8	73%	52%	50%	61%	3%	15/1	20-25	48%	67%	7%
48. Lee University (TN)	54	2.8	78%	51%	50%	56%	6%	17/1	21-28	51%	87%	8%
48. University of North Florida*	54	2.9	81%	56%	54%	27%	10%	19/1	21-26	40%	65%	5%
48. West Virginia Wesleyan College	54	2.7	70%	58%	50%	55%	0.3%	13/1	20-25	54%	77%	17%
48. William Carey University (MS)	54	2.6	78%	36%	46%	72%	2%	13/1	21-27[3]	53%	38%	3%
52. Coastal Carolina University (SC)*	53	3.0	66%	48%	42%	38%	2%	17/1	20-25	33%	61%	10%
52. Jacksonville University (FL)	53	2.8	70%	54%	42%	74%	1%	12/1	19-25[2]	N/A	56%	5%
52. Keiser University (FL)†	53	1.9	82%[8]	28%	72%	N/A	N/A	N/A	N/A[2]	N/A	N/A	N/A
52. Marymount University (VA)	53	2.8	76%	56%	52%	49%	0.2%	13/1	860-1085[2]	31%[5]	91%	4%
52. Mississippi Univ. for Women*	53	2.9	71%	49%	47%	66%	4%	14/1	18-24	58%	99%	10%
57. Brenau University (GA)	52	2.7	66%	47%	43%	80%	1%	10/1	860-1030[2]	N/A	36%	3%
57. Columbia College (SC)	52	2.5	72%	47%	50%	82%	0%	13/1	18-24	48%	87%	10%
57. Palm Beach Atlantic University (FL)	52	2.7	74%	55%	51%	64%	1%	12/1	930-1170	N/A	93%	3%
57. Univ. of Tennessee–Chattanooga*	52	3.1	71%	52%	44%	41%	9%	19/1	21-26	N/A	78%	5%
61. Bob Jones University (SC)	51	2.1	81%[8]	48%	60%	70%	7%	12/1	23-26	36%[5]	58%	7%
61. Lenoir-Rhyne University (NC)	51	2.7	69%	50%	48%	59%	0%	13/1	870-1090	N/A	70%	12%
61. Morehead State University (KY)*	51	2.7	69%	50%	46%	53%	4%	18/1	20-26	51%	86%	8%
61. Saint Leo University (FL)*	51	2.7	70%	43%	40%	48%	0%	14/1	20-26[2]	32%	70%	5%
61. University of North Georgia*	51	2.9	81%	50%	54%	29%	3%	21/1	1000-1190	56%	66%	7%
66. Carson-Newman University (TN)	50	2.8	69%	54%	49%	60%	0.2%	13/1	20-26	N/A	63%	7%
66. U. of South Florida–St. Petersburg*	50	2.8	69%	46%	36%	26%	9%	16/1	990-1180	52%	43%	18%
68. Arkansas State University[1]*	49	2.8	75%[8]	40%	37%[8]	49%[4]	5%[4]	17/1[4]	21-26[4]	49%[4]	70%[4]	10%[4]
68. Bryan College (TN)	49	2.3	69%	53%	57%	70%	3%	14/1	21-26	52%	42%	7%
68. Piedmont College (GA)	49	2.4	69%	43%	50%	73%	0%	11/1	860-1090	36%	57%	5%
68. Southern Adventist University (TN)	49	2.4	77%	54%	49%	65%	6%	14/1	20-26	N/A	60%	12%
72. University of Central Arkansas*	48	2.8	71%	52%	42%	46%	3%	17/1	20-27	47%	90%	7%
73. Anderson University (SC)	47	2.8	75%	52%	53%	43%	12%	17/1	21-26	55%	54%	6%
73. Austin Peay State University (TN)*	47	3.0	69%	43%	40%	50%	5%	18/1	19-24[2]	37%	89%	3%
73. Eastern Kentucky University*	47	2.9	71%	50%	45%	41%	4%	16/1	19-25	42%	86%	4%
73. Florida Gulf Coast University*	47	3.0	78%	50%	46%	19%	16%	21/1	22-26	39%	56%	5%
73. Northern Kentucky University*	47	2.9	69%	49%	38%	35%	4%	19/1	20-26	34%	91%	5%
78. Belhaven University (MS)	46	2.7	65%	43%	36%	87%	1%	11/1	20-23	43%[4]	43%	4%
78. University of Charleston (WV)	46	3.0	65%	54%	40%	67%	1%	14/1	18-24	N/A	52%	6%
80. Lincoln Memorial University[1] (TN)	45	2.5	69%[8]	53%	44%[8]	N/A	N/A	N/A	20-28[4]	N/A	74%[4]	5%[4]
80. North Carolina Central Univ.*	45	2.5	78%	34%	43%	37%	4%	16/1	810-940	22%	67%	13%
80. North Greenville University (SC)	45	2.3	74%	50%	57%	75%	0.1%	14/1	20-29[3]	40%	59%	3%
80. St. Thomas University (FL)	45	2.5	65%	42%	41%	70%	0%	12/1	840-1050	27%[5]	54%	2%
80. Thomas More College (KY)	45	2.4	67%	57%	50%	65%	1%	16/1	20-24	31%[4]	89%	11%
85. Methodist University (NC)	44	2.5	62%[8]	43%	39%	65%	0%	11/1	18-23	37%	55%	11%
85. University of North Alabama*	44	2.8	74%	51%	43%	44%	4%	20/1	19-25	N/A	52%	5%
87. Elizabeth City State Univ. (NC)*	42	2.1	70%	30%	37%	70%	1%	13/1	790-950	3%	57%	N/A

Note: Key to footnotes Page 101

Rank	School (State) (*Public)	Overall score	Peer assessment score (5.0=highest)	Average first-year student retention rate	2016 graduation rate Predicted	2016 graduation rate Actual	% of classes under 20 ('16)	% of classes of 50 or more ('16)	Student/ faculty ratio ('16)	SAT/ACT 25th-75th percentile** ('16)	Freshmen in top 25% of HS class ('16)	Accept- ance rate ('16)	Average alumni giving rate
87.	Pfeiffer University[1] (NC)	42	2.3	66%[8]	43%	42%[8]	67%[4]	0%[4]	13/1[4]	805-1060[4]	28%[4]	47%[4]	N/A
89.	Charleston Southern University (SC)	41	2.7	66%	44%	36%	50%	1%	15/1	20-24	48%	61%	7%
89.	Francis Marion University (SC)*	41	2.6	68%	44%	40%	N/A	N/A	15/1	17-22[3]	46%	62%	3%
89.	Jacksonville State University (AL)*	41	2.8	74%	40%	35%	42%	6%	18/1	20-26[3]	41%	53%	8%
89.	King University (TN)	41	2.3	72%	47%	44%	73%	1%	13/1	19-24[9]	43%	51%	8%
89.	Midway University (KY)	41	2.1	80%[8]	34%	53%	N/A	N/A	14/1	18-23	49%	60%	N/A
89.	Troy University (AL)*	41	2.9	71%[8]	44%	39%	53%	6%	15/1	19-26	N/A	91%	N/A
95.	Alcorn State University (MS)*	40	2.5	73%	43%	31%	48%	2%	17/1	16-21	N/A	78%	10%
95.	Auburn University–Montgomery (AL)*	40	2.9	65%	46%	23%	48%	2%	14/1	19-24	44%	77%	3%
95.	Henderson State University (AR)*	40	2.6	59%	44%	34%	68%	1%	16/1	19-25	36%	62%	4%
95.	Lynn University (FL)	40	2.6	70%	55%	45%	46%	0.4%	20/1	870-1060[2]	14%[5]	82%	4%
95.	Nicholls State University (LA)*	40	2.6	68%[8]	50%	47%	40%	10%	17/1	20-24	40%	83%	6%
95.	Tusculum College (TN)	40	2.5	60%	35%	41%	70%	0.2%	15/1	18-23	N/A	74%	13%
101.	Montreat College (NC)	39	2.2	59%[8]	40%	36%	85%	1%	9/1	850-1060	28%	61%	3%[4]
102.	U. of North Carolina–Pembroke*	38	2.6	68%	38%	36%	45%	2%	16/1	18-21	32%	74%	4%
102.	Virginia State University*	38	2.4	67%[8]	24%	44%	N/A	N/A	13/1	730-900[3]	22%	94%	5%
104.	Arkansas Tech University*	37	2.5	69%	41%	38%	44%	6%	19/1	19-25[2]	36%	64%	3%
104.	McNeese State University (LA)*	37	2.6	68%	48%	41%	44%	8%	21/1	20-24	44%	65%	6%
106.	Albany State University (GA)*	36	2.3	71%	28%	31%	55%	1%	19/1	17-20[3]	32%	50%	6%
106.	Amridge University (AL)	36	2.0	N/A	32%	45%[6]	N/A	N/A	10/1[4]	N/A	N/A	N/A	N/A
106.	Campbellsville University (KY)	36	2.5	63%[8]	48%	36%	62%	1%	13/1	19-24	38%	70%	8%
106.	Columbus State University (GA)*	36	2.6	72%	44%	31%	47%	5%	17/1	860-1090	34%	53%	3%
106.	Cumberland University (TN)	36	2.4	66%	53%	55%	55%	4%	16/1[4]	19-23	34%[5]	49%	4%
106.	Faulkner University (AL)	36	2.6	55%	33%	30%	72%	1%	13/1	18-23	60%[5]	45%	2%
106.	Louisiana College (LA)	36	2.2	57%	46%	36%	72%	0.4%	12/1	18-23	27%	72%	1%
106.	Winston-Salem State Univ.[1] (NC)*	36	2.5	78%[8]	39%	46%[6]	N/A	N/A	14/1[4]	810-930[4]	N/A	59%[4]	N/A

School (State) (*Public)	Peer assessment score (5.0=highest)	Average first-year student retention rate	2016 graduation rate Predicted	2016 graduation rate Actual	% of classes under 20 ('16)	% of classes of 50 or more ('16)	Student/ faculty ratio ('16)	SAT/ACT 25th-75th percentile** ('16)	Freshmen in top 25% of HS class ('16)	Accept- ance rate ('16)	Average alumni giving rate
SCHOOLS RANKED 114 THROUGH 142 ARE LISTED HERE ALPHABETICALLY											
Alabama A&M University*	2.5	60%[8]	37%	27%	37%	3%	18/1	16-19	N/A	88%	9%
Alabama State University*	2.4	60%	31%	22%	43%[4]	0.3%[4]	17/1	15-19	9%[5]	46%	4%
Armstrong State University (GA)^	2.5	71%	43%	31%	45%	3%	17/1	890-1080	N/A	79%	5%
Bethel University (TN)	2.4	57%[8]	40%	35%	72%	0.2%	17/1	17-22[2]	23%	67%	N/A
Clayton State University (GA)*	2.4	70%	38%	33%	40%	3%	18/1	18-21	N/A	41%	2%
Concord University (WV)*	2.4	66%	43%	34%	66%	2%	15/1	19-24	47%	81%	4%
Delta State University[1] (MS)*	2.5	65%[8]	39%	34%[6]	N/A	N/A	14/1[4]	18-23[4]	N/A	87%[4]	N/A
Fairmont State University (WV)^	2.4	65%	40%	27%	56%	4%	14/1	18-23	35%	65%	N/A
Fayetteville State University (NC)*	2.4	73%	30%	32%	39%	2%	18/1	790-950	27%	59%	2%
Fort Valley State University (GA)*	2.2	68%	30%	30%	56%	3%	19/1	15-19	15%	26%	12%
Georgia Southwestern State University*	2.4	70%	44%	32%	44%	2%	18/1	870-1060	42%	68%	2%
Grambling State University (LA)*	2.4	66%	28%	36%	40%	8%	20/1	16-20[2]	23%	45%	N/A
Lindsey Wilson College (KY)	2.4	60%	36%	32%	59%	0%	12/1	19-24[2]	36%	73%	12%
Louisiana State U.–Shreveport*	2.6	65%	49%	33%[6]	56%	4%	20/1	N/A	N/A	89%	N/A
Mississippi Valley State Univ.*	2.2	64%[8]	19%	31%	59%	1%	15/1	15-19	N/A	84%	N/A
Norfolk State University (VA)*	2.3	75%[8]	33%	37%	56%	1%	17/1	620-860	17%	85%	N/A
Northwestern State U. of La.*	2.5	70%[8]	46%	41%	50%	5%	20/1	19-24	42%	58%	N/A
Savannah State University (GA)*	2.4	64%[8]	27%	27%	29%	0.1%	20/1	16-19[3]	N/A	51%	6%
South Carolina State University*	2.0	63%	32%	38%	61%	1%	17/1	14-17	25%	86%	6%
Southeastern Louisiana University*	2.5	63%	47%	37%	33%	6%	20/1	20-24	38%	88%	5%[4]
Southeastern University (FL)	2.3	68%	47%	41%	49%	5%	20/1	18-24[3]	28%	46%	7%[4]
Southern Arkansas University*	2.3	64%	42%	34%	38%	3%	19/1	18-24	38%	69%	6%
Southern Univ. and A&M College (LA)*	2.2	66%	22%	29%	N/A	N/A	16/1	16-20	7%	33%	N/A
Southern University–New Orleans*	2.2	53%	20%	16%	46%	0.3%	18/1	16-19	14%	12%	1%
Southern Wesleyan University[1] (SC)	2.3	69%[8]	38%	47%[6]	N/A	N/A	18/1[4]	N/A[2]	N/A	62%[4]	N/A
South University[1] (GA)	1.8	40%[8]	43%	8%[6]	N/A	N/A	14/1[4]	N/A[2]	N/A	N/A	N/A
Thomas University (GA)	1.9	58%[8]	39%	44%	N/A	N/A	10/1[4]	N/A[2]	N/A	47%	N/A
Union College[1] (KY)	2.5	59%[8]	41%	33%[6]	N/A	N/A	12/1[4]	18-23[4]	N/A	69%[4]	N/A
University of West Alabama*	2.5	62%	36%	29%	56%	3%	12/1	18-23	N/A	53%	3%

MIDWEST ▶

Rank School (State) (*Public)	Overall score	Peer assessment score (5.0=highest)	Average first-year student retention rate	2016 graduation rate Predicted	2016 graduation rate Actual	% of classes under 20 ('16)	% of classes of 50 or more ('16)	Student/ faculty ratio ('16)	SAT/ACT 25th-75th percentile** ('16)	Freshmen in top 25% of HS class ('16)	Accept-ance rate ('16)	Average alumni giving rate
1. Creighton University (NE)	100	4.2	90%	81%	79%	44%	8%	11/1	24-30	70%[5]	71%	12%
2. Butler University (IN)	97	4.0	91%	79%	74%	48%	4%	11/1	25-30	76%[5]	73%	20%
3. Drake University (IA)	94	3.9	88%	78%	78%	55%	5%	12/1	25-30[2]	68%	69%	12%
4. Valparaiso University (IN)	86	3.9	85%	71%	66%	43%	5%	13/1	23-29	62%	83%	16%
5. Xavier University (OH)	85	3.7	85%	70%	72%	41%	1%	12/1	23-28[3]	54%[5]	69%	14%
6. John Carroll University (OH)	84	3.4	86%	63%	76%	53%	0.1%	14/1	22-27	56%[5]	83%	14%
7. Bradley University (IL)	83	3.5	87%	70%	74%	56%	2%	12/1	22-28	61%	70%	9%
8. Truman State University (MO)*	82	3.7	88%	73%	72%	45%	1%	16/1	24-30	83%	68%	8%
9. University of Evansville (IN)	77	3.3	85%	72%	69%	62%	1%	11/1	23-29	68%	71%	12%
10. North Central College (IL)	74	3.1	79%	63%	69%	43%	0%	15/1	22-27	52%	59%	19%
11. Bethel University (MN)	72	3.0	85%	65%	74%	54%	3%	11/1	21-28	53%	82%	8%
11. Elmhurst College (IL)	72	3.2	81%	64%	69%	56%	1%	14/1	20-26	43%	70%	9%
11. Milwaukee School of Engineering	72	3.4	84%	76%	64%	37%	0%	16/1	25-30	N/A	66%	8%
11. Rockhurst University (MO)	72	3.1	86%	68%	72%	38%	1%	11/1	23-28	60%	74%	13%
11. St. Catherine University (MN)	72	3.2	81%	61%	64%	66%	2%	10/1	21-26	68%	69%	14%
16. Hamline University (MN)	71	3.3	81%	60%	59%	51%	2%	12/1	21-27	49%	70%	11%
16. Nebraska Wesleyan University	71	3.0	79%	67%	70%	69%	1%	12/1	21-27	23%	74%	17%
18. Baldwin Wallace University (OH)	70	3.0	81%	61%	67%	61%	1%	12/1	21-27[2]	47%	60%	8%
19. Dominican University (IL)	69	2.9	79%	57%	62%	61%	0%	11/1	20-25	56%	64%	15%
19. Franciscan U. of Steubenville (OH)	69	2.5	86%	65%	76%	56%	1%	14/1	22-28	50%[5]	79%	13%
19. Otterbein University (OH)	69	3.1	80%	61%	59%	64%	2%	12/1	21-26	57%	73%	13%
19. University of Detroit Mercy	69	2.9	82%	68%	68%	51%	3%	10/1	22-27	38%	78%	10%
23. Lewis University (IL)	68	2.8	82%	56%	61%	69%	0.3%	13/1	21-26	46%	59%	8%
23. Webster University (MO)	68	2.8	78%	63%	59%	89%	0%	9/1	21-27	42%[5]	47%	3%
25. University of Northern Iowa*	67	3.2	84%	59%	65%	34%	7%	17/1	20-25[3]	46%	82%	8%
26. Drury University (MO)	66	2.8	81%	73%	55%[6]	60%	0.2%	12/1	22-28	41%	70%	13%
26. Kettering University (MI)	66	2.9	93%	76%	53%	53%	1%	14/1	25-29	68%	72%	4%
26. St. Ambrose University (IA)	66	2.9	78%	57%	63%	72%	0.4%	11/1	20-25	41%	64%	6%
29. Augsburg College (MN)	64	3.1	78%	54%	57%	60%	0%	13/1	18-23	N/A	45%	8%
29. Grand Valley State University (MI)*	64	3.0	83%	59%	66%	24%	6%	17/1	21-26	44%	82%	5%
29. Indiana Wesleyan University	64	2.8	82%	61%	64%	65%	2%	14/1	21-27	53%	74%	7%
32. University of St. Francis (IL)	63	2.7	80%	57%	63%	64%	0%	12/1	20-26	40%[5]	49%	7%
33. Univ. of Wisconsin–La Crosse*	62	3.1	86%	68%	69%	26%	12%	19/1	23-27	59%	82%	4%
34. Capital University (OH)	61	2.7	75%	63%	59%	65%	2%	12/1	22-28[3]	46%	69%	8%
34. College of St. Scholastica (MN)	61	2.8	84%	59%	66%	48%	3%	15/1	21-26	52%	64%	5%
34. University of Indianapolis	61	3.1	75%	56%	55%	51%	1%	13/1	890-1120	51%	86%	11%
37. Univ. of Wisconsin–Eau Claire*	60	3.1	83%	63%	68%	22%	16%	22/1	22-26	47%	89%	8%
38. Anderson University (IN)	59	2.9	75%	56%	58%	69%	3%	11/1[4]	920-1140	51%	68%	8%
38. Bethel College (IN)	59	2.6	79%	48%	66%	62%	5%	12/1	910-1150	47%	98%	10%
38. Carroll University (WI)	59	2.9	79%	60%	63%	51%	5%	15/1	21-26	53%	72%	9%
38. Concordia University (NE)	59	2.7	77%	61%	67%	51%	2%	13/1	20-27	41%	73%	20%
38. Lawrence Technological Univ. (MI)	59	2.8	82%	70%	52%	73%	0.3%	11/1	22-29	53%	69%	4%
38. University of Findlay (OH)	59	2.7	80%[8]	63%	63%	57%	0.4%	16/1	20-25	45%	73%	9%
38. University of Michigan–Dearborn*	59	2.8	81%	59%	54%	33%	6%	17/1	22-27	57%	65%	8%
38. University of Minnesota–Duluth*	59	3.0	77%	59%	59%	38%	14%	18/1	22-26	42%	77%	6%
46. Baker University (KS)	58	2.5	78%	44%	55%	68%	0%	13/1	20-25	40%	78%	12%
47. Aquinas College (MI)	57	2.7	79%	54%	53%	67%	0.2%	11/1	21-26	N/A	75%	14%
47. Marian University (IN)	57	2.7	75%	54%	56%	61%	3%	13/1	900-1140	38%	59%	15%
47. St. Mary's Univ. of Minnesota	57	2.7	77%	58%	61%	74%	0%	20/1	20-26	38%[5]	79%	8%
47. Univ. of Northwestern–St. Paul (MN)	57	2.5	81%[8]	54%	65%[6]	N/A	N/A	N/A	21-27[4]	49%[4]	87%[4]	16%[4]
51. Concordia University Wisconsin	56	2.7	74%	50%	56%	60%	2%	11/1	21-27[3]	46%	63%	3%
51. Eastern Illinois University*	56	2.5	75%	53%	57%	47%	3%	14/1	18-24	33%	47%	4%
51. Robert Morris University (IL)	56	2.4	48%	31%	70%	48%	1%	21/1	16-22[2]	15%	74%	1%
54. Alverno College (WI)	55	3.0	72%	40%	42%	79%	0%	10/1	18-22	38%	74%	11%
54. Morningside College (IA)	55	2.4	73%	55%	54%	60%	0%	13/1	20-26	45%	57%	22%
54. Mount Mercy University (IA)	55	2.4	78%	58%	58%	59%	1%	14/1	18-24	44%	62%	12%
54. Olivet Nazarene University (IL)	55	2.7	76%	61%	57%	43%	8%	15/1	19-26	52%	73%	13%
54. Univ. of Wisconsin–Stevens Point*	55	2.9	76%	56%	64%	33%	5%	20/1	20-25[9]	38%	77%	5%
54. Ursuline College (OH)	55	2.5	67%	49%	52%	88%	0%	7/1	19-24	47%	90%	14%
60. Heidelberg University (OH)†	54	2.7	69%	53%	49%	66%	1%	11/1	19-25	N/A	79%	18%
61. Muskingum University (OH)	53	2.5	70%	52%	54%	73%	0.4%	12/1	19-24[3]	37%	77%	14%
61. Univ. of Wisconsin–Whitewater*	53	2.9	80%	51%	57%	31%	6%	21/1	20-25	28%	81%	8%
61. Western Illinois University*	53	2.6	68%	50%	53%	50%	3%	15/1	18-23	30%	59%	4%

Note: Key to footnotes Page 101

Rank	School (State) (*Public)	Overall score	Peer assessment score (5.0=highest)	Average first-year student retention rate	2016 graduation rate		% of classes under 20 ('16)	% of classes of 50 or more ('16)	Student/ faculty ratio ('16)	SAT/ACT 25th-75th percentile** ('16)	Freshmen in top 25% of HS class ('16)	Accept- ance rate ('16)	Average alumni giving rate
					Predicted	Actual							
64.	Spring Arbor University (MI)	52	2.6	78%	50%	54%	60%	2%	14/1	19-25	41%	71%	9%
64.	St. Xavier University (IL)	52	2.9	74%	54%	51%	42%	2%	14/1	19-24	50%	75%	6%
64.	Univ. of Illinois–Springfield*	52	2.8	76%	60%	50%	51%	2%	14/1	20-26	43%	65%	5%
64.	Univ. of Nebraska–Kearney*	52	2.7	80%	52%	57%	50%	3%	14/1	19-25	43%	85%	8%
64.	Walsh University (OH)	52	2.4	78%	51%	58%	75%	0%	14/1	19-25[9]	40%	78%	10%
64.	Winona State University (MN)*	52	2.8	78%	54%	59%	33%	8%	18/1	20-25	32%	60%	8%
70.	Fontbonne University (MO)	51	2.5	77%	54%	52%	90%	0%	10/1	20-25	N/A	90%	4%
70.	Southern Illinois U.–Edwardsville*	51	2.8	72%	58%	47%	37%	11%	20/1	20-26	40%	89%	3%
70.	University of Wisconsin–Stout*	51	2.9	75%	51%	54%	32%	1%	19/1	19-25	28%	88%	3%
73.	McKendree University (IL)	50	2.5	74%	55%	52%	74%	0%	14/1	20-24	36%	68%	7%
73.	Univ. of Wisconsin–Oshkosh*	50	2.8	77%	53%	54%	43%	8%	18/1	20-24[3]	35%	65%	4%
75.	Concordia University Chicago†	49	2.6	65%	54%	48%	79%	0%	15/1	19-24	40%	50%	7%
75.	Judson University (IL)	49	2.3	73%	57%	64%	77%	0.3%	9/1	19-24	31%	75%	4%
75.	Malone University (OH)	49	2.3	72%	52%	53%	65%	1%	11/1	19-25	37%	73%	8%
75.	MidAmerica Nazarene U. (KS)	49	2.3	71%[8]	39%	54%	75%	2%	17/1	18-25[2]	N/A	52%	8%
75.	North Park University (IL)	49	2.7	78%	54%	53%	60%[4]	2%[4]	11/1[4]	18-24	N/A	94%	N/A
75.	University of Saint Francis (IN)	49	2.7	70%	49%	55%	66%	0.3%	11/1	900-1090	43%	97%	5%
75.	University of Sioux Falls (SD)	49	2.5	69%	54%	53%	65%	1%	13/1	20-25	43%	91%	3%
75.	William Woods University (MO)	49	2.4	75%	53%	54%	81%	0%	11/1	19-25	55%	88%	9%
83.	Ferris State University (MI)*	48	2.7	76%	49%	47%	42%	3%	16/1	19-25[9]	N/A	78%	2%
83.	Northern Michigan University*	48	2.9	74%	52%	47%	36%	6%	21/1	19-25[3]	N/A	76%	4%
83.	Pittsburg State University (KS)*	48	2.6	74%	47%	51%	51%	6%	17/1	19-24	46%	87%	7%
83.	Quincy University[1] (IL)	48	2.5	70%[8]	49%	50%[8]	64%[4]	0.3%[4]	14/1[4]	19-24[4]	32%[4]	63%[4]	13%[4]
87.	College of St. Mary (NE)	47	2.4	78%	47%	40%	69%	0.4%	8/1	19-25	42%	60%	11%
87.	Grace College and Seminary (IN)	47	2.2	80%	58%	61%	55%	4%	22/1	930-1170[3]	52%	78%	15%
87.	Mount St. Joseph University (OH)	47	2.3	69%	51%	52%	65%	0.3%	11/1	19-24	30%	88%	9%

MIDWEST ▶

Rank School (State) (*Public)	Overall score	Peer assessment score (5.0=highest)	Average first-year student retention rate	2016 graduation rate Predicted	2016 graduation rate Actual	% of classes under 20 ('16)	% of classes of 50 or more ('16)	Student/ faculty ratio ('16)	SAT/ACT 25th-75th percentile** ('16)	Freshmen in top 25% of HS class ('16)	Accept- ance rate ('16)	Average alumni giving rate
87. Northwest Missouri State Univ.*	47	2.7	70%	51%	49%	47%	8%	21/1	20-25	40%	74%	8%
87. Stephens College (MO)	47	2.4	67%	57%	50%	78%	0%	9/1	20-25	44%	61%	10%
87. University of Central Missouri*	47	2.7	70%	49%	50%	47%	4%	19/1	20-25[2]	36%	98%	N/A
93. Madonna University (MI)	46	2.4	82%	59%	60%	69%	2%	11/1	18-23	43%[4]	75%	2%
93. Mount Vernon Nazarene U. (OH)	46	2.2	78%	52%	57%	69%	2%	14/1	20-25	51%	74%	6%
93. Southeast Missouri State Univ.*	46	2.7	73%	53%	49%	43%	4%	21/1	20-25[3]	44%	83%	5%
93. Tiffin University (OH)	46	2.5	64%	21%	44%	48%	0%	14/1	17-22[9]	26%	60%	4%
93. Univ. of Wisconsin–River Falls*	46	2.7	74%	52%	54%	37%	7%	18/1	20-25	36%	72%	6%
93. Washburn University (KS)*	46	2.8	68%	50%	36%[8]	48%	2%	12/1	19-25	35%	100%	12%[4]
99. Greenville University (IL)	45	2.3	69%	48%	47%	57%	4%	14/1	18-25	38%	58%	15%
99. Minnesota State Univ.–Mankato*	45	2.8	74%	50%	51%	31%	9%	23/1	20-24[3]	27%	62%	5%
99. Mount Mary University (WI)	45	2.3	74%	47%	46%	82%	0.4%	12/1	18-23	51%	56%	N/A
99. Northern State University (SD)*	45	2.4	70%	50%	50%	68%	2%	20/1	19-24	28%	89%	10%
99. University of Michigan–Flint*	45	2.6	73%	49%	37%	53%	2%	14/1	19-26	42%	65%	1%
99. Univ. of Wisconsin–Green Bay*	45	2.9	75%	57%	50%	31%	8%	22/1	20-25	N/A	92%	4%
99. Univ. of Wisconsin–Platteville*	45	2.8	77%	52%	53%	23%	6%	22/1	20-25	40%	79%	N/A
106. Concordia University–St. Paul (MN)	44	2.7	72%	45%	51%	68%	0%	17/1	18-24[3]	27%	56%	5%
106. Missouri State Univ.[1]*	44	2.7	77%[8]	56%	53%[6]	N/A	N/A	21/1[4]	21-26[4]	N/A	86%[4]	N/A
106. Ohio Dominican University	44	2.6	69%	45%	37%	63%	0%	13/1	19-24	31%	52%	5%
109. Bemidji State University (MN)*	43	2.6	68%	48%	46%	39%	9%	19/1	20-24	19%	64%	6%
109. Rockford University (IL)	43	2.3	64%	51%	49%	79%	0%	10/1	19-24	N/A	54%	8%
109. Roosevelt University (IL)	43	2.4	63%	44%	40%	56%	1%	10/1	19-24	46%[5]	73%	5%
109. University of Dubuque (IA)	43	2.6	66%[8]	44%	46%	80%	0.4%	13/1	17-22[3]	14%	76%	8%
109. University of Mary (ND)	43	2.4	75%	53%	54%	67%	5%	15/1	20-26[3]	51%	84%	1%
109. Wayne State College (NE)*	43	2.4	67%	45%	48%	50%	1%	18/1	18-25[2]	30%	100%	11%
115. Cornerstone University (MI)	42	2.3	77%	52%	53%	56%	2%	14/1	18-25	39%	63%	3%
115. Mount Marty College (SD)	42	2.1	70%	50%	44%	81%	0%	11/1	19-23	45%[4]	65%	7%
115. Viterbo University[1] (WI)	42	2.7	77%[8]	48%	49%[6]	N/A	N/A	11/1[4]	21-26[4]	N/A	66%[4]	N/A
118. Dakota State University (SD)*	41	2.4	70%	52%	37%	53%	1%	17/1	19-25	25%	83%	8%
118. Minnesota State Univ.–Moorhead*	41	2.6	72%	48%	41%	41%	7%	19/1	20-25	28%	60%	5%
118. Siena Heights University (MI)	41	2.5	67%	46%	46%	80%	0%	13/1	19-22[2]	29%	72%	4%[4]
118. St. Cloud State University (MN)*	41	2.7	71%	48%	44%	42%	4%	20/1	18-24	19%	85%	3%
122. Davenport University (MI)	40	2.1	71%	29%	43%	74%	0%	12/1	19-23[2]	N/A	78%	1%
122. Emporia State University (KS)*	40	2.7	72%	49%	44%	47%	5%	18/1	19-25[9]	33%	87%	8%
122. Evangel University (MO)	40	2.2	73%[8]	47%	54%	N/A	N/A	14/1[4]	20-26	N/A	75%	N/A
122. Marian University (WI)	40	2.3	69%	45%	45%	76%	0%	12/1	17-23	26%	77%	5%

School (State) (*Public)	Peer assessment score (5.0=highest)	Average first-year student retention rate	2016 graduation rate Predicted	2016 graduation rate Actual	% of classes under 20 ('16)	% of classes of 50 or more ('16)	Student/ faculty ratio ('16)	SAT/ACT 25th-75th percentile** ('16)	Freshmen in top 25% of HS class ('16)	Accept- ance rate ('16)	Average alumni giving rate
SCHOOLS RANKED 126 THROUGH 165 ARE LISTED HERE ALPHABETICALLY											
Aurora University[1] (IL)	2.4	71%[8]	47%	57%[6]	N/A	N/A	17/1[4]	19-23[4]	N/A	77%[4]	4%[7]
Avila University[1] (MO)	2.4	72%[8]	48%	51%[6]	N/A	N/A	10/1[4]	18-24[4]	N/A	51%[4]	N/A
Black Hills State University (SD)*	2.5	61%[8]	44%	36%	N/A	N/A	20/1	19-24	9%	47%	N/A
Calumet College of St. Joseph (IN)	2.1	56%	37%	26%	72%	1%	11/1	15-21[2]	20%	30%	3%
Chicago State University[1]*	1.7	55%[8]	34%	17%[6]	N/A	N/A	11/1[4]	16-20[4]	N/A	21%[4]	N/A
Columbia College Chicago[1]	2.5	69%[8]	48%	42%[6]	N/A	N/A	12/1[4]	N/A[2]	N/A	88%[4]	N/A
DeVry University (IL)	1.5	N/A	35%	24%	91%	0%	17/1	N/A[2]	N/A	N/A	N/A
Fort Hays State University (KS)*	2.4	70%[8]	38%	35%	47%	4%	16/1	18-24[2]	31%	91%	N/A
Friends University (KS)	2.2	66%	39%	39%	76%	2%	10/1	19-24	38%	55%	9%
Governors State University (IL)*	2.1	53%[8]	N/A	N/A	64%	0.4%	13/1	17-21	30%	42%	N/A
Graceland University (IA)	2.1	64%	53%	43%	66%	1%	14/1	18-24	27%	48%	17%
Indiana University East*	2.3	66%	38%	32%	66%	2%	14/1	830-1040	27%	60%	6%
Indiana University Northwest*	2.5	67%	35%	23%	45%	6%	14/1	820-1010	32%	76%	5%
Indiana U.–Purdue U.–Fort Wayne*	2.8	65%	44%	24%	50%	4%	14/1	860-1080	35%	71%	N/A
Indiana University–South Bend*	2.6	65%	40%	28%	41%	3%	14/1	840-1050	29%	77%	5%
Indiana University Southeast*	2.5	62%	41%	31%	51%	1%	14/1	17-23	31%	84%	6%
Lake Erie College (OH)	2.0	69%	50%	45%	69%	0.4%	14/1	18-22[2]	24%	63%	7%
Lakeland University[1] (WI)	2.1	73%[8]	47%	52%[6]	N/A	N/A	15/1[4]	16-22[4]	N/A	96%[4]	N/A

Note: Key to footnotes Page 101.

CONTINUED (SCHOOLS RANKED 126 THROUGH 165 ARE LISTED HERE ALPHABETICALLY)

School (State) (*Public)	Peer assessment score (5.0=highest)	Average first-year student retention rate	2016 graduation rate Predicted	2016 graduation rate Actual	% of classes under 20 ('16)	% of classes of 50 or more ('16)	Student/ faculty ratio ('16)	SAT/ACT 25th-75th percentile** ('16)	Freshmen in top 25% of HS class ('16)	Accept- ance rate ('16)	Average alumni giving rate
Lincoln University (MO)*	2.1	52%	44%	22%	51%	2%	15/1	15-20	24%	N/A	8%
Lourdes University (OH)	2.2	64%	35%	28%	65%	0%	11/1	18-24	29%	89%	5%
Marygrove College[1] (MI)	2.3	50%[8]	24%	26%[6]	N/A	N/A	8/1[4]	14-18[4]	N/A	57%[4]	4%
Metropolitan State University[1] (MN)*	2.2	68%[8]	45%	33%[6]	N/A	N/A	17/1[4]	N/A[2]	N/A	100%[4]	2%[7]
Minot State University (ND)*	2.3	70%	54%	43%	N/A	N/A	12/1	18-23	22%	60%	4%
Missouri Baptist University[1]	2.1	60%[8]	49%	41%[6]	N/A	N/A	18/1[4]	18-23[4]	N/A	57%[4]	N/A
Newman University (KS)	2.3	72%	56%	51%	66%	1%	11/1	20-27[9]	44%	58%	5%
Northeastern Illinois University*	2.3	59%	47%	24%	51%	0.4%	16/1	16-20	18%	71%	2%
Notre Dame College of Ohio[1]	2.3	62%[8]	47%	38%[6]	N/A	N/A	14/1[4]	17-21[4]	N/A	91%[4]	N/A
Park University (MO)	2.3	57%[8]	50%	23%	90%[4]	0%[4]	15/1	N/A[2]	35%[4]	85%	1%[4]
Purdue University–Northwest (IN)*	2.8	61%[8]	48%	28%	46%	4%	19/1	860-1070	34%	54%	N/A
Saginaw Valley State Univ. (MI)*	2.5	70%	49%	38%	36%	2%	17/1	20-25	41%	76%	3%[4]
Silver Lake College (WI)	2.0	71%[8]	43%	44%	N/A	N/A	8/1	14-22[2]	N/A	55%	N/A
Southwest Baptist University[1] (MO)	2.2	66%[8]	44%	47%[6]	N/A	N/A	15/1[4]	20-26[4]	N/A	90%[4]	N/A
Southwestern College (KS)	2.1	65%	55%	38%	80%	2%	10/1	18-23	31%	92%	4%
Southwest Minnesota State University*	2.4	68%	52%	50%	43%	3%	17/1	18-23	20%	54%	10%
University of Southern Indiana*	2.5	71%	44%	38%	39%	5%	17/1	890-1080	37%	92%	3%
University of St. Mary (KS)	2.4	72%	43%	34%	73%	1%	11/1	19-24[3]	34%[4]	49%	N/A
Upper Iowa University	2.1	61%	39%	44%	89%	0%	17/1	17-24	27%	94%	3%
William Penn University[1] (IA)	2.0	59%[8]	37%	32%[6]	N/A	N/A	16/1[4]	N/A[2]	N/A	58%[4]	N/A
Youngstown State University (OH)*	2.4	72%	36%	31%	40%	6%	17/1	18-25	34%	67%	5%

WEST ▶

Rank School (State) (*Public)	Overall score	Peer assessment score (5.0=highest)	Average first-year student retention rate	2016 graduation rate Predicted	2016 graduation rate Actual	% of classes under 20 ('16)	% of classes of 50 or more ('16)	Student/ faculty ratio ('16)	SAT/ACT 25th-75th percentile** ('16)	Freshmen in top 25% of HS class ('16)	Accept- ance rate ('16)	Average alumni giving rate
1. Trinity University (TX)	100	4.1	89%	87%	77%	60%	1%	9/1	1160-1370	75%	41%	15%
2. Santa Clara University (CA)	99	4.0	96%	83%	89%	44%	1%	11/1	28-32	85%[5]	48%	20%
3. Loyola Marymount University (CA)	90	3.8	90%	78%	83%	54%	1%	10/1	1120-1330	73%[5]	54%	20%
4. Gonzaga University (WA)	87	3.9	93%	76%	84%	40%	2%	12/1	1110-1300	69%[5]	67%	15%
5. Chapman University (CA)	80	3.6	90%	82%	79%	46%	3%	14/1	1110-1300	81%[5]	54%	8%
6. University of Portland (OR)	79	3.7	91%	74%	82%	34%	1%	12/1	1080-1320	75%[5]	61%	12%
7. Seattle University	76	3.5	86%	73%	75%	61%	1%	12/1	1070-1290	64%[9]	61%	7%
8. Whitworth University (WA)	75	3.6	86%	70%	73%	61%	1%	11/1	1000-1260[2]	60%[5]	89%	15%
9. Mills College (CA)	74	3.2	78%	69%	66%	71%	0.4%	10/1	920-1230[2]	64%[5]	84%	18%
9. St. Mary's College of California	74	3.4	88%	69%	73%	70%	0%	11/1	950-1160	N/A	80%	10%
11. Cal. Poly. State U.–San Luis Obispo*	73	3.9	94%	75%	83%	15%	13%	19/1	26-31[3]	88%[5]	29%	4%
12. University of Redlands (CA)	72	3.2	87%	66%	74%	68%	0.1%	13/1	980-1190	55%	75%	12%
13. University of Dallas	70	3.4	80%	72%	70%	65%	3%	11/1	1040-1290[3]	61%[5]	80%	14%
14. California Lutheran University	69	3.3	84%	67%	73%	56%	1%	14/1	990-1080	68%[5]	64%	14%
15. St. Edward's University (TX)	68	3.4	83%	63%	64%	59%	0.1%	14/1	1010-1200	60%	74%	8%
16. Pacific Lutheran University (WA)	66	3.2	82%	69%	71%	52%	3%	11/1	980-1230	85%[5]	77%	10%
17. Point Loma Nazarene University (CA)	65	3.2	86%	71%	71%	39%	2%	15/1	1030-1240	66%	69%	8%
18. Abilene Christian University (TX)	63	3.4	77%	68%	62%	43%	8%	14/1	21-27	56%	85%	9%
19. Western Washington University*	61	3.4	83%	62%	70%	34%	16%	19/1	990-1220	56%[5]	83%	4%
19. Westminster College (UT)	61	3.0	77%	66%	62%	72%	0%	9/1	22-27	52%	94%	13%
21. St. Mary's Univ. of San Antonio	60	3.1	75%	58%	55%	56%	1%	11/1	950-1130	55%	78%	10%
22. Pacific University (OR)	58	3.0	80%	67%	58%	63%	3%	11/1	1010-1230	N/A	79%	10%
23. George Fox University (OR)	56	3.2	81%	63%	64%	47%	2%	14/1	980-1220	59%[5]	79%	4%
23. LeTourneau University (TX)	56	3.0	77%	61%	53%	66%	2%	14/1	1030-1280[2]	55%[5]	44%	7%
23. N.M. Inst. of Mining and Tech.*	56	3.1	77%	78%	49%	56%	6%	11/1	23-29	64%	23%	N/A
26. University of St. Thomas (TX)	55	3.0	83%	65%	60%	60%	0%	10/1	990-1175	57%	77%	8%
27. Oklahoma City University	54	3.0	82%	71%	62%	72%	2%	11/1	23-30[3]	54%	72%	5%
27. Regis University (CO)	54	3.2	80%	62%	68%	60%	1%	14/1	22-26	39%[5]	57%	4%
29. Mount Saint Mary's University (CA)	53	2.9	79%	48%	65%	63%	0.1%	14/1	820-1020[2]	35%	86%	12%
30. Dominican University of California	51	2.7	84%	64%	68%	62%	0.2%	9/1	918-1123	57%[5]	78%	N/A
31. California Baptist University	50	3.0	78%	47%	60%	54%	5%	18/1	850-1100	41%	73%	2%
31. Calif. State Poly. Univ.–Pomona*	50	3.5	90%	44%	69%	14%	13%	23/1	900-1160[3]	N/A	59%	2%
33. Evergreen State College (WA)*	49	3.3	70%	47%	56%	36%	9%	21/1	920-1180	26%[5]	97%	4%
33. Hardin-Simmons University (TX)	49	2.9	67%	59%	52%	71%	1%	12/1	19-24	53%	88%	9%

WEST ▶

Rank	School (State) (*Public)	Overall score	Peer assessment score (5.0=highest)	Average first-year student retention rate	2016 graduation rate Predicted	2016 graduation rate Actual	% of classes under 20 ('16)	% of classes of 50 or more ('16)	Student/faculty ratio ('16)	SAT/ACT 25th-75th percentile** ('16)	Freshmen in top 25% of HS class ('16)	Acceptance rate ('16)	Average alumni giving rate
35.	San Jose State University (CA)*	48	3.2	87%	49%	62%	22%	14%	26/1	920-1150	N/A	53%	2%
35.	Univ. of Colo.–Colorado Springs*	48	3.2	69%	53%	47%	40%	7%	18/1	20-26	36%	93%	4%
37.	California State Univ.–Chico*	47	2.9	86%	59%	69%	25%	14%	24/1	880-1100	76%[5]	67%	4%[7]
37.	The Master's U. and Seminary (CA)	47	2.5	85%	61%	69%	74%	7%	10/1	950-1210	49%[5]	83%	10%
39.	California State U.–Long Beach*	46	3.2	90%	57%	66%	23%	9%	26/1	930-1160	N/A	32%	2%[7]
40.	Chaminade Univ. of Honolulu	45	2.7	75%	37%	56%	59%	0.3%	11/1	870-1060	48%	91%	3%
41.	Concordia University (CA)	44	2.7	76%	50%	54%	58%	0.2%	18/1	907-1160	49%[5]	65%	4%
41.	Fresno Pacific University (CA)	44	2.5	79%	39%	64%	67%	2%	13/1	850-1060	56%	68%	N/A
41.	Notre Dame de Namur University (CA)	44	2.6	77%	44%	50%	73%	0%	12/1	800-1018	25%[5]	97%	12%
44.	Central Washington University*	42	3.0	77%	49%	52%	37%	4%	18/1	960-1150[3]	N/A	79%	2%
44.	La Sierra University[1] (CA)	42	2.4	77%[8]	49%	53%[8]	72%[4]	2%[4]	14/1[4]	840-1030[4]	42%[4]	45%[4]	3%[4]
44.	Saint Martin's University (WA)	42	2.6	80%	55%	55%	69%	0%	12/1	895-1150[3]	51%	95%	4%
47.	California State U.–Monterey Bay*	41	2.8	82%	49%	55%	20%	7%	27/1	840-1060	51%	35%	2%
47.	Humboldt State University (CA)*	41	2.8	74%	48%	46%	32%	13%	23/1	890-1140[2]	50%	76%	5%
47.	Northwest Nazarene University (ID)	41	2.5	76%	48%	49%	61%	4%	16/1	910-1170	49%	95%	12%
47.	Oklahoma Christian U.	41	2.7	78%	62%	47%	59%	7%	13/1	21-28[3]	55%	61%	14%
47.	Oral Roberts University (OK)	41	2.4	80%	55%	56%	62%	5%	16/1	19-24	36%	58%	8%
47.	Univ. of the Incarnate Word (TX)	41	2.8	74%	49%	57%	57%	2%	14/1	850-940	36%	92%	5%
47.	Walla Walla University (WA)	41	2.8	79%[8]	60%	51%	60%	6%	15/1	920-1210	40%[4]	62%	N/A
54.	Univ. of Mary Hardin-Baylor (TX)	40	2.9	69%	53%	48%	44%	5%	19/1	920-1120[3]	47%	79%	6%
55.	California State U.–Stanislaus*	39	2.7	85%	37%	57%	23%	7%	22/1	790-1000[2]	N/A	74%	1%
55.	Holy Names University (CA)	39	2.3	72%	46%	45%	74%	0%	6/1	820-990	40%[5]	49%	9%
57.	Alaska Pacific University	38	2.3	60%[8]	58%	48%	96%	0%	8/1	21-26[2]	N/A	55%	N/A
57.	Sonoma State University (CA)*	38	2.9	81%	53%	61%	24%	19%	24/1	880-1080	N/A	76%	1%
59.	California State U.–Los Angeles*	37	3.0	82%	25%	46%	19%	9%	25/1	780-980[2]	N/A	64%	2%
59.	Hawaii Pacific University	37	2.9	69%	62%	42%	58%	1%	12/1	900-1090	53%	75%	1%
59.	Texas Wesleyan University	37	2.7	56%	51%	32%	64%	0%	17/1	925-1070	38%	41%	7%
59.	Vanguard Univ. of Southern California	37	2.4	76%	48%	56%	65%	4%	13/1	830-1030	29%	70%	8%
63.	Calif. State U.–San Bernardino*	36	2.7	87%	34%	55%	21%	20%	28/1	780-980[2]	N/A	58%	2%
63.	Northwest University (WA)	36	2.5	79%	51%	50%	62%	4%	7/1	940-1190	N/A	93%	N/A
63.	University of Houston–Clear Lake*	36	2.7	74%[8]	N/A	N/A	28%	6%	15/1	930-1110	44%	65%	6%
66.	California State U.–Channel Islands[1]*	35	2.8	78%[8]	45%	57%[6]	N/A	N/A	22/1[4]	N/A[2]	N/A	68%[4]	N/A
66.	Corban University (OR)	35	2.2	79%	55%	58%	63%	1%	13/1	950-1170	33%	35%	3%
66.	University of Hawaii–Hilo[1]*	35	2.9	66%[8]	54%	38%[8]	49%[4]	2%[4]	12/1[4]	830-1050[4]	50%[4]	71%[4]	N/A
66.	Woodbury University (CA)	35	2.2	79%	44%	44%	82%	0%	8/1	860-1115[2]	N/A	66%	2%
70.	California State U.–Sacramento*	34	3.0	82%[8]	40%	49%	18%	16%	25/1	930-1050[2]	N/A	72%	3%
70.	Houston Baptist University	34	2.6	67%	55%	44%	49%	1%	16/1	940-1140	56%[5]	35%	4%[4]
70.	Texas A&M International University*	34	2.8	81%	40%	41%	32%	17%	20/1	820-1020	54%	54%	2%
73.	California State U.–Northridge*	33	3.1	78%	39%	50%	13%	14%	27/1	800-1030	N/A	48%	5%[7]
73.	Stephen F. Austin State Univ. (TX)*	33	3.0	70%	47%	44%	28%	10%	20/1	870-1090	41%	62%	3%
73.	Western Oregon University*	33	2.7	71%	44%	39%	52%	2%	14/1	840-1070[2]	35%	88%	3%[4]
76.	California State Univ.–San Marcos*	32	2.8	82%	46%	54%	14%	8%	26/1	860-1060	N/A	73%	1%[7]
76.	Southern Oregon University*	32	2.7	70%	50%	40%	46%	4%	21/1	900-1130	N/A	78%	1%
76.	Southern Utah University*	32	2.6	66%	55%	39%	42%	7%	19/1	20-26	48%	72%	4%
76.	University of Alaska–Anchorage*	32	2.8	71%	55%	25%	58%	3%	12/1	17-24[2]	32%[5]	82%	4%
76.	University of Central Oklahoma*	32	2.9	64%	49%	38%	41%	1%	18/1	19-24	35%	94%	1%
81.	Lubbock Christian University (TX)	31	2.5	70%	48%	39%	68%	3%	12/1	19-25[3]	43%	100%	5%
81.	Oklahoma Wesleyan University	31	2.5	54%	51%	44%	82%	3%	14/1	16-22[3]	4%	73%	16%
81.	Prescott College (AZ)	31	2.4	71%	42%	31%	99%	1%	9/1	920-1200	N/A	68%	N/A
81.	Simpson University (CA)	31	2.2	78%	43%	47%	74%	2%	11/1	860-1105	51%	52%	3%
81.	West Texas A&M University*	31	2.7	66%	48%	45%	35%	10%	20/1	18-24	43%	60%	3%
86.	Eastern Washington University*	30	2.7	76%[8]	45%	46%	40%	11%	21/1	850-1080	N/A	95%	N/A
86.	Our Lady of the Lake University (TX)	30	2.5	61%	45%	39%	63%	0%	10/1	830-1010	33%	55%	13%
86.	Weber State University (UT)*	30	2.9	66%	49%	35%	47%	6%	20/1	18-24[2]	29%	100%	2%
86.	Western State Colorado University*	30	2.5	69%	50%	45%	61%	0.1%	19/1	19-25	18%	92%	N/A
90.	University of Texas–Tyler*	29	2.8	62%	56%	39%	32%	11%	25/1	950-1150	39%[5]	69%	1%[4]
91.	Midwestern State University (TX)*	28	2.5	70%[8]	51%	42%	41%	13%	18/1	870-1080	36%	74%	5%[4]
91.	Northwest Christian University (OR)	28	2.1	68%	44%	49%	73%	2%	13/1	863-1080	N/A	67%	5%[4]
91.	U. of Texas of the Permian Basin*	28	2.5	69%	53%	34%	32%	12%	24/1	850-1060	50%	81%	13%
94.	California State Univ.–Bakersfield*	27	2.7	72%[8]	30%	42%	33%	8%	26/1	800-1010[2]	N/A	100%	1%[7]
95.	University of North Texas–Dallas*	26	2.7	68%[8]	N/A	N/A	45%	0.2%	12/1	820-985	45%	68%	N/A

Note: Key to footnotes Page 101

School (State) (*Public)	Peer assessment score (5.0=highest)	Average first-year student retention rate	2016 graduation rate Predicted	2016 graduation rate Actual	% of classes under 20 ('16)	% of classes of 50 or more ('16)	Student/faculty ratio ('16)	SAT/ACT 25th–75th percentile** ('16)	Freshmen in top 25% of HS class ('16)	Acceptance rate ('16)	Average alumni giving rate
SCHOOLS RANKED 96 THROUGH 126 ARE LISTED HERE ALPHABETICALLY											
Adams State University[1] (CO)*	2.4	56%[8]	33%	26%[6]	N/A	N/A	14/1[4]	17-23[4]	N/A	64%[4]	N/A
Angelo State University[1] (TX)*	2.3	60%[8]	46%	32%[6]	23%[4]	10%[4]	23/1[4]	18-23[4]	31%[4]	77%[4]	2%[4]
California State U.–Dominguez Hills*	2.5	81%	33%	42%	22%	9%	21/1	760-940[2]	N/A	75%	1%
California State Univ.–East Bay*	2.7	79%	42%	48%	15%	16%	23/1	770-990[9]	N/A	70%	N/A
Cameron University (OK)*	2.2	62%	39%	21%	46%	1%	19/1	17-22[2]	14%	100%	3%
Colorado Christian University[1]	2.6	73%[8]	45%	41%[6]	N/A	N/A	15/1[4]	N/A[2]	N/A	N/A	N/A
Colorado State University–Pueblo*	2.7	64%	32%	32%	55%	6%	16/1	18-23	33%	96%	2%
Concordia University Texas[1]	2.4	62%[8]	50%	36%[6]	N/A	N/A	9/1[4]	890-1090[4]	N/A	82%[4]	N/A
East Central University[1] (OK)*	2.2	64%[8]	38%	35%[6]	N/A	N/A	18/1[4]	18-23[4]	N/A	46%[4]	N/A
Eastern New Mexico University[1]*	2.5	58%[8]	38%	29%[6]	N/A	N/A	19/1[4]	17-23[4]	N/A	50%[4]	N/A
Eastern Oregon University*	2.4	63%	40%	31%	68%	4%	16/1	830-1040	35%	97%	1%
Hope International University (CA)	2.0	76%	34%	39%	71%	0%	14/1	820-1040	30%	32%	7%
Langston University (OK)*	2.0	64%[8]	26%	18%	N/A	N/A	17/1	N/A	N/A	52%	N/A
Metropolitan State Univ. of Denver*	2.8	66%	34%	27%	37%	1%	17/1	17-23[3]	19%	64%	N/A
Montana State Univ.–Billings*	2.7	56%	43%	36%	53%	3%	17/1	18-22[2]	27%	100%	N/A
New Mexico Highlands University*	2.3	50%[8]	37%	18%[6]	77%	1%	14/1[4]	15-20[2]	17%	100%	N/A
Northeastern State University (OK)*	2.5	64%	43%	27%	49%	3%	17/1	19-24[3]	48%	94%	2%
Northwestern Oklahoma State U.*	2.3	57%	40%	26%	54%	1%	14/1	18-23	31%	44%	4%
Sierra Nevada College (NV)	2.2	66%[0]	52%	34%	82%	0%	10/1	850-1050[3]	32%	51%	N/A
Southeastern Oklahoma State U.*	2.4	60%	44%	26%	52%	2%	20/1	18-23	45%	77%	2%
Southern Nazarene University[1] (OK)	2.5	54%[8]	46%	46%[6]	N/A	N/A	14/1[4]	N/A	N/A	N/A	N/A
Southwestern Assemblies of God University[1] (TX)	2.3	71%[8]	42%	39%[6]	N/A	N/A	14/1[4]	18-23[4]	N/A	28%[4]	1%[4]
Southwestern Oklahoma State U.*	2.4	68%	44%	35%	42%	6%	19/1	18-24[2]	48%	91%	N/A
Sul Ross State University[1] (TX)*	2.2	55%[8]	34%	24%[6]	62%[4]	3%[4]	16/1[4]	740-940[4]	20%[4]	80%[4]	N/A
Tarleton State University (TX)*	2.5	69%	42%	43%	32%	9%	20/1	850-1060	23%	74%	4%[7]
Texas A&M University–Texarkana[1]*	2.6	49%[8]	N/A	N/A	N/A	N/A	9/1[4]	19-24[4]	N/A	71%[4]	N/A
University of Alaska–Southeast[1]*	2.2	64%[8]	60%	17%[6]	N/A	N/A	12/1[4]	N/A[2]	N/A	49%[4]	N/A
University of Houston–Downtown*	2.5	66%	39%	16%	32%	2%	20/1	820-990	32%	83%	1%
University of Houston–Victoria*	2.5	50%[8]	39%	18%	43%	7%	18/1	780-1000[9]	18%[5]	53%	3%[7]
University of the Southwest[1] (NM)	2.2	52%[8]	44%	12%[6]	N/A	N/A	17/1[4]	N/A	N/A	N/A	N/A
Wayland Baptist University (TX)	2.1	49%	46%	24%	84%	0.2%	8/1	17-22	30%	100%	1%

The Top Public Regional Universities ▶

NORTH
Rank School (State)

1. College of New Jersey
2. SUNY–Geneseo
3. SUNY Polytechnic Institute
4. Massachusetts Maritime Academy
5. CUNY–Baruch College
6. Rutgers University–Camden (NJ)
7. CUNY–Hunter College
7. SUNY–New Paltz
9. Ramapo College of New Jersey
10. CUNY–Queens College
10. Stockton University (NJ)
10. Towson University (MD)
13. SUNY College–Cortland
13. SUNY College–Oneonta
13. SUNY–Oswego

SOUTH
Rank School (State)

1. The Citadel (SC)
2. James Madison University (VA)
3. Appalachian State University (NC)
4. Christopher Newport Univ. (VA)
5. College of Charleston (SC)
6. U. of North Carolina–Wilmington
7. Univ. of Mary Washington (VA)
8. Winthrop University (SC)
9. Longwood University (VA)
10. Georgia College & State Univ.
11. Murray State University (KY)
11. Western Kentucky University
13. University of Montevallo (AL)
14. Western Carolina University (NC)
15. Marshall University (WV)
15. Radford University (VA)

MIDWEST
Rank School (State)

1. Truman State University (MO)
2. University of Northern Iowa
3. Grand Valley State University (MI)
4. Univ. of Wisconsin–La Crosse
5. Univ. of Wisconsin–Eau Claire
6. University of Michigan–Dearborn
6. University of Minnesota–Duluth
8. Eastern Illinois University
9. Univ. of Wisconsin–Stevens Point
10. Univ. of Wisconsin–Whitewater
10. Western Illinois University
12. Univ. of Illinois–Springfield
12. Univ. of Nebraska–Kearney
15. Winona State University (MN)
15. Southern Illinois U.–Edwardsville
15. University of Wisconsin–Stout

WEST
Rank School (State)

1. California Polytechnic State University–San Luis Obispo
2. Western Washington University
3. N.M. Inst. of Mining and Tech.
4. Calif. State Poly. Univ.–Pomona
5. Evergreen State College (WA)
6. San Jose State University (CA)
6. Univ. of Colo.–Colorado Springs
8. California State Univ.–Chico
9. California State U.–Long Beach
10. Central Washington University
11. California State U.–Monterey Bay
11. Humboldt State University (CA)
13. California State U.–Stanislaus
14. Sonoma State University (CA)
15. California State U.–Los Angeles

Footnotes:
1. School refused to fill out U.S. News statistical survey. Data that appear are from school in previous years or from another source such as the National Center for Education Statistics.
2. SAT and/or ACT not required by school for some or all applicants.
3. In reporting SAT/ACT scores, the school did not include all students for whom it had scores or refused to tell U.S. News whether all students with scores had been included.
4. Data reported to U.S. News in previous years.
5. Data based on fewer than 51 percent of enrolled freshmen.
6. Some or all data reported to the National Center for Education Statistics.
7. Data reported to the Council for Aid to Education.

8. This rate, normally based on four years of data, is given here for fewer than four years because school didn't report rate for the most recent year or years to U.S. News.
9. SAT and/or ACT may not be required by school for some or all applicants, and in reporting SAT/ACT scores, the school did not include all students for whom it had scores or refused to tell U.S. News whether all students with scores had been included.
**The SAT scores used in the rankings and published in this guidebook are for the "old" SAT test taken prior to March 2016.
† School's Carnegie classification has changed. It appeared in a different U.S. News ranking category last year.
N/A means not available.

Best Regional Colleges

What Is a Regional College?

These schools focus almost entirely on the undergraduate experience and offer a broad range of programs in the liberal arts (which account for fewer than half of bachelor's degrees granted) and in fields such as business, nursing and education. They grant few graduate degrees. Because most of the 324 colleges in the category draw heavily from nearby states, they are ranked by region: North, South, Midwest, West.

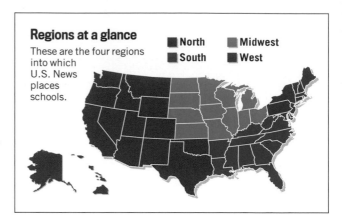

Regions at a glance
These are the four regions into which U.S. News places schools.

■ North ■ Midwest
■ South ■ West

NORTH ▶

Rank School (State) (*Public)	Overall score	Peer assessment score (5.0=highest)	Average first-year student retention rate	2016 graduation rate Predicted	2016 graduation rate Actual	% of classes under 20 ('16)	% of classes of 50 or more ('16)	Student/ faculty ratio ('16)	SAT/ACT 25th-75th percentile** ('16)	Freshmen in top 25% of HS class ('16)	Accept- ance rate ('16)	Average alumni giving rate
1. Cooper Union (NY)	100	4.1	96%[8]	85%	82%[8]	70%[4]	1%[4]	9/1[4]	1240-1510[4]	90%[4]	13%[4]	18%[4]
2. U.S. Coast Guard Acad. (CT)*	96	4.3	92%	78%	78%	78%	0%	6/1	1170-1340	79%	21%	N/A
3. U.S. Merchant Marine Acad. (NY)*	88	4.0	92%	73%	76%	45%	0.3%	13/1	26-30	68%[4]	15%	N/A
4. Messiah College (PA)	73	3.4	87%	69%	76%	48%	2%	13/1	1020-1260	62%	80%	12%
5. Maine Maritime Academy*	72	3.6	82%	53%	62%	53%	0%	13/1	950-1140	43%[5]	72%	18%
6. Cedar Crest College (PA)	60	3.3	74%	56%	56%	79%	1%	10/1	880-1090	55%	66%	13%
7. Colby-Sawyer College (NH)	55	3.2	75%[8]	44%	59%	65%	0.4%	12/1	950-1140[2]	N/A	90%	10%
8. St. Francis College (NY)	50	3.0	79%	38%	52%	56%	0.3%	16/1	830-1030	N/A	64%	11%
8. University of Maine–Farmington*	50	2.9	74%	41%	56%	64%	1%	13/1	870-1128[2]	42%	80%	2%
8. Vaughn Col. of Aeron. and Tech. (NY)	50	2.9	74%	43%	53%	73%	0%	14/1	904-1129	N/A	79%	4%
11. Wilson College (PA)	49	2.8	68%	56%	59%	85%	0%	10/1	810-1030[2]	49%	58%	17%
12. Cazenovia College (NY)	47	2.9	72%	44%	43%	82%	0%	12/1	843-1090[2]	35%	90%	7%
13. Pennsylvania College of Technology*	45	3.1	74%	48%	34%	61%	0%	14/1	840-1050[2]	22%	67%	1%
14. SUNY College of Technology–Alfred*	43	2.9	82%	43%	56%	44%	2%	18/1	830-1060[2]	N/A	72%	2%
15. Farmingdale State College–SUNY*	42	3.0	81%	48%	53%	23%	1%	20/1	880-1060	24%[5]	58%	0.4%
16. Unity College (ME)	41	2.8	73%	47%	58%	43%	1%	15/1	960-1188[2]	32%[5]	93%	2%
17. SUNY College of A&T–Cobleskill*	40	2.8	74%	38%	44%[6]	43%	3%	17/1	910-1100[2]	21%	78%	4%
17. SUNY College of Technology–Delhi*	40	2.9	71%	36%	52%	46%	3%	17/1	840-1030[2]	17%[5]	66%	5%
19. Concordia College (NY)	37	2.8	75%[8]	36%	54%	N/A	N/A	9/1	830-1010[2]	35%[5]	71%	7%
19. La Roche College (PA)	37	2.5	73%[8]	37%	55%	65%	0%	13/1	810-1020	30%[5]	92%	4%
19. Vermont Technical College*	37	2.7	76%	47%	44%	61%	11%	13/1	820-1050[9]	26%	70%	1%
22. Dean College (MA)	36	2.9	69%	38%	34%	61%	0%	16/1	740-980[2]	N/A	91%	6%
22. Paul Smith's College (NY)	36	2.9	71%[8]	38%	40%	53%	5%	15/1	860-1100[2]	22%[5]	82%	10%
24. Castleton University[1] (VT)*	34	2.8	72%[8]	41%	50%[6]	N/A	N/A	12/1[4]	850-1063[4]	N/A	97%[4]	N/A
25. SUNY Col. of Technology–Canton*	33	2.8	77%	31%	39%	38%	2%	18/1	800-1030[2]	17%	83%	2%
26. Keystone College (PA)	32	2.7	67%	31%	38%[8]	65%	1%	13/1	780-970[2]	N/A	98%	4%
26. Mount Aloysius College (PA)	32	2.8	N/A	34%	37%[6]	78%	0%	11/1	870-1030[3]	N/A	73%[4]	N/A
26. Mount Ida College (MA)	32	2.6	61%	38%	43%	77%	0%	13/1	790-1020[2]	N/A	68%	2%
29. Morrisville State College (NY)*	30	2.8	69%	37%	30%	61%	0%	16/1	750-970[9]	16%[5]	77%	3%
29. Univ. of Maine–Presque Isle*	30	2.6	62%	46%	35%	76%	0%	16/1	770-1030[2]	13%	77%	1%
31. University of Maine–Fort Kent*	27	2.6	67%	33%	31%	61%	3%	19/1	790-985[2]	24%	96%	5%
32. Fisher College (MA)	26	2.4	59%	28%	46%	74%[4]	0%[4]	17/1	690-880[2]	N/A	67%	N/A
33. CUNY–York College*	25	2.7	74%[8]	29%	30%	28%	9%	16/1	770-950	N/A	64%	N/A
33. Lyndon State College[1] (VT)*	25	2.8	65%[8]	35%	36%[6]	N/A	N/A	14/1[4]	840-1060[4]	N/A	98%[4]	N/A
35. University of Valley Forge (PA)	24	2.3	74%[8]	39%	35%	80%	4%	13/1	N/A[2]	N/A	79%	N/A
36. CUNY–New York City Col. of Tech.*	23	2.7	77%	29%	25%	31%	0%	16/1	740-940[2]	N/A	75%	1%
36. Newbury College (MA)	23	2.6	62%[8]	39%	34%[6]	71%	0%	13/1	780-1030[2]	N/A	81%	1%

Note: Key to footnotes, Page 107.

NORTH ▶

School (State) (*Public)	Peer assessment score (5.0=highest)	Average first-year student retention rate	2016 graduation rate Predicted	2016 graduation rate Actual	% of classes under 20 ('16)	% of classes of 50 or more ('16)	Student/faculty ratio ('16)	SAT/ACT 25th-75th percentile** ('16)	Freshmen in top 25% of HS class ('16)	Accept-ance rate ('16)	Average alumni giving rate
SCHOOLS RANKED 38 THROUGH 48 ARE LISTED HERE ALPHABETICALLY											
Bay State College[1] (MA)	2.2	N/A	36%	25%[6]	68%[4]	0%[4]	N/A	N/A[2]	N/A	N/A	N/A
Becker College[1] (MA)	2.6	68%[8]	36%	27%[6]	N/A	N/A	17/1[4]	900-1110[4]	N/A	67%[4]	N/A
Central Pennsylvania College	2.5	54%	30%	38%	67%	0%	9/1	660-910[9]	N/A	67%	0.4%
College of St. Joseph[1] (VT)	2.7	64%[8]	37%	25%[6]	97%[4]	0%[4]	N/A	783-923[4]	10%[4]	70%[4]	N/A
CUNY–Medgar Evers College*	2.5	N/A	29%	9%	5%	2%	18/1	710-870[9]	N/A	98%	N/A
Five Towns College (NY)	2.5	68%	34%	34%[6]	79%[4]	0%[4]	15/1	770-980[4]	16%[4]	55%	N/A
Mitchell College[1] (CT)	2.4	81%[8]	43%	41%[6]	N/A	N/A	14/1[4]	N/A[2]	N/A	74%[4]	N/A
New England Institute of Technology (RI)	2.5	N/A	N/A	N/A	N/A	N/A	13/1	N/A[2]	N/A	N/A	N/A
Southern Vermont College	2.8	64%[8]	34%	20%	N/A	N/A	14/1	770-990	12%	63%	N/A
University of Maine–Augusta*	3.1	53%	35%	14%	76%[4]	0.3%[4]	16/1[4]	780-1000[4]	N/A	97%[4]	0.3%[4]
Wesley College (DE)	3.1	52%[8]	42%	22%	N/A	N/A	15/1	740-930	16%	60%	N/A

SOUTH ▶

Rank School (State) (*Public)	Overall score	Peer assessment score (5.0=highest)	Average first-year student retention rate	2016 graduation rate Predicted	2016 graduation rate Actual	% of classes under 20 ('16)	% of classes of 50 or more ('16)	Student/faculty ratio ('16)	SAT/ACT 25th-75th percentile** ('16)	Freshmen in top 25% of HS class ('16)	Accept-ance rate ('16)	Average alumni giving rate
1. High Point University (NC)	100	3.7	79%	58%	64%	50%	1%	15/1	995-1200	46%[5]	79%	11%
2. Flagler College (FL)	90	3.6	70%	51%	60%	56%	0%	16/1	960-1150	N/A	55%	14%
3. University of the Ozarks[1] (AR)	82	3.5	70%[8]	56%	46%[8]	68%[4]	1%[4]	13/1[4]	20-25[4]	39%[4]	97%[4]	14%[4]
4. Catawba College (NC)	79	3.1	72%	47%	52%	77%	0.4%	13/1	18-24[9]	39%	47%	14%
5. University of Mobile (AL)	71	3.3	75%	48%	48%	62%	0.3%	13/1	19-25	53%	62%	1%
6. Univ. of South Carolina–Aiken*	70	3.3	68%	45%	43%	49%	1%	15/1	18-23	40%	66%	5%
7. Alice Lloyd College (KY)†	68	3.2	64%	40%	34%	50%	2%	17/1	18-25	43%	4%	45%
8. Barton College (NC)	65	2.7	71%	41%	52%	65%	0%	11/1	17-23	32%	41%	8%
8. Belmont Abbey College (NC)	65	3.2	62%	41%	44%	66%	0%	16/1	880-1090[2]	N/A	97%	6%
8. Blue Mountain College (MS)	65	2.7	71%	45%	51%	70%	1%	13/1	18-23	42%	48%	7%
8. Coker College (SC)	65	3.0	66%[8]	44%	48%	75%	0%	13/1	18-22[3]	30%	59%	N/A
8. Kentucky Wesleyan College	65	3.0	65%	50%	38%	85%[4]	0.3%[4]	13/1	20-26[4]	N/A	60%	13%
13. Huntingdon College (AL)	64	2.9	65%	50%	39%	59%	0.3%	14/1	19-24	29%	57%	29%
14. U. of South Carolina–Upstate*	63	3.1	71%	42%	42%	59%	1%	15/1	18-22	37%	56%	2%
15. Tennessee Wesleyan University	62	2.8	68%[8]	41%	44%	69%	3%	12/1	19-25	48%[5]	58%	7%
16. Lander University (SC)*	60	2.9	67%	32%	43%	43%	3%	17/1	17-23	38%	62%	9%
17. Averett University (VA)	59	2.8	60%	35%	43%	76%	0%	11/1	810-1010	23%	57%	3%
17. Newberry College (SC)	59	2.8	69%	44%	44%	61%	1%	12/1	17-23[3]	36%	60%	16%
19. Lees-McRae College (NC)	57	2.9	62%	36%	38%	80%	0%	12/1	18-23[2]	27%	63%	10%
19. University of Mount Olive (NC)	57	2.7	64%	36%	51%	73%	0%	15/1	17-22[2]	N/A	48%	3%[4]
21. Brevard College[1] (NC)	56	3.0	58%[8]	43%	41%[8]	68%[4]	0%[4]	11/1[4]	840-1060[4]	18%[4]	41%[4]	7%[4]
21. Florida Memorial University	56	2.7	68%[8]	21%	39%	61%[4]	0%[4]	16/1	16-19[9]	N/A	23%	N/A
21. Toccoa Falls College (GA)	56	2.6	71%	39%	47%	65%	1%	15/1	830-1080	28%	54%	3%
24. Mars Hill University (NC)	55	2.9	57%	36%	34%	75%	0.2%	11/1	17-22[3]	25%	57%	13%
25. Bennett College (NC)	54	2.4	53%	30%	42%	72%	0%	11/1	623-778[2]	10%	98%	27%
26. Alderson Broaddus University (WV)	53	2.7	56%	48%	49%	66%	4%	17/1	18-23	27%	41%	10%
26. Welch College (TN)	53	2.4	71%	46%	45%	90%	1%	8/1	17-25	52%	64%	14%
28. Brescia University (KY)	52	2.8	62%	42%	27%	93%	0%	8/1	20-26	N/A	47%	12%
28. Oakwood University[1] (AL)	52	2.9	76%[8]	39%	41%[6]	N/A	N/A	N/A	N/A	N/A	47%[4]	N/A
28. Pensacola State College (FL)*	52	2.9	70%[8]	N/A	N/A	64%	0.2%	21/1	780-1020[2]	N/A	100%	5%
28. Reinhardt University (GA)	52	2.8	60%	40%	33%	74%	0%	12/1	18-23	26%	87%	5%
28. South Florida State College*	52	2.8	N/A	41%	45%	69%	0%	N/A	N/A[2]	N/A	100%	N/A
33. Kentucky State University*	51	2.7	54%	36%	21%	76%	0.3%	12/1	17-21[3]	26%	53%	4%[4]
33. Shorter University (GA)	51	3.0	64%[8]	44%	37%	N/A	N/A	N/A	18-23[3]	N/A	61%	N/A
35. Williams Baptist College (AR)	50	2.7	56%[8]	40%	35%	66%	0%	12/1	19-24	36%	60%	4%
36. Everglades University (FL)	49	2.4	51%	21%	52%	88%	0%	13/1	N/A[2]	N/A	74%	N/A
37. Univ. of South Carolina–Beaufort†	48	2.9	55%	37%	24%	52%	3%	16/1	18-24	31%	65%	3%[4]
37. West Liberty University (WV)*	48	2.5	69%	38%	42%	65%	1%	13/1	18-23	33%	72%	3%
39. Limestone College (SC)	47	2.4	56%	43%	36%	68%	0%	13/1	19-23[2]	19%	52%	6%[4]
40. Ohio Valley University (WV)	46	2.4	53%	43%	30%	80%	0%	10/1	18-23[2]	29%	64%	10%
41. Bluefield College (VA)	45	2.6	56%	37%	32%	69%	0%	14/1	790-1010	25%	85%	7%
41. Emmanuel College (GA)	45	2.6	62%	34%	28%	65%	0%	13/1	790-1070	N/A	41%	5%
41. Point University (GA)	45	2.6	59%[8]	32%	34%	73%	2%	18/1	17-22[2]	N/A	51%	N/A
44. Greensboro College (NC)	44	2.8	55%[8]	36%	44%	N/A	N/A	N/A	N/A	N/A	36%	10%[7]
45. Warner University (FL)	43	2.5	60%	31%	32%	66%	0%	17/1	17-20[2]	18%	25%	2%

SOUTH ▶

Rank School (State) (*Public)	Overall score	Peer assessment score (5.0=highest)	Average first-year student retention rate	2016 graduation rate		% of classes under 20 ('16)	% of classes of 50 or more ('16)	Student/ faculty ratio ('16)	SAT/ACT 25th-75th percentile** ('16)	Freshmen in top 25% of HS class ('16)	Accept-ance rate ('16)	Average alumni giving rate
				Predicted	Actual							
46. Ferrum College (VA)	42	2.8	53%	32%	30%	58%	0%	16/1	770-960[2]	12%	72%	6%
46. North Carolina Wesleyan College	42	2.7	54%	30%	21%	71%	0%	15/1	16-23[2]	30%	62%	3%
48. Central Baptist College (AR)	41	2.5	65%	37%	29%	74%	0%	14/1	19-25	34%	62%	7%
48. Kentucky Christian University[1]	41	2.7	59%[8]	44%	39%[6]	N/A	N/A	12/1[4]	19-23[4]	N/A	36%[4]	N/A
50. Bluefield State College (WV)*	39	2.5	61%	36%	26%	87%	0%	14/1	17-22	42%[5]	83%	4%
50. Chowan University (NC)	39	2.8	49%	23%	23%	50%	0.3%	16/1	720-895	11%	58%	17%
50. Georgia Gwinnett College*	39	3.0	67%	29%	17%	34%	0%	18/1	810-1040	14%	89%	3%
50. St. Augustine's University (NC)	39	2.3	49%	28%	43%	54%	0%	13/1	630-830	N/A	73%	6%
50. Univ. of Arkansas–Pine Bluff*	39	2.6	65%	30%	23%	54%	4%	15/1	16-21	39%	42%	7%
55. College of Coastal Georgia*	35	2.7	60%	29%	24%	43%	1%	19/1	800-1000	N/A	95%	1%
55. University of Holy Cross[1] (LA)	35	2.7	69%[8]	34%	31%[6]	N/A	N/A	10/1[4]	N/A[2]	N/A	100%[4]	N/A
57. Glenville State College (WV)*	34	2.5	65%	35%	23%	62%	1%	18/1	16-22	24%	69%	3%
57. Truett McConnell University (GA)	34	2.5	64%	34%	42%	62%	11%	18/1	860-1053	32%	91%	2%
57. Webber International University (FL)	34	2.6	50%	34%	27%	53%	0%	24/1	17-21	16%	50%	N/A

School (State) (*Public)	Peer assessment score (5.0=highest)	Average first-year student retention rate	2016 graduation rate		% of classes under 20 ('16)	% of classes of 50 or more ('16)	Student/ faculty ratio ('16)	SAT/ACT 25th-75th percentile** ('16)	Freshmen in top 25% of HS class ('16)	Accept-ance rate ('16)	Average alumni giving rate
			Predicted	Actual							
SCHOOLS RANKED 60 THROUGH 79 ARE LISTED HERE ALPHABETICALLY											
Abraham Baldwin Agricultural College[1] (GA)*	2.6	60%[8]	32%	20%[6]	N/A	N/A	22/1[4]	830-1040[4]	N/A	77%[4]	N/A
Arkansas Baptist College	2.1	47%[8]	35%	1%	57%	0%	22/1	17-19[2]	N/A	28%	N/A
Atlanta Metropolitan State College (GA)*	2.1	60%[8]	N/A	N/A	N/A	N/A	17/1	17-21[2]	N/A	19%	1%
Benedict College[1] (SC)	2.3	60%[8]	22%	29%[6]	N/A	N/A	18/1[4]	N/A[2]	N/A	N/A	N/A
Brewton-Parker College[1] (GA)	2.3	51%[8]	29%	17%[6]	N/A	N/A	13/1[4]	N/A[2]	N/A	N/A	N/A
Chipola College[1] (FL)*	2.6	N/A	N/A	N/A	N/A	N/A	15/1[4]	N/A[2]	N/A	N/A	N/A
Crowley's Ridge College[1] (AR)	2.2	60%[8]	32%	22%[6]	N/A	N/A	10/1[4]	N/A[2]	N/A	N/A	N/A
East Georgia State College[1]*	2.3	N/A	N/A	N/A	N/A	N/A	N/A	N/A[2]	N/A	59%[4]	N/A
Edward Waters College[1] (FL)	2.2	47%[8]	21%	20%[6]	N/A	N/A	15/1[4]	14-18[4]	N/A	54%[4]	N/A
Florida College	2.5	N/A	47%	14%[6]	68%	3%	13/1	20-26[3]	N/A	79%	39%[4]
Gordon State College (GA)*	2.5	N/A	N/A	N/A	N/A	N/A	20/1	750-970[3]	N/A	41%	N/A
Indian River State College (FL)*	2.8	N/A	N/A	N/A	36%	1%	N/A	N/A[2]	N/A	100%	N/A
Lane College[1] (TN)	2.5	51%[8]	19%	29%[8]	42%[4]	1%[4]	21/1[4]	14-17[4]	30%[4]	55%[4]	N/A
LeMoyne-Owen College (TN)	2.5	47%[8]	23%	14%	75%	0%	12/1	13-17[4]	N/A	100%[4]	N/A
Livingstone College (NC)	2.3	54%	20%	25%	51%	1%	15/1	13-17[3]	6%	48%	10%
Middle Georgia State University*	2.7	67%[8]	32%	33%	N/A	N/A	N/A	N/A[2]	N/A	85%	N/A
Rust College (MS)	2.5	57%[8]	23%	23%[6]	N/A	N/A	21/1	13-17	N/A	N/A	N/A
Shaw University (NC)	2.2	44%[8]	25%	28%[6]	49%	3%	19/1	640-820	4%	49%	N/A
University of Arkansas–Fort Smith[1]*	2.8	64%[8]	38%	25%[6]	N/A	N/A	19/1[4]	N/A	N/A	56%[4]	N/A
Voorhees College[1] (SC)	2.4	49%[8]	20%	33%[6]	N/A	N/A	12/1[4]	N/A[2]	N/A	93%[4]	N/A

MIDWEST ▶

Rank School (State) (*Public)	Overall score	Peer assessment score (5.0=highest)	Average first-year student retention rate	2016 graduation rate		% of classes under 20 ('16)	% of classes of 50 or more ('16)	Student/ faculty ratio ('16)	SAT/ACT 25th-75th percentile** ('16)	Freshmen in top 25% of HS class ('16)	Accept-ance rate ('16)	Average alumni giving rate
				Predicted	Actual							
1. Calvin College (MI)	100	4.0	86%	71%	77%	33%	1%	13/1	23-29[2]	57%	75%	21%
2. Taylor University (IN)	98	3.8	87%	70%	76%	60%	5%	13/1	22-29	64%[5]	80%	20%
3. Augustana University (SD)	91	3.7	83%	70%	71%	51%	3%	11/1	23-29	53%	69%	14%
4. Ohio Northern University	89	3.4	86%	76%	74%	60%	1%	11/1	23-28	57%	64%	13%
5. College of the Ozarks (MO)	88	3.6	80%	52%	69%	56%	3%	14/1	21-25[3]	66%	14%	20%
6. Goshen College (IN)	86	3.4	79%	62%	68%	66%	0%	10/1	930-1253	52%	68%	21%
7. Cottey College (MO)	85	2.9	75%[8]	57%	72%	92%	0%	7/1	21-26	35%[5]	68%	3%
8. Dordt College (IA)	83	3.2	83%	58%	69%	62%	4%	13/1	21-27	42%	76%	22%
8. Marietta College (OH)	83	3.2	70%	61%	61%	79%	0%	10/1	21-26	53%	61%	17%
10. Northwestern College (IA)	81	3.3	80%	66%	64%	66%	1%	11/1	21-28	47%	66%	19%
11. Millikin University (IL)†	80	3.6	76%	56%	60%	67%	1%	11/1	19-26	39%	64%	12%
11. University of Mount Union (OH)	80	3.5	77%	54%	59%	51%	0.4%	13/1	20-26[2]	50%	77%	18%
13. Benedictine College (KS)	77	3.4	78%	53%	63%	60%	1%	14/1	21-28	42%[5]	98%	23%
13. Cedarville University (OH)	77	3.2	86%	72%	72%	62%	5%	13/1	23-29	68%[5]	69%	11%
13. Loras College (IA)	77	3.3	81%	62%	71%	44%	0.3%	12/1	20-25	36%	92%	20%
16. Huntington University (IN)	75	3.2	80%	53%	65%	74%	1%	13/1	900-1150	45%	90%	15%
17. Clarke University (IA)	71	2.9	74%	54%	61%	74%	1%	8/1	20-25	40%	65%	14%

Note: Key to footnotes, Page 107.

MIDWEST ▶

Rank	School (State) (*Public)	Overall score	Peer assessment score (5.0=highest)	Average first-year student retention rate	2016 graduation rate		% of classes under 20 ('16)	% of classes of 50 or more ('16)	Student/ faculty ratio ('16)	SAT/ACT 25th–75th percentile** ('16)	Freshmen in top 25% of HS class ('16)	Accept- ance rate ('16)	Average alumni giving rate
					Predicted	Actual							
17.	Hastings College (NE)	71	3.1	69%	52%	58%	62%	0.2%	12/1	19-26	45%	64%	19%
17.	Wisconsin Lutheran College	71	2.8	76%	56%	61%	72%	0.3%	10/1	21-27	46%	90%	16%
20.	Adrian College (MI)	70	3.2	65%	55%	53%	68%	0%	12/1	19-24	56%	58%	11%
20.	Trinity Christian College (IL)	70	3.1	81%	56%	59%	63%	0.4%	11/1	20-27	35%	70%	12%
22.	Saint Mary-of-the-Woods Col. (IN)	66	3.1	77%	46%	46%	97%	0%	6/1	820-1030	31%[4]	73%	23%
23.	Trine University (IN)	65	3.3	74%	57%	57%	49%	0.2%	13/1	20-27	46%	77%	8%
24.	Buena Vista University (IA)	62	3.0	73%	65%	53%	76%	0%	9/1	19-26	40%	64%	6%
25.	Manchester University (IN)	60	3.1	69%	51%	57%	49%	1%	14/1	865-1090[2]	34%	71%	18%
26.	Eureka College (IL)	58	2.7	70%	50%	52%	71%	0%	13/1	19-25	25%	65%	17%
27.	Bluffton University (OH)	56	2.7	68%	47%	49%	67%	0%	11/1	19-24	32%	50%	10%
27.	Central Methodist University (MO)	56	2.9	63%	57%	45%	65%	2%	12/1	20-24	38%	61%	7%
27.	University of Jamestown (ND)	56	3.2	71%	51%	50%	50%	3%	13/1	20-25[3]	39%	57%	14%
30.	Dakota Wesleyan University (SD)	55	2.9	73%	41%	47%	60%	1%	12/1	19-24	30%	73%	13%
31.	Briar Cliff University (IA)	53	2.9	68%	45%	44%	67%	4%	14/1	18-24	25%	15%	12%

UNITED STATES
COAST GUARD
ACADEMY

MIDWEST ▶

Rank School (State) (*Public)	Overall score	Peer assessment score (5.0=highest)	Average first-year student retention rate	2016 graduation rate		% of classes under 20 ('16)	% of classes of 50 or more ('16)	Student/faculty ratio ('16)	SAT/ACT 25th-75th percentile** ('16)	Freshmen in top 25% of HS class ('16)	Acceptance rate ('16)	Average alumni giving rate
				Predicted	Actual							
31. Union College (NE)	53	2.6	74%	53%	47%[6]	70%	1%	11/1	18-26	25%[4]	64%	21%
33. University of Minnesota–Crookston*	52	2.7	68%	45%	54%	63%	1%	16/1	20-24[3]	29%	68%	5%[4]
33. Valley City State University (ND)*	52	2.8	69%	46%	35%	76%	0%	11/1	18-24	N/A	98%	10%
35. Defiance College (OH)	51	2.7	57%	45%	42%	75%[4]	0%[4]	11/1	18-22	22%	58%	10%
36. Univ. of Wisconsin–Superior*	50	2.9	68%	51%	43%	59%	2%	13/1	19-24	23%	69%	5%
37. Blackburn College (IL)	49	2.6	67%	47%	42%	73%	1%	13/1	18-23	28%	54%	16%
37. Culver-Stockton College (MO)	49	2.8	69%	49%	47%	60%	0%	15/1	18-23	24%	58%	17%
39. Grand View University (IA)	46	2.6	70%	44%	48%	69%	0.4%	13/1	18-23	35%	97%	4%
39. McPherson College (KS)	46	2.6	60%	50%	37%	80%	1%	13/1	19-24[2]	28%	53%	7%
39. Oakland City University (IN)	46	2.1	71%	43%	47%	94%	0%	12/1	18-24[2]	28%	33%	9%
42. Ottawa University (KS)	45	2.6	62%	46%	47%	67%	1%	18/1	18-23[2]	28%	41%	13%
43. Tabor College (KS)	44	2.5	60%	45%	48%	69%	1%	10/1	18-24	28%	56%	8%
44. Olivet College (MI)	42	2.6	63%	39%	50%	57%	2%	16/1	18-23	N/A	50%	7%
45. Kansas Wesleyan University	41	2.5	62%	46%	41%	69%	2%	10/1	19-24	34%	55%	11%
45. Lake Superior State University (MI)*	41	2.7	69%[8]	45%	43%	51%	6%	16/1	20-25[2]	39%	91%	2%
45. Mayville State University (ND)*	41	2.6	55%	42%	28%	77%	1%	15/1	18-23	N/A	38%	15%
45. Wilmington College[1] (OH)	41	2.8	71%[8]	43%	46%[6]	N/A	N/A	17/1[4]	19-22[4]	N/A	93%[4]	10%[7]
49. Bethany College (KS)	38	2.4	59%	49%	42%	68%	1%	11/1	18-23	29%	65%	11%
49. York College[1] (NE)	38	2.4	67%[8]	41%	36%[6]	81%[4]	0%[4]	15/1[4]	16-20[4]	22%[4]	46%[4]	N/A
51. Dickinson State University (ND)*	37	2.5	56%	52%	30%	79%	1%	10/1	17-24[9]	N/A	72%	1%
51. North Central University (MN)	37	2.4	73%	39%	48%	N/A	N/A	17/1	18-24	25%[5]	61%	4%
53. Crown College (MN)	36	2.3	68%[8]	43%	47%	51%	4%	18/1	19-25	N/A	54%	2%
54. Iowa Wesleyan University	35	2.2	50%	34%	26%	77%	0%	14/1	17-21	20%	51%	7%
54. Midland University[1] (NE)	35	2.6	59%[8]	41%	47%[6]	N/A	N/A	16/1[4]	18-23[4]	N/A	61%[4]	5%[4]
56. Dunwoody College of Tech. (MN)	34	2.3	61%[8]	N/A	N/A	86%	0%	11/1	N/A[2]	38%	79%	3%
56. MacMurray College (IL)	34	2.3	69%	37%	23%	70%	1%	12/1	18-22	31%	57%	14%
56. Maranatha Baptist University (WI)	34	2.1	69%	52%	49%	72%	4%	11/1	19-26	24%[5]	68%	N/A
59. Grace University[1] (NE)	33	2.1	78%[8]	41%	46%[6]	N/A	N/A	12/1[4]	19-24[4]	N/A	59%[4]	N/A
59. Kuyper College[1] (MI)	33	2.0	63%[8]	42%	54%[6]	N/A	N/A	12/1[4]	19-24[3]	N/A	71%[4]	N/A
59. Missouri Southern State University*	33	2.6	64%	35%	30%	49%[4]	0%[4]	20/1	18-24	39%[4]	94%	10%[4]

School (State) (*Public)	Peer assessment score (5.0=highest)	Average first-year student retention rate	2016 graduation rate		% of classes under 20 ('16)	% of classes of 50 or more ('16)	Student/faculty ratio ('16)	SAT/ACT 25th-75th percentile** ('16)	Freshmen in top 25% of HS class ('16)	Acceptance rate ('16)	Average alumni giving rate
			Predicted	Actual							
SCHOOLS RANKED 62 THROUGH 80 ARE LISTED HERE ALPHABETICALLY											
Bismarck State College (ND)*	2.4	N/A	N/A	N/A	N/A	N/A	14/1	17-22[2]	15%	100%	2%
Central Christian College (KS)	1.9	59%	34%	23%	55%	1%	12/1	17-22[2]	23%[4]	54%	12%
Central State University (OH)*	1.9	50%	27%	26%	57%	2%	13/1	15-18	20%	42%	23%
Finlandia University[1] (MI)	2.1	57%[8]	28%	33%[6]	N/A	N/A	11/1[4]	16-21[4]	N/A	46%[4]	N/A
Grace Bible College (MI)	1.8	63%[8]	26%	28%	79%	1%	10/1	17-23	33%	81%	10%
Hannibal-LaGrange University (MO)	2.3	58%[8]	43%	40%	83%	0.3%	14/1	N/A	N/A	N/A	4%
Harris-Stowe State University (MO)*	2.0	47%	26%	6%	88%[4]	0%[4]	16/1	14-19	15%	55%	1%[4]
Indiana University–Kokomo*	2.5	63%	32%	39%	53%	2%	15/1	830-1030	25%	69%	7%
Kendall College (IL)	2.3	61%	38%	17%	72%	1%	9/1	18-21[9]	N/A	84%	N/A
Lincoln College[1] (IL)	2.2	45%[8]	22%	10%[6]	N/A	N/A	16/1[4]	15-19[4]	N/A	52%[4]	N/A
Missouri Valley College[1]	2.1	44%[8]	33%	27%[6]	N/A	N/A	14/1[4]	N/A	37%[4]	46%[4]	N/A
Missouri Western State University[1]*	2.6	63%[8]	37%	32%[6]	N/A	N/A	15/1[4]	N/A[2]	N/A	N/A	6%[7]
Ohio Christian University	2.5	63%[8]	24%	32%[6]	N/A	N/A	10/1[4]	N/A[2]	N/A	N/A	N/A
Rochester College[1] (MI)	2.5	60%[8]	38%	39%[6]	N/A	N/A	12/1[4]	17-23[4]	N/A	58%[4]	N/A
Shawnee State University (OH)*	2.1	61%	36%	28%	63%	1%	16/1	18-24[2]	12%	74%	0.5%[4]
Sterling College[1] (KS)	2.3	71%[8]	42%	41%[6]	N/A	N/A	N/A	N/A	20%[4]	41%[4]	N/A
Urbana University[1] (OH)	2.3	47%[8]	42%	34%[6]	N/A	N/A	20/1[4]	18-23[4]	N/A	91%[4]	N/A
Waldorf College[1] (IA)	2.1	52%[8]	32%	35%[6]	N/A	N/A	23/1[4]	18-22[4]	N/A	66%[4]	N/A
Wilberforce University[1] (OH)	2.2	60%[8]	27%	41%[6]	N/A	N/A	8/1[4]	14-18[4]	N/A	55%[4]	N/A

WEST ▶

Rank School (State) (*Public)	Overall score	Peer assessment score (5.0=highest)	Average first-year student retention rate	2016 graduation rate		% of classes under 20 ('16)	% of classes of 50 or more ('16)	Student/faculty ratio ('16)	SAT/ACT 25th-75th percentile** ('16)	Freshmen in top 25% of HS class ('16)	Acceptance rate ('16)	Average alumni giving rate
				Predicted	Actual							
1. Carroll College (MT)	100	3.4	80%	61%	66%	65%	1%	12/1	22-28	62%[5]	71%	15%
2. Texas Lutheran University	90	3.4	70%	51%	52%	65%	0%	13/1	880-1070	51%	43%	15%
3. California State U.–Maritime Academy*	87	3.2	83%	58%	63%	13%	2%	16/1	970-1193	N/A	68%	6%

WEST ▶

Rank School (State) (*Public)	Overall score	Peer assessment score (5.0=highest)	Average first-year student retention rate	2016 graduation rate		% of classes under 20 ('16)	% of classes of 50 or more ('16)	Student/ faculty ratio ('16)	SAT/ACT 25th–75th percentile** ('16)	Freshmen in top 25% of HS class ('16)	Acceptance rate ('16)	Average alumni giving rate
				Predicted	Actual							
3. Montana Tech of the Univ. of Mont.*	87	3.6	72%	62%	45%	61%	7%	14/1	22-26	56%	89%	13%
3. Oklahoma Baptist University	87	3.4	77%	59%	57%	70%	3%	13/1	21-26	58%	60%	6%
6. Oregon Inst. of Technology*	84	3.6	75%	49%	47%	59%	2%	15/1	920-1160	56%	73%	4%
7. William Jessup University (CA)	83	3.2	78%	52%	65%	68%	0.4%	12/1	800-1140	40%	73%	6%
8. University of Montana–Western*	75	3.3	68%	31%	52%	61%	0%	19/1	17-22[3]	23%	73%	3%
9. Rocky Mountain College (MT)	71	3.0	70%	50%	48%	75%	1%	11/1	20-24	39%	62%	8%
9. Warner Pacific College[1] (OR)	71	3.1	67%[8]	45%	43%[6]	74%[4]	1%[4]	11/1[4]	800-1070[4]	7%[4]	94%[4]	4%[4]
11. San Diego Christian College	70	3.2	68%	36%	52%	82%	0%	11/1	860-1050[2]	25%	53%	N/A
12. McMurry University (TX)	64	3.0	57%	42%	36%	76%	1%	12/1	18-22	39%	48%	10%
13. Brigham Young University–Idaho[1]	62	3.3	68%[8]	43%	51%[6]	N/A	N/A	25/1[4]	20-25[4]	N/A	100%[4]	N/A
13. Howard Payne University (TX)	62	2.9	57%	43%	41%	73%	0.3%	10/1	830-1030	32%	88%	8%
15. Marymount California University	60	3.6	65%	53%	34%	64%	0.4%	16/1	820-1020[2]	N/A	76%	0.3%
16. Arizona Christian University[1] (AZ)	59	2.7	64%[8]	42%	49%[8]	80%[4]	2%[4]	16/1[4]	19-23[4]	N/A	51%[4]	N/A
16. East Texas Baptist University	59	3.0	60%	44%	38%	55%	1%	15/1	18-22	36%	51%	3%
18. Brigham Young University–Hawaii[1]	58	3.1	61%[8]	48%	48%[6]	N/A	N/A	15/1[4]	22-26[4]	N/A	36%[4]	N/A
19. St. Gregory's University (OK)	57	3.0	57%[8]	40%	41%	90%	0.4%	11/1[4]	17-23[2]	17%[5]	42%	N/A
20. Southwestern Adventist Univ. (TX)	53	2.5	71%[8]	43%	37%	75%	2%	12/1	830-1030	26%	50%	7%
21. Southwestern Christian U.[1] (OK)	49	2.7	51%[8]	30%	47%[6]	N/A	N/A	13/1[4]	17-24[4]	N/A	48%[4]	N/A
22. University of Great Falls[1] (MT)	48	2.8	68%[8]	38%	34%[4]	67%[4]	0%[4]	14/1[4]	17-22[4]	N/A	84%[4]	N/A
23. Lewis-Clark State College (ID)*	43	3.1	59%[8]	35%	26%	74%	1%	14/1	810-1030[9]	20%	100%	N/A
24. Colorado Mesa University*	40	2.9	68%	33%	36%	48%	7%	21/1	18-24	27%	83%	2%
25. University of Hawaii–West Oahu[1]*	37	2.9	67%[8]	52%	31%[6]	N/A	N/A	19/1[4]	N/A[2]	N/A	70%[4]	N/A

School (State) (*Public)	Peer assessment score (5.0=highest)	Average first-year student retention rate	2016 graduation rate		% of classes under 20 ('16)	% of classes of 50 or more ('16)	Student/ faculty ratio ('16)	SAT/ACT 25th–75th percentile** ('16)	Freshmen in top 25% of HS class ('16)	Acceptance rate ('16)	Average alumni giving rate
			Predicted	Actual							
SCHOOLS RANKED 26 THROUGH 33 ARE LISTED HERE ALPHABETICALLY											
Bacone College[1] (OK)	2.1	32%[8]	26%	8%[6]	N/A	N/A	15/1[4]	15-20[4]	N/A	42%[4]	N/A
Huston-Tillotson University (TX)	2.6	57%[8]	30%	22%	75%[4]	0%[4]	15/1[4]	690-920	N/A	36%	N/A
Jarvis Christian College (TX)	2.0	54%	24%	15%	62%	10%	20/1	650-843	10%	8%	4%
Montana State Univ.–Northern[1]*	2.7	60%[8]	35%	25%[6]	N/A	N/A	14/1[4]	16-21[4]	N/A	100%[4]	N/A
Oklahoma Panhandle State Univ.*	2.4	59%[8]	36%	40%	N/A	N/A	14/1	N/A[2]	N/A	N/A	N/A
Oklahoma State U. Institute of Tech.–Okmulgee*	2.7	57%	39%	32%	78%	0.2%	14/1	16-21	23%	40%	1%
Rogers State University (OK)*	2.8	66%	43%	34%	49%	1%	19/1	19-21	33%	79%	N/A
Wiley College[1] (TX)	2.1	52%[8]	20%	20%[6]	N/A	N/A	18/1[4]	N/A[2]	N/A	N/A	N/A

The Top Public Regional Colleges ▶

NORTH
Rank School (State)

1. U.S. Coast Guard Acad. (CT)
2. U.S. Merchant Marine Acad. (NY)
3. Maine Maritime Academy
4. University of Maine–Farmington
5. Pennsylvania College of Technology

SOUTH
Rank School (State)

1. Univ. of South Carolina–Aiken
2. U. of South Carolina–Upstate
3. Lander University (SC)
4. Pensacola State College (FL)
4. South Florida State College

MIDWEST
Rank School (State)

1. University of Minnesota–Crookston
1. Valley City State University (ND)
3. Univ. of Wisconsin–Superior
4. Lake Superior State University (MI)
4. Mayville State University (ND)

WEST
Rank School (State)

1. California State University–Maritime Academy
1. Montana Tech of the Univ. of Mont.
3. Oregon Inst. of Technology
4. University of Montana–Western
5. Lewis-Clark State College (ID)

Footnotes:
1. School refused to fill out U.S. News statistical survey. Data that appear are from school in previous years or from another source such as the National Center for Education Statistics.
2. SAT and/or ACT not required by school for some or all applicants.
3. In reporting SAT/ACT scores, the school did not include all students for whom it had scores or refused to tell U.S. News whether all students with scores had been included.
4. Data reported to U.S. News in previous years.
5. Data based on fewer than 51 percent of enrolled freshmen.
6. Some or all data reported to the National Center for Education Statistics.
7. Data reported to the Council for Aid to Education.

8. This rate, normally based on four years of data, is given here for fewer than four years because school didn't report rate for the most recent year or years to U.S. News.
9. SAT and/or ACT may not be required by school for some or all applicants, and in reporting SAT/ACT scores, the school did not include all students for whom it had scores, or refused to tell U.S. News whether all students with scores had been included.
**The SAT scores used in the rankings and published in this guidebook are for the "old" SAT test taken prior to March 2016.
† School's Carnegie classification has changed. It appeared in a different U.S. News ranking category last year.
N/A means not available.

Best Historically Black Colleges

Increasingly, the nation's top historically black colleges and universities are an appealing option for applicants of all races; many HBCUs, in fact, now actively recruit Hispanic, international and white students in addition to African-American high school graduates. Which schools offer the best undergraduate education? U.S. News each year surveys administrators at the HBCUs, asking the president, provost and admissions dean at each to rate the academic quality of all other HBCUs with which they are familiar.

In addition to the two most recent years of survey results, reflected in the peer assessment score, the rankings below are based on nearly all the same ranking indicators (although weighted slightly differently) as those used in ranking the regional universities. These include graduation and retention rates, high school class standing, admission test scores, and the strength of the faculty, among others.

To be part of the universe, a school must be designated by the Department of Education as an HBCU, be a baccalaureate-granting institution that enrolls primarily first-year, first-time students, and have been part of this year's Best Colleges survey and ranking process. If an HBCU is unranked in the 2018 Best Colleges rankings, it is also unranked here; reasons that schools are not ranked vary, but include a school's policy not to use test scores in admissions decisions.

There are 80 HBCUs, and 74 were ranked. HBCUs in the top three-quarters are numerically ranked, and those in the bottom quarter are listed alphabetically. For more detail, visit usnews.com/hbcu.

Key Measures

Graduation and retention rates	27.5%
Peer assessment	25%
Faculty resources	20%
Student selectivity	12.5%
Financial resources	10%
Alumni giving	5%

Rank School (State) (*Public)	Overall score	Peer assessment score (5.0=highest)	Average first-year student retention rate	Average graduation rate	% of classes under 20 ('16)	% of classes of 50 or more ('16)	Student/ faculty ratio ('16)	% of faculty who are full time ('16)	SAT/ACT 25th-75th percentile** ('16)	Freshmen in top 25% of HS class ('16)	Accept- ance rate ('16)	Average alumni giving rate
1. Spelman College (GA)	100	4.6	90%	74%	62%	1%	11/1	87%	980-1170	73%[5]	36%	35%
2. Howard University (DC)	91	4.5	86%	61%	55%	5%	7/1	91%	1040-1240[3]	60%[5]	30%	10%
3. Hampton University (VA)	80	4.4	77%	66%[6]	51%	6%	9/1	92%	860-1040[2]	51%	65%	16%
4. Morehouse College (GA)	75	4.3	81%	52%	50%	1%	12/1	91%	19-24	37%[5]	66%	11%
5. Xavier University of Louisiana	71	4.1	72%	42%	54%	4%	14/1	96%	20-26	58%	62%	19%
6. Florida A&M University*	69	3.8	83%	40%	36%	12%	15/1	93%	19-24	48%[5]	31%	6%
6. Tuskegee University[1] (AL)	69	4.0	72%[8]	45%[6]	57%[4]	9%[4]	14/1[4]	98%[4]	18-23[4]	60%[4]	53%[4]	10%[4]
8. North Carolina A&T State Univ.*	61	4.1	77%	45%[6]	26%	10%	19/1	83%	850-1010	25%	54%	8%
9. Claflin University (SC)	60	3.8	74%	41%[6]	64%	2%	13/1	86%	830-950	30%	42%	50%
9. Fisk University (TN)	60	3.6	78%	44%[6]	70%	0.4%	11/1	84%	17-22	39%[5]	78%	21%
11. Dillard University (LA)	57	3.6	70%	40%[6]	57%	1%	13/1	77%	18-22	32%[5]	38%	15%
12. Tougaloo College (MS)	56	3.2	74%	50%[6]	66%	1%	9/1	96%	16-24	37%	52%	22%
13. Delaware State University*	54	3.6	70%	41%	44%	3%	16/1	87%	820-970	30%	41%	10%
13. North Carolina Central Univ.*	54	3.8	78%	43%	37%	4%	16/1	86%	810-940	22%	67%	13%
15. Jackson State University (MS)*	50	3.7	75%[8]	40%[6]	40%	10%	18/1	83%	16-24	N/A	69%	N/A
16. Clark Atlanta University	49	3.6	65%	39%	33%	7%	19/1	84%	18-21	30%	72%	N/A
16. Morgan State University (MD)*	49	3.7	75%	32%[6]	42%	2%	13/1	85%	800-990	N/A	60%	11%
18. Johnson C. Smith University (NC)	46	3.3	64%	46%	77%	0.2%	11/1	76%	740-915	20%	45%	16%
19. Alcorn State University (MS)*	45	3.1	73%	35%[6]	48%	2%	17/1	88%	16-21	N/A	78%	10%
20. Univ. of Maryland–Eastern Shore*	43	3.3	67%	35%	56%	3%	14/1	86%	790-950	N/A	38%	3%
21. Alabama A&M University*	42	3.4	60%[8]	31%[6]	37%	3%	18/1	89%	16-19	N/A	88%	9%
22. Bowie State University (MD)*	41	3.2	74%	36%[6]	46%	1%	16/1	77%	810-960	N/A	41%	6%
23. Fayetteville State University (NC)*	40	3.2	73%	33%	39%	2%	18/1	88%	790-950	27%	59%	2%
23. Lincoln University (PA)*	40	2.9	74%	42%[6]	22%	0%	12/1	68%	750-925	25%	87%	7%
25. Bethune-Cookman University (FL)	39	3.3	64%	40%[6]	47%	2%	15/1	87%	15-18	33%	44%	7%
25. Prairie View A&M University (TX)*	39	3.3	67%	35%[6]	21%	10%	18/1	93%	750-940	13%	85%	N/A
27. Albany State University (GA)*	38	3.0	71%	36%[6]	55%	1%	19/1	92%	17-20[3]	32%	50%	6%
27. Bennett College (NC)	38	3.0	53%	44%	72%	0%	11/1	86%	623-778	10%	98%	27%
27. Norfolk State University (VA)*	38	3.4	75%[8]	35%[6]	56%	1%	17/1	86%	620-860	17%	85%	N/A

Note: Key to footnotes, Page 101.

Rank	School (State) (*Public)	Overall score	Peer assessment score (5.0=highest)	Average first-year student retention rate	Average graduation rate	% of classes under 20 ('16)	% of classes of 50 or more ('16)	Student/faculty ratio ('16)	% of faculty who are full time ('16)	SAT/ACT 25th-75th percentile** ('16)	Freshmen in top 25% of HS class ('16)	Acceptance rate ('16)	Average alumni giving rate
27.	Winston-Salem State Univ.[1] (NC)*	38	3.3	78%[8]	46%[6]	N/A	N/A	14/1[4]	87%[4]	810-930[4]	N/A	59%[4]	N/A
31.	Elizabeth City State Univ. (NC)*	37	2.6	70%	39%	70%	1%	13/1	98%	790-950	3%	57%	N/A
31.	Philander Smith College (AR)	37	2.8	66%	41%[6]	64%	3%	16/1	78%	14-19	24%	52%	5%
31.	Virginia State University*	37	3.3	67%[8]	46%[6]	N/A	N/A	13/1	81%	730-900[3]	22%	94%	5%
34.	Florida Memorial University	36	2.9	68%[8]	38%[6]	61%[4]	0%[4]	16/1	90%	16-19[9]	N/A	23%	N/A
34.	Fort Valley State University (GA)*	36	2.8	68%	30%[6]	56%	3%	19/1	80%	15-19	15%	26%	12%
34.	Oakwood University[1] (AL)	36	3.2	76%[8]	41%[6]	N/A	N/A	N/A	N/A	N/A	N/A	47%[4]	N/A
34.	Tennessee State University*	36	3.5	47%[8]	34%[6]	78%	2%	14/1	82%	16-20	N/A	53%	N/A
38.	Alabama State University*	34	3.2	60%	25%[6]	43%[4]	0.3%[4]	17/1	83%	15-19	9%[5]	46%	4%
38.	Kentucky State University*	34	2.8	54%	20%	76%	0.3%	12/1	99%	17-21[3]	26%	53%	4%[4]
38.	Southern U. and A&M College (LA)*	34	3.0	66%	32%	N/A	N/A	16/1	91%	16-20	7%	33%	N/A
38.	Univ. of Arkansas–Pine Bluff*	34	3.0	65%	26%	54%	4%	15/1	92%	16-21	39%	42%	7%
42.	South Carolina State University*	31	2.7	63%	37%	61%	1%	17/1	88%	14-17	25%	86%	6%
42.	West Virginia State University*	31	2.9	57%	25%[6]	56%	1%	14/1	80%	17-22	N/A	96%	4%
44.	Central State University (OH)*	30	2.8	50%	23%	57%	2%	13/1	75%	15-18	20%	42%	23%
44.	Grambling State University (LA)*	30	3.0	66%	33%[6]	40%	8%	20/1	99%	16-20	23%	45%	N/A
46.	Bluefield State College (WV)*	29	2.8	61%	22%[6]	87%	0%	14/1	84%	17-22	42%[5]	83%	4%
47.	Lincoln University (MO)*	28	2.8	52%	22%	51%	2%	15/1	87%	15-20	24%	N/A	8%
47.	Mississippi Valley State Univ.*	28	2.8	64%[8]	27%[6]	59%	1%	15/1	87%	15-19	N/A	84%	N/A
47.	Texas Southern University*	28	3.1	51%	17%	37%	14%	18/1	86%	715-900	21%	51%	2%[4]
50.	Coppin State University[1] (MD)*	26	2.8	69%[8]	17%[6]	52%[4]	2%[4]	13/1[4]	75%[4]	810-970[4]	N/A	37%[4]	N/A
50.	St. Augustine's University (NC)	26	2.7	49%	35%[6]	N/A	N/A	13/1	83%	630-830	N/A	73%	6%
52.	Savannah State University (GA)*	25	3.0	64%[8]	28%	29%	0.1%	20/1	94%	16-19[3]	N/A	51%	6%
53.	Univ. of the District of Columbia*	24	2.9	59%	25%	65%	0%	N/A	61%	700-910[3]	N/A	54%	1%
53.	Virginia Union University	24	3.0	57%	32%	53%	0.2%	15/1	78%	700-890	22%	41%	8%
55.	Southern University–New Orleans*	23	2.8	53%	13%[6]	46%	0.3%	18/1	86%	16-19	14%	12%	1%
55.	Wilberforce University[1] (OH)	23	2.6	60%[8]	41%[6]	N/A	N/A	8/1[4]	56%[4]	14-18[4]	N/A	55%[4]	N/A

School (State) (*Public)	Peer assessment score (5.0=highest)	Average first-year student retention rate	Average graduation rate	% of classes under 20 ('16)	% of classes of 50 or more ('16)	Student/faculty ratio ('16)	% of faculty who are full time ('16)	SAT/ACT 25th-75th percentile** ('16)	Freshmen in top 25% of HS class ('16)	Acceptance rate ('16)	Average alumni giving rate
SCHOOLS RANKED 57 THROUGH 74 ARE LISTED HERE ALPHABETICALLY											
Allen University[1] (SC)	2.4	52%[8]	23%[6]	N/A	N/A	15/1[4]	100%[4]	N/A[2]	N/A	N/A	N/A
Arkansas Baptist College	2.3	47%[8]	6%[6]	57%	0%	22/1	71%	17-19[2]	N/A	28%	N/A
Benedict College[1] (SC)	2.9	60%[8]	29%[6]	N/A	N/A	18/1[4]	88%[4]	N/A[2]	N/A	N/A	N/A
Cheyney U. of Pennsylvania*	2.4	54%[8]	21%[6]	N/A	N/A	N/A	75%	650-860	N/A	46%	N/A
Edward Waters College[1] (FL)	2.4	47%[8]	20%[6]	N/A	N/A	15/1[4]	81%[4]	14-18[4]	N/A	54%[4]	N/A
Harris-Stowe State University (MO)*	2.6	47%	8%	88%[4]	0%[4]	16/1	46%	14-19	15%	55%	1%[4]
Huston-Tillotson University (TX)	2.7	57%[8]	25%[6]	75%[4]	0%[4]	15/1[4]	77%[4]	690-920	N/A	36%	N/A
Jarvis Christian College (TX)	2.5	54%	14%	62%	10%	20/1	74%	650-843	10%	8%	4%
Lane College[1] (TN)	2.7	51%[8]	29%[8]	42%[4]	1%[4]	21/1[4]	97%[4]	14-17[4]	30%[4]	55%[4]	N/A
Langston University (OK)*	2.9	64%[8]	19%[6]	N/A	N/A	17/1	N/A	N/A	N/A	52%	N/A
LeMoyne-Owen College (TN)	2.5	47%[8]	16%[6]	75%	0%	12/1	68%	13-17[4]	N/A	100%[4]	N/A
Livingstone College (NC)	2.5	54%	23%	51%	1%	15/1	97%	13-17[3]	6%	48%	10%
Paine College[1] (GA)	2.2	52%[8]	20%[6]	N/A	N/A	9/1[4]	93%[4]	14-17[4]	N/A	31%[4]	N/A
Rust College (MS)	2.8	57%[8]	23%[6]	N/A	N/A	21/1	98%	13-17	N/A	N/A	N/A
Shaw University (NC)	2.7	44%[8]	28%[6]	49%	3%	19/1	78%	640-820	4%	49%	N/A
Stillman College[1] (AL)	2.6	63%[8]	23%[6]	N/A	N/A	15/1[4]	100%[4]	14-21[4]	N/A	57%[4]	N/A
Voorhees College[1] (SC)	2.6	49%[8]	33%[6]	N/A	N/A	12/1[4]	91%[4]	N/A[2]	N/A	93%[4]	N/A
Wiley College[1] (TX)	2.8	52%[8]	20%[6]	N/A	N/A	18/1[4]	84%[4]	N/A[2]	N/A	N/A	N/A

Sources: Statistical data from the schools. Peer assessment data collected by Ipsos Public Affairs.

Best Business Programs

Each year, U.S. News ranks undergraduate business programs accredited by the Association to Advance Collegiate Schools of Business; the results are based solely on surveys of B-school deans and senior faculty. Participants were asked to rate the quality of business programs with which they're familiar on a scale of 1 (marginal) to 5 (distinguished);

38.4 percent of those canvassed responded to the most recent survey conducted in the spring of 2017. Two years of data were used to calculate the peer assessment score. Deans and faculty members also were asked to nominate the 10 best programs in a number of specialty areas; the five schools receiving the most mentions in the 2017 survey appear on page 116.

Top Programs ▶

Rank	School (State) (*Public)	Peer assessment score (5.0=highest)
1.	University of Pennsylvania (Wharton)	4.8
2.	Massachusetts Inst. of Technology (Sloan)	4.6
3.	University of California–Berkeley (Haas)*	4.5
3.	University of Michigan–Ann Arbor (Ross)*	4.5
5.	New York University (Stern)	4.3
5.	University of Texas–Austin (McCombs)*	4.3
7.	Carnegie Mellon University (Tepper) (PA)	4.2
7.	Cornell University (Dyson) (NY)	4.2
7.	U. of N. Carolina–Chapel Hill (Kenan-Flagler)*	4.2
7.	University of Virginia (McIntire)*	4.2
11.	Indiana University–Bloomington (Kelley)*	4.1
11.	University of Notre Dame (Mendoza) (IN)	4.1
11.	Univ. of Southern California (Marshall)	4.1
14.	Washington University in St. Louis (Olin)	4.0
15.	Emory University (Goizueta) (GA)	3.8
15.	Georgetown University (McDonough) (DC)	3.8
15.	Ohio State University–Columbus (Fisher)*	3.8
15.	U. of Illinois–Urbana-Champaign*	3.8
15.	Univ. of Minnesota–Twin Cities (Carlson)*	3.8
15.	Univ. of Wisconsin–Madison*	3.8
21.	Pennsylvania State U.–Univ. Park (Smeal)*	3.7
21.	University of Arizona (Eller)*	3.7
21.	Univ. of Maryland–College Park*	3.7
24.	Arizona State University–Tempe (Carey)*	3.6
24.	Boston College (Carroll)	3.6
24.	Michigan State University (Broad)*	3.6
24.	Purdue U.–West Lafayette (Krannert) (IN)*	3.6
24.	University of Florida (Warrington)*	3.6
24.	University of Georgia (Terry)*	3.6
24.	University of Washington (Foster)*	3.6
31.	Babson College (MA)	3.5
31.	Brigham Young Univ.–Provo (Marriott) (UT)	3.5
31.	Case Western Reserve U. (Weatherhead) (OH)	3.5
31.	Georgia Institute of Technology (Scheller)*	3.5
31.	Texas A&M Univ.–College Station (Mays)*	3.5
31.	University of California–Irvine (Merage)*	3.5
31.	University of Colorado–Boulder (Leeds)*	3.5
31.	University of Iowa (Tippie)*	3.5
31.	University of Pittsburgh*	3.5
40.	Boston University	3.4
40.	Wake Forest University (NC)	3.4
42.	College of William & Mary (Mason) (VA)*	3.3
42.	George Washington University (DC)	3.3
42.	Syracuse University (Whitman) (NY)	3.3
45.	Florida State University*	3.2
45.	Miami University–Oxford (Farmer) (OH)*	3.2
45.	Pepperdine University (CA)	3.2
45.	Southern Methodist University (Cox) (TX)	3.2
45.	Temple University (Fox) (PA)*	3.2
45.	Tulane University (Freeman) (LA)	3.2
45.	United States Air Force Acad. (CO)*	3.2
45.	University of Alabama (Culverhouse)*	3.2
45.	University of Arkansas (Walton)*	3.2
45.	Univ. of California–San Diego (Rady)*	3.2
45.	University of Connecticut*	3.2
45.	University of Kansas*	3.2
45.	Univ. of Massachusetts–Amherst (Isenberg)*	3.2
45.	Univ. of Nebraska–Lincoln*	3.2
45.	Univ. of South Carolina (Moore)*	3.2
45.	University of Tennessee (Haslam)*	3.2
45.	University of Utah (Eccles)*	3.2
45.	Villanova University (PA)	3.2
45.	Virginia Tech (Pamplin)*	3.2
64.	Auburn University (Harbert) (AL)*	3.1
64.	Baylor University (Hankamer) (TX)	3.1
64.	Bentley University (MA)	3.1
64.	CUNY–Baruch College (Zicklin)*	3.1
64.	Fordham University (Gabelli) (NY)	3.1
64.	Georgia State University (Robinson)*	3.1
64.	Northeastern U. (D'Amore-McKim) (MA)	3.1
64.	Rensselaer Polytechnic Inst. (Lally) (NY)	3.1
64.	Rochester Inst. of Technology (Saunders) (NY)	3.1
64.	Santa Clara University (Leavey) (CA)	3.1
64.	University of Miami (FL)	3.1
64.	University of Oklahoma (Price)*	3.1
64.	University of Oregon (Lundquist)*	3.1
64.	University of Texas–Dallas (Jindal)*	3.1
78.	Clemson University (SC)*	3.0
78.	DePaul University (Driehaus) (IL)	3.0
78.	George Mason University (VA)*	3.0
78.	Iowa State University*	3.0
78.	Loyola University Chicago (Quinlan)	3.0
78.	Rutgers University–New Brunswick (NJ)*	3.0
78.	Texas Christian University (Neeley)	3.0
78.	University at Buffalo–SUNY*	3.0
78.	Univ. of California–Riverside*	3.0
78.	University of Delaware (Lerner)*	3.0
78.	University of Illinois–Chicago*	3.0
78.	University of Kentucky (Gatton)*	3.0
78.	Univ. of Missouri (Trulaske)*	3.0
91.	American University (Kogod) (DC)	2.9
91.	Brandeis University (MA)	2.9
91.	Colorado State University*	2.9
91.	Creighton University (NE)	2.9
91.	Lehigh University (PA)	2.9
91.	Loyola Marymount University (CA)	2.9
91.	Marquette University (WI)	2.9
91.	North Carolina State U.–Raleigh (Poole)*	2.9
91.	Oklahoma State University (Spears)*	2.9
91.	Rutgers University–Newark (NJ)*	2.9
91.	Saint Louis University (Cook)	2.9
91.	San Diego State University*	2.9
91.	U.S. Coast Guard Acad. (CT)*	2.9
91.	University of Cincinnati (Lindner)*	2.9
91.	University of Colorado–Denver*	2.9
91.	University of Denver (Daniels)	2.9
91.	University of Houston (Bauer)*	2.9
91.	University of Richmond (Robins) (VA)	2.9
109.	Drexel University (LeBow) (PA)	2.8
109.	Gonzaga University (WA)	2.8
109.	James Madison University (VA)*	2.8
109.	Kansas State University*	2.8
109.	Louisiana State Univ.–Baton Rouge (Ourso)*	2.8
109.	Loyola University Maryland (Sellinger)	2.8
109.	Seton Hall University (Stillman) (NJ)	2.8
109.	St. Joseph's University (Haub) (PA)	2.8
109.	Texas Tech University (Rawls)*	2.8
109.	University at Albany–SUNY*	2.8
109.	University of Alabama–Birmingham (Collat)*	2.8
109.	University of Hawaii–Manoa (Shidler)*	2.8
109.	University of Louisville (KY)*	2.8
109.	University of Mississippi*	2.8
109.	U. of North Carolina–Charlotte (Belk)*	2.8
109.	University of San Diego	2.8
109.	University of San Francisco	2.8
109.	Univ. of Wisconsin–Milwaukee (Lubar)*	2.8
109.	Washington State University (Carson)*	2.8
128.	Binghamton University–SUNY*	2.7
128.	Bucknell University (PA)	2.7
128.	Butler University (IN)	2.7
128.	Cal. Poly. State U.–San Luis Obispo (Orfalea)*	2.7
128.	California State U.–Los Angeles*	2.7
128.	Elon University (Love) (NC)	2.7
128.	Hofstra University (Zarb) (NY)	2.7
128.	Howard University (DC)	2.7
128.	Kennesaw State University (Coles) (GA)*	2.7
128.	Ohio University*	2.7
128.	Oregon State University*	2.7
128.	Rollins College (FL)	2.7
128.	Rutgers University–Camden (NJ)*	2.7
128.	Seattle University (Albers)	2.7

Top Programs ▶

Rank School (State) (*Public)	Peer assessment score (5.0=highest)
128. University of Central Florida*	2.7
128. Univ. of Colo.–Colorado Springs*	2.7
128. University of Memphis (Fogelman)*	2.7
128. University of New Mexico (Anderson)*	2.7
128. University of St. Thomas (Opus) (MN)	2.7
128. University of Texas–Arlington*	2.7
128. Virginia Commonwealth University*	2.7
128. Washington and Lee U. (Williams) (VA)	2.7
128. Xavier University (Williams) (OH)	2.7
151. Ball State University (Miller) (IN)*	2.6
151. Calif. State Poly. Univ.–Pomona*	2.6
151. California State U.–Fullerton (Mihaylo)*	2.6
151. Chapman University (Argyros) (CA)	2.6
151. The Citadel (SC)*	2.6
151. Duquesne University (Palumbo) (PA)	2.6
151. Fairfield University (Dolan) (CT)	2.6
151. Florida International University*	2.6
151. Kent State University (OH)*	2.6
151. Mississippi State University*	2.6
151. Northern Illinois University*	2.6
151. Pace University (Lubin) (NY)	2.6
151. Providence College (RI)	2.6
151. Purdue University–Northwest (IN)*	2.6
151. Quinnipiac University (CT)	2.6
151. San Jose State University (Lucas) (CA)*	2.6

Rank School (State) (*Public)	Peer assessment score (5.0=highest)
151. University of Idaho*	2.6
151. Univ. of Massachusetts–Boston*	2.6
151. U. of Massachusetts–Dartmouth (Charlton)*	2.6
151. University of Minnesota–Duluth (Labovitz)*	2.6
151. Univ. of Missouri–Kansas City (Bloch)*	2.6
151. Univ. of Missouri–St. Louis*	2.6
151. University of Montana*	2.6
151. University of Nebraska–Omaha*	2.6
151. University of New Hampshire (Paul)*	2.6
151. U. of North Carolina–Greensboro (Bryan)*	2.6
151. University of Portland (Pamplin) (OR)	2.6
151. University of Rhode Island*	2.6
151. Univ. of Tennessee–Chattanooga*	2.6
151. University of Vermont*	2.6
151. West Virginia University*	2.6
151. Worcester Polytechnic Inst. (MA)	2.6
183. Boise State University (ID)*	2.5
183. Bowling Green State University (OH)*	2.5
183. Bradley University (Foster) (IL)	2.5
183. Bryant University (RI)	2.5
183. Clarkson University (NY)	2.5
183. Clark University (MA)	2.5
183. Drake University (IA)	2.5
183. Georgia College & State Univ. (Bunting)*	2.5
183. John Carroll University (Roler) (OH)	2.5

Rank School (State) (*Public)	Peer assessment score (5.0=highest)
183. Loyola University New Orleans	2.5
183. Northern Arizona University (Franke)*	2.5
183. Old Dominion University (Strome) (VA)*	2.5
183. Portland State University (OR)*	2.5
183. San Francisco State University*	2.5
183. Southern Illinois U.–Carbondale*	2.5
183. Stevens Institute of Technology (NJ)	2.5
183. St. John's University (Tobin) (NY)	2.5
183. University of Alabama–Huntsville*	2.5
183. Univ. of Arkansas–Little Rock*	2.5
183. University of Baltimore (Merrick)*	2.5
183. University of Dayton (OH)	2.5
183. University of Evansville (Schroeder) (IN)	2.5
183. University of Michigan–Dearborn*	2.5
183. University of Nevada–Las Vegas (Lee)*	2.5
183. U. of North Carolina–Asheville*	2.5
183. U. of North Carolina–Wilmington (Cameron)*	2.5
183. University of Scranton (Kania) (PA)	2.5
183. University of South Florida (Muma)*	2.5
183. University of Tulsa (Collins) (OK)	2.5
183. University of Wyoming^	2.5
183. Utah State University (Huntsman)*	2.5
183. Valparaiso University (IN)	2.5
183. Western Michigan University (Haworth)*	2.5

Note: Peer assessment survey conducted by Ipsos Public Affairs. To be ranked in a specialty, an undergraduate business school may have either a program or course offerings in that subject area. Extended undergraduate business rankings can be found at usnews.com/bestcolleges.

Best in the Specialties ▶

(*Public)

ACCOUNTING
1. **University of Texas–Austin** (McCombs)*
2. **U. of Illinois–Urbana-Champaign***
3. **Brigham Young Univ.–Provo** (Marriott) (UT)
4. **University of Pennsylvania** (Wharton)
5. **University of Michigan–Ann Arbor** (Ross)*

ENTREPRENEURSHIP
1. **Babson College** (MA)
2. **Massachusetts Inst. of Technology** (Sloan)
3. **Indiana University–Bloomington** (Kelley)*
3. **University of California–Berkeley** (Haas)*
5. **University of Pennsylvania** (Wharton)

FINANCE
1. **University of Pennsylvania** (Wharton)
2. **New York University** (Stern)
3. **Massachusetts Inst. of Technology** (Sloan)
4. **University of Michigan–Ann Arbor** (Ross)*
5. **University of Texas–Austin** (McCombs)*

INSURANCE/RISK MANAGEMENT
1. **University of Pennsylvania** (Wharton)
2. **University of Georgia** (Terry)*
3. **Univ. of Wisconsin–Madison***
4. **St. Joseph's University** (Haub) (PA)
5. **Georgia State University** (Robinson)*

INTERNATIONAL BUSINESS
1. **Univ. of South Carolina** (Moore)*
2. **University of Pennsylvania** (Wharton)
3. **New York University** (Stern)
4. **Georgetown University** (McDonough) (DC)
5. **University of California–Berkeley** (Haas)*

MANAGEMENT
1. **University of Michigan–Ann Arbor** (Ross)*
2. **University of Pennsylvania** (Wharton)
3. **University of California–Berkeley** (Haas)*
4. **U. of North Carolina–Chapel Hill** (Kenan-Flagler)*
5. **University of Virginia** (McIntire)*

MANAGEMENT INFORMATION SYSTEMS
1. **Massachusetts Inst. of Technology** (Sloan)
2. **Carnegie Mellon University** (Tepper) (PA)
3. **University of Arizona** (Eller)*
4. **Univ. of Minnesota–Twin Cities** (Carlson)*
5. **University of Texas–Austin** (McCombs)*

MARKETING
1. **University of Pennsylvania** (Wharton)
2. **University of Michigan–Ann Arbor** (Ross)*
3. **New York University** (Stern)
4. **University of Texas–Austin** (McCombs)*
5. **University of California–Berkeley** (Haas)*

PRODUCTION/OPERATIONS MANAGEMENT
1. **Massachusetts Inst. of Technology** (Sloan)
2. **University of Pennsylvania** (Wharton)
3. **Carnegie Mellon University** (Tepper) (PA)
4. **University of Michigan–Ann Arbor** (Ross)*
5. **Purdue Univ.–West Lafayette** (Krannert) (IN)*

QUANTITATIVE ANALYSIS/METHODS
1. **Massachusetts Inst. of Technology** (Sloan)
2. **Carnegie Mellon University** (Tepper) (PA)
3. **University of Pennsylvania** (Wharton)
4. **University of California–Berkeley** (Haas)*
5. **New York University** (Stern)

REAL ESTATE
1. **University of Pennsylvania** (Wharton)
2. **University of California–Berkeley** (Haas)*
3. **Univ. of Wisconsin–Madison***
4. **New York University** (Stern)
5. **University of Georgia** (Terry)*

SUPPLY CHAIN MANAGEMENT/LOGISTICS
1. **Michigan State University** (Broad)*
2. **Massachusetts Inst. of Technology** (Sloan)
3. **University of Tennessee** (Haslam)*
4. **Arizona State University–Tempe** (Carey)*
4. **Pennsylvania State U.–Univ. Park** (Smeal)*

Best Engineering Programs

On these pages, U.S. News ranks undergraduate engineering programs accredited by ABET. The rankings are based solely on surveys of engineering deans and senior faculty at accredited programs. Participants were asked to rate programs with which they're familiar on a scale from 1 (marginal) to 5 (distinguished); the two most recent years' survey results were used to calculate the peer assessment score. Students who prefer a program that focuses on its undergrads can use the list below of top institutions whose terminal engineering degree is a bachelor's or master's; universities that grant doctorates in engineering, whose programs are ranked separately, may boast a wider range of offerings at the undergraduate level. For the spring 2017 surveys, 33 percent of those canvassed returned ratings of the group below; 52 percent did so for the doctorate group. Respondents were also asked to name 10 top programs in specialty areas; those mentioned most often in the 2017 survey alone appear here.

Top Programs ▶ AT ENGINEERING SCHOOLS WHOSE HIGHEST DEGREE IS A BACHELOR'S OR MASTER'S

Rank	School (State) (*Public)	Peer assessment score (5.0=highest)
1.	Harvey Mudd College (CA)	4.5
1.	Rose-Hulman Inst. of Tech. (IN)	4.5
3.	Franklin W. Olin Col. of Engineering (MA)	4.3
4.	United States Military Academy (NY)*	4.2
5.	United States Air Force Acad. (CO)*	4.1
5.	United States Naval Academy (MD)*	4.1
7.	Bucknell University (PA)	4.0
7.	Cal. Poly. State U.–San Luis Obispo*	4.0
9.	Cooper Union (NY)	3.8
10.	Milwaukee School of Engineering	3.6
10.	U.S. Coast Guard Acad. (CT)*	3.6
12.	Lafayette College (PA)	3.5
12.	University of San Diego	3.5
14.	Calif. State Poly. Univ.–Pomona*	3.4
14.	Embry-Riddle Aeronautical U.–Prescott (AZ)	3.4
14.	Kettering University (MI)	3.4
14.	Smith College (MA)	3.4
14.	Valparaiso University (IN)	3.4
19.	The Citadel (SC)*	3.3
19.	Gonzaga University (WA)	3.3
19.	Loyola Marymount University (CA)	3.3
19.	Rowan University (NJ)*	3.3
19.	San Jose State University (CA)*	3.3
19.	Swarthmore College (PA)	3.3

Rank	School (State) (*Public)	Peer assessment score (5.0=highest)
19.	U.S. Merchant Marine Acad. (NY)*	3.3
26.	Bradley University (IL)	3.2
26.	Purdue University–Northwest (IN)*	3.2
26.	Virginia Military Institute*	3.2
29.	LeTourneau University (TX)	3.1
29.	Miami University–Oxford (OH)*	3.1
29.	Ohio Northern University	3.1
29.	Penn State Univ.–Erie, Behrend Col.*	3.1
29.	Seattle University	3.1
29.	Trinity University (TX)	3.1
29.	Union College (NY)	3.1
29.	University of Portland (OR)	3.1
29.	University of St. Thomas (MN)	3.1
38.	Brigham Young University–Idaho	3.0
38.	Hofstra University (NY)	3.0
38.	James Madison University (VA)*	3.0
38.	Manhattan College (NY)	3.0
38.	Mercer University (GA)	3.0
38.	Oregon Inst. of Technology*	3.0
44.	California State U.–Los Angeles*	2.9
44.	California State U.–Northridge*	2.9
44.	Calvin College (MI)	2.9
44.	Cedarville University (OH)	2.9
44.	Dordt College (IA)	2.9

Rank	School (State) (*Public)	Peer assessment score (5.0=highest)
44.	Loyola University Maryland	2.9
44.	Seattle Pacific University	2.9
44.	SUNY Polytechnic Institute*	2.9
44.	Texas Christian University	2.9
44.	University of Minnesota–Duluth*	2.9
44.	University of the Pacific (CA)	2.9
44.	Univ. of Wisconsin–Platteville*	2.9
44.	Wentworth Inst. of Technology (MA)	2.9
57.	California State U.–Fullerton*	2.8
57.	California State U.–Maritime Academy*	2.8
57.	California State U.–Sacramento*	2.8
57.	Grand Valley State University (MI)*	2.8
57.	Grove City College (PA)	2.8
57.	Indiana U.-Purdue U.–Fort Wayne*	2.8
57.	Messiah College (PA)	2.8
57.	Minnesota State Univ.–Mankato*	2.8
57.	Montana Tech of the Univ. of Mont.*	2.8
57.	New York Inst. of Technology	2.8
57.	Northern Arizona University*	2.8
57.	Southern Illinois U.–Edwardsville*	2.8
57.	SUNY Maritime College*	2.8
57.	Trinity College (CT)	2.8
57.	University of Alaska–Anchorage*	2.8
57.	University of Hartford (CT)	2.8
57.	Western New England Univ. (MA)	2.8

Best in the Specialties ▶

(*Public)

AEROSPACE/AERONAUTICAL/ASTRONAUTICAL
1. Embry-Riddle Aeronautical U.–Prescott (AZ)
2. United States Air Force Acad. (CO)*
3. Cal. Poly. State U.–San Luis Obispo*

BIOMEDICAL/BIOMEDICAL ENGINEERING
1. Bucknell University (PA)

CHEMICAL
1. Bucknell University (PA)
1. Rose-Hulman Inst. of Tech. (IN)

CIVIL
1. United States Military Academy (NY)*
2. Cal. Poly. State U.–San Luis Obispo*
2. Rose-Hulman Inst. of Tech. (IN)
4. Calif. State Poly. Univ.–Pomona*
5. Bucknell University (PA)

COMPUTER ENGINEERING
1. Rose-Hulman Inst. of Tech. (IN)
2. Cal. Poly. State U.–San Luis Obispo*

ELECTRICAL/ELECTRONIC/COMMUNICATIONS
1. Rose-Hulman Inst. of Tech. (IN)
2. Franklin W. Olin College of Engineering (MA)
3. Cal. Poly. State U.–San Luis Obispo*
4. Harvey Mudd College (CA)
4. United States Military Academy (NY)*

MECHANICAL
1. Rose-Hulman Inst. of Tech. (IN)
2. Franklin W. Olin College of Engineering (MA)
3. Cal. Poly. State U.–San Luis Obispo*
4. Bucknell University (PA)
5. United States Military Academy (NY)*

Note: Peer assessment survey conducted by Ipsos Public Affairs. To be ranked in a specialty, a school may have either a program or course offerings in that subject area; ABET accreditation of that program is not needed. Extended rankings can be found at usnews.com/bestcolleges.

Top Programs ▶ AT ENGINEERING SCHOOLS WHOSE HIGHEST DEGREE IS A DOCTORATE

Rank	School (State) (*Public)	Peer assessment score (5.0=highest)	Rank	School (State) (*Public)	Peer assessment score (5.0=highest)	Rank	School (State) (*Public)	Peer assessment score (5.0=highest)
1.	Massachusetts Inst. of Technology	4.9	20.	University of Washington*	3.7	47.	Dartmouth College (NH)	3.2
2.	Stanford University (CA)	4.8	25.	Harvard University (MA)	3.6	47.	Lehigh University (PA)	3.2
3.	University of California–Berkeley*	4.7	25.	Univ. of Maryland–College Park*	3.6	49.	Boston University	3.1
4.	California Institute of Technology	4.6	25.	Univ. of Minnesota–Twin Cities*	3.6	49.	Colorado School of Mines*	3.1
4.	Georgia Institute of Technology*	4.6	25.	University of Pennsylvania	3.6	49.	Michigan State University*	3.1
6.	U. of Illinois–Urbana-Champaign*	4.4	25.	Univ. of Southern California	3.6	49.	Northeastern University (MA)	3.1
6.	University of Michigan–Ann Arbor*	4.4	30.	Ohio State University–Columbus*	3.5	49.	Rutgers University–New Brunswick (NJ)*	3.1
8.	Carnegie Mellon University (PA)	4.3	30.	Rensselaer Polytechnic Inst. (NY)	3.5	49.	University of Arizona*	3.1
8.	Purdue Univ.–West Lafayette (IN)*	4.3	30.	University of California–Davis*	3.5	49.	University of Pittsburgh*	3.1
10.	Cornell University (NY)	4.2	30.	University of Colorado–Boulder*	3.5	56.	Auburn University (AL)*	3.0
11.	Princeton University (NJ)	4.1	34.	North Carolina State U.–Raleigh*	3.4	56.	Clemson University (SC)*	3.0
11.	University of Texas–Austin*	4.1	34.	Univ. of California–Santa Barbara*	3.4	56.	Drexel University (PA)	3.0
13.	Northwestern University (IL)	4.0	34.	University of Florida*	3.4	56.	Tufts University (MA)	3.0
14.	Johns Hopkins University (MD)	3.9	34.	University of Virginia*	3.4	56.	University of Delaware*	3.0
14.	Texas A&M Univ.–College Station*	3.9	34.	Vanderbilt University (TN)	3.4	61.	Missouri Univ. of Science & Tech.*	2.9
14.	Univ. of Wisconsin–Madison*	3.9	34.	Yale University (CT)	3.4	61.	New York University	2.9
14.	Virginia Tech*	3.9	40.	Arizona State University–Tempe*	3.3	61.	Rochester Inst. of Technology (NY)	2.9
18.	Columbia University (NY)	3.8	40.	Brown University (RI)	3.3	61.	University of Connecticut*	2.9
18.	Univ. of California–Los Angeles*	3.8	40.	Case Western Reserve Univ. (OH)	3.3	61.	University of Iowa*	2.9
20.	Duke University (NC)	3.7	40.	Iowa State University*	3.3	61.	Univ. of Massachusetts–Amherst*	2.9
20.	Pennsylvania State U.–Univ. Park*	3.7	40.	University of California–Irvine*	3.3	61.	University of Tennessee*	2.9
20.	Rice University (TX)	3.7	40.	University of Notre Dame (IN)	3.3	61.	University of Utah*	2.9
20.	Univ. of California–San Diego*	3.7	40.	Washington University in St. Louis	3.3	61.	Worcester Polytechnic Inst. (MA)	2.9

Best in the Specialties ▶

(*Public)

AEROSPACE/AERONAUTICAL/ASTRONAUTICAL
1. Massachusetts Inst. of Technology
2. Georgia Institute of Technology*
2. University of Michigan–Ann Arbor*
4. Stanford University (CA)
5. California Institute of Technology

BIOLOGICAL/AGRICULTURAL
1. Iowa State University*
1. Purdue Univ.–West Lafayette (IN)*
1. Texas A&M Univ.–College Station*
4. Cornell University (NY)
4. U. of Illinois–Urbana-Champaign*

BIOMEDICAL/BIOMEDICAL ENGINEERING
1. Georgia Institute of Technology*
2. Johns Hopkins University (MD)
3. Massachusetts Inst. of Technology
4. Duke University (NC)
4. Stanford University (CA)

CHEMICAL
1. Massachusetts Inst. of Technology
2. University of California–Berkeley*
3. Georgia Institute of Technology*
4. Stanford University (CA)
5. Univ. of Wisconsin–Madison*

CIVIL
1. University of California–Berkeley*
2. Georgia Institute of Technology*
3. U. of Illinois–Urbana-Champaign*
4. University of Texas–Austin*
5. Massachusetts Inst. of Technology

COMPUTER ENGINEERING
1. Massachusetts Inst. of Technology
2. University of California–Berkeley*
3. Stanford University (CA)
4. Carnegie Mellon University (PA)
5. U. of Illinois–Urbana-Champaign*

ELECTRICAL/ELECTRONIC/COMMUNICATIONS
1. Massachusetts Inst. of Technology
2. Stanford University (CA)
3. University of California–Berkeley*
4. Georgia Institute of Technology*
5. University of Michigan–Ann Arbor*

ENVIRONMENTAL/ENVIRONMENTAL HEALTH
1. University of California–Berkeley*
2. Georgia Institute of Technology*
2. Stanford University (CA)
2. University of Michigan–Ann Arbor*
5. U. of Illinois–Urbana-Champaign*
5. University of Texas–Austin*

INDUSTRIAL/MANUFACTURING
1. Georgia Institute of Technology+
2. University of Michigan–Ann Arbor*
3. University of California–Berkeley*
4. Purdue Univ.–West Lafayette (IN)*
5. Stanford University (CA)
5. Univ. of Wisconsin–Madison*

MATERIALS
1. Massachusetts Inst. of Technology
2. University of California–Berkeley*
3. U. of Illinois–Urbana-Champaign*
4. University of Michigan–Ann Arbor*
5. Georgia Institute of Technology*

MECHANICAL
1. Massachusetts Inst. of Technology
2. Stanford University (CA)
3. Georgia Institute of Technology*
4. University of Michigan–Ann Arbor*
5. University of California–Berkeley*

PETROLEUM
1. Texas A&M Univ.–College Station*
2. University of Texas–Austin*
3. University of Oklahoma*
4. Colorado School of Mines*
4. Pennsylvania State U.–Univ. Park*
4. Texas Tech University*

Best
Online Degree Programs

When we surveyed colleges in 2016 about their online options, more than 300 schools reported having bachelor's programs that can be completed without showing up in person for class (though attendance may be required for testing, orientations or support services). These offerings, typically degree-completion programs aimed at working adults and community college grads, were evaluated on their success at engaging students, the credentials of their faculty, and the services and technologies made available remotely. The table below features some of the most significant ranking factors, such as the prevalence of faculty holding a Ph.D. or other terminal degree, class size, the percentages of new entrants who stayed enrolled and later graduated, and the debt load of recent graduates. The top half of programs are listed here. Ranks are determined by the institutions' rounded overall program scores, displayed below. To see the rest of the ranked online bachelor's programs and to read the full methodology, visit usnews.com/online. You'll also find detail-rich profile pages for each of the schools and (in case you want to plan ahead) rankings of online MBA programs and graduate programs in engineering, nursing, education and more.

(*Public, **For profit)

Rank	School	Overall program score	Average peer assessment score (5.0=highest)	'16 total program enrollment	'16 - '17 tuition[1]	'16 full-time faculty with Ph.D.	'16 average class size	'16 retention rate	'16 graduation rate[2]	% graduates with debt ('16)	Average debt of graduates ('16)
1.	Embry-Riddle Aeronautical U.–Worldwide (FL)	100	3.6	14,470	$365	67%	25	81%	27%	16%	$3,892
2.	Temple University* (PA)	95	3.6	181	$821	78%	25	83%	N/A	73%	$18,008
3.	University of Oklahoma*	94	3.3	1,302	$630	100%	17	83%	42%	31%	$2,758
4.	Arizona State University*	92	3.8	23,672	$500	67%	44	88%	N/A	68%	$26,611
5.	Western Kentucky University*	91	3.2	3,130	$496	59%	18	85%	52%	50%	$15,922
6.	California University of Pennsylvania*	90	2.9	2,422	$308	81%	32	86%	93%	54%	$5,390
6.	West Texas A&M University*	90	2.7	1,234	$295	76%	36	82%	68%	42%	$7,900
8.	California Baptist University	89	3.4	2,236	$547	72%	20	82%	N/A	89%	$32,586
8.	New England Institute of Technology (RI)	89	3.1	123	$230	68%	12	78%	N/A	71%	$17,557
8.	Ohio State University–Columbus*	89	3.4	307	$398	N/A	54	90%	97%	45%	$10,674
8.	Oregon State University*	89	3.6	4,651	$200	65%	31	79%	44%	67%	$25,740
8.	Pennsylvania State University–World Campus*	89	4.2	5,608	$542	56%	28	70%	40%	76%	$40,875
8.	University of Illinois–Chicago*	89	3.4	215	$519	38%	25	90%	92%	51%	$16,654
14.	Utah State University*	88	3.7	1,653	$310	57%	58	66%	61%	53%	$16,550
15.	Colorado State University–Global Campus*	87	3.5	10,670	$350	96%	14	71%	52%	58%	$25,064
15.	Daytona State College*	87	3.0	1,607	$550	75%	27	79%	65%	46%	$21,548
15.	Fort Hays State University* (KS)	87	3.1	7,813	$207	54%	24	88%	73%	24%	$24,035
15.	Savannah College of Art and Design (GA)	87	3.3	743	$782	37%	19	76%	45%	80%	$38,427
15.	Washington State University*	87	3.6	2,195	$569	74%	33	70%	51%	62%	$21,783
20.	University of Florida*	86	3.5	2,208	$500	70%	62	88%	70%	53%	$19,601
21.	Charleston Southern University (SC)	85	3.2	329	$490	73%	12	65%	54%	89%	$30,862
21.	Loyola University Chicago (IL)	85	3.3	367	$751	73%	18	82%	N/A	56%	$26,021
21.	University at Buffalo–SUNY*	85	3.4	88	$988	100%	37	93%	N/A	N/A	N/A
24.	CUNY School of Professional Studies*	84	3.1	1,665	$275	80%	17	60%	39%	59%	$7,096
24.	Siena Heights University (MI)	84	N/A	529	$495	70%	16	81%	87%	61%	$20,008
24.	University of Massachusetts–Amherst*	84	3.7	1,567	$385	67%	24	73%	63%	71%	$22,385
24.	University of Nebraska–Omaha*	84	3.3	205	$489	77%	24	85%	N/A	48%	$18,682
28.	Central Michigan University*	83	3.4	1,665	$405	77%	21	69%	30%	41%	$9,637
28.	Creighton University (NE)	83	3.4	126	$433	100%	14	80%	N/A	71%	$29,910
28.	Georgia College & State University*	83	3.1	17	$289	83%	15	80%	N/A	50%	$13,339
28.	Marist College (NY)	83	2.9	171	$650	55%	15	91%	70%	79%	$27,721
28.	Palm Beach Atlantic University (FL)	83	3.2	73	$475	72%	8	76%	35%	95%	$20,470
28.	Robert Morris University (PA)	83	2.7	574	$725	90%	12	79%	N/A	64%	$39,620
28.	Southeast Missouri State University*	83	3.1	843	$265	77%	25	76%	44%	50%	$7,343
28.	Wayne State University* (MI)	83	3.1	54	$428	100%	21	88%	N/A	85%	$28,973
36.	Ball State University* (IN)	82	3.4	1,103	$492	67%	32	81%	45%	61%	$28,347
36.	Florida State University*	82	3.6	491	$776	N/A	33	N/A	N/A	N/A	N/A
36.	Pace University (NY)	82	2.9	389	$555	94%	12	77%	60%	50%	$32,779
36.	Regent University (VA)	82	3.0	3,303	$395	78%	17	78%	36%	72%	$28,076
36.	SUNY College of Technology–Delhi*	82	3.1	994	$270	44%	17	66%	45%	40%	$18,879
36.	University of Arkansas*	82	3.1	688	$284	53%	40	78%	75%	57%	$16,780
36.	University of Central Florida*	82	3.6	11,264	$300	70%	68	83%	68%	58%	$21,878
36.	University of La Verne (CA)	82	2.9	348	$610	86%	19	86%	59%	83%	$31,565
36.	University of Nebraska–Lincoln*	82	3.4	26	$535	95%	23	90%	N/A	80%	$35,913

114 ▶ **More** @ usnews.com/bestcolleges

Note: Key to footnotes, Page 117.

(*Public, **For profit)

Rank	School	Overall program score	Average peer assessment score (5.0=highest)	'16 total program enrollment	'16 – '17 tuition[1]	'16 full-time faculty with Ph.D.	'16 average class size	'16 retention rate	'16 graduation rate[2]	% graduates with debt ('16)	Average debt of graduates ('16)
45.	Central Washington University*	81	3.4	1,349	$657	71%	23	78%	N/A	69%	$23,742
45.	City University of Seattle (WA)	81	3.2	2,562	$404	14%	11	73%	49%	N/A	$9,790
45.	Westfield State University* (MA)	81	N/A	146	$297	89%	22	91%	64%	67%	$15,017
48.	Colorado State University*	80	3.4	543	$444	69%	16	75%	N/A	69%	$27,517
48.	University of Denver (CO)	80	3.3	114	$594	N/A	7	88%	40%	65%	N/A
48.	University of Maine–Augusta*	80	3.1	3,558	$271	63%	21	76%	24%	74%	$26,289
48.	University of North Florida*	80	3.0	209	$285	85%	32	N/A	N/A	34%	$5,771
48.	University of Wisconsin–Milwaukee*	80	3.4	2,520	$337	79%	25	78%	N/A	77%	$33,234
48.	University of the Incarnate Word (TX)	80	2.6	1,686	$515	100%	21	70%	68%	77%	$22,722
54.	Florida International University*	79	3.1	3,533	$329	90%	38	100%	45%	60%	$14,759
54.	Indiana University– Online*	79	3.3	2,233	$310	63%	26	83%	50%	80%	$25,042
54.	Sam Houston State University* (TX)	79	2.8	2,209	$216	N/A	30	77%	N/A	67%	$22,567
54.	University of Illinois–Springfield*	79	3.5	999	$359	82%	22	76%	44%	54%	$23,702
54.	University of Massachusetts–Lowell*	79	3.5	2,061	$370	84%	25	82%	41%	56%	$29,452
59.	George Washington University (DC)	78	3.5	400	$570	40%	18	66%	56%	31%	$23,084
59.	Saint Leo University (FL)	78	2.8	6,398	$470	67%	16	82%	21%	66%	$34,842
59.	University of Georgia*	78	3.6	60	$562	N/A	17	78%	N/A	54%	$19,957
59.	University of Wisconsin–Platteville*	78	3.6	421	$370	N/A	15	66%	N/A	N/A	N/A
63.	Brandman University (CA)	77	2.8	1,197	$500	83%	26	69%	52%	72%	$29,414
63.	Concordia University Chicago (IL)	77	2.3	139	$505	70%	10	75%	N/A	92%	$22,992
63.	New Eng. Col. of Business and Finance** (MA)	77	N/A	813	$340	50%	18	90%	49%	60%	$41,200
63.	Old Dominion University* (VA)	77	3.1	5,919	$355	68%	40	81%	53%	N/A	N/A
63.	University of Alabama–Birmingham*	77	3.1	958	$746	76%	37	80%	N/A	43%	$13,406
68.	Florida Institute of Technology	76	3.2	2,657	$510	69%	19	71%	14%	82%	$44,680
68.	Lamar University* (TX)	76	2.5	1,848	$248	72%	32	61%	N/A	60%	$19,141
68.	Sacred Heart University (CT)	76	2.6	377	$560	50%	11	72%	70%	74%	$28,548
68.	Southern Illinois University–Edwardsville*	76	3.2	423	$696	45%	18	77%	N/A	31%	$13,618
68.	University of Louisiana–Lafayette*	76	3.4	1,700	$355	45%	41	71%	N/A	N/A	N/A
68.	University of Missouri–St. Louis*	76	3.2	97	$452	43%	21	91%	90%	48%	$4,763
68.	University of North Texas*	76	N/A	1,295	$274	77%	40	76%	N/A	46%	$11,897
68.	University of Wisconsin–Superior*	76	3.2	698	$305	33%	9	80%	28%	N/A	N/A
76.	Ferris State University* (MI)	75	3.0	897	$403	50%	18	75%	54%	56%	$17,760
76.	Missouri State University*	75	3.0	480	$285	68%	20	N/A	N/A	N/A	N/A
76.	SUNY College of Technology–Canton*	75	3.0	1,012	$680	57%	21	72%	54%	78%	$29,939
76.	University of North Carolina–Wilmington*	75	N/A	980	$668	59%	30	97%	N/A	39%	$15,988
76.	Western Carolina University* (NC)	75	3.1	1,207	$483	72%	20	76%	69%	43%	N/A
81.	California State University–Dominguez Hills*	74	2.8	599	$670	100%	18	82%	43%	38%	$18,581
81.	Clarion University of Pennsylvania*	74	N/A	578	$326	93%	25	10%	N/A	67%	$25,714
81.	Colorado Technical University**	74	2.8	26,330	$325	86%	30	86%	37%	79%	$28,785
81.	Concordia University–St. Paul (MN)	74	2.6	1,044	$420	63%	10	75%	74%	80%	$24,708
81.	Duquesne University (PA)	74	3.1	188	$846	73%	13	N/A	51%	46%	$33,706
81.	Fitchburg State University* (MA)	74	2.8	138	$366	44%	15	90%	71%	60%	N/A
81.	Northwestern College (IA)	74	3.2	20	$400	78%	7	80%	N/A	100%	$13,994
81.	University of Arizona*	74	3.2	244	$490	73%	30	N/A	N/A	60%	$17,307
81.	University of Massachusetts–Boston*	74	N/A	520	$559	N/A	30	82%	73%	55%	$20,407
81.	University of South Carolina–Aiken*	74	2.6	167	$825	73%	24	89%	65%	74%	$19,861
81.	University of Texas of the Permian Basin*	74	N/A	1,222	$229	71%	38	78%	N/A	81%	$3,679
92.	American Public University System** (WV)	73	2.6	57,909	$270	51%	6	52%	36%	31%	$26,298
92.	Ashland University (OH)	73	N/A	120	$405	75%	17	67%	N/A	26%	N/A
92.	Bellevue University (NE)	73	2.4	6,504	$410	45%	16	90%	51%	76%	$19,059
92.	Georgia Southern University*	73	2.7	756	$204	88%	38	70%	N/A	81%	$24,861
92.	McKendree University (IL)	73	N/A	396	$370	88%	14	85%	N/A	72%	$18,498
92.	St. Joseph's University (PA)	73	3.0	128	$573	100%	16	78%	N/A	68%	$19,276
92.	University of St. Francis (IL)	73	N/A	382	$599	64%	16	75%	61%	67%	$26,155
99.	Eastern Kentucky University*	72	2.8	2,196	$400	73%	18	76%	28%	90%	$31,031
99.	Granite State College* (NH)	72	N/A	2,139	$335	40%	13	83%	54%	72%	$19,780
99.	United States Sports Academy (AL)	72	2.6	273	$370	N/A	7	61%	54%	84%	$26,833
99.	University of Cincinnati* (OH)	72	3.1	2,333	$404	67%	39	77%	N/A	75%	$25,070
103.	Chatham University (PA)	71	2.3	117	$829	89%	12	52%	71%	70%	$13,818
103.	Columbia College (MO)	71	3.0	12,277	$290	74%	19	76%	9%	60%	$29,070
103.	Eastern Oregon University*	71	2.6	1,339	$218	68%	22	87%	52%	70%	$26,601
103.	Lindenwood University (MO)	71	2.2	147	$453	77%	17	61%	N/A	85%	$27,325
103.	North Carolina State University–Raleigh*	71	3.3	74	$632	85%	31	100%	48%	64%	$18,314
103.	Norwich University (VT)	71	3.2	1,095	$375	83%	10	81%	36%	19%	$12,269
103.	University of the Cumberlands (KY)	71	N/A	635	$199	63%	12	83%	N/A	77%	$11,501

BEST ONLINE DEGREE PROGRAMS

(*Public, **For profit)

Rank	School	Overall program score	Average peer assessment score (5.0=highest)	'16 total program enrollment	'16 - '17 tuition[1]	'16 full-time faculty with Ph.D.	'16 average class size	'16 retention rate	'16 graduation rate[2]	% graduates with debt ('16)	Average debt of graduates ('16)
110.	American InterContinental University** (IL)	70	N/A	15,959	$302	76%	26	82%	59%	81%	$30,230
110.	Drexel University (PA)	70	3.4	2,144	$572	71%	22	80%	32%	59%	$32,357
110.	Graceland University (IA)	70	N/A	226	$465	68%	10	91%	64%	80%	$18,211
110.	Indiana University-Purdue U.–Fort Wayne*	70	3.5	442	$367	65%	22	64%	N/A	76%	$25,208
110.	Slippery Rock University of Pennsylvania*	70	N/A	285	$308	100%	27	73%	58%	59%	$16,043
110.	Texas Tech University*	70	3.4	512	$250	28%	30	N/A	N/A	N/A	N/A
110.	University of Bridgeport (CT)	70	2.9	1,084	$515	80%	15	80%	N/A	N/A	N/A
110.	University of Wisconsin–Stout*	70	3.5	1,623	$334	59%	25	N/A	N/A	85%	$21,132
110.	Upper Iowa University	70	2.7	2,399	$430	52%	15	65%	50%	72%	$24,182
119.	Berkeley College** (NJ)	69	N/A	1,875	$825	61%	21	74%	30%	82%	$35,166
119.	Dallas Baptist University (TX)	69	3.0	1,173	$846	69%	13	N/A	N/A	N/A	N/A
119.	Johnson and Wales University (RI)	69	2.8	465	$366	49%	19	N/A	N/A	87%	N/A
119.	Linfield College (OR)	69	2.5	520	$480	83%	14	86%	64%	73%	$23,416
119.	Maranatha Baptist University (WI)	69	N/A	82	$386	46%	9	95%	N/A	56%	$13,226
119.	National University (CA)	69	2.1	10,521	$354	80%	15	62%	34%	76%	$21,649
119.	The Master's University (CA)	69	N/A	193	$360	73%	10	100%	N/A	N/A	N/A
126.	Adelphi University (NY)	68	2.2	17	$885	100%	155	10%	100%	N/A	N/A
126.	Bowling Green State University* (OH)	68	3.1	304	$390	78%	22	76%	N/A	59%	$26,203
126.	Lynn University (FL)	68	3.0	537	$295	70%	15	62%	56%	37%	$31,532
126.	Southwestern College (KS)	68	N/A	1,650	$455	100%	10	76%	52%	35%	$25,074
126.	St. Joseph's College New York	68	N/A	109	$495	82%	11	50%	N/A	42%	$26,803
126.	University of Southern Mississippi* (MS)	68	N/A	919	$340	59%	28	70%	N/A	71%	$24,500
132.	Cornerstone University (MI)	67	2.5	2,159	$410	60%	8	N/A	N/A	N/A	N/A
132.	Dakota Wesleyan University (SD)	67	N/A	170	$325	38%	17	N/A	N/A	36%	$6,827
132.	Lander University* (SC)	67	N/A	67	$846	50%	10	N/A	53%	N/A	N/A
132.	Peirce College (PA)	67	N/A	1,151	$578	76%	15	69%	56%	79%	N/A
132.	Southern New Hampshire University	67	3.1	61,810	$320	55%	21	84%	33%	80%	$35,041
132.	Texas A&M University–College Station*	67	N/A	64	$731	40%	86	69%	100%	N/A	N/A

Rank	School	Overall program score	Average peer assessment score (5.0=highest)	'16 total program enrollment	'16 - '17 tuition[1]	'16 full-time faculty with Ph.D.	'16 average class size	'16 retention rate	'16 graduation rate[2]	% graduates with debt ('16)	Average debt of graduates ('16)
132.	Union Institute and University (OH)	67	N/A	1,044	$510	43%	7	69%	99%	48%	$32,490
132.	University of Alaska–Fairbanks*	67	3.3	N/A	$212	42%	24	N/A	N/A	N/A	N/A
132.	University of Massachusetts–Dartmouth*	67	3.5	281	$322	82%	11	51%	N/A	N/A	N/A
132.	Utica College (NY)	67	2.8	901	$400	35%	22	79%	52%	54%	N/A
142.	California State University–East Bay*	66	2.8	519	$297	100%	27	N/A	N/A	N/A	N/A
142.	Herzing University (WI)	66	1.6	1,219	$550	21%	19	82%	32%	75%	$24,445
142.	Indiana State University*	66	3.2	1,354	$669	77%	23	N/A	N/A	91%	$25,014
142.	University of Toledo* (OH)	66	2.9	1,374	$774	69%	17	75%	35%	66%	$17,354
142.	University of Wisconsin–Green Bay*	66	3.3	1,611	$578	84%	27	76%	56%	66%	$24,067
142.	University of Wisconsin–Whitewater*	66	3.5	215	$389	N/A	25	65%	74%	N/A	N/A
148.	Champlain College (VT)	65	2.5	1,676	$641	N/A	14	73%	N/A	55%	$28,285
148.	Gallaudet University (DC)	65	3.2	N/A	$648	77%	12	50%	60%	N/A	N/A
148.	Goldfarb Sch. of Nursing at Barnes-Jewish Col. (MO)	65	N/A	33	$698	86%	15	97%	N/A	N/A	N/A
148.	Lee University (TN)	65	N/A	881	$202	100%	10	87%	6%	73%	$24,934
148.	Liberty University (VA)	65	2.7	42,135	$390	45%	22	74%	36%	73%	$31,095
148.	Southwestern Oklahoma State University*	65	N/A	500	$514	N/A	18	54%	59%	38%	$8,173
148.	University of Maine*	65	N/A	52	$349	N/A	10	87%	N/A	N/A	N/A
148.	Valley City State University* (ND)	65	3.2	N/A	$177	54%	11	N/A	N/A	N/A	N/A
156.	East Carolina University* (NC)	64	3.0	8,967	$687	71%	25	N/A	62%	62%	$23,303
156.	Kaplan University** (IA)	64	1.7	37,501	$371	55%	22	64%	24%	82%	$23,979
156.	Northwood University (MI)	64	2.7	340	$425	63%	17	61%	33%	71%	$33,746
156.	Oakland University* (MI)	64	N/A	254	$796	77%	24	74%	40%	N/A	N/A
156.	Post University** (CT)	64	2.5	10,474	$570	17%	16	65%	33%	54%	$32,032
156.	Regis University (CO)	64	2.8	2,377	$490	50%	12	83%	42%	68%	$36,724
156.	University of Missouri*	64	3.3	310	$355	81%	23	N/A	N/A	66%	$14,592
156.	University of West Florida*	64	3.2	1,355	$648	80%	30	N/A	N/A	N/A	N/A
156.	Wheeling Jesuit University (WV)	64	N/A	58	$390	89%	12	N/A	N/A	82%	$29,490

▶ Best Online Bachelor's Programs For Veterans

Which programs offer military veterans and active-duty service members the best distance education? To ensure academic quality, all schools included in this ranking had to first qualify for a spot by being in the top half of the Best Online Degree Programs ranking, above. They had to be housed in a regionally accredited institution and were judged on a multitude of factors, including program reputation, faculty credentials, student graduation rate and graduate debt load. Secondly, because veterans and active-duty members often wish to take full advantage of federal benefits designed to make their coursework less expensive, programs also had to be certified for the GI Bill and participate in the Yellow Ribbon Program or charge in-state tuition that can be fully covered by the GI Bill to veterans from out of state. A third criterion for being ranked is that a program must have enrolled a critical mass of students with military backgrounds. The undergraduate-level rankings require a total of 25 veterans and active-duty service members to be included. Qualifying programs were ranked in descending order based on their spot in the overall ranking.

Rank School (State)

1. Embry-Riddle Aeronautical University–Worldwide (FL)
2. University of Oklahoma*
3. Arizona State University*
4. Western Kentucky University*
5. California University of Pennsylvania*
5. West Texas A&M University*
7. Oregon State University*
7. Pennsylvania State University– World Campus*
9. Utah State University*
10. Colorado State University– Global Campus*
10. Daytona State College* (FL)
10. Fort Hays State University* (KS)

10. Washington State University*
14. University of Florida*
15. Charleston Southern University
16. CUNY School of Professional Studies*
16. Siena Heights University (MI)
16. University of Massachusetts– Amherst*
16. University of Nebraska–Omaha*
20. Central Michigan University*
20. Robert Morris University (PA)
20. Southeast Missouri State University*
23. Ball State University* (IN)
23. Florida State University*
23. Pace University (NY)

23. Regent University (VA)
23. University of Central Florida*
28. Central Washington University*
28. City University of Seattle (WA)
30. University of Maine–Augusta*
30. University of Wisconsin– Milwaukee*
32. Florida International University*
32. Indiana University– Online*
32. Sam Houston State University* (TX)
32. University of Illinois–Springfield*
32. University of Massachusetts– Lowell*
37. George Washington University (DC)
37. Saint Leo University (FL)
37. University of Wisconsin–Platteville*

40. Brandman University (CA)
40. University of Alabama– Birmingham*
42. Florida Institute of Technology
43. Ferris State University* (MI)
43. Missouri State University*
43. SUNY College of Technology– Canton*
43. University of North Carolina– Wilmington*
47. Colorado Technical University**
47. Concordia University–St. Paul
47. Duquesne University (PA)
47. University of Arizona*
47. University of Texas of the Permian Basin*

N/A=Data were not provided by the school. **1.** Tuition is reported on a per-credit-hour basis. Out-of-state tuition is listed for public institutions. **2.** Displayed here for standardization are six-year graduation rates.

Get Ready to Get In

PREPPING FOR
DRESS REHEARSAL
AT THE UNIVERSITY
OF PUGET SOUND

HOW TO
STAND
OUT IN THE FIELD

Here's some advice from admissions counselors on how you can impress them

by Arlene Weintraub

Aaron Bennington

HE BECAME A PAINTBALL REFEREE SO HE COULD PLAY FOR FREE. NOW AN OHIO WESLEYAN STUDENT, HE'S TRAVELED TO TOURNAMENTS AROUND THE WORLD.

NEWS YOU CAN USE

Aaron Bennington fell in love with the sport of competitive paintball at age 10, but his parents balked at the $800-plus cost of attending each tournament. So when he was 13, he started volunteering to referee in his hometown of Delaware, Ohio – a gig that allowed him to play for free and that got him noticed by national tournament organizers. By high school, Bennington was refereeing as many as 25 tournaments a year and traveling all over the world.

The unusual hobby and his resourcefulness also helped get him noticed at the college of his choice, Bennington thinks – Ohio Wesleyan University, where he is a sophomore majoring in international business and Spanish. "The experiences I had shaped how I am as a person," he says. Or as he put it in his college essay, he "walked along the equator in Ecuador, dove to the depths of the Caribbean to experience life underwater, and even experienced Hindu rituals in caves in Malaysia," all of which, he wrote, opened his mind and gave him "the utmost respect for differences around the world."

That kind of passion and determination is highly valued in the admissions office. Academics matter a lot, of course, but you'll need to find the right balance as you go through high school between hitting the books and pursuing activities outside the classroom that reflect who you are – and then figure out how to make that person shine through on your applications. That's especially important now, with highly selective colleges struggling to distinguish between thousands of entirely qualified applicants (and, in the case of Stanford, recently accepting a historic low of 4.65 percent of them). Don't get discouraged by scary headlines, though. Most

schools accept a much higher percentage, and even highly ranked colleges and universities may be more likely to welcome you with open arms than you think. Boston College took 32 percent of its 2017 applicants, for example. The University of Michigan admitted 24 percent, and George Washington University said "yes" to 41 percent of applicants.

Consultants and admissions counselors agree that students should start building their résumés in the ninth grade, with an eye toward being able to fill an application with fascinating facts. "We are going through these applications quickly. Grab our attention and show us what you're passionate about," advises Jeffrey Schiffman, director of admissions at Tulane University.

Here are the top strategies that worked for Bennington and other students:

Take your studies seriously

Admissions officers care a lot about your academic performance, but grades don't tell them the whole story. They devote much of their time to scrutinizing the course choices students make. Many students assume they should take every AP course available. But getting an A in one or two AP courses that fit your talents is better than B's in a bunch of courses that don't.

"If a student is taking a number of APs, that's great – but not if they're struggling," cautions Susan Dileno, vice president for enrollment at Ohio Wesleyan. "What we're really looking for is progression on particular topics. Do they excel in math? And if so, are they pushing the limits of what's offered at their school?"

Admissions officers view performance in the context of each student's goals, explains Andy Strickler, dean of admission and financial aid at Connecticut College. "A student with a stated desire in pre-med who's getting a B in AP bio is a red flag," he says. "But a self-described artist who happens to be taking AP bio, we'll look at that a little bit differently." He adds that students who attend schools offering just a few AP courses aren't compared to those who have, say, 20 to choose from (and it'll be clear, since your guidance counselor will send along a profile of your high school's offerings). Rather, they're judged based on how wisely they choose which advanced courses to take.

Sasha Voinov, who caught the attention of Duke University, chose science courses his school didn't even offer. He was unusual in that he studied at home through the Pennsylvania Cyber Charter School; wanting more challenge, he worked with the guidance counselors to create a program allowing students to take classes at nearby colleges. "On my applications, I highlighted the fact that I was passionate about science by going out of my way to take these advanced classes," says Voinov, who completed more than two years' worth of college-level biology, chemistry and math classes at the Community College of Allegheny County near his Pittsburgh home. After transferring from Duke to the University of Pittsburgh, he is now a senior majoring in neuroscience.

Taking classes at a local college while you're still in high school can be a great move, says Schiffman. "If a student truly excels in math and they're taking a multivariable calculus course at a local community college, absolutely we're going to be impressed."

Show that you're entrepreneurial (and a problem-solver)

The pathways you take outside of the classroom can give a sense of your ability to solve problems and use your skills in real-world settings.

Bennington's success breaking into paintball refereeing demonstrated both his seriousness of purpose in overcoming a big obstacle and an ability to turn a skill into an opportunity – the sort of entrepreneurial success story that college admissions counselors say they like to see. Even if you're not making money, you'll

Sasha Voinov

NOW A SENIOR AT PITTSBURGH, HE TURBOCHARGED HIS TRANSCRIPT WITH COMMUNITY COLLEGE COURSES AND CONVEYED HIS PASSION FOR MUSIC IN AN ESSAY.

turn heads if you find an internship related to your field of interest or show initiative by starting a club or business or a public service in your community, say.

This is especially beneficial if you're interested in business, says Stephanie Klein Wassink, founder of Winning Applications, a Wilton, Connecticut, admissions consulting firm. "You can even walk dogs," Klein Wassink suggests. "Have somebody work with you, have employees. That's possible in high school."

When Sara Camilli was a junior at Biotechnology High School in her hometown of Freehold, New Jersey, for example, she set her sights on the University of Richmond and started looking for a way to make her application pop among the many students who apply there with an interest in science, technology, engineering and math. Her solution: to team up with other students to

invent an app that uses facial-recognition technology to identify both endangered and invasive plant species. "When people take pictures on their phones, they often capture endangered species in the photographs, but the average person wouldn't know that," Camilli explains. "If you have the app running in the background, it can scan your pictures for plants, and if it spots endangered species, it alerts you and adds your location to a database."

Camilli's team entered a proposal in the Verizon Innovative App Challenge competition, and ended up winning $10,000 for the school to apply to STEM education initiatives. She's now a junior at Richmond majoring in biology and computer science.

Highlight your uniqueness – and depth

When listing your activities on applications, be sure to lead off with the most eye-catching and meaningful achievements."I'll get applications where the first one is National Honor Society, the second will be French club, the third will be an activity they did once, and the fourth one is that they're a world championship rodeo athlete," Schiffman says. "Why didn't they put the rodeo first?" Also, he notes, "I do not need to see all 10." Indeed, it doesn't pay to fill out every available space with extracurriculars that aren't distinctive. Your aim is to reveal what your true passions are, not to be joining for the sake of joining.

Barnard College freshman Katie Smith, for example, showed her passion for debate by highlighting her work with other students to establish a speech and debate team at her Falls Church, Virginia, high school, find a coach and get funding. She focused on building a public forum arm of the team that has groups of stu-

At the same time that you're demonstrating the depth of your interests, it's also valuable to show that there are other facets to your personality, notes college application coach Jessica Yeager. A 2008 Harvard graduate with a master's in engineering from the Massachusetts Institute of Technology, Yeager works at an engineering consulting firm in Boston and counsels high school students on the side about getting into college. When she was applying to college herself, for instance, she was able to point to her initiative in the realm of public service as well as her intention to major in engineering. Sophomore year, she'd formed a club that, among other projects, started a recycling program at the school. She also partnered with a local organization for foster families to plan a two-day resource fair. It helped her case, she thinks, that she could paint "a larger

Sara Camilli

A PRIZE-WINNING APP SHE HELPED DEVELOP USES FACIAL-RECOGNITION TECHNOLOGY TO IDENTIFY PLANTS. SHE'S NOW A BIO AND COMPUTER SCIENCE MAJOR AT RICHMOND.

dents arguing about current affairs "Crossfire"-style. Smith also became a coach and started a nonprofit called Open Access Debate that provides a database of source material that teams without a lot of funding can tap to build their cases.

"For the common app essay, I wrote about how my experience in debate shaped me as a person, and how starting the nonprofit helped my personal growth," Smith says. In a supplemental essay, she "drove home the point that I'm willing to go the extra mile."

Smith didn't have room in her essay to mention one more related accomplishment: that she also worked with her school principal to help develop a public speaking and debate course. So she made sure to describe that effort in the "additional information" section of her application. That's also a good place to address any personal struggles that have created weaknesses in your transcript, says Jayson Hodge, senior admissions officer at the University of Connecticut.

picture of someone who wants to do something for the environment and for the world in general – to improve it."

Besides science, Sasha Voinov displayed a passion for music, the topic of an essay. While studying classical piano throughout high school, he taught himself to produce and record music, which got him an internship at a recording studio. On top of her STEM initiative, Sara Camilli demonstrated an interest in making the world a better place by volunteering at her local senior center and as a tutor and assistant in a first-grade classroom.

One final, important tip: Show sincere interest in the schools you're applying to, including your safety schools. Attend information sessions, book a campus tour (perhaps even arranging for an overnight in the dorm), and spend time on each university's website. Thanks to technology, some colleges have started tracking which applicants are interacting with them in a convincing way. "Colleges are far more aware of where students are going on our websites and who's opening our e-mails," says Ohio Wesleyan's Dileno. Even when you're obviously qualified, failing to show true interest can be a black mark. ●

Wowing Admissions
With Your
Essay

Follow these tips from college admissions officials and you'll craft an essay that impresses them by revealing a sense of the real you

by Stacey Colino

EVEN IF YOU'RE SKILLED at writing high school papers and reports, that doesn't guarantee you'll automatically craft a stellar college admissions essay. A primary purpose of the essay and short responses, admissions officers say, is to allow you, the applicant, to share insights into your character and personality. At the same time, while the writing doesn't need to be Pulitzer-caliber prose, it should be grammatically correct and well-organized, and it should showcase your ability to clearly express your ideas. Reviewers look for how well you write "because it's a reflection of how you think," says Janet Lavin Rapelye, dean of admission at Princeton University.

That alone sets the bar pretty high. Adding to the challenge, some of the writing prompts are fairly intimidating: "What will be the best breakthrough – whether scientific, social, economic, or other – between now and 2025?" for example, or "Discuss an accomplishment, event or realization that sparked a period of personal growth and a new understanding of yourself or others." Admissions officers have to wade through thousands of these essays, so ideally you need to capture their attention – in a good way – from the start. If you follow these key steps, you'll be able to produce an effective essay that will impress the right people.

Choose your subject carefully. Often students feel pressure to write about a monumental life experience they've had, such as going on a service trip abroad or overcoming a significant obstacle like a major illness or sports injury.

But "the best essays are often the ones that tell a simple story or the writer's perspective on something that matters to them," says Ellen Kim, dean of undergraduate admissions at Johns Hopkins University. She and other admissions officers say some of the most memorable essays they've read were about ordinary experiences (working in a car shop or a bakery, for instance, or pretending to be a spy as a kid), personal passions (classical music, building robots or doing origami), or dealing with common fears (doing stand-up comedy despite having intense stage fright). In each case, a focused and detail-rich essay can reveal something important about the applicant, such as his or her level of self-reflection, curiosity, initiative or problem-solving skills.

Whatever subject you choose, make sure you fully answer the actual essay question or prompt – and make sure the response is about you, not just your inspiring grandfather or a winning or losing sports season. "Don't tell us what you think we want to hear; tell us who you are, what's important to you or what you will bring to your college community," advises Julie Kerich, director of admission at Franklin and Marshall College. If you're going to write about an influential person or event in your life, be sure to provide insights into how he,

your prose with highfalutin words you wouldn't normally use. That said, "You obviously don't want to be too casual because this is an essay that is representing you in the college admissions process," Kim notes. "Admissions committees know these are written by 17-year-olds and expect the essay to sound like one."

If you're playful or witty, for example, try to let that quality shine through. But it's wise to be judicious; what you think is amusing may not always be to an admissions officer. As you're writing, pay special attention to tone. "Overconfidence or cockiness in tone can really turn a reader off quickly," says Andy Strickler, dean of admission and financial aid at Connecticut College.

Think twice about mentioning touchy subjects. Certain topics such as religion, politics, sex and money "can prove to be problematic," Strickler says. It's unwise to go on a tirade about why the X political party can't be trusted, but if you worked on a political campaign or volunteered with a church organization and the experience inspired you to want to study political science or dedicate yourself to community service, that's worth sharing. Otherwise, your best bet is to steer clear of issues you wouldn't discuss on a first date or share with your grandmother.

Remember, you're trying to make a strong impression, and "sometimes there is a danger in being too honest," Strickler says. For example, if you reveal that you've been grappling with severe depression without providing sufficient insight into how you've worked to overcome it, that could elicit concern rather than admiration. On the other hand, if the disclosure explains why your grades were considerably lower during your freshman year than in 10th grade, or if you can use the experience to show how you overcame that challenge and grew into the person you are today, then "that is a story of resilience and determination," says Nakia Létang, associate director of undergraduate admission at Fairfield University. Létang recalls an effective essay about a young lady who was going to meet her birth mother for the first time. "While she could have

she or it shaped your personality and aspirations, the way you think and view the world. Remember, the purpose of the essay is to help admissions officers get to know you beyond your transcript, letters of recommendation and other materials.

Don't duplicate what's in the application. Rather than recounting achievements or academic credentials that admissions officers can see from other parts of your application, use your essay as a vehicle for venturing into new territory. "Don't write a résumé story," Kerich says. Some of the best essays create a more three-dimensional picture of an applicant that goes beyond stats and a roster of accomplishments to display the person's intellect, values, personality and interests.

Stay true to yourself. Even though you're trying to dazzle the admissions committee, the essay should be written in your authentic voice, not in a stiff or professorial style. "When we read formulaic prose that doesn't reveal your personality, we lose interest," says Meaghan Arena, vice president for enrollment management at SUNY Geneseo. "The essay is the only opportunity you'll have to tell us why you love math but are choosing to major in history or how a situation in your past has shaped the person you are today – so make sure to tell us your story in your way." Don't pepper

> "Don't write a résumé story." Instead, show off the real you.

ILLUSTRATION BY TOM GARRETT FOR USN&WR

USN&WR • BEST COLLEGES 127

expressed lots of anger in her essay," she says, "the overall message was one of hope and growth."

Give yourself plenty of time. As you're writing over the course of weeks or months, take time to fashion an opening sentence or paragraph that's intriguing and compelling and will grab the reader's attention. Don't rush or obsess about typos, grammar or flow at first, Kerich advises. Once you've completed a draft, put it aside for a few days. Then, reread it and revise it as you see fit. Proofread carefully, and don't just rely on spell check, which won't necessarily distinguish between their, they're and there, for example.

Once you think it's in good shape, share your essay with family members or teachers, and incorporate their suggestions if you think they're valuable while preserving your voice; guard against letting it morph into a parent's writing style. Also, read the essay aloud, so you can see if you're

Two Essays That Worked

What makes a college admissions essay successful? Below are two submissions that helped students get into Maryland's **Johns Hopkins University** with commentary from **Ellen Kim,** dean of undergraduate admissions, about what these applicants did right. Remember, Kim advises, that "what works in these essays works because of who the student is" and how it fits into the rest of the application. In other words, you'll want to apply these principles to a topic that reveals something intriguing about you.

> "This title is interesting," Kim says. "But it's up to students to decide whether they want to title an essay." If nothing brilliant comes to mind, then you can skip.

> The author takes a straightforward approach to starting, Kim says. "But you can tell you are going to get to know her."

> Many personal statements include short scenes, Kim notes. But the strongest essays are the ones that put those anecdotes toward a larger purpose, as the author does here. "She is helping us understand where she is in her journey with Italian," Kim says. "It's not just being descriptive for the sake of being descriptive."

> The author chose to write about something very accessible and approachable, Kim notes. "Everyone can relate to family heritage," she says. "It would have been very easy to talk about the members of the family, but she does a good job of making it say something about herself," which is the goal.

> In this paragraph, Kim says, "We learn not just about her intellectual appetite for something, but also about what she does when she is passionate."

More Than Thick Eyebrows

By Caroline

Rarely have I studied a topic that flows from my ears to my brain to my tongue as easily as the Italian language. The Italian blood that runs through me is more than the genetics that gave me my dark hair and thick eyebrows. It is the work of the generation that traveled from Istria in the north and Sicilia in the south, meeting through friends in Chicago, and encouraging their children to study hard and make a living for their future families. In time, that influence would be passed on to me; finding my grandfather's meticulously-written electricity notes circa 1935 – filled with drawings and words I did not yet understand – inspired me to take Italian at my own high school.

The moment I realized that my Italian heritage was wholly a part of me was a rather insignificant one, yet to me is one of the most remarkable realizations of my life. The summer after my second year of Italian study, I was driving in my car, listening to a young trio of Italian teenagers, *Il Volo*, meaning "The Flight." As one of the tenors sang a solo, *Ti voglio tanto bene*, I realized that I could understand every word he was singing. Though it was a simple declaration of love and devotion in a beautiful tune, what mattered was that I was not just listening to three cute teenagers sing a song. I was fully engaged with the words and could finally sing along.

After that moment, I sought out all the Italian I could get my hands on: watching *Cinema Paradiso* and *La Dolce Vita*, absorbing phrases of the language I felt I could now call my own. Even better, w that I felt confident enough in my skill that I could use it with my closest living Italian relative, my father's mother, *la mia nonna*. More than speaking the language, I discovered my family's past. In conversing with her and my father, I discovered that I will be only the third person in my paternal grandparents' family to attend college, that my grandmother had only a sixth-grade education, that my grandfather, despite never holding a degree in mathematics or physics, work for three decades on CTA train cars as an electrician. The marriage of my grandparents in 1952 represented a synthesis of the culture of northern and southern Italy and America.

Having now studied three full years of this language, I only want to consume more of it. I want to read Dante's *Divina Commedia* in its original vernacular, to watch my favorite Italian films without the subtitles, to sing every Italian refrain with fluid understanding of what the melody means, and to finally – finally! – visit my grandparents' childhood homes: the town of Trapani in Sicilia and the Istrian peninsula on the Adriatic coast. To me, the Italian language holds an essential connection to my past, but also a constant goal for the future. It is likely that I will never fully master the vernacular and colloquialisms, yet learning this language will stimulate me intellectually and culturally for life. Italian is a gift that I will hold dear forever, now, but there is still so much more to learn. I believe I can claim Italian as mine and I am glad that I received it so early in life.

> "This is a good way to close the essay, by describing why this matters to who she is as a person," Kim says.

repeatedly using the same word or if words are missing. "Attention to detail can be pivotal," Létang says.

A note of warning: If you're going to personalize the essay and explain how you're a great fit with School X, make sure you've got the details – and the name – correct and that the information doesn't instead apply to School Y. (Admissions officers say this is a common mistake.)

Ultimately, your essay should answer the question that's at the forefront of admissions officers' minds: What do we now know about this student that we didn't know before? "Oftentimes students get so wrapped up in the topic or story and forget to tie it back to a message to the committee about who they are," Kim says. Think of this as your chance to shine a spotlight on the real you. ●

String Theory
By Joanna

If string theory is really true, then the entire world is made up of strings, and I cannot tie a single one. This past summer, I applied for my very first job at a small, busy bakery and café in my neighborhood. I knew that if I were hired there, I would learn how to use a cash register, prepare sandwiches, and take cake orders. I imagined that my biggest struggle would be catering to demanding New Yorkers, but I never thought that it would be the benign act of tying a box that would become both my biggest obstacle and greatest teacher.

On my first day of work in late August, one of the bakery's employees hastily explained the procedure. It seemed simple: wrap the string around your hand, then wrap it three times around the box both ways, and knot it. I recited the anthem in my head, "three times, turn it, three times, knot" until it became my mantra. After observing multiple employees, it was clear that anyone tying the box could complete it in a matter of seconds. For weeks, I labored endlessly, only to watch the strong and small pieces of my pride unravel each time I tried.

As I rushed to discreetly shove half-tied cake boxes into plastic bags, I could not help but wonder what was wrong with me. I have learned Mozart arias, memorized the functional groups in organic chemistry, and calculated the anti-derivatives of functions that I will probably never use in real life – all with a modest amount of energy. For some reason though, after a month's effort, tying string around a cake box still left me in a quandary.

As the weeks progressed, my skills slowly began to improve. Of course there were days when I just wanted to throw all of the string in the trash and use Scotch tape; this sense of defeat was neither welcome nor wanted, but remarks like "Oh, you must be new" from snarky customers catapulted my determination to greater heights.

It should be more difficult to develop an internal pulse and sense of legato in a piece of music than it is to find the necessary rhythm required to tie a box, but this seemingly trivial task has clearly proven not to be trivial at all. The difficulties that I encountered trying to keep a single knot intact are proof of this. The lack of cooperation between my coordination and my understanding left me frazzled, but the satisfaction I felt when I successfully tied my first box was almost as great as any I had felt before.

Scientists developing string theory say that string can exist in a straight line, but it can also bend, oscillate, or break apart. I am thankful that the string I work with is not quite as temperamental, but I still cringe when someone asks for a chocolate mandel bread. Supposedly, the string suggested in string theory is responsible for unifying general relativity with quantum physics. The only thing I am responsible for when I use string is delivering someone's pie to them without the box falling apart. Tying a cake box may not be quantum physics, but it is just as crucial to holding together what matters.

I am beginning to realize that I should not be ashamed if it takes me longer to learn. I persist, and I continue to tie boxes every weekend at work. Even though I occasionally backslide into feelings of exasperation, I always rewrap the string around my hand and start over because I have learned that the most gratifying victories come from tenacity. If the universe really is comprised of strings, I am confident that I will be able to tie them together, even if I do have to keep my fingers crossed that knots hold up.

Students should try to grab the reader's attention at the first sentence. "Her opening paragraph is interesting," says Kim. "You read it, and you aren't sure what the essay is going to be about. It makes you curious about what she is going to tell you."

"A lot of times students feel like they need to write an essay about a life accomplishment or a life-changing event or something really extraordinary," Kim says. "But it's also possible to write a very effective personal statement about an ordinary thing. It's not the topic that has to be unique. It's what you say that has to be unique."

The author does a good job of providing a window into her thought process, Kim notes. "You also see how she responds to a challenge in a very approachable way."

In this instance, dropping in some academic references works with the theme of the essay, but students shouldn't think they have to follow suit, Kim cautions. It only works if it reinforces your central point.

This essay, like all strong essays, was well-written, clear and error-free, Kim notes. The writing felt natural - not as though the author was reaching for a thesaurus. "This should sound like you," she says.

Personal statements are called "personal" for a reason, Kim observes. They should tell the admissions committee something about the student. This essay does a good job of wrapping up the piece on a personal note.

A⁺ Schools for B Students

So you're a scholar with lots to offer and the GPA of a B student, and your heart is set on going to a great college. No problem. U.S. News has screened the universe of colleges and universities to identify those where nonsuperstars have a decent shot at being accepted and thriving – where spirit and hard work could make all the difference to the admissions office. To make this list, which is presented alphabetically, schools had to admit a meaningful proportion of applicants whose test scores and class standing put them in non-A territory (methodology, Page 133). Since many truly seek a broad and engaged student body, be sure to display your individuality and seriousness of purpose as you apply.

National Universities ▶

School (State) (*Public)	SAT/ACT 25th-75th percentile** ('16)	Average high school GPA ('16)	Freshmen in top 25% of class ('16)
Adelphi University (NY)	1010-1210[9]	3.6	64%[5]
American University (DC)	1150-1340[2]	3.7	68%[5]
Andrews University (MI)	21-29	3.5	41%
Arizona State University–Tempe*	22-28[2]	3.5	60%
Ashland University (OH)	20-25	3.4	41%
Auburn University (AL)*	24-30	3.9	62%
Ball State University (IN)*	990-1170[9]	3.5	46%
Baylor University (TX)	26-30	N/A	75%
Clarkson University (NY)	1080-1283	3.6	74%
Clark University (MA)	1110-1325[2]	3.7	74%[5]
Colorado State University*	22-28	3.6	49%
DePaul University (IL)	22-28[2]	3.6	53%[5]
Drexel University (PA)	1080-1300	3.7	69%[5]
Duquesne University (PA)	1055-1230[2]	3.7	56%
Edgewood College (WI)	21-25	3.4	46%
Florida Institute of Technology	1060-1260	3.6	60%[5]
Florida International University*	1030-1210	3.9	47%[5]
Florida State University*	25-29	N/A	77%
George Mason University (VA)*	1060-1250[2]	3.7	52%[5]
Hofstra University (NY)	1070-1260[2]	3.6	60%[5]
Howard University (DC)	1040-1240[3]	3.5	60%[5]
Indiana University–Bloomington*	1060-1290	3.7	72%[5]
Iowa State University*	22-28	3.6	55%
Kansas State University*	22-28[2]	3.5	47%
Kent State University (OH)*	21-25	3.4	41%
Lipscomb University (TN)	22-28	3.6	57%[5]
Louisiana State University–Baton Rouge*	23-28	3.4	51%
Louisiana Tech University*	21-27	3.7	50%
Loyola University Chicago	24-29	3.7	70%[5]
Marquette University (WI)	24-29	N/A	65%[5]
Maryville University of St. Louis	22-27[2]	3.6	59%
Mercer University (GA)	25-29	3.8	70%
Michigan State University*	24-29	3.7	68%[5]
Michigan Technological University*	25-30	3.7	62%
Mississippi State University*	21-28	3.4	56%
Montana State University*	21-28	3.4	43%
New Jersey Institute of Technology*	1110-1310[3]	3.5	61%[5]
The New School (NY)	1030-1280[2]	3.3	44%[5]
North Dakota State University*	21-26	3.4	40%
Nova Southeastern University (FL)	1000-1220	N/A	63%[5]
Ohio University*	21-26	3.5	42%
Oklahoma State University*	21-27	3.5	54%
Oregon State University*	990-1240	3.7	60%
Pennsylvania State University–U. Park*	1090-1300	3.6	77%[5]
Purdue University–West Lafayette (IN)*	1080-1330	3.7	77%[5]
Rochester Institute of Technology (NY)	1140-1330	N/A	73%
Rutgers University–New Brunswick (NJ)*	1110-1350	N/A	78%[5]
Saint Louis University	24-30	3.9	75%[5]
San Diego State University*	1000-1220	3.7	72%[5]
Seton Hall University (NJ)	1070-1250	3.6	59%[5]
SUNY Col. of Environmental Sci. and Forestry*	1070-1260	3.7	72%
Syracuse University (NY)	1090-1290	3.6	71%[5]
Temple University (PA)*	1050-1280[2]	3.6	58%[5]
Texas Christian University	25-30	N/A	74%[5]
Texas Tech University*	1020-1200	3.5	53%
Union University (TN)	23-30[3]	N/A	64%[5]
University at Buffalo–SUNY*	1070-1270	3.6	59%[5]
University of Alabama–Birmingham*	21-28	3.7	55%
University of Arizona*	21-27[2]	3.5	57%[5]
University of Arkansas*	23-29	3.7	54%
University of Central Florida*	1080-1270	3.9	71%
University of Cincinnati*	23-28	3.6	48%
University of Colorado–Boulder*	25-30	3.7	60%[5]
University of Dayton (OH)	24-29[3]	3.7	56%[5]
University of Delaware*	1090-1300	3.7	66%[5]
University of Houston*	1040-1250	N/A	66%
University of Illinois–Chicago*	21-27	3.3	60%
University of Iowa*	23-28	3.6	59%
University of Kansas*	23-29	3.6	58%
University of Kentucky*	22-28	3.7	57%[5]
University of Louisville (KY)*	22-29[3]	3.5	56%[5]
University of Maryland–Baltimore County*	1120-1320	N/A	51%
University of Massachusetts–Amherst*	1130-1330	3.8	74%[5]
University of Massachusetts–Lowell*	1070-1260[2]	3.6	56%[5]
University of Mississippi*	22-29[2]	3.6	50%
University of Missouri*	23-29	N/A	59%
University of Nebraska–Lincoln*	22-28	3.5	49%
University of Nevada–Reno*	21-26	3.6	54%
University of New Hampshire*	990-1200	3.5	50%
University of North Carolina–Charlotte*	22-26	3.9	59%
University of North Dakota*	21-26[3]	3.4	43%
University of Oklahoma*	23-29	3.6	66%
University of Oregon*	980-1220	3.6	60%[5]
University of Rhode Island*	990-1190[3]	3.5	47%
University of San Diego	26-30	3.9	77%[5]
University of San Francisco	1030-1250	3.4	64%[5]
University of South Carolina*	25-30	N/A	63%
University of South Florida*	1070-1250	3.9	72%
University of St. Thomas (MN)	24-29	3.6	53%[5]
University of the Pacific (CA)	1030-1300	3.5	40%[5]
University of Utah*	21-27	3.6	62%[5]
University of Vermont*	1100-1300	3.6	74%[5]

Note: Key to footnotes, Page 78.

School (State) (*Public)	SAT/ACT 25th-75th percentile** ('16)	Average high school GPA ('16)	Freshmen in top 25% of class ('16)
University of Wyoming*	21-27	3.5	48%
Virginia Commonwealth University*	980-1200[2]	3.6	47%
Virginia Tech*	1100-1320	3.9	78%
Wayne State University (MI)*	20-27	3.4	51%[5]
West Virginia University*	21-26	3.5	44%

National Liberal Arts Colleges ▶

School (State) (*Public)	SAT/ACT 25th-75th percentile** ('16)	Average high school GPA ('16)	Freshmen in top 25% of class ('16)
Agnes Scott College (GA)	24-30[2]	3.8	72%
Allegheny College (PA)	1070-1290[2]	3.7	66%[5]
Alma College (MI)	21-26	3.5	50%
Augustana College (IL)	23-28[2]	3.3	62%
Austin College (TX)	23-29	3.5	75%[5]
Beloit College (WI)	24-30[2]	3.3	62%[5]
Berea College (KY)	22-27	3.5	66%
Birmingham-Southern College (AL)	23-29[2]	3.7	58%
Carthage College (WI)	21-27[2]	3.3	51%[5]
Centenary College of Louisiana	22-28	3.5	52%
Central College (IA)	21-26	3.6	52%
Coe College (IA)	22-28	3.6	65%
College of St. Benedict (MN)	22-28	3.7	69%
College of the Atlantic (ME)	1110-1290[2]	3.5	70%[5]
College of Wooster (OH)	24-30	3.7	69%
Concordia College–Moorhead (MN)	22-28	3.5	55%
Cornell College (IA)	23-29[2]	3.5	41%[5]
Covenant College (GA)	24-29	3.7	58%[5]
DePauw University (IN)	24-29	3.8	75%[5]
Drew University (NJ)	1030-1250[2]	3.4	61%[5]
Elizabethtown College (PA)	990-1160	N/A	62%
Furman University (SC)	1120-1320[2]	N/A	77%
Goucher College (MD)	1000-1240[2]	3.1	47%[5]
Grove City College (PA)	1060-1325	3.6	67%
Gustavus Adolphus College (MN)	24-29[2]	3.6	63%
Hampden-Sydney College (VA)	1010-1230	3.6	40%
Hanover College (IN)	22-27	3.7	55%
Hobart and William Smith Colleges (NY)	1160-1350[2]	3.5	64%[5]
Hope College (MI)	23-29	3.7	55%
Illinois Wesleyan University	25-29	3.8	71%[5]
Juniata College (PA)	1040-1240[9]	3.7	75%[5]
Knox College (IL)	24-30[2]	N/A	71%[5]
Lake Forest College (IL)	24-29[2]	3.6	57%[5]
Luther College (IA)	23-28	3.7	52%
McDaniel College (MD)	980-1210	3.5	44%
Millsaps College (MS)	23-28	3.6	64%
Muhlenberg College (PA)	1130-1320[2]	3.3	71%[5]
New College of Florida*	1140-1350	N/A	73%
Ohio Wesleyan University	22-28[2]	3.4	45%
Presbyterian College (SC)	20-27[2]	3.5	62%
Ripon College (WI)	21-26	3.4	47%
Salem College (NC)	21-27	3.9	78%
Siena College (NY)	980-1200[2]	3.5	56%
Simpson College (IA)	21-27	N/A	56%
Skidmore College (NY)	1120-1330[2]	N/A	71%[5]
Southwestern University (TX)	1050-1280	N/A	73%
Spelman College (GA)	980-1170	3.5	73%[5]

School (State) (*Public)	SAT/ACT 25th-75th percentile** ('16)	Average high school GPA ('16)	Freshmen in top 25% of class ('16)
St. Anselm College (NH)	1050-1220[2]	3.3	57%[5]
St. John's University (MN)	22-28	3.5	43%[5]
St. Lawrence University (NY)	1110-1300[2]	3.5	77%[5]
St. Mary's College (IN)	22-28	3.7	54%[5]
St. Michael's College (VT)	1100-1270[2]	3.2	49%
St. Norbert College (WI)	22-27	3.5	54%
Stonehill College (MA)	1000-1210[2]	3.3	58%
Susquehanna University (PA)	1010-1210[2]	3.5	51%
Transylvania University (KY)	25-30[2]	3.7	64%
University of Minnesota–Morris*	22-28	3.5	52%
University of North Carolina–Asheville*	23-28	3.5	54%
University of Puget Sound (WA)	1100-1330[2]	3.6	66%[5]
Ursinus College (PA)	1033-1290[2]	3.2	51%[5]
Virginia Military Institute*	1060-1240	3.6	46%
Wabash College (IN)	1020-1230	3.7	63%
Wartburg College (IA)	21-26	3.5	50%
Washington and Jefferson College (PA)	1070-1250[2]	3.7	59%
Washington College (MD)	1050-1260	3.6	73%[5]
Westmont College (CA)	1040-1280	3.8	65%[5]
Wheaton College (MA)	1050-1270[2]	3.5	54%[5]
Willamette University (OR)	1100-1330	3.9	74%[5]
William Jewell College (MO)	22-28[2]	3.7	55%
Wittenberg University (OH)	22-28[2]	3.4	40%
Wofford College (SC)	24-29	3.6	74%

Regional Universities ▶

School (State) (*Public)	SAT/ACT 25th-75th percentile** ('16)	Average high school GPA ('16)	Freshmen in top 25% of class ('16)
NORTH			
Arcadia University (PA)	1000-1210	3.6	59%
Bentley University (MA)	1150-1320	N/A	72%[5]
Bryant University (RI)	1085-1255[2]	3.5	49%[5]
Champlain College (VT)	1020-1240[3]	3.2	40%[5]
College of New Jersey*	1100-1300	N/A	76%[5]
CUNY–Baruch College*	1090-1310	3.3	76%
Emerson College (MA)	1120-1330	3.7	70%[5]
Endicott College (MA)	1000-1150[2]	3.3	42%[5]
Fairfield University (CT)	1110-1270[2]	3.5	67%[5]
Ithaca College (NY)	1090-1280[2]	N/A	57%[5]
Le Moyne College (NY)	1000-1210[2]	3.5	54%
Loyola University Maryland	1100-1280[2]	3.4	68%[5]
Manhattan College (NY)	1000-1210[3]	N/A	60%[5]
Marist College (NY)	1070-1270[2]	3.3	58%[5]
Molloy College (NY)	980-1170	3.0	56%[5]
Nazareth College (NY)	980-1190[2]	3.5	58%
Providence College (RI)	1030-1240[2]	3.4	69%[5]
Quinnipiac University (CT)	980-1190	3.4	62%
Salisbury University (MD)*	1080-1230[9]	3.7	55%[5]
Salve Regina University (RI)	1020-1180[2]	3.3	45%
Simmons College (MA)	1080-1260	3.4	71%[5]
St. Joseph's University (PA)	1050-1230[2]	3.6	50%[5]
SUNY–Geneseo*	1090-1300	3.7	74%[5]
SUNY Maritime College*	1030-1210	N/A	50%[5]
SUNY–New Paltz*	1010-1200	3.6	58%[5]
SUNY–Oswego*	1010-1180[3]	3.5	50%
SUNY–Plattsburgh*	990-1210[3]	3.3	52%[5]

Regional Universities (continued)

School (State) (*Public)	SAT/ACT 25th-75th percentile** ('16)	Average high school GPA ('16)	Freshmen in top 25% of class ('16)
SUNY Polytechnic Institute*	990-1230[3]	N/A	63%
Towson University (MD)*	980-1160	3.6	42%[5]
University of Scranton (PA)	1030-1220	3.5	62%[5]
Wagner College (NY)	1030-1230[2]	3.6	61%[5]

SOUTH

School (State) (*Public)	SAT/ACT 25th-75th percentile** ('16)	Average high school GPA ('16)	Freshmen in top 25% of class ('16)
Appalachian State University (NC)*	23-27	3.6	57%
Asbury University (KY)	21-28	3.6	59%
Bellarmine University (KY)	22-27	3.5	52%[5]
Belmont University (TN)	24-29	3.7	60%[5]
Berry College (GA)	24-29[3]	3.7	69%
Christian Brothers University (TN)	22-27	3.7	63%
Christopher Newport University (VA)*	1060-1250[2]	3.8	54%

School (State) (*Public)	SAT/ACT 25th-75th percentile** ('16)	Average high school GPA ('16)	Freshmen in top 25% of class ('16)
College of Charleston (SC)*	22-27	3.9	52%
Elon University (NC)	1100-1280	N/A	62%[5]
Embry-Riddle Aeronautical U. (FL)	1000-1240[2]	3.7	50%
Florida Southern College	24-29	3.7	60%[5]
Freed-Hardeman University (TN)	21-27	3.6	59%[5]
Harding University (AR)	22-28	3.6	42%
John Brown University (AR)	23-29[2]	3.7	62%[5]
Lee University (TN)	21-28	3.6	51%
Loyola University New Orleans	23-29	3.6	55%[5]
Milligan College (TN)	22-27	3.7	65%
Rollins College (FL)	1120-1290[2]	3.3	67%[5]
Samford University (AL)	23-29	3.6	57%[5]
Stetson University (FL)	1040-1250[2]	3.9	59%

GONZAGA UNIVERSITY

School (State) (*Public)	SAT/ACT 25th-75th percentile** ('16)	Average high school GPA ('16)	Freshmen in top 25% of class ('16)
University of Mary Washington (VA)*	1010-1210[2]	3.6	46%
U. of North Carolina–Wilmington*	22-26	N/A	61%
University of North Florida*	21-26	3.8	40%
University of North Georgia*	1000-1190	3.6	56%
William Carey University (MS)	21-27[3]	3.6	53%

MIDWEST

School (State) (*Public)	SAT/ACT	Average high school GPA	Freshmen in top 25%
Baker University (KS)	20-25	3.4	40%
Baldwin Wallace University (OH)	21-27[2]	3.5	47%
Bethel University (MN)	21-28	3.5	53%
Bradley University (IL)	22-28	3.7	61%
Butler University (IN)	25-30	3.8	76%[5]
Capital University (OH)	22-28[3]	3.5	46%
Carroll University (WI)	21-26	N/A	53%
College of St. Scholastica (MN)	21-26	3.5	52%
Concordia University (NE)	20-27	3.5	41%
Creighton University (NE)	24-30	3.8	70%[5]
Dominican University (IL)	20-25	3.7	56%
Drake University (IA)	25-30[2]	3.7	68%
Drury University (MO)	22-28	3.6	41%
Elmhurst College (IL)	20-26	3.5	43%
Franciscan U. of Steubenville (OH)	22-28	3.6	50%[5]
Grand Valley State University (MI)*	21-26	3.5	44%
Hamline University (MN)	21-27	3.5	49%
Indiana Wesleyan University	21-27	3.6	53%
John Carroll University (OH)	22-27	3.6	56%[5]
Kettering University (MI)	25-29	3.7	68%
Lawrence Technological U. (MI)	22-29	3.5	53%
Lewis University (IL)	21-26	3.4	46%
Mount Vernon Nazarene U. (OH)	20-26	3.6	51%
North Central College (IL)	22-27	3.6	52%
Otterbein University (OH)	21-26	3.6	57%
Rockhurst University (MO)	23-28	3.7	60%
St. Ambrose University (IA)	20-25	3.3	41%
St. Catherine University (MN)	21-26	3.6	68%
University of Evansville (IN)	23-29	3.7	68%
University of Findlay (OH)	20-25	3.5	45%
University of Illinois–Springfield^	20-26	3.4	43%
University of Mary (ND)	20-26[3]	3.6	51%
University of Michigan–Dearborn*	22-27	3.6	57%
University of Minnesota–Duluth*	22-26	3.5	42%
University of Northern Iowa*	20-25[3]	3.5	46%
University of St. Francis (IL)	20-26	3.4	40%[5]
University of Wisconsin–Eau Claire*	22-26	N/A	47%
University of Wisconsin–La Crosse*	23-27	N/A	59%
University of Wisconsin–Platteville*	20-25	N/A	40%
Valparaiso University (IN)	23-29	3.7	62%
Webster University (MO)	21-27	3.4	42%[5]
Xavier University (OH)	23-28[3]	3.7	54%[5]

WEST

School (State) (*Public)	SAT/ACT	Average high school GPA	Freshmen in top 25%
Abilene Christian University (TX)	21-27	3.6	56%
California Lutheran University	990-1080	3.7	68%[5]
George Fox University (OR)	980-1220	3.6	59%[5]
Gonzaga University (WA)	1110-1300	3.8	69%[5]
LeTourneau University (TX)	1030-1280[2]	3.6	55%[5]
Loyola Marymount University (CA)	1120-1330	3.7	73%[5]

School (State) (*Public)	SAT/ACT 25th-75th percentile** ('16)	Average high school GPA ('16)	Freshmen in top 25% of class ('16)
New Mexico Inst. of Mining & Technology*	23-29	3.7	64%
Oklahoma Christian University	21-28[3]	3.6	55%
Oklahoma City University	23-30[3]	3.7	54%
Point Loma Nazarene University (CA)	1030-1240	3.8	66%
Seattle University	1070-1290	3.6	64%[5]
St. Edward's University (TX)	1010-1200	N/A	60%
University of Dallas	1040-1290[3]	3.8	61%[5]
University of Portland (OR)	1080-1320	3.6	75%[5]
University of Redlands (CA)	980-1190	3.5	55%
University of St. Thomas (TX)	990-1175	3.6	57%
Western Washington University*	990-1220	3.4	56%[5]
Westminster College (UT)	22-27	3.5	52%
Whitworth University (WA)	1000-1260[2]	3.8	60%[5]

Regional Colleges ▶

School (State) (*Public)	SAT/ACT 25th-75th percentile** ('16)	Average high school GPA ('16)	Freshmen in top 25% of class ('16)
NORTH			
Messiah College (PA)	1020-1260	3.8	62%
U.S. Coast Guard Academy (CT)*	1170-1340	3.8	79%
SOUTH			
High Point University (NC)	995-1200	3.3	46%[5]
MIDWEST			
Augustana University (SD)	23-29	3.8	53%
Benedictine College (KS)	21-28	3.4	42%[5]
Calvin College (MI)	23-29[2]	3.7	57%
Cedarville University (OH)	23-29	3.7	68%[5]
College of the Ozarks (MO)	21-25[3]	3.7	66%
Dordt College (IA)	21-27	3.6	42%
Northwestern College (IA)	21-28	3.6	47%
Ohio Northern University	23-28	3.7	57%
Taylor University (IN)	22-29	3.7	64%[5]
University of Mount Union (OH)	20-26[2]	3.4	50%
Wisconsin Lutheran College	21-27	3.4	46%
WEST			
Carroll College (MT)	22-28	3.6	62%[5]
Oklahoma Baptist University	21-26	3.7	58%

Methodology: To be eligible, national universities, liberal arts colleges, regional universities and regional colleges all had to be numerically ranked among the top three-quarters of their peer groups in the 2018 Best Colleges rankings. They had to admit a meaningful proportion of non-A students, as indicated by fall 2016 admissions data on SAT Critical Reading and Math or Composite ACT scores and high school class standing. The cutoffs were: The 75th percentile for the SAT had to be less than or equal to 1,350; the 25th percentile, greater than or equal to 980. The ACT composite range: less than or equal to 30 and greater than or equal to 20. The proportion of freshmen from the top 10 percent of their high school class had to be less than or equal to 50 percent (for national universities and liberal arts colleges only); for all schools, the proportion of freshmen from the top 25 percent of their high school class had to be less than or equal to 80 percent, and greater than or equal to 40 percent. Average freshman retention rates for all schools had to be greater than or equal to 75 percent. Average high school GPA itself was not used in the calculations identifying the A-plus schools. N/A means not available.

WE DID IT!

How eight high school seniors got accepted

by Lindsay Cates

TACKLING COLLEGE APPLICATIONS, on top of classes, work, sports and extracurriculars, certainly raises the excitement level senior year. And then there's the suspense of waiting to get accepted and making a choice. For an inside look at the process, U.S. News visited Floral Park Memorial High School on Long Island in April to see how several seniors got it all done – and got in. With dozens of colleges in nearby New York City, a number have headed for the Big Apple, while others answered a craving for a change of scenery. The public school's 1,400-student population is diverse: 55 percent white, 14 percent Hispanic, 17 percent Asian, and 14 percent African-American. Ninety-eight percent of students continue their education at two- or four-year colleges. Floral Park offers 17 Advanced Placement courses and, unlike many schools, measures GPA on a scale of 100 versus 4.0. Here, eight seniors share secrets for success – and what they'd tackle differently if given a do-over:

Ashish James

Sometimes students feel the pull of a calling. James knew he wanted to study nursing to honor his older brother, an aspiring nurse, who passed away in a car accident in 2011. Originally James considered exploring New York state for school, maybe heading north to the The College at Brockport; in the end, he realized he couldn't part with Long Island's proximity to New York City – a place he says "has it all." Once he'd decided to stay local, he focused on affordability and a good nursing program.

He applied to Molloy College and Adelphi University, and was accepted on the spot to both schools during on-campus interviews in January. Satisfied, he didn't apply elsewhere and decided Molloy was the best fit. James aspires to work in an intensive care unit, given his strong interest in helping people needing immediate care. Next up? A possible master's in nursing.

GPA: 83.80
SAT: 600 math, 560 evidence-based reading and writing
Extracurriculars: Football; The American Legion: Boys State (a selective military leadership program), Leo Club youth organization.
Interview tactic: "Just the truth." He was transparent about who he is and why the school appealed.
Essay: Losing a brother "definitely changed me." He explained how the loss motivated him to improve academically and socially in high school, and to live out the nursing dreams his brother no longer could.
Stressor: Paying for school. Sorting out scholarships and financial aid was trickier than he imagined.
Do-over: Researching scholarships sooner and applying for more of them.

Advice: Have a support system. "Take breathers," his best friend counseled when James got frustrated with the process.

Elizabeth Talero

For Talero, applying to schools was "a balancing act." The daughter of Colombian immigrants with "traditional" family values, Talero juggled cooking, cleaning and helping at home with schoolwork, extra-curriculars and college applications. Her initial instinct was to get away from New York, but after visiting the University of Vermont on a trip for minority students, a dose of culture shock led her to explore schools closer to home. Scientifically inclined, Talero's dream job is to work as a zoo veterinarian, treating exotic animals, especially reptiles and amphibians.

She earned acceptances at Macaulay Honors College at CUNY, Fordham University and SUNY–Oswego – all in New York – as well as the University of Vermont and the University of Scranton in Pennsylvania. She was wait-listed at Barnard and denied by Tufts. She weighed cost, programs offered, distance from home and diversity before choosing Macaulay Honors College. Also a talented artist, she hopes to tack on at least a minor in art (her favorite medium is colored pencil) in addition to her science studies.

GPA: 93.06
SAT/ACT: 540

math; 670 evidence-based reading and writing/32
Extracurriculars: President of Science Olympiad (silver and bronze medalist), president of Photo Club, vice president of National Art Honor Society, vice president of Drama Club, actor in the school musical; Girl Scout Gold Award winner; employed as a mother's helper.
Winning combo: Extracurriculars paired with good grades are what she believes caught the attention of admissions officers. She hopes they "saw that I can take on the world."
Essay: As a kid, Talero wondered why her brothers got to do things she didn't in their traditional household, so she starting acting and dressing like a boy herself. Her essay chronicled her transformation from a rebellious young girl to a woman who still thinks gender-specific norms are "dumb" but can love doing makeup as a way to express her art.
Bonus: She submitted an art portfolio to Barnard, Tufts and Macaulay Honors.
Good move: Staying overnight during campus visits. "Once you're there, that's when it hits you."
Cost: Macaulay Honors College is tuition-free. Her parents will help with room and board, but she plans to become a resident

> Have a support system and take breathers to squash stress.

Ashish James

assistant to pitch in.
Helpful resources:
Fastweb.com to search
for scholarships, and her
guidance counselor.
Advice: "Space yourself
out" doing applications.
Procrastination clobbered
some of her friends.

Sydnie Jaime

An art and design lover,
Jaime felt at home when
she visited the Fashion
Institute of Technology in
New York City. Initially
interested in studying
photography, she narrowed
her focus to advertising
and communications
design as her college search
progressed. Jaime got
her applications in early,
then took more time to
complete accompanying art
portfolios. Each portfolio
included 10 to 12 pieces
of her best photography
and web design work.

In addition, Jaime stayed
active in her community
through PEARLS Club,
a minority women's
leadership group at Floral
Park Memorial. Her high
school achievements and
artistic talent won Jaime
acceptances at every
school she applied to:
City College of New York,
FIT, Farmingdale State
College, New York Institute
of Technology, Temple
University in Pennsylvania
and Rider University in New
Jersey. She wanted a school
with a community feel – and
that was cost-friendly. FIT
had both, not to mention
ample opportunities to land
art and design internships
in the city. Jaime hopes to
someday launch her own
design business and thinks
FIT can help her get there.
GPA: 87.71
SAT: 600 math;
570 evidence-based
reading and writing
Extracurriculars: President
of PEARLS Club, secretary
of the Class Board,
National Honor Society,

Superintendent's Student
Advisory Council.
Essay: Finding friends as an
introvert and gaining self-

> Stay
> overnight.
> When you're
> there, that's
> when it hits
> you.

confidence
though PEARLS Club.
FIT required three
additional essays and
three art projects
(on top of her
portfolio) for the
communications
design major.
Smart move: Keep-
ing a notebook of
essay questions,
deadlines and
weekly to-do
lists, helping
her stay on
track and
manage her
time wisely.
Regret: Not
applying
to more
"reach"
schools.
**Hardest
step:** Pull-
ing together
her portfolio
despite dis-
tractions. At
the time, her
family home
was alive
with rela-
tives from
Jamaica.
"It was
fun but
stressful."
Money:
Financial
aid

from FIT and work-study
will cover most of her
$4,690 in-state tuition.
Cherry on top: Acceptance
letters were "validation of
years of hard work."
Advice: "Work hard and

> Don't just
> stick to
> "safe"
> schools.

Elizabeth
Talero

Sydnie
Jaime

It's not where you go to college, but what you make of it.

stick to what your dreams are." Be open to tips from those who have gone through the application process.

Dylan Slavin

A politics and debate enthusiast, Slavin envisions becoming a lawyer or politician. When not debating during high school, he quarterbacked the marching band as drum major, an activity that helped shape who he is today. Come time to think about college, he visited several New York schools including Adelphi University, Long Island University and Farmingdale State College but sent applications to just four in-state top choices.

He was accepted at Nassau Community College and St. John's University; wait-listed at Fordham; denied by NYU. Cost was his biggest concern. He decided to start at Nassau Community College and then transfer to a more competitive school. This strategy will help him cut costs (he's paying for college himself out of pocket) but still get a good education. He plans to major in English and minor in politics or economics.
GPA: 90.63
SAT: 550 math, 640 evidence-based reading and writing
Extracurriculars: Drum major of the marching band, jazz band, Music Honor Society, Battle of the Bands (he plays five instruments); waiting tables.
Essay: A personal reflection on how his parents' decision to live near and take care of his grandparents gave him an appreciation for those who go out of their way to help others. The aspiring English major enjoyed the writing portions of his applications and thinks having a unique personal story helped him stand out.
Influencers: Teachers. One

in seventh grade "ignited his passion" for politics. Recently, when he was struggling with the college decision, that same teacher told him "it's not where you go to college, but what you make of it." Those words gave him courage to start at community college.

Advice: If you're invested in college, establish a good work ethic now. "Be thinking about your future and put in the 100 percent to get there."

Luke deArmas

On top of being Floral Park Memorial's top graduate, deArmas lent his time as a volunteer firefighter and played varsity soccer. He even helped lead the team to its first county championship his junior year. His stellar grades and extracurricular involvement scored him entry to all nine schools he applied to, but Vanderbilt University was a top choice from the get-go. DeArmas knew the type of school he was looking for: a place with strong academic programs (but not cutthroat), and somewhere he could have fun, too.

He was accepted to Binghamton University–SUNY and Fordham University in New York; Tulane University in New Orleans; the University of North Carolina–Chapel Hill; Clemson University and the University of South Carolina; Vanderbilt in Nashville; the University of Miami; and Lehigh

Dylan Slavin

University in Pennsylvania. Vanderbilt's warm climate, strong computer science and engineering programs, and generous financial aid package sealed the deal. "At other schools it was give-and-take, but Vanderbilt had everything," he says. He'll study computer engineering and is already considering grad school in the field.
GPA: 98.58
ACT: 33
Extracurriculars: Varsity soccer, editor-in-chief of The Shield school newspaper, National Honor Society; treasurer of Future Business Leaders of America, Relay For Life, The American Legion: Boys State (a selec-

tive military leadership program), volunteer firefighter.
Essay: "I wanted to take time to make it great." He focused on how the discipline and communication skills needed as a firefighter prepared him for the demands of college.
Good move: He had all his apps done by mid-October for the early action deadlines, leaving more time to balance sports, school and volunteering.
College visits: He did them all junior year, freeing up time to focus on applications senior year.
Regret: Avoiding more competitive schools, maybe Ivy League. "But I didn't want to be one of those kids who applied to all those schools."
Resources: He used The Princeton Review, U.S. News' college rankings, and Niche.com for research, in addition to browsing school websites.
Advice: His guidance counselor suggested he check the flexibility of programs in case he decides to switch majors.

Jacqueline Tam

Tam was as diligent in her college search as she was in her schoolwork and extracurriculars throughout high school. She started visiting schools her junior year, and took notes on her smartphone to remember the differences in curriculums and activities offered. Not only a talented viola and volleyball player, Tam worked her way up to leadership positions in several clubs, her favorite being president of the school chamber orchestra.

Drawn to colder climates, she applied to 11 Northeast schools and was accepted at Boston University and Northeastern University, also in Boston; New York University, Stony Brook University, Rensselaer Polytechnic Institute and Rochester Institute of Technology in New York; and Wesleyan University in Connecticut. She was waitlisted at Williams College in Massachusetts and Cornell University in New York; denied by Massachusetts Institute of Technology and Tufts University in Boston. Her decision came down to scholarship money and program quality. Ultimately, Northeastern University's co-op program and urban campus swayed her. She'll attend its College of Computer and Information Science, pursuing a combined computer science and mathematics degree.

> **Visit colleges junior year to focus on apps senior year.**

GPA: 97.10

SAT: 800 math, 700 evidence-based reading and writing

Extracurriculars: President of chamber orchestra, president of Mathletes, principal violist in district orchestra, captain of varsity volleyball team, treasurer of National Honor Society, JV softball and Chess Club; teaching yo-yo to kids at a Chinese school.

Interviews: Tam jumped at every school interview opportunity to learn more about each campus and get advice.

Regrets: Rushing the essays. She ended up writing about her experience in orchestra, a club where she felt she belonged and could mentor younger musicians.

Lifeline: Her parents. They guided her through the process and made sure she had her apps in early. Ultimately, they left the decision up to her.

Most fun: "Going on tours and exploring college campuses. Some were tucked away in parts of the city you wouldn't normally go."

Advice: Get involved in the high school community and clubs. "It's the best way to ensure you get good recommendation letters."

Emmanuel Betancourth

Resilience is what Betancourth says got him to college. His parents divorced when he was young, and the recession was hard on his family. His self-esteem was sagging and he felt like an outsider, he says, until he joined the high school football team. Not only was he smiling in the hallways, but he was starting to consider college. November of senior year, he got serious about his applications – a timeline he admits was last-minute and stressful. Affordability, solid computer and information technology programs, outdoorsy surroundings, and a New York ZIP code were his must-haves.

He was accepted to SUNY Polytechnic Institute, Marist College and Rochester Institute of Technology, but was denied by Binghamton University–SUNY. Betancourth chose RIT after loving the vibe at accepted-students day. "People were having fun ... it just felt like a college experience," he says. The modern buildings, F1 car club, and potential internship opportunities he could score impressed him. His goal? Learning the ropes of network and data administration, while picking up computer coding skills at the tech school.

GPA: 88.78

SAT: 600 math; 580 evidence-based reading and writing

Extracurriculars: Varsity football. "Even if you don't have much in common with people, you can rally around the football."

Essay: Transformation-themed. "I did a 180" after joining the football team.

Big help: Tapping professors at schools and programs of interest. Hearing them talk about opportunities in computing security, video games and software engineering enticed him.

Cost: "Definitely a big issue." Financial aid will cover most of the $54,758 price tag for tuition and room and board.

Sleuth work: He browsed Facebook profiles of current students to get an inside scoop on campus life. On visits, he snagged school newspapers to see what students were talking about.

> **Jump at every college interview opportunity.**

Jacqueline Tam

Luke deArmas

Best part: Seeing campuses in action.
Advice: "Be open to trying something new, and if cost is an issue, get a job to start saving money now."

Reach out to professors in programs that interest you.

Dayna Cardalena

Cardalena focused on schools with nursing programs from day one. After her mother died of breast cancer in 2013, she moved in with her aunt and uncle, five siblings and two cousins; come application time, she craved the "space" of leaving New York for college. The loss fortified her desire to succeed, motivating her to enroll in AP classes and stay involved in extracurriculars. She wanted admissions reviewers to see her dedication and involvement in spite of her tough situation. She sent applications to 11 nursing and pharmacy schools (completing them all by the Nov. 1 early action deadline).

She was welcomed by St. John's University's pharmacy program in New York, and the nursing programs at Quinnipiac University and Sacred Heart University in Connecticut; Adelphi University and Pace University–Pleasantville in New York; James Madison University in Virginia; and the University of New Hampshire. At University of Kentucky and University of Rhode Island she was accepted, but not into nursing. She was denied by the University of Massachusetts–Amherst and Fairfield University in Connecticut. The application process opened her eyes to possibilities beyond nursing, and she is now considering education or social work. After visiting a cousin at JMU, she fell in love with the warmer climate and liked that she could pursue nursing or do other things if she changed her mind.

GPA: 90.18
SAT/ACT: 670 math; 420 evidence-based reading and writing/20
Extracurriculars: Line captain of the kickline team, National Honor Society, Spanish Honor Society, District Sports Night.
Essay: She connected key principles of kickline (smile, pointed toes, straight posture, strong connections) to being strong in life through tough times.
Good move: Being unafraid to ask teachers for extra help when needed. Forming those connections helped her when it came time to secure rec letters and application assistance.
Bold choice: She chose JMU despite her family wanting her to stay close.
Regret: Applying almost exclusively to nursing schools.
Advice: Take guidance with a grain of salt. A counselor dashed her interest in pharmacy after doubting she'd get into any programs. Since St. John's pharmacy program did accept her; she wishes she had applied to more. ●

If you encounter naysayers, keep going.

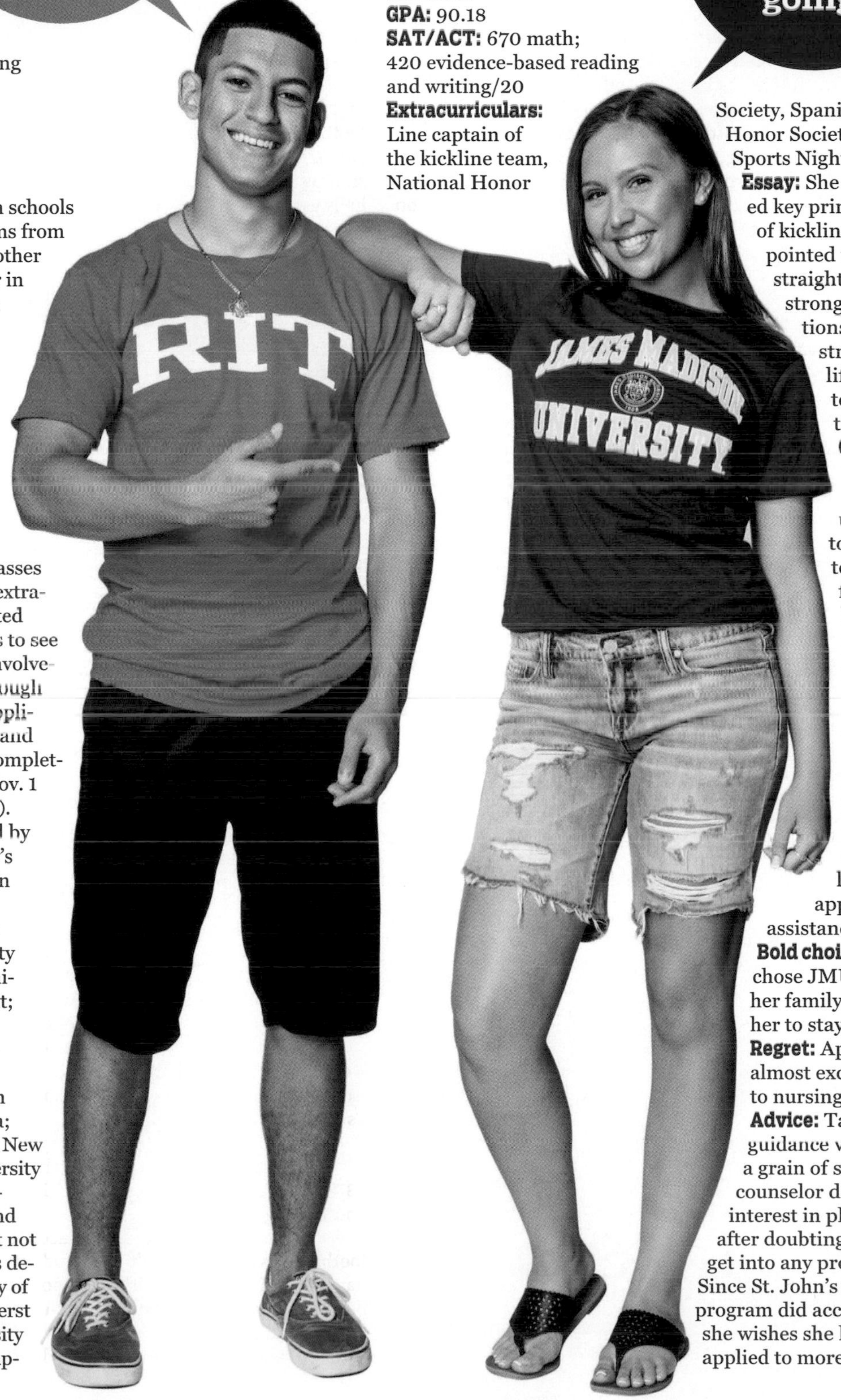

Emmanuel Betancourth   Dayna Cardalena

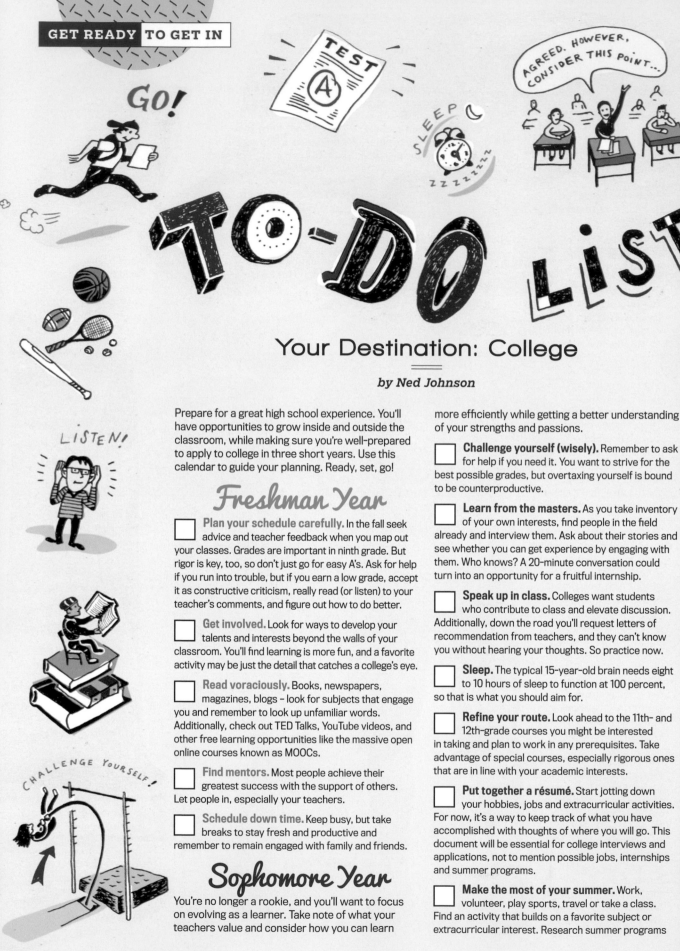

TO-DO LIST

Your Destination: College

by Ned Johnson

Prepare for a great high school experience. You'll have opportunities to grow inside and outside the classroom, while making sure you're well-prepared to apply to college in three short years. Use this calendar to guide your planning. Ready, set, go!

Freshman Year

☐ **Plan your schedule carefully.** In the fall seek advice and teacher feedback when you map out your classes. Grades are important in ninth grade. But rigor is key, too, so don't just go for easy A's. Ask for help if you run into trouble, but if you earn a low grade, accept it as constructive criticism, really read (or listen) to your teacher's comments, and figure out how to do better.

☐ **Get involved.** Look for ways to develop your talents and interests beyond the walls of your classroom. You'll find learning is more fun, and a favorite activity may be just the detail that catches a college's eye.

☐ **Read voraciously.** Books, newspapers, magazines, blogs – look for subjects that engage you and remember to look up unfamiliar words. Additionally, check out TED Talks, YouTube videos, and other free learning opportunities like the massive open online courses known as MOOCs.

☐ **Find mentors.** Most people achieve their greatest success with the support of others. Let people in, especially your teachers.

☐ **Schedule down time.** Keep busy, but take breaks to stay fresh and productive and remember to remain engaged with family and friends.

Sophomore Year

You're no longer a rookie, and you'll want to focus on evolving as a learner. Take note of what your teachers value and consider how you can learn more efficiently while getting a better understanding of your strengths and passions.

☐ **Challenge yourself (wisely).** Remember to ask for help if you need it. You want to strive for the best possible grades, but overtaxing yourself is bound to be counterproductive.

☐ **Learn from the masters.** As you take inventory of your own interests, find people in the field already and interview them. Ask about their stories and see whether you can get experience by engaging with them. Who knows? A 20-minute conversation could turn into an opportunity for a fruitful internship.

☐ **Speak up in class.** Colleges want students who contribute to class and elevate discussion. Additionally, down the road you'll request letters of recommendation from teachers, and they can't know you without hearing your thoughts. So practice now.

☐ **Sleep.** The typical 15-year-old brain needs eight to 10 hours of sleep to function at 100 percent, so that is what you should aim for.

☐ **Refine your route.** Look ahead to the 11th- and 12th-grade courses you might be interested in taking and plan to work in any prerequisites. Take advantage of special courses, especially rigorous ones that are in line with your academic interests.

☐ **Put together a résumé.** Start jotting down your hobbies, jobs and extracurricular activities. For now, it's a way to keep track of what you have accomplished with thoughts of where you will go. This document will be essential for college interviews and applications, not to mention possible jobs, internships and summer programs.

☐ **Make the most of your summer.** Work, volunteer, play sports, travel or take a class. Find an activity that builds on a favorite subject or extracurricular interest. Research summer programs

or internships to give yourself the opportunity to go beyond the scope of your regular high school classes.

☐ **Determine your testing strategy.** Use your PSAT scores and other practice test experiences to get a better sense of where you stand and identify the best test for you (i.e., SAT vs. ACT). Organize yourself and set up a test-prep plan.

Junior Year

Essays and testing and APs, oh my! Your grades, test scores and activities junior year constitute a big chunk of what colleges consider for admission, so prepare for your exams and do your best in class.

☐ **Plan your testing calendar.** Talk with your parents and guidance counselor about which exams to take and when. If your 10th-grade scores on the PSAT put you in reach of a National Merit Scholarship, it might be wise to spend concentrated time prepping. Then take the SAT or ACT in winter or early spring. In May or June the SAT Subject Tests (required by some colleges) are also an option in areas where you shine or in subjects you covered junior year. If you're enrolled in an AP or honors course now, consider taking one of the practice AP tests offered by the College Board.

☐ **Do a deeper dive into activities.** Look for extracurriculars you enjoy in and out of school that show you work hard, are dedicated, play well with others and can assume leadership roles.

☐ **Build your college list in the spring.** Once you receive your test scores, talk to a counselor and put together a list of target schools, reaches and safeties. Use apps to aid your research. Explore college websites and resources like ed.gov/finaid and usnews.com/bestcolleges. While you're online, be sure to clean up your social media (e.g., Instagram, Facebook, Twitter). It's likely to get a look from the college admissions folks.

☐ **Make campus visits.** Spring break and summer vacation are ideal times to check out a few campuses. Attend college fairs and talk with the people behind the tables. They can give you a feel for their school and some good future contacts.

☐ **Ask for recommendations.** Right after spring break, ask two teachers if they are willing to write letters on your behalf. Choose teachers with whom you have a good relationship and who will effectively communicate your academic and personal qualities. You will want people who can offer different perspectives on your performance.

☐ **Write.** Procrastination doesn't make for a good college essay. Aim to have first drafts done by Labor Day of senior year. Share them with an English teacher or counselor.

Senior Year

Colleges consider senior-year transcripts, so don't clock off. You'll need to be especially busy in the fall

☐ **Finish testing.** If necessary, you can retake the SAT, ACT or Subject Tests. The early fall test dates give you time to apply early. Be sure to check deadlines and admissions testing policy of all of your schools. Are they test-optional or do they require the SAT or ACT (and, if so, do you also need the optional written essays for the ACT or SAT or the SAT Subject Tests)?

☐ **Know your deadlines.** Many colleges have multiple deadline options. Consider the implications of early decision, early action, rolling, regular and other deadlines and plan accordingly.

☐ **Apply.** Fill out applications carefully. Review a copy of your transcript. Have you displayed an upward trend that should be discussed? Does an anomaly need context? Discuss with your counselor.

☐ **Follow up.** Check that your colleges have received records and recs from your high school, and have your SAT or ACT scores sent from the testing organization. A month from the date you submit your application, call the college and confirm that your file is complete.

☐ **Confirm aid rules.** Check with each college for specific financial aid application requirements. Dates and forms may vary.

☐ **Make a choice.** Try to visit or even revisit the colleges where you've been accepted. Talk with alumni, attend an accepted-student reception. Then make your college choice official by sending in your deposit. Done!

Ned Johnson is founder of and tutor-geek at PrepMatters (prepmatters.com) where, along with colleagues, he torments teens with test prep, educational counseling and general attempts to help them thrive. He also is co-author of "Conquering the SAT: How Parents Can Help Teens Overcome the Pressure and Succeed."

WHY I PICKED...

...Furman University

Greenville, South Carolina

> **WHEN I FIRST** saw Furman, I was intrigued by its stunning campus tucked away at the base of the Blue Ridge Mountains and its commitment to engaged learning. As a first-generation college student, I had to pay for my education. So I looked for schools that would offer me grants and the chance to explore my many interests, including politics, history, numbers and theater. Furman, I found, could give me all of this.

For example, through the school's Riley Institute, which is committed to finding bipartisan solutions to the education gap and diversity in South Carolina, I could help organize events with political leaders. I also joined Furman's Heller Service Corps, which each year sends over 1,800 students into Greenville County to work on community projects. I helped put on a dance for exceptional adults and "adopted" a grandparent.

I got to originate a role in "Pomp & Circumstance," a play written by a Furman alum. I spent a semester abroad in Brussels, where I combined my passion for politics and numbers by interning for the chair of the budgetary control committee in the European Parliament. Going to Furman was absolutely the right decision for me. ●

FURMAN UNIVERSITY

Nathan Mathai, '17

❝
I got to originate a role in a play written by a Furman alum.

TAKING A BREAK BY FURMAN'S 30-ACRE LAKE

6
UMN is a public university with award-winning professors.

Raven Ziegler, '17

...U. of Minnesota Twin Cities

Minneapolis/St. Paul

➤ **UMN, A PUBLIC RESEARCH** university with award-winning professors, attracted me because it offers students outstanding opportunities to pursue their passions by volunteering, studying abroad, interning and conducting research. As someone interested in international law and helping oppressed groups, I was eager to capitalize on the practical experiences UMN offers. For example, I interned at Minnesota's largest county attorney's office and, drawing on my Lakota Sioux heritage, I volunteered locally to teach the Dakota language to Native American youth.

UNIVERSITY OF MINNESOTA

UMN also enabled me to spend six months at the University of Cape Town in South Africa studying international relations and foreign policy. While there, I studied a student-led movement pushing to restructure the educational system, which many felt was still mired in its apartheid roots. I later incorporated my experiences into my senior thesis on the plight of indigenous communities and how reparations could alleviate poverty in South Africa.

UMN offers so many opportunities to students. A friend of mine, for example, got help in setting up a university-based community veterinarian clinic in rural communities. The university helped me better understand global crises, build networks and understand how to use these networks to find solutions. ●

...Trinity University

San Antonio

➤ **VISITING TRINITY, I TOURED** the Center for the Sciences and Innovation, the school's state-of-the-art research and teaching facilities for engineering and science. It was impressive, but so was our guide, the head of the neuroscience department, who struck me with his commitment to his students' success. Faculty-student engagement is a real strength at Trinity. Professors hold extensive office hours, offer review sessions and make themselves available for extra help. Many courses are discussion-based, even in the sciences, where students can explore how research was handled, a real plus for me as a future physician. Undergraduate research is encouraged. My faculty mentor helped me design my own project on visual processing in the lizard brain that I got funded through a Trinity fellowship and a grant.

Maria Jaramillo, '17

Since the school is located in downtown San Antonio, I was able to enjoy the city while still finding quiet spots to retreat to if needed. Groups regularly put on cultural events like the Indian Student Association's Diwali (the festival of lights) celebration, which enriched the diversity of my college experience. While the care of my professors and mentors kept me on track for medical school, my fellow students helped me grow. ●

6
My faculty mentor helped me design my own project on visual processing in the lizard brain.

COURTESY OF TRINITY UNIVERSITY

5

Finding the Money

ELON UNIVERSITY

9

Things You Need to Know to Get a

GREAT DEAL

Understanding a few key facts about how aid is awarded will raise the odds of a generous package

by Arlene Weintraub

NEWS YOU CAN USE Want your share of the $150 billion Uncle Sam will be handing out in financial aid as you head off to college? And a portion of the money your school has set aside for its own awards? There are a multitude of details to consider when you're angling for aid, from meeting application deadlines to the complicated calculations schools make to arrive at their offers. Here are our top tips for navigating your way to success.

You must fill out the aid forms (and do it early)

THE FREE APPLICATION FOR FEDERAL student aid is a must-do for anyone hoping for help from the government. It asks parents for information about their own assets and those of their applicant and shoots back the "expected family contri-

bution" that colleges use to assemble packages. It's essential to fill out this form as early as possible during senior year, because many schools award money on a first-come-first-served basis. In 2016, the FAFSA calendar moved up by three months, so those who will be freshmen in the fall of 2018 can tackle the form as early as Oct. 1 of this year.

There are other changes to the FAFSA process that are important to understand, too. First, you no longer have to plug in figures from your most recent tax return. Previously, families typically had to estimate the numbers and then correct them after their return was finished. Now you can instead use what's called prior-prior year tax information. So if you're applying in the fall of 2017 for the 2018-19 school year, you will use your 2016 tax information.

Be aware that some savings and investments that previously would not have counted against you in calculating your expected contribution may be included in the future. The amount of these so-called protected assets that families can hold without being penalized varies according to the age and marital status of the parents, but overall it's on a downward trend. For example, for a student whose

Paige Adams
Kennesaw State University

One Family's Strategy: Be a Landlord

Paige Adams, who graduated from Kennesaw State University near Atlanta this year, had 80 percent of her $7,000-a-year tuition paid for by the HOPE Scholarship she won from the state of Georgia for those with GPAs of at least 3.0, with another award covering the rest. Her other expenses? Before the start of freshman year, she looked for a way to live near the university without incurring thousands of dollars in housing fees.

Adams' mother and stepfather have a home just seven miles from campus, but they wanted to support her quest for independence. So the family came up with an innovative solution: Adams found a 1,200-square-foot two-bedroom townhouse near campus that had gone into foreclosure, they snapped it up for $36,000 in cash, and Adams took charge of finding a roommate to help cover utilities, property taxes and maintenance. The $500 per month her roommate paid in rent covered most of that, with her parents helping out some, too. It worked out so well that when Adams headed to veterinary school at the University of Georgia after graduation, her parents bought her another home near the Athens campus.

Adams says that being a homeowner has offered her other benefits. "I learned a lot about making basic repairs in the house and keeping everything clean outside and inside," says Adams. During her time living in the townhome, she landscaped the backyard, repaired faucets and changed out air filters and light bulbs. Her Athens house is a standalone three-bedroom, and she will have a roommate, but she says she's ready for the responsibility of a bigger home. "Most of my friends don't know how to set up appointments with pest control and the air conditioning guy. This has made me more independent."

Her stepfather, Bruce Ailion, happens to be a real estate broker in Atlanta, but he says parents need no special training to use property ownership as a strategy for saving money on college. And it can pay off even after a child's graduation, depending on the location and purchase price - even if you have to take out a home loan. "If you lock in a 4 percent interest rate for a long period of time, you can make money on the money you borrow" by taking in renters, says Ailion, who held on to the townhome near Kennesaw State and has rented it out for $1,250 a month. He estimates its value now at $99,000 to $105,000. –A.W.

eldest parent is 48, the limit plummeted from $30,300 in 2015-16 to $20,200 for 2017-18. "The protection allowance has declined or stayed flat for years," says Beth V. Walker, founder of the Center for College Solutions in Colorado Springs and author of "Never Pay Retail for College."

That said, there are some simple ways to plan your finances that should work to your advantage. You can balance any capital gains you report on your return with capital losses, avoid exercising stock options in the tax year that will be reflected on your FAFSA, and be strategic about taking distributions from 529 savings plans. Distributions from 529 plans that are owned by aunts, uncles or grandparents have to be reported as untaxed income, which can affect financial aid. Distributions from 529 plans owned by parents or students, on the other hand, won't count against you. Walker also recommends investing in "financial aid invisible assets," such as life insurance policies and annuities.

Heads up that you may need to fill out a second form as well as the FAFSA: the College Board's CSS/Financial Aid Profile. The CSS is a much more in-depth form required by about 300 colleges and scholarship programs to help these institutions determine which families should get their own nonfederal money. It's often due even earlier than the FAFSA, so be aware of each school's deadline.

The FAFSA doesn't require families to report the value of their home or retirement accounts; the Profile does. It gets at the value of a business and "splits out income, so you can see, for example, whether there is income or losses from a business," says Sara Beth Holman, director of financial aid at Lawrence University in Wisconsin. The CSS also takes into account factors like the cost of living in big cities vs. rural areas and allows for a larger proportion of income to be protected than the FAFSA does.

Nathan Fink
Belmont University

An elite private college might cost less than State U.

SOME PRIVATE INSTITUTIONS are struggling to compete for talented students – a trend that applicants can take advantage of, advises Jeff Thomas, CEO of Stratus Admissions Counseling. "Many private schools are offering more discounts in the form of scholarships," he says.

In fact, while public universities are struggling with tight budgets, tuition "discounting" by private colleges in the form of grants and scholarships reached an all-time high in the 2016-17 school year, according to a report from the National Association of College and University Business Officers. The average discount rate was 49 percent for full-time freshmen, up from 48 percent the previous year. For all undergraduates, the discount rate rose from 43 percent to 44.2 percent. Colleges and universities with the largest endowments were most likely to provide aid to financially strapped students.

Many schools are also going out of their way to address the growing student debt burden. Toward that end, a few schools have opted to become "no loan" universities, meaning their pockets are deep enough to meet your full need without any loans. Northwestern University joined the ranks of no-loan schools in 2016, announcing that it would be eliminating loans for incoming undergrads thanks to more than $147 million in gifts and endowment earnings. Other schools with no-loan or minimal-loan policies include the University of Chicago, Davidson College in North Carolina, Vanderbilt University in Tennessee, and all of the Ivy League schools.

But you need to do your homework. "While it's great that a select few colleges with resources are investing in their students, it's still important for students and parents to read the fine print and understand what 'no-loan' actually means," says Kevin Fudge, director of consumer advocacy and ombudsman at American Student Assistance, a nonprofit that educates students on the financial aspects of obtaining a college degree. "Sometimes 'no-loan' only ap-

One student's strategy: Become a franchisee

When students at Belmont University in Nashville attend the college's basketball games, they flock to a food cart called Maui Wowi Hawaiian Coffees & Smoothies, staffed by fellow student Nathan Fink. For Fink, the opportunity to dole out Kona coffee and black raspberry smoothies to thirsty classmates is more than a fun way to make some pocket change – it's helping him pay his way through college.

"There's the potential to make $1,000 in a weekend," Fink says of the food cart, which he was introduced to by his dad, who bought into the Maui Wowi franchise in 2013 and operates some carts near their home in Mayville, Wisconsin. "I was watching him do it, and I was helping out at events and making smoothies. I made use of that experience to get started on my own." Fink and his father tracked down a retired franchisee in Nashville who was no longer using the cart and worked out a deal to take it over. In addition to college events, Fink brings the cart to local high school softball and volleyball tournaments.

A sophomore majoring in economics and music business, Fink got a $7,000-per-year scholarship from his high school and $11,000 in aid from Belmont. So his take-home earnings from Maui Wowi are essential for helping cover $30,000 annually for tuition plus living expenses. He took out $5,500 in federal loans for freshman year – but that was so he could use some of his savings to invest in the franchise. Now that his Maui Wowi cart has taken off, he expects he won't need any more loans.

There are other advantages to operating a food cart, Fink adds. "Maui Wowi is great for college students, because pretty much all the work happens on the weekends," he says. "So I have all week available for school." –A.W.

plies to freshman year; there's no guarantee the student won't have to borrow later on down the road."

full need as determined by the FAFSA form. Others will not offer enough to cover all the costs that exceed the EFC, forcing the family to figure out how to manage even more than their expected contribution.

Your family "need" may not be what you think

COLLEGES DETERMINE HOW MUCH AID students need based on the gap between the cost of attending the school and the expected family contribution. Many families are shocked to realize that they're expected to contribute $15,000 or $20,000 a year, and that the amount is not part of their need. It's also quite possible that each school a student applies to will decide what to do about his or her need completely differently than the others do. Some schools will come up with a package that meets a family's

It's important to understand how packaging works

IT GOES WITHOUT SAYING that the more free money you can get in the form of grants and scholarships, the better. So you want to pay close attention to the components of your aid offers and not just focus on the bottom line. The typical package consists of scholarships from the school, if any, plus money from government sources such as the Pell Grant for low-income students, the Stafford loan

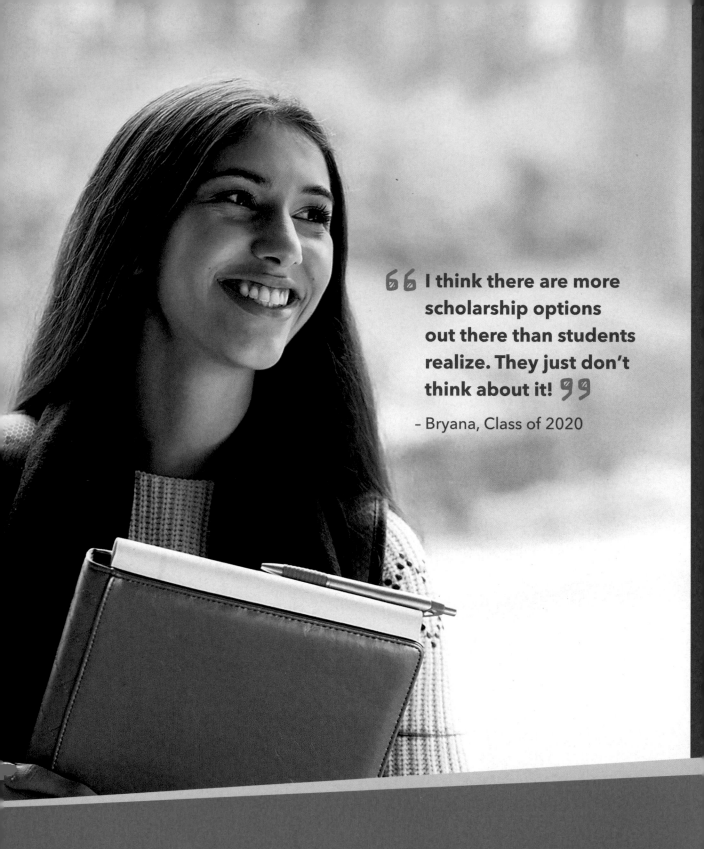

> **I think there are more scholarship options out there than students realize. They just don't think about it!**

– Bryana, Class of 2020

Access 5 million (yes, million) scholarships with Scholarship Search.

You read that right. With our Scholarship Search tool, you'll get access to more than 5 million college scholarships, worth up to $24 billion.

All scholarships are verified.

Each and every scholarship we add to Scholarship Search is vetted and approved, and we add new scholarships daily.

Get personalized results.

We'll match you with scholarships that fit your skills, activities and interests. It's all based on the profile you'll fill out when you register.

You could win $1,000 for college.

Everyone who registers for our college planning tools can enter to win the $1,000 Plan for College℠ Sweepstakes.* We draw one winner each month.

Register for Scholarship Search at SallieMae.com/Scholarship

* No purchase necessary. Void where prohibited. Odds of winning depend on the number of entries received. See official rules at SallieMae.com/SweepstakesRules.

and other loans that don't have to be repaid until after college, and the offer of a work-study job on campus. Parents might also be offered the opportunity to borrow up to the full cost of college via a PLUS loan.

But colleges can choose how they mix and match the funding sources for particular students. So if a college really wants that oboe-playing, straight-A student to fill an opening for an oboist in the school orchestra, her $20,000 package might include $3,000 in federal grants, $7,000 in scholarships, and $10,000 in loans while a kid who has the same GPA but plays volleyball instead is offered $2,000 in federal grants, $6,000 in scholarships, and $12,000 in loans.

Besides making the most of your talents as you search for scholarships, it's a good idea to apply to a handful of schools where your academic credentials will stand out. Those schools are good bets to make attractive aid offers.

Your external scholarships might count against you

REGARDLESS OF HOW RICH the aid package offered by your dream school is, experts advise supplementing your award by applying for scholarships from companies, churches and the many other groups that offer them – provided your target schools endorse that strategy. The online search tool Scholarships.com lists over 3.7 million scholarships and grants. Apply for these opportunities every year of college, counselors advise.

But you do need to ensure there won't be ramifications, says Kevin Ladd, Scholarships.com's chief operating officer. Federal law requires that universities lower aid packages when the sum from all sources is $300 or more above a family's calculated need. Be sure to ask about all outside scholarship policies. "Always make sure that the school you're going to isn't going to take whatever you win and use it to supplant the scholarships and grants they offer," Ladd says.

Pell Grants aren't affected, he notes, and many colleges will work with you to first apply the outside scholarship funding to any unmet need. Then they often use it to reduce your loan burden before lowering their initial offer.

You can look for ways to save on costs beyond tuition

ROOM, BOARD, BOOKS and incidental expenses make up a substantial portion of college costs. Room and board expenses for four-year public colleges during the 2016-17 school year rose 2.9 percent on average to $10,440,

according to the College Board. Those costs at private four-year colleges were up 3 percent to $11,890.

"You can often shave your bill by carefully considering the various options available at your chosen university," notes Rose Pasenelli, director of financial aid and scholarships at San Diego State University.

One example: You might forgo a meal plan that covers a fixed number of meals per week and opt for a flexible alternative such as a "declining balance" account. Such plans allow you to deposit money into an account that is tapped with a debit card at eateries around campus. "We've found that a lot of students want flexibility when it comes to their meals," said Pasenelli. "Why pay for meals they are not going to eat?"

Work-study can pay off in more ways than one

ABOUT 3,400 UNIVERSITIES receive federal funding to provide work-study jobs, which eligible students are offered as part of their aid package. And some schools provide "co-op" opportunities, cooperative education jobs at partnering companies that allow students to earn money, gain credits, and get experience in their field.

These programs provide not just a funding boost but also valuable real-world practice that can kick-start a career. Work-study jobs may be available on or off campus and are often related to your area of study. Students earn at least the federal minimum wage and possibly more if the job requires special skills. The amount you can earn is limited by your aid award, though: Financial aid officers will determine how many hours you can work each week based on how much work-study funding per semester you're allotted. President Donald Trump has proposed cutting federal funding for work-study from nearly $1 billion in 2017 to just $500 million in 2018, though it's unclear that he has enough support in Congress to get those cuts passed. You'll indicate so on your FAFSA if you're interested in the opportunity.

Students who attend a school with co-ops, which typically involve periods of work interspersed with periods of class time so that the lessons learned build on each other, needn't worry about it affecting their financial aid going forward. "Because you're on a prearranged agreement between a company and the school, the earnings you get paid can be excluded from your earnings on the FAFSA," says Linda Fontaine, assistant director of financial aid at Michigan Technological University.

Alex Ball, a Michigan Tech student who will graduate in 2018, opted for a full-year co-op in 2015 at a maker of auto supplies. It pushed his graduation back a year, but in addition to earning some credits and $60,000, "it gave me hands-on experience," says Ball, who is majoring in materials science and engineering and minoring

One student's strategy: Live at home and get a job

Shortly after Ivy Bryan started at the City University of New York in Brooklyn in 2016, she began looking for work to help cover her $3,000-per-semester tuition. She wanted to build on experience she'd gained in high school doing e-commerce marketing for a record company, but found that employers weren't taking her seriously on LinkedIn or any of the major job sites because of her age. Then she found WayUp, a company that matches college students and new grads with companies looking to hire young talent.

Bryan landed a spot right away working remotely for HoneyColony, a California-based online source of natural plant-based foods and supplements. She was promoted within six months from branding assistant responsible for maintaining the company's social media presence, among other duties, to inventory manager creating and managing purchase orders. Between working 20 hours a week and saving money by living at home in Brooklyn, Bryan predicts she will get through college without needing financial aid. "Transportation, any books that I need - the job basically covers most of that," says Bryan, who is majoring in film and women's studies.

Granted, the schedule isn't easy, she admits. She logs on to get her work done between classes and sometimes while commuting on the train. After she gets home, it's time for homework. "I get stressed sometimes, but I find a way to manage it all," Bryan says. The challenge "is about figuring out how to work independently and get things done as fast as possible by myself. That's important for building my management skills."

WayUp features millions of postings and counts more than 3.5 million young users, with over 300,000 employers whose openings appear on the site. About 1 in 3 applicants finds a job, according to the company. For Bryan, the flexibility of remote work has been a big boon. "If I need to work in the middle of the night," she says, "I can." –A.W.

---

in manufacturing. "In one class we learned about how inducing an electric current in a metal coil will create a magnetic field," he recalls. "When I got to this co-op, it showed me that what I was studying applied to the real world."

If you must borrow, it's best to choose federal loans first

IN GENERAL, FEDERAL LOANS offer the most attractive features. They don't have to be repaid until after graduation, they have fixed rates, and most are eligible for repayment plans that base monthly payments on income. And in some cases, the government will eventually forgive the loan, canceling the repayment requirement for people who have worked in public service careers for 10 years, for example. In recent years, private lenders have started to offer fixed-rate student loans and flexible repayment options, too, though the most favorable terms might require a parent to co-sign.

Students with demonstrated need can get subsidized federal Stafford loans, meaning the government pays the interest while you're in college. Students without demonstrated need can take out federal Stafford loans that aren't subsidized, meaning the interest will accumulate. The current cap for Stafford loans for freshmen who rely on their parents financially is $5,500, of which $3,500 can be subsidized. Freshmen who are not dependents can borrow up to $9,500. The caps increase in subsequent years.

Then there are Pell Grants, which may become even more desirable under President Trump. In May 2017, as part of his 2017 budget, he proposed year-round eligibility for Pell grants, making it possible for students to use them to take summer courses. Congress also bumped up the maximum grant amount from $5,815 to $5,920.

You can appeal your package (respectfully)

WHEN A FINANCIAL AID OFFER doesn't measure up to what other universities are dangling, you may well be able to successfully appeal for more money. Many colleges and universities are willing to compete for students they want and are open to hearing about a better offer from another institution. "A lot of schools routinely hold back 10 to 15 percent of their merit-based scholarship budget strictly for the sake of negotiating in April with the savvy families that come back and ask" for a better package, Walker says.

And if your circumstances have changed since you filled out the FAFSA, perhaps because of a job loss or onerous medical expense, financial aid officers certainly want to hear from you. Be specific about your reasons for wanting more. And it's best to be polite. You're unlikely to get happy cooperation from a demanding phone call.

"When you contact the financial aid office, it can be helpful to paint a picture of your financial reality. Explain just what your financial aid gap is, and help the office to understand exactly what this gap means for you and your family," advises Carolina Martín, executive director of Students Rising Above, a Bay Area nonprofit that supports low-income first-generation students in succeeding in college. "A well-written and timely letter, with a direct ask specifying what you need, can really act in your favor. Students need to show that they are truly enthusiastic about attending that school." ●

SAVING BY TAKING A TEST

IF YOU MISSED the boat to cut time and tuition by racking up Advanced Placement and International Baccalaureate credits, you may be able to accomplish similar savings with a College Board testing program known as CLEP, designed to let students earn credit for subjects they already know.

Maybe you're a history buff, or fluent in Spanish. Maybe you learned bookkeeping to help out an employer, or got a crash course in government when you worked on a political campaign. Depending on the policies of your college, you may be able to earn credit in any of those areas through the College-Level Examination Program, perhaps with minimal studying depending on the depth of your existing knowledge. Your cost: just $85 per test to save potentially thousands. As with other College Board tests, there are CLEP testing dates and locations throughout the year and around the country.

"Do it!" says Andrea Burton, testing officer at McNeese State University in Louisiana, which awarded 870 CLEP credit hours to 270 students enrolling this fall. McNeese allows students to amass up to 45 hours of CLEP credit toward an undergraduate degree, though Burton says most submit scores for only one test. Most popular at McNeese is English composition, followed by calculus and pre-algebra.

The College Board says 2,900 schools, including both community colleges and four-year colleges and universities, give credit for a passing score on at least some of the 33 CLEP exams. As with AP tests, a "passing" score can vary from school to school and from course to course, though 50, equivalent to a C, is typical. Most schools post CLEP guidelines on their websites – if they're not there, give the admissions office a call.

Fine print. Many selective schools may not give CLEP credit. But schools that do, at least to some degree, include the University of Massachusetts–Amherst, the University of Wisconsin, the University of Arizona and North Carolina State. If you transfer away from a school that has awarded you CLEP credits, make sure they will be accepted by the school you're transferring to. In short, read the fine print.

At Brandman University in California, 28 CLEP tests are considered the equivalent of specific courses, and students can use additional exams to get general education credit, says Sean Nemeth, associate vice chancellor of enrollment services. Brandman's 4,000 undergrads skew older than average and have more work experience. For the 2016-17 school year, 141 students received CLEP credit, and Nemeth says it's the eighth most common source of transfer credit overall.

Both Nemeth and Burton advise doing some preparation, taking advantage of review books, online review courses, and practice tests.

–Elizabeth Gardner

Textbooks 2.0

Digital texts may save you comparison shopping and money

by Courtney Rubin

AS A STUDENT at Indiana University, one thing Ellie Boyer learned was how to buy textbooks as cheaply as possible – and each year she got better at it. Freshman year book bill: about $1,000. Senior year: about $300.

"I had it down to a science," says Boyer, a 2017 graduate in marketing. She used a combination of book-deal sites, what she could read free from Google Books – and the university's increasingly popular eTexts initiative.

ETexts is one of several attempts by universities to shelve the traditional (and costly) textbook in favor of a fee, usually per course, for students to access readings digitally on any device with a browser. The model is variously called "all students acquire," "day one access" "digital direct access" and "inclusive access." Fees vary based on the type of course. But according to RedShelf, a firm that works with 550 colleges and universities, its average e-book recently was $60. Traditional textbooks often cost more than $200, according to a 2016 report from U.S. PIRG (Public Interest Research Groups.)

Used books can be still cheaper. Boyer has snagged a $200 book for $12 and an $80 one for $6, whereas the cheapest e-textbooks are still about $20. But there are advantages to the digital version that go beyond price.

For one thing, digital books aren't a problem to hunt down; IU participants get all required materials automatically. There's no worry about what might have changed between, say, the edition the professor is using and the one you bought used, and the books are full-text searchable and printable until you graduate.

For-profit universities have been using this model for years, bundling the cost of course materials into tuition. What paved the way at traditional universities was a Department of Education decision in 2015 to amend the rules about what schools can include in their tuition-and-fee structure so that course materials can be in that structure if available at a discount and if students can opt out. According to RedShelf, just five of its university customers included the cost in tuition in 2015-16; in 2016-17, the number hit 100. Other customers let faculty decide which courses will have a digital material option.

The company has experienced 300 to 400 percent growth every year since its inception, says Tim Haitaian, chief financial officer and a co-founder. And college bookstores are quite literally buying in: the National Association of College Stores is one of the company's investors. "The bookstore sees this as a method of keeping themselves relevant," Haitaian says.

RedShelf earns a percentage on the delivery of materials, but Indiana University makes nothing from the service, according to the school's vice president for information technology, Brad Wheeler, who is also a professor in the business school. This past academic year, 53,000 students from the eight IU campuses had at least one of these texts, which the university estimates helped them save at least $3.5 million. The initiative will soon spread to fellow members of the Unizin Consortium, a collaboration of large research universities intent on improving the education environment with digital technology.

For the record, all of the materials can be printed – something student groups Wheeler consulted insisted on. The idea made book publishers nervous, but they assented.

"Seven years in, and students don't print," Wheeler laughs. "We have the analytics. Nobody prints." ●

Finding THE MONEY

Great Schools, Great Prices

Which colleges and universities offer students the best value? The calculation used here takes into account a school's academic quality based on its U.S. News Best Colleges ranking and the 2016-17 net cost of attendance for a student who received the average level of need-based financial aid. The higher the quality of the program and the lower the cost, the better the deal. Only schools in the top half of their U.S. News ranking categories are included because U.S. News considers the most significant values to be among colleges that perform well academically.

National Universities ▶

Rank	School (State) (*Public)	% receiving grants based on need ('16)	Average cost after receiving grants based on need ('16)	Average discount from total cost ('16)
1.	Princeton University (NJ)	60%	$16,793	74%
2.	Harvard University (MA)	55%	$16,338	76%
3.	Yale University (CT)	50%	$18,385	73%
4.	Stanford University (CA)	47%	$19,296	71%
5.	Massachusetts Inst. of Technology	58%	$20,331	69%
6.	Columbia University (NY)	48%	$21,041	71%
7.	Dartmouth College (NH)	50%	$23,312	67%
8.	California Institute of Technology	51%	$23,973	64%
9.	U. of North Carolina–Chapel Hill*	41%	$17,815	64%
10.	Duke University (NC)	41%	$23,374	67%
11.	Brigham Young Univ.–Provo (UT)	38%	$13,186	27%
12.	Vanderbilt University (TN)	46%	$23,323	64%
13.	University of Pennsylvania	47%	$25,441	63%
14.	Brown University (RI)	41%	$24,482	64%
15.	University of Chicago	42%	$27,767	61%
16.	Rice University (TX)	37%	$23,996	61%
17.	Emory University (GA)	42%	$24,264	63%
18.	Cornell University (NY)	44%	$28,068	59%
19.	Johns Hopkins University (MD)	45%	$30,067	56%
20.	University of Notre Dame (IN)	47%	$29,653	56%
21.	Northwestern University (IL)	43%	$31,087	56%
22.	Washington University in St. Louis	41%	$29,245	58%
23.	Wake Forest University (NC)	30%	$24,241	64%
24.	University of Rochester (NY)	51%	$28,476	58%
25.	Tufts University (MA)	34%	$27,034	60%
26.	Georgetown University (DC)	34%	$29,667	58%
27.	Brandeis University (MA)	47%	$29,288	57%
28.	Lehigh University (PA)	38%	$25,376	60%
29.	Clark University (MA)	62%	$27,702	48%
30.	University of Virginia*	28%	$28,079	53%
31.	Rensselaer Polytechnic Inst. (NY)	61%	$35,125	49%
32.	New Jersey Inst. of Technology*	35%	$18,674	63%
33.	Carnegie Mellon University (PA)	40%	$33,550	51%
34.	Boston College	35%	$30,170	56%
35.	Pepperdine University (CA)	51%	$32,416	53%
36.	Clarkson University (NY)	79%	$33,669	48%
37.	St. John Fisher College (NY)	81%	$28,750	38%
38.	Illinois Institute of Technology	62%	$29,116	53%
39.	Mercer University (GA)	67%	$26,615	48%
40.	Univ. of Southern California	33%	$33,112	52%
41.	Rochester Inst. of Technology (NY)	70%	$31,793	40%
42.	Duquesne University (PA)	65%	$29,185	42%
43.	Texas A&M Univ.–College Station*	41%	$26,376	42%
44.	Saint Louis University	51%	$28,328	49%
45.	Case Western Reserve Univ. (OH)	48%	$35,248	44%
46.	North Carolina State U.–Raleigh*	41%	$25,623	37%
47.	Syracuse University (NY)	48%	$33,912	46%
48.	Villanova University (PA)	44%	$35,459	46%
49.	Worcester Polytechnic Inst. (MA)	62%	$39,995	36%
50.	University of Michigan–Ann Arbor*	25%	$32,856	46%

National Liberal Arts Colleges ▶

Rank	School (State) (*Public)	% receiving grants based on need ('16)	Average cost after receiving grants based on need ('16)	Average discount from total cost ('16)
1.	Williams College (MA)	50%	$19,545	71%
2.	Amherst College (MA)	55%	$19,256	72%
3.	Pomona College (CA)	56%	$19,040	72%
4.	Wellesley College (MA)	62%	$21,788	67%
5.	Swarthmore College (PA)	54%	$21,024	68%
6.	Vassar College (NY)	64%	$21,104	69%
7.	Soka University of America (CA)	87%	$20,944	56%
8.	Middlebury College (VT)	43%	$21,497	68%
9.	Principia College (IL)	70%	$14,563	65%
10.	Washington and Lee University (VA)	42%	$21,208	67%
11.	Grinnell College (IA)	68%	$24,394	62%
12.	Davidson College (NC)	48%	$22,700	65%
13.	Bowdoin College (ME)	45%	$23,384	64%
14.	Colgate University (NY)	37%	$21,566	68%
15.	Colby College (ME)	42%	$22,371	66%
16.	Haverford College (PA)	50%	$23,365	66%
17.	College of the Atlantic (ME)	83%	$19,780	64%
18.	Smith College (MA)	58%	$24,861	63%
19.	Hamilton College (NY)	48%	$24,425	63%
20.	University of Richmond (VA)	41%	$23,106	63%
21.	Macalester College (MN)	68%	$27,115	58%
22.	Agnes Scott College (GA)	74%	$23,316	55%
23.	Carleton College (MN)	56%	$28,108	58%
24.	Wesleyan University (CT)	41%	$25,220	63%
25.	Knox College (IL)	77%	$23,959	56%
26.	Bates College (ME)	43%	$25,072	62%
27.	Bryn Mawr College (PA)	53%	$26,295	61%
28.	Franklin and Marshall College (PA)	53%	$25,261	63%
29.	Claremont McKenna College (CA)	39%	$26,940	61%
30.	Thomas Aquinas College (CA)	64%	$21,441	40%
31.	Centre College (KY)	55%	$23,580	55%
32.	Colorado College	31%	$23,949	64%
33.	Trinity College (CT)	46%	$24,128	65%
34.	St. John's College (MD)	74%	$27,573	57%
35.	Barnard College (NY)	39%	$25,329	63%
36.	Gustavus Adolphus College (MN)	68%	$22,979	58%
37.	Hollins University (VA)	82%	$23,434	55%
38.	DePauw University (IN)	60%	$26,049	57%
39.	Bard College (NY)	67%	$28,808	58%
40.	St. Olaf College (MN)	64%	$26,147	54%

Methodology: The rankings were based on the following three variables: **1.** Ratio of quality to price: a school's overall score in the latest Best Colleges rankings divided by the net cost to a student receiving the average need-based scholarship or grant. The higher the ratio of rank to the discounted cost (tuition, fees, room and board, and other expenses less average need-based scholarship or grant), the better the value. **2.** Percentage of all undergrads receiving need-based scholarships or grants during the 2016-17 school year. **3.** Average discount: percentage of a school's total costs for 2016-17 school year covered by the average need-based scholarship or grant to undergrads. For public institutions, 2016-17 out-of-state tuition and percentage of out-of-state students receiving need-based scholarships or grants were used. Only those schools ranked in the top half of their U.S. News ranking categories were considered. Ranks are determined by standardizing scores achieved by every school in each of the three variables and weighting those scores. Ratio of quality to price accounted for 60 percent of the overall score; percentage of undergrads receiving need-based grants, for 25 percent; and average discount, for 15 percent. The school with the most total weighted points became No. 1 in its category.

Regional Universities ▶

Rank School (State) (*Public)	% receiving grants based on need ('16)	Average cost after receiving grants based on need ('16)	Average discount from total cost ('16)
NORTH			
1. Gallaudet University (DC)	80%	$15,660	57%
2. CUNY–Brooklyn College*	71%	$12,328	29%
3. Geneva College (PA)	81%	$20,608	45%
4. Bentley University (MA)	43%	$32,116	49%
5. St. Bonaventure University (NY)	73%	$25,401	45%
6. Le Moyne College (NY)	82%	$27,334	44%
7. Mercyhurst University (PA)	70%	$23,096	53%
8. St. Joseph's College New York	65%	$20,012	34%
9. Canisius College (NY)	76%	$27,067	47%
10. Gannon University (PA)	76%	$24,684	46%
11. Hood College (MD)	80%	$27,649	48%
12. Providence College (RI)	47%	$36,430	42%
13. Ithaca College (NY)	66%	$34,131	43%
14. Lebanon Valley College (PA)	84%	$29,125	47%
15. Niagara University (NY)	71%	$25,180	45%
SOUTH			
1. Xavier University of Louisiana	63%	$13,203	63%
2. Coastal Carolina University (SC)*	20%	$13,218	66%
3. William Carey University (MS)	96%	$15,645	38%
4. Harding University (AR)	58%	$18,988	34%
5. Berry College (GA)	70%	$25,899	47%
6. Milligan College (TN)	82%	$22,375	47%
7. Bob Jones University (SC)	70%	$16,377	37%
8. West Virginia Wesleyan College	79%	$19,510	56%
9. Loyola University New Orleans	71%	$28,136	50%
10. Converse College (SC)	79%	$22,041	34%
11. Appalachian State University (NC)*	22%	$22,904	32%
12. Mississippi College	48%	$19,482	37%
13. University of Montevallo (AL)*	47%	$19,691	45%
14. Christian Brothers University (TN)	67%	$21,934	47%
15. Stetson University (FL)	69%	$31,603	47%
MIDWEST			
1. Valparaiso University (IN)	74%	$24,890	51%
2. Truman State University (MO)*	37%	$20,193	26%
3. University of Evansville (IN)	61%	$22,362	54%
4. Grand Valley State University (MI)*	3%	$16,583	39%
5. Dominican University (IL)	88%	$24,156	45%
6. Creighton University (NE)	52%	$31,138	40%
7. John Carroll University (OH)	70%	$29,238	46%
8. Drury University (MO)	63%	$22,185	41%
9. Drake University (IA)	58%	$30,877	38%
10. Concordia University (NE)	75%	$21,234	47%
11. Milwaukee School of Engineering	75%	$26,349	47%
12. Rockhurst University (MO)	70%	$26,006	48%
13. Elmhurst College (IL)	77%	$26,476	45%
14. Baldwin Wallace University (OH)	73%	$25,341	43%
15. Bradley University (IL)	63%	$28,451	37%
WEST			
1. Trinity University (TX)	45%	$25,888	53%
2. Mills College (CA)	78%	$27,218	57%
3. St. Mary's Univ. of San Antonio	70%	$21,711	48%
4. University of Dallas	61%	$27,354	49%
5. Whitworth University (WA)	68%	$29,882	46%
6. Pacific Lutheran University (WA)	74%	$28,529	46%
7. Gonzaga University (WA)	53%	$33,362	40%
8. Westminster College (UT)	59%	$24,943	45%
9. Abilene Christian University (TX)	67%	$26,624	43%
10. University of St. Thomas (TX)	63%	$23,989	47%
11. LeTourneau University (TX)	70%	$25,143	41%
12. Northwest Nazarene University (ID)	37%	$17,040	56%
13. California Lutheran University	69%	$31,689	45%
14. Santa Clara University (CA)	32%	$38,755	41%
15. Seattle University	50%	$34,814	40%

Regional Colleges ▶

Rank School (State) (*Public)	% receiving grants based on need ('16)	Average cost after receiving grants based on need ('16)	Average discount from total cost ('16)
NORTH			
1. Cazenovia College (NY)	90%	$19,167	60%
2. Cedar Crest College (PA)	91%	$24,633	50%
3. Messiah College (PA)	72%	$28,991	38%
4. Colby-Sawyer College (NH)	74%	$26,769	52%
5. Wilson College (PA)	87%	$25,947	32%
6. University of Maine–Farmington*	16%	$21,492	30%
7. Paul Smith's College (NY)	88%	$21,967	44%
8. Unity College (ME)	83%	$25,273	35%
9. Maine Maritime Academy*	11%	$33,729	16%
10. Concordia College (NY)	70%	$25,221	45%
SOUTH			
1. Blue Mountain College (MS)	79%	$11,275	45%
2. Alice Lloyd College (KY)	91%	$14,501	41%
3. Kentucky Wesleyan College	96%	$20,615	43%
4. Alderson Broaddus University (WV)	83%	$16,876	55%
5. Tennessee Wesleyan University	79%	$18,714	46%
6. Flagler College (FL)	59%	$23,698	26%
7. Newberry College (SC)	87%	$20,260	48%
8. Huntingdon College (AL)	76%	$22,114	41%
9. Averett University (VA)	86%	$22,795	49%
10. Barton College (NC)	87%	$26,169	41%
MIDWEST			
1. College of the Ozarks (MO)	92%	$13,934	53%
2. Cottey College (MO)	69%	$13,456	55%
3. Augustana University (SD)	58%	$19,234	53%
4. Ohio Northern University	79%	$22,708	49%
5. Blackburn College (IL)	91%	$15,512	49%
6. Eureka College (IL)	71%	$15,494	52%
7. Goshen College (IN)	73%	$23,516	48%
8. Clarke University (IA)	87%	$23,543	47%
9. Loras College (IA)	73%	$22,299	47%
10. Manchester University (IN)	85%	$20,382	53%
WEST			
1. Texas Lutheran University	78%	$20,928	49%
2. Carroll College (MT)	65%	$27,008	43%
3. Rocky Mountain College (MT)	73%	$21,083	46%
4. William Jessup University (CA)	82%	$26,336	41%
5. University of Montana–Western*	74%	$21,829	22%
6. Howard Payne University (TX)	84%	$22,149	42%
7. McMurry University (TX)	83%	$23,484	41%
8. Oklahoma Baptist University	55%	$31,146	18%
9. Montana Tech of the Univ. of Mont.*	24%	$29,050	16%
10. Warner Pacific College (OR)	59%	$28,231	19%

The Payback Picture

With tuition rising and financial aid budgets shrinking, many undergrads have to borrow their way to a degree. U.S. News has compiled a list of the schools whose class of 2016 graduated with the heaviest and lightest debt loads. The data include loans taken out by students from their colleges, from private financial institutions, and from federal, state and local governments. Loans directly to parents are not included. The first data column indicates what percentage of the class graduated owing money and, by extrapolation, what percentage graduated debt-free. "Average amount of debt" refers to the cumulative amount borrowed by students who incurred debt; it's not an average for all students.

MOST DEBT

National Universities ▶

School (State) (*Public)	% of grads with debt	Average amount of debt
Catholic University of America (DC)	70%	$46,779
Baylor University (TX)	53%	$44,540
Duquesne University (PA)	59%	$41,272
Boston University	51%	$41,098
New Jersey Inst. of Technology*	64%	$40,967
Clark Atlanta University	91%	$40,393
University of St. Thomas (MN)	64%	$40,307
Robert Morris University (PA)	82%	$39,431
Barry University (FL)	72%	$39,255
Wichita State University (KS)*	61%	$39,122
Indiana Univ. of Pennsylvania*	83%	$38,956
University of New Hampshire*	79%	$38,799
University of Pittsburgh*	65%	$38,612
Rochester Inst. of Technology (NY)	76%	$38,198
Syracuse University (NY)	63%	$37,753

National Liberal Arts Colleges ▶

School (State) (*Public)	% of grads with debt	Average amount of debt
St. John's University (MN)	66%	$40,272
Pacific Union College (CA)	80%	$40,263
Wartburg College (IA)	75%	$39,794
College of St. Benedict (MN)	71%	$39,536
Roanoke College (VA)	77%	$39,175
Johnson C. Smith University (NC)	79%	$38,732
Hartwick College (NY)	79%	$38,662
Ursinus College (PA)	74%	$38,537
Saint Vincent College (PA)	76%	$38,493
Spelman College (GA)	77%	$38,361
Albion College (MI)	68%	$38,356
St. Michael's College (VT)	72%	$38,226
Albright College (PA)	89%	$38,196
Grove City College (PA)	54%	$37,655
Wabash College (IN)	89%	$37,495

Regional Universities ▶

School (State) (*Public)	% of grads with debt	Average amount of debt
NORTH		
Fairleigh Dickinson Univ. (NJ)	76%	$53,702
Metropolitan College of New York	95%	$49,357
Alvernia University (PA)	87%	$49,277
Delaware Valley University (PA)	84%	$47,640
Quinnipiac University (CT)	71%	$47,217
SOUTH		
Northwestern State U. of La.*	64%	$41,500
Coastal Carolina University (SC)*	79%	$37,982
Wheeling Jesuit University (WV)	71%	$37,762
Amridge University (AL)	100%	$36,284
Queens University of Charlotte (NC)	76%	$36,059
MIDWEST		
University of Findlay (OH)	79%	$45,400
Alverno College (WI)	88%	$41,044
Otterbein University (OH)	77%	$40,937
College of St. Scholastica (MN)	77%	$40,774
Rockford University (IL)	84%	$40,313
WEST		
Woodbury University (CA)	83%	$41,211
St. Mary's Univ. of San Antonio	77%	$39,883
Hardin-Simmons University (TX)	66%	$39,597
LeTourneau University (TX)	69%	$38,988
Trinity University (TX)	45%	$38,605

Regional Colleges ▶

School (State) (*Public)	% of grads with debt	Average amount of debt
NORTH		
Maine Maritime Academy*	87%	$52,434
Dean College (MA)	83%	$48,728
Mount Ida College (MA)	80%	$44,097
Messiah College (PA)	70%	$39,617
Paul Smith's College (NY)	83%	$39,553
SOUTH		
Kentucky State University*	87%	$36,323
High Point University (NC)	58%	$35,897
Averett University (VA)	81%	$35,659
Bluefield College (VA)	78%	$34,510
Huntingdon College (AL)	81%	$33,503
MIDWEST		
Mayville State University (ND)*	100%	$48,128
Eureka College (IL)	88%	$42,248
Ohio Northern University	78%	$42,212
Iowa Wesleyan University	72%	$41,503
Adrian College (MI)	85%	$38,842
WEST		
McMurry University (TX)	82%	$38,844
Texas Lutheran University	73%	$37,337
Howard Payne University (TX)	75%	$37,164
Warner Pacific College (OR)	80%	$36,916
East Texas Baptist University	82%	$34,048

Note: Student debt data are as of August 25, 2017.

LEAST DEBT

National Universities ▷

School (State) (*Public)	% of grads with debt	Average amount of debt
Princeton University (NJ)	18%	$8,908
Yale University (CT)	14%	$13,625
Brigham Young Univ.–Provo (UT)	26%	$15,158
University of Texas–Arlington*	83%	$15,559
Harvard University (MA)	23%	$16,702
Dartmouth College (NH)	48%	$17,849
California Institute of Technology	33%	$18,219
California State Univ.–Fresno*	51%	$18,221
University of California–Berkeley*	37%	$18,789
Maryville Univ. of St. Louis	84%	$19,266
University of California–Davis*	53%	$19,276
University of Colorado–Denver*	54%	$19,378
Florida International University*	50%	$19,915
San Diego State University*	49%	$19,969
Tennessee Technological Univ.*	53%	$20,134
Northwestern University (IL)	42%	$20,308
University of Texas–Dallas*	35%	$20,432
University of California–Irvine*	58%	$20,466
Boston College	50%	$20,481
San Francisco State University*	50%	$20,716
U. of North Carolina–Chapel Hill*	42%	$20,852
Univ. of Maryland–Eastern Shore*	57%	$21,000
Univ. of California–Santa Barbara*	53%	$21,001
University of California–Merced*	73%	$21,009
University of Texas–El Paso*	58%	$21,021

National Liberal Arts Colleges ▷

School (State) (*Public)	% of grads with debt	Average amount of debt
Berea College (KY)	65%	$7,062
Wellesley College (MA)	48%	$13,415
Williams College (MA)	43%	$15,496
New College of Florida*	35%	$16,577
Thomas Aquinas College (CA)	85%	$16,986
Whitman College (WA)	38%	$18,089
Vassar College (NY)	44%	$18,462
Amherst College (MA)	22%	$18,662
Middlebury College (VT)	45%	$18,736
Pomona College (CA)	36%	$18,738
Grinnell College (IA)	50%	$18,780
Haverford College (PA)	29%	$18,932
Sarah Lawrence College (NY)	35%	$19,772
Scripps College (CA)	39%	$20,205
Davidson College (NC)	26%	$20,431
University of Virginia–Wise*	55%	$20,576
Colorado College	41%	$20,742
Louisiana State University–Alexandria*	58%	$20,817
Principia College (IL)	63%	$21,260
Colgate University (NY)	34%	$21,427
Hamilton College (NY)	45%	$21,491
Pitzer College (CA)	38%	$21,569
Barnard College (NY)	42%	$22,015
U. of North Carolina–Asheville*	53%	$22,026
Tougaloo College (MS)	74%	$22,160

Regional Universities ▷

School (State) (*Public)	% of grads with debt	Average amount of debt
NORTH		
CUNY–Lehman College*	30%	$9,227
CUNY–Brooklyn College*	17%	$10,743
Gallaudet University (DC)	61%	$15,767
East Stroudsburg Univ. of Pa.*	72%	$20,531
Univ. of the District of Columbia*	67%	$22,964
SOUTH		
University of North Georgia*	46%	$10,062
University of North Florida*	50%	$18,685
Belhaven University (MS)	76%	$18,889
Hampton University (VA)	73%	$19,093
Elizabeth City State Univ. (NC)*	86%	$19,631
MIDWEST		
Northeastern Illinois University*	55%	$16,247
Emporia State University (KS)*	62%	$20,433
Mount Vernon Nazarene U. (OH)	82%	$21,564
Indiana University Southeast*	71%	$22,612
Southern Illinois U.–Edwardsville*	62%	$23,168
WEST		
California State Univ.–Bakersfield*	91%	$11,437
Texas A&M University–Texarkana*	66%	$13,274
California State U.–Long Beach*	44%	$15,917
Southwestern Oklahoma State U.*	46%	$16,268
California State U.–Los Angeles*	50%	$16,362

Regional Colleges ▷

School (State) (*Public)	% of grads with debt	Average amount of debt
NORTH		
U.S. Merchant Marine Acad. (NY)*	24%	$3,880
Farmingdale State College–SUNY*	45%	$20,786
Univ. of Maine–Presque Isle*	73%	$22,934
St. Francis College (NY)	59%	$22,977
SUNY College of Technology–Delhi*	98%	$23,637
SOUTH		
Alice Lloyd College (KY)	68%	$10,714
Truett McConnell University (GA)	67%	$15,542
Newberry College (SC)	76%	$18,566
Blue Mountain College (MS)	65%	$19,695
Williams Baptist College (AR)	70%	$19,904
MIDWEST		
Tabor College (KS)	65%	$13,597
Cottey College (MO)	64%	$20,287
Maranatha Baptist University (WI)	69%	$21,521
Valley City State University (ND)*	86%	$24,281
Sterling College (KS)	91%	$24,347
WEST		
Oklahoma Baptist University	58%	$24,451
William Jessup University (CA)	73%	$24,656
Colorado Mesa University*	65%	$25,575
Oregon Inst. of Technology*	71%	$26,716
Montana Tech of the Univ. of Mont.*	56%	$27,193

Show up ready on test day.

Official SAT® Practice from the College Board and Khan Academy®—it's free, personalized, and online. Students who spent 6–8 hours on Official SAT Practice improved their scores by an average of 90 points from the PSAT/NMSQT® to the SAT. Get started today!

satpractice.org

WHY I PICKED...

...Hamilton College

Clinton, New York

STATUE OF ALEXANDER HAMILTON, FOR WHOM THE COLLEGE WAS NAMED

➤ **I WAS THE FIRST** in my family to attend college and had no idea what I wanted to major in. Hamilton, a small, 205-year-old liberal arts school, appealed to me as it really pushes students to broaden themselves. It starts with the school's open curriculum, which doesn't require students to meet course requirements until they declare a major. I tested my interests in classes like biology, government and philosophy until settling on sociology with minors in economics and Spanish.

Kureem Nugent, '18

> **Hamilton also offers grants so students can pursue research.**

Hamilton also offers grants so students, regardless of major, can pursue research on their own or with professors. These projects have ranged from studying geological outcroppings in the remote Western Desert of Egypt to examining the experience of Utica, New York's, refugee community with ESL education.

Hamilton emphasizes a "Know Thyself" philosophy that encourages students to further explore their interests and talents through extracurricular opportunities. This past summer, for example, I led a six-day wilderness adventure trip in the Adirondack Mountains for 10 freshmen as part of their orientation. Seeing the value of Hamilton's approach to learning has led me to want to pursue my own career in higher education. ●

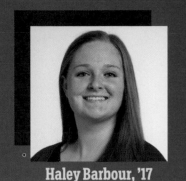

'Drake helped me get short internships with Yahoo, CNN and Fusion.

Haley Barbour, '17

...Drake University

Des Moines, Iowa

➤ **I CHOSE DRAKE** because of the flexibility it offers students to shape their academic programs to fit their goals and to take advantage of valuable experiences outside of class. Knowing that I wanted to study political science/ international relations, I felt from my research that Drake was the best place for me. Located in Des Moines, the school has front-row seats for the "first-in-the-nation" Iowa presidential caucuses. Everyone, regardless of major, tends to get involved during caucus season. In my case, Drake helped me get short internships with Yahoo, CNN and Fusion to see how they covered the caucuses. I also helped organize conferences, town halls and a presidential debate. Drake even let me take a semester off to work full time for Hillary Clinton in 2016.

DRAKE UNIVERSITY

Drake offers students many other immersive experiences. For instance, the school's study abroad program covers some 70 countries, and I was able to spend a semester in Amman, Jordan, studying Arabic and Middle Eastern politics. Every step of the way I found that my faculty adviser and the administration were eager to help me find ways to get experiences that overlapped with my coursework, which has opened so many doors for me. ●

...Valparaiso University

Valparaiso, Indiana

➤ **WHEN SEARCHING FOR** a school with an undergraduate meteorology program, I was drawn to Valparaiso's emphasis on experiential learning. Who wouldn't want to do things like launch a weather balloon at 3 a.m. in a blizzard to more precisely predict snowfall, or use the school's own radar to provide daily weather forecasts? I joined a school-sponsored storm-chasing team and one summer got within two miles of a tornado in Lamar, Colorado. Senior year, I was able to conduct undergraduate research based on historic storms of the Great Lakes region and to present my findings at a student forum.

Valpo excels at offering professional development opportunities. For example, I was able to intern with respected television meteorologists in Birmingham and Chicago. Students can also find many ways to serve and build leadership skills through Valpo's 250 clubs. I've done choreography for a dance showcase, acted in an improv troupe, and served as president of a meteorology club. Best of all, students here help each other. We have a great peer tutoring program, and it helped me get through the heavy math and physics for my major, keeping me on my path to become a meteorologist. ●

Elyse Smith, '17

' I joined a school-sponsored storm-chasing team.

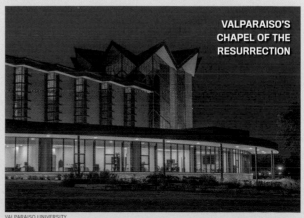

VALPARAISO'S CHAPEL OF THE RESURRECTION

VALPARAISO UNIVERSITY

HEADSHOTS FROM LEFT: NANCY L. FORD; DRAKE UNIVERSITY; BRENDAN JOHNSON

Parenting From Afar

A Guide for Mom and Dad to Surviving Freshman Year

by Stacey Colino

THE PROSPECT OF A CHILD heading off to college often fills parents with hope, excitement – and more than a few twinges of fear, given headlines about such scary realities as extreme drinking and sexual assault and normal insecurities about watching a child leave the nest. You won't be able to step in and head off trouble (and you may not even know it if trouble happens). But you can take steps to help your young adult assess risks and navigate sticky situations. "Your role is changing – you're not in charge anymore. You're stepping into the role of coach," says Karen Levin Coburn, senior consultant in residence at Washington University in St. Louis and author of "Letting Go: A Parents' Guide to Understanding the College Years." "There are safety nets to deal with all of these things, but your child has to be willing to use the resources that are available."

It's smart to have an open conversation well before drop-off day about your concerns, expectations and lines of communication. Parents are often shocked to discover that, even when they're paying the bills, federal privacy laws limit their access to information about their college kids' grades, physical and mental health and other aspects of their lives. When her daughter went to a large university on the West Coast, Jill Perel, a Florida therapist, was horrified that the young woman was hospitalized with the flu in 2010 without anybody from campus alerting her parents. "The RA took her to the ER, but the school left it to my child to let me know how sick she was," Perel recalls. "She was hospitalized for several days and not in a position to fend for herself." But most colleges have procedures students can follow to allow parents access to key information.

Rest assured: Assuming you manage this transition wisely, you'll still be able

> "A lot of students experience homesickness or separation anxiety."

to guide from afar. "College students are trying to distance themselves from their parents," says Jonathan Sauls, dean of students at the University of North Carolina–Chapel Hill. "But parents will continue to be the greatest influence on their kids for the next four years." What follows is a look at the realities behind parents' fears, with tips on how to help kids handle them.

Your kid is apt to get **homesick** and possibly **depressed.**

"A lot of students experience homesickness or separation anxiety, especially in the first six to eight weeks," Sauls notes. In fact, it's such a rite of passage that you shouldn't be surprised if your child calls in misery, wanting to come home. The best thing you can do is to listen and be supportive without opening an escape hatch. Run-of-the-mill homesickness usually lifts once freshmen become engaged in their classes and activities. It's a good idea to suggest joining a club or other group that will provide a social network, and participating

Perhaps the course load is too heavy, or a tutor or study group is called for.

in any programs the residence hall and student life team offer to help new students bond quickly with each other and with faculty. Counseling centers often create support groups to help students deal with homesickness.

Constantly talking and texting with your child in an effort to do the problem-solving may only make matters worse. "Part of being a college student is becoming more independent and autonomous," says Rachel Annunziato, an associate professor of psychology at Fordham University. It's in a homesick student's best interests "to learn to secure resources and build connections."

On the other hand, depression and anxiety may well require action. "It's hard to know how much to intervene," says one Maryland mother who wanted to give her daughter "as much space as possible" but realized she had to step in when the young woman, who was being treated for depression, began missing classes and staying in her room. Her parents asked for her permission to speak with her mental health team, and were advised to come to campus to discuss the wisdom of a break from college. After a year off to regain her footing, the student returned to campus, graduated, and has since pursued graduate study.

This young woman has plenty of company. According to the 2016 American College Health Association National College Health Assessment, which surveyed 33,512 students at 51 colleges and universities, 38 percent of students admitted they had felt so depressed that it was difficult for them to function at some time in the previous 12 months, and 61 percent felt overwhelming anxiety.

If anxiety or depression is already an issue, parents should help set up a plan to continue care and make sure needed support will be in place, Coburn advises. If you don't hear from your child for an unusually long time or become aware he or she is avoiding class, contact the dean of students. Colleges can do a wellness check to gauge how your child is doing and whether a referral to a psychologist or psychiatrist seems wise. You might also suggest your child and a roommate or friend exchange home phone numbers so each can alert the other's family of an illness or an accident.

Your kid may **struggle academically.**

Many freshmen, accustomed to getting very high grades in high school, experience an abrupt awakening as

they're challenged at a whole new level. For one thing, they "often don't realize how much self-directed study is involved," Sauls says. The 2016 health assessment survey found that 48 percent of responding students found academics to be traumatic or very difficult to handle. As a parent, your best bet is to acknowledge the struggle and encourage turning to advisers, professors or the tutoring center for guidance. Perhaps the course load is too heavy, or a tutor or study group is called for.

Parents often find the academic transition difficult because their access to information about their student's performance is limited by law, explains Chelsea Petree, director of Parent and Family Programs at the Rochester Institute of Technology. The Family Educational Rights and Privacy Act gives students control of their educational records, including grades and financial information. So it's conceivable you wouldn't know that anything is wrong until there's a change in status, such as a suspension or academic probation, notes Avis Hinkson, dean of Barnard College.

If your child is open with you about the struggle, steel yourself to avoid micromanaging, experts advise. And "don't panic if your student is panicking," Petree says. Parents typically get an SOS when kids "are the most raw and emotional," and generally students can work out their issues once they calm down, she says. Coburn agrees:

"Be open to the idea that your child is likely to go through a period of being stressed. Sometimes they need to vent, and parents need to be able to tolerate that. Listen and be supportive."

There may be
roommate problems.

These days, incoming college students often bond with their roommates online before the school year starts. But "the way students present themselves online is often very different from the way they are to live with," Coburn says. It helps if parents temper expectations by noting that a roommate does not have to become a best friend; the goal is to live together in a respectful way.

When tensions arise, good communication and negotiation skills will be key to a happy resolution. Parents can offer coaching but shouldn't intervene, Sauls says. Encourage your son or daughter to speak directly to the roommate about what's not working, using "I" statements that avoid accusations. For example, your child could say, "I'd rather you not use my stuff without asking." Caution against being passive-aggressive, Sauls advises. "Don't send an email when you're sitting across the room from each other, and don't let issues fester."

If your child's efforts to improve a situation don't help, you might suggest turning to a resi-

"Don't send an email when you're sitting across the room from each other, and don't let issues fester."

dent adviser for advice or mediation. Switching roommates may be an option if all else fails. But your child will undoubtedly be expected to exhaust other possible remedies first – a good mindset to develop.

Count on it: There will be lots of **excessive drinking.**

According to the health assessment survey, 64 percent of college students admitted to consuming alcohol within the previous 30 days, and 18 percent reported having seven or more drinks the last time they "partied." Researchers at the University of Michigan reported earlier this year that 10 percent of 19- and 20-year-olds surveyed had had 10 or more drinks on one occasion.

"It's so much more intense than when par-

You might ask: What will you do if you've reached the point where you've had enough?

ents were in college," says J. Davidson Porter, vice president of student affairs at Tulane University. "Assume this is going to happen. Quashing a sense of invincibility in an 18-to-20-year-old is pretty difficult."

Rather than crossing your fingers and simply hoping for the best, it's wise to start a candid conversation – not a lecture – about the alcohol and drug use your child is likely to encounter and be clear about how your child might best behave in such situations and handle safety issues and transportation. You might, for example, caution against consuming punch or a proffered drink that could have been doctored. You might ask: What do you plan to do if you're at a party and realize your friends are drinking too much, or you've reached the point where you've had enough? (Good answers: Leave the party, preferably with a friend, and switch to water.) Signal that the door is open, Coburn says. "Let them know they can always call you."

Sexual assault
is a risk to both sexes.

Reported statistics vary. But nearly 25 percent of women in the U.S. said they'd been sexually assaulted during college in a 2015 survey involving 92,306 undergraduates at 27 institutions for the Association of American Universities. The 2016 health assessment survey revealed that 11 percent of female students and 4 percent of males experienced sexual touching without their consent during the previous year. The vast majority of assaults occur between two people who know each other, and many involve alcohol or drugs, campus authorities say.

The good news is that the risk has become a frequent topic of discussion on campuses in the years since the Department of Education during the Obama administration began holding schools to account for the way they handle reports of assault and investigations. Whatever may happen to those rules in the future, many colleges and universities have stepped up their prevention efforts – teaching bystander intervention skills, for example, so people who witness problematic encounters learn how to step in to avert harm in a direct but nonconfrontational way. Women and men can watch out for each other at parties and have a plan for extricating themselves from problematic situations. Students also should not be shy about tapping the school's security force and taking precautions like not walking home alone at night.

But fending off obvious predators is not the only concern. It's also vital to make sure students understand what it means to have a healthy relationship and the concept of consent. In more day-to-day interactions, judgments about assaults having occurred increasingly hinge on whether there was explicit consent. "It must be active; it cannot be assumed," says Dwayne Todd, vice president for student engagement and success and dean of students at Ohio Wesleyan University. You might ask your child: How can you make sure you have consent? Or that you give it? Not only should both parties make sure they have explicit permission, but ideally, before any encounter, they should wait till they are sober, thereby lowering the risk of any misunderstanding. ●

2018 EDITION

DIRECTORY OF COLLEGES AND UNIVERSITIES

INSIDE

The latest facts and figures on over
1,600 American colleges and universities,
including schools' U.S. News rankings

New data on tuition, admissions, the
makeup of the undergraduate student body,
popular majors and financial aid

Statistical profiles of freshman classes, including
entrance exam scores and high school class standing

Using the Directory

How to interpret the statistics in the following entries on more than 1,600 American colleges and universities – and how to get the most out of them

The snapshots of colleges and universities presented here, alphabetized by state, contain a wealth of helpful information on everything from the most popular majors offered to the stats on the freshman class that arrived in the fall of 2016. The statistics were collected in the spring and summer of 2017 and are as of Aug. 21, 2017; they are explained in detail below. A school whose name has been footnoted did not return the U.S. News statistical questionnaire, so limited data appear. If a college did not reply to a particular question, you'll see N/A, for "not available." By tapping our online directory at usnews.com/collegesearch, you can experiment with a customized search of our database that allows you to pick schools based on major, location and other criteria. To find a school of interest in the rankings tables, consult the index at the back of the book.

EXAMPLE

Fairfield University

Fairfield CT
1— (203) 254-4100
2— **U.S. News ranking:** Reg. U. (N), No. 3
3— **Website:** www.fairfield.edu
4— **Admissions email:** admis@fairfield.edu
5— **Private;** founded 1942
Affiliation: Roman Catholic
6— **Freshman admissions:** more selective; 2016-2017: 11,055 applied, 6,795 accepted. Neither SAT nor ACT required. SAT 25/75 percentile: 1110-1270. High school rank: 35% in top tenth, 67% in top quarter, 93% in top half
7— **Early decision deadline:** 11/15, notification date: 12/15
Early action deadline: 11/1, notification date: 12/20
8— **Application deadline (fall):** 1/15
9— **Undergraduate student body:** 3,803 full time, 229 part time; 39% male, 61% female; 0% American Indian, 2% Asian, 2% black, 8% Hispanic, 1% multiracial, 0% Pacific Islander, 77% white, 3% international; 29% from in state; 72% live on campus; N/A of students in fraternities, N/A in sororities
10— **Most popular majors:** 38% Business, Management, Marketing, and Related Support Services, 11% Health Professions and Related Programs, 10% Communication, Journalism, and Related Programs, 9% Social Sciences, 8% Psychology
11— **Expenses:** 2017-2018: $47,165; room/board: $14,280
12— **Financial aid:** (203) 254-4000; 46% of undergrads determined to have financial need; average aid package $33,012

1. TELEPHONE NUMBER
This number reaches the admissions office.

2. U.S. NEWS RANKING
The abbreviation indicates which category of institution the school falls into: National Universities (Nat. U.), National Liberal Arts Colleges (Nat. Lib. Arts), Regional Universities (Reg. U.), or Regional Colleges (Reg. Coll.). The regional universities and regional colleges are further divided by region: North (N), South (S), Midwest (MidW), and West (W). "Business" refers to business specialty schools, and "Engineering" refers to engineering specialty schools. "Arts" refers to schools devoted to the fine and performing arts.

Next, you'll find the school's 2018 rank within its category. Schools falling in the top three-fourths of their categories are ranked numerically. Those ranked in the bottom 25 percent of their respective category are listed alphabetically. But remember: You cannot compare school ranks in different categories; U.S. News ranks schools only against their peers. Specialty schools that focus on business, engineering and the arts aren't ranked and are listed as unranked. Also unranked are schools with fewer than 200 students, a high percentage of older or part-time students, that don't use SAT or ACT test scores for admission decisions or that have received a very small number of peer assessment votes in a survey conducted in spring 2017.

3. WEBSITE
Visit the school's website to research programs, take a virtual tour, or submit an application.

You can also find a link to each site at usnews.com.

4. ADMISSIONS EMAIL
You can use this email address to request information or to submit an application.

5. TYPE/AFFILIATION
Is the school public, private or for-profit? Affiliated with a religious denomination?

6. FRESHMAN ADMISSIONS
How competitive is the admissions process at this institution? Schools are designated "most selective," "more selective," "selective," "less selective" or "least selective." The more selective a school, the harder it will probably be to get in. All of the admissions statistics reported are for the class that entered in the fall of 2016. The 25/75 percentiles for the SAT Math and Critical Reading or ACT Composite show the range in which half the students scored: 25 percent of students scored at or below the lower end, and 75 percent scored at or below the upper end. If a school reported the averages and not the 25/75 percentiles, the average score is listed. The test score that is published represents the test that the greatest percentage of entering students took. The SAT scores used in the rankings and published in this book are for the test taken prior to March 2016.

7. EARLY DECISION/ EARLY ACTION DEADLINES
Applicants who plan to take the early decision route to fall 2018 enrollment will have to meet the deadline listed for the school. If the school offers an early action option, the applica-

tion deadline and notification date are also shown.

8. APPLICATION DEADLINE
The date shown is the regular admission deadline for the academic year starting in the fall of 2018. "Rolling" means the school makes admissions decisions as applications come in until the class is filled.

9. UNDERGRADUATE STUDENT BODY
This section gives the breakdown of full-time vs. part-time students, male and female enrollment, ethnic makeup of the student body, in-state and out-of-state students, percentage living on campus, and percentage in fraternities and sororities. Figures are for 2016-2017.

10. MOST POPULAR MAJORS
The five most popular majors appear, along with the percentage majoring in each among 2016 graduates with a bachelor's degree.

11. EXPENSES
The first figure represents tuition (including required fees); next is total room and board. Figures are for the 2017-2018 academic year; if data are not available, we use figures for the 2016-2017 academic year. For public schools, we list both in-state and out-of-state tuition.

12. FINANCIAL AID
The percentage of undergrads determined to have financial need and the amount of the average package (grants, loans and jobs) in 2016-2017. We also provide the phone number of the financial aid office.

ALABAMA

Alabama Agricultural and Mechanical University

Normal AL
(256) 372-5245
U.S. News ranking: Reg. U. (S), second tier
Website: www.aamu.edu
Admissions email: admissions@aamu.edu
Public; founded 1875
Affiliation: Other
Freshman admissions: less selective; 2016-2017: 7,558 applied, 6,652 accepted. Either SAT or ACT required. ACT 25/75 percentile: 16-19. High school rank: N/A
Early decision deadline: N/A, notification date: N/A
Early action deadline: N/A, notification date: N/A
Application deadline (fall): 7/15
Undergraduate student body: 4,436 full time, 415 part time; 43% male, 57% female; 0% American Indian, 0% Asian, 91% black, 1% Hispanic, 4% multiracial, 0% Pacific Islander, 3% white, 1% international
Most popular majors: Information not available
Expenses: 2016-2017: $9,366 in state, $17,496 out of state; room/board: $8,830
Financial aid: (256) 372-5400

Alabama State University

Montgomery AL
(334) 229-4291
U.S. News ranking: Reg. U. (S), second tier
Website: www.alasu.edu
Admissions email: admissions@alasu.edu
Public; founded 1887
Freshman admissions: less selective; 2016-2017: 9,053 applied, 4,155 accepted. Either SAT or ACT required. ACT 25/75 percentile: 15-19. High school rank: 9% in top tenth, 9% in top quarter, 41% in top half
Early decision deadline: N/A, notification date: N/A
Early action deadline: N/A, notification date: N/A
Application deadline (fall): 7/30
Undergraduate student body: 4,368 full time, 359 part time; 38% male, 62% female; 0% American Indian, 0% Asian, 93% black, 1% Hispanic, 1% multiracial, 0% Pacific Islander, 1% white, 2% international; 66% from in state; 44% live on campus; 5% of students in fraternities, 7% in sororities
Most popular majors: 14% Criminal Justice/Safety Studies, 12% Rehabilitation and Therapeutic Professions, Other, 10% Speech Communication and Rhetoric, 7% Biology/Biological Sciences, General, 6% Social Work
Expenses: 2017-2018: $9,220 in state, $16,156 out of state; room/board: $5,422
Financial aid: (334) 229-4712; 87% of undergrads determined to have financial need; average aid package $19,409

Amridge University

Montgomery AL
(888) 790-8080
U.S. News ranking: Reg. U. (S), No. 106
Website: www.amridgeuniversity.edu
Admissions email: admissions@amridgeuniversity.edu
Private; founded 1967
Freshman admissions: less selective; 2016-2017: N/A applied, N/A accepted. Either SAT or ACT required. SAT 25/75 percentile: N/A. High school rank: N/A
Early decision deadline: N/A, notification date: N/A
Early action deadline: N/A, notification date: N/A
Application deadline (fall): rolling
Undergraduate student body: 135 full time, 159 part time; 39% male, 61% female; 0% American Indian, 0% Asian, 24% black, 1% Hispanic, 0% multiracial, 0% Pacific Islander, 16% white, 0% international
Most popular majors: 44% Bible/Biblical Studies, 27% Business/Corporate Communications, 12% Business Administration and Management, General, 10% Human Development and Family Studies, General, 5% Criminal Justice/Law Enforcement Administration
Expenses: 2017-2018: $12,630; room/board: N/A
Financial aid: (334) 387-7523; 98% of undergrads determined to have financial need; average aid package $9,097

Athens State University

Athens AL
(256) 233-8217
U.S. News ranking: Reg. Coll. (S), unranked
Website: www.athens.edu/
Public; founded 1822
Freshman admissions: least selective; 2016-2017: N/A applied, N/A accepted. Neither SAT nor ACT required. SAT 25/75 percentile: N/A. High school rank: N/A
Early decision deadline: N/A, notification date: N/A
Early action deadline: N/A, notification date: N/A
Application deadline (fall): N/A
Undergraduate student body: 1,212 full time, 1,813 part time; 34% male, 66% female; 1% American Indian, 1% Asian, 13% black, 2% Hispanic, 2% multiracial, 0% Pacific Islander, 78% white, 0% international
Most popular majors: 17% Business Administration and Management, General, 13% Accounting, 13% Elementary Education and Teaching, 5% Computer and Information Sciences, General, 5% Liberal Arts and Sciences/Liberal Studies
Expenses: 2016-2017: $6,480 in state, $12,210 out of state; room/board: $0
Financial aid: (256) 233-8161; 75% of undergrads determined to have financial need; average aid package $9,669

Auburn University

Auburn AL
(334) 844-6425
U.S. News ranking: Nat. U., No. 103
Website: www.auburn.edu
Admissions email: admissions@auburn.edu
Public; founded 1856
Freshman admissions: more selective; 2016-2017: 18,256 applied, 14,704 accepted. Either SAT or ACT required. ACT 25/75 percentile: 24-30. High school rank: 30% in top tenth, 62% in top quarter, 90% in top half
Early decision deadline: N/A, notification date: N/A
Early action deadline: 2/1, notification date: 10/15
Application deadline (fall): 6/1
Undergraduate student body: 20,396 full time, 2,262 part time; 51% male, 49% female; 1% American Indian, 3% Asian, 7% black, 3% Hispanic, 1% multiracial, 0% Pacific Islander, 83% white, 2% international; 66% from in state; 20% live on campus; 28% of students in fraternities, 43% in sororities
Most popular majors: 21% Business, Management, Marketing, and Related Support Services, 19% Engineering, 9% Education, 7% Biological and Biomedical Sciences, 7% Health Professions and Related Programs
Expenses: 2017-2018: $10,968 in state, $29,640 out of state; room/board: $13,332
Financial aid: (334) 844-4634; 36% of undergrads determined to have financial need; average aid package $10,851

Auburn University–Montgomery

Montgomery AL
(334) 244-3611
U.S. News ranking: Reg. U. (S), No. 95
Website: www.aum.edu
Admissions email: vsamuel@aum.edu
Public; founded 1967
Freshman admissions: selective; 2016-2017: 2,905 applied, 2,225 accepted. Either SAT or ACT required. ACT 25/75 percentile: 19-24. High school rank: 16% in top tenth, 44% in top quarter, 80% in top half
Early decision deadline: N/A, notification date: N/A
Early action deadline: N/A, notification date: N/A
Application deadline (fall): 8/15
Undergraduate student body: 3,095 full time, 1,178 part time; 36% male, 64% female; 1% American Indian, 2% Asian, 36% black, 1% Hispanic, 3% multiracial, 0% Pacific Islander, 51% white, 4% international; 94% from in state; 23% live on campus; 2% of students in fraternities, N/A in sororities
Most popular majors: 26% Health Professions and Related Programs, 20% Business, Management, Marketing, and Related Support Services, 7% Psychology, 5% Biological and Biomedical Sciences, 4% Education
Expenses: 2017-2018: $9,910 in state, $21,310 out of state; room/board: $5,780

Birmingham-Southern College

Birmingham AL
(205) 226-4696
U.S. News ranking: Nat. Lib. Arts, No. 123
Website: www.bsc.edu
Admissions email: admission@bsc.edu
Private; founded 1856
Affiliation: United Methodist
Freshman admissions: more selective; 2016-2017: 3,722 applied, 1,801 accepted. Neither SAT nor ACT required. ACT 25/75 percentile: 23-29. High school rank: 30% in top tenth, 58% in top quarter, 86% in top half
Early decision deadline: N/A, notification date: N/A
Early action deadline: 11/15, notification date: 12/15
Application deadline (fall): 5/1
Undergraduate student body: 1,284 full time, 10 part time; 49% male, 51% female; 1% American Indian, 5% Asian, 12% black, 2% Hispanic, 1% multiracial, 0% Pacific Islander, 79% white, 0% international; 56% from in state; 61% live on campus; 37% of students in fraternities, 55% in sororities
Most popular majors: 22% Business Administration and Management, General, 14% Biology/Biological Sciences, General, 7% Psychology, General, 6% Mathematics, General, 5% History, General
Expenses: 2017-2018: $35,792; room/board: $12,050
Financial aid: (205) 226-4688; 56% of undergrads determined to have financial need; average aid package $32,233

Concordia College[1]

Selma AL
(334) 874-5700
U.S. News ranking: Reg. Coll. (S), unranked
Website: www.ccal.edu/
Admissions email: admission@ccal.edu
Private; founded 1922
Application deadline (fall): N/A
Undergraduate student body: N/A full time, N/A part time
Expenses: 2016-2017: $10,320; room/board: $5,700
Financial aid: (334) 874-5700

Faulkner University

Montgomery AL
(334) 386-7200
U.S. News ranking: Reg. U. (S), No. 106
Website: www.faulkner.edu
Admissions email: admissions@faulkner.edu
Private; founded 1942
Affiliation: Churches of Christ
Freshman admissions: selective; 2016-2017: 2,446 applied, 1,110 accepted. Either SAT or ACT required. ACT 25/75 percentile: 18-23. High school rank: 12% in top tenth, 60% in top quarter, 84% in top half

Financial aid: (334) 244-3571; 67% of undergrads determined to have financial need; average aid package $7,189

Birmingham-Southern College

(see entry above)

Early decision deadline: N/A, notification date: N/A
Early action deadline: N/A, notification date: N/A
Application deadline (fall): 8/1
Undergraduate student body: 1,779 full time, 804 part time; 40% male, 60% female; 0% American Indian, 0% Asian, 50% black, 2% Hispanic, 2% multiracial, 0% Pacific Islander, 41% white, 2% international; 98% from in state; 28% live on campus; 13% of students in fraternities, 9% in sororities
Most popular majors: 39% Business Administration and Management, General, 16% Criminal Justice/Safety Studies, 16% Human Resources Management/Personnel Administration, General, 8% Business/Commerce, General, 4% Sport and Fitness Administration/Management
Expenses: 2017-2018: $20,970; room/board: $7,400
Financial aid: (334) 386-7195; 69% of undergrads determined to have financial need; average aid package $6,325

Huntingdon College

Montgomery AL
(334) 833-4497
U.S. News ranking: Reg. Coll. (S), No. 13
Website: www.huntingdon.edu
Admissions email: admiss@huntingdon.edu
Private; founded 1854
Freshman admissions: selective; 2016-2017: 1,716 applied, 974 accepted. Either SAT or ACT required. ACT 25/75 percentile: 19-24. High school rank: 8% in top tenth, 29% in top quarter, 63% in top half
Early decision deadline: N/A, notification date: N/A
Early action deadline: N/A, notification date: N/A
Application deadline (fall): rolling
Undergraduate student body: 881 full time, 267 part time; 51% male, 49% female; 1% American Indian, 0% Asian, 21% black, 4% Hispanic, 4% multiracial, 0% Pacific Islander, 64% white, 0% international; 81% from in state; 62% live on campus; 18% of students in fraternities, 46% in sororities
Most popular majors: 43% Business, Management, Marketing, and Related Support Services, 12% Parks, Recreation, Leisure, and Fitness Studies, 9% Biological and Biomedical Sciences, 6% Education, 5% Psychology
Expenses: 2017-2018: $26,400; room/board: $9,500
Financial aid: (334) 833-4428; 76% of undergrads determined to have financial need; average aid package $18,551

Jacksonville State University

Jacksonville AL
(256) 782-5268
U.S. News ranking: Reg. U. (S), No. 89
Website: www.jsu.edu
Admissions email: info@jsu.edu
Public; founded 1883

Freshman admissions: selective; 2016-2017: 4,979 applied, 2,643 accepted. Either SAT or ACT required. ACT 25/75 percentile: 20-26. High school rank: 17% in top tenth, 41% in top quarter, 73% in top half
Early decision deadline: N/A, notification date: N/A
Early action deadline: N/A, notification date: N/A
Application deadline (fall): rolling
Undergraduate student body: 5,480 full time, 2,081 part time; 43% male, 57% female; 1% American Indian, 1% Asian, 19% black, 1% Hispanic, 0% multiracial, 0% Pacific Islander, 72% white, 3% international; 83% from in state; 26% live on campus; 12% of students in fraternities, 17% in sororities
Most popular majors: 22% Registered Nursing/Registered Nurse, 8% Elementary Education and Teaching, 6% Business Administration and Management, General, 6% Criminal Justice/Safety Studies, 5% Liberal Arts and Sciences/Liberal Studies
Expenses: 2017-2018: $9,525 in state, $18,525 out of state; room/board: $7,128
Financial aid: (256) 782-5006; 87% of undergrads determined to have financial need; average aid package $9,592

Judson College[1]
Marion AL
(800) 447-9472
U.S. News ranking: Nat. Lib. Arts, second tier
Website: www.judson.edu/
Admissions email: admissions@judson.edu
Private
Application deadline (fall): N/A
Undergraduate student body: N/A full time, N/A part time
Expenses: 2016-2017: $17,376; room/board: $9,978
Financial aid: N/A

Miles College[1]
Birmingham AL
U.S. News ranking: Reg. Coll. (S), unranked
Website: www.miles.edu
Admissions email: admissions@mail.miles.edu
Private
Application deadline (fall): N/A
Undergraduate student body: N/A full time, N/A part time
Expenses: 2016-2017: $11,604; room/board: $7,042
Financial aid: N/A

Oakwood University[1]
Huntsville AL
(256) 726-7356
U.S. News ranking: Reg. Coll. (S), No. 28
Website: www.oakwood.edu
Admissions email: admissions@oakwood.edu
Private; founded 1896
Application deadline (fall): N/A
Undergraduate student body: N/A full time, N/A part time
Expenses: 2016-2017: $16,750; room/board: $9,700
Financial aid: N/A

Samford University
Birmingham AL
(800) 888-7218
U.S. News ranking: Reg. U. (S), No. 3
Website: www.samford.edu
Admissions email: admission@samford.edu
Private; founded 1841
Affiliation: Baptist
Freshman admissions: more selective; 2016-2017: 3,446 applied, 3,149 accepted. Either SAT or ACT required. ACT 25/75 percentile: 23-29. High school rank: 31% in top tenth, 57% in top quarter, 84% in top half
Early decision deadline: N/A, notification date: N/A
Early action deadline: N/A, notification date: N/A
Application deadline (fall): N/A
Undergraduate student body: 3,207 full time, 134 part time; 35% male, 65% female; 0% American Indian, 1% Asian, 7% black, 4% Hispanic, 2% multiracial, 0% Pacific Islander, 83% white, 2% international; 33% from in state; 70% live on campus; 36% of students in fraternities, 57% in sororities
Most popular majors: 28% Health Professions and Related Programs, 18% Business, Management, Marketing, and Related Support Services, 7% Communication, Journalism, and Related Programs, 6% Visual and Performing Arts, 5% Parks, Recreation, Leisure, and Fitness Studies
Expenses: 2017-2018: $30,490; room/board: $10,280
Financial aid: (205) 726-2905; 40% of undergrads determined to have financial need; average aid package $19,644

Spring Hill College
Mobile AL
(251) 380-3030
U.S. News ranking: Nat. Lib. Arts, second tier
Website: www.shc.edu
Admissions email: admit@shc.edu
Private; founded 1830
Freshman admissions: more selective; 2016-2017: 8,534 applied, 3,715 accepted. Either SAT or ACT required. ACT 25/75 percentile: 22-27. High school rank: 27% in top tenth, 60% in top quarter, 90% in top half
Early decision deadline: N/A, notification date: N/A
Early action deadline: N/A, notification date: N/A
Application deadline (fall): 7/15
Undergraduate student body: 1,382 full time, 14 part time; 37% male, 63% female; 1% American Indian, 1% Asian, 15% black, 3% Hispanic, 5% multiracial, 0% Pacific Islander, 69% white, 3% international; 39% from in state; 75% live on campus; 34% of students in fraternities, 38% in sororities
Most popular majors: 23% Business, Management, Marketing, and Related Support Services, 12% Psychology, 11% Biological and Biomedical Sciences, 11% Communication, Journalism, and Related Programs, 8% Social Sciences

Expenses: 2017-2018: $37,584; room/board: $13,070
Financial aid: (800) 548-7886; 70% of undergrads determined to have financial need; average aid package $32,092

Stillman College[1]
Tuscaloosa AL
(205) 366-8837
U.S. News ranking: Nat. Lib. Arts, second tier
Website: www.stillman.edu
Admissions email: admissions@stillman.edu
Private; founded 1876
Application deadline (fall): rolling
Undergraduate student body: N/A full time, N/A part time
Expenses: 2016-2017: $10,418; room/board: $7,394
Financial aid: (205) 366-8817

Talladega College[1]
Talladega AL
U.S. News ranking: Reg. Coll. (S), unranked
Website: www.talladega.edu
Admissions email: admissions@talladega.edu
Private
Application deadline (fall): N/A
Undergraduate student body: N/A full time, N/A part time
Expenses: 2016-2017: $12,340; room/board: $6,504
Financial aid: N/A

Troy University
Troy AL
(334) 670-3179
U.S. News ranking: Reg. U. (S), No. 89
Website: www.troy.edu/
Admissions email: admit@troy.edu
Public; founded 1887
Freshman admissions: selective; 2016-2017: 6,101 applied, 5,545 accepted. Either SAT or ACT required. ACT 25/75 percentile: 19-26. High school rank: N/A
Early decision deadline: N/A, notification date: N/A
Early action deadline: N/A, notification date: N/A
Application deadline (fall): rolling
Undergraduate student body: 9,040 full time, 5,203 part time; 40% male, 60% female; 1% American Indian, 3% Asian, 30% black, 3% Hispanic, 3% multiracial, 0% Pacific Islander, 51% white, 5% international; 67% from in state; 32% live on campus; 13% of students in fraternities, 15% in sororities
Most popular majors: 30% Business, Management, Marketing, and Related Support Services, 14% Psychology, 12% Homeland Security, Law Enforcement, Firefighting and Related Protective Services, 7% Education, 5% Public Administration and Social Service Professions
Expenses: 2017-2018: $12,155 in state, $22,267 out of state; room/board: N/A
Financial aid: (334) 670-3182; 68% of undergrads determined to have financial need; average aid package $4,394

Tuskegee University[1]
Tuskegee AL
(334) 727-8500
U.S. News ranking: Reg. U. (S), No. 27
Website: www.tuskegee.edu
Admissions email: admiweb@tusk.edu
Private; founded 1881
Application deadline (fall): rolling
Undergraduate student body: N/A full time, N/A part time
Expenses: 2017-2018: $22,235; room/board: $9,650
Financial aid: (334) 727-8088; 78% of undergrads determined to have financial need; average aid package $19,550

University of Alabama
Tuscaloosa AL
(205) 348-5666
U.S. News ranking: Nat. U., No. 110
Website: www.ua.edu
Admissions email: admissions@ua.edu
Public; founded 1831
Freshman admissions: more selective; 2016-2017: 38,237 applied, 20,107 accepted. Either SAT or ACT required. ACT 25/75 percentile: 23-31. High school rank: 37% in top tenth, 58% in top quarter, 82% in top half
Early decision deadline: N/A, notification date: N/A
Early action deadline: N/A, notification date: N/A
Application deadline (fall): rolling
Undergraduate student body: 29,220 full time, 3,343 part time; 44% male, 56% female; 0% American Indian, 1% Asian, 10% black, 4% Hispanic, 3% multiracial, 0% Pacific Islander, 78% white, 2% international; 43% from in state; 26% live on campus; 27% of students in fraternities, 42% in sororities
Most popular majors: 30% Business, Management, Marketing, and Related Support Services, 10% Communication, Journalism, and Related Programs, 10% Engineering, 9% Health Professions and Related Programs, 7% Education
Expenses: 2017-2018: $10,780 in state, $28,100 out of state; room/board: $9,974
Financial aid: (205) 348-6756; 42% of undergrads determined to have financial need; average aid package $16,204

University of Alabama–Birmingham
Birmingham AL
(205) 934-8221
U.S. News ranking: Nat. U., No. 159
Website: www.uab.edu
Admissions email: chooseuab@uab.edu
Public; founded 1969
Freshman admissions: more selective; 2016-2017: 5,838 applied, 5,212 accepted. Either SAT or ACT required. ACT 25/75 percentile: 21-28. High school rank: 28% in top tenth, 55% in top quarter, 83% in top half
Early decision deadline: N/A, notification date: N/A

Early action deadline: N/A, notification date: N/A
Application deadline (fall): rolling
Undergraduate student body: 8,971 full time, 3,398 part time; 41% male, 59% female; 0% American Indian, 6% Asian, 26% black, 3% Hispanic, 4% multiracial, 0% Pacific Islander, 58% white, 2% international; 89% from in state; 22% live on campus; 8% of students in fraternities, 10% in sororities
Most popular majors: 24% Health Professions and Related Programs, 21% Business, Management, Marketing, and Related Support Services, 9% Education, 8% Psychology, 7% Biological and Biomedical Sciences
Expenses: 2017-2018: $10,410 in state, $23,790 out of state; room/board: $11,682
Financial aid: (205) 934-8223; 61% of undergrads determined to have financial need; average aid package $10,971

University of Alabama–Huntsville
Huntsville AL
(256) 824-6070
U.S. News ranking: Nat. U., No. 216
Website: www.uah.edu
Admissions email: uahadmissions@uah.edu
Public; founded 1950
Freshman admissions: more selective; 2016-2017: 4,545 applied, 3,467 accepted. Either SAT or ACT required. ACT 25/75 percentile: 25-31. High school rank: 29% in top tenth, 56% in top quarter, 85% in top half
Early decision deadline: N/A, notification date: N/A
Early action deadline: N/A, notification date: N/A
Application deadline (fall): 8/17
Undergraduate student body: 5,257 full time, 1,250 part time; 58% male, 42% female; 1% American Indian, 4% Asian, 11% black, 4% Hispanic, 2% multiracial, 0% Pacific Islander, 72% white, 3% international; 84% from in state; 25% live on campus; 7% of students in fraternities, 8% in sororities
Most popular majors: 26% Engineering, 23% Business, Management, Marketing, and Related Support Services, 19% Health Professions and Related Programs, 6% Biological and Biomedical Sciences, 5% Computer and Information Sciences and Support Services
Expenses: 2017-2018: $10,280 in state, $21,480 out of state; room/board: $9,748
Financial aid: (256) 824-6650; 51% of undergrads determined to have financial need; average aid package $10,713

University of Mobile
Mobile AL
(251) 442-2222
U.S. News ranking: Reg. Coll. (S), No. 5
Website: www.umobile.edu
Admissions email: umenrollment@umobile.edu
Private; founded 1961
Affiliation: Baptist

Freshman admissions: selective; 2016-2017: 935 applied, 579 accepted. Either SAT or ACT required. ACT 25/75 percentile: 19-25. High school rank: 23% in top tenth, 53% in top quarter, 80% in top half
Early decision deadline: N/A, notification date: N/A
Early action deadline: N/A, notification date: N/A
Application deadline (fall): rolling
Undergraduate student body: 1,241 full time, 135 part time; 37% male, 63% female; 1% American Indian, 1% Asian, 19% black, 3% Hispanic, 3% multiracial, 0% Pacific Islander, 53% white, 4% international; 82% from in state; 50% live on campus; N/A of students in fraternities, N/A in sororities
Most popular majors: 21% Business, Management, Marketing, and Related Support Services, 15% Health Professions and Related Programs, 9% Multi/Interdisciplinary Studies, 6% Education, 5% Visual and Performing Arts
Expenses: 2017-2018: $22,006; room/board: $9,600
Financial aid: (251) 442-2239; 84% of undergrads determined to have financial need; average aid package $17,739

University of Montevallo
Montevallo AL
(205) 665-6030
U.S. News ranking: Reg. U. (S), No. 38
Website: www.montevallo.edu
Admissions email: admissions@montevallo.edu
Public; founded 1896
Freshman admissions: selective; 2016-2017: 2,334 applied, 1,527 accepted. Either SAT or ACT required. ACT 25/75 percentile: 20-26. High school rank: N/A
Early decision deadline: N/A, notification date: N/A
Early action deadline: N/A, notification date: N/A
Application deadline (fall): 8/15
Undergraduate student body: 2,178 full time, 231 part time; 32% male, 68% female; 0% American Indian, 1% Asian, 15% black, 4% Hispanic, 3% multiracial, 0% Pacific Islander, 71% white, 1% international; 91% from in state; 48% live on campus; 16% of students in fraternities, 18% in sororities
Most popular majors: Information not available
Expenses: 2017-2018: $12,400 in state, $25,030 out of state; room/board: $7,612
Financial aid: (205) 665-6050; 66% of undergrads determined to have financial need; average aid package $11,100

University of North Alabama
Florence AL
(256) 765-4608
U.S. News ranking: Reg. U. (S), No. 85
Website: www.una.edu
Admissions email: admissions@una.edu

Public; founded 1830
Freshman admissions: selective; 2016-2017: 4,761 applied, 2,457 accepted. Either SAT or ACT required. ACT 25/75 percentile: 19-25. High school rank: N/A
Early decision deadline: N/A, notification date: N/A
Early action deadline: N/A, notification date: N/A
Application deadline (fall): rolling
Undergraduate student body: 5,163 full time, 1,150 part time; 41% male, 59% female; 1% American Indian, 1% Asian, 14% black, 3% Hispanic, 3% multiracial, 0% Pacific Islander, 72% white, 3% international; 82% from in state; 25% live on campus; 9% of students in fraternities, 15% in sororities
Most popular majors: 20% Business, Management, Marketing, and Related Support Services, 16% Health Professions and Related Programs, 11% Education, 6% Parks, Recreation, Leisure, and Fitness Studies, 6% Social Sciences
Expenses: 2016-2017: $10,872 in state, $18,792 out of state; room/board: $3,642
Financial aid: (256) 765-4279; 52% of undergrads determined to have financial need; average aid package $7,972

University of South Alabama
Mobile AL
(251) 460-6141
U.S. News ranking: Nat. U., second tier
Website: www.southalabama.edu
Admissions email: recruitment@southalabama.edu
Public; founded 1963
Freshman admissions: selective; 2016-2017: 6,401 applied, 5,097 accepted. Neither SAT nor ACT required. ACT 25/75 percentile: 20-26. High school rank: N/A
Early decision deadline: N/A, notification date: N/A
Early action deadline: N/A, notification date: N/A
Application deadline (fall): 7/15
Undergraduate student body: 9,604 full time, 2,157 part time; 46% male, 54% female; 1% American Indian, 3% Asian, 22% black, 3% Hispanic, 3% multiracial, 0% Pacific Islander, 57% white, 9% international; 82% from in state; 27% live on campus; N/A of students in fraternities, N/A in sororities
Most popular majors: 17% Registered Nursing/Registered Nurse, 5% Health/Medical Preparatory Programs, Other, 5% Multi/Interdisciplinary Studies, 5% Physical Education Teaching and Coaching, 4% Speech Communication and Rhetoric
Expenses: 2017-2018: $10,005 in state, $19,586 out of state; room/board: $8,460
Financial aid: (800) 305-6828; 62% of undergrads determined to have financial need; average aid package $9,708

University of West Alabama
Livingston AL
(205) 652-3578
U.S. News ranking: Reg. U. (S), second tier
Website: www.uwa.edu
Admissions email: admissions@uwa.edu
Public; founded 1835
Freshman admissions: selective; 2016-2017: 1,032 applied, 548 accepted. Either SAT or ACT required. ACT 25/75 percentile: 18-23. High school rank: N/A
Early decision deadline: N/A, notification date: N/A
Early action deadline: N/A, notification date: N/A
Application deadline (fall): rolling
Undergraduate student body: 1,722 full time, 256 part time; 45% male, 55% female; 0% American Indian, 0% Asian, 41% black, 2% Hispanic, 2% multiracial, 0% Pacific Islander, 45% white, 6% international; 80% from in state; 44% live on campus; 10% of students in fraternities, 14% in sororities
Most popular majors: 17% Multi-/Interdisciplinary Studies, Other, 10% Teacher Education, Multiple Levels, 9% Physical Education Teaching and Coaching, 7% Biology/Biological Sciences, General, 7% Kinesiology and Exercise Science
Expenses: 2017-2018: $8,876 in state, $16,162 out of state; room/board: $6,640
Financial aid: (205) 652-3576; 76% of undergrads determined to have financial need; average aid package $10,833

ALASKA

Alaska Pacific University
Anchorage AK
(800) 252-7528
U.S. News ranking: Reg. U. (W), No. 57
Website: www.alaskapacific.edu
Admissions email: admissions@alaskapacific.edu
Private; founded 1957
Freshman admissions: selective; 2016-2017: 474 applied, 261 accepted. Neither SAT nor ACT required. ACT 25/75 percentile: 21-26. High school rank: N/A
Early decision deadline: N/A, notification date: N/A
Early action deadline: N/A, notification date: N/A
Application deadline (fall): rolling
Undergraduate student body: 209 full time, 85 part time; 37% male, 63% female; 15% American Indian, 2% Asian, 4% black, 1% Hispanic, 13% multiracial, 1% Pacific Islander, 53% white, 0% international
Most popular majors: Information not available
Expenses: 2016-2017: $20,380; room/board: $7,260
Financial aid: (907) 564-8342

University of Alaska–Anchorage
Anchorage AK
(907) 786-1480
U.S. News ranking: Reg. U. (W), No. 76
Website: www.uaa.alaska.edu
Admissions email: admissions@alaska.edu
Public; founded 1954
Freshman admissions: selective; 2016-2017: 3,714 applied, 3,062 accepted. Neither SAT nor ACT required. ACT 25/75 percentile: 17-24. High school rank: 12% in top tenth, 32% in top quarter, 61% in top half
Early decision deadline: N/A, notification date: N/A
Early action deadline: N/A, notification date: N/A
Application deadline (fall): 6/15
Undergraduate student body: 7,079 full time, 8,624 part time; 42% male, 58% female; 6% American Indian, 8% Asian, 4% black, 8% Hispanic, 12% multiracial, 1% Pacific Islander, 56% white, 2% international; 91% from in state; N/A live on campus; N/A of students in fraternities, N/A in sororities
Most popular majors: 21% Business, Management, Marketing, and Related Support Services, 15% Health Professions and Related Programs, 7% Engineering, 7% Psychology, 6% Education
Expenses: 2017-2018: $7,398 in state, $22,788 out of state; room/board: $11,962
Financial aid: (907) 786-1517; 53% of undergrads determined to have financial need; average aid package $9,404

University of Alaska–Fairbanks
Fairbanks AK
(000) 478 1823
U.S. News ranking: Nat. U., No. 207
Website: www.uaf.edu
Admissions email: admissions@uaf.edu
Public; founded 1917
Freshman admissions: selective; 2016-2017: 1,557 applied, 1,144 accepted. Either SAT or ACT required. ACT 25/75 percentile: 19-26. High school rank: 19% in top tenth, 43% in top quarter, 69% in top half
Early decision deadline: N/A, notification date: N/A
Early action deadline: N/A, notification date: N/A
Application deadline (fall): 6/15
Undergraduate student body: 3,189 full time, 4,050 part time; 43% male, 57% female; 14% American Indian, 1% Asian, 2% black, 7% Hispanic, 4% multiracial, 0% Pacific Islander, 43% white, 1% international; 86% from in state; 37% live on campus; N/A of students in fraternities, N/A in sororities
Most popular majors: 10% Biology/Biological Sciences, General, 7% Business Administration and Management, General, 6% Accounting, 6% Psychology, General, 5% Mechanical Engineering

Expenses: 2017-2018: $8,144 in state, $23,534 out of state; room/board: $8,530
Financial aid: (888) 474-7256; 53% of undergrads determined to have financial need; average aid package $8,074

University of Alaska–Southeast[1]
Juneau AK
U.S. News ranking: Reg. U. (W), second tier
Website: www.uas.alaska.edu
Admissions email: admissions@uas.alaska.edu
Public
Application deadline (fall): N/A
Undergraduate student body: N/A full time, N/A part time
Expenses: 2016-2017: $8,415 in state, $22,550 out of state; room/board: $9,200
Financial aid: N/A

ARIZONA

Arizona Christian University[1]
Phoenix AZ
(602) 386-4100
U.S. News ranking: Reg. Coll. (W), No. 16
Website: arizonachristian.edu/
Admissions email: admissions@arizonachristian.edu
Private; founded 1960
Affiliation: Undenominational
Application deadline (fall): 8/15
Undergraduate student body: N/A full time, N/A part time
Expenses: 2016-2017: $23,896; room/board: $10,080
Financial aid: (602) 386-4115

Arizona State University–Tempe
Tempe AZ
(480) 965-7788
U.S. News ranking: Nat. U., No. 115
Website: www.asu.edu
Admissions email: admissions@asu.edu
Public; founded 1885
Freshman admissions: more selective; 2016-2017: 24,764 applied, 20,431 accepted. Neither SAT nor ACT required. ACT 25/75 percentile: 22-28. High school rank: 30% in top tenth, 60% in top quarter, 88% in top half
Early decision deadline: N/A, notification date: N/A
Early action deadline: N/A, notification date: N/A
Undergraduate student body: 38,946 full time, 3,531 part time; 57% male, 43% female; 1% American Indian, 7% Asian, 4% black, 20% Hispanic, 4% multiracial, 0% Pacific Islander, 51% white, 13% international; 74% from in state; 21% live on campus; 9% of students in fraternities, 17% in sororities
Most popular majors: 23% Business, Management, Marketing, and Related Support Services, 12% Engineering, 9% Biological and Biomedical Sciences, 9% Social Sciences, 8% Visual and Performing Arts

Expenses: 2017-2018: $10,792 in state, $27,372 out of state; room/board: $12,209
Financial aid: (855) 278-5080; 54% of undergrads determined to have financial need; average aid package $15,226

Frank Lloyd Wright School of Architecture
Scottsdale AZ
(480) 627-5345
U.S. News ranking: Arts, unranked
Website: www.taliesin.edu/
Admissions email: admissions@taliesin.edu
Private; founded 1932
Freshman admissions: least selective; 2016-2017: N/A applied, N/A accepted. Neither SAT nor ACT required. SAT 25/75 percentile: N/A. High school rank: N/A
Early decision deadline: N/A, notification date: N/A
Early action deadline: N/A, notification date: N/A
Application deadline (fall): 4/1
Undergraduate student body: 0 full time, 0 part time; N/A% male, N/A% female; N/A American Indian, N/A Asian, N/A black, N/A Hispanic, N/A multiracial, N/A Pacific Islander, N/A white, N/A international
Most popular majors: Information not available
Expenses: 2016-2017: $40,500; room/board: N/A
Financial aid: N/A

Grand Canyon University[1]
Phoenix AZ
(800) 800-9776
U.S. News ranking: Nat. U., second tier
Website: apply.gcu.edu
Admissions email: golopes@gcu.edu
For-profit; founded 1949
Application deadline (fall): rolling
Undergraduate student body: N/A full time, N/A part time
Expenses: 2016-2017: $17,050; room/board: $8,550
Financial aid: (602) 639-6600

Northcentral University
San Diego AZ
(888) 327-2877
U.S. News ranking: Nat. U., unranked
Website: www.ncu.edu
Admissions email: admissions@ncu.edu
For-profit; founded 1996
Affiliation: Other
Freshman admissions: least selective; 2016-2017: N/A applied, N/A accepted. Neither SAT nor ACT required. SAT 25/75 percentile: N/A. High school rank: N/A
Early decision deadline: N/A, notification date: N/A
Early action deadline: N/A, notification date: N/A
Application deadline (fall): rolling

Undergraduate student body: 12 full time, 121 part time; 35% male, 65% female; 1% American Indian, 2% Asian, 16% black, 12% Hispanic, 2% multiracial, 0% Pacific Islander, 41% white, 0% international
Most popular majors: Information not available
Expenses: 2016-2017: $10,368; room/board: N/A
Financial aid: (888) 896-5112

Northern Arizona University
Flagstaff AZ
(928) 523-5511
U.S. News ranking: Nat. U., second tier
Website: www.nau.edu
Admissions email: admissions@nau.edu
Public; founded 1899
Freshman admissions: selective; 2016-2017: 36,511 applied, 28,495 accepted. Neither SAT nor ACT required. SAT 25/75 percentile: 940-1160. High school rank: 21% in top tenth, 51% in top quarter, 83% in top half
Early decision deadline: N/A, notification date: N/A
Early action deadline: N/A, notification date: N/A
Application deadline (fall): rolling
Undergraduate student body: 21,494 full time, 5,012 part time; 41% male, 59% female; 3% American Indian, 2% Asian, 3% black, 23% Hispanic, 6% multiracial, 0% Pacific Islander, 58% white, 4% international; 71% from in state; 43% live on campus; 3% of students in fraternities, 4% in sororities
Most popular majors: 19% Business, Management, Marketing, and Related Support Services, 13% Health Professions and Related Programs, 11% Liberal Arts and Sciences, General Studies and Humanities, 9% Education, 8% Social Sciences
Expenses: 2017-2018: $11,059 in state, $24,841 out of state; room/board: $9,944
Financial aid: (928) 523-4951

Prescott College
Prescott AZ
(877) 350-2100
U.S. News ranking: Reg. U. (W), No. 81
Website: www.prescott.edu/
Admissions email: admissions@prescott.edu
Private; founded 1966
Freshman admissions: selective; 2016-2017: 314 applied, 215 accepted. Either SAT or ACT required. SAT 25/75 percentile: 920-1200. High school rank: N/A
Early decision deadline: 12/1, notification date: 12/15
Early action deadline: N/A, notification date: N/A
Application deadline (fall): rolling
Undergraduate student body: 267 full time, 89 part time; 40% male, 60% female; 4% American Indian, 1% Asian, 1% black, 7% Hispanic, 7% multiracial, 0% Pacific Islander, 71% white, 1% international; 28% from in state; 16% live on campus; N/A of students in fraternities, N/A in sororities

Most popular majors: Information not available
Expenses: 2017-2018: $30,641; room/board: $9,322
Financial aid: (928) 350-1111; 68% of undergrads determined to have financial need; average aid package $20,132

Southwest University of Visual Arts[1]
Tucson AZ
U.S. News ranking: Arts, unranked
Website: www.suva.edu/
Admissions email: N/A
For-profit
Application deadline (fall): N/A
Undergraduate student body: N/A full time, N/A part time
Expenses: 2016-2017: $23,069; room/board: N/A
Financial aid: N/A

University of Arizona
Tucson AZ
(520) 621-3237
U.S. News ranking: Nat. U., No. 124
Website: www.arizona.edu
Admissions email: admissions@arizona.edu
Public; founded 1885
Freshman admissions: selective; 2016-2017: 36,166 applied, 28,433 accepted. Neither SAT nor ACT required. ACT 25/75 percentile: 21-27. High school rank: 28% in top tenth, 57% in top quarter, 84% in top half
Early decision deadline: N/A, notification date: N/A
Early action deadline: N/A, notification date: N/A
Application deadline (fall): 5/1
Undergraduate student body: 29,341 full time, 4,731 part time; 48% male, 52% female; 1% American Indian, 5% Asian, 4% black, 26% Hispanic, 4% multiracial, 0% Pacific Islander, 51% white, 7% international; 68% from in state; 20% live on campus; N/A of students in fraternities, N/A in sororities
Most popular majors: 15% Business, Management, Marketing, and Related Support Services, 10% Biological and Biomedical Sciences, 9% Social Sciences, 7% Health Professions and Related Programs, 7% Psychology
Expenses: 2017-2018: $11,644 in state, $32,449 out of state; room/board: $11,300
Financial aid: (520) 621-1858; 51% of undergrads determined to have financial need; average aid package $12,620

University of Phoenix[1]
Phoenix AZ
U.S. News ranking: Nat. U., unranked
Website: www.phoenix.edu
Admissions email: N/A
For-profit
Application deadline (fall): N/A
Undergraduate student body: N/A full time, N/A part time
Expenses: 2016-2017: $9,690; room/board: N/A
Financial aid: N/A

ARKANSAS

Arkansas Baptist College
Little Rock AR
(501) 420-1234
U.S. News ranking: Reg. Coll. (S), second tier
Website: www.arkansasbaptist.edu
Admissions email: admissions@arkansasbaptist.edu
Private; founded 1884
Affiliation: Baptist
Freshman admissions: least selective; 2016-2017: 1,233 applied, 349 accepted. Neither SAT nor ACT required. ACT 25/75 percentile: 17-19. High school rank: N/A
Early decision deadline: N/A, notification date: N/A
Early action deadline: N/A, notification date: N/A
Application deadline (fall): rolling
Undergraduate student body: 753 full time, 125 part time; 69% male, 31% female; 0% American Indian, 0% Asian, 94% black, 1% Hispanic, 0% multiracial, 0% Pacific Islander, 5% white, 0% international; 57% from in state; 51% live on campus; 1% of students in fraternities, 0% in sororities
Most popular majors: 24% Corrections and Criminal Justice, Other, 24% Public Administration and Social Service Professions, 16% Urban Education and Leadership, 13% Business Administration and Management, General, 11% Religion/Religious Studies
Expenses: 2017-2018: $8,760; room/board: $4,412
Financial aid: (501) 420-1223; 94% of undergrads determined to have financial need; average aid package $12,270

Arkansas State University[1]
State University AR
(870) 972-3024
U.S. News ranking: Reg. U. (S), No. 68
Website: www.astate.edu
Admissions email: admissions@astate.edu
Public; founded 1909
Application deadline (fall): 8/22
Undergraduate student body: N/A full time, N/A part time
Expenses: 2016-2017: $8,200 in state, $14,260 out of state; room/board: $8,540
Financial aid: (870) 972-2310

Arkansas Tech University
Russellville AR
(479) 968-0343
U.S. News ranking: Reg. U. (S), No. 104
Website: www.atu.edu
Admissions email: tech.enroll@atu.edu
Public; founded 1909
Freshman admissions: selective; 2016-2017: 5,232 applied, 3,344 accepted. Either SAT or ACT required. ACT 25/75 percentile: 19-25. High school rank: 14% in top tenth, 36% in top quarter, 68% in top half

Early decision deadline: N/A, notification date: N/A
Early action deadline: N/A, notification date: N/A
Application deadline (fall): rolling
Undergraduate student body: 6,785 full time, 4,268 part time; 45% male, 55% female; 1% American Indian, 1% Asian, 9% black, 6% Hispanic, 3% multiracial, 0% Pacific Islander, 76% white, 4% international; 96% from in state; 31% live on campus; 8% of students in fraternities, 8% in sororities
Most popular majors: 19% Multi-/Interdisciplinary Studies, Other, 11% Registered Nursing/Registered Nurse, 6% Business Administration and Management, General, 5% Crisis/Emergency/Disaster Management, 5% Early Childhood Education and Teaching
Expenses: 2017-2018: $8,880 in state, $15,660 out of state; room/board: $7,654
Financial aid: (479) 968-0399; 69% of undergrads determined to have financial need; average aid package $9,302

Central Baptist College
Conway AR
(501) 329-6873
U.S. News ranking: Reg. Coll. (S), No. 48
Website: www.cbc.edu
Admissions email: admissions@cbc.edu
Private; founded 1952
Freshman admissions: selective; 2016-2017: 318 applied, 197 accepted. Either SAT or ACT required. ACT 25/75 percentile: 19-25. High school rank: 12% in top tenth, 34% in top quarter, 58% in top half
Early decision deadline: N/A, notification date: N/A
Early action deadline: N/A, notification date: N/A
Application deadline (fall): 8/10
Undergraduate student body: 630 full time, 194 part time; 53% male, 47% female; 1% American Indian, 0% Asian, 21% black, 3% Hispanic, 1% multiracial, 0% Pacific Islander, 70% white, 3% international; N/A from in state; 19% live on campus; 0% of students in fraternities, 0% in sororities
Most popular majors: 16% Psychology, General, 14% Bible/Biblical Studies, 11% Organizational Behavior Studies, 8% Business, Management, Marketing, and Related Support Services, Other, 7% General Studies
Expenses: 2017-2018: $15,750; room/board: $7,500
Financial aid: (501) 205-8809; 83% of undergrads determined to have financial need; average aid package $10,720

Crowley's Ridge College[1]
Paragould AR
U.S. News ranking: Reg. Coll. (S), second tier
Private
Application deadline (fall): N/A

Undergraduate student body: N/A full time, N/A part time
Expenses: 2016-2017: $12,500; room/board: $6,300
Financial aid: N/A

Harding University
Searcy AR
(800) 477-4407
U.S. News ranking: Reg. U. (S), No. 23
Website: www.harding.edu
Admissions email: admissions@harding.edu
Private; founded 1924
Affiliation: Churches of Christ
Freshman admissions: more selective; 2016-2017: 2,184 applied, 1,663 accepted. Either SAT or ACT required. ACT 25/75 percentile: 22-28. High school rank: 24% in top tenth, 42% in top quarter, 61% in top half
Early decision deadline: N/A, notification date: N/A
Early action deadline: 11/15, notification date: N/A
Application deadline (fall): rolling
Undergraduate student body: 4,143 full time, 276 part time; 44% male, 56% female; 1% American Indian, 1% Asian, 4% black, 3% Hispanic, 2% multiracial, 0% Pacific Islander, 82% white, 6% international; 32% from in state, 71% live on campus; 0% of students in fraternities, 0% in sororities
Most popular majors: 15% Business, Management, Marketing, and Related Support Services, 14% Education, 12% Health Professions and Related Programs, 7% Liberal Arts and Sciences, General Studies and Humanities, 6% Parks, Recreation, Leisure, and Fitness Studies
Expenses: 2017-2018: $19,190; room/board: $6,894
Financial aid: (501) 279-4257; 62% of undergrads determined to have financial need; average aid package $17,325

Henderson State University
Arkadelphia AR
(870) 230-5028
U.S. News ranking: Reg. U. (S), No. 95
Website: www.hsu.edu/admissions
Admissions email: admissions@hsu.edu
Public; founded 1890
Freshman admissions: selective; 2016-2017: 3,388 applied, 2,106 accepted. Either SAT or ACT required. ACT 25/75 percentile: 19-25. High school rank: 15% in top tenth, 36% in top quarter, 69% in top half
Early decision deadline: N/A, notification date: N/A
Early action deadline: N/A, notification date: N/A
Application deadline (fall): rolling
Undergraduate student body: 2,791 full time, 261 part time; 43% male, 57% female; 0% American Indian, 1% Asian, 23% black, 4% Hispanic, 3% multiracial, 0% Pacific Islander, 66% white, 1% international; 86% from in state; 53% live on campus; N/A of students in fraternities, N/A in sororities

Most popular majors: 18% Business, Management, Marketing, and Related Support Services, 14% Education, 13% Liberal Arts and Sciences, General Studies and Humanities, 8% Visual and Performing Arts, 7% Psychology
Expenses: 2017-2018: $8,311 in state, $9,961 out of state; room/board: $7,640
Financial aid: (870) 230-5148; 55% of undergrads determined to have financial need; average aid package $8,719

Hendrix College
Conway AR
(800) 277-9017
U.S. News ranking: Nat. Lib. Arts, No. 76
Website: www.hendrix.edu
Admissions email: adm@hendrix.edu
Private; founded 1876
Freshman admissions: more selective; 2016-2017: 1,830 applied, 1,411 accepted. Either SAT or ACT required. ACT 25/75 percentile: 26-32. High school rank: 49% in top tenth, 72% in top quarter, 89% in top half
Early decision deadline: N/A, notification date: N/A
Early action deadline: 11/15, notification date: 12/15
Application deadline (fall): 6/1
Undergraduate student body: 1,314 full time, 7 part time; 47% male, 53% female; 1% American Indian, 5% Asian, 6% black, 5% Hispanic, 3% multiracial, 0% Pacific Islander, 76% white, 4% international; 54% from in state; 94% live on campus; 0% of students in fraternities, 0% in sororities
Most popular majors: 20% Social Sciences, 11% Biological and Biomedical Sciences, 11% Psychology, 9% English Language and Literature/Letters, 8% History
Expenses: 2017-2018: $44,070; room/board: $11,926
Financial aid: (501) 450-1368; 69% of undergrads determined to have financial need; average aid package $35,223

John Brown University
Siloam Springs AR
(479) 524-7454
U.S. News ranking: Reg. U. (S), No. 17
Website: www.jbu.edu
Admissions email: jbuinfo@jbu.edu
Private; founded 1919
Freshman admissions: more selective; 2016-2017: 1,206 applied, 930 accepted. Neither SAT nor ACT required. ACT 25/75 percentile: 23-29. High school rank: 30% in top tenth, 62% in top quarter, 84% in top half
Early decision deadline: N/A, notification date: N/A
Early action deadline: N/A, notification date: N/A
Application deadline (fall): rolling
Undergraduate student body: 1,521 full time, 496 part time; 42% male, 58% female; 2% American Indian, 2% Asian, 3% black, 6% Hispanic, 3% multiracial, 0% Pacific Islander, 75% white,

6% international; 53% from in state; 58% live on campus; N/A of students in fraternities, N/A in sororities
Most popular majors: 48% Business, Management, Marketing, and Related Support Services, 9% Visual and Performing Arts, 7% Education, 7% Family and Consumer Sciences/Human Sciences, 4% Engineering
Expenses: 2017-2018: $26,144; room/board: $9,040
Financial aid: (479) 524-7424; 45% of undergrads determined to have financial need; average aid package $19,535

Lyon College
Batesville AR
(800) 423-2542
U.S. News ranking: Nat. Lib. Arts, second tier
Website: www.lyon.edu
Admissions email: admissions@lyon.edu
Private; founded 1872
Affiliation: Presbyterian Church (USA)
Freshman admissions: more selective; 2016-2017: 1,776 applied, 1,054 accepted. Either SAT or ACT required. ACT 25/75 percentile: 22-26. High school rank: 23% in top tenth, 58% in top quarter, 89% in top half
Early decision deadline: N/A, notification date: N/A
Early action deadline: N/A, notification date: N/A
Application deadline (fall): rolling
Undergraduate student body: 673 full time, 17 part time; 53% male, 47% female; 2% American Indian, 2% Asian, 6% black, 8% Hispanic, 0% multiracial, 0% Pacific Islander, 73% white, 3% international; 69% from in state; 74% live on campus; 27% of students in fraternities, 23% in sororities
Most popular majors: 26% Biological and Biomedical Sciences, 24% Psychology, 12% Business, Management, Marketing, and Related Support Services, 12% History, 8% Mathematics and Statistics
Expenses: 2017-2018: $27,340; room/board: $8,780
Financial aid: (870) 307-7250; 75% of undergrads determined to have financial need; average aid package $21,216

Ouachita Baptist University
Arkadelphia AR
(870) 245-5110
U.S. News ranking: Nat. Lib. Arts, second tier
Website: www.obu.edu
Admissions email: admissions@obu.edu
Private; founded 1886
Affiliation: Southern Baptist
Freshman admissions: more selective; 2016-2017: 1,712 applied, 1,145 accepted. Either SAT or ACT required. ACT 25/75 percentile: 21-28. High school rank: 34% in top tenth, 62% in top quarter, 84% in top half
Early decision deadline: N/A, notification date: N/A

Early action deadline: N/A, notification date: N/A
Application deadline (fall): rolling
Undergraduate student body: 1,469 full time, 25 part time; 47% male, 53% female; 1% American Indian, 1% Asian, 8% black, 4% Hispanic, 0% multiracial, 0% Pacific Islander, 84% white, 2% international; 67% from in state; 95% live on campus; 24% of students in fraternities, 35% in sororities
Most popular majors: 19% Business, Management, Marketing, and Related Support Services, 13% Biological and Biomedical Sciences, 9% Communication, Journalism, and Related Programs, 9% Visual and Performing Arts, 8% Education
Expenses: 2017-2018: $25,870; room/board: $7,630
Financial aid: (870) 245-5316; 61% of undergrads determined to have financial need; average aid package $22,754

Philander Smith College
Little Rock AR
(501) 370-5221
U.S. News ranking: Nat. Lib. Arts, second tier
Website: www.philander.edu
Admissions email: admissions@philander.edu
Private; founded 1877
Affiliation: United Methodist
Freshman admissions: less selective; 2016-2017: 3,330 applied, 1,730 accepted. Either SAT or ACT required. ACT 25/75 percentile: 14-19. High school rank: 8% in top tenth, 24% in top quarter, 45% in top half
Early decision deadline: N/A, notification date: N/A
Early action deadline: N/A, notification date: N/A
Application deadline (fall): rolling
Undergraduate student body: 725 full time, 40 part time; 38% male, 62% female; 0% American Indian, 0% Asian, 92% black, 1% Hispanic, 2% multiracial, 0% Pacific Islander, 0% white, 3% international
Most popular majors: 36% Business Administration and Management, General, 17% Biology/Biological Sciences, General, 11% Psychology, General, 5% English Language and Literature, General, 5% Sociology
Expenses: 2016-2017: $12,414; room/board: $9,064
Financial aid: (501) 370-5380

Southern Arkansas University
Magnolia AR
(870) 235-4040
U.S. News ranking: Reg. U. (S), second tier
Website: www.saumag.edu
Admissions email: muleriders@saumag.edu
Public; founded 1909
Freshman admissions: selective; 2016-2017: 3,460 applied, 2,392 accepted. Either SAT or ACT required. ACT 25/75 percentile: 18-24. High school

rank: 15% in top tenth, 38% in top quarter, 70% in top half
Early decision deadline: N/A, notification date: N/A
Early action deadline: N/A, notification date: N/A
Application deadline (fall): 8/27
Undergraduate student body: 2,834 full time, 452 part time; 45% male, 55% female; 1% American Indian, 1% Asian, 27% black, 3% Hispanic, 0% multiracial, 1% Pacific Islander, 64% white, 3% international; 78% from in state; 54% live on campus; 1% of students in fraternities, 1% in sororities
Most popular majors: 19% Business, Management, Marketing, and Related Support Services, 14% Health Professions and Related Programs, 10% Education, 8% Psychology, 6% Biological and Biomedical Sciences
Expenses: 2016-2017: $8,196 in state, $11,856 out of state; room/board: $6,560
Financial aid: N/A

University of Arkansas
Fayetteville AR
(800) 377-8632
U.S. News ranking: Nat. U., No. 133
Website: www.uark.edu
Admissions email: uofa@uark.edu
Public; founded 1871
Freshman admissions: more selective; 2016-2017: 21,539 applied, 13,613 accepted. Either SAT or ACT required. ACT 25/75 percentile: 23-29. High school rank: 25% in top tenth, 54% in top quarter, 85% in top half
Early decision deadline: N/A, notification date: N/A
Early action deadline: 11/1, notification date: 12/15
Application deadline (fall): 8/1
Undergraduate student body: 19,853 full time, 2,695 part time; 47% male, 53% female; 1% American Indian, 2% Asian, 5% black, 8% Hispanic, 3% multiracial, 0% Pacific Islander, 77% white, 3% international; 56% from in state; 26% live on campus; 21% of students in fraternities, 38% in sororities
Most popular majors: 23% Business, Management, Marketing, and Related Support Services, 10% Engineering, 8% Health Professions and Related Programs, 8% Social Sciences, 6% Communication, Journalism, and Related Programs
Expenses: 2017-2018: $9,062 in state, $24,308 out of state; room/board: $10,704
Financial aid: (479) 575-3806; 42% of undergrads determined to have financial need; average aid package $9,440

University of Arkansas–Fort Smith[1]
Fort Smith AR
(479) 788-7120
U.S. News ranking: Reg. Coll. (S), second tier
Website: www.uafortsmith.edu/Home/Index
Public; founded 1928

Application deadline (fall): rolling
Undergraduate student body: N/A full time, N/A part time
Expenses: 2016-2017: $5,390 in state, $12,038 out of state; room/board: $8,242
Financial aid: N/A

University of Arkansas–Little Rock
Little Rock AR
(501) 569-3127
U.S. News ranking: Nat. U., second tier
Website: www.ualr.edu/
Admissions email: admissions@ualr.edu
Public; founded 1927
Freshman admissions: selective; 2016-2017: 2,708 applied, 2,085 accepted. Either SAT or ACT required. ACT 25/75 percentile: 19-25. High school rank: 14% in top tenth, 40% in top quarter, 72% in top half
Early decision deadline: N/A, notification date: N/A
Early action deadline: N/A, notification date: N/A
Application deadline (fall): 8/9
Undergraduate student body: 5,146 full time, 4,228 part time; 36% male, 64% female; 0% American Indian, 2% Asian, 27% black, 8% Hispanic, 10% multiracial, 0% Pacific Islander, 50% white, 2% international
Most popular majors: 19% Health Professions and Related Programs, 17% Business, Management, Marketing, and Related Support Services, 8% Homeland Security, Law Enforcement, Firefighting and Related Protective Services, 7% Psychology, 4% Biological and Biomedical Sciences
Expenses: 2017-2018: $8,401 in state, $19,797 out of state; room/board: $9,218
Financial aid: (501) 569-3035; 76% of undergrads determined to have financial need; average aid package $12,616

University of Arkansas–Monticello[1]
Monticello AR
U.S. News ranking: Reg. U. (S), unranked
Website: www.uamont.edu
Admissions email: admissions@uamont.edu
Public
Application deadline (fall): N/A
Undergraduate student body: N/A full time, N/A part time
Expenses: 2016-2017: $7,210 in state, $13,060 out of state; room/board: $6,338
Financial aid: N/A

University of Arkansas–Pine Bluff
Pine Bluff AR
(870) 575-8492
U.S. News ranking: Reg. Coll. (S), No. 50
Website: www.uapb.edu/
Admissions email: owasoyop@uapb.edu
Public; founded 1873
Freshman admissions: less selective; 2016-2017: 6,353 applied, 2,664 accepted. Either

SAT or ACT required. ACT 25/75 percentile: 16-21. High school rank: 20% in top tenth, 39% in top quarter, 69% in top half
Early decision deadline: N/A, notification date: N/A
Early action deadline: N/A, notification date: N/A
Application deadline (fall): rolling
Undergraduate student body: 2,502 full time, 219 part time; 41% male, 59% female; 0% American Indian, 1% Asian, 91% black, 2% Hispanic, 1% multiracial, 0% Pacific Islander, 4% white, 1% international; 62% from in state; 53% live on campus; 9% of students in fraternities, 8% in sororities
Most popular majors: 15% Biology/Biological Sciences, General, 15% Criminal Justice/Safety Studies, 9% Business Administration and Management, General, 7% General Studies, 6% Physical Education Teaching and Coaching
Expenses: 2017-2018: $7,336 in state, $13,666 out of state; room/board: $7,673
Financial aid: (870) 575-8302; 89% of undergrads determined to have financial need; average aid package $12,831

University of Central Arkansas
Conway AR
(501) 450-3128
U.S. News ranking: Reg. U. (S), No. 72
Website: www.uca.edu
Admissions email: admissions@uca.edu
Public; founded 1907
Freshman admissions: selective; 2016-2017: 4,922 applied, 4,419 accepted. Either SAT or ACT required. ACT 25/75 percentile: 20-27. High school rank: 18% in top tenth, 47% in top quarter, 79% in top half
Early decision deadline: N/A, notification date: N/A
Early action deadline: N/A, notification date: N/A
Application deadline (fall): rolling
Undergraduate student body: 8,010 full time, 1,606 part time; 41% male, 59% female; 1% American Indian, 2% Asian, 17% black, 5% Hispanic, 4% multiracial, 0% Pacific Islander, 66% white, 5% international; 92% from in state; N/A live on campus; 20% of students in fraternities, 21% in sororities
Most popular majors: 26% Business, Management, Marketing, and Related Support Services, 25% Health Professions and Related Programs, 6% Biological and Biomedical Sciences, 6% Parks, Recreation, Leisure, and Fitness Studies, 6% Psychology
Expenses: 2017-2018: $8,524 in state, $15,047 out of state; room/board: $6,518
Financial aid: (501) 450-3140

University of the Ozarks[1]
Clarksville AR
(479) 979-1227
U.S. News ranking: Reg. Coll. (S), No. 3
Website: www.ozarks.edu

Admissions email: admiss@ozarks.edu
Private; founded 1834
Application deadline (fall): rolling
Undergraduate student body: N/A full time, N/A part time
Expenses: 2016-2017: $23,750; room/board: $7,100
Financial aid: (479) 979-1221

Williams Baptist College
Walnut Ridge AR
(800) 722-4434
U.S. News ranking: Reg. Coll. (S), No. 35
Website: www. williamsbaptistcollege.com
Admissions email: admissions@wbcoll.edu
Private; founded 1941
Affiliation: Southern Baptist
Freshman admissions: selective; 2016-2017: 662 applied, 400 accepted. Either SAT or ACT required. ACT 25/75 percentile: 19-24. High school rank: 12% in top tenth, 36% in top quarter, 70% in top half
Early decision deadline: N/A, notification date: N/A
Early action deadline: N/A, notification date: N/A
Application deadline (fall): rolling
Undergraduate student body: 423 full time, 35 part time; 51% male, 49% female; 0% American Indian, 0% Asian, 12% black, 4% Hispanic, 1% multiracial, 0% Pacific Islander, 76% white, 6% international; 73% from in state; 73% live on campus; 0% of students in fraternities, 0% in sororities
Most popular majors: 20% Liberal Arts and Sciences/Liberal Studies, 20% Psychology, General, 13% Bible/Biblical Studies, 12% Elementary Education and Teaching, 9% Business Administration and Management, General
Expenses: 2017-2018: $17,320; room/board: $7,600
Financial aid: (870) 759-4112; 60% of undergrads determined to have financial need; average aid package $19,240

CALIFORNIA

Academy of Art University
San Francisco CA
(800) 544-2787
U.S. News ranking: Arts, unranked
Website: www.academyart.edu/
Admissions email: admissions@academyart.edu
For-profit; founded 1929
Freshman admissions: least selective; 2016-2017: 2,761 applied, 2,761 accepted. Neither SAT nor ACT required. SAT 25/75 percentile: N/A. High school rank: N/A
Early decision deadline: N/A, notification date: N/A
Early action deadline: N/A, notification date: N/A
Application deadline (fall): rolling
Undergraduate student body: 4,827 full time, 3,476 part time; 43% male, 57% female; 0% American Indian, 7% Asian, 7% black, 12% Hispanic, 3% multiracial, 1% Pacific Islander, 20% white,

29% international; 59% from in state; 15% live on campus; N/A of students in fraternities, N/A in sororities
Most popular majors: 14% Fashion/Apparel Design, 13% Animation, Interactive Technology, Video Graphics and Special Effects, 10% Illustration, 8% Cinematography and Film/Video Production, 8% Photography
Expenses: 2017-2018: $26,490; room/board: $15,792
Financial aid: (415) 618-6190; 41% of undergrads determined to have financial need; average aid package $11,808

Alliant International University
San Diego CA
(858) 635-4772
U.S. News ranking: Nat. U., unranked
Website: www.alliant.edu
Admissions email: admissions@alliant.edu
Private; founded 1969
Freshman admissions: least selective; 2016-2017: N/A applied, N/A accepted. Neither SAT nor ACT required. SAT 25/75 percentile: N/A. High school rank: N/A
Early decision deadline: N/A, notification date: N/A
Early action deadline: N/A, notification date: N/A
Application deadline (fall): rolling
Undergraduate student body: 129 full time, 1,135 part time; 46% male, 54% female; N/A American Indian, N/A Asian, N/A black, N/A Hispanic, N/A multiracial, N/A Pacific Islander, N/A white, N/A international
Most popular majors: 58% Business Administration and Management, General, 26% Psychology, General, 7% Criminal Justice/Law Enforcement Administration
Expenses: 2017-2018: $17,510; room/board: N/A
Financial aid: (858) 635-4700

American Jewish University[1]
Bel-Air CA
(310) 440-1247
U.S. News ranking: Nat. Lib. Arts, second tier
Website: www.aju.edu
Admissions email: admissions@aju.edu
Private; founded 1947
Application deadline (fall): rolling
Undergraduate student body: N/A full time, N/A part time
Expenses: 2017-2018: $30,938; room/board: $16,528
Financial aid: (310) 476-9777; 83% of undergrads determined to have financial need; average aid package $29,215

Argosy University[1]
Orange CA
U.S. News ranking: Nat. U., unranked
Website: www.argosy.edu/
Admissions email: N/A
For-profit
Application deadline (fall): N/A
Undergraduate student body: N/A full time, N/A part time

Expenses: 2016-2017: $13,152; room/board: N/A
Financial aid: N/A

Art Center College of Design
Pasadena CA
(626) 396-2373
U.S. News ranking: Arts, unranked
Website: www.artcenter.edu
Admissions email: admissions@artcenter.edu
Private; founded 1930
Freshman admissions: least selective; 2016-2017: N/A applied, N/A accepted. Neither SAT nor ACT required. SAT 25/75 percentile: N/A. High school rank: N/A
Early decision deadline: N/A, notification date: N/A
Early action deadline: N/A, notification date: N/A
Application deadline (fall): rolling
Undergraduate student body: 1,649 full time, 259 part time; 48% male, 52% female; 0% American Indian, 35% Asian, 1% black, 12% Hispanic, 4% multiracial, 0% Pacific Islander, 16% white, 29% international
Most popular majors: 32% Illustration, 15% Graphic Design, 9% Automotive Engineering Technology/Technician, 8% Engineering-Related Fields, Other, 8% Photography
Expenses: 2016-2017: $40,596; room/board: N/A
Financial aid: (626) 396-2215

Ashford University[1]
San Diego CA
(866) 711-1700
U.S. News ranking: Reg. U. (W), unranked
Website: www.ashford.edu
Admissions email: admissions@ashford.edu
For-profit
Application deadline (fall): N/A
Undergraduate student body: N/A full time, N/A part time
Expenses: 2016-2017: $11,032; room/board: $7,162
Financial aid: N/A

Azusa Pacific University
Azusa CA
(800) 825-5278
U.S. News ranking: Nat. U., No. 187
Website: www.apu.edu
Admissions email: admissions@apu.edu
Private; founded 1899
Freshman admissions: selective; 2016-2017: 6,605 applied, 5,517 accepted. Either SAT or ACT required. SAT 25/75 percentile: 930-1160. High school rank: N/A
Early decision deadline: N/A, notification date: N/A
Early action deadline: 11/15, notification date: 1/15
Application deadline (fall): 6/1
Undergraduate student body: 5,259 full time, 511 part time; 34% male, 66% female; 0% American Indian, 9% Asian, 5% black, 31% Hispanic, 8% multiracial, 1% Pacific Islander, 41% white, 3% international; 81% from in

state; 67% live on campus; 0% of students in fraternities, 0% in sororities
Most popular majors: 28% Health Professions and Related Programs, 15% Business, Management, Marketing, and Related Support Services, 10% Psychology, 8% Education, 8% Liberal Arts and Sciences, General Studies and Humanities
Expenses: 2017-2018: $36,120; room/board: N/A
Financial aid: (888) 788-6090

Biola University
La Mirada CA
(562) 903-4752
U.S. News ranking: Nat. U., No. 159
Website: www.biola.edu
Admissions email: admissions@biola.edu
Private; founded 1908
Affiliation: Multiple Protestant Denomination
Freshman admissions: selective; 2016-2017: 4,393 applied, 2,849 accepted. Either SAT or ACT required. SAT 25/75 percentile: 950-1220. High school rank: 30% in top tenth, 59% in top quarter, 88% in top half
Early decision deadline: 11/15, notification date: 1/15
Early action deadline: 11/15, notification date: 1/15
Application deadline (fall): rolling
Undergraduate student body: 3,947 full time, 144 part time; 36% male, 64% female; 0% American Indian, 17% Asian, 2% black, 20% Hispanic, 6% multiracial, 0% Pacific Islander, 48% white, 3% international; 74% from in state; 65% live on campus; 0% of students in fraternities, 0% in sororities
Most popular majors: 15% Business, Management, Marketing, and Related Support Services, 12% Communication, Journalism, and Related Programs, 11% Visual and Performing Arts, 9% Psychology, 8% Theology and Religious Vocations
Expenses: 2017-2018: $38,448; room/board: $10,238
Financial aid: (562) 903-4742; 67% of undergrads determined to have financial need; average aid package $20,321

Brandman University
Irvine CA
(800) 746-0082
U.S. News ranking: Reg. U. (W), unranked
Website: www.brandman.edu
Admissions email: apply@brandman.edu
Private; founded 1958
Affiliation: Other
Freshman admissions: least selective; 2016-2017: 52 applied, 43 accepted. Neither SAT nor ACT required. SAT 25/75 percentile: N/A. High school rank: N/A
Early decision deadline: N/A, notification date: N/A
Early action deadline: N/A, notification date: N/A
Application deadline (fall): rolling
Undergraduate student body: 1,118 full time, 2,468 part time; 39% male, 61% female; 1% American Indian, 4% Asian, 10% black, 25% Hispanic, 4% multiracial,

2% Pacific Islander, 48% white, 0% international; 81% from in state; 0% live on campus; N/A of students in fraternities, N/A in sororities
Most popular majors: 17% Organizational Leadership, 17% Psychology, General, 14% Business Administration and Management, General, 10% Criminal Justice/Safety Studies, 10% Liberal Arts and Sciences/Liberal Studies
Expenses: 2017-2018: $15,540; room/board: N/A
Financial aid: (800) 746-0082; 68% of undergrads determined to have financial need; average aid package $7,774

California Baptist University
Riverside CA
(877) 228-8866
U.S. News ranking: Reg. U. (W), No. 31
Website: www.calbaptist.edu
Admissions email: admissions@calbaptist.edu
Private; founded 1950
Affiliation: Southern Baptist
Freshman admissions: selective; 2016-2017: 4,971 applied, 3,610 accepted. Either SAT or ACT required. SAT 25/75 percentile: 850 1100. High school rank: 15% in top tenth, 41% in top quarter, 76% in top half
Early decision deadline: N/A, notification date: N/A
Early action deadline: 12/15, notification date: 1/31
Application deadline (fall): rolling
Undergraduate student body: 5,885 full time, 1,052 part time; 37% male, 63% female; 1% American Indian, 5% Asian, 8% black, 36% Hispanic, 6% multiracial, 1% Pacific Islander, 38% white, 2% international; 93% from in state; 39% live on campus; 0% of students in fraternities, 0% in sororities
Most popular majors: 14% Business/Commerce, General, 11% Registered Nursing/Registered Nurse, 10% Psychology, General, 7% Kinesiology and Exercise Science, 5% Liberal Arts and Sciences/Liberal Studies
Expenses: 2017-2018: $32,256; room/board: $8,630
Financial aid: (951) 343-4235; 87% of undergrads determined to have financial need; average aid package $17,879

California College of the Arts
San Francisco CA
(800) 447-1278
U.S. News ranking: Arts, unranked
Website: www.cca.edu
Admissions email: enroll@cca.edu
Private; founded 1907
Freshman admissions: selective; 2016-2017: 1,896 applied, 1,531 accepted. Neither SAT nor ACT required. SAT 25/75 percentile: 895-1200. High school rank: N/A
Early decision deadline: N/A, notification date: N/A
Early action deadline: N/A, notification date: N/A
Application deadline (fall): rolling

Undergraduate student body: 1,442 full time, 86 part time; 36% male, 64% female; 0% American Indian, 18% Asian, 6% black, 12% Hispanic, 0% multiracial, 1% Pacific Islander, 23% white, 35% international; 65% from in state; N/A live on campus; N/A of students in fraternities, N/A in sororities
Most popular majors: 75% Visual and Performing Arts, 10% Architecture and Related Services, 10% Communications Technologies/Technicians and Support Services, 3% Precision Production, 2% English Language and Literature/Letters
Expenses: 2017-2018: $47,266; room/board: $12,697
Financial aid: (415) 703-9573; 50% of undergrads determined to have financial need; average aid package $30,706

California Institute of Integral Studies[1]
San Francisco CA
(415) 575-6100
U.S. News ranking: Nat. U., unranked
Website: www.ciis.edu
Private; founded 1968
Application deadline (fall): N/A
Undergraduate student body: N/A full time, N/A part time
Expenses: 2016-2017: $28,467; room/board: N/A
Financial aid: N/A

California Institute of Technology
Pasadena CA
(626) 395-6341
U.S. News ranking: Nat. U., No. 10
Website: www.caltech.edu
Admissions email: ugadmissions@caltech.edu
Private; founded 1891
Freshman admissions: most selective; 2016-2017: 6,855 applied, 553 accepted. Either SAT or ACT required. SAT 25/75 percentile: 1510-1600. High school rank: 97% in top tenth, 100% in top quarter, 100% in top half
Early decision deadline: N/A, notification date: N/A
Early action deadline: 11/1, notification date: 12/15
Application deadline (fall): 1/3
Undergraduate student body: 979 full time, 0 part time; 59% male, 41% female; 0% American Indian, 43% Asian, 1% black, 12% Hispanic, 6% multiracial, 0% Pacific Islander, 29% white, 9% international; 34% from in state; 86% live on campus; N/A of students in fraternities, N/A in sororities
Most popular majors: 37% Engineering, 23% Computer and Information Sciences and Support Services, 18% Physical Sciences, 14% Mathematics and Statistics, 7% Biological and Biomedical Sciences
Expenses: 2017-2018: $49,908; room/board: $14,796
Financial aid: (626) 395-6280; 51% of undergrads determined to have financial need; average aid package $46,095

California Institute of the Arts
Valencia CA
(661) 255-1050
U.S. News ranking: Arts, unranked
Website: www.calarts.edu
Admissions email: admiss@calarts.edu
Private; founded 1961
Freshman admissions: least selective; 2016-2017: 2,250 applied, 532 accepted. Neither SAT nor ACT required. SAT 25/75 percentile: N/A. High school rank: N/A
Early decision deadline: N/A, notification date: N/A
Early action deadline: N/A, notification date: N/A
Application deadline (fall): N/A
Undergraduate student body: 943 full time, 16 part time; 42% male, 58% female; 1% American Indian, 11% Asian, 6% black, 12% Hispanic, 10% multiracial, 0% Pacific Islander, 40% white, 16% international
Most popular majors: Information not available
Expenses: 2016-2017: $45,646; room/board: $11,363
Financial aid: (661) 253-7869

California Lutheran University
Thousand Oaks CA
(877) 258-3678
U.S. News ranking: Reg. U. (W), No. 14
Website: www.callutheran.edu
Admissions email: admissions@callutheran.edu
Private; founded 1959
Affiliation: Evangelical Lutheran Church
Freshman admissions: more selective; 2016-2017: 6,013 applied, 3,860 accepted. Either SAT or ACT required. SAT 25/75 percentile: 990-1080. High school rank: 32% in top tenth, 68% in top quarter, 93% in top half
Early decision deadline: N/A, notification date: N/A
Early action deadline: 11/1, notification date: 1/15
Application deadline (fall): N/A
Undergraduate student body: 2,768 full time, 124 part time; 43% male, 57% female; 0% American Indian, 5% Asian, 3% black, 29% Hispanic, 7% multiracial, 0% Pacific Islander, 48% white, 3% international; 89% from in state; 53% live on campus; N/A of students in fraternities, N/A in sororities
Most popular majors: 22% Business, Management, Marketing, and Related Support Services, 15% Communication, Journalism, and Related Programs, 12% Psychology, 8% Biological and Biomedical Sciences, 7% Parks, Recreation, Leisure, and Fitness Studies
Expenses: 2017-2018: $41,363; room/board: $13,320
Financial aid: (805) 493-3139; 70% of undergrads determined to have financial need; average aid package $30,400

California Polytechnic State University–San Luis Obispo
San Luis Obispo CA
(805) 756-2311
U.S. News ranking: Reg. U. (W), No. 11
Website: www.calpoly.edu/
Admissions email: admissions@calpoly.edu
Public; founded 1901
Freshman admissions: more selective; 2016-2017: 48,162 applied, 14,202 accepted. Either SAT or ACT required. ACT 25/75 percentile: 26-31. High school rank: 56% in top tenth, 88% in top quarter, 99% in top half
Early decision deadline: 10/31, notification date: 12/15
Early action deadline: N/A, notification date: N/A
Application deadline (fall): 11/30
Undergraduate student body: 19,703 full time, 723 part time; 53% male, 47% female; 0% American Indian, 13% Asian, 1% black, 16% Hispanic, 7% multiracial, 0% Pacific Islander, 57% white, 2% international; 86% from in state; 35% live on campus; 7% of students in fraternities, 12% in sororities
Most popular majors: 27% Engineering, 13% Agriculture, Agriculture Operations, and Related Sciences, 12% Business, Management, Marketing, and Related Support Services, 6% Biological and Biomedical Sciences, 6% Parks, Recreation, Leisure, and Fitness Studies
Expenses: 2017-2018: $9,432 in state, $21,312 out of state; room/board: $13,115
Financial aid: (805) 756-2927; 42% of undergrads determined to have financial need; average aid package $10,141

California State Polytechnic University–Pomona
Pomona CA
(909) 869-5299
U.S. News ranking: Reg. U. (W), No. 31
Website: www.cpp.edu
Admissions email: admissions@cpp.edu
Public; founded 1938
Freshman admissions: selective; 2016-2017: 32,917 applied, 19,474 accepted. Either SAT or ACT required. SAT 25/75 percentile: 900-1160. High school rank: N/A
Early decision deadline: N/A, notification date: N/A
Early action deadline: N/A, notification date: N/A
Application deadline (fall): 11/30
Undergraduate student body: 21,148 full time, 2,585 part time; 55% male, 45% female; 0% American Indian, 23% Asian, 3% black, 42% Hispanic, 4% multiracial, 0% Pacific Islander, 18% white, 6% international; 99% from in state; 10% live on campus; 2% of students in fraternities, 1% in sororities
Most popular majors: 25% Business Administration and Management, General, 8% Hospitality Administration/Management, General, 4%

Civil Engineering, General, 4% Mechanical Engineering, 3% Health and Physical Education/Fitness, General
Expenses: 2017-2018: $7,297 in state, $19,177 out of state; room/board: $14,514
Financial aid: (909) 869-3704; 68% of undergrads determined to have financial need; average aid package $10,345

California State University–Bakersfield
Bakersfield CA
(661) 654-3036
U.S. News ranking: Reg. U. (W), No. 94
Website: www.csub.edu
Admissions email: admissions@csub.edu
Public
Freshman admissions: less selective; 2016-2017: 5,756 applied, 5,756 accepted. Neither SAT nor ACT required. SAT 25/75 percentile: 800-1010. High school rank: N/A
Early decision deadline: N/A, notification date: N/A
Early action deadline: 11/30, notification date: 3/1
Application deadline (fall): 3/1
Undergraduate student body: 7,083 full time, 1,010 part time; 40% male, 60% female; 1% American Indian, 7% Asian, 6% black, 55% Hispanic, 3% multiracial, 0% Pacific Islander, 18% white, 6% international; 99% from in state; 4% live on campus; 4% of students in fraternities, 3% in sororities
Most popular majors: 31% Liberal Arts and Sciences, General Studies and Humanities, 13% Education, 10% Social Sciences, 8% English Language and Literature/Letters, 8% Psychology
Expenses: 2017-2018: $8,550 in state, $18,054 out of state; room/board: $13,230
Financial aid: (661) 654-3016; 81% of undergrads determined to have financial need; average aid package $4,278

California State University–Channel Islands[1]
Camarillo CA
(805) 437-8500
U.S. News ranking: Reg. U. (W), No. 66
Website: www.csuci.edu
Public
Application deadline (fall): N/A
Undergraduate student body: N/A full time, N/A part time
Expenses: 2016-2017: $6,547 in state, $17,707 out of state; room/board: $16,146
Financial aid: N/A

California State University–Chico
Chico CA
(530) 898-4428
U.S. News ranking: Reg. U. (W), No. 37
Website: www.csuchico.edu
Admissions email: info@csuchico.edu
Public; founded 1887

Freshman admissions: selective; 2016-2017: 23,124 applied, 15,393 accepted. Either SAT or ACT required. SAT 25/75 percentile: 880-1100. High school rank: 35% in top tenth, 76% in top quarter, 100% in top half
Early decision deadline: N/A, notification date: N/A
Early action deadline: N/A, notification date: N/A
Application deadline (fall): 11/30
Undergraduate student body: 14,819 full time, 1,652 part time; 47% male, 53% female; 1% American Indian, 6% Asian, 2% black, 31% Hispanic, 5% multiracial, 0% Pacific Islander, 44% white, 4% international; 99% from in state; 0% live on campus; 1% of students in fraternities, 1% in sororities
Most popular majors: Biological and Biomedical Sciences, Business, Management, Marketing, and Related Support Services, Health Professions and Related Programs, Psychology, Social Sciences
Expenses: 2017-2018: $8,616 in state, $19,776 out of state; room/board: $12,824
Financial aid: (530) 898-6451; 72% of undergrads determined to have financial need; average aid package $16,081

California State University–Dominguez Hills
Carson CA
(310) 243-3300
U.S. News ranking: Reg. U. (W), second tier
Website: www.csudh.edu
Admissions email: info@csudh.edu
Public; founded 1960
Freshman admissions: least selective; 2016-2017: 10,615 applied, 7,974 accepted. Neither SAT nor ACT required. SAT 25/75 percentile: 760-940. High school rank: N/A
Early decision deadline: N/A, notification date: N/A
Early action deadline: N/A, notification date: N/A
Application deadline (fall): rolling
Undergraduate student body: 9,311 full time, 3,321 part time; 37% male, 63% female; 0% American Indian, 10% Asian, 13% black, 60% Hispanic, 3% multiracial, 0% Pacific Islander, 7% white, 4% international; 100% from in state; 5% live on campus; 1% of students in fraternities, 1% in sororities
Most popular majors: 19% Business, Management, Marketing, and Related Support Services, 13% Health Professions and Related Programs, 11% Psychology, 10% Social Sciences, 7% Homeland Security, Law Enforcement, Firefighting and Related Protective Services
Expenses: 2017-2018: $7,922 in state, $17,426 out of state; room/board: $11,404
Financial aid: (310) 243-3189; 76% of undergrads determined to have financial need; average aid package $6,199

California State University–East Bay
Hayward CA
(510) 885-2784
U.S. News ranking: Reg. U. (W), second tier
Website: www.csueastbay.edu
Admissions email: admissions@csueastbay.edu
Public; founded 1957
Freshman admissions: least selective; 2016-2017: 15,670 applied, 10,930 accepted. Neither SAT nor ACT required. SAT 25/75 percentile: 770-990. High school rank: N/A
Early decision deadline: N/A, notification date: N/A
Early action deadline: N/A, notification date: N/A
Application deadline (fall): 11/30
Undergraduate student body: 11,535 full time, 1,805 part time; 39% male, 61% female; 0% American Indian, 24% Asian, 11% black, 33% Hispanic, 6% multiracial, 1% Pacific Islander, 16% white, 6% international; 99% from in state; N/A live on campus; N/A of students in fraternities, N/A in sororities
Most popular majors: 19% Business Administration and Management, General, 18% Health Professions and Related Programs, 9% Social Sciences, General, 8% Psychology, General, 6% Public Administration and Social Service Professions, Other
Expenses: 2017-2018: $6,834 in state, $18,714 out of state; room/board: $14,184
Financial aid: (510) 885-2784; 67% of undergrads determined to have financial need; average aid package $10,778

California State University–Fresno
Fresno CA
(559) 278-2191
U.S. News ranking: Nat. U., No. 223
Website: www.csufresno.edu
Admissions email: lyager@csufresno.edu
Public; founded 1911
Freshman admissions: selective; 2016-2017: 18,731 applied, 10,030 accepted. Either SAT or ACT required. SAT 25/75 percentile: 800-1010. High school rank: 15% in top tenth, 80% in top quarter, 100% in top half
Early decision deadline: N/A, notification date: N/A
Early action deadline: N/A, notification date: N/A
Application deadline (fall): 11/30
Undergraduate student body: 18,194 full time, 3,334 part time; 42% male, 58% female; 0% American Indian, 14% Asian, 3% black, 50% Hispanic, 3% multiracial, 0% Pacific Islander, 20% white, 6% international; 99% from in state; 4% live on campus; 6% of students in fraternities, 7% in sororities
Most popular majors: 13% Business, Management, Marketing, and Related Support Services, 12% Health Professions

and Related Programs, 8% Psychology, 7% Homeland Security, Law Enforcement, Firefighting and Related Protective Services, 7% Liberal Arts and Sciences, General Studies and Humanities
Expenses: 2017-2018: $6,583 in state, $17,929 out of state; room/board: $9,704
Financial aid: (559) 278-2182; 75% of undergrads determined to have financial need; average aid package $10,770

California State University–Fullerton
Fullerton CA
(657) 278-7788
U.S. News ranking: Nat. U., No. 202
Website: www.fullerton.edu
Admissions email: admissions@fullerton.edu
Public; founded 1957
Freshman admissions: selective; 2016-2017: 44,493 applied, 21,459 accepted. Either SAT or ACT required. SAT 25/75 percentile: 920-1120. High school rank: 20% in top tenth, 68% in top quarter, 97% in top half
Early decision deadline: N/A, notification date: N/A
Early action deadline: N/A, notification date: N/A
Application deadline (fall): 11/30
Undergraduate student body: 27,994 full time, 6,582 part time; 44% male, 56% female; 0% American Indian, 21% Asian, 2% black, 42% Hispanic, 4% multiracial, 0% Pacific Islander, 20% white, 6% international; 99% from in state; N/A live on campus; N/A of students in fraternities, N/A in sororities
Most popular majors: 26% Business, Management, Marketing, and Related Support Services, 12% Communication, Journalism, and Related Programs, 10% Health Professions and Related Programs, 7% Psychology, 6% Social Sciences
Expenses: 2017-2018: $6,850 in state, $17,460 out of state; room/board: $15,642
Financial aid: (657) 278-5254; 67% of undergrads determined to have financial need; average aid package $7,772

California State University–Long Beach
Long Beach CA
(562) 985-5471
U.S. News ranking: Reg. U. (W), No. 39
Website: www.csulb.edu
Public; founded 1949
Freshman admissions: selective; 2016-2017: 60,732 applied, 19,711 accepted. Either SAT or ACT required. SAT 25/75 percentile: 930-1160. High school rank: N/A
Early decision deadline: N/A, notification date: N/A
Early action deadline: N/A, notification date: N/A
Application deadline (fall): 11/30

Undergraduate student body: 27,905 full time, 4,341 part time; 44% male, 56% female; 0% American Indian, 22% Asian, 4% black, 40% Hispanic, 5% multiracial, 0% Pacific Islander, 18% white, 7% international; 94% from in state; 3% live on campus; N/A of students in fraternities, N/A in sororities
Most popular majors: 15% Business, Management, Marketing, and Related Support Services, 10% Communication, Journalism, and Related Programs, 10% Health Professions and Related Programs, 10% Social Sciences, 7% Family and Consumer Sciences/Human Sciences
Expenses: 2017-2018: $6,524 in state, $16,196 out of state; room/board: $12,644
Financial aid: (562) 985-8403; 77% of undergrads determined to have financial need; average aid package $13,529

California State University–Los Angeles
Los Angeles CA
(323) 343-3901
U.S. News ranking: Reg. U. (W), No. 59
Website: www.calstatela.edu
Admissions email: admission@calstatela.edu
Public; founded 1947
Freshman admissions: less selective; 2016-2017: 35,429 applied, 22,567 accepted. Neither SAT nor ACT required. SAT 25/75 percentile: 780-980. High school rank: N/A
Early decision deadline: N/A, notification date: N/A
Early action deadline: N/A, notification date: N/A
Application deadline (fall): 11/30
Undergraduate student body: 20,022 full time, 4,037 part time; 42% male, 58% female; 0% American Indian, 14% Asian, 4% black, 64% Hispanic, 2% multiracial, 0% Pacific Islander, 7% white, 6% international; N/A from in state; 4% live on campus; 2% of students in fraternities, 3% in sororities
Most popular majors: 19% Business, Management, Marketing, and Related Support Services, 14% Health Professions and Related Programs, 13% Social Sciences, 7% Communication, Journalism, and Related Programs, 6% Psychology
Expenses: 2017-2018: $6,613 in state, $18,513 out of state; room/board: $13,356
Financial aid: (323) 343-6260; 88% of undergrads determined to have financial need; average aid package $10,811

California State University–Maritime Academy
Vallejo CA
(707) 654-1330
U.S. News ranking: Reg. Coll. (W), No. 3
Website: www.csum.edu
Admissions email: admission@csum.edu

Public; founded 1929
Freshman admissions: selective; 2016-2017: 1,217 applied, 830 accepted. Either SAT or ACT required. SAT 25/75 percentile: 970-1193. High school rank: N/A
Early decision deadline: N/A, notification date: N/A
Early action deadline: 10/31, notification date: 12/15
Application deadline (fall): 11/30
Undergraduate student body: 1,075 full time, 32 part time; 83% male, 17% female; 0% American Indian, 10% Asian, 2% black, 19% Hispanic, 12% multiracial, 1% Pacific Islander, 49% white, 1% international; 87% from in state; 67% live on campus; 0% of students in fraternities, 0% in sororities
Most popular majors: 27% Transportation and Materials Moving, 21% Engineering, 21% Engineering Technologies and Engineering-Related Fields, 19% Business, Management, Marketing, and Related Support Services, 12% Multi/ Interdisciplinary Studies
Expenses: 2016-2017: $6,808 in state, $17,968 out of state; room/ board: $11,670
Financial aid: N/A

California State University– Monterey Bay

Seaside CA
(831) 582-3783
U.S. News ranking: Reg. U. (W), No. 47
Website: www.csumb.edu
Admissions email: admissions@csumb.edu
Public; founded 1994
Freshman admissions: selective; 2016-2017: 16,258 applied, 5,729 accepted. Either SAT or ACT required. SAT 25/75 percentile: 840-1060. High school rank: 16% in top tenth, 51% in top quarter, 89% in top half
Early decision deadline: N/A, notification date: N/A
Early action deadline: N/A, notification date: N/A
Application deadline (fall): 11/30
Undergraduate student body: 6,241 full time, 682 part time; 38% male, 62% female; 1% American Indian, 6% Asian, 7% black, 38% Hispanic, 7% multiracial, 1% Pacific Islander, 31% white, 5% international; 98% from in state; N/A live on campus; 3% of students in fraternities, 4% in sororities
Most popular majors: 16% Liberal Arts and Sciences, General Studies and Humanities, 14% Psychology, 13% Business, Management, Marketing, and Related Support Services, 13% Parks, Recreation, Leisure, and Fitness Studies, 6% Computer and Information Sciences and Support Services
Expenses: 2017-2018: $6,379 in state, $17,539 out of state; room/ board: $11,930
Financial aid: (831) 582-4136; 69% of undergrads determined to have financial need; average aid package $11,277

California State University– Northridge

Northridge CA
(818) 677-3700
U.S. News ranking: Reg. U. (W), No. 73
Website: www.csun.edu
Admissions email: admissions.records@csun.edu
Public; founded 1958
Freshman admissions: less selective; 2016-2017: 32,913 applied, 15,876 accepted. Either SAT or ACT required. SAT 25/75 percentile: 800-1030. High school rank: N/A
Early decision deadline: N/A, notification date: N/A
Early action deadline: N/A, notification date: N/A
Application deadline (fall): 11/30
Undergraduate student body: 28,969 full time, 6,583 part time; 46% male, 54% female; 0% American Indian, 11% Asian, 5% black, 46% Hispanic, 3% multiracial, 0% Pacific Islander, 22% white, 9% international
Most popular majors: Information not available
Expenses: 2017-2018: $6,569 in state, $17,729 out of state; room/ board: $10,272
Financial aid: (818) 677-4085; 78% of undergrads determined to have financial need; average aid package $18,142

California State University– Sacramento

Sacramento CA
(916) 278-3901
U.S. News ranking: Reg. U. (W), No. 70
Website: www.csus.edu
Admissions email: outreach@csus.edu
Public; founded 1947
Freshman admissions: less selective; 2016-2017: 23,944 applied, 17,224 accepted. Neither SAT nor ACT required. SAT 25/75 percentile: 930-1050. High school rank: N/A
Early decision deadline: N/A, notification date: N/A
Early action deadline: N/A, notification date: N/A
Application deadline (fall): 11/30
Undergraduate student body: 23,170 full time, 4,706 part time; 44% male, 56% female; 0% American Indian, 21% Asian, 6% black, 30% Hispanic, 6% multiracial, 1% Pacific Islander, 27% white, 3% international; 99% from in state; 6% live on campus; 4% of students in fraternities, 5% in sororities
Most popular majors: 14% Business, Management, Marketing, and Related Support Services, 11% Social Sciences, 8% Communication, Journalism, and Related Programs, 8% Homeland Security, Law Enforcement, and Related Protective Services, 8% Parks, Recreation, Leisure, and Fitness Studies
Expenses: 2017-2018: $7,204 in state, $19,084 out of state; room/ board: $11,856

Financial aid: (916) 278-6980; 76% of undergrads determined to have financial need; average aid package $10,618

California State University– San Bernardino

San Bernardino CA
(909) 537-5188
U.S. News ranking: Reg. U. (W), No. 63
Website: www.csusb.edu
Admissions email: moreinfo@csusb.edu
Public; founded 1962
Freshman admissions: less selective; 2016-2017: 15,740 applied, 9,152 accepted. Neither SAT nor ACT required. SAT 25/75 percentile: 780-980. High school rank: N/A
Early decision deadline: N/A, notification date: N/A
Early action deadline: N/A, notification date: 5/1
Application deadline (fall): rolling
Undergraduate student body: 16,474 full time, 1,979 part time; 40% male, 60% female; 0% American Indian, 6% Asian, 6% black, 63% Hispanic, 3% multiracial, 0% Pacific Islander, 13% white, 7% international; 100% from in state; 7% live on campus; 1% of students in fraternities, 1% in sororities
Most popular majors: 24% Business, Management, Marketing, and Related Support Services, 13% Psychology, 10% Social Sciences, 8% Health Professions and Related Programs, 8% Homeland Security, Law Enforcement, Firefighting and Related Protective Services
Expenses: 2017-2018: $6,601 in state, $13,009 out of state; room/ board: $12,066
Financial aid: (909) 537-7651; 84% of undergrads determined to have financial need; average aid package $9,430

California State University– San Marcos

San Marcos CA
(760) 750-4848
U.S. News ranking: Reg. U. (W), No. 76
Website: www.csusm.edu
Admissions email: apply@csusm.edu
Public; founded 1989
Freshman admissions: less selective; 2016-2017: 12,872 applied, 9,402 accepted. Either SAT or ACT required. SAT 25/75 percentile: 860-1060. High school rank: N/A
Early decision deadline: N/A, notification date: N/A
Early action deadline: N/A, notification date: N/A
Application deadline (fall): 11/30
Undergraduate student body: 10,466 full time, 2,096 part time; 39% male, 61% female; 0% American Indian, 10% Asian, 3% black, 42% Hispanic, 5% multiracial, 0% Pacific Islander,

29% white, 5% international; 100% from in state; 15% live on campus; N/A of students in fraternities, N/A in sororities
Most popular majors: 19% Business, Management, Marketing, and Related Support Services, 16% Social Sciences, 10% Health Professions and Related Programs, 8% Family and Consumer Sciences/Human Sciences, 7% Psychology
Expenses: 2017-2018: $7,364 in state, $16,292 out of state; room/ board: $13,240
Financial aid: (760) 750-4881; 69% of undergrads determined to have financial need; average aid package $10,677

California State University– Stanislaus

Turlock CA
(209) 667-3070
U.S. News ranking: Reg. U. (W), No. 55
Website: www.csustan.edu
Admissions email: Outreach_Help_ Desk@csustan.edu
Public; founded 1957
Freshman admissions: less selective; 2016-2017: 7,618 applied, 5,663 accepted. Neither SAT nor ACT required. SAT 25/75 percentile: 790-1000. High school rank: N/A
Early decision deadline: N/A, notification date: N/A
Early action deadline: N/A, notification date: N/A
Application deadline (fall): 11/30
Undergraduate student body: 7,217 full time, 1,403 part time; 35% male, 65% female; 0% American Indian, 10% Asian, 2% black, 51% Hispanic, 4% multiracial, 1% Pacific Islander, 23% white, 4% international; 97% from in state; 0% live on campus; 6% of students in fraternities, 6% in sororities
Most popular majors: 22% Business Administration and Management, General, 13% Psychology, General, 10% Liberal Arts and Sciences/Liberal Studies, 8% Criminal Justice/Safety Studies, 6% Sociology
Expenses: 2017-2018: $7,038 in state, $18,918 out of state; room/ board: $8,670
Financial aid: (209) 667-3337; 79% of undergrads determined to have financial need; average aid package $11,739

Chapman University

Orange CA
(888) 282-7759
U.S. News ranking: Reg. U. (W), No. 5
Website: www.chapman.edu
Admissions email: admit@chapman.edu
Private; founded 1861
Affiliation: Christian Church (Disciples of Christ)
Freshman admissions: more selective; 2016-2017: 12,821 applied, 6,927 accepted. Either SAT or ACT required. SAT 25/75 percentile: 1110-1300. High school rank: 38% in top tenth, 81% in top quarter, 96% in top half

Early decision deadline: N/A, notification date: N/A
Early action deadline: 11/1, notification date: 1/10
Application deadline (fall): 1/15
Undergraduate student body: 6,130 full time, 280 part time; 40% male, 60% female; 0% American Indian, 11% Asian, 2% black, 15% Hispanic, 7% multiracial, 0% Pacific Islander, 57% white, 4% international; 68% from in state; 34% live on campus; 25% of students in fraternities, 40% in sororities
Most popular majors: 20% Business Administration and Management, General, 8% Cinematography and Film/Video Production, 7% Psychology, General, 7% Speech Communication and Rhetoric, 5% Business/Corporate Communications
Expenses: 2017-2018: $50,594; room/board: $14,910
Financial aid: (714) 997-6741; 56% of undergrads determined to have financial need; average aid package $32,471

Claremont McKenna College

Claremont CA
(909) 621-8088
U.S. News ranking: Nat. Lib. Arts, No. 8
Website: www.claremontmckenna.edu
Admissions email: admission@cmc.edu
Private; founded 1946
Freshman admissions: most selective; 2016-2017: 6,342 applied, 599 accepted. Either SAT or ACT required. ACT 25/75 percentile: 31-33. High school rank: 68% in top tenth, 100% in top quarter, 100% in top half
Early decision deadline: 11/1, notification date: 12/15
Early action deadline: N/A, notification date: N/A
Application deadline (fall): 1/1
Undergraduate student body: 1,346 full time, 1 part time; 51% male, 49% female; 0% American Indian, 10% Asian, 5% black, 14% Hispanic, 6% multiracial, 0% Pacific Islander, 42% white, 17% international; 44% from in state; 97% live on campus; N/A of students in fraternities, N/A in sororities
Most popular majors: 33% Economics, General, 14% Political Science and Government, General, 12% International Relations and Affairs, 11% Psychology, General, 9% Accounting
Expenses: 2017-2018: $52,825; room/board: $16,220
Financial aid: (909) 621-8356; 40% of undergrads determined to have financial need; average aid package $46,129

Cogswell Polytechnical College

San Jose CA
(408) 498-5160
U.S. News ranking: Reg. Coll. (W), unranked
Website: www. cogswell.edu
Admissions email: admissions@cogswell.edu
Private; founded 1887
Freshman admissions: selective; 2016-2017: 281 applied, 232 accepted. Neither SAT nor ACT required. SAT 25/75 percentile: 970-1177. High school rank: N/A
Early decision deadline: N/A, notification date: N/A
Early action deadline: 12/1, notification date: 12/1
Application deadline (fall): rolling
Undergraduate student body: 487 full time, 169 part time; 71% male, 29% female; 1% American Indian, 20% Asian, 5% black, 21% Hispanic, 9% multiracial, 1% Pacific Islander, 36% white, 0% international; 93% from in state; 16% live on campus; N/A of students in fraternities, N/A in sororities
Most popular majors: 44% Animation, Interactive Technology, Video Graphics and Special Effects, 24% Music Technology, 14% Computer Programming/Programmer, General, 6% Modeling, Virtual Environments and Simulation, 5% Game and Interactive Media Design
Expenses: 2016-2017: $19,096; room/board: $12,415
Financial aid: (408) 541-0100

Concordia University

Irvine CA
(949) 214-3010
U.S. News ranking: Reg. U. (W), No. 41
Website: www.cui.edu
Admissions email: admission@cui.edu
Private; founded 1972
Freshman admissions: selective; 2016-2017: 3,839 applied, 2,497 accepted. Either SAT or ACT required. SAT 25/75 percentile: 907-1160. High school rank: 19% in top tenth, 49% in top quarter, 78% in top half
Early decision deadline: N/A, notification date: N/A
Early action deadline: 12/1, notification date: 12/15
Application deadline (fall): rolling
Undergraduate student body: 1,777 full time, 148 part time; 36% male, 64% female; 0% American Indian, 7% Asian, 4% black, 23% Hispanic, 5% multiracial, 0% Pacific Islander, 48% white, 4% international; 85% from in state; 47% live on campus; N/A of students in fraternities, N/A in sororities
Most popular majors: 19% Business Administration and Management, General, 17% Registered Nursing/Registered Nurse, 10% Liberal Arts and Sciences/Liberal Studies, 10% Psychology, General, 7% Health and Physical Education/Fitness, General

Expenses: 2017-2018: $34,100; room/board: $10,760
Financial aid: (949) 214-3066; 71% of undergrads determined to have financial need; average aid package $21,103

Dominican University of California

San Rafael CA
(415) 485-3204
U.S. News ranking: Reg. U. (W), No. 30
Website: www.dominican.edu
Admissions email: enroll@dominican.edu
Private; founded 1890
Freshman admissions: selective; 2016-2017: 2,049 applied, 1,593 accepted. Either SAT or ACT required. SAT 25/75 percentile: 918-1123. High school rank: 25% in top tenth, 57% in top quarter, 84% in top half
Early decision deadline: N/A, notification date: N/A
Early action deadline: N/A, notification date: N/A
Application deadline (fall): rolling
Undergraduate student body: 1,225 full time, 166 part time; 27% male, 73% female; 1% American Indian, 23% Asian, 5% black, 20% Hispanic, 7% multiracial, 1% Pacific Islander, 34% white, 1% international; 91% from in state; 35% live on campus; N/A of students in fraternities, N/A in sororities
Most popular majors: 40% Health Professions and Related Programs, 15% Business, Management, Marketing, and Related Support Services, 14% Biological and Biomedical Sciences, 10% Psychology, 5% Communication, Journalism, and Related Programs
Expenses: 2017-2018: $44,690; room/board: $14,650
Financial aid: (415) 257-1350; 78% of undergrads determined to have financial need; average aid package $28,594

Fashion Institute of Design & Merchandising

Los Angeles CA
(800) 624-1200
U.S. News ranking: Arts, unranked
Website: fidm.edu/
Admissions email: admissions@fidm.edu
Private; founded 1969
Freshman admissions: least selective; 2016-2017: 2,016 applied, 842 accepted. Neither SAT nor ACT required. SAT 25/75 percentile: N/A. High school rank: N/A
Early decision deadline: N/A, notification date: N/A
Early action deadline: 6/30, notification date: 8/1
Application deadline (fall): rolling
Undergraduate student body: 2,802 full time, 331 part time; 11% male, 89% female; 1% American Indian, 11% Asian, 5% black, 22% Hispanic, 3% multiracial, 1% Pacific Islander, 35% white, 16% international; 73% from in state; N/A live on campus; N/A of students in fraternities, N/A in sororities

Most popular majors: 92% Business, Management, Marketing, and Related Support Services, Other, 4% Fashion/Apparel Design, 3% Marketing/Marketing Management, General, 1% Apparel and Textile Marketing Management, 1% Costume Design
Expenses: 2016-2017: $31,760; room/board: N/A
Financial aid: N/A

Fresno Pacific University

Fresno CA
(559) 453-2039
U.S. News ranking: Reg. U. (W), No. 41
Website: www.fresno.edu
Admissions email: ugadmis@fresno.edu
Private; founded 1944
Freshman admissions: selective; 2016-2017: 644 applied, 441 accepted. Either SAT or ACT required. SAT 25/75 percentile: 850-1060. High school rank: 26% in top tenth, 56% in top quarter, 90% in top half
Early decision deadline: N/A, notification date: N/A
Early action deadline: N/A, notification date: N/A
Application deadline (fall): 7/31
Undergraduate student body: 2,077 full time, 362 part time; 29% male, 71% female; 2% American Indian, 7% Asian, 8% black, 28% Hispanic, 1% multiracial, 1% Pacific Islander, 46% white, 1% international; 97% from in state; 45% live on campus; 0% of students in fraternities, 0% in sororities
Most popular majors: 24% Education, 10% Liberal Arts and Sciences, General Studies and Humanities, 8% Psychology, 8% Public Administration and Social Service Professions, 5% Mathematics and Statistics
Expenses: 2016-2017: $29,170; room/board: $8,060
Financial aid: (559) 453-7137; 86% of undergrads determined to have financial need; average aid package $21,383

Golden Gate University

San Francisco CA
(415) 442-7800
U.S. News ranking: Reg. U. (W), unranked
Website: www.ggu.edu/apply
Admissions email: maguilar@ggu.edu
Private; founded 1901
Affiliation: Other
Freshman admissions: least selective; 2016-2017: N/A applied, N/A accepted. Neither SAT nor ACT required. SAT 25/75 percentile: N/A. High school rank: N/A
Early decision deadline: N/A, notification date: N/A
Early action deadline: N/A, notification date: N/A
Application deadline (fall): N/A
Undergraduate student body: 125 full time, 297 part time; 50% male, 50% female; 0% American Indian, 11% Asian, 10% black,

20% Hispanic, 3% multiracial, 3% Pacific Islander, 25% white, 3% international
Most popular majors: 94% Business Administration and Management, General, 2% Accounting, 2% Information Science/Studies, 1% Computer/Information Technology Services Administration and Management, Other
Expenses: 2017-2018: $19,970; room/board: N/A
Financial aid: (415) 442-6632; 44% of undergrads determined to have financial need; average aid package $4,716

Harvey Mudd College

Claremont CA
(909) 621-8011
U.S. News ranking: Nat. Lib. Arts, No. 12
Website: www.hmc.edu
Admissions email: admission@hmc.edu
Private; founded 1955
Freshman admissions: most selective; 2016-2017: 4,180 applied, 538 accepted. Either SAT or ACT required. SAT 25/75 percentile: 1420-1580. High school rank: 88% in top tenth, 95% in top quarter, 98% in top half
Early decision deadline: 11/15, notification date: 12/15
Early action deadline: N/A, notification date: N/A
Application deadline (fall): 1/5
Undergraduate student body: 829 full time, 0 part time; 54% male, 46% female; 0% American Indian, 19% Asian, 3% black, 16% Hispanic, 10% multiracial, 0% Pacific Islander, 36% white, 11% international; 44% from in state; N/A live on campus; 0% of students in fraternities, 0% in sororities
Most popular majors: 30% Engineering, 22% Computer and Information Sciences and Support Services, 16% Physical Sciences, 12% Multi/Interdisciplinary Studies, 10% Mathematics and Statistics
Expenses: 2017-2018: $54,886; room/board: $17,592
Financial aid: (909) 621-8055; 51% of undergrads determined to have financial need; average aid package $42,799

Holy Names University

Oakland CA
(510) 436-1351
U.S. News ranking: Reg. U. (W), No. 55
Website: www.hnu.edu
Admissions email: admissions@hnu.edu
Private; founded 1868
Affiliation: Roman Catholic
Freshman admissions: less selective; 2016-2017: 972 applied, 472 accepted. Either SAT or ACT required. SAT 25/75 percentile: 820-990. High school rank: 11% in top tenth, 40% in top quarter, 75% in top half
Early decision deadline: N/A, notification date: N/A

Early action deadline: N/A, notification date: N/A
Application deadline (fall): rolling
Undergraduate student body: 455 full time, 71 part time; 35% male, 65% female; 0% American Indian, 10% Asian, 21% black, 42% Hispanic, 2% multiracial, 3% Pacific Islander, 17% white, 4% international; 93% from in state; 51% live on campus; N/A of students in fraternities, N/A in sororities
Most popular majors: 22% Health Professions and Related Programs, 17% Business, Management, Marketing, and Related Support Services, 17% Psychology, 14% Parks, Recreation, Leisure, and Fitness Studies, 9% Liberal Arts and Sciences, General Studies and Humanities
Expenses: 2017-2018: $38,188; room/board: $12,808
Financial aid: (510) 436-1348; 91% of undergrads determined to have financial need; average aid package $28,373

Hope International University

Fullerton CA
(888) 352-4673
U.S. News ranking: Reg. U. (W), second tier
Website: www.hiu.edu
Admissions email: admissions@hiu.edu
Private; founded 1928
Affiliation: Christian Churches and Churches of Christ
Freshman admissions: less selective; 2016-2017: 1,006 applied, 323 accepted. Either SAT or ACT required. SAT 25/75 percentile: 820-1040. High school rank: 6% in top tenth, 30% in top quarter, 70% in top half
Early decision deadline: N/A, notification date: N/A
Early action deadline: N/A, notification date: N/A
Application deadline (fall): rolling
Undergraduate student body: 627 full time, 226 part time; 44% male, 56% female; 1% American Indian, 3% Asian, 8% black, 25% Hispanic, 13% multiracial, 0% Pacific Islander, 44% white, 1% international; 92% from in state; 41% live on campus; N/A of students in fraternities, N/A in sororities
Most popular majors: 26% Business Administration and Management, General, 23% Theological and Ministerial Studies, Other, 16% Human Development and Family Studies, General, 10% English Language and Literature, General, 9% Psychology, General
Expenses: 2017-2018: $31,800; room/board: $9,930
Financial aid: (714) 879-3901; 85% of undergrads determined to have financial need; average aid package $20,777

Humboldt State University

Arcata CA
(707) 826-4402
U.S. News ranking: Reg. U. (W),
No. 47
Website: www.humboldt.edu
Admissions email:
hsuinfo@humboldt.edu
Public; founded 1913
Freshman admissions: selective;
2016-2017: 12,967 applied,
9,895 accepted. Neither SAT
nor ACT required. SAT 25/75
percentile: 890-1140. High school
rank: 15% in top tenth, 50% in
top quarter, 80% in top half
Early decision deadline: N/A,
notification date: N/A
Early action deadline: N/A,
notification date: N/A
Application deadline (fall): 11/30
Undergraduate student body: 7,492
full time, 476 part time; 44%
male, 56% female; 1% American
Indian, 3% Asian, 3% black,
35% Hispanic, 7% multiracial,
0% Pacific Islander, 43% white,
1% international; 94% from in
state; 25% live on campus; 2%
of students in fraternities, 2% in
sororities
Most popular majors: 8% Biology/
Biological Sciences, General,
8% Business Administration and
Management, General, 7% Liberal
Arts and Sciences/Liberal Studies,
7% Psychology, General, 5%
Health and Physical Education/
Fitness, General
Expenses: 2017-2018: $7,492 in
state, $19,372 out of state; room/
board $13,056
Financial aid: (707) 826-4321;
78% of undergrads determined to
have financial need; average aid
package $13,650

Humphreys College[1]

Stockton CA
(209) 478-0800
U.S. News ranking: Reg. Coll. (W),
unranked
Website: www.humphreys.edu
Admissions email: ugadmission@
humphreys.edu
Private
Application deadline (fall): N/A
Undergraduate student body: N/A
full time, N/A part time
Expenses: 2016-2017: $14,004;
room/board: N/A
Financial aid: N/A

John F. Kennedy University[1]

Pleasant Hill CA
U.S. News ranking: Reg. U. (W),
unranked
Website: www.jfku.edu
Admissions email: proginfo@
jfku.edu
Private; founded 1964
Application deadline (fall): N/A
Undergraduate student body: N/A
full time, N/A part time
Expenses: 2016-2017: $23,400;
room/board: N/A
Financial aid: N/A

John Paul the Great Catholic University

Escondido CA
(858) 653-6740
U.S. News ranking: Reg. Coll. (W),
unranked
Website: jpcatholic.edu/
For-profit; founded 2006
Affiliation: Roman Catholic
Freshman admissions: selective;
2016-2017: 204 applied, 200
accepted. Either SAT or ACT
required. SAT 25/75 percentile:
910-1200. High school rank:
13% in top tenth, 29% in top
quarter, 81% in top half
Early decision deadline: N/A,
notification date: N/A
Early action deadline: N/A,
notification date: N/A
Application deadline (fall): rolling
Undergraduate student body: 210
full time, 17 part time; 53%
male, 47% female; 0% American
Indian, 4% Asian, 0% black,
23% Hispanic, 4% multiracial,
0% Pacific Islander, 54% white,
2% international; 47% from in
state; 79% live on campus; N/A
of students in fraternities, N/A in
sororities
Most popular majors: 82%
Visual and Performing Arts,
18% Business, Management,
Marketing, and Related Support
Services
Expenses: 2017-2018: $24,900;
room/board: $8,100
Financial aid: (858) 653-6740

La Sierra University[1]

Riverside CA
(951) 785-2176
U.S. News ranking: Reg. U. (W),
No. 44
Website: www.lasierra.edu
Admissions email: admissions@
lasierra.edu
Private; founded 1922
Application deadline (fall): 7/1
Undergraduate student body: N/A
full time, N/A part time
Expenses: 2016-2017: $31,590;
room/board: $8,100
Financial aid: (951) 785-2175

Laguna College of Art and Design

Laguna Beach CA
(949) 376-6000
U.S. News ranking: Arts, unranked
Website: www.lcad.edu/
Admissions email:
admissions@lcad.edu
Private; founded 1961
Freshman admissions: least
selective; 2016-2017: 472
applied, 186 accepted. Neither
SAT nor ACT required. SAT 25/75
percentile: N/A. High school
rank: N/A
Early decision deadline: N/A,
notification date: N/A
Early action deadline: 2/1,
notification date: N/A
Application deadline (fall): 8/1
Undergraduate student body: 496
full time, 71 part time; 37%
male, 63% female; 1% American
Indian, 21% Asian, 1% black,
19% Hispanic, 2% multiracial,
1% Pacific Islander, 54% white,
1% international

Most popular majors: 35%
Animation, Interactive Technology,
Video Graphics and Special
Effects, 25% Game and
Interactive Media Design, 20%
Illustration, 15% Graphic Design,
5% Fine/Studio Arts, General
Expenses: 2017-2018: $29,800;
room/board: $9,700
Financial aid: (949) 376-6000;
95% of undergrads determined to
have financial need; average aid
package $14,714

Loyola Marymount University

Los Angeles CA
(310) 338-2750
U.S. News ranking: Reg. U. (W),
No. 3
Website: www.lmu.edu
Admissions email:
admission@lmu.edu
Private; founded 1911
Affiliation: Roman Catholic
Freshman admissions: more
selective; 2016-2017: 13,506
applied, 7,276 accepted. Either
SAT or ACT required. SAT 25/75
percentile: 1120-1330. High
school rank: 39% in top tenth,
73% in top quarter, 98% in
top half
Early decision deadline: 11/1,
notification date: 12/1
Early action deadline: 11/1,
notification date: 12/20
Application deadline (fall): 1/15
Undergraduate student body: 6,044
full time, 217 part time; 44%
male, 56% female; 0% American
Indian, 11% Asian, 6% black,
21% Hispanic, 8% multiracial,
0% Pacific Islander, 44% white,
10% international; 74% from in
state; 52% live on campus; 17%
of students in fraternities, 33%
in sororities
Most popular majors: 28%
Business, Management,
Marketing, and Related Support
Services, 13% Social Sciences,
13% Visual and Performing
Arts, 8% Psychology, 7%
Communication, Journalism, and
Related Programs
Expenses: 2017-2018: $46,136;
room/board: $14,690
Financial aid: (310) 338-2753;
54% of undergrads determined to
have financial need; average aid
package $28,497

Marymount California University

Rancho Palos Verdes CA
(310) 303-7311
U.S. News ranking: Reg. Coll. (W),
No. 15
Website:
www.marymountcalifornia.edu
Admissions email: admissions@
marymountcalifornia.edu
Private; founded 1933
Affiliation: Roman Catholic
Freshman admissions: less
selective; 2016-2017: 1,755
applied, 1,337 accepted. Neither
SAT nor ACT required. SAT 25/75
percentile: 820-1020. High
school rank: N/A
Early decision deadline: N/A,
notification date: N/A

Early action deadline: N/A,
notification date: N/A
Application deadline (fall): rolling
Undergraduate student body: 882
full time, 60 part time; 50%
male, 50% female; 0% American
Indian, 5% Asian, 8% black,
39% Hispanic, 2% multiracial,
0% Pacific Islander, 20% white,
18% international; 90% from in
state; 32% live on campus; 0%
of students in fraternities, 0% in
sororities
Most popular majors: 37%
Business Administration and
Management, General, 30%
Liberal Arts and Sciences/Liberal
Studies, 24% Psychology, General,
9% Digital Communication and
Media/Multimedia
Expenses: 2016-2017: $35,309;
room/board: $14,262
Financial aid: (310) 303-7217

The Master's University and Seminary

Santa Clarita CA
(800) 568-6248
U.S. News ranking: Reg. U. (W),
No. 37
Website: www.masters.edu
Admissions email: admissions@
masters.edu
Private; founded 1927
Affiliation: Other
Freshman admissions: selective;
2016-2017: 446 applied, 371
accepted. Either SAT or ACT
required. SAT 25/75 percentile:
950-1210. High school rank:
26% in top tenth, 49% in top
quarter, 74% in top half
Early decision deadline: N/A,
notification date: N/A
Early action deadline: 11/15,
notification date: 12/22
Application deadline (fall): rolling
Undergraduate student body: 952
full time, 438 part time; 53%
male, 47% female; 0% American
Indian, 6% Asian, 3% black,
9% Hispanic, 7% multiracial,
0% Pacific Islander, 66% white,
4% international; 64% from in
state; 82% live on campus; N/A
of students in fraternities, N/A in
sororities
Most popular majors: 22%
Business, Management,
Marketing, and Related Support
Services, 16% Theology and
Religious Vocations, 13%
Communication, Journalism,
and Related Programs, 12%
Liberal Arts and Sciences,
General Studies and Humanities,
8% Biological and Biomedical
Sciences
Expenses: 2017-2018: $33,040;
room/board: $10,550
Financial aid: (661) 362-2290;
82% of undergrads determined to
have financial need; average aid
package $23,183

Menlo College

Atherton CA
(800) 556-3656
U.S. News ranking: Business,
unranked
Website: www.menlo.edu
Admissions email:
admissions@menlo.edu
Private; founded 1927
Freshman admissions: selective;
2016-2017: 2,195 applied, 897

accepted. Neither SAT nor ACT
required. SAT 25/75 percentile:
920-1116. High school rank: N/A
Early decision deadline: N/A,
notification date: N/A
Early action deadline: 11/15,
notification date: 1/15
Application deadline (fall): 4/1
Undergraduate student body: 758
full time, 19 part time; 55%
male, 45% female; 1% American
Indian, 10% Asian, 6% black,
23% Hispanic, 9% multiracial,
2% Pacific Islander, 26% white,
14% international; 81% from in
state; 60% live on campus; N/A
of students in fraternities, N/A in
sororities
Most popular majors: 28%
Marketing/Marketing Management,
General, 18% Accounting, 14%
Finance, General, 8% Psychology,
General
Expenses: 2017-2018: $41,350;
room/board: $13,680
Financial aid: (650) 543-3855;
61% of undergrads determined to
have financial need; average aid
package $31,413

Mills College

Oakland CA
(510) 430-2135
U.S. News ranking: Reg. U. (W),
No. 9
Website: www.mills.edu
Admissions email:
admission@mills.edu
Private; founded 1852
Freshman admissions: selective;
2016-2017: 1,052 applied, 888
accepted. Neither SAT nor ACT
required. SAT 25/75 percentile:
920-1230. High school rank:
25% in top tenth, 64% in top
quarter, 96% in top half
Early decision deadline: N/A,
notification date: N/A
Early action deadline: 11/15,
notification date: 12/1
Application deadline (fall): 1/15
Undergraduate student body: 775
full time, 33 part time; 0% male,
100% female; 0% American
Indian, 9% Asian, 9% black,
27% Hispanic, 8% multiracial,
0% Pacific Islander, 45% white,
1% international; 81% from in
state; 60% live on campus; N/A
of students in fraternities, N/A in
sororities
Most popular majors: 27% Social
Sciences, 15% English Language
and Literature/Letters, 12%
Visual and Performing Arts, 9%
Psychology, 7% Biological and
Biomedical Sciences
Expenses: 2017-2018: $45,907;
room/board: $13,528
Financial aid: (510) 430-2039;
84% of undergrads determined to
have financial need; average aid
package $42,502

Minerva Schools at Keck Graduate Institute[1]

San Francisco CA
U.S. News ranking: Reg. Coll. (W),
unranked
Admissions email: admissions@
minerva.kgi.edu
Private
Application deadline (fall): N/A

Undergraduate student body: N/A full time, N/A part time
Expenses: N/A
Financial aid: N/A

Mount Saint Mary's University
Los Angeles CA
(310) 954-4250
U.S. News ranking: Reg. U. (W), No. 29
Website: www.msmu.edu
Admissions email: admissions@msmu.edu
Private; founded 1925
Affiliation: Roman Catholic
Freshman admissions: less selective; 2016-2017: 2,486 applied, 2,136 accepted. Neither SAT nor ACT required. SAT 25/75 percentile: 820-1020. High school rank: 11% in top tenth, 35% in top quarter, 76% in top half
Early decision deadline: N/A, notification date: N/A
Early action deadline: 12/1, notification date: 1/30
Application deadline (fall): 8/1
Undergraduate student body: 2,184 full time, 647 part time; 7% male, 93% female; 0% American Indian, 15% Asian, 6% black, 63% Hispanic, 2% multiracial, 1% Pacific Islander, 9% white, 1% international; 98% from in state; 21% live on campus; N/A of students in fraternities, N/A in sororities
Most popular majors: 32% Health Professions and Related Programs, 10% Social Sciences, 6% Business, Management, Marketing, and Related Support Services, 4% Family and Consumer Sciences/Human Sciences, 4% Public Administration and Social Service Professions
Expenses: 2016-2017: $37,722; room/board: $11,451
Financial aid: (310) 954-4190

National University[1]
La Jolla CA
(800) 628-8648
U.S. News ranking: Reg. U. (W), unranked
Website: www.nu.edu
Admissions email: advisor@nu.edu
Private; founded 1971
Application deadline (fall): rolling
Undergraduate student body: N/A full time, N/A part time
Expenses: 2016-2017: $13,016; room/board: N/A
Financial aid: (858) 642-8513

NewSchool of Architecture and Design
San Diego CA
(619) 684-8828
U.S. News ranking: Arts, unranked
Website: newschoolarch.edu/
Admissions email: fguidali@newschoolarch.edu
For-profit; founded 1980
Freshman admissions: least selective; 2016-2017: 109 applied, 108 accepted. Neither SAT nor ACT required. SAT 25/75 percentile: N/A. High school rank: N/A
Early decision deadline: N/A, notification date: N/A

Early action deadline: N/A, notification date: N/A
Application deadline (fall): rolling
Undergraduate student body: 391 full time, 23 part time; 67% male, 33% female; 0% American Indian, 8% Asian, 1% black, 34% Hispanic, 3% multiracial, 0% Pacific Islander, 23% white, 27% international
Most popular majors: Information not available
Expenses: 2016-2017: $26,463; room/board: N/A
Financial aid: (619) 684-8803

Notre Dame de Namur University
Belmont CA
(650) 508-3600
U.S. News ranking: Reg. U. (W), No. 41
Website: www.ndnu.edu
Admissions email: admissions@ndnu.edu
Private; founded 1851
Freshman admissions: less selective; 2016-2017: 1,234 applied, 1,193 accepted. Either SAT or ACT required. SAT 25/75 percentile: 800-1018. High school rank: 6% in top tenth, 25% in top quarter, 58% in top half
Early decision deadline: N/A, notification date: N/A
Early action deadline: 12/1, notification date: 12/15
Application deadline (fall): rolling
Undergraduate student body: 740 full time, 242 part time; 34% male, 66% female; 1% American Indian, 13% Asian, 7% black, 40% Hispanic, 5% multiracial, 3% Pacific Islander, 23% white, 5% international
Most popular majors: 23% Business, Management, Marketing, and Related Support Services, 15% Psychology, 11% Public Administration and Social Service Professions, 8% Biological and Biomedical Sciences, 8% Communication, Journalism, and Related Programs
Expenses: 2017-2018: $34,196; room/board: $13,656
Financial aid: (650) 508-3741; 79% of undergrads determined to have financial need; average aid package $25,084

Occidental College
Los Angeles CA
(323) 259-2700
U.S. News ranking: Nat. Lib. Arts, No. 44
Website: www.oxy.edu
Admissions email: admission@oxy.edu
Private; founded 1887
Freshman admissions: more selective; 2016-2017: 6,409 applied, 2,936 accepted. Either SAT or ACT required. SAT 25/75 percentile: 1200-1420. High school rank: 52% in top tenth, 83% in top quarter, 98% in top half
Early decision deadline: 11/15, notification date: 12/15
Early action deadline: N/A, notification date: N/A
Application deadline (fall): 1/15

Undergraduate student body: 2,045 full time, 17 part time; 43% male, 57% female; 0% American Indian, 14% Asian, 5% black, 15% Hispanic, 8% multiracial, 0% Pacific Islander, 50% white, 6% international; 51% from in state; 79% live on campus; N/A of students in fraternities, N/A in sororities
Most popular majors: 12% Economics, General, 8% Biology/Biological Sciences, General, 8% International Relations and Affairs, 6% Psychology, General, 6% Sociology
Expenses: 2017-2018: $52,838; room/board: $14,968
Financial aid: (323) 259-2548; 56% of undergrads determined to have financial need; average aid package $47,127

Otis College of Art and Design[1]
Los Angeles CA
U.S. News ranking: Arts, unranked
Website: www.otis.edu
Admissions email: admissions@otis.edu
Private; founded 1918
Application deadline (fall): N/A
Undergraduate student body: N/A full time, N/A part time
Expenses: 2016-2017: $44,020; room/board: $14,258
Financial aid: (310) 665-6898

Pacific Union College
Angwin CA
(707) 965-6336
U.S. News ranking: Nat. Lib. Arts, second tier
Website: www.puc.edu
Admissions email: enroll@puc.edu
Private; founded 1882
Affiliation: Seventh Day Adventist
Freshman admissions: selective; 2016-2017: 2,157 applied, 1,004 accepted. Either SAT or ACT required. SAT 25/75 percentile: 860-1110. High school rank: N/A
Early decision deadline: 12/1, notification date: 8/1
Early action deadline: N/A, notification date: N/A
Application deadline (fall): N/A
Undergraduate student body: 1,286 full time, 149 part time; 39% male, 61% female; 0% American Indian, 18% Asian, 9% black, 24% Hispanic, 7% multiracial, 1% Pacific Islander, 23% white, 3% international; 83% from in state; 74% live on campus; 0% of students in fraternities, 0% in sororities
Most popular majors: 23% Registered Nursing/Registered Nurse, 10% Business/Commerce, General, 8% Health and Physical Education/Fitness, General, 7% Biology/Biological Sciences, General, 6% Health Communication
Expenses: 2017-2018: $29,469; room/board: $8,148
Financial aid: (707) 965-7200; 81% of undergrads determined to have financial need; average aid package $25,507

Pepperdine University
Malibu CA
(310) 506-4392
U.S. News ranking: Nat. U., No. 46
Website: www.pepperdine.edu
Admissions email: admission-seaver@pepperdine.edu
Private; founded 1937
Affiliation: Churches of Christ
Freshman admissions: more selective; 2016-2017: 11,111 applied, 4,097 accepted. Either SAT or ACT required. SAT 25/75 percentile: 1110-1330. High school rank: 49% in top tenth, 90% in top quarter, 98% in top half
Early decision deadline: N/A, notification date: N/A
Early action deadline: N/A, notification date: N/A
Application deadline (fall): 1/5
Undergraduate student body: 3,222 full time, 320 part time; 41% male, 59% female; 0% American Indian, 11% Asian, 5% black, 14% Hispanic, 5% multiracial, 0% Pacific Islander, 48% white, 11% international; 54% from in state; 56% live on campus; 24% of students in fraternities, 32% in sororities
Most popular majors: 27% Business, Management, Marketing, and Related Support Services, 19% Communication, Journalism, and Related Programs, 11% Social Sciences, 8% Psychology, 7% Multi/Interdisciplinary Studies
Expenses: 2017-2018: $51,992; room/board: $14,870
Financial aid: (310) 506-4301; 51% of undergrads determined to have financial need; average aid package $40,113

Pitzer College
Claremont CA
(909) 621-8129
U.S. News ranking: Nat. Lib. Arts, No. 33
Website: www.pitzer.edu
Admissions email: admission@pitzer.edu
Private; founded 1963
Freshman admissions: more selective; 2016-2017: 4,142 applied, 569 accepted. Neither SAT nor ACT required. SAT 25/75 percentile: 1300-1450. High school rank: 54% in top tenth, 80% in top quarter, 98% in top half
Early decision deadline: 11/15, notification date: 12/18
Early action deadline: N/A, notification date: N/A
Application deadline (fall): 1/1
Undergraduate student body: 1,056 full time, 33 part time; 44% male, 56% female; 0% American Indian, 9% Asian, 5% black, 15% Hispanic, 10% multiracial, 0% Pacific Islander, 46% white, 9% international; 48% from in state; 73% live on campus; 0% of students in fraternities, 0% in sororities
Most popular majors: 23% Social Sciences, 12% Multi/Interdisciplinary Studies, 10% Natural Resources and Conservation, 9% Biological and Biomedical Sciences, 8% Psychology

Expenses: 2016-2017: $50,430; room/board: $15,762
Financial aid: (909) 621-8208; 39% of undergrads determined to have financial need; average aid package $45,338

Point Loma Nazarene University
San Diego CA
(619) 849-2273
U.S. News ranking: Reg. U. (W), No. 17
Website: www.pointloma.edu
Admissions email: admissions@pointloma.edu
Private; founded 1902
Affiliation: Church of the Nazarene
Freshman admissions: more selective; 2016-2017: 3,162 applied, 2,195 accepted. Either SAT or ACT required. SAT 25/75 percentile: 1030-1240. High school rank: 29% in top tenth, 66% in top quarter, 91% in top half
Early decision deadline: N/A, notification date: N/A
Early action deadline: 11/15, notification date: 12/21
Application deadline (fall): 2/15
Undergraduate student body: 2,592 full time, 461 part time; 35% male, 65% female; 0% American Indian, 6% Asian, 2% black, 24% Hispanic, 7% multiracial, 1% Pacific Islander, 55% white, 1% international; 83% from in state; 56% live on campus; N/A of students in fraternities, N/A in sororities
Most popular majors: 25% Business, Management, Marketing, and Related Support Services, 23% Health Professions and Related Programs, 9% Psychology, 8% Biological and Biomedical Sciences, 6% Visual and Performing Arts
Expenses: 2017-2018: $34,600; room/board: $10,150
Financial aid: (619) 849-2495; 66% of undergrads determined to have financial need; average aid package $22,624

Pomona College
Claremont CA
(909) 621-8134
U.S. News ranking: Nat. Lib. Arts, No. 6
Website: www.pomona.edu
Admissions email: admissions@pomona.edu
Private; founded 1887
Freshman admissions: most selective; 2016-2017: 8,102 applied, 765 accepted. Either SAT or ACT required. SAT 25/75 percentile: 1340-1540. High school rank: 92% in top tenth, 99% in top quarter, 100% in top half
Early decision deadline: 11/1, notification date: 12/15
Early action deadline: N/A, notification date: N/A
Application deadline (fall): 1/1
Undergraduate student body: 1,651 full time, 9 part time; 49% male, 51% female; 0% American Indian, 14% Asian, 8% black, 15% Hispanic, 7% multiracial,

0% Pacific Islander, 38% white, 11% international; 30% from in state; 98% live on campus; 5% of students in fraternities, 0% in sororities
Most popular majors: 21% Social Sciences, 16% Biological and Biomedical Sciences, 10% Mathematics and Statistics, 10% Physical Sciences, 8% Computer and Information Sciences and Support Services
Expenses: 2017-2018: $51,075; room/board: $16,150
Financial aid: (909) 621-8205; 56% of undergrads determined to have financial need; average aid package $51,134

Providence Christian College[1]
Pasadena CA
(866) 323-0233
U.S. News ranking: Nat. Lib. Arts, second tier
Website: www.providencecc.net/
Private; founded 2003
Application deadline (fall): rolling
Undergraduate student body: N/A full time, N/A part time
Expenses: 2016-2017: $28,164; room/board: $8,408
Financial aid: N/A

San Diego Christian College
Santee CA
(800) 676-2242
U.S. News ranking: Reg. Coll. (W), No. 11
Website: www.sdcc.edu/
Admissions email: admissions@sdcc.edu
Private; founded 1970
Affiliation: Undenominational
Freshman admissions: selective; 2016-2017: 379 applied, 202 accepted. Neither SAT nor ACT required. SAT 25/75 percentile: 860-1050. High school rank: 9% in top tenth, 25% in top quarter, 50% in top half
Early decision deadline: N/A, notification date: N/A
Early action deadline: 12/1, notification date: 1/15
Application deadline (fall): rolling
Undergraduate student body: 518 full time, 177 part time; 47% male, 53% female; 1% American Indian, 2% Asian, 10% black, 26% Hispanic, 6% multiracial, 2% Pacific Islander, 45% white, 1% international; 79% from in state; 20% live on campus; 0% of students in fraternities, 0% in sororities
Most popular majors: 20% Business Administration and Management, General, 19% Human Development and Family Studies, General, 14% Theological and Ministerial Studies, Other, 10% Psychology, General, 7% Kinesiology and Exercise Science
Expenses: 2016-2017: $29,550; room/board: $10,974
Financial aid: N/A

San Diego State University
San Diego CA
(619) 594-6336
U.S. News ranking: Nat. U., No. 140
Website: www.sdsu.edu

Admissions email: admissions@sdsu.edu
Public; founded 1897
Freshman admissions: more selective; 2016-2017: 60,691 applied, 20,943 accepted. Either SAT or ACT required. SAT 25/75 percentile: 1000-1220. High school rank: 31% in top tenth, 72% in top quarter, 96% in top half
Early decision deadline: N/A, notification date: N/A
Early action deadline: N/A, notification date: N/A
Application deadline (fall): 11/30
Undergraduate student body: 26,788 full time, 3,065 part time; 46% male, 54% female; 0% American Indian, 14% Asian, 4% black, 31% Hispanic, 7% multiracial, 0% Pacific Islander, 33% white, 7% international; 91% from in state; 15% live on campus; 8% of students in fraternities, 9% in sororities
Most popular majors: 19% Business, Management, Marketing, and Related Support Services, 11% Social Sciences, 9% Health Professions and Related Programs, 8% Psychology, 7% Engineering
Expenses: 2017-2018: $7,460 in state, $19,340 out of state; room/board: $15,966
Financial aid: (619) 594-6323; 55% of undergrads determined to have financial need; average aid package $11,400

San Francisco Art Institute
San Francisco CA
(800) 345-7324
U.S. News ranking: Arts, unranked
Website: www.sfai.edu
Admissions email: admissions@sfai.edu
Private; founded 1871
Freshman admissions: selective; 2016-2017: 352 applied, 326 accepted. Neither SAT nor ACT required. SAT 25/75 percentile: 960-1250. High school rank: N/A
Early decision deadline: N/A, notification date: N/A
Early action deadline: 11/15, notification date: 12/12
Application deadline (fall): rolling
Undergraduate student body: 312 full time, 26 part time; 38% male, 62% female; 1% American Indian, 5% Asian, 4% black, 16% Hispanic, 9% multiracial, 0% Pacific Islander, 43% white, 20% international; 59% from in state; 34% live on campus; 0% of students in fraternities, 0% in sororities
Most popular majors: 38% Painting, 22% Photography, 11% Printmaking, 8% Sculpture, 8% Visual and Performing Arts, Other
Expenses: 2017-2018: $44,778; room/board: $11,500
Financial aid: (415) 749-4520; 55% of undergrads determined to have financial need; average aid package $15,441

San Francisco Conservatory of Music
San Francisco CA
(800) 899-7326
U.S. News ranking: Arts, unranked
Website: www.sfcm.edu
Admissions email: admit@sfcm.edu
Private; founded 1917
Freshman admissions: least selective; 2016-2017: 424 applied, 177 accepted. Neither SAT nor ACT required. SAT 25/75 percentile: N/A. High school rank: N/A
Early decision deadline: N/A, notification date: N/A
Early action deadline: N/A, notification date: N/A
Application deadline (fall): 12/1
Undergraduate student body: 186 full time, 2 part time; 55% male, 45% female; 1% American Indian, 7% Asian, 4% black, 6% Hispanic, 11% multiracial, 0% Pacific Islander, 32% white, 34% international; 52% from in state; 61% live on campus; 0% of students in fraternities, 0% in sororities
Most popular majors: 36% Voice and Opera, 21% Stringed Instruments, 18% Keyboard Instruments, 8% Musicology and Ethnomusicology, 8% Percussion Instruments
Expenses: 2017-2018: $44,810; room/board: $16,060
Financial aid: (415) 503-6214; 69% of undergrads determined to have financial need; average aid package $35,305

San Francisco State University
San Francisco CA
(415) 338-6486
U.S. News ranking: Nat. U., second tier
Website: www.sfsu.edu
Admissions email: ugadmit@sfsu.edu
Public; founded 1899
Freshman admissions: less selective; 2016-2017: 36,223 applied, 24,704 accepted. Either SAT or ACT required. SAT 25/75 percentile: 860-1090. High school rank: N/A
Early decision deadline: N/A, notification date: N/A
Early action deadline: N/A, notification date: N/A
Application deadline (fall): 11/30
Undergraduate student body: 21,515 full time, 4,430 part time; 44% male, 56% female; 0% American Indian, 28% Asian, 5% black, 31% Hispanic, 6% multiracial, 0% Pacific Islander, 19% white, 6% international; 99% from in state; 15% live on campus; N/A of students in fraternities, N/A in sororities
Most popular majors: 26% Business, Management, Marketing, and Related Support Services, 9% Social Sciences, 8% Visual and Performing Arts, 7% Biological and Biomedical Sciences, 7% Communication, Journalism, and Related Programs
Expenses: 2017-2018: $7,254 in state, $19,134 out of state; room/board: $13,248

Financial aid: (415) 338-7000; 70% of undergrads determined to have financial need; average aid package $15,082

San Jose State University
San Jose CA
(408) 283-7500
U.S. News ranking: Reg. U. (W), No. 35
Website: www.sjsu.edu/Admissions/
Admissions email: admissions@sjsu.edu
Public; founded 1857
Freshman admissions: selective; 2016-2017: 31,555 applied, 16,862 accepted. Either SAT or ACT required. SAT 25/75 percentile: 920-1150. High school rank: N/A
Early decision deadline: N/A, notification date: N/A
Early action deadline: N/A, notification date: N/A
Application deadline (fall): 11/30
Undergraduate student body: 21,613 full time, 4,819 part time; 52% male, 48% female; 0% American Indian, 36% Asian, 3% black, 26% Hispanic, 5% multiracial, 0% Pacific Islander, 18% white, 7% international; 99% from in state; 14% live on campus; N/A of students in fraternities, N/A in sororities
Most popular majors: 23% Business, Management, Marketing, and Related Support Services, 12% Engineering, 8% Health Professions and Related Programs, 7% Visual and Performing Arts, 6% Psychology
Expenses: 2017-2018: $9,700 in state, $13,859 out of state; room/board: $15,594
Financial aid: (408) 924-6086; 63% of undergrads determined to have financial need; average aid package $18,142

Santa Clara University
Santa Clara CA
(408) 554-4700
U.S. News ranking: Reg. U. (W), No. 2
Website: www.scu.edu
Admissions email: Admission@scu.edu
Private; founded 1851
Affiliation: Roman Catholic
Freshman admissions: more selective; 2016-2017: 15,834 applied, 7,648 accepted. Either SAT or ACT required. ACT 25/75 percentile: 28-32. High school rank: 51% in top tenth, 85% in top quarter, 98% in top half
Early decision deadline: 11/1, notification date: 12/31
Early action deadline: 11/1, notification date: 12/31
Application deadline (fall): 1/7
Undergraduate student body: 5,353 full time, 85 part time; 50% male, 50% female; 0% American Indian, 17% Asian, 3% black, 17% Hispanic, 7% multiracial, 0% Pacific Islander, 49% white, 4% international; 72% from in state; 55% live on campus; 0% of students in fraternities, 0% in sororities

Most popular majors: 23% Business, Management, Marketing, and Related Support Services, 16% Social Sciences, 15% Engineering, 9% Communication, Journalism, and Related Programs, 7% Biological and Biomedical Sciences
Expenses: 2017-2018: $49,858; room/board: $14,490
Financial aid: (408) 551-1000; 45% of undergrads determined to have financial need; average aid package $34,298

Scripps College
Claremont CA
(909) 621-8149
U.S. News ranking: Nat. Lib. Arts, No. 26
Website: www.scrippscollege.edu/
Admissions email: admission@scrippscollege.edu
Private; founded 1926
Freshman admissions: more selective; 2016-2017: 3,032 applied, 903 accepted. Either SAT or ACT required. SAT 25/75 percentile: 1290-1440. High school rank: 67% in top tenth, 90% in top quarter, 100% in top half
Early decision deadline: 11/15, notification date: 12/15
Early action deadline: N/A, notification date: N/A
Application deadline (fall): 1/1
Undergraduate student body: 1,030 full time, 9 part time; 0% male, 100% female; 0% American Indian, 15% Asian, 4% black, 11% Hispanic, 6% multiracial, 0% Pacific Islander, 52% white, 5% international; 47% from in state; 100% live on campus; 0% of students in fraternities, 0% in sororities
Most popular majors: 20% Social Sciences, 14% Biological and Biomedical Sciences, 13% Visual and Performing Arts, 10% Psychology, 8% Area, Ethnic, Cultural, Gender, and Group Studies
Expenses: 2017-2018: $52,966; room/board: $16,294
Financial aid: (909) 621-8275; 36% of undergrads determined to have financial need; average aid package $43,167

Simpson University
Redding CA
(530) 226-4606
U.S. News ranking: Reg. U. (W), No. 81
Website: www.simpsonu.edu
Admissions email: admissions@simpsonu.edu
Private; founded 1921
Affiliation: Christ and Missionary Alliance Church
Freshman admissions: selective; 2016-2017: 627 applied, 327 accepted. Either SAT or ACT required. SAT 25/75 percentile: 860-1105. High school rank: 19% in top tenth, 51% in top quarter, 78% in top half
Early decision deadline: N/A, notification date: N/A
Early action deadline: N/A, notification date: N/A
Application deadline (fall): 8/1
Undergraduate student body: 741 full time, 49 part time; 34% male, 66% female; 3% American Indian, 4% Asian, 4% black,

16% Hispanic, 3% multiracial, 1% Pacific Islander, 59% white, 1% international; 88% from in state; 41% live on campus; 0% of students in fraternities, 0% in sororities
Most popular majors: 22% Psychology, General, 13% Liberal Arts and Sciences/Liberal Studies, 11% Registered Nursing/ Registered Nurse, 7% Business Administration and Management, General, 7% Organizational Behavior Studies
Expenses: 2017-2018: $27,700; room/board: $8,350
Financial aid: (530) 226-4621; 85% of undergrads determined to have financial need; average aid package $17,174

Soka University of America
Aliso Viejo CA
(888) 600-7652
U.S. News ranking: Nat. Lib. Arts, No. 39
Website: www.soka.edu
Admissions email: admission@soka.edu
Private; founded 1987
Freshman admissions: more selective; 2016-2017: 500 applied, 192 accepted. Either SAT or ACT required. SAT 25/75 percentile: 1070-1370. High school rank: 22% in top tenth, 73% in top quarter, 100% in top half
Early decision deadline: N/A, notification date: N/A
Early action deadline: 11/1, notification date: 12/1
Application deadline (fall): 1/15
Undergraduate student body: 417 full time, 2 part time; 38% male, 62% female; 0% American Indian, 15% Asian, 4% black, 10% Hispanic, 5% multiracial, 0% Pacific Islander, 20% white, 43% international; 68% from in state; 99% live on campus; 0% of students in fraternities, 0% in sororities
Most popular majors: 100% Liberal Arts and Sciences/Liberal Studies
Expenses: 2017-2018: $31,776; room/board: $12,166
Financial aid: (949) 480-4000; 87% of undergrads determined to have financial need; average aid package $37,302

Sonoma State University
Rohnert Park CA
(707) 664-2778
U.S. News ranking: Reg. U. (W), No. 57
Website: www.sonoma.edu
Admissions email: student.outreach@sonoma.edu
Public; founded 1960
Freshman admissions: selective; 2016-2017: 16,487 applied, 12,575 accepted. Either SAT or ACT required. SAT 25/75 percentile: 880-1080. High school rank: N/A
Early decision deadline: N/A, notification date: N/A
Early action deadline: N/A, notification date: N/A
Application deadline (fall): 11/30
Undergraduate student body: 7,795 full time, 811 part time; 37% male, 63% female; 0% American

Indian, 5% Asian, 2% black, 31% Hispanic, 7% multiracial, 0% Pacific Islander, 46% white, 2% international; N/A from in state; 23% live on campus; N/A of students in fraternities, N/A in sororities
Most popular majors: 18% Business Administration and Management, General, 13% Sociology, 10% Psychology, General, 8% Liberal Arts and Sciences/Liberal Studies, 5% Multi-/Interdisciplinary Studies, Other
Expenses: 2017-2018: $7,724 in state, $19,604 out of state; room/board: $13,554
Financial aid: (707) 664-2389; 61% of undergrads determined to have financial need; average aid package $10,085

Southern California Institute of Architecture[1]
Los Angeles CA
U.S. News ranking: Arts, unranked
Website: www.sciarc.edu
Admissions email: admissions@sciarc.edu
Private
Application deadline (fall): N/A
Undergraduate student body: N/A full time, N/A part time
Expenses: 2016-2017: $42,900; room/board: N/A
Financial aid: N/A

St. Mary's College of California
Moraga CA
(925) 631-4224
U.S. News ranking: Reg. U. (W), No. 9
Website: www.stmarys-ca.edu
Admissions email: smcadmit@stmarys-ca.edu
Private; founded 1863
Freshman admissions: selective; 2016-2017: 4,711 applied, 3,787 accepted. Either SAT or ACT required. SAT 25/75 percentile: 950-1160. High school rank: N/A
Early decision deadline: N/A, notification date: N/A
Early action deadline: 11/15, notification date: 1/15
Application deadline (fall): 2/1
Undergraduate student body: 2,597 full time, 205 part time; 40% male, 60% female; 1% American Indian, 14% Asian, 6% black, 25% Hispanic, 0% multiracial, 2% Pacific Islander, 46% white, 2% international; 89% from in state; 59% live on campus; 0% of students in fraternities, 0% in sororities
Most popular majors: 27% Business, Management, Marketing, and Related Support Services, 12% Psychology, 10% Social Sciences, 9% Communication, Journalism, and Related Programs, 9% Liberal Arts and Sciences, General Studies and Humanities
Expenses: 2017-2018: $45,686; room/board: $15,370
Financial aid: (925) 631-4370; 68% of undergrads determined to have financial need; average aid package $31,609

Stanford University
Stanford CA
(650) 723-2091
U.S. News ranking: Nat. U., No. 5
Website: www.stanford.edu
Admissions email: admission@stanford.edu
Private; founded 1885
Freshman admissions: most selective; 2016-2017: 43,997 applied, 2,118 accepted. Either SAT or ACT required. SAT 25/75 percentile: 1380-1580. High school rank: 95% in top tenth, 99% in top quarter, 100% in top half
Early decision deadline: N/A, notification date: N/A
Early action deadline: 11/1, notification date: 12/15
Application deadline (fall): 1/3
Undergraduate student body: 7,034 full time, 0 part time; 51% male, 49% female; 1% American Indian, 21% Asian, 6% black, 16% Hispanic, 10% multiracial, 0% Pacific Islander, 36% white, 9% international; 42% from in state; 92% live on campus; 19% of students in fraternities, 25% in sororities
Most popular majors: 14% Computer and Information Sciences and Support Services, 9% Multi/Interdisciplinary Studies, 6% Biological and Biomedical Sciences, 6% Engineering, 6% Social Sciences
Expenses: 2017-2018: $49,617; room/board: $15,112
Financial aid: (650) 723-3058; 47% of undergrads determined to have financial need; average aid package $51,000

Thomas Aquinas College
Santa Paula CA
(800) 634-9797
U.S. News ranking: Nat. Lib. Arts, No. 58
Website: www.thomasaquinas.edu
Admissions email: admissions@thomasaquinas.edu
Private; founded 1971
Affiliation: Roman Catholic
Freshman admissions: more selective; 2016-2017: 193 applied, 144 accepted. Either SAT or ACT required. SAT 25/75 percentile: 1140-1360. High school rank: 25% in top tenth, 50% in top quarter, 75% in top half
Early decision deadline: N/A, notification date: N/A
Early action deadline: N/A, notification date: N/A
Application deadline (fall): rolling
Undergraduate student body: 389 full time, 0 part time; 51% male, 49% female; 0% American Indian, 2% Asian, 0% black, 15% Hispanic, 7% multiracial, 0% Pacific Islander, 71% white, 3% international; 38% from in state; 99% live on campus; 0% of students in fraternities, 0% in sororities
Most popular majors: 100% Liberal Arts and Sciences, General Studies and Humanities
Expenses: 2017-2018: $24,500; room/board: $7,950
Financial aid: (805) 421-5936; 75% of undergrads determined to have financial need; average aid package $20,738

Trident University International[1]
Cypress CA
U.S. News ranking: Nat. U., unranked
Website: www.trident.edu
Admissions email: N/A
For-profit
Application deadline (fall): N/A
Undergraduate student body: N/A full time, N/A part time
Expenses: 2016-2017: $9,000; room/board: N/A
Financial aid: N/A

United States University[1]
Chula Vista CA
U.S. News ranking: Reg. Coll. (W), unranked
Admissions email: N/A
For-profit
Application deadline (fall): N/A
Undergraduate student body: N/A full time, N/A part time
Expenses: 2016-2017: N/A; room/board: N/A
Financial aid: N/A

University of California–Berkeley
Berkeley CA
(510) 642-3175
U.S. News ranking: Nat. U., No. 21
Website: www.berkeley.edu
Public; founded 1868
Freshman admissions: most selective; 2016-2017: 82,581 applied, 13,507 accepted. Either SAT or ACT required. SAT 25/75 percentile: 1300-1530. High school rank: 98% in top tenth, 100% in top quarter, 100% in top half
Early decision deadline: N/A, notification date: N/A
Early action deadline: N/A, notification date: N/A
Application deadline (fall): 11/30
Undergraduate student body: 28,107 full time, 1,204 part time; 48% male, 52% female; 0% American Indian, 35% Asian, 2% black, 15% Hispanic, 4% multiracial, 0% Pacific Islander, 26% white, 13% international; 86% from in state; 26% live on campus; 10% of students in fraternities, 10% in sororities
Most popular majors: 19% Social Sciences, 12% Engineering, 11% Biological and Biomedical Sciences, 6% Multi/Interdisciplinary Studies, 5% Mathematics and Statistics
Expenses: 2017-2018: $14,098 in state, $42,112 out of state; room/board: $17,274
Financial aid: (510) 642-7117; 57% of undergrads determined to have financial need; average aid package $20,066

University of California–Davis
Davis CA
(530) 752-2971
U.S. News ranking: Nat. U., No. 46
Website: www.ucdavis.edu
Admissions email: undergraduateadmissions@ucdavis.edu
Public; founded 1905

Freshman admissions: more selective; 2016-2017: 67,472 applied, 28,617 accepted. Either SAT or ACT required. SAT 25/75 percentile: 1050-1330. High school rank: 100% in top tenth, 100% in top quarter, 100% in top half
Early decision deadline: N/A, notification date: N/A
Early action deadline: N/A, notification date: N/A
Application deadline (fall): 11/30
Undergraduate student body: 29,111 full time, 435 part time; 41% male, 59% female; 0% American Indian, 30% Asian, 2% black, 20% Hispanic, 5% multiracial, 0% Pacific Islander, 27% white, 13% international; 95% from in state; 25% live on campus; N/A of students in fraternities, N/A in sororities
Most popular majors: 19% Biological and Biomedical Sciences, 17% Social Sciences, 14% Psychology, 11% Engineering, 6% Agriculture, Agriculture Operations, and Related Sciences
Expenses: 2017-2018: $14,382 in state, $42,396 out of state; room/board: $16,136
Financial aid: (530) 752-2396; 62% of undergrads determined to have financial need; average aid package $21,194

University of California–Irvine
Irvine CA
(949) 824-6703
U.S. News ranking: Nat. U., No. 42
Website: www.uci.edu
Admissions email: admissions@uci.edu
Public; founded 1965
Freshman admissions: more selective; 2016-2017: 77,810 applied, 31,631 accepted. Either SAT or ACT required. SAT 25/75 percentile: 1060-1330. High school rank: 98% in top tenth, 100% in top quarter, 100% in top half
Early decision deadline: N/A, notification date: N/A
Early action deadline: N/A, notification date: N/A
Application deadline (fall): 11/30
Undergraduate student body: 26,889 full time, 442 part time; 47% male, 53% female; 0% American Indian, 36% Asian, 2% black, 26% Hispanic, 4% multiracial, 0% Pacific Islander, 14% white, 16% international; 97% from in state; 41% live on campus; N/A of students in fraternities, N/A in sororities
Most popular majors: 9% Biology/Biological Sciences, General, 8% Public Health, Other, 8% Social Psychology, 7% Business/Managerial Economics, 4% Criminology
Expenses: 2017-2018: $15,516 in state, $43,530 out of state; room/board: $14,829
Financial aid: (949) 824-5337; 65% of undergrads determined to have financial need; average aid package $23,022

University of California–Los Angeles

Los Angeles CA
(310) 825-3101
U.S. News ranking: Nat. U., No. 21
Website: www.ucla.edu/
Admissions email: ugadm@saonet.ucla.edu
Public; founded 1919
Freshman admissions: most selective; 2016-2017: 97,121 applied, 17,474 accepted. Either SAT or ACT required. SAT 25/75 percentile: 1160-1460. High school rank: 97% in top tenth, 100% in top quarter, 100% in top half
Early decision deadline: N/A, notification date: N/A
Early action deadline: N/A, notification date: N/A
Application deadline (fall): 11/30
Undergraduate student body: 30,343 full time, 530 part time; 43% male, 57% female; 3% American Indian, 0% Asian, 0% black, 22% Hispanic, 5% multiracial, 27% Pacific Islander, 29% white, 12% international; 89% from in state; N/A live on campus; 13% of students in fraternities, 13% in sororities
Most popular majors: 7% Social Sciences, 6% Psychology, 6% Social Sciences, 5% Biological and Biomedical Sciences
Expenses: 2017-2018: $13,256 in state, $41,270 out of state; room/board: $15,441
Financial aid: (310) 206-0401; 55% of undergrads determined to have financial need; average aid package $22,998

University of California–Merced

Merced CA
(866) 270-7301
U.S. News ranking: Nat. U., No. 165
Website: www.ucmerced.edu
Admissions email: admissions@ucmerced.edu
Public; founded 2005
Freshman admissions: less selective; 2016-2017: 20,888 applied, 15,492 accepted. Either SAT or ACT required. SAT 25/75 percentile: 860-1070. High school rank: N/A
Early decision deadline: N/A, notification date: N/A
Early action deadline: N/A, notification date: N/A
Application deadline (fall): 11/30
Undergraduate student body: 6,741 full time, 74 part time; 49% male, 51% female; 0% American Indian, 21% Asian, 5% black, 51% Hispanic, 3% multiracial, 1% Pacific Islander, 11% white, 7% international; 100% from in state; 36% live on campus; 7% of students in fraternities, 8% in sororities
Most popular majors: 20% Biological and Biomedical Sciences, 19% Psychology, 17% Engineering, 17% Social Sciences, 10% Business, Management, Marketing, and Related Support Services

Expenses: 2017-2018: $13,598 in state, $41,612 out of state; room/board: $15,923
Financial aid: (209) 228-7178; 89% of undergrads determined to have financial need; average aid package $24,792

University of California–Riverside

Riverside CA
(951) 827-3411
U.S. News ranking: Nat. U., No. 124
Website: www.ucr.edu
Admissions email: admissions@ucr.edu
Public; founded 1954
Freshman admissions: more selective; 2016-2017: 42,629 applied, 28,280 accepted. Either SAT or ACT required. SAT 25/75 percentile: 940-1190. High school rank: 94% in top tenth, 100% in top quarter, 100% in top half
Early decision deadline: N/A, notification date: N/A
Early action deadline: N/A, notification date: N/A
Application deadline (fall): 11/30
Undergraduate student body: 19,544 full time, 255 part time; 46% male, 54% female; 0% American Indian, 34% Asian, 4% black, 41% Hispanic, 6% multiracial, 0% Pacific Islander, 12% white, 2% international; 99% from in state; 34% live on campus; 5% of students in fraternities, 9% in sororities
Most popular majors: 22% Social Sciences, 15% Biological and Biomedical Sciences, 15% Business, Management, Marketing, and Related Support Services, 10% Psychology, 9% Engineering
Expenses: 2017-2018: $13,917 in state, $41,931 out of state; room/board: $15,500
Financial aid: (951) 827-7249; 80% of undergrads determined to have financial need; average aid package $22,301

University of California–San Diego

La Jolla CA
(858) 534-4831
U.S. News ranking: Nat. U., No. 42
Website: www.ucsd.edu/
Admissions email: admissionsinfo@ucsd.edu
Public; founded 1960
Freshman admissions: most selective; 2016-2017: 84,209 applied, 30,273 accepted. Either SAT or ACT required. SAT 25/75 percentile: 1140-1420. High school rank: 100% in top tenth, 100% in top quarter, 100% in top half
Early decision deadline: N/A, notification date: N/A
Early action deadline: N/A, notification date: N/A
Application deadline (fall): 11/30
Undergraduate student body: 27,698 full time, 429 part time; 52% male, 48% female; 0% American Indian, 39% Asian, 2% black, 16% Hispanic, 0% multiracial, 0% Pacific Islander, 19% white, 19% international;

94% from in state; 39% live on campus; 10% of students in fraternities, 10% in sororities
Most popular majors: 21% Biology, General, 13% Economics, 9% Computer Engineering, 6% Psychology, General, 5% Communication and Media Studies
Expenses: 2017-2018: $16,183 in state, $44,197 out of state; room/board: $13,254
Financial aid: (858) 534-4480; 55% of undergrads determined to have financial need; average aid package $22,499

University of California–Santa Barbara

Santa Barbara CA
(805) 893-2485
U.S. News ranking: Nat. U., No. 37
Website: www.ucsb.edu
Admissions email: admissions@sa.ucsb.edu
Public; founded 1909
Freshman admissions: most selective; 2016-2017: 77,098 applied, 27,580 accepted. Either SAT or ACT required. SAT 25/75 percentile: 1140-1390. High school rank: 100% in top tenth, 100% in top quarter, 100% in top half
Early decision deadline: N/A, notification date: N/A
Early action deadline: N/A, notification date: N/A
Application deadline (fall): 11/30
Undergraduate student body: 21,198 full time, 376 part time; 47% male, 53% female; 0% American Indian, 21% Asian, 2% black, 26% Hispanic, 6% multiracial, 0% Pacific Islander, 34% white, 8% international; 95% from in state; 39% live on campus; 2% of students in fraternities, 4% in sororities
Most popular majors: 26% Social Sciences, 9% Biological and Biomedical Sciences, 8% Psychology, 7% Communication, Journalism, and Related Programs, 5% Visual and Performing Arts
Expenses: 2017-2018: $14,409 in state, $42,423 out of state; room/board: $16,218
Financial aid: (805) 893-2432; 60% of undergrads determined to have financial need; average aid package $22,544

University of California–Santa Cruz

Santa Cruz CA
(831) 459-4008
U.S. News ranking: Nat. U., No. 81
Website: www.ucsc.edu
Admissions email: admissions@ucsc.edu
Public; founded 1965
Freshman admissions: more selective; 2016-2017: 49,185 applied, 28,884 accepted. Either SAT or ACT required. SAT 25/75 percentile: 1060-1300. High school rank: 96% in top tenth, 100% in top quarter, 100% in top half
Early decision deadline: N/A, notification date: N/A
Early action deadline: N/A, notification date: N/A

Application deadline (fall): 11/30
Undergraduate student body: 16,509 full time, 453 part time; 49% male, 51% female; 0% American Indian, 22% Asian, 2% black, 30% Hispanic, 8% multiracial, 0% Pacific Islander, 32% white, 4% international; 97% from in state; 53% live on campus; 4% of students in fraternities, 8% in sororities
Most popular majors: 12% Psychology, General, 6% Business/Managerial Economics, 6% Cell/Cellular and Molecular Biology, 6% Sociology, 5% Environmental Studies
Expenses: 2017-2018: $14,028 in state, $42,042 out of state; room/board: $16,055
Financial aid: (831) 459-2963; 65% of undergrads determined to have financial need; average aid package $24,821

University of La Verne

La Verne CA
(800) 876-4858
U.S. News ranking: Nat. U., No. 159
Website: www.laverne.edu
Admissions email: admission@laverne.edu
Private; founded 1891
Freshman admissions: selective; 2016-2017: 8,072 applied, 3,879 accepted. Either SAT or ACT required. SAT 25/75 percentile: 930-1130. High school rank: 18% in top tenth, 54% in top quarter, 86% in top half
Early decision deadline: N/A, notification date: N/A
Early action deadline: N/A, notification date: N/A
Application deadline (fall): rolling
Undergraduate student body: 2,715 full time, 94 part time; 42% male, 58% female; 0% American Indian, 6% Asian, 5% black, 53% Hispanic, 5% multiracial, 1% Pacific Islander, 23% white, 6% international; 96% from in state; 29% live on campus; 8% of students in fraternities, 12% in sororities
Most popular majors: 25% Business, Management, Marketing, and Related Support Services, 14% Social Sciences, 11% Communication, Journalism, and Related Programs, 11% Education, 11% Psychology
Expenses: 2017-2018: $41,450; room/board: $13,140
Financial aid: (800) 649-0160; 83% of undergrads determined to have financial need; average aid package $31,389

University of Redlands

Redlands CA
(800) 455-5064
U.S. News ranking: Reg. U. (W), No. 12
Website: www.redlands.edu
Admissions email: admissions@redlands.edu
Private; founded 1907
Freshman admissions: selective; 2016-2017: 4,562 applied, 3,410 accepted. Either SAT

or ACT required. SAT 25/75 percentile: 980-1190. High school rank: 22% in top tenth, 55% in top quarter, 88% in top half
Early decision deadline: N/A, notification date: N/A
Early action deadline: 11/15, notification date: 1/15
Application deadline (fall): 1/15
Undergraduate student body: 2,497 full time, 740 part time; 44% male, 56% female; 1% American Indian, 6% Asian, 4% black, 28% Hispanic, 5% multiracial, 1% Pacific Islander, 47% white, 2% international
Most popular majors: Information not available
Expenses: 2017-2018: $48,072; room/board: $13,862
Financial aid: (909) 748-8266

University of San Diego

San Diego CA
(619) 260-4506
U.S. News ranking: Nat. U., No. 90
Website: www.SanDiego.edu
Admissions email: admissions@SanDiego.edu
Private; founded 1949
Freshman admissions: more selective; 2016-2017: 14,413 applied, 7,406 accepted. Either SAT or ACT required. ACT 25/75 percentile: 26-30. High school rank: 39% in top tenth, 77% in top quarter, 97% in top half
Early decision deadline: N/A, notification date: N/A
Early action deadline: N/A, notification date: N/A
Application deadline (fall): 12/15
Undergraduate student body: 5,499 full time, 212 part time; 46% male, 54% female; 0% American Indian, 7% Asian, 3% black, 19% Hispanic, 6% multiracial, 0% Pacific Islander, 52% white, 8% international; 52% from in state; 44% live on campus; 24% of students in fraternities, 31% in sororities
Most popular majors: 40% Business, Management, Marketing, and Related Support Services, 12% Biological and Biomedical Sciences, 12% Social Sciences, 8% Communication, Journalism, and Related Programs, 8% Engineering
Expenses: 2017-2018: $47,708; room/board: $12,630
Financial aid: (619) 260-4720; 51% of undergrads determined to have financial need; average aid package $33,913

University of San Francisco

San Francisco CA
(415) 422-6563
U.S. News ranking: Nat. U., No. 110
Website: www.usfca.edu
Admissions email: admission@usfca.edu
Private; founded 1855
Affiliation: Roman Catholic
Freshman admissions: more selective; 2016-2017: 15,414 applied, 10,901 accepted. Either SAT or ACT required. SAT 25/75 percentile: 1030-1250. High school rank: 25% in top tenth, 64% in top quarter, 92% in top half

Early decision deadline: 11/1, notification date: 12/1
Early action deadline: 11/1, notification date: 12/14
Application deadline (fall): 1/15
Undergraduate student body: 6,450 full time, 295 part time; 38% male, 62% female; 0% American Indian, 22% Asian, 3% black, 21% Hispanic, 7% multiracial, 1% Pacific Islander, 26% white, 18% international; 77% from in state; 37% live on campus; 3% of students in fraternities, 11% in sororities
Most popular majors: 13% Business Administration and Management, General, 11% Registered Nursing/Registered Nurse, 9% Finance, General, 7% Psychology, General, 6% Marketing/Marketing Management, General
Expenses: 2017-2018: $46,250; room/board: $14,330
Financial aid: (415) 422-2624; 55% of undergrads determined to have financial need; average aid package $35,963

University of Southern California

Los Angeles CA
(213) 740-1111
U.S. News ranking: Nat. U., No. 21
Website: www.usc.edu/
Admissions email: admitusc@usc.edu
Private; founded 1880
Freshman admissions: most selective; 2016-2017: 54,280 applied, 9,022 accepted. Either SAT or ACT required. SAT 25/75 percentile: 1280-1500. High school rank: 88% in top tenth, 96% in top quarter, 100% in top half
Early decision deadline: N/A, notification date: N/A
Early action deadline: N/A, notification date: N/A
Application deadline (fall): 1/15
Undergraduate student body: 18,195 full time, 909 part time; 48% male, 52% female; 0% American Indian, 21% Asian, 4% black, 14% Hispanic, 5% multiracial, 0% Pacific Islander, 40% white, 14% international; 67% from in state; 30% live on campus; 26% of students in fraternities, 27% in sororities
Most popular majors: 25% Business, Management, Marketing, and Related Support Services, 12% Social Sciences, 12% Visual and Performing Arts, 10% Engineering, 9% Communication, Journalism, and Related Programs
Expenses: 2017-2018: $54,259; room/board: $14,885
Financial aid: (213) 740-4444; 36% of undergrads determined to have financial need; average aid package $49,696

University of the Antelope Valley[1]

Lancaster CA
U.S. News ranking: Reg. Coll. (W), unranked
Website: www.uav.edu
Admissions email: N/A
Public
Application deadline (fall): N/A

Undergraduate student body: N/A full time, N/A part time
Expenses: 2016-2017: $13,100 in state, $13,100 out of state; room/board: $9,900
Financial aid: N/A

University of the Pacific

Stockton CA
(209) 946-2011
U.S. News ranking: Nat. U., No. 110
Website: www.pacific.edu
Admissions email: admissions@pacific.edu
Private; founded 1851
Freshman admissions: more selective; 2016-2017: 8,870 applied, 5,853 accepted. Either SAT or ACT required. SAT 25/75 percentile: 1030-1300. High school rank: 37% in top tenth, 40% in top quarter, 92% in top half
Early decision deadline: N/A, notification date: N/A
Early action deadline: 11/15, notification date: 1/15
Application deadline (fall): 8/15
Undergraduate student body: 3,384 full time, 99 part time; 47% male, 53% female; 0% American Indian, 37% Asian, 3% black, 19% Hispanic, 5% multiracial, 0% Pacific Islander, 25% white, 6% international; 93% from in state; 44% live on campus; 9% of students in fraternities, 13% in sororities
Most popular majors: 16% Business Administration and Management, General, 13% Biology/Biological Sciences, General, 13% Engineering, General
Expenses: 2017-2018: $46,346; room/board: $13,356
Financial aid: (209) 946-2421; 69% of undergrads determined to have financial need; average aid package $32,595

University of the West

Rosemead CA
(855) 468-9378
U.S. News ranking: Reg. Coll. (W), unranked
Website: www.uwest.edu
Admissions email: admission@uwest.edu
Private; founded 1991
Freshman admissions: least selective; 2016-2017: 221 applied, 213 accepted. Neither SAT nor ACT required. SAT 25/75 percentile: N/A. High school rank: N/A
Early decision deadline: N/A, notification date: N/A
Early action deadline: N/A, notification date: N/A
Application deadline (fall): 5/1
Undergraduate student body: 151 full time, 6 part time; 39% male, 61% female; 1% American Indian, 8% Asian, 1% black, 46% Hispanic, 2% multiracial, 0% Pacific Islander, 6% white, 37% international
Most popular majors: 68% Business Administration and Management, General, 15% Psychology, General, 10% General Studies, 7% English Language and Literature, General

Expenses: 2017-2018: $11,990; room/board: $7,514
Financial aid: (626) 571-8811

Vanguard University of Southern California

Costa Mesa CA
(800) 722-6279
U.S. News ranking: Reg. U. (W), No. 59
Website: www.vanguard.edu
Admissions email: admissions@vanguard.edu
Private; founded 1920
Affiliation: Assemblies of God Church
Freshman admissions: less selective; 2016-2017: 1,418 applied, 996 accepted. Either SAT or ACT required. SAT 25/75 percentile: 830-1030. High school rank: 11% in top tenth, 29% in top quarter, 70% in top half
Early decision deadline: N/A, notification date: N/A
Early action deadline: 12/1, notification date: 1/15
Application deadline (fall): 8/1
Undergraduate student body: 1,447 full time, 344 part time; 34% male, 66% female; 0% American Indian, 3% Asian, 6% black, 37% Hispanic, 4% multiracial, 1% Pacific Islander, 44% white, 1% international; 89% from in state; 51% live on campus; 0% of students in fraternities, 0% in sororities
Most popular majors: 20% Psychology, General, 19% Business Administration and Management, General, 12% Nursing Administration, 7% Kinesiology and Exercise Science, 6% Speech Communication and Rhetoric
Expenses: 2016-2017: $31,430; room/board: $9,310
Financial aid: (714) 966-5490

Westmont College

Santa Barbara CA
(805) 565-6000
U.S. News ranking: Nat. Lib. Arts, No. 96
Website: www.westmont.edu
Admissions email: admissions@westmont.edu
Private; founded 1937
Freshman admissions: more selective; 2016-2017: 2,001 applied, 1,656 accepted. Either SAT or ACT required. SAT 25/75 percentile: 1040-1280. High school rank: 36% in top tenth, 65% in top quarter, 93% in top half
Early decision deadline: N/A, notification date: N/A
Early action deadline: 11/15, notification date: 12/1
Application deadline (fall): rolling
Undergraduate student body: 1,291 full time, 7 part time; 39% male, 61% female; 1% American Indian, 7% Asian, 2% black, 16% Hispanic, 6% multiracial, 0% Pacific Islander, 62% white, 3% international; 75% from in state; 86% live on campus; 0% of students in fraternities, 0% in sororities

Most popular majors: 16% Kinesiology and Exercise Science, 14% Business/Managerial Economics, 11% Biology/Biological Sciences, General, 7% Psychology, General, 6% Speech Communication and Rhetoric
Expenses: 2017-2018: $44,044; room/board: $13,886
Financial aid: (805) 565-6063; 66% of undergrads determined to have financial need; average aid package $32,102

Whittier College

Whittier CA
(562) 907-4238
U.S. News ranking: Nat. Lib. Arts, No. 128
Website: www.whittier.edu
Admissions email: admission@whittier.edu
Private; founded 1887
Freshman admissions: selective; 2016-2017: 5,146 applied, 3,574 accepted. Neither SAT nor ACT required. SAT 25/75 percentile: 920-1130. High school rank: 24% in top tenth, 36% in top quarter, 86% in top half
Early decision deadline: N/A, notification date: N/A
Early action deadline: 11/15, notification date: 12/30
Application deadline (fall): rolling
Undergraduate student body: 1,579 full time, 36 part time; 43% male, 57% female; 0% American Indian, 7% Asian, 4% black, 47% Hispanic, 6% multiracial, 0% Pacific Islander, 31% white, 3% international; 80% from in state; 50% live on campus; N/A of students in fraternities, N/A in sororities
Most popular majors: 20% Business, Management, Marketing, and Related Support Services, 16% Social Sciences, 11% Parks, Recreation, Leisure, and Fitness Studies, 9% Psychology, 7% Biological and Biomedical Sciences
Expenses: 2017-2018: $46,120; room/board: $13,310
Financial aid: (562) 907-4285; 78% of undergrads determined to have financial need; average aid package $35,665

William Jessup University

Rocklin CA
(916) 577-2222
U.S. News ranking: Reg. Coll. (W), No. 7
Website: www.jessup.edu
Admissions email: admissions@jessup.edu
Private; founded 1939
Freshman admissions: selective; 2016-2017: 742 applied, 538 accepted. Either SAT or ACT required. SAT 25/75 percentile: 800-1140. High school rank: 22% in top tenth, 40% in top quarter, 72% in top half
Early decision deadline: N/A, notification date: N/A
Early action deadline: N/A, notification date: N/A
Application deadline (fall): 8/18

Undergraduate student body: 995 full time, 170 part time; 40% male, 60% female; 1% American Indian, 4% Asian, 6% black, 19% Hispanic, 2% multiracial, 1% Pacific Islander, 60% white, 2% international; 90% from in state; 64% live on campus; N/A of students in fraternities, N/A in sororities
Most popular majors: 30% Psychology, 26% Business, Management, Marketing, and Related Support Services, 13% Theology and Religious Vocations, 8% Education, 4% English Language and Literature/Letters
Expenses: 2017-2018: $30,550; room/board: $10,950
Financial aid: (916) 577-2232; 83% of undergrads determined to have financial need; average aid package $21,232

Woodbury University

Burbank CA
(818) 767-0888
U.S. News ranking: Reg. U. (W), No. 66
Website: www.woodbury.edu
Admissions email: info@woodbury.edu
Private; founded 1884
Freshman admissions: selective; 2016-2017: 1,487 applied, 985 accepted. Either SAT or ACT required. SAT 25/75 percentile: 860-1115. High school rank: N/A
Early decision deadline: N/A, notification date: N/A
Early action deadline: N/A, notification date: N/A
Application deadline (fall): rolling
Undergraduate student body: 973 full time, 162 part time; 52% male, 48% female; 0% American Indian, 9% Asian, 3% black, 29% Hispanic, 2% multiracial, 1% Pacific Islander, 32% white, 24% international; 95% from in state; 30% live on campus; 7% of students in fraternities, 8% in sororities
Most popular majors: Information not available
Expenses: 2017-2018: $38,460; room/board: $11,133
Financial aid: (818) 252-5273; 84% of undergrads determined to have financial need; average aid package $23,976

COLORADO

Adams State University[1]

Alamosa CO
(800) 824-6494
U.S. News ranking: Reg. U. (W), second tier
Website: www.adams.edu
Admissions email: ascadmit@adams.edu
Public
Application deadline (fall): N/A
Undergraduate student body: N/A full time, N/A part time
Expenses: 2016-2017: $9,153 in state, $20,169 out of state; room/board: $8,550
Financial aid: N/A

Art Institute of Colorado[1]
Denver CO
U.S. News ranking: Arts, unranked
Website: www.artinstitutes.edu/denver/
Admissions email: N/A
For-profit
Application deadline (fall): N/A
Undergraduate student body: N/A full time, N/A part time
Expenses: 2016-2017: $17,628; room/board: N/A
Financial aid: N/A

Colorado Christian University[1]
Lakewood CO
(303) 963-3200
U.S. News ranking: Reg. U. (W), second tier
Website: www.ccu.edu
Admissions email: admission@ccu.edu
Private
Application deadline (fall): N/A
Undergraduate student body: N/A full time, N/A part time
Expenses: 2016-2017: $29,360; room/board: $10,316
Financial aid: N/A

Colorado College
Colorado Springs CO
(719) 389-6344
U.S. News ranking: Nat. Lib. Arts, No. 23
Website: www.ColoradoCollege.edu
Admissions email: admission@ColoradoCollege.edu
Private; founded 1874
Freshman admissions: most selective; 2016-2017: 7,894 applied, 1,262 accepted. Neither SAT nor ACT required. ACT 25/75 percentile: 28-32. High school rank: 69% in top tenth, 90% in top quarter, 100% in top half
Early decision deadline: 11/10, notification date: 12/15
Early action deadline: 11/10, notification date: 12/20
Application deadline (fall): 1/15
Undergraduate student body: 2,084 full time, 17 part time; 46% male, 54% female; 1% American Indian, 4% Asian, 3% black, 9% Hispanic, 9% multiracial, 0% Pacific Islander, 66% white, 8% international; 17% from in state; 75% live on campus; N/A of students in fraternities, N/A in sororities
Most popular majors: 10% Economics, General, 7% Ecology and Evolutionary Biology, 7% Political Science and Government, General, 4% International Economics
Expenses: 2017-2018: $53,238; room/board: $12,076
Financial aid: (719) 389-6651; 33% of undergrads determined to have financial need; average aid package $46,024

Colorado Mesa University
Grand Junction CO
(970) 248-1875
U.S. News ranking: Reg. Coll. (W), No. 24
Website: www.coloradomesa.edu/
Admissions email: admissions@coloradomesa.edu

Public; founded 1925
Freshman admissions: selective; 2016-2017: 7,152 applied, 5,918 accepted. Either SAT or ACT required. ACT 25/75 percentile: 18-24. High school rank: 11% in top tenth, 27% in top quarter, 58% in top half
Early decision deadline: N/A, notification date: N/A
Early action deadline: N/A, notification date: N/A
Application deadline (fall): rolling
Undergraduate student body: 7,277 full time, 2,318 part time; 46% male, 54% female; 1% American Indian, 2% Asian, 2% black, 18% Hispanic, 4% multiracial, 1% Pacific Islander, 69% white, 1% international; 86% from in state; 23% live on campus; N/A of students in fraternities, N/A in sororities
Most popular majors: 18% Business/Commerce, General, 17% Kinesiology and Exercise Science, 11% Registered Nursing/Registered Nurse, 8% Biology/Biological Sciences, General, 7% Criminal Justice/Safety Studies
Expenses: 2017-2018: $8,972 in state, $21,782 out of state; room/board: $10,735
Financial aid: (970) 248-1396; 64% of undergrads determined to have financial need; average aid package $9,206

Colorado Mountain College
Glenwood Springs CO
(970) 945-8691
U.S. News ranking: Reg. Coll. (W), unranked
Admissions email: joinus@coloradomtn.edu
Public; founded 1967
Freshman admissions: least selective, 2016-2017: 2,326 applied, 1,053 accepted. Neither SAT nor ACT required. SAT 25/75 percentile: N/A. High school rank: N/A
Early decision deadline: N/A, notification date: N/A
Early action deadline: N/A, notification date: N/A
Application deadline (fall): rolling
Undergraduate student body: 1,823 full time, 3,983 part time; 45% male, 55% female; 0% American Indian, 1% Asian, 1% black, 22% Hispanic, 2% multiracial, 0% Pacific Islander, 67% white, 0% international; 88% from in state; N/A live on campus; N/A of students in fraternities; N/A in sororities
Most popular majors: 53% Business, Management, Marketing, and Related Support Services, 36% Multi/Interdisciplinary Studies, 10% Health Professions and Related Programs
Expenses: 2017-2018: $6,360 in state, $13,200 out of state; room/board: $9,280
Financial aid: N/A

Colorado School of Mines
Golden CO
(303) 273-3220
U.S. News ranking: Nat. U., No. 75
Website: www.mines.edu
Admissions email: admissions@mines.edu
Public; founded 1874
Freshman admissions: most selective; 2016-2017: 12,284 applied, 4,957 accepted. Either SAT or ACT required. ACT 25/75 percentile: 29-32. High school rank: 56% in top tenth, 90% in top quarter, 99% in top half
Early decision deadline: N/A, notification date: N/A
Early action deadline: N/A, notification date: N/A
Application deadline (fall): 5/1
Undergraduate student body: 4,397 full time, 215 part time; 72% male, 28% female; 0% American Indian, 5% Asian, 1% black, 7% Hispanic, 5% multiracial, 0% Pacific Islander, 74% white, 6% international; 62% from in state; 28% live on campus; 11% of students in fraternities, 24% in sororities
Most popular majors: 88% Engineering, 6% Computer and Information Sciences and Support Services, 3% Mathematics and Statistics, 2% Physical Sciences, 1% Social Sciences
Expenses: 2017-2018: $18,386 in state, $37,436 out of state; room/board: $11,897
Financial aid: (303) 273-3207; 47% of undergrads determined to have financial need; average aid package $14,039

Colorado State University
Fort Collins CO
(970) 491-6909
U.S. News ranking: Nat. U., No. 124
Website: www.colostate.edu
Admissions email: admissions@colostate.edu
Public; founded 1870
Freshman admissions: more selective; 2016-2017: 21,992 applied, 17,080 accepted. Either SAT or ACT required. ACT 25/75 percentile: 22-28. High school rank: 21% in top tenth, 49% in top quarter, 84% in top half
Early decision deadline: N/A, notification date: N/A
Early action deadline: 12/1, notification date: 2/1
Application deadline (fall): 5/1
Undergraduate student body: 21,977 full time, 3,200 part time; 48% male, 52% female; 0% American Indian, 2% Asian, 2% black, 12% Hispanic, 3% multiracial, 0% Pacific Islander, 73% white, 4% international; 77% from in state; 29% live on campus; 9% of students in fraternities, 13% in sororities
Most popular majors: 14% Business, Management, Marketing, and Related Support Services, 10% Biological and Biomedical Sciences, 9% Family and Consumer Sciences/Human Sciences, 9% Social Sciences, 8% Engineering

---

Expenses: 2017-2018: $11,632 in state, $29,140 out of state; room/board: $12,208
Financial aid: (970) 491-6321; 49% of undergrads determined to have financial need; average aid package $11,098

Colorado State University–Pueblo
Pueblo CO
(719) 549-2461
U.S. News ranking: Reg. U. (W), second tier
Website: www.csupueblo.edu
Admissions email: info@colostate-pueblo.edu
Public; founded 1933
Freshman admissions: selective; 2016-2017: 7,131 applied, 6,873 accepted. Either SAT or ACT required. ACT 25/75 percentile: 18-23. High school rank: 11% in top tenth, 33% in top quarter, 66% in top half
Early decision deadline: N/A, notification date: N/A
Early action deadline: N/A, notification date: N/A
Application deadline (fall): 8/1
Undergraduate student body: 3,436 full time, 1,588 part time; 47% male, 53% female; 0% American Indian, 1% Asian, 7% black, 33% Hispanic, 6% multiracial, 0% Pacific Islander, 48% white, 2% international; 84% from in state; 21% live on campus; 1% of students in fraternities, 1% in sororities
Most popular majors: 11% Business/Commerce, General, 11% Sociology, 9% Registered Nursing/Registered Nurse, 8% Mass Communication/Media Studies, 7% Kinesiology and Exercise Science
Expenses: 2017-2018: $10,090 in state, $25,547 out of state; room/board: $10,210
Financial aid: (719) 549-2753; 78% of undergrads determined to have financial need; average aid package $11,140

Colorado Technical University[1]
Colorado Springs CO
U.S. News ranking: Reg. U. (W), unranked
Website: www.coloradotech.edu
Admissions email: info@ctuonline.edu
For-profit
Application deadline (fall): N/A
Undergraduate student body: N/A full time, N/A part time
Expenses: 2016-2017: $10,540; room/board: N/A
Financial aid: N/A

Fort Lewis College
Durango CO
(970) 247-7184
U.S. News ranking: Nat. Lib. Arts, second tier
Website: www.fortlewis.edu
Admissions email: admission@fortlewis.edu
Public; founded 1911

Freshman admissions: selective; 2016-2017: 4,164 applied, 3,836 accepted. Either SAT or ACT required. ACT 25/75 percentile: 19-24. High school rank: 9% in top tenth, 27% in top quarter, 64% in top half
Early decision deadline: N/A, notification date: N/A
Early action deadline: 1/15, notification date: 3/15
Application deadline (fall): 8/1
Undergraduate student body: 3,178 full time, 378 part time; 50% male, 50% female; 26% American Indian, 1% Asian, 1% black, 11% Hispanic, 8% multiracial, 0% Pacific Islander, 50% white, 1% international; 49% from in state; 39% live on campus; N/A of students in fraternities, N/A in sororities
Most popular majors: 21% Business, Management, Marketing, and Related Support Services, 11% Social Sciences, 9% Parks, Recreation, Leisure, and Fitness Studies, 8% Psychology, 8% Visual and Performing Arts
Expenses: 2017-2018: $8,630 in state, $18,764 out of state; room/board: $9,416
Financial aid: (970) 247-7142; 54% of undergrads determined to have financial need; average aid package $16,298

Metropolitan State University of Denver
Denver CO
(303) 556-3058
U.S. News ranking: Reg. U. (W), second tier
Website: www.msudenver.edu
Admissions email: askmetro@msudenver.edu
Public; founded 1963
Freshman admissions: less selective; 2016-2017: 7,228 applied, 4,641 accepted. Either SAT or ACT required. ACT 25/75 percentile: 17-23. High school rank: 5% in top tenth, 19% in top quarter, 52% in top half
Early decision deadline: N/A, notification date: N/A
Early action deadline: N/A, notification date: N/A
Application deadline (fall): 7/1
Undergraduate student body: 12,483 full time, 7,457 part time; 46% male, 54% female; 1% American Indian, 4% Asian, 6% black, 24% Hispanic, 4% multiracial, 0% Pacific Islander, 56% white, 1% international; 97% from in state; N/A live on campus; N/A of students in fraternities, N/A in sororities
Most popular majors: 6% Criminal Justice/Safety Studies, 5% Biology/Biological Sciences, General, 5% Psychology, General, 4% Accounting, 4% Business Administration and Management, General
Expenses: 2017-2018: $7,352 in state, $20,149 out of state; room/board: N/A
Financial aid: (303) 556-4741; 66% of undergrads determined to have financial need; average aid package $8,590

Naropa University

Boulder CO
(303) 546-3572
U.S. News ranking: Reg. U. (W),
unranked
Website: www.naropa.edu
Admissions email: admissions@
naropa.edu
Private; founded 1974
Freshman admissions: least
selective; 2016-2017: 139
applied, 139 accepted. Neither
SAT nor ACT required. SAT 25/75
percentile: N/A. High school
rank: N/A
Early decision deadline: N/A,
notification date: N/A
Early action deadline: N/A,
notification date: N/A
Application deadline (fall): rolling
Undergraduate student body: 348
full time, 34 part time; 33%
male, 67% female; 1% American
Indian, 2% Asian, 1% black,
9% Hispanic, 8% multiracial,
0% Pacific Islander, 64% white,
3% international; 41% from in
state; 16% live on campus; N/A
of students in fraternities, N/A in
sororities
Most popular majors: 39%
Psychology, General, 13% Multi-/
Interdisciplinary Studies, Other,
13% Visual and Performing Arts,
General, 11% Environmental
Studies, 8% English Language
and Literature, General
Expenses: 2017-2018: $31,790;
room/board: $11,880
Financial aid: (303) 546-3509;
68% of undergrads determined to
have financial need; average aid
package $37,041

Regis University

Denver CO
(303) 458-4900
U.S. News ranking: Reg. U. (W),
No. 27
Website: www.regis.edu
Admissions email:
ruadmissions@regis.edu
Private; founded 1877
Freshman admissions: selective;
2016-2017: 6,756 applied,
3,823 accepted. Either SAT
or ACT required. ACT 25/75
percentile: 22-26. High school
rank: 16% in top tenth, 39% in
top quarter, 90% in top half
Early decision deadline: N/A,
notification date: N/A
Early action deadline: N/A,
notification date: N/A
Application deadline (fall): 8/1
Undergraduate student body: 2,362
full time, 1,708 part time; 40%
male, 60% female; 0% American
Indian, 5% Asian, 5% black,
20% Hispanic, 4% multiracial,
0% Pacific Islander, 58% white,
1% international; 62% from in
state; N/A live on campus; 0%
of students in fraternities, 0% in
sororities
Most popular majors: 33% Health
Professions and Related Programs,
25% Business, Management,
Marketing, and Related Support
Services, 7% Computer and
Information Sciences and Support
Services, 6% Psychology, 5%
Biological and Biomedical
Sciences
Expenses: 2017-2018: $34,450;
room/board: $10,420

Rocky Mountain College of Art and Design[1]

Lakewood CO
U.S. News ranking: Arts, unranked
Website: www.rmcad.edu/
Admissions email: admissions@
rmcad.edu
For-profit; founded 1963
Application deadline (fall): N/A
Undergraduate student body: N/A
full time, N/A part time
Expenses: 2016-2017: $17,170;
room/board: N/A
Financial aid: (303) 225-8551

United States Air Force Academy

USAF Academy CO
(800) 443-9266
U.S. News ranking: Nat. Lib. Arts,
No. 26
Website: academyadmissions.com
Admissions email:
rr_webmail@usafa.edu
Public; founded 1954
Freshman admissions: most
selective; 2016-2017: 9,894
applied, 1,492 accepted. Either
SAT or ACT required. ACT 25/75
percentile: 27-33. High school
rank: 52% in top tenth, 81% in
top quarter, 97% in top half
Early decision deadline: N/A,
notification date: N/A
Early action deadline: N/A,
notification date: N/A
Application deadline (fall): 12/31
Undergraduate student body:
4,237 full time, 0 part time; 75%
male, 25% female; 0% American
Indian, 5% Asian, 6% black, 11%
Hispanic, 7% multiracial, 1%
Pacific Islander, 62% white, 1%
international
Most popular majors: 36%
Engineering, 18% Social
Sciences, 17% Business,
Management, Marketing, and
Related Support Services, 7%
Multi/Interdisciplinary Studies,
5% Biological and Biomedical
Sciences
Expenses: N/A
Financial aid: N/A

University of Colorado–Boulder

Boulder CO
(303) 492-6301
U.S. News ranking: Nat. U., No. 90
Website: www.colorado.edu
Admissions email:
apply@colorado.edu
Public; founded 1876
Freshman admissions: more
selective; 2016-2017: 34,047
applied, 26,087 accepted. Either
SAT or ACT required. ACT 25/75
percentile: 25-30. High school
rank: 29% in top tenth, 60% in
top quarter, 90% in top half
Early decision deadline: N/A,
notification date: N/A
Early action deadline: 11/15,
notification date: 2/1
Application deadline (fall): 1/15

Undergraduate student body:
25,727 full time, 2,119 part
time; 56% male, 44% female;
0% American Indian, 5% Asian,
2% black, 11% Hispanic, 5%
multiracial, 0% Pacific Islander,
69% white, 7% international;
59% from in state; 29% live
on campus; 12% of students in
fraternities, 20% in sororities
Most popular majors: 14%
Biological and Biomedical
Sciences, 14% Social Sciences,
13% Business, Management,
Marketing, and Related Support
Services, 11% Engineering, 10%
Communication, Journalism, and
Related Programs
Expenses: 2017-2018: $11,531
in state, $35,079 out of state;
room/board: $13,590
Financial aid: (303) 492-5091;
35% of undergrads determined to
have financial need; average aid
package $16,838

University of Colorado– Colorado Springs

Colorado Springs CO
(719) 255-3383
U.S. News ranking: Reg. U. (W),
No. 35
Website: www.uccs.edu
Admissions email:
admrecor@uccs.edu
Public; founded 1965
Freshman admissions: selective;
2016-2017: 9,664 applied,
8,972 accepted. Either SAT
or ACT required. ACT 25/75
percentile: 20-26. High school
rank: 14% in top tenth, 36% in
top quarter, 71% in top half
Early decision deadline: N/A,
notification date: N/A
Early action deadline: N/A,
notification date: N/A
Application deadline (fall): rolling
Undergraduate student body: 7,927
full time, 2,487 part time; 48%
male, 52% female; 0% American
Indian, 3% Asian, 4% black,
17% Hispanic, 7% multiracial,
0% Pacific Islander, 65% white,
1% international; 88% from in
state; 16% live on campus; 2%
of students in fraternities, 2% in
sororities
Most popular majors: 21%
Business, Management,
Marketing, and Related Support
Services, 14% Health Professions
and Related Programs, 11% Social
Sciences, 9% Communication,
Journalism, and Related Programs,
9% Psychology
Expenses: 2017-2018: $10,201
in state, $24,181 out of state;
room/board: $10,100
Financial aid: (719) 255-3460

University of Colorado–Denver

Denver CO
(303) 556-2704
U.S. News ranking: Nat. U.,
No. 207
Website: www.ucdenver.edu
Admissions email:
admissions@ucdenver.edu
Public; founded 1912

Freshman admissions: selective;
2016-2017: 12,252 applied,
7,415 accepted. Either SAT
or ACT required. ACT 25/75
percentile: 21-26. High school
rank: 14% in top tenth, 49% in
top quarter, 82% in top half
Early decision deadline: N/A,
notification date: N/A
Early action deadline: N/A,
notification date: N/A
Application deadline (fall): rolling
Undergraduate student body: 8,530
full time, 6,092 part time; 45%
male, 55% female; 0% American
Indian, 10% Asian, 5% black,
20% Hispanic, 5% multiracial,
0% Pacific Islander, 49% white,
8% international; 91% from in
state; 0% live on campus; N/A
of students in fraternities, N/A in
sororities
Most popular majors: 17%
Business, Management,
Marketing, and Related Support
Services, 17% Health Professions
and Related Programs, 13%
Social Sciences, 10% Biological
and Biomedical Sciences, 10%
Visual and Performing Arts
Expenses: 2017-2018: $11,019
in state, $31,209 out of state;
room/board: $11,358
Financial aid: (303) 556-2886;
50% of undergrads determined to
have financial need; average aid
package $9,946

University of Denver

Denver CO
(303) 871-2036
U.S. News ranking: Nat. U., No. 87
Website: www.du.edu
Admissions email:
admission@du.edu
Private; founded 1864
Freshman admissions: more
selective; 2016-2017: 20,322
applied, 10,867 accepted. Either
SAT or ACT required. ACT 25/75
percentile: 26-31. High school
rank: 42% in top tenth, 74% in
top quarter, 96% in top half
Early decision deadline: 11/1,
notification date: 12/15
Early action deadline: 11/1,
notification date: 1/15
Application deadline (fall): 1/15
Undergraduate student body: 5,491
full time, 263 part time; 46%
male, 54% female; 0% American
Indian, 4% Asian, 2% black,
10% Hispanic, 4% multiracial,
0% Pacific Islander, 69% white,
8% international; 38% from in
state; 45% live on campus; 24%
of students in fraternities, 29%
in sororities
Most popular majors: 30%
Business, Management,
Marketing, and Related Support
Services, 17% Social Sciences,
8% Communication, Journalism,
and Related Programs, 8%
Psychology, 7% Biological and
Biomedical Sciences
Expenses: 2017-2018: $48,669;
room/board: $12,612
Financial aid: (303) 871-4857;
41% of undergrads determined to
have financial need; average aid
package $37,109

University of Northern Colorado

Greeley CO
(970) 351-2881
U.S. News ranking: Nat. U.,
second tier
Website: www.unco.edu
Admissions email:
admissions@unco.edu
Public; founded 1890
Freshman admissions: selective;
2016-2017: 6,784 applied,
6,124 accepted. Either SAT
or ACT required. ACT 25/75
percentile: 19-25. High school
rank: 13% in top tenth, 38% in
top quarter, 73% in top half
Early decision deadline: N/A,
notification date: N/A
Early action deadline: N/A,
notification date: N/A
Application deadline (fall): 8/1
Undergraduate student body: 8,331
full time, 1,172 part time; 36%
male, 64% female; 0% American
Indian, 2% Asian, 4% black,
19% Hispanic, 4% multiracial,
0% Pacific Islander, 58% white,
1% international; 85% from in
state; 37% live on campus; 7%
of students in fraternities, 7% in
sororities
Most popular majors: 15% Health
Professions and Related Programs,
13% Multi/Interdisciplinary
Studies, 11% Business,
Management, Marketing, and
Related Support Services, 8%
Parks, Recreation, Leisure, and
Fitness Studies, 8% Psychology
Expenses: 2017-2018: $8,888 in
state, $20,474 out of state; room/
board: $10,770
Financial aid: (970) 351-2502;
62% of undergrads determined to
have financial need; average aid
package $10,831

Western State Colorado University

Gunnison CO
(800) 876-5309
U.S. News ranking: Reg. U. (W),
No. 86
Website: www.western.edu
Admissions email: discover@
western.edu
Public; founded 1901
Freshman admissions: selective;
2016-2017: 2,191 applied,
2,013 accepted. Either SAT
or ACT required. ACT 25/75
percentile: 19-25. High school
rank: 6% in top tenth, 18% in top
quarter, 50% in top half
Early decision deadline: N/A,
notification date: N/A
Early action deadline: N/A,
notification date: N/A
Application deadline (fall): rolling
Undergraduate student body: 1,939
full time, 556 part time; 58%
male, 42% female; 1% American
Indian, 1% Asian, 3% black,
11% Hispanic, 4% multiracial,
0% Pacific Islander, 73% white,
0% international; 70% from in
state; 38% live on campus; 0%
of students in fraternities, 0% in
sororities
Most popular majors: 26%
Business, Management,
Marketing, and Related Support
Services, 15% Parks, Recreation,
Leisure, and Fitness Studies, 10%

Financial aid: (303) 964-5758;
68% of undergrads determined to
have financial need; average aid
package $27,284

Social Sciences, 9% Biological and Biomedical Sciences, 6% Natural Resources and Conservation
Expenses: 2017-2018: $9,802 in state, $21,274 out of state; room/board: $9,546
Financial aid: N/A; 57% of undergrads determined to have financial need; average aid package $9,806

CONNECTICUT

Albertus Magnus College
New Haven CT
(800) 578-9160
U.S. News ranking: Reg. U. (N), No. 116
Website: www.albertus.edu
Admissions email: admissions@albertus.edu
Private; founded 1925
Freshman admissions: less selective; 2016-2017: 666 applied, 418 accepted. Either SAT or ACT required. SAT 25/75 percentile: 820-950. High school rank: N/A
Early decision deadline: N/A, notification date: N/A
Early action deadline: N/A, notification date: N/A
Application deadline (fall): rolling
Undergraduate student body: 1,034 full time, 186 part time; 33% male, 67% female; 0% American Indian, 0% Asian, 34% black, 18% Hispanic, 1% multiracial, 0% Pacific Islander, 36% white, 2% international; N/A from in state; 15% live on campus; N/A of students in fraternities, N/A in sororities
Most popular majors: Information not available
Expenses: 2017-2018: $31,140; room/board. $13,000
Financial aid: (203) 773-8508; 88% of undergrads determined to have financial need; average aid package $15,110

Central Connecticut State University
New Britain CT
(860) 832 2278
U.S. News ranking: Reg. U. (N), No. 94
Website: www.ccsu.edu
Admissions email: admissions@ccsu.edu
Public; founded 1849
Freshman admissions: selective; 2016-2017: 7,810 applied, 4,687 accepted. Either SAT or ACT required. SAT 25/75 percentile: 900-1100. High school rank: 9% in top tenth, 32% in top quarter, 69% in top half
Early decision deadline: N/A, notification date: N/A
Early action deadline: N/A, notification date: N/A
Application deadline (fall): 5/1
Undergraduate student body: 7,539 full time, 1,999 part time; 54% male, 46% female; 0% American Indian, 4% Asian, 12% black, 14% Hispanic, 3% multiracial, 0% Pacific Islander, 63% white, 2% international; 96% from in state; 24% live on campus; 0% of students in fraternities, 0% in sororities

Most popular majors: 23% Business, Management, Marketing, and Related Support Services, 14% Social Sciences, 8% Psychology, 6% Biological and Biomedical Sciences, 6% Education
Expenses: 2017-2018: $10,225 in state, $21,683 out of state; room/board: $11,816
Financial aid: (860) 832-2203; 79% of undergrads determined to have financial need; average aid package $12,267

Charter Oak State College
New Britain CT
(860) 515-3701
U.S. News ranking: Nat. Lib. Arts, unranked
Website: www.charteroak.edu
Admissions email: admissions@charteroak.edu
Public; founded 1973
Freshman admissions: least selective; 2016-2017: N/A applied, N/A accepted. Neither SAT nor ACT required. SAT 25/75 percentile: N/A. High school rank: N/A
Early decision deadline: N/A, notification date: N/A
Early action deadline: N/A, notification date: N/A
Application deadline (fall): rolling
Undergraduate student body: 313 full time, 1,220 part time; 32% male, 68% female; 1% American Indian, 1% Asian, 17% black, 15% Hispanic, 2% multiracial, 0% Pacific Islander, 58% white, 1% international; 80% from in state; 0% live on campus; N/A of students in fraternities, N/A in sororities
Most popular majors: 83% Liberal Arts and Sciences/Liberal Studies, 8% Health/Health Care Administration/Management, 7% Business Administration and Management, General, 2% Psychology, General
Expenses: 2017-2018: $9,771 in state, $12,591 out of state; room/board: N/A
Financial aid: (860) 515-3703

Connecticut College
New London CT
(860) 439-2200
U.S. News ranking: Nat. Lib. Arts, No. 46
Website: www.conncoll.edu
Admissions email: admission@conncoll.edu
Private; founded 1911
Freshman admissions: more selective; 2016-2017: 5,879 applied, 2,065 accepted. Neither SAT nor ACT required. SAT 25/75 percentile: 1230-1398. High school rank: 45% in top tenth, 79% in top quarter, 97% in top half
Early decision deadline: 11/15, notification date: 12/15
Early action deadline: N/A, notification date: N/A
Application deadline (fall): 1/1
Undergraduate student body: 1,819 full time, 46 part time; 37% male, 63% female; 0% American Indian, 4% Asian, 4% black, 9% Hispanic, 3% multiracial,

0% Pacific Islander, 70% white, 7% international; 19% from in state; 97% live on campus; 0% of students in fraternities, 0% in sororities
Most popular majors: 16% Economics, General, 14% Psychology, General, 8% Biology/Biological Sciences, General, 6% Political Science and Government, General, 5% International Relations and Affairs
Expenses: 2017-2018: $52,850; room/board: $14,590
Financial aid: (860) 439-2058; 57% of undergrads determined to have financial need; average aid package $40,891

Eastern Connecticut State University
Willimantic CT
(860) 465-5286
U.S. News ranking: Reg. U. (N), No. 86
Website: www.easternct.edu
Admissions email: admissions@easternct.edu
Public; founded 1889
Freshman admissions: selective; 2016-2017: 5,863 applied, 3,395 accepted. Neither SAT nor ACT required. SAT 25/75 percentile: 950-1120. High school rank: 11% in top tenth, 37% in top quarter, 78% in top half
Early decision deadline: N/A, notification date: N/A
Early action deadline: N/A, notification date: N/A
Application deadline (fall): rolling
Undergraduate student body: 4,292 full time, 879 part time; 44% male, 56% female; 0% American Indian, 2% Asian, 8% black, 11% Hispanic, 3% multiracial, 0% Pacific Islander, 66% white, 1% international; 6% from in state; 52% live on campus; N/A of students in fraternities, N/A in sororities
Most popular majors: 18% Business, Management, Marketing, and Related Support Services, 10% Liberal Arts and Sciences, General Studies and Humanities, 10% Psychology, 10% Social Sciences, 9% Communication, Journalism, and Related Programs
Expenses: 2017-2018: $10,919 in state, $22,377 out of state; room/board: $13,050
Financial aid: (860) 465-5205; 69% of undergrads determined to have financial need; average aid package $9,941

Fairfield University
Fairfield CT
(203) 254-4100
U.S. News ranking: Reg. U. (N), No. 3
Website: www.fairfield.edu
Admissions email: admis@fairfield.edu
Private; founded 1942
Affiliation: Roman Catholic
Freshman admissions: more selective; 2016-2017: 11,055 applied, 6,795 accepted. Neither SAT nor ACT required. SAT 25/75 percentile: 1110-1270. High school rank: 35% in top tenth, 67% in top quarter, 93% in top half

Early decision deadline: 11/15, notification date: 12/15
Early action deadline: 11/1, notification date: 12/20
Application deadline (fall): 1/15
Undergraduate student body: 3,803 full time, 229 part time; 39% male, 61% female; 0% American Indian, 2% Asian, 2% black, 8% Hispanic, 1% multiracial, 0% Pacific Islander, 77% white, 3% international; 29% from in state; 72% live on campus; N/A of students in fraternities, N/A in sororities
Most popular majors: 38% Business, Management, Marketing, and Related Support Services, 11% Health Professions and Related Programs, 10% Communication, Journalism, and Related Programs, 9% Social Sciences, 8% Psychology
Expenses: 2017-2018: $47,165; room/board: $14,280
Financial aid: (203) 254-4000; 46% of undergrads determined to have financial need; average aid package $33,012

Lincoln College of New England–Southington[1]
Southington CT
U.S. News ranking: Reg. Coll. (N), unranked
Admissions email: N/A
For-profit
Application deadline (fall): N/A
Undergraduate student body: N/A full time, N/A part time
Expenses: 2016-2017: $20,050; room/board: $11,300
Financial aid: N/A

Mitchell College[1]
New London CT
U.S. News ranking: Reg. Coll. (N), second tier
Website: www.mitchell.edu
Admissions email: admissions@mitchell.edu
Private
Application deadline (fall): N/A
Undergraduate student body: N/A full time, N/A part time
Expenses: 2016-2017: $31,780; room/board: $12,500
Financial aid: N/A

Post University
Waterbury CT
(203) 596-4520
U.S. News ranking: Reg. U. (N), second tier
Website: www.post.edu
Admissions email: admissions@post.edu
For-profit; founded 1890
Freshman admissions: less selective; 2016-2017: 4,507 applied, 1,835 accepted. Neither SAT nor ACT required. SAT 25/75 percentile: 770-1000. High school rank: N/A
Early decision deadline: N/A, notification date: N/A
Early action deadline: N/A, notification date: N/A
Application deadline (fall): rolling
Undergraduate student body: 2,566 full time, 4,493 part time; 38% male, 62% female; 1% American

Indian, 1% Asian, 24% black, 7% Hispanic, 6% multiracial, 0% Pacific Islander, 41% white, 0% international; 53% from in state; 20% live on campus; 0% of students in fraternities, 0% in sororities
Most popular majors: 44% Business Administration and Management, General, 9% Accounting, 8% Criminal Justice/Safety Studies, 6% Management Information Systems, General, 6% Psychology, General
Expenses: 2017-2018: $29,550; room/board: $11,600
Financial aid: (800) 345-2562; 79% of undergrads determined to have financial need; average aid package $11,756

Quinnipiac University
Hamden CT
(203) 582-8600
U.S. News ranking: Reg. U. (N), No. 13
Website: www.qu.edu
Admissions email: admissions@qu.edu
Private; founded 1929
Freshman admissions: selective; 2016-2017: 23,492 applied, 17,957 accepted. Either SAT or ACT required. SAT 25/75 percentile: 980-1190. High school rank: 27% in top tenth, 62% in top quarter, 92% in top half
Early decision deadline: 11/1, notification date: 12/1
Early action deadline: N/A, notification date. N/A
Application deadline (fall): 2/1
Undergraduate student body: 6,784 full time, 315 part time; 39% male, 61% female; 0% American Indian, 3% Asian, 5% black, 9% Hispanic, 2% multiracial, 0% Pacific Islander, 76% white, 2% international; 25% from in state; 80% live on campus; 24% of students in fraternities, 30% in sororities
Most popular majors: 34% Health Professions and Related Programs, 21% Business, Management, Marketing, and Related Support Services, 14% Communication, Journalism, and Related Programs, 5% Biological and Biomedical Sciences, 5% Psychology
Expenses: 2017-2018: $46,780; room/board: $14,190
Financial aid: (203) 582-8750; 63% of undergrads determined to have financial need; average aid package $27,228

Sacred Heart University
Fairfield CT
(203) 371-7880
U.S. News ranking: Reg. U. (N), No. 41
Website: www.sacredheart.edu
Admissions email: enroll@sacredheart.edu
Private; founded 1963
Affiliation: Roman Catholic
Freshman admissions: selective; 2016-2017: 10,017 applied, 5,731 accepted. Neither SAT nor ACT required. SAT 25/75 percentile: 1040-1200. High school rank: 8% in top tenth, 31% in top quarter, 68% in top half

Early decision deadline: 12/1, notification date: 12/15
Early action deadline: 12/15, notification date: 1/31
Application deadline (fall): rolling
Undergraduate student body: 4,794 full time, 634 part time; 36% male, 64% female; 0% American Indian, 2% Asian, 4% black, 10% Hispanic, 2% multiracial, 0% Pacific Islander, 73% white, 1% international; 37% from in state; 51% live on campus; 15% of students in fraternities, 36% in sororities
Most popular majors: 33% Business, Management, Marketing, and Related Support Services, 27% Health Professions and Related Programs, 10% Psychology, 5% Communication, Journalism, and Related Programs, 5% Homeland Security, Law Enforcement, Firefighting and Related Protective Services
Expenses: 2017-2018: $39,820; room/board: $14,770
Financial aid: (203) 371-7980; 67% of undergrads determined to have financial need; average aid package $20,275

Southern Connecticut State University

New Haven CT
(203) 392-5644
U.S. News ranking: Reg. U. (N), No. 130
Website: www.southernct.edu/
Admissions email: information@southernct.edu
Public; founded 1893
Freshman admissions: less selective; 2016-2017: 8,625 applied, 5,479 accepted. Either SAT or ACT required. SAT 25/75 percentile: 830-1030. High school rank: 1% in top tenth, 8% in top quarter, 39% in top half
Early decision deadline: N/A, notification date: N/A
Early action deadline: N/A, notification date: N/A
Application deadline (fall): rolling
Undergraduate student body: 6,830 full time, 1,133 part time; 38% male, 62% female; 0% American Indian, 4% Asian, 17% black, 14% Hispanic, 3% multiracial, 0% Pacific Islander, 55% white, 1% international; 96% from in state; 33% live on campus; 1% of students in fraternities, 1% in sororities
Most popular majors: 13% Business Administration and Management, General, 13% Liberal Arts and Sciences/Liberal Studies, 10% Psychology, General, 6% Public Health, General, 6% Registered Nursing/Registered Nurse
Expenses: 2017-2018: $10,537 in state, $21,995 out of state; room/board: $11,975
Financial aid: (203) 392-5222; 67% of undergrads determined to have financial need; average aid package $14,501

Trinity College

Hartford CT
(860) 297-2180
U.S. News ranking: Nat. Lib. Arts, No. 44
Website: www.trincoll.edu
Admissions email: admissions.office@trincoll.edu
Private; founded 1823
Freshman admissions: more selective; 2016-2017: 6,073 applied, 2,062 accepted. Neither SAT nor ACT required. SAT 25/75 percentile: 1210-1370. High school rank: 50% in top tenth, 78% in top quarter, 96% in top half
Early decision deadline: 11/15, notification date: 12/15
Early action deadline: N/A, notification date: N/A
Application deadline (fall): 1/1
Undergraduate student body: 2,159 full time, 100 part time; 51% male, 49% female; 0% American Indian, 4% Asian, 6% black, 8% Hispanic, 3% multiracial, 0% Pacific Islander, 65% white, 10% international
Most popular majors: 16% Political Science and Government, General, 12% Economics, General, 7% English Language and Literature, General, 6% Psychology, General, 5% Public Policy Analysis, General
Expenses: 2017-2018: $54,770; room/board: $14,200
Financial aid: (860) 428-2048; 48% of undergrads determined to have financial need; average aid package $47,679

United States Coast Guard Academy

New London CT
(800) 883-8724
U.S. News ranking: Reg. Coll. (N), No. 2
Website: www.uscga.edu
Admissions email: admissions@uscga.edu
Public; founded 1932
Freshman admissions: more selective; 2016-2017: 2,028 applied, 433 accepted. Either SAT or ACT required. SAT 25/75 percentile: 1170-1340. High school rank: 41% in top tenth, 79% in top quarter, 97% in top half
Early decision deadline: N/A, notification date: N/A
Early action deadline: 10/15, notification date: 2/1
Application deadline (fall): 1/15
Undergraduate student body: 988 full time, 0 part time; 64% male, 36% female; 0% American Indian, 6% Asian, 6% black, 9% Hispanic, 9% multiracial, 0% Pacific Islander, 67% white, 2% international
Most popular majors: 37% Engineering, 18% Business, Management, Marketing, and Related Support Services, 16% Social Sciences, 15% Biological and Biomedical Sciences, 14% Mathematics and Statistics
Expenses: 2017-2018: $978 in state, $978 out of state; room/board: $0
Financial aid: N/A

University of Bridgeport

Bridgeport CT
(203) 576-4552
U.S. News ranking: Reg. U. (N), second tier
Website: www.bridgeport.edu
Admissions email: admit@bridgeport.edu
Private; founded 1927
Freshman admissions: less selective; 2016-2017: 6,969 applied, 4,027 accepted. Either SAT or ACT required. SAT 25/75 percentile: 840-1010. High school rank: 13% in top tenth, 44% in top quarter, 62% in top half
Early decision deadline: N/A, notification date: N/A
Early action deadline: N/A, notification date: N/A
Application deadline (fall): rolling
Undergraduate student body: 2,140 full time, 801 part time; 37% male, 63% female; 1% American Indian, 3% Asian, 34% black, 20% Hispanic, 3% multiracial, 0% Pacific Islander, 23% white, 14% international; 63% from in state; 44% live on campus; 2% of students in fraternities, 2% in sororities
Most popular majors: 18% Business/Commerce, General, 14% Psychology, General, 11% General Studies, 8% Public Administration and Social Service Professions, 6% Dental Hygiene/Hygienist
Expenses: 2017-2018: $32,250; room/board: $13,590
Financial aid: (203) 576-4568; 81% of undergrads determined to have financial need; average aid package $24,676

University of Connecticut

Storrs CT
(860) 486-3137
U.S. News ranking: Nat. U., No. 56
Website: www.uconn.edu
Admissions email: beahusky@uconn.edu
Public; founded 1881
Freshman admissions: more selective; 2016-2017: 35,980 applied, 17,560 accepted. Either SAT or ACT required. SAT 25/75 percentile: 1130-1340. High school rank: 51% in top tenth, 84% in top quarter, 98% in top half
Early decision deadline: N/A, notification date: N/A
Early action deadline: N/A, notification date: N/A
Application deadline (fall): 1/15
Undergraduate student body: 18,655 full time, 669 part time; 50% male, 50% female; 0% American Indian, 11% Asian, 6% black, 10% Hispanic, 3% multiracial, 0% Pacific Islander, 60% white, 6% international; 78% from in state; 67% live on campus; 12% of students in fraternities, 17% in sororities
Most popular majors: 13% Business, Management, Marketing, and Related Support Services, 13% Health Professions and Related Programs, 11% Social Sciences, 10% Engineering, 9% Biological and Biomedical Sciences

Expenses: 2017-2018: $14,880 in state, $36,948 out of state; room/board: $12,514
Financial aid: (860) 486-2819; 55% of undergrads determined to have financial need; average aid package $14,404

University of Hartford

West Hartford CT
(860) 768-4296
U.S. News ranking: Nat. U., No. 176
Website: www.hartford.edu
Admissions email: admission@hartford.edu
Private; founded 1877
Freshman admissions: selective; 2016-2017: 15,526 applied, 11,168 accepted. Either SAT or ACT required. SAT 25/75 percentile: 920-1160. High school rank: N/A
Early decision deadline: N/A, notification date: N/A
Early action deadline: 11/15, notification date: 12/1
Application deadline (fall): rolling
Undergraduate student body: 4,508 full time, 642 part time; 49% male, 51% female; 0% American Indian, 3% Asian, 16% black, 13% Hispanic, 3% multiracial, 0% Pacific Islander, 55% white, 6% international; 49% from in state; 65% live on campus; 17% of students in fraternities, 21% in sororities
Most popular majors: 23% Visual and Performing Arts, 14% Health Professions and Related Programs, 13% Engineering, 11% Business, Management, Marketing, and Related Support Services, 7% Communication, Journalism, and Related Programs
Expenses: 2017-2018: $38,910; room/board: $12,346
Financial aid: (860) 768-4296; 73% of undergrads determined to have financial need; average aid package $22,084

University of New Haven

West Haven CT
(203) 932-7319
U.S. News ranking: Reg. U. (N), No. 94
Website: www.newhaven.edu
Admissions email: admissions@newhaven.edu
Private; founded 1920
Freshman admissions: selective; 2016-2017: 10,720 applied, 8,633 accepted. Either SAT or ACT required. SAT 25/75 percentile: 930-1140. High school rank: 14% in top tenth, 41% in top quarter, 76% in top half
Early decision deadline: 12/1, notification date: 12/15
Early action deadline: 12/15, notification date: 1/15
Application deadline (fall): rolling
Undergraduate student body: 4,552 full time, 384 part time; 50% male, 50% female; 0% American Indian, 3% Asian, 11% black, 10% Hispanic, 2% multiracial, 0% Pacific Islander, 62% white, 8% international; 43% from in state; 53% live on campus; N/A of students in fraternities, N/A in sororities

Most popular majors: 43% Homeland Security, Law Enforcement, Firefighting and Related Protective Services, 11% Business, Management, Marketing, and Related Support Services, 10% Engineering, 8% Visual and Performing Arts, 5% Psychology
Expenses: 2017-2018: $38,170; room/board: $15,610
Financial aid: (203) 932-7315; 75% of undergrads determined to have financial need; average aid package $22,746

University of St. Joseph

West Hartford CT
(860) 231-5216
U.S. News ranking: Reg. U. (N), No. 78
Website: www.usj.edu
Admissions email: admissions@usj.edu
Private; founded 1932
Affiliation: Roman Catholic
Freshman admissions: selective; 2016-2017: 743 applied, 647 accepted. Neither SAT nor ACT required. SAT 25/75 percentile: 830-1100. High school rank: 21% in top tenth, 53% in top quarter, 93% in top half
Early decision deadline: N/A, notification date: N/A
Early action deadline: N/A, notification date: N/A
Application deadline (fall): rolling
Undergraduate student body: 726 full time, 168 part time; 3% male, 97% female; 0% American Indian, 5% Asian, 16% black, 16% Hispanic, 1% multiracial, 0% Pacific Islander, 55% white, 1% international; 96% from in state; 29% live on campus; 0% of students in fraternities, 0% in sororities
Most popular majors: 41% Health Professions and Related Programs, 15% Public Administration and Social Service Professions, 10% Psychology, 8% Family and Consumer Sciences/Human Sciences, 7% Biological and Biomedical Sciences
Expenses: 2017-2018: $38,033; room/board: $11,095
Financial aid: (860) 231-5245; 90% of undergrads determined to have financial need; average aid package $25,455

Wesleyan University

Middletown CT
(860) 685-3000
U.S. News ranking: Nat. Lib. Arts, No. 21
Website: www.wesleyan.edu
Admissions email: admissions@wesleyan.edu
Private; founded 1831
Freshman admissions: most selective; 2016-2017: 11,928 applied, 2,129 accepted. Neither SAT nor ACT required. SAT 25/75 percentile: 1250-1480. High school rank: 69% in top tenth, 87% in top quarter, 98% in top half
Early decision deadline: 11/15, notification date: 12/15
Early action deadline: N/A, notification date: N/A

Application deadline (fall): 1/1
Undergraduate student body: 2,918 full time, 53 part time; 46% male, 54% female; 0% American Indian, 7% Asian, 7% black, 10% Hispanic, 5% multiracial, 0% Pacific Islander, 55% white, 10% international; 8% from in state; 100% live on campus; 4% of students in fraternities, 1% in sororities
Most popular majors: 10% Economics, General, 9% Psychology, General, 8% Political Science and Government, General, 6% English Language and Literature, General, 6% Physiological Psychology/Psychobiology
Expenses: 2017-2018: $52,474; room/board: $15,456
Financial aid: (860) 685-2800; 44% of undergrads determined to have financial need; average aid package $47,077

Western Connecticut State University
Danbury CT
(203) 837-9000
U.S. News ranking: Reg. U. (N), No. 120
Website: www.wcsu.edu
Admissions email: admissions@wcsu.edu
Public; founded 1903
Freshman admissions: selective; 2016-2017: 5,484 applied, 3,665 accepted. Neither SAT nor ACT required. SAT 25/75 percentile: 880-1090. High school rank: 7% in top tenth, 25% in top quarter, 61% in top half
Early decision deadline: N/A, notification date: N/A
Early action deadline: N/A, notification date: N/A
Application deadline (fall): rolling
Undergraduate student body: 4,116 full time, 1,065 part time; 40% male, 52% female; 0% American Indian, 4% Asian, 11% black, 18% Hispanic, 3% multiracial, 0% Pacific Islander, 60% white, 0% international; 94% from in state; 32% live on campus; 3% of students in fraternities, 5% in sororities
Most popular majors: 21% Business, Management, Marketing, and Related Support Services, 13% Health Professions and Related Programs, 13% Homeland Security, Law Enforcement, Firefighting and Related Protective Services, 9% Communication, Journalism, and Related Programs, 9% Psychology
Expenses: 2017-2018: $10,418 in state, $21,876 out of state; room/board: $12,622
Financial aid: (203) 837-8580; 69% of undergrads determined to have financial need; average aid package $8,593

Yale University
New Haven CT
(203) 432-9300
U.S. News ranking: Nat. U., No. 3
Website: www.yale.edu/
Admissions email: student.questions@yale.edu
Private; founded 1701
Freshman admissions: most selective; 2016-2017: 31,445 applied, 1,988 accepted. Either

SAT or ACT required. SAT 25/75 percentile: 1420-1600. High school rank: 94% in top tenth, 99% in top quarter, 100% in top half
Early decision deadline: N/A, notification date: N/A
Early action deadline: 11/1, notification date: 12/15
Application deadline (fall): 1/1
Undergraduate student body: 5,469 full time, 3 part time; 51% male, 49% female; 1% American Indian, 17% Asian, 7% black, 12% Hispanic, 6% multiracial, 0% Pacific Islander, 46% white, 11% international; 7% from in state; 83% live on campus; N/A of students in fraternities, N/A in sororities
Most popular majors: 15% Economics, General, 9% Political Science and Government, General, 7% History, General, 7% Psychology, General, 6% Cell/Cellular and Molecular Biology
Expenses: 2017-2018: $51,400; room/board: $15,500
Financial aid: (203) 432-2700; 50% of undergrads determined to have financial need; average aid package $52,894

DELAWARE

Delaware State University
Dover DE
(302) 857-6353
U.S. News ranking: Reg. U. (N), No. 130
Website: www.desu.edu
Admissions email: admissions@desu.edu
Public; founded 1891
Freshman admissions: less selective; 2016-2017: 8,529 applied, 3,467 accepted. Either SAT or ACT required. SAT 25/75 percentile: 820-970. High school rank: 10% in top tenth, 30% in top quarter, 64% in top half
Early decision deadline: N/A, notification date: N/A
Early action deadline: N/A, notification date: N/A
Application deadline (fall): rolling
Undergraduate student body: 3,593 full time, 400 part time; 36% male, 64% female; 0% American Indian, 1% Asian, 75% black, 7% Hispanic, 5% multiracial, 0% Pacific Islander, 10% white, 2% international; 53% from in state; 59% live on campus; 3% of students in fraternities, 3% in sororities
Most popular majors: 13% Parks, Recreation, Leisure, and Fitness Studies, 12% Business, Management, Marketing, and Related Support Services, 11% Communication, Journalism, and Related Programs, 10% Social Sciences, 9% Health Professions and Related Programs
Expenses: 2017-2018: $7,868 in state, $16,904 out of state; room/board: $11,054
Financial aid: (302) 857-6250; 83% of undergrads determined to have financial need; average aid package $11,234

Goldey-Beacom College[1]
Wilmington DE
U.S. News ranking: Business, unranked
Website: www.gbc.edu
Admissions email: admissions@gbc.edu
Private; founded 1886
Application deadline (fall): N/A
Undergraduate student body: N/A full time, N/A part time
Expenses: 2016-2017: $23,400; room/board: $7,699
Financial aid: (302) 225-6265

University of Delaware
Newark DE
(302) 831-8123
U.S. News ranking: Nat. U., No. 81
Website: www.udel.edu/
Admissions email: admissions@udel.edu
Public; founded 1743
Freshman admissions: more selective; 2016-2017: 24,456 applied, 15,879 accepted. Either SAT or ACT required. SAT 25/75 percentile: 1090-1300. High school rank: 31% in top tenth, 66% in top quarter, 92% in top half
Early decision deadline: N/A, notification date: N/A
Early action deadline: N/A, notification date: N/A
Application deadline (fall): 1/15
Undergraduate student body: 16,953 full time, 1,421 part time; 42% male, 58% female; 0% American Indian, 5% Asian, 5% black, 8% Hispanic, 3% multiracial, 0% Pacific Islander, 73% white, 4% international; 38% from in state; 40% live on campus; 18% of students in fraternities, 24% in sororities
Most popular majors: 16% Business, Management, Marketing, and Related Support Services, 15% Health Professions and Related Programs, 15% Social Sciences, 7% Engineering, 5% Biological and Biomedical Sciences
Expenses: 2017-2018: $12,830 in state, $32,250 out of state; room/board: $12,068
Financial aid: (302) 831-0520; 48% of undergrads determined to have financial need; average aid package $12,963

Wesley College
Dover DE
(302) 736-2400
U.S. News ranking: Reg. Coll. (N), second tier
Website: www.wesley.edu
Admissions email: admissions@wesley.edu
Private; founded 1873
Affiliation: United Methodist
Freshman admissions: least selective; 2016-2017: 3,463 applied, 2,094 accepted. Either SAT or ACT required. SAT 25/75 percentile: 740-930. High school rank: 6% in top tenth, 16% in top quarter, 47% in top half
Early decision deadline: N/A, notification date: N/A
Early action deadline: N/A, notification date: N/A

Application deadline (fall): 4/30
Undergraduate student body: 1,305 full time, 40 part time; 44% male, 56% female; 0% American Indian, 1% Asian, 43% black, 6% Hispanic, 6% multiracial, 1% Pacific Islander, 39% white, 0% international
Most popular majors: 15% Registered Nursing/Registered Nurse, 13% Kinesiology and Exercise Science, 12% Business Administration and Management, General, 11% Psychology, General, 8% Legal Assistant/Paralegal
Expenses: 2016-2017: $25,646; room/board: $11,244
Financial aid: (302) 736-2483

Wilmington University
New Castle DE
(302) 328-9407
U.S. News ranking: Nat. U., unranked
Website: www.wilmu.edu
Admissions email: undergradadmissions@wilmu.edu
Private; founded 1967
Freshman admissions: least selective; 2016-2017: 1,760 applied, 1,759 accepted. Neither SAT nor ACT required. SAT 25/75 percentile: N/A. High school rank: N/A
Early decision deadline: N/A, notification date: N/A
Early action deadline: N/A, notification date: N/A
Application deadline (fall): rolling
Undergraduate student body: 3,570 full time, 5,303 part time; 35% male, 65% female; 2% American Indian, 2% Asian, 27% black, 4% Hispanic, 0% multiracial, 0% Pacific Islander, 55% white, 2% international; 66% from in state; 0% live on campus; N/A of students in fraternities, N/A in sororities
Most popular majors: 22% Nursing Practice, 12% Business Administration and Management, General, 10% Behavioral Sciences, 7% Criminal Justice/Law Enforcement Administration, 6% Psychology, General
Expenses: 2017-2018: $10,940; room/board: N/A
Financial aid: (302) 356-4636

DISTRICT OF COLUMBIA

American University
Washington DC
(202) 885-6000
U.S. News ranking: Nat. U., No. 69
Website: www.american.edu
Admissions email: admissions@american.edu
Private; founded 1893
Freshman admissions: more selective; 2016-2017: 19,325 applied, 5,008 accepted. Neither SAT nor ACT required. SAT 25/75 percentile: 1150-1340. High school rank: 35% in top tenth, 68% in top quarter, 94% in top half
Early decision deadline: 11/15, notification date: 12/31
Early action deadline: N/A, notification date: N/A

Application deadline (fall): 1/15
Undergraduate student body: 7,545 full time, 356 part time; 37% male, 63% female; 0% American Indian, 7% Asian, 7% black, 13% Hispanic, 5% multiracial, 0% Pacific Islander, 59% white, 7% international; 18% from in state; N/A live on campus; 24% of students in fraternities, 32% in sororities
Most popular majors: 25% International Relations and Affairs, 14% Business Administration and Management, General, 8% Political Science and Government, General, 6% Mass Communication/Media Studies, 4% Multi-/Interdisciplinary Studies, Other
Expenses: 2017-2018: $46,615; room/board: $14,702
Financial aid: (202) 885-6500; 53% of undergrads determined to have financial need; average aid package $31,064

The Catholic University of America
Washington DC
(800) 673-2772
U.S. News ranking: Nat. U., No. 120
Website: www.cua.edu
Admissions email: cua-admissions@cua.edu
Private; founded 1887
Affiliation: Roman Catholic
Freshman admissions: selective; 2016-2017: 5,926 applied, 4,714 accepted. Neither SAT nor ACT required. SAT 25/75 percentile: 1040-1250. High school rank: N/A
Early decision deadline: 11/15, notification date: 12/20
Early action deadline: 11/1, notification date: 12/20
Application deadline (fall): 1/15
Undergraduate student body: 3,096 full time, 145 part time; 45% male, 55% female; 0% American Indian, 4% Asian, 5% black, 13% Hispanic, 5% multiracial, 0% Pacific Islander, 65% white, 5% international; 4% from in state; 56% live on campus; 0% of students in fraternities, 1% in sororities
Most popular majors: 10% Political Science and Government, General, 10% Psychology, General, 8% Registered Nursing/Registered Nurse, 7% Architecture, 6% Mechanical Engineering
Expenses: 2017-2018: $44,060; room/board: $14,316
Financial aid: (202) 319-5307; 55% of undergrads determined to have financial need; average aid package $29,024

Gallaudet University
Washington DC
(202) 651-5750
U.S. News ranking: Reg. U. (N), No. 22
Website: www.gallaudet.edu
Admissions email: admissions.office@gallaudet.edu
Private; founded 1864
Freshman admissions: less selective; 2016-2017: 511 applied, 338 accepted. Either SAT or ACT required. ACT 25/75

percentile: 14-20. High school rank: N/A
Early decision deadline: N/A, notification date: N/A
Early action deadline: N/A, notification date: N/A
Undergraduate student body: 1,082 full time, 39 part time; 48% male, 52% female; 1% American Indian, 4% Asian, 16% black, 10% Hispanic, 4% multiracial, 1% Pacific Islander, 53% white, 7% international; 3% from in state; 82% live on campus; 7% of students in fraternities, 6% in sororities
Most popular majors: 11% Business, Management, Marketing, and Related Support Services, 11% Communication, Journalism, and Related Programs, 11% Foreign Languages, Literatures, and Linguistics, 9% Parks, Recreation, Leisure, and Fitness Studies, 8% Psychology
Expenses: 2017-2018: $16,558; room/board: $14,038
Financial aid: (202) 651-5290; 82% of undergrads determined to have financial need; average aid package $21,472

George Washington University
Washington DC
(202) 994-6040
U.S. News ranking: Nat. U., No. 56
Website: www.gwu.edu
Admissions email: gwadm@gwu.edu
Private; founded 1821
Freshman admissions: more selective; 2016-2017: 25,488 applied, 10,249 accepted. Neither SAT nor ACT required. SAT 25/75 percentile: 1180-1390. High school rank: 55% in top tenth, 85% in top quarter, 98% in top half
Early decision deadline: 11/1, notification date: 12/15
Early action deadline: N/A, notification date: N/A
Application deadline (fall): 1/1
Undergraduate student body: 10,430 full time, 1,074 part time; 43% male, 57% female; 0% American Indian, 10% Asian, 7% black, 9% Hispanic, 4% multiracial, 0% Pacific Islander, 54% white, 11% international; 3% from in state; 65% live on campus; 18% of students in fraternities, 26% in sororities
Most popular majors: 34% Social Sciences, 18% Business, Management, Marketing, and Related Support Services, 9% Health Professions and Related Programs, 5% Communication, Journalism, and Related Programs, 5% Engineering
Expenses: 2017-2018: $53,518; room/board: $13,000
Financial aid: (202) 994-6620; 46% of undergrads determined to have financial need; average aid package $45,233

Georgetown University
Washington DC
(202) 687-3600
U.S. News ranking: Nat. U., No. 20
Website: www.georgetown.edu
Admissions email: guadmiss@georgetown.edu
Private; founded 1789
Affiliation: Roman Catholic
Freshman admissions: most selective; 2016-2017: 19,997 applied, 3,369 accepted. Either SAT or ACT required. SAT 25/75 percentile: 1320-1520. High school rank: 91% in top tenth, 97% in top quarter, 99% in top half
Early decision deadline: N/A, notification date: N/A
Early action deadline: 11/1, notification date: 12/15
Application deadline (fall): 1/10
Undergraduate student body: 7,056 full time, 397 part time; 44% male, 56% female; 0% American Indian, 10% Asian, 6% black, 9% Hispanic, 5% multiracial, 0% Pacific Islander, 56% white, 12% international; 4% from in state; 78% live on campus; N/A of students in fraternities, N/A in sororities
Most popular majors: 38% Social Sciences, 18% Business, Management, Marketing, and Related Support Services, 6% Biological and Biomedical Sciences, 6% Health Professions and Related Programs, 6% Multi/Interdisciplinary Studies
Expenses: 2017-2018: $52,300; room/board: $16,036
Financial aid: (202) 687-4547; 38% of undergrads determined to have financial need; average aid package $48,999

Howard University
Washington DC
(202) 806-2755
U.S. News ranking: Nat. U., No. 110
Website: www.howard.edu
Admissions email: admission@howard.edu
Private; founded 1867
Freshman admissions: selective; 2016-2017: 18,225 applied, 5,468 accepted. Either SAT or ACT required. SAT 25/75 percentile: 1040-1240. High school rank: 28% in top tenth, 60% in top quarter, 89% in top half
Early decision deadline: N/A, notification date: N/A
Early action deadline: 11/1, notification date: 12/20
Application deadline (fall): 2/15
Undergraduate student body: 5,575 full time, 324 part time; 33% male, 67% female; 0% American Indian, 1% Asian, 90% black, 1% Hispanic, 0% multiracial, 0% Pacific Islander, 1% white, 7% international; 5% from in state; 61% live on campus; 3% of students in fraternities, 5% in sororities
Most popular majors: 14% Physical Sciences, 13% Business, Management, Marketing, and Related Support Services, 11% Communication, Journalism, and

Related Programs, 11% Social Sciences, 9% Biological and Biomedical Sciences
Expenses: 2017-2018: $25,697; room/board: $13,390
Financial aid: (202) 806-2850; 80% of undergrads determined to have financial need; average aid package $14,601

Strayer University[1]
Washington DC
(202) 408-2400
U.S. News ranking: Reg. U. (N), unranked
Website: www.strayer.edu
Admissions email: mzm@strayer.edu
For-profit; founded 1892
Application deadline (fall): N/A
Undergraduate student body: N/A full time, N/A part time
Expenses: 2016-2017: $12,975; room/board: N/A
Financial aid: N/A

Trinity Washington University[1]
Washington DC
(202) 884-9400
U.S. News ranking: Reg. U. (N), second tier
Website: www.trinitydc.edu
Admissions email: admissions@trinitydc.edu
Private
Application deadline (fall): N/A
Undergraduate student body: N/A full time, N/A part time
Expenses: 2016-2017: $23,250; room/board: $10,334
Financial aid: N/A

University of the District of Columbia
Washington DC
(202) 274-5010
U.S. News ranking: Reg. U. (N), second tier
Website: www.udc.edu/
Public; founded 1976
Freshman admissions: least selective; 2016-2017: 2,551 applied, 1,377 accepted. Either SAT or ACT required. SAT 25/75 percentile: 700-910. High school rank: N/A
Early decision deadline: N/A, notification date: N/A
Early action deadline: N/A, notification date: N/A
Application deadline (fall): rolling
Undergraduate student body: 1,798 full time, 2,152 part time; 43% male, 57% female; 0% American Indian, 2% Asian, 58% black, 11% Hispanic, 2% multiracial, 0% Pacific Islander, 3% white, 14% international
Most popular majors: 11% Business Administration, Management and Operations, Other, 10% Human Development and Family Studies, General, 6% Accounting, 6% Psychology, General, 6% Public Health, General
Expenses: 2016-2017: $5,612 in state, $11,756 out of state; room/board: $16,425
Financial aid: (202) 274-6053; 61% of undergrads determined to have financial need; average aid package $8,794

University of the Potomac
Washington DC
(202) 274-2303
U.S. News ranking: Business, unranked
Website: www.potomac.edu
Admissions email: admissions@potomac.edu
For-profit; founded 1991
Freshman admissions: least selective; 2016-2017: N/A applied, N/A accepted. Neither SAT nor ACT required. SAT 25/75 percentile: N/A. High school rank: N/A
Early decision deadline: N/A, notification date: N/A
Early action deadline: N/A, notification date: N/A
Application deadline (fall): rolling
Undergraduate student body: 120 full time, 8 part time; 65% male, 35% female; 2% American Indian, 3% Asian, 54% black, 2% Hispanic, 2% multiracial, 2% Pacific Islander, 18% white, 9% international
Most popular majors: Information not available
Expenses: 2016-2017: $13,884; room/board: N/A
Financial aid: N/A

FLORIDA

Ave Maria University[1]
Ave Maria FL
(877) 283-8648
U.S. News ranking: Nat. Lib. Arts, second tier
Website: www.avemaria.edu
Private; founded 2003
Application deadline (fall): rolling
Undergraduate student body: N/A full time, N/A part time
Expenses: 2016-2017: $19,128; room/board: $10,492
Financial aid: (239) 280-2423

Barry University
Miami Shores FL
(305) 899-3100
U.S. News ranking: Nat. U., second tier
Website: www.barry.edu
Admissions email: admissions@mail.barry.edu
Private; founded 1940
Freshman admissions: less selective; 2016-2017: 4,982 applied, 3,070 accepted. Either SAT or ACT required. SAT 25/75 percentile: 850-1010. High school rank: N/A
Early decision deadline: N/A, notification date: N/A
Early action deadline: N/A, notification date: N/A
Application deadline (fall): rolling
Undergraduate student body: 2,924 full time, 617 part time; 39% male, 61% female; 0% American Indian, 1% Asian, 29% black, 31% Hispanic, 2% multiracial, 0% Pacific Islander, 19% white, 8% international; 79% from in state; 30% live on campus; N/A of students in fraternities, N/A in sororities

Most popular majors: 23% Health Professions and Related Programs, 22% Business, Management, Marketing, and Related Support Services, 11% Public Administration and Social Service Professions, 9% Biological and Biomedical Sciences, 7% Computer and Information Sciences and Support Services
Expenses: 2017-2018: $29,700; room/board: $11,100
Financial aid: (800) 899-3673; 76% of undergrads determined to have financial need; average aid package $20,983

Beacon College[1]
Leesburg FL
U.S. News ranking: Reg. Coll. (S), unranked
Website: www.beaconcollege.edu/
Admissions email: admissions@beaconcollege.edu
Private
Application deadline (fall): N/A
Undergraduate student body: N/A full time, N/A part time
Expenses: 2016-2017: $36,172; room/board: $10,690
Financial aid: N/A

Bethune-Cookman University
Daytona Beach FL
(800) 448-0228
U.S. News ranking: Nat. Lib. Arts, second tier
Website: www.bethune.cookman.edu
Admissions email: admissions@cookman.edu
Private; founded 1904
Freshman admissions: least selective; 2016-2017: 11,900 applied, 5,259 accepted. Either SAT or ACT required. ACT 25/75 percentile: 15-18. High school rank: 13% in top tenth, 33% in top quarter, 67% in top half
Early decision deadline: N/A, notification date: N/A
Early action deadline: N/A, notification date: N/A
Application deadline (fall): rolling
Undergraduate student body: 3,584 full time, 212 part time; 40% male, 60% female; 0% American Indian, 0% Asian, 79% black, 3% Hispanic, 2% multiracial, 0% Pacific Islander, 2% white, 2% international; 73% from in state; 66% live on campus; 3% of students in fraternities, 5% in sororities
Most popular majors: 17% Liberal Arts and Sciences/Liberal Studies, 14% Corrections and Criminal Justice, Other, 12% Psychology, General, 10% Business Administration and Management, General, 7% Mass Communication/Media Studies
Expenses: 2017-2018: $14,410; room/board: $8,710
Financial aid: (386) 481-2620; 95% of undergrads determined to have financial need; average aid package $13,302

Broward College[1]
Fort Lauderdale FL
U.S. News ranking: Reg. Coll. (S), unranked
Admissions email: N/A
Public
Application deadline (fall): N/A
Undergraduate student body: N/A full time, N/A part time
Expenses: 2017-2018: $3,417 in state, $7,749 out of state; room/board: N/A
Financial aid: (954) 201-7000; 57% of undergrads determined to have financial need; average aid package $3,314

Chipola College[1]
Marianna FL
(850) 718-2211
U.S. News ranking: Reg. Coll. (S), second tier
Website: www.chipola.edu
Public
Application deadline (fall): N/A
Undergraduate student body: N/A full time, N/A part time
Expenses: 2016-2017: $3,120 in state, $8,950 out of state; room/board: $4,560
Financial aid: N/A

College of Central Florida
Ocala FL
(352) 854-2322
U.S. News ranking: Reg. Coll. (S), unranked
Website: www.cf.edu
Admissions email: admiss@cf.edu
Public; founded 1957
Freshman admissions: least selective; 2016-2017: 3,398 applied, 1,685 accepted. Neither SAT nor ACT required. SAT 25/75 percentile: N/A. High school rank: N/A
Early decision deadline: N/A, notification date: N/A
Early action deadline: N/A, notification date: N/A
Application deadline (fall): 8/12
Undergraduate student body: 3,100 full time, 4,275 part time; 38% male, 62% female; 1% American Indian, 2% Asian, 15% black, 14% Hispanic, 4% multiracial, 0% Pacific Islander, 60% white, 2% international
Most popular majors: Information not available
Expenses: 2017-2018: $3,210 in state, $12,660 out of state; room/board: N/A
Financial aid: (352) 854-2322; 45% of undergrads determined to have financial need; average aid package $1,897

Daytona State College[1]
Daytona Beach FL
U.S. News ranking: Reg. Coll. (S), unranked
Website: www.daytonastate.edu
Admissions email: N/A
Public; founded 1957
Application deadline (fall): N/A
Undergraduate student body: N/A full time, N/A part time
Expenses: 2016-2017: $3,112 in state, $12,001 out of state; room/board: N/A
Financial aid: N/A

Eastern Florida State College
Cocoa FL
U.S. News ranking: Reg. Coll. (S), unranked
Website: www.easternflorida.edu
Public; founded 1960
Freshman admissions: least selective; 2016-2017: N/A applied, N/A accepted. Neither SAT nor ACT required. SAT 25/75 percentile: N/A. High school rank: N/A
Early decision deadline: N/A, notification date: N/A
Early action deadline: N/A, notification date: N/A
Application deadline (fall): rolling
Undergraduate student body: 5,524 full time, 10,301 part time; 40% male, 60% female; N/A American Indian, N/A Asian, N/A black, N/A Hispanic, N/A multiracial, N/A Pacific Islander, N/A white, N/A international
Most popular majors: 49% Liberal Arts and Sciences/Liberal Studies, Business Administration, Management and Operations
Expenses: 2016-2017: $2,496 in state, $9,739 out of state; room/board: N/A
Financial aid: N/A

Eckerd College
St. Petersburg FL
(727) 864-8331
U.S. News ranking: Nat. Lib. Arts, No. 128
Website: www.eckerd.edu
Admissions email: admissions@eckerd.edu
Private; founded 1958
Affiliation: Presbyterian Church (USA)
Freshman admissions: selective; 2016-2017: 4,603 applied, 3,320 accepted. Either SAT or ACT required. ACT 25/75 percentile: 22-28. High school rank: N/A
Early decision deadline: N/A, notification date: N/A
Early action deadline: 11/15, notification date: 12/15
Application deadline (fall): rolling
Undergraduate student body: 1,808 full time, 36 part time; 35% male, 65% female; 0% American Indian, 2% Asian, 3% black, 8% Hispanic, 3% multiracial, 0% Pacific Islander, 78% white, 5% international; 25% from in state; 88% live on campus; 0% of students in fraternities, 0% in sororities
Most popular majors: 15% Environmental Studies, 13% Marine Biology and Biological Oceanography, 11% Psychology, General, 9% Biology/Biological Sciences, General, 9% Communication and Media Studies
Expenses: 2017-2018: $43,044; room/board: $11,706
Financial aid: (727) 864-8334; 60% of undergrads determined to have financial need; average aid package $34,291

Edward Waters College[1]
Jacksonville FL
(904) 470-8200
U.S. News ranking: Reg. Coll. (S), second tier
Website: www.ewc.edu
Admissions email: admissions@ewc.edu
Private
Application deadline (fall): N/A
Undergraduate student body: N/A full time, N/A part time
Expenses: 2016-2017: $13,525; room/board: $7,282
Financial aid: N/A

Embry-Riddle Aeronautical University
Daytona Beach FL
(800) 862-2416
U.S. News ranking: Reg. U. (S), No. 12
Website: www.embryriddle.edu
Admissions email: dbadmit@erau.edu
Private; founded 1926
Freshman admissions: selective; 2016-2017: 4,901 applied, 3,466 accepted. Neither SAT nor ACT required. SAT 25/75 percentile: 1000-1240. High school rank: 22% in top tenth, 50% in top quarter, 80% in top half
Early decision deadline: N/A, notification date: N/A
Early action deadline: N/A, notification date: N/A
Application deadline (fall): rolling
Undergraduate student body: 5,017 full time, 430 part time; 80% male, 20% female; 0% American Indian, 5% Asian, 6% black, 4% Hispanic, 9% multiracial, 0% Pacific Islander, 54% white, 13% international; 36% from in state; 39% live on campus; N/A of students in fraternities, N/A in sororities
Most popular majors: 40% Transportation and Materials Moving, 35% Engineering, 6% Business, Management, Marketing, and Related Support Services, 6% Homeland Security, Law Enforcement, Firefighting and Related Protective Services, 4% Mechanic and Repair Technologies/Technicians
Expenses: 2017-2018: $34,822; room/board: $11,100
Financial aid: (386) 226-6300; 61% of undergrads determined to have financial need; average aid package $17,938

Everglades University
Boca Raton FL
(888) 772-6077
U.S. News ranking: Reg. Coll. (S), No. 36
Website: www.evergladesuniversity.edu
Private; founded 2002
Freshman admissions: less selective; 2016-2017: 1,474 applied, 1,096 accepted. Neither SAT nor ACT required. SAT 25/75 percentile: N/A. High school rank: N/A
Early decision deadline: N/A, notification date: N/A

Early action deadline: N/A, notification date: N/A
Application deadline (fall): rolling
Undergraduate student body: 2,089 full time, 0 part time; 49% male, 51% female; 1% American Indian, 1% Asian, 17% black, 16% Hispanic, 3% multiracial, 0% Pacific Islander, 55% white, 0% international; N/A from in state; 0% live on campus; 0% of students in fraternities, 0% in sororities
Most popular majors: 50% Alternative and Complementary Medicine and Medical Systems, Other, 21% Construction Management, 20% Aeronautics/Aviation/Aerospace Science and Technology, General, 4% Business Administration and Management, General, 4% Natural Resources/Conservation, General
Expenses: 2017-2018: $17,000; room/board: N/A
Financial aid: (561) 912-1211

Flagler College
St. Augustine FL
(800) 304-4208
U.S. News ranking: Reg. Coll. (S), No. 2
Website: www.flagler.edu
Admissions email: admiss@flagler.edu
Private; founded 1968
Freshman admissions: selective; 2016-2017: 4,794 applied, 2,639 accepted. Either SAT or ACT required. SAT 25/75 percentile: 960-1150. High school rank: N/A
Early decision deadline: 11/1, notification date: 11/15
Early action deadline: N/A, notification date: N/A
Application deadline (fall): 3/1
Undergraduate student body: 2,539 full time, 75 part time; 37% male, 63% female; 0% American Indian, 1% Asian, 4% black, 5% Hispanic, 2% multiracial, 0% Pacific Islander, 78% white, 3% international; 41% from in state; 38% live on campus; N/A of students in fraternities, N/A in sororities
Most popular majors: 22% Business, Management, Marketing, and Related Support Services, 14% Communication, Journalism, and Related Programs, 11% Visual and Performing Arts, 10% Psychology, 10% Social Sciences
Expenses: 2017-2018: $18,300; room/board: $10,680
Financial aid: (904) 819-6225; 61% of undergrads determined to have financial need; average aid package $12,151

Florida A&M University
Tallahassee FL
(850) 599-3796
U.S. News ranking: Nat. U., No. 207
Website: www.famu.edu
Admissions email: ugradmissions@famu.edu
Public; founded 1887
Freshman admissions: selective; 2016-2017: 6,988 applied, 2,174 accepted. Either SAT or ACT required. ACT 25/75 percentile: 19-24. High school

rank: 16% in top tenth, 48% in top quarter, 85% in top half
Early decision deadline: N/A, notification date: N/A
Early action deadline: N/A, notification date: N/A
Application deadline (fall): 5/15
Undergraduate student body: 6,623 full time, 1,146 part time; 35% male, 65% female; 0% American Indian, 1% Asian, 90% black, 2% Hispanic, 3% multiracial, 0% Pacific Islander, 3% white, 1% international; 87% from in state; 22% live on campus; 0% of students in fraternities, 0% in sororities
Most popular majors: 24% Health Professions and Related Programs, 12% Multi/Interdisciplinary Studies, 9% Business, Management, Marketing, and Related Support Services, 8% Homeland Security, Law Enforcement, Firefighting and Related Protective Services, 6% Social Sciences
Expenses: 2017-2018: $5,785 in state, $17,725 out of state; room/board: $10,058
Financial aid: (850) 599-3730; 85% of undergrads determined to have financial need; average aid package $13,113

Florida Atlantic University
Boca Raton FL
(561) 297-3040
U.S. News ranking: Nat. U., second tier
Website: www.fau.edu
Admissions email: Admissions@fau.edu
Public; founded 1961
Freshman admissions: selective; 2016-2017: 15,907 applied, 9,509 accepted. Either SAT or ACT required. SAT 25/75 percentile: 960 1160. High school rank: 15% in top tenth, 45% in top quarter, 83% in top half
Early decision deadline: N/A, notification date: N/A
Early action deadline: N/A, notification date: N/A
Application deadline (fall): 5/1
Undergraduate student body: 16,092 full time, 9,310 part time; 44% male, 56% female; 0% American Indian, 4% Asian, 20% black, 27% Hispanic, 4% multiracial, 0% Pacific Islander, 42% white, 3% international; 95% from in state; 17% live on campus; 4% of students in fraternities, 6% in sororities
Most popular majors: 19% Business, Management, Marketing, and Related Support Services, 8% Health Professions and Related Programs, 8% Homeland Security, Law Enforcement, Firefighting and Related Protective Services, 7% Biological and Biomedical Sciences, 7% Psychology
Expenses: 2017-2018: $6,039 in state, $21,595 out of state; room/board: $11,906
Financial aid: (561) 297-3531; 61% of undergrads determined to have financial need; average aid package $13,345

Florida College
Temple Terrace FL
(800) 326-7655
U.S. News ranking: Reg. Coll. (S), second tier
Website: www.floridacollege.edu/
Private; founded 1946
Freshman admissions: selective; 2016-2017: 284 applied, 223 accepted. Either SAT or ACT required. ACT 25/75 percentile: 20-26. High school rank: N/A
Early decision deadline: N/A, notification date: N/A
Early action deadline: N/A, notification date: N/A
Application deadline (fall): 8/25
Undergraduate student body: 517 full time, 16 part time; 49% male, 51% female; 1% American Indian, 0% Asian, 6% black, 7% Hispanic, 5% multiracial, 0% Pacific Islander, 77% white, 4% international
Most popular majors: Information not available
Expenses: 2017-2018: $17,042; room/board: $8,420
Financial aid: (813) 988-5131; 67% of undergrads determined to have financial need; average aid package $10,644

Florida Gateway College[1]
Lake City FL
U.S. News ranking: Reg. Coll. (S), unranked
Admissions email: N/A
Public
Application deadline (fall): N/A
Undergraduate student body: N/A full time, N/A part time
Expenses: 2016-2017: $3,100 in state, $11,747 out of state; room/board: N/A
Financial aid: N/A

Florida Gulf Coast University
Fort Myers FL
(239) 590-7878
U.S. News ranking: Reg. U. (S), No. 73
Website: www.fgcu.edu
Admissions email: admissions@fgcu.edu
Public; founded 1991
Freshman admissions: selective; 2016-2017: 15,152 applied, 8,508 accepted. Either SAT or ACT required. ACT 25/75 percentile: 22-26. High school rank: 14% in top tenth, 39% in top quarter, 77% in top half
Early decision deadline: N/A, notification date: N/A
Early action deadline: N/A, notification date: N/A
Application deadline (fall): 5/1
Undergraduate student body: 10,810 full time, 2,901 part time; 44% male, 56% female; 0% American Indian, 2% Asian, 7% black, 20% Hispanic, 3% multiracial, 0% Pacific Islander, 65% white, 2% international; 89% from in state; 35% live on campus; 10% of students in fraternities, 15% in sororities
Most popular majors: 8% Resort Management, 6% Mass Communication/Media Studies, 6% Psychology, General, 5%

Business Administration and Management, General, 5% Criminal Justice/Safety Studies
Expenses: 2017-2018: $6,118 in state, $24,255 out of state; room/board: $8,619
Financial aid: (239) 590-1210; 48% of undergrads determined to have financial need; average aid package $10,260

Florida Institute of Technology
Melbourne FL
(800) 888-4348
U.S. News ranking: Nat. U., No. 151
Website: www.fit.edu
Admissions email: admission@fit.edu
Private; founded 1958
Freshman admissions: more selective; 2016-2017: 9,503 applied, 5,828 accepted. Either SAT or ACT required. SAT 25/75 percentile: 1060-1260. High school rank: 33% in top tenth, 60% in top quarter, 89% in top half
Early decision deadline: N/A, notification date: N/A
Early action deadline: N/A, notification date: N/A
Application deadline (fall): rolling
Undergraduate student body: 3,286 full time, 343 part time; 70% male, 30% female; 0% American Indian, 2% Asian, 6% black, 7% Hispanic, 2% multiracial, 0% Pacific Islander, 44% white, 33% international; 51% from in state; 45% live on campus; 8% of students in fraternities, 3% in sororities
Most popular majors: 11% Mechanical Engineering, 9% Aerospace, Aeronautical and Astronautical/Space Engineering, 7% Aviation/Airway Management and Operations, 6% Electrical and Electronics Engineering, 5% Civil Engineering, General
Expenses: 2017-2018: $41,240; room/board: $12,880
Financial aid: (321) 674-8070; 51% of undergrads determined to have financial need; average aid package $36,720

Florida International University
Miami FL
(305) 348-2363
U.S. News ranking: Nat. U., No. 216
Website: www.fiu.edu
Admissions email: admiss@fiu.edu
Public; founded 1972
Freshman admissions: more selective; 2016-2017: 17,218 applied, 8,498 accepted. Either SAT or ACT required. SAT 25/75 percentile: 1030-1210. High school rank: 18% in top tenth, 47% in top quarter, 83% in top half
Early decision deadline: N/A, notification date: N/A
Early action deadline: N/A, notification date: N/A
Undergraduate student body: 26,335 full time, 19,478 part time; 44% male, 56% female; 0% American Indian, 3% Asian,

12% black, 67% Hispanic, 3% multiracial, 0% Pacific Islander, 9% white, 6% international; 97% from in state; 8% live on campus; N/A of students in fraternities, N/A in sororities
Most popular majors: 28% Business, Management, Marketing, and Related Support Services, 12% Psychology, 8% Social Sciences, 7% Communication, Journalism, and Related Programs, 6% Biological and Biomedical Sciences
Expenses: 2017-2018: $6,558 in state, $18,956 out of state; room/board: $10,846
Financial aid: (305) 348-2333; 70% of undergrads determined to have financial need; average aid package $8,370

Florida Memorial University
Miami FL
(305) 626-3750
U.S. News ranking: Reg. Coll. (S), No. 21
Website: www.fmuniv.edu/
Admissions email: admit@fmuniv.edu
Private; founded 1879
Affiliation: Baptist
Freshman admissions: less selective; 2016-2017: 5,560 applied, 1,268 accepted. Neither SAT nor ACT required. ACT 25/75 percentile: 16-19. High school rank: N/A
Early decision deadline: 4/1, notification date: 4/1
Early action deadline: N/A, notification date: N/A
Application deadline (fall): rolling
Undergraduate student body: 1,231 full time, 49 part time; 37% male, 63% female; 0% American Indian, 0% Asian, 71% black, 7% Hispanic, 1% multiracial, 0% Pacific Islander, 1% white, 12% international
Most popular majors: 14% Criminal Justice/Law Enforcement Administration, 13% Psychology, General, 12% Special Education and Teaching, Other, 11% Accounting and Finance, 11% Social Work
Expenses: 2017-2018: $15,536; room/board: $6,734
Financial aid: (305) 626-3745; 78% of undergrads determined to have financial need; average aid package $10,133

Florida National University– Main Campus
Hialeah FL
(305) 821-3333
U.S. News ranking: Reg. Coll. (S), unranked
Website: www.fnu.edu/
Admissions email: rlopez@fnu.edu
For-profit; founded 1988
Freshman admissions: least selective; 2016-2017: 1,566 applied, 1,556 accepted. Neither SAT nor ACT required. SAT 25/75 percentile: N/A. High school rank: N/A
Early decision deadline: N/A, notification date: N/A
Early action deadline: N/A, notification date: N/A

Application deadline (fall): N/A
Undergraduate student body: 2,517 full time, 674 part time; 27% male, 73% female; 0% American Indian, 0% Asian, 3% black, 82% Hispanic, 1% multiracial, 0% Pacific Islander, 2% white, 12% international
Most popular majors: 51% High School/Secondary Diplomas and Certificates, 14% Health Professions and Related Programs, 13% Business, Management, Marketing, and Related Support Services, 12% Homeland Security, Law Enforcement, Firefighting and Related Protective Services, 9% Business, Management, Marketing, and Related Support Services
Expenses: 2017-2018: $13,900; room/board: N/A
Financial aid: (305) 821-3333; 90% of undergrads determined to have financial need

Florida SouthWestern State College
Fort Myers FL
(800) 749-2322
U.S. News ranking: Reg. Coll. (S), unranked
Website: www.fsw.edu/
Public; founded 1962
Freshman admissions: least selective; 2016-2017: 5,769 applied, 4,663 accepted. Neither SAT nor ACT required. SAT 25/75 percentile: N/A. High school rank: N/A
Early decision deadline: N/A, notification date: N/A
Early action deadline: N/A, notification date: N/A
Application deadline (fall): 8/17
Undergraduate student body: 5,708 full time, 10,908 part time; 39% male, 61% female; 0% American Indian, 2% Asian, 10% black, 29% Hispanic, 2% multiracial, 0% Pacific Islander, 48% white, 2% international; 96% from in state; 2% live on campus; N/A of students in fraternities, N/A in sororities
Most popular majors: 37% Health Professions and Related Programs, 36% Business, Management, Marketing, and Related Support Services, 17% Education, 9% Homeland Security, Law Enforcement, Firefighting and Related Protective Services
Expenses: 2016-2017: $3,401 in state, $10,715 out of state; room/board: $8,860
Financial aid: (239) 489-9336

Florida Southern College
Lakeland FL
(863) 680-4131
U.S. News ranking: Reg. U. (S), No. 19
Website: www.flsouthern.edu
Admissions email: fscadm@flsouthern.edu
Private; founded 1883
Freshman admissions: more selective; 2016-2017: 6,192 applied, 2,820 accepted. Either SAT or ACT required. ACT 25/75 percentile: 24-29. High school rank: 29% in top tenth, 60% in top quarter, 89% in top half

Early decision deadline: 11/1, notification date: 12/1
Early action deadline: N/A, notification date: N/A
Application deadline (fall): rolling
Undergraduate student body: 2,319 full time, 67 part time; 37% male, 63% female; 1% American Indian, 2% Asian, 5% black, 11% Hispanic, 2% multiracial, 0% Pacific Islander, 74% white, 4% international; 64% from in state; 87% live on campus; 29% of students in fraternities, 35% in sororities
Most popular majors: 21% Business Administration, Management and Operations, 10% Registered Nursing, Nursing Administration, Nursing Research and Clinical Nursing, 7% Biology, General, 7% Psychology, General, 7% Teacher Education and Professional Development, Specific Levels and Methods
Expenses: 2017-2018: $34,774; room/board: $11,204
Financial aid: (863) 680-4140; 67% of undergrads determined to have financial need; average aid package $26,342

Florida State College– Jacksonville[1]
Jacksonville FL
U.S. News ranking: Reg. Coll. (S), unranked
Website: www.fscj.edu
Admissions email: N/A
Public
Application deadline (fall): N/A
Undergraduate student body: N/A full time, N/A part time
Expenses: 2016-2017: $2,878 in state, $9,992 out of state; room/board: N/A
Financial aid: N/A

Florida State University
Tallahassee FL
(850) 644-6200
U.S. News ranking: Nat. U., No. 81
Website: www.fsu.edu
Admissions email: admissions@admin.fsu.edu
Public; founded 1851
Freshman admissions: more selective; 2016-2017: 29,027 applied, 16,840 accepted. Either SAT or ACT required. ACT 25/75 percentile: 25-29. High school rank: 41% in top tenth, 77% in top quarter, 98% in top half
Early decision deadline: N/A, notification date: N/A
Early action deadline: N/A, notification date: N/A
Application deadline (fall): 2/7
Undergraduate student body: 29,282 full time, 3,647 part time; 45% male, 55% female; 0% American Indian, 2% Asian, 8% black, 20% Hispanic, 3% multiracial, 0% Pacific Islander, 63% white, 1% international; 90% from in state; 18% live on campus; 19% of students in fraternities, 26% in sororities
Most popular majors: 7% Psychology, General, 6% Criminal Justice/Safety Studies, 5% English Language and Literature, General, 5% Finance, General, 4% Biology/Biological Sciences, General

Expenses: 2017-2018: $6,507 in state, $21,673 out of state; room/board: $10,458
Financial aid: (850) 644-5716; 50% of undergrads determined to have financial need; average aid package $11,761

Gulf Coast State College[1]
Panama City FL
U.S. News ranking: Reg. Coll. (S), unranked
Admissions email: N/A
Public
Application deadline (fall): N/A
Undergraduate student body: N/A full time, N/A part time
Expenses: 2017-2018: $2,370 in state, $7,685 out of state; room/board: N/A
Financial aid: (850) 872-3845

Hodges University[1]
Naples FL
(239) 513-1122
U.S. News ranking: Reg. U. (S), unranked
Website: www.hodges.edu
Admissions email: admit@hodges.edu
Private; founded 1990
Application deadline (fall): rolling
Undergraduate student body: N/A full time, N/A part time
Expenses: 2016-2017: $16,400; room/board: N/A
Financial aid: (239) 938-7765

Indian River State College
Fort Pierce FL
(772) 462-7460
U.S. News ranking: Reg. Coll. (S), second tier
Website: www.irsc.edu
Public
Freshman admissions: less selective; 2016-2017: 1,789 applied, 1,789 accepted. Neither SAT nor ACT required. SAT 25/75 percentile: N/A. High school rank: N/A
Early decision deadline: N/A, notification date: N/A
Early action deadline: N/A, notification date: N/A
Application deadline (fall): rolling
Undergraduate student body: 6,138 full time, 12,106 part time; 40% male, 60% female; 0% American Indian, 1% Asian, 17% black, 22% Hispanic, 2% multiracial, 0% Pacific Islander, 53% white, 1% international
Most popular majors: Information not available
Expenses: 2017-2018: $2,640 in state, $9,890 out of state; room/board: $5,700
Financial aid: (772) 462-7450; average aid package $4,680

Jacksonville University
Jacksonville FL
(800) 225-2027
U.S. News ranking: Reg. U. (S), No. 52
Website: www.ju.edu/index.php
Admissions email: admiss@ju.edu
Private; founded 1934

Freshman admissions: selective; 2016-2017: 4,858 applied, 2,708 accepted. Neither SAT nor ACT required. ACT 25/75 percentile: 19-25. High school rank: N/A
Early decision deadline: N/A, notification date: N/A
Early action deadline: N/A, notification date: N/A
Application deadline (fall): 7/1
Undergraduate student body: 2,113 full time, 776 part time; 38% male, 62% female; 1% American Indian, 2% Asian, 14% black, 9% Hispanic, 3% multiracial, 0% Pacific Islander, 47% white, 6% international; 67% from in state; 37% live on campus; 3% of students in fraternities, 3% in sororities
Most popular majors: 53% Health Professions and Related Programs, 13% Business, Management, Marketing, and Related Support Services, 9% Social Sciences, 5% Visual and Performing Arts, 4% Parks, Recreation, Leisure, and Fitness Studies
Expenses: 2017-2018: $35,260; room/board: $13,950
Financial aid: (904) 256-7062; 86% of undergrads determined to have financial need; average aid package $22,584

Keiser University
Ft. Lauderdale FL
(954) 776-4456
U.S. News ranking: Reg. U. (S), No. 52
Website: www.keiseruniversity.edu
Private; founded 1977
Freshman admissions: less selective; 2016-2017: N/A applied, N/A accepted. Neither SAT nor ACT required. SAT 25/75 percentile: N/A. High school rank: N/A
Early decision deadline: N/A, notification date: N/A
Early action deadline: N/A, notification date: N/A
Application deadline (fall): rolling
Undergraduate student body: 11,524 full time, 6,648 part time; 31% male, 69% female; 1% American Indian, 2% Asian, 21% black, 32% Hispanic, 3% multiracial, 0% Pacific Islander, 37% white, 1% international
Most popular majors: 21% Business Administration and Management, General, 12% Multi/Interdisciplinary Studies, 10% Criminal Justice/Safety Studies, 7% Health Services Administration, 7% Registered Nursing/Registered Nurse
Expenses: 2017-2018: $28,768; room/board: $11,240
Financial aid: (954) 776-4476; 93% of undergrads determined to have financial need; average aid package $5,512

Lake-Sumter State College[1]
Leesburg FL
U.S. News ranking: Reg. Coll. (S), unranked
Public
Application deadline (fall): N/A
Undergraduate student body: N/A full time, N/A part time

Expenses: 2016-2017: $3,172 in state, $13,276 out of state; room/board: N/A
Financial aid: N/A

Lynn University
Boca Raton FL
(561) 237-7900
U.S. News ranking: Reg. U. (S), No. 95
Website: www.lynn.edu
Admissions email: admission@lynn.edu
Private; founded 1962
Freshman admissions: less selective; 2016-2017: 3,514 applied, 2,872 accepted. Neither SAT nor ACT required. SAT 25/75 percentile: 870-1060. High school rank: 2% in top tenth, 14% in top quarter, 44% in top half
Early decision deadline: N/A, notification date: N/A
Early action deadline: 11/15, notification date: 12/15
Application deadline (fall): 3/1
Undergraduate student body: 1,950 full time, 145 part time; 51% male, 49% female; 0% American Indian, 1% Asian, 9% black, 16% Hispanic, 1% multiracial, 0% Pacific Islander, 45% white, 21% international; 47% from in state; 47% live on campus; 6% of students in fraternities, 6% in sororities
Most popular majors: 48% Business, Management, Marketing, and Related Support Services, 13% Communication, Journalism, and Related Programs, 8% Psychology, 7% Homeland Security, Law Enforcement, Firefighting and Related Protective Services, 7% Visual and Performing Arts
Expenses: 2017-2018: $36,557; room/board: $11,970
Financial aid: (561) 237-7973; 43% of undergrads determined to have financial need; average aid package $22,404

Miami Dade College[1]
Miami FL
U.S. News ranking: Reg. Coll. (S), unranked
Website: www.mdc.edu/
Admissions email: mdcinfo@mdc.edu
Public
Application deadline (fall): N/A
Undergraduate student body: N/A full time, N/A part time
Expenses: 2016-2017: $2,834 in state, $9,661 out of state; room/board: N/A
Financial aid: N/A

Miami International University of Art & Design[1]
Miami FL
U.S. News ranking: Arts, unranked
Website: www.aimiu.aii.edu/
Admissions email: N/A
For-profit
Application deadline (fall): N/A
Undergraduate student body: N/A full time, N/A part time
Expenses: 2016-2017: $17,700; room/board: $7,800
Financial aid: N/A

New College of Florida
Sarasota FL
(941) 487-5000
U.S. News ranking: Nat. Lib. Arts, No. 101
Website: www.ncf.edu
Admissions email: admissions@ncf.edu
Public; founded 1960
Freshman admissions: more selective; 2016-2017: 1,417 applied, 1,010 accepted. Either SAT or ACT required. SAT 25/75 percentile: 1140-1350. High school rank: 35% in top tenth, 73% in top quarter, 96% in top half
Early decision deadline: N/A, notification date: N/A
Early action deadline: 11/1, notification date: 4/1
Application deadline (fall): 4/15
Undergraduate student body: 861 full time, 0 part time; 38% male, 62% female; 0% American Indian, 3% Asian, 3% black, 18% Hispanic, 4% multiracial, 0% Pacific Islander, 69% white, 2% international; 85% from in state; 77% live on campus; 0% of students in fraternities, 0% in sororities
Most popular majors: 12% Biology/Biological Sciences, General, 10% Chemistry, General, 8% Psychology, General, 6% Political Science and Government, General, 4% Economics, General
Expenses: 2017-2018: $6,916 in state, $29,944 out of state; room/board: $9,264
Financial aid: (941) 487-5000; 55% of undergrads determined to have financial need; average aid package $13,458

Northwest Florida State College[1]
Niceville FL
U.S. News ranking: Reg. Coll. (S), unranked
Website: www.owcc.cc.fl.us/
Admissions email: N/A
Public
Application deadline (fall): N/A
Undergraduate student body: N/A full time, N/A part time
Expenses: 2016-2017: $3,123 in state, $11,940 out of state; room/board: N/A
Financial aid: N/A

Nova Southeastern University
Ft. Lauderdale FL
(954) 262-8000
U.S. News ranking: Nat. U., No. 198
Website: www.nova.edu
Admissions email: admissions@nova.edu
Private; founded 1964
Freshman admissions: more selective; 2016-2017: 6,532 applied, 3,432 accepted. Either SAT or ACT required. SAT 25/75 percentile: 1000-1220. High school rank: 30% in top tenth, 63% in top quarter, 88% in top half
Early decision deadline: 11/1, notification date: N/A
Early action deadline: 11/1, notification date: N/A

Application deadline (fall): 2/1
Undergraduate student body: 3,051 full time, 1,244 part time; 30% male, 70% female; 0% American Indian, 10% Asian, 16% black, 30% Hispanic, 2% multiracial, 0% Pacific Islander, 33% white, 6% international; 82% from in state; 25% live on campus; 7% of students in fraternities, 6% in sororities
Most popular majors: 44% Health Professions and Related Programs, 19% Biological and Biomedical Sciences, 11% Business, Management, Marketing, and Related Support Services, 8% Psychology, 3% Education
Expenses: 2017-2018: $29,940; room/board: $12,550
Financial aid: N/A; 74% of undergrads determined to have financial need; average aid package $28,480

Palm Beach Atlantic University
West Palm Beach FL
(888) 468-6722
U.S. News ranking: Reg. U. (S), No. 57
Website: www.pba.edu
Admissions email: admit@pba.edu
Private; founded 1968
Affiliation: Interdenominational
Freshman admissions: selective; 2016-2017: 1,449 applied, 1,353 accepted. Either SAT or ACT required. SAT 25/75 percentile: 930-1170. High school rank: N/A
Early decision deadline: N/A, notification date: N/A
Early action deadline: 3/31, notification date: 4/15
Application deadline (fall): rolling
Undergraduate student body: 2,300 full time, 626 part time; 35% male, 65% female; 1% American Indian, 2% Asian, 12% black, 16% Hispanic, 3% multiracial, 0% Pacific Islander, 62% white, 4% international; 66% from in state; 49% live on campus; 0% of students in fraternities, 0% in sororities
Most popular majors: 27% Business, Management, Marketing, and Related Support Services, 16% Psychology, 12% Health Professions and Related Programs, 10% Theology and Religious Vocations, 6% Communication, Journalism, and Related Programs
Expenses: 2017-2018: $29,950; room/board: $9,770
Financial aid: (561) 803-2629; 71% of undergrads determined to have financial need; average aid package $20,358

Palm Beach State College[1]
Lake Worth FL
U.S. News ranking: Reg. Coll. (S), unranked
Public
Application deadline (fall): N/A
Undergraduate student body: N/A full time, N/A part time
Expenses: 2016-2017: $2,444 in state, $8,732 out of state; room/board: N/A
Financial aid: N/A

Pensacola State College

Pensacola FL
(850) 484-2544
U.S. News ranking: Reg. Coll. (S), No. 28
Website: www.pensacolastate.edu
Admissions email: askus@pensacolastate.edu
Public; founded 1948
Affiliation: Other
Freshman admissions: least selective; 2016-2017: 3,576 applied, 3,576 accepted. Neither SAT nor ACT required. SAT 25/75 percentile: 780-1020. High school rank: N/A
Early decision deadline: N/A, notification date: N/A
Early action deadline: N/A, notification date: N/A
Application deadline (fall): rolling
Undergraduate student body: 3,576 full time, 6,067 part time; 39% male, 61% female; 1% American Indian, 3% Asian, 17% black, 7% Hispanic, 5% multiracial, 1% Pacific Islander, 64% white, 0% international
Most popular majors: 74% Business, Management, Marketing, and Related Support Services, 26% Health Professions and Related Programs
Expenses: 2017-2018: $3,137 in state, $12,593 out of state; room/board: N/A
Financial aid: (850) 484-1708

Polk State College[1]

Winter Haven FL
U.S. News ranking: Reg. Coll. (S), unranked
Public
Application deadline (fall): N/A
Undergraduate student body: N/A full time, N/A part time
Expenses: 2016-2017: $3,366 in state, $12,272 out of state; room/board: N/A
Financial aid: N/A

Ringling College of Art and Design

Sarasota FL
(800) 255-7695
U.S. News ranking: Arts, unranked
Website: www.ringling.edu
Admissions email: admissions@ringling.edu
Private; founded 1931
Freshman admissions: least selective; 2016-2017: 1,782 applied, 1,369 accepted. Neither SAT nor ACT required. SAT 25/75 percentile: N/A. High school rank: N/A
Early decision deadline: N/A, notification date: N/A
Early action deadline: 10/1, notification date: 12/15
Application deadline (fall): rolling
Undergraduate student body: 1,270 full time, 71 part time; 35% male, 65% female; 1% American Indian, 8% Asian, 3% black, 16% Hispanic, 3% multiracial, 0% Pacific Islander, 47% white, 16% international; 54% from in state; 72% live on campus; 0% of students in fraternities, 0% in sororities

Most popular majors: 30% Illustration, 21% Animation, Interactive Technology, Video Graphics and Special Effects, 11% Game and Interactive Media Design, 10% Cinematography and Film/Video Production, 5% Graphic Design
Expenses: 2017-2018: $44,560; room/board: $14,600
Financial aid: (941) 359-7532; 67% of undergrads determined to have financial need; average aid package $24,503

Rollins College

Winter Park FL
(407) 646-2161
U.S. News ranking: Reg. U. (S), No. 2
Website: www.rollins.edu
Admissions email: admission@rollins.edu
Private; founded 1885
Freshman admissions: more selective; 2016-2017: 5,445 applied, 3,301 accepted. Neither SAT nor ACT required. SAT 25/75 percentile: 1120-1290. High school rank: 36% in top tenth, 67% in top quarter, 88% in top half
Early decision deadline: 11/15, notification date: 12/15
Early action deadline: N/A, notification date: N/A
Application deadline (fall): 2/15
Undergraduate student body: 1,935 full time, 7 part time; 40% male, 60% female; 0% American Indian, 3% Asian, 3% black, 14% Hispanic, 3% multiracial, 0% Pacific Islander, 64% white, 10% international; 75% from in state; 61% live on campus; 10% of students in fraternities, 11% in sororities
Most popular majors: 21% Business, Management, Marketing, and Related Support Services, 17% Construction Trades, 13% Communication, Journalism, and Related Programs, 9% Psychology, 8% Visual and Performing Arts
Expenses: 2017-2018: $48,335; room/board: $14,730
Financial aid: (407) 646-2395; 51% of undergrads determined to have financial need; average aid package $39,204

Saint Johns River State College[1]

Palatka FL
U.S. News ranking: Reg. Coll. (S), unranked
Public
Application deadline (fall): N/A
Undergraduate student body: N/A full time, N/A part time
Expenses: 2016-2017: $2,880 in state, $10,399 out of state; room/board: N/A
Financial aid: N/A

Saint Leo University

Saint Leo FL
(800) 334-5532
U.S. News ranking: Reg. U. (S), No. 61
Website: www.saintleo.edu
Admissions email: admission@saintleo.edu
Private; founded 1889

Affiliation: Roman Catholic
Freshman admissions: selective; 2016-2017: 4,501 applied, 3,139 accepted. Neither SAT nor ACT required. ACT 25/75 percentile: 20-26. High school rank: 12% in top tenth, 32% in top quarter, 72% in top half
Early decision deadline: N/A, notification date: N/A
Early action deadline: N/A, notification date: N/A
Application deadline (fall): rolling
Undergraduate student body: 2,192 full time, 72 part time; 43% male, 57% female; 0% American Indian, 2% Asian, 14% black, 19% Hispanic, 2% multiracial, 0% Pacific Islander, 43% white, 12% international; 70% from in state; 67% live on campus; 9% of students in fraternities, 16% in sororities
Most popular majors: 23% Business, Management, Marketing, and Related Support Services, 13% Computer and Information Sciences and Support Services, 12% Homeland Security, Law Enforcement, Firefighting and Related Protective Services, 10% Social Sciences, 9% Parks, Recreation, Leisure, and Fitness Studies
Expenses: 2017-2018: $21,970; room/board: $10,570
Financial aid: (800) 240-7658; 71% of undergrads determined to have financial need; average aid package $20,298

Santa Fe College[1]

Gainesville FL
U.S. News ranking: Reg. Coll. (S), unranked
Admissions email: N/A
Public
Application deadline (fall): N/A
Undergraduate student body: N/A full time, N/A part time
Expenses: 2016-2017: $2,563 in state, $9,189 out of state; room/board: N/A
Financial aid: N/A

Seminole State College of Florida

Sanford FL
(407) 708-2380
U.S. News ranking: Reg. Coll. (S), unranked
Website: www.seminolestate.edu
Admissions email: admissions@seminolestate.edu
Public; founded 1965
Freshman admissions: least selective; 2016-2017: N/A applied, N/A accepted. Neither SAT nor ACT required. SAT 25/75 percentile: N/A. High school rank: N/A
Early decision deadline: N/A, notification date: N/A
Early action deadline: N/A, notification date: N/A
Application deadline (fall): N/A
Undergraduate student body: 5,927 full time, 11,861 part time; 44% male, 56% female; 0% American Indian, 3% Asian, 16% black, 24% Hispanic, 3% multiracial, 0% Pacific Islander, 49% white, 2% international

Most popular majors: 37% Liberal Arts and Sciences/Liberal Studies, 3% Registered Nursing/Registered Nurse, 1% Automobile/Automotive Mechanics Technology/Technician, 1% Emergency Medical Technology/Technician (EMT Paramedic), 1% Respiratory Care Therapy/Therapist
Expenses: 2016-2017: $3,131 in state, $11,456 out of state; room/board: N/A
Financial aid: N/A

South Florida State College

Avon Park FL
U.S. News ranking: Reg. Coll. (S), No. 28
Website: www.southflorida.edu
Admissions email: deborah.fuschetti@southflorida.edu
Public; founded 1966
Freshman admissions: less selective; 2016-2017: 2,722 applied, 2,722 accepted. Neither SAT nor ACT required. SAT 25/75 percentile: N/A. High school rank: N/A
Early decision deadline: N/A, notification date: N/A
Early action deadline: N/A, notification date: N/A
Application deadline (fall): rolling
Undergraduate student body: 900 full time, 1,759 part time; 38% male, 62% female; 0% American Indian, 2% Asian, 11% black, 34% Hispanic, 1% multiracial, 0% Pacific Islander, 49% white, 2% international
Most popular majors: Information not available
Expenses: 2016-2017: $3,165 in state, $11,859 out of state; room/board: N/A
Financial aid: N/A

Southeastern University

Lakeland FL
(800) 500-8760
U.S. News ranking: Reg. U. (S), second tier
Website: www.seu.edu
Admissions email: admission@seu.edu
Private; founded 1935
Freshman admissions: less selective; 2016-2017: 4,061 applied, 1,862 accepted. Either SAT or ACT required. ACT 25/75 percentile: 18-24. High school rank: 9% in top tenth, 28% in top quarter, 57% in top half
Early decision deadline: N/A, notification date: N/A
Early action deadline: N/A, notification date: N/A
Application deadline (fall): 5/1
Undergraduate student body: 3,888 full time, 1,167 part time; 43% male, 57% female; 0% American Indian, 1% Asian, 16% black, 19% Hispanic, 0% multiracial, 1% Pacific Islander, 59% white, 2% international; 63% from in state; 43% live on campus; N/A of students in fraternities, N/A in sororities

Most popular majors: 25% Theology and Religious Vocations, 21% Business, Management, Marketing, and Related Support Services, 8% Education, 7% Communication, Journalism, and Related Programs, 7% Public Administration and Social Service Professions
Expenses: 2017-2018: $24,160; room/board: $9,450
Financial aid: (863) 667-5306; 80% of undergrads determined to have financial need; average aid package $15,184

St. Petersburg College[1]

St. Petersburg FL
U.S. News ranking: Reg. Coll. (S), unranked
Website: www.spcollege.edu/
Admissions email: information@spcollege.edu
Public
Application deadline (fall): N/A
Undergraduate student body: N/A full time, N/A part time
Expenses: 2016-2017: $3,385 in state, $11,667 out of state; room/board: N/A
Financial aid: N/A

St. Thomas University

Miami Gardens FL
(305) 628-6546
U.S. News ranking: Reg. U. (S), No. 80
Website: www.stu.edu
Admissions email: signup@stu.edu
Private; founded 1961
Affiliation: Roman Catholic
Freshman admissions: less selective; 2016-2017: 1,672 applied, 905 accepted. Either SAT or ACT required. SAT 25/75 percentile: 840-1050. High school rank: 13% in top tenth, 27% in top quarter, 54% in top half
Early decision deadline: N/A, notification date: N/A
Early action deadline: N/A, notification date: N/A
Application deadline (fall): rolling
Undergraduate student body: 840 full time, 3,440 part time; 39% male, 61% female; N/A American Indian, N/A Asian, N/A black, N/A Hispanic, N/A multiracial, N/A Pacific Islander, N/A white, N/A international
Most popular majors: Information not available
Expenses: 2016-2017: $28,800; room/board: $11,700
Financial aid: (305) 474-6960

State College of Florida–Manatee-Sarasota[1]

Bradenton FL
U.S. News ranking: Reg. Coll. (S), unranked
Admissions email: N/A
Public
Application deadline (fall): N/A
Undergraduate student body: N/A full time, N/A part time
Expenses: 2016-2017: $3,074 in state, $11,606 out of state; room/board: N/A
Financial aid: N/A

Stetson University
DeLand FL
(800) 688-0101
U.S. News ranking: Reg. U. (S), No. 6
Website: www.stetson.edu
Admissions email: admissions@stetson.edu
Private; founded 1883
Freshman admissions: more selective; 2016-2017: 12,130 applied, 7,957 accepted. Neither SAT nor ACT required. SAT 25/75 percentile: 1040-1250. High school rank: 24% in top tenth, 59% in top quarter, 86% in top half
Early decision deadline: N/A, notification date: N/A
Early action deadline: N/A, notification date: N/A
Application deadline (fall): N/A
Undergraduate student body: 3,048 full time, 41 part time; 42% male, 58% female; 0% American Indian, 2% Asian, 8% black, 15% Hispanic, 3% multiracial, 0% Pacific Islander, 64% white, 5% international; 68% from in state; 65% live on campus; 30% of students in fraternities, 35% in sororities
Most popular majors: 30% Business, Management, Marketing, and Related Support Services, 11% Psychology, 8% Social Sciences, 8% Visual and Performing Arts, 7% Biological and Biomedical Sciences
Expenses: 2017-2018: $44,480; room/board: $12,684
Financial aid: (386) 822-7120; 70% of undergrads determined to have financial need; average aid package $34,778

University of Central Florida
Orlando FL
(407) 823-3000
U.S. News ranking: Nat. U., No. 171
Website: www.ucf.edu
Admissions email: admission@ucf.edu
Public; founded 1963
Freshman admissions: more selective, 2016-2017: 34,886 applied, 17,441 accepted. Either SAT or ACT required. SAT 25/75 percentile: 1080-1270. High school rank: 33% in top tenth, 71% in top quarter, 97% in top half
Early decision deadline: N/A, notification date: N/A
Early action deadline: N/A, notification date: N/A
Application deadline (fall): 5/1
Undergraduate student body: 38,454 full time, 17,322 part time; 45% male, 55% female; 0% American Indian, 6% Asian, 11% black, 25% Hispanic, 4% multiracial, 0% Pacific Islander, 51% white, 1% international; 94% from in state; 19% live on campus; 5% of students in fraternities, 7% in sororities
Most popular majors: 21% Business, Management, Marketing, and Related Support Services, 16% Health Professions and Related Programs, 9% Psychology, 8% Education, 7% Engineering

Expenses: 2017-2018: $6,368 in state, $22,467 out of state; room/board: $10,011
Financial aid: (407) 823-2827; 63% of undergrads determined to have financial need; average aid package $8,744

University of Florida
Gainesville FL
(352) 392-1365
U.S. News ranking: Nat. U., No. 42
Public; founded 1853
Freshman admissions: more selective; 2016-2017: 30,118 applied, 13,835 accepted. Either SAT or ACT required. SAT 25/75 percentile: 1180-1370. High school rank: 73% in top tenth, 95% in top quarter, 100% in top half
Early decision deadline: N/A, notification date: N/A
Early action deadline: N/A, notification date: N/A
Application deadline (fall): 3/31
Undergraduate student body: 31,014 full time, 3,540 part time; 45% male, 55% female; 0% American Indian, 8% Asian, 6% black, 21% Hispanic, 3% multiracial, 1% Pacific Islander, 56% white, 2% international; 94% from in state; 24% live on campus; 21% of students in fraternities, 25% in sororities
Most popular majors: 13% Engineering, 12% Business, Management, Marketing, and Related Support Services, 11% Biological and Biomedical Sciences, 11% Social Sciences, 8% Communication, Journalism, and Related Programs
Expenses: 2017-2018: $6,381 in state, $28,658 out of state; room/board: $9,910
Financial aid: (352) 392-6684; 47% of undergrade determined to have financial need; average aid package $13,100

University of Miami
Coral Gables FL
(305) 284-4323
U.S. News ranking: Nat. U., No. 46
Website: www.miami.edu
Admissions email: admission@miami.edu
Private; founded 1925
Freshman admissions: more selective; 2016-2017: 32,525 applied, 12,266 accepted. Either SAT or ACT required. ACT 25/75 percentile: 28-32. High school rank: 60% in top tenth, 85% in top quarter, 95% in top half
Early decision deadline: 11/1, notification date: 12/20
Early action deadline: 11/1, notification date: 1/20
Application deadline (fall): 1/1
Undergraduate student body: 10,221 full time, 628 part time; 48% male, 52% female; 0% American Indian, 5% Asian, 8% black, 23% Hispanic, 3% multiracial, 0% Pacific Islander, 43% white, 14% international; 42% from in state; 38% live on campus; 19% of students in fraternities, 19% in sororities

Most popular majors: 20% Business, Management, Marketing, and Related Support Services, 15% Biological and Biomedical Sciences, 12% Social Sciences, 10% Health Professions and Related Programs, 9% Communication, Journalism, and Related Programs
Expenses: 2017-2018: $48,484; room/board: $13,666
Financial aid: (305) 284-6000; 42% of undergrads determined to have financial need; average aid package $43,227

University of North Florida
Jacksonville FL
(904) 620-2624
U.S. News ranking: Reg. U. (S), No. 48
Website: www.unf.edu
Admissions email: admissions@unf.edu
Public; founded 1965
Freshman admissions: selective; 2016-2017: 11,346 applied, 7,322 accepted. Either SAT or ACT required. ACT 25/75 percentile: 21-26. High school rank: 14% in top tenth, 40% in top quarter, 74% in top half
Early decision deadline: N/A, notification date: N/A
Early action deadline: N/A, notification date: N/A
Application deadline (fall): rolling
Undergraduate student body: 9,702 full time, 4,144 part time; 44% male, 56% female; 0% American Indian, 4% Asian, 10% black, 11% Hispanic, 5% multiracial, 0% Pacific Islander, 67% white, 1% international; 96% from in state; 25% live on campus; N/A of students in fraternities, N/A of sororities
Most popular majors: 19% Business, Management, Marketing, and Related Support Services, 18% Health Professions and Related Programs, 9% Psychology, 7% Communication, Journalism, and Related Programs, 6% Social Sciences
Expenses: 2017-2018: $6,394 in state, $20,112 out of state; room/board: $9,772
Financial aid: (904) 620-5555; 53% of undergrads determined to have financial need; average aid package $8,050

University of South Florida
Tampa FL
(813) 974-3350
U.S. News ranking: Nat. U., No. 140
Website: www.usf.edu
Admissions email: admission@admin.usf.edu
Public; founded 1956
Freshman admissions: more selective; 2016-2017: 28,623 applied, 13,349 accepted. Either SAT or ACT required. SAT 25/75 percentile: 1070-1250. High school rank: 35% in top tenth, 72% in top quarter, 94% in top half
Early decision deadline: N/A, notification date: N/A
Early action deadline: N/A, notification date: N/A

Application deadline (fall): 3/15
Undergraduate student body: 24,013 full time, 7,448 part time; 46% male, 54% female; 0% American Indian, 7% Asian, 10% black, 21% Hispanic, 4% multiracial, 0% Pacific Islander, 50% white, 6% international; 94% from in state; 24% live on campus; 7% of students in fraternities, 10% in sororities
Most popular majors: 20% Health Professions and Related Programs, 16% Business, Management, Marketing, and Related Support Services, 12% Biological and Biomedical Sciences, 12% Social Sciences, 6% Psychology
Expenses: 2017-2018: $6,410 in state, $17,324 out of state; room/board: $9,700
Financial aid: (813) 974-4700; 63% of undergrads determined to have financial need; average aid package $10,242

University of South Florida–St. Petersburg
St. Petersburg FL
(727) 873-4142
U.S. News ranking: Reg. U. (S), No. 66
Website: www.usfsp.edu
Admissions email: admissions@usfsp.edu
Public; founded 1965
Freshman admissions: more selective; 2016-2017: 5,749 applied, 2,469 accepted. Either SAT or ACT required. SAT 25/75 percentile: 990-1180. High school rank: 19% in top tenth, 52% in top quarter, 86% in top half
Early decision deadline: N/A, notification date: N/A
Early action deadline: 11/15, notification date: 12/1
Application deadline (fall): 4/15
Undergraduate student body: 2,705 full time, 1,468 part time; 38% male, 62% female; 0% American Indian, 4% Asian, 8% black, 16% Hispanic, 4% multiracial, 0% Pacific Islander, 64% white, 1% international; 95% from in state; 18% live on campus; 0% of students in fraternities, 0% in sororities
Most popular majors: 31% Business, Management, Marketing, and Related Support Services, 16% Social Sciences, 14% Psychology, 12% Biological and Biomedical Sciences, 7% Education
Expenses: 2017-2018: $5,821 in state, $16,735 out of state; room/board: $9,400
Financial aid: (727) 873-4128; 70% of undergrads determined to have financial need; average aid package $10,380

University of Tampa
Tampa FL
(888) 646-2738
U.S. News ranking: Reg. U. (S), No. 21
Website: www.ut.edu
Admissions email: admissions@ut.edu
Private; founded 1931

Freshman admissions: selective; 2016-2017: 19,947 applied, 9,634 accepted. Either SAT or ACT required. SAT 25/75 percentile: 990-1160. High school rank: 16% in top tenth, 46% in top quarter, 84% in top half
Early decision deadline: N/A, notification date: N/A
Early action deadline: 11/15, notification date: 12/15
Application deadline (fall): rolling
Undergraduate student body: 7,124 full time, 258 part time; 42% male, 58% female; 0% American Indian, 2% Asian, 5% black, 12% Hispanic, 3% multiracial, 0% Pacific Islander, 60% white, 11% international; 34% from in state; 52% live on campus; 16% of students in fraternities, 25% in sororities
Most popular majors: 32% Business, Management, Marketing, and Related Support Services, 11% Social Sciences, 10% Communication, Journalism, and Related Programs, 8% Health Professions and Related Programs, 7% Visual and Performing Arts
Expenses: 2017-2018: $28,426; room/board: $10,502
Financial aid: (813) 253-6219; 59% of undergrads determined to have financial need; average aid package $16,715

University of West Florida
Pensacola FL
(850) 474-2230
U.S. News ranking: Nat. U., second tier
Website: uwf.edu
Admissions email: admissions@uwf.edu
Public; founded 1963
Freshman admissions: selective; 2016-2017: 7,475 applied, 3,052 accepted. Either SAT or ACT required. ACT 25/75 percentile: 21-26. High school rank: 12% in top tenth, 36% in top quarter, 74% in top half
Early decision deadline: N/A, notification date: N/A
Early action deadline: N/A, notification date: N/A
Application deadline (fall): 6/1
Undergraduate student body: 7,117 full time, 2,965 part time; 43% male, 57% female; 1% American Indian, 3% Asian, 13% black, 9% Hispanic, 5% multiracial, 0% Pacific Islander, 65% white, 2% international; 91% from in state; 16% live on campus; N/A of students in fraternities, N/A in sororities
Most popular majors: 21% Health Professions and Related Programs, 13% Business, Management, Marketing, and Related Support Services, 10% Social Sciences, 6% Communication, Journalism, and Related Programs, 6% Parks, Recreation, Leisure, and Fitness Studies
Expenses: 2017-2018: $9,014 in state, $21,895 out of state; room/board: $9,354
Financial aid: (850) 474-3145; 66% of undergrads determined to have financial need; average aid package $8,006

Valencia College[1]
Orlando FL
U.S. News ranking: Reg. Coll. (S), unranked
Admissions email: N/A
Public
Application deadline (fall): N/A
Undergraduate student body: N/A full time, N/A part time
Expenses: 2016-2017: $2,474 in state, $9,383 out of state; room/board: N/A
Financial aid: N/A

Warner University
Lake Wales FL
(800) 309-9563
U.S. News ranking: Reg. Coll. (S), No. 45
Website: www.warner.edu
Admissions email: admissions@warner.edu
Private; founded 1964
Affiliation: Church of God
Freshman admissions: less selective; 2016-2017: 1,082 applied, 273 accepted. Neither SAT nor ACT required. ACT 25/75 percentile: 17-20. High school rank: 4% in top tenth, 18% in top quarter, 45% in top half
Early decision deadline: N/A, notification date: N/A
Early action deadline: N/A, notification date: N/A
Application deadline (fall): rolling
Undergraduate student body: 835 full time, 112 part time; 54% male, 46% female; 0% American Indian, 0% Asian, 38% black, 14% Hispanic, 3% multiracial, 0% Pacific Islander, 42% white, 3% international; 95% from in state; 40% live on campus; 0% of students in fraternities, 0% in sororities
Most popular majors: 22% Elementary Education and Teaching, 17% Business Administration, Management and Operations, Other, 9% Business Administration and Management, General, 9% Sport and Fitness Administration/Management, 6% Theology/Theological Studies
Expenses: 2017-2018: $29,864; room/board: $8,348
Financial aid: (863) 638-7202; 96% of undergrads determined to have financial need; average aid package $15,558

Webber International University
Babson Park FL
(800) 741-1844
U.S. News ranking: Reg. Coll. (S), No. 57
Website: www.webber.edu
Admissions email: admissions@webber.edu
Private; founded 1927
Freshman admissions: less selective; 2016-2017: 717 applied, 355 accepted. Either SAT or ACT required. ACT 25/75 percentile: 17-21. High school rank: 5% in top tenth, 16% in top quarter, 65% in top half
Early decision deadline: N/A, notification date: N/A
Early action deadline: N/A, notification date: N/A
Application deadline (fall): 8/1

Undergraduate student body: 628 full time, 34 part time; 69% male, 31% female; 0% American Indian, 0% Asian, 26% black, 14% Hispanic, 0% multiracial, 0% Pacific Islander, 37% white, 22% international; 86% from in state; 50% live on campus; 0% of students in fraternities, 0% in sororities
Most popular majors: 64% Business, Management, Marketing, and Related Support Services, 20% Parks, Recreation, Leisure, and Fitness Studies, 13% Homeland Security, Law Enforcement, Firefighting and Related Protective Services, 1% Computer and Information Sciences and Support Services
Expenses: 2017-2018: $25,358; room/board: $8,942
Financial aid: (863) 638-2930; 73% of undergrads determined to have financial need; average aid package $19,825

GEORGIA

Abraham Baldwin Agricultural College[1]
Tifton GA
(800) 733-3653
U.S. News ranking: Reg. Coll. (S), second tier
Website: www.abac.edu/
Public; founded 1908
Application deadline (fall): 8/1
Undergraduate student body: N/A full time, N/A part time
Expenses: 2016-2017: $3,453 in state, $10,060 out of state; room/board: $7,372
Financial aid: (229) 391-4985

Agnes Scott College
Decatur GA
(800) 868-8602
U.S. News ranking: Nat. Lib. Arts, No. 61
Website: www.agnesscott.edu
Admissions email: admission@agnesscott.edu
Private; founded 1889
Affiliation: Presbyterian Church (USA)
Freshman admissions: more selective; 2016-2017: 1,399 applied, 905 accepted. Neither SAT nor ACT required. ACT 25/75 percentile: 24-30. High school rank: 43% in top tenth, 72% in top quarter, 92% in top half
Early decision deadline: 11/1, notification date: 12/1
Early action deadline: 11/15, notification date: 12/15
Application deadline (fall): 5/1
Undergraduate student body: 917 full time, 10 part time; 1% male, 99% female; 0% American Indian, 8% Asian, 30% black, 10% Hispanic, 6% multiracial, 0% Pacific Islander, 35% white, 9% international; 52% from in state; 86% live on campus; N/A of students in fraternities, N/A in sororities
Most popular majors: 15% Biological and Biomedical Sciences, 15% Social Sciences, 12% English Language and Literature/Letters, 12% Health Professions and Related Programs, 12% Psychology

Expenses: 2017-2018: $39,960; room/board: $11,970
Financial aid: (404) 471-6395; 74% of undergrads determined to have financial need; average aid package $35,349

Albany State University
Albany GA
(229) 430-4646
U.S. News ranking: Reg. U. (S), No. 106
Website: www.asurams.edu/
Admissions email: admissions@asurams.edu
Public; founded 1903
Freshman admissions: less selective; 2016-2017: 2,915 applied, 1,448 accepted. Either SAT or ACT required. ACT 25/75 percentile: 17-20. High school rank: 11% in top tenth, 32% in top quarter, 70% in top half
Early decision deadline: N/A, notification date: N/A
Early action deadline: N/A, notification date: N/A
Application deadline (fall): 7/1
Undergraduate student body: 2,194 full time, 400 part time; 34% male, 66% female; 0% American Indian, 0% Asian, 90% black, 2% Hispanic, 1% multiracial, 0% Pacific Islander, 5% white, 0% international; N/A from in state; 39% live on campus; N/A of students in fraternities, N/A in sororities
Most popular majors: 24% Business, Management, Marketing, and Related Support Services, 20% Education, 14% Homeland Security, Law Enforcement, Firefighting and Related Protective Services, 9% Public Administration and Social Service Professions, 6% Health Professions and Related Programs
Expenses: 2017-2018: $6,726 in state, $19,802 out of state; room/board: $7,788
Financial aid: (229) 430-4650; 83% of undergrads determined to have financial need; average aid package $2,535

Armstrong State University
Savannah GA
(912) 344-2503
U.S. News ranking: Reg. U. (S), second tier
Website: www.armstrong.edu
Admissions email: admissions.info@armstrong.edu
Public; founded 1935
Freshman admissions: selective; 2016-2017: 2,168 applied, 1,702 accepted. Either SAT or ACT required. SAT 25/75 percentile: 890-1080. High school rank: N/A
Early decision deadline: N/A, notification date: N/A
Early action deadline: N/A, notification date: N/A
Application deadline (fall): 7/1
Undergraduate student body: 4,737 full time, 1,660 part time; 34% male, 66% female; 0% American Indian, 4% Asian, 26% black, 8% Hispanic, 5% multiracial, 0% Pacific Islander, 56% white,

1% international; 92% from in state; 21% live on campus; N/A of students in fraternities, N/A in sororities
Most popular majors: 44% Health Professions and Related Programs, 9% Biological and Biomedical Sciences, 9% Education, 9% Liberal Arts and Sciences, General Studies and Humanities, 5% Social Sciences
Expenses: 2017-2018: $5,360 in state, $15,616 out of state; room/board: $10,750
Financial aid: (912) 344-3166; 74% of undergrads determined to have financial need

Art Institute of Atlanta[1]
Atlanta GA
U.S. News ranking: Arts, unranked
Website: www.artinstitutes.edu/atlanta/
Admissions email: aiaadm@aii.edu
For-profit
Application deadline (fall): N/A
Undergraduate student body: N/A full time, N/A part time
Expenses: 2016-2017: $17,592; room/board: N/A
Financial aid: N/A

Atlanta Metropolitan State College
Atlanta GA
(404) 756-4004
U.S. News ranking: Reg. Coll. (S), second tier
Website: www.Atlm.edu
Admissions email: admissions@atlm.edu
Public; founded 1974
Freshman admissions: less selective; 2016-2017: 1,294 applied, 242 accepted. Neither SAT nor ACT required. ACT 25/75 percentile: 17-21. High school rank: N/A
Early decision deadline: N/A, notification date: N/A
Early action deadline: N/A, notification date: N/A
Application deadline (fall): rolling
Undergraduate student body: 1,145 full time, 1,638 part time; 36% male, 64% female; 0% American Indian, 1% Asian, 92% black, 2% Hispanic, 2% multiracial, 0% Pacific Islander, 1% white, 1% international
Most popular majors: 18% Business Administration and Management, General, 13% Criminal Justice/Law Enforcement Administration, 13% Teacher Education, Multiple Levels, 9% Pre-Nursing Studies, 8% Clinical Psychology
Expenses: 2016-2017: $3,250 in state, $9,588 out of state; room/board: N/A
Financial aid: N/A

Augusta University
Augusta GA
(706) 721-2725
U.S. News ranking: Nat. U., second tier
Website: www.augusta.edu/
Admissions email: admissions@augusta.edu
Public; founded 1828

Freshman admissions: less selective; 2016-2017: N/A applied, N/A accepted. Either SAT or ACT required. SAT 25/75 percentile: N/A. High school rank: N/A
Early decision deadline: N/A, notification date: N/A
Early action deadline: N/A, notification date: N/A
Application deadline (fall): N/A
Undergraduate student body: 4,133 full time, 1,000 part time; 36% male, 64% female; N/A American Indian, N/A Asian, N/A black, N/A Hispanic, N/A multiracial, N/A Pacific Islander, N/A white, N/A international
Most popular majors: 20% Registered Nursing/Registered Nurse, 7% Psychology, General, 6% Kinesiology and Exercise Science, 5% Speech Communication and Rhetoric, 4% Biology/Biological Sciences, General
Expenses: 2017-2018: $8,634 in state, $23,606 out of state; room/board: $14,620
Financial aid: (706) 737-1524; 60% of undergrads determined to have financial need; average aid package $2,390

Berry College
Mount Berry GA
(706) 236-2215
U.S. News ranking: Reg. U. (S), No. 8
Website: www.berry.edu
Admissions email: admissions@berry.edu
Private; founded 1902
Freshman admissions: selective; 2016-2017: 3,477 applied, 2,159 accepted. Either SAT or ACT required. ACT 25/75 percentile: 24-29. High school rank: 33% in top tenth, 69% in top quarter, 93% in top half
Early decision deadline: 11/1, notification date: 12/1
Early action deadline: 11/1, notification date: 12/15
Application deadline (fall): 7/21
Undergraduate student body: 2,050 full time, 23 part time; 40% male, 60% female; 0% American Indian, 1% Asian, 4% black, 7% Hispanic, 3% multiracial, 0% Pacific Islander, 81% white, 0% international; 67% from in state; 86% live on campus; N/A of students in fraternities, N/A in sororities
Most popular majors: 21% Biological and Biomedical Sciences, 16% Business, Management, Marketing, and Related Support Services, 10% Psychology, 7% Communication, Journalism, and Related Programs, 7% Education
Expenses: 2017-2018: $35,176; room/board: $12,260
Financial aid: (706) 236-1714; 70% of undergrads determined to have financial need; average aid package $27,248

Brenau University
Gainesville GA
(770) 534-6100
U.S. News ranking: Reg. U. (S), No. 57
Website: www.brenau.edu
Admissions email: admissions@brenau.edu

Private; founded 1878
Freshman admissions: selective; 2016-2017: 1,975 applied, 704 accepted. Neither SAT nor ACT required. SAT 25/75 percentile: 860-1030. High school rank: N/A
Early decision deadline: N/A, notification date: N/A
Early action deadline: N/A, notification date: N/A
Application deadline (fall): rolling
Undergraduate student body: 1,038 full time, 615 part time; 10% male, 90% female; 0% American Indian, 2% Asian, 33% black, 9% Hispanic, 3% multiracial, 0% Pacific Islander, 48% white, 3% international; 95% from in state; 24% live on campus; 0% of students in fraternities, 9% in sororities
Most popular majors: 42% Health Professions and Related Programs, 20% Business, Management, Marketing, and Related Support Services, 14% Visual and Performing Arts, 9% Education, 4% Liberal Arts and Sciences, General Studies and Humanities
Expenses: 2017-2018: $28,510; room/board: $12,418
Financial aid: (770) 534-6176; 82% of undergrads determined to have financial need; average aid package $21,389

Brewton-Parker College[1]
Mount Vernon GA
(912) 583-3265
U.S. News ranking: Reg. Coll. (S), second tier
Website: www.bpc.edu
Admissions email: admissions@bpc.edu
Private; founded 1904
Application deadline (fall): rolling
Undergraduate student body: N/A full time, N/A part time
Expenses: 2016 2017: $16,960; room/board: $7,980
Financial aid: N/A

Clark Atlanta University
Atlanta GA
(800) 688-3228
U.S. News ranking: Nat. U., second tier
Website: www.cau.edu
Admissions email: cauadmissions@cau.edu
Private; founded 1988
Freshman admissions: less selective; 2016-2017: 10,733 applied, 7,711 accepted. Either SAT or ACT required. ACT 25/75 percentile: 18-21. High school rank: 9% in top tenth, 30% in top quarter, 69% in top half
Early decision deadline: N/A, notification date: N/A
Early action deadline: N/A, notification date: N/A
Application deadline (fall): 6/1
Undergraduate student body: 2,986 full time, 107 part time; 29% male, 71% female; 0% American Indian, 0% Asian, 83% black, 0% Hispanic, 0% multiracial, 0% Pacific Islander, 0% white, 4% international; 35% from in state; 62% live on campus; 2% of students in fraternities, 3% in sororities

Most popular majors: 20% Communication, Journalism, and Related Programs, 19% Business, Management, Marketing, and Related Support Services, 12% Visual and Performing Arts, 11% Biological and Biomedical Sciences, 10% Psychology
Expenses: 2017-2018: $23,082; room/board: $10,878
Financial aid: (404) 880-8111; 88% of undergrads determined to have financial need; average aid package $7,324

Clayton State University
Morrow GA
(678) 466-4115
U.S. News ranking: Reg. U. (S), second tier
Website: www.clayton.edu
Admissions email: ccsu-info@mail.clayton.edu
Public; founded 1969
Freshman admissions: selective; 2016-2017: 2,295 applied, 939 accepted. Either SAT or ACT required. ACT 25/75 percentile: 18-21. High school rank: N/A
Early decision deadline: N/A, notification date: N/A
Early action deadline: N/A, notification date: N/A
Application deadline (fall): 7/1
Undergraduate student body: 3,636 full time, 2,919 part time; 31% male, 69% female; 0% American Indian, 5% Asian, 66% black, 5% Hispanic, 3% multiracial, 0% Pacific Islander, 16% white, 1% international; 97% from in state; 15% live on campus; N/A of students in fraternities, N/A in sororities
Most popular majors: 13% Liberal Arts and Sciences/ Liberal Studies, 12% Registered Nursing/Registered Nurse, 10% Community Psychology, 10% Hospital and Health Care Facilities Administration/Management, 6% Office Management and Supervision
Expenses: 2017-2018: $6,410 in state, $19,486 out of state; room/ board: $10,156
Financial aid: (678) 466-4185; 87% of undergrads determined to have financial need; average aid package $9,489

College of Coastal Georgia
Brunswick GA
(912) 279-5730
U.S. News ranking: Reg. Coll. (S), No. 55
Website: www.ccga.edu
Admissions email: admiss@ccga.edu
Public; founded 1961
Freshman admissions: less selective; 2016-2017: 1,544 applied, 1,470 accepted. Either SAT or ACT required. SAT 25/75 percentile: 800-1000. High school rank: N/A
Early decision deadline: N/A, notification date: N/A
Early action deadline: N/A, notification date: N/A
Application deadline (fall): rolling

Undergraduate student body: 2,165 full time, 1,364 part time; 34% male, 66% female; 0% American Indian, 1% Asian, 20% black, 6% Hispanic, 5% multiracial, 0% Pacific Islander, 64% white, 1% international; 94% from in state; 45% live on campus; N/A of students in fraternities, N/A in sororities
Most popular majors: 26% Registered Nursing/Registered Nurse, 18% Business/Commerce, General, 13% Psychology, General, 11% Early Childhood Education and Teaching, 9% Biology/Biological Sciences, General
Expenses: 2017-2018: $4,648 in state, $13,070 out of state; room/ board: $9,850
Financial aid: (912) 279-5722; 61% of undergrads determined to have financial need; average aid package $10,826

Columbus State University
Columbus GA
(706) 507-8800
U.S. News ranking: Reg. U. (S), No. 106
Website: www.columbusstate.edu
Admissions email: admissions@ columbusstate.edu
Public; founded 1958
Freshman admissions: selective; 2016-2017: 3,160 applied, 1,680 accepted. Either SAT or ACT required. SAT 25/75 percentile: 860-1090. High school rank: 11% in top tenth, 34% in top quarter, 65% in top half
Early decision deadline: N/A, notification date: N/A
Early action deadline: N/A, notification date: N/A
Application deadline (fall): 6/30
Undergraduate student body: 4,834 full time, 1,955 part time; 41% male, 59% female; 0% American Indian, 2% Asian, 38% black, 6% Hispanic, 2% multiracial, 0% Pacific Islander, 50% white, 1% international; 84% from in state; 20% live on campus; 5% of students in fraternities, 5% in sororities
Most popular majors: 26% Health Professions and Related Programs, 16% Business, Management, Marketing, and Related Support Services, 10% Education, 6% Visual and Performing Arts, 5% Communication, Journalism, and Related Programs
Expenses: 2017-2018: $7,200 in state, $20,682 out of state; room/ board: $10,550
Financial aid: (706) 507-8898; 72% of undergrads determined to have financial need; average aid package $9,309

Covenant College
Lookout Mountain GA
(706) 820-2398
U.S. News ranking: Nat. Lib. Arts, No. 168
Website: www.covenant.edu
Admissions email: admissions@ covenant.edu
Private; founded 1955
Affiliation: The Presbyterian Church in America

Freshman admissions: more selective; 2016-2017: 612 applied, 589 accepted. Either SAT or ACT required. ACT 25/75 percentile: 24-29. High school rank: 26% in top tenth, 58% in top quarter, 85% in top half
Early decision deadline: N/A, notification date: N/A
Early action deadline: 11/1, notification date: 12/15
Application deadline (fall): 2/1
Undergraduate student body: 973 full time, 32 part time; 45% male, 55% female; 0% American Indian, 1% Asian, 3% black, 3% Hispanic, 3% multiracial, 0% Pacific Islander, 86% white, 3% international; 27% from in state; 84% live on campus; 0% of students in fraternities, 0% in sororities
Most popular majors: 16% Social Sciences, 11% Education, 10% English Language and Literature/Letters, 10% Visual and Performing Arts, 9% Business, Management, Marketing, and Related Support Services
Expenses: 2017-2018: $33,170; room/board: $9,910
Financial aid: (706) 419-1104; 65% of undergrads determined to have financial need; average aid package $27,907

Dalton State College[1]
Dalton GA
U.S. News ranking: Reg. Coll. (S), unranked
Website: www.daltonstate.edu/
Admissions email: N/A
Public
Application deadline (fall): N/A
Undergraduate student body: N/A full time, N/A part time
Expenses: 2016-2017: $3,503 in state, $10,100 out of state; room/ board: $8,128
Financial aid: N/A

East Georgia State College[1]
Swainsboro GA
U.S. News ranking: Reg. Coll. (S), second tier
Public
Application deadline (fall): 8/15
Undergraduate student body: N/A full time, N/A part time
Expenses: 2016-2017: $3,067 in state, $9,142 out of state; room/ board: $8,523
Financial aid: N/A

Emmanuel College
Franklin Springs GA
(800) 860-8800
U.S. News ranking: Reg. Coll. (S), No. 41
Website: www.ec.edu
Admissions email: admissions@ec.edu
Private; founded 1919
Affiliation: Pentecostal Holiness Church
Freshman admissions: less selective; 2016-2017: 1,386 applied, 562 accepted. Either SAT or ACT required. SAT 25/75 percentile: 790-1070. High school rank: N/A

Early decision deadline: N/A, notification date: N/A
Early action deadline: N/A, notification date: N/A
Application deadline (fall): 8/1
Undergraduate student body: 796 full time, 124 part time; 52% male, 48% female; 0% American Indian, 0% Asian, 14% black, 7% Hispanic, 3% multiracial, 1% Pacific Islander, 68% white, 6% international
Most popular majors: 25% Parks, Recreation, Leisure, and Fitness Studies, 12% Education, 11% Business, Management, Marketing, and Related Support Services, 10% Psychology, 10% Theology and Religious Vocations
Expenses: 2017-2018: $19,710; room/board: $7,480
Financial aid: (706) 245-2844; 76% of undergrads determined to have financial need; average aid package $15,648

Emory University
Atlanta GA
(404) 727-6036
U.S. News ranking: Nat. U., No. 21
Website: www.emory.edu
Admissions email: admission@emory.edu
Private; founded 1836
Affiliation: United Methodist
Freshman admissions: most selective; 2016-2017: 19,924 applied, 5,039 accepted. Either SAT or ACT required. SAT 25/75 percentile: 1290-1500. High school rank: 83% in top tenth, 98% in top quarter, 100% in top half
Early decision deadline: 11/1, notification date: 12/15
Early action deadline: N/A, notification date: N/A
Application deadline (fall): 1/1
Undergraduate student body: 6,714 full time, 147 part time; 41% male, 59% female; 0% American Indian, 18% Asian, 9% black, 9% Hispanic, 4% multiracial, 0% Pacific Islander, 42% white, 16% international; 21% from in state; 64% live on campus; 27% of students in fraternities, 33% in sororities
Most popular majors: 15% Business Administration and Management, General, 10% Biology/Biological Sciences, General, 9% Economics, General, 7% Neuroscience, 7% Registered Nursing/Registered Nurse
Expenses: 2017-2018: $49,392; room/board: $13,894
Financial aid: (404) 727-6039; 45% of undergrads determined to have financial need; average aid package $44,168

Fort Valley State University
Fort Valley GA
(478) 825-6307
U.S. News ranking: Reg. U. (S), second tier
Website: www.fvsu.edu
Admissions email: admissap@mail.fvsu.edu
Public; founded 1895
Freshman admissions: less selective; 2016-2017: 6,371 applied, 1,686 accepted. Either

SAT or ACT required. ACT 25/75 percentile: 15-19. High school rank: 2% in top tenth, 15% in top quarter, 46% in top half
Early decision deadline: N/A, notification date: N/A
Early action deadline: N/A, notification date: N/A
Application deadline (fall): 7/19
Undergraduate student body: 1,997 full time, 255 part time; 42% male, 58% female; 0% American Indian, 0% Asian, 94% black, 0% Hispanic, 0% multiracial, 0% Pacific Islander, 2% white, 0% international; 95% from in state; 52% live on campus; 0% of students in fraternities, 0% in sororities
Most popular majors: 14% Health Professions and Related Programs, 11% Homeland Security, Law Enforcement, Firefighting and Related Protective Services, 11% Psychology, 9% Physical Sciences, 8% Biological and Biomedical Sciences
Expenses: 2017-2018: $6,664 in state, $19,740 out of state; room/board: $8,278
Financial aid: (478) 825-6363; 100% of undergrads determined to have financial need; average aid package $7,041

Georgia College & State University
Milledgeville GA
(478) 445-1283
U.S. News ranking: Reg. U. (S), No. 31
Website: www.gcsu.edu
Admissions email: admissions@gcsu.edu
Public; founded 1889
Freshman admissions: selective; 2016-2017: 3,980 applied, 3,364 accepted. Either SAT or ACT required. ACT 25/75 percentile: 22-26. High school rank: N/A
Early decision deadline: N/A, notification date: N/A
Early action deadline: 11/1, notification date: 1/1
Application deadline (fall): 4/1
Undergraduate student body: 5,555 full time, 492 part time; 39% male, 61% female; 0% American Indian, 2% Asian, 5% black, 5% Hispanic, 3% multiracial, 0% Pacific Islander, 84% white, 1% international; 99% from in state; 33% live on campus; 7% of students in fraternities, 12% in sororities
Most popular majors: 9% Business Administration and Management, General, 9% Registered Nursing/Registered Nurse, 8% Journalism, 8% Marketing/Marketing Management, General
Expenses: 2017-2018: $9,346 in state, $28,060 out of state; room/board: $12,538
Financial aid: (478) 445-5149; 50% of undergrads determined to have financial need; average aid package $10,428

Georgia Gwinnett College
Lawrenceville GA
(877) 704-4422
U.S. News ranking: Reg. Coll. (S), No. 50
Website: www.ggc.edu
Public; founded 2005
Freshman admissions: less selective; 2016-2017: 3,705 applied, 3,293 accepted. Either SAT or ACT required. SAT 25/75 percentile: 810-1040. High school rank: 3% in top tenth, 14% in top quarter, 41% in top half
Early decision deadline: N/A, notification date: N/A
Early action deadline: N/A, notification date: N/A
Application deadline (fall): 6/1
Undergraduate student body: 8,154 full time, 3,898 part time; 44% male, 56% female; 0% American Indian, 10% Asian, 34% black, 18% Hispanic, 4% multiracial, 0% Pacific Islander, 32% white, 2% international; 99% from in state; 6% live on campus; N/A of students in fraternities, N/A in sororities
Most popular majors: 36% Business/Commerce, General, 11% Biology/Biological Sciences, General, 11% Psychology, General, 10% Early Childhood Education and Teaching, 9% Information Technology
Expenses: 2017-2018: $5,634 in state, $16,348 out of state; room/board: $12,870
Financial aid: (678) 407-5701; 75% of undergrads determined to have financial need; average aid package $14,668

Georgia Institute of Technology
Atlanta GA
(404) 894-4154
U.S. News ranking: Nat. U., No. 34
Website: admission.gatech.edu/information/
Admissions email: admission@gatech.edu
Public; founded 1885
Freshman admissions: most selective; 2016-2017: 30,528 applied, 7,868 accepted. Either SAT or ACT required. SAT 25/75 percentile: 1320-1500. High school rank: 87% in top tenth, 97% in top quarter, 99% in top half
Early decision deadline: N/A, notification date: N/A
Early action deadline: 10/15, notification date: 1/10
Application deadline (fall): 1/1
Undergraduate student body: 13,815 full time, 1,674 part time; 63% male, 37% female; 0% American Indian, 20% Asian, 7% black, 7% Hispanic, 4% multiracial, 0% Pacific Islander, 50% white, 10% international; 66% from in state; 53% live on campus; 23% of students in fraternities, 31% in sororities
Most popular majors: 63% Engineering, 12% Business, Management, Marketing, and Related Support Services, 11% Computer and Information Sciences and Support Services, 4% Biological and Biomedical Sciences, 2% Physical Sciences

Expenses: 2017-2018: $12,418 in state, $33,014 out of state; room/board: $14,126
Financial aid: (404) 894-4160; 41% of undergrads determined to have financial need; average aid package $9,223

Georgia Southern University
Statesboro GA
(912) 478-5391
U.S. News ranking: Nat. U., second tier
Website: www.georgiasouthern.edu/
Admissions email: admissions@georgiasouthern.edu
Public; founded 1906
Freshman admissions: selective; 2016-2017: 9,834 applied, 6,348 accepted. Either SAT or ACT required. ACT 25/75 percentile: 22-26. High school rank: 18% in top tenth, 47% in top quarter, 78% in top half
Early decision deadline: N/A, notification date: N/A
Early action deadline: N/A, notification date: N/A
Application deadline (fall): 5/1
Undergraduate student body: 15,976 full time, 2,029 part time; 49% male, 51% female; 0% American Indian, 2% Asian, 26% black, 5% Hispanic, 2% multiracial, 0% Pacific Islander, 62% white, 2% international; 96% from in state; 27% live on campus; 14% of students in fraternities, 19% in sororities
Most popular majors: 19% Business, Management, Marketing, and Related Support Services, 10% Parks, Recreation, Leisure, and Fitness Studies, 8% Liberal Arts and Sciences, General Studies and Humanities, 7% Engineering, 6% Psychology
Expenses: 2017-2018: $6,796 in state, $18,692 out of state; room/board: $9,800
Financial aid: (912) 478-5413; 65% of undergrads determined to have financial need; average aid package $10,404

Georgia Southwestern State University
Americus GA
(229) 928-1273
U.S. News ranking: Reg. U. (S), second tier
Website: www.gsw.edu
Admissions email: admissions@gsw.edu
Public; founded 1906
Freshman admissions: selective; 2016-2017: 1,389 applied, 947 accepted. Either SAT or ACT required. SAT 25/75 percentile: 870-1060. High school rank: 15% in top tenth, 42% in top quarter, 75% in top half
Early decision deadline: N/A, notification date: N/A
Early action deadline: N/A, notification date: N/A
Application deadline (fall): 7/21
Undergraduate student body: 1,769 full time, 789 part time; 38% male, 62% female; 0% American Indian, 1% Asian, 27% black, 4% Hispanic, 2% multiracial,

0% Pacific Islander, 63% white, 2% international; 96% from in state; 32% live on campus; 10% of students in fraternities, 10% in sororities
Most popular majors: 18% Business Administration and Management, General, 17% Registered Nursing/Registered Nurse, 13% Accounting, 10% Adult and Continuing Education and Teaching, 10% Psychology, General
Expenses: 2017-2018: $6,332 in state, $19,408 out of state; room/board: $7,910
Financial aid: (229) 928-1378; 73% of undergrads determined to have financial need; average aid package $9,480

Georgia State University
Atlanta GA
(404) 413-2500
U.S. News ranking: Nat. U., No. 223
Website: www.gsu.edu
Admissions email: admissions@gsu.edu
Public; founded 1913
Freshman admissions: selective; 2016-2017: 17,467 applied, 9,212 accepted. Either SAT or ACT required. SAT 25/75 percentile: 950-1180. High school rank: 17% in top tenth, 45% in top quarter, 82% in top half
Early decision deadline: N/A, notification date: N/A
Early action deadline: 11/16, notification date: 1/30
Application deadline (fall): 3/1
Undergraduate student body: 19,371 full time, 6,084 part time; 41% male, 59% female; 0% American Indian, 13% Asian, 42% black, 10% Hispanic, 6% multiracial, 0% Pacific Islander, 25% white, 2% international; 95% from in state; 21% live on campus; N/A of students in fraternities, N/A in sororities
Most popular majors: 25% Business, Management, Marketing, and Related Support Services, 10% Social Sciences, 9% Psychology, 8% Visual and Performing Arts, 7% Biological and Biomedical Sciences
Expenses: 2017-2018: $10,858 in state, $29,432 out of state; room/board: $14,392
Financial aid: (404) 413-2600; 79% of undergrads determined to have financial need; average aid package $11,461

Gordon State College
Barnesville GA
(678) 359-5021
U.S. News ranking: Reg. Coll. (S), second tier
Website: www.gordonstate.edu/
Admissions email: admissions@gordonstate.edu
Public; founded 1852
Freshman admissions: less selective; 2016-2017: 2,718 applied, 1,122 accepted. Either SAT or ACT required. SAT 25/75 percentile: 750-970. High school rank: N/A
Early decision deadline: N/A, notification date: N/A

Early action deadline: N/A, notification date: N/A
Application deadline (fall): rolling
Undergraduate student body: 2,492 full time, 1,409 part time; 34% male, 66% female; N/A American Indian, N/A Asian, N/A black, N/A Hispanic, N/A multiracial, N/A Pacific Islander, N/A white, N/A international
Most popular majors: 36% Registered Nursing/Registered Nurse, 18% Public Administration and Social Service Professions, 17% Elementary Education and Teaching, 15% Biology/Biological Sciences, General, 7% English Language and Literature, General
Expenses: 2017-2018: $4,164 in state, $12,422 out of state; room/board: $8,101
Financial aid: (678) 359-5990

Kennesaw State University
Kennesaw GA
(770) 423-6300
U.S. News ranking: Nat. U., second tier
Website: www.kennesaw.edu
Admissions email: ksuadmit@kennesaw.edu
Public; founded 1963
Freshman admissions: selective; 2016-2017: 15,122 applied, 8,847 accepted. Either SAT or ACT required. ACT 25/75 percentile: 21-26. High school rank: 21% in top tenth, 53% in top quarter, 81% in top half
Early decision deadline: N/A, notification date: N/A
Early action deadline: N/A, notification date: N/A
Application deadline (fall): 5/5
Undergraduate student body: 24,412 full time, 7,754 part time; 52% male, 48% female; 0% American Indian, 5% Asian, 21% black, 9% Hispanic, 4% multiracial, 0% Pacific Islander, 57% white, 2% international; 90% from in state; 15% live on campus; 5% of students in fraternities, 10% in sororities
Most popular majors: 20% Business, Management, Marketing, and Related Support Services, 9% Computer and Information Sciences and Support Services, 8% Communication, Journalism, and Related Programs, 7% Education, 7% Social Sciences
Expenses: 2017-2018: $7,432 in state, $21,158 out of state; room/board: $11,467
Financial aid: (770) 423-6074; 74% of undergrads determined to have financial need; average aid package $8,426

LaGrange College
LaGrange GA
(706) 880-8005
U.S. News ranking: Nat. Lib. Arts, second tier
Website: www.lagrange.edu
Admissions email: admission@lagrange.edu
Private; founded 1831
Affiliation: United Methodist
Freshman admissions: selective; 2016-2017: 1,568 applied, 905 accepted. Either SAT or ACT

required. ACT 25/75 percentile: 20-24. High school rank: 15% in top tenth, 41% in top quarter, 72% in top half
Early decision deadline: N/A, notification date: N/A
Early action deadline: N/A, notification date: N/A
Application deadline (fall): rolling
Undergraduate student body: 854 full time, 52 part time; 51% male, 49% female; 0% American Indian, 1% Asian, 23% black, 1% Hispanic, 2% multiracial, 0% Pacific Islander, 71% white, 1% international; 17% from in state; 62% live on campus; 23% of students in fraternities, 40% in sororities
Most popular majors: 19% Registered Nursing/Registered Nurse, 9% Business Administration and Management, General, 8% Kinesiology and Exercise Science, 7% Biology/Biological Sciences, General, 7% Psychology, General
Expenses: 2017-2018: $29,450; room/board: $11,740
Financial aid: (706) 880-8249; 82% of undergrads determined to have financial need; average aid package $25,146

Mercer University
Macon GA
(478) 301-2650
U.S. News ranking: Nat. U., No. 133
Website: www.mercer.edu
Admissions email: admissions@mercer.edu
Private; founded 1833
Freshman admissions: more selective; 2016-2017: 4,836 applied, 3,354 accepted. Either SAT or ACT required. ACT 25/75 percentile: 25-29. High school rank: 39% in top tenth, 70% in top quarter, 92% in top half
Early decision deadline: N/A, notification date: N/A
Early action deadline: 11/1, notification date: 11/15
Application deadline (fall): 7/1
Undergraduate student body: 4,035 full time, 671 part time; 38% male, 62% female; 0% American Indian, 6% Asian, 30% black, 5% Hispanic, 3% multiracial, 0% Pacific Islander, 48% white, 3% international; 81% from in state; 78% live on campus; 21% of students in fraternities, 27% in sororities
Most popular majors: 20% Business, Management, Marketing, and Related Support Services, 14% Biological and Biomedical Sciences, 14% Engineering, 10% Social Sciences, 7% Psychology
Expenses: 2017-2018: $36,000; room/board: $12,153
Financial aid: (478) 301-2226; 67% of undergrads determined to have financial need; average aid package $34,952

Middle Georgia State University
Macon GA
(800) 272-7619
U.S. News ranking: Reg. Coll. (S), second tier
Website: www.mga.edu/

Admissions email: admissions@mga.edu
Public; founded 2013
Freshman admissions: less selective; 2016-2017: 6,026 applied, 5,099 accepted. Neither SAT nor ACT required. SAT 25/75 percentile: N/A. High school rank: N/A
Early decision deadline: N/A, notification date: N/A
Early action deadline: N/A, notification date: N/A
Application deadline (fall): 7/16
Undergraduate student body: 4,769 full time, 2,873 part time; 42% male, 58% female; N/A American Indian, N/A Asian, N/A black, N/A Hispanic, N/A multiracial, N/A Pacific Islander, N/A white, N/A international; 97% from in state; 21% live on campus; N/A of students in fraternities, N/A in sororities
Most popular majors: Information not available
Expenses: 2016-2017: $3,890 in state, $10,919 out of state; room/board: $7,870
Financial aid: N/A

Morehouse College
Atlanta GA
(470) 639-0391
U.S. News ranking: Nat. Lib. Arts, No. 160
Website: www.morehouse.edu
Admissions email: admissions@morehouse.edu
Private; founded 1867
Freshman admissions: selective; 2016-2017: 3,186 applied, 2,105 accepted. Either SAT or ACT required. ACT 25/75 percentile: 19-24. High school rank: 15% in top tenth, 37% in top quarter, 71% in top half
Early decision deadline: 11/1, notification date: 12/15
Early action deadline: 11/1, notification date: 12/15
Application deadline (fall): 2/15
Undergraduate student body: 2,020 full time, 88 part time; 100% male, 0% female; 0% American Indian, 0% Asian, 95% black, 1% Hispanic, 0% multiracial, 0% Pacific Islander, 0% white, 2% international; 29% from in state; 74% live on campus; 3% of students in fraternities, N/A in sororities
Most popular majors: 22% Business, Management, Marketing, and Related Support Services, 21% Social Sciences, 13% Biological and Biomedical Sciences, 7% English Language and Literature/Letters, 6% Psychology
Expenses: 2017-2018: $27,278; room/board: $13,557
Financial aid: (404) 215-2639; 82% of undergrads determined to have financial need; average aid package $21,187

Oglethorpe University[1]
Atlanta GA
(404) 364-8307
U.S. News ranking: Nat. Lib. Arts, second tier
Website: www.oglethorpe.edu
Admissions email: admission@oglethorpe.edu
Private; founded 1835
Application deadline (fall): rolling

Undergraduate student body: N/A full time, N/A part time
Expenses: 2016-2017: $35,280; room/board: $12,710
Financial aid: (404) 364-8355

Paine College[1]
Augusta GA
(706) 821-8320
U.S. News ranking: Nat. Lib. Arts, second tier
Website: www.paine.edu
Admissions email: admissions@paine.edu
Private; founded 1882
Application deadline (fall): 7/15
Undergraduate student body: N/A full time, N/A part time
Expenses: 2016-2017: $14,224; room/board: $6,662
Financial aid: N/A

Piedmont College
Demorest GA
(800) 277-7020
U.S. News ranking: Reg. U. (S), No. 68
Website: www.piedmont.edu
Admissions email: ugrad@piedmont.edu
Private; founded 1897
Affiliation: United Church of Christ
Freshman admissions: selective; 2016-2017: 1,335 applied, 763 accepted. Either SAT or ACT required. SAT 25/75 percentile: 860-1090. High school rank: 15% in top tenth, 36% in top quarter, 73% in top half
Early decision deadline: N/A, notification date: N/A
Early action deadline: N/A, notification date: N/A
Application deadline (fall): 7/1
Undergraduate student body: 1,177 full time, 118 part time; 36% male, 64% female; 1% American Indian, 2% Asian, 9% black, 7% Hispanic, 3% multiracial, 0% Pacific Islander, 69% white, 0% international; 92% from in state; 69% live on campus; N/A of students in fraternities, N/A in sororities
Most popular majors: 35% Health Professions and Related Programs, 16% Education, 13% Business, Management, Marketing, and Related Support Services, 7% Psychology, 6% Visual and Performing Arts
Expenses: 2017-2018: $24,468; room/board: $9,870
Financial aid: (706) 776-0114; 82% of undergrads determined to have financial need; average aid package $19,224

Point University
West Point GA
(706) 385-1202
U.S. News ranking: Reg. Coll. (S), No. 41
Website: www.point.edu
Admissions email: admissions@point.edu
Private; founded 1937
Freshman admissions: less selective; 2016-2017: 1,184 applied, 609 accepted. Neither SAT nor ACT required. ACT 25/75 percentile: 17-22. High school rank: N/A

Early decision deadline: N/A, notification date: N/A
Early action deadline: N/A, notification date: N/A
Application deadline (fall): 8/1
Undergraduate student body: 1,366 full time, 588 part time; 47% male, 53% female; 0% American Indian, 0% Asian, 34% black, 6% Hispanic, 5% multiracial, 0% Pacific Islander, 47% white, 2% international; 63% from in state; 41% live on campus; 0% of students in fraternities, 0% in sororities
Most popular majors: Information not available
Expenses: 2017-2018: $20,600; room/board: $7,900
Financial aid: (706) 385-1462; 77% of undergrads determined to have financial need; average aid package $2,500

Reinhardt University
Waleska GA
(770) 720-5526
U.S. News ranking: Reg. Coll. (S), No. 28
Website: www.reinhardt.edu/
Admissions email: admissions@reinhardt.edu
Private; founded 1883
Affiliation: United Methodist
Freshman admissions: less selective; 2016-2017: 1,275 applied, 1,115 accepted. Either SAT or ACT required. ACT 25/75 percentile: 18-23. High school rank: 9% in top tenth, 26% in top quarter, 56% in top half
Early decision deadline: N/A, notification date: N/A
Early action deadline: N/A, notification date: N/A
Application deadline (fall): 8/15
Undergraduate student body: 1,257 full time, 117 part time; 54% male, 46% female; 1% American Indian, 1% Asian, 22% black, 7% Hispanic, 2% multiracial, 0% Pacific Islander, 63% white, 0% international
Most popular majors: Information not available
Expenses: 2017-2018: $22,422; room/board: $8,266
Financial aid: (770) 720-5667; 68% of undergrads determined to have financial need; average aid package $14,219

Savannah College of Art and Design
Savannah GA
(912) 525-5100
U.S. News ranking: Arts, unranked
Website: www.scad.edu
Admissions email: admission@scad.edu
Private; founded 1978
Freshman admissions: selective; 2016-2017: 11,723 applied, 8,329 accepted. Either SAT or ACT required. SAT 25/75 percentile: 950-1190. High school rank: N/A
Early decision deadline: N/A, notification date: N/A
Early action deadline: N/A, notification date: N/A
Application deadline (fall): rolling
Undergraduate student body: 8,825 full time, 1,748 part time; 33% male, 67% female; 1% American

Indian, 5% Asian, 10% black, 8% Hispanic, 0% multiracial, 0% Pacific Islander, 52% white, 21% international; 21% from in state; 42% live on campus; N/A of students in fraternities, N/A in sororities
Most popular majors: 10% Animation, Interactive Technology, Video Graphics and Special Effects, 9% Graphic Design, 7% Apparel and Textile Marketing Management, 6% Fashion/Apparel Design, 6% Illustration
Expenses: 2017-2018: $35,910; room/board: $14,244
Financial aid: (912) 525-5100; 50% of undergrads determined to have financial need; average aid package $17,818

Savannah State University
Savannah GA
(912) 358-4338
U.S. News ranking: Reg. U. (S), second tier
Website: www.savannahstate.edu
Admissions email: admissions@savannahstate.edu
Public; founded 1890
Freshman admissions: least selective; 2016-2017: 4,332 applied, 2,200 accepted. Either SAT or ACT required. SAT 25/75 percentile: 16-19. High school rank: N/A
Early decision deadline: N/A, notification date: N/A
Early action deadline: N/A, notification date: N/A
Application deadline (fall): 7/15
Undergraduate student body: 4,132 full time, 640 part time; 40% male, 60% female; 0% American Indian, 0% Asian, 88% black, 6% Hispanic, 3% multiracial, 0% Pacific Islander, 1% white, 1% international; 87% from in state; 56% live on campus; N/A of students in fraternities, N/A in sororities
Most popular majors: 15% Homeland Security, Law Enforcement, Firefighting and Related Protective Services, Other, 14% Biology/Biological Sciences, General, 14% Business Administration and Management, General, 10% Journalism, 8% Political Science and Government, General
Expenses: 2017-2018: $3,367 in state, $9,905 out of state; room/board: N/A
Financial aid: (912) 358-4162

Shorter University
Rome GA
(800) 868-6980
U.S. News ranking: Reg. Coll. (S), No. 33
Website: su.shorter.edu
Admissions email: admissions@shorter.edu
Private; founded 1873
Affiliation: Baptist
Freshman admissions: less selective; 2016-2017: 1,820 applied, 1,113 accepted. Either SAT or ACT required. ACT 25/75 percentile: 18-23. High school rank: N/A
Early decision deadline: N/A, notification date: N/A

Early action deadline: N/A, notification date: N/A
Application deadline (fall): N/A
Undergraduate student body: 1,214 full time, 205 part time; 45% male, 55% female; 0% American Indian, 0% Asian, 27% black, 5% Hispanic, 3% multiracial, 0% Pacific Islander, 61% white, 3% international
Most popular majors: Biology/Biological Sciences, General, Early Childhood Education and Teaching, General Studies, Registered Nursing/Registered Nurse, Sport and Fitness Administration/Management
Expenses: 2017-2018: $21,730; room/board: $9,400
Financial aid: (706) 233-7227

South Georgia State College

Douglas GA
(912) 260-4206
U.S. News ranking: Reg. Coll. (S), unranked
Website: www.sgsc.edu/future-students/1592.cms
Private
Freshman admissions: least selective; 2016-2017: N/A applied, N/A accepted. Neither SAT nor ACT required. SAT 25/75 percentile: N/A. High school rank: N/A
Early decision deadline: N/A, notification date: N/A
Early action deadline: N/A, notification date: N/A
Application deadline (fall): rolling
Undergraduate student body: 1,638 full time, 904 part time; 37% male, 63% female; 0% American Indian, 1% Asian, 34% black, 6% Hispanic, 2% multiracial, 0% Pacific Islander, 56% white, 1% international
Most popular majors: Information not available
Expenses: 2016-2017: N/A; room/board: $8,250
Financial aid: N/A

South University[1]

Savannah GA
(912) 201-8000
U.S. News ranking: Reg. U. (S), second tier
Website: www.southuniversity.edu
Admissions email: cshall@southuniversity.edu
Private
Application deadline (fall): N/A
Undergraduate student body: N/A full time, N/A part time
Expenses: 2016-2017: $17,016; room/board: N/A
Financial aid: N/A

Spelman College

Atlanta GA
(800) 982-2411
U.S. News ranking: Nat. Lib. Arts, No. 61
Website: www.spelman.edu
Admissions email: admiss@spelman.edu
Private; founded 1881
Freshman admissions: more selective; 2016-2017: 7,864 applied, 2,810 accepted. Either SAT or ACT required. SAT 25/75 percentile: 980-1170. High school rank: 38% in top tenth, 73% in top quarter, 93% in top half

Early decision deadline: 11/1, notification date: 12/15
Early action deadline: 11/15, notification date: 12/31
Application deadline (fall): 2/1
Undergraduate student body: 2,061 full time, 64 part time; 0% male, 100% female; 1% American Indian, 0% Asian, 97% black, 0% Hispanic, 1% multiracial, 0% Pacific Islander, 0% white, 1% international; 28% from in state; 67% live on campus; N/A of students in fraternities, 2% in sororities
Most popular majors: 20% Psychology, General, 11% Biology/Biological Sciences, General, 11% Economics, General, 9% Political Science and Government, General, 7% English Language and Literature, General
Expenses: 2017-2018: $28,181; room/board: $13,461
Financial aid: (404) 270-5212; 82% of undergrads determined to have financial need; average aid package $16,900

Thomas University

Thomasville GA
(229) 227-6934
U.S. News ranking: Reg. U. (S), second tier
Website: www.thomasu.edu
Admissions email: rgagliano@thomasu.edu
Private; founded 1950
Freshman admissions: less selective; 2016-2017: 416 applied, 197 accepted. Neither SAT nor ACT required. SAT 25/75 percentile: N/A. High school rank: N/A
Early decision deadline: N/A, notification date: N/A
Early action deadline: N/A, notification date: N/A
Application deadline (fall): rolling
Undergraduate student body: 465 full time, 304 part time; 45% male, 55% female; N/A American Indian, N/A Asian, N/A black, N/A Hispanic, N/A multiracial, N/A Pacific Islander, N/A white, N/A international
Most popular majors: Information not available
Expenses: 2016-2017: $16,940; room/board: $9,820
Financial aid: (229) 226-1621

Toccoa Falls College

Toccoa Falls GA
(888) 785-5624
U.S. News ranking: Reg. Coll. (S), No. 21
Website: www.tfc.edu
Admissions email: admissions@tfc.edu
Private; founded 1907
Affiliation: Christ and Missionary Alliance Church
Freshman admissions: selective; 2016-2017: 881 applied, 477 accepted. Either SAT or ACT required. SAT 25/75 percentile: 830-1080. High school rank: 12% in top tenth, 28% in top quarter, 64% in top half
Early decision deadline: N/A, notification date: N/A
Early action deadline: N/A, notification date: N/A
Application deadline (fall): rolling

Undergraduate student body: 793 full time, 459 part time; 43% male, 57% female; 1% American Indian, 8% Asian, 8% black, 5% Hispanic, 2% multiracial, 0% Pacific Islander, 76% white, 1% international; 77% from in state; 39% live on campus; 0% of students in fraternities, 0% in sororities
Most popular majors: 18% Counseling Psychology, 13% Missions/Missionary Studies and Missiology, 9% Religious Education, 7% Bible/Biblical Studies, 7% Communication and Media Studies
Expenses: 2017-2018: $22,104; room/board: $7,934
Financial aid: (706) 886-7299; 87% of undergrads determined to have financial need

Truett McConnell University

Cleveland GA
(706) 865-2134
U.S. News ranking: Reg. Coll. (S), No. 57
Website: truett.edu/
Admissions email: admissions@truett.edu
Private; founded 1946
Affiliation: Southern Baptist
Freshman admissions: less selective; 2016-2017: 543 applied, 492 accepted. Either SAT or ACT required. SAT 25/75 percentile: 860-1053. High school rank: 9% in top tenth, 32% in top quarter, 60% in top half
Early decision deadline: N/A, notification date: N/A
Early action deadline: N/A, notification date: N/A
Application deadline (fall): 8/1
Undergraduate student body: 740 full time, 1,412 part time; 44% male, 56% female; 0% American Indian, 0% Asian, 8% black, 6% Hispanic, 0% multiracial, 0% Pacific Islander, 81% white, 2% international; 91% from in state; 70% live on campus; 0% of students in fraternities, 0% in sororities
Most popular majors: 26% Business, Management, Marketing, and Related Support Services, 24% Health Professions and Related Programs, 14% Psychology, 14% Theology and Religious Vocations, 9% Education
Expenses: 2017-2018: $19,480; room/board: $7,400
Financial aid: (706) 865-2134; 83% of undergrads determined to have financial need; average aid package $15,321

University of Georgia

Athens GA
(706) 542-8776
U.S. News ranking: Nat. U., No. 54
Website: www.admissions.uga.edu
Admissions email: adm-info@uga.edu
Public; founded 1785
Freshman admissions: more selective; 2016-2017: 22,694 applied, 12,232 accepted. Either SAT or ACT required. SAT 25/75 percentile: 1140-1340. High school rank: 55% in top tenth, 91% in top quarter, 99% in top half

Early decision deadline: N/A, notification date: N/A
Early action deadline: 10/15, notification date: 12/1
Application deadline (fall): 1/15
Undergraduate student body: 26,328 full time, 1,623 part time; 43% male, 57% female; 0% American Indian, 10% Asian, 8% black, 6% Hispanic, 4% multiracial, 0% Pacific Islander, 70% white, 2% international; 92% from in state; 32% live on campus; 20% of students in fraternities, 31% in sororities
Most popular majors: 7% Finance, General, 7% Psychology, General, 6% Biology/Biological Sciences, General, 4% Marketing/Marketing Management, General, 3% International Relations and Affairs
Expenses: 2017-2018: $11,818 in state, $30,392 out of state; room/board: $10,060
Financial aid: (706) 542-6147; 44% of undergrads determined to have financial need; average aid package $11,997

University of North Georgia

Dahlonega GA
(706) 864-1800
U.S. News ranking: Reg. U. (S), No. 61
Website: ung.edu/
Admissions email: admissions-dah@ung.edu
Public; founded 1873
Freshman admissions: selective; 2016-2017: 5,634 applied, 3,736 accepted. Either SAT or ACT required. SAT 25/75 percentile: 1000-1190. High school rank: 21% in top tenth, 56% in top quarter, 92% in top half
Early decision deadline: N/A, notification date: N/A
Early action deadline: 11/15, notification date: 12/15
Application deadline (fall): 2/15
Undergraduate student body: 12,567 full time, 5,137 part time; 44% male, 56% female; 0% American Indian, 3% Asian, 4% black, 11% Hispanic, 3% multiracial, 0% Pacific Islander, 75% white, 2% international; 95% from in state; 15% live on campus; 4% of students in fraternities, 6% in sororities
Most popular majors: 22% Business, Management, Marketing, and Related Support Services, 20% Education, 11% Health Professions and Related Programs, 7% Biological and Biomedical Sciences, 6% Psychology
Expenses: 2017-2018: $7,336 in state, $21,148 out of state; room/board: $10,440
Financial aid: (706) 864-1412; 56% of undergrads determined to have financial need; average aid package $8,598

University of West Georgia

Carrollton GA
(678) 839-5600
U.S. News ranking: Nat. U., second tier
Website: www.westga.edu
Admissions email: admiss@westga.edu

Public; founded 1906
Freshman admissions: less selective; 2016-2017: 7,974 applied, 4,712 accepted. Either SAT or ACT required. SAT 25/75 percentile: 870-1020. High school rank: N/A
Early decision deadline: N/A, notification date: N/A
Early action deadline: N/A, notification date: N/A
Application deadline (fall): 6/1
Undergraduate student body: 9,084 full time, 2,071 part time; 36% male, 64% female; 0% American Indian, 1% Asian, 38% black, 5% Hispanic, 4% multiracial, 0% Pacific Islander, 49% white, 1% international; 96% from in state; 29% live on campus; 8% of students in fraternities, 8% in sororities
Most popular majors: 25% Business, Management, Marketing, and Related Support Services, 17% Social Sciences, 12% Health Professions and Related Programs, 10% Education, 9% Psychology
Expenses: 2017-2018: $7,188 in state, $20,406 out of state; room/board: $9,652
Financial aid: (678) 839-6421; 75% of undergrads determined to have financial need; average aid package $8,852

Valdosta State University

Valdosta GA
(229) 333-5791
U.S. News ranking: Nat. U., second tier
Website: www.valdosta.edu
Admissions email: admissions@valdosta.edu
Public; founded 1906
Freshman admissions: selective; 2016-2017: 5,108 applied, 3,327 accepted. Either SAT or ACT required. SAT 25/75 percentile: 890-1060. High school rank: N/A
Early decision deadline: N/A, notification date: N/A
Early action deadline: N/A, notification date: N/A
Application deadline (fall): 6/15
Undergraduate student body: 7,185 full time, 1,595 part time; 40% male, 60% female; 0% American Indian, 1% Asian, 37% black, 6% Hispanic, 4% multiracial, 0% Pacific Islander, 49% white, 3% international; 90% from in state; 27% live on campus; 2% of students in fraternities, 3% in sororities
Most popular majors: 22% Business, Management, Marketing, and Related Support Services, 9% Communication, Journalism, and Related Programs, 9% Education, 9% Health Professions and Related Programs, 7% Psychology
Expenses: 2017-2018: $6,410 in state, $17,196 out of state; room/board: $7,900
Financial aid: (229) 333-5935; 66% of undergrads determined to have financial need; average aid package $16,647

Wesleyan College
Macon GA
(800) 447-6610
U.S. News ranking: Nat. Lib. Arts,
No. 141
Website: www.wesleyancollege.edu
Admissions email: admissions@
wesleyancollege.edu
Private; founded 1836
Affiliation: United Methodist
Freshman admissions: selective;
2016-2017: 842 applied, 317
accepted. Either SAT or ACT
required. SAT 25/75 percentile:
930-1118. High school rank:
22% in top tenth, 49% in top
quarter, 86% in top half
Early decision deadline: 11/15,
notification date: 12/15
Early action deadline: N/A,
notification date: N/A
Application deadline (fall): 7/1
Undergraduate student body: 494
full time, 136 part time; 2%
male, 98% female; 0% American
Indian, 2% Asian, 27% black,
6% Hispanic, 3% multiracial,
0% Pacific Islander, 42% white,
18% international; 89% from in
state; 60% live on campus; 0%
of students in fraternities, 0% in
sororities
Most popular majors: 21%
Registered Nursing/Registered
Nurse, 11% Accounting, 10%
Advertising, 9% Music, General,
6% Biology/Biological Sciences,
General
Expenses: 2017-2018: $22,370;
room/board: $9,570
Financial aid: (478) 757-5167;
78% of undergrads determined to
have financial need; average aid
package $20,567

Young Harris College
Young Harris GA
(706) 379-3111
U.S. News ranking: Nat. Lib. Arts,
second tier
Website: www.yhc.edu
Admissions email:
cpdaniels@yhc.edu
Private; founded 1886
Affiliation: United Methodist
Freshman admissions: selective;
2016-2017: 2,333 applied,
1,284 accepted. Either SAT
or ACT required. SAT 25/75
percentile: 880-1120. High school
rank: 14% in top tenth, 36% in
top quarter, 75% in top half
Early decision deadline: N/A,
notification date: N/A
Early action deadline: N/A,
notification date: N/A
Application deadline (fall): rolling
Undergraduate student body: 1,109
full time, 91 part time; 44%
male, 56% female; 0% American
Indian, 1% Asian, 6% black,
4% Hispanic, 3% multiracial,
0% Pacific Islander, 75% white,
7% international; 8% from in
state; 80% live on campus; 5%
of students in fraternities, 8% in
sororities
Most popular majors: 30%
Business Administration and
Management, General, 18%
Biology/Biological Sciences,
General, 7% Communication
and Media Studies, 7% Early
Childhood Education and
Teaching, 6% Psychology, General

Expenses: 2016-2017: $29,012;
room/board: $10,464
Financial aid: N/A

HAWAII

Brigham Young University–Hawaii[1]
Laie Oahu HI
(808) 293-3738
U.S. News ranking: Reg. Coll. (W),
No. 18
Website: www.byuh.edu
Admissions email:
admissions@byuh.edu
Private
Application deadline (fall): N/A
Undergraduate student body: N/A
full time, N/A part time
Expenses: 2016-2017: $5,240;
room/board: $6,050
Financial aid: N/A

Chaminade University of Honolulu
Honolulu HI
(808) 735-4735
U.S. News ranking: Reg. U. (W),
No. 40
Website: www.chaminade.edu
Admissions email: admissions@
chaminade.edu
Private; founded 1955
Affiliation: Roman Catholic
Freshman admissions: selective;
2016-2017: 842 applied, 769
accepted. Either SAT or ACT
required. SAT 25/75 percentile:
870-1060. High school rank:
23% in top tenth, 48% in top
quarter, 81% in top half
Early decision deadline: N/A,
notification date: N/A
Early action deadline: N/A,
notification date: N/A
Application deadline (fall): rolling
Undergraduate student body: 1,150
full time, 33 part time; 29%
male, 71% female; 1% American
Indian, 39% Asian, 3% black,
5% Hispanic, 13% multiracial,
21% Pacific Islander, 13% white,
1% international; 70% from in
state; 24% live on campus; 0%
of students in fraternities, 0% in
sororities
Most popular majors: 24%
Criminal Justice/Safety Studies,
21% Registered Nursing/
Registered Nurse, 11% Business
Administration and Management,
General, 10% Psychology,
General, 9% Biology/Biological
Sciences, General
Expenses: 2017-2018: $24,514;
room/board: $13,100
Financial aid: (808) 735-4780;
70% of undergrads determined to
have financial need; average aid
package $19,111

Hawaii Pacific University
Honolulu HI
(808) 544-0238
U.S. News ranking: Reg. U. (W),
No. 59
Website: www.hpu.edu
Admissions email:
admissions@hpu.edu
Private; founded 1965

Freshman admissions: selective;
2016-2017: 5,452 applied,
4,109 accepted. Either SAT
or ACT required. SAT 25/75
percentile: 900-1090. High school
rank: 24% in top tenth, 53% in
top quarter, 86% in top half
Early decision deadline: N/A,
notification date: N/A
Early action deadline: 11/15,
notification date: 12/31
Application deadline (fall): rolling
Undergraduate student body: 2,553
full time, 883 part time; 42%
male, 58% female; 1% American
Indian, 17% Asian, 5% black,
15% Hispanic, 14% multiracial,
2% Pacific Islander, 27% white,
11% international; 56% from in
state; 13% live on campus; N/A
of students in fraternities, N/A in
sororities
Most popular majors: 29%
Business, Management,
Marketing, and Related Support
Services, 23% Health Professions
and Related Programs, 9%
Biological and Biomedical
Sciences, 7% Communication,
Journalism, and Related Programs,
7% Psychology
Expenses: 2017-2018: $24,500;
room/board: $14,204
Financial aid: (808) 544-0253;
55% of undergrads determined to
have financial need; average aid
package $15,142

University of Hawaii–Hilo[1]
Hilo HI
(800) 897-4456
U.S. News ranking: Reg. U. (W),
No. 66
Website: www.uhh.hawaii.edu
Admissions email:
uhhadm@hawaii.edu
Public; founded 1947
Application deadline (fall): 7/1
Undergraduate student body: N/A
full time, N/A part time
Expenses: 2016-2017: $7,650 in
state, $20,610 out of state; room/
board: $10,418
Financial aid: (808) 932-7449

University of Hawaii–Manoa
Honolulu HI
(808) 956-8975
U.S. News ranking: Nat. U.,
No. 159
Website: www.manoa.hawaii.edu/
Admissions email:
ar-info@hawaii.edu
Public; founded 1907
Freshman admissions: selective;
2016-2017: 7,861 applied,
6,296 accepted. Either SAT
or ACT required. SAT 25/75
percentile: 970-1190. High school
rank: 26% in top tenth, 55% in
top quarter, 87% in top half
Early decision deadline: N/A,
notification date: N/A
Early action deadline: N/A,
notification date: N/A
Application deadline (fall): 3/1
Undergraduate student body:
10,871 full time, 2,261 part
time; 44% male, 56% female;
0% American Indian, 41% Asian,
2% black, 2% Hispanic, 16%
multiracial, 17% Pacific Islander,

19% white, 3% international;
74% from in state; 24% live
on campus; 1% of students in
fraternities, 1% in sororities
Most popular majors: 20%
Business, Management,
Marketing, and Related Support
Services, 8% Health Professions
and Related Programs, 7%
Biological and Biomedical
Sciences, 7% Engineering, 7%
Social Sciences
Expenses: 2016-2017: $11,732
in state, $33,764 out of state;
room/board: $13,030
Financial aid: (808) 956-7251

University of Hawaii–Maui College[1]
Kahului HI
U.S. News ranking: Reg. Coll. (W),
unranked
Website: www.maui.hawaii.edu/
Admissions email: N/A
Public
Application deadline (fall): N/A
Undergraduate student body: N/A
full time, N/A part time
Expenses: 2016-2017: $3,150 in
state, $8,286 out of state; room/
board: N/A
Financial aid: N/A

University of Hawaii–West Oahu[1]
Kapolei HI
U.S. News ranking: Reg. Coll. (W),
No. 25
Website: www.uhwo.hawaii.edu
Admissions email:
uhwo.admissions@hawaii.edu
Public; founded 1976
Application deadline (fall): N/A
Undergraduate student body: N/A
full time, N/A part time
Expenses: 2016-2017: $7,440 in
state, $20,400 out of state; room/
board: N/A
Financial aid: (808) 689-2900

IDAHO

Boise State University
Boise ID
(208) 426-1156
U.S. News ranking: Nat. U.,
second tier
Website: www.BoiseState.edu
Admissions email:
bsuinfo@boisestate.edu
Public; founded 1932
Freshman admissions: selective;
2016-2017: 8,330 applied,
6,808 accepted. Neither SAT
nor ACT required. SAT 25/75
percentile: 910-1150. High school
rank: 13% in top tenth, 38% in
top quarter, 73% in top half
Early decision deadline: N/A,
notification date: N/A
Early action deadline: N/A,
notification date: N/A
Application deadline (fall): rolling
Undergraduate student body:
12,375 full time, 7,834 part
time; 46% male, 54% female;
0% American Indian, 2% Asian,
2% black, 12% Hispanic, 4%
multiracial, 0% Pacific Islander,
74% white, 4% international;
N/A from in state; 17% live
on campus; N/A of students in
fraternities, N/A in sororities

Most popular majors: 21% Health
Professions and Related Programs,
18% Business, Management,
Marketing, and Related Support
Services, 7% Communication,
Journalism, and Related Programs,
7% Social Sciences, 6%
Psychology
Expenses: 2017-2018: $7,326 in
state, $22,642 out of state; room/
board: $10,042
Financial aid: (208) 426-1664;
59% of undergrads determined to
have financial need; average aid
package $9,578

Brigham Young University–Idaho[1]
Rexburg ID
(208) 496-1036
U.S. News ranking: Reg. Coll. (W),
No. 13
Website: www.byui.edu
Admissions email:
admissions@byui.edu
Private
Application deadline (fall): N/A
Undergraduate student body: N/A
full time, N/A part time
Expenses: 2016-2017: $3,920;
room/board: $4,312
Financial aid: N/A

College of Idaho
Caldwell ID
(800) 224-3246
U.S. News ranking: Nat. Lib. Arts,
No. 168
Website: www.collegeofidaho.edu
Admissions email: admissions@
collegeofidaho.edu
Private; founded 1891
Freshman admissions: selective;
2016-2017: 975 applied, 827
accepted. Neither SAT nor ACT
required. ACT 25/75 percentile:
21-27. High school rank: 23%
in top tenth, 27% in top quarter,
74% in top half
Early decision deadline: N/A,
notification date: N/A
Early action deadline: 11/16,
notification date: 12/21
Application deadline (fall): 2/16
Undergraduate student body: 918
full time, 44 part time; 50%
male, 50% female; 1% American
Indian, 2% Asian, 2% black,
13% Hispanic, 4% multiracial,
1% Pacific Islander, 66% white,
7% international; 29% from in
state; 61% live on campus; 12%
of students in fraternities, 16%
in sororities
Most popular majors: 15%
Business, Management,
Marketing, and Related Support
Services, 12% Health Professions
and Related Programs, 12%
Psychology, 10% Biological and
Biomedical Sciences, 9% Social
Sciences
Expenses: 2017-2018: $28,755;
room/board: $9,654
Financial aid: (208) 459-5307;
67% of undergrads determined to
have financial need; average aid
package $23,822

Idaho State University[1]
Pocatello ID
U.S. News ranking: Nat. U., unranked
Website: www.isu.edu
Admissions email: info@isu.edu
Public
Application deadline (fall): N/A
Undergraduate student body: N/A full time, N/A part time
Expenses: 2016-2017: $6,956 in state, $21,023 out of state; room/board: $6,663
Financial aid: N/A

Lewis-Clark State College
Lewiston ID
(208) 792-2210
U.S. News ranking: Reg. Coll. (W), No. 23
Website: www.lcsc.edu
Admissions email: admissions@lcsc.edu
Public; founded 1893
Freshman admissions: least selective; 2016-2017: 1,573 applied, 1,569 accepted. Neither SAT nor ACT required. SAT 25/75 percentile: 810-1030. High school rank: 6% in top tenth, 20% in top quarter, 48% in top half
Early decision deadline: N/A, notification date: N/A
Early action deadline: N/A, notification date: N/A
Application deadline (fall): 8/8
Undergraduate student body: 2,290 full time, 1,634 part time; 38% male, 62% female; 3% American Indian, 1% Asian, 1% black, 3% Hispanic, 3% multiracial, 0% Pacific Islander, 83% white, 2% international; 81% from in state; 5% live on campus; N/A of students in fraternities, N/A in sororities
Most popular majors: 23% Business, Management, Marketing, and Related Support Services, 22% Health Professions and Related Programs, 8% Education, 7% Parks, Recreation, Leisure, and Fitness Studies, 6% Public Administration and Social Service Professions
Expenses: 2017-2018: $6,334 in state, $17,834 out of state; room/board: N/A
Financial aid: (208) 792-2224; 68% of undergrads determined to have financial need; average aid package $10,773

Northwest Nazarene University
Nampa ID
(208) 467-8000
U.S. News ranking: Reg. U. (W), No. 47
Website: www.nnu.edu
Admissions email: Admissions@nnu.edu
Private; founded 1913
Freshman admissions: selective; 2016-2017: 956 applied, 910 accepted. Either SAT or ACT required. SAT 25/75 percentile: 910-1170. High school rank: 19% in top tenth, 49% in top quarter, 80% in top half
Early decision deadline: N/A, notification date: N/A

Early action deadline: 11/15, notification date: 12/15
Application deadline (fall): 8/15
Undergraduate student body: 1,324 full time, 334 part time; 49% male, 51% female; 1% American Indian, 2% Asian, 2% black, 6% Hispanic, 14% multiracial, 0% Pacific Islander, 65% white, 4% international; 57% from in state; 70% live on campus; N/A of students in fraternities, N/A in sororities
Most popular majors: 26% Business, Management, Marketing, and Related Support Services, 12% Education, 10% Health Professions and Related Programs, 8% Liberal Arts and Sciences, General Studies and Humanities, 6% Biological and Biomedical Sciences
Expenses: 2017-2018: $29,000; room/board: $7,000
Financial aid: (208) 467-8347; 78% of undergrads determined to have financial need; average aid package $22,119

University of Idaho
Moscow ID
(888) 884-3246
U.S. News ranking: Nat. U., No. 171
Website: www.uidaho.edu/admissions
Admissions email: admissions@uidaho.edu
Public; founded 1889
Freshman admissions: selective; 2016-2017: 5,953 applied, 4,518 accepted. Either SAT or ACT required. SAT 25/75 percentile: 930-1170. High school rank: 19% in top tenth, 44% in top quarter, 73% in top half
Early decision deadline: N/A, notification date: N/A
Early action deadline: N/A, notification date: N/A
Application deadline (fall): 8/1
Undergraduate student body: 7,269 full time, 2,317 part time; 51% male, 49% female; 1% American Indian, 1% Asian, 1% black, 10% Hispanic, 4% multiracial, 0% Pacific Islander, 75% white, 5% international; 78% from in state; 36% live on campus; 21% of students in fraternities, 22% in sororities
Most popular majors: 6% Psychology, General, 4% Business Administration and Management, General, 4% General Studies, 4% Marketing/Marketing Management, General, 4% Mechanical Engineering
Expenses: 2017-2018: $7,488 in state, $23,812 out of state; room/board: $8,670
Financial aid: (208) 885-6312; 64% of undergrads determined to have financial need; average aid package $13,631

ILLINOIS

American Academy of Art[1]
Chicago IL
U.S. News ranking: Arts, unranked
Website: www.aaart.edu
Admissions email: N/A
For-profit
Application deadline (fall): N/A

Undergraduate student body: N/A full time, N/A part time
Expenses: 2016-2017: $32,220; room/board: N/A
Financial aid: N/A

American InterContinental University[1]
Hoffman Estates IL
U.S. News ranking: Reg. U. (Mid. W), unranked
Website: www.aiuniv.edu
Admissions email: N/A
For-profit
Application deadline (fall): N/A
Undergraduate student body: N/A full time, N/A part time
Expenses: 2016-2017: $10,966; room/board: N/A
Financial aid: N/A

Augustana College
Rock Island IL
(800) 798-8100
U.S. News ranking: Nat. Lib. Arts, No. 101
Website: www.augustana.edu
Admissions email: admissions@augustana.edu
Private; founded 1860
Affiliation: Evangelical Lutheran Church
Freshman admissions: more selective; 2016-2017: 6,587 applied, 3,400 accepted. Neither SAT nor ACT required. ACT 25/75 percentile: 23-28. High school rank: 29% in top tenth, 62% in top quarter, 90% in top half
Early decision deadline: 11/1, notification date: 11/15
Early action deadline: 11/1, notification date: 12/1
Application deadline (fall): rolling
Undergraduate student body: 2,523 full time, 14 part time; 43% male, 57% female; 0% American Indian, 2% Asian, 4% black, 10% Hispanic, 3% multiracial, 0% Pacific Islander, 75% white, 5% international; 85% from in state; 71% live on campus; 26% of students in fraternities, 39% in sororities
Most popular majors: 18% Biology/Biological Sciences, General, 12% Business Administration and Management, General, 7% Communication Sciences and Disorders, General, 7% Psychology, General, 6% Speech Communication and Rhetoric
Expenses: 2017-2018: $40,908; room/board: $10,314
Financial aid: (309) 794-7207; 77% of undergrads determined to have financial need; average aid package $30,840

Aurora University[1]
Aurora IL
(800) 742-5281
U.S. News ranking: Reg. U. (Mid. W), second tier
Website: www.aurora.edu
Admissions email: admission@aurora.edu
Private
Application deadline (fall): N/A
Undergraduate student body: N/A full time, N/A part time
Expenses: 2016-2017: $22,830; room/board: $9,366
Financial aid: N/A

Benedictine University
Lisle IL
(630) 829-6300
U.S. News ranking: Nat. U., No. 223
Website: www.ben.edu
Admissions email: admissions@ben.edu
Private; founded 1887
Affiliation: Roman Catholic
Freshman admissions: selective; 2016-2017: 2,139 applied, 1,569 accepted. Either SAT or ACT required. ACT 25/75 percentile: 20-26. High school rank: 13% in top tenth, 41% in top quarter, 73% in top half
Early decision deadline: N/A, notification date: N/A
Early action deadline: N/A, notification date: N/A
Application deadline (fall): rolling
Undergraduate student body: 2,708 full time, 463 part time; 44% male, 56% female; 0% American Indian, 16% Asian, 8% black, 15% Hispanic, 0% multiracial, 1% Pacific Islander, 45% white, 1% international; N/A from in state; N/A live on campus; 0% of students in fraternities, 0% in sororities
Most popular majors: 31% Business, Management, Marketing, and Related Support Services, 27% Health Professions and Related Programs, 9% Psychology, 7% Biological and Biomedical Sciences, 5% Social Sciences
Expenses: 2017-2018: $33,900; room/board: $9,200
Financial aid: N/A; 79% of undergrads determined to have financial need; average aid package $21,842

Blackburn College
Carlinville IL
(800) 233-3550
U.S. News ranking: Reg. Coll. (Mid. W), No. 37
Website: www.blackburn.edu
Admissions email: alisha.kapp@blackburn.edu
Private; founded 1837
Affiliation: Presbyterian Church (USA)
Freshman admissions: selective; 2016-2017: 1,001 applied, 539 accepted. Either SAT or ACT required. ACT 25/75 percentile: 18-23. High school rank: 13% in top tenth, 28% in top quarter, 64% in top half
Early decision deadline: N/A, notification date: N/A
Early action deadline: N/A, notification date: N/A
Application deadline (fall): rolling
Undergraduate student body: 572 full time, 24 part time; 46% male, 54% female; 0% American Indian, 1% Asian, 12% black, 3% Hispanic, 4% multiracial, 0% Pacific Islander, 77% white, 1% international; 89% from in state; 69% live on campus; N/A of students in fraternities, N/A in sororities
Most popular majors: 16% Biology/Biological Sciences, General, 10% Business Administration, Management and Operations,

Other, 10% Criminal Justice/Safety Studies, 8% Elementary Education and Teaching, 8% Psychology, General
Expenses: 2017-2018: $21,992; room/board: $7,884
Financial aid: (217) 854-5511; 94% of undergrads determined to have financial need; average aid package $18,805

Bradley University
Peoria IL
(309) 677-1000
U.S. News ranking: Reg. U. (Mid. W), No. 7
Website: www.bradley.edu
Admissions email: admissions@bradley.edu
Private; founded 1897
Freshman admissions: more selective; 2016-2017: 9,786 applied, 6,832 accepted. Either SAT or ACT required. ACT 25/75 percentile: 22-28. High school rank: 27% in top tenth, 61% in top quarter, 90% in top half
Early decision deadline: N/A, notification date: N/A
Early action deadline: N/A, notification date: N/A
Application deadline (fall): rolling
Undergraduate student body: 4,278 full time, 195 part time; 49% male, 51% female; 0% American Indian, 3% Asian, 5% black, 7% Hispanic, 2% multiracial, 0% Pacific Islander, 57% white, 1% international; 83% from in state; 62% live on campus; 30% of students in fraternities, 29% in sororities
Most popular majors: 19% Business, Management, Marketing, and Related Support Services, 19% Engineering, 13% Health Professions and Related Programs, 9% Communication, Journalism, and Related Programs, 8% Education
Expenses: 2017-2018: $32,930; room/board: $10,310
Financial aid: (309) 677-3089; 65% of undergrads determined to have financial need; average aid package $22,141

Chicago State University[1]
Chicago IL
(773) 995-2513
U.S. News ranking: Reg. U. (Mid. W), second tier
Website: www.csu.edu
Admissions email: ug-admissions@csu.edu
Public; founded 1867
Application deadline (fall): rolling
Undergraduate student body: N/A full time, N/A part time
Expenses: 2016-2017: $10,252 in state, $17,212 out of state; room/board: $8,724
Financial aid: N/A; 97% of undergrads determined to have financial need; average aid package $14,511

Columbia College Chicago[1]

Chicago IL
(312) 344-7130
U.S. News ranking: Reg. U.
(Mid. W), second tier
Website: www.colum.edu
Admissions email:
admissions@colum.edu
Private
Application deadline (fall): N/A
Undergraduate student body: N/A
full time, N/A part time
Expenses: 2016-2017: $25,334;
room/board: $13,298
Financial aid: N/A

Concordia University Chicago

River Forest IL
(877) 282-4422
U.S. News ranking: Reg. U.
(Mid. W), No. 75
Website: www.cuchicago.edu/
Admissions email: admission@
cuchicago.edu
Private; founded 1864
Affiliation: Lutheran Church–
Missouri Synod
Freshman admissions: selective;
2016-2017: 4,802 applied,
2,386 accepted. Either SAT
or ACT required. ACT 25/75
percentile: 19-24. High school
rank: 15% in top tenth, 40% in
top quarter, 72% in top half
Early decision deadline: N/A,
notification date: N/A
Early action deadline: N/A,
notification date: N/A
Application deadline (fall): rolling
Undergraduate student body: 1,357
full time, 173 part time; 43%
male, 57% female; 0% American
Indian, 2% Asian, 13% black,
27% Hispanic, 3% multiracial,
0% Pacific Islander, 52% white,
2% international; 74% from in
state; 34% live on campus; 0%
of students in fraternities, 0% in
sororities
Most popular majors: 21%
Education, 15% Business,
Management, Marketing, and
Related Support Services, 14%
Health Professions and Related
Programs, 10% Parks, Recreation,
Leisure, and Fitness Studies, 7%
Psychology
Expenses: 2017-2018: $31,562;
room/board: $9,448
Financial aid: (708) 209-3113;
85% of undergrads determined to
have financial need; average aid
package $21,774

DePaul University

Chicago IL
(312) 362-8300
U.S. News ranking: Nat. U.,
No. 120
Website: www.depaul.edu
Admissions email:
admission@depaul.edu
Private; founded 1898
Affiliation: Roman Catholic
Freshman admissions: more
selective; 2016-2017: 22,502
applied, 15,695 accepted. Neither
SAT nor ACT required. ACT 25/75
percentile: 22-28. High school
rank: 23% in top tenth, 53% in
top quarter, 85% in top half
Early decision deadline: N/A,
notification date: N/A

Early action deadline: 11/15,
notification date: 1/15
Application deadline (fall): 2/1
Undergraduate student body:
13,168 full time, 2,239 part
time; 47% male, 53% female;
0% American Indian, 9% Asian,
8% black, 18% Hispanic, 4%
multiracial, 0% Pacific Islander,
54% white, 4% international;
77% from in state; 18% live
on campus; 5% of students in
fraternities, 12% in sororities
Most popular majors: 31%
Business, Management,
Marketing, and Related Support
Services, 12% Communication,
Journalism, and Related Programs,
9% Liberal Arts and Sciences,
General Studies and Humanities,
8% Computer and Information
Sciences and Support Services,
8% Social Sciences
Expenses: 2017-2018: $39,010;
room/board: $13,797
Financial aid: (312) 362-8520;
69% of undergrads determined to
have financial need; average aid
package $22,381

DeVry University

Downers Grove IL
U.S. News ranking: Reg. U.
(Mid. W), second tier
Website: www.devry.edu
For-profit; founded 1931
Freshman admissions: less
selective; 2016-2017: N/A
applied, N/A accepted. Neither
SAT nor ACT required. SAT 25/75
percentile: N/A. High school
rank: N/A
Early decision deadline: N/A,
notification date: N/A
Early action deadline: N/A,
notification date: N/A
Application deadline (fall): rolling
Undergraduate student body:
10,232 full time, 16,905 part
time; 50% male, 50% female;
0% American Indian, 5% Asian,
20% black, 19% Hispanic, 1%
multiracial, 1% Pacific Islander,
42% white, 1% international;
78% from in state; N/A live
on campus; N/A of students in
fraternities, N/A in sororities
Most popular majors: 50%
Business, Management,
Marketing, and Related Support
Services, 20% Computer and
Information Sciences and Support
Services, 5% Engineering
Technologies and Engineering-
Related Fields, 2% Homeland
Security, Law Enforcement,
Firefighting and Related Protective
Services, 1% Health Professions
and Related Programs
Expenses: 2016-2017: $19,948;
room/board: $10,908
Financial aid: N/A

Dominican University

River Forest IL
(708) 524-6800
U.S. News ranking: Reg. U.
(Mid. W), No. 19
Website: www.dom.edu/
Admissions email:
domadmis@dom.edu
Private; founded 1901
Affiliation: Roman Catholic

Freshman admissions: selective;
2016-2017: 4,568 applied,
2,911 accepted. Either SAT
or ACT required. ACT 25/75
percentile: 20-25. High school
rank: 26% in top tenth, 56% in
top quarter, 85% in top half
Early decision deadline: N/A,
notification date: N/A
Early action deadline: N/A,
notification date: N/A
Application deadline (fall): 7/1
Undergraduate student body: 2,105
full time, 201 part time; 33%
male, 67% female; 0% American
Indian, 3% Asian, 7% black,
48% Hispanic, 1% multiracial,
0% Pacific Islander, 35% white,
3% international; 94% from in
state; 26% live on campus; 0%
of students in fraternities, 0% in
sororities
Most popular majors: 13%
Business Administration and
Management, General, 8%
Nutrition Sciences, 7% Natural
Sciences, 7% Psychology,
General, 6% Pre-Medicine/Pre-
Medical Studies
Expenses: 2017-2018: $32,530;
room/board: $9,942
Financial aid: (708) 524-6950;
88% of undergrads determined to
have financial need; average aid
package $23,524

East-West University[1]

Chicago IL
(312) 939-0111
U.S. News ranking: Nat. Lib. Arts,
second tier
Website: www.eastwest.edu
Admissions email:
seeyou@eastwest.edu
Private; founded 1980
Application deadline (fall): rolling
Undergraduate student body: N/A
full time, N/A part time
Expenses: 2016-2017: $20,820;
room/board: N/A
Financial aid: N/A

Eastern Illinois University

Charleston IL
(877) 581-2348
U.S. News ranking: Reg. U.
(Mid. W), No. 51
Website: www.eiu.edu
Admissions email:
admissions@eiu.edu
Public; founded 1895
Freshman admissions: selective;
2016-2017: 8,420 applied,
3,947 accepted. Either SAT
or ACT required. ACT 25/75
percentile: 18-24. High school
rank: 13% in top tenth, 33% in
top quarter, 69% in top half
Early decision deadline: N/A,
notification date: N/A
Early action deadline: N/A,
notification date: N/A
Application deadline (fall): 8/15
Undergraduate student body: 5,133
full time, 824 part time; 39%
male, 61% female; 0% American
Indian, 1% Asian, 19% black,
7% Hispanic, 2% multiracial,
0% Pacific Islander, 67% white,
2% international; 94% from in
state; 38% live on campus; 16%
of students in fraternities, 20%
in sororities

Most popular majors: 14%
Business, Management,
Marketing, and Related Support
Services, 13% Education, 11%
Parks, Recreation, Leisure,
and Fitness Studies, 9%
Communication, Journalism, and
Related Programs, 9% Liberal Arts
and Sciences, General Studies and
Humanities
Expenses: 2017-2018: $11,678
in state, $13,868 out of state;
room/board: $9,736
Financial aid: (217) 581-3713;
67% of undergrads determined to
have financial need; average aid
package $9,187

Elmhurst College

Elmhurst IL
(630) 617-3400
U.S. News ranking: Reg. U.
(Mid. W), No. 11
Website: www.elmhurst.edu
Admissions email:
admit@elmhurst.edu
Private; founded 1871
Affiliation: United Church of Christ
Freshman admissions: selective;
2016-2017: 3,528 applied,
2,486 accepted. Either SAT
or ACT required. ACT 25/75
percentile: 20-26. High school
rank: 17% in top tenth, 43% in
top quarter, 74% in top half
Early decision deadline: N/A,
notification date: N/A
Early action deadline: N/A,
notification date: N/A
Application deadline (fall): rolling
Undergraduate student body: 2,712
full time, 144 part time; 41%
male, 59% female; 0% American
Indian, 6% Asian, 6% black,
19% Hispanic, 3% multiracial,
0% Pacific Islander, 64% white,
0% international; 91% from in
state; 31% live on campus; 5%
of students in fraternities, 9% in
sororities
Most popular majors: 24%
Business, Management,
Marketing, and Related Support
Services, 13% Health Professions
and Related Programs, 9%
Psychology, 8% Education, 8%
Visual and Performing Arts
Expenses: 2017-2018: $36,370;
room/board: $10,344
Financial aid: (630) 617-3015;
77% of undergrads determined to
have financial need; average aid
package $26,073

Eureka College

Eureka IL
(309) 467-6350
U.S. News ranking: Reg. Coll.
(Mid. W), No. 26
Website: www.eureka.edu
Admissions email:
admissions@eureka.edu
Private; founded 1855
Affiliation: Christian Church
(Disciples of Christ)
Freshman admissions: selective;
2016-2017: 1,046 applied, 675
accepted. Either SAT or ACT
required. ACT 25/75 percentile:
19-25. High school rank: 8% in
top tenth, 25% in top quarter,
66% in top half
Early decision deadline: N/A,
notification date: N/A
Early action deadline: N/A,
notification date: N/A

Application deadline (fall): 8/1
Undergraduate student body: 645
full time, 27 part time; 49%
male, 51% female; 1% American
Indian, 1% Asian, 5% black, 3%
Hispanic, 3% multiracial, 0%
Pacific Islander, 85% white, 1%
international; 94% from in state;
65% live on campus; 39% of
students in fraternities, 31% in
sororities
Most popular majors: 18%
Business Administration and
Management, General, 12%
Psychology, General, 11%
Elementary Education and
Teaching, 7% Accounting, 7%
History, Other
Expenses: 2017-2018: $25,390;
room/board: $9,370
Financial aid: (309) 467-6311;
71% of undergrads determined to
have financial need; average aid
package $18,087

Governors State University

University Park IL
(708) 534-4490
U.S. News ranking: Reg. U.
(Mid. W), second tier
Website: www.govst.edu/
Admissions email:
admission@govst.edu
Public; founded 1969
Freshman admissions: selective;
2016-2017: 1,176 applied, 499
accepted. Either SAT or ACT
required. ACT 25/75 percentile:
17-21. High school rank: 11%
in top tenth, 30% in top quarter,
66% in top half
Early decision deadline: 11/15,
notification date: 12/15
Early action deadline: 11/15,
notification date: 12/15
Application deadline (fall): 4/1
Undergraduate student body: 1,925
full time, 1,592 part time; 36%
male, 64% female; 0% American
Indian, 1% Asian, 39% black,
12% Hispanic, 2% multiracial,
0% Pacific Islander, 34% white,
1% international; 99% from in
state; 7% live on campus; 0%
of students in fraternities, 0% in
sororities
Most popular majors: 17% Health
Professions and Related Programs,
17% Liberal Arts and Sciences,
General Studies and Humanities,
16% Business, Management,
Marketing, and Related Support
Services, 12% Psychology,
10% Homeland Security, Law
Enforcement, Firefighting and
Related Protective Services
Expenses: 2017-2018: $10,516
in state, $18,586 out of state;
room/board: $9,868
Financial aid: (708) 534-4480;
78% of undergrads determined to
have financial need; average aid
package $10,462

Greenville University

Greenville IL
(618) 664-7100
U.S. News ranking: Reg. U.
(Mid. W), No. 99
Website: www.greenville.edu
Admissions email: admissions@
greenville.edu
Private; founded 1892
Affiliation: Free Methodist

Freshman admissions: selective; 2016-2017: 1,093 applied, 632 accepted. Either SAT or ACT required. ACT 25/75 percentile: 18-25. High school rank: 15% in top tenth, 38% in top quarter, 75% in top half
Early decision deadline: N/A, notification date: N/A
Early action deadline: N/A, notification date: N/A
Application deadline (fall): rolling
Undergraduate student body: 919 full time, 75 part time; 50% male, 50% female; 0% American Indian, 1% Asian, 11% black, 5% Hispanic, 1% multiracial, 0% Pacific Islander, 68% white, 3% international; 67% from in state; 78% live on campus; 0% of students in fraternities, 0% in sororities
Most popular majors: 22% Business, Management, Marketing, and Related Support Services, 19% Education, 12% Visual and Performing Arts, 9% Biological and Biomedical Sciences, 6% Theology and Religious Vocations
Expenses: 2017-2018: $26,356; room/board: $8,922
Financial aid: (618) 664-7108; 83% of undergrads determined to have financial need; average aid package $20,519

Illinois College
Jacksonville IL
(217) 245-3030
U.S. News ranking: Nat. Lib. Arts, No. 138
Website: www.ic.edu
Admissions email: admissions@mail.ic.edu
Private; founded 1829
Freshman admissions: selective; 2016-2017: 4,462 applied, 2,411 accepted. Neither SAT nor ACT required. ACT 25/75 percentile: 19-24. High school rank: 17% in top tenth, 48% in top quarter, 83% in top half
Early decision deadline: N/A, notification date: N/A
Early action deadline: 12/1, notification date: 12/23
Application deadline (fall): rolling
Undergraduate student body: 955 full time, 3 part time; 47% male, 53% female; 0% American Indian, 1% Asian, 12% black, 9% Hispanic, 4% multiracial, 0% Pacific Islander, 69% white, 4% international; 85% from in state; 85% live on campus; 0% of students in fraternities, 0% in sororities
Most popular majors: 20% Biological and Biomedical Sciences, 14% Business, Management, Marketing, and Related Support Services, 10% English Language and Literature/ Letters, 10% Psychology, 10% Social Sciences
Expenses: 2017-2018: $32,140; room/board: $9,190
Financial aid: (217) 245-3035; 84% of undergrads determined to have financial need; average aid package $27,034

Illinois Institute of Art–Chicago[1]
Chicago IL
U.S. News ranking: Arts, unranked
Website: www.artinstitutes.edu/chicago/
Admissions email: N/A
For-profit
Application deadline (fall): N/A
Undergraduate student body: N/A full time, N/A part time
Expenses: 2016-2017: $17,484; room/board: $6,377
Financial aid: N/A

Illinois Institute of Technology
Chicago IL
(800) 448-2329
U.S. News ranking: Nat. U., No. 103
Website: admissions.iit.edu/ undergraduate/apply
Admissions email: admission@iit.edu
Private; founded 1890
Freshman admissions: more selective; 2016-2017: 4,288 applied, 2,449 accepted. Either SAT or ACT required. ACT 25/75 percentile: 26-31. High school rank: 60% in top tenth, 91% in top quarter, 99% in top half
Early decision deadline: N/A, notification date: N/A
Early action deadline: N/A, notification date: N/A
Application deadline (fall): 8/1
Undergraduate student body: 2,712 full time, 232 part time; 70% male, 30% female; 0% American Indian, 14% Asian, 6% black, 17% Hispanic, 3% multiracial, 0% Pacific Islander, 35% white, 22% international; 78% from in state; 68% live on campus; 11% of students in fraternities, 15% in sororities
Most popular majors: 52% Engineering, 17% Architecture and Related Services, 10% Computer and Information Sciences and Support Services, 6% Business, Management, Marketing, and Related Support Services, 4% Engineering Technologies and Engineering-Related Fields
Expenses: 2017-2018: $45,864; room/board: $11,840
Financial aid: (312) 567-6917; 62% of undergrads determined to have financial need; average aid package $38,963

Illinois State University
Normal IL
(309) 438-2181
U.S. News ranking: Nat. U., No. 159
Website: illinoisstate.edu/
Admissions email: admissions@ilstu.edu
Public; founded 1857
Freshman admissions: selective; 2016-2017: 12,078 applied, 10,735 accepted. ACT required. ACT 25/75 percentile: 21-26. High school rank: N/A
Early decision deadline: N/A, notification date: N/A
Early action deadline: N/A, notification date: N/A

Application deadline (fall): N/A
Undergraduate student body: 17,456 full time, 1,187 part time; 45% male, 55% female; 0% American Indian, 2% Asian, 8% black, 10% Hispanic, 3% multiracial, 0% Pacific Islander, 76% white, 0% international; 98% from in state; 32% live on campus; 11% of students in fraternities, 17% in sororities
Most popular majors: 21% Business, Management, Marketing, and Related Support Services, 15% Education, 8% Health Professions and Related Programs, 7% Social Sciences, 6% Communication, Journalism, and Related Programs
Expenses: 2017-2018: $14,061 in state, $25,168 out of state; room/board: $9,948
Financial aid: (309) 438-2231; 61% of undergrads determined to have financial need; average aid package $10,177

Illinois Wesleyan University
Bloomington IL
(800) 332-2498
U.S. News ranking: Nat. Lib. Arts, No. 71
Website: www.iwu.edu
Admissions email: iwuadmit@iwu.edu
Private; founded 1850
Freshman admissions: more selective; 2016-2017: 3,841 applied, 2,236 accepted. Either SAT or ACT required. ACT 25/75 percentile: 25-29. High school rank: 34% in top tenth, 71% in top quarter, 96% in top half
Early decision deadline: N/A, notification date: N/A
Early action deadline: 11/1, notification date: 12/15
Application deadline (fall): rolling
Undergraduate student body: 1,766 full time, 5 part time; 46% male, 54% female; 0% American Indian, 4% Asian, 4% black, 7% Hispanic, 3% multiracial, 0% Pacific Islander, 71% white, 9% international; 86% from in state; 77% live on campus; 36% of students in fraternities, 32% in sororities
Most popular majors: 11% Biology/Biological Sciences, General, 10% Accounting, 10% Business/Commerce, General, 9% Psychology, General, 9% Registered Nursing/Registered Nurse
Expenses: 2017-2018: $45,856; room/board: $10,574
Financial aid: (309) 556-3096; 62% of undergrads determined to have financial need; average aid package $32,607

Judson University
Elgin IL
(847) 628-2510
U.S. News ranking: Reg. U. (Mid. W), No. 75
Website: www.judsonu.edu
Admissions email: admissions@judsonu.edu
Private; founded 1963
Affiliation: American Baptist

Freshman admissions: selective; 2016-2017: 676 applied, 506 accepted. Either SAT or ACT required. ACT 25/75 percentile: 19-24. High school rank: 19% in top tenth, 31% in top quarter, 58% in top half
Early decision deadline: N/A, notification date: N/A
Early action deadline: N/A, notification date: N/A
Application deadline (fall): rolling
Undergraduate student body: 777 full time, 346 part time; 41% male, 59% female; 0% American Indian, 2% Asian, 10% black, 17% Hispanic, 2% multiracial, 0% Pacific Islander, 54% white, 4% international; 78% from in state; 65% live on campus; N/A of students in fraternities, N/A in sororities
Most popular majors: 32% Business, Management, Marketing, and Related Support Services, 11% Social Sciences, 11% Visual and Performing Arts, 9% Architecture and Related Services, 7% Education
Expenses: 2017-2018: $29,434; room/board: $9,840
Financial aid: (847) 628-2531; 75% of undergrads determined to have financial need; average aid package $10,726

Kendall College
Chicago IL
(877) 588-8860
U.S. News ranking: Reg. Coll. (Mid. W), second tier
Website: www.kendall.edu
Admissions email: Kendalladmissions@kendall.edu
For-profit; founded 1934
Freshman admissions: least selective; 2016-2017: 154 applied, 129 accepted. Neither SAT nor ACT required. ACT 25/75 percentile: 18-21. High school rank: N/A
Early decision deadline: N/A, notification date: N/A
Early action deadline: N/A, notification date: N/A
Application deadline (fall): rolling
Undergraduate student body: 717 full time, 483 part time; 26% male, 75% female; 0% American Indian, 3% Asian, 17% black, 17% Hispanic, 2% multiracial, 0% Pacific Islander, 42% white, 18% international
Most popular majors: 29% Hospitality Administration/ Management, General, 26% Early Childhood Education and Teaching, 25% Culinary Arts/ Chef Training, 12% Baking and Pastry Arts/Baker/Pastry Chef, 8% Business/Commerce, General
Expenses: 2017-2018: $19,828; room/board: N/A
Financial aid: (312) 752-2194; 63% of undergrads determined to have financial need; average aid package $16,522

Knox College
Galesburg IL
(800) 678-5669
U.S. News ranking: Nat. Lib. Arts, No. 71
Website: www.knox.edu
Admissions email: admission@knox.edu
Private; founded 1837

Freshman admissions: more selective; 2016-2017: 3,514 applied, 2,292 accepted. Neither SAT nor ACT required. ACT 25/75 percentile: 24-30. High school rank: 46% in top tenth, 71% in top quarter, 95% in top half
Early decision deadline: 11/1, notification date: 11/15
Early action deadline: 12/1, notification date: 11/15
Application deadline (fall): 1/15
Undergraduate student body: 1,327 full time, 30 part time; 41% male, 59% female; 0% American Indian, 6% Asian, 8% black, 15% Hispanic, 5% multiracial, 0% Pacific Islander, 49% white, 14% international; 56% from in state; 90% live on campus; 35% of students in fraternities, 19% in sororities
Most popular majors: 11% Creative Writing, 9% Economics, General, 9% Psychology, General, 8% Biology/Biological Sciences, General, 8% Education, General
Expenses: 2017-2018: $44,958; room/board: $9,696
Financial aid: (309) 341-7149; 79% of undergrads determined to have financial need; average aid package $36,532

Lake Forest College
Lake Forest IL
(847) 735-5000
U.S. News ranking: Nat. Lib. Arts, No. 101
Website: www.lakeforest.edu
Admissions email: admissions@ lakeforest.edu
Private; founded 1857
Freshman admissions: more selective; 2016-2017: 4,227 applied, 2,407 accepted. Neither SAT nor ACT required. ACT 25/75 percentile: 24-29. High school rank: 33% in top tenth, 57% in top quarter, 86% in top half
Early decision deadline: 11/15, notification date: 12/15
Early action deadline: 11/15, notification date: 12/15
Application deadline (fall): 2/15
Undergraduate student body: 1,524 full time, 16 part time; 43% male, 57% female; 0% American Indian, 6% Asian, 6% black, 16% Hispanic, 3% multiracial, 0% Pacific Islander, 58% white, 8% international; 64% from in state; 73% live on campus; 19% of students in fraternities, 21% in sororities
Most popular majors: 21% Social Sciences, 15% Library Science, 13% Business, Management, Marketing, and Related Support Services, 8% Communication, Journalism, and Related Programs, 6% Foreign Languages, Literatures, and Linguistics
Expenses: 2016-2017: $44,116; room/board: $9,810
Financial aid: (847) 735-5015

Lewis University
Romeoville IL
(800) 897-9000
U.S. News ranking: Reg. U. (Mid. W), No. 23
Website: www.lewisu.edu
Admissions email: admissions@lewisu.edu
Private; founded 1932
Affiliation: Roman Catholic

Freshman admissions: selective; 2016-2017: 6,199 applied, 3,669 accepted. Either SAT or ACT required. ACT 25/75 percentile: 21-26. High school rank: 20% in top tenth, 46% in top quarter, 83% in top half
Early decision deadline: N/A, notification date: N/A
Early action deadline: N/A, notification date: N/A
Application deadline (fall): rolling
Undergraduate student body: 3,744 full time, 809 part time; 47% male, 53% female; 0% American Indian, 4% Asian, 6% black, 19% Hispanic, 3% multiracial, 0% Pacific Islander, 62% white, 1% international; 92% from in state; 24% live on campus; 1% of students in fraternities, 2% in sororities
Most popular majors: 16% Registered Nursing/Registered Nurse, 11% Criminal Justice/Safety Studies, 9% Business Administration and Management, General, 7% Psychology, General, 6% Aviation/Airway Management and Operations
Expenses: 2017-2018: $31,250; room/board: $10,460
Financial aid: (815) 836-5263; 77% of undergrads determined to have financial need; average aid package $24,080

Lincoln College[1]
Lincoln IL
(800) 569-0556
U.S. News ranking: Reg. Coll. (Mid. W), second tier
Website: www.lincolncollege.edu
Admissions email: admission@lincolncollege.edu
Private; founded 1865
Application deadline (fall): rolling
Undergraduate student body: N/A full time, N/A part time
Expenses: 2016-2017: $17,700, room/board: $7,100
Financial aid: (217) 732-3155

Loyola University Chicago
Chicago IL
(800) 262-2373
U.S. News ranking: Nat. U., No. 103
Website: www.luc.edu
Admissions email: admission@luc.edu
Private; founded 1870
Affiliation: Roman Catholic
Freshman admissions: more selective; 2016-2017: 22,712 applied, 16,482 accepted. Either SAT or ACT required. ACT 25/75 percentile: 24-29. High school rank: 34% in top tenth, 70% in top quarter, 92% in top half
Early decision deadline: N/A, notification date: N/A
Early action deadline: N/A, notification date: N/A
Application deadline (fall): rolling
Undergraduate student body: 10,362 full time, 767 part time; 34% male, 66% female; 0% American Indian, 12% Asian, 5% black, 15% Hispanic, 4% multiracial, 0% Pacific Islander, 56% white, 5% international; 65% from in state; 40% live on campus; 10% of students in fraternities, 15% in sororities

Most popular majors: 20% Business, Management, Marketing, and Related Support Services, 15% Biological and Biomedical Sciences, 13% Health Professions and Related Programs, 10% Psychology, 10% Social Sciences
Expenses: 2017-2018: $42,828; room/board: $14,080
Financial aid: (773) 508-7704; 66% of undergrads determined to have financial need; average aid package $33,514

MacMurray College
Jacksonville IL
(217) 479-7056
U.S. News ranking: Reg. Coll. (Mid. W), No. 56
Website: www.mac.edu
Admissions email: admissions@mac.edu
Private; founded 1846
Affiliation: United Methodist
Freshman admissions: selective; 2016-2017: 1,076 applied, 612 accepted. Either SAT or ACT required. ACT 25/75 percentile: 18-22. High school rank: 9% in top tenth, 31% in top quarter, 67% in top half
Early decision deadline: N/A, notification date: N/A
Early action deadline: N/A, notification date: N/A
Application deadline (fall): 8/15
Undergraduate student body: 531 full time, 21 part time; 50% male, 50% female; 0% American Indian, 0% Asian, 10% black, 6% Hispanic, 3% multiracial, 0% Pacific Islander, 75% white, 0% international; N/A from in state; 60% live on campus; N/A of students in fraternities, N/A in sororities
Most popular majors: 22% Criminal Justice/Law Enforcement Administration, 21% Registered Nursing/Registered Nurse, 17% Business Administration and Management, General, 14% Homeland Security, 8% Sport and Fitness Administration/Management
Expenses: 2017-2018: $26,100; room/board: $8,925
Financial aid: (217) 479-7041; 91% of undergrads determined to have financial need; average aid package $21,506

McKendree University
Lebanon IL
(618) 537-6831
U.S. News ranking: Reg. U. (Mid. W), No. 73
Website: www.mckendree.edu
Admissions email: inquiry@mckendree.edu
Private; founded 1828
Affiliation: United Methodist
Freshman admissions: selective; 2016-2017: 2,283 applied, 1,556 accepted. Either SAT or ACT required. ACT 25/75 percentile: 20-24. High school rank: 11% in top tenth, 36% in top quarter, 76% in top half
Early decision deadline: N/A, notification date: N/A
Early action deadline: N/A, notification date: N/A
Application deadline (fall): rolling

Undergraduate student body: 1,823 full time, 438 part time; 46% male, 54% female; 1% American Indian, 1% Asian, 14% black, 5% Hispanic, 3% multiracial, 0% Pacific Islander, 65% white, 3% international; 73% from in state; 78% live on campus; 3% of students in fraternities, 21% in sororities
Most popular majors: 20% Business Administration and Management, General, 20% Registered Nursing/Registered Nurse, 6% Accounting, 6% Human Resources Management/Personnel Administration, General, 6% Psychology, General
Expenses: 2017-2018: $29,640; room/board: $9,350
Financial aid: (618) 537-6532; 79% of undergrads determined to have financial need; average aid package $21,543

Midstate College[1]
Peoria IL
U.S. News ranking: Reg. Coll. (Mid. W), unranked
Website: www.midstate.edu/
Admissions email: jauer@midstate.edu
For-profit
Application deadline (fall): N/A
Undergraduate student body: N/A full time, N/A part time
Expenses: 2016-2017: $16,230; room/board: N/A
Financial aid: N/A

Millikin University
Decatur IL
(217) 424-6210
U.S. News ranking: Reg. Coll. (Mid. W), No. 11
Website: www.millikin.edu
Admissions email: admis@millikin.edu
Private; founded 1901
Affiliation: Presbyterian
Freshman admissions: selective; 2016-2017: 3,608 applied, 2,302 accepted. Either SAT or ACT required. ACT 25/75 percentile: 19-26. High school rank: 16% in top tenth, 39% in top quarter, 67% in top half
Early decision deadline: N/A, notification date: N/A
Early action deadline: N/A, notification date: N/A
Application deadline (fall): rolling
Undergraduate student body: 1,824 full time, 146 part time; 42% male, 58% female; 0% American Indian, 1% Asian, 14% black, 6% Hispanic, 4% multiracial, 0% Pacific Islander, 71% white, 2% international; 84% from in state; 58% live on campus; 23% of students in fraternities, 31% in sororities
Most popular majors: 24% Business, Management, Marketing, and Related Support Services, 17% Visual and Performing Arts, 12% Health Professions and Related Programs, 9% Education, 6% Communication, Journalism, and Related Programs
Expenses: 2017-2018: $33,066; room/board: $11,082
Financial aid: (217) 424-6317; 83% of undergrads determined to have financial need; average aid package $24,386

Monmouth College
Monmouth IL
(800) 747-2687
U.S. News ranking: Nat. Lib. Arts, No. 147
Website: www.monmouthcollege.edu/admissions
Admissions email: admissions@monmouthcollege.edu
Private; founded 1853
Freshman admissions: selective; 2016-2017: 3,248 applied, 1,690 accepted. Either SAT or ACT required. ACT 25/75 percentile: 19-26. High school rank: 15% in top tenth, 36% in top quarter, 70% in top half
Early decision deadline: N/A, notification date: N/A
Early action deadline: N/A, notification date: N/A
Application deadline (fall): rolling
Undergraduate student body: 1,128 full time, 19 part time; 48% male, 52% female; 0% American Indian, 2% Asian, 10% black, 11% Hispanic, 3% multiracial, 0% Pacific Islander, 63% white, 7% international; 89% from in state; 93% live on campus; 21% of students in fraternities, 33% in sororities
Most popular majors: 23% Business, Management, Marketing, and Related Support Services, 13% Communication, Journalism, and Related Programs, 8% Parks, Recreation, Leisure, and Fitness Studies, 7% Biological and Biomedical Sciences, 7% Psychology
Expenses: 2017-2018: $36,400; room/board: $8,620
Financial aid: (309) 457-2129; 82% of undergrads determined to have financial need; average aid package $31,972

National Louis University[1]
Chicago IL
(888) 658-8632
U.S. News ranking: Nat. U., second tier
Website: www.nl.edu
Admissions email: nluinfo@nl.edu
Private
Application deadline (fall): N/A
Undergraduate student body: N/A full time, N/A part time
Expenses: 2016-2017: $10,380; room/board: N/A
Financial aid: N/A

North Central College
Naperville IL
(630) 637-5800
U.S. News ranking: Reg. U. (Mid. W), No. 10
Website: www.northcentralcollege.edu
Admissions email: admissions@noctrl.edu
Private; founded 1861
Freshman admissions: more selective; 2016-2017: 6,860 applied, 4,072 accepted. Either SAT or ACT required. ACT 25/75 percentile: 22-27. High school rank: 20% in top tenth, 52% in top quarter, 83% in top half
Early decision deadline: N/A, notification date: N/A
Early action deadline: N/A, notification date: N/A

Application deadline (fall): rolling
Undergraduate student body: 2,545 full time, 171 part time; 47% male, 53% female; 0% American Indian, 3% Asian, 4% black, 13% Hispanic, 3% multiracial, 0% Pacific Islander, 68% white, 2% international; 93% from in state; 56% live on campus; N/A of students in fraternities, N/A in sororities
Most popular majors: 11% Psychology, 11% Social Sciences, 9% Visual and Performing Arts, 8% Parks, Recreation, Leisure, and Fitness Studies, 7% Communication, Journalism, and Related Programs
Expenses: 2017-2018: $37,749; room/board: $10,650
Financial aid: (630) 637-5600; 78% of undergrads determined to have financial need; average aid package $24,522

North Park University
Chicago IL
(773) 244-5500
U.S. News ranking: Reg. U. (Mid. W), No. 75
Website: www.northpark.edu
Admissions email: admissions@northpark.edu
Private; founded 1891
Affiliation: Evangelical Covenant Church of America
Freshman admissions: selective; 2016-2017: 1,923 applied, 1,813 accepted. Either SAT or ACT required. ACT 25/75 percentile: 18-24. High school rank: N/A
Early decision deadline: N/A, notification date: N/A
Early action deadline: N/A, notification date: N/A
Application deadline (fall): 7/1
Undergraduate student body: 1,871 full time, 232 part time; 37% male, 63% female; 0% American Indian, 7% Asian, 8% black, 24% Hispanic, 4% multiracial, 2% Pacific Islander, 46% white, 6% international
Most popular majors: Information not available
Expenses: 2016-2017: $27,210; room/board: $9,310
Financial aid: N/A

Northeastern Illinois University
Chicago IL
(773) 442-4000
U.S. News ranking: Reg. U. (Mid. W), second tier
Website: www.neiu.edu
Admissions email: admrec@neiu.edu
Public; founded 1867
Affiliation: Other
Freshman admissions: less selective; 2016-2017: 6,203 applied, 4,405 accepted. Either SAT or ACT required. ACT 25/75 percentile: 16-20. High school rank: 4% in top tenth, 18% in top quarter, 45% in top half
Early decision deadline: N/A, notification date: N/A
Early action deadline: N/A, notification date: N/A
Application deadline (fall): 8/1

Undergraduate student body: 4,321 full time, 3,344 part time; 44% male, 56% female; 0% American Indian, 9% Asian, 11% black, 38% Hispanic, 2% multiracial, 0% Pacific Islander, 31% white, 5% international; 1% from in state; 3% live on campus; 1% of students in fraternities, 1% in sororities
Most popular majors: 12% Liberal Arts and Sciences, General Studies and Humanities, 12% Multi/Interdisciplinary Studies, 11% Public Administration and Social Service Professions, 9% Education, 9% Social Sciences
Expenses: 2017-2018: $13,420 in state, $24,739 out of state; room/board: $14,424
Financial aid: (773) 442-5010; 68% of undergrads determined to have financial need; average aid package $8,549

Northern Illinois University
DeKalb IL
(815) 753-0446
U.S. News ranking: Nat. U., second tier
Website: www.niu.edu/
Admissions email: admissions@niu.edu
Public; founded 1895
Freshman admissions: selective; 2016-2017: 14,958 applied, 7,757 accepted. Either SAT or ACT required. ACT 25/75 percentile: 19-25. High school rank: 12% in top tenth, 36% in top quarter, 71% in top half
Early decision deadline: N/A, notification date: N/A
Early action deadline: N/A, notification date: N/A
Application deadline (fall): 8/1
Undergraduate student body: 12,343 full time, 1,736 part time; 51% male, 49% female; 0% American Indian, 5% Asian, 16% black, 17% Hispanic, 4% multiracial, 0% Pacific Islander, 56% white, 2% international; 97% from in state; 26% live on campus; 5% of students in fraternities, 4% in sororities
Most popular majors: 7% Speech Communication and Rhetoric, 6% Psychology, General, 6% Registered Nursing/Registered Nurse, 5% Health/Medical Preparatory Programs, Other, 4% Accounting
Expenses: 2017-2018: $14,352 in state, $23,817 out of state; room/board: $10,880
Financial aid: (815) 753-1300; 72% of undergrads determined to have financial need; average aid package $12,946

Northwestern University
Evanston IL
(847) 491-7271
U.S. News ranking: Nat. U., No. 11
Website: www.northwestern.edu
Admissions email: ug-admission@ northwestern.edu
Private; founded 1851
Freshman admissions: most selective; 2016-2017: 35,100 applied, 3,743 accepted. Either SAT or ACT required. ACT 25/75

percentile: 32-34. High school rank: 91% in top tenth, 100% in top quarter, 100% in top half
Early decision deadline: 11/1, notification date: 12/15
Early action deadline: N/A, notification date: N/A
Application deadline (fall): 1/1
Undergraduate student body: 8,216 full time, 137 part time; 50% male, 50% female; 0% American Indian, 17% Asian, 6% black, 12% Hispanic, 5% multiracial, 0% Pacific Islander, 48% white, 10% international; 33% from in state; 50% live on campus; 29% of students in fraternities, 32% in sororities
Most popular majors: 15% Economics, General, 6% Biology/ Biological Sciences, General, 6% Psychology, General, 5% Journalism, 5% Political Science and Government, General
Expenses: 2017-2018: $52,678; room/board: $16,047
Financial aid: (847) 491-7400; 44% of undergrads determined to have financial need; average aid package $45,505

Olivet Nazarene University
Bourbonnais IL
(815) 939-5011
U.S. News ranking: Reg. U. (Mid. W), No. 54
Website: www.olivet.edu
Admissions email: admissions@olivet.edu
Private; founded 1907
Affiliation: Church of the Nazarene
Freshman admissions: selective; 2016-2017: 4,168 applied, 3,046 accepted. Either SAT or ACT required. ACT 25/75 percentile: 19-26. High school rank: 24% in top tenth, 52% in top quarter, 80% in top half
Early decision deadline: N/A, notification date: N/A
Early action deadline: N/A, notification date: N/A
Application deadline (fall): 8/1
Undergraduate student body: 3,019 full time, 339 part time; 40% male, 60% female; 0% American Indian, 2% Asian, 8% black, 7% Hispanic, 2% multiracial, 0% Pacific Islander, 79% white, 1% international; 65% from in state; 70% live on campus; 0% of students in fraternities, 0% in sororities
Most popular majors: 31% Registered Nursing/Registered Nurse, 7% Business Administration and Management, General, 4% Elementary Education and Teaching, 4% Psychology, General, 4% Social Work
Expenses: 2017-2018: $34,940; room/board: $7,900
Financial aid: (815) 939-5249; 81% of undergrads determined to have financial need; average aid package $26,483

Principia College
Elsah IL
(618) 374-5181
U.S. News ranking: Nat. Lib. Arts, No. 112
Website: www.principiacollege.edu
Admissions email: collegeadmissions@principia.edu

Private; founded 1910
Affiliation: Other
Freshman admissions: selective; 2016-2017: 165 applied, 150 accepted. Either SAT or ACT required. SAT 25/75 percentile: 970-1240. High school rank: 11% in top tenth, 43% in top quarter, 71% in top half
Early decision deadline: N/A, notification date: N/A
Early action deadline: N/A, notification date: N/A
Application deadline (fall): 7/25
Undergraduate student body: 462 full time, 17 part time; 49% male, 51% female; 0% American Indian, 1% Asian, 2% black, 4% Hispanic, 1% multiracial, 0% Pacific Islander, 72% white, 16% international; 2% from in state; 98% live on campus; 0% of students in fraternities, 0% in sororities
Most popular majors: 16% Business Administration and Management, General, 15% Sociology and Anthropology, 12% Mass Communication/Media Studies, 11% Fine/Studio Arts, General, 8% Education, General
Expenses: 2017-2018: $28,920; room/board: $11,430
Financial aid: (618) 374-5187; 70% of undergrads determined to have financial need; average aid package $31,415

Quincy University[1]
Quincy IL
(217) 228-5210
U.S. News ranking: Reg. U. (Mid. W), No. 83
Website: www.quincy.edu
Admissions email: admissions@quincy.edu
Private; founded 1860
Application deadline (fall): rolling
Undergraduate student body: N/A full time, N/A part time
Expenses: 2016-2017: $27,128; room/board: $10,000
Financial aid: (217) 228-5260

Robert Morris University
Chicago IL
(312) 935-4400
U.S. News ranking: Reg. U. (Mid. W), No. 51
Website: www.robertmorris.edu/
Admissions email: enroll@robertmorris.edu
Private; founded 1913
Freshman admissions: less selective; 2016-2017: 2,621 applied, 1,937 accepted. Neither SAT nor ACT required. ACT 25/75 percentile: 16-22. High school rank: 4% in top tenth, 15% in top quarter, 45% in top half
Early decision deadline: N/A, notification date: N/A
Early action deadline: N/A, notification date: N/A
Application deadline (fall): rolling
Undergraduate student body: 2,253 full time, 99 part time; 54% male, 46% female; 0% American Indian, 3% Asian, 25% black, 31% Hispanic, 2% multiracial, 0% Pacific Islander, 36% white, 1% international; 88% from in state; 10% live on campus; N/A of students in fraternities, N/A in sororities

Most popular majors: 64% Business, Management, Marketing, and Related Support Services, 26% Multi/ Interdisciplinary Studies, 7% Computer and Information Sciences and Support Services, 3% Visual and Performing Arts
Expenses: 2017-2018: $27,180; room/board: $14,187
Financial aid: (312) 935-4078; 67% of undergrads determined to have financial need; average aid package $17,131

Rockford University
Rockford IL
(815) 226-4050
U.S. News ranking: Reg. U. (Mid. W), No. 109
Website: www.rockford.edu
Admissions email: Admissions@ Rockford.edu
Private; founded 1847
Freshman admissions: selective; 2016-2017: 3,013 applied, 1,640 accepted. Either SAT or ACT required. ACT 25/75 percentile: 19-24. High school rank: N/A
Early decision deadline: N/A, notification date: N/A
Early action deadline: N/A, notification date: N/A
Application deadline (fall): 8/15
Undergraduate student body: 945 full time, 141 part time; 43% male, 57% female; 0% American Indian, 2% Asian, 10% black, 14% Hispanic, 3% multiracial, 0% Pacific Islander, 68% white, 3% international; 89% from in state; 37% live on campus; 0% of students in fraternities, 0% in sororities
Most popular majors: 31% Health Professions and Related Programs, 20% Business, Management, Marketing, and Related Support Services, 9% Education, 8% Social Sciences, 7% Biological and Biomedical Sciences
Expenses: 2017-2018: $30,050; room/board: $8,420
Financial aid: (815) 226-3385; 90% of undergrads determined to have financial need; average aid package $20,548

Roosevelt University
Chicago IL
(877) 277-5978
U.S. News ranking: Reg. U. (Mid. W), No. 109
Website: www.roosevelt.edu
Admissions email: admission@ roosevelt.edu
Private; founded 1945
Freshman admissions: selective; 2016-2017: 5,993 applied, 4,393 accepted. Either SAT or ACT required. ACT 25/75 percentile: 19-24. High school rank: 8% in top tenth, 46% in top quarter, 62% in top half
Early decision deadline: N/A, notification date: N/A
Early action deadline: N/A, notification date: N/A
Application deadline (fall): rolling
Undergraduate student body: 2,263 full time, 495 part time; 36% male, 64% female; 0% American Indian, 5% Asian, 18% black,

24% Hispanic, 3% multiracial, 0% Pacific Islander, 45% white, 4% international; 85% from in state; 22% live on campus; N/A of students in fraternities, 2% in sororities
Most popular majors: 36% Business, Management, Marketing, and Related Support Services, 13% Psychology, 8% Visual and Performing Arts, 7% Biological and Biomedical Sciences, 5% Social Sciences
Expenses: 2017-2018: $28,963; room/board: $12,927
Financial aid: (312) 341-3868; 94% of undergrads determined to have financial need; average aid package $75

School of the Art Institute of Chicago
Chicago IL
(312) 629-6100
U.S. News ranking: Arts, unranked
Website: www.saic.edu
Admissions email: admiss@saic.edu
Private; founded 1866
Freshman admissions: selective; 2016-2017: 5,244 applied, 3,111 accepted. Either SAT or ACT required. ACT 25/75 percentile: 22-27. High school rank: N/A
Early decision deadline: N/A, notification date: N/A
Early action deadline: 11/15, notification date: 12/25
Application deadline (fall): 4/15
Undergraduate student body: 2,681 full time, 168 part time; 27% male, 73% female; 0% American Indian, 11% Asian, 3% black, 11% Hispanic, 3% multiracial, 0% Pacific Islander, 35% white, 32% international
Most popular majors: Information not available
Expenses: 2017-2018: $47,420; room/board: $13,500
Financial aid: (312) 629-6600

Southern Illinois University– Carbondale
Carbondale IL
(618) 536-4405
U.S. News ranking: Nat. U., No. 216
Website: www.siu.edu
Admissions email: admissions@siu.edu
Public; founded 1869
Freshman admissions: selective; 2016-2017: 9,084 applied, 6,977 accepted. Either SAT or ACT required. ACT 25/75 percentile: 19-25. High school rank: 11% in top tenth, 31% in top quarter, 60% in top half
Early decision deadline: N/A, notification date: N/A
Early action deadline: N/A, notification date: N/A
Application deadline (fall): 5/1
Undergraduate student body: 10,554 full time, 1,628 part time; 55% male, 45% female; 0% American Indian, 2% Asian, 17% black, 9% Hispanic, 3% multiracial, 0% Pacific Islander,

65% white, 4% international; 83% from in state; 26% live on campus; 9% of students in fraternities, 8% in sororities
Most popular majors: 13% Education, 9% Business, Management, Marketing, and Related Support Services, 8% Engineering Technologies and Engineering-Related Fields, 8% Health Professions and Related Programs, 6% Social Sciences
Expenses: 2017-2018: $13,936 in state, $13,936 out of state; room/board: $10,622
Financial aid: (618) 453-4613; 70% of undergrads determined to have financial need; average aid package $14,946

Southern Illinois University–Edwardsville

Edwardsville IL
(618) 650-3705
U.S. News ranking: Reg. U. (Mid. W), No. 70
Website: www.siue.edu
Admissions email: admissions@siue.edu
Public; founded 1957
Freshman admissions: selective; 2016-2017: 7,274 applied, 6,496 accepted. Either SAT or ACT required. ACT 25/75 percentile: 20-26. High school rank: 17% in top tenth, 40% in top quarter, 73% in top half
Early decision deadline: N/A, notification date: N/A
Early action deadline: N/A, notification date: N/A
Application deadline (fall): 5/2
Undergraduate student body: 9,908 full time, 1,812 part time; 47% male, 53% female; 0% American Indian, 2% Asian, 14% black, 4% Hispanic, 3% multiracial, 0% Pacific Islander, 73% white, 1% international; 88% from in state; 26% live on campus; N/A of students in fraternities, N/A in sororities
Most popular majors: 15% Registered Nursing/Registered Nurse, 9% Business Administration and Management, General, 7% Psychology, General, 6% Biology/Biological Sciences, General, 4% Criminal Justice/Safety Studies
Expenses: 2017-2018: $11,491 in state, $25,118 out of state; room/board: $9,481
Financial aid: (618) 650-3880; 65% of undergrads determined to have financial need; average aid package $11,702

St. Augustine College[1]

Chicago IL
U.S. News ranking: Reg. Coll. (Mid. W), unranked
Website: www.staugustinecollege. edu/index.asp
Admissions email: info@staugustine.edu
Private
Application deadline (fall): N/A
Undergraduate student body: N/A full time, N/A part time
Expenses: 2016-2017: $13,200; room/board: N/A
Financial aid: N/A

St. Xavier University

Chicago IL
(773) 298-3050
U.S. News ranking: Reg. U. (Mid. W), No. 64
Website: www.sxu.edu
Admissions email: admission@sxu.edu
Private; founded 1846
Affiliation: Roman Catholic
Freshman admissions: selective; 2016-2017: 8,315 applied, 6,257 accepted. Either SAT or ACT required. ACT 25/75 percentile: 19-24. High school rank: 22% in top tenth, 50% in top quarter, 86% in top half
Early decision deadline: N/A, notification date: N/A
Early action deadline: N/A, notification date: N/A
Application deadline (fall): rolling
Undergraduate student body: 2,601 full time, 353 part time; 35% male, 65% female; 0% American Indian, 3% Asian, 13% black, 35% Hispanic, 3% multiracial, 0% Pacific Islander, 42% white, 0% international; 96% from in state; 16% live on campus; 0% of students in fraternities, 0% in sororities
Most popular majors: 23% Health Professions and Related Programs, 17% Business, Management, Marketing, and Related Support Services, 9% Biological and Biomedical Sciences, 9% Psychology, 8% Education
Expenses: 2017-2018: $33,380; room/board: $11,340
Financial aid: (773) 298-3073; 88% of undergrads determined to have financial need; average aid package $26,223

Trinity Christian College

Palos Heights IL
(800) 748-0085
U.S. News ranking: Reg. Coll. (Mid. W), No. 20
Website: www.trnty.edu
Admissions email: admissions@trnty.edu
Private; founded 1959
Affiliation: Other
Freshman admissions: selective; 2016-2017: 884 applied, 619 accepted. Either SAT or ACT required. ACT 25/75 percentile: 20-27. High school rank: 8% in top tenth, 35% in top quarter, 75% in top half
Early decision deadline: N/A, notification date: N/A
Early action deadline: N/A, notification date: N/A
Application deadline (fall): rolling
Undergraduate student body: 955 full time, 238 part time; 33% male, 67% female; 0% American Indian, 2% Asian, 9% black, 14% Hispanic, 2% multiracial, 0% Pacific Islander, 68% white, 2% international; 70% from in state; 45% live on campus; 0% of students in fraternities, 0% in sororities
Most popular majors: 27% Education, 18% Business, Management, Marketing, and Related Support Services, 15% Health Professions and Related Programs, 5% Psychology, 5% Public Administration and Social Service Professions

Expenses: 2017-2018: $28,450; room/board: $9,680
Financial aid: (708) 239-4872; 78% of undergrads determined to have financial need; average aid package $19,593

Trinity International University

Deerfield IL
(800) 822-3225
U.S. News ranking: Nat. U., second tier
Website: www.tiu.edu
Admissions email: tcadmissions@tiu.edu
Private; founded 1897
Affiliation: Evangelical Free Church of America
Freshman admissions: selective; 2016-2017: 356 applied, 315 accepted. Either SAT or ACT required. ACT 25/75 percentile: 19-26. High school rank: N/A
Early decision deadline: N/A, notification date: N/A
Early action deadline: N/A, notification date: N/A
Application deadline (fall): rolling
Undergraduate student body: 719 full time, 357 part time; 51% male, 49% female; N/A American Indian, N/A Asian, N/A black, N/A Hispanic, N/A multiracial, N/A Pacific Islander, N/A white, N/A international
Most popular majors: 26% Religious Education, 14% Psychology, General, 8% Business/Commerce, General, 7% Sport and Fitness Administration/Management, 6% Elementary Education and Teaching
Expenses: 2017-2018: $30,750; room/board: $9,240
Financial aid: (847) 317-8060; 80% of undergrads determined to have financial need; average aid package $24,780

University of Chicago

Chicago IL
(773) 702-8650
U.S. News ranking: Nat. U., No. 3
Website: www.uchicago.edu
Admissions email: collegeadmissions@uchicago.edu
Private; founded 1890
Freshman admissions: most selective; 2016-2017: 31,484 applied, 2,499 accepted. Either SAT or ACT required. SAT 25/75 percentile: 1450-1600. High school rank: 98% in top tenth, 100% in top quarter, 100% in top half
Early decision deadline: 11/1, notification date: 12/18
Early action deadline: 11/1, notification date: 12/18
Application deadline (fall): 1/1
Undergraduate student body: 5,918 full time, 23 part time; 52% male, 48% female; 0% American Indian, 18% Asian, 5% black, 11% Hispanic, 4% multiracial, 0% Pacific Islander, 44% white, 12% international; 19% from in state; 56% live on campus; 8% of students in fraternities, 12% in sororities

Most popular majors: 20% Economics, General, 9% Biology/Biological Sciences, General, 8% Mathematics, General, 7% Political Science and Government, General, 6% Public Policy Analysis, General
Expenses: 2017-2018: $54,825; room/board: $15,726
Financial aid: (773) 702-8666; 43% of undergrads determined to have financial need; average aid package $49,967

University of Illinois–Chicago

Chicago IL
(312) 996-4350
U.S. News ranking: Nat. U., No. 145
Website: www.uic.edu
Admissions email: uicadmit@uic.edu
Public; founded 1965
Freshman admissions: more selective; 2016-2017: 17,931 applied, 13,196 accepted. Either SAT or ACT required. ACT 25/75 percentile: 21-27. High school rank: 27% in top tenth, 60% in top quarter, 91% in top half
Early decision deadline: N/A, notification date: N/A
Early action deadline: 11/1, notification date: 12/1
Application deadline (fall): 1/15
Undergraduate student body: 16,517 full time, 1,442 part time; 50% male, 50% female; 0% American Indian, 22% Asian, 8% black, 31% Hispanic, 3% multiracial, 0% Pacific Islander, 32% white, 3% international; 97% from in state; 14% live on campus; 3% of students in fraternities, 4% in sororities
Most popular majors: 15% Business, Management, Marketing, and Related Support Services, 14% Biological and Biomedical Sciences, 13% Psychology, 12% Engineering, 8% Health Professions and Related Programs
Expenses: 2017-2018: $14,816 in state, $27,672 out of state; room/board: $10,882
Financial aid: (312) 996-5563; 76% of undergrads determined to have financial need; average aid package $14,569

University of Illinois–Springfield

Springfield IL
(217) 206-4847
U.S. News ranking: Reg. U. (Mid. W), No. 64
Website: www.uis.edu
Admissions email: admissions@uis.edu
Public; founded 1969
Freshman admissions: selective; 2016-2017: 1,467 applied, 958 accepted. Either SAT or ACT required. ACT 25/75 percentile: 20-26. High school rank: 17% in top tenth, 43% in top quarter, 80% in top half
Early decision deadline: N/A, notification date: N/A
Early action deadline: N/A, notification date: N/A
Application deadline (fall): rolling

Undergraduate student body: 1,913 full time, 1,046 part time; 49% male, 51% female; 0% American Indian, 4% Asian, 15% black, 8% Hispanic, 3% multiracial, 0% Pacific Islander, 64% white, 5% international; 87% from in state; 31% live on campus; 3% of students in fraternities, 3% in sororities
Most popular majors: 24% Business Administration and Management, General, 16% Computer Science, 9% Psychology, General, 7% Criminal Justice/Safety Studies, 6% Communication and Media Studies
Expenses: 2017-2018: $11,423 in state, $20,948 out of state; room/board: $9,760
Financial aid: (217) 206-6724; 66% of undergrads determined to have financial need; average aid package $13,326

University of Illinois–Urbana-Champaign

Champaign IL
(217) 333-0302
U.S. News ranking: Nat. U., No. 52
Website: illinois.edu
Admissions email: ugradadmissions@illinois.edu
Public; founded 1867
Freshman admissions: more selective; 2016-2017: 38,093 applied, 22,881 accepted. Either SAT or ACT required. ACT 25/75 percentile: 26-32. High school rank: 49% in top tenth, 82% in top quarter, 99% in top half
Early decision deadline: N/A, notification date: N/A
Early action deadline: 11/1, notification date: 12/16
Application deadline (fall): 12/1
Undergraduate student body: 32,540 full time, 1,392 part time; 55% male, 45% female; 0% American Indian, 18% Asian, 6% black, 10% Hispanic, 3% multiracial, 0% Pacific Islander, 47% white, 16% international; 86% from in state; 50% live on campus; 21% of students in fraternities, 27% in sororities
Most popular majors: 19% Engineering, 13% Business, Management, Marketing, and Related Support Services, 9% Social Sciences, 7% Biological and Biomedical Sciences, 7% Communication, Journalism, and Related Programs
Expenses: 2017-2018: $15,868 in state, $31,988 out of state; room/board: $11,308
Financial aid: (217) 333-0100; 46% of undergrads determined to have financial need; average aid package $16,635

University of St. Francis

Joliet IL
(800) 735-7500
U.S. News ranking: Reg. U. (Mid. W), No. 32
Website: www.stfrancis.edu
Admissions email: admissions@stfrancis.edu
Private; founded 1920
Affiliation: Roman Catholic

Freshman admissions: selective; 2016-2017: 1,560 applied, 768 accepted. Either SAT or ACT required. ACT 25/75 percentile: 20-26. High school rank: 16% in top tenth, 40% in top quarter, 76% in top half
Early decision deadline: N/A, notification date: N/A
Early action deadline: N/A, notification date: N/A
Application deadline (fall): 8/1
Undergraduate student body: 1,301 full time, 61 part time; 38% male, 62% female; 0% American Indian, 2% Asian, 8% black, 20% Hispanic, 3% multiracial, 0% Pacific Islander, 63% white, 3% international; 95% from in state; 28% live on campus; N/A of students in fraternities, 1% in sororities
Most popular majors: 28% Health Professions and Related Programs, 13% Business, Management, Marketing, and Related Support Services, 9% Biological and Biomedical Sciences, 9% Public Administration and Social Service Professions, 7% Education
Expenses: 2017-2018: $31,470; room/board: $9,358
Financial aid: (815) 740-3403; 85% of undergrads determined to have financial need; average aid package $22,637

VanderCook College of Music
Chicago IL
(800) 448-2655
U.S. News ranking: Arts, unranked
Website: www.vandercook.edu
Admissions email: admissions@vandercook.edu
Private; founded 1909
Freshman admissions: selective; 2016-2017: 51 applied, 46 accepted. Either SAT or ACT required. ACT 25/75 percentile: 20-25. High school rank: 0% in top tenth, 29% in top quarter, 57% in top half
Early decision deadline: N/A, notification date: N/A
Early action deadline: N/A, notification date: N/A
Application deadline (fall): rolling
Undergraduate student body: 102 full time, 31 part time; 53% male, 47% female; 0% American Indian, 1% Asian, 7% black, 22% Hispanic, 5% multiracial, 0% Pacific Islander, 58% white, 2% international; 76% from in state; 19% live on campus; N/A of students in fraternities, N/A in sororities
Most popular majors: 100% Music Teacher Education
Expenses: 2016-2017: $27,180; room/board: N/A
Financial aid: (312) 567-1137

Western Illinois University
Macomb IL
(309) 298-3157
U.S. News ranking: Reg. U. (Mid. W), No. 61
Website: www.wiu.edu
Admissions email: admissions@wiu.edu
Public; founded 1899

Freshman admissions: selective; 2016-2017: 10,191 applied, 6,059 accepted. Either SAT or ACT required. ACT 25/75 percentile: 18-23. High school rank: 9% in top tenth, 30% in top quarter, 67% in top half
Early decision deadline: N/A, notification date: N/A
Early action deadline: N/A, notification date: N/A
Application deadline (fall): 5/15
Undergraduate student body: 7,482 full time, 1,061 part time; 49% male, 51% female; 0% American Indian, 1% Asian, 21% black, 12% Hispanic, 3% multiracial, 0% Pacific Islander, 60% white, 2% international; 88% from in state; 46% live on campus; 14% of students in fraternities, 14% in sororities
Most popular majors: 19% Criminal Justice/Law Enforcement Administration, 14% Business Administration and Management, General, 11% Liberal Arts and Sciences, General Studies and Humanities, Other, 7% Parks, Recreation and Leisure Facilities Management, General, 6% Speech Communication and Rhetoric
Expenses: 2017-2018: $11,267 in state, $11,267 out of state; room/board: $9,830
Financial aid: (309) 298-2446; 75% of undergrads determined to have financial need; average aid package $11,646

Wheaton College
Wheaton IL
(800) 222-2419
U.S. News ranking: Nat. Lib. Arts, No. 63
Website: www.wheaton.edu
Admissions email: admissions@wheaton.edu
Private; founded 1860
Affiliation: Protestant, not specified
Freshman admissions: more selective; 2016-2017: 1,850 applied, 1,455 accepted. Either SAT or ACT required. ACT 25/75 percentile: 27-32. High school rank: 48% in top tenth, 76% in top quarter, 94% in top half
Early decision deadline: N/A, notification date: N/A
Early action deadline: 11/1, notification date: 12/31
Application deadline (fall): 1/10
Undergraduate student body: 2,400 full time, 56 part time; 47% male, 53% female; 0% American Indian, 9% Asian, 3% black, 6% Hispanic, 4% multiracial, 0% Pacific Islander, 75% white, 3% international; 24% from in state; 88% live on campus; N/A of students in fraternities, N/A in sororities
Most popular majors: 11% Business, Management, Marketing, and Related Support Services, 8% Biological and Biomedical Sciences, 7% English Language and Literature/Letters, 6% Health Professions and Related Programs, 6% Psychology
Expenses: 2017-2018: $35,190; room/board: $9,806
Financial aid: (630) 752-5021; 55% of undergrads determined to have financial need; average aid package $24,946

INDIANA

Anderson University
Anderson IN
(765) 641-4088
U.S. News ranking: Reg. U. (Mid. W), No. 38
Website: www.anderson.edu
Admissions email: info@anderson.edu
Private; founded 1917
Affiliation: Church of God
Freshman admissions: selective; 2016-2017: 2,590 applied, 1,753 accepted. Either SAT or ACT required. SAT 25/75 percentile: 920-1140. High school rank: 20% in top tenth, 51% in top quarter, 75% in top half
Early decision deadline: N/A, notification date: N/A
Early action deadline: N/A, notification date: N/A
Application deadline (fall): rolling
Undergraduate student body: 1,591 full time, 292 part time; 40% male, 60% female; 1% American Indian, 2% Asian, 9% black, 2% Hispanic, 0% multiracial, 0% Pacific Islander, 80% white, 2% international
Most popular majors: 19% Business, Management, Marketing, and Related Support Services, 15% Health Professions and Related Programs, 12% Education, 8% Visual and Performing Arts, 6% Parks, Recreation, Leisure, and Fitness Studies
Expenses: 2017-2018: $29,710; room/board: $9,740
Financial aid: (765) 641-4180; 80% of undergrads determined to have financial need; average aid package $16,900

Ball State University
Muncie IN
(765) 285-8300
U.S. News ranking: Nat. U., No. 187
Website: www.bsu.edu
Admissions email: askus@bsu.edu
Public; founded 1918
Freshman admissions: selective; 2016-2017: 24,735 applied, 15,398 accepted. Neither SAT nor ACT required. SAT 25/75 percentile: 990-1170. High school rank: 17% in top tenth, 46% in top quarter, 86% in top half
Early decision deadline: N/A, notification date: N/A
Early action deadline: N/A, notification date: N/A
Application deadline (fall): 8/10
Undergraduate student body: 15,110 full time, 1,901 part time; 40% male, 60% female; 0% American Indian, 1% Asian, 8% black, 4% Hispanic, 3% multiracial, 0% Pacific Islander, 81% white, 2% international; 86% from in state; 43% live on campus; 15% of students in fraternities, 17% in sororities
Most popular majors: 17% Business, Management, Marketing, and Related Support Services, 14% Communication, Journalism, and Related Programs, 10% Health Professions and Related Programs, 7% Education, 6% Liberal Arts and Sciences, General Studies and Humanities

Expenses: 2017-2018: $9,848 in state, $25,938 out of state; room/board: $10,038
Financial aid: (765) 285-5600; 68% of undergrads determined to have financial need; average aid package $12,659

Bethel College
Mishawaka IN
(800) 422-4101
U.S. News ranking: Reg. U. (Mid. W), No. 38
Website: www.bethelcollege.edu
Admissions email: admissions@bethelcollege.edu
Private; founded 1947
Affiliation: Missionary Church Inc
Freshman admissions: selective; 2016-2017: 1,168 applied, 1,142 accepted. Either SAT or ACT required. SAT 25/75 percentile: 910-1150. High school rank: 21% in top tenth, 47% in top quarter, 76% in top half
Early decision deadline: N/A, notification date: N/A
Early action deadline: N/A, notification date: N/A
Application deadline (fall): rolling
Undergraduate student body: 1,128 full time, 260 part time; 36% male, 64% female; 0% American Indian, 2% Asian, 11% black, 7% Hispanic, 5% multiracial, 0% Pacific Islander, 73% white, 1% international; 72% from in state; 52% live on campus; N/A of students in fraternities, N/A in sororities
Most popular majors: 16% Business, Management, Marketing, and Related Support Services, 13% Health Professions and Related Programs, 12% Liberal Arts and Sciences, General Studies and Humanities, 12% Theology and Religious Vocations, 7% Public Administration and Social Service Professions
Expenses: 2017-2018: $28,030; room/board: $8,800
Financial aid: (574) 807-7415

Butler University
Indianapolis IN
(317) 940-8150
U.S. News ranking: Reg. U. (Mid. W), No. 2
Website: www.butler.edu
Admissions email: admission@butler.edu
Private; founded 1855
Freshman admissions: more selective; 2016-2017: 12,937 applied, 9,406 accepted. Either SAT or ACT required. ACT 25/75 percentile: 25-30. High school rank: 46% in top tenth, 76% in top quarter, 95% in top half
Early decision deadline: N/A, notification date: N/A
Early action deadline: 11/1, notification date: 12/20
Application deadline (fall): 2/1
Undergraduate student body: 4,199 full time, 91 part time; 40% male, 60% female; 0% American Indian, 3% Asian, 4% black, 4% Hispanic, 3% multiracial, 0% Pacific Islander, 82% white, 1% international; 45% from in state; 68% live on campus; 24% of students in fraternities, 36% in sororities

Most popular majors: 32% Business, Management, Marketing, and Related Support Services, 11% Communication, Journalism, and Related Programs, 8% Education, 8% Health Professions and Related Programs, 8% Visual and Performing Arts
Expenses: 2017-2018: $40,175; room/board: $12,947
Financial aid: (317) 940-8200; 61% of undergrads determined to have financial need; average aid package $24,536

Calumet College of St. Joseph
Whiting IN
(219) 473-4295
U.S. News ranking: Reg. U. (Mid. W), second tier
Website: www.ccsj.edu
Admissions email: admissions@ccsj.edu
Private; founded 1951
Freshman admissions: less selective; 2016-2017: 628 applied, 191 accepted. Neither SAT nor ACT required. ACT 25/75 percentile: 15-21. High school rank: 6% in top tenth, 20% in top quarter, 47% in top half
Early decision deadline: N/A, notification date: N/A
Early action deadline: N/A, notification date: N/A
Application deadline (fall): rolling
Undergraduate student body: 489 full time, 295 part time; 55% male, 45% female; 0% American Indian, 1% Asian, 22% black, 31% Hispanic, 1% multiracial, 0% Pacific Islander, 44% white, 0% international; 51% from in state; 0% live on campus; N/A of students in fraternities, N/A in sororities
Most popular majors: 40% Criminal Justice/Safety Studies, 25% Business Administration, Management and Operations, Other, 8% Biology/Biological Sciences, General, 4% English Language and Literature, General, 3% Liberal Arts and Sciences, General Studies and Humanities, Other
Expenses: 2017-2018: $18,620; room/board: N/A
Financial aid: (219) 473-4379; 82% of undergrads determined to have financial need; average aid package $12,971

DePauw University
Greencastle IN
(765) 658-4006
U.S. News ranking: Nat. Lib. Arts, No. 53
Website: www.depauw.edu
Admissions email: admission@depauw.edu
Private; founded 1837
Freshman admissions: more selective; 2016-2017: 4,845 applied, 3,167 accepted. Either SAT or ACT required. ACT 25/75 percentile: 24-29. High school rank: 45% in top tenth, 75% in top quarter, 97% in top half
Early decision deadline: 11/1, notification date: 12/1
Early action deadline: 12/1, notification date: 1/15
Application deadline (fall): 2/1

Undergraduate student body: 2,190 full time, 35 part time; 47% male, 53% female; 0% American Indian, 3% Asian, 6% black, 5% Hispanic, 6% multiracial, 0% Pacific Islander, 69% white, 8% international; 37% from in state; 98% live on campus; 75% of students in fraternities, 65% in sororities
Most popular majors: 22% Social Sciences, 12% Communication, Journalism, and Related Programs, 9% Biological and Biomedical Sciences, 9% English Language and Literature/Letters, 8% Computer and Information Sciences and Support Services
Expenses: 2017-2018: $47,838; room/board: $12,529
Financial aid: (765) 658-4030; 60% of undergrads determined to have financial need; average aid package $39,790

Earlham College
Richmond IN
U.S. News ranking: Nat. Lib. Arts, No. 68
Website: www.earlham.edu/admissions
Admissions email: admission@earlham.edu
Private; founded 1847
Affiliation: Friends
Freshman admissions: more selective; 2016-2017: 2,917 applied, 1,681 accepted. Neither SAT nor ACT required. SAT 25/75 percentile: 1130-1380. High school rank: 36% in top tenth, 67% in top quarter, 93% in top half
Early decision deadline: 11/1, notification date: 12/1
Early action deadline: 1/15, notification date: 2/15
Application deadline (fall): 2/15
Undergraduate student body: 1,024 full time, 7 part time; 44% male, 56% female; 1% American Indian, 6% Asian, 12% black, 7% Hispanic, 0% multiracial, 0% Pacific Islander, 50% white, 23% international; 20% from in state; 96% live on campus; 0% of students in fraternities, 0% in sororities
Most popular majors: 17% Biology, General, 11% Fine and Studio Arts, 9% Business Administration, Management and Operations, 9% Multi/Interdisciplinary Studies, Other, 8% Psychology, General
Expenses: 2017-2018: $45,750; room/board: $9,920
Financial aid: (765) 983-1217; 86% of undergrads determined to have financial need; average aid package $39,223

Franklin College
Franklin IN
(317) 738-8062
U.S. News ranking: Nat. Lib. Arts, No. 147
Website: www.franklincollege.edu
Admissions email: admissions@franklincollege.edu
Private; founded 1834
Affiliation: American Baptist
Freshman admissions: selective; 2016-2017: 1,479 applied, 1,152 accepted. Either SAT or ACT required. SAT 25/75 percentile: 850-1080. High school rank: 26% in top tenth, 54% in top quarter, 85% in top half

Early decision deadline: N/A, notification date: N/A
Early action deadline: N/A, notification date: N/A
Application deadline (fall): rolling
Undergraduate student body: 961 full time, 55 part time; 48% male, 52% female; 0% American Indian, 1% Asian, 5% black, 3% Hispanic, 4% multiracial, 0% Pacific Islander, 84% white, 1% international; 92% from in state; 73% live on campus; 25% of students in fraternities, 45% in sororities
Most popular majors: 15% Business/Commerce, General, 11% Biology/Biological Sciences, General, 11% Journalism, 9% Education, 8% Psychology, General
Expenses: 2017-2018: $30,920; room/board: $9,630
Financial aid: (317) 738-8073; 84% of undergrads determined to have financial need; average aid package $23,805

Goshen College
Goshen IN
(574) 535-7535
U.S. News ranking: Reg. Coll. (Mid. W), No. 6
Website: www.goshen.edu
Admissions email: admissions@goshen.edu
Private; founded 1894
Affiliation: Mennonite Church
Freshman admissions: selective; 2016-2017: 1,004 applied, 687 accepted. Either SAT or ACT required. SAT 25/75 percentile: 930-1253. High school rank: 24% in top tenth, 52% in top quarter, 87% in top half
Early decision deadline: N/A, notification date: N/A
Early action deadline: N/A, notification date: N/A
Application deadline (fall): 8/15
Undergraduate student body: 741 full time, 59 part time; 40% male, 60% female; 0% American Indian, 2% Asian, 4% black, 18% Hispanic, 2% multiracial, 0% Pacific Islander, 64% white, 9% international; 60% from in state; 53% live on campus; N/A of students in fraternities, N/A in sororities
Most popular majors: 20% Health Professions and Related Programs, 10% Business, Management, Marketing, and Related Support Services, 9% Biological and Biomedical Sciences, 9% Education, 8% Visual and Performing Arts
Expenses: 2017-2018: $33,200; room/board: $10,500
Financial aid: (574) 535-7525; 75% of undergrads determined to have financial need; average aid package $25,976

Grace College and Seminary
Winona Lake IN
(574) 372-5100
U.S. News ranking: Reg. U. (Mid. W), No. 87
Website: www.grace.edu
Admissions email: enroll@grace.edu
Private; founded 1948
Affiliation: Other

Freshman admissions: selective; 2016-2017: 4,177 applied, 3,276 accepted. Either SAT or ACT required. SAT 25/75 percentile: 930-1170. High school rank: 24% in top tenth, 52% in top quarter, 80% in top half
Early decision deadline: N/A, notification date: N/A
Early action deadline: 12/1, notification date: 12/20
Application deadline (fall): 3/1
Undergraduate student body: 1,521 full time, 413 part time; 44% male, 56% female; 0% American Indian, 1% Asian, 6% black, 5% Hispanic, 3% multiracial, 0% Pacific Islander, 80% white, 1% international; 75% from in state; 52% live on campus; 0% of students in fraternities, 0% in sororities
Most popular majors: 17% Business Administration and Management, General, 7% General Studies, 7% Psychology, General, 6% Clinical, Counseling and Applied Psychology, Other, 4% Criminal Justice/Safety Studies
Expenses: 2017-2018: $23,930; room/board: $8,782
Financial aid: (574) 372-5100; 80% of undergrads determined to have financial need; average aid package $13,610

Hanover College
Hanover IN
(812) 866-7021
U.S. News ranking: Nat. Lib. Arts, No. 112
Website: www.hanover.edu
Admissions email: admission@hanover.edu
Private; founded 1827
Freshman admissions: selective; 2016-2017: 3,696 applied, 2,119 accepted. Either SAT or ACT required. ACT 25/75 percentile: 22-27. High school rank: 25% in top tenth, 55% in top quarter, 91% in top half
Early decision deadline: N/A, notification date: N/A
Early action deadline: 12/1, notification date: 12/20
Application deadline (fall): rolling
Undergraduate student body: 1,084 full time, 6 part time; 43% male, 57% female; 1% American Indian, 1% Asian, 5% black, 3% Hispanic, 1% multiracial, 0% Pacific Islander, 81% white, 4% international; 68% from in state; 93% live on campus; 42% of students in fraternities, 31% in sororities
Most popular majors: 9% Psychology, General, 8% Economics, General, 7% Kinesiology and Exercise Science, 7% Speech Communication and Rhetoric, 6% Elementary Education and Teaching
Expenses: 2017-2018: $36,520; room/board: $11,230
Financial aid: (812) 866-7029; 77% of undergrads determined to have financial need; average aid package $29,386

Holy Cross College[1]
Notre Dame IN
(574) 239-8400
U.S. News ranking: Nat. Lib. Arts, second tier
Website: www.hcc-nd.edu/home
Admissions email: admissions@hcc-nd.edu
Private; founded 1966
Application deadline (fall): rolling
Undergraduate student body: N/A full time, N/A part time
Expenses: 2017-2018: $29,734; room/board: $11,002
Financial aid: (574) 239-8362; 62% of undergrads determined to have financial need; average aid package $22,200

Huntington University
Huntington IN
(800) 642-6493
U.S. News ranking: Reg. Coll. (Mid. W), No. 16
Website: www.huntington.edu
Admissions email: admissions@huntington.edu
Private; founded 1897
Affiliation: Other
Freshman admissions: selective; 2016-2017: 789 applied, 709 accepted. Either SAT or ACT required. SAT 25/75 percentile: 900-1150. High school rank: 20% in top tenth, 45% in top quarter, 70% in top half
Early decision deadline: N/A, notification date: N/A
Early action deadline: N/A, notification date: N/A
Application deadline (fall): 8/1
Undergraduate student body: 871 full time, 125 part time; 45% male, 55% female; 0% American Indian, 0% Asian, 2% black, 5% Hispanic, 3% multiracial, 0% Pacific Islander, 84% white, 5% international; 67% from in state; 78% live on campus; 0% of students in fraternities, 0% in sororities
Most popular majors: 10% Film/Cinema/Video Studies, 9% Business Administration and Management, General, 9% Registered Nursing/Registered Nurse, 5% Psychology, General, 5% Special Education and Teaching, General
Expenses: 2017-2018: $25,540; room/board: $8,456
Financial aid: (800) 642-6493; 78% of undergrads determined to have financial need; average aid package $22,123

Indiana Institute of Technology[1]
Fort Wayne IN
(800) 937-2448
U.S. News ranking: Business, unranked
Website: www.indianatech.edu
Admissions email: admissions@indianatech.edu
Private; founded 1930
Application deadline (fall): rolling
Undergraduate student body: N/A full time, N/A part time
Expenses: 2017-2018: $26,370; room/board: $11,132
Financial aid: (260) 422-5561; 83% of undergrads determined to have financial need; average aid package $17,004

Indiana State University
Terre Haute IN
(812) 237-2121
U.S. News ranking: Nat. U., second tier
Website: www.indstate.edu/
Admissions email: admissions@indstate.edu
Public; founded 1865
Freshman admissions: less selective; 2016-2017: 11,101 applied, 9,534 accepted. Either SAT or ACT required. SAT 25/75 percentile: 790-1020. High school rank: 9% in top tenth, 25% in top quarter, 62% in top half
Early decision deadline: N/A, notification date: N/A
Early action deadline: N/A, notification date: N/A
Application deadline (fall): 8/15
Undergraduate student body: 9,364 full time, 1,838 part time; 46% male, 54% female; 0% American Indian, 1% Asian, 19% black, 4% Hispanic, 4% multiracial, 0% Pacific Islander, 65% white, 6% international; 83% from in state; 36% live on campus; 15% of students in fraternities, 13% in sororities
Most popular majors: 16% Business, Management, Marketing, and Related Support Services, 13% Health Professions and Related Programs, 12% Social Sciences, 10% Engineering Technologies and Engineering-Related Fields, 8% Education
Expenses: 2017-2018: $8,916 in state, $19,454 out of state; room/board: $9,883
Financial aid: (800) 841-4744; 73% of undergrads determined to have financial need; average aid package $11,138

Indiana University East
Richmond IN
(765) 973-8208
U.S. News ranking: Reg. U. (Mid. W), second tier
Website: www.iue.edu
Admissions email: applynow@iue.edu
Public; founded 1971
Freshman admissions: less selective; 2016-2017: 1,226 applied, 739 accepted. Either SAT or ACT required. SAT 25/75 percentile: 830-1040. High school rank: 8% in top tenth, 27% in top quarter, 67% in top half
Early decision deadline: N/A, notification date: N/A
Early action deadline: N/A, notification date: N/A
Application deadline (fall): rolling
Undergraduate student body: 1,868 full time, 2,419 part time; 36% male, 64% female; 0% American Indian, 1% Asian, 4% black, 3% Hispanic, 3% multiracial, 0% Pacific Islander, 86% white, 1% international; 76% from in state; 0% live on campus; N/A of students in fraternities, N/A in sororities

Most popular majors: 26% Business, Management, Marketing, and Related Support Services, 18% Health Professions and Related Programs, 11% Psychology, 9% Liberal Arts and Sciences, General Studies and Humanities, 6% Homeland Security, Law Enforcement, Firefighting and Related Protective Services
Expenses: 2017-2018: $7,207 in state, $19,038 out of state; room/board: N/A
Financial aid: (765) 973-8206; 77% of undergrads determined to have financial need; average aid package $8,872

Indiana University Northwest

Gary IN
(219) 980-6991
U.S. News ranking: Reg. U. (Mid. W), second tier
Website: www.iun.edu
Admissions email: admit@iun.edu
Public; founded 1948
Freshman admissions: less selective; 2016-2017: 1,723 applied, 1,306 accepted. Either SAT or ACT required. SAT 25/75 percentile: 820-1010. High school rank: 13% in top tenth, 32% in top quarter, 72% in top half
Early decision deadline: N/A, notification date: N/A
Early action deadline: N/A, notification date: N/A
Application deadline (fall): rolling
Undergraduate student body: 2,776 full time, 2,468 part time; 34% male, 66% female; 0% American Indian, 2% Asian, 16% black, 22% Hispanic, 3% multiracial, 0% Pacific Islander, 55% white, 0% international; 97% from in state; 0% live on campus; N/A of students in fraternities, N/A in sororities
Most popular majors: 26% Health Professions and Related Programs, 14% Liberal Arts and Sciences, General Studies and Humanities, 11% Business, Management, Marketing, and Related Support Services, 8% Homeland Security, Law Enforcement, Firefighting and Related Protective Services, 8% Psychology
Expenses: 2017-2018: $7,207 in state, $19,038 out of state; room/board: N/A
Financial aid: (219) 980-6778; 68% of undergrads determined to have financial need; average aid package $8,454

Indiana University Southeast

New Albany IN
(812) 941-2212
U.S. News ranking: Reg. U. (Mid. W), second tier
Website: www.ius.edu
Admissions email: admissions@ius.edu
Public; founded 1941
Freshman admissions: less selective; 2016-2017: 2,177 applied, 1,829 accepted. Either SAT or ACT required. ACT 25/75 percentile: 17-23. High school rank: 10% in top tenth, 31% in top quarter, 67% in top half
Early decision deadline: N/A, notification date: N/A
Early action deadline: N/A, notification date: N/A
Undergraduate student body: 3,326 full time, 2,160 part time; 40% male, 60% female; 0% American Indian, 1% Asian, 7% black, 3% Hispanic, 3% multiracial, 0% Pacific Islander, 84% white, 0% international; 70% from in state; 7% live on campus; 6% of students in fraternities, 5% in sororities
Most popular majors: 20% Business, Management, Marketing, and Related Support Services, 15% Health Professions and Related Programs, 12% Education, 9% Liberal Arts and Sciences, General Studies and Humanities, 9% Psychology
Expenses: 2017-2018: $7,207 in state, $19,038 out of state; room/board: N/A
Financial aid: (812) 941-2246; 67% of undergrads determined to have financial need; average aid package $8,298

Indiana University–Bloomington

Bloomington IN
(812) 855-0661
U.S. News ranking: Nat. U., No. 90
Website: www.iub.edu
Admissions email: iuadmit@indiana.edu
Public; founded 1820
Freshman admissions: more selective; 2016-2017: 34,646 applied, 27,272 accepted. Either SAT or ACT required. SAT 25/75 percentile: 1060-1290. High school rank: 35% in top tenth, 72% in top quarter, 96% in top half
Early decision deadline: N/A, notification date: N/A
Early action deadline: N/A, notification date: N/A
Application deadline (fall): rolling
Undergraduate student body: 32,005 full time, 7,179 part time; 49% male, 51% female; 0% American Indian, 5% Asian, 4% black, 6% Hispanic, 4% multiracial, 0% Pacific Islander, 70% white, 11% international; 67% from in state; 35% live on campus; 25% of students in fraternities, 21% in sororities
Most popular majors: 19% Business, Management, Marketing, and Related Support Services, 9% Communication, Journalism, and Related Programs, 8% Biological and Biomedical Sciences, 8% Parks, Recreation, Leisure, and Fitness Studies, 7% Social Sciences
Expenses: 2017-2018: $10,533 in state, $34,845 out of state; room/board: $10,258
Financial aid: (812) 855-6500; 41% of undergrads determined to have financial need; average aid package $13,515

Indiana University–Kokomo

Kokomo IN
(765) 455-9217
U.S. News ranking: Reg. Coll. (Mid. W), second tier
Website: www.iuk.edu
Admissions email: iuadmiss@iuk.edu
Public; founded 1945
Freshman admissions: less selective; 2016-2017: 1,513 applied, 1,046 accepted. Either SAT or ACT required. SAT 25/75 percentile: 830-1030. High school rank: 7% in top tenth, 25% in top quarter, 63% in top half
Early decision deadline: N/A, notification date: N/A
Early action deadline: N/A, notification date: N/A
Application deadline (fall): rolling
Undergraduate student body: 2,089 full time, 1,888 part time; 34% male, 66% female; 0% American Indian, 1% Asian, 4% black, 5% Hispanic, 3% multiracial, 0% Pacific Islander, 84% white, 1% international; 99% from in state; 0% live on campus; N/A of students in fraternities, N/A in sororities
Most popular majors: 39% Health Professions and Related Programs, 12% Liberal Arts and Sciences, General Studies and Humanities, 10% Business, Management, Marketing, and Related Support Services, 7% Communication, Journalism, and Related Programs, 7% Homeland Security, Law Enforcement, Firefighting and Related Protective Services
Expenses: 2017-2018: $7,207 in state, $19,038 out of state; room/board: N/A
Financial aid: (765) 455-9216; 71% of undergrads determined to have financial need; average aid package $8,644

Indiana University–South Bend

South Bend IN
(574) 520-4839
U.S. News ranking: Reg. U. (Mid. W), second tier
Website: www.iusb.edu
Admissions email: admissions@iusb.edu
Public; founded 1922
Freshman admissions: less selective; 2016-2017: 2,451 applied, 1,888 accepted. Either SAT or ACT required. SAT 25/75 percentile: 840-1050. High school rank: 10% in top tenth, 29% in top quarter, 65% in top half
Early decision deadline: N/A, notification date: N/A
Early action deadline: N/A, notification date: N/A
Application deadline (fall): rolling
Undergraduate student body: 3,815 full time, 2,838 part time; 39% male, 61% female; 0% American Indian, 1% Asian, 8% black, 10% Hispanic, 4% multiracial, 0% Pacific Islander, 73% white, 3% international; 96% from in state; 8% live on campus; N/A of students in fraternities, N/A in sororities
Most popular majors: 20% Business, Management, Marketing, and Related Support Services, 17% Health Professions and Related Programs, 14% Liberal Arts and Sciences, General Studies and Humanities, 8% Communication, Journalism, and Related Programs, 6% Education
Expenses: 2017-2018: $7,207 in state, $19,038 out of state; room/board: N/A
Financial aid: (574) 520-4357; 72% of undergrads determined to have financial need; average aid package $8,945

Indiana University-Purdue University–Fort Wayne

Fort Wayne IN
(260) 481-6812
U.S. News ranking: Reg. U. (Mid. W), second tier
Website: www.ipfw.edu
Admissions email: ask@ipfw.edu
Public; founded 1964
Freshman admissions: selective; 2016-2017: 4,666 applied, 3,295 accepted. Either SAT or ACT required. SAT 25/75 percentile: 860-1080. High school rank: 10% in top tenth, 35% in top quarter, 72% in top half
Early decision deadline: N/A, notification date: N/A
Early action deadline: N/A, notification date: N/A
Application deadline (fall): 8/1
Undergraduate student body: 6,384 full time, 5,069 part time; 44% male, 56% female; 0% American Indian, 3% Asian, 5% black, 6% Hispanic, 3% multiracial, 0% Pacific Islander, 81% white, 2% international; 94% from in state; 10% live on campus; 0% of students in fraternities, 1% in sororities
Most popular majors: 18% Business, Management, Marketing, and Related Support Services, 14% Health Professions and Related Programs, 14% Liberal Arts and Sciences, General Studies and Humanities, 7% Engineering Technologies and Engineering-Related Fields, 6% Education
Expenses: 2016-2017: $8,213 in state, $19,727 out of state; room/board: $9,340
Financial aid: (260) 481-6820

Indiana University-Purdue University–Indianapolis

Indianapolis IN
(317) 274-4591
U.S. News ranking: Nat. U., No. 192
Website: www.iupui.edu
Admissions email: apply@iupui.edu
Public; founded 1969
Freshman admissions: selective; 2016-2017: 13,301 applied, 9,839 accepted. Either SAT or ACT required. SAT 25/75 percentile: 890-1130. High school rank: 16% in top tenth, 45% in top quarter, 87% in top half
Early decision deadline: N/A, notification date: N/A
Early action deadline: N/A, notification date: N/A
Application deadline (fall): 5/1
Undergraduate student body: 17,389 full time, 4,359 part time; 44% male, 56% female; 0% American Indian, 4% Asian, 10% black, 7% Hispanic, 4% multiracial, 0% Pacific Islander, 71% white, 4% international; 97% from in state; 12% live on campus; 3% of students in fraternities, 5% in sororities
Most popular majors: 19% Health Professions and Related Programs, 17% Business, Management, Marketing, and Related Support Services, 8% Liberal Arts and Sciences, General Studies and Humanities, 5% Engineering, 5% Public Administration and Social Service Professions
Expenses: 2017-2018: $9,334 in state, $29,806 out of state; room/board: $8,745
Financial aid: (311) 274-4162; 67% of undergrads determined to have financial need; average aid package $11,048

Indiana Wesleyan University

Marion IN
(866) 468-6498
U.S. News ranking: Reg. U. (Mid. W), No. 29
Website: www.indwes.edu
Admissions email: admissions@indwes.edu
Private; founded 1920
Freshman admissions: selective; 2016-2017: 3,323 applied, 2,455 accepted. Either SAT or ACT required. ACT 25/75 percentile: 21-27. High school rank: 27% in top tenth, 53% in top quarter, 85% in top half
Early decision deadline: N/A, notification date: N/A
Early action deadline: N/A, notification date: N/A
Application deadline (fall): rolling
Undergraduate student body: 2,618 full time, 164 part time; 34% male, 66% female; 0% American Indian, 1% Asian, 3% black, 4% Hispanic, 3% multiracial, 0% Pacific Islander, 82% white, 1% international; 54% from in state; 82% live on campus; 0% of students in fraternities, 0% in sororities
Most popular majors: 29% Health Professions and Related Programs, 12% Theology and Religious Vocations, 11% Education, 10% Business, Management, Marketing, and Related Support Services, 5% Psychology
Expenses: 2017-2018: $25,980; room/board: $8,312
Financial aid: (765) 677-2115; 77% of undergrads determined to have financial need; average aid package $27,709

Manchester University

North Manchester IN
(800) 852-3648
U.S. News ranking: Reg. Coll. (Mid. W), No. 25
Website: www.manchester.edu
Admissions email: admitinfo@manchester.edu

Private; founded 1889
Affiliation: Church of Brethren
Freshman admissions: selective;
2016-2017: 2,431 applied,
1,715 accepted. Neither SAT
nor ACT required. SAT 25/75
percentile: 865-1090. High school
rank: 13% in top tenth, 34% in
top quarter, 75% in top half
Early decision deadline: N/A,
notification date: N/A
Early action deadline: N/A,
notification date: N/A
Application deadline (fall): rolling
Undergraduate student body: 1,250
full time, 22 part time; 48%
male, 52% female; 0% American
Indian, 2% Asian, 7% black,
6% Hispanic, 4% multiracial,
0% Pacific Islander, 77% white,
4% international; 88% from in
state; 78% live on campus; N/A
of students in fraternities, N/A in
sororities
Most popular majors: 29%
Business, Management,
Marketing, and Related Support
Services, 11% Parks, Recreation,
Leisure, and Fitness Studies, 9%
Education, 8% Health Professions
and Related Programs, 6% Social
Sciences
Expenses: 2017-2018: $31,660;
room/board: $9,880
Financial aid: (260) 982-5237;
86% of undergrads determined to
have financial need; average aid
package $28,495

Marian University
Indianapolis IN
(317) 955-6300
U.S. News ranking: Reg. U.
(Mid. W), No. 47
Website: www.marian.edu
Admissions email: admissions@
marian.edu
Private; founded 1851
Affiliation: Roman Catholic
Freshman admissions: selective;
2016-2017: 2,181 applied,
1,297 accepted. Either SAT
or ACT required. SAT 25/75
percentile: 900-1140. High school
rank: 14% in top tenth, 38% in
top quarter, 74% in top half
Early decision deadline: N/A,
notification date: N/A
Early action deadline: N/A,
notification date: N/A
Application deadline (fall): 8/1
Undergraduate student body: 1,764
full time, 383 part time; 39%
male, 61% female; 0% American
Indian, 2% Asian, 12% black,
5% Hispanic, 3% multiracial,
0% Pacific Islander, 73% white,
1% international; 79% from in
state; 37% live on campus; 0%
of students in fraternities, 0% in
sororities
Most popular majors: 48% Health
Professions and Related Programs,
23% Business, Management,
Marketing, and Related Support
Services, 5% Biological and
Biomedical Sciences, 5%
Education, 4% Parks, Recreation,
Leisure, and Fitness Studies
Expenses: 2017-2018: $33,000;
room/board: $10,206
Financial aid: (317) 955-6040;
80% of undergrads determined to
have financial need; average aid
package $25,874

Martin University[1]
Indianapolis IN
U.S. News ranking: Nat. Lib. Arts,
unranked
Website: www.martin.edu
Admissions email: admissions@
martin.edu
Private
Application deadline (fall): N/A
Undergraduate student body: N/A
full time, N/A part time
Expenses: 2016-2017: $12,536;
room/board: N/A
Financial aid: N/A

Oakland City University
Oakland City IN
(800) 737-5125
U.S. News ranking: Reg. Coll.
(Mid. W), No. 39
Website: www.oak.edu
Admissions email:
admission@oak.edu
Private; founded 1885
Affiliation: General Baptist
Freshman admissions: selective;
2016-2017: 628 applied, 208
accepted. Neither SAT nor ACT
required. ACT 25/75 percentile:
18-24. High school rank: 10%
in top tenth, 28% in top quarter,
53% in top half
Early decision deadline: N/A,
notification date: N/A
Early action deadline: N/A,
notification date: N/A
Application deadline (fall): rolling
Undergraduate student body: 540
full time, 730 part time; 43%
male, 57% female; 0% American
Indian, 0% Asian, 7% black,
3% Hispanic, 1% multiracial,
0% Pacific Islander, 72% white,
4% international; 80% from in
state; 36% live on campus; N/A
of students in fraternities, N/A in
sororities
Most popular majors: 35%
Business, Management,
Marketing, and Related Support
Services, 24% Homeland Security,
Law Enforcement, Firefighting and
Related Protective Services, 15%
Education, 5% Philosophy and
Religious Studies, 4% Psychology
Expenses: 2017-2018: $23,700;
room/board: $9,450
Financial aid: (812) 749-1225

Purdue University–Northwest
Hammond IN
(219) 989-2213
U.S. News ranking: Reg. U.
(Mid. W), second tier
Website: www.pnw.edu/
Admissions email:
admissons@pnw.edu
Public; founded 2016
Freshman admissions: selective;
2016-2017: 5,785 applied,
3,134 accepted. Either SAT
or ACT required. SAT 25/75
percentile: 860-1070. High school
rank: 12% in top tenth, 34% in
top quarter, 73% in top half
Early decision deadline: N/A,
notification date: N/A
Early action deadline: N/A,
notification date: N/A
Application deadline (fall): 8/1

Undergraduate student body:
Undergraduate student body: 6,620
full time, 7,765 part time; 41%
male, 59% female; 0% American
Indian, 2% Asian, 10% black,
17% Hispanic, 3% multiracial,
0% Pacific Islander, 62% white,
4% international; 91% from in
state; 5% live on campus; 1%
of students in fraternities, 1% in
sororities
Most popular majors: 39% Health
Professions and Related Programs,
17% Business, Management,
Marketing, and Related Support
Services, 8% Engineering
Technologies and Engineering-
Related Fields, 5% Engineering,
4% Psychology
Expenses: 2017-2018: $8,324 in
state, $17,872 out of state; room/
board: $7,597
Financial aid: (855) 608-4600;
67% of undergrads determined to
have financial need; average aid
package $7,874

Purdue University–West Lafayette
West Lafayette IN
(765) 494-1776
U.S. News ranking: Nat. U., No. 56
Website: www.purdue.edu
Admissions email:
admissions@purdue.edu
Public; founded 1869
Freshman admissions: more
selective; 2016-2017: 48,775
applied, 27,226 accepted. Either
SAT or ACT required. SAT 25/75
percentile: 1080-1330. High
school rank: 43% in top tenth,
77% in top quarter, 97% in
top half
Early decision deadline: N/A,
notification date: N/A
Early action deadline: 11/1,
notification date: 12/12
Application deadline (fall): rolling
Undergraduate student body:
28,712 full time, 1,331 part
time; 58% male, 42% female;
0% American Indian, 7% Asian,
3% black, 5% Hispanic, 2%
multiracial, 0% Pacific Islander,
63% white, 17% international;
64% from in state; 41% live
on campus; 18% of students in
fraternities, 22% in sororities
Most popular majors: 23%
Engineering, 18% Business,
Management, Marketing, and
Related Support Services, 11%
Liberal Arts and Sciences,
General Studies and Humanities,
9% Agriculture, Agriculture
Operations, and Related Sciences,
5% Engineering Technologies and
Engineering-Related Fields
Expenses: 2017-2018: $10,002
in state, $28,804 out of state;
room/board: $10,030
Financial aid: (765) 494-5050;
42% of undergrads determined to
have financial need; average aid
package $13,852

Rose-Hulman Institute of Technology
Terre Haute IN
(812) 877-8213
U.S. News ranking: Engineering,
unranked
Website: www.rose-hulman.edu
Admissions email: admissions@
rose-hulman.edu
Private; founded 1874

Freshman admissions:
Freshman admissions: more
selective; 2016-2017: 4,241
applied, 2,590 accepted. Either
SAT or ACT required. ACT 25/75
percentile: 27-32. High school
rank: 62% in top tenth, 92% in
top quarter, 99% in top half
Early decision deadline: N/A,
notification date: N/A
Early action deadline: 11/1,
notification date: 12/15
Application deadline (fall): 2/1
Undergraduate student body: 2,180
full time, 22 part time; 75%
male, 25% female; 0% American
Indian, 4% Asian, 2% black, 4%
Hispanic, 4% multiracial, 0%
Pacific Islander, 71% white, 13%
international; 35% from in state;
60% live on campus; 35% of
students in fraternities, 36% in
sororities
Most popular majors: 36%
Mechanical Engineering, 12%
Chemical Engineering, 10%
Electrical and Electronics
Engineering, 8% Civil Engineering,
General, 8% Computer Science
Expenses: 2017-2018: $45,747;
room/board: $14,061
Financial aid: (812) 877-8672;
60% of undergrads determined to
have financial need; average aid
package $29,940

Saint Mary-of-the-Woods College
St. Mary-of-the-Woods IN
(800) 926-7692
U.S. News ranking: Reg. Coll.
(Mid. W), No. 22
Website: www.smwc.edu
Admissions email:
admission@smwc.edu
Private; founded 1840
Affiliation: Roman Catholic
Freshman admissions: less
selective; 2016-2017: 367
applied, 268 accepted. Either
SAT or ACT required. SAT 25/75
percentile: 820-1030. High
school rank: N/A
Early decision deadline: N/A,
notification date: N/A
Early action deadline: N/A,
notification date: N/A
Application deadline (fall): rolling
Undergraduate student body: 427
full time, 262 part time; 7%
male, 93% female; 1% American
Indian, 1% Asian, 5% black,
2% Hispanic, 2% multiracial,
0% Pacific Islander, 79% white,
1% international; 76% from in
state; 57% live on campus; 0%
of students in fraternities, 0% in
sororities
Most popular majors: 22%
Business, Management,
Marketing, and Related Support
Services, 22% Education,
19% Health Professions and
Related Programs, 8% Public
Administration and Social Service
Professions, 7% Psychology
Expenses: 2017-2018: $29,510;
room/board: $10,914
Financial aid: (812) 535-5110;
97% of undergrads determined to
have financial need; average aid
package $21,115

St. Mary's College
Notre Dame IN
(574) 284-4587
U.S. News ranking: Nat. Lib. Arts,
No. 101
Website: www.saintmarys.edu
Admissions email: admission@
saintmarys.edu
Private; founded 1844
Affiliation: Roman Catholic
Freshman admissions: selective;
2016-2017: 1,771 applied,
1,446 accepted. Either SAT
or ACT required. ACT 25/75
percentile: 22-28. High school
rank: 18% in top tenth, 54% in
top quarter, 89% in top half
Early decision deadline: 11/15,
notification date: 12/15
Early action deadline: N/A,
notification date: N/A
Application deadline (fall): rolling
Undergraduate student body:
1,569 full time, 56 part time; 1%
male, 99% female; 0% American
Indian, 2% Asian, 2% black,
11% Hispanic, 3% multiracial,
0% Pacific Islander, 77% white,
2% international; 27% from in
state; 86% live on campus; 0%
of students in fraternities, 0% in
sororities
Most popular majors: 15%
Registered Nursing/Registered
Nurse, 11% Business
Administration and Management,
General, 10% Biology/
Biological Sciences, General,
9% Communication Disorders
Sciences and Services, Other,
9% Communication and Media
Studies
Expenses: 2017-2018: $40,800;
room/board: $12,100
Financial aid: (574) 284-4557;
69% of undergrads determined to
have financial need; average aid
package $33,468

Taylor University
Upland IN
(765) 998-5134
U.S. News ranking: Reg. Coll.
(Mid. W), No. 2
Website: www.taylor.edu
Admissions email:
admissions_u@taylor.edu
Private; founded 1846
Affiliation: Interdenominational
Freshman admissions: more
selective; 2016-2017: 1,775
applied, 1,413 accepted. Either
SAT or ACT required. ACT 25/75
percentile: 22-29. High school
rank: 38% in top tenth, 64% in
top quarter, 88% in top half
Early decision deadline: N/A,
notification date: N/A
Early action deadline: N/A,
notification date: N/A
Application deadline (fall): rolling
Undergraduate student body: 1,826
full time, 305 part time; 43%
male, 57% female; 1% American
Indian, 3% Asian, 3% black,
4% Hispanic, 0% multiracial,
0% Pacific Islander, 83% white,
6% international; 41% from in
state; 89% live on campus; N/A
of students in fraternities, N/A in
sororities
Most popular majors: 15%
Business, Management,
Marketing, and Related Support
Services, 9% Parks, Recreation,

Leisure, and Fitness Studies, 7% Communication, Journalism, and Related Programs, 7% Visual and Performing Arts, 6% Education
Expenses: 2017-2018: $32,885; room/board: $9,245
Financial aid: (765) 998-5358; 59% of undergrads determined to have financial need; average aid package $21,985

Trine University
Angola IN
(260) 665-4100
U.S. News ranking: Reg. Coll. (Mid. W), No. 23
Website: www.trine.edu
Admissions email: admit@trine.edu
Private; founded 1884
Freshman admissions: selective; 2016-2017: 2,890 applied, 2,217 accepted. Either SAT or ACT required. ACT 25/75 percentile: 20-27. High school rank: 15% in top tenth, 46% in top quarter, 82% in top half
Early decision deadline: N/A, notification date: N/A
Early action deadline: N/A, notification date: N/A
Application deadline (fall): 8/1
Undergraduate student body: 1,729 full time, 1,643 part time; 57% male, 43% female; 1% American Indian, 3% Asian, 6% black, 16% Hispanic, 5% multiracial, 0% Pacific Islander, 52% white, 12% international
Most popular majors: 37% Engineering, General, 19% Business, Management, Marketing, and Related Support Services, 13% Kinesiology and Exercise Science, 10% CAD/CADD Drafting and/or Design Technology/ Technician, 8% Criminal Justice/ Law Enforcement Administration
Expenses: 2017-2018: $31,540; room/board: $10,570
Financial aid: (260) 665-4438; 86% of undergrads determined to have financial need; average aid package $27,021

University of Evansville
Evansville IN
(812) 488-2468
U.S. News ranking: Reg. U. (Mid. W), No. 9
Website: www.evansville.edu
Admissions email: admission@ evansville.edu
Private; founded 1854
Freshman admissions: more selective; 2016-2017: 4,033 applied, 2,859 accepted. Either SAT or ACT required. ACT 25/75 percentile: 23-29. High school rank: 34% in top tenth, 68% in top quarter, 90% in top half
Early decision deadline: N/A, notification date: N/A
Early action deadline: 12/1, notification date: 12/15
Application deadline (fall): rolling
Undergraduate student body: 2,186 full time, 162 part time; 45% male, 55% female; 0% American Indian, 2% Asian, 3% black, 4% Hispanic, 2% multiracial, 0% Pacific Islander, 71% white, 15% international; 61% from in state; 61% live on campus; 31% of students in fraternities, 31% in sororities

Most popular majors: 14% Business, Management, Marketing, and Related Support Services, 10% Parks, Recreation, Leisure, and Fitness Studies, 10% Visual and Performing Arts, 8% Engineering, 7% Social Sciences
Expenses: 2017-2018: $35,396; room/board: $12,160
Financial aid: (812) 488-2364; 63% of undergrads determined to have financial need; average aid package $28,569

University of Indianapolis
Indianapolis IN
(317) 788-3216
U.S. News ranking: Reg. U. (Mid. W), No. 34
Website: www.uindy.edu
Admissions email: admissions@uindy.edu
Private; founded 1902
Affiliation: United Methodist
Freshman admissions: selective; 2016-2017: 7,301 applied, 6,291 accepted. Either SAT or ACT required. SAT 25/75 percentile: 890-1120. High school rank: 21% in top tenth, 51% in top quarter, 85% in top half
Early decision deadline: N/A, notification date: N/A
Early action deadline: N/A, notification date: N/A
Application deadline (fall): rolling
Undergraduate student body: 3,589 full time, 757 part time; 36% male, 64% female; 0% American Indian, 2% Asian, 9% black, 5% Hispanic, 3% multiracial, 0% Pacific Islander, 68% white, 8% international; 91% from in state; 42% live on campus; 0% of students in fraternities, 0% in sororities
Most popular majors: 20% Registered Nursing/Registered Nurse, 9% Business Administration and Management, General, 9% Psychology, General, 7% Kinesiology and Exercise Science, 7% Liberal Arts and Sciences/Liberal Studies
Expenses: 2017-2018: $28,390; room/board: $10,724
Financial aid: (317) 788-3217; 72% of undergrads determined to have financial need; average aid package $20,785

University of Notre Dame
Notre Dame IN
(574) 631-7505
U.S. News ranking: Nat. U., No. 18
Website: www.nd.edu
Admissions email: admissions@nd.edu
Private; founded 1842
Affiliation: Roman Catholic
Freshman admissions: most selective; 2016-2017: 19,505 applied, 3,654 accepted. Either SAT or ACT required. ACT 25/75 percentile: 32-35. High school rank: 91% in top tenth, 98% in top quarter, 100% in top half
Early decision deadline: N/A, notification date: N/A
Early action deadline: 11/1, notification date: 12/21
Application deadline (fall): 1/1

Undergraduate student body: 8,514 full time, 16 part time; 53% male, 47% female; 0% American Indian, 5% Asian, 4% black, 11% Hispanic, 5% multiracial, 0% Pacific Islander, 69% white, 6% international; 7% from in state; 79% live on campus; N/A of students in fraternities, N/A in sororities
Most popular majors: 10% Finance, General, 6% Accounting, 6% Economics, General, 5% Political Science and Government, General, 5% Psychology, General
Expenses: 2017-2018: $51,505; room/board: $14,890
Financial aid: (574) 631-6436; 48% of undergrads determined to have financial need; average aid package $47,884

University of Saint Francis
Fort Wayne IN
(260) 399-8000
U.S. News ranking: Reg. U. (Mid. W), No. 75
Website: www.sf.edu
Admissions email: admis@sf.edu
Private; founded 1890
Affiliation: Roman Catholic
Freshman admissions: selective; 2016-2017: 977 applied, 945 accepted. Either SAT or ACT required. SAT 25/75 percentile: 900-1090. High school rank: 18% in top tenth, 43% in top quarter, 76% in top half
Early decision deadline: N/A, notification date: N/A
Early action deadline: N/A, notification date: N/A
Application deadline (fall): rolling
Undergraduate student body: 1,475 full time, 335 part time; 28% male, 72% female; 0% American Indian, 1% Asian, 7% black, 8% Hispanic, 2% multiracial, 0% Pacific Islander, 80% white, 1% international; 91% from in state; 20% live on campus; 0% of students in fraternities, 0% in sororities
Most popular majors: 54% Health Professions and Related Programs, 13% Visual and Performing Arts, 9% Business, Management, Marketing, and Related Support Services, 5% Biological and Biomedical Sciences, 4% Psychology
Expenses: 2017-2018: $29,430; room/board: $9,090
Financial aid: (260) 399-8003; 87% of undergrads determined to have financial need; average aid package $19,864

University of Southern Indiana
Evansville IN
(812) 464-1765
U.S. News ranking: Reg. U. (Mid. W), second tier
Website: www.usi.edu
Admissions email: enroll@usi.edu
Public; founded 1965
Freshman admissions: selective; 2016-2017: 4,552 applied, 4,183 accepted. Either SAT or ACT required. SAT 25/75 percentile: 890-1080. High school rank: 14% in top tenth, 37% in top quarter, 75% in top half

Early decision deadline: N/A, notification date: N/A
Early action deadline: N/A, notification date: N/A
Application deadline (fall): 8/15
Undergraduate student body: 6,705 full time, 1,251 part time; 38% male, 62% female; 0% American Indian, 1% Asian, 4% black, 3% Hispanic, 2% multiracial, 0% Pacific Islander, 87% white, 2% international; 88% from in state; 31% live on campus; 9% of students in fraternities, 10% in sororities
Most popular majors: 26% Health Professions and Related Programs, 16% Business, Management, Marketing, and Related Support Services, 7% Education, 6% Communication, Journalism, and Related Programs, 6% Psychology
Expenses: 2017-2018: $7,605 in state, $17,847 out of state; room/ board: $8,896
Financial aid: (812) 464-1767; 62% of undergrads determined to have financial need; average aid package $9,507

Valparaiso University
Valparaiso IN
(888) 468-2576
U.S. News ranking: Reg. U. (Mid. W), No. 4
Website: www.valpo.edu
Admissions email: undergrad. admission@valpo.edu
Private; founded 1859
Freshman admissions: more selective; 2016-2017: 7,484 applied, 6,205 accepted. Either SAT or ACT required. ACT 25/75 percentile: 23-29. High school rank: 31% in top tenth, 62% in top quarter, 91% in top half
Early decision deadline: N/A, notification date: N/A
Early action deadline: N/A, notification date: N/A
Application deadline (fall): rolling
Undergraduate student body: 3,242 full time, 52 part time; 46% male, 54% female; 0% American Indian, 2% Asian, 6% black, 9% Hispanic, 3% multiracial, 0% Pacific Islander, 72% white, 5% international; 43% from in state; 63% live on campus; 25% of students in fraternities, 22% in sororities
Most popular majors: 16% Registered Nursing/Registered Nurse, 6% Mechanical Engineering, 5% Atmospheric Sciences and Meteorology, General, 5% Biology/Biological Sciences, General, 5% Finance, General
Expenses: 2017-2018: $38,760; room/board: $11,400
Financial aid: (219) 464-5304; 74% of undergrads determined to have financial need; average aid package $29,200

Vincennes University[1]
Vincennes IN
(800) 742-9198
U.S. News ranking: Reg. Coll. (Mid. W), unranked
Website: www.vinu.edu
Public; founded 1801
Application deadline (fall): rolling
Undergraduate student body: N/A full time, N/A part time

Expenses: 2016-2017: $5,575 in state, $13,184 out of state; room/ board: $9,332
Financial aid: (812) 888-4361

Wabash College
Crawfordsville IN
(800) 345-5385
U.S. News ranking: Nat. Lib. Arts, No. 65
Website: www.wabash.edu
Admissions email: admissions@ wabash.edu
Private; founded 1832
Freshman admissions: more selective; 2016-2017: 1,284 applied, 804 accepted. Either SAT or ACT required. SAT 25/75 percentile: 1020-1230. High school rank: 29% in top tenth, 63% in top quarter, 92% in top half
Early decision deadline: 10/15, notification date: 11/16
Early action deadline: 11/1, notification date: 12/7
Application deadline (fall): 1/15
Undergraduate student body: 843 full time, 0 part time; 100% male, 0% female; 0% American Indian, 1% Asian, 6% black, 8% Hispanic, 2% multiracial, 0% Pacific Islander, 72% white, 7% international; 77% from in state; 91% live on campus; 65% of students in fraternities, N/A in sororities
Most popular majors: 12% Political Science and Government, General, 11% History, General, 9% Biology/ Biological Sciences, General, 9% English Language and Literature, General, 8% Experimental Psychology
Expenses: 2017-2018: $42,250; room/board: $9,850
Financial aid: (765) 361-6370; 73% of undergrads determined to have financial need; average aid package $34,144

IOWA

Briar Cliff University
Sioux City IA
(712) 279-5200
U.S. News ranking: Reg. Coll. (Mid. W), No. 31
Website: www.briarcliff.edu
Admissions email: admissions@ briarcliff.edu
Private; founded 1930
Affiliation: Roman Catholic
Freshman admissions: selective; 2016-2017: 1,491 applied, 226 accepted. Either SAT or ACT required. ACT 25/75 percentile: 18-24. High school rank: 11% in top tenth, 25% in top quarter, 72% in top half
Early decision deadline: N/A, notification date: N/A
Early action deadline: N/A, notification date: N/A
Application deadline (fall): rolling
Undergraduate student body: 797 full time, 320 part time; 44% male, 56% female; 2% American Indian, 1% Asian, 9% black, 15% Hispanic, 1% multiracial, 1% Pacific Islander, 66% white, 5% international; 60% from in state; 44% live on campus; 0% of students in fraternities, 0% in sororities

Most popular majors: 31% Health Professions and Related Programs, 22% Business, Management, Marketing, and Related Support Services, 9% Parks, Recreation, Leisure, and Fitness Studies, 7% Education, 5% Biological and Biomedical Sciences
Expenses: 2017-2018: $29,606; room/board: $8,640
Financial aid: N/A; 83% of undergrads determined to have financial need; average aid package $30,582

Buena Vista University
Storm Lake IA
(800) 383-9600
U.S. News ranking: Reg. Coll. (Mid. W), No. 24
Website: www.bvu.edu
Admissions email: admissions@bvu.edu
Private; founded 1891
Affiliation: Presbyterian Church (USA)
Freshman admissions: selective; 2016-2017: 1,256 applied, 800 accepted. Either SAT or ACT required. ACT 25/75 percentile: 19-26. High school rank: 16% in top tenth, 40% in top quarter, 79% in top half
Early decision deadline: N/A, notification date: N/A
Early action deadline: N/A, notification date: N/A
Application deadline (fall): rolling
Undergraduate student body: 784 full time, 11 part time; 49% male, 51% female; 0% American Indian, 2% Asian, 3% black, 7% Hispanic, 4% multiracial, 0% Pacific Islander, 75% white, 5% international; 79% from in state; 90% live on campus; 0% of students in fraternities, 0% in sororities
Most popular majors: 25% Business, Management, Marketing, and Related Support Services, 16% Education, 11% Biological and Biomedical Sciences, 8% Parks, Recreation, Leisure, and Fitness Studies, 6% Visual and Performing Arts
Expenses: 2017-2018: $32,854; room/board: $9,490
Financial aid: (712) 749-2164; 81% of undergrads determined to have financial need; average aid package $28,121

Central College
Pella IA
(641) 628-5286
U.S. News ranking: Nat. Lib. Arts, No. 128
Website: www.central.edu
Admissions email: admission@central.edu
Private; founded 1853
Freshman admissions: more selective; 2016-2017: 3,899 applied, 2,863 accepted. Either SAT or ACT required. ACT 25/75 percentile: 21-26. High school rank: 23% in top tenth, 52% in top quarter, 88% in top half
Early decision deadline: N/A, notification date: N/A
Early action deadline: N/A, notification date: N/A
Application deadline (fall): 8/15

Undergraduate student body: 1,204 full time, 44 part time; 48% male, 52% female; 0% American Indian, 1% Asian, 3% black, 4% Hispanic, 1% multiracial, 0% Pacific Islander, 88% white, 0% international; 75% from in state; 89% live on campus; 1% of students in fraternities, 1% in sororities
Most popular majors: 21% Biological and Biomedical Sciences, 13% Business, Management, Marketing, and Related Support Services, 11% Education, 10% Social Sciences, 7% Psychology
Expenses: 2017-2018: $35,930; room/board: $9,980
Financial aid: (641) 628-5336; 81% of undergrads determined to have financial need; average aid package $30,404

Clarke University
Dubuque IA
(563) 588-6316
U.S. News ranking: Reg. Coll. (Mid. W), No. 17
Website: www.clarke.edu
Admissions email: admissions@clarke.edu
Private; founded 1843
Affiliation: Roman Catholic
Freshman admissions: selective; 2016-2017: 1,172 applied, 761 accepted. Either SAT or ACT required. ACT 25/75 percentile: 20-25. High school rank: 12% in top tenth, 40% in top quarter, 75% in top half
Early decision deadline: N/A, notification date: N/A
Early action deadline: N/A, notification date: N/A
Application deadline (fall): rolling
Undergraduate student body: 732 full time, 69 part time; 34% male, 66% female; 0% American Indian, 1% Asian, 5% black, 6% Hispanic, 2% multiracial, 1% Pacific Islander, 82% white, 1% international; 50% from in state; 60% live on campus; N/A of students in fraternities, N/A in sororities
Most popular majors: 19% Psychology, General, 18% Registered Nursing/Registered Nurse, 11% Business Administration and Management, General, 10% Elementary Education and Teaching, 6% Athletic Training/Trainer
Expenses: 2017-2018: $31,950; room/board: $9,400
Financial aid: (563) 588-6327; 87% of undergrads determined to have financial need; average aid package $26,183

Coe College
Cedar Rapids IA
(319) 399-8500
U.S. News ranking: Nat. Lib. Arts, No. 123
Website: www.coe.edu
Admissions email: admission@coe.edu
Private; founded 1851
Freshman admissions: more selective; 2016-2017: 6,725 applied, 3,359 accepted. Either SAT or ACT required. ACT 25/75 percentile: 22-28. High school rank: 30% in top tenth, 65% in top quarter, 89% in top half

Early decision deadline: N/A, notification date: N/A
Early action deadline: 12/10, notification date: 1/20
Application deadline (fall): 3/1
Undergraduate student body: 1,344 full time, 65 part time; 43% male, 57% female; 0% American Indian, 2% Asian, 7% black, 9% Hispanic, 3% multiracial, 0% Pacific Islander, 73% white, 3% international; 47% from in state; 86% live on campus; 24% of students in fraternities, 26% in sororities
Most popular majors: 18% Business, Management, Marketing, and Related Support Services, 12% Psychology, 9% Biological and Biomedical Sciences, 9% Social Sciences, 7% Communication, Journalism, and Related Programs
Expenses: 2017-2018: $42,430; room/board: $9,140
Financial aid: (319) 399-8540; 84% of undergrads determined to have financial need; average aid package $33,486

Cornell College
Mount Vernon IA
(800) 747-1112
U.S. News ranking: Nat. Lib. Arts, No. 87
Website: www.cornellcollege.edu
Admissions email: admissions@cornellcollege.edu
Private; founded 1853
Affiliation: United Methodist
Freshman admissions: more selective; 2016-2017: 1,965 applied, 1,394 accepted. Neither SAT nor ACT required. ACT 25/75 percentile: 23-29. High school rank: 19% in top tenth, 41% in top quarter, 76% in top half
Early decision deadline: 11/1, notification date: 12/15
Early action deadline: 12/1, notification date: 2/1
Application deadline (fall): 2/1
Undergraduate student body: 973 full time, 1 part time; 50% male, 50% female; 1% American Indian, 3% Asian, 5% black, 12% Hispanic, 3% multiracial, 0% Pacific Islander, 67% white, 5% international; 19% from in state; 93% live on campus; 21% of students in fraternities, 39% in sororities
Most popular majors: 12% Psychology, 9% Biological and Biomedical Sciences, 9% English Language and Literature/Letters, 9% Parks, Recreation, Leisure, and Fitness Studies, 7% Computer and Information Sciences and Support Services
Expenses: 2017-2018: $40,880; room/board: $9,110
Financial aid: (319) 895-4216; 72% of undergrads determined to have financial need; average aid package $31,933

Dordt College
Sioux Center IA
(800) 343-6738
U.S. News ranking: Reg. Coll. (Mid. W), No. 8
Website: www.dordt.edu
Admissions email: admissions@dordt.edu
Private; founded 1955
Affiliation: Christian Reformed Church

Freshman admissions: selective; 2016-2017: 1,344 applied, 1,015 accepted. Either SAT or ACT required. ACT 25/75 percentile: 21-27. High school rank: 17% in top tenth, 42% in top quarter, 72% in top half
Early decision deadline: N/A, notification date: N/A
Early action deadline: N/A, notification date: N/A
Application deadline (fall): 8/16
Undergraduate student body: 1,377 full time, 77 part time; 52% male, 48% female; 0% American Indian, 1% Asian, 1% black, 2% Hispanic, 7% multiracial, 0% Pacific Islander, 73% white, 8% international; 40% from in state; 90% live on campus; 0% of students in fraternities, 0% in sororities
Most popular majors: 19% Business/Commerce, General, 18% Elementary Education and Teaching, 9% Engineering, General, 7% Chiropractic, 6% Agricultural Business and Management, General
Expenses: 2017-2018: $30,000; room/board: $9,140
Financial aid: (712) 722-6082; 67% of undergrads determined to have financial need; average aid package $25,564

Drake University
Des Moines IA
(800) 443-7253
U.S. News ranking: Reg. U. (Mid. W), No. 3
Website: www.drake.edu
Admissions email: admission@drake.edu
Private; founded 1881
Freshman admissions: more selective; 2016-2017: 4,959 applied, 3,419 accepted. Neither SAT nor ACT required. ACT 25/75 percentile: 25-30. High school rank: 37% in top tenth, 68% in top quarter, 95% in top half
Early decision deadline: N/A, notification date: N/A
Early action deadline: N/A, notification date: N/A
Application deadline (fall): rolling
Undergraduate student body: 3,102 full time, 165 part time; 43% male, 57% female; 0% American Indian, 3% Asian, 4% black, 4% Hispanic, 2% multiracial, 0% Pacific Islander, 79% white, 7% international; 31% from in state; 70% live on campus; 36% of students in fraternities, 29% in sororities
Most popular majors: 31% Business, Management, Marketing, and Related Support Services, 11% Communication, Journalism, and Related Programs, 8% Biological and Biomedical Sciences, 8% Education, 7% Social Sciences
Expenses: 2017-2018: $39,062; room/board: $10,158
Financial aid: (515) 271-2905; 59% of undergrads determined to have financial need; average aid package $27,171

Graceland University
Lamoni IA
(866) 472-2352
U.S. News ranking: Reg. U. (Mid. W), second tier
Website: www.graceland.edu
Admissions email: admissions@graceland.edu
Private; founded 1895
Affiliation: Other
Freshman admissions: selective; 2016-2017: 2,440 applied, 1,181 accepted. Either SAT or ACT required. ACT 25/75 percentile: 18-24. High school rank: 10% in top tenth, 27% in top quarter, 67% in top half
Early decision deadline: N/A, notification date: N/A
Early action deadline: N/A, notification date: N/A
Application deadline (fall): rolling
Undergraduate student body: 1,166 full time, 280 part time; 41% male, 59% female; 0% American Indian, 1% Asian, 10% black, 12% Hispanic, 4% multiracial, 1% Pacific Islander, 62% white, 3% international; 27% from in state; 70% live on campus; 0% of students in fraternities, 0% in sororities
Most popular majors: 27% Health Professions and Related Programs, 20% Education, 15% Business, Management, Marketing, and Related Support Services, 7% Parks, Recreation, Leisure, and Fitness Studies, 4% Psychology
Expenses: 2017-2018: $28,110; room/board: $8,480
Financial aid: (641) 784-5117; 80% of undergrads determined to have financial need; average aid package $22,282

Grand View University
Des Moines IA
(515) 263-2810
U.S. News ranking: Reg. Coll. (Mid. W), No. 39
Website: admissions.grandview.edu/
Admissions email: admissions@grandview.edu
Private; founded 1896
Freshman admissions: selective; 2016-2017: 886 applied, 856 accepted. Either SAT or ACT required. ACT 25/75 percentile: 18-23. High school rank: 16% in top tenth, 35% in top quarter, 67% in top half
Early decision deadline: N/A, notification date: N/A
Early action deadline: N/A, notification date: N/A
Application deadline (fall): 8/15
Undergraduate student body: 1,643 full time, 267 part time; 45% male, 55% female; 0% American Indian, 3% Asian, 8% black, 4% Hispanic, 4% multiracial, 0% Pacific Islander, 70% white, 2% international; 93% from in state; 45% live on campus; 0% of students in fraternities, 0% in sororities
Most popular majors: 25% Business, Management, Marketing, and Related Support Services, 11% Health Professions and Related Programs, 10% Parks, Recreation, Leisure, and Fitness Studies, 7% Public Administration and Social Service Professions, 6% Education

Expenses: 2017-2018: $26,516; room/board: $8,834
Financial aid: (515) 263-2853; 82% of undergrads determined to have financial need; average aid package $19,738

Grinnell College

Grinnell IA
(800) 247-0113
U.S. News ranking: Nat. Lib. Arts, No. 18
Website: www.grinnell.edu
Admissions email: admission@grinnell.edu
Private; founded 1846
Freshman admissions: most selective; 2016-2017: 7,370 applied, 1,488 accepted. Either SAT or ACT required. ACT 25/75 percentile: 30-33. High school rank: 66% in top tenth, 91% in top quarter, 99% in top half
Early decision deadline: 11/15, notification date: 12/15
Early action deadline: N/A, notification date: N/A
Application deadline (fall): 1/15
Undergraduate student body: 1,658 full time, 41 part time; 45% male, 55% female; 0% American Indian, 8% Asian, 6% black, 8% Hispanic, 5% multiracial, 0% Pacific Islander, 52% white, 18% international; 18% from in state; N/A live on campus; 0% of students in fraternities, 0% in sororities
Most popular majors: 24% Social Sciences, 17% Biological and Biomedical Sciences, 9% English Language and Literature/Letters, 9% Foreign Languages, Literatures, and Linguistics, 8% Computer and Information Sciences and Support Services
Expenses: 2017-2018: $50,464; room/board: $12,400
Financial aid: (641) 269-3250; 68% of undergrads determined to have financial need; average aid package $45,717

Iowa State University

Ames IA
(515) 294-2592
U.S. News ranking: Nat. U., No. 115
Website: www.iastate.edu
Admissions email: admissions@iastate.edu
Public; founded 1858
Freshman admissions: more selective; 2016-2017: 19,433 applied, 17,002 accepted. Either SAT or ACT required. ACT 25/75 percentile: 22-28. High school rank: 22% in top tenth, 55% in top quarter, 92% in top half
Early decision deadline: N/A, notification date: N/A
Early action deadline: N/A, notification date: N/A
Application deadline (fall): rolling
Undergraduate student body: 28,872 full time, 1,799 part time; 57% male, 43% female; 0% American Indian, 3% Asian, 3% black, 5% Hispanic, 2% multiracial, 0% Pacific Islander, 75% white, 7% international; 69% from in state; 33% live on campus; 13% of students in fraternities, 21% in sororities

Most popular majors: 20% Business, Management, Marketing, and Related Support Services, 20% Engineering, 12% Agriculture, Agriculture Operations, and Related Sciences, 6% Biological and Biomedical Sciences, 5% Family and Consumer Sciences/Human Sciences
Expenses: 2017-2018: $8,420 in state, $22,256 out of state; room/board: $8,762
Financial aid: (515) 294-2223; 50% of undergrads determined to have financial need; average aid package $11,923

Iowa Wesleyan University

Mount Pleasant IA
(319) 385-6231
U.S. News ranking: Reg. Coll. (Mid. W), No. 54
Website: www.iw.edu
Admissions email: admit@iw.edu
Private; founded 1842
Affiliation: United Methodist
Freshman admissions: selective; 2016-2017: 5,413 applied, 2,746 accepted. Either SAT or ACT required. ACT 25/75 percentile: 17-21. High school rank: 5% in top tenth, 20% in top quarter, 54% in top half
Early decision deadline: N/A, notification date: N/A
Early action deadline: N/A, notification date: N/A
Application deadline (fall): N/A
Undergraduate student body: 479 full time, 41 part time; 47% male, 53% female; 1% American Indian, 0% Asian, 16% black, 6% Hispanic, 5% multiracial, 1% Pacific Islander, 39% white, 12% international
Most popular majors: 20% Registered Nursing/Registered Nurse, 19% Elementary Education and Teaching, 18% Business Administration and Management, General, 6% Psychology, General
Expenses: 2017-2018: $30,500; room/board: $10,500
Financial aid: (319) 385-6242; 84% of undergrads determined to have financial need; average aid package $18,701

Kaplan University[1]

Davenport IA
U.S. News ranking: Reg. U. (Mid. W), unranked
Website: www.kaplan.edu
Admissions email: N/A
For-profit
Application deadline (fall): N/A
Undergraduate student body: N/A full time, N/A part time
Expenses: 2016-2017: $14,325; room/board: N/A
Financial aid: N/A

Loras College

Dubuque IA
(800) 245-6727
U.S. News ranking: Reg. Coll. (Mid. W), No. 13
Website: www.loras.edu
Admissions email: admission@loras.edu
Private; founded 1839
Affiliation: Roman Catholic

Freshman admissions: selective; 2016-2017: 1,269 applied, 1,172 accepted. Either SAT or ACT required. ACT 25/75 percentile: 20-25. High school rank: 15% in top tenth, 36% in top quarter, 76% in top half
Early decision deadline: N/A, notification date: N/A
Early action deadline: N/A, notification date: N/A
Application deadline (fall): rolling
Undergraduate student body: 1,400 full time, 63 part time; 53% male, 47% female; 0% American Indian, 1% Asian, 2% black, 7% Hispanic, 2% multiracial, 0% Pacific Islander, 83% white, 1% international; 40% from in state; 65% live on campus; 5% of students in fraternities, 4% in sororities
Most popular majors: 7% Accounting, 7% Sport and Fitness Administration/Management, 6% Elementary Education and Teaching, 6% Marketing/Marketing Management, General, 6% Public Relations/Image Management
Expenses: 2017-2018: $32,886; room/board: $7,840
Financial aid: (563) 588-7817; 73% of undergrads determined to have financial need; average aid package $26,390

Luther College

Decorah IA
(563) 387-1287
U.S. News ranking: Nat. Lib. Arts, No. 87
Website: www.luther.edu
Admissions email: admissions@luther.edu
Private; founded 1861
Affiliation: Evangelical Lutheran Church
Freshman admissions: more selective; 2016-2017: 3,856 applied, 2,608 accepted. Either SAT or ACT required. ACT 25/75 percentile: 23-28. High school rank: 23% in top tenth, 52% in top quarter, 84% in top half
Early decision deadline: N/A, notification date: N/A
Early action deadline: N/A, notification date: N/A
Application deadline (fall): rolling
Undergraduate student body: 2,131 full time, 38 part time; 45% male, 55% female; 0% American Indian, 2% Asian, 2% black, 5% Hispanic, 2% multiracial, 0% Pacific Islander, 82% white, 7% international; 35% from in state; 89% live on campus; 1% of students in fraternities, 2% in sororities
Most popular majors: 17% Biology/Biological Sciences, General, 13% Business Administration and Management, General, 9% Music, General, 9% Psychology, General, 5% English Language and Literature, General
Expenses: 2017-2018: $41,020; room/board: $8,970
Financial aid: (563) 387-1018; 77% of undergrads determined to have financial need; average aid package $33,407

Maharishi University of Management[1]

Fairfield IA
U.S. News ranking: Reg. U. (Mid. W), unranked
Website: www.mum.edu
Admissions email: admissions@mum.edu
Private
Application deadline (fall): N/A
Undergraduate student body: N/A full time, N/A part time
Expenses: 2016-2017: $27,530; room/board: $7,400
Financial aid: N/A

Morningside College

Sioux City IA
(712) 274-5111
U.S. News ranking: Reg. U. (Mid. W), No. 54
Website: www.morningside.edu
Admissions email: mscadm@morningside.edu
Private; founded 1894
Affiliation: United Methodist
Freshman admissions: selective; 2016-2017: 4,561 applied, 2,597 accepted. Either SAT or ACT required. ACT 25/75 percentile: 20-26. High school rank: 17% in top tenth, 45% in top quarter, 72% in top half
Early decision deadline: N/A, notification date: N/A
Early action deadline: N/A, notification date: N/A
Application deadline (fall): rolling
Undergraduate student body: 1,295 full time, 26 part time; 46% male, 54% female; 1% American Indian, 1% Asian, 2% black, 7% Hispanic, 3% multiracial, 0% Pacific Islander, 78% white, 5% international; 62% from in state; 46% live on campus; 5% of students in fraternities, 2% in sororities
Most popular majors: 20% Business, Management, Marketing, and Related Support Services, 16% Education, 13% Biological and Biomedical Sciences, 10% Health Professions and Related Programs, 7% Visual and Performing Arts
Expenses: 2017-2018: $30,390; room/board: $9,390
Financial aid: (712) 274-5159; 80% of undergrads determined to have financial need; average aid package $23,298

Mount Mercy University

Cedar Rapids IA
(319) 368-6460
U.S. News ranking: Reg. U. (Mid. W), No. 54
Website: www.mtmercy.edu
Admissions email: admission@mtmercy.edu
Private; founded 1928
Affiliation: Roman Catholic
Freshman admissions: selective; 2016-2017: 1,288 applied, 797 accepted. Either SAT or ACT required. ACT 25/75 percentile: 18-24. High school rank: 15% in top tenth, 44% in top quarter, 76% in top half
Early decision deadline: N/A, notification date: N/A
Early action deadline: N/A, notification date: N/A

Application deadline (fall): rolling
Undergraduate student body: 1,046 full time, 534 part time; 31% male, 69% female; 1% American Indian, 2% Asian, 7% black, 2% Hispanic, 2% multiracial, 0% Pacific Islander, 79% white, 4% international; 86% from in state; 42% live on campus; N/A of students in fraternities, N/A in sororities
Most popular majors: 27% Registered Nursing/Registered Nurse, 13% Business/Commerce, General, 6% Business Administration and Management, General, 5% Criminal Justice/Law Enforcement Administration, 5% Human Resources Management/Personnel Administration, General
Expenses: 2017-2018: $30,582; room/board: $9,166
Financial aid: (319) 368-6467; 76% of undergrads determined to have financial need; average aid package $23,169

Northwestern College

Orange City IA
(800) 747-4757
U.S. News ranking: Reg. Coll. (Mid. W), No. 10
Website: www.nwciowa.edu
Admissions email: admissions@nwciowa.edu
Private; founded 1882
Affiliation: Reformed Church in America
Freshman admissions: more selective; 2016-2017: 2,199 applied, 1,441 accepted. Either SAT or ACT required. ACT 25/75 percentile: 21-28. High school rank: 24% in top tenth, 47% in top quarter, 78% in top half
Early decision deadline: N/A, notification date: N/A
Early action deadline: N/A, notification date: N/A
Application deadline (fall): rolling
Undergraduate student body: 1,045 full time, 54 part time; 44% male, 56% female; 0% American Indian, 1% Asian, 2% black, 5% Hispanic, 2% multiracial, 0% Pacific Islander, 82% white, 4% international; 55% from in state; 89% live on campus; 0% of students in fraternities, 0% in sororities
Most popular majors: 18% Business Administration and Management, General, 18% Elementary Education and Teaching, 12% Registered Nursing/Registered Nurse, 7% Biology/Biological Sciences, General, 6% Drama and Dramatics/Theatre Arts, General
Expenses: 2017-2018: $30,200; room/board: $9,000
Financial aid: (712) 707-7131; 73% of undergrads determined to have financial need; average aid package $24,635

Simpson College

Indianola IA
(515) 961-1624
U.S. News ranking: Nat. Lib. Arts, No. 147
Website: www.simpson.edu
Admissions email: admiss@simpson.edu
Private; founded 1860
Affiliation: United Methodist

Freshman admissions: selective; 2016-2017: 1,265 applied, 1,081 accepted. Either SAT or ACT required. ACT 25/75 percentile: 21-27. High school rank: 26% in top tenth, 56% in top quarter, 87% in top half **Early decision deadline:** N/A, notification date: N/A **Early action deadline:** N/A, notification date: N/A **Application deadline (fall):** rolling **Undergraduate student body:** 1,379 full time, 164 part time; 44% male, 56% female; 0% American Indian, 1% Asian, 2% black, 4% Hispanic, 2% multiracial, 0% Pacific Islander, 86% white, 0% international; 79% from in state; 87% live on campus; 24% of students in fraternities, 21% in sororities **Most popular majors:** 13% Business/Commerce, General, 8% Criminal Justice/Safety Studies, 7% Psychology, General, 6% Accounting, 5% Biology/Biological Sciences, General **Expenses:** 2017-2018: $37,663; room/board: $7,963 **Financial aid:** (515) 961-1596; 82% of undergrads determined to have financial need; average aid package $27,950

St. Ambrose University

Davenport IA
(563) 333-6300
U.S. News ranking: Reg. U. (Mid. W), No. 26
Website: www.sau.edu
Admissions email: admit@sau.edu
Private; founded 1882
Affiliation: Roman Catholic
Freshman admissions: selective; 2016-2017: 4,426 applied, 2,814 accepted. Either SAT or ACT required. ACT 25/75 percentile: 20-25. High school rank: 16% in top tenth, 41% in top quarter, 72% in top half **Early decision deadline:** N/A, notification date: N/A **Early action deadline:** N/A, notification date: N/A **Application deadline (fall):** rolling **Undergraduate student body:** 2,188 full time, 210 part time; 43% male, 57% female; 0% American Indian, 1% Asian, 4% black, 7% Hispanic, 2% multiracial, 0% Pacific Islander, 78% white, 3% international; 40% from in state; 64% live on campus; 0% of students in fraternities, 0% in sororities **Most popular majors:** 21% Business, Management, Marketing, and Related Support Services, 13% Health Professions and Related Programs, 13% Parks, Recreation, Leisure, and Fitness Studies, 11% Psychology, 6% Education **Expenses:** 2017-2018: $30,016; room/board: $10,164 **Financial aid:** (563) 333-6318; 67% of undergrads determined to have financial need; average aid package $22,153

University of Dubuque

Dubuque IA
(563) 589-3200
U.S. News ranking: Reg. U. (Mid. W), No. 109
Website: www.dbq.edu
Admissions email: admssns@dbq.edu
Private; founded 1852
Affiliation: Presbyterian Church (USA)
Freshman admissions: less selective; 2016-2017: 1,662 applied, 1,258 accepted. Either SAT or ACT required. ACT 25/75 percentile: 17-22. High school rank: 5% in top tenth, 14% in top quarter, 42% in top half **Early decision deadline:** N/A, notification date: N/A **Early action deadline:** N/A, notification date: N/A **Application deadline (fall):** rolling **Undergraduate student body:** 1,679 full time, 245 part time; 59% male, 41% female; 0% American Indian, 2% Asian, 14% black, 9% Hispanic, 3% multiracial, 0% Pacific Islander, 61% white, 6% international; 43% from in state; 48% live on campus; 2% of students in fraternities, 2% in sororities **Most popular majors:** 19% Business Administration and Management, General, 9% Marketing/Marketing Management, General, 7% Kinesiology and Exercise Science, 6% Elementary Education and Teaching, 5% Registered Nursing/Registered Nurse **Expenses:** 2017-2018: $29,710; room/board: $9,450 **Financial aid:** (563) 589-3125; 88% of undergrads determined to have financial need; average aid package $24,999

University of Iowa

Iowa City IA
(319) 335-3847
U.S. News ranking: Nat. U., No. 78
Website: www.uiowa.edu
Admissions email: admissions@uiowa.edu
Public; founded 1847
Freshman admissions: more selective; 2016-2017: 28,494 applied, 23,967 accepted. Either SAT or ACT required. ACT 25/75 percentile: 23-28. High school rank: 28% in top tenth, 59% in top quarter, 91% in top half **Early decision deadline:** N/A, notification date: N/A **Early action deadline:** N/A, notification date: N/A **Application deadline (fall):** 5/1 **Undergraduate student body:** 20,868 full time, 3,608 part time; 47% male, 53% female; 0% American Indian, 4% Asian, 3% black, 8% Hispanic, 3% multiracial, 0% Pacific Islander, 69% white, 11% international; 65% from in state; 26% live on campus; 13% of students in fraternities, 18% in sororities **Most popular majors:** 19% Business, Management, Marketing, and Related Support Services, 12% Parks, Recreation, Leisure, and Fitness Studies, 9% Social Sciences, 8% Communication, Journalism, and Related Programs, 7% Engineering

Expenses: 2017-2018: $8,575 in state, $28,813 out of state; room/board: $10,108 **Financial aid:** (319) 335-1450; 48% of undergrads determined to have financial need; average aid package $15,593

University of Northern Iowa

Cedar Falls IA
(800) 772-2037
U.S. News ranking: Reg. U. (Mid. W), No. 25
Website: uni.edu/
Public; founded 1876
Freshman admissions: selective; 2016-2017: 5,287 applied, 4,346 accepted. Either SAT or ACT required. ACT 25/75 percentile: 20-25. High school rank: 17% in top tenth, 46% in top quarter, 81% in top half **Early decision deadline:** N/A, notification date: N/A **Early action deadline:** N/A, notification date: N/A **Application deadline (fall):** 8/15 **Undergraduate student body:** 9,146 full time, 958 part time; 43% male, 57% female; 0% American Indian, 1% Asian, 3% black, 4% Hispanic, 2% multiracial, 0% Pacific Islander, 83% white, 4% international; 94% from in state; 41% live on campus; 4% of students in fraternities, 8% in sororities **Most popular majors:** 19% Business, Management, Marketing, and Related Support Services, 17% Education, 8% Communication, Journalism, and Related Programs, 7% Parks, Recreation, Leisure, and Fitness Studies, 6% Social Sciences **Expenses:** 2017-2018: $8,483 in state, $19,025 out of state; room/board: $8,782 **Financial aid:** (319) 273-2722; 60% of undergrads determined to have financial need; average aid package $8,363

Upper Iowa University

Fayette IA
(563) 425-5281
U.S. News ranking: Reg. U. (Mid. W), second tier
Website: www.uiu.edu
Admissions email: admission@uiu.edu
Private; founded 1857
Freshman admissions: selective; 2016-2017: 1,121 applied, 1,056 accepted. Either SAT or ACT required. ACT 25/75 percentile: 17-24. High school rank: 22% in top tenth, 27% in top quarter, 57% in top half **Early decision deadline:** N/A, notification date: N/A **Early action deadline:** N/A, notification date: N/A **Application deadline (fall):** rolling **Undergraduate student body:** 2,236 full time, 1,755 part time; 38% male, 62% female; 0% American Indian, 1% Asian, 20% black, 6% Hispanic, 2% multiracial, 0% Pacific Islander, 66% white, 2% international; 45% from in state; 10% live on campus; 10% of students in fraternities, 10% in sororities

William Penn University[1]

Oskaloosa IA
(641) 673-1012
U.S. News ranking: Reg. U. (Mid. W), second tier
Website: www.wmpenn.edu
Admissions email: admissions@wmpenn.edu
Private
Application deadline (fall): N/A

Most popular majors: 37% Business Administration and Management, General, 17% Psychology, General, 12% Health/Health Care Administration/Management, 10% Public Administration, 9% Criminology **Expenses:** 2016-2017: $28,890; room/board: $8,120 **Financial aid:** (563) 425-5276

Waldorf College[1]

Forest City IA
(641) 585-8112
U.S. News ranking: Reg. Coll. (Mid. W), second tier
Website: www.waldorf.edu
Admissions email: admissions@waldorf.edu
For-profit
Application deadline (fall): N/A **Undergraduate student body:** N/A full time, N/A part time **Expenses:** 2016-2017: $21,260; room/board: $7,246 **Financial aid:** N/A

Wartburg College

Waverly IA
(319) 352-8264
U.S. News ranking: Nat. Lib. Arts, No. 128
Website: www.wartburg.edu
Admissions email: admissions@wartburg.edu
Private; founded 1852
Affiliation: Evangelical Lutheran Church
Freshman admissions: selective; 2016-2017: 4,028 applied, 2,749 accepted. Either SAT or ACT required. ACT 25/75 percentile: 21-26. High school rank: 24% in top tenth, 50% in top quarter, 79% in top half **Early decision deadline:** N/A, notification date: N/A **Early action deadline:** 12/1, notification date: N/A **Application deadline (fall):** rolling **Undergraduate student body:** 1,434 full time, 48 part time; 48% male, 52% female; 0% American Indian, 1% Asian, 5% black, 4% Hispanic, 3% multiracial, 0% Pacific Islander, 75% white, 8% international; 71% from in state; 85% live on campus; N/A of students in fraternities, N/A in sororities **Most popular majors:** 23% Business/Commerce, General, 20% Biology/Biological Sciences, General, 12% Elementary Education and Teaching, 8% Mass Communication/Media Studies, 5% Psychology, General **Expenses:** 2017-2018: $39,730; room/board: $9,748 **Financial aid:** (319) 352-8262; 72% of undergrads determined to have financial need; average aid package $30,575

Undergraduate student body: N/A full time, N/A part time **Expenses:** 2016-2017: $24,510; room/board: $6,666 **Financial aid:** N/A

KANSAS

Baker University

Baldwin City KS
(800) 873-4282
U.S. News ranking: Reg. U. (Mid. W), No. 46
Website: www.bakeru.edu
Admissions email: admission@bakeru.edu
Private; founded 1858
Affiliation: United Methodist
Freshman admissions: selective; 2016-2017: 899 applied, 699 accepted. Either SAT or ACT required. ACT 25/75 percentile: 20-25. High school rank: 12% in top tenth, 40% in top quarter, 76% in top half **Early decision deadline:** N/A, notification date: N/A **Early action deadline:** N/A, notification date: N/A **Application deadline (fall):** rolling **Undergraduate student body:** 848 full time, 296 part time; 51% male, 49% female; 2% American Indian, 0% Asian, 11% black, 8% Hispanic, 3% multiracial, 1% Pacific Islander, 69% white, 2% international; 65% from in state; 80% live on campus; 35% of students in fraternities, 46% in sororities **Most popular majors:** 21% Business Administration and Management, General, 13% Kinesiology and Exercise Science, 7% Elementary Education and Teaching, 6% Biology/Biological Sciences, General, 6% Psychology, General **Expenses:** 2017-2018: $28,880; room/board: $8,310 **Financial aid:** (785) 594-4595; 79% of undergrads determined to have financial need; average aid package $25,372

Benedictine College

Atchison KS
(800) 467-5340
U.S. News ranking: Reg. Coll. (Mid. W), No. 13
Website: www.benedictine.edu
Admissions email: bcadmiss@benedictine.edu
Private; founded 1859
Affiliation: Roman Catholic
Freshman admissions: selective; 2016-2017: 2,182 applied, 2,132 accepted. Either SAT or ACT required. ACT 25/75 percentile: 21-28. High school rank: 19% in top tenth, 42% in top quarter, 67% in top half **Early decision deadline:** N/A, notification date: N/A **Early action deadline:** N/A, notification date: N/A **Application deadline (fall):** rolling **Undergraduate student body:** 1,927 full time, 322 part time; 46% male, 54% female; 0% American Indian, 1% Asian, 3% black, 6% Hispanic, 0% multiracial, 0% Pacific Islander, 77% white, 2% international; 23% from in state; 81% live on campus; 0% of students in fraternities, 0% in sororities

Most popular majors: 19% Business, Management, Marketing, and Related Support Services, 16% Education, 9% Social Sciences, 8% Theology and Religious Vocations, 6% Health Professions and Related Programs
Expenses: 2017-2018: $28,480; room/board: $9,820
Financial aid: (913) 360-7484; 64% of undergrads determined to have financial need; average aid package $22,440

Bethany College
Lindsborg KS
(800) 826-2281
U.S. News ranking: Reg. Coll. (Mid. W), No. 49
Website: www.bethanylb.edu
Admissions email: admissions@bethanylb.edu
Private; founded 1881
Affiliation: Evangelical Lutheran Church
Freshman admissions: selective; 2016-2017: 1,399 applied, 904 accepted. Either SAT or ACT required. ACT 25/75 percentile: 18-23. High school rank: 7% in top tenth, 29% in top quarter, 68% in top half
Early decision deadline: N/A, notification date: N/A
Early action deadline: N/A, notification date: N/A
Application deadline (fall): rolling
Undergraduate student body: 635 full time, 81 part time; 60% male, 40% female; 1% American Indian, 1% Asian, 18% black, 16% Hispanic, 3% multiracial, 1% Pacific Islander, 53% white, 8% international; 41% from in state; 76% live on campus; 18% of students in fraternities, 32% in sororities
Most popular majors: 17% Criminology, 14% Business, Management, Marketing, and Related Support Services, Other, 11% Biology/Biological Sciences, General, 10% Finance, General, 8% Elementary Education and Teaching
Expenses: 2016-2017: $26,660; room/board: $9,600
Financial aid: N/A

Bethel College
North Newton KS
(800) 522-1887
U.S. News ranking: Nat. Lib. Arts, second tier
Website: www.bethelks.edu
Admissions email: admissions@bethelks.edu
Private; founded 1887
Freshman admissions: selective; 2016-2017: 770 applied, 431 accepted. Either SAT or ACT required. ACT 25/75 percentile: 20-26. High school rank: 14% in top tenth, 43% in top quarter, 73% in top half
Early decision deadline: N/A, notification date: N/A
Early action deadline: N/A, notification date: N/A
Application deadline (fall): 8/1
Undergraduate student body: 441 full time, 19 part time; 50% male, 50% female; 1% American Indian, 1% Asian, 14% black,

6% Hispanic, 3% multiracial, 0% Pacific Islander, 71% white, 0% international; 64% from in state; 68% live on campus; 0% of students in fraternities, 0% in sororities
Most popular majors: 37% Health Professions and Related Programs, 11% Business, Management, Marketing, and Related Support Services, 8% Education, 8% Parks, Recreation, Leisure, and Fitness Studies, 7% Biological and Biomedical Sciences
Expenses: 2017-2018: $27,720; room/board: $9,270
Financial aid: (316) 284-5232; 87% of undergrads determined to have financial need; average aid package $25,636

Central Christian College
McPherson KS
(620) 241-0723
U.S. News ranking: Reg. Coll. (Mid. W), second tier
Website: www.centralchristian.edu/
Admissions email: admissions@centralchristian.edu
Private; founded 1884
Affiliation: Free Methodist
Freshman admissions: less selective; 2016-2017: 632 applied, 339 accepted. Neither SAT nor ACT required. ACT 25/75 percentile: 17-22. High school rank: N/A
Early decision deadline: N/A, notification date: N/A
Early action deadline: 11/30, notification date: 12/1
Application deadline (fall): rolling
Undergraduate student body: 791 full time, 222 part time; 49% male, 51% female; 2% American Indian, 1% Asian, 18% black, 12% Hispanic, 2% multiracial, 0% Pacific Islander, 57% white, 2% international; 50% from in state; 85% live on campus; 0% of students in fraternities, 0% in sororities
Most popular majors: 34% Homeland Security, Law Enforcement, Firefighting and Related Protective Services, 20% Business, Management, Marketing, and Related Support Services, 10% Leisure and Recreational Activities, 5% Philosophy and Religious Studies, 4% Psychology
Expenses: 2016-2017: $16,850; room/board: $7,950
Financial aid: N/A

Donnelly College
Kansas City KS
(913) 621-8700
U.S. News ranking: Reg. Coll. (Mid. W), unranked
Website: donnelly.edu
Admissions email: admissions@donnelly.edu
Private; founded 1949
Affiliation: Roman Catholic
Freshman admissions: least selective; 2016-2017: 664 applied, 664 accepted. Neither SAT nor ACT required. SAT 25/75 percentile: N/A. High school rank: N/A
Early decision deadline: N/A, notification date: N/A

Early action deadline: N/A, notification date: N/A
Application deadline (fall): rolling
Undergraduate student body: 236 full time, 82 part time; 27% male, 73% female; 1% American Indian, 5% Asian, 33% black, 45% Hispanic, 3% multiracial, 1% Pacific Islander, 9% white, 2% international
Most popular majors: 52% Liberal Arts and Sciences/Liberal Studies, 38% Licensed Practical/Vocational Nurse Training, 6% Non-Profit/Public/Organizational Management, 3% Information Technology, 1% Elementary Education and Teaching
Expenses: 2016-2017: $6,702; room/board: $7,520
Financial aid: N/A

Emporia State University
Emporia KS
(620) 341-5465
U.S. News ranking: Reg. U. (Mid. W), No. 122
Website: www.emporia.edu
Admissions email: go2esu@emporia.edu
Public; founded 1863
Freshman admissions: less selective; 2016-2017: 1,702 applied, 1,488 accepted. Neither SAT nor ACT required. ACT 25/75 percentile: 19-25. High school rank: 11% in top tenth, 33% in top quarter, 69% in top half
Early decision deadline: N/A, notification date: N/A
Early action deadline: N/A, notification date: N/A
Application deadline (fall): rolling
Undergraduate student body: 3,431 full time, 271 part time; 38% male, 62% female; 0% American Indian, 1% Asian, 6% black, 7% Hispanic, 8% multiracial, 0% Pacific Islander, 70% white, 7% international; 92% from in state; 29% live on campus; 10% of students in fraternities, 12% in sororities
Most popular majors: 26% Education, 16% Business, Management, Marketing, and Related Support Services, 11% Health Professions and Related Programs, 8% Liberal Arts and Sciences, General Studies and Humanities, 6% Social Sciences
Expenses: 2017-2018: $6,345 in state, $19,918 out of state; room/board: $8,684
Financial aid: (620) 341-5457; 61% of undergrads determined to have financial need; average aid package $9,163

Fort Hays State University
Hays KS
(800) 628-3478
U.S. News ranking: Reg. U. (Mid. W), second tier
Website: www.fhsu.edu
Admissions email: tigers@fhsu.edu
Public; founded 1902
Freshman admissions: selective; 2016-2017: 2,125 applied, 1,929 accepted. Neither SAT nor ACT required. ACT 25/75 percentile: 18-24. High school rank: 12% in top tenth, 31% in top quarter, 65% in top half

Early decision deadline: N/A, notification date: N/A
Early action deadline: N/A, notification date: N/A
Application deadline (fall): rolling
Undergraduate student body: 5,778 full time, 6,267 part time; 40% male, 60% female; 0% American Indian, 1% Asian, 4% black, 8% Hispanic, 2% multiracial, 0% Pacific Islander, 55% white, 29% international; 70% from in state; 11% live on campus; 4% of students in fraternities, 5% in sororities
Most popular majors: 43% Business, Management, Marketing, and Related Support Services, 12% Education, 10% Liberal Arts and Sciences, General Studies and Humanities, 8% Health Professions and Related Programs, 4% Computer and Information Sciences and Support Services
Expenses: 2017-2018: $5,009 in state, $14,832 out of state; room/board: $7,669
Financial aid: (785) 628-4408; 70% of undergrads determined to have financial need; average aid package $7,361

Friends University
Wichita KS
(316) 295-5100
U.S. News ranking: Reg. U. (Mid. W), second tier
Website: www.friends.edu
Admissions email: learn@friends.edu
Private; founded 1898
Freshman admissions: selective; 2016-2017: 749 applied, 412 accepted. Either SAT or ACT required. ACT 25/75 percentile: 19-24. High school rank: 16% in top tenth, 38% in top quarter, 70% in top half
Early decision deadline: N/A, notification date: N/A
Early action deadline: N/A, notification date: N/A
Application deadline (fall): rolling
Undergraduate student body: 920 full time, 272 part time; 46% male, 54% female; 1% American Indian, 1% Asian, 12% black, 7% Hispanic, 7% multiracial, 0% Pacific Islander, 65% white, 0% international; 78% from in state; 25% live on campus; 0% of students in fraternities, 0% in sororities
Most popular majors: 52% Business, Management, Marketing, and Related Support Services, 7% Computer and Information Sciences and Support Services, 7% Visual and Performing Arts, 6% Biological and Biomedical Sciences, 5% Psychology
Expenses: 2017-2018: $27,565; room/board: $7,740
Financial aid: (316) 295-5200; 79% of undergrads determined to have financial need; average aid package $16,394

Kansas State University
Manhattan KS
(785) 532-6250
U.S. News ranking: Nat. U., No. 145
Website: www.k-state.edu
Admissions email: k-state@k-state.edu
Public; founded 1863
Freshman admissions: selective; 2016-2017: 9,018 applied, 8,511 accepted. Neither SAT nor ACT required. ACT 25/75 percentile: 22-28. High school rank: 24% in top tenth, 47% in top quarter, 77% in top half
Early decision deadline: N/A, notification date: N/A
Early action deadline: N/A, notification date: N/A
Application deadline (fall): rolling
Undergraduate student body: 17,699 full time, 1,773 part time; 52% male, 48% female; 0% American Indian, 1% Asian, 4% black, 7% Hispanic, 3% multiracial, 0% Pacific Islander, 78% white, 5% international; 82% from in state; 23% live on campus; N/A of students in fraternities, N/A in sororities
Most popular majors: 18% Business, Management, Marketing, and Related Support Services, 13% Agriculture, Agriculture Operations, and Related Sciences, 10% Engineering, 8% Family and Consumer Sciences/Human Sciences, 8% Social Sciences
Expenses: 2016-2017: $9,874 in state, $24,775 out of state; room/board: $9,150
Financial aid: (785) 532-7626; 50% of undergrads determined to have financial need; average aid package $12,668

Kansas Wesleyan University
Salina KS
(785) 833-4305
U.S. News ranking: Reg. Coll. (Mid. W), No. 45
Website: www.kwu.edu
Admissions email: admissions@kwu.edu
Private; founded 1886
Affiliation: United Methodist
Freshman admissions: selective; 2016-2017: 805 applied, 440 accepted. Either SAT or ACT required. ACT 25/75 percentile: 19-24. High school rank: 15% in top tenth, 34% in top quarter, 75% in top half
Early decision deadline: N/A, notification date: N/A
Early action deadline: N/A, notification date: N/A
Application deadline (fall): rolling
Undergraduate student body: 638 full time, 55 part time; 56% male, 44% female; 0% American Indian, 1% Asian, 12% black, 15% Hispanic, 3% multiracial, 0% Pacific Islander, 66% white, 2% international; 47% from in state; 68% live on campus; 0% of students in fraternities, 0% in sororities

Most popular majors: 20% Business, Management, Marketing, and Related Support Services, 14% Parks, Recreation, Leisure, and Fitness Studies, 11% Health Professions and Related Programs, 10% Education, 8% Homeland Security, Law Enforcement, Firefighting and Related Protective Services
Expenses: 2016-2017: $28,000; room/board: $8,600
Financial aid: (785) 833-4319

McPherson College
McPherson KS
(800) 365-7402
U.S. News ranking: Reg. Coll. (Mid. W), No. 39
Website: www.mcpherson.edu
Admissions email: admissions@mcpherson.edu
Private; founded 1887
Affiliation: Church of Brethren
Freshman admissions: selective; 2016-2017: 922 applied, 485 accepted. Neither SAT nor ACT required. ACT 25/75 percentile: 19-24. High school rank: 12% in top tenth, 28% in top quarter, 59% in top half
Early decision deadline: N/A, notification date: N/A
Early action deadline: N/A, notification date: N/A
Application deadline (fall): 8/1
Undergraduate student body: 657 full time, 46 part time; 64% male, 36% female; 1% American Indian, 1% Asian, 11% black, 12% Hispanic, 2% multiracial, 0% Pacific Islander, 68% white, 2% international; 45% from in state; 75% live on campus; N/A of students in fraternities, N/A in sororities
Most popular majors: 19% Business Administration and Management, General, 19% Education, General, 12% Mechanical Engineering Related Technologies/Technicians, Other, 8% Public Administration and Social Service Professions, 7% Communication and Media Studies
Expenses: 2017-2018: $27,823; room/board: $8,311
Financial aid: (620) 242-0400

MidAmerica Nazarene University
Olathe KS
(913) 971-3380
U.S. News ranking: Reg. U. (Mid. W), No. 75
Website: www.mnu.edu
Admissions email: admissions@mnu.edu
Private; founded 1966
Affiliation: Church of the Nazarene
Freshman admissions: selective; 2016-2017: 1,077 applied, 558 accepted. Neither SAT nor ACT required. ACT 25/75 percentile: 18-25. High school rank: N/A
Early decision deadline: N/A, notification date: N/A
Early action deadline: N/A, notification date: N/A
Application deadline (fall): 8/1
Undergraduate student body: 1,001 full time, 308 part time; 42% male, 58% female; 1% American Indian, 1% Asian, 14% black,

2% Hispanic, 2% multiracial, 1% Pacific Islander, 63% white, 0% international; 57% from in state; 59% live on campus; 0% of students in fraternities, 0% in sororities
Most popular majors: 45% Health Professions and Related Programs, 31% Business, Management, Marketing, and Related Support Services, 6% Education
Expenses: 2017-2018: $29,670; room/board: $8,332
Financial aid: (913) 971-3298

Newman University
Wichita KS
(877) 639-6268
U.S. News ranking: Reg. U. (Mid. W), second tier
Website: www.newmanu.edu
Admissions email: admissions@newmanu.edu
Private; founded 1933
Affiliation: Roman Catholic
Freshman admissions: selective; 2016-2017: 1,331 applied, 769 accepted. Neither SAT nor ACT required. ACT 25/75 percentile: 20-27. High school rank: 17% in top tenth, 44% in top quarter, 74% in top half
Early decision deadline: N/A, notification date: N/A
Early action deadline: N/A, notification date: N/A
Application deadline (fall): rolling
Undergraduate student body: 1,001 full time, 1,534 part time; 38% male, 62% female; 1% American Indian, 5% Asian, 5% black, 15% Hispanic, 3% multiracial, 0% Pacific Islander, 63% white, 8% international; 86% from in state; 26% live on campus; N/A of students in fraternities, N/A in sororities
Most popular majors: 22% Health Professions and Related Programs, 17% Biological and Biomedical Sciences, 17% Education, 14% Business, Management, Marketing, and Related Support Services, 5% Multi/Interdisciplinary Studies
Expenses: 2017-2018: $29,092; room/board: $8,022
Financial aid: (316) 942-4291; 77% of undergrads determined to have financial need; average aid package $12,607

Ottawa University
Ottawa KS
(785) 242-5200
U.S. News ranking: Reg. Coll. (Mid. W), No. 42
Website: www.ottawa.edu
Admissions email: admiss@ottawa.edu
Private; founded 1865
Affiliation: American Baptist
Freshman admissions: selective; 2016-2017: 1,002 applied, 410 accepted. Neither SAT nor ACT required. ACT 25/75 percentile: 18-23. High school rank: 8% in top tenth, 28% in top quarter, 61% in top half
Early decision deadline: N/A, notification date: N/A
Early action deadline: N/A, notification date: N/A
Application deadline (fall): 8/15

Undergraduate student body: 614 full time, 16 part time; 60% male, 40% female; 5% American Indian, 1% Asian, 13% black, 3% Hispanic, 3% multiracial, 0% Pacific Islander, 61% white, 0% international; 59% from in state; 69% live on campus; N/A of students in fraternities, N/A in sororities
Most popular majors: 15% Kinesiology and Exercise Science, 14% Business Administration and Management, General, 10% Biology/Biological Sciences, General, 10% Elementary Education and Teaching, 9% Public Administration and Social Service Professions
Expenses: 2017-2018: $28,550; room/board: $9,770
Financial aid: (602) 749-5120; 82% of undergrads determined to have financial need; average aid package $12,343

Pittsburg State University
Pittsburg KS
(800) 854-7488
U.S. News ranking: Reg. U. (Mid. W), No. 83
Website: www.pittstate.edu
Admissions email: psuadmit@pittstate.edu
Public; founded 1903
Freshman admissions: selective; 2016-2017: 2,503 applied, 2,186 accepted. Either SAT or ACT required. ACT 25/75 percentile: 19-24. High school rank: 31% in top tenth, 46% in top quarter, 74% in top half
Early decision deadline: N/A, notification date: N/A
Early action deadline: N/A, notification date: N/A
Application deadline (fall): rolling
Undergraduate student body: 5,342 full time, 563 part time; 52% male, 48% female; 1% American Indian, 1% Asian, 4% black, 5% Hispanic, 6% multiracial, 0% Pacific Islander, 79% white, 3% international; 70% from in state; 19% live on campus; N/A of students in fraternities, N/A in sororities
Most popular majors: 19% Business, Management, Marketing, and Related Support Services, 14% Engineering Technologies and Engineering-Related Fields, 13% Education, 9% Health Professions and Related Programs, 6% Liberal Arts and Sciences, General Studies and Humanities
Expenses: 2017-2018: $7,100 in state, $18,152 out of state; room/board: $7,700
Financial aid: (620) 235-4240; 88% of undergrads determined to have financial need; average aid package $6,926

Southwestern College
Winfield KS
(620) 229-6236
U.S. News ranking: Reg. U. (Mid. W), second tier
Website: www.sckans.edu
Admissions email: scadmit@sckans.edu
Private; founded 1885
Affiliation: United Methodist

Freshman admissions: selective; 2016-2017: 395 applied, 364 accepted. Either SAT or ACT required. ACT 25/75 percentile: 18-23. High school rank: 8% in top tenth, 31% in top quarter, 69% in top half
Early decision deadline: N/A, notification date: N/A
Early action deadline: N/A, notification date: N/A
Application deadline (fall): 8/25
Undergraduate student body: 513 full time, 713 part time; 60% male, 40% female; 2% American Indian, 1% Asian, 11% black, 8% Hispanic, 4% multiracial, 0% Pacific Islander, 46% white, 4% international; 41% from in state; 30% live on campus; N/A of students in fraternities, N/A in sororities
Most popular majors: 42% Business, Management, Marketing, and Related Support Services, 12% Homeland Security, Law Enforcement, Firefighting and Related Protective Services, 11% Computer and Information Sciences and Support Services, 8% Education, 7% Health Professions and Related Programs
Expenses: 2017-2018: $28,750; room/board: $7,520
Financial aid: (620) 229-6387; 79% of undergrads determined to have financial need; average aid package $23,249

Sterling College[1]
Sterling KS
(800) 346-1017
U.S. News ranking: Reg. Coll. (Mid. W), second tier
Website: www.sterling.edu
Admissions email: admissions@sterling.edu
Private; founded 1887
Application deadline (fall): rolling
Undergraduate student body: N/A full time, N/A part time
Expenses: 2017-2018: $24,985, room/board: $7,266
Financial aid: (620) 278-4226; 85% of undergrads determined to have financial need; average aid package $22,213

Tabor College
Hillsboro KS
(620) 947-3121
U.S. News ranking: Reg. Coll. (Mid. W), No. 43
Website: www.tabor.edu
Admissions email: admissions@tabor.edu
Private; founded 1908
Affiliation: Mennonite Brethren Church
Freshman admissions: selective; 2016-2017: 631 applied, 353 accepted. Either SAT or ACT required. ACT 25/75 percentile: 18-24. High school rank: 12% in top tenth, 28% in top quarter, 61% in top half
Early decision deadline: N/A, notification date: N/A
Early action deadline: N/A, notification date: N/A
Application deadline (fall): rolling
Undergraduate student body: 523 full time, 147 part time; 54% male, 46% female; 1% American Indian, 0% Asian, 10% black,

13% Hispanic, 4% multiracial, 0% Pacific Islander, 66% white, 4% international; 47% from in state; N/A live on campus; 0% of students in fraternities, 0% in sororities
Most popular majors: 29% Health Professions and Related Programs, 17% Business, Management, Marketing, and Related Support Services, 12% Parks, Recreation, Leisure, and Fitness Studies, 9% Education, 8% Psychology
Expenses: 2017-2018: $27,220; room/board: $9,555
Financial aid: (620) 947-3121; 74% of undergrads determined to have financial need; average aid package $22,111

University of Kansas
Lawrence KS
(785) 864-3911
U.S. News ranking: Nat. U., No. 115
Website: www.ku.edu/
Admissions email: adm@ku.edu
Public; founded 1865
Freshman admissions: more selective; 2016-2017: 15,015 applied, 13,965 accepted. Either SAT or ACT required. ACT 25/75 percentile: 23-29. High school rank: 26% in top tenth, 58% in top quarter, 88% in top half
Early decision deadline: N/A, notification date: N/A
Early action deadline: N/A, notification date: N/A
Application deadline (fall): rolling
Undergraduate student body: 17,141 full time, 2,121 part time; 49% male, 51% female; 0% American Indian, 5% Asian, 4% black, 8% Hispanic, 5% multiracial, 0% Pacific Islander, 72% white, 6% international; 73% from in state; 25% live on campus; 19% of students in fraternities, 26% in sororities
Most popular majors: 16% Business, Management, Marketing, and Related Support Services, 12% Health Professions and Related Programs, 10% Engineering, 9% Communication, Journalism, and Related Programs, 6% Visual and Performing Arts
Expenses: 2017-2018: $10,824 in state, $26,592 out of state; room/board: $10,060
Financial aid: (785) 864-4700; 48% of undergrads determined to have financial need; average aid package $15,156

University of St. Mary
Leavenworth KS
(913) 758-6118
U.S. News ranking: Reg. U. (Mid. W), second tier
Website: www.stmary.edu
Admissions email: admiss@stmary.edu
Private; founded 1923
Freshman admissions: selective; 2016-2017: 888 applied, 439 accepted. Either SAT or ACT required. ACT 25/75 percentile: 19-24. High school rank: N/A
Early decision deadline: N/A, notification date: N/A
Early action deadline: N/A, notification date: N/A
Application deadline (fall): rolling

Undergraduate student body: 648 full time, 189 part time; 43% male, 57% female; 0% American Indian, 1% Asian, 9% black, 20% Hispanic, 4% multiracial, 1% Pacific Islander, 58% white, 1% international
Most popular majors: Information not available
Expenses: 2016-2017: $26,650; room/board: $7,940
Financial aid: (913) 758-6172

Washburn University
Topeka KS
(785) 670-1030
U.S. News ranking: Reg. U. (Mid. W), No. 93
Website: www.washburn.edu
Admissions email: admissions@washburn.edu
Public; founded 1865
Freshman admissions: selective; 2016-2017: 1,678 applied, 1,671 accepted. ACT required. ACT 25/75 percentile: 19-25. High school rank: 13% in top tenth, 35% in top quarter, 65% in top half
Early decision deadline: N/A, notification date: N/A
Early action deadline: N/A, notification date: N/A
Application deadline (fall): 8/1
Undergraduate student body: 3,866 full time, 1,914 part time; 40% male, 60% female; 1% American Indian, 1% Asian, 6% black, 10% Hispanic, 4% multiracial, 0% Pacific Islander, 64% white, 4% international; 92% from in state; 18% live on campus; 9% of students in fraternities, 9% in sororities
Most popular majors: 26% Health Professions and Related Programs, 18% Business, Management, Marketing, and Related Support Services, 7% Education, 6% Communication, Journalism, and Related Programs, 6% Homeland Security, Law Enforcement, Firefighting and Related Protective Services
Expenses: 2017-2018: $8,300 in state, $18,620 out of state; room/board: $7,527
Financial aid: (785) 670-2770; 61% of undergrads determined to have financial need; average aid package $9,580

Wichita State University
Wichita KS
(316) 978-3085
U.S. News ranking: Nat. U., second tier
Website: www.wichita.edu
Admissions email: admissions@wichita.edu
Public; founded 1895
Freshman admissions: selective; 2016-2017: 6,306 applied, 5,797 accepted. Neither SAT nor ACT required. ACT 25/75 percentile: 21-27. High school rank: 19% in top tenth, 44% in top quarter, 80% in top half
Early decision deadline: N/A, notification date: N/A
Early action deadline: N/A, notification date: N/A
Application deadline (fall): rolling

Undergraduate student body: 8,687 full time, 3,136 part time; 47% male, 53% female; 1% American Indian, 7% Asian, 6% black, 11% Hispanic, 4% multiracial, 0% Pacific Islander, 61% white, 7% international; 92% from in state; 10% live on campus; 1% of students in fraternities, 1% in sororities
Most popular majors: 19% Business, Management, Marketing, and Related Support Services, 15% Health Professions and Related Programs, 13% Engineering, 9% Education, 6% Psychology
Expenses: 2017-2018: $8,312 in state, $17,270 out of state; room/board: $6,280
Financial aid: (316) 978-3430; 39% of undergrads determined to have financial need; average aid package $5,900

KENTUCKY

Alice Lloyd College
Pippa Passes KY
(888) 280-4252
U.S. News ranking: Reg. Coll. (S), No. 7
Website: www.alc.edu
Admissions email: admissions@alc.edu
Private; founded 1923
Freshman admissions: selective; 2016-2017: 6,337 applied, 262 accepted. Either SAT or ACT required. ACT 25/75 percentile: 18-25. High school rank: 16% in top tenth, 43% in top quarter, 80% in top half
Early decision deadline: N/A, notification date: N/A
Early action deadline: N/A, notification date: N/A
Application deadline (fall): 7/1
Undergraduate student body: 572 full time, 27 part time; 46% male, 54% female; 0% American Indian, 0% Asian, 1% black, 1% Hispanic, 0% multiracial, 0% Pacific Islander, 95% white, 0% international; 75% from in state; 80% live on campus; 0% of students in fraternities, 0% in sororities
Most popular majors: 15% Parks, Recreation, Leisure, and Fitness Studies, 13% Biological and Biomedical Sciences, 13% History, 12% Business, Management, Marketing, and Related Support Services, 12% Social Sciences
Expenses: 2017-2018: $12,050; room/board: $6,550
Financial aid: (606) 368-6058; 92% of undergrads determined to have financial need; average aid package $13,775

Asbury University
Wilmore KY
(800) 888-1818
U.S. News ranking: Reg. U. (S), No. 15
Website: www.asbury.edu
Admissions email: admissions@asbury.edu
Private; founded 1890
Affiliation: Other Protestant
Freshman admissions: more selective; 2016-2017: 1,285 applied, 895 accepted. Either SAT or ACT required. ACT 25/75

percentile: 21-28. High school rank: 28% in top tenth, 59% in top quarter, 85% in top half
Early decision deadline: N/A, notification date: N/A
Early action deadline: N/A, notification date: N/A
Application deadline (fall): rolling
Undergraduate student body: 1,301 full time, 323 part time; 39% male, 61% female; 0% American Indian, 1% Asian, 4% black, 4% Hispanic, 0% multiracial, 0% Pacific Islander, 82% white, 3% international; 52% from in state; 95% live on campus; 0% of students in fraternities, 0% in sororities
Most popular majors: 11% Elementary Education and Teaching, 11% Radio, Television, and Digital Communication, Other, 8% Equestrian/Equine Studies, 5% Business/Commerce, General, 5% Psychology, General
Expenses: 2016-2017: $28,630; room/board: $6,748
Financial aid: N/A

Bellarmine University
Louisville KY
(502) 272-7100
U.S. News ranking: Reg. U. (S), No. 15
Website: www.bellarmine.edu
Admissions email: admissions@bellarmine.edu
Private; founded 1950
Affiliation: Roman Catholic
Freshman admissions: selective; 2016-2017: 6,212 applied, 5,122 accepted. Either SAT or ACT required. ACT 25/75 percentile: 22-27. High school rank: 19% in top tenth, 52% in top quarter, 88% in top half
Early decision deadline: N/A, notification date: N/A
Early action deadline: 11/1, notification date: 11/15
Application deadline (fall): 8/15
Undergraduate student body: 2,476 full time, 174 part time; 36% male, 64% female; 0% American Indian, 2% Asian, 4% black, 3% Hispanic, 3% multiracial, 0% Pacific Islander, 82% white, 1% international; 70% from in state; 41% live on campus; 1% of students in fraternities, 1% in sororities
Most popular majors: 27% Health Professions and Related Programs, 13% Business, Management, Marketing, and Related Support Services, 11% Psychology, 7% Biological and Biomedical Sciences, 6% Parks, Recreation, Leisure, and Fitness Studies
Expenses: 2017-2018: $40,350; room/board: $12,182
Financial aid: (502) 272-7300; 79% of undergrads determined to have financial need; average aid package $30,651

Berea College
Berea KY
(859) 985-3500
U.S. News ranking: Nat. Lib. Arts, No. 68
Website: www.berea.edu
Admissions email: admissions@berea.edu
Private; founded 1855

Freshman admissions: more selective; 2016-2017: 1,741 applied, 572 accepted. Either SAT or ACT required. ACT 25/75 percentile: 22-27. High school rank: 23% in top tenth, 66% in top quarter, 96% in top half
Early decision deadline: N/A, notification date: N/A
Early action deadline: N/A, notification date: N/A
Application deadline (fall): 4/30
Undergraduate student body: 1,616 full time, 49 part time; 44% male, 56% female; 0% American Indian, 2% Asian, 15% black, 9% Hispanic, 6% multiracial, 0% Pacific Islander, 59% white, 8% international; 47% from in state; 97% live on campus; N/A of students in fraternities, N/A in sororities
Most popular majors: 10% Business, Management, Marketing, and Related Support Services, 8% Visual and Performing Arts, 7% Education, 7% English Language and Literature/Letters, 7% Family and Consumer Sciences/Human Sciences
Expenses: 2017-2018: $560; room/board: $6,534
Financial aid: (859) 985-3313; 100% of undergrads determined to have financial need; average aid package $32,460

Brescia University
Owensboro KY
(270) 686-4241
U.S. News ranking: Reg. Coll. (S), No. 28
Website: www.brescia.edu
Admissions email: admissions@brescia.edu
Private; founded 1950
Affiliation: Roman Catholic
Freshman admissions: selective; 2016-2017: 4,438 applied, 2,094 accepted. Either SAT or ACT required. ACT 25/75 percentile: 20-26. High school rank: N/A
Early decision deadline: N/A, notification date: N/A
Early action deadline: N/A, notification date: N/A
Application deadline (fall): rolling
Undergraduate student body: 711 full time, 219 part time; 25% male, 75% female; 0% American Indian, 1% Asian, 10% black, 4% Hispanic, 0% multiracial, 0% Pacific Islander, 52% white, 2% international
Most popular majors: Audiology/Audiologist and Speech-Language Pathology/Pathologist, Business/Commerce, General, Liberal Arts and Sciences/Liberal Studies, Psychology, General, Social Work
Expenses: 2017-2018: $21,984; room/board: $9,050
Financial aid: (270) 686-4253; 76% of undergrads determined to have financial need; average aid package $12,375

Campbellsville University
Campbellsville KY
(270) 789-5220
U.S. News ranking: Reg. U. (S), No. 106
Website: www.campbellsville.edu
Admissions email: admissions@campbellsville.edu
Private; founded 1906
Freshman admissions: selective; 2016-2017: 2,966 applied, 2,072 accepted. Either SAT or ACT required. ACT 25/75 percentile: 19-24. High school rank: 15% in top tenth, 38% in top quarter, 72% in top half
Early decision deadline: N/A, notification date: N/A
Early action deadline: N/A, notification date: N/A
Application deadline (fall): rolling
Undergraduate student body: 1,998 full time, 1,351 part time; 42% male, 58% female; 0% American Indian, 0% Asian, 13% black, 3% Hispanic, 2% multiracial, 0% Pacific Islander, 71% white, 10% international; 85% from in state; 46% live on campus; 0% of students in fraternities, 0% in sororities
Most popular majors: 20% Business/Commerce, General, 11% Criminal Justice/Law Enforcement Administration, 8% Social Work, 7% Early Childhood Education and Teaching, 5% Registered Nursing/Registered Nurse
Expenses: 2017-2018: $25,400; room/board: $9,000
Financial aid: (270) 789-5013; 89% of undergrads determined to have financial need; average aid package $19,624

Centre College
Danville KY
(859) 238-5350
U.S. News ranking: Nat. Lib. Arts, No. 46
Website: www.centre.edu
Admissions email: admission@centre.edu
Private; founded 1819
Affiliation: Presbyterian
Freshman admissions: more selective; 2016-2017: 2,595 applied, 1,927 accepted. Either SAT or ACT required. ACT 25/75 percentile: 26-31. High school rank: 62% in top tenth, 88% in top quarter, 97% in top half
Early decision deadline: 11/15, notification date: 12/15
Early action deadline: 12/1, notification date: 1/15
Application deadline (fall): 1/15
Undergraduate student body: 1,428 full time, 2 part time; 49% male, 51% female; 0% American Indian, 5% Asian, 5% black, 4% Hispanic, 3% multiracial, 0% Pacific Islander, 76% white, 7% international; 57% from in state; 98% live on campus; 40% of students in fraternities, 43% in sororities
Most popular majors: 21% Economics, General, 9% Biology/Biological Sciences, General, 7% History, General, 6% Physiological Psychology/Psychobiology, 6% Political Science and Government, General

Expenses: 2017-2018: $40,500; room/board: $10,180
Financial aid: (859) 238-5365; 56% of undergrads determined to have financial need; average aid package $32,001

Eastern Kentucky University
Richmond KY
(800) 465-9191
U.S. News ranking: Reg. U. (S), No. 73
Website: www.eku.edu
Admissions email: admissions@eku.edu
Public; founded 1906
Freshman admissions: selective; 2016-2017: 8,086 applied, 6,983 accepted. Either SAT or ACT required. ACT 25/75 percentile: 19-25. High school rank: 18% in top tenth, 42% in top quarter, 72% in top half
Early decision deadline: N/A, notification date: N/A
Early action deadline: N/A, notification date: N/A
Application deadline (fall): 8/1
Undergraduate student body: 11,010 full time, 3,283 part time; 43% male, 57% female; 0% American Indian, 1% Asian, 6% black, 3% Hispanic, 3% multiracial, 0% Pacific Islander, 85% white, 1% international
Most popular majors: 10% Liberal Arts and Sciences, General Studies and Humanities, 8% Homeland Security, Law Enforcement, Firefighting and Related Protective Services, 7% Health Professions and Related Programs, 6% Psychology, 4% Engineering Technologies and Engineering-Related Fields
Expenses: 2017-2018: $9,296 in state, $19,074 out of state; room/board: $9,624
Financial aid: (859) 622-2361; 72% of undergrads determined to have financial need; average aid package $10,962

Georgetown College
Georgetown KY
(502) 863-8009
U.S. News ranking: Nat. Lib. Arts, No. 147
Website: www.georgetowncollege.edu
Admissions email: admissions@georgetowncollege.edu
Private; founded 1829
Freshman admissions: selective; 2016-2017: 2,486 applied, 1,403 accepted. Either SAT or ACT required. ACT 25/75 percentile: 20-26. High school rank: N/A
Early decision deadline: N/A, notification date: N/A
Early action deadline: N/A, notification date: N/A
Application deadline (fall): 8/15
Undergraduate student body: 917 full time, 112 part time; 45% male, 55% female; 0% American Indian, 1% Asian, 9% black, 2% Hispanic, 4% multiracial, 0% Pacific Islander, 79% white, 1% international

Most popular majors: 14% Communication and Media Studies, Other, 10% Kinesiology and Exercise Science, 8% Business/Commerce, General, 7% Biology/Biological Sciences, General, 5% Political Science and Government, General
Expenses: 2016-2017: $35,650; room/board: $9,050
Financial aid: N/A

Kentucky Christian University[1]
Grayson KY
(800) 522-3181
U.S. News ranking: Reg. Coll. (S), No. 48
Website: www.kcu.edu
Admissions email: knights@kcu.edu
Private; founded 1919
Application deadline (fall): 8/1
Undergraduate student body: N/A full time, N/A part time
Expenses: 2016-2017: $18,560; room/board: $8,000
Financial aid: (606) 474-3226

Kentucky State University
Frankfort KY
(800) 325-1716
U.S. News ranking: Reg. Coll. (S), No. 33
Website: www.kysu.edu
Admissions email: admissions@kysu.edu
Public; founded 1886
Freshman admissions: less selective; 2016-2017: 2,003 applied, 1,057 accepted. Either SAT or ACT required. ACT 25/75 percentile: 17-21. High school rank: 4% in top tenth, 26% in top quarter, 58% in top half
Early decision deadline: N/A, notification date: N/A
Early action deadline: N/A, notification date: N/A
Application deadline (fall): 7/31
Undergraduate student body: 1,049 full time, 519 part time; 39% male, 61% female; 1% American Indian, 1% Asian, 57% black, 2% Hispanic, 3% multiracial, 0% Pacific Islander, 29% white, 0% international; 68% from in state; 35% live on campus; 2% of students in fraternities, 4% in sororities
Most popular majors: 10% Criminal Justice/Police Science, 9% Liberal Arts and Sciences/Liberal Studies, 9% Psychology, General, 9% Registered Nursing/Registered Nurse, 8% Business Administration and Management, General
Expenses: 2017-2018: $8,184 in state, $19,638 out of state; room/board: $6,690
Financial aid: (502) 597-5759; 50% of undergrads determined to have financial need; average aid package $11,792

Kentucky Wesleyan College
Owensboro KY
(800) 999-0592
U.S. News ranking: Reg. Coll. (S), No. 8
Website: www.kwc.edu
Admissions email: admissions@kwc.edu
Private; founded 1858
Affiliation: United Methodist
Freshman admissions: selective; 2016-2017: 995 applied, 600 accepted. Either SAT or ACT required. ACT 25/75 percentile: 20-26. High school rank: N/A
Early decision deadline: N/A, notification date: N/A
Early action deadline: N/A, notification date: N/A
Application deadline (fall): rolling
Undergraduate student body: 663 full time, 122 part time; 49% male, 51% female; 0% American Indian, 1% Asian, 16% black, 1% Hispanic, 0% multiracial, 0% Pacific Islander, 73% white, 0% international
Most popular majors: Information not available
Expenses: 2017-2018: $25,070; room/board: $8,750
Financial aid: (270) 852-3130; 96% of undergrads determined to have financial need; average aid package $19,380

Lindsey Wilson College
Columbia KY
(270) 384-8100
U.S. News ranking: Reg. U. (S), second tier
Website: www.lindsey.edu
Admissions email: admissions@lindsey.edu
Private; founded 1903
Affiliation: United Methodist
Freshman admissions: selective; 2016-2017: 2,771 applied, 2,032 accepted. Neither SAT nor ACT required. ACT 25/75 percentile: 19-24. High school rank: 12% in top tenth, 36% in top quarter, 70% in top half
Early decision deadline: N/A, notification date: N/A
Early action deadline: N/A, notification date: N/A
Application deadline (fall): rolling
Undergraduate student body: 2,005 full time, 138 part time; 40% male, 60% female; 0% American Indian, 0% Asian, 9% black, 1% Hispanic, 2% multiracial, 0% Pacific Islander, 67% white, 0% international; 82% from in state; 48% live on campus; N/A of students in fraternities, N/A in sororities
Most popular majors: 49% Public Administration and Social Service Professions, 12% Business Administration and Management, General, 5% Criminal Justice/Safety Studies, 4% Registered Nursing/Registered Nurse, 4% Speech Communication and Rhetoric
Expenses: 2017-2018: $24,246; room/board: $9,300
Financial aid: (270) 384-8022; 94% of undergrads determined to have financial need; average aid package $19,723

Midway University
Midway KY
(800) 755-0031
U.S. News ranking: Reg. U. (S), No. 89
Website: www.midway.edu
Admissions email: admissions@midway.edu
Private; founded 1847
Affiliation: Christian Church (Disciples of Christ)
Freshman admissions: selective; 2016-2017: 499 applied, 301 accepted. Either SAT or ACT required. ACT 25/75 percentile: 18-23. High school rank: 18% in top tenth, 49% in top quarter, 95% in top half
Early decision deadline: N/A, notification date: N/A
Early action deadline: N/A, notification date: N/A
Application deadline (fall): rolling
Undergraduate student body: 749 full time, 256 part time; 20% male, 80% female; 0% American Indian, 1% Asian, 9% black, 4% Hispanic, 3% multiracial, 0% Pacific Islander, 77% white, 4% international
Most popular majors: 29% Business/Commerce, General, 14% Health/Health Care Administration/Management, 11% Psychology, General, 10% Registered Nursing/Registered Nurse, 8% Equestrian/Equine Studies
Expenses: 2016-2017: $23,350; room/board: $8,400
Financial aid: (859) 846-5304

Morehead State University
Morehead KY
(606) 783-2000
U.S. News ranking: Reg. U. (S), No. 61
Website: www.moreheadstate.edu
Admissions email: admissions@moreheadstate.edu
Public; founded 1887
Freshman admissions: selective; 2016-2017: 4,327 applied, 3,702 accepted. Either SAT or ACT required. ACT 25/75 percentile: 20-26. High school rank: 22% in top tenth, 51% in top quarter, 83% in top half
Early decision deadline: N/A, notification date: N/A
Early action deadline: N/A, notification date: N/A
Application deadline (fall): rolling
Undergraduate student body: 5,963 full time, 3,791 part time; 40% male, 60% female; 0% American Indian, 0% Asian, 4% black, 2% Hispanic, 2% multiracial, 0% Pacific Islander, 88% white, 3% international; 87% from in state; 41% live on campus; 6% of students in fraternities, 8% in sororities
Most popular majors: 10% General Studies, 8% Social Work, 5% Registered Nursing/Registered Nurse, 4% Agriculture, Agriculture Operations, and Related Sciences, 4% Special Education and Teaching, General
Expenses: 2017-2018: $8,950 in state, $13,746 out of state; room/board: $9,436

Financial aid: (606) 783-2011; 74% of undergrads determined to have financial need; average aid package $11,197

Murray State University
Murray KY
(270) 809-3741
U.S. News ranking: Reg. U. (S), No. 32
Website: www.murraystate.edu
Admissions email: msu.admissions@murraystate.edu
Public; founded 1922
Freshman admissions: selective; 2016-2017: 6,479 applied, 5,530 accepted. Either SAT or ACT required. ACT 25/75 percentile: 21-27. High school rank: 21% in top tenth, 48% in top quarter, 76% in top half
Early decision deadline: N/A, notification date: N/A
Early action deadline: N/A, notification date: N/A
Application deadline (fall): 8/15
Undergraduate student body: 6,980 full time, 1,906 part time; 42% male, 58% female; 0% American Indian, 1% Asian, 7% black, 2% Hispanic, 2% multiracial, 0% Pacific Islander, 81% white, 4% international; 68% from in state; 33% live on campus; 19% of students in fraternities, 19% in sororities
Most popular majors: 14% Health Professions and Related Programs, 12% Business, Management, Marketing, and Related Support Services, 10% Education, 9% Engineering Technologies and Engineering-Related Fields, 8% Liberal Arts and Sciences, General Studies and Humanities
Expenses: 2017-2018: $8,820 in state, $23,820 out of state; room/board: $8,906
Financial aid: (270) 809-2596; 65% of undergrads determined to have financial need; average aid package $11,517

Northern Kentucky University
Highland Heights KY
(859) 572-5220
U.S. News ranking: Reg. U. (S), No. 73
Website: www.nku.edu/
Admissions email: beanorse@nku.edu
Public; founded 1968
Freshman admissions: selective; 2016-2017: 6,059 applied, 5,519 accepted. Either SAT or ACT required. ACT 25/75 percentile: 20-26. High school rank: 11% in top tenth, 34% in top quarter, 67% in top half
Early decision deadline: N/A, notification date: N/A
Early action deadline: N/A, notification date: N/A
Application deadline (fall): 8/22
Undergraduate student body: 9,193 full time, 3,196 part time; 43% male, 57% female; 0% American Indian, 1% Asian, 7% black, 3% Hispanic, 2% multiracial, 0% Pacific Islander, 82% white, 3% international; 67% from in state; 15% live on campus; 9% of students in fraternities, 14% in sororities

Most popular majors: 8% Organizational Behavior Studies, 6% Registered Nursing/Registered Nurse, 4% Accounting, 4% Information Technology, 4% Social Work
Expenses: 2017-2018: $9,744 in state, $19,104 out of state; room/board: $7,960
Financial aid: (859) 572-5143; 65% of undergrads determined to have financial need; average aid package $10,368

Spalding University[1]

Louisville KY
(502) 585-7111
U.S. News ranking: Nat. U., second tier
Website: www.spalding.edu
Admissions email: admissions@spalding.edu
Private; founded 1814
Application deadline (fall): rolling
Undergraduate student body: N/A full time, N/A part time
Expenses: 2016-2017: $24,388; room/board: $7,900
Financial aid: N/A

Sullivan University[1]

Louisville KY
U.S. News ranking: Reg. U. (S), unranked
Website: www.sullivan.edu
Admissions email: admissions@sullivan.edu
Private
Application deadline (fall): N/A
Undergraduate student body: N/A full time, N/A part time
Expenses: 2016-2017: $19,740; room/board: $9,810
Financial aid: N/A

Thomas More College

Crestview Hills KY
(800) 825-4557
U.S. News ranking: Reg. U. (S), No. 80
Website: www.thomasmore.edu
Admissions email: admissions@thomasmore.edu
Private; founded 1921
Affiliation: Roman Catholic
Freshman admissions: selective; 2016-2017: 2,401 applied, 2,139 accepted. Either SAT or ACT required. ACT 25/75 percentile: 20-24. High school rank: N/A
Early decision deadline: N/A, notification date: N/A
Early action deadline: N/A, notification date: N/A
Application deadline (fall): rolling
Undergraduate student body: 1,369 full time, 452 part time; 47% male, 53% female; 0% American Indian, 1% Asian, 7% black, 3% Hispanic, 4% multiracial, 0% Pacific Islander, 78% white, 1% international; 53% from in state; 31% live on campus; 1% of students in fraternities, 1% in sororities
Most popular majors: 36% Business Administration and Management, General, 17% Registered Nursing/Registered Nurse, 8% Biology/Biological Sciences, General, 4% Criminal Justice/Safety Studies

Expenses: 2017-2018: $30,270; room/board: $8,300
Financial aid: (859) 344-3506; 77% of undergrads determined to have financial need; average aid package $20,739

Transylvania University

Lexington KY
(859) 233-8242
U.S. News ranking: Nat. Lib. Arts, No. 87
Website: www.transy.edu
Admissions email: admissions@transy.edu
Private; founded 1780
Affiliation: Christian Church (Disciples of Christ)
Freshman admissions: more selective; 2016-2017: 1,216 applied, 1,153 accepted. Neither SAT nor ACT required. ACT 25/75 percentile: 25-30. High school rank: 36% in top tenth, 64% in top quarter, 92% in top half
Early decision deadline: N/A, notification date: N/A
Early action deadline: 12/1, notification date: 1/15
Application deadline (fall): rolling
Undergraduate student body: 953 full time, 10 part time; 42% male, 58% female; 0% American Indian, 1% Asian, 4% black, 6% Hispanic, 3% multiracial, 0% Pacific Islander, 79% white, 4% international; 74% from in state; 65% live on campus; 50% of students in fraternities, 54% in sororities
Most popular majors: 11% Business/Commerce, General, 10% Biology/Biological Sciences, General, 7% Psychology, General, 6% Spanish Language and Literature, 5% Kinesiology and Exercise Science
Expenses: 2017-2018: $37,290; room/board: $10,160
Financial aid: (859) 233-8239; 66% of undergrads determined to have financial need; average aid package $28,085

Union College[1]

Barbourville KY
U.S. News ranking: Reg. U. (S), second tier
Website: www.unionky.edu
Admissions email: enroll@unionky.edu
Private
Application deadline (fall): N/A
Undergraduate student body: N/A full time, N/A part time
Expenses: 2016-2017: $25,060; room/board: $7,325
Financial aid: (606) 546-1223

University of Kentucky

Lexington KY
(859) 257-2000
U.S. News ranking: Nat. U., No. 133
Website: www.uky.edu
Admissions email: admissions@uky.edu
Public; founded 1865
Freshman admissions: more selective; 2016-2017: 20,480 applied, 18,593 accepted. Either

SAT or ACT required. ACT 25/75 percentile: 22-28. High school rank: 30% in top tenth, 57% in top quarter, 86% in top half
Early decision deadline: N/A, notification date: N/A
Early action deadline: 12/1, notification date: N/A
Application deadline (fall): 2/15
Undergraduate student body: 20,833 full time, 1,788 part time; 46% male, 54% female; 0% American Indian, 3% Asian, 8% black, 4% Hispanic, 4% multiracial, 0% Pacific Islander, 76% white, 3% international; 69% from in state; N/A live on campus; 18% of students in fraternities, 30% in sororities
Most popular majors: 5% Education, 4% Biological and Biomedical Sciences, 4% Business, Management, Marketing, and Related Support Services, 4% Health Professions and Related Programs
Expenses: 2017-2018: $11,922 in state, $28,046 out of state; room/board: $12,858
Financial aid: (859) 257-3172; 52% of undergrads determined to have financial need; average aid package $12,245

University of Louisville

Louisville KY
(502) 852-6531
U.S. News ranking: Nat. U., No. 165
Website: www.louisville.edu
Admissions email: admitme@louisville.edu
Public; founded 1798
Freshman admissions: selective; 2016-2017: 10,165 applied, 7,377 accepted. Either SAT or ACT required. ACT 25/75 percentile: 22-29. High school rank: 29% in top tenth, 56% in top quarter, 84% in top half
Early decision deadline: N/A, notification date: N/A
Early action deadline: N/A, notification date: N/A
Application deadline (fall): 8/21
Undergraduate student body: 12,434 full time, 3,393 part time; 49% male, 51% female; 0% American Indian, 4% Asian, 11% black, 4% Hispanic, 5% multiracial, 0% Pacific Islander, 75% white, 1% international; 82% from in state; 32% live on campus; 21% of students in fraternities, 19% in sororities
Most popular majors: 14% Business, Management, Marketing, and Related Support Services, 11% Engineering, 10% Health Professions and Related Programs, 10% Parks, Recreation, Leisure, and Fitness Studies, 8% Education
Expenses: 2017-2018: $11,264 in state, $26,286 out of state; room/board: $8,700
Financial aid: (502) 852-5511; 60% of undergrads determined to have financial need; average aid package $11,864

University of Pikeville

Pikeville KY
(606) 218-5251
U.S. News ranking: Nat. Lib. Arts, second tier
Website: www.upike.edu/
Admissions email: wewantyou@upike.edu
Private; founded 1889
Affiliation: Presbyterian Church (USA)
Freshman admissions: less selective; 2016-2017: 2,437 applied, 2,437 accepted. Either SAT or ACT required. ACT 25/75 percentile: 17-22. High school rank: 10% in top tenth, 27% in top quarter, 61% in top half
Early decision deadline: N/A, notification date: N/A
Early action deadline: N/A, notification date: N/A
Application deadline (fall): rolling
Undergraduate student body: 1,129 full time, 529 part time; 47% male, 53% female; 0% American Indian, 1% Asian, 10% black, 2% Hispanic, 0% multiracial, 0% Pacific Islander, 85% white, 2% international; 80% from in state; 53% live on campus; 3% of students in fraternities, 3% in sororities
Most popular majors: 17% Business, Management, Marketing, and Related Support Services, 16% Biological and Biomedical Sciences, 11% Psychology, 10% Communication, Journalism, and Related Programs, 8% Public Administration and Social Service Professions
Expenses: 2017-2018: $20,350; room/board: $7,500
Financial aid: (606) 218-5254; 93% of undergrads determined to have financial need; average aid package $18,612

University of the Cumberlands

Williamsburg KY
(800) 343-1609
U.S. News ranking: Nat. U., second tier
Website: www.ucumberlands.edu
Admissions email: admiss@ucumberlands.edu
Private; founded 1888
Affiliation: Baptist
Freshman admissions: selective; 2016-2017: 2,326 applied, 1,656 accepted. Either SAT or ACT required. ACT 25/75 percentile: 19-25. High school rank: 14% in top tenth, 42% in top quarter, 71% in top half
Early decision deadline: N/A, notification date: N/A
Early action deadline: N/A, notification date: N/A
Application deadline (fall): 8/31
Undergraduate student body: 1,780 full time, 1,302 part time; 44% male, 56% female; 0% American Indian, 0% Asian, 5% black, 2% Hispanic, 2% multiracial, 0% Pacific Islander, 77% white, 4% international; 68% from in state; 75% live on campus; N/A of students in fraternities, N/A in sororities
Most popular majors: 21% Business/Commerce, General, 15% Psychology, General, 11% Criminal Justice/Safety Studies,

10% Public Administration and Social Service Professions, 7% Biology/Biological Sciences, General
Expenses: 2016-2017: $23,000; room/board: $9,000
Financial aid: (606) 539-4239

Western Kentucky University

Bowling Green KY
(270) 745-2551
U.S. News ranking: Reg. U. (S), No. 32
Website: www.wku.edu
Admissions email: admission@wku.edu
Public; founded 1906
Freshman admissions: selective; 2016-2017: 9,693 applied, 9,113 accepted. Either SAT or ACT required. ACT 25/75 percentile: 19-26. High school rank: 22% in top tenth, 44% in top quarter, 72% in top half
Early decision deadline: N/A, notification date: N/A
Early action deadline: N/A, notification date: N/A
Application deadline (fall): 8/1
Undergraduate student body: 13,160 full time, 4,435 part time; 42% male, 58% female; 0% American Indian, 1% Asian, 10% black, 3% Hispanic, 3% multiracial, 0% Pacific Islander, 77% white, 5% international; 80% from in state; 33% live on campus; 15% of students in fraternities, 17% in sororities
Most popular majors: 10% General Studies, 8% Registered Nursing/Registered Nurse, 4% Biology/Biological Sciences, General, 4% Business Administration and Management, General, 4% Elementary Education and Teaching
Expenses: 2017-2018: $10,202 in state, $25,512 out of state; room/board: $8,104
Financial aid: (270) 745-2755; 62% of undergrads determined to have financial need; average aid package $14,282

LOUISIANA

Centenary College of Louisiana

Shreveport LA
(800) 234-4448
U.S. News ranking: Nat. Lib. Arts, No. 147
Website: www.centenary.edu
Admissions email: admission@centenary.edu
Private; founded 1825
Affiliation: United Methodist
Freshman admissions: more selective; 2016-2017: 886 applied, 569 accepted. Either SAT or ACT required. ACT 25/75 percentile: 22-28. High school rank: 25% in top tenth, 52% in top quarter, 86% in top half
Early decision deadline: N/A, notification date: N/A
Early action deadline: 12/15, notification date: 1/15
Application deadline (fall): rolling

Undergraduate student body:
472 full time, 9 part time; 43% male, 57% female; 1% American Indian, 3% Asian, 16% black, 7% Hispanic, 6% multiracial, 0% Pacific Islander, 65% white, 1% international; 55% from in state; 89% live on campus; N/A of students in fraternities, N/A in sororities
Most popular majors: 22% Biology/Biological Sciences, General, 16% Business Administration and Management, General, 9% Communication and Media Studies, 9% Psychology, General, 6% Music, General
Expenses: 2017-2018: $35,900; room/board: $13,150
Financial aid: (318) 869-5137; 79% of undergrads determined to have financial need; average aid package $27,996

Dillard University
New Orleans LA
(800) 216 6637
U.S. News ranking: Nat. Lib. Arts, second tier
Website: www.dillard.edu
Admissions email: admissions@dillard.edu
Private; founded 1869
Affiliation: United Methodist
Freshman admissions: selective; 2016-2017: 5,995 applied, 2,285 accepted. Either SAT or ACT required. ACT 25/75 percentile: 18-22. High school rank: 14% in top tenth, 32% in top quarter, 63% in top half
Early decision deadline: N/A, notification date: N/A
Early action deadline: N/A, notification date: N/A
Application deadline (fall): 8/1
Undergraduate student body: 1,179 full time, 82 part time; 27% male, 73% female; 0% American Indian, 0% Asian, 89% black, 0% Hispanic, 0% multiracial, 0% Pacific Islander, 1% white, 2% international
Most popular majors: 18% Public Health, General, 17% Registered Nursing/Registered Nurse, 9% Biology/Biological Sciences, General, 9% Business Administration and Management, General, 7% Sociology
Expenses: 2017-2018: $18,711; room/board: $9,985
Financial aid: (504) 816-4864; 96% of undergrads determined to have financial need; average aid package $17,150

Grambling State University
Grambling LA
(318) 274-6183
U.S. News ranking: Reg. U. (S), second tier
Website: www.gram.edu/
Admissions email: admissions@gram.edu
Public; founded 1901
Freshman admissions: less selective; 2016-2017: 6,340 applied, 2,862 accepted. Either SAT or ACT required. ACT 25/75 percentile: 16-20. High school rank: 6% in top tenth, 23% in top quarter, 57% in top half
Early decision deadline: N/A, notification date: N/A

Early action deadline: N/A, notification date: N/A
Application deadline (fall): 8/15
Undergraduate student body: 3,598 full time, 285 part time; 43% male, 57% female; 0% American Indian, 0% Asian, 91% black, 1% Hispanic, 2% multiracial, 0% Pacific Islander, 1% white, 5% international; 70% from in state; 33% live on campus; N/A of students in fraternities, N/A in sororities
Most popular majors: 24% Criminal Justice/Safety Studies, 11% Social Work, 7% Registered Nursing/Registered Nurse, 5% Biology/Biological Sciences, General, 5% Mass Communication/Media Studies
Expenses: 2017-2018: $7,443 in state, $16,466 out of state; room/board: $9,934
Financial aid: (318) 274-6328; 93% of undergrads determined to have financial need; average aid package $3,731

Louisiana College
Pineville LA
(318) 487-7259
U.S. News ranking: Reg. U. (S), No. 106
Website: www.lacollege.edu
Admissions email: admissions@lacollege.edu
Private; founded 1906
Affiliation: Southern Baptist
Freshman admissions: selective; 2016-2017: 755 applied, 545 accepted. Either SAT or ACT required. ACT 25/75 percentile: 18-23. High school rank: 13% in top tenth, 27% in top quarter, 65% in top half
Early decision deadline: N/A, notification date: N/A
Early action deadline: N/A, notification date: N/A
Application deadline (fall): rolling
Undergraduate student body: 830 full time, 79 part time; 54% male, 46% female; 1% American Indian, 1% Asian, 29% black, 2% Hispanic, 1% multiracial, 0% Pacific Islander, 62% white, 3% international; 90% from in state; N/A live on campus; N/A of students in fraternities, N/A in sororities
Most popular majors: 33% Health Professions and Related Programs, 10% Parks, Recreation, Leisure, and Fitness Studies, 8% Education, 7% Multi/Interdisciplinary Studies, 6% Homeland Security, Law Enforcement, Firefighting and Related Protective Services
Expenses: 2017-2018: $16,000; room/board: $5,274
Financial aid: (318) 487-7387; 80% of undergrads determined to have financial need; average aid package $11,801

Louisiana State University–Alexandria
Alexandria LA
(318) 473-6417
U.S. News ranking: Nat. Lib. Arts, second tier
Website: www.lsua.edu
Admissions email: admissions@lsua.edu
Public; founded 1960

Freshman admissions: selective; 2016-2017: 2,101 applied, 655 accepted. Either SAT or ACT required. ACT 25/75 percentile: 18-23. High school rank: 11% in top tenth, 33% in top quarter, 71% in top half
Early decision deadline: N/A, notification date: N/A
Early action deadline: N/A, notification date: N/A
Application deadline (fall): 8/1
Undergraduate student body: 1,850 full time, 1,427 part time; 33% male, 67% female; 5% American Indian, 1% Asian, 19% black, 3% Hispanic, 3% multiracial, 0% Pacific Islander, 65% white, 4% international; 97% from in state; 9% live on campus; 0% of students in fraternities, 0% in sororities
Most popular majors: 23% Liberal Arts and Sciences, General Studies and Humanities, 19% Business, Management, Marketing, and Related Support Services, 8% Health Professions and Related Programs, 8% Psychology, 7% History
Expenses: 2016-2017: $6,668 in state, $15,708 out of state; room/board: $7,950
Financial aid: (318) 473-6477; 61% of undergrads determined to have financial need; average aid package $5,647

Louisiana State University–Baton Rouge
Baton Rouge LA
(225) 578-1175
U.S. News ranking: Nat. U., No. 133
Website: www.lsu.edu
Admissions email: admissions@lsu.edu
Public; founded 1860
Freshman admissions: more selective; 2016-2017: 18,122 applied, 13,843 accepted. Either SAT or ACT required. ACT 25/75 percentile: 23-28. High school rank: 25% in top tenth, 51% in top quarter, 81% in top half
Early decision deadline: N/A, notification date: N/A
Early action deadline: N/A, notification date: N/A
Application deadline (fall): 4/15
Undergraduate student body: 23,212 full time, 2,906 part time; 48% male, 52% female; 0% American Indian, 4% Asian, 12% black, 6% Hispanic, 2% multiracial, 0% Pacific Islander, 72% white, 2% international; 83% from in state; 24% live on campus; 16% of students in fraternities, 28% in sororities
Most popular majors: 22% Business, Management, Marketing, and Related Support Services, 13% Engineering, 10% Education, 7% Biological and Biomedical Sciences, 6% Communication, Journalism, and Related Programs
Expenses: 2017-2018: $11,374 in state, $28,051 out of state; room/board: $11,750
Financial aid: (225) 578-3103; 46% of undergrads determined to have financial need; average aid package $16,020

Louisiana State University–Shreveport
Shreveport LA
(318) 797-5061
U.S. News ranking: Reg. U. (S), second tier
Website: www.lsus.edu
Admissions email: admissions@pilot.lsus.edu
Public; founded 1967
Freshman admissions: less selective; 2016-2017: 691 applied, 612 accepted. Either SAT or ACT required. SAT 25/75 percentile: N/A. High school rank: N/A
Early decision deadline: N/A, notification date: N/A
Early action deadline: N/A, notification date: N/A
Application deadline (fall): rolling
Undergraduate student body: 1,677 full time, 934 part time; 40% male, 60% female; 0% American Indian, 2% Asian, 23% black, 4% Hispanic, 4% multiracial, 0% Pacific Islander, 56% white, 2% international; 95% from in state; 0% live on campus; 1% of students in fraternities, 1% in sororities
Most popular majors: 21% Business, Management, Marketing, and Related Support Services, 12% Liberal Arts and Sciences, General Studies and Humanities, 10% Psychology, 9% Education, 8% Biological and Biomedical Sciences
Expenses: 2016-2017: $7,146 in state, $20,300 out of state; room/board: N/A
Financial aid: N/A

Louisiana Tech University
Ruston LA
(318) 257-3036
U.S. News ranking: Nat. U., No. 216
Website: www.latech.edu
Admissions email: bulldog@latech.edu
Public; founded 1894
Freshman admissions: more selective; 2016-2017: 7,227 applied, 4,567 accepted. Either SAT or ACT required. ACT 25/75 percentile: 21-27. High school rank: 25% in top tenth, 50% in top quarter, 81% in top half
Early decision deadline: N/A, notification date: N/A
Early action deadline: N/A, notification date: N/A
Application deadline (fall): rolling
Undergraduate student body: 7,850 full time, 3,431 part time; 52% male, 48% female; 0% American Indian, 1% Asian, 14% black, 4% Hispanic, 3% multiracial, 0% Pacific Islander, 69% white, 2% international; 89% from in state; 8% live on campus; 14% of students in fraternities, 9% in sororities
Most popular majors: 18% Business, Management, Marketing, and Related Support Services, 13% Engineering, 6% Education, 6% Health Professions and Related Programs, 5% Biological and Biomedical Sciences

Expenses: 2017-2018: $9,525 in state, $18,438 out of state; room/board: $7,890
Financial aid: (318) 257-2641; 59% of undergrads determined to have financial need; average aid package $11,308

Loyola University New Orleans
New Orleans LA
(800) 456-9652
U.S. News ranking: Reg. U. (S), No. 10
Website: www.loyno.edu
Admissions email: admit@loyno.edu
Private; founded 1912
Affiliation: Roman Catholic
Freshman admissions: more selective; 2016-2017: 5,160 applied, 3,496 accepted. Either SAT or ACT required. ACT 25/75 percentile: 23-29. High school rank: 27% in top tenth, 55% in top quarter, 85% in top half
Early decision deadline: N/A, notification date: N/A
Early action deadline: N/A, notification date: N/A
Application deadline (fall): rolling
Undergraduate student body: 2,338 full time, 145 part time; 39% male, 61% female; 0% American Indian, 3% Asian, 16% black, 17% Hispanic, 5% multiracial, 0% Pacific Islander, 52% white, 2% international; 43% from in state; 49% live on campus; 11% of students in fraternities, 20% in sororities
Most popular majors: 12% Music Management, 9% Psychology, General, 8% Speech Communication and Rhetoric, 6% Criminology, 5% Business Administration and Management, General
Expenses: 2017-2018: $39,242; room/board: $13,214
Financial aid: (504) 865-3231; 72% of undergrads determined to have financial need; average aid package $32,315

McNeese State University
Lake Charles LA
(337) 475-5504
U.S. News ranking: Reg. U. (S), No. 104
Website: www.mcneese.edu
Admissions email: admissions@mcneese.edu
Public; founded 1939
Freshman admissions: selective; 2016-2017: 3,160 applied, 2,044 accepted. Either SAT or ACT required. ACT 25/75 percentile: 20-24. High school rank: 18% in top tenth, 44% in top quarter, 77% in top half
Early decision deadline: N/A, notification date: N/A
Early action deadline: N/A, notification date: N/A
Application deadline (fall): 8/14
Undergraduate student body: 5,468 full time, 1,493 part time; 40% male, 60% female; 0% American Indian, 2% Asian, 18% black, 3% Hispanic, 3% multiracial, 0% Pacific Islander, 67% white, 7% international; 91% from in state; 12% live on campus; N/A of students in fraternities, N/A in sororities

Most popular majors: 13% Registered Nursing/Registered Nurse, 10% General Studies, 8% Engineering, General, 5% Accounting, 5% Psychology, General
Expenses: 2016-2017: $7,290 in state, $18,366 out of state; room/board: $8,014
Financial aid: (337) 475-5065

Nicholls State University
Thibodaux LA
(985) 448-4507
U.S. News ranking: Reg. U. (S), No. 95
Website: www.nicholls.edu
Admissions email: nicholls@nicholls.edu
Public; founded 1948
Freshman admissions: selective; 2016-2017: 2,734 applied, 2,260 accepted. Either SAT or ACT required. ACT 25/75 percentile: 20-24. High school rank: 16% in top tenth, 40% in top quarter, 74% in top half
Early decision deadline: N/A, notification date: N/A
Early action deadline: N/A, notification date: N/A
Application deadline (fall): rolling
Undergraduate student body: 4,605 full time, 1,042 part time; 36% male, 64% female; 2% American Indian, 1% Asian, 21% black, 4% Hispanic, 3% multiracial, 0% Pacific Islander, 67% white, 1% international; 95% from in state; 24% live on campus; 12% of students in fraternities, 15% in sororities
Most popular majors: 26% Business, Management, Marketing, and Related Support Services, 19% Health Professions and Related Programs, 14% Multi/Interdisciplinary Studies, 8% Education, 6% Psychology
Expenses: 2017-2018: $7,276 in state, $20,562 out of state; room/board: $7,200
Financial aid: (985) 448-4047; 65% of undergrads determined to have financial need; average aid package $10,110

Northwestern State University of Louisiana
Natchitoches LA
(800) 426-3754
U.S. News ranking: Reg. U. (S), second tier
Website: www.nsula.edu
Admissions email: admissions@nsula.edu
Public; founded 1884
Freshman admissions: selective; 2016-2017: 5,535 applied, 3,235 accepted. Either SAT or ACT required. ACT 25/75 percentile: 19-24. High school rank: 16% in top tenth, 42% in top quarter, 77% in top half
Early decision deadline: N/A, notification date: N/A
Early action deadline: N/A, notification date: N/A
Application deadline (fall): 8/1

Undergraduate student body: 5,224 full time, 3,476 part time; 31% male, 69% female; 2% American Indian, 1% Asian, 32% black, 6% Hispanic, 4% multiracial, 0% Pacific Islander, 53% white, 2% international; 87% from in state; 15% live on campus; N/A of students in fraternities, N/A in sororities
Most popular majors: 27% Health Professions and Related Programs, 11% Liberal Arts and Sciences, General Studies and Humanities, 10% Business, Management, Marketing, and Related Support Services, 8% Biological and Biomedical Sciences, 8% Psychology
Expenses: 2017-2018: $7,620 in state, $18,408 out of state; room/board: $8,684
Financial aid: N/A; 73% of undergrads determined to have financial need; average aid package $13,863

Southeastern Louisiana University
Hammond LA
(985) 549-5637
U.S. News ranking: Reg. U. (S), second tier
Website: www.southeastern.edu
Admissions email: admissions@southeastern.edu
Public; founded 1925
Freshman admissions: selective; 2016-2017: 4,226 applied, 3,722 accepted. Either SAT or ACT required. ACT 25/75 percentile: 20-24. High school rank: 14% in top tenth, 38% in top quarter, 71% in top half
Early decision deadline: N/A, notification date: N/A
Early action deadline: N/A, notification date: N/A
Application deadline (fall): 8/1
Undergraduate student body: 9,020 full time, 4,539 part time; 38% male, 62% female; 0% American Indian, 1% Asian, 20% black, 8% Hispanic, 6% multiracial, 0% Pacific Islander, 63% white, 2% international; 95% from in state; 21% live on campus; 6% of students in fraternities, 7% in sororities
Most popular majors: 20% Business, Management, Marketing, and Related Support Services, 14% Education, 13% Health Professions and Related Programs, 12% Liberal Arts and Sciences, General Studies and Humanities, 5% Engineering Technologies and Engineering-Related Fields
Expenses: 2016-2017: $7,773 in state, $20,251 out of state; room/board: $7,510
Financial aid: (985) 549-2030; 62% of undergrads determined to have financial need; average aid package $9,479

Southern University and A&M College
Baton Rouge LA
(225) 771-2430
U.S. News ranking: Reg. U. (S), second tier
Website: www.subr.edu/
Admissions email: admit@subr.edu
Public; founded 1880

Freshman admissions: less selective; 2016-2017: 3,781 applied, 1,235 accepted. Either SAT or ACT required. ACT 25/75 percentile: 16-20. High school rank: 2% in top tenth, 7% in top quarter, 34% in top half
Early decision deadline: N/A, notification date: N/A
Early action deadline: N/A, notification date: N/A
Application deadline (fall): 7/1
Undergraduate student body: 4,582 full time, 765 part time; 35% male, 65% female; 0% American Indian, 0% Asian, 93% black, 1% Hispanic, 2% multiracial, 0% Pacific Islander, 3% white, 1% international
Most popular majors: 21% Health Professions and Related Programs, 13% Business, Management, Marketing, and Related Support Services, 11% Homeland Security, Law Enforcement, Firefighting and Related Protective Services, 7% Psychology, 6% Engineering
Expenses: 2016-2017: $9,332 in state, $19,332 out of state; room/board: $8,370
Financial aid: N/A

Southern University–New Orleans
New Orleans LA
(504) 286-5314
U.S. News ranking: Reg. U. (S), second tier
Website: www.suno.edu
Public; founded 1956
Freshman admissions: less selective; 2016-2017: 1,903 applied, 220 accepted. Either SAT or ACT required. ACT 25/75 percentile: 16-19. High school rank: 3% in top tenth, 14% in top quarter, 40% in top half
Early decision deadline: N/A, notification date: N/A
Early action deadline: N/A, notification date: N/A
Application deadline (fall): N/A
Undergraduate student body: 1,371 full time, 610 part time; 27% male, 73% female; N/A American Indian, N/A Asian, N/A black, N/A Hispanic, N/A multiracial, N/A Pacific Islander, N/A white, N/A international
Most popular majors: Information not available
Expenses: 2016-2017: $6,421 in state, $15,322 out of state; room/board: $8,780
Financial aid: (504) 286-5263

Tulane University
New Orleans LA
(504) 865-5731
U.S. News ranking: Nat. U., No. 40
Website: www.tulane.edu
Admissions email: undergrad.admission@tulane.edu
Private; founded 1834
Freshman admissions: most selective; 2016-2017: 32,006 applied, 8,162 accepted. Either SAT or ACT required. ACT 25/75 percentile: 29-33. High school rank: 61% in top tenth, 87% in top quarter, 96% in top half
Early decision deadline: N/A, notification date: N/A
Early action deadline: 11/15, notification date: 11/15

Application deadline (fall): 1/15
Undergraduate student body: 6,349 full time, 28 part time; 42% male, 58% female; 0% American Indian, 4% Asian, 4% black, 6% Hispanic, 4% multiracial, 0% Pacific Islander, 76% white, 3% international; 24% from in state; 47% live on campus; 30% of students in fraternities, 50% in sororities
Most popular majors: 24% Business, Management, Marketing, and Related Support Services, 15% Social Sciences, 11% Biological and Biomedical Sciences, 9% Health Professions and Related Programs, 6% Communication, Journalism, and Related Programs
Expenses: 2017-2018: $52,960; room/board: $14,536
Financial aid: (504) 865-5723; 32% of undergrads determined to have financial need; average aid package $45,124

University of Holy Cross[1]
New Orleans LA
(504) 398-2175
U.S. News ranking: Reg. Coll. (S), No. 55
Website: www.olhcc.edu
Admissions email: admissions@olhcc.edu
Private
Application deadline (fall): N/A
Undergraduate student body: N/A full time, N/A part time
Expenses: 2016-2017: $11,632; room/board: N/A
Financial aid: (504) 398-2143

University of Louisiana–Lafayette
Lafayette LA
(337) 482-6553
U.S. News ranking: Nat. U., second tier
Website: www.louisiana.edu
Admissions email: enroll@louisiana.edu
Public; founded 1898
Freshman admissions: more selective; 2016-2017: 11,450 applied, 5,945 accepted. Either SAT or ACT required. ACT 25/75 percentile: 21-26. High school rank: 21% in top tenth, 47% in top quarter, 76% in top half
Early decision deadline: N/A, notification date: N/A
Early action deadline: N/A, notification date: N/A
Application deadline (fall): rolling
Undergraduate student body: 12,875 full time, 3,123 part time; 43% male, 57% female; 0% American Indian, 2% Asian, 20% black, 5% Hispanic, 1% multiracial, 0% Pacific Islander, 63% white, 2% international; 61% from in state; 19% live on campus; 9% of students in fraternities, 12% in sororities
Most popular majors: 22% Health Professions and Related Programs, 14% Business, Management, Marketing, and Related Support Services, 13% Education, 9% Engineering, 9% Liberal Arts and Sciences, General Studies and Humanities

Expenses: 2016-2017: $9,346 in state, $23,074 out of state; room/board: $9,998
Financial aid: (337) 482-6506; 62% of undergrads determined to have financial need; average aid package $9,503

University of Louisiana–Monroe
Monroe LA
(318) 342-7777
U.S. News ranking: Nat. U., second tier
Website: www.ulm.edu
Admissions email: admissions@ulm.edu
Public; founded 1931
Freshman admissions: selective; 2016-2017: 3,965 applied, 3,428 accepted. Either SAT or ACT required. ACT 25/75 percentile: 19-25. High school rank: 25% in top tenth, 53% in top quarter, 87% in top half
Early decision deadline: N/A, notification date: N/A
Early action deadline: N/A, notification date: N/A
Application deadline (fall): rolling
Undergraduate student body: 5,208 full time, 2,570 part time; 37% male, 63% female; 0% American Indian, 2% Asian, 25% black, 2% Hispanic, 2% multiracial, 0% Pacific Islander, 62% white, 4% international; 83% from in state; 31% live on campus; N/A of students in fraternities, N/A in sororities
Most popular majors: 7% Business Administration and Management, General, 7% General Studies, 7% Pharmacy, 6% Kinesiology and Exercise Science, 6% Pharmacy, Pharmaceutical Sciences, and Administration, Other
Expenses: 2016-2017: $8,281 in state, $20,381 out of state; room/board: $6,963
Financial aid: (318) 342-5329; 58% of undergrads determined to have financial need; average aid package $10,823

University of New Orleans
New Orleans LA
(504) 280-6595
U.S. News ranking: Nat. U., second tier
Website: www.uno.edu
Admissions email: admissions@uno.edu
Public; founded 1958
Freshman admissions: selective; 2016-2017: 3,409 applied, 2,047 accepted. Either SAT or ACT required. ACT 25/75 percentile: 20-24. High school rank: 12% in top tenth, 35% in top quarter, 67% in top half
Early decision deadline: N/A, notification date: N/A
Early action deadline: N/A, notification date: N/A
Application deadline (fall): 8/10
Undergraduate student body: 4,684 full time, 1,758 part time; 49% male, 51% female; 0% American Indian, 8% Asian, 16% black, 12% Hispanic, 4% multiracial, 0% Pacific Islander, 53% white, 4% international; 95% from in state; 9% live on campus; 2% of students in fraternities, 3% in sororities

Most popular majors: 29% Business, Management, Marketing, and Related Support Services, 12% Engineering, 10% Visual and Performing Arts, 9% Multi/Interdisciplinary Studies, 9% Psychology
Expenses: 2017-2018: $8,694 in state, $13,530 out of state; room/board: $10,575
Financial aid: (504) 280-6501; 74% of undergrads determined to have financial need; average aid package $10,007

Xavier University of Louisiana
New Orleans LA
(504) 520-7388
U.S. News ranking: Reg. U. (S), No. 25
Website: www.xula.edu
Admissions email: apply@xula.edu
Private; founded 1915
Affiliation: Roman Catholic
Freshman admissions: selective; 2016-2017: 6,640 applied, 4,084 accepted. Either SAT or ACT required. ACT 25/75 percentile: 20-26. High school rank: 32% in top tenth, 58% in top quarter, 80% in top half
Early decision deadline: N/A, notification date: N/A
Early action deadline: N/A, notification date: N/A
Application deadline (fall): 7/1
Undergraduate student body: 2,201 full time, 126 part time; 27% male, 73% female; 0% American Indian, 9% Asian, 78% black, 3% Hispanic, 3% multiracial, 0% Pacific Islander, 3% white, 2% international; 56% from in state; 48% live on campus; 1% of students in fraternities, 2% in sororities
Most popular majors: 37% Biology, General, 14% Chemistry, General, 6% Business/Commerce, General, 6% Communication and Media Studies
Expenses: 2017-2018: $23,606; room/board: $8,784
Financial aid: (504) 520-7835; 75% of undergrads determined to have financial need; average aid package $19,478

MAINE

Bates College
Lewiston ME
(855) 228-3755
U.S. News ranking: Nat. Lib. Arts, No. 23
Website: www.bates.edu
Admissions email: admission@bates.edu
Private; founded 1855
Freshman admissions: more selective; 2016-2017: 5,356 applied, 1,213 accepted. Neither SAT nor ACT required. SAT 25/75 percentile: 1150-1390. High school rank: 61% in top tenth, 88% in top quarter, 98% in top half
Early decision deadline: 11/15, notification date: 12/20
Early action deadline: N/A, notification date: N/A
Application deadline (fall): 1/1

Undergraduate student body: 1,780 full time, 0 part time; 49% male, 51% female; 0% American Indian, 4% Asian, 6% black, 9% Hispanic, 4% multiracial, 0% Pacific Islander, 70% white, 7% international
Most popular majors: 27% Social Sciences, 13% Biological and Biomedical Sciences, 9% Psychology, 7% English Language and Literature/Letters, 6% Mathematics and Statistics
Expenses: 2017-2018: $52,042; room/board: $14,678
Financial aid: (207) 786-6096; 43% of undergrads determined to have financial need; average aid package $45,494

Bowdoin College
Brunswick ME
(207) 725-3100
U.S. News ranking: Nat. Lib. Arts, No. 3
Website: www.bowdoin.edu
Admissions email: admissions@bowdoin.edu
Private; founded 1794
Affiliation: Other
Freshman admissions: most selective; 2016-2017: 6,799 applied, 1,009 accepted. Neither SAT nor ACT required. SAT 25/75 percentile: 1290-1510. High school rank: 80% in top tenth, 97% in top quarter, 100% in top half
Early decision deadline: 11/15, notification date: 12/15
Early action deadline: N/A, notification date: N/A
Application deadline (fall): 1/1
Undergraduate student body: 1,801 full time, 5 part time; 50% male, 50% female; 0% American Indian, 6% Asian, 6% black, 11% Hispanic, 7% multiracial, 0% Pacific Islander, 64% white, 5% international; 10% from in state; 88% live on campus; N/A of students in fraternities, N/A in sororities
Most popular majors: 19% Political Science and Government, General, 13% Economics, General, 8% Biology/Biological Sciences, General, 8% Mathematics, General, 7% English Language and Literature, General
Expenses: 2017-2018: $51,848; room/board: $14,132
Financial aid: (207) 725-3146; 45% of undergrads determined to have financial need; average aid package $44,088

Colby College
Waterville ME
(800) 723-3032
U.S. News ranking: Nat. Lib. Arts, No. 12
Website: www.colby.edu
Admissions email: admissions@colby.edu
Private; founded 1813
Freshman admissions: most selective; 2016-2017: 9,833 applied, 1,840 accepted. Neither SAT nor ACT required. SAT 25/75 percentile: 1260-1460. High school rank: 76% in top tenth, 93% in top quarter, 99% in top half

Early decision deadline: 11/15, notification date: 12/15
Early action deadline: N/A, notification date: N/A
Application deadline (fall): 1/1
Undergraduate student body: 1,879 full time, 0 part time; 48% male, 52% female; 0% American Indian, 6% Asian, 4% black, 7% Hispanic, 5% multiracial, 0% Pacific Islander, 62% white, 11% international; 12% from in state; 95% live on campus; 0% of students in fraternities, 0% in sororities
Most popular majors: 24% Social Sciences, 12% Biological and Biomedical Sciences, 8% Natural Resources and Conservation, 7% Multi/Interdisciplinary Studies, 7% Psychology
Expenses: 2017-2018: $53,120; room/board: $13,660
Financial aid: (207) 859-4832; 42% of undergrads determined to have financial need; average aid package $45,306

College of the Atlantic
Bar Harbor ME
(800) 528-0025
U.S. News ranking: Nat. Lib. Arts, No. 93
Website: www.coa.edu/
Admissions email: inquiry@coa.edu
Private; founded 1969
Freshman admissions: selective; 2016-2017: 485 applied, 314 accepted. Neither SAT nor ACT required. SAT 25/75 percentile: 1110-1290. High school rank: 27% in top tenth, 70% in top quarter, 87% in top half
Early decision deadline: 12/1, notification date: 12/15
Early action deadline: N/A, notification date: N/A
Application deadline (fall): 2/1
Undergraduate student body: 312 full time, 26 part time; 27% male, 73% female; 0% American Indian, 3% Asian, 1% black, 5% Hispanic, 2% multiracial, 0% Pacific Islander, 67% white, 21% international; 25% from in state; 45% live on campus; 0% of students in fraternities, 0% in sororities
Most popular majors: Information not available
Expenses: 2017-2018: $43,542; room/board: $9,747
Financial aid: (207) 801-5645; 84% of undergrads determined to have financial need; average aid package $40,946

Husson University
Bangor ME
(207) 941-7100
U.S. News ranking: Reg. U. (N), second tier
Website: www.husson.edu
Admissions email: admit@husson.edu
Private; founded 1898
Freshman admissions: less selective; 2016-2017: 2,460 applied, 1,974 accepted. Either SAT or ACT required. SAT 25/75 percentile: 860-1070. High school rank: 10% in top tenth, 39% in top quarter, 77% in top half
Early decision deadline: N/A, notification date: N/A

Early action deadline: N/A, notification date: N/A
Application deadline (fall): 8/15
Undergraduate student body: 2,339 full time, 495 part time; 45% male, 55% female; 1% American Indian, 1% Asian, 4% black, 2% Hispanic, 2% multiracial, 0% Pacific Islander, 86% white, 3% international; 78% from in state; 39% live on campus; 3% of students in fraternities, 4% in sororities
Most popular majors: 30% Business Administration, Management and Operations, 24% Health Professions and Related Programs, 11% Criminal Justice and Corrections, 10% Communications Technologies/Technicians and Support Services, 4% Psychology, General
Expenses: 2017-2018: $17,561; room/board: $9,498
Financial aid: (207) 941-7156; 85% of undergrads determined to have financial need; average aid package $12,592

Maine College of Art[1]
Portland ME
(800) 699-1509
U.S. News ranking: Arts, unranked
Website: www.meca.edu
Admissions email: admissions@meca.edu
Private; founded 1882
Application deadline (fall): rolling
Undergraduate student body: N/A full time, N/A part time
Expenses: 2016-2017: $32,872; room/board: $11,186
Financial aid: (207) 699-5073

Maine Maritime Academy
Castine ME
(207) 326-2206
U.S. News ranking: Reg. Coll. (N), No. 5
Website: www.mainemaritime.edu
Admissions email: admissions@mma.edu
Public; founded 1941
Freshman admissions: selective; 2016-2017: 865 applied, 627 accepted. Either SAT or ACT required. SAT 25/75 percentile: 950-1140. High school rank: 13% in top tenth, 43% in top quarter, 76% in top half
Early decision deadline: N/A, notification date: N/A
Early action deadline: 11/30, notification date: 2/1
Application deadline (fall): 3/1
Undergraduate student body: 983 full time, 37 part time; 85% male, 15% female; 0% American Indian, 1% Asian, 1% black, 2% Hispanic, 0% multiracial, 0% Pacific Islander, 88% white, 0% international; 72% from in state; 65% live on campus; 0% of students in fraternities, 0% in sororities
Most popular majors: 33% Engineering Technologies and Engineering-Related Fields, Other, 30% Naval Architecture and Marine Engineering, 23% Marine Science/Merchant Marine Officer, 1% Biological and Biomedical Sciences, Other, 1% International Business/Trade/Commerce

Expenses: 2017-2018: $18,408 in state, $26,628 out of state; room/board: $10,110
Financial aid: (207) 326-2339; 69% of undergrads determined to have financial need; average aid package $9,263

St. Joseph's College[1]
Standish ME
(207) 893-7746
U.S. News ranking: Reg. U. (N), No. 136
Website: www.sjcme.edu
Admissions email: admission@sjcme.edu
Private
Application deadline (fall): N/A
Undergraduate student body: N/A full time, N/A part time
Expenses: 2016-2017: $33,600; room/board: $12,890
Financial aid: N/A

Thomas College[1]
Waterville ME
(800) 339-7001
U.S. News ranking: Reg. U. (N), second tier
Website: www.thomas.edu
Admissions email: admiss@thomas.edu
Private; founded 1894
Application deadline (fall): rolling
Undergraduate student body: N/A full time, N/A part time
Expenses: 2017-2018: $26,110; room/board: $10,930
Financial aid: (207) 859-1105; 88% of undergrads determined to have financial need; average aid package $20,932

Unity College
Unity ME
(800) 624-1024
U.S. News ranking: Reg. Coll. (N), No. 16
Website: www.unity.edu
Admissions email: admissions@unity.edu
Private; founded 1965
Freshman admissions: selective; 2016-2017: 991 applied, 920 accepted. Neither SAT nor ACT required. SAT 25/75 percentile: 960-1188. High school rank: 7% in top tenth, 32% in top quarter, 68% in top half
Early decision deadline: N/A, notification date: N/A
Early action deadline: 12/15, notification date: 9/1
Application deadline (fall): rolling
Undergraduate student body: 705 full time, 24 part time; 49% male, 51% female; 2% American Indian, 2% Asian, 1% black, 2% Hispanic, 3% multiracial, 0% Pacific Islander, 86% white, 0% international; 30% from in state; 69% live on campus; 0% of students in fraternities, 0% in sororities
Most popular majors: 29% Wildlife, Fish and Wildlands Science and Management, 24% Natural Resources Law Enforcement and Protective Services, 11% Wildlife Biology
Expenses: 2017-2018: $27,850; room/board: $10,400
Financial aid: (207) 509-7235; 83% of undergrads determined to have financial need; average aid package $20,247

University of Maine
Orono ME
(877) 486-2364
U.S. News ranking: Nat. U.,
No. 181
Website: www.umaine.edu
Admissions email:
umaineadmissions@maine.edu
Public; founded 1865
Freshman admissions: selective;
2016-2017: 12,952 applied,
11,625 accepted. Either SAT
or ACT required. SAT 25/75
percentile: 950-1190. High school
rank: 18% in top tenth, 42% in
top quarter, 76% in top half
Early decision deadline: N/A,
notification date: N/A
Early action deadline: 12/1,
notification date: 1/15
Application deadline (fall): 2/1
Undergraduate student body: 8,125
full time, 1,198 part time; 53%
male, 47% female; 1% American
Indian, 2% Asian, 2% black,
3% Hispanic, 3% multiracial,
0% Pacific Islander, 84% white,
2% international; 70% from in
state; 39% live on campus; N/A
of students in fraternities, N/A in
sororities
Most popular majors: 15%
Business, Management,
Marketing, and Related Support
Services, 15% Engineering, 8%
Education, 7% Health Professions
and Related Programs, 7% Social
Sciences
Expenses: 2017-2018: $10,902
in state, $30,282 out of state;
room/board: $10,144
Financial aid: (207) 581-1324;
68% of undergrads determined to
have financial need; average aid
package $16,723

University of Maine–Augusta
Augusta ME
(207) 621-3465
U.S. News ranking: Reg. Coll. (N),
second tier
Website: www.uma.edu
Admissions email:
umaadm@maine.edu
Public; founded 1965
Freshman admissions: least
selective; 2016-2017: N/A
applied, N/A accepted. Neither
SAT nor ACT required. SAT 25/75
percentile: 780-1000. High
school rank: N/A
Early decision deadline: N/A,
notification date: N/A
Early action deadline: N/A,
notification date: N/A
Application deadline (fall): 9/1
Undergraduate student body: 1,436
full time, 2,980 part time; 28%
male, 72% female; 2% American
Indian, 1% Asian, 1% black, 2%
Hispanic, 3% multiracial, 0%
Pacific Islander, 87% white, 0%
international
Most popular majors: Information
not available
Expenses: 2016-2017: $7,448 in
state, $16,688 out of state; room/
board: N/A
Financial aid: (207) 621-3141

University of Maine–Farmington
Farmington ME
(207) 778-7050
U.S. News ranking: Reg. Coll. (N),
No. 8
Website: www.farmington.edu
Admissions email: umfadmit@
maine.edu
Public; founded 1864
Freshman admissions: selective;
2016-2017: 1,880 applied,
1,512 accepted. Neither SAT
nor ACT required. SAT 25/75
percentile: 870-1128. High school
rank: 13% in top tenth, 42% in
top quarter, 79% in top half
Early decision deadline: N/A,
notification date: N/A
Early action deadline: 11/15,
notification date: 12/15
Application deadline (fall): rolling
Undergraduate student body: 1,662
full time, 120 part time; 34%
male, 66% female; 0% American
Indian, 1% Asian, 2% black,
2% Hispanic, 2% multiracial,
0% Pacific Islander, 88% white,
0% international; 84% from in
state; 50% live on campus; N/A
of students in fraternities, N/A in
sororities
Most popular majors: 34%
Education, 13% Health
Professions and Related Programs,
13% Psychology, 8% Business,
Management, Marketing, and
Related Support Services, 8%
English Language and Literature/
Letters
Expenses: 2017-2018: $9,458 in
state, $19,026 out of state; room/
board: $9,334
Financial aid: (207) 778-7100;
79% of undergrads determined to
have financial need; average aid
package $13,881

University of Maine–Fort Kent
Fort Kent ME
(207) 834-7600
U.S. News ranking: Reg. Coll. (N),
No. 31
Website: www.umfk.maine.edu
Admissions email: umfkadm@
maine.edu
Public; founded 1878
Freshman admissions: least
selective; 2016-2017: 411
applied, 394 accepted. Neither
SAT nor ACT required. SAT 25/75
percentile: 790-985. High school
rank: 9% in top tenth, 24% in top
quarter, 68% in top half
Early decision deadline: N/A,
notification date: N/A
Early action deadline: N/A,
notification date: N/A
Application deadline (fall): rolling
Undergraduate student body: 668
full time, 1,236 part time; 31%
male, 69% female; 1% American
Indian, 1% Asian, 4% black,
2% Hispanic, 3% multiracial,
0% Pacific Islander, 76% white,
9% international; 83% from in
state; 20% live on campus; 1%
of students in fraternities, 2% in
sororities
Most popular majors: 57% Health
Professions and Related Programs,
12% Business, Management,
Marketing, and Related Support

Services, 11% Social Sciences,
5% Liberal Arts and Sciences,
General Studies and Humanities,
5% Public Administration and
Social Service Professions
Expenses: 2017-2018: $7,965 in
state, $12,075 out of state; room/
board: $7,910
Financial aid: (207) 834-7607;
74% of undergrads determined to
have financial need; average aid
package $11,403

University of Maine–Machias[1]
Machias ME
(888) 468-6866
U.S. News ranking: Nat. Lib. Arts,
second tier
Website: machias.edu/
Admissions email:
ummadmissions@maine.edu
Public; founded 1909
Application deadline (fall): 8/15
Undergraduate student body: N/A
full time, N/A part time
Expenses: 2016-2017: $7,530 in
state, $19,350 out of state; room/
board: $8,466
Financial aid: N/A

University of Maine–Presque Isle
Presque Isle ME
(207) 768-9532
U.S. News ranking: Reg. Coll. (N),
No. 29
Website: www.umpi.edu
Admissions email: admissions@
umpi.edu
Public; founded 1903
Freshman admissions: least
selective; 2016-2017: 1,491
applied, 1,141 accepted. Neither
SAT nor ACT required. SAT 25/75
percentile: 770-1030. High
school rank: 2% in top tenth, 13%
in top quarter, 42% in top half
Early decision deadline: N/A,
notification date: N/A
Early action deadline: N/A,
notification date: N/A
Application deadline (fall): rolling
Undergraduate student body: 726
full-time, 600 part time; 38%
male, 62% female; 3% American
Indian, 1% Asian, 3% black,
2% Hispanic, 4% multiracial,
0% Pacific Islander, 79% white,
7% international; 91% from in
state; 38% live on campus; N/A
of students in fraternities, N/A in
sororities
Most popular majors: 14%
Psychology, General, 12% Liberal
Arts and Sciences/Liberal Studies,
9% Business Administration
and Management, General, 6%
Corrections and Criminal Justice,
Other, 6% Multicultural Education
Expenses: 2017-2018: $7,884 in
state, $11,994 out of state; room/
board: $8,264
Financial aid: (207) 768-9511;
76% of undergrads determined to
have financial need; average aid
package $11,665

University of New England
Biddeford ME
(800) 477-4863
U.S. News ranking: Reg. U. (N),
No. 78
Website: www.une.edu
Admissions email:
admissions@une.edu
Private; founded 1831
Freshman admissions: selective;
2016-2017: 4,883 applied,
4,056 accepted. Either SAT
or ACT required. SAT 25/75
percentile: 940-1150. High
school rank: N/A
Early decision deadline: N/A,
notification date: N/A
Early action deadline: 12/1,
notification date: 12/31
Application deadline (fall): 2/15
Undergraduate student body: 2,374
full time, 1,873 part time; 25%
male, 75% female; 0% American
Indian, 4% Asian, 1% black,
0% Hispanic, 1% multiracial,
0% Pacific Islander, 83% white,
1% international; 30% from in
state; 65% live on campus; N/A
of students in fraternities, N/A in
sororities
Most popular majors: 42% Health
Professions and Related Programs,
27% Biological and Biomedical
Sciences, 6% Parks, Recreation,
Leisure, and Fitness Studies,
5% Business, Management,
Marketing, and Related Support
Services, 4% Psychology
Expenses: 2017-2018: $36,530;
room/board: $13,580
Financial aid: (207) 602-2342;
83% of undergrads determined to
have financial need

University of Southern Maine
Portland ME
(207) 780-5670
U.S. News ranking: Reg. U. (N),
second tier
Website: www.usm.maine.edu
Admissions email:
admitusm@maine.edu
Public; founded 1878
Freshman admissions: selective;
2016-2017: 4,111 applied,
3,299 accepted. Either SAT
or ACT required. SAT 25/75
percentile: 870-1090. High school
rank: 10% in top tenth, 37% in
top quarter, 75% in top half
Early decision deadline: N/A,
notification date: N/A
Early action deadline: N/A,
notification date: N/A
Application deadline (fall): rolling
Undergraduate student body: 3,750
full time, 2,439 part time; 42%
male, 58% female; 1% American
Indian, 2% Asian, 5% black, 3%
Hispanic, 3% multiracial, 0%
Pacific Islander, 81% white, 1%
international
Most popular majors: 21%
Business, Management,
Marketing, and Related Support
Services, 17% Health Professions
and Related Programs, 12% Social
Sciences, 6% Communication,
Journalism, and Related Programs,
5% Psychology
Expenses: 2017-2018: $9,220 in
state, $22,030 out of state; room/
board: $9,200

Financial aid: (207) 780-5250;
75% of undergrads determined to
have financial need; average aid
package $13,894

MARYLAND

Bowie State University
Bowie MD
(301) 860-3415
U.S. News ranking: Reg. U. (N),
second tier
Website: www.bowiestate.edu
Admissions email:
ugradadmissions@bowiestate.edu
Public; founded 1865
Freshman admissions: less
selective; 2016-2017: 6,720
applied, 2,775 accepted. Either
SAT or ACT required. SAT 25/75
percentile: 810-960. High school
rank: N/A
Early decision deadline: N/A,
notification date: N/A
Early action deadline: N/A,
notification date: N/A
Application deadline (fall): rolling
Undergraduate student body: 3,939
full time, 772 part time; 38%
male, 62% female; 0% American
Indian, 1% Asian, 83% black,
4% Hispanic, 5% multiracial,
0% Pacific Islander, 3% white,
1% international; 98% from in
state; 50% live on campus; 25%
of students in fraternities, 30%
in sororities
Most popular majors: Information
not available
Expenses: 2017-2018: $8,064 in
state, $18,653 out of state; room/
board: $10,546
Financial aid: (301) 860-3540

Capitol Technology University[1]
Laurel MD
U.S. News ranking: Engineering,
unranked
Website: www.captechu.edu/
Admissions email: N/A
Private
Application deadline (fall): N/A
Undergraduate student body: N/A
full time, N/A part time
Expenses: 2016-2017: $24,272;
room/board: $12,624
Financial aid: (301) 369-2324

Coppin State University[1]
Baltimore MD
(410) 951-3600
U.S. News ranking: Reg. U. (N),
second tier
Website: www.coppin.edu
Admissions email: admissions@
coppin.edu
Public; founded 1900
Application deadline (fall): rolling
Undergraduate student body: N/A
full time, N/A part time
Expenses: 2016-2017: $7,438 in
state, $13,168 out of state; room/
board: $9,752
Financial aid: N/A

Frostburg State University
Frostburg MD
(301) 687-4201
U.S. News ranking: Reg. U. (N), No. 120
Website: www.frostburg.edu
Admissions email: fsuadmissions@frostburg.edu
Public; founded 1898
Freshman admissions: selective; 2016-2017: 4,228 applied, 2,652 accepted. Either SAT or ACT required. SAT 25/75 percentile: 860-1060. High school rank: 12% in top tenth, 31% in top quarter, 63% in top half
Early decision deadline: 12/15, notification date: N/A
Early action deadline: N/A, notification date: N/A
Application deadline (fall): rolling
Undergraduate student body: 4,141 full time, 743 part time; 48% male, 52% female; 0% American Indian, 2% Asian, 32% black, 6% Hispanic, 5% multiracial, 0% Pacific Islander, 53% white, 1% international; 94% from in state; 29% live on campus; N/A of students in fraternities, N/A in sororities
Most popular majors: 14% Registered Nursing/Registered Nurse, 10% Business Administration and Management, General, 9% Psychology, General, 6% Criminal Justice/Safety Studies, 5% Liberal Arts and Sciences/Liberal Studies
Expenses: 2017-2018: $8,914 in state, $22,262 out of state; room/board: $10,298
Financial aid: (301) 687-4301; 66% of undergrads determined to have financial need; average aid package $9,743

Goucher College
Baltimore MD
(410) 337-6100
U.S. News ranking: Nat. Lib. Arts, No. 112
Website: www.goucher.edu
Admissions email: admissions@goucher.edu
Private; founded 1885
Freshman admissions: selective; 2016-2017: 3,443 applied, 2,728 accepted. Neither SAT nor ACT required. SAT 25/75 percentile: 1000-1240. High school rank: 13% in top tenth, 47% in top quarter, 76% in top half
Early decision deadline: 11/15, notification date: 12/15
Early action deadline: 12/1, notification date: 2/1
Application deadline (fall): 8/1
Undergraduate student body: 1,444 full time, 29 part time; 32% male, 68% female; 0% American Indian, 4% Asian, 13% black, 6% Hispanic, 6% multiracial, 0% Pacific Islander, 62% white, 3% international; 28% from in state; 84% live on campus; 0% of students in fraternities, 0% in sororities
Most popular majors: 15% Social Sciences, 14% Psychology, 12% Visual and Performing Arts, 8% English Language and Literature/Letters, 8% Foreign Languages, Literatures, and Linguistics

Expenses: 2017-2018: $43,440; room/board: $12,670
Financial aid: (410) 337-6141; 68% of undergrads determined to have financial need; average aid package $34,502

Hood College
Frederick MD
(800) 922-1599
U.S. News ranking: Reg. U. (N), No. 28
Website: www.hood.edu
Admissions email: admission@hood.edu
Private; founded 1893
Affiliation: United Church of Christ
Freshman admissions: selective; 2016-2017: 1,727 applied, 1,218 accepted. Neither SAT nor ACT required. SAT 25/75 percentile: 900-1100. High school rank: 17% in top tenth, 46% in top quarter, 82% in top half
Early decision deadline: N/A, notification date: N/A
Early action deadline: N/A, notification date: N/A
Application deadline (fall): rolling
Undergraduate student body: 1,090 full time, 84 part time; 39% male, 61% female; 0% American Indian, 3% Asian, 14% black, 10% Hispanic, 5% multiracial, 0% Pacific Islander, 61% white, 2% international; 76% from in state; 52% live on campus; N/A of students in fraternities, N/A in sororities
Most popular majors: 16% Business, Management, Marketing, and Related Support Services, 9% Communication, Journalism, and Related Programs, 8% Biological and Biomedical Sciences, 8% Psychology, 8% Social Sciences
Expenses: 2017-2018: $37,960; room/board: $12,580
Financial aid: (301) 696-3411; 80% of undergrads determined to have financial need; average aid package $29,186

Johns Hopkins University
Baltimore MD
(410) 516-8171
U.S. News ranking: Nat. U., No. 11
Website: www.jhu.edu
Admissions email: gotojhu@jhu.edu
Private; founded 1876
Freshman admissions: most selective; 2016-2017: 27,094 applied, 3,234 accepted. Either SAT or ACT required. SAT 25/75 percentile: 1420-1570. High school rank: 94% in top tenth, 99% in top quarter, 100% in top half
Early decision deadline: 11/1, notification date: 12/15
Early action deadline: N/A, notification date: N/A
Application deadline (fall): 1/1
Undergraduate student body: 5,696 full time, 421 part time; 48% male, 52% female; 0% American Indian, 24% Asian, 6% black, 13% Hispanic, 5% multiracial, 0% Pacific Islander, 37% white, 11% international; 12% from in state; 48% live on campus; 22% of students in fraternities, 33% in sororities

Most popular majors: 10% Public Health, General, 9% Bioengineering and Biomedical Engineering, 7% Cell/Cellular and Molecular Biology, 7% Neuroscience, 6% International Relations and Affairs
Expenses: 2017-2018: $52,170; room/board: $15,410
Financial aid: (410) 516-8028; 48% of undergrads determined to have financial need; average aid package $40,048

Loyola University Maryland
Baltimore MD
(410) 617-5012
U.S. News ranking: Reg. U. (N), No. 4
Website: www.loyola.edu
Admissions email: admissions@loyola.edu
Private; founded 1852
Affiliation: Roman Catholic
Freshman admissions: selective; 2016-2017: 12,727 applied, 8,340 accepted. Neither SAT nor ACT required. SAT 25/75 percentile: 1100-1280. High school rank: 29% in top tenth, 68% in top quarter, 93% in top half
Early decision deadline: 11/1, notification date: 12/15
Early action deadline: 11/15, notification date: 1/15
Application deadline (fall): 1/15
Undergraduate student body: 4,050 full time, 54 part time; 43% male, 57% female; 0% American Indian, 4% Asian, 5% black, 10% Hispanic, 3% multiracial, 0% Pacific Islander, 77% white, 1% international; 18% from in state; 81% live on campus; 0% of students in fraternities, 0% in sororities
Most popular majors: 35% Business, Management, Marketing, and Related Support Services, 11% Communication, Journalism, and Related Programs, 11% Social Sciences, 7% Psychology, 6% Health Professions and Related Programs
Expenses: 2017-2018: $47,725; room/board: $14,150
Financial aid: (410) 617-2576; 55% of undergrads determined to have financial need; average aid package $35,294

Maryland Institute College of Art
Baltimore MD
(410) 225-2222
U.S. News ranking: Arts, unranked
Website: www.mica.edu
Admissions email: admissions@mica.edu
Private; founded 1826
Freshman admissions: selective; 2016-2017: 3,475 applied, 1,984 accepted. Either SAT or ACT required. SAT 25/75 percentile: 1020-1290. High school rank: N/A
Early decision deadline: 11/1, notification date: 12/1
Early action deadline: N/A, notification date: N/A
Application deadline (fall): 2/1

Undergraduate student body: 1,654 full time, 25 part time; 26% male, 74% female; 0% American Indian, 13% Asian, 6% black, 4% Hispanic, 11% multiracial, 0% Pacific Islander, 45% white, 18% international
Most popular majors: Information not available
Expenses: 2017-2018: $46,990; room/board: $12,860
Financial aid: (410) 225-2285

McDaniel College
Westminster MD
(800) 638-5005
U.S. News ranking: Nat. Lib. Arts, No. 134
Website: www.mcdaniel.edu
Admissions email: admissions@mcdaniel.edu
Private; founded 1867
Freshman admissions: selective; 2016-2017: 2,403 applied, 1,876 accepted. Either SAT or ACT required. SAT 25/75 percentile: 980-1210. High school rank: 22% in top tenth, 44% in top quarter, 78% in top half
Early decision deadline: 11/1, notification date: 12/1
Early action deadline: 12/15, notification date: 1/15
Application deadline (fall): 2/1
Undergraduate student body: 1,525 full time, 34 part time; 49% male, 51% female; 0% American Indian, 4% Asian, 15% black, 7% Hispanic, 3% multiracial, 0% Pacific Islander, 65% white, 0% international; 65% from in state; 82% live on campus; 15% of students in fraternities, 18% in sororities
Most popular majors: 14% Social Sciences, 13% Parks, Recreation, Leisure, and Fitness Studies, 11% Business, Management, Marketing, and Related Support Services, 10% Psychology, 9% Biological and Biomedical Sciences
Expenses: 2017-2018: $41,800; room/board: $11,110
Financial aid: (410) 857-2233; 75% of undergrads determined to have financial need; average aid package $35,192

Morgan State University
Baltimore MD
(800) 332-6674
U.S. News ranking: Nat. U., second tier
Website: www.morgan.edu
Admissions email: admissions@morgan.edu
Public; founded 1867
Freshman admissions: less selective; 2016-2017: 6,049 applied, 3,653 accepted. SAT required. SAT 25/75 percentile: 800-990. High school rank: N/A
Early decision deadline: N/A, notification date: N/A
Early action deadline: 11/15, notification date: 2/15
Application deadline (fall): 2/15
Undergraduate student body: 5,739 full time, 623 part time; 49% male, 51% female; 0% American Indian, 1% Asian, 77% black, 3% Hispanic, 3% multiracial,

0% Pacific Islander, 2% white, 11% international; 89% from in state; N/A live on campus; N/A of students in fraternities, N/A in sororities
Most popular majors: 22% Business, Management, Marketing, and Related Support Services, 21% Psychology, 13% Engineering, 12% Family and Consumer Sciences/Human Sciences, 9% Communications Technologies/Technicians and Support Services
Expenses: 2017-2018: $7,767 in state, $17,833 out of state; room/board: $10,650
Financial aid: (443) 885-3170; 81% of undergrads determined to have financial need; average aid package $11,021

Mount St. Mary's University
Emmitsburg MD
(800) 448-4347
U.S. News ranking: Reg. U. (N), No. 25
Website: www.msmary.edu
Admissions email: admissions@msmary.edu
Private; founded 1808
Affiliation: Roman Catholic
Freshman admissions: selective; 2016-2017: 6,086 applied, 3,745 accepted. Either SAT or ACT required. SAT 25/75 percentile: 940-1160. High school rank: 17% in top tenth, 38% in top quarter, 68% in top half
Early decision deadline: N/A, notification date: N/A
Early action deadline: 12/1, notification date: 12/25
Application deadline (fall): 3/1
Undergraduate student body: 1,629 full time, 100 part time; 46% male, 54% female; 0% American Indian, 3% Asian, 13% black, 10% Hispanic, 4% multiracial, 0% Pacific Islander, 68% white, 1% international; 55% from in state; 80% live on campus; N/A of students in fraternities, N/A in sororities
Most popular majors: 24% Business/Commerce, General, 13% Criminology, 7% Accounting, 6% Biology/Biological Sciences, General, 6% Research and Experimental Psychology, Other
Expenses: 2017-2018: $40,550; room/board: $12,830
Financial aid: (301) 447-8364; 71% of undergrads determined to have financial need; average aid package $26,219

Notre Dame of Maryland University
Baltimore MD
(410) 532-5330
U.S. News ranking: Reg. U. (N), No. 56
Website: www.ndm.edu
Admissions email: admiss@ndm.edu
Private; founded 1895
Affiliation: Roman Catholic
Freshman admissions: selective; 2016-2017: 822 applied, 499 accepted. Neither SAT nor ACT required. SAT 25/75 percentile: 960-1140. High school rank: 30% in top tenth, 69% in top quarter, 94% in top half

Early decision deadline: N/A, notification date: N/A
Early action deadline: N/A, notification date: N/A
Application deadline (fall): rolling
Undergraduate student body: 515 full time, 359 part time; 5% male, 95% female; 1% American Indian, 8% Asian, 27% black, 7% Hispanic, 1% multiracial, 0% Pacific Islander, 52% white, 2% international; 91% from in state; 23% live on campus; 0% of students in fraternities, 0% in sororities
Most popular majors: 64% Registered Nursing/Registered Nurse, 8% Liberal Arts and Sciences, General Studies and Humanities, Other, 7% Multi-/Interdisciplinary Studies, Other, 5% Biology/Biological Sciences, General, 3% Business Administration and Management, General
Expenses: 2016-2017: $35,019; room/board: $11,446
Financial aid: (410) 532-5369

Salisbury University
Salisbury MD
(410) 543-6161
U.S. News ranking: Reg. U. (N), No. 78
Website: www.salisbury.edu/
Admissions email: admissions@salisbury.edu
Public; founded 1925
Freshman admissions: selective; 2016-2017: 8,307 applied, 5,477 accepted. Neither SAT nor ACT required. SAT 25/75 percentile: 1080-1230. High school rank: 21% in top tenth, 55% in top quarter, 86% in top half
Early decision deadline: 11/15, notification date: 12/15
Early action deadline: 12/1, notification date: 1/15
Application deadline (fall): 1/15
Undergraduate student body: 7,250 full time, 611 part time; 43% male, 57% female; 1% American Indian, 3% Asian, 14% black, 4% Hispanic, 3% multiracial, 0% Pacific Islander, 70% white, 2% international; 86% from in state; 40% live on campus; 10% of students in fraternities, 10% in sororities
Most popular majors: 16% Business, Management, Marketing, and Related Support Services, 11% Education, 9% Communication, Journalism, and Related Programs, 9% Health Professions and Related Programs, 7% Parks, Recreation, Leisure, and Fitness Studies
Expenses: 2016-2017: $9,364 in state, $17,776 out of state; room/board: $11,350
Financial aid: (410) 543-6165; 53% of undergrads determined to have financial need; average aid package $8,246

St. John's College
Annapolis MD
(410) 626-2522
U.S. News ranking: Nat. Lib. Arts, No. 53
Website: sjc.edu
Admissions email: annapolis.admissions@sjc.edu
Private; founded 1696

Freshman admissions: more selective; 2016-2017: 612 applied, 326 accepted. Neither SAT nor ACT required. SAT 25/75 percentile: 1180-1440. High school rank: 33% in top tenth, 64% in top quarter, 88% in top half
Early decision deadline: N/A, notification date: N/A
Early action deadline: 1/15, notification date: 2/15
Application deadline (fall): rolling
Undergraduate student body: 432 full time, 2 part time; 55% male, 45% female; 0% American Indian, 4% Asian, 1% black, 5% Hispanic, 2% multiracial, 0% Pacific Islander, 69% white, 18% international; 22% from in state; 78% live on campus; 0% of students in fraternities, 0% in sororities
Most popular majors: 100% Liberal Arts and Sciences/Liberal Studies
Expenses: 2017-2018: $51,795; room/board: $12,234
Financial aid: (410) 626-2502; 75% of undergrads determined to have financial need; average aid package $41,603

St. Mary's College of Maryland
St. Marys City MD
(800) 492-7181
U.S. News ranking: Nat. Lib. Arts, No. 96
Website: www.smcm.edu
Admissions email: admissions@smcm.edu
Public; founded 1840
Freshman admissions: selective; 2016-2017: 1,767 applied, 1,413 accepted. Either SAT or ACT required. SAT 25/75 percentile: 1000-1250. High school rank: N/A
Early decision deadline: N/A, notification date: N/A
Early action deadline: 11/15, notification date: 12/20
Application deadline (fall): 2/15
Undergraduate student body: 1,587 full time, 56 part time; 43% male, 57% female; 0% American Indian, 4% Asian, 9% black, 9% Hispanic, 5% multiracial, 0% Pacific Islander, 69% white, 0% international; 93% from in state; 83% live on campus; 0% of students in fraternities, 0% in sororities
Most popular majors: 14% Psychology, General, 12% Biology/Biological Sciences, General, 11% Economics, General, 7% English Language and Literature, General, 7% Political Science and Government, General
Expenses: 2017-2018: $14,496 in state, $29,948 out of state; room/board: $12,816
Financial aid: (240) 895-3000; 51% of undergrads determined to have financial need; average aid package $13,095

Stevenson University
Stevenson MD
(877) 468-6852
U.S. News ranking: Reg. U. (N), No. 86
Website: www.stevenson.edu/
Admissions email: admissions@stevenson.edu
Private; founded 1947

Freshman admissions: selective; 2016-2017: 5,856 applied, 3,558 accepted. Either SAT or ACT required. SAT 25/75 percentile: 910-1130. High school rank: 17% in top tenth, 43% in top quarter, 80% in top half
Early decision deadline: N/A, notification date: N/A
Early action deadline: N/A, notification date: N/A
Application deadline (fall): rolling
Undergraduate student body: 3,065 full time, 556 part time; 34% male, 66% female; 0% American Indian, 3% Asian, 27% black, 5% Hispanic, 5% multiracial, 0% Pacific Islander, 56% white, 0% international; 80% from in state; 43% live on campus; 0% of students in fraternities, 2% in sororities
Most popular majors: 25% Health Professions and Related Programs, 18% Business, Management, Marketing, and Related Support Services, 9% Computer and Information Sciences and Support Services, 7% Education, 7% Homeland Security, Law Enforcement, Firefighting and Related Protective Services
Expenses: 2017-2018: $35,490; room/board: $12,922
Financial aid: (443) 334-3200; 79% of undergrads determined to have financial need; average aid package $21,222

Towson University
Towson MD
(410) 704-2113
U.S. News ranking: Reg. U. (N), No. 41
Website: www.towson.edu
Admissions email: admissions@towson.edu
Public; founded 1866
Freshman admissions: selective; 2016-2017: 11,897 applied, 8,773 accepted. Either SAT or ACT required. SAT 25/75 percentile: 980-1160. High school rank: 17% in top tenth, 42% in top quarter, 78% in top half
Early decision deadline: N/A, notification date: N/A
Early action deadline: N/A, notification date: N/A
Application deadline (fall): 1/17
Undergraduate student body: 16,893 full time, 2,305 part time; 40% male, 60% female; 0% American Indian, 6% Asian, 19% black, 7% Hispanic, 5% multiracial, 0% Pacific Islander, 59% white, 2% international; 86% from in state; 26% live on campus; 11% of students in fraternities, 12% in sororities
Most popular majors: 14% Business, Management, Marketing, and Related Support Services, 13% Health Professions and Related Programs, 11% Social Sciences, 10% Communication, Journalism, and Related Programs, 10% Education
Expenses: 2017-2018: $9,694 in state, $22,140 out of state; room/board: $12,184
Financial aid: (410) 704-4236; 55% of undergrads determined to have financial need; average aid package $10,178

United States Naval Academy
Annapolis MD
(410) 293-1858
U.S. News ranking: Nat. Lib. Arts, No. 21
Website: www.usna.edu
Admissions email: webmail@usna.edu
Public; founded 1845
Freshman admissions: more selective; 2016-2017: 17,043 applied, 1,355 accepted. Either SAT or ACT required. SAT 25/75 percentile: 1170-1390. High school rank: 59% in top tenth, 83% in top quarter, 95% in top half
Early decision deadline: N/A, notification date: N/A
Early action deadline: N/A, notification date: N/A
Application deadline (fall): 1/31
Undergraduate student body: 4,526 full time, 0 part time; 74% male, 26% female; 0% American Indian, 7% Asian, 7% black, 11% Hispanic, 8% multiracial, 0% Pacific Islander, 64% white, 1% international; 6% from in state; 100% live on campus; 0% of students in fraternities, 0% in sororities
Most popular majors: 11% Political Science and Government, General, 10% Economics, General, 10% Systems Engineering, 7% History, General, 7% Mechanical Engineering
Expenses: 2017-2018: $0 in state, $0 out of state; room/board: N/A
Financial aid: N/A

University of Baltimore
Baltimore MD
(410) 837-4777
U.S. News ranking: Reg. U. (N), second tier
Website: www.ubalt.edu
Admissions email: admissions@ubalt.edu
Public; founded 1925
Freshman admissions: less selective; 2016-2017: 426 applied, 354 accepted. Either SAT or ACT required. SAT 25/75 percentile: 810-1030. High school rank: N/A
Early decision deadline: N/A, notification date: N/A
Early action deadline: N/A, notification date: N/A
Application deadline (fall): rolling
Undergraduate student body: 1,995 full time, 1,227 part time; 42% male, 58% female; 0% American Indian, 5% Asian, 48% black, 4% Hispanic, 4% multiracial, 0% Pacific Islander, 33% white, 2% international; 96% from in state; N/A live on campus; N/A of students in fraternities, N/A in sororities
Most popular majors: 37% Business/Commerce, General, 12% Criminal Justice/Police Science, 7% Health Services Administration, 6% Animation, Interactive Technology, Video Graphics and Special Effects, 4% Psychology, General
Expenses: 2017-2018: $8,824 in state, $20,704 out of state; room/board: N/A

Financial aid: (410) 837-4779; 54% of undergrads determined to have financial need; average aid package $4,108

University of Maryland University College
Adelphi MD
(800) 888-8682
U.S. News ranking: Reg. U. (N), unranked
Website: www.umuc.edu/
Admissions email: enroll@umuc.edu
Public; founded 1947
Freshman admissions: least selective; 2016-2017: 1,981 applied, 1,981 accepted. Neither SAT nor ACT required. SAT 25/75 percentile: N/A. High school rank: N/A
Early decision deadline: N/A, notification date: N/A
Early action deadline: N/A, notification date: N/A
Application deadline (fall): rolling
Undergraduate student body: 9,530 full time, 34,689 part time; 56% male, 44% female; 1% American Indian, 5% Asian, 26% black, 13% Hispanic, 4% multiracial, 1% Pacific Islander, 41% white, 1% international; 40% from in state; N/A live on campus; N/A of students in fraternities, N/A in sororities
Most popular majors: 42% Computer and Information Sciences and Support Services, 23% Business, Management, Marketing, and Related Support Services, 7% Homeland Security, Law Enforcement, Firefighting and Related Protective Services, 7% Psychology, 5% Social Sciences
Expenses: 2017-2018: $7,176 in state, $12,336 out of state; room/board: N/A
Financial aid: (301) 985-7510; 60% of undergrads determined to have financial need; average aid package $7,217

University of Maryland–Baltimore County
Baltimore MD
(410) 455-2291
U.S. News ranking: Nat. U., No. 159
Website: www.umbc.edu
Admissions email: admissions@umbc.edu
Public; founded 1966
Freshman admissions: more selective; 2016-2017: 10,812 applied, 6,144 accepted. Either SAT or ACT required. SAT 25/75 percentile: 1120-1320. High school rank: 24% in top tenth, 51% in top quarter, 81% in top half
Early decision deadline: N/A, notification date: N/A
Early action deadline: 11/1, notification date: 12/15
Application deadline (fall): 2/1
Undergraduate student body: 9,484 full time, 1,658 part time; 55% male, 45% female; 0% American Indian, 21% Asian, 18% black,

7% Hispanic, 4% multiracial, 0% Pacific Islander, 43% white, 4% international; 95% from in state; 35% live on campus; 3% of students in fraternities, 6% in sororities
Most popular majors: 17% Biological and Biomedical Sciences, 16% Computer and Information Sciences and Support Services, 12% Psychology, 12% Social Sciences, 9% Engineering
Expenses: 2017-2018: $11,518 in state, $25,654 out of state; room/board: $11,836
Financial aid: (410) 455-1517; 54% of undergrads determined to have financial need; average aid package $10,448

University of Maryland–College Park
College Park MD
(301) 314-8385
U.S. News ranking: Nat. U., No. 61
Website: www.maryland.edu
Admissions email: ApplyMaryland@umd.edu
Public; founded 1856
Freshman admissions: more selective; 2016-2017: 30,272 applied, 14,538 accepted. Either SAT or ACT required. SAT 25/75 percentile: 1210-1420. High school rank: 71% in top tenth, 89% in top quarter, 98% in top half
Early decision deadline: N/A, notification date: N/A
Early action deadline: 11/1, notification date: 1/31
Application deadline (fall): 1/20
Undergraduate student body: 26,350 full time, 2,122 part time; 53% male, 47% female; 0% American Indian, 16% Asian, 13% black, 10% Hispanic, 4% multiracial, 0% Pacific Islander, 51% white, 4% international; 79% from in state, 40% live on campus; 15% of students in fraternities, 14% in sororities
Most popular majors: 7% Biology/ Biological Sciences, General, 5% Computer Engineering, General, 5% Criminology, 5% Economics, General, 5% Finance, General
Expenses: 2017-2018: $10,399 in state, $33,606 out of state; room/board: $12,082
Financial aid: (301) 314-9000; 41% of undergrads determined to have financial need; average aid package $12,319

University of Maryland–Eastern Shore
Princess Anne MD
(410) 651-6410
U.S. News ranking: Nat. U., second tier
Website: www.umes.edu
Admissions email: umesadmissions@umes.edu
Public; founded 1886
Freshman admissions: less selective; 2016-2017: 10,415 applied, 3,994 accepted. Either SAT or ACT required. SAT 25/75 percentile: 790-950. High school rank: N/A

Early decision deadline: N/A, notification date: N/A
Early action deadline: N/A, notification date: N/A
Application deadline (fall): 6/30
Undergraduate student body: 2,918 full time, 360 part time; 45% male, 55% female; 0% American Indian, 1% Asian, 76% black, 3% Hispanic, 7% multiracial, 0% Pacific Islander, 10% white, 3% international; 82% from in state; 45% live on campus; N/A of students in fraternities, N/A in sororities
Most popular majors: 18% Business Administration and Management, General, 14% Biology/Biological Sciences, General, 13% Criminal Justice/ Police Science, 8% Family and Consumer Sciences/ Human Sciences, General, 7% Rehabilitation and Therapeutic Professions, Other
Expenses: 2017-2018: $8,042 in state, $18,048 out of state; room/ board: $9,623
Financial aid: (410) 651-6172; 82% of undergrads determined to have financial need; average aid package $14,681

Washington Adventist University
Takoma Park MD
(301) 891-4000
U.S. News ranking: Reg. U. (N), second tier
Website: www.wau.edu
Admissions email: enroll@wau.edu
Private; founded 1904
Affiliation: Seventh Day Adventist
Freshman admissions: least selective; 2016-2017: 1,978 applied, 666 accepted. Neither SAT nor ACT required. SAT 25/75 percentile: 720-1000. High school rank: N/A
Early decision deadline: N/A, notification date: N/A
Early action deadline: N/A, notification date: N/A
Application deadline (fall): 8/1
Undergraduate student body: 698 full time, 213 part time; 41% male, 59% female; N/A American Indian, N/A Asian, N/A black, N/A Hispanic, N/A multiracial, N/A Pacific Islander, N/A white, N/A international
Most popular majors: Information not available
Expenses: 2017-2018: $23,400; room/board: $8,930
Financial aid: (301) 891-4005; 95% of undergrads determined to have financial need; average aid package $10,500

Washington College
Chestertown MD
(410) 778-7700
U.S. News ranking: Nat. Lib. Arts, No. 96
Website: www.washcoll.edu
Admissions email: wc_admissions@ washcoll.edu
Private; founded 1782
Freshman admissions: more selective; 2016-2017: 6,720 applied, 3,295 accepted. Either SAT or ACT required. SAT 25/75 percentile: 1050-1260. High school rank: 40% in top tenth, 73% in top quarter, 94% in top half

Early decision deadline: 11/15, notification date: 12/15
Early action deadline: 12/1, notification date: 1/15
Application deadline (fall): 2/15
Undergraduate student body: 1,458 full time, 21 part time; 44% male, 56% female; 1% American Indian, 3% Asian, 7% black, 5% Hispanic, 1% multiracial, 0% Pacific Islander, 69% white, 11% international; 47% from in state; 85% live on campus; 6% of students in fraternities, 10% in sororities
Most popular majors: 26% Social Sciences, 14% Business, Management, Marketing, and Related Support Services, 11% Biological and Biomedical Sciences, 9% Psychology, 8% English Language and Literature/ Letters
Expenses: 2016-2017: $43,850; room/board: $10,612
Financial aid: (410) 778-7214

MASSACHUSETTS

American International College
Springfield MA
(413) 205-3201
U.S. News ranking: Nat. U., second tier
Website: www.aic.edu
Admissions email: inquiry@aic.edu
Private; founded 1885
Freshman admissions: less selective; 2016-2017: N/A applied, N/A accepted. Either SAT or ACT required. SAT 25/75 percentile: 790-980. High school rank: N/A
Early decision deadline: N/A, notification date: N/A
Early action deadline: N/A, notification date: N/A
Application deadline (fall): rolling
Undergraduate student body: 1,347 full time, 77 part time; 40% male, 60% female; 0% American Indian, 1% Asian, 25% black, 16% Hispanic, 2% multiracial, 1% Pacific Islander, 38% white, 4% international
Most popular majors: Information not available
Expenses: 2016-2017: $33,140; room/board: $13,490
Financial aid: (413) 205-3521

Amherst College
Amherst MA
(413) 542-2328
U.S. News ranking: Nat. Lib. Arts, No. 2
Website: www.amherst.edu
Admissions email: admission@ amherst.edu
Private; founded 1821
Freshman admissions: most selective; 2016-2017: 8,406 applied, 1,161 accepted. Either SAT or ACT required. SAT 25/75 percentile: 1360-1560. High school rank: 87% in top tenth, 96% in top quarter, 99% in top half
Early decision deadline: 11/15, notification date: 12/15
Early action deadline: N/A, notification date: N/A
Application deadline (fall): 1/1

Undergraduate student body: 1,849 full time, 0 part time; 50% male, 50% female; 0% American Indian, 14% Asian, 12% black, 14% Hispanic, 5% multiracial, 0% Pacific Islander, 43% white, 9% international; 13% from in state; 98% live on campus; 0% of students in fraternities, 0% in sororities
Most popular majors: 17% Economics, General, 14% Mathematics, General, 13% Psychology, General, 11% English Language and Literature, General, 10% Political Science and Government, General
Expenses: 2017-2018: $54,310; room/board: $14,190
Financial aid: (413) 542-2296; 55% of undergrads determined to have financial need; average aid package $51,775

Anna Maria College
Paxton MA
(508) 849-3360
U.S. News ranking: Reg. U. (N), second tier
Website: www.annamaria.edu
Admissions email: admissions@ annamaria.edu
Private; founded 1946
Affiliation: Roman Catholic
Freshman admissions: less selective; 2016-2017: 1,631 applied, 1,349 accepted. Neither SAT nor ACT required. SAT 25/75 percentile: N/A. High school rank: N/A
Early decision deadline: N/A, notification date: N/A
Early action deadline: N/A, notification date: N/A
Application deadline (fall): rolling
Undergraduate student body: 780 full time, 278 part time; 39% male, 61% female; 1% American Indian, 1% Asian, 13% black, 10% Hispanic, 1% multiracial, 0% Pacific Islander, 65% white, 0% international; 73% from in state; 44% live on campus; N/A of students in fraternities, N/A in sororities
Most popular majors: 46% Health Professions and Related Programs, 27% Homeland Security, Law Enforcement, Firefighting and Related Protective Services
Expenses: 2017-2018: $37,130; room/board: $13,890
Financial aid: (508) 849-3363; 87% of undergrads determined to have financial need; average aid package $28,771

Assumption College
Worcester MA
(866) 477-7776
U.S. News ranking: Reg. U. (N), No. 28
Website: www.assumption.edu
Admissions email: admiss@ assumption.edu
Private; founded 1904
Freshman admissions: selective; 2016-2017: 4,559 applied, 3,544 accepted. Neither SAT nor ACT required. SAT 25/75 percentile: 1010-1200. High school rank: 14% in top tenth, 38% in top quarter, 78% in top half

Early decision deadline: 11/1, notification date: 12/15
Early action deadline: 11/1, notification date: 12/15
Application deadline (fall): 2/15
Undergraduate student body: 1,964 full time, 25 part time; 42% male, 58% female; 0% American Indian, 2% Asian, 6% black, 7% Hispanic, 2% multiracial, 0% Pacific Islander, 75% white, 2% international; 65% from in state; 87% live on campus; N/A of students in fraternities, N/A in sororities
Most popular majors: 15% Rehabilitation Science, 10% Biology/Biological Sciences, General, 9% English Language and Literature, General, 8% Psychology, General, 6% Teacher Education, Multiple Levels
Expenses: 2017-2018: $36,260; room/board: $12,196
Financial aid: (508) 767-7158; 74% of undergrads determined to have financial need; average aid package $26,539

Babson College
Babson Park MA
(781) 239-5522
U.S. News ranking: Business, unranked
Website: www.babson.edu
Admissions email: ugradadmission@babson.edu
Private; founded 1919
Freshman admissions: more selective; 2016-2017: 7,648 applied, 1,881 accepted. Either SAT or ACT required. SAT 25/75 percentile: 1170-1370. High school rank: N/A
Early decision deadline: 11/1, notification date: 12/15
Early action deadline: 11/1, notification date: 1/1
Application deadline (fall): 1/4
Undergraduate student body: 2,283 full time, 0 part time; 52% male, 48% female; 0% American Indian, 12% Asian, 5% black, 10% Hispanic, 2% multiracial, 0% Pacific Islander, 38% white, 27% international; 28% from in state; 79% live on campus; 16% of students in fraternities, 27% in sororities
Most popular majors: 23% Finance, General, 15% Marketing/ Marketing Management, General, 11% Economics, General, 7% Entrepreneurship/Entrepreneurial Studies, 7% Management Sciences and Quantitative Methods
Expenses: 2017-2018: $49,664; room/board: $15,838
Financial aid: (781) 239-4015; 42% of undergrads determined to have financial need; average aid package $40,358

Bard College at Simon's Rock[1]
Great Barrington MA
(800) 234-7186
U.S. News ranking: Nat. Lib. Arts, No. 147
Website: www.simons-rock.edu
Admissions email: admit@simons-rock.edu
Private; founded 1966
Application deadline (fall): 5/1

Undergraduate student body: N/A full time, N/A part time
Expenses: 2016-2017: $51,797; room/board: $14,060
Financial aid: (413) 528-7297

Bay Path University

Longmeadow MA
(413) 565-1331
U.S. News ranking: Reg. U. (N), No. 102
Website: www.baypath.edu
Admissions email: admiss@baypath.edu
Private; founded 1897
Freshman admissions: selective; 2016-2017: 1,542 applied, 924 accepted. Neither SAT nor ACT required. SAT 25/75 percentile: 845-1065. High school rank: 15% in top tenth, 44% in top quarter, 76% in top half
Early decision deadline: N/A, notification date: N/A
Early action deadline: 12/15, notification date: 1/2
Application deadline (fall): 8/1
Undergraduate student body: 1,415 full time, 478 part time; 0% male, 100% female; 0% American Indian, 2% Asian, 13% black, 19% Hispanic, 3% multiracial, 0% Pacific Islander, 57% white, 1% international; 59% from in state; 45% live on campus; N/A of students in fraternities, N/A in sororities
Most popular majors: 28% Business, Management, Marketing, and Related Support Services, 21% Psychology, 13% Education, 11% Health Professions and Related Programs, 8% Homeland Security, Law Enforcement, Firefighting and Related Protective Services
Expenses: 2017-2018: $33,557; room/board: $12,799
Financial aid: (413) 565-1345; 90% of undergrads determined to have financial need; average aid package $26,392

Bay State College[1]

Boston MA
(617) 217-9000
U.S. News ranking: Reg. Coll. (N), second tier
Website: www.baystate.edu
For-profit; founded 1946
Application deadline (fall): rolling
Undergraduate student body: N/A full time, N/A part time
Expenses: 2016-2017: $27,750; room/board: $13,000
Financial aid: (617) 217-9003

Becker College[1]

Worcester MA
(877) 523-2537
U.S. News ranking: Reg. Coll. (N), second tier
Website: www.beckercollege.edu
Admissions email: admissions@beckercollege.edu
Private; founded 1784
Application deadline (fall): rolling
Undergraduate student body: N/A full time, N/A part time
Expenses: 2016-2017: $37,272; room/board: $12,850
Financial aid: (508) 373-9430

Bentley University

Waltham MA
(781) 891-2244
U.S. News ranking: Reg. U. (N), No. 2
Website: www.bentley.edu
Admissions email: ugadmission@bentley.edu
Private; founded 1917
Freshman admissions: more selective; 2016-2017: 8,281 applied, 3,836 accepted. Either SAT or ACT required. SAT 25/75 percentile: 1150-1320. High school rank: 32% in top tenth, 72% in top quarter, 96% in top half
Early decision deadline: 11/15, notification date: 12/31
Early action deadline: N/A, notification date: N/A
Application deadline (fall): 1/7
Undergraduate student body: 4,140 full time, 82 part time; 59% male, 41% female; 0% American Indian, 8% Asian, 3% black, 8% Hispanic, 2% multiracial, 0% Pacific Islander, 62% white, 14% international; 43% from in state; 80% live on campus; 12% of students in fraternities, 15% in sororities
Most popular majors: 18% Finance, General, 17% Business, Management, Marketing, and Related Support Services, Other, 15% Marketing/Marketing Management, General, 11% Accounting, 11% Accounting and Finance
Expenses: 2017-2018: $48,000; room/board: $15,720
Financial aid: (781) 891-3441; 44% of undergrads determined to have financial need; average aid package $36,226

Berklee College of Music

Boston MA
(800) 237-5533
U.S. News ranking: Arts, unranked
Website: www.berklee.edu
Admissions email: admissions@berklee.edu
Private; founded 1945
Freshman admissions: least selective; 2016-2017: 9,224 applied, 3,121 accepted. Neither SAT or ACT required. SAT 25/75 percentile: N/A. High school rank: N/A
Early decision deadline: N/A, notification date: N/A
Early action deadline: 11/1, notification date: 1/31
Application deadline (fall): 1/15
Undergraduate student body: 4,875 full time, 1,108 part time; 63% male, 37% female; 0% American Indian, 4% Asian, 5% black, 9% Hispanic, 3% multiracial, 0% Pacific Islander, 37% white, 30% international; 11% from in state; 29% live on campus; 0% of students in fraternities, 0% in sororities
Most popular majors: 92% Visual and Performing Arts, 6% Health Professions and Related Programs, 2% Education
Expenses: 2017-2018: $42,750; room/board: $18,180
Financial aid: (617) 747-2274; 33% of undergrads determined to have financial need; average aid package $18,827

Boston Architectural College

Boston MA
(617) 585-0123
U.S. News ranking: Arts, unranked
Website: www.the-bac.edu
Admissions email: admissions@the-bac.edu
Private; founded 1889
Freshman admissions: least selective; 2016-2017: 50 applied, 50 accepted. Neither SAT nor ACT required. SAT 25/75 percentile: N/A. High school rank: N/A
Early decision deadline: N/A, notification date: N/A
Early action deadline: N/A, notification date: N/A
Application deadline (fall): rolling
Undergraduate student body: 305 full time, 60 part time; 56% male, 44% female; 0% American Indian, 8% Asian, 7% black, 13% Hispanic, 4% multiracial, 0% Pacific Islander, 39% white, 20% international
Most popular majors: 50% Architecture, 40% Environmental Design/Architecture, 5% Interior Architecture, 5% Landscape Architecture
Expenses: 2017-2018: $21,174; room/board: $13,280
Financial aid: (617) 585-0183; 45% of undergrads determined to have financial need; average aid package $11,624

Boston College

Chestnut Hill MA
(617) 552-3100
U.S. News ranking: Nat. U., No. 32
Website: www.bc.edu
Private; founded 1863
Affiliation: Roman Catholic
Freshman admissions: most selective; 2016-2017: 28,956 applied, 9,017 accepted. Either SAT or ACT required. SAT 25/75 percentile: 1260-1460. High school rank: 80% in top tenth, 95% in top quarter, 99% in top half
Early decision deadline: N/A, notification date: N/A
Early action deadline: 11/1, notification date: 12/25
Application deadline (fall): 1/1
Undergraduate student body: 9,309 full time, 0 part time; 46% male, 54% female; 0% American Indian, 10% Asian, 4% black, 10% Hispanic, 3% multiracial, 0% Pacific Islander, 63% white, 7% international; 26% from in state; 82% live on campus; 0% of students in fraternities, 0% in sororities
Most popular majors: 12% Economics, General, 11% Finance, General, 8% Biology/Biological Sciences, General, 7% Psychology, General, 6% Speech Communication and Rhetoric
Expenses: 2017-2018: $53,346; room/board: $14,142
Financial aid: (617) 552-3300; 40% of undergrads determined to have financial need; average aid package $41,102

Boston Conservatory[1]

Boston MA
U.S. News ranking: Arts, unranked
Website: www.bostonconservatory.edu
Admissions email: admissions@bostonconservatory.edu
Private
Application deadline (fall): N/A
Undergraduate student body: N/A full time, N/A part time
Expenses: 2017-2018: $44,735; room/board: $11,820
Financial aid: N/A

Boston University

Boston MA
(617) 353-2300
U.S. News ranking: Nat. U., No. 37
Website: www.bu.edu
Admissions email: admissions@bu.edu
Private; founded 1839
Freshman admissions: most selective; 2016-2017: 57,441 applied, 16,907 accepted. Either SAT or ACT required. SAT 25/75 percentile: 1220-1420. High school rank: 63% in top tenth, 91% in top quarter, 99% in top half
Early decision deadline: 11/1, notification date: 12/15
Early action deadline: N/A, notification date: N/A
Application deadline (fall): 1/2
Undergraduate student body: 16,627 full time, 1,317 part time; 39% male, 61% female; 0% American Indian, 14% Asian, 4% black, 11% Hispanic, 4% multiracial, 0% Pacific Islander, 41% white, 22% international; 20% from in state; 75% live on campus; 5% of students in fraternities, 15% in sororities
Most popular majors: 20% Business, Management, Marketing, and Related Support Services, 14% Social Sciences, 13% Communication, Journalism, and Related Programs, 9% Health Professions and Related Programs, 8% Engineering
Expenses: 2017-2018: $52,082; room/board: $15,270
Financial aid: (617) 353-2965; 36% of undergrads determined to have financial need; average aid package $40,232

Brandeis University

Waltham MA
(781) 736-3500
U.S. News ranking: Nat. U., No. 34
Website: www.brandeis.edu
Admissions email: admissions@brandeis.edu
Private; founded 1948
Freshman admissions: most selective; 2016-2017: 11,351 applied, 3,796 accepted. Either SAT or ACT required. SAT 25/75 percentile: 1270-1480. High school rank: 72% in top tenth, 95% in top quarter, 100% in top half
Early decision deadline: 11/1, notification date: 12/15
Early action deadline: N/A, notification date: N/A
Application deadline (fall): 1/1

Undergraduate student body: 3,591 full time, 17 part time; 42% male, 58% female; 0% American Indian, 13% Asian, 5% black, 8% Hispanic, 3% multiracial, 0% Pacific Islander, 46% white, 21% international; 28% from in state; 78% live on campus; 0% of students in fraternities, 0% in sororities
Most popular majors: 10% Business/Commerce, General, 10% Economics, General, 9% Biology/Biological Sciences, General, 8% Psychology, General, 6% Health Policy Analysis
Expenses: 2017-2018: $53,582; room/board: $14,906
Financial aid: (791) 736-3700; 50% of undergrads determined to have financial need; average aid package $43,803

Bridgewater State University

Bridgewater MA
(508) 531-1237
U.S. News ranking: Reg. U. (N), No. 102
Website: www.bridgew.edu/admissions
Admissions email: admission@bridgew.edu
Public; founded 1840
Freshman admissions: less selective; 2016-2017: 6,007 applied, 4,863 accepted. Neither SAT nor ACT required. SAT 25/75 percentile: 890-1090. High school rank: N/A
Early decision deadline: N/A, notification date: N/A
Early action deadline: 11/15, notification date: 12/15
Application deadline (fall): rolling
Undergraduate student body: 7,826 full time, 1,736 part time; 41% male, 59% female; 0% American Indian, 2% Asian, 10% black, 7% Hispanic, 4% multiracial, 0% Pacific Islander, 76% white, 0% international; 96% from in state; 42% live on campus; N/A of students in fraternities, N/A in sororities
Most popular majors: 19% Education, 16% Business, Management, Marketing, and Related Support Services, 12% Homeland Security, Law Enforcement, Firefighting and Related Protective Services, 11% Psychology, 7% Communication, Journalism, and Related Programs
Expenses: 2017-2018: $9,870 in state, $16,010 out of state; room/board: $12,750
Financial aid: (508) 531-2685; 70% of undergrads determined to have financial need; average aid package $8,343

Cambridge College[1]

Cambridge MA
U.S. News ranking: Reg. U. (N), unranked
Website: www.cambridgecollege.edu
Admissions email: N/A
Private; founded 1971
Application deadline (fall): N/A
Undergraduate student body: N/A full time, N/A part time
Expenses: 2016-2017: $14,436; room/board: $8,000
Financial aid: (617) 873-0440

Clark University
Worcester MA
(508) 793-7431
U.S. News ranking: Nat. U., No. 81
Website: www.clarku.edu
Admissions email: admissions@clarku.edu
Private; founded 1887
Freshman admissions: more selective; 2016-2017: 7,914 applied, 4,331 accepted. Neither SAT nor ACT required. SAT 25/75 percentile: 1110-1325. High school rank: 36% in top tenth, 74% in top quarter, 96% in top half
Early decision deadline: 11/1, notification date: 12/15
Early action deadline: 11/1, notification date: 12/15
Application deadline (fall): 1/15
Undergraduate student body: 2,223 full time, 66 part time; 39% male, 61% female; 0% American Indian, 7% Asian, 4% black, 7% Hispanic, 2% multiracial, 0% Pacific Islander, 57% white, 14% international; 38% from in state; 69% live on campus; 0% of students in fraternities, 0% in sororities
Most popular majors: 19% Psychology, 8% Business Administration, Management and Operations, 7% Economics, 7% Political Science and Government, 6% Biology, General
Expenses: 2017-2018: $44,400; room/board: $8,860
Financial aid: (508) 793-7478; 64% of undergrads determined to have financial need; average aid package $36,022

College of Our Lady of the Elms
Chicopee MA
(800) 255-3567
U.S. News ranking: Reg. U. (N), No. 102
Website: www.elms.edu
Admissions email: admissions@elms.edu
Private; founded 1928
Affiliation: Roman Catholic
Freshman admissions: less selective; 2016-2017: 684 applied, 523 accepted. Either SAT or ACT required. SAT 25/75 percentile: 840-1055. High school rank: N/A
Early decision deadline: N/A, notification date: N/A
Early action deadline: N/A, notification date: N/A
Application deadline (fall): rolling
Undergraduate student body: 954 full time, 234 part time; 25% male, 75% female; 0% American Indian, 2% Asian, 8% black, 12% Hispanic, 0% multiracial, 0% Pacific Islander, 57% white, 1% international; 78% from in state; 31% live on campus; N/A of students in fraternities, N/A in sororities
Most popular majors: 48% Health Professions and Related Programs, 13% Business, Management, Marketing, and Related Support Services, 13% Public Administration and Social Service Professions, 6% Education, 5% Psychology

College of the Holy Cross
Worcester MA
(508) 793-2443
U.S. News ranking: Nat. Lib. Arts, No. 33
Website: www.holycross.edu
Admissions email: admissions@holycross.edu
Private; founded 1843
Affiliation: Roman Catholic
Freshman admissions: more selective; 2016-2017: 6,693 applied, 2,574 accepted. Neither SAT nor ACT required. SAT 25/75 percentile: 1220-1370. High school rank: 61% in top tenth, 87% in top quarter, 100% in top half
Early decision deadline: 12/15, notification date: N/A
Early action deadline: N/A, notification date: N/A
Application deadline (fall): 1/15
Undergraduate student body: 2,910 full time, 31 part time; 49% male, 51% female; 0% American Indian, 5% Asian, 4% black, 10% Hispanic, 3% multiracial, 0% Pacific Islander, 70% white, 3% international; 40% from in state; 89% live on campus; 0% of students in fraternities, 0% in sororities
Most popular majors: 33% Social Sciences, 13% Psychology, 9% Foreign Languages, Literatures, and Linguistics, 9% Physical Sciences, 7% English Language and Literature/Letters
Expenses: 2017-2018: $50,630; room/board: $13,690
Financial aid: (508) 793-2265; 50% of undergrads determined to have financial need; average aid package $39,079

Curry College
Milton MA
(800) 669-0686
U.S. News ranking: Reg. U. (N), second tier
Website: www.curry.edu
Admissions email: adm@curry.edu
Private; founded 1879
Freshman admissions: less selective; 2016-2017: 6,143 applied, 5,442 accepted. Neither SAT nor ACT required. SAT 25/75 percentile: 840-1040. High school rank: 4% in top tenth, 16% in top quarter, 48% in top half
Early decision deadline: N/A, notification date: N/A
Early action deadline: 12/1, notification date: 12/15
Application deadline (fall): rolling
Undergraduate student body: 2,111 full time, 577 part time; 41% male, 59% female; 0% American Indian, 2% Asian, 10% black, 6% Hispanic, 2% multiracial, 0% Pacific Islander, 67% white, 2% international; 76% from in state; 57% live on campus; N/A of students in fraternities, N/A in sororities

Most popular majors: 44% Health Professions and Related Programs, 13% Business, Management, Marketing, and Related Support Services, 12% Homeland Security, Law Enforcement, Firefighting and Related Protective Services, 11% Communication, Journalism, and Related Programs, 7% Psychology
Expenses: 2017-2018: $38,596; room/board: $14,735
Financial aid: (617) 333-2354; 75% of undergrads determined to have financial need; average aid package $27,281

Dean College
Franklin MA
(508) 541-1508
U.S. News ranking: Reg. Coll. (N), No. 22
Website: www.dean.edu
Admissions email: admissions@dean.edu
Private; founded 1865
Freshman admissions: least selective; 2016-2017: 2,832 applied, 2,570 accepted. Neither SAT nor ACT required. SAT 25/75 percentile: 740-980. High school rank: N/A
Early decision deadline: N/A, notification date: N/A
Early action deadline: 12/1, notification date: 1/15
Application deadline (fall): rolling
Undergraduate student body: 1,132 full time, 207 part time; 47% male, 53% female; 0% American Indian, 1% Asian, 15% black, 8% Hispanic, 5% multiracial, 0% Pacific Islander, 50% white, 6% international; 55% from in state; 87% live on campus; N/A of students in fraternities, N/A in sororities
Most popular majors: 41% Business Administration and Management, General, 41% Visual and Performing Arts, General, 10% Liberal Arts and Sciences/Liberal Studies, 5% Psychology, General, 1% English Language and Literature, General
Expenses: 2017-2018: $38,090; room/board: $16,346
Financial aid: (508) 541-1518; 74% of undergrads determined to have financial need; average aid package $27,345

Eastern Nazarene College
Quincy MA
(617) 745-3711
U.S. News ranking: Reg. U. (N), second tier
Website: www.enc.edu
Admissions email: admissions@enc.edu
Private; founded 1918
Affiliation: Church of the Nazarene
Freshman admissions: selective; 2016-2017: 1,045 applied, 692 accepted. Either SAT or ACT required. SAT 25/75 percentile: 820-1110. High school rank: 11% in top tenth, 34% in top quarter, 67% in top half
Early decision deadline: N/A, notification date: N/A
Early action deadline: N/A, notification date: N/A
Application deadline (fall): rolling

Undergraduate student body: 656 full time, 128 part time; 40% male, 60% female; 0% American Indian, 2% Asian, 22% black, 13% Hispanic, 4% multiracial, 0% Pacific Islander, 52% white, 2% international; 65% from in state; 50% live on campus; 0% of students in fraternities, 0% in sororities
Most popular majors: 38% Business Administration and Management, General, 10% Biology/Biological Sciences, General, 8% Elementary Education and Teaching, 8% Psychology, General, 7% Social Work
Expenses: 2017-2018: $31,780; room/board: $9,334
Financial aid: (617) 745-3712; 91% of undergrads determined to have financial need; average aid package $22,151

Emerson College
Boston MA
(617) 824-8600
U.S. News ranking: Reg. U. (N), No. 7
Website: www.emerson.edu
Admissions email: admission@emerson.edu
Private; founded 1880
Freshman admissions: more selective; 2016-2017: 9,149 applied, 4,397 accepted. Either SAT or ACT required. SAT 25/75 percentile: 1120-1330. High school rank: 34% in top tenth, 70% in top quarter, 95% in top half
Early decision deadline: N/A, notification date: N/A
Early action deadline: 11/1, notification date: 12/15
Application deadline (fall): 1/15
Undergraduate student body: 3,733 full time, 57 part time; 40% male, 60% female; 0% American Indian, 4% Asian, 3% black, 11% Hispanic, 4% multiracial, 0% Pacific Islander, 67% white, 8% international; 32% from in state; 57% live on campus; 2% of students in fraternities, 3% in sororities
Most popular majors: 51% Visual and Performing Arts, 16% Communication, Journalism, and Related Programs, 15% Business, Management, Marketing, and Related Support Services, 14% English Language and Literature/Letters, 2% Health Professions and Related Programs
Expenses: 2017-2018: $42,908; room/board: $16,320
Financial aid: (617) 824-8655; 55% of undergrads determined to have financial need; average aid package $21,848

Emmanuel College
Boston MA
(617) 735-9715
U.S. News ranking: Nat. Lib. Arts, second tier
Website: www.emmanuel.edu
Admissions email: enroll@emmanuel.edu
Private; founded 1919
Affiliation: Roman Catholic

Freshman admissions: selective; 2016-2017: 6,223 applied, 4,443 accepted. Neither SAT nor ACT required. SAT 25/75 percentile: 1030-1200. High school rank: N/A
Early decision deadline: N/A, notification date: N/A
Early action deadline: 11/1, notification date: 12/15
Application deadline (fall): 2/15
Undergraduate student body: 1,834 full time, 178 part time; 26% male, 74% female; 0% American Indian, 4% Asian, 5% black, 10% Hispanic, 3% multiracial, 0% Pacific Islander, 71% white, 2% international; 56% from in state; 70% live on campus; N/A of students in fraternities, N/A in sororities
Most popular majors: 15% Biological and Biomedical Sciences, 12% Business, Management, Marketing, and Related Support Services, 12% Psychology, 9% Social Sciences, 8% Education
Expenses: 2017-2018: $38,844; room/board: $14,628
Financial aid: (617) 735-9938; 81% of undergrads determined to have financial need; average aid package $26,986

Endicott College
Beverly MA
(978) 921-1000
U.S. News ranking: Reg. U. (N), No. 34
Website: www.endicott.edu
Admissions email: admission@endicott.edu
Private; founded 1939
Freshman admissions: selective; 2016-2017: 3,619 applied, 2,850 accepted. Neither SAT nor ACT required. SAT 25/75 percentile: 1000-1150. High school rank: 10% in top tenth, 42% in top quarter, 79% in top half
Early decision deadline: N/A, notification date: N/A
Early action deadline: N/A, notification date: N/A
Application deadline (fall): 2/15
Undergraduate student body: 2,897 full time, 393 part time; 39% male, 61% female; 0% American Indian, 1% Asian, 3% black, 5% Hispanic, 1% multiracial, 0% Pacific Islander, 82% white, 2% international; 48% from in state; 91% live on campus; 0% of students in fraternities, 0% in sororities
Most popular majors: 17% Business Administration and Management, General, 12% Registered Nursing/Registered Nurse, 7% Education, Other, 7% Hospitality Administration/Management, General, 7% Sport and Fitness Administration/Management
Expenses: 2017-2018: $32,154; room/board: $14,900
Financial aid: (978) 232-2060; 61% of undergrads determined to have financial need; average aid package $21,634

Fisher College
Boston MA
(617) 236-8818
U.S. News ranking: Reg. Coll. (N), No. 32
Website: www.fisher.edu
Admissions email: admissions@fisher.edu
Private; founded 1903
Freshman admissions: least selective; 2016-2017: 3,109 applied, 2,096 accepted. Neither SAT nor ACT required. SAT 25/75 percentile: 690-880. High school rank: N/A
Early decision deadline: N/A, notification date: N/A
Early action deadline: N/A, notification date: N/A
Application deadline (fall): rolling
Undergraduate student body: 1,171 full time, 825 part time; 26% male, 74% female; 0% American Indian, 1% Asian, 12% black, 10% Hispanic, 2% multiracial, 0% Pacific Islander, 29% white, 9% international; 78% from in state; 16% live on campus; 0% of students in fraternities, 0% in sororities
Most popular majors: 26% Business, Management, Marketing, and Related Support Services, 10% Public Administration and Social Service Professions, 6% Health Professions and Related Programs, 5% Communication, Journalism, and Related Programs, 3% Homeland Security, Law Enforcement, Firefighting and Related Protective Services
Expenses: 2017-2018: $30,499; room/board: $15,768
Financial aid: (617) 236-8821; 70% of undergrads determined to have financial need; average aid package $20,048

Fitchburg State University
Fitchburg MA
(978) 665-3144
U.S. News ranking: Reg. U. (N), No. 137
Website: www.fitchburgstate.edu
Admissions email: admissions@fitchburgstate.edu
Public; founded 1894
Freshman admissions: selective; 2016-2017: 3,566 applied, 2,662 accepted. Either SAT or ACT required. SAT 25/75 percentile: 890-1090. High school rank: N/A
Early decision deadline: N/A, notification date: N/A
Early action deadline: N/A, notification date: N/A
Application deadline (fall): rolling
Undergraduate student body: 3,428 full time, 734 part time; 47% male, 53% female; 0% American Indian, 2% Asian, 10% black, 11% Hispanic, 3% multiracial, 0% Pacific Islander, 71% white, 0% international; 92% from in state; 57% live on campus; 1% of students in fraternities, 3% in sororities
Most popular majors: 13% Business, Management, Marketing, and Related Support Services, 13% Health Professions and Related Programs, 13%

Visual and Performing Arts, 9% Biological and Biomedical Sciences, 8% Homeland Security, Law Enforcement, Firefighting and Related Protective Services
Expenses: 2017-2018: $10,175 in state, $16,255 out of state; room/board: N/A
Financial aid: (978) 665-3302; 67% of undergrads determined to have financial need; average aid package $10,590

Framingham State University
Framingham MA
(508) 626-4500
U.S. News ranking: Reg. U. (N), No. 126
Website: www.framingham.edu
Admissions email: admissions@framingham.edu
Public; founded 1839
Freshman admissions: selective; 2016-2017: 6,204 applied, 4,021 accepted. Either SAT or ACT required. SAT 25/75 percentile: 890-1090. High school rank: 6% in top tenth, 26% in top quarter, 63% in top half
Early decision deadline: N/A, notification date: N/A
Early action deadline: 11/15, notification date: 12/15
Application deadline (fall): rolling
Undergraduate student body: 3,701 full time, 636 part time; 39% male, 61% female; 0% American Indian, 3% Asian, 11% black, 12% Hispanic, 4% multiracial, 0% Pacific Islander, 69% white, 0% international
Most popular majors: 18% Business, Management, Marketing, and Related Support Services, 18% Social Sciences, 12% Family and Consumer Sciences/Human Sciences, 10% Psychology, 8% Communications Technologies/Technicians and Support Services
Expenses: 2016-2017: $9,340 in state, $15,420 out of state; room/board: $11,244
Financial aid: N/A

Franklin W. Olin College of Engineering
Needham MA
(781) 292-2222
U.S. News ranking: Engineering, unranked
Website: www.olin.edu/
Admissions email: info@olin.edu
Private; founded 1997
Freshman admissions: more selective; 2016-2017: 1,296 applied, 132 accepted. Either SAT or ACT required. SAT 25/75 percentile: 1400-1580. High school rank: N/A
Early decision deadline: N/A, notification date: N/A
Early action deadline: N/A, notification date: N/A
Application deadline (fall): 1/1
Undergraduate student body: 340 full time, 38 part time; 51% male, 49% female; 0% American Indian, 14% Asian, 1% black, 6% Hispanic, 7% multiracial,

0% Pacific Islander, 54% white, 8% international; 14% from in state; 100% live on campus; 0% of students in fraternities, 0% in sororities
Most popular majors: 40% Electrical and Electronics Engineering, 31% Engineering, General, 29% Mechanical Engineering
Expenses: 2017-2018: $49,280; room/board: $16,300
Financial aid: (781) 292-2215; 45% of undergrads determined to have financial need; average aid package $44,286

Gordon College
Wenham MA
(866) 464-6736
U.S. News ranking: Nat. Lib. Arts, No. 168
Website: www.gordon.edu
Admissions email: admissions@gordon.edu
Private; founded 1889
Affiliation: Other
Freshman admissions: selective; 2016-2017: 2,714 applied, 2,496 accepted. Either SAT or ACT required. SAT 25/75 percentile: 890-1210. High school rank: 27% in top tenth, 58% in top quarter, 87% in top half
Early decision deadline: N/A, notification date: N/A
Early action deadline: 11/15, notification date: 12/1
Application deadline (fall): 8/1
Undergraduate student body: 1,574 full time, 83 part time; 37% male, 63% female; 0% American Indian, 5% Asian, 5% black, 7% Hispanic, 4% multiracial, 0% Pacific Islander, 69% white, 9% international; 35% from in state; 86% live on campus; 0% of students in fraternities, 0% in sororities
Most popular majors: 9% Business/Commerce, General, 7% English Language and Literature, General, 7% Social Work, 6% Psychology, General, 5% Speech Communication and Rhetoric
Expenses: 2017-2018: $36,740; room/board: $11,000
Financial aid: (800) 343-1379; 65% of undergrads determined to have financial need; average aid package $24,414

Hampshire College[1]
Amherst MA
U.S. News ranking: Nat. Lib. Arts, unranked
Website: www.hampshire.edu
Admissions email: admissions@hampshire.edu
Private; founded 1965
Application deadline (fall): N/A
Undergraduate student body: N/A full time, N/A part time
Expenses: 2016-2017: $50,238; room/board: $13,274
Financial aid: (413) 559-5739

Harvard University
Cambridge MA
(617) 495-1551
U.S. News ranking: Nat. U., No. 2
Website: www.harvard.edu
Admissions email: college@fas.harvard.edu
Private; founded 1636

Freshman admissions: most selective; 2016-2017: 39,041 applied, 2,110 accepted. Either SAT or ACT required. SAT 25/75 percentile: 1430-1600. High school rank: 95% in top tenth, 99% in top quarter, 100% in top half
Early decision deadline: N/A, notification date: N/A
Early action deadline: 11/1, notification date: 12/16
Application deadline (fall): 1/1
Undergraduate student body: 6,710 full time, 0 part time; 53% male, 47% female; 0% American Indian, 20% Asian, 7% black, 11% Hispanic, 7% multiracial, 0% Pacific Islander, 41% white, 12% international; 16% from in state; 98% live on campus; N/A of students in fraternities, N/A in sororities
Most popular majors: 30% Social Sciences, General, 14% Biology/Biological Sciences, General, 11% Mathematics, General, 8% History, General, 7% Physical Sciences
Expenses: 2017-2018: $48,949; room/board: $16,660
Financial aid: (617) 495-1581; 55% of undergrads determined to have financial need; average aid package $53,048

Lasell College
Newton MA
(617) 243-2225
U.S. News ranking: Reg. U. (N), No. 130
Website: www.lasell.edu
Admissions email: info@lasell.edu
Private; founded 1851
Freshman admissions: less selective; 2016-2017: 3,221 applied, 2,450 accepted. Neither SAT nor ACT required. SAT 25/75 percentile: 870-1060. High school rank: N/A
Early decision deadline: N/A, notification date: N/A
Early action deadline: 11/15, notification date: 12/1
Application deadline (fall): rolling
Undergraduate student body: 1,747 full time, 41 part time; 35% male, 65% female; 0% American Indian, 2% Asian, 5% black, 9% Hispanic, 2% multiracial, 0% Pacific Islander, 71% white, 6% international; 58% from in state; 75% live on campus; 0% of students in fraternities, 0% in sororities
Most popular majors: 11% Speech Communication and Rhetoric, 10% Fashion Merchandising, 9% Criminology, 8% Sport and Fitness Administration/Management, 6% Psychology, General
Expenses: 2017-2018: $34,600; room/board: $14,800
Financial aid: (617) 243-2227; 77% of undergrads determined to have financial need; average aid package $26,531

Lesley University
Cambridge MA
(617) 349-8800
U.S. News ranking: Nat. U., No. 181
Website: www.lesley.edu
Admissions email: admissions@lesley.edu
Private; founded 1909

Freshman admissions: selective; 2016-2017: 3,386 applied, 2,158 accepted. Either SAT or ACT required. SAT 25/75 percentile: 960-1170. High school rank: N/A
Early decision deadline: N/A, notification date: N/A
Early action deadline: 12/1, notification date: 12/23
Application deadline (fall): 7/15
Undergraduate student body: 1,541 full time, 388 part time; 23% male, 77% female; 0% American Indian, 4% Asian, 7% black, 12% Hispanic, 4% multiracial, 0% Pacific Islander, 64% white, 2% international; 65% from in state; 43% live on campus; 0% of students in fraternities, 0% in sororities
Most popular majors: 21% Psychology, 15% Liberal Arts and Sciences, General Studies and Humanities, 15% Visual and Performing Arts, 9% Education, 8% English Language and Literature/Letters
Expenses: 2017-2018: $26,550; room/board: $15,750
Financial aid: (617) 349-8760; 68% of undergrads determined to have financial need; average aid package $16,470

Massachusetts College of Art and Design
Boston MA
(617) 879-7222
U.S. News ranking: Arts, unranked
Website: www.massart.edu
Admissions email: admissions@massart.edu
Public; founded 1873
Freshman admissions: selective; 2016-2017: 1,531 applied, 1,085 accepted. Neither SAT nor ACT required. SAT 25/75 percentile: 970-1200. High school rank: N/A
Early decision deadline: N/A, notification date: N/A
Early action deadline: 12/1, notification date: 1/5
Application deadline (fall): 2/1
Undergraduate student body: 1,560 full time, 275 part time; 29% male, 71% female; 0% American Indian, 8% Asian, 4% black, 10% Hispanic, 1% multiracial, 0% Pacific Islander, 63% white, 5% international; 67% from in state; 39% live on campus; N/A of students in fraternities, N/A in sororities
Most popular majors: 15% Illustration, 12% Graphic Design, 10% Film/Video and Photographic Arts, Other, 8% Industrial and Product Design, 7% Painting
Expenses: 2017-2018: $12,700 in state, $34,400 out of state; room/board: $13,500
Financial aid: (617) 879-7849; 67% of undergrads determined to have financial need; average aid package $12,552

Massachusetts College of Liberal Arts

North Adams MA
(413) 662-5410
U.S. News ranking: Nat. Lib. Arts, second tier
Website: www.mcla.edu
Admissions email: admissions@mcla.edu
Public; founded 1894
Freshman admissions: selective; 2016-2017: 2,013 applied, 1,552 accepted. Either SAT or ACT required. SAT 25/75 percentile: 890-1130. High school rank: 17% in top tenth, 42% in top quarter, 72% in top half
Early decision deadline: N/A, notification date: N/A
Early action deadline: 12/1, notification date: 12/15
Application deadline (fall): rolling
Undergraduate student body: 1,255 full time, 189 part time; 37% male, 63% female; 0% American Indian, 2% Asian, 9% black, 7% Hispanic, 3% multiracial, 0% Pacific Islander, 74% white, 1% international; 74% from in state; 60% live on campus; N/A of students in fraternities, N/A in sororities
Most popular majors: 18% Business, Management, Marketing, and Related Support Services, 13% English Language and Literature/Letters, 11% Biological and Biomedical Sciences, 11% Social Sciences, 10% Multi/Interdisciplinary Studies
Expenses: 2017/2018: $1,030 in state, $9,975 out of state; room/board: N/A
Financial aid: (413) 662-5219; 76% of undergrads determined to have financial need; average aid package $15,633

Massachusetts Institute of Technology

Cambridge MA
(617) 253-3400
U.S. News ranking: Nat. U., No. 5
Website: web.mit.edu/
Admissions email: admissions@mit.edu
Private; founded 1861
Freshman admissions: most selective; 2016-2017: 19,020 applied, 1,511 accepted. Either SAT or ACT required. SAT 25/75 percentile: 1460-1590. High school rank: 97% in top tenth, 100% in top quarter, 100% in top half
Early decision deadline: N/A, notification date: N/A
Early action deadline: 11/1, notification date: 12/20
Application deadline (fall): 1/1
Undergraduate student body: 4,476 full time, 48 part time; 54% male, 46% female; 0% American Indian, 26% Asian, 6% black, 15% Hispanic, 7% multiracial, 0% Pacific Islander, 35% white, 10% international; 10% from in state; 94% live on campus; 46% of students in fraternities, 34% in sororities

Most popular majors: 38% Engineering, 25% Computer and Information Sciences and Support Services, 9% Mathematics and Statistics, 8% Biological and Biomedical Sciences, 8% Physical Sciences
Expenses: 2017-2018: $49,892; room/board: $14,720
Financial aid: (617) 258-8600; 60% of undergrads determined to have financial need; average aid package $47,329

Massachusetts Maritime Academy

Buzzards Bay MA
(800) 544-3411
U.S. News ranking: Reg. U. (N), No. 18
Website: www.maritime.edu
Admissions email: admissions@maritime.edu
Public; founded 1891
Freshman admissions: selective; 2016-2017: 825 applied, 664 accepted. Either SAT or ACT required. SAT 25/75 percentile: 950-1150. High school rank: N/A
Early decision deadline: N/A, notification date: N/A
Early action deadline: 11/1, notification date: 12/31
Application deadline (fall): rolling
Undergraduate student body: 1,605 full time, 72 part time; 87% male, 13% female; 0% American Indian, 1% Asian, 1% black, 4% Hispanic, 3% multiracial, 0% Pacific Islander, 87% white, 1% international; 79% from in state; 95% live on campus; 0% of students in fraternities, 0% in sororities
Most popular majors: 34% Naval Architecture and Marine Engineering, 21% Marine Science/Merchant Marine Officer, 14% Engineering, Other
Expenses: 2017-2018: $8,381 in state, $25,007 out of state; room/board: $12,306
Financial aid: (508) 830-5087; 56% of undergrads determined to have financial need; average aid package $12,188

Merrimack College

North Andover MA
(978) 837-5100
U.S. News ranking: Reg. U. (N), No. 56
Website: www.merrimack.edu
Admissions email: Admission@Merrimack.edu
Private; founded 1947
Affiliation: Roman Catholic
Freshman admissions: selective; 2016-2017: 8,214 applied, 6,728 accepted. Neither SAT nor ACT required. SAT 25/75 percentile: 900-1090. High school rank: 5% in top tenth, 24% in top quarter, 59% in top half
Early decision deadline: 11/15, notification date: 12/15
Early action deadline: 1/15, notification date: 2/15
Application deadline (fall): 2/15
Undergraduate student body: 3,313 full time, 135 part time; 48% male, 52% female; 0% American Indian, 1% Asian, 3% black, 6% Hispanic, 2% multiracial,

0% Pacific Islander, 76% white, 3% international; 70% from in state; 75% live on campus; 1% of students in fraternities, 7% in sororities
Most popular majors: 28% Business, Management, Marketing, and Related Support Services, 14% Family and Consumer Sciences/Human Sciences, 11% Health Professions and Related Programs, 6% Education, 5% Homeland Security, Law Enforcement, Firefighting and Related Protective Services
Expenses: 2017-2018: $40,190; room/board: $15,225
Financial aid: (978) 837-5186; 71% of undergrads determined to have financial need; average aid package $23,143

Montserrat College of Art[1]

Beverly MA
U.S. News ranking: Arts, unranked
Website: www.montserrat.edu
Admissions email: admissions@montserrat.edu
Private; founded 1970
Application deadline (fall): N/A
Undergraduate student body: N/A full time, N/A part time
Expenses: 2016-2017: $30,800; room/board: $9,250
Financial aid: (978) 921-4242

Mount Holyoke College

South Hadley MA
(413) 538-2023
U.S. News ranking: Nat. Lib. Arts, No. 36
Website: www.mtholyoke.edu
Admissions email: admission@mtholyoke.edu
Private; founded 1837
Freshman admissions: more selective; 2016-2017: 3,543 applied, 1,849 accepted. Neither SAT nor ACT required. SAT 25/75 percentile: 1220-1460. High school rank: 49% in top tenth, 88% in top quarter, 97% in top half
Early decision deadline: 11/15, notification date: 1/1
Early action deadline: N/A, notification date: N/A
Application deadline (fall): 1/15
Undergraduate student body: 2,162 full time, 37 part time; 0% male, 100% female; 0% American Indian, 11% Asian, 5% black, 8% Hispanic, 3% multiracial, 0% Pacific Islander, 45% white, 27% international; 25% from in state; 95% live on campus; 0% of students in fraternities, 0% in sororities
Most popular majors: 12% Biology/Biological Sciences, General, 11% Psychology, General, 9% Economics, General, 8% English Language and Literature, General, 6% International Relations and Affairs
Expenses: 2017-2018: $47,940; room/board: $14,060
Financial aid: (413) 538-2291; 52% of undergrads determined to have financial need; average aid package $37,763

Mount Ida College

Newton MA
(617) 928-4535
U.S. News ranking: Reg. Coll. (N), No. 26
Website: www.mountida.edu
Admissions email: admissions@mountida.edu
Private; founded 1899
Affiliation: African Methodist Episcopal
Freshman admissions: less selective; 2016-2017: 2,338 applied, 1,597 accepted. Neither SAT nor ACT required. SAT 25/75 percentile: 790-1020. High school rank: N/A
Early decision deadline: N/A, notification date: N/A
Early action deadline: N/A, notification date: N/A
Application deadline (fall): rolling
Undergraduate student body: 1,295 full time, 62 part time; 31% male, 69% female; 0% American Indian, 3% Asian, 10% black, 11% Hispanic, 4% multiracial, 0% Pacific Islander, 63% white, 5% international; 66% from in state; 62% live on campus; 0% of students in fraternities, 0% in sororities
Most popular majors: 21% Veterinary/Animal Health Technology/Technician and Veterinary Assistant, 15% Business Administration and Management, General, 13% Dental Hygiene/Hygienist, 7% Criminal Justice/Law Enforcement Administration, 5% Forensic Science and Technology
Expenses: 2017-2018: $35,720; room/board: $13,680
Financial aid: (617) 928-4099; 82% of undergrads determined to have financial need; average aid package $25,503

National Graduate School of Quality Management[1]

Falmouth MA
(800) 838-2580
U.S. News ranking: Business, unranked
Website: www.ngs.edu
Private; founded 1993
Application deadline (fall): N/A
Undergraduate student body: N/A full time, N/A part time
Expenses: 2016-2017: $11,200; room/board: N/A
Financial aid: N/A

New England College of Business and Finance[1]

Boston MA
U.S. News ranking: Business, unranked
Website: www.necb.edu/
For-profit; founded 1909
Application deadline (fall): N/A
Undergraduate student body: N/A full time, N/A part time
Expenses: 2016-2017: $11,240; room/board: N/A
Financial aid: N/A

New England Conservatory of Music[1]

Boston MA
(617) 585-1101
U.S. News ranking: Arts, unranked
Website: www.newenglandconservatory.edu
Admissions email: admission@newenglandconservatory.edu
Private; founded 1867
Application deadline (fall): 12/1
Undergraduate student body: N/A full time, N/A part time
Expenses: 2017-2018: $46,930; room/board: $15,700
Financial aid: (617) 585-1110; 44% of undergrads determined to have financial need; average aid package $28,741

New England Institute of Art[1]

Brookline MA
U.S. News ranking: Arts, unranked
Website: www.artinstitutes.edu/boston/
Admissions email: N/A
For-profit
Application deadline (fall): N/A
Undergraduate student body: N/A full time, N/A part time
Expenses: 2016-2017: $18,540; room/board: N/A
Financial aid: N/A

Newbury College

Brookline MA
(617) 730-7007
U.S. News ranking: Reg. Coll. (N), No. 36
Website: www.newbury.edu/
Admissions email: admissions@newbury.edu
Private; founded 1962
Freshman admissions: least selective; 2016-2017: 2,439 applied, 1,986 accepted. Neither SAT nor ACT required. SAT 25/75 percentile: 780-1030. High school rank: N/A
Early decision deadline: N/A, notification date: N/A
Early action deadline: N/A, notification date: N/A
Application deadline (fall): 8/1
Undergraduate student body: 675 full time, 76 part time; 42% male, 58% female; 0% American Indian, 7% Asian, 36% black, 16% Hispanic, 0% multiracial, 0% Pacific Islander, 38% white, 3% international; 82% from in state; 37% live on campus; 0% of students in fraternities, 0% in sororities
Most popular majors: 18% Business Administration and Management, General, 9% Corrections and Criminal Justice, Other, 8% Hospitality Administration/Management, General, 8% Interior Design, 7% Sport and Fitness Administration/Management
Expenses: 2017-2018: $34,470; room/board: $14,500
Financial aid: (617) 730-7102; 92% of undergrads determined to have financial need; average aid package $25,843

Nichols College

Dudley MA
(800) 470-3379
U.S. News ranking: Business, unranked
Website: www.nichols.edu/
Admissions email: admissions@nichols.edu
Private; founded 1815
Freshman admissions: less selective; 2016-2017: 2,311 applied, 1,934 accepted. Neither SAT nor ACT required. SAT 25/75 percentile: 830-1040. High school rank: 6% in top tenth, 20% in top quarter, 54% in top half
Early decision deadline: N/A, notification date: N/A
Early action deadline: 12/1, notification date: N/A
Application deadline (fall): rolling
Undergraduate student body: 1,160 full time, 109 part time; 60% male, 40% female; 0% American Indian, 1% Asian, 7% black, 7% Hispanic, 3% multiracial, 0% Pacific Islander, 80% white, 1% international; 58% from in state; 82% live on campus; N/A of students in fraternities, N/A in sororities
Most popular majors: 25% Business/Commerce, General, 12% Sport and Fitness Administration/Management, 11% Accounting, 10% Marketing/Marketing Management, General, 9% Finance, General
Expenses: 2017-2018: $34,000; room/board: $13,800
Financial aid: (508) 213-2340; 82% of undergrads determined to have financial need; average aid package $28,591

Northeastern University

Boston MA
(617) 373-2200
U.S. News ranking: Nat. U., No. 40
Website: www.northeastern.edu/
Admissions email: admissions@northeastern.edu
Private; founded 1898
Freshman admissions: most selective; 2016-2017: 51,063 applied, 14,747 accepted. Either SAT or ACT required. ACT 25/75 percentile: 31-34. High school rank: 76% in top tenth, 94% in top quarter, 99% in top half
Early decision deadline: 11/1, notification date: 12/15
Early action deadline: 11/1, notification date: 2/1
Application deadline (fall): 1/1
Undergraduate student body: 13,444 full time, 29 part time; 49% male, 51% female; 0% American Indian, 13% Asian, 4% black, 7% Hispanic, 4% multiracial, 0% Pacific Islander, 47% white, 20% international; 28% from in state; 45% live on campus; 11% of students in fraternities, 19% in sororities
Most popular majors: 26% Business, Management, Marketing, and Related Support Programs, 17% Engineering, 13% Health Professions and Related Programs, 10% Social Sciences, 8% Biological and Biomedical Sciences

Expenses: 2017-2018: $49,497; room/board: $16,240
Financial aid: (617) 373-3190; 37% of undergrads determined to have financial need; average aid package $31,140

Pine Manor College

Chestnut Hill MA
(617) 731-7111
U.S. News ranking: Nat. Lib. Arts, second tier
Website: www.pmc.edu
Admissions email: admission@pmc.edu
Private; founded 1911
Freshman admissions: less selective; 2016-2017: 782 applied, 582 accepted. Either SAT or ACT required. SAT 25/75 percentile: N/A. High school rank: N/A
Early decision deadline: N/A, notification date: N/A
Early action deadline: N/A, notification date: N/A
Application deadline (fall): rolling
Undergraduate student body: 454 full time, 7 part time; 49% male, 51% female; 1% American Indian, 3% Asian, 42% black, 17% Hispanic, 10% multiracial, 0% Pacific Islander, 7% white, 2% international
Most popular majors: 20% Biology/Biological Sciences, General, 20% Business Administration and Management, General, 17% Psychology, General, 15% Early Childhood Education and Teaching, 15% Sociology
Expenses: 2016-2017: $28,780; room/board: $13,280
Financial aid: (617) 731-7000

Salem State University

Salem MA
(978) 542-6200
U.S. News ranking: Reg. U. (N), No. 137
Website: www.salemstate.edu
Admissions email: admissions@salemstate.edu
Public; founded 1854
Freshman admissions: less selective; 2016-2017: 6,139 applied, 4,517 accepted. Neither SAT nor ACT required. SAT 25/75 percentile: 890-1090. High school rank: N/A
Early decision deadline: N/A, notification date: N/A
Early action deadline: 11/15, notification date: 1/1
Application deadline (fall): rolling
Undergraduate student body: 5,864 full time, 1,482 part time; 38% male, 62% female; 0% American Indian, 3% Asian, 10% black, 14% Hispanic, 3% multiracial, 0% Pacific Islander, 65% white, 3% international; 97% from in state; 32% live on campus; N/A of students in fraternities, N/A in sororities
Most popular majors: 22% Business, Management, Marketing, and Related Support Services, 12% Health Professions and Related Programs, 9% Homeland Security, Law Enforcement, Firefighting and Related Protective Services, 9% Psychology, 8% Education

Expenses: 2016-2017: $9,736 in state, $16,148 out of state; room/board: $12,892
Financial aid: N/A

Simmons College

Boston MA
(617) 521-2051
U.S. News ranking: Reg. U. (N), No. 14
Website: www.simmons.edu
Admissions email: ugadm@simmons.edu
Private; founded 1899
Freshman admissions: more selective; 2016-2017: 3,362 applied, 2,139 accepted. Either SAT or ACT required. SAT 25/75 percentile: 1080-1260. High school rank: 26% in top tenth, 71% in top quarter, 89% in top half
Early decision deadline: N/A, notification date: N/A
Early action deadline: 11/1, notification date: 12/15
Application deadline (fall): 2/1
Undergraduate student body: 1,594 full time, 207 part time; 0% male, 100% female; 0% American Indian, 9% Asian, 7% black, 7% Hispanic, 4% multiracial, 0% Pacific Islander, 66% white, 2% international; 60% from in state; 60% live on campus; 0% of students in fraternities, 0% in sororities
Most popular majors: 33% Health Professions and Related Programs, 9% Business, Management, Marketing, and Related Support Services, 9% Parks, Recreation, Leisure, and Fitness Studies, 8% Social Sciences, 7% Biological and Biomedical Sciences
Expenses: 2016-2017: $38,590; room/board: $14,500
Financial aid: (617) 521-2001

Smith College

Northampton MA
(413) 585-2500
U.S. News ranking: Nat. Lib. Arts, No. 12
Website: www.smith.edu
Admissions email: admission@smith.edu
Private; founded 1871
Freshman admissions: most selective; 2016-2017: 5,254 applied, 1,956 accepted. Neither SAT nor ACT required. SAT 25/75 percentile: 1230-1480. High school rank: 71% in top tenth, 93% in top quarter, 100% in top half
Early decision deadline: 11/15, notification date: 12/15
Early action deadline: N/A, notification date: N/A
Application deadline (fall): 1/15
Undergraduate student body: 2,503 full time, 11 part time; 0% male, 100% female; 0% American Indian, 12% Asian, 6% black, 10% Hispanic, 5% multiracial, 0% Pacific Islander, 45% white, 14% international; 20% from in state; 96% live on campus; 0% of students in fraternities, 0% in sororities
Most popular majors: 10% Research and Experimental Psychology, Other, 8% Economics, General, 8% Political Science and

Government, General, 5% Biology/Biological Sciences, General, 5% English Language and Literature, General
Expenses: 2017-2018: $50,044; room/board: $16,730
Financial aid: (413) 585-2530; 60% of undergrads determined to have financial need; average aid package $48,115

Springfield College

Springfield MA
(413) 748-3136
U.S. News ranking: Reg. U. (N), No. 25
Website: www.springfield.edu
Admissions email: admissions@springfieldcollege.edu
Private; founded 1885
Freshman admissions: selective; 2016-2017: 3,616 applied, 2,383 accepted. Either SAT or ACT required. SAT 25/75 percentile: 900-1120. High school rank: 18% in top tenth, 41% in top quarter, 76% in top half
Early decision deadline: 12/1, notification date: 2/1
Early action deadline: N/A, notification date: N/A
Application deadline (fall): 4/1
Undergraduate student body: 2,091 full time, 19 part time; 50% male, 50% female; 0% American Indian, 1% Asian, 6% black, 7% Hispanic, 2% multiracial, 0% Pacific Islander, 80% white, 3% international; 41% from in state; 85% live on campus; N/A of students in fraternities, N/A in sororities
Most popular majors: 10% Physical Education Teaching and Coaching, 8% Kinesiology and Exercise Science, 8% Sport and Fitness Administration/Management, 7% Business Administration and Management, General, 7% Physical Therapy/Therapist
Expenses: 2017-2018: $36,535; room/board: $12,240
Financial aid: (413) 748-3108; 82% of undergrads determined to have financial need; average aid package $26,866

Stonehill College

Easton MA
(508) 565-1373
U.S. News ranking: Nat. Lib. Arts, No. 111
Website: www.stonehill.edu
Admissions email: admission@stonehill.edu
Private; founded 1948
Affiliation: Roman Catholic
Freshman admissions: selective; 2016-2017: 6,362 applied, 4,639 accepted. Neither SAT nor ACT required. SAT 25/75 percentile: 1000-1210. High school rank: 20% in top tenth, 58% in top quarter, 90% in top half
Early decision deadline: 12/1, notification date: 12/31
Early action deadline: 11/1, notification date: 12/31
Application deadline (fall): 1/15
Undergraduate student body: 2,455 full time, 26 part time; 40% male, 60% female; 0% American Indian, 2% Asian, 5% black,

5% Hispanic, 2% multiracial, 0% Pacific Islander, 83% white, 1% international; 60% from in state; 90% live on campus; 0% of students in fraternities, 0% in sororities
Most popular majors: 23% Business, Management, Marketing, and Related Support Services, 17% Social Sciences, 13% Biological and Biomedical Sciences, 11% Psychology, 7% Communication, Journalism, and Related Programs
Expenses: 2017-2018: $41,300; room/board: $15,760
Financial aid: (508) 565-1088; 66% of undergrads determined to have financial need; average aid package $30,606

Suffolk University

Boston MA
(617) 573-8460
U.S. News ranking: Nat. U., No. 181
Website: www.suffolk.edu
Admissions email: admission@suffolk.edu
Private; founded 1906
Freshman admissions: selective; 2016-2017: 8,624 applied, 7,271 accepted. Either SAT or ACT required. SAT 25/75 percentile: 910-1150. High school rank: 19% in top tenth, 46% in top quarter, 79% in top half
Early decision deadline: N/A, notification date: N/A
Early action deadline: 11/15, notification date: 12/15
Application deadline (fall): 2/15
Undergraduate student body: 5,004 full time, 286 part time; 45% male, 55% female; 0% American Indian, 8% Asian, 6% black, 11% Hispanic, 2% multiracial, 0% Pacific Islander, 44% white, 22% international; 68% from in state; 25% live on campus; N/A of students in fraternities, N/A in sororities
Most popular majors: 47% Business, Management, Marketing, and Related Support Services, 14% Communication, Journalism, and Related Programs, 13% Social Sciences, 6% Biological and Biomedical Sciences, 5% Psychology
Expenses: 2017-2018: $37,270; room/board: $16,576
Financial aid: (617) 573-8470; 57% of undergrads determined to have financial need; average aid package $31,105

Tufts University

Medford MA
(617) 627-3170
U.S. News ranking: Nat. U., No. 29
Website: www.tufts.edu
Admissions email: undergraduate.admissions@tufts.edu
Private; founded 1852
Freshman admissions: more selective; 2016-2017: 20,223 applied, 2,889 accepted. Either SAT or ACT required. ACT 25/75 percentile: 31-34. High school rank: N/A
Early decision deadline: 11/1, notification date: 12/15
Early action deadline: N/A, notification date: N/A
Application deadline (fall): 1/1

Undergraduate student body: 5,435 full time, 73 part time; 50% male, 50% female; 0% American Indian, 12% Asian, 4% black, 7% Hispanic, 5% multiracial, 0% Pacific Islander, 56% white, 10% international; 26% from in state; 62% live on campus; 16% of students in fraternities, 17% in sororities
Most popular majors: 27% Social Sciences, 10% Engineering, 8% Biological and Biomedical Sciences, 7% Multi/Interdisciplinary Studies, 6% Computer and Information Sciences and Support Services
Expenses: 2017-2018: $54,318; room/board: $14,054
Financial aid: (617) 627-2000; 37% of undergrads determined to have financial need; average aid package $43,325

University of Massachusetts–Amherst
Amherst MA
(413) 545-0222
U.S. News ranking: Nat. U., No. 75
Website: www.umass.edu
Admissions email: mail@admissions.umass.edu
Public; founded 1863
Freshman admissions: more selective; 2016-2017: 40,703 applied, 24,275 accepted. Either SAT or ACT required. SAT 25/75 percentile: 1130-1330. High school rank: 34% in top tenth, 74% in top quarter, 97% in top half
Early decision deadline: N/A, notification date: N/A
Early action deadline: 11/1, notification date: 12/31
Application deadline (fall): rolling
Undergraduate student body: 21,460 full time, 1,913 part time; 51% male, 49% female; 0% American Indian, 10% Asian, 4% black, 6% Hispanic, 3% multiracial, 0% Pacific Islander, 66% white, 5% international; 81% from in state; 60% live on campus; 9% of students in fraternities, 10% in sororities
Most popular majors: 14% Business, Management, Marketing, and Related Support Services, 12% Social Sciences, 10% Biological and Biomedical Sciences, 9% Health Professions and Related Programs, 8% Psychology
Expenses: 2017-2018: $15,596 in state, $33,662 out of state; room/board: $12,258
Financial aid: (413) 545-0801; 56% of undergrads determined to have financial need; average aid package $17,083

University of Massachusetts–Boston
Boston MA
(617) 287-6100
U.S. News ranking: Nat. U., No. 202
Website: www.umb.edu
Admissions email: undergrad.admissions@umb.edu
Public; founded 1964

Freshman admissions: selective; 2016-2017: 9,886 applied, 6,774 accepted. Neither SAT nor ACT required. SAT 25/75 percentile: 960-1180. High school rank: 15% in top tenth, 42% in top quarter, 79% in top half
Early decision deadline: N/A, notification date: N/A
Early action deadline: 11/1, notification date: 12/31
Application deadline (fall): 3/1
Undergraduate student body: 9,283 full time, 3,564 part time; 47% male, 53% female; 0% American Indian, 13% Asian, 16% black, 14% Hispanic, 3% multiracial, 0% Pacific Islander, 35% white, 12% international; 95% from in state; N/A live on campus; N/A of students in fraternities, N/A in sororities
Most popular majors: 19% Business, Management, Marketing, and Related Support Services, 15% Health Professions and Related Programs, 11% Psychology, 11% Social Sciences, 7% Biological and Biomedical Sciences
Expenses: 2017-2018: $13,828 in state, $32,985 out of state; room/board: N/A
Financial aid: (617) 287-6300; 65% of undergrads determined to have financial need; average aid package $15,856

University of Massachusetts–Dartmouth
North Dartmouth MA
(508) 999-8605
U.S. News ranking: Nat. U., No. 207
Website: www.umassd.edu
Admissions email: admissions@umassd.edu
Public; founded 1895
Freshman admissions: selective; 2016-2017: 8,211 applied, 6,242 accepted. Either SAT or ACT required. SAT 25/75 percentile: 910-1130. High school rank: N/A
Early decision deadline: N/A, notification date: N/A
Early action deadline: 11/18, notification date: 12/15
Application deadline (fall): rolling
Undergraduate student body: 6,011 full time, 988 part time; 51% male, 49% female; 0% American Indian, 4% Asian, 15% black, 9% Hispanic, 4% multiracial, 0% Pacific Islander, 62% white, 2% international; 94% from in state; 55% live on campus; N/A of students in fraternities, N/A in sororities
Most popular majors: 30% Business, Management, Marketing, and Related Support Services, 12% Engineering, 12% Health Professions and Related Programs, 10% Social Sciences, 8% Psychology
Expenses: 2017-2018: $13,571 in state, $28,285 out of state; room/board: $12,936
Financial aid: (508) 999-8643; 71% of undergrads determined to have financial need; average aid package $17,213

University of Massachusetts–Lowell
Lowell MA
(978) 934-3931
U.S. News ranking: Nat. U., No. 156
Website: www.uml.edu
Admissions email: admissions@uml.edu
Public; founded 1894
Freshman admissions: more selective; 2016-2017: 11,231 applied, 6,771 accepted. Neither SAT nor ACT required. SAT 25/75 percentile: 1070-1260. High school rank: 25% in top tenth, 56% in top quarter, 89% in top half
Early decision deadline: N/A, notification date: N/A
Early action deadline: 11/1, notification date: 12/10
Application deadline (fall): 2/1
Undergraduate student body: 10,019 full time, 3,620 part time; 62% male, 38% female; 0% American Indian, 9% Asian, 6% black, 11% Hispanic, 3% multiracial, 0% Pacific Islander, 63% white, 4% international; 90% from in state; 37% live on campus; N/A of students in fraternities, N/A in sororities
Most popular majors: 18% Business, Management, Marketing, and Related Support Services, 18% Engineering, 12% Health Professions and Related Programs, 11% Computer and Information Sciences and Support Services, 9% Homeland Security, Law Enforcement, Firefighting and Related Protective Services
Expenses: 2017-2018: $14,800 in state, $31,865 out of state; room/board: N/A
Financial aid: (978) 934-4220; 58% of undergrads determined to have financial need; average aid package $15,810

Wellesley College
Wellesley MA
(781) 283-2270
U.S. News ranking: Nat. Lib. Arts, No. 3
Website: www.wellesley.edu
Admissions email: admission@wellesley.edu
Private; founded 1870
Freshman admissions: most selective; 2016-2017: 4,854 applied, 1,388 accepted. Either SAT or ACT required. SAT 25/75 percentile: 1310-1500. High school rank: 81% in top tenth, 97% in top quarter, 100% in top half
Early decision deadline: 11/1, notification date: 12/15
Early action deadline: N/A, notification date: N/A
Application deadline (fall): 1/15
Undergraduate student body: 2,212 full time, 135 part time; 2% male, 98% female; 0% American Indian, 24% Asian, 6% black, 12% Hispanic, 7% multiracial, 0% Pacific Islander, 40% white, 12% international; 16% from in state; 98% live on campus; N/A of students in fraternities, N/A in sororities

Most popular majors: 25% Social Sciences, 11% Biological and Biomedical Sciences, 10% Psychology, 8% Foreign Languages, Literatures, and Linguistics, 7% Area, Ethnic, Cultural, Gender, and Group Studies
Expenses: 2017-2018: $51,148; room/board: $15,836
Financial aid: (781) 283-2360; 63% of undergrads determined to have financial need; average aid package $47,527

Wentworth Institute of Technology
Boston MA
(617) 989-4000
U.S. News ranking: Reg. U. (N), No. 71
Website: www.wit.edu
Admissions email: admissions@wit.edu
Private; founded 1904
Freshman admissions: selective; 2016-2017: 7,556 applied, 5,333 accepted. Either SAT or ACT required. SAT 25/75 percentile: 1010-1220. High school rank: N/A
Early decision deadline: N/A, notification date: N/A
Early action deadline: N/A, notification date: N/A
Application deadline (fall): rolling
Undergraduate student body: 3,888 full time, 89 part time; 80% male, 20% female; 0% American Indian, 8% Asian, 4% black, 3% Hispanic, 6% multiracial, 0% Pacific Islander, 63% white, 9% international; 65% from in state; 52% live on campus; 0% of students in fraternities, 0% in sororities
Most popular majors: 25% Architecture and Related Services, 25% Engineering Technologies and Engineering-Related Fields, 14% Engineering, 13% Computer and Information Sciences and Support Services, 12% Business, Management, Marketing, and Related Support Services
Expenses: 2017-2018: $32,954; room/board: $13,844
Financial aid: (617) 989-4020; 70% of undergrads determined to have financial need; average aid package $23,788

Western New England University
Springfield MA
(413) 782-1321
U.S. News ranking: Reg. U. (N), No. 64
Website: www.wne.edu
Admissions email: learn@wne.edu
Private; founded 1919
Freshman admissions: selective; 2016-2017: 6,399 applied, 5,094 accepted. Neither SAT nor ACT required. SAT 25/75 percentile: 990-1190. High school rank: 11% in top tenth, 39% in top quarter, 74% in top half
Early decision deadline: N/A, notification date: N/A
Early action deadline: N/A, notification date: N/A
Application deadline (fall): rolling

Undergraduate student body: 2,580 full time, 144 part time; 62% male, 38% female; 0% American Indian, 3% Asian, 6% black, 8% Hispanic, 2% multiracial, 0% Pacific Islander, 73% white, 3% international; 52% from in state; 62% live on campus; N/A of students in fraternities, N/A in sororities
Most popular majors: 25% Business, Management, Marketing, and Related Support Services, 19% Engineering, 8% Psychology, 7% Homeland Security, Law Enforcement, Firefighting and Related Protective Services, 6% Biological and Biomedical Sciences
Expenses: 2017-2018: $35,740; room/board: $13,442
Financial aid: (413) 796-2080; 78% of undergrads determined to have financial need; average aid package $25,735

Westfield State University
Westfield MA
(413) 572-5218
U.S. News ranking: Reg. U. (N), No. 116
Website: www.westfield.ma.edu
Admissions email: admissions@westfield.ma.edu
Public; founded 1839
Freshman admissions: less selective; 2016-2017: 4,740 applied, 3,695 accepted. Either SAT or ACT required. SAT 25/75 percentile: 890-1090. High school rank: 8% in top tenth, 27% in top quarter, 61% in top half
Early decision deadline: N/A, notification date: N/A
Early action deadline: N/A, notification date: N/A
Application deadline (fall): 4/1
Undergraduate student body: 4,982 full time, 628 part time; 46% male, 54% female; 0% American Indian, 2% Asian, 5% black, 9% Hispanic, 5% multiracial, 0% Pacific Islander, 76% white, 0% international; 93% from in state; 54% live on campus; 0% of students in fraternities, 0% in sororities
Most popular majors: 15% Liberal Arts and Sciences, General Studies and Humanities, 13% Business, Management, Marketing, and Related Support Services, 13% Homeland Security, Law Enforcement, Firefighting and Related Protective Services, 10% Education, 9% Psychology
Expenses: 2017-2018: $9,715 in state, $15,795 out of state; room/board: $10,689
Financial aid: (413) 572-8530; 64% of undergrads determined to have financial need; average aid package $8,386

Wheaton College
Norton MA
(508) 286-8251
U.S. News ranking: Nat. Lib. Arts, No. 76
Website: www.wheatoncollege.edu
Admissions email: admission@wheatoncollege.edu
Private; founded 1834

Freshman admissions: more selective; 2016-2017: 4,478 applied, 2,779 accepted. Neither SAT nor ACT required. SAT 25/75 percentile: 1050-1270. High school rank: 27% in top tenth, 54% in top quarter, 85% in top half
Early decision deadline: 11/1, notification date: 12/15
Early action deadline: 11/1, notification date: 1/15
Application deadline (fall): 1/1
Undergraduate student body: 1,638 full time, 13 part time; 38% male, 62% female; 0% American Indian, 5% Asian, 6% black, 7% Hispanic, 3% multiracial, 0% Pacific Islander, 65% white, 12% international; 40% from in state; 97% live on campus; N/A of students in fraternities, N/A in sororities
Most popular majors: 18% Social Sciences, 14% Biological and Biomedical Sciences, 13% Visual and Performing Arts, 12% Psychology, 8% Business, Management, Marketing, and Related Support Services
Expenses: 2017-2018: $50,850; room/board: $12,968
Financial aid: (508) 286-8232; 64% of undergrads determined to have financial need; average aid package $37,725

Wheelock College
Boston MA
(617) 879-2206
U.S. News ranking: Reg. U. (N), No. 97
Website: www.wheelock.edu
Admissions email: undergrad@wheelock.edu
Private; founded 1888
Freshman admissions: less selective; 2016-2017: 1,305 applied, 1,095 accepted. Either SAT or ACT required. SAT 25/75 percentile: 800-1015. High school rank: 4% in top tenth, 10% in top quarter, 50% in top half
Early decision deadline: N/A, notification date: N/A
Early action deadline: 12/1, notification date: 12/20
Application deadline (fall): 5/1
Undergraduate student body: 713 full time, 13 part time; 18% male, 82% female; 0% American Indian, 4% Asian, 15% black, 12% Hispanic, 4% multiracial, 0% Pacific Islander, 58% white, 2% international; 63% from in state; 60% live on campus; 0% of students in fraternities, 0% in sororities
Most popular majors: 37% Psychology, 26% Education, 13% Public Administration and Social Service Professions, 6% Visual and Performing Arts, 5% Family and Consumer Sciences/Human Sciences
Expenses: 2017-2018: $36,200; room/board: $14,975
Financial aid: N/A; 84% of undergrads determined to have financial need; average aid package $25,647

Williams College
Williamstown MA
(413) 597-2211
U.S. News ranking: Nat. Lib. Arts, No. 1
Website: www.williams.edu
Admissions email: admission@williams.edu
Private; founded 1793
Freshman admissions: most selective; 2016-2017: 6,985 applied, 1,230 accepted. Either SAT or ACT required. SAT 25/75 percentile: 1330-1540. High school rank: 91% in top tenth, 98% in top quarter, 99% in top half
Early decision deadline: 11/15, notification date: 12/15
Early action deadline: N/A, notification date: N/A
Application deadline (fall): 1/1
Undergraduate student body: 2,043 full time, 33 part time; 51% male, 49% female; 0% American Indian, 13% Asian, 7% black, 12% Hispanic, 6% multiracial, 0% Pacific Islander, 53% white, 8% international; 12% from in state; 93% live on campus; N/A of students in fraternities, N/A in sororities
Most popular majors: 21% Economics, General, 12% Mathematics, General, 11% Biology/Biological Sciences, General, 10% English Language and Literature, General, 10% Psychology, General
Expenses: 2017-2018: $53,550; room/board: $14,150
Financial aid: (413) 597-4181; 50% of undergrads determined to have financial need; average aid package $51,890

Worcester Polytechnic Institute
Worcester MA
(508) 831-5286
U.S. News ranking: Nat. U., No. 61
Website: www.wpi.edu/admissions
Admissions email: admissions@wpi.edu
Private; founded 1865
Freshman admissions: more selective; 2016-2017: 10,468 applied, 5,071 accepted. Neither SAT nor ACT required. SAT 25/75 percentile: 1200-1400. High school rank: 65% in top tenth, 92% in top quarter, 99% in top half
Early decision deadline: N/A, notification date: N/A
Early action deadline: 1/1, notification date: 2/10
Application deadline (fall): 2/1
Undergraduate student body: 4,275 full time, 157 part time; 66% male, 34% female; 0% American Indian, 4% Asian, 3% black, 9% Hispanic, 3% multiracial, 0% Pacific Islander, 63% white, 11% international; 43% from in state; 57% live on campus; 28% of students in fraternities, 45% in sororities
Most popular majors: 22% Mechanical Engineering, 10% Electrical and Electronics Engineering, 9% Chemical Engineering, 8% Bioengineering and Biomedical Engineering, 8% Computer Science

Expenses: 2017-2018: $48,628; room/board: $14,218
Financial aid: (508) 831-5469; 64% of undergrads determined to have financial need; average aid package $35,618

Worcester State University
Worcester MA
(508) 929-8040
U.S. News ranking: Reg. U. (N), No. 116
Website: www.worcester.edu
Admissions email: admissions@worcester.edu
Public; founded 1874
Freshman admissions: selective; 2016-2017: 3,876 applied, 2,735 accepted. Either SAT or ACT required. SAT 25/75 percentile: 890-1100. High school rank: N/A
Early decision deadline: N/A, notification date: N/A
Early action deadline: 11/15, notification date: 12/15
Application deadline (fall): 5/1
Undergraduate student body: 4,033 full time, 1,348 part time; 40% male, 60% female; 0% American Indian, 4% Asian, 8% black, 11% Hispanic, 3% multiracial, 0% Pacific Islander, 68% white, 1% international; 96% from in state; 30% live on campus; 0% of students in fraternities, 0% in sororities
Most popular majors: 21% Health Professions and Related Programs, 16% Business, Management, Marketing, and Related Support Services, 15% Psychology, 9% Homeland Security, Law Enforcement, Firefighting and Related Protective Services, 7% Biological and Biomedical Sciences
Expenses: 2017-2018: $10,017 in state, $15,612 out of state; room/board: $12,006
Financial aid: (508) 929-8058; 63% of undergrads determined to have financial need; average aid package $12,226

MICHIGAN

Adrian College
Adrian MI
(800) 877-2246
U.S. News ranking: Reg. Coll. (Mid. W), No. 20
Website: www.adrian.edu
Admissions email: admissions@adrian.edu
Private; founded 1859
Affiliation: United Methodist
Freshman admissions: selective; 2016-2017: 5,622 applied, 3,284 accepted. Either SAT or ACT required. ACT 25/75 percentile: 19-24. High school rank: 26% in top tenth, 56% in top quarter, 86% in top half
Early decision deadline: N/A, notification date: N/A
Early action deadline: N/A, notification date: N/A
Application deadline (fall): rolling
Undergraduate student body: 1,604 full time, 48 part time; 52% male, 48% female; 0% American Indian, 0% Asian, 7% black, 6% Hispanic, 4% multiracial,

0% Pacific Islander, 70% white, 0% international; 81% from in state; 86% live on campus; 21% of students in fraternities, 20% in sororities
Most popular majors: 23% Business, Management, Marketing, and Related Support Services, 19% Parks, Recreation, Leisure, and Fitness Studies, 10% Biological and Biomedical Sciences, 9% Visual and Performing Arts, 8% Education
Expenses: 2017-2018: $36,010; room/board: $10,988
Financial aid: (888) 876-0194; 85% of undergrads determined to have financial need; average aid package $27,294

Albion College
Albion MI
(800) 858-6770
U.S. News ranking: Nat. Lib. Arts, No. 128
Website: www.albion.edu/
Admissions email: admission@albion.edu
Private; founded 1835
Affiliation: United Methodist
Freshman admissions: selective; 2016-2017: 3,338 applied, 2,412 accepted. Either SAT or ACT required. ACT 25/75 percentile: 20-26. High school rank: N/A
Early decision deadline: 12/1, notification date: 11/1
Early action deadline: N/A, notification date: N/A
Application deadline (fall): rolling
Undergraduate student body: 1,393 full time, 25 part time; 48% male, 52% female; 0% American Indian, 3% Asian, 9% black, 7% Hispanic, 3% multiracial, 0% Pacific Islander, 71% white, 2% international; 83% from in state; 93% live on campus; 37% of students in fraternities, 30% in sororities
Most popular majors: 16% Biology/Biological Sciences, General, 13% Psychology, General, 12% Business Administration and Management, General, 8% Economics, General, 6% Kinesiology and Exercise Science
Expenses: 2017-2018: $43,050; room/board: $12,210
Financial aid: (517) 629-0440; 75% of undergrads determined to have financial need; average aid package $35,866

Alma College
Alma MI
(800) 321-2562
U.S. News ranking: Nat. Lib. Arts, No. 141
Website: www.alma.edu
Admissions email: admissions@alma.edu
Private; founded 1886
Affiliation: Presbyterian Church (USA)
Freshman admissions: selective; 2016-2017: 4,695 applied, 3,184 accepted. Either SAT or ACT required. ACT 25/75 percentile: 21-26. High school rank: 18% in top tenth, 50% in top quarter, 84% in top half
Early decision deadline: N/A, notification date: N/A

Early action deadline: N/A, notification date: N/A
Application deadline (fall): rolling
Undergraduate student body: 1,379 full time, 72 part time; 42% male, 58% female; 0% American Indian, 1% Asian, 4% black, 5% Hispanic, 2% multiracial, 0% Pacific Islander, 78% white, 1% international; 92% from in state; 91% live on campus; 19% of students in fraternities, 20% in sororities
Most popular majors: 16% Business, Management, Marketing, and Related Support Services, 12% Education, 10% Psychology, 9% Biological and Biomedical Sciences, 9% Health Professions and Related Programs
Expenses: 2017-2018: $38,768; room/board: $10,642
Financial aid: (989) 463-7347; 84% of undergrads determined to have financial need; average aid package $26,369

Andrews University
Berrien Springs MI
(800) 253-2874
U.S. News ranking: Nat. U., No. 192
Website: www.andrews.edu
Admissions email: enroll@andrews.edu
Private; founded 1874
Affiliation: Seventh Day Adventist
Freshman admissions: more selective; 2016-2017: 2,417 applied, 977 accepted. Either SAT or ACT required. ACT 25/75 percentile: 21-29. High school rank: 20% in top tenth, 41% in top quarter, 69% in top half
Early decision deadline: N/A, notification date: N/A
Early action deadline: N/A, notification date: N/A
Application deadline (fall): rolling
Undergraduate student body: 1,373 full time, 315 part time; 46% male, 54% female; 0% American Indian, 15% Asian, 19% black, 15% Hispanic, 4% multiracial, 0% Pacific Islander, 27% white, 17% international; 36% from in state; 60% live on campus; N/A of students in fraternities, N/A in sororities
Most popular majors: 18% Health Professions and Related Programs, 9% Business, Management, Marketing, and Related Support Services, 7% Biological and Biomedical Sciences, 6% Visual and Performing Arts, 5% Public Administration and Social Service Professions
Expenses: 2017-2018: $28,436; room/board: $9,078
Financial aid: (269) 471-3334; 61% of undergrads determined to have financial need; average aid package $29,204

Aquinas College
Grand Rapids MI
(616) 632-2900
U.S. News ranking: Reg. U. (Mid. W), No. 47
Website: www.aquinas.edu
Admissions email: admissions@aquinas.edu
Private; founded 1886
Affiliation: Roman Catholic

Freshman admissions: selective; 2016-2017: 2,085 applied, 1,558 accepted. Either SAT or ACT required. ACT 25/75 percentile: 21-26. High school rank: N/A
Early decision deadline: N/A, notification date: N/A
Early action deadline: N/A, notification date: N/A
Application deadline (fall): rolling
Undergraduate student body: 1,416 full time, 238 part time; 39% male, 61% female; 0% American Indian, 1% Asian, 3% black, 6% Hispanic, 2% multiracial, 0% Pacific Islander, 79% white, 2% international; 94% from in state; 46% live on campus; N/A of students in fraternities, N/A in sororities
Most popular majors: 20% Business, Management, Marketing, and Related Support Services, 9% Social Sciences, 8% Biological and Biomedical Sciences, 6% Parks, Recreation, Leisure, and Fitness Studies, 6% Psychology
Expenses: 2017-2018: $31,244; room/board: $9,070
Financial aid: (616) 632-2894; 76% of undergrads determined to have financial need; average aid package $22,824

Baker College of Flint[1]
Flint MI
U.S. News ranking: Reg. Coll. (Mid. W), unranked
Website: www.baker.edu
Admissions email: troy.crowe@baker.edu
Private
Application deadline (fall): N/A
Undergraduate student body: N/A full time, N/A part time
Expenses: 2016-2017: $9,000; room/board: $5,400
Financial aid: N/A

Calvin College
Grand Rapids MI
(616) 526-6106
U.S. News ranking: Reg. Coll. (Mid. W), No. 1
Website: www.calvin.edu
Admissions email: admissions@calvin.edu
Private; founded 1876
Affiliation: Christian Reformed Church
Freshman admissions: more selective; 2016-2017: 3,981 applied, 2,970 accepted. Neither SAT nor ACT required. ACT 25/75 percentile: 23-29. High school rank: 32% in top tenth, 57% in top quarter, 84% in top half
Early decision deadline: N/A, notification date: N/A
Early action deadline: N/A, notification date: N/A
Application deadline (fall): 8/15
Undergraduate student body: 3,602 full time, 205 part time; 46% male, 54% female; 0% American Indian, 4% Asian, 3% black, 4% Hispanic, 4% multiracial, 0% Pacific Islander, 73% white, 11% international; 56% from in state; 60% live on campus; 0% of students in fraternities, 0% in sororities

Most popular majors: 9% Engineering, General, 7% Business Administration and Management, General, 7% Psychology, General, 7% Registered Nursing/Registered Nurse, 6% Biology/Biological Sciences, General
Expenses: 2017-2018: $33,100; room/board: $9,990
Financial aid: (616) 526-6134; 61% of undergrads determined to have financial need; average aid package $22,846

Central Michigan University
Mount Pleasant MI
(989) 774-3076
U.S. News ranking: Nat. U., No. 207
Website: www.cmich.edu
Admissions email: cmuadmit@cmich.edu
Public; founded 1892
Freshman admissions: selective; 2016-2017: 18,875 applied, 13,594 accepted. Either SAT or ACT required. ACT 25/75 percentile: 20-25. High school rank: 14% in top tenth, 39% in top quarter, 74% in top half
Early decision deadline: N/A, notification date: N/A
Early action deadline: 5/1, notification date: N/A
Application deadline (fall): 7/1
Undergraduate student body: 17,202 full time, 2,721 part time; 43% male, 57% female; 1% American Indian, 1% Asian, 9% black, 4% Hispanic, 4% multiracial, 0% Pacific Islander, 78% white, 2% international; 95% from in state; 37% live on campus; 9% of students in fraternities, 11% in sororities
Most popular majors: 26% Business, Management, Marketing, and Related Support Services, 9% Education, 9% Psychology, 8% Communication, Journalism, and Related Programs, 8% Parks, Recreation, Leisure, and Fitness Studies
Expenses: 2017-2018: $12,510 in state, $23,670 out of state; room/board: $9,736
Financial aid: N/A; 59% of undergrads determined to have financial need; average aid package $13,708

Cleary University
Howell MI
(800) 686-1883
U.S. News ranking: Business, unranked
Website: www.cleary.edu
Admissions email: admissions@cleary.edu
Private; founded 1883
Freshman admissions: least selective; 2016-2017: 289 applied, 158 accepted. Either SAT or ACT required. SAT 25/75 percentile: N/A. High school rank: N/A
Early decision deadline: N/A, notification date: N/A
Early action deadline: N/A, notification date: N/A
Application deadline (fall): 8/24

Undergraduate student body: 257 full time, 218 part time; 49% male, 51% female; 0% American Indian, 1% Asian, 5% black, 2% Hispanic, 0% multiracial, 0% Pacific Islander, 79% white, 2% international
Most popular majors: Information not available
Expenses: 2017-2018: $19,600; room/board: $9,600
Financial aid: (517) 338-3015

College for Creative Studies[1]
Detroit MI
U.S. News ranking: Arts, unranked
Website: www.collegeforcreativestudies.edu
Admissions email: admissions@collegeforcreativestudies.edu
Private; founded 1906
Application deadline (fall): N/A
Undergraduate student body: N/A full time, N/A part time
Expenses: 2016-2017: $40,840; room/board: $8,650
Financial aid: (313) 664-7495

Cornerstone University
Grand Rapids MI
(616) 949-5300
U.S. News ranking: Reg. U. (Mid. W), No. 115
Website: www.cornerstone.edu
Admissions email: admissions@cornerstone.edu
Private; founded 1941
Affiliation: Interdenominational
Freshman admissions: selective; 2016-2017: 2,892 applied, 1,834 accepted. Either SAT or ACT required. ACT 25/75 percentile: 18-25. High school rank: 18% in top tenth, 39% in top quarter, 75% in top half
Early decision deadline: N/A, notification date: N/A
Early action deadline: N/A, notification date: N/A
Application deadline (fall): rolling
Undergraduate student body: 1,363 full time, 493 part time; 39% male, 61% female; 1% American Indian, 1% Asian, 13% black, 4% Hispanic, 1% multiracial, 0% Pacific Islander, 77% white, 3% international; 75% from in state; 61% live on campus; 0% of students in fraternities, 0% in sororities
Most popular majors: 44% Business, Management, Marketing, and Related Support Services, 13% Psychology, 10% Theology and Religious Vocations, 8% Education, 6% Communication, Journalism, and Related Programs
Expenses: 2017-2018: $27,520; room/board: $9,030
Financial aid: (616) 222-1424; 79% of undergrads determined to have financial need; average aid package $20,891

Davenport University
Grand Rapids MI
(866) 925-3884
U.S. News ranking: Reg. U. (Mid. W), No. 122
Website: www.davenport.edu
Admissions email: Davenport.Admissions@davenport.edu
Private; founded 1866
Freshman admissions: selective; 2016-2017: 2,606 applied, 2,042 accepted. Neither SAT nor ACT required. ACT 25/75 percentile: 19-23. High school rank: N/A
Early decision deadline: N/A, notification date: N/A
Early action deadline: N/A, notification date: N/A
Application deadline (fall): rolling
Undergraduate student body: 2,378 full time, 3,399 part time; 43% male, 57% female; 1% American Indian, 2% Asian, 13% black, 3% Hispanic, 3% multiracial, 0% Pacific Islander, 69% white, 2% international; 95% from in state; 14% live on campus; 0% of students in fraternities, 0% in sororities
Most popular majors: 22% Business Administration and Management, General, 12% Health/Health Care Administration/Management, 11% Business/Commerce, General, 8% Accounting, 7% Registered Nursing/Registered Nurse
Expenses: 2017-2018: $21,662; room/board: $9,902
Financial aid: (616) 732-1132

Eastern Michigan University
Ypsilanti MI
(734) 487-3060
U.S. News ranking: Nat. U., second tier
Website: www.emich.edu/
Admissions email: admissions@emich.edu
Public; founded 1849
Freshman admissions: selective; 2016-2017: 14,736 applied, 10,769 accepted. Either SAT or ACT required. ACT 25/75 percentile: 19-25. High school rank: 13% in top tenth, 39% in top quarter, 75% in top half
Early decision deadline: N/A, notification date: N/A
Early action deadline: N/A, notification date: N/A
Application deadline (fall): rolling
Undergraduate student body: 12,846 full time, 4,695 part time; 41% male, 59% female; 0% American Indian, 3% Asian, 20% black, 5% Hispanic, 4% multiracial, 0% Pacific Islander, 64% white, 2% international; 90% from in state; 21% live on campus; N/A of students in fraternities, N/A in sororities
Most popular majors: 19% Business, Management, Marketing, and Related Support Services, 14% Health Professions and Related Programs, 10% Education, 7% Social Sciences, 6% Public Administration and Social Service Professions

Expenses: 2017-2018: $11,530 in state, $11,530 out of state; room/board: $9,854
Financial aid: (734) 487-1048; 69% of undergrads determined to have financial need; average aid package $8,785

Ferris State University
Big Rapids MI
(231) 591-2100
U.S. News ranking: Reg. U. (Mid. W), No. 83
Website: www.ferris.edu
Admissions email: admissions@ferris.edu
Public; founded 1884
Freshman admissions: selective; 2016-2017: 10,883 applied, 8,455 accepted. Neither SAT nor ACT required. ACT 25/75 percentile: 19-25. High school rank: N/A
Early decision deadline: N/A, notification date: N/A
Early action deadline: N/A, notification date: N/A
Application deadline (fall): rolling
Undergraduate student body: 8,785 full time, 4,081 part time; 47% male, 53% female; 1% American Indian, 2% Asian, 7% black, 5% Hispanic, 3% multiracial, 0% Pacific Islander, 80% white, 1% international; 93% from in state; 26% live on campus; 2% of students in fraternities, 2% in sororities
Most popular majors: 8% Criminal Justice/Law Enforcement Administration, 6% Pharmacy, 6% Registered Nursing/Registered Nurse, 4% Business Administration and Management, General, 4% Elementary Education and Teaching
Expenses: 2017-2018: $12,180 in state, $18,270 out of state; room/board: $9,894
Financial aid: (231) 591-2110; 70% of undergrads determined to have financial need; average aid package $11,350

Finlandia University[1]
Hancock MI
(906) 487-7274
U.S. News ranking: Reg. Coll. (Mid. W), second tier
Website: www.finlandia.edu
Admissions email: admissions@finlandia.edu
Private; founded 1896
Affiliation: Evangelical Lutheran Church
Application deadline (fall): N/A
Undergraduate student body: N/A full time, N/A part time
Expenses: 2016-2017: $22,758; room/board: $8,800
Financial aid: N/A

Grace Bible College
Grand Rapids MI
(616) 538-2330
U.S. News ranking: Reg. Coll. (Mid. W), second tier
Website: www.gbcol.edu
Admissions email: enrollment@gbcol.edu
Private; founded 1939
Affiliation: Other
Freshman admissions: selective; 2016-2017: 313 applied, 252 accepted. Either SAT or ACT required. ACT 25/75 percentile:

17-23. High school rank: 5% in top tenth, 33% in top quarter, 43% in top half
Early decision deadline: N/A, notification date: N/A
Early action deadline: N/A, notification date: N/A
Application deadline (fall): rolling
Undergraduate student body: 945 full time, 55 part time; 46% male, 54% female; 1% American Indian, 1% Asian, 27% black, 6% Hispanic, 6% multiracial, 0% Pacific Islander, 54% white, 0% international; 91% from in state; 58% live on campus; 0% of students in fraternities, 0% in sororities
Most popular majors: 31% Public Administration and Social Service Professions, 29% Music, Other, 13% Bible/Biblical Studies, 9% Business Administration and Management, General, 9% Early Childhood Education and Teaching
Expenses: 2016-2017: $12,644; room/board: $7,500
Financial aid: N/A

Grand Valley State University
Allendale MI
(800) 748-0246
U.S. News ranking: Reg. U. (Mid. W), No. 29
Website: www.gvsu.edu
Admissions email: admissions@gvsu.edu
Public; founded 1960
Freshman admissions: selective; 2016-2017: 17,104 applied, 13,972 accepted. Either SAT or ACT required. ACT 25/75 percentile: 21-26. High school rank: 16% in top tenth, 44% in top quarter, 84% in top half
Early decision deadline: N/A, notification date: N/A
Early action deadline: N/A, notification date: N/A
Application deadline (fall): 5/1
Undergraduate student body: 19,668 full time, 2,541 part time; 42% male, 58% female; 0% American Indian, 2% Asian, 5% black, 5% Hispanic, 3% multiracial, 0% Pacific Islander, 82% white, 1% international; 94% from in state; 28% live on campus; N/A of students in fraternities, N/A in sororities
Most popular majors: 19% Business, Management, Marketing, and Related Support Services, 19% Health Professions and Related Programs, 8% Education, 7% Communication, Journalism, and Related Programs, 6% Psychology
Expenses: 2017-2018: $11,994 in state, $17,064 out of state; room/board: $9,000
Financial aid: (616) 331-3234; 57% of undergrads determined to have financial need; average aid package $9,698

Hillsdale College
Hillsdale MI
(517) 607-2327
U.S. News ranking: Nat. Lib. Arts, No. 71
Website: www.hillsdale.edu
Admissions email: admissions@hillsdale.edu
Private; founded 1844
Affiliation: Undenominational

Freshman admissions: more selective; 2016-2017: 1,934 applied, 874 accepted. Either SAT or ACT required. ACT 25/75 percentile: 28-32. High school rank: N/A
Early decision deadline: 11/1, notification date: 12/1
Early action deadline: N/A, notification date: N/A
Application deadline (fall): 4/1
Undergraduate student body: 1,440 full time, 46 part time; 50% male, 50% female; 0% American Indian, 0% Asian, 0% black, 0% Hispanic, 0% multiracial, 0% Pacific Islander, 0% white, 0% international; 35% from in state; 69% live on campus; 29% of students in fraternities, 34% in sororities
Most popular majors: 12% English Language and Literature, General, 11% History, General, 10% Economics, General, 9% Biology/Biological Sciences, General, 9% Finance, General
Expenses: 2017-2018: $26,742; room/board: $10,610
Financial aid: (517) 607-2350; 52% of undergrads determined to have financial need; average aid package $15,776

Hope College
Holland MI
(616) 395-7850
U.S. News ranking: Nat. Lib. Arts, No. 106
Website: www.hope.edu
Admissions email: admissions@hope.edu
Private; founded 1866
Affiliation: Christian Reformed Church
Freshman admissions: more selective; 2016-2017: 3,899 applied, 3,291 accepted. Either SAT or ACT required. ACT 25/75 percentile: 23-29. High school rank: 26% in top tenth, 55% in top quarter, 84% in top half
Early decision deadline: N/A, notification date: N/A
Early action deadline: 11/1, notification date: 11/24
Application deadline (fall): rolling
Undergraduate student body: 3,039 full time, 195 part time; 39% male, 61% female; N/A American Indian, N/A Asian, N/A black, N/A Hispanic, N/A multiracial, N/A Pacific Islander, N/A white, N/A international; 70% from in state; 71% live on campus; 6% of students in fraternities, 11% in sororities
Most popular majors: 12% Psychology, General, 11% Business Administration and Management, General, 7% Biology/Biological Sciences, General, 6% Registered Nursing/Registered Nurse, 5% Speech Communication and Rhetoric
Expenses: 2017-2018: $32,780; room/board: $10,000
Financial aid: (616) 395-7765; 56% of undergrads determined to have financial need; average aid package $25,792

Jackson College[1]
Jackson MI
U.S. News ranking: Reg. Coll. (Mid. W), unranked
Admissions email: N/A
Public
Application deadline (fall): N/A
Undergraduate student body: N/A full time, N/A part time
Expenses: 2016-2017: $5,640 in state, $7,440 out of state; room/board: $8,100
Financial aid: N/A

Kalamazoo College
Kalamazoo MI
(800) 253-3602
U.S. News ranking: Nat. Lib. Arts, No. 76
Website: www.kzoo.edu
Admissions email: admission@kzoo.edu
Private; founded 1833
Freshman admissions: more selective; 2016-2017: 3,626 applied, 2,381 accepted. Neither SAT nor ACT required. ACT 25/75 percentile: 26-30. High school rank: 52% in top tenth, 81% in top quarter, 95% in top half
Early decision deadline: 11/15, notification date: 12/1
Early action deadline: 11/15, notification date: 12/20
Application deadline (fall): 1/15
Undergraduate student body: 1,437 full time, 6 part time; 44% male, 56% female; 0% American Indian, 7% Asian, 6% black, 10% Hispanic, 5% multiracial, 0% Pacific Islander, 59% white, 8% international; 67% from in state; 53% live on campus; 0% of students in fraternities, 0% in sororities
Most popular majors: 17% Social Sciences, 14% Physical Sciences, 13% Biological and Biomedical Sciences, 11% Psychology, 9% Foreign Languages, Literatures, and Linguistics
Expenses: 2017-2018: $46,692; room/board: $9,390
Financial aid: N/A; 68% of undergrads determined to have financial need; average aid package $37,979

Kettering University
Flint MI
(800) 955-4464
U.S. News ranking: Reg. U. (Mid. W), No. 26
Website: www.kettering.edu
Admissions email: admissions@kettering.edu
Private; founded 1919
Freshman admissions: more selective; 2016-2017: 2,251 applied, 1,617 accepted. Either SAT or ACT required. ACT 25/75 percentile: 25-29. High school rank: 31% in top tenth, 68% in top quarter, 93% in top half
Early decision deadline: N/A, notification date: N/A
Early action deadline: 11/15, notification date: 12/15
Application deadline (fall): rolling
Undergraduate student body: 1,783 full time, 122 part time; 82% male, 18% female; 0% American Indian, 4% Asian, 3% black,

5% Hispanic, 3% multiracial, 0% Pacific Islander, 76% white, 4% international; 84% from in state; 40% live on campus; 39% of students in fraternities, 32% in sororities
Most popular majors: 84% Engineering, 8% Computer and Information Sciences and Support Services, 4% Business, Management, Marketing, and Related Support Services, 2% Biological and Biomedical Sciences, 2% Mathematics and Statistics
Expenses: 2016-2017: $39,790; room/board: $7,780
Financial aid: N/A

Kuyper College[1]
Grand Rapids MI
(800) 511-3749
U.S. News ranking: Reg. Coll. (Mid. W), No. 59
Website: www.kuyper.edu
Admissions email: admissions@kuyper.edu
Private
Application deadline (fall): N/A
Undergraduate student body: N/A full time, N/A part time
Expenses: 2016-2017: $20,342; room/board: $7,280
Financial aid: N/A

Lake Superior State University
Sault Ste. Marie MI
(906) 635-2231
U.S. News ranking: Reg. Coll. (Mid. W), No. 45
Website: www.lssu.edu
Admissions email: admissions@lssu.edu
Public; founded 1946
Freshman admissions: selective; 2016-2017: 1,460 applied, 1,325 accepted. Neither SAT nor ACT required. ACT 25/75 percentile: 20-25. High school rank: 16% in top tenth, 39% in top quarter, 76% in top half
Early decision deadline: N/A, notification date: N/A
Early action deadline: N/A, notification date: N/A
Application deadline (fall): rolling
Undergraduate student body: 1,811 full time, 288 part time; 49% male, 51% female; 8% American Indian, 0% Asian, 1% black, 2% Hispanic, 0% multiracial, 0% Pacific Islander, 80% white, 7% international
Most popular majors: 31% Homeland Security, Law Enforcement, Firefighting and Related Protective Services, 15% Health Professions and Related Programs, 12% Business, Management, Marketing, and Related Support Services, 8% Parks, Recreation, Leisure, and Fitness Studies, 3% Biological and Biomedical Sciences
Expenses: 2017-2018: $11,427 in state, $11,427 out of state; room/board: $9,594
Financial aid: (906) 635-2677; 69% of undergrads determined to have financial need; average aid package $11,325

Lawrence Technological University
Southfield MI
(248) 204-3160
U.S. News ranking: Reg. U. (Mid. W), No. 38
Website: www.ltu.edu
Admissions email: admissions@ltu.edu
Private; founded 1932
Freshman admissions: more selective; 2016-2017: 2,318 applied, 1,607 accepted. Either SAT or ACT required. ACT 25/75 percentile: 22-29. High school rank: 26% in top tenth, 53% in top quarter, 83% in top half
Early decision deadline: N/A, notification date: N/A
Early action deadline: N/A, notification date: N/A
Application deadline (fall): rolling
Undergraduate student body: 1,711 full time, 453 part time; 72% male, 28% female; 0% American Indian, 2% Asian, 6% black, 2% Hispanic, 2% multiracial, 0% Pacific Islander, 64% white, 16% international; 94% from in state; 35% live on campus; 10% of students in fraternities, 18% in sororities
Most popular majors: 36% Engineering, General, 22% Architecture, 11% Computer Science, 9% Business Administration and Management, General, 8% Design and Visual Communications, General
Expenses: 2017-2018: $32,130; room/board: $9,500
Financial aid: (248) 204-2280; 59% of undergrads determined to have financial need; average aid package $24,386

Madonna University
Livonia MI
(734) 432-5339
U.S. News ranking: Reg. U. (Mid. W), No. 93
Website: www.madonna.edu
Admissions email: admissions@madonna.edu
Private; founded 1937
Affiliation: Roman Catholic
Freshman admissions: selective; 2016-2017: 843 applied, 635 accepted. Either SAT or ACT required. ACT 25/75 percentile: 18-23. High school rank: N/A
Early decision deadline: 12/1, notification date: 1/15
Early action deadline: N/A, notification date: N/A
Application deadline (fall): N/A
Undergraduate student body: 1,353 full time, 1,276 part time; 32% male, 68% female; 0% American Indian, 1% Asian, 12% black, 5% Hispanic, 3% multiracial, 0% Pacific Islander, 61% white, 16% international; 99% from in state; 11% live on campus; N/A of students in fraternities, N/A in sororities
Most popular majors: 29% Business, Management, Marketing, and Related Support Services, 22% Health Professions and Related Programs, 15% Homeland Security, Law Enforcement,

Firefighting and Related Protective Services, 4% Biological and Biomedical Sciences, 4% Public Administration and Social Service Professions
Expenses: 2017-2018: $20,700; room/board: $9,750
Financial aid: (734) 432-5662; 71% of undergrads determined to have financial need; average aid package $11,397

Marygrove College[1]
Detroit MI
(313) 927-1240
U.S. News ranking: Reg. U. (Mid. W), second tier
Website: www.marygrove.edu
Admissions email: info@marygrove.edu
Private
Application deadline (fall): rolling
Undergraduate student body: N/A full time, N/A part time
Expenses: 2016-2017: $22,064; room/board: $7,100
Financial aid: N/A

Michigan State University
East Lansing MI
(517) 355-8332
U.S. News ranking: Nat. U., No. 81
Website: www.msu.edu
Admissions email: admis@msu.edu
Public; founded 1855
Freshman admissions: more selective; 2016-2017: 37,480 applied, 24,641 accepted. Either SAT or ACT required. ACT 25/75 percentile: 24-29. High school rank: 30% in top tenth, 68% in top quarter, 95% in top half
Early decision deadline: N/A, notification date: N/A
Early action deadline: N/A, notification date: N/A
Application deadline (fall): rolling
Undergraduate student body: 35,447 full time, 3,643 part time; 49% male, 51% female; 0% American Indian, 5% Asian, 7% black, 4% Hispanic, 3% multiracial, 0% Pacific Islander, 67% white, 12% international; 86% from in state; 39% live on campus; 12% of students in fraternities, 11% in sororities
Most popular majors: 18% Business, Management, Marketing, and Related Support Services, 13% Communication, Journalism, and Related Programs, 11% Social Sciences, 10% Biological and Biomedical Sciences, 8% Engineering
Expenses: 2017-2018: $14,460 in state, $39,405 out of state; room/board: $9,976
Financial aid: (517) 353-5940; 47% of undergrads determined to have financial need; average aid package $13,202

Michigan Technological University
Houghton MI
(906) 487-2335
U.S. News ranking: Nat. U., No. 124
Website: www.mtu.edu
Admissions email: mtu4u@mtu.edu
Public; founded 1885

Freshman admissions: more selective; 2016-2017: 5,589 applied, 4,272 accepted. Either SAT or ACT required. ACT 25/75 percentile: 25-30. High school rank: 29% in top tenth, 62% in top quarter, 90% in top half
Early decision deadline: N/A, notification date: N/A
Early action deadline: N/A, notification date: N/A
Application deadline (fall): rolling
Undergraduate student body: 5,460 full time, 369 part time; 73% male, 27% female; 0% American Indian, 1% Asian, 1% black, 2% Hispanic, 3% multiracial, 0% Pacific Islander, 87% white, 3% international; 77% from in state; 47% live on campus; 8% of students in fraternities, 14% in sororities
Most popular majors: 63% Engineering, 7% Business, Management, Marketing, and Related Support Services, 6% Computer and Information Sciences and Support Services, 4% Biological and Biomedical Sciences, 4% Engineering Technologies and Engineering-Related Fields
Expenses: 2017-2018: $15,074 in state, $32,318 out of state; room/board: $10,477
Financial aid: (906) 487-2622; 64% of undergrads determined to have financial need; average aid package $14,423

Northern Michigan University
Marquette MI
(906) 227-2650
U.S. News ranking: Reg. U. (Mid. W), No. 83
Website: www.nmu.edu
Admissions email: admissions@nmu.edu
Public; founded 1899
Freshman admissions: selective; 2016-2017: 5,345 applied, 4,056 accepted. Either SAT or ACT required. ACT 25/75 percentile: 19-25. High school rank: N/A
Early decision deadline: N/A, notification date: N/A
Early action deadline: N/A, notification date: N/A
Application deadline (fall): rolling
Undergraduate student body: 6,296 full time, 786 part time; 45% male, 55% female; 2% American Indian, 1% Asian, 2% black, 3% Hispanic, 4% multiracial, 0% Pacific Islander, 86% white, 1% international; 80% from in state; 41% live on campus; N/A of students in fraternities, N/A in sororities
Most popular majors: 14% Health Professions and Related Programs, 12% Business, Management, Marketing, and Related Support Services, 10% Biological and Biomedical Sciences, 10% Visual and Performing Arts, 9% Education
Expenses: 2017-2018: $10,240 in state, $15,736 out of state; room/board: $10,328
Financial aid: (906) 227-2327; 66% of undergrads determined to have financial need; average aid package $9,962

Northwestern Michigan College[1]
Traverse City MI
U.S. News ranking: Reg. Coll. (Mid. W), unranked
Admissions email: N/A
Public
Application deadline (fall): N/A
Undergraduate student body: N/A full time, N/A part time
Expenses: 2016-2017: $6,630 in state, $8,501 out of state; room/board: $9,350
Financial aid: N/A

Northwood University
Midland MI
(989) 837-4273
U.S. News ranking: Business, unranked
Website: www.northwood.edu
Admissions email: miadmit@northwood.edu
Private; founded 1959
Freshman admissions: selective; 2016-2017: 2,265 applied, 1,636 accepted. Either SAT or ACT required. ACT 25/75 percentile: 20-24. High school rank: 8% in top tenth, 29% in top quarter, 63% in top half
Early decision deadline: N/A, notification date: N/A
Early action deadline: N/A, notification date: N/A
Application deadline (fall): rolling
Undergraduate student body: 1,394 full time, 48 part time; 64% male, 36% female; 0% American Indian, 0% Asian, 6% black, 3% Hispanic, 2% multiracial, 0% Pacific Islander, 73% white, 7% international; 87% from in state; 30% live on campus; 9% of students in fraternities, 14% in sororities
Most popular majors: 23% Marketing/Marketing Management, General, 14% Business Administration and Management, General, 12% Accounting, 10% Sport and Fitness Administration/Management, 9% Finance, General
Expenses: 2016-2017: $25,130; room/board: $9,880
Financial aid: (989) 837-4301

Oakland University
Rochester MI
(248) 370-3360
U.S. News ranking: Nat. U., second tier
Website: www.oakland.edu
Admissions email: visit@oakland.edu
Public; founded 1957
Freshman admissions: selective; 2016-2017: 10,688 applied, 9,229 accepted. Either SAT or ACT required. ACT 25/75 percentile: 20-27. High school rank: 18% in top tenth, 47% in top quarter, 77% in top half
Early decision deadline: N/A, notification date: N/A
Early action deadline: N/A, notification date: N/A
Application deadline (fall): 8/1
Undergraduate student body: 12,968 full time, 3,600 part time; 43% male, 57% female; 0% American Indian, 5% Asian, 8% black, 3% Hispanic,

3% multiracial, 0% Pacific Islander, 75% white, 2% international; 99% from in state; 16% live on campus; N/A of students in fraternities, N/A in sororities
Most popular majors: 23% Health Professions and Related Programs, 18% Business, Management, Marketing, and Related Support Services, 8% Communication, Journalism, and Related Programs, 6% Psychology, 5% Engineering
Expenses: 2017-2018: $13,406 in state, $24,735 out of state; room/board: $9,910
Financial aid: (248) 370-2550; 61% of undergrads determined to have financial need; average aid package $13,924

Olivet College
Olivet MI
(800) 456-7189
U.S. News ranking: Reg. Coll. (Mid. W), No. 44
Website: www.olivetcollege.edu
Admissions email: admissions@olivetcollege.edu
Private; founded 1844
Affiliation: United Church of Christ
Freshman admissions: selective; 2016-2017: 2,654 applied, 1,316 accepted. Either SAT or ACT required. ACT 25/75 percentile: 18-23. High school rank: N/A
Early decision deadline: N/A, notification date: N/A
Early action deadline: N/A, notification date: N/A
Application deadline (fall): 8/31
Undergraduate student body: 951 full time, 94 part time; 59% male, 41% female; 0% American Indian, 1% Asian, 16% black, 5% Hispanic, 5% multiracial, 0% Pacific Islander, 70% white, 1% international
Most popular majors: 14% Criminal Justice/Safety Studies, 12% Insurance, 11% Sport and Fitness Administration/Management, 10% Business Administration and Management, General, 7% Journalism
Expenses: 2017-2018: $26,695; room/board: $9,310
Financial aid: (269) 749-7645; 93% of undergrads determined to have financial need; average aid package $18,885

Rochester College[1]
Rochester Hills MI
(248) 218-2031
U.S. News ranking: Reg. Coll. (Mid. W), second tier
Website: www.rc.edu
Admissions email: admissions@rc.edu
Private; founded 1959
Application deadline (fall): rolling
Undergraduate student body: N/A full time, N/A part time
Expenses: 2016-2017: $21,662; room/board: $6,952
Financial aid: (248) 218-2038

Saginaw Valley State University
University Center MI
(989) 964-4200
U.S. News ranking: Reg. U. (Mid. W), second tier
Website: www.svsu.edu

Admissions email: admissions@svsu.edu
Public; founded 1963
Freshman admissions: selective; 2016-2017: 6,699 applied, 5,083 accepted. Either SAT or ACT required. ACT 25/75 percentile: 20-25. High school rank: 17% in top tenth, 41% in top quarter, 75% in top half
Early decision deadline: N/A, notification date: N/A
Early action deadline: N/A, notification date: N/A
Application deadline (fall): rolling
Undergraduate student body: 6,988 full time, 1,409 part time; 42% male, 58% female; 0% American Indian, 1% Asian, 9% black, 4% Hispanic, 2% multiracial, 0% Pacific Islander, 72% white, 6% international; 98% from in state; 30% live on campus; 3% of students in fraternities, 3% in sororities
Most popular majors: 18% Business, Management, Marketing, and Related Support Services, 17% Health Professions and Related Programs, 7% Homeland Security, Law Enforcement, Firefighting and Related Protective Services, 7% Public Administration and Social Service Professions, 6% Education
Expenses: 2016-2017: $9,345 in state, $21,947 out of state; room/board: $8,520
Financial aid: (989) 964-4900; 66% of undergrads determined to have financial need

Siena Heights University
Adrian MI
(517) 264-7180
U.S. News ranking: Reg. U. (Mid. W), No. 118
Website: www.sienaheights.edu
Admissions email: admissions@sienaheights.edu
Private; founded 1919
Affiliation: Roman Catholic
Freshman admissions: selective; 2016-2017: 1,800 applied, 1,291 accepted. Neither SAT nor ACT required. ACT 25/75 percentile: 19-22. High school rank: 0% in top tenth, 29% in top quarter, 62% in top half
Early decision deadline: N/A, notification date: N/A
Early action deadline: N/A, notification date: N/A
Application deadline (fall): 8/1
Undergraduate student body: 1,327 full time, 1,080 part time; 41% male, 59% female; 1% American Indian, 1% Asian, 12% black, 6% Hispanic, 2% multiracial, 0% Pacific Islander, 61% white, 2% international
Most popular majors: 13% Business Administration and Management, General, 7% Community Organization and Advocacy, 7% Radiologic Technology/Science - Radiographer, 7% Registered Nursing/Registered Nurse, 5% Criminal Justice/Safety Studies
Expenses: 2017-2018: $25,932; room/board: $10,390
Financial aid: (517) 264-7110

Spring Arbor University

Spring Arbor MI
(800) 968-0011
U.S. News ranking: Reg. U. (Mid. W), No. 64
Website: www.arbor.edu/
Admissions email: admissions@arbor.edu
Private; founded 1873
Affiliation: Free Methodist
Freshman admissions: selective; 2016-2017: 1,623 applied, 1,160 accepted. Either SAT or ACT required. ACT 25/75 percentile: 19-25. High school rank: 17% in top tenth, 41% in top quarter, 72% in top half
Early decision deadline: N/A, notification date: N/A
Early action deadline: N/A, notification date: N/A
Application deadline (fall): 8/1
Undergraduate student body: 1,559 full time, 644 part time; 33% male, 67% female; 0% American Indian, 1% Asian, 10% black, 4% Hispanic, 3% multiracial, 0% Pacific Islander, 76% white, 1% international; 88% from in state; 72% live on campus; 0% of students in fraternities, 0% in sororities
Most popular majors: 9% Teacher Education and Professional Development, Specific Subject Areas, 8% Psychology, General, 6% Health and Physical Education/Fitness, General, 6% Social Work, 5% Business Administration and Management, General
Expenses: 2017-2018: $27,750; room/board: $9,640
Financial aid: (517) 750-6463; 84% of undergrads determined to have financial need; average aid package $23,256

University of Detroit Mercy

Detroit MI
(313) 993-1245
U.S. News ranking: Reg. U. (Mid. W), No. 19
Website: www.udmercy.edu
Admissions email: admissions@udmercy.edu
Private; founded 1877
Affiliation: Roman Catholic
Freshman admissions: selective; 2016-2017: 4,542 applied, 3,561 accepted. Either SAT or ACT required. ACT 25/75 percentile: 22-27. High school rank: 26% in top tenth, 38% in top quarter, 87% in top half
Early decision deadline: 11/1, notification date: 12/1
Early action deadline: N/A, notification date: N/A
Application deadline (fall): 3/1
Undergraduate student body: 2,165 full time, 481 part time; 36% male, 64% female; 0% American Indian, 6% Asian, 13% black, 5% Hispanic, 3% multiracial, 0% Pacific Islander, 62% white, 6% international; 95% from in state; 31% live on campus; 3% of students in fraternities, 4% in sororities
Most popular majors: 46% Registered Nursing/Registered Nurse, 19% Biology/Biological Sciences, General, 6% Business Administration and Management,

General, 4% Architecture, 4% Dental Hygiene/Hygienist
Expenses: 2017-2018: $41,158; room/board: $9,452
Financial aid: (313) 993-3354; 69% of undergrads determined to have financial need; average aid package $33,808

University of Michigan–Ann Arbor

Ann Arbor MI
(734) 764-7433
U.S. News ranking: Nat. U., No. 28
Website: umich.edu
Public; founded 1817
Freshman admissions: most selective; 2016-2017: 55,504 applied, 15,871 accepted. Either SAT or ACT required. ACT 25/75 percentile: 29-33. High school rank: 74% in top tenth, 95% in top quarter, 100% in top half
Early decision deadline: N/A, notification date: N/A
Early action deadline: 11/1, notification date: 12/24
Application deadline (fall): 2/1
Undergraduate student body: 27,969 full time, 1,014 part time; 50% male, 50% female; 0% American Indian, 14% Asian, 4% black, 5% Hispanic, 4% multiracial, 0% Pacific Islander, 61% white, 7% international; 60% from in state; 33% live on campus; 17% of students in fraternities, 24% in sororities
Most popular majors: 7% Business Administration and Management, General, 7% Experimental Psychology, 6% Economics, General, 5% Physiological Psychology/Psychobiology, 4% Computer and Information Sciences, General
Expenses: 2017-2018: $14,826 in state, $47,476 out of state; room/board: $11,198
Financial aid: (734) 763-4119; 38% of undergrads determined to have financial need; average aid package $24,323

University of Michigan–Dearborn

Dearborn MI
(313) 593-5100
U.S. News ranking: Reg. U. (Mid. W), No. 38
Website: umdearborn.edu/
Admissions email: umd-admissions@umich.edu
Public; founded 1959
Freshman admissions: more selective; 2016-2017: 5,328 applied, 3,448 accepted. Either SAT or ACT required. ACT 25/75 percentile: 22-27. High school rank: 27% in top tenth, 57% in top quarter, 89% in top half
Early decision deadline: N/A, notification date: N/A
Early action deadline: N/A, notification date: N/A
Application deadline (fall): 9/6
Undergraduate student body: 4,985 full time, 2,156 part time; 52% male, 48% female; 0% American Indian, 8% Asian, 9% black, 6% Hispanic, 3% multiracial, 0% Pacific Islander, 68% white, 2% international; 96% from in state; N/A live on campus; 3% of students in fraternities, 4% in sororities

Most popular majors: 20% Business, Management, Marketing, and Related Support Services, 15% Engineering, 11% Psychology, 10% Biological and Biomedical Sciences, 8% Social Sciences
Expenses: 2017-2018: $12,472 in state, $24,706 out of state; room/board: N/A
Financial aid: (313) 593-5300; 65% of undergrads determined to have financial need; average aid package $11,053

University of Michigan–Flint

Flint MI
(810) 762-3300
U.S. News ranking: Reg. U. (Mid. W), No. 99
Website: www.umflint.edu
Admissions email: admissions@umflint.edu
Public; founded 1956
Freshman admissions: selective; 2016-2017: 4,033 applied, 2,627 accepted. Either SAT or ACT required. ACT 25/75 percentile: 19-26. High school rank: 16% in top tenth, 42% in top quarter, 76% in top half
Early decision deadline: N/A, notification date: N/A
Early action deadline: N/A, notification date: N/A
Application deadline (fall): 8/18
Undergraduate student body: 3,844 full time, 2,741 part time; 39% male, 61% female; 1% American Indian, 2% Asian, 14% black, 4% Hispanic, 3% multiracial, 0% Pacific Islander, 68% white, 5% international; 98% from in state; 6% live on campus; 4% of students in fraternities, 4% in sororities
Most popular majors: 34% Health Professions and Related Programs, 18% Business, Management, Marketing, and Related Support Services, 8% Psychology, 7% Biological and Biomedical Sciences, 5% Public Administration and Social Service Professions
Expenses: 2017-2018: $11,334 in state, $21,654 out of state; room/board: $8,437
Financial aid: (810) 762-3444

Walsh College of Accountancy and Business Administration[1]

Troy MI
(248) 823-1610
U.S. News ranking: Business, unranked
Website: www.walshcollege.edu
Admissions email: admissions@walshcollege.edu
Private; founded 1922
Application deadline (fall): N/A
Undergraduate student body: N/A full time, N/A part time
Expenses: 2016-2017: $13,200; room/board: N/A
Financial aid: N/A

Wayne State University

Detroit MI
(313) 577-2100
U.S. News ranking: Nat. U., No. 223
Website: www.wayne.edu/
Admissions email: studentservice@wayne.edu
Public; founded 1868
Freshman admissions: more selective; 2016-2017: 13,309 applied, 8,997 accepted. Either SAT or ACT required. ACT 25/75 percentile: 20-27. High school rank: 24% in top tenth, 51% in top quarter, 79% in top half
Early decision deadline: N/A, notification date: N/A
Early action deadline: N/A, notification date: N/A
Application deadline (fall): 8/1
Undergraduate student body: 12,041 full time, 5,239 part time; 44% male, 56% female; 0% American Indian, 9% Asian, 17% black, 5% Hispanic, 4% multiracial, 0% Pacific Islander, 58% white, 2% international; 99% from in state; 13% live on campus; N/A of students in fraternities, N/A in sororities
Most popular majors: 12% Psychology, General, 6% Biology/Biological Sciences, General, 4% Health Professions and Related Clinical Sciences, Other, 4% Organizational Behavior Studies, 4% Social Work
Expenses: 2016-2017: $13,278 in state, $28,590 out of state; room/board: $9,747
Financial aid: (313) 577-2100; 73% of undergrads determined to have financial need; average aid package $11,073

Western Michigan University

Kalamazoo MI
(269) 387-2000
U.S. News ranking: Nat. U., No. 207
Website: wmich.edu/
Admissions email: ask-wmu@wmich.edu
Public; founded 1903
Freshman admissions: selective; 2016-2017: 13,613 applied, 11,205 accepted. Either SAT or ACT required. ACT 25/75 percentile: 19-25. High school rank: 12% in top tenth, 32% in top quarter, 69% in top half
Early decision deadline: N/A, notification date: N/A
Early action deadline: N/A, notification date: N/A
Application deadline (fall): rolling
Undergraduate student body: 15,048 full time, 3,265 part time; 50% male, 50% female; 0% American Indian, 2% Asian, 13% black, 6% Hispanic, 4% multiracial, 0% Pacific Islander, 71% white, 4% international; 92% from in state; 27% live on campus; 7% of students in fraternities, 8% in sororities
Most popular majors: 20% Business, Management, Marketing, and Related Support Services, 11% Health Professions and Related Programs, 8% Multi/Interdisciplinary Studies, 6% Education, 6% Engineering

Expenses: 2017-2018: $11,943 in state, $14,699 out of state; room/board: $9,848
Financial aid: (269) 387-6000; 66% of undergrads determined to have financial need; average aid package $13,687

MINNESOTA

Augsburg College

Minneapolis MN
(612) 330-1001
U.S. News ranking: Reg. U. (Mid. W), No. 29
Website: www.augsburg.edu
Admissions email: admissions@augsburg.edu
Private; founded 1869
Freshman admissions: selective; 2016-2017: 3,487 applied, 1,574 accepted. Either SAT or ACT required. ACT 25/75 percentile: 18-23. High school rank: N/A
Early decision deadline: N/A, notification date: N/A
Early action deadline: N/A, notification date: N/A
Application deadline (fall): 8/1
Undergraduate student body: 2,085 full time, 465 part time; 46% male, 54% female; 1% American Indian, 7% Asian, 11% black, 7% Hispanic, 2% multiracial, 0% Pacific Islander, 47% white, 3% international; 88% from in state; 38% live on campus; N/A of students in fraternities, N/A in sororities
Most popular majors: 28% Business, Management, Marketing, and Related Support Services, 13% Health Professions and Related Programs, 9% Social Sciences, 8% Psychology, 7% Education
Expenses: 2016-2017: $36,415; room/board: $9,628
Financial aid: N/A

Bemidji State University

Bemidji MN
(218) 755-2040
U.S. News ranking: Reg. U. (Mid. W), No. 109
Website: www.bemidjistate.edu
Admissions email: admissions@bemidjistate.edu
Public; founded 1919
Freshman admissions: selective; 2016-2017: 4,137 applied, 2,651 accepted. Either SAT or ACT required. ACT 25/75 percentile: 20-24. High school rank: 7% in top tenth, 19% in top quarter, 36% in top half
Early decision deadline: N/A, notification date: N/A
Early action deadline: N/A, notification date: N/A
Application deadline (fall): rolling
Undergraduate student body: 3,437 full time, 1,358 part time; 43% male, 57% female; 3% American Indian, 1% Asian, 2% black, 3% Hispanic, 4% multiracial, 0% Pacific Islander, 84% white, 2% international; 90% from in state; 29% live on campus; N/A of students in fraternities, N/A in sororities

Most popular majors: 21% Business, Management, Marketing, and Related Support Services, 20% Health Professions and Related Programs, 10% Education, 9% Engineering Technologies and Engineering-Related Fields, 7% Biological and Biomedical Sciences
Expenses: 2017-2018: $8,644 in state; $8,644 out of state; room/board: $8,162
Financial aid: (218) 755-4142; 61% of undergrads determined to have financial need; average aid package $9,845

Bethany Lutheran College
Mankato MN
(507) 344-7331
U.S. News ranking: Nat. Lib. Arts, second tier
Website: www.blc.edu
Admissions email: admiss@blc.edu
Private; founded 1927
Affiliation: Evangelical Lutheran Church
Freshman admissions: selective; 2016-2017: 328 applied, 264 accepted. Either SAT or ACT required. ACT 25/75 percentile: 20-27. High school rank: 9% in top tenth, 40% in top quarter, 68% in top half
Early decision deadline: N/A, notification date: N/A
Early action deadline: N/A, notification date: N/A
Application deadline (fall): 7/1
Undergraduate student body: 514 full time, 73 part time; 43% male, 57% female; 0% American Indian, 0% Asian, 3% black, 3% Hispanic, 2% multiracial, 0% Pacific Islander, 84% white, 6% international; 77% from in state; 69% live on campus; 0% of students in fraternities, 0% in sororities
Most popular majors: 17% Business, Management, Marketing, and Related Programs, 11% Communication, Journalism, and Related Programs, 10% Biological and Biomedical Sciences, 9% Visual and Performing Arts, 8% Psychology
Expenses: 2017-2018: $26,830; room/board: $8,100
Financial aid: (507) 344-7328; 80% of undergrads determined to have financial need; average aid package $21,236

Bethel University
St. Paul MN
(800) 255-8706
U.S. News ranking: Reg. U. (Mid. W), No. 11
Website: www.bethel.edu
Admissions email: undergrad-admissions@bethel.edu
Private; founded 1871
Affiliation: Baptist
Freshman admissions: more selective; 2016-2017: 1,798 applied, 1,481 accepted. Either SAT or ACT required. ACT 25/75 percentile: 21-28. High school rank: 29% in top tenth, 53% in top quarter, 84% in top half
Early decision deadline: N/A, notification date: N/A

Early action deadline: N/A, notification date: N/A
Application deadline (fall): rolling
Undergraduate student body: 2,454 full time, 511 part time; 38% male, 62% female; 0% American Indian, 3% Asian, 4% black, 5% Hispanic, 3% multiracial, 0% Pacific Islander, 72% white, 0% international; 80% from in state; 68% live on campus; N/A of students in fraternities, N/A in sororities
Most popular majors: 17% Business, Management, Marketing, and Related Support Services, 14% Health Professions and Related Programs, 12% Education, 8% Communication, Journalism, and Related Programs, 7% Social Sciences
Expenses: 2017-2018: $36,200; room/board: $10,340
Financial aid: (651) 638-6241; 73% of undergrads determined to have financial need; average aid package $27,371

Capella University[1]
Minneapolis MN
U.S. News ranking: Nat. U., unranked
Website: www.capella.edu
Admissions email: admissionsoffice@capella.edu
For-profit
Application deadline (fall): N/A
Undergraduate student body: N/A full time, N/A part time
Expenses: 2016-2017: $13,998; room/board: N/A
Financial aid: N/A

Carleton College
Northfield MN
(507) 222-4190
U.S. News ranking: Nat. Lib. Arts, No. 8
Website: www.carleton.edu
Admissions email: admissions@carleton.edu
Private; founded 1866
Freshman admissions: most selective; 2016-2017: 6,485 applied, 1,467 accepted. Either SAT or ACT required. ACT 25/75 percentile: 30-33. High school rank: 75% in top tenth, 93% in top quarter, 100% in top half
Early decision deadline: 11/15, notification date: 12/15
Early action deadline: N/A, notification date: N/A
Application deadline (fall): 1/15
Undergraduate student body: 2,087 full time, 18 part time; 49% male, 51% female; 0% American Indian, 9% Asian, 4% black, 7% Hispanic, 6% multiracial, 0% Pacific Islander, 62% white, 10% international; 17% from in state; 97% live on campus; 0% of students in fraternities, 0% in sororities
Most popular majors: 20% Social Sciences, 12% Physical Sciences, 10% Biological and Biomedical Sciences, 10% Computer and Information Sciences and Support Services, 10% Visual and Performing Arts
Expenses: 2017-2018: $52,782; room/board: $13,632
Financial aid: (507) 222-4138; 56% of undergrads determined to have financial need; average aid package $45,763

College of St. Benedict
St. Joseph MN
(320) 363-5060
U.S. News ranking: Nat. Lib. Arts, No. 87
Website: www.csbsju.edu
Admissions email: admissions@csbsju.edu
Private; founded 1913
Affiliation: Roman Catholic
Freshman admissions: more selective; 2016-2017: 2,042 applied, 1,631 accepted. Either SAT or ACT required. ACT 25/75 percentile: 22-28. High school rank: 36% in top tenth, 69% in top quarter, 93% in top half
Early decision deadline: N/A, notification date: N/A
Early action deadline: 11/15, notification date: 12/15
Application deadline (fall): N/A
Undergraduate student body: 1,939 full time, 19 part time; 0% male, 100% female; 1% American Indian, 6% Asian, 3% black, 7% Hispanic, 1% multiracial, 0% Pacific Islander, 78% white, 4% international; 84% from in state; 89% live on campus; N/A of students in fraternities, N/A in sororities
Most popular majors: 11% Biology/Biological Sciences, General, 11% Registered Nursing/Registered Nurse, 11% Rhetoric and Composition, 10% Psychology, General, 9% Nutrition Sciences
Expenses: 2017-2018: $43,738; room/board: $10,742
Financial aid: (320) 363-5388; 74% of undergrads determined to have financial need; average aid package $35,174

College of St. Scholastica
Duluth MN
(218) 723-6046
U.S. News ranking: Reg. U. (Mid. W), No. 34
Website: www.css.edu
Admissions email: admissions@css.edu
Private; founded 1912
Affiliation: Roman Catholic
Freshman admissions: selective; 2016-2017: 3,232 applied, 2,059 accepted. Either SAT or ACT required. ACT 25/75 percentile: 21-26. High school rank: 22% in top tenth, 52% in top quarter, 77% in top half
Early decision deadline: N/A, notification date: N/A
Early action deadline: N/A, notification date: N/A
Application deadline (fall): rolling
Undergraduate student body: 2,255 full time, 586 part time; 28% male, 72% female; 1% American Indian, 2% Asian, 3% black, 3% Hispanic, 3% multiracial, 0% Pacific Islander, 83% white, 3% international; 85% from in state; 51% live on campus; N/A of students in fraternities, N/A in sororities
Most popular majors: 49% Health Professions and Related Programs, 15% Business, Management, Marketing, and Related Support Services, 10% Biological and Biomedical Sciences, 7% Psychology, 7% Public Administration and Social Service Professions

Expenses: 2017-2018: $36,212; room/board: $9,522
Financial aid: (218) 723-6725; 78% of undergrads determined to have financial need; average aid package $24,815

Concordia College–Moorhead
Moorhead MN
(800) 699-9897
U.S. News ranking: Nat. Lib. Arts, No. 117
Website: www.concordiacollege.edu
Admissions email: admissions@cord.edu
Private; founded 1891
Affiliation: Evangelical Lutheran Church
Freshman admissions: more selective; 2016-2017: 3,741 applied, 2,435 accepted. Either SAT or ACT required. ACT 25/75 percentile: 22-28. High school rank: 27% in top tenth, 55% in top quarter, 82% in top half
Early decision deadline: N/A, notification date: N/A
Early action deadline: N/A, notification date: N/A
Application deadline (fall): rolling
Undergraduate student body: 2,066 full time, 48 part time; 41% male, 59% female; 1% American Indian, 1% Asian, 2% black, 2% Hispanic, 2% multiracial, 0% Pacific Islander, 84% white, 3% international; 70% from in state; 62% live on campus; 0% of students in fraternities, 0% in sororities
Most popular majors: 17% Business, Management, Marketing, and Related Support Services, 13% Education, 10% Biological and Biomedical Sciences, 7% Communication, Journalism, and Related Programs, 6% Health Professions and Related Programs
Expenses: 2017-2018: $38,978; room/board: $8,040
Financial aid: (218) 299-3010; 72% of undergrads determined to have financial need; average aid package $29,519

Concordia University–St. Paul
St. Paul MN
(651) 641-8230
U.S. News ranking: Reg. U. (Mid. W), No. 106
Website: www.csp.edu
Admissions email: admissions@csp.edu
Private; founded 1893
Affiliation: Lutheran Church–Missouri Synod
Freshman admissions: selective; 2016-2017: 1,704 applied, 949 accepted. Either SAT or ACT required. ACT 25/75 percentile: 18-24. High school rank: 6% in top tenth, 27% in top quarter, 60% in top half
Early decision deadline: N/A, notification date: N/A
Early action deadline: N/A, notification date: N/A
Application deadline (fall): 8/1

Undergraduate student body: 1,393 full time, 1,266 part time; 40% male, 60% female; 0% American Indian, 8% Asian, 12% black, 4% Hispanic, 4% multiracial, 0% Pacific Islander, 65% white, 5% international; 76% from in state; 21% live on campus; N/A of students in fraternities, N/A in sororities
Most popular majors: 16% Business Administration and Management, General, 13% Kinesiology and Exercise Science, 6% Marketing/Marketing Management, General, 5% Accounting, 5% Psychology, General
Expenses: 2017-2018: $21,750; room/board: $8,750
Financial aid: (651) 603-6300; 72% of undergrads determined to have financial need; average aid package $14,088

Crown College
St. Bonifacius MN
(952) 446-4142
U.S. News ranking: Reg. Coll. (Mid. W), No. 53
Website: www.crown.edu
Admissions email: admissions@crown.edu
Private; founded 1916
Affiliation: Christ and Missionary Alliance Church
Freshman admissions: selective; 2016-2017: 763 applied, 413 accepted. Either SAT or ACT required. ACT 25/75 percentile: 19-25. High school rank: N/A
Early decision deadline: N/A, notification date: N/A
Early action deadline: N/A, notification date: N/A
Application deadline (fall): 8/20
Undergraduate student body: 730 full time, 329 part time; 45% male, 55% female; 1% American Indian, 7% Asian, 7% black, 7% Hispanic, 2% multiracial, 0% Pacific Islander, 73% white, 3% international; 43% from in state; 76% live on campus; 0% of students in fraternities, 0% in sororities
Most popular majors: 15% Business Administration and Management, General, 15% Religious Education, 10% Counseling Psychology, 7% Communication and Media Studies, Other, 7% Registered Nursing/Registered Nurse
Expenses: 2017-2018: $25,430; room/board: $8,490
Financial aid: (952) 446-4177; 83% of undergrads determined to have financial need; average aid package $17,545

Dunwoody College of Technology
Minneapolis MN
(800) 292-4625
U.S. News ranking: Reg. Coll. (Mid. W), No. 56
Website: www.dunwoody.edu
Admissions email: admissions@dunwoody.edu
Private; founded 1914
Freshman admissions: less selective; 2016-2017: 889 applied, 703 accepted. Neither SAT nor ACT required. SAT 25/75

percentile: N/A. High school rank: 15% in top tenth, 38% in top quarter, 76% in top half
Early decision deadline: N/A, notification date: N/A
Early action deadline: N/A, notification date: N/A
Application deadline (fall): rolling
Undergraduate student body: 1,062 full time, 202 part time; 84% male, 16% female; 0% American Indian, 7% Asian, 5% black, 3% Hispanic, 4% multiracial, 0% Pacific Islander, 76% white, 0% international
Most popular majors: 32% Business Administration and Management, General, 21% Interior Design, 7% Computer Science, 4% Manufacturing Engineering
Expenses: 2017-2018: $21,937; room/board: N/A
Financial aid: (612) 381-3347; 82% of undergrads determined to have financial need; average aid package $8,939

Gustavus Adolphus College
St. Peter MN
(507) 933-7676
U.S. News ranking: Nat. Lib. Arts, No. 85
Website: gustavus.edu
Admissions email: admission@gustavus.edu
Private; founded 1862
Affiliation: Evangelical Lutheran Church
Freshman admissions: more selective; 2016-2017: 4,801 applied, 3,111 accepted. Neither SAT nor ACT required. ACT 25/75 percentile: 24-29. High school rank: 29% in top tenth, 63% in top quarter, 94% in top half
Early decision deadline: N/A, notification date: N/A
Early action deadline: 11/1, notification date: 11/15
Application deadline (fall): 4/1
Undergraduate student body: 2,200 full time, 30 part time; 46% male, 54% female; 0% American Indian, 4% Asian, 2% black, 5% Hispanic, 3% multiracial, 0% Pacific Islander, 80% white, 5% international; 82% from in state; 97% live on campus; 17% of students in fraternities, 13% in sororities
Most popular majors: 15% Business, Management, Marketing, and Related Support Services, 14% Social Sciences, 10% Biological and Biomedical Sciences, 10% Psychology, 8% Education
Expenses: 2017-2018: $44,080; room/board: $9,670
Financial aid: (507) 933-7527; 70% of undergrads determined to have financial need; average aid package $36,349

Hamline University
St. Paul MN
(651) 523-2207
U.S. News ranking: Reg. U. (Mid. W), No. 16
Website: www.hamline.edu
Admissions email: admission@hamline.edu
Private; founded 1854
Affiliation: United Methodist

Freshman admissions: selective; 2016-2017: 4,252 applied, 2,989 accepted. Either SAT or ACT required. ACT 25/75 percentile: 21-27. High school rank: 16% in top tenth, 49% in top quarter, 84% in top half
Early decision deadline: 11/1, notification date: 11/15
Early action deadline: 12/1, notification date: N/A
Application deadline (fall): rolling
Undergraduate student body: 2,090 full time, 94 part time; 40% male, 60% female; 0% American Indian, 6% Asian, 6% black, 8% Hispanic, 7% multiracial, 0% Pacific Islander, 70% white, 1% international; 80% from in state; 39% live on campus; N/A of students in fraternities, N/A in sororities
Most popular majors: 16% Business, Management, Marketing, and Related Support Services, 13% Social Sciences, 11% Psychology, 9% Multi/Interdisciplinary Studies, 8% English Language and Literature/Letters
Expenses: 2017-2018: $40,332; room/board: $10,156
Financial aid: (651) 523-3000; 84% of undergrads determined to have financial need; average aid package $29,877

Macalester College
St. Paul MN
(651) 696-6357
U.S. News ranking: Nat. Lib. Arts, No. 26
Website: www.macalester.edu
Admissions email: admissions@macalester.edu
Private; founded 1874
Freshman admissions: most selective; 2016-2017: 5,946 applied, 2,206 accepted. Either SAT or ACT required. ACT 25/75 percentile: 29-33. High school rank: 69% in top tenth, 94% in top quarter, 99% in top half
Early decision deadline: 11/15, notification date: 12/15
Early action deadline: N/A, notification date: N/A
Application deadline (fall): 1/15
Undergraduate student body: 2,108 full time, 38 part time; 40% male, 60% female; 0% American Indian, 7% Asian, 3% black, 6% Hispanic, 5% multiracial, 0% Pacific Islander, 64% white, 14% international; 17% from in state; 60% live on campus; N/A of students in fraternities, N/A in sororities
Most popular majors: 23% Social Sciences, 11% Biological and Biomedical Sciences, 9% Foreign Languages, Literatures, and Linguistics, 9% Mathematics and Statistics, 9% Physical Sciences
Expenses: 2017-2018: $52,464; room/board: $11,672
Financial aid: (651) 696-6214; 68% of undergrads determined to have financial need; average aid package $43,969

Metropolitan State University[1]
St. Paul MN
(651) 772-7600
U.S. News ranking: Reg. U. (Mid. W), second tier
Website: www.metrostate.edu
Admissions email: admissions@metrostate.edu
Public
Application deadline (fall): N/A
Undergraduate student body: N/A full time, N/A part time
Expenses: 2016-2017: $7,566 in state, $14,394 out of state; room/board: N/A
Financial aid: N/A

Minneapolis College of Art and Design
Minneapolis MN
(612) 874-3760
U.S. News ranking: Arts, unranked
Website: www.mcad.edu
Admissions email: admissions@mcad.edu
Private; founded 1886
Freshman admissions: selective; 2016-2017: 636 applied, 415 accepted. Either SAT or ACT required. ACT 25/75 percentile: 20-26. High school rank: N/A
Early decision deadline: N/A, notification date: N/A
Early action deadline: 12/1, notification date: 12/15
Application deadline (fall): 4/1
Undergraduate student body: 686 full time, 17 part time; 29% male, 71% female; 2% American Indian, 7% Asian, 5% black, 6% Hispanic, 2% multiracial, 0% Pacific Islander, 65% white, 3% international; 53% from in state; 38% live on campus; 0% of students in fraternities, 0% in sororities
Most popular majors: 84% Visual and Performing Arts, 5% Precision Production, 4% Business, Management, Marketing, and Related Support Services, 4% Communications Technologies/Technicians and Support Services
Expenses: 2017-2018: $37,812; room/board: $7,550
Financial aid: (612) 874-3733; 80% of undergrads determined to have financial need; average aid package $26,642

Minnesota State University–Mankato
Mankato MN
(507) 389-1822
U.S. News ranking: Reg. U. (Mid. W), No. 99
Website: www.mnsu.edu
Admissions email: admissions@mnsu.edu
Public; founded 1868
Freshman admissions: selective; 2016-2017: 11,428 applied, 7,141 accepted. ACT required. ACT 25/75 percentile: 20-24. High school rank: 7% in top tenth, 27% in top quarter, 67% in top half
Early decision deadline: N/A, notification date: N/A
Early action deadline: N/A, notification date: N/A
Application deadline (fall): rolling

Undergraduate student body: 11,009 full time, 2,183 part time; 47% male, 53% female; 0% American Indian, 4% Asian, 5% black, 4% Hispanic, 3% multiracial, 0% Pacific Islander, 75% white, 7% international; 84% from in state; 23% live on campus; N/A of students in fraternities, N/A in sororities
Most popular majors: 8% Registered Nursing/Registered Nurse, 5% Business Administration and Management, General, 5% Psychology, General, 4% Biology/Biological Sciences, General, 4% Health and Physical Education/Fitness, General
Expenses: 2016-2017: $7,859 in state, $15,602 out of state; room/board: $8,716
Financial aid: (507) 389-1419; 54% of undergrads determined to have financial need; average aid package $9,396

Minnesota State University–Moorhead
Moorhead MN
(800) 593-7246
U.S. News ranking: Reg. U. (Mid. W), No. 118
Website: www.mnstate.edu
Admissions email: admissions@mnstate.edu
Public; founded 1887
Freshman admissions: selective; 2016-2017: 4,261 applied, 2,540 accepted. Either SAT or ACT required. ACT 25/75 percentile: 20-25. High school rank: 9% in top tenth, 28% in top quarter, 59% in top half
Early decision deadline: N/A, notification date: N/A
Early action deadline: N/A, notification date: N/A
Application deadline (fall): rolling
Undergraduate student body: 4,283 full time, 922 part time; 40% male, 60% female; 1% American Indian, 1% Asian, 3% black, 3% Hispanic, 3% multiracial, 0% Pacific Islander, 78% white, 8% international; 67% from in state; 24% live on campus; 1% of students in fraternities, 2% in sororities
Most popular majors: 15% Business, Management, Marketing, and Related Support Services, 15% Education, 12% Health Professions and Related Programs, 11% Visual and Performing Arts, 7% Communication, Journalism, and Related Programs
Expenses: 2017-2018: $8,144 in state, $15,260 out of state; room/board: $8,310
Financial aid: (218) 477-2251; 59% of undergrads determined to have financial need; average aid package $3,208

North Central University
Minneapolis MN
(800) 289-6222
U.S. News ranking: Reg. Coll. (Mid. W), No. 51
Website: www.northcentral.edu
Admissions email: admissions@northcentral.edu
Private; founded 1930
Affiliation: Assemblies of God Church

Freshman admissions: selective; 2016-2017: 1,023 applied, 629 accepted. Either SAT or ACT required. ACT 25/75 percentile: 18-24. High school rank: 11% in top tenth, 25% in top quarter, 68% in top half
Early decision deadline: N/A, notification date: N/A
Early action deadline: N/A, notification date: N/A
Application deadline (fall): rolling
Undergraduate student body: 881 full time, 38 part time; 42% male, 58% female; 0% American Indian, 2% Asian, 4% black, 5% Hispanic, 3% multiracial, 0% Pacific Islander, 75% white, 1% international; 49% from in state; 84% live on campus; N/A of students in fraternities, N/A in sororities
Most popular majors: 9% Elementary Education and Teaching, 8% Business Administration and Management, General, 8% Intercultural/Multicultural and Diversity Studies, 8% Pastoral Studies/Counseling, 7% Human Development and Family Studies, General
Expenses: 2017-2018: $23,480; room/board: $7,130
Financial aid: (612) 343-4485; 84% of undergrads determined to have financial need; average aid package $17,819

Southwest Minnesota State University
Marshall MN
(507) 537-6286
U.S. News ranking: Reg. U. (Mid. W), second tier
Website: www.smsu.edu
Admissions email: smsu.admissions@smsu.edu
Public; founded 1963
Freshman admissions: selective; 2016-2017: 1,884 applied, 1,021 accepted. Either SAT or ACT required. ACT 25/75 percentile: 18-23. High school rank: 5% in top tenth, 20% in top quarter, 50% in top half
Early decision deadline: N/A, notification date: N/A
Early action deadline: N/A, notification date: N/A
Application deadline (fall): 9/1
Undergraduate student body: 2,034 full time, 4,776 part time; 42% male, 58% female; 1% American Indian, 3% Asian, 7% black, 3% Hispanic, 0% multiracial, 0% Pacific Islander, 76% white, 8% international
Most popular majors: 30% Business, Management, Marketing, and Related Support Services, 20% Education, 10% Parks, Recreation, Leisure, and Fitness Studies, 5% Psychology
Expenses: 2017-2018: $8,338 in state, $8,338 out of state; room/board: $8,286
Financial aid: (507) 537-6281; 65% of undergrads determined to have financial need; average aid package $9,027

St. Catherine University
St. Paul MN
(800) 945-4599
U.S. News ranking: Reg. U. (Mid. W), No. 11
Website: www.stkate.edu
Admissions email: admissions@stkate.edu
Private; founded 1905
Affiliation: Roman Catholic
Freshman admissions: selective; 2016-2017: 2,853 applied, 1,979 accepted. Either SAT or ACT required. ACT 25/75 percentile: 21-26. High school rank: 26% in top tenth, 68% in top quarter, 95% in top half
Early decision deadline: N/A, notification date: N/A
Early action deadline: N/A, notification date: N/A
Application deadline (fall): rolling
Undergraduate student body: 2,038 full time, 1,138 part time; 4% male, 96% female; 1% American Indian, 12% Asian, 11% black, 8% Hispanic, 3% multiracial, 0% Pacific Islander, 62% white, 1% international; 88% from in state; 41% live on campus; 0% of students in fraternities, 0% in sororities
Most popular majors: 35% Registered Nursing/Registered Nurse, 6% Public Health, General, 6% Social Work, 4% Business Administration and Management, General, 4% Psychology, General
Expenses: 2017-2018: $38,349; room/board: $9,196
Financial aid: (651) 690-6061; 86% of undergrads determined to have financial need; average aid package $35,162

St. Cloud State University
St. Cloud MN
(320) 308-2244
U.S. News ranking: Reg. U. (Mid. W), No. 118
Website: www.stcloudstate.edu
Admissions email: scsu4u@stcloudstate.edu
Public; founded 1869
Freshman admissions: selective; 2016-2017: 6,986 applied, 5,946 accepted. Either SAT or ACT required. ACT 25/75 percentile: 18-24. High school rank: 5% in top tenth, 19% in top quarter, 46% in top half
Early decision deadline: N/A, notification date: N/A
Early action deadline: N/A, notification date: N/A
Application deadline (fall): 8/11
Undergraduate student body: 8,837 full time, 4,399 part time; 47% male, 53% female; 0% American Indian, 7% Asian, 7% black, 3% Hispanic, 3% multiracial, 0% Pacific Islander, 70% white, 9% international; 91% from in state; 19% live on campus; 2% of students in fraternities, 3% in sororities
Most popular majors: 5% Multi-/Interdisciplinary Studies, Other, 4% Business Administration and Management, General, 4% Criminal Justice/Safety Studies, 4% Finance, General, 4% Psychology, General

Expenses: 2016-2017: $7,910 in state, $15,828 out of state; room/board: $8,230
Financial aid: (320) 308-2047; 60% of undergrads determined to have financial need; average aid package $11,835

St. John's University
Collegeville MN
(320) 363-5060
U.S. News ranking: Nat. Lib. Arts, No. 85
Website: www.csbsju.edu
Admissions email: admissions@csbsju.edu
Private; founded 1857
Affiliation: Roman Catholic
Freshman admissions: selective; 2016-2017: 1,659 applied, 1,279 accepted. Either SAT or ACT required. ACT 25/75 percentile: 22-28. High school rank: 19% in top tenth, 43% in top quarter, 82% in top half
Early decision deadline: N/A, notification date: N/A
Early action deadline: 11/15, notification date: 12/15
Application deadline (fall): N/A
Undergraduate student body: 1,737 full time, 17 part time; 100% male, 0% female; 1% American Indian, 3% Asian, 5% black, 8% Hispanic, 0% multiracial, 0% Pacific Islander, 79% white, 4% international; 80% from in state; 90% live on campus; N/A of students in fraternities, N/A in sororities
Most popular majors: 22% Business Administration and Management, General, 14% Accounting, 8% Economics, General, 7% Biology/Biological Sciences, General, 6% Computer Science
Expenses: 2017-2018: $43,356; room/board: $10,116
Financial aid: (320) 363-2189; 69% of undergrads determined to have financial need; average aid package $32,176

St. Mary's University of Minnesota
Winona MN
(507) 457-1700
U.S. News ranking: Reg. U. (Mid. W), No. 47
Website: www.smumn.edu
Admissions email: admissions@smumn.edu
Private; founded 1912
Freshman admissions: selective; 2016-2017: 1,686 applied, 1,336 accepted. Either SAT or ACT required. ACT 25/75 percentile: 20-26. High school rank: 8% in top tenth, 38% in top quarter, 70% in top half
Early decision deadline: N/A, notification date: N/A
Early action deadline: N/A, notification date: N/A
Application deadline (fall): 5/1
Undergraduate student body: 1,168 full time, 422 part time; 46% male, 54% female; 0% American Indian, 2% Asian, 6% black, 5% Hispanic, 1% multiracial, 0% Pacific Islander, 58% white, 3% international; 71% from in state; 84% live on campus; 4% of students in fraternities, 3% in sororities

Most popular majors: 11% Business Administration and Management, General, 8% Marketing/Marketing Management, General, 6% Criminal Justice/Police Science, 6% Health/Health Care Administration/Management, 6% Human Resources Management/Personnel Administration, General
Expenses: 2017-2018: $33,560; room/board: $8,880
Financial aid: (612) 238-4552; 72% of undergrads determined to have financial need; average aid package $25,847

St. Olaf College
Northfield MN
(507) 786-3025
U.S. News ranking: Nat. Lib. Arts, No. 57
Website: wp.stolaf.edu/
Admissions email: admissions@stolaf.edu
Private; founded 1874
Freshman admissions: more selective; 2016-2017: 6,041 applied, 2,704 accepted. Either SAT or ACT required. ACT 25/75 percentile: 26-31. High school rank: 44% in top tenth, 77% in top quarter, 94% in top half
Early decision deadline: 11/15, notification date: 12/15
Early action deadline: N/A, notification date: N/A
Application deadline (fall): 1/15
Undergraduate student body: 2,990 full time, 50 part time; 44% male, 56% female; 0% American Indian, 6% Asian, 2% black, 6% Hispanic, 3% multiracial, 0% Pacific Islander, 73% white, 8% international; 45% from in state; 94% live on campus; N/A of students in fraternities, N/A in sororities
Most popular majors: 17% Social Sciences, 12% Biological and Biomedical Sciences, 11% Visual and Performing Arts, 9% Mathematics and Statistics, 8% Physical Sciences
Expenses: 2017-2018: $46,000; room/board: $10,430
Financial aid: (507) 786-3706; 64% of undergrads determined to have financial need; average aid package $37,224

University of Minnesota–Crookston
Crookston MN
(800) 232-6466
U.S. News ranking: Reg. Coll. (Mid. W), No. 33
Website: www.crk.umn.edu
Admissions email: UMCinfo@umn.edu
Public; founded 1966
Freshman admissions: selective; 2016-2017: 1,288 applied, 878 accepted. Either SAT or ACT required. ACT 25/75 percentile: 20-24. High school rank: 8% in top tenth, 29% in top quarter, 61% in top half
Early decision deadline: N/A, notification date: N/A
Early action deadline: N/A, notification date: N/A
Application deadline (fall): rolling
Undergraduate student body: 1,187 full time, 1,489 part time; 47% male, 53% female; 1% American Indian, 3% Asian, 6% black,

4% Hispanic, 2% multiracial, 0% Pacific Islander, 77% white, 5% international; 70% from in state; 33% live on campus; 1% of students in fraternities, N/A in sororities
Most popular majors: 38% Business, Management, Marketing, and Related Support Services, 22% Agriculture, Agriculture Operations, and Related Sciences, 11% Health Professions and Related Programs, 8% Natural Resources and Conservation, 6% Multi/Interdisciplinary Studies
Expenses: 2017-2018: $12,202 in state, $12,202 out of state; room/board: $7,658
Financial aid: (218) 281-6510; 65% of undergrads determined to have financial need; average aid package $11,692

University of Minnesota–Duluth
Duluth MN
(218) 726-7171
U.S. News ranking: Reg. U. (Mid. W), No. 38
Website: www.d.umn.edu
Admissions email: umdadmis@d.umn.edu
Public; founded 1947
Freshman admissions: selective; 2016-2017: 7,973 applied, 6,105 accepted. Either SAT or ACT required. ACT 25/75 percentile: 22-26. High school rank: 17% in top tenth, 42% in top quarter, 85% in top half
Early decision deadline: N/A, notification date: N/A
Early action deadline: N/A, notification date: N/A
Application deadline (fall): 6/15
Undergraduate student body: 8,755 full time, 1,212 part time; 53% male, 47% female; 1% American Indian, 3% Asian, 2% black, 3% Hispanic, 3% multiracial, 0% Pacific Islander, 85% white, 2% international; 88% from in state; 32% live on campus; N/A of students in fraternities, N/A in sororities
Most popular majors: 19% Business, Management, Marketing, and Related Support Services, 13% Engineering, 11% Biological and Biomedical Sciences, 8% Social Sciences, 7% Education
Expenses: 2017-2018: $1,328 in state, $18,462 out of state; room/board: $7,608
Financial aid: (218) 726-8000; 57% of undergrads determined to have financial need; average aid package $12,743

University of Minnesota–Morris
Morris MN
(888) 866-3382
U.S. News ranking: Nat. Lib. Arts, No. 141
Website: www.morris.umn.edu
Admissions email: admissions@morris.umn.edu
Public; founded 1959
Freshman admissions: more selective; 2016-2017: 3,414 applied, 1,982 accepted. Either SAT or ACT required. ACT 25/75 percentile: 22-28. High school

rank: 20% in top tenth, 52% in top quarter, 88% in top half
Early decision deadline: N/A, notification date: N/A
Early action deadline: N/A, notification date: N/A
Application deadline (fall): 3/15
Undergraduate student body: 1,646 full time, 125 part time; 44% male, 56% female; 6% American Indian, 3% Asian, 2% black, 5% Hispanic, 12% multiracial, 0% Pacific Islander, 60% white, 11% international; 87% from in state; 56% live on campus; N/A of students in fraternities, N/A in sororities
Most popular majors: 12% Biology/Biological Sciences, General, 11% Economics, General, 10% Psychology, General, 7% Business Administration and Management, General, 7% Computer Science
Expenses: 2017-2018: $13,072 in state, $15,092 out of state; room/board: $8,150
Financial aid: (320) 589-6046; 63% of undergrads determined to have financial need; average aid package $12,633

University of Minnesota–Twin Cities
Minneapolis MN
(800) 752-1000
U.S. News ranking: Nat. U., No. 69
Website: twin-cities.umn.edu/
Public; founded 1851
Freshman admissions: more selective; 2016-2017: 49,129 applied, 21,820 accepted. Either SAT or ACT required. ACT 25/75 percentile: 26-31. High school rank: 48% in top tenth, 85% in top quarter, 99% in top half
Early decision deadline: N/A, notification date: N/A
Early action deadline: N/A, notification date: N/A
Application deadline (fall): rolling
Undergraduate student body: 29,567 full time, 5,304 part time; 48% male, 52% female; 0% American Indian, 9% Asian, 4% black, 4% Hispanic, 4% multiracial, 0% Pacific Islander, 69% white, 9% international; 73% from in state; 22% live on campus; N/A of students in fraternities, N/A in sororities
Most popular majors: 12% Social Sciences, 11% Biological and Biomedical Sciences, 11% Engineering, 9% Business, Management, Marketing, and Related Support Services, 7% Psychology
Expenses: 2017-2018: $14,417 in state, $26,603 out of state; room/board: $9,852
Financial aid: (800) 400-8636; 48% of undergrads determined to have financial need; average aid package $13,153

University of Northwestern–St. Paul
St. Paul MN
(800) 827-6827
U.S. News ranking: Reg. U. (Mid. W), No. 47
Website: www.unwsp.edu
Admissions email: reerickson@unwsp.edu
Private; founded 1902

Affiliation: Undenominational
Freshman admissions: selective; 2016-2017: N/A applied, N/A accepted. Either SAT or ACT required. ACT 25/75 percentile: 21-27. High school rank: N/A
Early decision deadline: N/A, notification date: N/A
Early action deadline: N/A, notification date: N/A
Application deadline (fall): 8/1
Undergraduate student body: 1,987 full time, 1,254 part time; 39% male, 61% female; 0% American Indian, 4% Asian, 4% black, 4% Hispanic, 3% multiracial, 0% Pacific Islander, 83% white, 1% international
Most popular majors: Information not available
Expenses: 2016-2017: $29,370; room/board: $9,060
Financial aid: (651) 631-5321

University of St. Thomas
St. Paul MN
(651) 962-6150
U.S. News ranking: Nat. U., No. 115
Website: www.stthomas.edu
Admissions email: admissions@stthomas.edu
Private; founded 1885
Affiliation: Roman Catholic
Freshman admissions: more selective; 2016-2017: 6,221 applied, 5,142 accepted. Either SAT or ACT required. ACT 25/75 percentile: 24-29. High school rank: 25% in top tenth, 53% in top quarter, 87% in top half
Early decision deadline: N/A, notification date: N/A
Early action deadline: 11/1, notification date: 12/15
Application deadline (fall): rolling
Undergraduate student body: 5,849 full time, 262 part time; 54% male, 46% female; 0% American Indian, 4% Asian, 3% black, 4% Hispanic, 3% multiracial, 0% Pacific Islander, 82% white, 3% international; 81% from in state; 40% live on campus; N/A of students in fraternities, N/A in sororities
Most popular majors: 37% Business, Management, Marketing, and Related Support Services, 5% Communication, Journalism, and Related Programs, 4% Biological and Biomedical Sciences, 4% Engineering, 4% Health Professions and Related Programs
Expenses: 2017-2018: $41,133; room/board: $10,054
Financial aid: (651) 962-6168; 56% of undergrads determined to have financial need; average aid package $26,846

Walden University[1]
Minneapolis MN
U.S. News ranking: Nat. U., unranked
Website: www.waldenu.edu/
Admissions email: N/A
For-profit; founded 1970
Application deadline (fall): N/A
Undergraduate student body: N/A full time, N/A part time
Expenses: 2016-2017: $12,075; room/board: N/A
Financial aid: (443) 537-1719

Winona State University
Winona MN
(507) 457-5100
U.S. News ranking: Reg. U. (Mid. W), No. 64
Website: www.winona.edu
Admissions email: admissions@winona.edu
Public; founded 1858
Freshman admissions: selective; 2016-2017: 7,476 applied, 4,467 accepted. Either SAT or ACT required. ACT 25/75 percentile: 20-25. High school rank: 10% in top tenth, 32% in top quarter, 70% in top half
Early decision deadline: N/A, notification date: N/A
Early action deadline: N/A, notification date: N/A
Application deadline (fall): 7/16
Undergraduate student body: 6,697 full time, 959 part time; 37% male, 63% female; 0% American Indian, 2% Asian, 3% black, 3% Hispanic, 2% multiracial, 0% Pacific Islander, 86% white, 3% international; 71% from in state; 29% live on campus; N/A of students in fraternities, N/A in sororities
Most popular majors: 22% Business, Management, Marketing, and Related Support Services, 19% Health Professions and Related Programs, 10% Education, 8% Parks, Recreation, Leisure, and Fitness Studies, 6% Communication, Journalism, and Related Programs
Expenses: 2017-2018: $9,379 in state, $15,302 out of state; room/board: $8,730
Financial aid: (507) 457-2800; 58% of undergrads determined to have financial need; average aid package $8,099

MISSISSIPPI

Alcorn State University
Lorman MS
(601) 877-6147
U.S. News ranking: Reg. U. (S), No. 95
Website: www.alcorn.edu
Admissions email: ksampson@alcorn.edu
Public; founded 1871
Freshman admissions: less selective; 2016-2017: 2,078 applied, 1,630 accepted. Either SAT or ACT required. ACT 25/75 percentile: 16-21. High school rank: 0% in top tenth, 0% in top quarter, 79% in top half
Early decision deadline: N/A, notification date: N/A
Early action deadline: N/A, notification date: N/A
Application deadline (fall): rolling
Undergraduate student body: 2,589 full time, 236 part time; 36% male, 64% female; 0% American Indian, 0% Asian, 92% black, 1% Hispanic, 2% multiracial, 0% Pacific Islander, 3% white, 2% international; 76% from in state; 64% live on campus; N/A of students in fraternities, N/A in sororities

Most popular majors: 17% Biological and Biomedical Sciences, 10% Liberal Arts and Sciences, General Studies and Humanities, 9% Health Professions and Related Programs, 7% Business, Management, Marketing, and Related Support Services, 7% Public Administration and Social Service Professions
Expenses: 2017-2018: $6,888 in state, $6,888 out of state; room/board: $9,731
Financial aid: (601) 877-6190; 51% of undergrads determined to have financial need; average aid package $7,516

Belhaven University
Jackson MS
(601) 968-5940
U.S. News ranking: Reg. U. (S), No. 78
Website: www.belhaven.edu
Admissions email: admission@belhaven.edu
Private; founded 1883
Affiliation: Presbyterian
Freshman admissions: selective; 2016-2017: 2,474 applied, 1,053 accepted. Either SAT or ACT required. ACT 25/75 percentile: 20-23. High school rank: N/A
Early decision deadline: N/A, notification date: N/A
Early action deadline: N/A, notification date: N/A
Application deadline (fall): rolling
Undergraduate student body: 1,331 full time, 1,307 part time; 34% male, 66% female; 1% American Indian, 1% Asian, 47% black, 5% Hispanic, 2% multiracial, 0% Pacific Islander, 36% white, 2% international; 72% from in state; 25% live on campus; 0% of students in fraternities, 0% in sororities
Most popular majors: 31% Business, Management, Marketing, and Related Support Services, 13% Social Sciences, 10% Health Professions and Related Programs, 10% Visual and Performing Arts, 9% Parks, Recreation, Leisure, and Fitness Studies
Expenses: 2017-2018: $24,250; room/board: $8,000
Financial aid: (601) 968-5933; 84% of undergrads determined to have financial need; average aid package $15,744

Blue Mountain College
Blue Mountain MS
(662) 685-4161
U.S. News ranking: Reg. Coll. (S), No. 8
Website: www.bmc.edu
Admissions email: admissions@bmc.edu
Private; founded 1873
Affiliation: Southern Baptist
Freshman admissions: selective; 2016-2017: 386 applied, 185 accepted. Either SAT or ACT required. ACT 25/75 percentile: 18-23. High school rank: 15% in top tenth, 42% in top quarter, 71% in top half
Early decision deadline: N/A, notification date: N/A

Early action deadline: N/A, notification date: N/A
Application deadline (fall): rolling
Undergraduate student body: 495 full time, 49 part time; 45% male, 55% female; 1% American Indian, 0% Asian, 10% black, 2% Hispanic, 1% multiracial, 0% Pacific Islander, 84% white, 2% international; 79% from in state; 59% live on campus; 0% of students in fraternities, 0% in sororities
Most popular majors: 17% Business Administration and Management, General, 17% Psychology, General, 14% Elementary Education and Teaching, 12% Kinesiology and Exercise Science, 11% Biology/Biological Sciences, General
Expenses: 2017-2018: $11,760; room/board: $6,294
Financial aid: (662) 685-4771; 81% of undergrads determined to have financial need; average aid package $11,230

Delta State University[1]
Cleveland MS
(662) 846-4018
U.S. News ranking: Reg. U. (S), second tier
Website: www.deltastate.edu
Admissions email: admissions@deltastate.edu
Public; founded 1924
Application deadline (fall): 8/1
Undergraduate student body: N/A full time, N/A part time
Expenses: 2016-2017: $6,418 in state, $6,418 out of state; room/board: $7,374
Financial aid: (662) 846-4670

Jackson State University
Jackson MS
(601) 979-2100
U.S. News ranking: Nat. U., second tier
Website: www.jsums.edu
Admissions email: admappl@jsums.edu
Public; founded 1877
Freshman admissions: less selective; 2016-2017: 8,516 applied, 5,857 accepted. Either SAT or ACT required. ACT 25/75 percentile: 16-24. High school rank: N/A
Early decision deadline: N/A, notification date: N/A
Early action deadline: N/A, notification date: N/A
Application deadline (fall): 9/2
Undergraduate student body: 6,507 full time, 985 part time; 37% male, 63% female; 0% American Indian, 0% Asian, 92% black, 1% Hispanic, 1% multiracial, 0% Pacific Islander, 4% white, 2% international; N/A from in state; 36% live on campus; 1% of students in fraternities, 1% in sororities
Most popular majors: 19% Biological and Biomedical Sciences, 16% Physical Sciences, 9% Homeland Security, Law Enforcement, Firefighting and Related Protective Services, 7% Engineering, 5% Psychology
Expenses: 2016-2017: $7,261 in state, $17,614 out of state; room/board: $10,078

Financial aid: (601) 979-2227; 86% of undergrads determined to have financial need; average aid package $12,324

Millsaps College
Jackson MS
(601) 974-1050
U.S. News ranking: Nat. Lib. Arts, No. 87
Website: www.millsaps.edu
Admissions email: admissions@millsaps.edu
Private; founded 1890
Freshman admissions: more selective; 2016-2017: 4,269 applied, 2,525 accepted. Either SAT or ACT required. ACT 25/75 percentile: 23-28. High school rank: 30% in top tenth, 64% in top quarter, 86% in top half
Early decision deadline: N/A, notification date: N/A
Early action deadline: 11/15, notification date: 1/15
Application deadline (fall): 7/1
Undergraduate student body: 795 full time, 14 part time; 51% male, 49% female; 1% American Indian, 4% Asian, 14% black, 4% Hispanic, 0% multiracial, 0% Pacific Islander, 71% white, 4% international; 45% from in state; 90% live on campus; 61% of students in fraternities, 59% in sororities
Most popular majors: 28% Biological and Biomedical Sciences, 25% Business, Management, Marketing, and Related Support Services, 12% Social Sciences, 7% Psychology, 5% History
Expenses: 2017-2018: $38,930; room/board: $13,400
Financial aid: (601) 974-1220; 63% of undergrads determined to have financial need; average aid package $33,569

Mississippi College
Clinton MS
(601) 925-3800
U.S. News ranking: Reg. U. (S), No. 32
Website: www.mc.edu
Admissions email: admissions@mc.edu
Private; founded 1826
Affiliation: Southern Baptist
Freshman admissions: selective; 2016-2017: 2,175 applied, 1,076 accepted. Either SAT or ACT required. ACT 25/75 percentile: 21-28. High school rank: 34% in top tenth, 66% in top quarter, 86% in top half
Early decision deadline: N/A, notification date: N/A
Early action deadline: N/A, notification date: N/A
Application deadline (fall): rolling
Undergraduate student body: 2,804 full time, 341 part time; 37% male, 63% female; 1% American Indian, 2% Asian, 18% black, 3% Hispanic, 1% multiracial, 0% Pacific Islander, 68% white, 6% international; 73% from in state; 63% live on campus; 22% of students in fraternities, 36% in sororities
Most popular majors: 13% Registered Nursing/Registered Nurse, 8% Business Administration and Management,

General, 8% Kinesiology and Exercise Science, 6% Biomedical Sciences, General, 6% Elementary Education and Teaching
Expenses: 2017-2018: $17,392; room/board: $9,610
Financial aid: (601) 925-3212; 51% of undergrads determined to have financial need; average aid package $16,184

Mississippi State University
Mississippi State MS
(662) 325-2224
U.S. News ranking: Nat. U., No. 171
Website: www.msstate.edu
Admissions email: admit@ admissions.msstate.edu
Public; founded 1878
Freshman admissions: more selective; 2016-2017: 13,930 applied, 9,866 accepted. Either SAT or ACT required. ACT 25/75 percentile: 21-28. High school rank: 28% in top tenth, 56% in top quarter, 83% in top half
Early decision deadline: N/A, notification date: N/A
Early action deadline: N/A, notification date: N/A
Application deadline (fall): rolling
Undergraduate student body: 16,695 full time, 1,395 part time; 50% male, 50% female; 0% American Indian, 1% Asian, 20% black, 3% Hispanic, 2% multiracial, 0% Pacific Islander, 72% white, 1% international; 70% from in state; 28% live on campus; 18% of students in fraternities, 25% in sororities
Most popular majors: 17% Business, Management, Marketing, and Related Support Services, 15% Engineering, 8% Education, 8% Parks, Recreation, Leisure, and Fitness Studies, 6% Multi/Interdisciplinary Studies
Expenses: 2017-2018: $8,138 in state, $22,358 out of state; room/board: $9,614
Financial aid: (662) 325-2450; 63% of undergrads determined to have financial need; average aid package $14,539

Mississippi University for Women
Columbus MS
(662) 329-7106
U.S. News ranking: Reg. U. (S), No. 52
Website: www.muw.edu
Admissions email: admissions@muw.edu
Public; founded 1884
Freshman admissions: selective; 2016-2017: 750 applied, 741 accepted. Either SAT or ACT required. ACT 25/75 percentile: 18-24. High school rank: 24% in top tenth, 58% in top quarter, 87% in top half
Early decision deadline: N/A, notification date: N/A
Early action deadline: N/A, notification date: N/A
Application deadline (fall): rolling
Undergraduate student body: 2,116 full time, 629 part time; 19% male, 81% female; 1% American

Indian, 0% Asian, 38% black, 0% Hispanic, 1% multiracial, 0% Pacific Islander, 53% white, 6% international; 90% from in state; 24% live on campus; 9% of students in fraternities, 12% in sororities
Most popular majors: 59% Registered Nursing/Registered Nurse, 4% Business Administration and Management, General, 3% Liberal Arts and Sciences/Liberal Studies, 3% Public Health Education and Promotion, 3% Speech-Language Pathology/Pathologist
Expenses: 2017-2018: $6,614 in state, $18,155 out of state; room/board: $7,032
Financial aid: (662) 329-7114; 74% of undergrads determined to have financial need; average aid package $9,245

Mississippi Valley State University
Itta Bena MS
(662) 254-3344
U.S. News ranking: Reg. U. (S), second tier
Website: www.mvsu.edu
Admissions email: admsn@mvsu.edu
Public; founded 1950
Freshman admissions: least selective; 2016-2017: 2,605 applied, 2,200 accepted. Either SAT or ACT required. ACT 25/75 percentile: 15-19. High school rank: N/A
Early decision deadline: N/A, notification date: N/A
Early action deadline: N/A, notification date: N/A
Application deadline (fall): 8/17
Undergraduate student body: 1,744 full time, 267 part time; 40% male, 60% female; 0% American Indian, 0% Asian, 91% black, 1% Hispanic, 1% multiracial, 0% Pacific Islander, 3% white, 0% international; 72% from in state; 52% live on campus; 3% of students in fraternities, 4% in sororities
Most popular majors: 13% Business, Management, Marketing, and Related Support Services, 13% Education, 13% Public Administration and Social Service Professions, 12% Homeland Security, Law Enforcement, Firefighting and Related Protective Services, 12% Parks, Recreation, Leisure, and Fitness Studies
Expenses: 2016-2017: $6,116 in state, $6,116 out of state; room/board: $7,394
Financial aid: N/A

Rust College
Holly Springs MS
(662) 252-8000
U.S. News ranking: Reg. Coll. (S), second tier
Website: www.rustcollege.edu
Admissions email: admissions@rustcollege.edu
Private; founded 1866
Affiliation: United Methodist
Freshman admissions: least selective; 2016-2017: N/A applied, N/A accepted. ACT required. ACT 25/75 percentile: 13-17. High school rank: N/A

Early decision deadline: N/A, notification date: N/A
Early action deadline: N/A, notification date: N/A
Application deadline (fall): rolling
Undergraduate student body: 872 full time, 132 part time; 40% male, 60% female; 0% American Indian, 0% Asian, 96% black, 0% Hispanic, 0% multiracial, 0% Pacific Islander, 1% white, 2% international
Most popular majors: 29% Biology/Biological Sciences, General, 12% Business Administration and Management, General, 12% Child Care and Support Services Management, 0% Broadcast Journalism, 0% Computer Science
Expenses: 2016-2017: $9,500; room/board: $4,100
Financial aid: (662) 252-8000

Tougaloo College
Tougaloo MS
(601) 977-7768
U.S. News ranking: Nat. Lib. Arts, second tier
Website: www.tougaloo.edu
Admissions email: information@mail.tougaloo.edu
Private; founded 1869
Affiliation: United Church of Christ
Freshman admissions: selective; 2016-2017: 2,284 applied, 1,183 accepted. Either SAT or ACT required. ACT 25/75 percentile: 16-24. High school rank: 22% in top tenth, 37% in top quarter, 52% in top half
Early decision deadline: N/A, notification date: N/A
Early action deadline: 11/1, notification date: 11/15
Application deadline (fall): 7/1
Undergraduate student body: 812 full time, 31 part time; 34% male, 66% female; N/A American Indian, N/A Asian, N/A black, N/A Hispanic, N/A multiracial, N/A Pacific Islander, N/A white, N/A international; 81% from in state; 68% live on campus; 11% of students in fraternities, 5% in sororities
Most popular majors: 19% Sociology, 14% Biology/Biological Sciences, General, 11% Mass Communication/Media Studies, 11% Psychology, General, 10% Economics, General
Expenses: 2017-2018: $10,600; room/board: $6,330
Financial aid: (601) 977-7769; 95% of undergrads determined to have financial need; average aid package $12,500

University of Mississippi
University MS
(662) 915-7226
U.S. News ranking: Nat. U., No. 145
Website: www.olemiss.edu
Admissions email: admissions@olemiss.edu
Public; founded 1844
Freshman admissions: more selective; 2016-2017: 17,918 applied, 14,029 accepted. Neither SAT nor ACT required. ACT 25/75 percentile: 22-29. High school rank: 25% in top tenth, 50% in top quarter, 80% in top half

Early decision deadline: N/A, notification date: N/A
Early action deadline: N/A, notification date: N/A
Application deadline (fall): rolling
Undergraduate student body: 17,852 full time, 1,361 part time; 44% male, 56% female; 0% American Indian, 2% Asian, 13% black, 3% Hispanic, 2% multiracial, 0% Pacific Islander, 78% white, 1% international; 56% from in state; 29% live on campus; 33% of students in fraternities, 42% in sororities
Most popular majors: 7% General Studies, 6% Accounting, 6% Marketing/Marketing Management, General, 5% Digital Communication and Media/Multimedia, 5% Elementary Education and Teaching
Expenses: 2017-2018: $8,290 in state, $23,554 out of state; room/board: $10,502
Financial aid: (662) 915-5788; 50% of undergrads determined to have financial need; average aid package $10,202

University of Southern Mississippi
Hattiesburg MS
(601) 266-5000
U.S. News ranking: Nat. U., second tier
Website: www.usm.edu/admissions
Admissions email: admissions@usm.edu
Public; founded 1910
Freshman admissions: selective; 2016-2017: 5,180 applied, 3,115 accepted. Either SAT or ACT required. ACT 25/75 percentile: 20-26. High school rank: N/A
Early decision deadline: N/A, notification date: N/A
Early action deadline: N/A, notification date: N/A
Application deadline (fall): rolling
Undergraduate student body: 10,246 full time, 1,533 part time; 37% male, 63% female; 0% American Indian, 1% Asian, 29% black, 3% Hispanic, 2% multiracial, 0% Pacific Islander, 61% white, 2% international; 84% from in state; 25% live on campus; 10% of students in fraternities, 14% in sororities
Most popular majors: 8% Registered Nursing/Registered Nurse, 7% Psychology, General, 6% Elementary Education and Teaching, 4% Biology/Biological Sciences, General, 4% Business Administration and Management, General
Expenses: 2017-2018: $7,854 in state, $9,854 out of state; room/board: $9,012
Financial aid: (601) 266-4774; 75% of undergrads determined to have financial need; average aid package $12,868

William Carey University
Hattiesburg MS
(601) 318-6103
U.S. News ranking: Reg. U. (S), No. 48
Website: www.wmcarey.edu
Admissions email: admissions@wmcarey.edu
Private; founded 1892

Affiliation: Southern Baptist
Freshman admissions: selective; 2016-2017: 1,110 applied, 421 accepted. Either SAT or ACT required. ACT 25/75 percentile: 21-27. High school rank: 33% in top tenth, 53% in top quarter, 81% in top half
Early decision deadline: N/A, notification date: N/A
Early action deadline: N/A, notification date: N/A
Application deadline (fall): rolling
Undergraduate student body: 1,648 full time, 1,160 part time; 38% male, 62% female; 1% American Indian, 1% Asian, 31% black, 2% Hispanic, 0% multiracial, 0% Pacific Islander, 60% white, 4% international; 91% from in state; 18% live on campus; N/A of students in fraternities, 2% in sororities
Most popular majors: 24% Psychology, General, 16% Elementary Education and Teaching, 14% Registered Nursing/Registered Nurse, 13% Business Administration and Management, General, 10% Biology/Biological Sciences, General
Expenses: 2017-2018: $12,300; room/board: $4,320
Financial aid: (601) 318-6153; 96% of undergrads determined to have financial need; average aid package $17,000

MISSOURI

Avila University[1]
Kansas City MO
(816) 501-2400
U.S. News ranking: Reg. U. (Mid. W), second tier
Website: www.Avila.edu
Admissions email: admissions@mail.avila.edu
Private
Application deadline (fall): N/A
Undergraduate student body: N/A full time, N/A part time
Expenses: 2016-2017: $27,312; room/board: $8,420
Financial aid: N/A

Central Methodist University
Fayette MO
(660) 248-6251
U.S. News ranking: Reg. Coll. (Mid. W), No. 27
Website: www.centralmethodist.edu
Admissions email: admissions@centralmethodist.edu
Private; founded 1854
Affiliation: United Methodist
Freshman admissions: selective; 2016-2017: 1,365 applied, 833 accepted. Either SAT or ACT required. ACT 25/75 percentile: 20-24. High school rank: 14% in top tenth, 38% in top quarter, 75% in top half
Early decision deadline: N/A, notification date: N/A
Early action deadline: N/A, notification date: N/A
Application deadline (fall): 8/20
Undergraduate student body: 1,062 full time, 32 part time; 48% male, 52% female; 0% American Indian, 0% Asian, 8% black,

3% Hispanic, 3% multiracial, 0% Pacific Islander, 77% white, 6% international; 89% from in state; 56% live on campus; 21% of students in fraternities, 20% in sororities
Most popular majors: 20% Health Professions and Related Programs, 18% Education, 9% Biological and Biomedical Sciences, 8% Business, Management, Marketing, and Related Support Services, 8% Homeland Security, Law Enforcement, Firefighting and Related Protective Services
Expenses: 2017-2018: $23,770; room/board: $7,730
Financial aid: (660) 248-6245; 80% of undergrads determined to have financial need; average aid package $19,890

College of the Ozarks
Point Lookout MO
(800) 222-0525
U.S. News ranking: Reg. Coll. (Mid. W), No. 5
Website: www.cofo.edu
Admissions email: admiss4@cofo.edu
Private; founded 1906
Affiliation: Other
Freshman admissions: selective; 2016-2017: 2,896 applied, 413 accepted. Either SAT or ACT required. ACT 25/75 percentile: 21-25. High school rank: 28% in top tenth, 66% in top quarter, 94% in top half
Early decision deadline: N/A, notification date: N/A
Early action deadline: N/A, notification date: N/A
Application deadline (fall): rolling
Undergraduate student body: 1,499 full time, 13 part time; 45% male, 55% female; 0% American Indian, 1% Asian, 1% black, 2% Hispanic, 2% multiracial, 0% Pacific Islander, 92% white, 1% international; 100% from in state; 90% live on campus; 0% of students in fraternities, 0% in sororities
Most popular majors: 15% Education, 11% Health Professions and Related Programs, 10% Business, Management, Marketing, and Related Support Services, 7% Agriculture, Agriculture Operations, and Related Sciences, 5% Homeland Security, Law Enforcement, Firefighting and Related Protective Services
Expenses: 2017-2018: $19,130; room/board: $7,100
Financial aid: (417) 690-3292; 92% of undergrads determined to have financial need; average aid package $20,163

Columbia College[1]
Columbia MO
(573) 875-7352
U.S. News ranking: Reg. U. (Mid. W), unranked
Website: www.ccis.edu
Admissions email: admissions@ccis.edu
Private; founded 1851
Application deadline (fall): rolling
Undergraduate student body: N/A full time, N/A part time
Expenses: 2016-2017: $20,936; room/board: $6,302
Financial aid: (573) 875-7390

Cottey College
Nevada MO
(888) 526-8839
U.S. News ranking: Reg. Coll. (Mid. W), No. 7
Website: www.cottey.edu
Admissions email: enrollmgt@cottey.edu
Private; founded 1884
Freshman admissions: selective; 2016-2017: 356 applied, 243 accepted. Either SAT or ACT required. ACT 25/75 percentile: 21-26. High school rank: 15% in top tenth, 35% in top quarter, 55% in top half
Early decision deadline: N/A, notification date: N/A
Early action deadline: N/A, notification date: N/A
Application deadline (fall): rolling
Undergraduate student body: 279 full time, 9 part time; 0% male, 100% female; 1% American Indian, 1% Asian, 5% black, 10% Hispanic, 5% multiracial, 0% Pacific Islander, 63% white, 15% international; 20% from in state; 97% live on campus; 0% of students in fraternities, 0% in sororities
Most popular majors: 26% Psychology, 20% Business, Management, Marketing, and Related Support Services, 17% English Language and Literature/Letters, 14% Natural Resources and Conservation, 14% Social Sciences
Expenses: 2017-2018: $20,200; room/board: $7,400
Financial aid: (417) 667-8181; 69% of undergrads determined to have financial need; average aid package $19,905

Culver-Stockton College
Canton MO
(800) 537-1883
U.S. News ranking: Reg. Coll. (Mid. W), No. 37
Website: www.culver.edu
Admissions email: admission@culver.edu
Private; founded 1853
Affiliation: Christian Church (Disciples of Christ)
Freshman admissions: selective; 2016-2017: 3,305 applied, 1,921 accepted. Either SAT or ACT required. ACT 25/75 percentile: 18-23. High school rank: 6% in top tenth, 24% in top quarter, 61% in top half
Early decision deadline: N/A, notification date: N/A
Early action deadline: N/A, notification date: N/A
Application deadline (fall): rolling
Undergraduate student body: 944 full time, 114 part time; 49% male, 51% female; 0% American Indian, 1% Asian, 12% black, 5% Hispanic, 3% multiracial, 0% Pacific Islander, 72% white, 7% international; 52% from in state; 73% live on campus; 37% of students in fraternities, 39% in sororities
Most popular majors: 18% Management Information Systems, General, 14% Psychology, General, 12% Sport and Fitness Administration/Management, 7% Biology/Biological Sciences,

General, 6% Criminal Justice/Law Enforcement Administration
Expenses: 2017-2018: $26,040; room/board: $8,310
Financial aid: (573) 288-6307; 81% of undergrads determined to have financial need; average aid package $19,954

Drury University
Springfield MO
(417) 873-7205
U.S. News ranking: Reg. U. (Mid. W), No. 26
Website: www.drury.edu
Admissions email: druryad@drury.edu
Private; founded 1873
Freshman admissions: more selective; 2016-2017: 1,563 applied, 1,088 accepted. Either SAT or ACT required. ACT 25/75 percentile: 22-28. High school rank: 21% in top tenth, 41% in top quarter, 79% in top half
Early decision deadline: N/A, notification date: N/A
Early action deadline: N/A, notification date: N/A
Application deadline (fall): rolling
Undergraduate student body: 1,342 full time, 28 part time; 46% male, 54% female; 0% American Indian, 1% Asian, 3% black, 3% Hispanic, 3% multiracial, 0% Pacific Islander, 78% white, 10% international; 85% from in state; 65% live on campus; 21% of students in fraternities, 25% in sororities
Most popular majors: 23% Business, Management, and Related Support Services, 12% Biological and Biomedical Sciences, 11% Visual and Performing Arts, 9% Social Sciences, 8% Physical Sciences
Expenses: 2017-2018: $27,005; room/board: $8,036
Financial aid: (417) 873-7312; 63% of undergrads determined to have financial need; average aid package $19,616

Evangel University
Springfield MO
(800) 382-6435
U.S. News ranking: Reg. U. (Mid. W), No. 122
Website: www.evangel.edu
Admissions email: admissions@evangel.edu
Private; founded 1955
Affiliation: Assemblies of God Church
Freshman admissions: selective; 2016-2017: 1,123 applied, 846 accepted. Either SAT or ACT required. ACT 25/75 percentile: 20-26. High school rank: N/A
Early decision deadline: N/A, notification date: N/A
Early action deadline: N/A, notification date: N/A
Application deadline (fall): rolling
Undergraduate student body: 1,473 full time, 154 part time; 45% male, 55% female; 1% American Indian, 2% Asian, 4% black, 4% Hispanic, 3% multiracial, 0% Pacific Islander, 81% white, 1% international
Most popular majors: Information not available
Expenses: 2017-2018: $22,582; room/board: $8,118

Financial aid: (417) 865-2811; 84% of undergrads determined to have financial need; average aid package $16,755

Fontbonne University
St. Louis MO
(314) 889-1400
U.S. News ranking: Reg. U. (Mid. W), No. 70
Website: www.fontbonne.edu
Admissions email: admissions@fontbonne.edu
Private; founded 1923
Affiliation: Roman Catholic
Freshman admissions: selective; 2016-2017: 477 applied, 427 accepted. Either SAT or ACT required. ACT 25/75 percentile: 20-25. High school rank: N/A
Early decision deadline: N/A, notification date: N/A
Early action deadline: N/A, notification date: N/A
Application deadline (fall): rolling
Undergraduate student body: 825 full time, 143 part time; 34% male, 66% female; 0% American Indian, 1% Asian, 14% black, 2% Hispanic, 2% multiracial, 0% Pacific Islander, 71% white, 7% international; 76% from in state; 34% live on campus; N/A of students in fraternities, N/A in sororities
Most popular majors: 9% Business Administration and Management, General, 4% Psychology, General, 4% Social Work, 4% Special Education and Teaching, General, 4% Speech-Language Pathology/Pathologist
Expenses: 2017-2018: $25,460; room/board: $9,590
Financial aid: (314) 889-1414; 79% of undergrads determined to have financial need; average aid package $15,640

Hannibal-LaGrange University
Hannibal MO
(800) 454-1119
U.S. News ranking: Reg. Coll. (Mid. W), second tier
Website: www.hlg.edu
Admissions email: admissions@hlg.edu
Private; founded 1858
Affiliation: Southern Baptist
Freshman admissions: less selective; 2016-2017: N/A applied, N/A accepted. Either SAT or ACT required. SAT 25/75 percentile: N/A. High school rank: N/A
Early decision deadline: N/A, notification date: N/A
Early action deadline: N/A, notification date: N/A
Application deadline (fall): 8/27
Undergraduate student body: 729 full time, 308 part time; 38% male, 62% female; 0% American Indian, 0% Asian, 3% black, 3% Hispanic, 2% multiracial, 0% Pacific Islander, 83% white, 8% international
Most popular majors: Business Administration and Management, General, Criminal Justice/Safety Studies, Elementary Education and Teaching, Organizational Leadership, Registered Nursing/Registered Nurse

Expenses: 2016-2017: $21,810; room/board: $7,608
Financial aid: N/A

Harris-Stowe State University
St. Louis MO
(314) 340-3300
U.S. News ranking: Reg. Coll. (Mid. W), second tier
Website: www.hssu.edu
Admissions email: admissions@hssu.edu
Public; founded 1857
Freshman admissions: least selective; 2016-2017: 4,266 applied, 2,337 accepted. Either SAT or ACT required. ACT 25/75 percentile: 14-19. High school rank: 3% in top tenth, 15% in top quarter, 44% in top half
Early decision deadline: N/A, notification date: N/A
Early action deadline: N/A, notification date: N/A
Application deadline (fall): rolling
Undergraduate student body: 1,159 full time, 305 part time; 33% male, 67% female; 0% American Indian, 1% Asian, 80% black, 3% Hispanic, 2% multiracial, 0% Pacific Islander, 6% white, 0% international; 79% from in state; 17% live on campus; N/A of students in fraternities, N/A in sororities
Most popular majors: 37% Business, Management, Marketing, and Related Support Services, 24% Education, 20% Homeland Security, Law Enforcement, Firefighting and Related Protective Services, 8% Health Professions and Related Programs, 7% Biological and Biomedical Sciences
Expenses: 2017-2018: $5,220 in state, $9,853 out of state; room/board: $9,250
Financial aid: (314) 340-3502; 97% of undergrads determined to have financial need; average aid package $10,140

Kansas City Art Institute[1]
Kansas City MO
U.S. News ranking: Arts, unranked
Website: www.kcai.edu
Admissions email: admiss@kcai.edu
Private; founded 1885
Application deadline (fall): N/A
Undergraduate student body: N/A full time, N/A part time
Expenses: 2016-2017: $36,450; room/board: $10,240
Financial aid: (816) 802-3448

Lincoln University
Jefferson City MO
(573) 681-4357
U.S. News ranking: Reg. U. (Mid. W), second tier
Website: www.lincolnu.edu
Admissions email: admissions@lincolnu.edu
Public; founded 1866
Freshman admissions: less selective; 2016-2017: N/A applied, N/A accepted. Either SAT or ACT required. ACT 25/75 percentile: 15-20. High school

rank: 5% in top tenth, 24% in top quarter, 56% in top half
Early decision deadline: N/A, notification date: N/A
Early action deadline: N/A, notification date: N/A
Application deadline (fall): rolling
Undergraduate student body: 1,851 full time, 767 part time; 43% male, 57% female; 1% American Indian, 1% Asian, 53% black, 2% Hispanic, 4% multiracial, 0% Pacific Islander, 34% white, 2% international; 76% from in state; 43% live on campus; N/A of students in fraternities, N/A in sororities
Most popular majors: 12% Liberal Arts and Sciences/Liberal Studies, 10% Business Administration and Management, General, 9% Criminal Justice/Law Enforcement Administration, 7% Elementary Education and Teaching, 6% Psychology, General
Expenses: 2016-2017: $7,488 in state, $13,878 out of state; room/board: $6,560
Financial aid: (573) 681-5032; 82% of undergrads determined to have financial need; average aid package $11,908

Lindenwood University
St. Charles MO
(636) 949-4949
U.S. News ranking: Nat. U., second tier
Website: www.lindenwood.edu
Admissions email: admissions@lindenwood.edu
Private; founded 1827
Freshman admissions: selective; 2016-2017: 4,039 applied, 2,209 accepted. Neither SAT nor ACT required. ACT 25/75 percentile: 20-25. High school rank: 15% in top tenth, 36% in top quarter, 71% in top half
Early decision deadline: N/A, notification date: N/A
Early action deadline: N/A, notification date: N/A
Application deadline (fall): rolling
Undergraduate student body: 6,794 full time, 755 part time; 46% male, 54% female; 0% American Indian, 1% Asian, 13% black, 4% Hispanic, 3% multiracial, 0% Pacific Islander, 55% white, 12% international; 63% from in state; 55% live on campus; 4% of students in fraternities, 4% in sororities
Most popular majors: 20% Business/Commerce, General, 9% Criminal Justice/Safety Studies, 5% Elementary Education and Teaching, 5% Human Resources Management/Personnel Administration, General, 4% Kinesiology and Exercise Science
Expenses: 2017-2018: $16,960; room/board: $8,800
Financial aid: (636) 949-4923; 56% of undergrads determined to have financial need; average aid package $9,635

Maryville University of St. Louis
St Louis MO
(800) 627-9855
U.S. News ranking: Nat. U., No. 165
Website: www.maryville.edu
Admissions email: admissions@maryville.edu
Private; founded 1872
Freshman admissions: selective; 2016-2017: 1,846 applied, 1,713 accepted. Neither SAT nor ACT required. ACT 25/75 percentile: 22-27. High school rank: 28% in top tenth, 59% in top quarter, 85% in top half
Early decision deadline: N/A, notification date: N/A
Early action deadline: N/A, notification date: N/A
Application deadline (fall): 8/15
Undergraduate student body: 2,147 full time, 820 part time; 33% male, 67% female; 0% American Indian, 3% Asian, 8% black, 4% Hispanic, 2% multiracial, 0% Pacific Islander, 73% white, 5% international; 76% from in state; 25% live on campus; 0% of students in fraternities, 0% in sororities
Most popular majors: 38% Health Professions and Related Programs, 25% Business, Management, Marketing, and Related Support Services, 11% Psychology, 5% Biological and Biomedical Sciences, 5% Visual and Performing Arts
Expenses: 2017-2018: $28,470; room/board: $10,088
Financial aid: (314) 529-9361; 68% of undergrads determined to have financial need; average aid package $19,215

Missouri Baptist University[1]
St. Louis MO
(314) 434-2290
U.S. News ranking: Reg. U. (Mid. W), second tier
Website: www.mobap.edu
Admissions email: admissions@mobap.edu
Private; founded 1964
Application deadline (fall): rolling
Undergraduate student body: N/A full time, N/A part time
Expenses: 2016-2017: $24,924; room/board: $9,940
Financial aid: (314) 744-7639

Missouri Southern State University
Joplin MO
(417) 781-6778
U.S. News ranking: Reg. Coll. (Mid. W), No. 59
Website: www.mssu.edu
Admissions email: admissions@mssu.edu
Public; founded 1937
Freshman admissions: selective; 2016-2017: 2,599 applied, 2,452 accepted. Either SAT or ACT required. ACT 25/75 percentile: 18-24. High school rank: N/A
Early decision deadline: N/A, notification date: N/A
Early action deadline: N/A, notification date: N/A

Application deadline (fall): rolling
Undergraduate student body: 4,460 full time, 1,657 part time; 42% male, 58% female; 3% American Indian, 2% Asian, 7% black, 6% Hispanic, 2% multiracial, 0% Pacific Islander, 76% white, 3% international
Most popular majors: Information not available
Expenses: 2016-2017: $5,877 in state, $11,283 out of state; room/board: $6,627
Financial aid: (417) 659-5422; 57% of undergrads determined to have financial need; average aid package $10,826

Missouri State University[1]
Springfield MO
(800) 492-7900
U.S. News ranking: Reg. U. (Mid. W), No. 106
Website: www.missouristate.edu
Admissions email: info@missouristate.edu
Public; founded 1906
Application deadline (fall): 7/20
Undergraduate student body: N/A full time, N/A part time
Expenses: 2016-2017: $7,060 in state, $14,110 out of state; room/board: $8,288
Financial aid: (417) 836-5262

Missouri University of Science & Technology
Rolla MO
(573) 341-4165
U.S. News ranking: Nat. U., No. 165
Website: www.mst.edu
Admissions email: admissions@mst.edu
Public; founded 1870
Freshman admissions: more selective; 2016-2017: 4,166 applied, 3,305 accepted. Either SAT or ACT required. ACT 25/75 percentile: 25-31. High school rank: 33% in top tenth, 78% in top quarter, 97% in top half
Early decision deadline: N/A, notification date: N/A
Early action deadline: N/A, notification date: N/A
Application deadline (fall): 7/1
Undergraduate student body: 6,215 full time, 694 part time; 77% male, 23% female; 0% American Indian, 3% Asian, 3% black, 3% Hispanic, 3% multiracial, 0% Pacific Islander, 80% white, 4% international; 83% from in state; 30% live on campus; N/A of students in fraternities, N/A in sororities
Most popular majors: 65% Engineering, 10% Computer and Information Sciences and Support Services, 5% Physical Sciences, 4% Biological and Biomedical Sciences, 4% Engineering Technologies and Engineering-Related Fields
Expenses: 2017-2018: $1,379 in state, $27,701 out of state; room/board: N/A
Financial aid: (573) 341-4282

Missouri Valley College[1]
Marshall MO
(660) 831-4114
U.S. News ranking: Reg. Coll. (Mid. W), second tier
Website: www.moval.edu
Admissions email: admissions@moval.edu
Private; founded 1889
Affiliation: Presbyterian
Application deadline (fall): rolling
Undergraduate student body: N/A full time, N/A part time
Expenses: 2016-2017: $19,750; room/board: $7,700
Financial aid: N/A

Missouri Western State University[1]
St. Joseph MO
(816) 271-4266
U.S. News ranking: Reg. Coll. (Mid. W), second tier
Website: www.missouriwestern.edu
Admissions email: admission@missouriwestern.edu
Public; founded 1969
Application deadline (fall): rolling
Undergraduate student body: N/A full time, N/A part time
Expenses: 2016-2017: $7,330 in state, $13,070 out of state; room/board: $8,700
Financial aid: (816) 271-4361

Northwest Missouri State University
Maryville MO
(800) 633-1175
U.S. News ranking: Reg. U. (Mid. W), No. 87
Website: www.nwmissouri.edu
Admissions email: admissions@nwmissouri.edu
Public; founded 1905
Freshman admissions: selective; 2016-2017: 5,382 applied, 3,986 accepted. Either SAT or ACT required. ACT 25/75 percentile: 20-25. High school rank: 14% in top tenth, 40% in top quarter, 75% in top half
Early decision deadline: N/A, notification date: N/A
Early action deadline: N/A, notification date: N/A
Application deadline (fall): rolling
Undergraduate student body: 4,918 full time, 710 part time; 43% male, 57% female; 0% American Indian, 1% Asian, 6% black, 4% Hispanic, 3% multiracial, 0% Pacific Islander, 80% white, 4% international; 70% from in state; 37% live on campus; 12% of students in fraternities, 18% in sororities
Most popular majors: 20% Business, Management, Marketing, and Related Support Services, 19% Education, 11% Psychology, 9% Agriculture, Agriculture Operations, and Related Sciences, 7% Communication, Journalism, and Related Programs
Expenses: 2017-2018: $9,571 in state, $16,135 out of state; room/board: $8,714
Financial aid: (660) 562-1138; 67% of undergrads determined to have financial need; average aid package $9,731

Park University
Parkville MO
(877) 505-1059
U.S. News ranking: Reg. U. (Mid. W), second tier
Website: www.park.edu
Admissions email: enrollmentservices@park.edu
Private; founded 1875
Freshman admissions: less selective; 2016-2017: 4,152 applied, 3,511 accepted. Neither SAT nor ACT required. SAT 25/75 percentile: N/A. High school rank: N/A
Early decision deadline: N/A, notification date: N/A
Early action deadline: N/A, notification date: N/A
Application deadline (fall): 8/1
Undergraduate student body: 3,931 full time, 5,926 part time; 52% male, 48% female; 1% American Indian, 2% Asian, 19% black, 17% Hispanic, 3% multiracial, 1% Pacific Islander, 48% white, 3% international
Most popular majors: 49% Business, Management, Marketing, and Related Support Services, 17% Psychology, 10% Homeland Security, Law Enforcement, Firefighting and Related Protective Services, 8% Computer and Information Sciences and Support Services, 5% Health Professions and Related Programs
Expenses: 2017-2018: $12,470; room/board: $4,000
Financial aid: (816) 584-6250

Ranken Technical College[1]
Saint Louis MO
U.S. News ranking: Reg. Coll. (Mid. W), unranked
Website: www.ranken.edu
Admissions email: N/A
Private
Application deadline (fall): N/A
Undergraduate student body: N/A full time, N/A part time
Expenses: 2016-2017: $14,457; room/board: $5,200
Financial aid: N/A

Rockhurst University
Kansas City MO
(816) 501-4100
U.S. News ranking: Reg. U. (Mid. W), No. 11
Website: www.rockhurst.edu
Admissions email: admissions@rockhurst.edu
Private; founded 1910
Affiliation: Russian Orthodox
Freshman admissions: more selective; 2016-2017: 3,038 applied, 2,250 accepted. Either SAT or ACT required. ACT 25/75 percentile: 23-28. High school rank: 30% in top tenth, 60% in top quarter, 89% in top half
Early decision deadline: N/A, notification date: N/A
Early action deadline: N/A, notification date: N/A
Application deadline (fall): rolling
Undergraduate student body: 1,409 full time, 633 part time; 39% male, 61% female; 0% American Indian, 3% Asian, 4% black,

8% Hispanic, 4% multiracial, 0% Pacific Islander, 72% white, 1% international; 57% from in state; 53% live on campus; 36% of students in fraternities, 54% in sororities
Most popular majors: 21% Health Professions and Related Programs, 20% Business, Management, Marketing, and Related Support Services, 11% Biological and Biomedical Sciences, 11% Psychology, 10% Parks, Recreation, Leisure, and Fitness Studies
Expenses: 2017-2018: $36,590; room/board: $9,360
Financial aid: (816) 501-4831; 70% of undergrads determined to have financial need; average aid package $27,237

Saint Louis University
St. Louis MO
(314) 977-2500
U.S. News ranking: Nat. U., No. 94
Website: www.slu.edu
Admissions email: admission@slu.edu
Private; founded 1818
Affiliation: Roman Catholic
Freshman admissions: more selective; 2016-2017: 12,737 applied, 8,258 accepted. Either SAT or ACT required. ACT 25/75 percentile: 24-30. High school rank: 41% in top tenth, 75% in top quarter, 93% in top half
Early decision deadline: N/A, notification date: N/A
Early action deadline: N/A, notification date: N/A
Application deadline (fall): 8/20
Undergraduate student body: 6,747 full time, 707 part time; 41% male, 59% female; 0% American Indian, 9% Asian, 6% black, 5% Hispanic, 4% multiracial, 0% Pacific Islander, 68% white, 5% international; 42% from in state; 46% live on campus; 15% of students in fraternities, 25% in sororities
Most popular majors: 30% Health Professions and Related Programs, 25% Business, Management, Marketing, and Related Support Services, 7% Engineering, 6% Biological and Biomedical Sciences, 6% Parks, Recreation, Leisure, and Fitness Studies
Expenses: 2017-2018: $42,166; room/board: $10,996
Financial aid: (314) 977-2350; 54% of undergrads determined to have financial need; average aid package $29,596

Southeast Missouri State University
Cape Girardeau MO
(573) 651-2590
U.S. News ranking: Reg. U. (Mid. W), No. 93
Website: www.semo.edu
Admissions email: admissions@semo.edu
Public; founded 1873
Freshman admissions: selective; 2016-2017: 5,184 applied, 4,293 accepted. Either SAT or ACT required. ACT 25/75 percentile: 20-25. High school rank: 18% in top tenth, 44% in top quarter, 77% in top half

Early decision deadline: N/A, notification date: N/A
Early action deadline: N/A, notification date: N/A
Application deadline (fall): 7/1
Undergraduate student body: 7,896 full time, 2,797 part time; 43% male, 57% female; 0% American Indian, 1% Asian, 10% black, 2% Hispanic, 1% multiracial, 0% Pacific Islander, 78% white, 7% international; 81% from in state; 32% live on campus; 15% of students in fraternities, 21% in sororities
Most popular majors: 9% Liberal Arts and Sciences, General Studies and Humanities, 8% Teacher Education and Professional Development, Specific Levels and Methods, 7% Communication and Media Studies, 7% Registered Nursing, Nursing Administration, Nursing Research and Clinical Nursing, 5% Teacher Education and Professional Development, Specific Subject Areas
Expenses: 2017-2018: $7,185 in state, $12,720 out of state; room/board: $8,715
Financial aid: (573) 651-2253; 61% of undergrads determined to have financial need; average aid package $9,168

Southwest Baptist University[1]
Bolivar MO
(800) 526-5859
U.S. News ranking: Reg. U. (Mid. W), second tier
Website: www.sbuniv.edu
Admissions email: dcrowder@sbuniv.edu
Private
Application deadline (fall): N/A
Undergraduate student body: N/A full time, N/A part time
Expenses: 2016-2017: $22,508; room/board: $7,460
Financial aid: N/A

Stephens College
Columbia MO
(800) 876-7207
U.S. News ranking: Reg. U. (Mid. W), No. 87
Website: www.stephens.edu
Admissions email: apply@stephens.edu
Private; founded 1833
Freshman admissions: selective; 2016-2017: 1,168 applied, 713 accepted. Either SAT or ACT required. ACT 25/75 percentile: 20-25. High school rank: 14% in top tenth, 44% in top quarter, 79% in top half
Early decision deadline: 12/31, notification date: 11/1
Early action deadline: 12/31, notification date: 12/31
Application deadline (fall): rolling
Undergraduate student body: 607 full time, 122 part time; 1% male, 99% female; 1% American Indian, 2% Asian, 13% black, 4% Hispanic, 6% multiracial, 0% Pacific Islander, 69% white, 0% international; 63% from in state; 76% live on campus; N/A of students in fraternities, N/A in sororities

Most popular majors: 19% Counselor Education/School Counseling and Guidance Services, 7% Fashion Merchandising, 7% Health Information/Medical Records Administration/Administrator, 6% Acting, 6% Organizational Leadership
Expenses: 2017-2018: $30,344; room/board: $10,424
Financial aid: (573) 876-7106; 76% of undergrads determined to have financial need; average aid package $10,000

Truman State University
Kirksville MO
(660) 785-4114
U.S. News ranking: Reg. U. (Mid. W), No. 8
Website: www.truman.edu
Admissions email: admissions@truman.edu
Public; founded 1867
Freshman admissions: more selective; 2016-2017: 5,178 applied, 3,505 accepted. Either SAT or ACT required. ACT 25/75 percentile: 24-30. High school rank: 52% in top tenth, 83% in top quarter, 97% in top half
Early decision deadline: N/A, notification date: N/A
Early action deadline: N/A, notification date: N/A
Application deadline (fall): rolling
Undergraduate student body: 5,187 full time, 852 part time; 41% male, 59% female; 0% American Indian, 3% Asian, 4% black, 3% Hispanic, 3% multiracial, 0% Pacific Islander, 79% white, 7% international; 81% from in state; 46% live on campus; 4% of students in fraternities, 6% in sororities
Most popular majors: 10% Business Administration and Management, General, 10% Kinesiology and Exercise Science, 9% Biology/Biological Sciences, General, 8% Psychology, General, 7% English Language and Literature, General
Expenses: 2017-2018: $7,656 in state, $14,440 out of state; room/board: $8,630
Financial aid: (660) 785-4130; 50% of undergrads determined to have financial need; average aid package $12,376

University of Central Missouri
Warrensburg MO
(660) 543-4290
U.S. News ranking: Reg. U. (Mid. W), No. 87
Website: www.ucmo.edu
Admissions email: admit@ucmo.edu
Public; founded 1871
Freshman admissions: selective; 2016-2017: 3,941 applied, 3,866 accepted. Neither SAT nor ACT required. ACT 25/75 percentile: 20-25. High school rank: 11% in top tenth, 36% in top quarter, 71% in top half
Early decision deadline: N/A, notification date: N/A
Early action deadline: N/A, notification date: N/A

Application deadline (fall): rolling
Undergraduate student body: 7,858 full time, 1,928 part time; 44% male, 56% female; 0% American Indian, 1% Asian, 11% black, 4% Hispanic, 4% multiracial, 0% Pacific Islander, 77% white, 2% international; 89% from in state; 34% live on campus; 13% of students in fraternities, 16% in sororities
Most popular majors: 15% Health Professions and Related Programs, 14% Education, 12% Business, Management, Marketing, and Related Support Services, 10% Engineering Technologies and Engineering-Related Fields, 9% Homeland Security, Law Enforcement, Firefighting and Related Protective Services
Expenses: 2017-2018: $7,520 in state, $14,150 out of state; room/board: $8,536
Financial aid: N/A; 61% of undergrads determined to have financial need; average aid package $8,621

University of Missouri
Columbia MO
(573) 882-7786
U.S. News ranking: Nat. U., No. 120
Website: www.missouri.edu
Admissions email: mu4u@missouri.edu
Public; founded 1839
Freshman admissions: more selective; 2016-2017: 21,107 applied, 15,767 accepted. Either SAT or ACT required. ACT 25/75 percentile: 23-29. High school rank: 30% in top tenth, 59% in top quarter, 89% in top half
Early decision deadline: N/A, notification date: N/A
Early action deadline: N/A, notification date: N/A
Application deadline (fall): rolling
Undergraduate student body: 24,124 full time, 1,774 part time; 48% male, 52% female; 0% American Indian, 2% Asian, 8% black, 4% Hispanic, 3% multiracial, 0% Pacific Islander, 79% white, 4% international; 77% from in state; 24% live on campus; 23% of students in fraternities, 33% in sororities
Most popular majors: 15% Business, Management, Marketing, and Related Support Services, 14% Health Professions and Related Programs, 12% Communication, Journalism, and Related Programs, 9% Engineering, 5% Biological and Biomedical Sciences
Expenses: 2017-2018: $9,817 in state, $26,506 out of state; room/board: $10,676
Financial aid: (573) 882-7506; 47% of undergrads determined to have financial need; average aid package $11,696

University of Missouri–Kansas City
Kansas City MO
(816) 235-1111
U.S. News ranking: Nat. U., No. 216
Website: www.umkc.edu
Admissions email: admit@umkc.edu
Public; founded 1929

Freshman admissions: selective; 2016-2017: 5,138 applied, 3,179 accepted. Either SAT or ACT required. ACT 25/75 percentile: 21-28. High school rank: 31% in top tenth, 56% in top quarter, 84% in top half
Early decision deadline: N/A, notification date: N/A
Early action deadline: N/A, notification date: N/A
Application deadline (fall): rolling
Undergraduate student body: 6,669 full time, 5,039 part time; 42% male, 58% female; 0% American Indian, 7% Asian, 15% black, 9% Hispanic, 4% multiracial, 0% Pacific Islander, 57% white, 5% international; 81% from in state; 22% live on campus; 3% of students in fraternities, 4% in sororities
Most popular majors: 18% Business/Commerce, General, 17% Registered Nursing/Registered Nurse, 10% Liberal Arts and Sciences/Liberal Studies, 7% Chemistry, General, 6% Psychology, General
Expenses: 2017-2018: $9,734 in state, $25,999 out of state; room/board: $10,150
Financial aid: (816) 235-5511; 63% of undergrads determined to have financial need; average aid package $9,810

University of Missouri–St. Louis
St. Louis MO
(314) 516-5451
U.S. News ranking: Nat. U., second tier
Website: www.umsl.edu
Admissions email: admissions@umsl.edu
Public; founded 1963
Freshman admissions: more selective; 2016-2017: 1,947 applied, 1,375 accepted. Either SAT or ACT required. ACT 25/75 percentile: 21-27. High school rank: 26% in top tenth, 53% in top quarter, 84% in top half
Early decision deadline: N/A, notification date: N/A
Early action deadline: N/A, notification date: N/A
Application deadline (fall): 9/8
Undergraduate student body: 5,434 full time, 8,489 part time; 43% male, 57% female; 0% American Indian, 5% Asian, 18% black, 3% Hispanic, 3% multiracial, 0% Pacific Islander, 63% white, 3% international; 89% from in state; 9% live on campus; 1% of students in fraternities, 1% in sororities
Most popular majors: 23% Business, Management, Marketing, and Related Support Services, 11% Health Professions and Related Programs, 11% Social Sciences, 8% Education, 7% Psychology
Expenses: 2017-2018: $10,275 in state, $27,327 out of state; room/board: $9,363
Financial aid: (314) 516-5508; 70% of undergrads determined to have financial need; average aid package $11,633

Washington University in St. Louis

St. Louis MO
(800) 638-0700
U.S. News ranking: Nat. U., No. 18
Website: www.wustl.edu
Admissions email: admissions@wustl.edu
Private; founded 1853
Freshman admissions: most selective; 2016-2017: 29,197 applied, 4,827 accepted. Either SAT or ACT required. ACT 25/75 percentile: 32-34. High school rank: 86% in top tenth, 98% in top quarter, 100% in top half
Early decision deadline: 11/1, notification date: 12/15
Early action deadline: N/A, notification date: N/A
Application deadline (fall): 1/2
Undergraduate student body: 6,915 full time, 625 part time; 47% male, 53% female; 0% American Indian, 18% Asian, 7% black, 8% Hispanic, 4% multiracial, 0% Pacific Islander, 53% white, 8% international; 8% from in state; 77% live on campus; 30% of students in fraternities, 30% in sororities
Most popular majors: 19% Engineering, 13% Business, Management, Marketing, and Related Support Services, 12% Social Sciences, 11% Biological and Biomedical Sciences, 9% Psychology
Expenses: 2017-2018: $51,533; room/board: $16,006
Financial aid: (888) 547-6670; 42% of undergrads determined to have financial need; average aid package $43,722

Webster University

St. Louis MO
(314) 246-7800
U.S. News ranking: Reg. U. (Mid. W), No. 23
Website: www.webster.edu
Admissions email: admit@webster.edu
Private; founded 1915
Freshman admissions: more selective; 2016-2017: 2,630 applied, 1,225 accepted. Either SAT or ACT required. ACT 25/75 percentile: 21-27. High school rank: 13% in top tenth, 42% in top quarter, 76% in top half
Early decision deadline: N/A, notification date: N/A
Early action deadline: N/A, notification date: N/A
Application deadline (fall): 8/1
Undergraduate student body: 2,231 full time, 390 part time; 46% male, 54% female; 0% American Indian, 2% Asian, 12% black, 5% Hispanic, 4% multiracial, 0% Pacific Islander, 65% white, 4% international; 72% from in state; 33% live on campus; 0% of students in fraternities, 3% in sororities
Most popular majors: 22% Business, Management, Marketing, and Related Support Services, 20% Visual and Performing Arts, 13% Communication, Journalism, and Related Programs, 7% Computer and Information Sciences and Support Services, 6% Social Sciences

Expenses: 2017-2018: $27,100; room/board: $11,050
Financial aid: (800) 983-4623; 74% of undergrads determined to have financial need; average aid package $22,542

Westminster College

Fulton MO
(800) 475-3361
U.S. News ranking: Nat. Lib. Arts, No. 147
Website: www.westminster-mo.edu
Admissions email: admissions@westminster-mo.edu
Private; founded 1851
Freshman admissions: selective; 2016-2017: 1,661 applied, 1,082 accepted. Either SAT or ACT required. ACT 25/75 percentile: 21-26. High school rank: N/A
Early decision deadline: N/A, notification date: N/A
Early action deadline: N/A, notification date: N/A
Application deadline (fall): rolling
Undergraduate student body: 867 full time, 9 part time; 56% male, 44% female; 1% American Indian, 2% Asian, 7% black, 4% Hispanic, 1% multiracial, 0% Pacific Islander, 71% white, 10% international
Most popular majors: 29% Business, Management, Marketing, and Related Support Services, 13% Biological and Biomedical Sciences, 13% Education, 5% Computer and Information Sciences and Support Services, 5% Parks, Recreation, Leisure, and Fitness Studies
Expenses: 2016-2017: $24,540; room/board: $9,480
Financial aid: (573) 592-5364

William Jewell College

Liberty MO
(888) 253-9355
U.S. News ranking: Nat. Lib. Arts, No. 147
Website: www.jewell.edu
Admissions email: admission@william.jewell.edu
Private; founded 1849
Freshman admissions: more selective; 2016-2017: 2,081 applied, 1,063 accepted. Neither SAT nor ACT required. ACT 25/75 percentile: 22-28. High school rank: 25% in top tenth, 55% in top quarter, 89% in top half
Early decision deadline: N/A, notification date: N/A
Early action deadline: N/A, notification date: N/A
Application deadline (fall): 8/15
Undergraduate student body: 977 full time, 15 part time; 42% male, 58% female; 0% American Indian, 1% Asian, 4% black, 4% Hispanic, 4% multiracial, 0% Pacific Islander, 79% white, 5% international; 61% from in state; 87% live on campus; 40% of students in fraternities, 40% in sororities
Most popular majors: 33% Health Professions and Related Programs, 17% Business, Management, Marketing, and Related Support Services, 9% Psychology, 7% Education, 6% Physical Sciences

Expenses: 2017-2018: $33,620; room/board: $9,640
Financial aid: (816) 415-5977; 69% of undergrads determined to have financial need; average aid package $28,073

William Woods University

Fulton MO
(573) 592-4221
U.S. News ranking: Reg. U. (Mid. W), No. 75
Website: www.williamwoods.edu
Admissions email: admissions@williamwoods.edu
Private; founded 1870
Affiliation: Other
Freshman admissions: selective; 2016-2017: 682 applied, 599 accepted. Either SAT or ACT required. ACT 25/75 percentile: 19-25. High school rank: 40% in top tenth, 55% in top quarter, 80% in top half
Early decision deadline: N/A, notification date: N/A
Early action deadline: N/A, notification date: N/A
Application deadline (fall): rolling
Undergraduate student body: 834 full time, 139 part time; 26% male, 74% female; 1% American Indian, 1% Asian, 4% black, 5% Hispanic, 2% multiracial, 0% Pacific Islander, 81% white, 4% international; 61% from in state; 63% live on campus; 43% of students in fraternities, 45% in sororities
Most popular majors: 16% Equestrian/Equine Studies, 15% Business Administration and Management, General, 14% Sign Language Interpretation and Translation, 11% Sport and Fitness Administration/Management, 10% Education, General
Expenses: 2017-2018: $23,260; room/board: $9,400
Financial aid: (573) 592-4255; 82% of undergrads determined to have financial need; average aid package $17,620

MONTANA

Carroll College

Helena MT
(406) 447-4384
U.S. News ranking: Reg. Coll. (W), No. 1
Website: www.carroll.edu
Admissions email: admission@carroll.edu
Private; founded 1909
Affiliation: Roman Catholic
Freshman admissions: more selective; 2016-2017: 3,005 applied, 2,148 accepted. Either SAT or ACT required. ACT 25/75 percentile: 22-28. High school rank: 29% in top tenth, 62% in top quarter, 87% in top half
Early decision deadline: N/A, notification date: N/A
Early action deadline: 12/1, notification date: 1/1
Application deadline (fall): 5/1
Undergraduate student body: 1,324 full time, 49 part time; 41% male, 59% female; 1% American Indian, 1% Asian, 0% black, 6% Hispanic, 3% multiracial,

0% Pacific Islander, 80% white, 1% international; 44% from in state; 60% live on campus; N/A of students in fraternities, N/A in sororities
Most popular majors: 30% Health Professions and Related Programs, 12% Biological and Biomedical Sciences, 12% Business, Management, Marketing, and Related Support Services, 8% Education, 8% Social Sciences
Expenses: 2017-2018: $34,480; room/board: $9,608
Financial aid: (406) 447-5425; 65% of undergrads determined to have financial need; average aid package $25,029

Montana State University

Bozeman MT
(406) 994-2452
U.S. News ranking: Nat. U., No. 207
Website: www.montana.edu
Admissions email: admissions@montana.edu
Public; founded 1893
Freshman admissions: selective; 2016-2017: 15,996 applied, 13,256 accepted. Either SAT or ACT required. ACT 25/75 percentile: 21-28. High school rank: 20% in top tenth, 43% in top quarter, 74% in top half
Early decision deadline: N/A, notification date: N/A
Early action deadline: N/A, notification date: N/A
Application deadline (fall): rolling
Undergraduate student body: 12,248 full time, 2,152 part time; 55% male, 45% female; 2% American Indian, 1% Asian, 1% black, 4% Hispanic, 2% multiracial, 0% Pacific Islander, 84% white, 3% international; 61% from in state; 25% live on campus; 2% of students in fraternities, 2% in sororities
Most popular majors: 16% Engineering, 10% Business, Management, Marketing, and Related Support Services, 10% Health Professions and Related Programs, 9% Family and Consumer Sciences/Human Sciences, 8% Biological and Biomedical Sciences
Expenses: 2017-2018: $7,031 in state, $23,042 out of state; room/board: $8,900
Financial aid: (406) 994-2845; 46% of undergrads determined to have financial need; average aid package $11,297

Montana State University–Billings

Billings MT
(406) 657-2158
U.S. News ranking: Reg. U. (W), second tier
Website: www.msubillings.edu
Admissions email: admissions@msubillings.edu
Public; founded 1927
Freshman admissions: less selective; 2016-2017: 1,478 applied, 1,476 accepted. Neither SAT nor ACT required. ACT 25/75 percentile: 18-22. High school rank: 10% in top tenth, 27% in top quarter, 63% in top half

0% Pacific Islander, 80% white, 1% international; 44% from in state; 60% live on campus; N/A of students in fraternities, N/A in sororities
Most popular majors: 30% Health Professions and Related Programs, 12% Biological and Biomedical Sciences, 12% Business, Management, Marketing, and Related Support Services, 8% Education, 8% Social Sciences
Expenses: 2017-2018: $34,480; room/board: $9,608
Financial aid: (406) 447-5425; 65% of undergrads determined to have financial need; average aid package $25,029

Early decision deadline: N/A, notification date: N/A
Early action deadline: N/A, notification date: N/A
Application deadline (fall): rolling
Undergraduate student body: 2,500 full time, 1,472 part time; 40% male, 60% female; 4% American Indian, 1% Asian, 1% black, 6% Hispanic, 3% multiracial, 0% Pacific Islander, 81% white, 2% international; 91% from in state; 12% live on campus; 0% of students in fraternities, 0% in sororities
Most popular majors: 28% Business, Management, Marketing, and Related Support Services, 21% Education, 9% Psychology, 7% Liberal Arts and Sciences, General Studies and Humanities, 6% Parks, Recreation, Leisure, and Fitness Studies
Expenses: 2017-2018: $5,833 in state, $18,598 out of state; room/board: $7,730
Financial aid: (406) 657-2188; 59% of undergrads determined to have financial need; average aid package $6,981

Montana State University–Northern[1]

Havre MT
(406) 265-3704
U.S. News ranking: Reg. Coll. (W), second tier
Website: www.msun.edu
Admissions email: admissions@msun.edu
Public
Application deadline (fall): rolling
Undergraduate student body: N/A full time, N/A part time
Expenses: 2016-2017: $5,371 in state, $17,681 out of state; room/board: $6,300
Financial aid: N/A

Montana Tech of the University of Montana

Butte MT
(406) 496-4256
U.S. News ranking: Reg. Coll. (W), No. 3
Website: www.mtech.edu
Admissions email: enrollment@mtech.edu
Public; founded 1893
Freshman admissions: selective; 2016-2017: 894 applied, 795 accepted. Either SAT or ACT required. ACT 25/75 percentile: 22-26. High school rank: 26% in top tenth, 56% in top quarter, 86% in top half
Early decision deadline: N/A, notification date: N/A
Early action deadline: N/A, notification date: N/A
Application deadline (fall): rolling
Undergraduate student body: 2,076 full time, 518 part time; 63% male, 37% female; 2% American Indian, 1% Asian, 1% black, 2% Hispanic, 0% multiracial, 0% Pacific Islander, 77% white, 11% international; 80% from in state; 10% live on campus; N/A of students in fraternities, N/A in sororities

Most popular majors: 31% Petroleum Engineering, 13% Engineering, General, 7% Chiropractic, 7% Occupational Health and Industrial Hygiene, 5% Registered Nursing/Registered Nurse
Expenses: 2017-2018: $7,139 in state, $21,969 out of state; room/board: $9,350
Financial aid: (406) 496-4256; 53% of undergrads determined to have financial need; average aid package $11,159

Rocky Mountain College
Billings MT
(406) 657-1026
U.S. News ranking: Reg. Coll. (W), No. 9
Website: www.rocky.edu
Admissions email: admissions@rocky.edu
Private; founded 1878
Affiliation: Presbyterian Church (USA)
Freshman admissions: selective; 2016-2017: 1,545 applied, 959 accepted. Either SAT or ACT required. ACT 25/75 percentile: 20-24. High school rank: 13% in top tenth, 39% in top quarter, 72% in top half
Early decision deadline: N/A, notification date: N/A
Early action deadline: N/A, notification date: N/A
Application deadline (fall): rolling
Undergraduate student body: 857 full time, 51 part time; 50% male, 50% female; 2% American Indian, 1% Asian, 2% black, 6% Hispanic, 4% multiracial, 1% Pacific Islander, 77% white, 4% international; 53% from in state; 45% live on campus; N/A of students in fraternities, N/A in sororities
Most popular majors: 23% Business, Management, Marketing, and Related Support Services, 15% Education, 14% Parks, Recreation, Leisure, and Fitness Studies, 8% Biological and Biomedical Sciences, 7% Transportation and Materials Moving
Expenses: 2017-2018: $27,566; room/board: $8,210
Financial aid: (406) 657-1031; 74% of undergrads determined to have financial need; average aid package $23,133

University of Great Falls[1]
Great Falls MT
(406) 791-5200
U.S. News ranking: Reg. Coll. (W), No. 22
Website: www.ugf.edu
Admissions email: enroll@ugf.edu
Private; founded 1932
Application deadline (fall): 9/1
Undergraduate student body: N/A full time, N/A part time
Expenses: 2016-2017: $24,184; room/board: $8,300
Financial aid: (406) 791-5235

University of Montana
Missoula MT
(800) 462-8636
U.S. News ranking: Nat. U., No. 207
Website: www.umt.edu
Admissions email: admiss@umontana.edu
Public; founded 1893
Freshman admissions: selective; 2016-2017: 6,660 applied, 6,156 accepted. Either SAT or ACT required. ACT 25/75 percentile: 20-26. High school rank: 17% in top tenth, 40% in top quarter, 71% in top half
Early decision deadline: N/A, notification date: N/A
Early action deadline: N/A, notification date: N/A
Application deadline (fall): rolling
Undergraduate student body: 7,857 full time, 2,220 part time; 45% male, 55% female; 3% American Indian, 1% Asian, 1% black, 5% Hispanic, 4% multiracial, 0% Pacific Islander, 79% white, 2% international; 72% from in state; 36% live on campus; 6% of students in fraternities, 6% in sororities
Most popular majors: 19% Business, Management, Marketing, and Related Support Services, 12% Social Sciences, 11% Visual and Performing Arts, 9% Natural Resources and Conservation, 8% Education
Expenses: 2017-2018: $7,063 in state, $24,943 out of state; room/board: $9,178
Financial aid: (406) 243-5504; 58% of undergrads determined to have financial need; average aid package $14,092

University of Montana–Western
Dillon MT
(877) 683-7331
U.S. News ranking: Reg. Coll. (W), No. 8
Website: www.umwestern.edu
Admissions email: admissions@umwestern.edu
Public; founded 1893
Freshman admissions: less selective; 2016-2017: 785 applied, 574 accepted. Either SAT or ACT required. ACT 25/75 percentile: 17-22. High school rank: 7% in top tenth, 23% in top quarter, 51% in top half
Early decision deadline: N/A, notification date: N/A
Early action deadline: N/A, notification date: N/A
Application deadline (fall): rolling
Undergraduate student body: 1,232 full time, 273 part time; 39% male, 61% female; 3% American Indian, 1% Asian, 1% black, 4% Hispanic, 2% multiracial, 0% Pacific Islander, 86% white, 0% international; 76% from in state; 27% live on campus; N/A of students in fraternities, N/A in sororities
Most popular majors: 33% Education, 19% Business/Commerce, General, 8% Biology/Biological Sciences, General, 6% Health and Physical Education/Fitness, General, 5% Environmental Science

Expenses: 2017-2018: $5,502 in state, $16,644 out of state; room/board: $7,744
Financial aid: (406) 683-7893; 75% of undergrads determined to have financial need; average aid package $3,423

NEBRASKA

Bellevue University[1]
Bellevue NE
U.S. News ranking: Reg. U. (Mid. W), unranked
Website: www.bellevue.edu
Admissions email: info@bellevue.edu
Private
Application deadline (fall): N/A
Undergraduate student body: N/A full time, N/A part time
Expenses: 2017-2018: $7,365; room/board: $6,399
Financial aid: (402) 557-7095

Chadron State College[1]
Chadron NE
U.S. News ranking: Reg. U. (Mid. W), unranked
Website: www.csc.edu
Admissions email: inquire@csc.edu
Public; founded 1911
Application deadline (fall): N/A
Undergraduate student body: N/A full time, N/A part time
Expenses: 2016-2017: $6,510 in state, $6,540 out of state; room/board: $7,164
Financial aid: N/A

College of St. Mary
Omaha NE
(402) 399-2407
U.S. News ranking: Reg. U. (Mid. W), No. 87
Website: www.csm.edu
Admissions email: enroll@csm.edu
Private; founded 1923
Freshman admissions: selective; 2016-2017: 323 applied, 195 accepted. Either SAT or ACT required. ACT 25/75 percentile: 19-25. High school rank: 14% in top tenth, 42% in top quarter, 76% in top half
Early decision deadline: N/A, notification date: N/A
Early action deadline: N/A, notification date: N/A
Application deadline (fall): rolling
Undergraduate student body: 717 full time, 43 part time; 0% male, 100% female; 1% American Indian, 2% Asian, 8% black, 13% Hispanic, 2% multiracial, 0% Pacific Islander, 72% white, 1% international; 77% from in state; 37% live on campus; 0% of students in fraternities, N/A in sororities
Most popular majors: 35% Occupational Therapy/Therapist, 33% Registered Nursing/Registered Nurse, 12% Elementary Education and Teaching, 6% Business Administration and Management, General, 5% Biology/Biological Sciences, General
Expenses: 2017-2018: $19,950; room/board: $7,550

Financial aid: (402) 399-2415; 84% of undergrads determined to have financial need; average aid package $21,409

Concordia University
Seward NE
(800) 535-5494
U.S. News ranking: Reg. U. (Mid. W), No. 38
Website: www.cune.edu
Admissions email: admiss@cune.edu
Private; founded 1894
Affiliation: Lutheran Church–Missouri Synod
Freshman admissions: selective; 2016-2017: 1,396 applied, 1,023 accepted. Either SAT or ACT required. ACT 25/75 percentile: 20-27. High school rank: 18% in top tenth, 41% in top quarter, 68% in top half
Early decision deadline: N/A, notification date: N/A
Early action deadline: N/A, notification date: N/A
Application deadline (fall): 8/1
Undergraduate student body: 1,205 full time, 589 part time; 47% male, 53% female; 0% American Indian, 1% Asian, 4% black, 6% Hispanic, 0% multiracial, 0% Pacific Islander, 76% white, 2% international; 46% from in state; 71% live on campus; 0% of students in fraternities, 0% in sororities
Most popular majors: 31% Education, 16% Business, Management, Marketing, and Related Support Services, 11% Theology and Religious Vocations, 8% Biological and Biomedical Sciences, 7% Psychology
Expenses: 2017-2018: $31,000; room/board: $8,100
Financial aid: (402) 643-7270; 75% of undergrads determined to have financial need; average aid package $23,520

Creighton University
Omaha NE
(800) 282-5835
U.S. News ranking: Reg. U. (Mid. W), No. 1
Website: www.creighton.edu
Admissions email: admissions@creighton.edu
Private; founded 1878
Affiliation: Roman Catholic
Freshman admissions: more selective; 2016-2017: 10,352 applied, 7,315 accepted. Either SAT or ACT required. ACT 25/75 percentile: 24-30. High school rank: 35% in top tenth, 70% in top quarter, 91% in top half
Early decision deadline: N/A, notification date: N/A
Early action deadline: 11/1, notification date: N/A
Application deadline (fall): 2/15
Undergraduate student body: 3,981 full time, 222 part time; 43% male, 57% female; 0% American Indian, 9% Asian, 2% black, 8% Hispanic, 4% multiracial, 0% Pacific Islander, 70% white, 3% international; 24% from in state; 58% live on campus; 37% of students in fraternities, 56% in sororities

Most popular majors: 22% Business, Management, Marketing, and Related Support Services, 22% Health Professions and Related Programs, 10% Biological and Biomedical Sciences, 7% Psychology, 7% Social Sciences
Expenses: 2017-2018: $38,750; room/board: $10,702
Financial aid: (402) 280-2731; 54% of undergrads determined to have financial need; average aid package $27,537

Doane University
Crete NE
(402) 826-8222
U.S. News ranking: Nat. Lib. Arts, No. 158
Website: www.doane.edu
Admissions email: admissions@doane.edu
Private; founded 1872
Freshman admissions: selective; 2016-2017: 1,972 applied, 1,496 accepted. Either SAT or ACT required. ACT 25/75 percentile: 21-26. High school rank: 11% in top tenth, 44% in top quarter, 91% in top half
Early decision deadline: N/A, notification date: N/A
Early action deadline: N/A, notification date: N/A
Application deadline (fall): rolling
Undergraduate student body: 1,038 full time, 9 part time; 51% male, 49% female; 0% American Indian, 1% Asian, 3% black, 8% Hispanic, 3% multiracial, 0% Pacific Islander, 81% white, 2% international; 77% from in state; 78% live on campus; 21% of students in fraternities, 25% in sororities
Most popular majors: 21% Education, 12% Social Sciences, 11% Biological and Biomedical Sciences, 11% Business, Management, Marketing, and Related Support Services, 9% Visual and Performing Arts
Expenses: 2017-2018: $32,250; room/board: $9,090
Financial aid: (402) 826-8260; 76% of undergrads determined to have financial need; average aid package $23,742

Grace University[1]
Omaha NE
(402) 449-2831
U.S. News ranking: Reg. Coll. (Mid. W), No. 59
Website: www.graceuniversity.edu
Admissions email: admissions@graceuniversity.edu
Private
Application deadline (fall): N/A
Undergraduate student body: N/A full time, N/A part time
Expenses: 2016-2017: $21,928; room/board: $7,558
Financial aid: N/A

Hastings College
Hastings NE
(800) 532-7642
U.S. News ranking: Reg. Coll. (Mid. W), No. 17
Website: www.hastings.edu
Admissions email: hcadmissions@hastings.edu
Private; founded 1882
Affiliation: Presbyterian

Freshman admissions: selective; 2016-2017: 1,722 applied, 1,101 accepted. Either SAT or ACT required. ACT 25/75 percentile: 19-26. High school rank: 18% in top tenth, 45% in top quarter, 71% in top half **Early decision deadline:** N/A, notification date: N/A **Early action deadline:** N/A, notification date: N/A **Application deadline (fall):** rolling **Undergraduate student body:** 1,108 full time, 73 part time; 50% male, 50% female; 0% American Indian, 1% Asian, 3% black, 7% Hispanic, 3% multiracial, 1% Pacific Islander, 81% white, 2% international; 68% from in state; 70% live on campus; 27% of students in fraternities, 27% in sororities **Most popular majors:** 20% Education, 19% Business, Management, Marketing, and Related Support Services, 10% Biological and Biomedical Sciences, 9% Social Sciences, 8% Psychology **Expenses:** 2017-2018: $29,200; room/board: $9,400 **Financial aid:** (402) 461-7431; 72% of undergrads determined to have financial need; average aid package $23,484

Midland University[1]
Fremont NE
(402) 941-6501
U.S. News ranking: Reg. Coll. (Mid. W), No. 54
Website: www.midlandu.edu/
Admissions email: admissions@midlandu.edu
Private; founded 1883
Application deadline (fall): rolling
Undergraduate student body: N/A full time, N/A part time
Expenses: 2016-2017: $30,430; room/board: $8,038
Financial aid: N/A

Nebraska Wesleyan University
Lincoln NE
(402) 465-2218
U.S. News ranking: Reg. U. (Mid. W), No. 16
Website: www.nebrwesleyan.edu/ undergraduate/how-apply
Admissions email: admissions@nebrwesleyan.edu
Private; founded 1887
Affiliation: United Methodist
Freshman admissions: selective; 2016-2017: 1,803 applied, 1,341 accepted. Either SAT or ACT required. ACT 25/75 percentile: 21-27. High school rank: 19% in top tenth, 23% in top quarter, 81% in top half **Early decision deadline:** 12/1, notification date: N/A **Early action deadline:** N/A, notification date: N/A **Application deadline (fall):** 8/15 **Undergraduate student body:** 1,586 full time, 230 part time; 42% male, 58% female; 0% American Indian, 2% Asian, 3% black, 7% Hispanic, 3% multiracial, 0% Pacific Islander, 83% white, 1% international; 83% from in state; 46% live on campus; 15% of students in fraternities, 24% in sororities

Most popular majors: 18% Health Professions and Related Programs, 14% Business, Management, Marketing, and Related Support Services, 10% Biological and Biomedical Sciences, 9% Parks, Recreation, Leisure, and Fitness Studies, 8% Education **Expenses:** 2017-2018: $32,894; room/board: $9,150 **Financial aid:** (402) 465-2167; 74% of undergrads determined to have financial need; average aid package $21,474

Peru State College[1]
Peru NE
U.S. News ranking: Reg. U. (Mid. W), unranked
Website: www.peru.edu
Admissions email: admissions@peru.edu
Public
Application deadline (fall): N/A
Undergraduate student body: N/A full time, N/A part time
Expenses: 2016-2017: $7,243 in state, $7,243 out of state; room/board: $7,488
Financial aid: N/A

Union College
Lincoln NE
(800) 228-4600
U.S. News ranking: Reg. Coll. (Mid. W), No. 31
Website: www.ucollege.edu
Admissions email: ucenroll@ucollege.edu
Private; founded 1891
Freshman admissions: selective; 2016-2017: 1,811 applied, 1,150 accepted. Either SAT or ACT required. ACT 25/75 percentile: 18-26. High school rank: N/A
Early decision deadline: N/A, notification date: N/A
Early action deadline: N/A, notification date: N/A
Application deadline (fall): 8/1
Undergraduate student body: 698 full time, 107 part time; 41% male, 59% female; 0% American Indian, 4% Asian, 7% black, 21% Hispanic, 5% multiracial, 1% Pacific Islander, 52% white, 9% international; 17% from in state; 63% live on campus; 0% of students in fraternities, 0% in sororities
Most popular majors: 28% Health Professions and Related Programs, 13% Biological and Biomedical Sciences, 12% Business, Management, Marketing, and Related Support Services, 8% Education, 5% Computer and Information Sciences and Support Services
Expenses: 2017-2018: $23,070; room/board: $6,926
Financial aid: (402) 486-2505; 71% of undergrads determined to have financial need; average aid package $17,578

University of Nebraska–Kearney
Kearney NE
(308) 865-8526
U.S. News ranking: Reg. U. (Mid. W), No. 64
Website: www.unk.edu
Admissions email: admissionsug@unk.edu

Public; founded 1903
Freshman admissions: selective; 2016-2017: 2,815 applied, 2,395 accepted. Either SAT or ACT required. ACT 25/75 percentile: 19-25. High school rank: 18% in top tenth, 43% in top quarter, 74% in top half **Early decision deadline:** N/A, notification date: N/A **Early action deadline:** N/A, notification date: N/A **Application deadline (fall):** 9/1 **Undergraduate student body:** 4,255 full time, 801 part time; 43% male, 57% female; 0% American Indian, 1% Asian, 2% black, 11% Hispanic, 2% multiracial, 0% Pacific Islander, 79% white, 5% international; 92% from in state; 35% live on campus; 14% of students in fraternities, 17% in sororities **Most popular majors:** 14% Business Administration and Management, General, 13% Elementary Education and Teaching, 8% Operations Management and Supervision, 7% Parks, Recreation and Leisure Studies, 5% Criminal Justice/Safety Studies **Expenses:** 2017-2018: $7,326 in state, $14,106 out of state; room/board: $9,688 **Financial aid:** (308) 865-8520; 65% of undergrads determined to have financial need; average aid package $10,456

University of Nebraska–Lincoln
Lincoln NE
(800) 742-8800
U.S. News ranking: Nat. U., No. 124
Website: www.unl.edu
Admissions email: Admissions@unl.edu
Public; founded 1869
Freshman admissions: more selective; 2016-2017: 11,193 applied, 8,425 accepted. Either SAT or ACT required. ACT 25/75 percentile: 22-28. High school rank: 24% in top tenth, 49% in top quarter, 83% in top half **Early decision deadline:** N/A, notification date: N/A **Early action deadline:** N/A, notification date: N/A **Application deadline (fall):** 5/1 **Undergraduate student body:** 19,381 full time, 1,452 part time; 52% male, 48% female; 0% American Indian, 3% Asian, 3% black, 6% Hispanic, 3% multiracial, 0% Pacific Islander, 76% white, 8% international; 77% from in state; 39% live on campus; 19% of students in fraternities, 24% in sororities **Most popular majors:** 23% Business, Management, Marketing, and Related Support Services, 10% Engineering, 9% Agriculture, Agriculture Operations, and Related Sciences, 8% Communication, Journalism, and Related Programs, 8% Family and Consumer Sciences/Human Sciences **Expenses:** 2017-2018: $8,690 in state, $23,256 out of state; room/board: $11,234

Financial aid: (402) 472-2030; 43% of undergrads determined to have financial need; average aid package $13,668

University of Nebraska–Omaha
Omaha NE
(402) 554-2393
U.S. News ranking: Nat. U., second tier
Website: www.unomaha.edu
Admissions email: unoadmissions@unomaha.edu
Public; founded 1908
Freshman admissions: selective; 2016-2017: 5,549 applied, 4,799 accepted. Either SAT or ACT required. ACT 25/75 percentile: 19-26. High school rank: 15% in top tenth, 40% in top quarter, 74% in top half **Early decision deadline:** N/A, notification date: N/A **Early action deadline:** N/A, notification date: N/A **Application deadline (fall):** 8/1 **Undergraduate student body:** 9,880 full time, 2,656 part time; 48% male, 52% female; 0% American Indian, 4% Asian, 6% black, 12% Hispanic, 4% multiracial, 0% Pacific Islander, 67% white, 4% international; 91% from in state; 13% live on campus; 2% of students in fraternities, 2% in sororities **Most popular majors:** 10% Criminal Justice/Safety Studies, 6% Business Administration and Management, General, 6% Elementary Education and Teaching, 6% Psychology, General, 5% Marketing/Marketing Management, General **Expenses:** 2017-2018: $8,205 in state, $22,035 out of state; room/board: $9,406 **Financial aid:** (402) 554-3408; 58% of undergrads determined to have financial need; average aid package $9,464

Wayne State College
Wayne NE
(800) 228-9972
U.S. News ranking: Reg. U. (Mid. W), No. 109
Website: www.wsc.edu/
Admissions email: admit1@wsc.edu
Public; founded 1909
Freshman admissions: selective; 2016-2017: 1,764 applied, 1,764 accepted. Neither SAT nor ACT required. ACT 25/75 percentile: 18-25. High school rank: 12% in top tenth, 30% in top quarter, 60% in top half **Early decision deadline:** N/A, notification date: N/A **Early action deadline:** N/A, notification date: N/A **Application deadline (fall):** 8/21 **Undergraduate student body:** 2,455 full time, 382 part time; 43% male, 57% female; 1% American Indian, 1% Asian, 3% black, 8% Hispanic, 2% multiracial, 0% Pacific Islander, 82% white, 0% international; 85% from in state; 38% live on campus; N/A of students in fraternities, N/A in sororities

Most popular majors: 26% Education, 18% Business, Management, and Related Support Services, 10% Psychology, 8% Homeland Security, Law Enforcement, Firefighting and Related Protective Services, 8% Parks, Recreation, Leisure, and Fitness Studies **Expenses:** 2017-2018: $6,824 in state, $11,984 out of state; room/board: $7,430 **Financial aid:** (402) 375-7230; 70% of undergrads determined to have financial need; average aid package $9,181

York College[1]
York NE
(800) 950-9675
U.S. News ranking: Reg. Coll. (Mid. W), No. 49
Website: www.york.edu
Admissions email: enroll@york.edu
Private; founded 1890
Application deadline (fall): 8/31
Undergraduate student body: N/A full time, N/A part time
Expenses: N/A
Financial aid: (402) 363-5624

NEVADA

College of Southern Nevada[1]
Las Vegas NV
U.S. News ranking: Reg. Coll. (W), unranked
Website: www.csn.edu
Admissions email: N/A
Public; founded 1971
Application deadline (fall): N/A
Undergraduate student body: N/A full time, N/A part time
Expenses: 2016-2017: $2,910 in state, $9,555 out of state; room/board: N/A
Financial aid: N/A

Great Basin College[1]
Elko NV
U.S. News ranking: Reg. Coll. (W), unranked
Website: www.gbcnv.edu
Admissions email: N/A
Public
Application deadline (fall): N/A
Undergraduate student body: N/A full time, N/A part time
Expenses: 2016-2017: $2,910 in state, $9,555 out of state; room/board: $6,800
Financial aid: N/A

Nevada State College[1]
Henderson NV
(702) 992-2130
U.S. News ranking: Reg. Coll. (W), unranked
Website: nsc.nevada.edu
Public; founded 2002
Application deadline (fall): rolling
Undergraduate student body: N/A full time, N/A part time
Expenses: 2016-2017: $5,001 in state, $16,114 out of state; room/board: N/A
Financial aid: N/A

Sierra Nevada College

Incline Village NV
(866) 412-4636
U.S. News ranking: Reg. U. (W),
second tier
Website: www.sierranevada.edu
Admissions email: admissions@
sierranevada.edu
Private; founded 1969
Freshman admissions: less
selective; 2016-2017: 851
applied, 438 accepted. Either
SAT or ACT required. SAT 25/75
percentile: 850-1050. High school
rank: 15% in top tenth, 32% in
top quarter, 58% in top half
Early decision deadline: N/A,
notification date: N/A
Early action deadline: N/A,
notification date: N/A
Application deadline (fall): 8/26
Undergraduate student body: 464
full time, 15 part time; 58%
male, 42% female; 3% American
Indian, 4% Asian, 3% black,
4% Hispanic, 0% multiracial,
2% Pacific Islander, 75% white,
1% international; 15% from in
state; 40% live on campus; N/A
of students in fraternities, N/A in
sororities
Most popular majors: 50%
Business, Management,
Marketing, and Related
Support Services, 19% Multi/
Interdisciplinary Studies, 11%
Psychology, 4% Visual and
Performing Arts, 2% English
Language and Literature/Letters
Expenses: 2017-2018: $32,639;
room/board: $12,764
Financial aid: (775) 831-1314;
66% of undergrads determined to
have financial need; average aid
package $27,099

University of Nevada–Las Vegas

Las Vegas NV
(702) 774-8658
U.S. News ranking: Nat. U.,
second tier
Website: www.unlv.edu
Admissions email:
admissions@unlv.edu
Public; founded 1957
Freshman admissions: selective;
2016-2017: 8,533 applied,
7,064 accepted. Either SAT
or ACT required. ACT 25/75
percentile: 19-24. High school
rank: 20% in top tenth, 52% in
top quarter, 82% in top half
Early decision deadline: N/A,
notification date: N/A
Early action deadline: N/A,
notification date: N/A
Application deadline (fall): 7/1
Undergraduate student body:
18,322 full time, 6,392 part
time; 44% male, 56% female;
0% American Indian, 16% Asian,
8% black, 28% Hispanic, 10%
multiracial, 1% Pacific Islander,
33% white, 4% international;
89% from in state; 7% live
on campus; 8% of students in
fraternities, 9% in sororities
Most popular majors: 30%
Business, Management,
Marketing, and Related Support
Services, 8% Psychology, 6%
Health Professions and Related
Programs, 6% Homeland Security,
Law Enforcement, Firefighting and
Related Protective Services, 6%
Social Sciences

Expenses: 2017-2018: $7,310 in
state, $21,498 out of state; room/
board: $10,806
Financial aid: (702) 895-3424;
64% of undergrads determined to
have financial need; average aid
package $8,335

University of Nevada–Reno

Reno NV
(775) 784-4700
U.S. News ranking: Nat. U.,
No. 202
Website: www.unr.edu
Admissions email:
asknevada@unr.edu
Public; founded 1864
Freshman admissions: selective;
2016-2017: 9,644 applied,
7,986 accepted. Either SAT
or ACT required. ACT 25/75
percentile: 21-26. High school
rank: 23% in top tenth, 54% in
top quarter, 87% in top half
Early decision deadline: N/A,
notification date: N/A
Early action deadline: 11/1,
notification date: 11/15
Application deadline (fall): 4/7
Undergraduate student body:
15,769 full time, 2,422 part
time; 47% male, 53% female;
1% American Indian, 7% Asian,
3% black, 20% Hispanic, 6%
multiracial, 1% Pacific Islander,
59% white, 1% international;
70% from in state; 15% live
on campus; N/A of students in
fraternities, N/A in sororities
Most popular majors: 17%
Business, Management,
Marketing, and Related Support
Services, 12% Health Professions
and Related Programs, 11%
Engineering, 10% Social
Sciences, 9% Biological and
Biomedical Sciences
Expenses: 2017-2018: $7,599 in
state, $21,787 out of state; room/
board: $10,940
Financial aid: (775) 784-4666;
53% of undergrads determined to
have financial need; average aid
package $11,600

Western Nevada College[1]

Carson City NV
U.S. News ranking: Reg. Coll. (W),
unranked
Website: www.wnc.edu
Admissions email: N/A
Public; founded 1971
Application deadline (fall): N/A
Undergraduate student body: N/A
full time, N/A part time
Expenses: 2016-2017: $2,910 in
state, $9,555 out of state; room/
board: N/A
Financial aid: N/A

NEW HAMPSHIRE

Colby-Sawyer College

New London NH
(800) 272-1015
U.S. News ranking: Reg. Coll. (N),
No. 7
Website: colby-sawyer.edu/
Admissions email: admissions@
colby-sawyer.edu
Private
Freshman admissions: selective;
2016-2017: 1,978 applied,

1,786 accepted. Neither SAT
nor ACT required. SAT 25/75
percentile: 950-1140. High
school rank: N/A
Early decision deadline: N/A,
notification date: N/A
Early action deadline: 12/1,
notification date: 12/15
Application deadline (fall): rolling
Undergraduate student body: 1,013
full time, 82 part time; 31%
male, 69% female; 1% American
Indian, 2% Asian, 6% black, 3%
Hispanic, 0% multiracial, 0%
Pacific Islander, 70% white, 8%
international
Most popular majors: 11%
Business Administration
and Management, General,
10% Registered Nursing/
Registered Nurse, 9% Biology/
Biological Sciences, General,
8% Psychology, General, 6%
Kinesiology and Exercise Science
Expenses: 2017-2018: $41,186;
room/board: $13,650
Financial aid: (603) 526-3717;
75% of undergrads determined to
have financial need; average aid
package $33,354

Dartmouth College

Hanover NH
(603) 646-2875
U.S. News ranking: Nat. U., No. 11
Website: www.dartmouth.edu
Admissions email: admissions.
office@dartmouth.edu
Private; founded 1769
Freshman admissions: most
selective; 2016-2017: 20,675
applied, 2,190 accepted. Either
SAT or ACT required. SAT 25/75
percentile: 1350-1560. High
school rank: 93% in top tenth,
99% in top quarter, 100% in
top half
Early decision deadline: 11/1,
notification date: 12/15
Early action deadline: N/A,
notification date: N/A
Application deadline (fall): 1/1
Undergraduate student body: 4,270
full time, 40 part time; 50%
male, 50% female; 2% American
Indian, 15% Asian, 7% black,
9% Hispanic, 5% multiracial, 0%
Pacific Islander, 50% white, 8%
international; 2% from in state;
87% live on campus; 43% of
students in fraternities, 47% in
sororities
Most popular majors: 35%
Social Sciences, 10% Biological
and Biomedical Sciences, 8%
Engineering, 6% History, 6%
Psychology
Expenses: 2017-2018: $52,950;
room/board: $15,159
Financial aid: (603) 646-2451;
52% of undergrads determined to
have financial need; average aid
package $49,141

Franklin Pierce University

Rindge NH
(800) 437-0048
U.S. News ranking: Reg. U. (N),
second tier
Website: www.franklinpierce.edu/
Admissions email: admissions@
franklinpierce.edu
Private; founded 1962
Freshman admissions: less
selective; 2016-2017: 6,506
applied, 5,295 accepted. Neither
SAT nor ACT required. SAT 25/75

percentile: 870-1070. High school
rank: 13% in top tenth, 30% in
top quarter, 52% in top half
Early decision deadline: N/A,
notification date: N/A
Early action deadline: N/A,
notification date: N/A
Application deadline (fall): rolling
Undergraduate student body: 1,582
full time, 170 part time; 45%
male, 55% female; 0% American
Indian, 1% Asian, 7% black,
8% Hispanic, 2% multiracial,
0% Pacific Islander, 73% white,
3% international; 18% from in
state; 90% live on campus; 0%
of students in fraternities, 0% in
sororities
Most popular majors: 20%
Business, Management,
Marketing, and Related Support
Services, 15% Health Professions
and Related Programs, 12%
Homeland Security, Law
Enforcement, Firefighting and
Related Protective Services, 8%
Psychology, 7% Biological and
Biomedical Sciences
Expenses: 2017-2018: $34,995;
room/board: $13,082
Financial aid: (603) 899-4186;
83% of undergrads determined to
have financial need; average aid
package $24,632

Granite State College

Concord NH
(603) 513-1391
U.S. News ranking: Reg. Coll. (N),
unranked
Website: www.granite.edu
Admissions email: gsc.admissions@
granite.edu
Public; founded 1972
Freshman admissions: least
selective; 2016-2017: 254
applied, 254 accepted. Neither
SAT nor ACT required. SAT 25/75
percentile: N/A. High school
rank: N/A
Early decision deadline: N/A,
notification date: N/A
Early action deadline: N/A,
notification date: N/A
Application deadline (fall): rolling
Undergraduate student body: 933
full time, 921 part time; 26%
male, 74% female; 0% American
Indian, 1% Asian, 3% black,
4% Hispanic, 2% multiracial,
0% Pacific Islander, 84% white,
0% international; 81% from in
state; N/A live on campus; N/A
of students in fraternities, N/A in
sororities
Most popular majors: 25%
Business, Management,
Marketing, and Related
Support Services, 21% Multi/
Interdisciplinary Studies,
17% Psychology, 12% Health
Professions and Related Programs,
7% Education
Expenses: 2017-2018: $7,593 in
state, $8,505 out of state; room/
board: N/A
Financial aid: (603) 513-1392;
75% of undergrads determined to
have financial need; average aid
package $6,769

Keene State College

Keene NH
(603) 358-2276
U.S. News ranking: Reg. U. (N),
No. 71
Website: www.keene.edu
Admissions email:
admissions@keene.edu

Public; founded 1909
Freshman admissions: less
selective; 2016-2017: 5,466
applied, 4,511 accepted. Either
SAT or ACT required. SAT 25/75
percentile: 880-1070. High
school rank: 5% in top tenth, 28%
in top quarter, 58% in top half
Early decision deadline: N/A,
notification date: N/A
Early action deadline: N/A,
notification date: N/A
Application deadline (fall): 4/1
Undergraduate student body: 4,004
full time, 86 part time; 45%
male, 55% female; 0% American
Indian, 1% Asian, 1% black,
4% Hispanic, 2% multiracial,
0% Pacific Islander, 87% white,
0% international; 43% from in
state; 53% live on campus; 5%
of students in fraternities, 8% in
sororities
Most popular majors: 13%
Education, 13% Engineering
Technologies and Engineering-
Related Fields, 12% Health
Professions and Related Programs,
11% Psychology, 9% Visual and
Performing Arts
Expenses: 2017-2018: $13,868
in state, $22,614 out of state;
room/board: $10,736
Financial aid: (603) 358-2058;
66% of undergrads determined to
have financial need; average aid
package $12,285

New England College

Henniker NH
(800) 521-7642
U.S. News ranking: Reg. U. (N),
second tier
Website: www.nec.edu
Admissions email:
admission@nec.edu
Private; founded 1946
Freshman admissions: least
selective; 2016-2017: 4,204
applied, 4,163 accepted. Neither
SAT nor ACT required. SAT 25/75
percentile: 790-1060. High
school rank: 1% in top tenth, 11%
in top quarter, 41% in top half
Early decision deadline: N/A,
notification date: N/A
Early action deadline: N/A,
notification date: N/A
Application deadline (fall): rolling
Undergraduate student body: 1,730
full time, 26 part time; 41%
male, 59% female; 1% American
Indian, 1% Asian, 24% black,
8% Hispanic, 2% multiracial,
0% Pacific Islander, 53% white,
4% international; 18% from in
state; 36% live on campus; 3%
of students in fraternities, 3% in
sororities
Most popular majors: 21%
Business, Management,
Marketing, and Related Support
Services, 15% Health Professions
and Related Programs, 12%
Multi/Interdisciplinary Studies,
12% Psychology, 10% Homeland
Security, Law Enforcement,
Firefighting and Related Protective
Services
Expenses: 2017-2018: $36,954;
room/board: $13,874
Financial aid: (603) 428-2436;
84% of undergrads determined to
have financial need; average aid
package $19,992

New Hampshire Institute of Art[1]
Manchester NH
U.S. News ranking: Arts, unranked
Admissions email: N/A
Private
Application deadline (fall): N/A
Undergraduate student body: N/A full time, N/A part time
Expenses: 2016-2017: $25,780; room/board: $10,980
Financial aid: N/A

Plymouth State University
Plymouth NH
(603) 535-2237
U.S. News ranking: Reg. U. (N), No. 115
Website: www.plymouth.edu
Admissions email: plymouthadmit@plymouth.edu
Public; founded 1871
Freshman admissions: less selective; 2016-2017: 6,864 applied, 5,407 accepted. Neither SAT nor ACT required. SAT 25/75 percentile: 880-1090. High school rank: 5% in top tenth, 20% in top quarter, 54% in top half
Early decision deadline: N/A, notification date: N/A
Early action deadline: N/A, notification date: N/A
Application deadline (fall): 4/1
Undergraduate student body: 3,935 full time, 190 part time; 50% male, 50% female; 0% American Indian, 2% Asian, 2% black, 1% Hispanic, 2% multiracial, 0% Pacific Islander, 83% white, 2% international; 55% from in state; 56% live on campus; 0% of students in fraternities, 3% in sororities
Most popular majors: 24% Business, Management, Marketing, and Related Support Services, 12% Education, 8% Homeland Security, Law Enforcement, Firefighting and Related Protective Services, 8% Parks, Recreation, Leisure, and Fitness Studies, 7% Communication, Journalism, and Related Programs
Expenses: 2017-2018: $13,770 in state, $22,230 out of state; room/board: $9,970
Financial aid: (603) 535-2338; 69% of undergrads determined to have financial need; average aid package $11,594

Rivier University[1]
Nashua NH
(603) 888-1311
U.S. News ranking: Reg. U. (N), second tier
Website: rivier.edu
Admissions email: admissions@rivier.edu
Private
Application deadline (fall): rolling
Undergraduate student body: N/A full time, N/A part time
Expenses: 2016-2017: $30,000; room/board: $11,610
Financial aid: N/A

Southern New Hampshire University
Manchester NH
(603) 645-9611
U.S. News ranking: Reg. U. (N), No. 86
Website: www.snhu.edu
Admissions email: admission@snhu.edu
Private; founded 1932
Freshman admissions: less selective; 2016-2017: 4,207 applied, 3,907 accepted. Neither SAT nor ACT required. SAT 25/75 percentile: 880-1100. High school rank: 10% in top tenth, 23% in top quarter, 54% in top half
Early decision deadline: N/A, notification date: N/A
Early action deadline: 11/15, notification date: 12/15
Application deadline (fall): rolling
Undergraduate student body: 2,935 full time, 85 part time; 47% male, 53% female; 0% American Indian, 2% Asian, 3% black, 4% Hispanic, 2% multiracial, 0% Pacific Islander, 77% white, 7% international; 47% from in state; 62% live on campus; 2% of students in fraternities, 2% in sororities
Most popular majors: 23% Business Administration and Management, General, 7% Psychology, General, 6% Computer and Information Sciences, General, 6% Marketing/Marketing Management, General, 5% Corrections and Criminal Justice, Other
Expenses: 2017-2018: $31,136; room/board: $12,278
Financial aid: (603) 626-9100; 71% of undergrads determined to have financial need; average aid package $23,425

St. Anselm College
Manchester NH
(603) 641-7500
U.S. News ranking: Nat. Lib. Arts, No. 106
Website: www.anselm.edu
Admissions email: admission@anselm.edu
Private; founded 1889
Affiliation: Roman Catholic
Freshman admissions: more selective; 2016-2017: 3,826 applied, 2,904 accepted. Neither SAT nor ACT required. SAT 25/75 percentile: 1050-1220. High school rank: 20% in top tenth, 57% in top quarter, 89% in top half
Early decision deadline: 12/1, notification date: 1/1
Early action deadline: 11/15, notification date: 1/15
Application deadline (fall): 2/1
Undergraduate student body: 1,876 full time, 54 part time; 39% male, 61% female; 0% American Indian, 1% Asian, 2% black, 3% Hispanic, 2% multiracial, 0% Pacific Islander, 88% white, 1% international; 23% from in state; 91% live on campus; 0% of students in fraternities, 0% in sororities
Most popular majors: 16% Registered Nursing/Registered Nurse, 10% Criminology, 8% Business/Commerce, General, 7% Speech Communication and Rhetoric, 6% Elementary Education and Teaching

Expenses: 2017-2018: $39,990; room/board: $14,146
Financial aid: (603) 641-7110; 70% of undergrads determined to have financial need; average aid package $26,687

Thomas More College of Liberal Arts[1]
Merrimack NH
U.S. News ranking: Nat. Lib. Arts, second tier
Website: www.thomasmorecollege.edu
Admissions email: admissions@thomasmorecollege.edu
Private
Application deadline (fall): N/A
Undergraduate student body: N/A full time, N/A part time
Expenses: 2016-2017: $20,400; room/board: $9,700
Financial aid: (603) 880-8308

University of New Hampshire
Durham NH
(603) 862-1360
U.S. News ranking: Nat. U., No. 103
Website: www.unh.edu
Admissions email: admissions@unh.edu
Public; founded 1866
Freshman admissions: selective; 2016-2017: 20,203 applied, 15,326 accepted. Either SAT or ACT required. SAT 25/75 percentile: 990-1200. High school rank: 19% in top tenth, 50% in top quarter, 88% in top half
Early decision deadline: N/A, notification date: N/A
Early action deadline: 11/15, notification date: 1/1
Application deadline (fall): 2/1
Undergraduate student body: 12,467 full time, 404 part time; 46% male, 54% female; 0% American Indian, 2% Asian, 1% black, 3% Hispanic, 2% multiracial, 0% Pacific Islander, 81% white, 3% international; 48% from in state; 55% live on campus; 11% of students in fraternities, 14% in sororities
Most popular majors: 18% Business Administration and Management, General, 8% Psychology, General, 6% Speech Communication and Rhetoric, 5% Biomedical Sciences, General, 4% English Language and Literature, General
Expenses: 2017-2018: $18,067 in state, $32,637 out of state; room/board: $11,266
Financial aid: (603) 862-3600; 67% of undergrads determined to have financial need; average aid package $23,451

NEW JERSEY

Berkeley College
Woodland Park NJ
(800) 446-5400
U.S. News ranking: Business, unranked
Website: www.berkeleycollege.edu
Admissions email: admissions@berkeleycollege.edu
For-profit; founded 1931

Freshman admissions: least selective; 2016-2017: N/A applied, N/A accepted. Neither SAT nor ACT required. SAT 25/75 percentile: N/A. High school rank: N/A
Early decision deadline: N/A, notification date: N/A
Early action deadline: N/A, notification date: N/A
Application deadline (fall): 8/28
Undergraduate student body: 2,788 full time, 831 part time; 29% male, 71% female; 0% American Indian, 2% Asian, 21% black, 37% Hispanic, 0% multiracial, 0% Pacific Islander, 14% white, 1% international; 97% from in state; N/A live on campus; N/A of students in fraternities, N/A in sororities
Most popular majors: 32% Business Administration and Management, General, 21% Criminal Justice/Law Enforcement Administration, 12% Fashion Merchandising, 11% Accounting, 11% Health/Health Care Administration/Management
Expenses: 2017-2018: $25,300; room/board: N/A
Financial aid: (973) 278-5400

Bloomfield College
Bloomfield NJ
(800) 848-4555
U.S. News ranking: Nat. Lib. Arts, second tier
Website: www.bloomfield.edu
Admissions email: admission@bloomfield.edu
Private; founded 1868
Affiliation: Presbyterian Church (USA)
Freshman admissions: least selective; 2016-2017: 3,623 applied, 2,231 accepted. Neither SAT nor ACT required. SAT 25/75 percentile: 760-940. High school rank: 7% in top tenth, 20% in top quarter, 50% in top half
Early decision deadline: N/A, notification date: N/A
Early action deadline: 12/1, notification date: 12/24
Application deadline (fall): 8/1
Undergraduate student body: 1,767 full time, 180 part time; 37% male, 63% female; 0% American Indian, 2% Asian, 50% black, 28% Hispanic, 1% multiracial, 1% Pacific Islander, 9% white, 4% international; 94% from in state; 28% live on campus; 4% of students in fraternities, 2% in sororities
Most popular majors: 17% Business, Management, Marketing, and Related Support Services, 17% Visual and Performing Arts, 16% Social Sciences, 15% Psychology, 8% Health Professions and Related Programs
Expenses: 2017-2018: $29,300; room/board: $11,700
Financial aid: (973) 748-9000; 93% of undergrads determined to have financial need; average aid package $27,426

Caldwell University
Caldwell NJ
(973) 618-3600
U.S. News ranking: Reg. U. (N), No. 102
Website: www.caldwell.edu
Admissions email: admissions@caldwell.edu
Private; founded 1939
Affiliation: Roman Catholic
Freshman admissions: less selective; 2016-2017: 2,831 applied, 2,418 accepted. Either SAT or ACT required. SAT 25/75 percentile: 850-1070. High school rank: 8% in top tenth, 32% in top quarter, 69% in top half
Early decision deadline: 12/1, notification date: 12/31
Early action deadline: 12/1, notification date: 12/31
Application deadline (fall): 4/1
Undergraduate student body: 1,446 full time, 191 part time; 30% male, 70% female; 0% American Indian, 3% Asian, 14% black, 17% Hispanic, 2% multiracial, 0% Pacific Islander, 38% white, 8% international; 91% from in state; 35% live on campus; 18% of students in fraternities, 17% in sororities
Most popular majors: 17% Psychology, General, 10% Business Administration and Management, General, 8% Registered Nursing/Registered Nurse, 7% Speech Communication and Rhetoric, 6% English Language and Literature, General
Expenses: 2017-2018: $33,900; room/board: $11,710
Financial aid: (973) 618-3221; 75% of undergrads determined to have financial need; average aid package $26,608

Centenary University
Hackettstown NJ
(800) 236-8679
U.S. News ranking: Reg. U. (N), No. 135
Website: www.centenaryuniversity.edu
Admissions email: admissions@centenaryuniversity.edu
Private; founded 1867
Affiliation: United Methodist
Freshman admissions: less selective; 2016-2017: 1,172 applied, 1,030 accepted. Either SAT or ACT required. SAT 25/75 percentile: 830-1050. High school rank: N/A
Early decision deadline: N/A, notification date: N/A
Early action deadline: N/A, notification date: N/A
Application deadline (fall): 8/15
Undergraduate student body: 1,237 full time, 281 part time; 38% male, 62% female; 0% American Indian, 2% Asian, 11% black, 12% Hispanic, 0% multiracial, 0% Pacific Islander, 57% white, 3% international
Most popular majors: 42% Business Administration and Management, General, 6% Art Teacher Education, 6% Criminal Justice/Safety Studies, 6% Fashion/Apparel Design, 5% Sociology
Expenses: 2017-2018: $32,580; room/board: $11,110
Financial aid: (908) 852-1400

College of New Jersey

Ewing NJ
(609) 771-2131
U.S. News ranking: Reg. U. (N), No. 4
Website: www.tcnj.edu
Admissions email: admiss@tcnj.edu
Public; founded 1855
Freshman admissions: more selective; 2016-2017: 11,825 applied, 5,778 accepted. Either SAT or ACT required. SAT 25/75 percentile: 1100-1300. High school rank: 40% in top tenth, 76% in top quarter, 98% in top half
Early decision deadline: 11/1, notification date: 12/1
Early action deadline: N/A, notification date: N/A
Application deadline (fall): 2/1
Undergraduate student body: 6,496 full time, 291 part time; 42% male, 58% female; 0% American Indian, 11% Asian, 6% black, 13% Hispanic, 0% multiracial, 0% Pacific Islander, 66% white, 0% international; 94% from in state; 58% live on campus; 14% of students in fraternities, 11% in sororities
Most popular majors: 20% Business Administration, Management and Operations, 17% Teacher Education and Professional Development, Specific Levels and Methods, 9% Psychology, General, 6% Biology, General, 6% Communication and Media Studies
Expenses: 2017-2018: $16,149 in state, $27,578 out of state; room/board: $13,200
Financial aid: (609) 771-2211; 52% of undergrads determined to have financial need; average aid package $10,955

College of St. Elizabeth

Morristown NJ
(973) 290-4700
U.S. News ranking: Reg. U. (N), No. 137
Website: www.cse.edu
Admissions email: apply@cse.edu
Private; founded 1899
Affiliation: Roman Catholic
Freshman admissions: least selective; 2016-2017: 1,633 applied, 1,082 accepted. Either SAT or ACT required. SAT 25/75 percentile: 716-928. High school rank: N/A
Early decision deadline: N/A, notification date: N/A
Early action deadline: N/A, notification date: N/A
Application deadline (fall): rolling
Undergraduate student body: 573 full time, 190 part time; 15% male, 85% female; 0% American Indian, 3% Asian, 34% black, 23% Hispanic, 3% multiracial, 0% Pacific Islander, 27% white, 3% international
Most popular majors: 45% Registered Nursing/Registered Nurse, 8% Multi-/Interdisciplinary Studies, Other, 7% Psychology, General, 5% Biology/Biological Sciences, General, 5% Business Administration and Management, General

Expenses: 2017-2018: $32,282; room/board: $12,744
Financial aid: (973) 290-4393

Drew University

Madison NJ
(973) 408-3739
U.S. News ranking: Nat. Lib. Arts, No. 112
Website: www.drew.edu
Admissions email: cadm@drew.edu
Private; founded 1867
Affiliation: United Methodist
Freshman admissions: more selective; 2016-2017: 3,494 applied, 1,997 accepted. Neither SAT nor ACT required. SAT 25/75 percentile: 1030-1250. High school rank: 27% in top tenth, 61% in top quarter, 85% in top half
Early decision deadline: 11/15, notification date: 12/15
Early action deadline: 1/15, notification date: 2/15
Application deadline (fall): 2/1
Undergraduate student body: 1,476 full time, 45 part time; 41% male, 59% female; 0% American Indian, 6% Asian, 9% black, 11% Hispanic, 5% multiracial, 0% Pacific Islander, 55% white, 8% international; 67% from in state; 78% live on campus; N/A of students in fraternities, N/A in sororities
Most popular majors: 14% Business Administration and Management, General, 9% Biology/Biological Sciences, General, 9% Psychology, General, 8% Drama and Dramatics/Theatre Arts, General, 7% Sociology
Expenses: 2017-2018: $49,168; room/board: $13,694
Financial aid: (973) 408-3112; 72% of undergrads determined to have financial need; average aid package $42,435

Fairleigh Dickinson University

Teaneck NJ
(800) 338-8803
U.S. News ranking: Reg. U. (N), No. 64
Website: www.fdu.edu
Admissions email: admissions@fdu.edu
Private; founded 1942
Freshman admissions: selective; 2016-2017: 8,274 applied, 6,451 accepted. Either SAT or ACT required. SAT 25/75 percentile: 920-1120. High school rank: 13% in top tenth, 38% in top quarter, 74% in top half
Early decision deadline: N/A, notification date: N/A
Early action deadline: N/A, notification date: N/A
Application deadline (fall): rolling
Undergraduate student body: 4,736 full time, 3,134 part time; 43% male, 57% female; 0% American Indian, 5% Asian, 11% black, 29% Hispanic, 2% multiracial, 0% Pacific Islander, 37% white, 4% international
Most popular majors: 32% Liberal Arts and Sciences, General Studies and Humanities, 15% Business, Management, Marketing, and Related Support Services, 10% Psychology,

5% Biological and Biomedical Sciences, 5% Health Professions and Related Programs
Expenses: 2017-2018: $40,704; room/board: $14,904
Financial aid: (973) 443-8700; 81% of undergrads determined to have financial need; average aid package $31,261

Felician University

Lodi NJ
(201) 559-6131
U.S. News ranking: Reg. U. (N), second tier
Website: www.felician.edu
Admissions email: admissions@felician.edu
Private; founded 1942
Affiliation: Roman Catholic
Freshman admissions: less selective; 2016-2017: 2,173 applied, 1,707 accepted. Either SAT or ACT required. SAT 25/75 percentile: 790-1010. High school rank: 7% in top tenth, 31% in top quarter, 62% in top half
Early decision deadline: N/A, notification date: N/A
Early action deadline: 11/15, notification date: 12/23
Application deadline (fall): rolling
Undergraduate student body: 1,433 full time, 215 part time; 28% male, 72% female; 1% American Indian, 5% Asian, 23% black, 30% Hispanic, 1% multiracial, 0% Pacific Islander, 29% white, 2% international; 90% from in state; 30% live on campus; 1% of students in fraternities, N/A in sororities
Most popular majors: 44% Health Professions and Related Programs, 14% Business, Management, Marketing, and Related Support Services, 8% Biological and Biomedical Sciences, 6% Education, 6% Multi/Interdisciplinary Studies
Expenses: 2017-2018: $33,650; room/board: $12,630
Financial aid: (201) 559-6040; 90% of undergrads determined to have financial need; average aid package $27,065

Georgian Court University

Lakewood NJ
(800) 458-8422
U.S. News ranking: Reg. U. (N), No. 137
Website: georgian.edu
Admissions email: admissions@georgian.edu
Private; founded 1908
Affiliation: Roman Catholic
Freshman admissions: less selective; 2016-2017: 1,609 applied, 1,198 accepted. Either SAT or ACT required. SAT 25/75 percentile: 850-1040. High school rank: 8% in top tenth, 24% in top quarter, 60% in top half
Early decision deadline: N/A, notification date: N/A
Early action deadline: 12/1, notification date: N/A
Application deadline (fall): 8/1
Undergraduate student body: 1,319 full time, 272 part time; 28% male, 72% female; 0% American Indian, 3% Asian, 12% black,

11% Hispanic, 2% multiracial, 0% Pacific Islander, 61% white, 1% international; 94% from in state; 30% live on campus; N/A of students in fraternities, N/A in sororities
Most popular majors: 25% Psychology, General, 8% English Language and Literature, General, 8% Registered Nursing/Registered Nurse, 6% Biology/Biological Sciences, General, 6% Criminal Justice/Safety Studies
Expenses: 2017-2018: $32,260; room/board: $10,808
Financial aid: (732) 987-2254; 86% of undergrads determined to have financial need; average aid package $28,364

Kean University

Union NJ
(908) 737-7100
U.S. News ranking: Reg. U. (N), No. 137
Website: www.kean.edu
Admissions email: admitme@kean.edu
Public; founded 1855
Freshman admissions: less selective; 2016-2017: 8,354 applied, 6,536 accepted. Either SAT or ACT required. SAT 25/75 percentile: 830-1010. High school rank: N/A
Early decision deadline: N/A, notification date: N/A
Early action deadline: 12/1, notification date: 1/1
Application deadline (fall): 8/15
Undergraduate student body: 9,239 full time, 2,573 part time; 39% male, 61% female; 0% American Indian, 5% Asian, 19% black, 27% Hispanic, 2% multiracial, 0% Pacific Islander, 35% white, 2% international; 98% from in state; 15% live on campus; N/A of students in fraternities, N/A in sororities
Most popular majors: 18% Psychology, General, 7% Biology/Biological Sciences, General, 7% Business Administration and Management, General, 6% Criminal Justice/Law Enforcement Administration, 6% Speech Communication and Rhetoric
Expenses: 2017-2018: $12,107 in state, $19,009 out of state; room/board: $13,513
Financial aid: (908) 737-3190; 71% of undergrads determined to have financial need; average aid package $10,497

Monmouth University

West Long Branch NJ
(800) 543-9671
U.S. News ranking: Reg. U. (N), No. 28
Website: www.monmouth.edu
Admissions email: admission@monmouth.edu
Private; founded 1933
Freshman admissions: selective; 2016-2017: 9,097 applied, 7,031 accepted. Either SAT or ACT required. SAT 25/75 percentile: 930-1120. High school rank: 14% in top tenth, 41% in top quarter, 75% in top half
Early decision deadline: N/A, notification date: N/A
Early action deadline: 12/1, notification date: 1/15
Application deadline (fall): 3/1

Undergraduate student body: 4,490 full time, 217 part time; 43% male, 57% female; 0% American Indian, 3% Asian, 5% black, 12% Hispanic, 2% multiracial, 0% Pacific Islander, 72% white, 1% international; 89% from in state; 41% live on campus; 16% of students in fraternities, 15% in sororities
Most popular majors: 22% Business, Management, Marketing, and Related Support Services, 11% Communication, Journalism, and Related Programs, 10% Education, 7% Health Professions and Related Programs, 7% Psychology
Expenses: 2017-2018: $36,733; room/board: $13,451
Financial aid: (732) 571-3463; 72% of undergrads determined to have financial need; average aid package $24,121

Montclair State University

Montclair NJ
(973) 655-4444
U.S. News ranking: Nat. U., No. 187
Website: www.montclair.edu
Admissions email: undergraduate.admissions@montclair.edu
Public; founded 1908
Freshman admissions: less selective; 2016-2017: 12,139 applied, 8,027 accepted. Neither SAT nor ACT required. SAT 25/75 percentile: 870-1070. High school rank: 11% in top tenth, 35% in top quarter, 77% in top half
Early decision deadline: N/A, notification date: N/A
Early action deadline: N/A, notification date: N/A
Application deadline (fall): 3/1
Undergraduate student body: 14,968 full time, 1,842 part time; 39% male, 61% female; 0% American Indian, 6% Asian, 12% black, 27% Hispanic, 3% multiracial, 0% Pacific Islander, 43% white, 1% international; 97% from in state; 30% live on campus; 35% of students in fraternities, 65% in sororities
Most popular majors: 15% Business Administration and Management, General, 11% Psychology, General, 7% Family and Consumer Sciences/Human Sciences, General, 5% Biology/Biological Sciences, General, 5% Multi-/Interdisciplinary Studies, Other
Expenses: 2017-2018: $12,454 in state, $20,566 out of state; room/board: N/A
Financial aid: (973) 655-7020; 71% of undergrads determined to have financial need; average aid package $9,290

New Jersey City University

Jersey City NJ
(888) 441-6528
U.S. News ranking: Reg. U. (N), second tier
Website: www.njcu.edu/
Admissions email: admissions@njcu.edu
Public; founded 1927

Freshman admissions: least selective; 2016-2017: 3,987 applied, 3,391 accepted. Either SAT or ACT required. SAT 25/75 percentile: 760-990. High school rank: 13% in top tenth, 32% in top quarter, 61% in top half
Early decision deadline: N/A, notification date: N/A
Early action deadline: N/A, notification date: N/A
Undergraduate student body: 5,166 full time, 1,497 part time; 41% male, 59% female; 0% American Indian, 8% Asian, 22% black, 38% Hispanic, 2% multiracial, 1% Pacific Islander, 23% white, 1% international; 99% from in state; 8% live on campus; N/A of students in fraternities, N/A in sororities
Most popular majors: 16% Registered Nursing/Registered Nurse, 11% Psychology, General, 10% Corrections and Criminal Justice, Other, 9% Business Administration and Management, General, 5% Accounting
Expenses: 2016-2017: $11,431 in state, $20,458 out of state; room/board: $12,446
Financial aid: (201) 200-3173; 87% of undergrads determined to have financial need; average aid package $10,213

New Jersey Institute of Technology
Newark NJ
(973) 596-3300
U.S. News ranking: Nat. U., No. 140
Website: www.njit.edu
Admissions email: admissions@njit.edu
Public; founded 1881
Freshman admissions: selective; 2016-2017: 7,222 applied, 4,283 accepted. Either SAT or ACT required. SAT 25/75 percentile: 1110-1310. High school rank: 31% in top tenth, 61% in top quarter, 88% in top half
Early decision deadline: N/A, notification date: N/A
Early action deadline: 11/11, notification date: 12/15
Application deadline (fall): 3/1
Undergraduate student body: 6,180 full time, 2,031 part time; 75% male, 25% female; 0% American Indian, 22% Asian, 8% black, 21% Hispanic, 3% multiracial, 0% Pacific Islander, 34% white, 5% international; 97% from in state; 22% live on campus; 6% of students in fraternities, 6% in sororities
Most popular majors: 37% Engineering, 19% Computer and Information Sciences and Support Services, 13% Engineering Technologies and Engineering-Related Fields, 12% Architecture and Related Services, 8% Business, Management, Marketing, and Related Support Services
Expenses: 2017-2018: $16,430 in state, $31,034 out of state; room/board: $13,700
Financial aid: (973) 596-3476; 72% of undergrads determined to have financial need; average aid package $13,200

Princeton University
Princeton NJ
(609) 258-3060
U.S. News ranking: Nat. U., No. 1
Website: www.princeton.edu
Admissions email: uaoffice@princeton.edu
Private; founded 1746
Freshman admissions: most selective; 2016-2017: 29,303 applied, 1,911 accepted. Either SAT or ACT required. SAT 25/75 percentile: 1400-1590. High school rank: 94% in top tenth, 99% in top quarter, 100% in top half
Early decision deadline: N/A, notification date: N/A
Early action deadline: 11/1, notification date: 12/15
Application deadline (fall): 1/1
Undergraduate student body: 5,251 full time, 149 part time; 52% male, 48% female; 0% American Indian, 21% Asian, 8% black, 10% Hispanic, 4% multiracial, 0% Pacific Islander, 44% white, 12% international; 18% from in state; 96% live on campus; N/A of students in fraternities, N/A in sororities
Most popular majors: 11% Public Policy Analysis, General, 9% Computer Engineering, General, 9% Econometrics and Quantitative Economics, 7% History, General, 6% Operations Research
Expenses: 2017-2018: $47,140; room/board: $15,610
Financial aid: (609) 258-3330; 60% of undergrads determined to have financial need; average aid package $49,502

Ramapo College of New Jersey
Mahwah NJ
(201) 684-7300
U.S. News ranking: Reg. U. (N), No. 37
Website: www.ramapo.edu
Admissions email: admissions@ramapo.edu
Public; founded 1969
Freshman admissions: selective; 2016-2017: 7,172 applied, 3,820 accepted. Either SAT or ACT required. SAT 25/75 percentile: 970-1190. High school rank: 11% in top tenth, 26% in top quarter, 52% in top half
Early decision deadline: 11/1, notification date: 12/5
Early action deadline: N/A, notification date: N/A
Application deadline (fall): 3/1
Undergraduate student body: 5,016 full time, 746 part time; 45% male, 55% female; 0% American Indian, 7% Asian, 5% black, 14% Hispanic, 1% multiracial, 0% Pacific Islander, 64% white, 2% international; 95% from in state; 47% live on campus; 9% of students in fraternities, 4% in sororities
Most popular majors: 15% Business Administration and Management, General, 11% Psychology, General, 9% Nursing Science, 8% Speech Communication and Rhetoric, 7% Accounting
Expenses: 2017-2018: $14,080 in state, $23,214 out of state; room/board: $12,180

Rider University
Lawrenceville NJ
(609) 896-5042
U.S. News ranking: Reg. U. (N), No. 34
Website: www.rider.edu
Admissions email: admissions@rider.edu
Private; founded 1865
Freshman admissions: selective; 2016-2017: 9,172 applied, 6,366 accepted. Either SAT or ACT required. SAT 25/75 percentile: 916-1110. High school rank: 15% in top tenth, 40% in top quarter, 75% in top half
Early decision deadline: N/A, notification date: N/A
Early action deadline: 11/15, notification date: 12/15
Application deadline (fall): rolling
Undergraduate student body: 3,639 full time, 421 part time; 41% male, 59% female; 0% American Indian, 5% Asian, 12% black, 14% Hispanic, 3% multiracial, 0% Pacific Islander, 61% white, 3% international; 77% from in state; 53% live on campus; 5% of students in fraternities, 10% in sororities
Most popular majors: 11% Accounting, 10% Psychology, General, 6% Finance, General, 5% Business Administration and Management, General, 5% Elementary Education and Teaching
Expenses: 2017-2018: $41,310; room/board: $14,700
Financial aid: (609) 896-5360; 74% of undergrads determined to have financial need; average aid package $28,684

Rowan University
Glassboro NJ
(856) 256-4200
U.S. News ranking: Nat. U., No. 171
Website: www.rowan.edu
Admissions email: admissions@rowan.edu
Public; founded 1923
Freshman admissions: selective; 2016-2017: 13,382 applied, 7,721 accepted. Either SAT or ACT required. SAT 25/75 percentile: 990-1210. High school rank: N/A
Early decision deadline: N/A, notification date: N/A
Early action deadline: N/A, notification date: N/A
Application deadline (fall): 3/1
Undergraduate student body: 12,731 full time, 1,613 part time; 54% male, 46% female; 0% American Indian, 5% Asian, 10% black, 10% Hispanic, 3% multiracial, 0% Pacific Islander, 67% white, 1% international; 95% from in state; 38% live on campus; 10% of students in fraternities, 8% in sororities
Most popular majors: 16% Business, Management, Marketing, and Related Support Services, 12% Biological and Biomedical Sciences, 12%

Rutgers University–New Brunswick
Piscataway NJ
(732) 932-4636
U.S. News ranking: Nat. U., No. 69
Website: www.rutgers.edu
Admissions email: admissions@ugadm.rutgers.edu
Public; founded 1766
Freshman admissions: more selective; 2016-2017: 36,677 applied, 20,884 accepted. Either SAT or ACT required. SAT 25/75 percentile: 1110-1350. High school rank: 41% in top tenth, 78% in top quarter, 97% in top half
Early decision deadline: N/A, notification date: N/A
Early action deadline: 11/1, notification date: 1/13
Application deadline (fall): 12/1
Undergraduate student body: 34,020 full time, 2,148 part time; 50% male, 50% female; 0% American Indian, 26% Asian, 8% black, 13% Hispanic,

---

Financial aid: (201) 684-7549; 55% of undergrads determined to have financial need; average aid package $11,031

Education, 9% Communication, Journalism, and Related Programs, 9% Psychology
Expenses: 2017-2018: $13,108 in state, $21,378 out of state; room/board: $11,948
Financial aid: (856) 256-4281; 65% of undergrads determined to have financial need; average aid package $10,011

Rutgers University–Camden
Camden NJ
(856) 225-6104
U.S. News ranking: Reg. U. (N), No. 25
Website: www.rutgers.edu/
Admissions email: camden@ugadm.rutgers.edu
Public; founded 1927
Freshman admissions: selective; 2016-2017: 8,725 applied, 5,016 accepted. Either SAT or ACT required. SAT 25/75 percentile: 890-1120. High school rank: 14% in top tenth, 44% in top quarter, 81% in top half
Early decision deadline: N/A, notification date: N/A
Early action deadline: N/A, notification date: N/A
Application deadline (fall): rolling
Undergraduate student body: 4,056 full time, 965 part time; 41% male, 59% female; 0% American Indian, 9% Asian, 17% black, 14% Hispanic, 4% multiracial, 0% Pacific Islander, 53% white, 1% international; 98% from in state; 13% live on campus; N/A of students in fraternities, N/A in sororities
Most popular majors: 18% Registered Nursing/Registered Nurse, 12% Psychology, General, 10% Business Administration and Management, General, 7% Accounting, 7% Criminal Justice/Safety Studies
Expenses: 2016-2017: $14,238 in state, $29,881 out of state; room/board: $11,900
Financial aid: (848) 932-7057; 88% of undergrads determined to have financial need; average aid package $12,810

3% multiracial, 0% Pacific Islander, 40% white, 8% international; 94% from in state; 44% live on campus; N/A of students in fraternities, N/A in sororities
Most popular majors: 7% Psychology, General, 5% Biology/Biological Sciences, General, 5% Kinesiology and Exercise Science, 5% Speech Communication and Rhetoric, 4% Public Health, General
Expenses: 2016-2017: $14,372 in state, $30,023 out of state; room/board: $12,260
Financial aid: (848) 932-7057; 53% of undergrads determined to have financial need; average aid package $13,796

Rutgers University–Newark
Newark NJ
(973) 353-5205
U.S. News ranking: Nat. U., No. 133
Website: www.newark.rutgers.edu/
Admissions email: admissions@ugadm.rutgers.edu
Public; founded 1908
Freshman admissions: selective; 2016-2017: 13,085 applied, 8,546 accepted. Either SAT or ACT required. SAT 25/75 percentile: 910-1100. High school rank: 20% in top tenth, 50% in top quarter, 85% in top half
Early decision deadline: N/A, notification date: N/A
Early action deadline: N/A, notification date: N/A
Application deadline (fall): rolling
Undergraduate student body: 6,680 full time, 1,490 part time; 46% male, 54% female; 0% American Indian, 20% Asian, 19% black, 28% Hispanic, 3% multiracial, 0% Pacific Islander, 24% white, 5% international; 98% from in state; 21% live on campus; N/A of students in fraternities, N/A in sororities
Most popular majors: 15% Accounting, 13% Psychology, General, 12% Criminal Justice/Safety Studies, 7% Biology/Biological Sciences, General, 7% Finance, General
Expenses: 2016-2017: $13,829 in state, $29,480 out of state; room/board: $13,059
Financial aid: (848) 932-7507; 78% of undergrads determined to have financial need; average aid package $14,141

Saint Peter's University
Jersey City NJ
(201) 761-7100
U.S. News ranking: Reg. U. (N), No. 97
Website: www.saintpeters.edu
Admissions email: admissions@saintpeters.edu
Private; founded 1872
Affiliation: Roman Catholic
Freshman admissions: less selective; 2016-2017: 4,611 applied, 3,425 accepted. Neither SAT nor ACT required. SAT 25/75 percentile: 830-1030. High school rank: 18% in top tenth, 46% in top quarter, 75% in top half
Early decision deadline: N/A, notification date: N/A

Early action deadline: 12/15, notification date: 1/30
Application deadline (fall): rolling
Undergraduate student body: 2,385 full time, 287 part time; 36% male, 64% female; 0% American Indian, 7% Asian, 23% black, 41% Hispanic, 2% multiracial, 1% Pacific Islander, 16% white, 2% international; 90% from in state; 30% live on campus; N/A of students in fraternities, N/A in sororities
Most popular majors: 22% Business, Management, Marketing, and Related Support Services, 15% Health Professions and Related Programs, 14% Biological and Biomedical Sciences, 8% Homeland Security, Law Enforcement, Firefighting and Related Protective Services, 7% Social Sciences
Expenses: 2017-2018: $36,402; room/board: $15,334
Financial aid: (201) 761-6071; 91% of undergrads determined to have financial need; average aid package $31,003

Seton Hall University

South Orange NJ
(800) 843-4255
U.S. News ranking: Nat. U., No. 124
Website: www.shu.edu
Admissions email: thehall@shu.edu
Private; founded 1856
Affiliation: Roman Catholic
Freshman admissions: more selective; 2016-2017: 15,427 applied, 10,321 accepted. Either SAT or ACT required. SAT 25/75 percentile: 1070-1250. High school rank: 34% in top tenth, 59% in top quarter, 89% in top half
Early decision deadline: N/A, notification date: N/A
Early action deadline: 11/15, notification date: 12/30
Application deadline (fall): rolling
Undergraduate student body: 5,494 full time, 462 part time; 45% male, 55% female; 0% American Indian, 10% Asian, 10% black, 18% Hispanic, 3% multiracial, 0% Pacific Islander, 50% white, 3% international
Most popular majors: 15% Registered Nursing/Registered Nurse, 9% Biology/Biological Sciences, General, 9% Humanities/Humanistic Studies, 6% Finance, General, 5% International Relations and Affairs
Expenses: 2017-2018: $40,588; room/board: $15,174
Financial aid: (973) 761-9350

Stevens Institute of Technology

Hoboken NJ
(201) 216-5194
U.S. News ranking: Nat. U., No. 69
Website: www.stevens.edu
Admissions email: admissions@stevens.edu
Private; founded 1870
Freshman admissions: most selective; 2016-2017: 7,409 applied, 2,898 accepted. Neither SAT nor ACT required. SAT 25/75 percentile: 1260-1440. High school rank: 65% in top tenth, 91% in top quarter, 100% in top half

Early decision deadline: 11/15, notification date: 12/15
Early action deadline: N/A, notification date: N/A
Application deadline (fall): 2/1
Undergraduate student body: 2,853 full time, 168 part time; 70% male, 30% female; 0% American Indian, 11% Asian, 2% black, 10% Hispanic, 0% multiracial, 0% Pacific Islander, 66% white, 5% international; 62% from in state; 68% live on campus; 46% of students in fraternities, 34% in sororities
Most popular majors: 27% Mechanical Engineering, 12% Business Administration and Management, General, 10% Civil Engineering, General, 9% Electrical and Electronics Engineering, 8% Chemical Engineering
Expenses: 2017-2018: $50,554; room/board: $14,400
Financial aid: (201) 216-8142; 64% of undergrads determined to have financial need; average aid package $29,204

Stockton University

Galloway NJ
(609) 652-4261
U.S. News ranking: Reg. U. (N), No. 41
Website: www.stockton.edu
Admissions email: admissions@stockton.edu
Public; founded 1969
Affiliation: Other
Freshman admissions: selective; 2016-2017: 4,826 applied, 3,713 accepted. Either SAT or ACT required. SAT 25/75 percentile: 960-1160. High school rank: 21% in top tenth, 52% in top quarter, 90% in top half
Early decision deadline: N/A, notification date: N/A
Early action deadline: N/A, notification date: N/A
Application deadline (fall): 5/1
Undergraduate student body: 7,416 full time, 438 part time; 41% male, 59% female; 0% American Indian, 6% Asian, 7% black, 12% Hispanic, 2% multiracial, 0% Pacific Islander, 70% white, 0% international; 99% from in state; 37% live on campus; 8% of students in fraternities, 8% in sororities
Most popular majors: 16% Business Administration and Management, General, 15% Health Professions and Related Programs, 10% Psychology, General, 9% Criminology, 7% Biology/Biological Sciences, General
Expenses: 2017-2018: $13,402 in state, $20,356 out of state; room/board: $12,120
Financial aid: (609) 652-4203; 71% of undergrads determined to have financial need; average aid package $16,344

Thomas Edison State University

Trenton NJ
(888) 442-8372
U.S. News ranking: Reg. U. (N), unranked
Website: www.tesu.edu
Admissions email: admissions@tesu.edu

Public; founded 1972
Freshman admissions: least selective; 2016-2017: N/A applied, N/A accepted. Neither SAT nor ACT required. SAT 25/75 percentile: N/A. High school rank: N/A
Early decision deadline: N/A, notification date: N/A
Early action deadline: N/A, notification date: N/A
Application deadline (fall): rolling
Undergraduate student body: 91 full time, 16,415 part time; 56% male, 44% female; 1% American Indian, 4% Asian, 15% black, 9% Hispanic, 2% multiracial, 1% Pacific Islander, 51% white, 1% international
Most popular majors: Information not available
Expenses: 2017-2018: $7,300 in state, $9,820 out of state; room/board: N/A
Financial aid: (609) 633-9658

William Paterson University of New Jersey

Wayne NJ
(973) 720-2125
U.S. News ranking: Reg. U. (N), No. 102
Website: www.wpunj.edu/
Admissions email: admissions@wpunj.edu
Public; founded 1855
Freshman admissions: less selective; 2016-2017: 10,791 applied, 8,162 accepted. Either SAT or ACT required. SAT 25/75 percentile: 890-1080. High school rank: N/A
Early decision deadline: N/A, notification date: N/A
Early action deadline: N/A, notification date: N/A
Application deadline (fall): 6/1
Undergraduate student body: 7,499 full time, 1,604 part time; 46% male, 54% female; 0% American Indian, 7% Asian, 17% black, 29% Hispanic, 3% multiracial, 0% Pacific Islander, 41% white, 1% international; 98% from in state; 24% live on campus; 2% of students in fraternities, 2% in sororities
Most popular majors: 21% Business, Management, Marketing, and Related Support Services, 11% Psychology, 10% Education, 9% Communication, Journalism, and Related Programs, 8% Social Sciences
Expenses: 2017-2018: $12,804 in state, $20,842 out of state; room/board: $11,218
Financial aid: (973) 720-3121; 74% of undergrads determined to have financial need; average aid package $10,524

NEW MEXICO

Eastern New Mexico University[1]

Portales NM
(505) 562-2178
U.S. News ranking: Reg. U. (W), second tier
Website: www.enmu.edu
Admissions email: admissions.office@enmu.edu
Public

Application deadline (fall): N/A
Undergraduate student body: N/A full time, N/A part time
Expenses: 2016-2017: $5,618 in state, $11,393 out of state; room/board: $6,910
Financial aid: N/A

New Mexico Highlands University

Las Vegas NM
(505) 454-3439
U.S. News ranking: Reg. U. (W), second tier
Website: www.nmhu.edu
Admissions email: admissions@nmhu.edu
Public; founded 1893
Freshman admissions: least selective; 2016-2017: 1,158 applied, 1,158 accepted. Neither SAT nor ACT required. ACT 25/75 percentile: 15-20. High school rank: 4% in top tenth, 17% in top quarter, 58% in top half
Early decision deadline: N/A, notification date: N/A
Early action deadline: N/A, notification date: N/A
Application deadline (fall): rolling
Undergraduate student body: 1,442 full time, 739 part time; 37% male, 63% female; 9% American Indian, 1% Asian, 5% black, 58% Hispanic, 2% multiracial, 1% Pacific Islander, 20% white, 5% international
Most popular majors: Information not available
Expenses: 2016-2017: $5,550 in state, $8,650 out of state; room/board: $7,235
Financial aid: (505) 454-3430; 77% of undergrads determined to have financial need; average aid package $1,811

New Mexico Institute of Mining and Technology

Socorro NM
(575) 835-5424
U.S. News ranking: Reg. U. (W), No. 23
Website: www.nmt.edu
Admissions email: Admission@nmt.edu
Public; founded 1889
Freshman admissions: more selective; 2016-2017: 1,663 applied, 390 accepted. Either SAT or ACT required. ACT 25/75 percentile: 23-29. High school rank: 35% in top tenth, 64% in top quarter, 86% in top half
Early decision deadline: N/A, notification date: N/A
Early action deadline: N/A, notification date: N/A
Application deadline (fall): 8/1
Undergraduate student body: 1,388 full time, 181 part time; 70% male, 30% female; 3% American Indian, 3% Asian, 2% black, 31% Hispanic, 5% multiracial, 0% Pacific Islander, 51% white, 3% international; 87% from in state; 45% live on campus; 0% of students in fraternities, 0% in sororities
Most popular majors: 26% Mechanical Engineering, 12% Petroleum Engineering, 10% Biology/Biological Sciences, General, 8% Chemical

Engineering, 6% Computer and Information Sciences, General
Expenses: 2017-2018: $7,183 in state, $20,991 out of state; room/board: $8,202
Financial aid: (575) 835-5333; 57% of undergrads determined to have financial need; average aid package $13,264

New Mexico State University

Las Cruces NM
(575) 646-3121
U.S. News ranking: Nat. U., No. 198
Website: www.nmsu.edu
Admissions email: admissions@nmsu.edu
Public; founded 1888
Freshman admissions: selective; 2016-2017: 7,618 applied, 4,541 accepted. Either SAT or ACT required. ACT 25/75 percentile: 18-24. High school rank: 22% in top tenth, 51% in top quarter, 83% in top half
Early decision deadline: N/A, notification date: N/A
Early action deadline: N/A, notification date: N/A
Application deadline (fall): rolling
Undergraduate student body: 9,874 full time, 2,153 part time; 46% male, 54% female; 2% American Indian, 1% Asian, 3% black, 56% Hispanic, 2% multiracial, 0% Pacific Islander, 28% white, 5% international; 75% from in state; 18% live on campus; 2% of students in fraternities, 2% in sororities
Most popular majors: 8% Criminal Justice/Safety Studies, 6% Liberal Arts and Sciences/Liberal Studies, 5% Registered Nursing/Registered Nurse, 4% Administrative Assistant and Secretarial Science, General, 4% Psychology, General
Expenses: 2017-2018: $7,122 in state, $22,701 out of state; room/board: $8,686
Financial aid: (575) 646-4105; 65% of undergrads determined to have financial need; average aid package $12,762

Northern New Mexico University[1]

Espanola NM
U.S. News ranking: Reg. Coll. (W), unranked
Website: www.nnmc.edu
Admissions email: N/A
Public
Application deadline (fall): N/A
Undergraduate student body: N/A full time, N/A part time
Expenses: 2016-2017: $2,280 in state, $6,516 out of state; room/board: N/A
Financial aid: N/A

Santa Fe University of Art and Design[1]

Santa Fe NM
(505) 473-6937
U.S. News ranking: Arts, unranked
Website: www.santafeuniversity.edu
Admissions email: admissions@santafeuniversity.edu
For-profit; founded 1859

Application deadline (fall): rolling
Undergraduate student body: N/A full time, N/A part time
Expenses: 2016-2017: $32,346; room/board: $8,946
Financial aid: (505) 473-6454

St. John's College
Santa Fe NM
(505) 984-6060
U.S. News ranking: Nat. Lib. Arts, No. 76
Website: www.sjc.edu/admissions-and-aid
Admissions email: santafe.admissions@sjc.edu
Private; founded 1696
Freshman admissions: more selective; 2016-2017: 298 applied, 187 accepted. Neither SAT nor ACT required. SAT 25/75 percentile: 1210-1490. High school rank: 52% in top tenth, 67% in top quarter, 90% in top half
Early decision deadline: N/A, notification date: N/A
Early action deadline: 1/15, notification date: 2/15
Application deadline (fall): rolling
Undergraduate student body: 320 full time, 6 part time; 56% male, 44% female; 0% American Indian, 3% Asian, 1% black, 9% Hispanic, 3% multiracial, 0% Pacific Islander, 57% white, 25% international; 11% from in state, 83% live on campus, N/A of students in fraternities, N/A in sororities
Most popular majors: 100% Liberal Arts and Sciences/Liberal Studies
Expenses: 2017-2018: $52,320; room/board: $11,486
Financial aid: (505) 984-6058; 88% of undergrads determined to have financial need; average aid package $40,988

University of New Mexico
Albuquerque NM
(505) 277-8900
U.S. News ranking: Nat. U., No. 192
Website: www.unm.edu
Admissions email: apply@unm.edu
Public; founded 1889
Freshman admissions: selective; 2016-2017: 15,266 applied, 7,150 accepted. Either SAT or ACT required. ACT 25/75 percentile: 19-25. High school rank: N/A
Early decision deadline: N/A, notification date: N/A
Early action deadline: N/A, notification date: N/A
Application deadline (fall): rolling
Undergraduate student body: 15,892 full time, 4,323 part time; 44% male, 56% female; 6% American Indian, 4% Asian, 2% black, 47% Hispanic, 3% multiracial, 0% Pacific Islander, 34% white, 2% international; 93% from in state; 6% live on campus; 5% of students in fraternities, 6% in sororities
Most popular majors: 14% Business, Management, Marketing, and Related Support Services, 12% Psychology, 9% Health Professions and Related Programs, 8% Biological and Biomedical Sciences, 8% Education

Expenses: 2017-2018: $7,150 in state, $22,412 out of state; room/board: $9,662
Financial aid: (505) 277-8900; 76% of undergrads determined to have financial need

University of the Southwest[1]
Hobbs NM
(575) 392-6563
U.S. News ranking: Reg. U. (W), second tier
Website: www.usw.edu
Admissions email: admissions@usw.edu
Private; founded 1962
Application deadline (fall): rolling
Undergraduate student body: N/A full time, N/A part time
Expenses: 2016-2017: $15,456; room/board: $7,310
Financial aid: N/A

Western New Mexico University[1]
Silver City NM
U.S. News ranking: Reg. U. (W), unranked
Website: www.wnmu.edu
Admissions email: admissions@wnmu.edu
Public; founded 1893
Application deadline (fall): N/A
Undergraduate student body: N/A full time, N/A part time
Expenses: 2016-2017: $5,906 in state, $13,806 out of state; room/board: $8,936
Financial aid: N/A

NEW YORK

Adelphi University
Garden City NY
(800) 233-5744
U.S. News ranking: Nat. U., No. 151
Website: www.adelphi.edu
Admissions email: admissions@adelphi.edu
Private; founded 1896
Freshman admissions: selective; 2016-2017: 11,863 applied, 8,339 accepted. Neither SAT nor ACT required. SAT 25/75 percentile: 1010-1210. High school rank: 31% in top tenth, 64% in top quarter, 89% in top half
Early decision deadline: N/A, notification date: N/A
Early action deadline: 12/1, notification date: 12/31
Application deadline (fall): rolling
Undergraduate student body: 4,742 full time, 463 part time; 31% male, 69% female; 0% American Indian, 10% Asian, 10% black, 16% Hispanic, 2% multiracial, 0% Pacific Islander, 52% white, 3% International; 93% from in state; 23% live on campus; 9% of students in fraternities, 8% in sororities
Most popular majors: 29% Registered Nursing/Registered Nurse, 6% Business Administration and Management, General, 6% Psychology, General, 5% Biology/Biological Sciences, General, 5% Social Sciences, General

Expenses: 2017-2018: $37,170; room/board: $15,120
Financial aid: (516) 877-3365; 68% of undergrads determined to have financial need; average aid package $21,500

Alfred University
Alfred NY
(800) 541-9229
U.S. News ranking: Reg. U. (N), No. 48
Website: www.alfred.edu
Admissions email: admissions@alfred.edu
Private; founded 1836
Freshman admissions: selective; 2016-2017: 3,897 applied, 2,447 accepted. Either SAT or ACT required. SAT 25/75 percentile: 910-1140. High school rank: 12% in top tenth, 41% in top quarter, 71% in top half
Early decision deadline: 12/1, notification date: 12/15
Early action deadline: N/A, notification date: N/A
Application deadline (fall): rolling
Undergraduate student body: 1,719 full time, 96 part time; 52% male, 48% female; 0% American Indian, 2% Asian, 10% black, 8% Hispanic, 3% multiracial, 0% Pacific Islander, 66% white, 2% international; 76% from in state, 75% live on campus, 0% of students in fraternities, 0% in sororities
Most popular majors: 22% Ceramic Arts and Ceramics, 11% Psychology, General, 6% Business Administration and Management, General, 6% Mechanical Engineering, 4% Biology/Biological Sciences, General
Expenses: 2017-2018: $32,264; room/board: $12,272
Financial aid: (607) 871-2150; 81% of undergrads determined to have financial need; average aid package $26,882

Bard College
Annandale on Hudson NY
(845) 758-7472
U.S. News ranking: Nat. Lib. Arts, No. 46
Website: www.bard.edu
Admissions email: admission@bard.edu
Private; founded 1860
Freshman admissions: more selective; 2016-2017: 5,181 applied, 2,912 accepted. Neither SAT nor ACT required. SAT 25/75 percentile: 1140-1370. High school rank: 43% in top tenth, 83% in top quarter, 94% in top half
Early decision deadline: 11/1, notification date: N/A
Early action deadline: 11/1, notification date: 1/1
Application deadline (fall): 1/1
Undergraduate student body: 1,917 full time, 78 part time; 42% male, 58% female; 1% American Indian, 6% Asian, 6% black, 3% Hispanic, 0% multiracial, 0% Pacific Islander, 61% white, 10% international; 34% from in state; 75% live on campus; 0% of students in fraternities, 0% in sororities

Most popular majors: 35% Visual and Performing Arts, 25% Social Sciences, 21% English Language and Literature/Letters, 18% Multi/Interdisciplinary Studies, 1% Business, Management, Marketing, and Related Support Services
Expenses: 2017-2018: $52,906; room/board: $15,066
Financial aid: (845) 758-7526; 68% of undergrads determined to have financial need; average aid package $44,760

Barnard College
New York NY
(212) 854-2014
U.S. News ranking: Nat. Lib. Arts, No. 26
Website: www.barnard.edu
Admissions email: admissions@barnard.edu
Private; founded 1889
Freshman admissions: most selective; 2016-2017: 7,071 applied, 1,184 accepted. Either SAT or ACT required. SAT 25/75 percentile: 1270-1470. High school rank: 81% in top tenth, 96% in top quarter, 100% in top half
Early decision deadline: 11/1, notification date: 12/15
Early action deadline: N/A, notification date: N/A
Application deadline (fall): 1/1
Undergraduate student body: 2,529 full time, 49 part time; 0% male, 100% female; 0% American Indian, 14% Asian, 6% black, 12% Hispanic, 6% multiracial, 0% Pacific Islander, 52% white, 8% international; 26% from in state; 91% live on campus; N/A of students in fraternities, N/A in sororities
Most popular majors: 27% Social Sciences, 12% Psychology, 11% Biological and Biomedical Sciences, 11% Visual and Performing Arts, 9% English Language and Literature/Letters
Expenses: 2017-2018: $52,662; room/board: $16,100
Financial aid: (212) 854-2154; 40% of undergrads determined to have financial need; average aid package $49,012

Berkeley College
New York NY
(800) 446-5400
U.S. News ranking: Business, unranked
Website: www.berkeleycollege.edu
Admissions email: admissions@berkeleycollege.edu
For-profit; founded 1931
Freshman admissions: least selective; 2016-2017: N/A applied, N/A accepted. Neither SAT nor ACT required. SAT 25/75 percentile: N/A. High school rank: N/A
Early decision deadline: N/A, notification date: N/A
Early action deadline: N/A, notification date: N/A
Application deadline (fall): 8/28
Undergraduate student body: 3,421 full time, 855 part time; 35% male, 65% female; 1% American Indian, 2% Asian, 25% black, 22% Hispanic, 0% multiracial, 0% Pacific Islander, 7% white,

12% international; 89% from in state; 2% live on campus; N/A of students in fraternities, N/A in sororities
Most popular majors: 27% Business Administration and Management, General, 16% Criminal Justice/Law Enforcement Administration, 15% Fashion Merchandising, 13% Health/Health Care Administration/Management, 9% International Business/Trade/Commerce
Expenses: 2017-2018: $25,300; room/board: $9,000
Financial aid: (212) 986-4343

Binghamton University–SUNY
Binghamton NY
(607) 777-2171
U.S. News ranking: Nat. U., No. 87
Website: www.binghamton.edu
Admissions email: admit@binghamton.edu
Public; founded 1946
Freshman admissions: more selective; 2016-2017: 32,139 applied, 13,056 accepted. Either SAT or ACT required. SAT 25/75 percentile: 1230-1400. High school rank: N/A
Early decision deadline: N/A, notification date: N/A
Early action deadline: 11/1, notification date: 1/15
Application deadline (fall): rolling
Undergraduate student body: 13,185 full time, 447 part time; 51% male, 49% female; 0% American Indian, 14% Asian, 5% black, 11% Hispanic, 2% multiracial, 0% Pacific Islander, 57% white, 9% international; 93% from in state; 52% live on campus; 14% of students in fraternities, 11% in sororities
Most popular majors: 16% Business Administration and Management, General, 12% Biology/Biological Sciences, General, 10% Engineering, General, 10% Psychology, General, 6% English Language and Literature, General
Expenses: 2017-2018: $9,523 in state, $24,403 out of state; room/board: $14,577
Financial aid: (607) 777-6358; 48% of undergrads determined to have financial need; average aid package $12,986

Boricua College
New York NY
(212) 694-1000
U.S. News ranking: Reg. Coll. (N), unranked
Website: www.boricuacollege.edu/
Admissions email: isanchez@boricuacollege.edu
Private; founded 1973
Freshman admissions: least selective; 2016-2017: 260 applied, 196 accepted. Neither SAT nor ACT required. SAT 25/75 percentile: N/A. High school rank: N/A
Early decision deadline: N/A, notification date: N/A
Early action deadline: N/A, notification date: N/A
Application deadline (fall): rolling

Undergraduate student body: 899 full time, 0 part time; 23% male, 77% female; N/A American Indian, N/A Asian, N/A black, N/A Hispanic, N/A multiracial, N/A Pacific Islander, N/A white, N/A international
Most popular majors: Business Administration and Management, General, Community Organization and Advocacy, Multicultural Education
Expenses: 2016-2017: $10,625; room/board: $5,750
Financial aid: N/A

CUNY–Baruch College
New York NY
(646) 312-1400
U.S. News ranking: Reg. U. (N), No. 20
Website: www.baruch.cuny.edu
Admissions email: admissions@baruch.cuny.edu
Public; founded 1919
Freshman admissions: more selective; 2016-2017: 20,789 applied, 6,377 accepted. Either SAT or ACT required. SAT 25/75 percentile: 1090-1310. High school rank: 47% in top tenth, 76% in top quarter, 93% in top half
Early decision deadline: 12/13, notification date: 1/7
Early action deadline: N/A, notification date: N/A
Application deadline (fall): 2/1
Undergraduate student body: 11,288 full time, 3,922 part time; 51% male, 49% female; 0% American Indian, 32% Asian, 9% black, 25% Hispanic, 1% multiracial, 0% Pacific Islander, 21% white, 11% international; 97% from in state; 2% live on campus; 0% of students in fraternities; 0% in sororities
Most popular majors: 23% Finance, General, 18% Accounting, 11% Sales, Distribution, and Marketing Operations, General, 10% Business/Corporate Communications, 6% Business Administration and Management, General
Expenses: 2017-2018: $7,551 in state, $18,021 out of state; room/board: $14,594
Financial aid: (646) 312-1399; 75% of undergrads determined to have financial need; average aid package $5,572

CUNY–Brooklyn College
Brooklyn NY
(718) 951-5001
U.S. News ranking: Reg. U. (N), No. 86
Website: www.brooklyn.cuny.edu
Admissions email: adminqry@brooklyn.cuny.edu
Public; founded 1930
Freshman admissions: selective; 2016-2017: 20,608 applied, 7,726 accepted. Either SAT or ACT required. SAT 25/75 percentile: 970-1180. High school rank: N/A
Early decision deadline: N/A, notification date: N/A
Early action deadline: N/A, notification date: N/A
Application deadline (fall): 2/1

Undergraduate student body: 10,198 full time, 4,208 part time; 41% male, 59% female; 0% American Indian, 19% Asian, 21% black, 23% Hispanic, 2% multiracial, 0% Pacific Islander, 31% white, 3% international; 98% from in state; 0% live on campus; 3% of students in fraternities, 3% in sororities
Most popular majors: 20% Business Administration and Management, General, 16% Psychology, General, 11% Accounting, 4% Biology/Biological Sciences, General, 4% Early Childhood Education and Teaching
Expenses: 2017-2018: $6,840 in state, $17,310 out of state; room/board: N/A
Financial aid: (718) 951-5051; 81% of undergrads determined to have financial need; average aid package $5,306

CUNY–City College
New York NY
(212) 650-6977
U.S. News ranking: Reg. U. (N), No. 56
Website: www.ccny.cuny.edu
Admissions email: admissions@ccny.cuny.edu
Public; founded 1847
Freshman admissions: selective; 2016-2017: 23,285 applied, 8,817 accepted. SAT required. SAT 25/75 percentile: 1035-1220. High school rank: N/A
Early decision deadline: N/A, notification date: N/A
Early action deadline: N/A, notification date: N/A
Application deadline (fall): 1/15
Undergraduate student body: 10,070 full time, 3,441 part time; 50% male, 50% female; 0% American Indian, 25% Asian, 16% black, 36% Hispanic, 2% multiracial, 0% Pacific Islander, 14% white, 6% international; 99% from in state; N/A live on campus; N/A of students in fraternities, N/A in sororities
Most popular majors: 15% Engineering, 12% Social Sciences, 10% Education, 10% Visual and Performing Arts, 6% English Language and Literature/Letters
Expenses: 2017-2018: $6,689 in state, $13,799 out of state; room/board: N/A
Financial aid: (212) 650-5824; 80% of undergrads determined to have financial need; average aid package $9,597

CUNY–College of Staten Island
Staten Island NY
(718) 982-2010
U.S. News ranking: Reg. U. (N), second tier
Website: www.csi.cuny.edu
Admissions email: admissions@csi.cuny.edu
Public; founded 1976
Freshman admissions: less selective; 2016-2017: 14,018 applied, 14,018 accepted. Either SAT or ACT required. SAT 25/75 percentile: 900-1100. High school rank: N/A
Early decision deadline: N/A, notification date: N/A

Early action deadline: N/A, notification date: N/A
Application deadline (fall): rolling
Undergraduate student body: 9,627 full time, 2,790 part time; 44% male, 56% female; 0% American Indian, 13% Asian, 16% black, 18% Hispanic, 0% multiracial, 0% Pacific Islander, 50% white, 3% international; 99% from in state; 3% live on campus; 0% of students in fraternities, 0% in sororities
Most popular majors: 19% Business, Management, Marketing, and Related Support Services, 19% Psychology, 11% Health Professions and Related Programs, 11% Social Sciences, 7% Education
Expenses: 2017-2018: $7,089 in state, $17,959 out of state; room/board: N/A
Financial aid: (718) 982-2030; 72% of undergrads determined to have financial need; average aid package $8,225

CUNY–Hunter College
New York NY
(212) 772-4490
U.S. News ranking: Reg. U. (N), No. 28
Website: www.hunter.cuny.edu
Admissions email: admissions@hunter.cuny.edu
Public; founded 1870
Freshman admissions: more selective; 2016-2017: 28,510 applied, 10,801 accepted. Either SAT or ACT required. SAT 25/75 percentile: 1060-1250. High school rank: N/A
Early decision deadline: N/A, notification date: N/A
Early action deadline: N/A, notification date: N/A
Application deadline (fall): 3/15
Undergraduate student body: 12,223 full time, 4,500 part time; 36% male, 64% female; 0% American Indian, 29% Asian, 12% black, 21% Hispanic, 0% multiracial, 0% Pacific Islander, 32% white, 6% international
Most popular majors: Information not available
Expenses: 2017-2018: $6,780 in state, $17,250 out of state; room/board: $10,573
Financial aid: (212) 772-4820; 72% of undergrads determined to have financial need; average aid package $8,137

CUNY–John Jay College of Criminal Justice
New York NY
(212) 237-8866
U.S. News ranking: Reg. U. (N), No. 111
Website: www.jjay.cuny.edu/
Admissions email: admissions@jjay.cuny.edu
Public; founded 1965
Freshman admissions: selective; 2016-2017: 13,899 applied, 4,692 accepted. Either SAT or ACT required. SAT 25/75 percentile: 860-1060. High school rank: N/A
Early decision deadline: N/A, notification date: N/A
Early action deadline: N/A, notification date: N/A

Application deadline (fall): rolling
Undergraduate student body: 9,831 full time, 2,843 part time; 44% male, 56% female; 0% American Indian, 11% Asian, 17% black, 50% Hispanic, 2% multiracial, 0% Pacific Islander, 17% white, 3% international; 96% from in state; N/A live on campus; N/A of students in fraternities, N/A in sororities
Most popular majors: 55% Criminal Justice/Law Enforcement Administration, 17% Forensic Psychology, 15% Social Sciences, 3% Legal Professions and Studies, 3% Public Administration
Expenses: 2017-2018: $7,070 in state, $17,940 out of state; room/board: N/A
Financial aid: (212) 237-8897; 77% of undergrads determined to have financial need; average aid package $8,589

CUNY–Lehman College
Bronx NY
(718) 960-8131
U.S. News ranking: Reg. U. (N), No. 137
Website: www.lehman.cuny.edu
Admissions email: undergraduate.admissions@lehman.cuny.edu
Public; founded 1968
Freshman admissions: less selective; 2016-2017: 14,318 applied, 4,651 accepted. Either SAT or ACT required. SAT 25/75 percentile: 860-1040. High school rank: N/A
Early decision deadline: N/A, notification date: N/A
Early action deadline: N/A, notification date: N/A
Application deadline (fall): 10/1
Undergraduate student body: 6,598 full time, 4,680 part time; 33% male, 67% female; 0% American Indian, 7% Asian, 30% black, 53% Hispanic, 0% multiracial, 0% Pacific Islander, 7% white, 3% international; 100% from in state; N/A live on campus; N/A of students in fraternities, N/A in sororities
Most popular majors: 20% Business, Management, Marketing, and Related Support Services, 19% Health Professions and Related Programs, 16% Social Sciences, 10% Psychology, 7% Public Administration and Social Service Professions
Expenses: 2017-2018: $6,230 in state, $13,040 out of state; room/board: N/A
Financial aid: (718) 960-8545; 84% of undergrads determined to have financial need; average aid package $4,640

CUNY–Medgar Evers College
Brooklyn NY
(718) 270-6024
U.S. News ranking: Reg. Coll. (N), second tier
Website: www.mec.cuny.edu
Admissions email: enroll@mec.cuny.edu
Public; founded 1969
Freshman admissions: least selective; 2016-2017: 10,105 applied, 9,864 accepted. Neither

SAT nor ACT required. SAT 25/75 percentile: 710-870. High school rank: N/A
Early decision deadline: N/A, notification date: N/A
Early action deadline: N/A, notification date: N/A
Application deadline (fall): rolling
Undergraduate student body: 4,760 full time, 2,059 part time; 28% male, 72% female; 0% American Indian, 2% Asian, 64% black, 14% Hispanic, 0% multiracial, 0% Pacific Islander, 1% white, 1% international
Most popular majors: Information not available
Expenses: 2016-2017: $6,756 in state, $13,866 out of state; room/board: N/A
Financial aid: (718) 270-6038

CUNY–New York City College of Technology
Brooklyn NY
(718) 260-5500
U.S. News ranking: Reg. Coll. (N), No. 36
Website: www.citytech.cuny.edu
Admissions email: admissions@citytech.cuny.edu
Public; founded 1946
Freshman admissions: least selective; 2016-2017: 16,846 applied, 12,554 accepted. Neither SAT nor ACT required. SAT 25/75 percentile: 740-940. High school rank: N/A
Early decision deadline: N/A, notification date: N/A
Early action deadline: N/A, notification date: N/A
Application deadline (fall): 2/1
Undergraduate student body: 10,912 full time, 6,370 part time; 55% male, 45% female; 0% American Indian, 20% Asian, 28% black, 34% Hispanic, 1% multiracial, 0% Pacific Islander, 11% white, 5% international; 95% from in state; N/A of students in fraternities, N/A in sororities
Most popular majors: 17% Health Professions and Related Programs, 15% Visual and Performing Arts, 14% Computer and Information Sciences and Support Services, 14% Engineering Technologies and Engineering-Related Fields, 13% Business, Management, Marketing, and Related Support Services
Expenses: 2016-2017: $6,669 in state, $13,779 out of state; room/board: N/A
Financial aid: N/A

CUNY–Queens College
Queens NY
(718) 997-5600
U.S. News ranking: Reg. U. (N), No. 41
Website: www.qc.cuny.edu/
Admissions email: admissions@qc.cuny.edu
Public; founded 1937
Freshman admissions: selective; 2016-2017: 18,142 applied, 7,499 accepted. Either SAT or ACT required. SAT 25/75 percentile: 1000-1180. High school rank: N/A

Early decision deadline: N/A, notification date: N/A
Early action deadline: N/A, notification date: N/A
Application deadline (fall): 2/1
Undergraduate student body: 11,693 full time, 4,633 part time; 45% male, 55% female; 0% American Indian, 28% Asian, 9% black, 28% Hispanic, 1% multiracial, 1% Pacific Islander, 27% white, 5% international; 99% from in state; 2% live on campus; 1% of students in fraternities, 1% in sororities
Most popular majors: 18% Psychology, General, 13% Accounting, General, 8% Economics, General, 7% Sociology, 5% Mass Communication/Media Studies
Expenses: 2017-2018: $6,938 in state, $17,408 out of state; room/board: $15,188
Financial aid: (718) 997-5102; 69% of undergrads determined to have financial need; average aid package $6,980

CUNY–York College
Jamaica NY
(718) 262-2165
U.S. News ranking: Reg. Coll. (N), No. 33
Website: www.york.cuny.edu
Admissions email: admissions@york.cuny.edu
Public; founded 1966
Freshman admissions: least selective; 2016-2017: 13,071 applied, 8,363 accepted. Either SAT or ACT required. SAT 25/75 percentile: 770-950. High school rank: N/A
Early decision deadline: N/A, notification date: N/A
Early action deadline: N/A, notification date: N/A
Application deadline (fall): 6/1
Undergraduate student body: 5,066 full time, 3,192 part time; 35% male, 65% female; 1% American Indian, 25% Asian, 41% black, 22% Hispanic, 0% multiracial, 0% Pacific Islander, 7% white, 5% international; 99% from in state; N/A live on campus; N/A of students in fraternities, N/A in sororities
Most popular majors: 22% Health Professions and Related Programs, 19% Psychology, 17% Business, Management, Marketing, and Related Support Services, 8% Public Administration and Social Service Professions, 8% Social Sciences
Expenses: 2017-2018: $6,748 in state, $17,218 out of state; room/board: N/A
Financial aid: (718) 262-2240; 85% of undergrads determined to have financial need; average aid package $7,738

Canisius College
Buffalo NY
(800) 843-1517
U.S. News ranking: Reg. U. (N), No. 22
Website: www.canisius.edu
Admissions email: admissions@canisius.edu
Private; founded 1870
Affiliation: Roman Catholic
Freshman admissions: selective; 2016-2017: 4,620 applied, 3,597 accepted. Either SAT or ACT required. SAT 25/75 percentile: 970-1190. High school rank: 24% in top tenth, 53% in top quarter, 85% in top half
Early decision deadline: N/A, notification date: N/A
Early action deadline: 11/1, notification date: 12/15
Application deadline (fall): rolling
Undergraduate student body: 2,474 full time, 121 part time; 48% male, 52% female; 0% American Indian, 2% Asian, 8% black, 7% Hispanic, 2% multiracial, 0% Pacific Islander, 73% white, 4% international; 90% from in state; 46% live on campus; 1% of students in fraternities, 1% in sororities
Most popular majors: 32% Business, Management, Marketing, and Related Support Services, 14% Biological and Biomedical Sciences, 10% Communication, Journalism, and Related Programs, 9% Psychology, 8% Social Sciences
Expenses: 2017-2018: $36,454; room/board: $13,218
Financial aid: (716) 888-2300; 77% of undergrads determined to have financial need; average aid package $30,597

Cazenovia College
Cazenovia NY
(800) 654-3210
U.S. News ranking: Reg. Coll. (N), No. 12
Website: www.cazenovia.edu
Admissions email: admission@cazenovia.edu
Private; founded 1824
Freshman admissions: less selective; 2016-2017: 1,730 applied, 1,555 accepted. Neither SAT nor ACT required. SAT 25/75 percentile: 843-1090. High school rank: 11% in top tenth, 35% in top quarter, 74% in top half
Early decision deadline: N/A, notification date: N/A
Early action deadline: N/A, notification date: N/A
Application deadline (fall): rolling
Undergraduate student body: 858 full time, 184 part time; 28% male, 72% female; 1% American Indian, 1% Asian, 8% black, 6% Hispanic, 2% multiracial, 0% Pacific Islander, 67% white, 1% international; 88% from in state; 77% live on campus; N/A of students in fraternities, N/A in sororities
Most popular majors: 30% Business, Management, Marketing, and Related Support Services, 25% Visual and Performing Arts, 15% Public Administration and Social Service Professions, 14% Homeland Security, Law Enforcement, Firefighting and Related Protective Services, 4% Psychology
Expenses: 2017-2018: $33,656; room/board: $14,210
Financial aid: (315) 655-7000; 90% of undergrads determined to have financial need; average aid package $33,202

Clarkson University
Potsdam NY
(800) 527-6577
U.S. News ranking: Nat. U., No. 124
Website: www.clarkson.edu
Admissions email: admission@clarkson.edu
Private; founded 1896
Freshman admissions: more selective; 2016-2017: 7,066 applied, 4,820 accepted. Either SAT or ACT required. SAT 25/75 percentile: 1080-1283. High school rank: 38% in top tenth, 74% in top quarter, 95% in top half
Early decision deadline: 12/1, notification date: 1/1
Early action deadline: N/A, notification date: N/A
Application deadline (fall): 1/15
Undergraduate student body: 3,203 full time, 65 part time; 70% male, 30% female; 0% American Indian, 3% Asian, 2% black, 5% Hispanic, 3% multiracial, 0% Pacific Islander, 83% white, 2% international; 73% from in state; 82% live on campus; 13% of students in fraternities, 14% in sororities
Most popular majors: 54% Engineering, General, 22% Business Administration and Management, General, 10% Biology/Biological Sciences, General, 3% Psychology, General, 2% Mathematics, General
Expenses: 2017-2018: $47,950; room/board: $14,794
Financial aid: (315) 268-6413; 80% of undergrads determined to have financial need; average aid package $41,810

Colgate University
Hamilton NY
(315) 228-7401
U.S. News ranking: Nat. Lib. Arts, No. 12
Website: www.colgate.edu
Admissions email: admission@colgate.edu
Private; founded 1819
Freshman admissions: most selective; 2016-2017: 8,394 applied, 2,416 accepted. Either SAT or ACT required. ACT 25/75 percentile: 30-33. High school rank: 72% in top tenth, 93% in top quarter, 99% in top half
Early decision deadline: 11/15, notification date: 12/15
Early action deadline: N/A, notification date: N/A
Application deadline (fall): 1/15
Undergraduate student body: 2,864 full time, 18 part time; 45% male, 55% female; 0% American Indian, 4% Asian, 5% black, 9% Hispanic, 4% multiracial, 0% Pacific Islander, 66% white, 9% international; 27% from in state; 90% live on campus; N/A of students in fraternities, N/A in sororities
Most popular majors: 10% Economics, General, 8% Political Science and Government, General, 6% English Language and Literature, General, 6% International Relations and Affairs, 6% Psychology, General
Expenses: 2017-2018: $53,980; room/board: $13,520

Financial aid: (315) 228-7431; 37% of undergrads determined to have financial need; average aid package $49,912

College at Brockport–SUNY
Brockport NY
(585) 395-2751
U.S. News ranking: Reg. U. (N), No. 64
Website: www.brockport.edu
Admissions email: admit@brockport.edu
Public; founded 1835
Freshman admissions: selective; 2016-2017: 9,211 applied, 5,096 accepted. Either SAT or ACT required. SAT 25/75 percentile: 920-1120. High school rank: 15% in top tenth, 40% in top quarter, 76% in top half
Early decision deadline: N/A, notification date: N/A
Early action deadline: N/A, notification date: N/A
Application deadline (fall): 8/1
Undergraduate student body: 6,375 full time, 753 part time; 44% male, 56% female; 0% American Indian, 2% Asian, 11% black, 7% Hispanic, 2% multiracial, 0% Pacific Islander, 71% white, 1% international; 98% from in state; 27% live on campus; 1% of students in fraternities, 1% in sororities
Most popular majors: 20% Health Professions and Related Programs, 14% Business, Management, Marketing, and Related Support Services, 12% Parks, Recreation, Leisure, and Fitness Studies, 8% Homeland Security, Law Enforcement, Firefighting and Related Protective Services, 7% Psychology
Expenses: 2017-2018: $7,928 in state, $17,778 out of state; room/board: $13,076
Financial aid: (585) 395-2501; 73% of undergrads determined to have financial need; average aid package $10,759

College of Mount St. Vincent
Bronx NY
(718) 405-3267
U.S. News ranking: Reg. U. (N), No. 120
Website: www.mountsaintvincent.edu
Admissions email: admissions.office@mountsaintvincent.edu
Private; founded 1847
Affiliation: Roman Catholic
Freshman admissions: least selective; 2016-2017: 2,667 applied, 2,471 accepted. Either SAT or ACT required. SAT 25/75 percentile: 780-980. High school rank: 8% in top tenth, 28% in top quarter, 62% in top half
Early decision deadline: N/A, notification date: N/A
Early action deadline: 11/15, notification date: 12/15
Application deadline (fall): rolling
Undergraduate student body: 1,589 full time, 113 part time; 30% male, 70% female; 0% American Indian, 9% Asian, 15% black, 40% Hispanic, 4% multiracial, 0% Pacific Islander, 25% white,

2% international; 88% from in state; 57% live on campus; 0% of students in fraternities, 0% in sororities
Most popular majors: 35% Health Professions and Related Programs, 20% Business, Management, Marketing, and Related Support Services, 11% Biological and Biomedical Sciences, 11% Social Sciences, 9% Psychology
Expenses: 2017-2018: $36,540; room/board: $9,500
Financial aid: (718) 405-3338; 77% of undergrads determined to have financial need; average aid package $20,861

College of New Rochelle
New Rochelle NY
(800) 933-5923
U.S. News ranking: Reg. U. (N), second tier
Website: www.cnr.edu
Admissions email: admission@cnr.edu
Private; founded 1904
Freshman admissions: selective; 2016-2017: 2,043 applied, 886 accepted. Either SAT or ACT required. SAT 25/75 percentile: 840-1020. High school rank: 16% in top tenth, 53% in top quarter, 77% in top half
Early decision deadline: N/A, notification date: N/A
Early action deadline: N/A, notification date: N/A
Application deadline (fall): rolling
Undergraduate student body: 935 full time, 273 part time; 13% male, 87% female; 0% American Indian, 7% Asian, 36% black, 28% Hispanic, 1% multiracial, 0% Pacific Islander, 15% white, 1% international
Most popular majors: Information not available
Expenses: 2017-2018: $36,618; room/board: $14,136
Financial aid: (914) 654-5225, 94% of undergrads determined to have financial need; average aid package $24,331

College of Saint Rose
Albany NY
(518) 454-5150
U.S. News ranking: Reg. U. (N), No. 91
Website: www.strose.edu
Admissions email: admit@strose.edu
Private; founded 1920
Freshman admissions: less selective; 2016-2017: 6,780 applied, 5,663 accepted. Neither SAT nor ACT required. SAT 25/75 percentile: 935-1140. High school rank: 9% in top tenth, 30% in top quarter, 70% in top half
Early decision deadline: N/A, notification date: N/A
Early action deadline: 12/1, notification date: 12/15
Application deadline (fall): 5/1
Undergraduate student body: 2,510 full time, 92 part time; 33% male, 67% female; 0% American Indian, 3% Asian, 13% black, 7% Hispanic, 8% multiracial, 0% Pacific Islander, 63% white, 2% international; 88% from in state; 49% live on campus; 0% of students in fraternities, 0% in sororities

Most popular majors: 22% Education, 16% Business, Management, Marketing, and Related Support Services, 11% Visual and Performing Arts, 8% Communication, Journalism, and Related Programs, 8% Health Professions and Related Programs
Expenses: 2017-2018: $31,654; room/board: $12,356
Financial aid: (518) 337-4915; 84% of undergrads determined to have financial need; average aid package $20,353

The College of Westchester[1]
White Plains NY
U.S. News ranking: Reg. Coll. (N), unranked
For-profit
Application deadline (fall): N/A
Undergraduate student body: N/A full time, N/A part time
Expenses: 2016-2017: $21,015; room/board: N/A
Financial aid: N/A

Columbia University
New York NY
(212) 854-2522
U.S. News ranking: Nat. U., No. 5
Website: www.columbia.edu
Admissions email: ugrad-ask@columbia.edu
Private; founded 1754
Freshman admissions: most selective; 2016-2017: 36,292 applied, 2,279 accepted. Either SAT or ACT required. SAT 25/75 percentile: 1430-1600. High school rank: 95% in top tenth, 99% in top quarter, 100% in top half
Early decision deadline: 11/1, notification date: 12/15
Early action deadline: N/A, notification date: N/A
Application deadline (fall): 1/1
Undergraduate student body: 6,113 full time, 0 part time; 52% male, 48% female; 2% American Indian, 23% Asian, 11% black, 12% Hispanic, 0% multiracial, 0% Pacific Islander, 34% white, 15% international; 24% from in state; 93% live on campus; 18% of students in fraternities, 16% in sororities
Most popular majors: 23% Social Sciences, 21% Engineering, 10% Biological and Biomedical Sciences, 6% Computer and Information Sciences and Support Services, 5% Visual and Performing Arts
Expenses: 2017-2018: $57,208; room/board: $13,618
Financial aid: (212) 854-3711; 49% of undergrads determined to have financial need; average aid package $55,535

Concordia College
Bronxville NY
(800) 937-2655
U.S. News ranking: Reg. Coll. (N), No. 19
Website: www.concordia-ny.edu
Admissions email: admission@concordia-ny.edu
Private; founded 1881
Affiliation: Lutheran Church–Missouri Synod
Freshman admissions: less selective; 2016-2017: 974 applied, 692 accepted. Neither

SAT nor ACT required. SAT 25/75 percentile: 830-1010. High school rank: 6% in top tenth, 35% in top quarter, 65% in top half
Early decision deadline: N/A, notification date: N/A
Early action deadline: 11/15, notification date: 12/15
Application deadline (fall): 8/15
Undergraduate student body: 812 full time, 117 part time; 35% male, 65% female; 0% American Indian, 4% Asian, 21% black, 24% Hispanic, 2% multiracial, 0% Pacific Islander, 32% white, 14% international
Most popular majors: Business Administration, Management and Operations
Expenses: 2017-2018: $31,600; room/board: $11,876
Financial aid: (914) 337-9300; 71% of undergrads determined to have financial need; average aid package $25,866

Cooper Union
New York NY
(212) 353-4120
U.S. News ranking: Reg. Coll. (N), No. 1
Website: www.cooper.edu
Admissions email: admissions@cooper.edu
Private; founded 1859
Freshman admissions: most selective; 2016-2017: N/A applied, N/A accepted. Either SAT or ACT required. SAT 25/75 percentile: 1240-1510. High school rank: N/A
Early decision deadline: 12/1, notification date: 12/22
Early action deadline: N/A, notification date: N/A
Application deadline (fall): 1/9
Undergraduate student body: 863 full time, 13 part time; 66% male, 34% female; N/A American Indian, N/A Asian, N/A black, N/A Hispanic, N/A multiracial, N/A Pacific Islander, N/A white, N/A international
Most popular majors: Information not available
Expenses: 2016-2017: $43,850; room/board: $15,910
Financial aid: (212) 353-4113

Cornell University
Ithaca NY
(607) 255-5241
U.S. News ranking: Nat. U., No. 14
Website: www.cornell.edu
Admissions email: admissions@cornell.edu
Private; founded 1865
Freshman admissions: most selective; 2016-2017: 44,965 applied, 6,337 accepted. Either SAT or ACT required. SAT 25/75 percentile: 1330-1530. High school rank: 90% in top tenth, 98% in top quarter, 100% in top half
Early decision deadline: 11/1, notification date: 12/15
Early action deadline: N/A, notification date: N/A
Application deadline (fall): 1/1
Undergraduate student body: 14,566 full time, 0 part time; 48% male, 52% female; 0% American Indian, 18% Asian,

6% black, 13% Hispanic, 5% multiracial, 0% Pacific Islander, 40% white, 10% international; 34% from in state; 54% live on campus; 25% of students in fraternities, 25% in sororities
Most popular majors: 17% Engineering, 15% Business, Management, Marketing, and Related Support Services, 14% Biological and Biomedical Sciences, 12% Agriculture, Agriculture Operations, and Related Sciences, 9% Social Sciences
Expenses: 2017-2018: $52,853; room/board: $14,380
Financial aid: (607) 255-5142; 45% of undergrads determined to have financial need; average aid package $46,339

D'Youville College
Buffalo NY
(716) 829-7600
U.S. News ranking: Reg. U. (N), second tier
Website: www.dyc.edu
Admissions email: admissions@dyc.edu
Private; founded 1908
Freshman admissions: selective; 2016-2017: 927 applied, 767 accepted. Either SAT or ACT required. SAT 25/75 percentile: 900-1090. High school rank: 10% in top tenth, 36% in top quarter, 88% in top half
Early decision deadline: N/A, notification date: N/A
Early action deadline: N/A, notification date: N/A
Application deadline (fall): rolling
Undergraduate student body: 1,334 full time, 382 part time; 25% male, 75% female; 0% American Indian, 4% Asian, 9% black, 4% Hispanic, 2% multiracial, 0% Pacific Islander, 74% white, 2% international; 77% from in state; 17% live on campus; 0% of students in fraternities, 0% in sororities
Most popular majors: 62% Health Professions and Related Programs, 11% Business, Management, Marketing, and Related Support Services, 11% Multi/Interdisciplinary Studies, 9% Biological and Biomedical Sciences, 4% Psychology
Expenses: 2017-2018: $25,710; room/board: $11,808
Financial aid: (716) 829-7500; 82% of undergrads determined to have financial need; average aid package $19,004

Daemen College
Amherst NY
(800) 462-7652
U.S. News ranking: Reg. U. (N), No. 130
Website: www.daemen.edu
Admissions email: admissions@daemen.edu
Private; founded 1947
Freshman admissions: selective; 2016-2017: 3,219 applied, 1,673 accepted. Neither SAT nor ACT required. SAT 25/75 percentile: 920-1160. High school rank: 28% in top tenth, 58% in top quarter, 89% in top half
Early decision deadline: N/A, notification date: N/A

Early action deadline: N/A, notification date: N/A
Application deadline (fall): rolling
Undergraduate student body: 1,621 full time, 372 part time; 29% male, 71% female; 0% American Indian, 2% Asian, 11% black, 7% Hispanic, 1% multiracial, 0% Pacific Islander, 74% white, 1% international; 94% from in state; 37% live on campus; 2% of students in fraternities, 5% in sororities
Most popular majors: 37% Registered Nursing/Registered Nurse, 19% Natural Sciences, 5% Health and Wellness, General, 5% Social Work, 4% Business Administration and Management, General
Expenses: 2017-2018: $27,990; room/board: $12,696
Financial aid: (716) 839-8254; 63% of undergrads determined to have financial need; average aid package $26,351

Dominican College
Orangeburg NY
(845) 848-7901
U.S. News ranking: Reg. U. (N), second tier
Website: www.dc.edu
Admissions email: admissions@dc.edu
Private; founded 1952
Freshman admissions: less selective; 2016-2017: 1,751 applied, 1,321 accepted. Either SAT or ACT required. SAT 25/75 percentile: 800-970. High school rank: N/A
Early decision deadline: N/A, notification date: N/A
Early action deadline: N/A, notification date: N/A
Application deadline (fall): rolling
Undergraduate student body: 1,330 full time, 148 part time; 33% male, 67% female; 0% American Indian, 6% Asian, 16% black, 30% Hispanic, 3% multiracial, 1% Pacific Islander, 35% white, 1% international; 78% from in state; 42% live on campus; N/A of students in fraternities, N/A in sororities
Most popular majors: 43% Health Professions and Related Programs, 11% Business, Management, Marketing, and Related Support Services, 11% Social Sciences, 9% Homeland Security, Law Enforcement, Firefighting and Related Protective Services, 5% Education
Expenses: 2017-2018: $28,448; room/board: $12,670
Financial aid: (845) 848-7818; 81% of undergrads determined to have financial need; average aid package $21,434

Elmira College
Elmira NY
(800) 935-6472
U.S. News ranking: Nat. Lib. Arts, No. 165
Website: www.elmira.edu
Admissions email: admissions@elmira.edu
Private; founded 1855
Freshman admissions: selective; 2016-2017: 2,096 applied, 1,722 accepted. Neither SAT

nor ACT required. SAT 25/75 percentile: 960-1150. High school rank: 20% in top tenth, 45% in top quarter, 69% in top half
Early decision deadline: N/A, notification date: N/A
Early action deadline: 10/15, notification date: 10/31
Application deadline (fall): rolling
Undergraduate student body: 974 full time, 127 part time; 30% male, 70% female; 0% American Indian, 2% Asian, 5% black, 4% Hispanic, 2% multiracial, 0% Pacific Islander, 78% white, 5% international; 62% from in state; 88% live on campus; 0% of students in fraternities, 0% in sororities
Most popular majors: 23% Business, Management, Marketing, and Related Support Services, 18% Health Professions and Related Programs, 14% Education, 9% Psychology, 6% Biological and Biomedical Sciences
Expenses: 2017-2018: $41,900; room/board: $12,000
Financial aid: (607) 735-1728; 83% of undergrads determined to have financial need; average aid package $30,976

Excelsior College[1]
Albany NY
U.S. News ranking: Reg. U. (N), unranked
Website: www.excelsior.edu
Admissions email: admissions@excelsior.edu
Private; founded 1971
Application deadline (fall): N/A
Undergraduate student body: N/A full time, N/A part time
Expenses: N/A
Financial aid: N/A

Farmingdale State College–SUNY
Farmingdale NY
(631) 420-2200
U.S. News ranking: Reg. Coll. (N), No. 15
Website: www.farmingdale.edu
Admissions email: admissions@farmingdale.edu
Public; founded 1912
Freshman admissions: selective; 2016-2017: 6,169 applied, 3,580 accepted. Either SAT or ACT required. SAT 25/75 percentile: 880-1060. High school rank: 6% in top tenth, 24% in top quarter, 65% in top half
Early decision deadline: N/A, notification date: N/A
Early action deadline: N/A, notification date: N/A
Application deadline (fall): 5/1
Undergraduate student body: 6,942 full time, 2,293 part time; 56% male, 44% female; 0% American Indian, 8% Asian, 10% black, 18% Hispanic, 2% multiracial, 0% Pacific Islander, 59% white, 2% international; 100% from in state; 6% live on campus; 3% of students in fraternities, 4% in sororities
Most popular majors: 21% Business, Management, Marketing, and Related Support Services, 14% Engineering Technologies and Engineering-

Related Fields, 12% Multi/Interdisciplinary Studies, 10% Health Professions and Related Programs, 10% Homeland Security, Law Enforcement, Firefighting and Related Protective Services
Expenses: 2017-2018: $8,076 in state, $17,726 out of state; room/board: $12,892
Financial aid: (631) 420-2328; 54% of undergrads determined to have financial need; average aid package $7,859

Fashion Institute of Technology
New York NY
(212) 217-3760
U.S. News ranking: Reg. U. (N), unranked
Website: www.fitnyc.edu
Admissions email: FITinfo@fitnyc.edu
Public; founded 1944
Freshman admissions: least selective; 2016-2017: 4,632 applied, 1,872 accepted. Neither SAT nor ACT required. SAT 25/75 percentile: N/A. High school rank: N/A
Early decision deadline: N/A, notification date: N/A
Early action deadline: N/A, notification date: N/A
Application deadline (fall): 1/1
Undergraduate student body: 7,395 full time, 1,701 part time, 15% male, 85% female; 0% American Indian, 10% Asian, 9% black, 18% Hispanic, 4% multiracial, 0% Pacific Islander, 46% white, 13% international; 68% from in state; 21% live on campus; 0% of students in fraternities, 0% in sororities
Most popular majors: 42% Business, Management, Marketing, and Related Support Services, 36% Visual and Performing Arts, 16% Communication, Journalism, and Related Programs, 4% Family and Consumer Sciences/Human Sciences, 1% Communications Technologies/Technicians and Support Services
Expenses: 2017-2018: $5,483 in state, $14,863 out of state; room/board: $13,945
Financial aid: (212) 217-3560; 51% of undergrads determined to have financial need; average aid package $11,804

Five Towns College
Dix Hills NY
(631) 424-7000
U.S. News ranking: Reg. Coll. (N), second tier
Website: www.ftc.edu
Admissions email: admissions@ftc.edu
For-profit; founded 1972
Freshman admissions: less selective; 2016-2017: 313 applied, 173 accepted. Neither SAT nor ACT required. SAT 25/75 percentile: 770-980. High school rank: N/A
Early decision deadline: 10/15, notification date: 11/1
Early action deadline: N/A, notification date: N/A

Application deadline (fall): rolling
Undergraduate student body: 623 full time, 45 part time; 66% male, 34% female; N/A American Indian, N/A Asian, N/A black, N/A Hispanic, N/A multiracial, N/A Pacific Islander, N/A white, N/A international
Most popular majors: Information not available
Expenses: 2017-2018: $19,590; room/board: $13,400
Financial aid: (631) 656-2168; 81% of undergrads determined to have financial need

Fordham University
New York NY
(800) 367-3426
U.S. News ranking: Nat. U., No. 61
Website: www.fordham.edu
Admissions email: enroll@fordham.edu
Private; founded 1841
Affiliation: Roman Catholic
Freshman admissions: more selective; 2016-2017: 44,816 applied, 20,268 accepted. Either SAT or ACT required. SAT 25/75 percentile: 1170-1370. High school rank: 46% in top tenth, 81% in top quarter, 98% in top half
Early decision deadline: 11/8, notification date: 12/19
Early action deadline: 11/8, notification date: 12/19
Application deadline (fall): 1/9
Undergraduate student body: 8,763 full time, 495 part time; 43% male, 57% female; 0% American Indian, 10% Asian, 4% black, 14% Hispanic, 3% multiracial, 0% Pacific Islander, 59% white, 8% international; 43% from in state; 51% live on campus; N/A of students in fraternities, N/A in sororities
Most popular majors: 12% Speech Communication and Rhetoric, 10% Business Administration and Management, General, 8% Psychology, General, 7% Finance, General, 6% Economics, General
Expenses: 2017-2018: $50,601; room/board: $17,445
Financial aid: N/A

Hamilton College
Clinton NY
(800) 843-2655
U.S. News ranking: Nat. Lib. Arts, No. 18
Website: www.hamilton.edu
Admissions email: admission@hamilton.edu
Private; founded 1812
Freshman admissions: most selective; 2016-2017: 5,230 applied, 1,364 accepted. Either SAT or ACT required. SAT 25/75 percentile: 1300-1480. High school rank: 65% in top tenth, 91% in top quarter, 98% in top half
Early decision deadline: 11/15, notification date: 12/15
Early action deadline: N/A, notification date: N/A
Application deadline (fall): 1/1
Undergraduate student body: 1,868 full time, 11 part time; 48% male, 52% female; 0% American Indian, 7% Asian, 4% black, 8% Hispanic, 3% multiracial, 0% Pacific Islander, 64% white, 7% international; 29% from in state; 100% live on campus; 26% of

students in fraternities, 18% in sororities
Most popular majors: 14% Economics, General, 8% Mathematics, General, 5% Biology/Biological Sciences, General, 5% Political Science and Government, General, 5% Research and Experimental Psychology, Other
Expenses: 2017-2018: $52,770; room/board: $13,400
Financial aid: (800) 859-4413; 48% of undergrads determined to have financial need; average aid package $47,003

Hartwick College
Oneonta NY
(607) 431-4150
U.S. News ranking: Nat. Lib. Arts, No. 165
Website: www.hartwick.edu
Admissions email: admissions@hartwick.edu
Private; founded 1797
Freshman admissions: selective; 2016-2017: 3,085 applied, 2,889 accepted. Neither SAT nor ACT required. SAT 25/75 percentile: 900-1090. High school rank: 9% in top tenth, 36% in top quarter, 71% in top half
Early decision deadline: 11/1, notification date: 11/15
Early action deadline: N/A, notification date: N/A
Application deadline (fall): rolling
Undergraduate student body: 1,362 full time, 34 part time; 40% male, 60% female; 0% American Indian, 2% Asian, 8% black, 8% Hispanic, 2% multiracial, 0% Pacific Islander, 65% white, 3% international; 77% from in state; 51% live on campus; 16% of students in fraternities, 18% in sororities
Most popular majors: 17% Business, Management, Marketing, and Related Support Services, 14% Biological and Biomedical Sciences, 13% Health Professions and Related Programs, 6% Social Sciences
Expenses: 2017-2018: $44,134; room/board: $12,093
Financial aid: (607) 431-4130; 84% of undergrads determined to have financial need; average aid package $33,725

Hilbert College[1]
Hamburg NY
U.S. News ranking: Reg. Coll. (N), unranked
Website: www.hilbert.edu/
Admissions email: admissions@hilbert.edu
Private
Application deadline (fall): N/A
Undergraduate student body: N/A full time, N/A part time
Expenses: 2016-2017: $21,300; room/board: $9,600
Financial aid: N/A

Hobart and William Smith Colleges
Geneva NY
(315) 781-3622
U.S. News ranking: Nat. Lib. Arts, No. 65
Website: www.hws.edu
Admissions email: admissions@hws.edu
Private; founded 1822

Freshman admissions: more selective; 2016-2017: 4,614 applied, 2,788 accepted. Neither SAT nor ACT required. SAT 25/75 percentile: 1160-1350. High school rank: 32% in top tenth, 64% in top quarter, 88% in top half
Early decision deadline: 11/15, notification date: 12/15
Early action deadline: N/A, notification date: N/A
Application deadline (fall): 2/1
Undergraduate student body: 2,246 full time, 16 part time; 50% male, 50% female; 0% American Indian, 4% Asian, 6% black, 5% Hispanic, 0% multiracial, 0% Pacific Islander, 73% white, 6% international; 40% from in state; 90% live on campus; 20% of students in fraternities, 0% in sororities
Most popular majors: 12% Economics, General, 12% Environmental Studies, 7% Mass Communication/Media Studies, 6% Architecture, 6% Psychology, General
Expenses: 2017-2018: $53,525; room/board: $13,525
Financial aid: (315) 781-3315; 63% of undergrads determined to have financial need; average aid package $36,731

Hofstra University
Hempstead NY
(516) 463-6700
U.S. News ranking: Nat. U., No. 132
Website: www.hofstra.edu
Admissions email: admission@hofstra.edu
Private; founded 1935
Freshman admissions: more selective; 2016-2017: 28,617 applied, 17,806 accepted. Neither SAT nor ACT required. SAT 25/75 percentile: 1070-1260. High school rank: 27% in top tenth, 60% in top quarter, 90% in top half
Early decision deadline: N/A, notification date: N/A
Early action deadline: 11/15, notification date: 12/15
Application deadline (fall): rolling
Undergraduate student body: 6,497 full time, 402 part time; 46% male, 54% female; 0% American Indian, 10% Asian, 8% black, 14% Hispanic, 2% multiracial, 1% Pacific Islander, 56% white, 5% international; 63% from in state; 46% live on campus; 7% of students in fraternities, 9% in sororities
Most popular majors: 7% Psychology, General, 6% Marketing/Marketing Management, General, 5% Accounting, 5% Public Relations/Image Management, 4% Finance, General
Expenses: 2017-2018: $43,960; room/board: $14,930
Financial aid: (516) 463-8000; 64% of undergrads determined to have financial need; average aid package $29,000

Houghton College
Houghton NY
(800) 777-2556
U.S. News ranking: Nat. Lib. Arts, No. 147
Website: www.houghton.edu

Admissions email: admission@houghton.edu
Private; founded 1883
Affiliation: Wesleyan
Freshman admissions: selective; 2016-2017: 852 applied, 810 accepted. Either SAT or ACT required. SAT 25/75 percentile: 963-1240. High school rank: 26% in top tenth, 51% in top quarter, 83% in top half
Early decision deadline: N/A, notification date: N/A
Early action deadline: 11/1, notification date: 12/1
Application deadline (fall): rolling
Undergraduate student body: 998 full time, 45 part time; 37% male, 63% female; 0% American Indian, 4% Asian, 4% black, 1% Hispanic, 5% multiracial, 0% Pacific Islander, 74% white, 6% international; 66% from in state; 90% live on campus; 0% of students in fraternities, 0% in sororities
Most popular majors: 9% Biology, General, 9% Business Administration, Management and Operations, 8% Communication and Media Studies, 8% Education, General, 7% Intercultural/Multicultural and Diversity Studies
Expenses: 2017-2018: $31,540; room/board: $9,018
Financial aid: (585) 567-9328; 80% of undergrads determined to have financial need; average aid package $25,443

Iona College
New Rochelle NY
(914) 633-2502
U.S. News ranking: Reg. U. (N), No. 75
Website: www.iona.edu
Admissions email: admissions@iona.edu
Private; founded 1940
Affiliation: Roman Catholic
Freshman admissions: selective; 2016-2017: 10,896 applied, 9,965 accepted. Either SAT or ACT required. SAT 25/75 percentile: 890-1100. High school rank: 10% in top tenth, 28% in top quarter, 58% in top half
Early decision deadline: N/A, notification date: N/A
Early action deadline: 12/1, notification date: 12/15
Application deadline (fall): 2/15
Undergraduate student body: 3,069 full time, 260 part time; 48% male, 52% female; 0% American Indian, 2% Asian, 10% black, 23% Hispanic, 2% multiracial, 0% Pacific Islander, 56% white, 3% international; 76% from in state; 45% live on campus; 3% of students in fraternities, 7% in sororities
Most popular majors: 38% Business, Management, Marketing, and Related Support Services, 14% Communication, Journalism, and Related Programs, 11% Psychology, 8% Homeland Security, Law Enforcement, Firefighting and Related Protective Services, 6% Health Professions and Related Programs
Expenses: 2017-2018: $37,682; room/board: $14,832
Financial aid: (914) 633-2497; 84% of undergrads determined to have financial need; average aid package $25,451

Ithaca College

Ithaca NY
(800) 429-4274
U.S. News ranking: Reg. U. (N),
No. 8
Website: www.ithaca.edu
Admissions email:
admission@ithaca.edu
Private; founded 1892
Freshman admissions: more
selective; 2016-2017: 14,380
applied, 10,054 accepted. Neither
SAT nor ACT required. SAT
25/75 percentile: 1090-1280.
High school rank: 27% in top
tenth, 57% in top quarter, 89%
in top half
Early decision deadline: 11/1,
notification date: 12/15
Early action deadline: 12/1,
notification date: 2/1
Application deadline (fall): 2/1
Undergraduate student body: 6,103
full time, 118 part time; 42%
male, 58% female; 0% American
Indian, 4% Asian, 6% black,
8% Hispanic, 3% multiracial,
0% Pacific Islander, 72% white,
2% international; 46% from in
state; 71% live on campus; 1%
of students in fraternities, 1% in
sororities
Most popular majors: 22%
Communication, Journalism, and
Related Programs, 17% Visual
and Performing Arts, 16% Health
Professions and Related Programs,
10% Business, Management,
Marketing, and Related Support
Services, 5% Biological and
Biomedical Sciences
Expenses: 2017-2018: $42,884;
room/board: $15,274
Financial aid: (607) 274-3131;
67% of undergrads determined to
have financial need; average aid
package $35,707

Jamestown Business College[1]

Jamestown NY
U.S. News ranking: Business,
unranked
For-profit
Application deadline (fall): N/A
Undergraduate student body: N/A
full time, N/A part time
Expenses: 2016-2017: $6,377;
room/board: N/A
Financial aid: N/A

Juilliard School

New York NY
(212) 799-5000
U.S. News ranking: Arts, unranked
Website: www.juilliard.edu
Admissions email: admissions@
juilliard.edu
Private; founded 1905
Freshman admissions: least
selective; 2016-2017: 2,533
applied, 166 accepted. Neither
SAT nor ACT required. SAT 25/75
percentile: N/A. High school
rank: N/A
Early decision deadline: N/A,
notification date: N/A
Early action deadline: N/A,
notification date: N/A
Application deadline (fall): 12/1
Undergraduate student body: 498
full time, 82 part time; 51%
male, 49% female; 0% American
Indian, 14% Asian, 5% black,
7% Hispanic, 6% multiracial,
0% Pacific Islander, 40% white,
26% international; 11% from in
state; 0% live on campus; 0%
of students in fraternities, 0% in
sororities
Most popular majors: 98% Visual
and Performing Arts
Expenses: 2017-2018: $41,410;
room/board: N/A
Financial aid: (212) 799-5000;
74% of undergrads determined to
have financial need; average aid
package $32,644

Keuka College

Keuka Park NY
(315) 279-5254
U.S. News ranking: Reg. U. (N),
No. 120
Website: www.keuka.edu
Admissions email: admissions@
keuka.edu
Private; founded 1890
Affiliation: American Baptist
Freshman admissions: less
selective; 2016-2017: 1,996
applied, 1,871 accepted. Neither
SAT nor ACT required. SAT 25/75
percentile: 840-1050. High school
rank: 10% in top tenth, 33% in
top quarter, 74% in top half
Early decision deadline: N/A,
notification date: N/A
Early action deadline: N/A,
notification date: N/A
Application deadline (fall): rolling
Undergraduate student body: 1,351
full time, 379 part time; 25%
male, 75% female; 1% American
Indian, 1% Asian, 9% black,
5% Hispanic, 2% multiracial,
0% Pacific Islander, 75% white,
2% international; 93% from in
state; 46% live on campus; N/A
of students in fraternities, N/A in
sororities
Most popular majors: 27%
Business, Management,
Marketing, and Related Support
Services, 27% Health Professions
and Related Programs, 21%
Public Administration and Social
Service Professions, 7% Homeland
Security, Law Enforcement,
Firefighting and Related Protective
Services, 6% Education
Expenses: 2017-2018: $31,071;
room/board: $11,452
Financial aid: (315) 279-5646;
93% of undergrads determined to
have financial need; average aid
package $20,333

The King's College

New York NY
(212) 659-3610
U.S. News ranking: Nat. Lib. Arts,
second tier
Website: www.tkc.edu/
Admissions email:
admissions@tkc.edu
Private; founded 1938
Affiliation: Undenominational
Freshman admissions: more
selective; 2016-2017: 2,672
applied, 1,092 accepted. Either
SAT or ACT required. ACT 25/75
percentile: 24-28. High school
rank: N/A
Early decision deadline: N/A,
notification date: N/A
Early action deadline: 11/15,
notification date: 12/15

Application deadline (fall): rolling
Undergraduate student body: 520
full time, 14 part time; 36%
male, 64% female; 0% American
Indian, 4% Asian, 6% black,
8% Hispanic, 1% multiracial,
1% Pacific Islander, 63% white,
3% international; 10% from in
state; N/A live on campus; N/A
of students in fraternities, N/A in
sororities
Most popular majors: 40%
Humanities/Humanistic
Studies, 37% Liberal Arts and
Sciences, General Studies and
Humanities, Other, 22% Business
Administration and Management,
General, 1% Finance, General
Expenses: 2017-2018: $35,400;
room/board: $16,652
Financial aid: (646) 237-8902;
71% of undergrads determined to
have financial need; average aid
package $25,427

LIM College

New York NY
(800) 677-1323
U.S. News ranking: Business,
unranked
Website: www.limcollege.edu
Admissions email: admissions@
limcollege.edu
For-profit; founded 1939
Freshman admissions: less
selective; 2016-2017: 1,055
applied, 986 accepted. Either
SAT or ACT required. SAT 25/75
percentile: 840-1013. High
school rank: N/A
Early decision deadline: N/A,
notification date: N/A
Early action deadline: 11/15,
notification date: 12/15
Application deadline (fall): rolling
Undergraduate student body:
1,400 full time, 99 part time; 8%
male, 92% female; 1% American
Indian, 7% Asian, 15% black,
10% Hispanic, 2% multiracial,
0% Pacific Islander, 54% white,
6% international; 41% from in
state; 25% live on campus; N/A
of students in fraternities, N/A in
sororities
Most popular majors: 91%
Business, Management,
Marketing, and Related Support
Services, 9% Visual and
Performing Arts
Expenses: 2017-2018: $26,395;
room/board: $20,350
Financial aid: (212) 752-1530

LIU Post

Brookville NY
(516) 299-2900
U.S. News ranking: Reg. U. (N),
No. 102
Website: www.liu.edu/post
Admissions email:
post-enroll@liu.edu
Private; founded 1954
Freshman admissions: selective;
2016-2017: 6,724 applied,
5,479 accepted. Either SAT
or ACT required. SAT 25/75
percentile: 920-1120. High school
rank: 10% in top tenth, 33% in
top quarter, 69% in top half
Early decision deadline: N/A,
notification date: N/A
Early action deadline: 12/1,
notification date: 12/31
Application deadline (fall): rolling
Undergraduate student body: 2,875
full time, 3,398 part time; 42%
male, 58% female; 0% American

Indian, 4% Asian, 12% black,
15% Hispanic, 2% multiracial,
0% Pacific Islander, 47% white,
8% international; 92% from in
state; 32% live on campus; 8%
of students in fraternities, 11%
in sororities
Most popular majors: 13%
Business Administration and
Management, General, 7%
Criminal Justice/Law Enforcement
Administration, 7% Psychology,
General, 6% Accounting, 5%
Health/Health Care Administration/
Management
Expenses: 2017-2018: $36,978;
room/board: $13,720
Financial aid: (516) 299-2553;
75% of undergrads determined to
have financial need; average aid
package $21,316

Le Moyne College

Syracuse NY
(315) 445-4300
U.S. News ranking: Reg. U. (N),
No. 17
Website: www.lemoyne.edu
Admissions email: admission@
lemoyne.edu
Private; founded 1946
Affiliation: Roman Catholic
Freshman admissions: selective;
2016-2017: 6,832 applied,
4,462 accepted. Neither SAT
nor ACT required. SAT 25/75
percentile: 1000-1210. High
school rank: 25% in top tenth,
54% in top quarter, 86% in
top half
Early decision deadline: N/A,
notification date: N/A
Early action deadline: 11/15,
notification date: 12/15
Application deadline (fall): rolling
Undergraduate student body: 2,534
full time, 363 part time; 39%
male, 61% female; 0% American
Indian, 2% Asian, 6% black,
5% Hispanic, 2% multiracial,
0% Pacific Islander, 79% white,
1% international; 95% from in
state; 57% live on campus; 0%
of students in fraternities, 0% in
sororities
Most popular majors: 18% Biology/
Biological Sciences, General,
13% Psychology, General, 9%
Accounting, 9% Registered
Nursing/Registered Nurse, 6%
Communication and Media
Studies
Expenses: 2017-2018: $33,905;
room/board: $13,400
Financial aid: (315) 445-4400;
82% of undergrads determined to
have financial need; average aid
package $26,170

Manhattan College

Riverdale NY
(718) 862-7200
U.S. News ranking: Reg. U. (N),
No. 15
Website: www.manhattan.edu
Admissions email:
admit@manhattan.edu
Private; founded 1853
Affiliation: Roman Catholic
Freshman admissions: selective;
2016-2017: 8,145 applied,
5,813 accepted. Either SAT
or ACT required. SAT 25/75
percentile: 1000-1210. High
school rank: 25% in top tenth,

60% in top quarter, 86% in
top half
Early decision deadline: 11/15,
notification date: 12/15
Early action deadline: N/A,
notification date: N/A
Application deadline (fall): rolling
Undergraduate student body: 3,444
full time, 193 part time; 55%
male, 45% female; 0% American
Indian, 5% Asian, 5% black,
21% Hispanic, 2% multiracial,
0% Pacific Islander, 57% white,
3% international; 69% from in
state; 57% live on campus; 2%
of students in fraternities, 3% in
sororities
Most popular majors: 26%
Engineering, 22% Business,
Management, Marketing, and
Related Support Services, 11%
Education, 8% Communication,
Journalism, and Related Programs
Expenses: 2016-2017: $40,345;
room/board: $15,010
Financial aid: (718) 862-7178

Manhattan School of Music[1]

New York NY
(917) 493-4436
U.S. News ranking: Arts, unranked
Website: msmnyc.edu/
Admissions email: admission@
msmnyc.edu
Private; founded 1917
Application deadline (fall): N/A
Undergraduate student body: N/A
full time, N/A part time
Expenses: 2016-2017: $44,600;
room/board: $16,000
Financial aid: (917) 493-4809

Manhattanville College

Purchase NY
(914) 323-5464
U.S. News ranking: Reg. U. (N),
No. 102
Website: www.mville.edu
Admissions email:
admissions@mville.edu
Private; founded 1841
Freshman admissions: selective;
2016-2017: 4,132 applied,
3,198 accepted. Neither SAT
nor ACT required. SAT 25/75
percentile: 950-1150. High school
rank: 12% in top tenth, 32% in
top quarter, 68% in top half
Early decision deadline: N/A,
notification date: N/A
Early action deadline: 12/1,
notification date: 12/31
Application deadline (fall): rolling
Undergraduate student body: 1,701
full time, 93 part time; 36%
male, 64% female; 0% American
Indian, 1% Asian, 8% black,
18% Hispanic, 2% multiracial,
0% Pacific Islander, 44% white,
8% international; 71% from in
state; 60% live on campus; 0%
of students in fraternities, 0% in
sororities
Most popular majors: 16%
Business Administration and
Management, General, 12%
Speech Communication and
Rhetoric, 10% Psychology,
General, 6% Finance, General, 5%
Sociology

Expenses: 2017-2018: $37,910; room/board: $14,520
Financial aid: (914) 323-5357; 73% of undergrads determined to have financial need; average aid package $27,769

Marist College
Poughkeepsie NY
(845) 575-3226
U.S. News ranking: Reg. U. (N), No. 9
Website: www.marist.edu
Admissions email: admissions@marist.edu
Private; founded 1929
Freshman admissions: more selective; 2016-2017: 11,087 applied, 4,545 accepted. Neither SAT nor ACT required. SAT 25/75 percentile: 1070-1270. High school rank: 24% in top tenth, 58% in top quarter, 89% in top half
Early decision deadline: 11/15, notification date: 12/15
Early action deadline: 11/15, notification date: 1/15
Application deadline (fall): 2/1
Undergraduate student body: 4,966 full time, 650 part time; 41% male, 59% female; 0% American Indian, 3% Asian, 4% black, 10% Hispanic, 2% multiracial, 0% Pacific Islander, 77% white, 2% international; 52% from in state; 61% live on campus; 3% of students in fraternities, 3% in sororities
Most popular majors: 30% Business/Commerce, General, 20% Communication and Media Studies, 13% Psychology, General, 7% Computer and Information Sciences, General, 5% Criminal Justice and Corrections
Expenses: 2017-2018: $36,780; room/board: $15,900
Financial aid: (845) 575 3230; 56% of undergrads determined to have financial need; average aid package $20,750

Marymount Manhattan College
New York NY
(212) 517-0430
U.S. News ranking: Nat. Lib. Arts, second tier
Website: www.mmm.edu
Admissions email: admissions@mmm.edu
Private; founded 1936
Freshman admissions: selective; 2016-2017: 5,265 applied, 4,118 accepted. Either SAT or ACT required. SAT 25/75 percentile: 930-1170. High school rank: N/A
Early decision deadline: N/A, notification date: N/A
Early action deadline: N/A, notification date: N/A
Application deadline (fall): rolling
Undergraduate student body: 1,841 full time, 228 part time; 23% male, 77% female; 1% American Indian, 4% Asian, 10% black, 17% Hispanic, 1% multiracial, 0% Pacific Islander, 58% white, 5% international; 40% from in state; 36% live on campus; 0% of students in fraternities, 0% in sororities
Most popular majors: 40% Visual and Performing Arts, 18% Communication, Journalism, and Related Programs, 12% Business,

Management, Marketing, and Related Support Services, 6% Psychology, 5% Multi/Interdisciplinary Studies
Expenses: 2017-2018: $31,950; room/board: $16,400
Financial aid: (212) 517-0500; 67% of undergrads determined to have financial need; average aid package $17,046

Medaille College[1]
Buffalo NY
(716) 880-2200
U.S. News ranking: Reg. U. (N), second tier
Website: www.medaille.edu
Admissions email: admissionsug@medaille.edu
Private; founded 1937
Application deadline (fall): rolling
Undergraduate student body: N/A full time, N/A part time
Expenses: 2016-2017: $27,276; room/board: $13,080
Financial aid: (716) 880-2256

Mercy College
Dobbs Ferry NY
(877) 637-2946
U.S. News ranking: Reg. U. (N), unranked
Website: www.mercy.edu
Admissions email: admissions@mercy.edu
Private; founded 1950
Freshman admissions: least selective; 2016-2017: 6,617 applied, 5,140 accepted. Neither SAT nor ACT required. SAT 25/75 percentile: N/A. High school rank: N/A
Early decision deadline: N/A, notification date: N/A
Early action deadline: 12/1, notification date: 1/2
Application deadline (fall): rolling
Undergraduate student body: 5,182 full time, 1,975 part time; 33% male, 67% female; 0% American Indian, 4% Asian, 24% black, 38% Hispanic, 1% multiracial, 0% Pacific Islander, 25% white, 2% international; 91% from in state; 12% live on campus; N/A of students in fraternities, N/A in sororities
Most popular majors: 25% Multi/Interdisciplinary Studies, 24% Health Professions and Related Programs, 14% Business, Management, Marketing, and Related Support Services, 12% Psychology, 7% Homeland Security, Law Enforcement, Firefighting and Related Protective Services
Expenses: 2017-2018: $18,714; room/board: $13,900
Financial aid: (888) 464-6737; 87% of undergrads determined to have financial need; average aid package $13,746

Metropolitan College of New York
New York NY
(212) 343-1234
U.S. News ranking: Reg. U. (N), second tier
Website: www.mcny.edu
Admissions email: admissions@mcny.edu
Private; founded 1964
Freshman admissions: less selective; 2016-2017: 252

applied, 99 accepted. Neither SAT nor ACT required. SAT 25/75 percentile: N/A. High school rank: N/A
Early decision deadline: N/A, notification date: N/A
Early action deadline: N/A, notification date: N/A
Application deadline (fall): rolling
Undergraduate student body: 621 full time, 76 part time; 26% male, 74% female; 0% American Indian, 3% Asian, 58% black, 24% Hispanic, 2% multiracial, 0% Pacific Islander, 4% white, 3% international; 96% from in state; N/A live on campus; N/A of students in fraternities, N/A in sororities
Most popular majors: 46% Public Administration and Social Service Professions, 27% Business, Management, Marketing, and Related Support Services, 22% Health Professions and Related Programs, 4% Social Sciences
Expenses: 2017-2018: $19,180; room/board: N/A
Financial aid: (212) 343-1234; 94% of undergrads determined to have financial need; average aid package $16,577

Molloy College
Rockville Centre NY
(516) 323-4000
U.S. News ranking: Reg. U. (N), No. 41
Website: www.molloy.edu
Admissions email: admissions@molloy.edu
Private; founded 1955
Freshman admissions: selective; 2016-2017: 4,030 applied, 3,100 accepted. Either SAT or ACT required. SAT 25/75 percentile: 980 1170. High school rank: 18% in top tenth, 56% in top quarter, 82% in top half
Early decision deadline: N/A, notification date: N/A
Early action deadline: 12/1, notification date: 12/15
Application deadline (fall): rolling
Undergraduate student body: 2,906 full time, 692 part time; 25% male, 75% female; 0% American Indian, 7% Asian, 12% black, 16% Hispanic, 1% multiracial, 0% Pacific Islander, 59% white, 0% international; 97% from in state; 8% live on campus; N/A of students in fraternities, N/A in sororities
Most popular majors: 49% Health Professions and Related Programs, 14% Business, Management, Marketing, and Related Support Services, 7% Education, 5% Biological and Biomedical Sciences, 5% Communication, Journalism, and Related Programs
Expenses: 2017-2018: $30,290; room/board: $14,560
Financial aid: (516) 323-4200; 81% of undergrads determined to have financial need; average aid package $16,123

Monroe College
Bronx NY
(800) 556-6676
U.S. News ranking: Reg. U. (N), second tier
Website: www.monroecollege.edu
Admissions email: admissions@monroecollege.edu

For-profit; founded 1933
Freshman admissions: least selective; 2016-2017: 5,153 applied, 2,736 accepted. Neither SAT nor ACT required. SAT 25/75 percentile: 718-1018. High school rank: N/A
Early decision deadline: N/A, notification date: N/A
Early action deadline: 12/15, notification date: 1/31
Application deadline (fall): rolling
Undergraduate student body: 4,355 full time, 1,533 part time; 37% male, 63% female; 0% American Indian, 2% Asian, 45% black, 37% Hispanic, 0% multiracial, 0% Pacific Islander, 3% white, 11% international; 92% from in state; 14% live on campus; 0% of students in fraternities, 0% in sororities
Most popular majors: 23% Criminal Justice/Law Enforcement Administration, 18% Business Administration and Management, General, 17% Health Services Administration, 12% Hospitality Administration/Management, General, 10% Accounting
Expenses: 2017-2018: $14,896; room/board: $10,130
Financial aid: (718) 933-6700; 92% of undergrads determined to have financial need; average aid package $12,928

Morrisville State College
Morrisville NY
(315) 684-6046
U.S. News ranking: Reg. Coll. (N), No. 29
Website: www.morrisville.edu
Admissions email: admissions@morrisville.edu
Public; founded 1908
Freshman admissions: least selective; 2016 2017: 4,031 applied, 3,118 accepted. Neither SAT nor ACT required. SAT 25/75 percentile: 750-970. High school rank: 2% in top tenth, 16% in top quarter, 49% in top half
Early decision deadline: N/A, notification date: N/A
Early action deadline: N/A, notification date: N/A
Application deadline (fall): 8/18
Undergraduate student body: 2,624 full time, 379 part time; 50% male, 50% female; 0% American Indian, 1% Asian, 19% black, 8% Hispanic, 2% multiracial, 0% Pacific Islander, 67% white, 1% international; 6% from in state; 55% live on campus; 0% of students in fraternities, 0% in sororities
Most popular majors: 22% Agriculture, Agriculture Operations, and Related Sciences, 19% Business, Management, Marketing, and Related Support Services, 17% Homeland Security, Law Enforcement, Firefighting and Related Protective Services, 13% Mechanic and Repair Technologies/Technicians, 12% Computer and Information Sciences and Support Services
Expenses: 2017-2018: $8,270 in state, $13,340 out of state; room/board: $15,600

Financial aid: (315) 684-6289; 84% of undergrads determined to have financial need; average aid package $9,682

Mount St. Mary College
Newburgh NY
(845) 569-3488
U.S. News ranking: Reg. U. (N), No. 126
Website: www.msmc.edu
Admissions email: admissions@msmc.edu
Private; founded 1959
Freshman admissions: selective; 2016-2017: 3,747 applied, 3,368 accepted. Either SAT or ACT required. SAT 25/75 percentile: 890-1070. High school rank: 7% in top tenth, 34% in top quarter, 74% in top half
Early decision deadline: N/A, notification date: N/A
Early action deadline: N/A, notification date: N/A
Application deadline (fall): 8/15
Undergraduate student body: 1,750 full time, 378 part time; 28% male, 72% female; 0% American Indian, 2% Asian, 8% black, 16% Hispanic, 2% multiracial, 0% Pacific Islander, 63% white, 0% international; 89% from in state; 47% live on campus; N/A of students in fraternities, N/A in sororities
Most popular majors: 28% Health Professions and Related Programs, 20% Business, Management, Marketing, and Related Support Services, 13% Psychology, 7% Communication, Journalism, and Related Programs, 7% History
Expenses: 2017-2018: $29,920; room/board: $14,528
Financial aid: (845) 569-3394; 81% of undergrads determined to have financial need; average aid package $19,472

Nazareth College
Rochester NY
(585) 389-2860
U.S. News ranking: Reg. U. (N), No. 28
Website: www.naz.edu
Admissions email: admissions@naz.edu
Private; founded 1924
Freshman admissions: selective; 2016-2017: 4,118 applied, 2,969 accepted. Neither SAT nor ACT required. SAT 25/75 percentile: 980-1190. High school rank: 24% in top tenth, 58% in top quarter, 89% in top half
Early decision deadline: 11/15, notification date: 12/15
Early action deadline: N/A, notification date: N/A
Application deadline (fall): 2/1
Undergraduate student body: 2,045 full time, 114 part time; 28% male, 72% female; 0% American Indian, 3% Asian, 7% black, 5% Hispanic, 2% multiracial, 0% Pacific Islander, 78% white, 2% international; 91% from in state; 55% live on campus; 0% of students in fraternities, 0% in sororities
Most popular majors: 24% Health Professions and Related Programs, 13% Education, 11% Business,

Management, Marketing, and Related Support Services, 10% Visual and Performing Arts, 9% Psychology
Expenses: 2016-2017: $32,424; room/board: $13,150
Financial aid: (585) 389-2310

The New School
New York NY
(800) 292-3040
U.S. News ranking: Nat. U., No. 133
Website: www.newschool.edu
Admissions email: admission@newschool.edu
Private; founded 1919
Freshman admissions: selective; 2016-2017: 9,003 applied, 5,410 accepted. Neither SAT nor ACT required. SAT 25/75 percentile: 1030-1280. High school rank: 18% in top tenth, 44% in top quarter, 77% in top half
Early decision deadline: 11/1, notification date: 12/20
Early action deadline: 11/1, notification date: N/A
Application deadline (fall): 1/15
Undergraduate student body: 6,184 full time, 830 part time; 26% male, 74% female; 0% American Indian, 9% Asian, 5% black, 12% Hispanic, 4% multiracial, 0% Pacific Islander, 33% white, 32% international; 26% from in state; 26% live on campus; N/A of students in fraternities, N/A in sororities
Most popular majors: 58% Visual and Performing Arts, 9% Social Sciences, 6% Business, Management, Marketing, and Related Support Services, 6% Communication, Journalism, and Related Programs, 5% Liberal Arts and Sciences, General Studies and Humanities
Expenses: 2017-2018: $47,330; room/board: $18,600
Financial aid: (212) 229-8930; 43% of undergrads determined to have financial need; average aid package $26,093

New York Institute of Technology
Old Westbury NY
(800) 345-6948
U.S. News ranking: Reg. U. (N), No. 47
Website: www.nyit.edu
Admissions email: admissions@nyit.edu
Private; founded 1955
Freshman admissions: selective; 2016-2017: 10,085 applied, 7,316 accepted. Either SAT or ACT required. SAT 25/75 percentile: 950-1180. High school rank: 22% in top tenth, 52% in top quarter, 88% in top half
Early decision deadline: N/A, notification date: N/A
Early action deadline: N/A, notification date: N/A
Application deadline (fall): rolling
Undergraduate student body: 3,172 full time, 403 part time; 64% male, 36% female; 0% American Indian, 16% Asian, 8% black,

15% Hispanic, 3% multiracial, 0% Pacific Islander, 23% white, 15% international; 87% from in state; 14% live on campus; 6% of students in fraternities, 5% in sororities
Most popular majors: 17% Engineering, 13% Business, Management, Marketing, and Related Support Services, 13% Health Professions and Related Programs, 12% Architecture and Related Services, 11% Communication, Journalism, and Related Programs
Expenses: 2017-2018: $35,870; room/board: $14,110
Financial aid: (516) 686-7680; 75% of undergrads determined to have financial need; average aid package $21,916

New York University
New York NY
(212) 998-4500
U.S. News ranking: Nat. U., No. 30
Website: www.nyu.edu
Admissions email: admissions@nyu.edu
Private; founded 1831
Freshman admissions: most selective; 2016-2017: 60,724 applied, 19,351 accepted. Neither SAT nor ACT required. SAT 25/75 percentile: 1250-1480. High school rank: 61% in top tenth, 87% in top quarter, 98% in top half
Early decision deadline: 11/1, notification date: 12/15
Early action deadline: N/A, notification date: N/A
Application deadline (fall): 1/1
Undergraduate student body: 24,888 full time, 1,247 part time; 43% male, 57% female; 0% American Indian, 20% Asian, 6% black, 13% Hispanic, 4% multiracial, 0% Pacific Islander, 32% white, 18% international; 38% from in state; 43% live on campus; 3% of students in fraternities, 7% in sororities
Most popular majors: 19% Visual and Performing Arts, 14% Social Sciences, 13% Business, Management, Marketing, and Related Support Services, 10% Liberal Arts and Sciences, General Studies and Humanities, 8% Health Professions and Related Programs
Expenses: 2017-2018: $50,464; room/board: $17,664
Financial aid: (212) 998-4444; 52% of undergrads determined to have financial need; average aid package $34,532

Niagara University
Niagara University NY
(716) 286-8700
U.S. News ranking: Reg. U. (N), No. 48
Website: www.niagara.edu
Admissions email: admissions@niagara.edu
Private; founded 1856
Affiliation: Roman Catholic
Freshman admissions: selective; 2016-2017: 3,359 applied, 2,784 accepted. Either SAT or ACT required. SAT 25/75 percentile: 930-1130. High

school rank: 17% in top tenth, 42% in top quarter, 75% in top half
Early decision deadline: N/A, notification date: N/A
Early action deadline: 12/15, notification date: N/A
Application deadline (fall): 8/30
Undergraduate student body: 2,950 full time, 186 part time; 38% male, 62% female; 1% American Indian, 1% Asian, 5% black, 4% Hispanic, 2% multiracial, 0% Pacific Islander, 72% white, 12% international; 91% from in state; 41% live on campus; 3% of students in fraternities, 4% in sororities
Most popular majors: 27% Education, 26% Business, Management, Marketing, and Related Support Services, 9% Health Professions and Related Programs, 9% Social Sciences, 6% Biological and Biomedical Sciences
Expenses: 2017-2018: $31,950; room/board: $12,950
Financial aid: (716) 286-8686; 72% of undergrads determined to have financial need; average aid package $25,326

Nyack College
Nyack NY
(800) 336-9225
U.S. News ranking: Reg. U. (N), second tier
Website: www.nyack.edu
Admissions email: admissions@nyack.edu
Private; founded 1882
Affiliation: Christ and Missionary Alliance Church
Freshman admissions: less selective; 2016-2017: 455 applied, 454 accepted. Neither SAT nor ACT required. SAT 25/75 percentile: 770-1026. High school rank: 8% in top tenth, 28% in top quarter, 55% in top half
Early decision deadline: N/A, notification date: N/A
Early action deadline: N/A, notification date: N/A
Application deadline (fall): rolling
Undergraduate student body: 1,179 full time, 272 part time; 38% male, 62% female; 1% American Indian, 7% Asian, 30% black, 32% Hispanic, 2% multiracial, 0% Pacific Islander, 20% white, 6% international; 68% from in state; 71% live on campus; N/A of students in fraternities, N/A in sororities
Most popular majors: 32% Business, Management, Marketing, and Related Support Services, 14% Multi/Interdisciplinary Studies, 9% Psychology, 9% Theology and Religious Vocations, 7% Health Professions and Related Programs
Expenses: 2017-2018: $25,350; room/board: $9,450
Financial aid: (800) 799-6248

Pace University
New York NY
(212) 346-1323
U.S. News ranking: Nat. U., No. 187
Website: www.pace.edu
Admissions email: infoctr@pace.edu
Private; founded 1906

Freshman admissions: selective; 2016-2017: 18,462 applied, 15,466 accepted. Neither SAT nor ACT required. SAT 25/75 percentile: 940-1160. High school rank: 15% in top tenth, 40% in top quarter, 75% in top half
Early decision deadline: 11/1, notification date: 12/1
Early action deadline: 12/1, notification date: 1/1
Application deadline (fall): 2/15
Undergraduate student body: 7,691 full time, 1,223 part time; 39% male, 61% female; 0% American Indian, 8% Asian, 11% black, 14% Hispanic, 4% multiracial, 0% Pacific Islander, 51% white, 10% international; 59% from in state; 41% live on campus; 2% of students in fraternities, 4% in sororities
Most popular majors: 33% Business, Management, Marketing, and Related Support Services, 12% Communication, Journalism, and Related Programs, 10% Health Professions and Related Programs, 10% Visual and Performing Arts, 9% Psychology
Expenses: 2017-2018: $44,036; room/board: $18,540
Financial aid: (877) 672-1830; 69% of undergrads determined to have financial need; average aid package $31,970

Paul Smith's College
Paul Smiths NY
(888) 873-6570
U.S. News ranking: Reg. Coll. (N), No. 22
Website: www.paulsmiths.edu
Admissions email: admissions@paulsmiths.edu
Private; founded 1946
Affiliation: Other
Freshman admissions: less selective; 2016-2017: 904 applied, 742 accepted. Neither SAT nor ACT required. SAT 25/75 percentile: 860-1100. High school rank: 6% in top tenth, 22% in top quarter, 49% in top half
Early decision deadline: N/A, notification date: N/A
Early action deadline: N/A, notification date: N/A
Application deadline (fall): rolling
Undergraduate student body: 844 full time, 7 part time; 65% male, 35% female; 0% American Indian, 0% Asian, 2% black, 6% Hispanic, 1% multiracial, 0% Pacific Islander, 81% white, 0% international; N/A from in state; N/A live on campus; 0% of students in fraternities, 0% in sororities
Most popular majors: 30% Natural Resources and Conservation, 18% Personal and Culinary Services, 10% Biological and Biomedical Sciences, 9% Physical Sciences, 4% Multi/Interdisciplinary Studies
Expenses: 2017-2018: $27,621; room/board: $11,870
Financial aid: (518) 327-6119; 88% of undergrads determined to have financial need; average aid package $22,662

Plaza College[1]
Forest Hills NY
U.S. News ranking: Reg. Coll. (N), unranked
Website: www.plazacollege.edu
Admissions email: N/A
For-profit; founded 1916
Application deadline (fall): N/A
Undergraduate student body: N/A full time, N/A part time
Expenses: 2016-2017: $12,450; room/board: N/A
Financial aid: N/A

Pratt Institute
Brooklyn NY
(718) 636-3514
U.S. News ranking: Arts, unranked
Website: www.pratt.edu
Admissions email: admissions@pratt.edu
Private; founded 1887
Freshman admissions: more selective; 2016-2017: 5,711 applied, 2,960 accepted. Either SAT or ACT required. SAT 25/75 percentile: 1090-1310. High school rank: N/A
Early decision deadline: N/A, notification date: N/A
Early action deadline: 11/1, notification date: 12/22
Application deadline (fall): 1/5
Undergraduate student body: 3,194 full time, 116 part time; 31% male, 69% female; 0% American Indian, 14% Asian, 4% black, 10% Hispanic, 3% multiracial, 0% Pacific Islander, 41% white, 27% international
Most popular majors: 20% Architecture, 12% Graphic Design, 9% Illustration, 9% Industrial and Product Design, 7% Interior Design
Expenses: 2017-2018: $50,038; room/board: $12,020
Financial aid: (718) 636-3599; 47% of undergrads determined to have financial need; average aid package $28,959

Purchase College–SUNY
Purchase NY
(914) 251-6300
U.S. News ranking: Nat. Lib. Arts, second tier
Website: www.purchase.edu
Admissions email: admissions@purchase.edu
Public; founded 1967
Freshman admissions: selective; 2016-2017: 6,762 applied, 2,942 accepted. Either SAT or ACT required. SAT 25/75 percentile: 970-1180. High school rank: N/A
Early decision deadline: N/A, notification date: N/A
Early action deadline: 11/15, notification date: 12/15
Application deadline (fall): 7/15
Undergraduate student body: 3,755 full time, 366 part time; 43% male, 57% female; 0% American Indian, 4% Asian, 11% black, 19% Hispanic, 5% multiracial, 0% Pacific Islander, 53% white, 2% international; 85% from in state; 67% live on campus; N/A of students in fraternities, N/A in sororities

Most popular majors: 48% Visual and Performing Arts, 16% Liberal Arts and Sciences, General Studies and Humanities, 8% Social Sciences, 6% Psychology, 5% Communication, Journalism, and Related Programs
Expenses: 2017-2018: $8,298 in state, $18,148 out of state; room/board: $12,952
Financial aid: (914) 251-6354; 62% of undergrads determined to have financial need; average aid package $9,795

Rensselaer Polytechnic Institute
Troy NY
(518) 276-6216
U.S. News ranking: Nat. U., No. 42
Website: www.rpi.edu
Admissions email: admissions@rpi.edu
Private; founded 1824
Freshman admissions: most selective; 2016-2017: 18,524 applied, 8,215 accepted. Either SAT or ACT required. SAT 25/75 percentile: 1280-1480. High school rank: 66% in top tenth, 93% in top quarter, 99% in top half
Early decision deadline: 11/1, notification date: 12/16
Early action deadline: N/A, notification date: N/A
Application deadline (fall): 2/1
Undergraduate student body: 6,246 full time, 19 part time; 68% male, 32% female; 0% American Indian, 11% Asian, 3% black, 9% Hispanic, 7% multiracial, 0% Pacific Islander, 57% white, 11% international, 34% from in state; 57% live on campus, 30% of students in fraternities, 16% in sororities
Most popular majors: 56% Engineering, 12% Computer and Information Sciences and Support Services, 5% Business, Management, Marketing, and Related Support Services, 4% Architecture and Related Services, 4% Biological and Biomedical Sciences
Expenses: 2017-2018: $52,305; room/board: $14,960
Financial aid: (518) 276-6813; 61% of undergrads determined to have financial need; average aid package $38,742

Roberts Wesleyan College
Rochester NY
(585) 594-6400
U.S. News ranking: Reg. U. (N), No. 78
Website: www.roberts.edu
Admissions email: admissions@roberts.edu
Private; founded 1866
Affiliation: Free Methodist
Freshman admissions: selective; 2016-2017: 1,270 applied, 822 accepted. Either SAT or ACT required. SAT 25/75 percentile: 960-1160. High school rank: 23% in top tenth, 54% in top quarter, 86% in top half
Early decision deadline: N/A, notification date: N/A

Early action deadline: N/A, notification date: N/A
Application deadline (fall): 8/20
Undergraduate student body: 1,207 full time, 109 part time; 31% male, 69% female; 0% American Indian, 2% Asian, 11% black, 5% Hispanic, 4% multiracial, 0% Pacific Islander, 73% white, 4% international; 85% from in state; 61% live on campus; 0% of students in fraternities, 0% in sororities
Most popular majors: 40% Health Professions and Related Programs, 18% Business, Management, Marketing, and Related Support Services, 9% Education, 6% Psychology, 5% Public Administration and Social Service Professions
Expenses: 2017-2018: $30,686; room/board: $10,430
Financial aid: (585) 594-6150; 84% of undergrads determined to have financial need; average aid package $21,746

Rochester Institute of Technology
Rochester NY
(585) 475-6631
U.S. News ranking: Nat. U., No. 97
Website: www.rit.edu
Admissions email: admissions@rit.edu
Private; founded 1829
Freshman admissions: more selective; 2016-2017: 19,824 applied, 10,889 accepted. Either SAT or ACT required. SAT 25/75 percentile: 1140-1330. High school rank: 39% in top tenth, 73% in top quarter, 94% in top half
Early decision deadline: 11/15, notification date: 12/15
Early action deadline: N/A, notification date: N/A
Application deadline (fall): rolling
Undergraduate student body: 11,279 full time, 1,131 part time; 66% male, 34% female; 0% American Indian, 8% Asian, 5% black, 8% Hispanic, 3% multiracial, 0% Pacific Islander, 66% white, 6% international; 54% from in state; 52% live on campus; 5% of students in fraternities, 6% in sororities
Most popular majors: 19% Engineering, 16% Computer and Information Sciences and Support Services, 13% Visual and Performing Arts, 12% Engineering Technologies and Engineering-Related Fields, 10% Business, Management, Marketing, and Related Support Services
Expenses: 2017-2018: $40,068; room/board: $12,666
Financial aid: (585) 475-2186; 74% of undergrads determined to have financial need; average aid package $26,000

The Sage Colleges
Troy NY
(888) 837-9724
U.S. News ranking: Reg. U. (N), No. 97
Website: www.sage.edu
Admissions email: tscadm@sage.edu
Private; founded 1916

Freshman admissions: selective; 2016-2017: 2,117 applied, 1,220 accepted. Neither SAT nor ACT required. SAT 25/75 percentile: 830-1060. High school rank: 16% in top tenth, 52% in top quarter, 86% in top half
Early decision deadline: N/A, notification date: N/A
Early action deadline: 12/1, notification date: 12/15
Application deadline (fall): rolling
Undergraduate student body: 1,278 full time, 195 part time; 20% male, 80% female; 0% American Indian, 4% Asian, 13% black, 8% Hispanic, 3% multiracial, 0% Pacific Islander, 65% white, 0% international; 92% from in state; 55% live on campus; N/A of students in fraternities, N/A in sororities
Most popular majors: 28% Health Professions and Related Programs, 13% Biological and Biomedical Sciences, 12% Business, Management, Marketing, and Related Support Services, 8% Psychology, 7% Visual and Performing Arts
Expenses: 2017-2018: $31,164; room/board: $12,408
Financial aid: (518) 244-4525; 91% of undergrads determined to have financial need

SUNY Buffalo State
Buffalo NY
(716) 878-4017
U.S. News ranking: Reg. U. (N), No. 120
Website: www.buffalostate.edu
Admissions email: admissions@buffalostate.edu
Public; founded 1871
Freshman admissions: less selective; 2016-2017: 13,715 applied, 8,787 accepted. Either SAT or ACT required. SAT 25/75 percentile: 770-980. High school rank: 9% in top tenth, 30% in top quarter, 66% in top half
Early decision deadline: N/A, notification date: N/A
Early action deadline: N/A, notification date: N/A
Application deadline (fall): rolling
Undergraduate student body: 7,598 full time, 884 part time; 44% male, 56% female; 1% American Indian, 3% Asian, 31% black, 13% Hispanic, 4% multiracial, 0% Pacific Islander, 47% white, 1% international; 99% from in state; 32% live on campus; 1% of students in fraternities, 1% in sororities
Most popular majors: 16% Business, Management, Marketing, and Related Support Services, 11% Education, 10% Homeland Security, Law Enforcement, Firefighting and Related Protective Services, 9% Social Sciences, 7% Visual and Performing Arts
Expenses: 2017-2018: $8,001 in state, $17,551 out of state; room/board: $13,656
Financial aid: (716) 878-4902; 88% of undergrads determined to have financial need; average aid package $17,677

SUNY College of Agriculture and Technology–Cobleskill
Cobleskill NY
(518) 255-5525
U.S. News ranking: Reg. Coll. (N), No. 17
Website: www.cobleskill.edu
Admissions email: admissionsoffice@cobleskill.edu
Public; founded 1911
Freshman admissions: selective; 2016-2017: 2,897 applied, 2,265 accepted. Neither SAT nor ACT required. SAT 25/75 percentile: 910-1100. High school rank: 4% in top tenth, 21% in top quarter, 53% in top half
Early decision deadline: N/A, notification date: N/A
Early action deadline: N/A, notification date: N/A
Application deadline (fall): rolling
Undergraduate student body: 2,197 full time, 107 part time; 47% male, 53% female; 0% American Indian, 2% Asian, 13% black, 5% Hispanic, 8% multiracial, 0% Pacific Islander, 70% white, 1% international; 93% from in state; 58% live on campus; N/A of students in fraternities, N/A in sororities
Most popular majors: 18% Animal Sciences, General, 17% Business Administration and Management, General, 10% Agricultural Business and Management, General, 9% Wildlife, Fish and Wildlands Science and Management, 7% Plant Sciences, General
Expenses: 2017-2018: $7,962 in state, $17,812 out of state; room/board: $13,442
Financial aid: (518) 255-5637; 77% of undergrads determined to have financial need; average aid package $7,422

SUNY College of Environmental Science and Forestry
Syracuse NY
(315) 470-6600
U.S. News ranking: Nat. U., No. 97
Website: www.esf.edu
Admissions email: esfinfo@esf.edu
Public; founded 1911
Freshman admissions: more selective; 2016-2017: 1,651 applied, 895 accepted. Either SAT or ACT required. SAT 25/75 percentile: 1070-1260. High school rank: 36% in top tenth, 72% in top quarter, 95% in top half
Early decision deadline: 12/1, notification date: 1/15
Early action deadline: N/A, notification date: N/A
Application deadline (fall): rolling
Undergraduate student body: 1,711 full time, 44 part time; 53% male, 47% female; 0% American Indian, 4% Asian, 2% black, 6% Hispanic, 3% multiracial, 0% Pacific Islander, 80% white, 2% international; 82% from in state; 35% live on campus; 2% of students in fraternities, 2% in sororities

Most popular majors: 43% Environmental Biology, 26% Natural Resources and Conservation, Other, 18% Engineering, General, 6% Landscape Architecture, 2% Chemistry, General
Expenses: 2017-2018: $8,240 in state, $18,090 out of state; room/board: $15,400
Financial aid: (315) 470-6670; 58% of undergrads determined to have financial need; average aid package $10,122

SUNY College of Technology–Alfred
Alfred NY
(800) 425-3733
U.S. News ranking: Reg. Coll. (N), No. 14
Website: www.alfredstate.edu
Admissions email: admissions@alfredstate.edu
Public; founded 1908
Freshman admissions: less selective; 2016-2017: 5,073 applied, 3,652 accepted. Neither SAT nor ACT required. SAT 25/75 percentile: 830-1060. High school rank: N/A
Early decision deadline: N/A, notification date: N/A
Early action deadline: N/A, notification date: N/A
Application deadline (fall): rolling
Undergraduate student body: 3,447 full time, 288 part time; 63% male, 37% female; 0% American Indian, 1% Asian, 13% black, 8% Hispanic, 2% multiracial, 0% Pacific Islander, 73% white, 1% international; 96% from in state; 66% live on campus; 4% of students in fraternities, 3% in sororities
Most popular majors: 48% Business, Management, Marketing, and Related Support Services, 28% Engineering Technologies and Engineering-Related Fields, 8% Computer and Information Sciences and Support Services, 5% Health Professions and Related Programs, 5% Homeland Security, Law Enforcement, Firefighting and Related Protective Services
Expenses: 2017-2018: $8,075 in state, $11,345 out of state; room/board: $11,820
Financial aid: (607) 587-3979; 80% of undergrads determined to have financial need; average aid package $11,156

SUNY College of Technology–Canton
Canton NY
(800) 388-7123
U.S. News ranking: Reg. Coll. (N), No. 25
Website: www.canton.edu/
Admissions email: admissions@canton.edu
Public; founded 1906
Freshman admissions: least selective; 2016-2017: 3,017 applied, 2,490 accepted. Neither SAT nor ACT required. SAT 25/75 percentile: 800-1030. High school rank: 4% in top tenth, 17% in top quarter, 51% in top half
Early decision deadline: N/A, notification date: N/A

Early action deadline: N/A, notification date: N/A
Application deadline (fall): rolling
Undergraduate student body: 2,676 full time, 565 part time; 43% male, 57% female; 2% American Indian, 1% Asian, 14% black, 11% Hispanic, 2% multiracial, 0% Pacific Islander, 67% white, 2% international; 97% from in state; 39% live on campus; 4% of students in fraternities, 4% in sororities
Most popular majors: 11% Registered Nursing/Registered Nurse, 10% Business Administration and Management, General, 9% Corrections and Criminal Justice, Other, 8% Business, Management, Marketing, and Related Support Services, Other, 7% Veterinary/Animal Health Technology/Technician and Veterinary Assistant
Expenses: 2017-2018: $8,200 in state, $17,850 out of state; room/board: $12,350
Financial aid: (315) 386-7616; 83% of undergrads determined to have financial need; average aid package $10,661

SUNY College of Technology–Delhi
Delhi NY
(607) 746-4550
U.S. News ranking: Reg. Coll. (N), No. 17
Website: www.delhi.edu/
Admissions email: enroll@delhi.edu
Public; founded 1913
Freshman admissions: less selective; 2016-2017: 5,218 applied, 3,423 accepted. Neither SAT nor ACT required. SAT 25/75 percentile: 840-1030. High school rank: 5% in top tenth, 17% in top quarter, 57% in top half
Early decision deadline: N/A, notification date: N/A
Early action deadline: N/A, notification date: N/A
Application deadline (fall): rolling
Undergraduate student body: 2,656 full time, 767 part time; 45% male, 55% female; 1% American Indian, 4% Asian, 17% black, 14% Hispanic, 0% multiracial, 0% Pacific Islander, 61% white, 0% international; 97% from in state; 50% live on campus; 10% of students in fraternities, 5% in sororities
Most popular majors: 46% Health Professions and Related Programs, 42% Business, Management, Marketing, and Related Support Services, 6% Homeland Security, Law Enforcement, Firefighting and Related Protective Services, 3% Architecture and Related Services, 2% Engineering Technologies and Engineering-Related Fields
Expenses: 2017-2018: $8,340 in state, $17,990 out of state; room/board: $11,980
Financial aid: (607) 746-4573; 79% of undergrads determined to have financial need; average aid package $10,501

SUNY College–Cortland
Cortland NY
(607) 753-4711
U.S. News ranking: Reg. U. (N), No. 48
Website: www2.cortland.edu/home/

Admissions email: admissions@cortland.edu
Public; founded 1868
Freshman admissions: selective; 2016-2017: 10,875 applied, 5,673 accepted. Neither SAT nor ACT required. SAT 25/75 percentile: 990-1140. High school rank: 11% in top tenth, 39% in top quarter, 88% in top half
Early decision deadline: N/A, notification date: N/A
Early action deadline: 11/15, notification date: 1/1
Application deadline (fall): rolling
Undergraduate student body: 6,187 full time, 117 part time; 44% male, 56% female; 0% American Indian, 1% Asian, 6% black, 12% Hispanic, 2% multiracial, 0% Pacific Islander, 73% white, 1% international; 96% from in state; N/A live on campus; N/A of students in fraternities, N/A in sororities
Most popular majors: 24% Education, 21% Parks, Recreation, Leisure, and Fitness Studies, 11% Social Sciences, 10% Health Professions and Related Programs, 7% Communication, Journalism, and Related Programs
Expenses: 2017-2018: $8,100 in state, $17,950 out of state; room/board: $12,410
Financial aid: (607) 753-4717; 64% of undergrads determined to have financial need; average aid package $14,563

SUNY College–Old Westbury
Old Westbury NY
(516) 876-3073
U.S. News ranking: Reg. U. (N), second tier
Website: www.oldwestbury.edu
Admissions email: enroll@oldwestbury.edu
Public; founded 1965
Freshman admissions: less selective; 2016-2017: 3,545 applied, 2,432 accepted. Either SAT or ACT required. SAT 25/75 percentile: 880-1060. High school rank: N/A
Early decision deadline: N/A, notification date: N/A
Early action deadline: N/A, notification date: N/A
Application deadline (fall): rolling
Undergraduate student body: 3,632 full time, 610 part time; 41% male, 59% female; 0% American Indian, 11% Asian, 28% black, 25% Hispanic, 3% multiracial, 0% Pacific Islander, 31% white, 0% international; 99% from in state; 18% live on campus; 2% of students in fraternities, 2% in sororities
Most popular majors: 17% Psychology, General, 11% Business Administration and Management, General, 9% Accounting, 9% Speech Communication and Rhetoric, 8% Social Sciences, General
Expenses: 2016-2017: $7,683 in state, $17,533 out of state; room/board: $11,020
Financial aid: N/A

SUNY College–Oneonta
Oneonta NY
(607) 436-2524
U.S. News ranking: Reg. U. (N), No. 48
Website: www.oneonta.edu
Admissions email: admissions@oneonta.edu
Public; founded 1889
Freshman admissions: selective; 2016-2017: 10,606 applied, 5,604 accepted. Either SAT or ACT required. SAT 25/75 percentile: 980-1160. High school rank: N/A
Early decision deadline: N/A, notification date: N/A
Early action deadline: 11/15, notification date: 12/1
Application deadline (fall): rolling
Undergraduate student body: 5,608 full time, 122 part time; 40% male, 60% female; 0% American Indian, 2% Asian, 4% black, 12% Hispanic, 2% multiracial, 0% Pacific Islander, 77% white, 1% international
Most popular majors: 12% Communication, Journalism, and Related Programs, 12% Education, 11% Business, Management, Marketing, and Related Support Services, 11% Family and Consumer Sciences/Human Sciences, 10% Psychology
Expenses: 2017-2018: $7,936 in state, $17,786 out of state; room/board: $12,658
Financial aid: (607) 436-2992; 57% of undergrads determined to have financial need; average aid package $9,837

SUNY College–Potsdam
Potsdam NY
(315) 267-2180
U.S. News ranking: Reg. U. (N), No. 91
Website: www.potsdam.edu
Admissions email: admissions@potsdam.edu
Public; founded 1816
Freshman admissions: selective; 2016-2017: 5,454 applied, 3,915 accepted. Neither SAT nor ACT required. SAT 25/75 percentile: 990-1210. High school rank: 14% in top tenth, 14% in top quarter, 62% in top half
Early decision deadline: N/A, notification date: N/A
Early action deadline: N/A, notification date: N/A
Application deadline (fall): rolling
Undergraduate student body: 3,321 full time, 95 part time; 42% male, 58% female; 2% American Indian, 2% Asian, 11% black, 14% Hispanic, 3% multiracial, 0% Pacific Islander, 62% white, 1% international; 96% from in state; 60% live on campus; 0% of students in fraternities, 3% in sororities
Most popular majors: 14% Education, 13% Visual and Performing Arts, 10% Business, Management, Marketing, and Related Support Services, 10% Social Sciences, 9% Psychology
Expenses: 2016-2017: $7,984 in state, $17,834 out of state; room/board: $12,420

Financial aid: (315) 267-2162; 74% of undergrads determined to have financial need; average aid package $16,045

SUNY Empire State College
Saratoga Springs NY
(518) 587-2100
U.S. News ranking: Reg. U. (N), unranked
Website: www.esc.edu
Admissions email: admissions@esc.edu
Public; founded 1971
Freshman admissions: least selective; 2016-2017: 904 applied, 690 accepted. Neither SAT nor ACT required. SAT 25/75 percentile: N/A. High school rank: N/A
Early decision deadline: N/A, notification date: N/A
Early action deadline: N/A, notification date: N/A
Application deadline (fall): rolling
Undergraduate student body: 3,841 full time, 6,350 part time; 38% male, 62% female; 1% American Indian, 2% Asian, 16% black, 13% Hispanic, 2% multiracial, 0% Pacific Islander, 60% white, 1% international; 95% from in state; 0% live on campus; 0% of students in fraternities, 0% in sororities
Most popular majors: 35% Business, Management, Marketing, and Related Support Services, 24% Public Administration and Social Service Professions, 8% Health Professions and Related Programs, 8% Psychology, 6% Physical Sciences
Expenses: 2016-2017: $6,985 in state, $16,835 out of state; room/board: N/A
Financial aid: N/A

SUNY Maritime College
Throggs Neck NY
(718) 409-7221
U.S. News ranking: Reg. U. (N), No. 62
Website: www.sunymaritime.edu
Admissions email: admissions@sunymaritime.edu
Public; founded 1874
Freshman admissions: selective; 2016-2017: 1,449 applied, 841 accepted. Either SAT or ACT required. SAT 25/75 percentile: 1030-1210. High school rank: 25% in top tenth, 50% in top quarter, 100% in top half
Early decision deadline: 11/1, notification date: 12/15
Early action deadline: N/A, notification date: N/A
Application deadline (fall): 1/31
Undergraduate student body: 1,590 full time, 45 part time; 88% male, 12% female; 0% American Indian, 5% Asian, 4% black, 13% Hispanic, 2% multiracial, 0% Pacific Islander, 71% white, 2% international; 76% from in state; 83% live on campus; N/A of students in fraternities, N/A in sororities

Most popular majors: 41% Marine Science/Merchant Marine Officer, 13% Business, Management, Marketing, and Related Support Services, Other, 11% Mechanical Engineering, 9% Electrical and Electronics Engineering, 9% Naval Architecture and Marine Engineering
Expenses: 2017-2018: $7,874 in state, $17,724 out of state; room/board: $12,134
Financial aid: (718) 409-7200; 52% of undergrads determined to have financial need; average aid package $4,508

SUNY Polytechnic Institute
Utica NY
(315) 792-7500
U.S. News ranking: Reg. U. (N), No. 15
Website: www.sunypoly.edu
Admissions email: admissions@sunypoly.edu
Public; founded 1966
Freshman admissions: selective; 2016-2017: 2,428 applied, 1,613 accepted. Either SAT or ACT required. SAT 25/75 percentile: 990-1230. High school rank: 30% in top tenth, 63% in top quarter, 94% in top half
Early decision deadline: N/A, notification date: N/A
Early action deadline: 11/15, notification date: 12/15
Application deadline (fall): 7/1
Undergraduate student body: 1,698 full time, 314 part time; 66% male, 34% female; 0% American Indian, 5% Asian, 5% black, 8% Hispanic, 3% multiracial, 0% Pacific Islander, 77% white, 1% international; 98% from in state; 41% live on campus; 0% of students in fraternities, 0% in sororities
Most popular majors: 13% Business Administration and Management, General, 13% Registered Nursing/Registered Nurse, 8% Computer and Information Sciences, General, 7% Mechanical Engineering/Mechanical Technology/Technician, 7% Psychology, General
Expenses: 2017-2018: $7,910 in state, $17,760 out of state; room/board: $13,620
Financial aid: (315) 792-7210; 67% of undergrads determined to have financial need; average aid package $10,449

SUNY–Fredonia
Fredonia NY
(800) 252-1212
U.S. News ranking: Reg. U. (N), No. 56
Website: www.fredonia.edu
Admissions email: admissions@fredonia.edu
Public; founded 1826
Freshman admissions: selective; 2016-2017: 5,381 applied, 3,355 accepted. Either SAT or ACT required. SAT 25/75 percentile: 900-1120. High school rank: 14% in top tenth, 38% in top quarter, 72% in top half
Early decision deadline: N/A, notification date: N/A

Early action deadline: N/A, notification date: N/A
Application deadline (fall): rolling
Undergraduate student body: 4,261 full time, 125 part time; 43% male, 57% female; 1% American Indian, 2% Asian, 7% black, 8% Hispanic, 3% multiracial, 0% Pacific Islander, 77% white, 2% international; 96% from in state; 48% live on campus; 3% of students in fraternities, 5% in sororities
Most popular majors: 15% Business, Management, Marketing, and Related Support Services, 15% Education, 12% Visual and Performing Arts, 9% Communication, Journalism, and Related Programs, 7% Psychology
Expenses: 2017-2018: $8,089 in state, $17,939 out of state; room/board: $12,490
Financial aid: (716) 673-3253; 70% of undergrads determined to have financial need; average aid package $10,936

SUNY–Geneseo

Geneseo NY
(585) 245-5571
U.S. News ranking: Reg. U. (N), No. 11
Website: www.geneseo.edu
Admissions email: admissions@geneseo.edu
Public; founded 1871
Freshman admissions: more selective; 2016-2017: 8,892 applied, 5,944 accepted. Either SAT or ACT required. SAT 25/75 percentile: 1090-1300. High school rank: 38% in top tenth, 74% in top quarter, 95% in top half
Early decision deadline: 11/15, notification date: 12/15
Early action deadline: N/A, notification date: N/A
Application deadline (fall): 1/1
Undergraduate student body: 5,316 full time, 115 part time; 41% male, 59% female; 0% American Indian, 6% Asian, 3% black, 8% Hispanic, 3% multiracial, 0% Pacific Islander, 75% white, 2% international; 98% from in state; 55% live on campus; 21% of students in fraternities, 30% in sororities
Most popular majors: 19% Social Sciences, 14% Biological and Biomedical Sciences, 14% Business, Management, Marketing, and Related Support Services, 13% Psychology, 10% Education
Expenses: 2017-2018: $8,408 in state, $18,058 out of state; room/board: $13,214
Financial aid: (585) 245-5731; 47% of undergrads determined to have financial need; average aid package $9,487

SUNY–New Paltz

New Paltz NY
(845) 257-3200
U.S. News ranking: Reg. U. (N), No. 28
Website: www.newpaltz.edu
Admissions email: admissions@newpaltz.edu
Public; founded 1828

Freshman admissions: selective; 2016-2017: 14,042 applied, 6,030 accepted. Either SAT or ACT required. SAT 25/75 percentile: 1010-1200. High school rank: 20% in top tenth, 58% in top quarter, 91% in top half
Early decision deadline: N/A, notification date: N/A
Early action deadline: 11/15, notification date: 12/15
Application deadline (fall): 4/1
Undergraduate student body: 6,198 full time, 519 part time; 38% male, 62% female; 0% American Indian, 6% Asian, 6% black, 18% Hispanic, 2% multiracial, 0% Pacific Islander, 63% white, 2% international; 97% from in state; 47% live on campus; 4% of students in fraternities, 4% in sororities
Most popular majors: 14% Business, Management, Marketing, and Related Support Services, 13% Social Sciences, 12% Communication, Journalism, and Related Programs, 12% Visual and Performing Arts, 10% Education
Expenses: 2017-2018: $7,833 in state, $17,683 out of state; room/board: $12,642
Financial aid: (845) 257-3256; 57% of undergrads determined to have financial need; average aid package $11,074

SUNY–Oswego

Oswego NY
(315) 312-2250
U.S. News ranking: Reg. U. (N), No. 48
Website: www.oswego.edu
Admissions email: admiss@oswego.edu
Public; founded 1861
Freshman admissions: selective; 2016-2017: 10,715 applied, 5,824 accepted. Either SAT or ACT required. SAT 25/75 percentile: 1010-1180. High school rank: 13% in top tenth, 50% in top quarter, 85% in top half
Early decision deadline: N/A, notification date: N/A
Early action deadline: 11/5, notification date: 12/15
Application deadline (fall): rolling
Undergraduate student body: 6,868 full time, 282 part time; 50% male, 50% female; 0% American Indian, 3% Asian, 8% black, 11% Hispanic, 3% multiracial, 0% Pacific Islander, 72% white, 2% international; 97% from in state; 60% live on campus; 7% of students in fraternities, 6% in sororities
Most popular majors: 11% Business Administration and Management, General, 7% Mass Communication/Media Studies, 6% Criminal Justice/Law Enforcement Administration, 5% Health and Wellness, General, 4% Psychology, General
Expenses: 2017-2018: $8,191 in state, $17,841 out of state; room/board: $13,740
Financial aid: (315) 312-2248; 66% of undergrads determined to have financial need; average aid package $11,154

SUNY–Plattsburgh

Plattsburgh NY
(888) 673-0012
U.S. News ranking: Reg. U. (N), No. 71
Website: www.plattsburgh.edu
Admissions email: admissions@plattsburgh.edu
Public; founded 1889
Freshman admissions: selective; 2016-2017: 9,404 applied, 4,799 accepted. Either SAT or ACT required. SAT 25/75 percentile: 990-1210. High school rank: 19% in top tenth, 52% in top quarter, 84% in top half
Early decision deadline: N/A, notification date: N/A
Early action deadline: N/A, notification date: N/A
Application deadline (fall): rolling
Undergraduate student body: 4,822 full time, 393 part time; 43% male, 57% female; 0% American Indian, 2% Asian, 8% black, 11% Hispanic, 2% multiracial, 0% Pacific Islander, 66% white, 6% international; 97% from in state; 50% live on campus; 9% of students in fraternities, 4% in sororities
Most popular majors: 22% Business, Management, Marketing, and Related Support Services, 12% Health Professions and Related Programs, 9% Communication, Journalism, and Related Programs, 9% Psychology, 8% Education
Expenses: 2017-2018: $7,950 in state, $17,800 out of state; room/board: $12,490
Financial aid: (518) 564-2072; 64% of undergrads determined to have financial need; average aid package $13,742

Sarah Lawrence College

Bronxville NY
(914) 395-2510
U.S. News ranking: Nat. Lib. Arts, No. 53
Website: www.slc.edu
Admissions email: slcadmit@sarahlawrence.edu
Private; founded 1926
Freshman admissions: more selective; 2016-2017: 3,183 applied, 1,589 accepted. Neither SAT nor ACT required. SAT 25/75 percentile: 1170-1400. High school rank: 40% in top tenth, 57% in top quarter, 91% in top half
Early decision deadline: 11/1, notification date: 12/15
Early action deadline: N/A, notification date: N/A
Application deadline (fall): 1/15
Undergraduate student body: 1,411 full time, 27 part time; 28% male, 72% female; 0% American Indian, 5% Asian, 4% black, 9% Hispanic, 7% multiracial, 0% Pacific Islander, 52% white, 14% international; 22% from in state; 84% live on campus; 0% of students in fraternities, 0% in sororities
Most popular majors: 100% Liberal Arts and Sciences, General Studies and Humanities
Expenses: 2017-2018: $54,010; room/board: $14,856

Financial aid: (914) 395-2570; 60% of undergrads determined to have financial need; average aid package $37,319

School of Visual Arts

New York NY
(212) 592-2100
U.S. News ranking: Arts, unranked
Website: www.sva.edu/admissions
Admissions email: admissions@sva.edu
For-profit; founded 1947
Freshman admissions: selective; 2016-2017: 3,805 applied, 2,833 accepted. Neither SAT nor ACT required. SAT 25/75 percentile: 940-1230. High school rank: N/A
Early decision deadline: N/A, notification date: N/A
Early action deadline: N/A, notification date: N/A
Application deadline (fall): N/A
Undergraduate student body: 3,505 full time, 262 part time; 33% male, 67% female; 0% American Indian, 14% Asian, 4% black, 12% Hispanic, 1% multiracial, 0% Pacific Islander, 26% white, 41% international
Most popular majors: Information not available
Expenses: 2017-2018: $38,000; room/board: $19,600
Financial aid: (212) 592-2030; 43% of undergrads determined to have financial need; average aid package $17,121

Siena College

Loudonville NY
(888) 287-4362
U.S. News ranking: Nat. Lib. Arts, No. 134
Website: www.siena.edu
Admissions email: admissions@siena.edu
Private; founded 1937
Affiliation: Roman Catholic
Freshman admissions: selective; 2016-2017: 9,704 applied, 5,835 accepted. Neither SAT nor ACT required. SAT 25/75 percentile: 980-1200. High school rank: 25% in top tenth, 56% in top quarter, 89% in top half
Early decision deadline: 12/1, notification date: 1/1
Early action deadline: 12/1, notification date: 1/7
Application deadline (fall): 2/15
Undergraduate student body: 3,062 full time, 124 part time; 48% male, 52% female; 0% American Indian, 4% Asian, 4% black, 8% Hispanic, 2% multiracial, 0% Pacific Islander, 79% white, 2% international; 81% from in state; 77% live on campus; 0% of students in fraternities, 0% in sororities
Most popular majors: 14% Accounting, 10% Administrative Assistant and Secretarial Science, General, 10% Psychology, General, 9% Biology/Biological Sciences, General, 7% Biology/Biological Sciences, General
Expenses: 2017-2018: $35,735; room/board: $14,550
Financial aid: (518) 783-2427; 79% of undergrads determined to have financial need; average aid package $29,737

Skidmore College

Saratoga Springs NY
(518) 580-5570
U.S. News ranking: Nat. Lib. Arts, No. 41
Website: www.skidmore.edu
Admissions email: admissions@skidmore.edu
Private; founded 1903
Freshman admissions: more selective; 2016-2017: 9,181 applied, 2,670 accepted. Neither SAT nor ACT required. SAT 25/75 percentile: 1120-1330. High school rank: 32% in top tenth, 71% in top quarter, 96% in top half
Early decision deadline: 11/15, notification date: 12/15
Early action deadline: N/A, notification date: N/A
Application deadline (fall): 1/15
Undergraduate student body: 2,643 full time, 37 part time; 40% male, 60% female; 0% American Indian, 5% Asian, 4% black, 9% Hispanic, 4% multiracial, 0% Pacific Islander, 64% white, 10% international; 33% from in state; 89% live on campus; 0% of students in fraternities, 0% in sororities
Most popular majors: 20% Social Sciences, 14% Business, Management, Marketing, and Related Support Services, 11% Visual and Performing Arts, 10% Psychology, 9% Biological and Biomedical Sciences
Expenses: 2017-2018: $52,446; room/board: $14,004
Financial aid: (518) 580-5750; 41% of undergrads determined to have financial need; average aid package $45,900

St. Bonaventure University

St. Bonaventure NY
(800) 462-5050
U.S. News ranking: Reg. U (N), No. 21
Website: www.sbu.edu
Admissions email: admissions@sbu.edu
Private; founded 1858
Affiliation: Roman Catholic
Freshman admissions: selective; 2016-2017: 2,871 applied, 1,892 accepted. Either SAT or ACT required. SAT 25/75 percentile: 930-1165. High school rank: 19% in top tenth, 46% in top quarter, 77% in top half
Early decision deadline: N/A, notification date: N/A
Early action deadline: N/A, notification date: N/A
Application deadline (fall): 7/1
Undergraduate student body: 1,592 full time, 68 part time; 51% male, 49% female; 0% American Indian, 4% Asian, 6% black, 8% Hispanic, 3% multiracial, 0% Pacific Islander, 69% white, 3% international; 72% from in state; 95% live on campus; 0% of students in fraternities, 0% in sororities
Most popular majors: 16% Accounting, 9% Journalism, 8% Biology/Biological Sciences, General, 8% Marketing/Marketing Management, General, 8% Sport and Fitness Administration/Management

Expenses: 2017-2018: $33,301; room/board: $11,815
Financial aid: (716) 375-2373; 74% of undergrads determined to have financial need; average aid package $26,057

St. Francis College

Brooklyn Heights NY
(718) 489-5200
U.S. News ranking: Reg. Coll. (N), No. 8
Website: www.sfc.edu
Admissions email: admissions@stfranciscollege.edu
Private; founded 1884
Freshman admissions: less selective; 2016-2017: 3,466 applied, 2,223 accepted. Either SAT or ACT required. SAT 25/75 percentile: 830-1030. High school rank: N/A
Early decision deadline: N/A, notification date: N/A
Early action deadline: N/A, notification date: N/A
Application deadline (fall): rolling
Undergraduate student body: 2,343 full time, 220 part time; 41% male, 59% female; 1% American Indian, 4% Asian, 19% black, 21% Hispanic, 3% multiracial, 1% Pacific Islander, 40% white, 6% international; 95% from in state; 6% live on campus; 7% of students in fraternities, 3% in sororities
Most popular majors: 17% Business Administration, Management and Operations, 14% Communication and Media Studies, 13% Biology, General, 10% Registered Nursing, Nursing Administration, Nursing Research and Clinical Nursing, 9% Psychology, General
Expenses: 2017-2018: $26,188; room/board: $14,250
Financial aid: (718) 489-5346; 76% of undergrads determined to have financial need; average aid package $15,350

St. John Fisher College

Rochester NY
(585) 385-8064
U.S. News ranking: Nat. U., No. 145
Website: www.sjfc.edu
Admissions email: admissions@sjfc.edu
Private; founded 1948
Affiliation: Roman Catholic
Freshman admissions: selective; 2016-2017: 4,551 applied, 2,937 accepted. Either SAT or ACT required. SAT 25/75 percentile: 970-1150. High school rank: 25% in top tenth, 53% in top quarter, 88% in top half
Early decision deadline: 12/1, notification date: 1/15
Early action deadline: N/A, notification date: N/A
Application deadline (fall): rolling
Undergraduate student body: 2,607 full time, 179 part time; 40% male, 60% female; 0% American Indian, 4% Asian, 4% black, 4% Hispanic, 2% multiracial, 0% Pacific Islander, 84% white, 0% international; 97% from in state; 50% live on campus; N/A of students in fraternities, N/A in sororities
Most popular majors: 26% Business, Management, Marketing, and Related Support Services, 26% Health Professions

and Related Programs, 10% Biological and Biomedical Sciences, 7% Communication, Journalism, and Related Programs, 7% Social Sciences
Expenses: 2017-2018: $33,120; room/board: $12,150
Financial aid: (585) 385-8042; 81% of undergrads determined to have financial need; average aid package $22,202

St. John's University

Queens NY
(718) 990-2000
U.S. News ranking: Nat. U., No. 165
Website: www.stjohns.edu/
Admissions email: admhelp@stjohns.edu
Private; founded 1870
Affiliation: Roman Catholic
Freshman admissions: selective; 2016-2017: 28,590 applied, 18,115 accepted. Neither SAT nor ACT required. SAT 25/75 percentile: 970-1180. High school rank: 18% in top tenth, 45% in top quarter, 77% in top half
Early decision deadline: N/A, notification date: N/A
Early action deadline: 11/1, notification date: N/A
Application deadline (fall): rolling
Undergraduate student body: 11,507 full time, 4,933 part time; 43% male, 57% female; 0% American Indian, 17% Asian, 17% black, 10% Hispanic, 5% multiracial, 0% Pacific Islander, 37% white, 6% international; 73% from in state; 28% live on campus; 3% of students in fraternities, 4% in sororities
Most popular majors: 23% Business, Management, Marketing, and Related Support Services, 11% Communication, Journalism, and Related Programs, 11% Health Professions and Related Programs, 8% Biological and Biomedical Sciences, 8% Homeland Security, Law Enforcement, Firefighting and Related Protective Services
Expenses: 2017-2018: $40,790; room/board: $17,020
Financial aid: (718) 990-5743; 80% of undergrads determined to have financial need; average aid package $26,295

St. Joseph's College New York

Brooklyn NY
(718) 940-5800
U.S. News ranking: Reg. U. (N), No. 71
Website: www.sjcny.edu
Admissions email: longislandas@sjcny.edu
Private; founded 1916
Freshman admissions: selective; 2016-2017: 3,673 applied, 2,453 accepted. Either SAT or ACT required. SAT 25/75 percentile: 900-1110. High school rank: N/A
Early decision deadline: N/A, notification date: N/A
Early action deadline: N/A, notification date: N/A
Application deadline (fall): 8/31
Undergraduate student body: 3,380 full time, 660 part time; 34% male, 66% female; 0% American Indian, 3% Asian, 9% black, 13% Hispanic, 2% multiracial, 0% Pacific Islander, 61% white, 0% international; 98% from in

state; 5% live on campus; N/A of students in fraternities, N/A in sororities
Most popular majors: 14% Special Education and Teaching, General, 13% Business Administration and Management, General, 7% Criminal Justice/Law Enforcement Administration, 7% Psychology, General, 6% Accounting
Expenses: 2017-2018: $26,560; room/board: N/A
Financial aid: (631) 687-2600; 78% of undergrads determined to have financial need; average aid package $15,176

St. Lawrence University

Canton NY
(315) 229-5261
U.S. News ranking: Nat. Lib. Arts, No. 58
Website: www.stlawu.edu
Admissions email: admissions@stlawu.edu
Private; founded 1856
Freshman admissions: more selective; 2016-2017: 5,874 applied, 2,519 accepted. Neither SAT nor ACT required. SAT 25/75 percentile: 1110-1300. High school rank: 45% in top tenth, 77% in top quarter, 92% in top half
Early decision deadline: 11/1, notification date: N/A
Early action deadline: N/A, notification date: N/A
Application deadline (fall): 2/1
Undergraduate student body: 2,345 full time, 32 part time; 45% male, 55% female; 0% American Indian, 2% Asian, 3% black, 4% Hispanic, 2% multiracial, 0% Pacific Islander, 79% white, 8% international; 41% from in state; 99% live on campus; 11% of students in fraternities, 16% in sororities
Most popular majors: 20% Economics, General, 12% Psychology, General, 11% Biology/Biological Sciences, General, 10% Mathematics, General, 9% Business/Commerce, General
Expenses: 2017-2018: $52,990; room/board: $13,656
Financial aid: (315) 229-5265; 61% of undergrads determined to have financial need; average aid package $41,517

St. Thomas Aquinas College

Sparkill NY
(845) 398-4100
U.S. News ranking: Reg. U. (N), No. 111
Website: www.stac.edu
Admissions email: admissions@stac.edu
Private; founded 1952
Freshman admissions: less selective; 2016-2017: 1,953 applied, 1,546 accepted. Either SAT or ACT required. SAT 25/75 percentile: 832-1057. High school rank: 5% in top tenth, 18% in top quarter, 68% in top half
Early decision deadline: N/A, notification date: N/A
Early action deadline: N/A, notification date: N/A
Application deadline (fall): rolling
Undergraduate student body: 1,130 full time, 591 part time; 44% male, 56% female; 0% American Indian, 3% Asian, 11% black,

24% Hispanic, 1% multiracial, 0% Pacific Islander, 50% white, 3% international; 80% from in state; 46% live on campus; 0% of students in fraternities, 0% in sororities
Most popular majors: 21% Business Administration and Management, General, 11% Criminal Justice/Law Enforcement Administration, 9% Psychology, General, 8% Biology/Biological Sciences, General, 7% Special Education and Teaching, General
Expenses: 2017-2018: $30,750; room/board: $12,750
Financial aid: (845) 398-4097; 75% of undergrads determined to have financial need; average aid package $17,100

Stony Brook University–SUNY

Stony Brook NY
(631) 632-6868
U.S. News ranking: Nat. U., No. 97
Website: www.stonybrook.edu
Admissions email: enroll@stonybrook.edu
Public; founded 1957
Freshman admissions: more selective; 2016-2017: 34,999 applied, 14,233 accepted. Either SAT or ACT required. SAT 25/75 percentile: 1150-1370. High school rank: 48% in top tenth, 80% in top quarter, 96% in top half
Early decision deadline: N/A, notification date: N/A
Early action deadline: N/A, notification date: N/A
Application deadline (fall): rolling
Undergraduate student body: 15,858 full time, 1,168 part time; 54% male, 46% female; 0% American Indian, 24% Asian, 7% black, 12% Hispanic, 2% multiracial, 0% Pacific Islander, 35% white, 14% international; 93% from in state; 51% live on campus; 3% of students in fraternities, 3% in sororities
Most popular majors: 12% Health Professions and Related Programs, 10% Biology/Biological Sciences, General, 8% Business Administration and Management, General, 8% Psychology, General, 5% Applied Mathematics, General
Expenses: 2017-2018: $9,257 in state, $26,297 out of state; room/board: $13,454
Financial aid: (631) 632-6840; 54% of undergrads determined to have financial need; average aid package $12,900

Syracuse University

Syracuse NY
(315) 443-3611
U.S. News ranking: Nat. U., No. 61
Website: www.syracuse.edu
Admissions email: orange@syr.edu
Private; founded 1870
Freshman admissions: more selective; 2016-2017: 30,923 applied, 16,179 accepted. Either SAT or ACT required. SAT 25/75 percentile: 1090-1290. High school rank: 36% in top tenth, 71% in top quarter, 94% in top half
Early decision deadline: 11/15, notification date: N/A
Early action deadline: N/A, notification date: N/A
Application deadline (fall): 1/1

Undergraduate student body: 14,607 full time, 611 part time; 46% male, 54% female; 1% American Indian, 7% Asian, 8% black, 10% Hispanic, 3% multiracial, 0% Pacific Islander, 56% white, 12% international; 41% from in state; 53% live on campus; 26% of students in fraternities, 36% in sororities
Most popular majors: 14% Business, Management, Marketing, and Related Support Services, 14% Communication, Journalism, and Related Programs, 13% Social Sciences, 9% Visual and Performing Arts, 8% Engineering
Expenses: 2017-2018: $46,755; room/board: $15,558
Financial aid: (315) 443-1513; 52% of undergrads determined to have financial need; average aid package $37,600

Touro College

New York NY
(212) 463-0400
U.S. News ranking: Reg. U. (N), second tier
Website: www.touro.edu/
Admissions email: lasadmit@touro.edu
Private; founded 1971
Freshman admissions: selective; 2016-2017: 1,578 applied, 817 accepted. Neither SAT nor ACT required. SAT 25/75 percentile: 960-1250. High school rank: N/A
Early decision deadline: N/A, notification date: N/A
Early action deadline: N/A, notification date: N/A
Application deadline (fall): rolling
Undergraduate student body: 4,983 full time, 2,104 part time; 29% male, 71% female; 0% American Indian, 3% Asian, 14% black, 10% Hispanic, 1% multiracial, 0% Pacific Islander, 60% white, 3% international; 87% from in state; 0% live on campus; 0% of students in fraternities, 0% in sororities
Most popular majors: 20% Psychology, 19% Health Professions and Related Programs, 17% Multi/Interdisciplinary Studies, 14% Business, Management, Marketing, and Related Support Services, 10% Biological and Biomedical Sciences
Expenses: 2017-2018: $19,870; room/board: $11,170
Financial aid: (646) 565-6000; 50% of undergrads determined to have financial need; average aid package $12,164

Union College

Schenectady NY
(888) 843-6688
U.S. News ranking: Nat. Lib. Arts, No. 36
Website: www.union.edu
Admissions email: admissions@union.edu
Private; founded 1795
Freshman admissions: more selective; 2016-2017: 6,648 applied, 2,453 accepted. Neither SAT nor ACT required. SAT 25/75 percentile: 1200-1390. High school rank: 67% in top tenth, 86% in top quarter, 98% in top half

Early decision deadline: 11/15, notification date: 12/15
Early action deadline: N/A, notification date: N/A
Application deadline (fall): 1/15
Undergraduate student body: 2,132 full time, 71 part time; 55% male, 45% female; 0% American Indian, 6% Asian, 4% black, 7% Hispanic, 3% multiracial, 0% Pacific Islander, 72% white, 8% international; 33% from in state; 90% live on campus; 35% of students in fraternities, 42% in sororities
Most popular majors: 16% Economics, General, 10% Mechanical Engineering, 10% Psychology, General, 6% Neuroscience, 6% Political Science and Government, General
Expenses: 2017-2018: $53,490; room/board: $13,119
Financial aid: (518) 388-6123; 52% of undergrads determined to have financial need; average aid package $42,155

United States Merchant Marine Academy
Kings Point NY
(516) 726-5391
U.S. News ranking: Reg. Coll. (N), No. 3
Website: www.usmma.edu
Admissions email: admissions@usmma.edu
Public; founded 1943
Freshman admissions: more selective; 2016-2017: 1,870 applied, 279 accepted. Either SAT or ACT required. ACT 25/75 percentile: 26-30. High school rank: N/A
Early decision deadline: N/A, notification date: N/A
Early action deadline: N/A, notification date: N/A
Application deadline (fall): 3/1
Undergraduate student body: 902 full time, 0 part time; 81% male, 19% female; 2% American Indian, 8% Asian, 3% black, 11% Hispanic, 0% multiracial, 0% Pacific Islander, 74% white, 1% international; N/A from in state; 100% live on campus; N/A of students in fraternities, N/A in sororities
Most popular majors: 34% Transportation and Materials Moving, Other, 30% Systems Engineering, 13% Engineering, Other, 12% Marine Science/Merchant Marine Officer, 11% Naval Architecture and Marine Engineering
Expenses: 2017-2018: $1,167 in state, $1,167 out of state; room/board: $0
Financial aid: (516) 726-5638; 12% of undergrads determined to have financial need; average aid package $8,069

United States Military Academy
West Point NY
(845) 938-4041
U.S. News ranking: Nat. Lib. Arts, No. 12
Website: www.usma.edu/SitePages/Home.aspx
Admissions email: admissions-info@usma.edu

Public; founded 1802
Freshman admissions: more selective; 2016-2017: 14,829 applied, 1,433 accepted. Either SAT or ACT required. SAT 25/75 percentile: 1180-1390. High school rank: 48% in top tenth, 75% in top quarter, 95% in top half
Early decision deadline: N/A, notification date: N/A
Early action deadline: N/A, notification date: N/A
Application deadline (fall): 2/28
Undergraduate student body: 4,389 full time, 0 part time; 80% male, 20% female; 1% American Indian, 6% Asian, 11% black, 12% Hispanic, 4% multiracial, 1% Pacific Islander, 64% white, 1% international; 6% from in state; 100% live on campus; 0% of students in fraternities, 0% in sororities
Most popular majors: 30% Engineering, 14% Social Sciences, 7% Business, Management, Marketing, and Related Support Services, 6% Computer and Information Sciences and Support Services, 6% Multi/Interdisciplinary Studies
Expenses: 2017-2018: $0 in state, $0 out of state; room/board: $0
Financial aid: N/A

University at Albany–SUNY
Albany NY
(518) 442-5435
U.S. News ranking: Nat. U., No. 151
Website: www.albany.edu
Admissions email: ugadmissions@albany.edu
Public; founded 1844
Freshman admissions: selective; 2016-2017: 23,799 applied, 12,944 accepted. Either SAT or ACT required. SAT 25/75 percentile: 1010-1170. High school rank: 16% in top tenth, 32% in top quarter, 83% in top half
Early decision deadline: 11/15, notification date: N/A
Early action deadline: 11/15, notification date: 11/15
Application deadline (fall): 3/1
Undergraduate student body: 12,421 full time, 718 part time; 51% male, 49% female; 0% American Indian, 9% Asian, 17% black, 16% Hispanic, 3% multiracial, 0% Pacific Islander, 47% white, 6% international; 95% from in state; 57% live on campus; 1% of students in fraternities, 2% in sororities
Most popular majors: 27% Social Sciences, 12% Biological and Biomedical Sciences, 12% Business, Management, Marketing, and Related Support Services, 12% English Language and Literature/Letters, 11% Psychology
Expenses: 2017-2018: $9,278 in state, $24,358 out of state; room/board: $13,464
Financial aid: (518) 442-3202; 66% of undergrads determined to have financial need; average aid package $11,046

University at Buffalo–SUNY
Buffalo NY
(716) 645-6900
U.S. News ranking: Nat. U., No. 97
Website: www.buffalo.edu
Admissions email: ub-admissions@buffalo.edu
Public; founded 1846
Freshman admissions: more selective; 2016-2017: 26,001 applied, 15,440 accepted. Either SAT or ACT required. SAT 25/75 percentile: 1070-1270. High school rank: 27% in top tenth, 59% in top quarter, 90% in top half
Early decision deadline: N/A, notification date: N/A
Early action deadline: 11/15, notification date: N/A
Application deadline (fall): rolling
Undergraduate student body: 18,876 full time, 1,535 part time; 57% male, 43% female; 0% American Indian, 14% Asian, 7% black, 7% Hispanic, 2% multiracial, 0% Pacific Islander, 48% white, 16% international; 97% from in state; 38% live on campus; 2% of students in fraternities, 2% in sororities
Most popular majors: 19% Business, Management, Marketing, and Related Support Services, 16% Social Sciences, 14% Engineering, 11% Psychology, 9% Biological and Biomedical Sciences
Expenses: 2017-2018: $9,770 in state, $26,270 out of state; room/board: $12,292
Financial aid: (716) 645-8232; 54% of undergrads determined to have financial need; average aid package $10,466

University of Rochester
Rochester NY
(585) 275-3221
U.S. News ranking: Nat. U., No. 34
Website: www.rochester.edu
Admissions email: admit@admissions.rochester.edu
Private; founded 1850
Freshman admissions: more selective; 2016-2017: 16,450 applied, 6,181 accepted. Neither SAT nor ACT required. SAT 25/75 percentile: 1250-1460. High school rank: 68% in top tenth, 90% in top quarter, 98% in top half
Early decision deadline: 11/1, notification date: 12/15
Early action deadline: N/A, notification date: N/A
Application deadline (fall): 1/5
Undergraduate student body: 6,170 full time, 216 part time; 50% male, 50% female; 0% American Indian, 11% Asian, 5% black, 7% Hispanic, 3% multiracial, 0% Pacific Islander, 47% white, 21% international; 41% from in state; 77% live on campus; 20% of students in fraternities, 21% in sororities
Most popular majors: 15% Social Sciences, 13% Engineering, 12% Health Professions and Related Programs, 11% Biological and Biomedical Sciences, 11% Psychology
Expenses: 2017-2018: $52,020; room/board: $15,398

Financial aid: (585) 275-3226; 52% of undergrads determined to have financial need; average aid package $44,425

Utica College
Utica NY
(315) 792-3006
U.S. News ranking: Reg. U. (N), No. 130
Website: www.utica.edu
Admissions email: admiss@utica.edu
Private; founded 1946
Freshman admissions: less selective; 2016-2017: 5,419 applied, 4,441 accepted. Neither SAT nor ACT required. SAT 25/75 percentile: 910-1120. High school rank: 11% in top tenth, 31% in top quarter, 68% in top half
Early decision deadline: 11/1, notification date: 12/15
Early action deadline: 11/15, notification date: 12/15
Application deadline (fall): rolling
Undergraduate student body: 2,758 full time, 792 part time; 39% male, 61% female; 0% American Indian, 3% Asian, 12% black, 10% Hispanic, 2% multiracial, 0% Pacific Islander, 67% white, 1% international; 81% from in state; 34% live on campus; 2% of students in fraternities, 2% in sororities
Most popular majors: 47% Health Professions and Related Programs, 21% Homeland Security, Law Enforcement, Firefighting and Related Protective Services, 6% Biological and Biomedical Sciences, 6% Communication, Journalism, and Related Programs, 6% Psychology
Expenses: 2017-2018: $20,676; room/board: $10,834
Financial aid: (315) 792-3215; 82% of undergrads determined to have financial need; average aid package $13,588

Vassar College
Poughkeepsie NY
(845) 437-7300
U.S. News ranking: Nat. Lib. Arts, No. 12
Website: www.vassar.edu
Admissions email: admissions@vassar.edu
Private; founded 1861
Freshman admissions: most selective; 2016-2017: 7,284 applied, 1,964 accepted. Either SAT or ACT required. SAT 25/75 percentile: 1330-1500. High school rank: 68% in top tenth, 93% in top quarter, 98% in top half
Early decision deadline: 11/15, notification date: 12/15
Early action deadline: N/A, notification date: N/A
Application deadline (fall): 1/1
Undergraduate student body: 2,405 full time, 19 part time; 43% male, 57% female; 0% American Indian, 12% Asian, 4% black, 11% Hispanic, 6% multiracial, 0% Pacific Islander, 58% white, 8% international; 25% from in state; 96% live on campus; 0% of students in fraternities, 0% in sororities
Most popular majors: 23% Social Sciences, 17% Biological and Biomedical Sciences, 10% Visual and Performing Arts, 8% English Language and Literature/Letters, 6% Psychology
Expenses: 2017-2018: $55,210; room/board: $12,900
Financial aid: (845) 437-5320; 64% of undergrads determined to have financial need; average aid package $50,820

Vaughn College of Aeronautics and Technology
Flushing NY
(718) 429-6600
U.S. News ranking: Reg. Coll. (N), No. 8
Website: www.vaughn.edu
Admissions email: admitme@vaughn.edu
Private; founded 1932
Freshman admissions: selective; 2016-2017: 800 applied, 635 accepted. Either SAT or ACT required. SAT 25/75 percentile: 904-1129. High school rank: N/A
Early decision deadline: N/A, notification date: N/A
Early action deadline: N/A, notification date: N/A
Application deadline (fall): rolling
Undergraduate student body: 1,275 full time, 205 part time; 87% male, 13% female; 0% American Indian, 10% Asian, 17% black, 34% Hispanic, 2% multiracial, 1% Pacific Islander, 13% white, 6% international; 89% from in state; 10% live on campus; 0% of students in fraternities, 0% in sororities
Most popular majors: 42% Aviation/Airway Management and Operations, 41% Mechanical Engineering/Mechanical Technology/Technician, 13% Mechanical Engineering, 3% Business Administration and Management, General, 1% Avionics Maintenance Technology/Technician
Expenses: 2017-2018: $24,777; room/board: $14,185
Financial aid: (718) 429-6600; 77% of undergrads determined to have financial need; average aid package $10,589

Villa Maria College[1]
Buffalo NY
U.S. News ranking: Reg. Coll. (N), unranked
Admissions email: N/A
Private
Application deadline (fall): N/A
Undergraduate student body: N/A full time, N/A part time
Expenses: 2016-2017: $21,080; room/board: N/A
Financial aid: N/A

Wagner College
Staten Island NY
(718) 390-3411
U.S. News ranking: Reg. U. (N), No. 37
Website: www.wagner.edu
Admissions email: admissions@wagner.edu
Private; founded 1883

Freshman admissions: selective; 2016-2017: 2,790 applied, 1,942 accepted. Neither SAT nor ACT required. SAT 25/75 percentile: 1030-1230. High school rank: 22% in top tenth, 61% in top quarter, 88% in top half
Early decision deadline: N/A, notification date: N/A
Early action deadline: 12/1, notification date: 1/5
Application deadline (fall): 2/15
Undergraduate student body: 1,757 full time, 39 part time; 36% male, 64% female; 0% American Indian, 3% Asian, 8% black, 11% Hispanic, 3% multiracial, 0% Pacific Islander, 66% white, 4% international; 48% from in state; 67% live on campus; 8% of students in fraternities, 12% in sororities
Most popular majors: 22% Health Professions and Related Programs, 19% Business, Management, Marketing, and Related Support Services, 14% Psychology, 10% Social Sciences, 9% Visual and Performing Arts
Expenses: 2017-2018: $45,380; room/board: $13,650
Financial aid: (718) 390-3122; 65% of undergrads determined to have financial need; average aid package $29,515

Webb Institute
Glen Cove NY
(516) 671-8355
U.S. News ranking: Engineering, unranked
Website: www.webb.edu
Admissions email: admissions@webb.edu
Private; founded 1889
Freshman admissions: more selective; 2016-2017: 116 applied, 34 accepted. Either SAT or ACT required. SAT 25/75 percentile: 1410-1490. High school rank: 63% in top tenth, 100% in top quarter, 100% in top half
Early decision deadline: 10/15, notification date: 12/15
Early action deadline: N/A, notification date: N/A
Application deadline (fall): 2/1
Undergraduate student body: 92 full time, 0 part time; 83% male, 17% female; 0% American Indian, 12% Asian, 0% black, 0% Hispanic, 9% multiracial, 0% Pacific Islander, 77% white, 0% international; 21% from in state; 100% live on campus; 0% of students in fraternities, 0% in sororities
Most popular majors: 100% Naval Architecture and Marine Engineering
Expenses: 2017-2018: $48,775; room/board: $14,750
Financial aid: (516) 403-5928; 29% of undergrads determined to have financial need; average aid package $52,650

Wells College[1]
Aurora NY
(800) 952-9355
U.S. News ranking: Nat. Lib. Arts, No. 168
Website: www.wells.edu/
Admissions email: admissions@wells.edu
Private; founded 1868

Application deadline (fall): 3/1
Undergraduate student body: N/A full time, N/A part time
Expenses: 2017-2018: $39,600; room/board: $13,730
Financial aid: (315) 364-3289; 94% of undergrads determined to have financial need; average aid package $36,135

Yeshiva University
New York NY
(212) 960-5277
U.S. News ranking: Nat. U., No. 94
Website: www.yu.edu
Admissions email: yuadmit@ymail.yu.edu
Private; founded 1886
Freshman admissions: more selective; 2016-2017: 1,673 applied, 849 accepted. Either SAT or ACT required. SAT 25/75 percentile: 1090-1360. High school rank: N/A
Early decision deadline: 11/1, notification date: 12/15
Early action deadline: N/A, notification date: N/A
Application deadline (fall): 2/1
Undergraduate student body: 2,628 full time, 86 part time; 55% male, 45% female; 0% American Indian, 0% Asian, 0% black, 0% Hispanic, 0% multiracial, 0% Pacific Islander, 94% white, 4% international; 37% from in state; 65% live on campus; N/A of students in fraternities, N/A in sororities
Most popular majors: 18% Business Administration and Management, General, 15% Biology/Biological Sciences, General, 13% Psychology, General, 12% Accounting, 5% Jewish/Judaic Studies
Expenses: 2017-2018: $42,000; room/board: $12,000
Financial aid: (212) 960-5399; 54% of undergrads determined to have financial need; average aid package $31,812

NORTH CAROLINA

Appalachian State University
Boone NC
(828) 262-2120
U.S. News ranking: Reg. U. (S), No. 9
Website: www.appstate.edu
Admissions email: admissions@appstate.edu
Public; founded 1899
Freshman admissions: more selective; 2016-2017: 13,202 applied, 9,020 accepted. Either SAT or ACT required. ACT 25/75 percentile: 23-27. High school rank: 19% in top tenth, 57% in top quarter, 92% in top half
Early decision deadline: N/A, notification date: N/A
Early action deadline: N/A, notification date: N/A
Application deadline (fall): 3/15
Undergraduate student body: 15,542 full time, 1,053 part time; 45% male, 55% female; 0% American Indian, 2% Asian, 4% black, 5% Hispanic, 3% multiracial, 0% Pacific Islander, 84% white, 0% international; 92% from in state; 34% live on campus; 11% of students in fraternities, 12% in sororities

Most popular majors: 19% Business, Management, Marketing, and Related Support Services, 11% Health Professions and Related Programs, 10% Education, 8% Communication, Journalism, and Related Programs, 7% Parks, Recreation, Leisure, and Fitness Studies
Expenses: 2017-2018: $7,136 in state, $21,652 out of state; room/board: $8,100
Financial aid: (828) 262-2190; 51% of undergrads determined to have financial need; average aid package $9,926

Barton College
Wilson NC
(800) 345-4973
U.S. News ranking: Reg. Coll. (S), No. 8
Website: www.barton.edu
Admissions email: enroll@barton.edu
Private; founded 1902
Freshman admissions: selective; 2016-2017: 2,828 applied, 1,156 accepted. Either SAT or ACT required. ACT 25/75 percentile: 17-23. High school rank: 14% in top tenth, 32% in top quarter, 69% in top half
Early decision deadline: N/A, notification date: N/A
Early action deadline: N/A, notification date: N/A
Application deadline (fall): rolling
Undergraduate student body: 903 full time, 85 part time; 30% male, 70% female; 1% American Indian, 1% Asian, 22% black, 7% Hispanic, 4% multiracial, 0% Pacific Islander, 54% white, 4% international; 84% from in state; 46% live on campus; 19% of students in fraternities, 15% in sororities
Most popular majors: 24% Health Professions and Related Programs, 15% Business, Management, Marketing, and Related Support Services, 9% Education, 6% Biological and Biomedical Sciences, 6% Multi/Interdisciplinary Studies
Expenses: 2017-2018: $29,998; room/board: $9,856
Financial aid: (252) 399-6371; 87% of undergrads determined to have financial need; average aid package $21,974

Belmont Abbey College
Belmont NC
(704) 461-6665
U.S. News ranking: Reg. Coll. (S), No. 8
Website: www. belmontabbeycollege.edu
Admissions email: admissions@bac.edu
Private; founded 1876
Affiliation: Roman Catholic
Freshman admissions: less selective; 2016-2017: 1,564 applied, 1,523 accepted. Neither SAT nor ACT required. SAT 25/75 percentile: 880-1090. High school rank: N/A
Early decision deadline: N/A, notification date: N/A
Early action deadline: N/A, notification date: N/A
Application deadline (fall): 8/1

Undergraduate student body: 1,406 full time, 117 part time; 47% male, 53% female; 0% American Indian, 2% Asian, 19% black, 1% Hispanic, 0% multiracial, 0% Pacific Islander, 55% white, 2% international
Most popular majors: Information not available
Expenses: 2017-2018: $18,500; room/board: $10,354
Financial aid: (704) 461-6719; 76% of undergrads determined to have financial need; average aid package $11,710

Bennett College
Greensboro NC
(336) 370-8624
U.S. News ranking: Reg. Coll. (S), No. 25
Website: www.bennett.edu
Admissions email: admiss@bennett.edu
Private; founded 1873
Affiliation: United Methodist
Freshman admissions: least selective; 2016-2017: 1,488 applied, 1,451 accepted. Either SAT or ACT required. SAT 25/75 percentile: 623-778. High school rank: 2% in top tenth, 10% in top quarter, 34% in top half
Early decision deadline: N/A, notification date: N/A
Early action deadline: N/A, notification date: N/A
Application deadline (fall): rolling
Undergraduate student body: 390 full time, 84 part time; 1% male, 99% female; 0% American Indian, 0% Asian, 85% black, 3% Hispanic, 3% multiracial, 0% Pacific Islander, 0% white, 0% international
Most popular majors: 22% Biology/Biological Sciences, General, 17% Social Work, 15% Multi-/Interdisciplinary Studies, Other, 10% Business Administration and Management, General, 10% Journalism, Other
Expenses: 2017-2018: $18,513; room/board: $8,114
Financial aid: (336) 517-2209; 99% of undergrads determined to have financial need

Brevard College[1]
Brevard NC
(828) 884-8300
U.S. News ranking: Reg. Coll. (S), No. 21
Website: www.brevard.edu
Admissions email: admissions@brevard.edu
Private; founded 1853
Application deadline (fall): rolling
Undergraduate student body: N/A full time, N/A part time
Expenses: 2016-2017: $27,790; room/board: $9,868
Financial aid: (828) 884-8287

Campbell University
Buies Creek NC
(910) 893-1200
U.S. News ranking: Reg. U. (S), No. 27
Website: www.campbell.edu
Admissions email: admissions@campbell.edu
Private; founded 1887

Freshman admissions: selective; 2016-2017: 6,558 applied, 5,312 accepted. Either SAT or ACT required. SAT 25/75 percentile: 920-1130. High school rank: 24% in top tenth, 53% in top quarter, 87% in top half
Early decision deadline: N/A, notification date: N/A
Early action deadline: N/A, notification date: N/A
Application deadline (fall): rolling
Undergraduate student body: 3,737 full time, 823 part time; 47% male, 53% female; 1% American Indian, 2% Asian, 18% black, 8% Hispanic, 3% multiracial, 0% Pacific Islander, 56% white, 2% international; 82% from in state; 41% live on campus; 2% of students in fraternities, 4% in sororities
Most popular majors: 8% Business Administration and Management, General, 8% Science Technologies/Technicians, Other, 7% Psychology, General, 7% Social Sciences, General, 6% Biology/Biological Sciences, General
Expenses: 2017-2018: $31,190; room/board: $11,150
Financial aid: (910) 893-1232; 76% of undergrads determined to have financial need; average aid package $23,385

Catawba College
Salisbury NC
(800) 228-2922
U.S. News ranking: Reg. Coll. (S), No. 4
Website: www.catawba.edu
Admissions email: admission@catawba.edu
Private; founded 1851
Affiliation: United Church of Christ
Freshman admissions: selective; 2016-2017: 2,528 applied, 1,190 accepted. Neither SAT nor ACT required. ACT 25/75 percentile: 18-24. High school rank: 11% in top tenth, 39% in top quarter, 77% in top half
Early decision deadline: N/A, notification date: N/A
Early action deadline: N/A, notification date: N/A
Application deadline (fall): rolling
Undergraduate student body: 1,243 full time, 54 part time; 46% male, 54% female; 0% American Indian, 1% Asian, 19% black, 7% Hispanic, 3% multiracial, 0% Pacific Islander, 67% white, 2% international; 79% from in state; 60% live on campus; 0% of students in fraternities, 0% in sororities
Most popular majors: 29% Business, Management, Marketing, and Related Support Services, 18% Education, 11% Parks, Recreation, Leisure, and Fitness Studies, 9% Biological and Biomedical Sciences, 6% Social Sciences
Expenses: 2017-2018: $29,920; room/board: $10,488
Financial aid: (704) 637-4416; 83% of undergrads determined to have financial need; average aid package $24,609

More @ usnews.com/bestcolleges

Chowan University

Murfreesboro NC
(252) 398-1236
U.S. News ranking: Reg. Coll. (S), No. 50
Website: www.chowan.edu
Admissions email: admission@chowan.edu
Private; founded 1848
Affiliation: Baptist
Freshman admissions: least selective; 2016-2017: 3,720 applied, 2,165 accepted. Either SAT or ACT required. SAT 25/75 percentile: 720-895. High school rank: 3% in top tenth, 11% in top quarter, 38% in top half
Early decision deadline: N/A, notification date: N/A
Early action deadline: N/A, notification date: N/A
Application deadline (fall): rolling
Undergraduate student body: 1,468 full time, 57 part time; 46% male, 54% female; 1% American Indian, 0% Asian, 70% black, 4% Hispanic, 4% multiracial, 0% Pacific Islander, 16% white, 3% International
Most popular majors: 21% Multi/Interdisciplinary Studies, Other, 15% Counseling Psychology, 12% Business Administration and Management, General, 8% Criminal Justice/Law Enforcement Administration, 7% Health and Physical Education/Fitness, General
Expenses: 2017-2018: $24,480; room/board: $9,200
Financial aid: (252) 398-6299; 96% of undergrads determined to have financial need; average aid package $22,580

Davidson College

Davidson NC
(800) 768-0380
U.S. News ranking: Nat. Lib. Arts, No. 10
Website: www.davidson.edu
Admissions email: admission@davidson.edu
Private; founded 1837
Freshman admissions: most selective; 2016-2017: 5,618 applied, 1,130 accepted. Either SAT or ACT required. ACT 25/75 percentile: 28-33. High school rank: 77% in top tenth, 95% in top quarter, 99% in top half
Early decision deadline: 11/15, notification date: 12/15
Early action deadline: N/A, notification date: N/A
Application deadline (fall): 1/2
Undergraduate student body: 1,796 full time, 0 part time; 51% male, 49% female; 1% American Indian, 5% Asian, 7% black, 7% Hispanic, 4% multiracial, 0% Pacific Islander, 67% white, 7% international; 23% from in state; 95% live on campus; 39% of students in fraternities, 70% in sororities
Most popular majors: 14% Biology/Biological Sciences, General, 12% Economics, General, 12% Political Science and Government, General, 11% Psychology, General, 9% English Language and Literature, General
Expenses: 2017-2018: $49,949; room/board: $13,954

Financial aid: (800) 768-0380; 49% of undergrads determined to have financial need; average aid package $45,001

Duke University

Durham NC
(919) 684-3214
U.S. News ranking: Nat. U., No. 9
Website: www.duke.edu/
Private; founded 1838
Freshman admissions: most selective; 2016-2017: 31,671 applied, 3,430 accepted. Either SAT or ACT required. SAT 25/75 percentile: 1380-1570. High school rank: 91% in top tenth, 97% in top quarter, 99% in top half
Early decision deadline: 11/1, notification date: 12/15
Early action deadline: N/A, notification date: N/A
Application deadline (fall): 1/3
Undergraduate student body: 6,577 full time, 32 part time; 50% male, 50% female; 1% American Indian, 22% Asian, 10% black, 8% Hispanic, 2% multiracial, 0% Pacific Islander, 46% white, 10% international
Most popular majors: 11% Biology/Biological Sciences, General, 11% Economics, General, 9% Public Policy Analysis, General, 7% Psychology, General, 6% Bioengineering and Biomedical Engineering
Expenses: 2017-2018: $53,744; room/board: $15,500
Financial aid: (919) 684-6225; 43% of undergrads determined to have financial need; average aid package $50,312

East Carolina University

Greenville NC
(252) 328-6640
U.S. News ranking: Nat. U., No. 207
Website: www.ecu.edu
Admissions email: admis@ecu.edu
Public; founded 1907
Freshman admissions: selective; 2016-2017: 17,135 applied, 12,049 accepted. Either SAT or ACT required. SAT 25/75 percentile: 970-1130. High school rank: 14% in top tenth, 42% in top quarter, 78% in top half
Early decision deadline: N/A, notification date: N/A
Early action deadline: N/A, notification date: N/A
Application deadline (fall): 3/1
Undergraduate student body: 19,754 full time, 3,215 part time; 44% male, 56% female; 1% American Indian, 3% Asian, 16% black, 6% Hispanic, 3% multiracial, 0% Pacific Islander, 68% white, 1% international
Most popular majors: 19% Business, Management, Marketing, and Related Support Services, 19% Health Professions and Related Programs, 9% Education, 6% Biological and Biomedical Sciences, 6% Communication, Journalism, and Related Programs
Expenses: 2017-2018: $7,143 in state, $23,420 out of state; room/board: $9,853

Elizabeth City State University

Elizabeth City NC
(252) 335-3305
U.S. News ranking: Reg. U. (S), No. 87
Website: www.ecsu.edu
Admissions email: admissions@mail.ecsu.edu
Public; founded 1891
Freshman admissions: least selective; 2016-2017: 1,566 applied, 895 accepted. Either SAT or ACT required. SAT 25/75 percentile: 790-950. High school rank: 1% in top tenth, 3% in top quarter, 36% in top half
Early decision deadline: N/A, notification date: N/A
Early action deadline: N/A, notification date: N/A
Application deadline (fall): 8/1
Undergraduate student body: 1,197 full time, 113 part time; 44% male, 56% female; 0% American Indian, 0% Asian, 72% black, 3% Hispanic, 1% multiracial, 0% Pacific Islander, 17% white, 0% international; 86% from in state; N/A live on campus; N/A of students in fraternities, N/A in sororities
Most popular majors: 14% Business, Management, Marketing, and Related Support Services, 10% Homeland Security, Law Enforcement, Firefighting and Related Protective Services, 8% Biological and Biomedical Sciences, 6% Public Administration and Social Service Professions, 6% Social Sciences
Expenses: 2017-2018: $5,466 in state, $18,610 out of state; room/board: $7,890
Financial aid: (252) 335-4850; 91% of undergrads determined to have financial need; average aid package $7,833

Elon University

Elon NC
(800) 334-8448
U.S. News ranking: Reg. U. (S), No. 1
Website: www.elon.edu
Admissions email: admissions@elon.edu
Private; founded 1889
Freshman admissions: more selective; 2016-2017: 10,098 applied, 6,103 accepted. Either SAT or ACT required. SAT 25/75 percentile: 1100-1280. High school rank: 29% in top tenth, 62% in top quarter, 89% in top half
Early decision deadline: 11/1, notification date: 12/1
Early action deadline: 11/10, notification date: 12/20
Application deadline (fall): 1/10
Undergraduate student body: 5,839 full time, 169 part time; 41% male, 59% female; 0% American Indian, 2% Asian, 5% black, 6% Hispanic, 3% multiracial, 0% Pacific Islander, 81% white, 2% international; 22% from in state; 63% live on campus; 20% of students in fraternities, 39% in sororities

Most popular majors: 34% Business/Commerce, General, 19% Communication and Media Studies, 6% Psychology, General, 5% Health and Physical Education/Fitness, 4% Biology, General
Expenses: 2017-2018: $34,273; room/board: $11,869
Financial aid: (336) 278-7640; 32% of undergrads determined to have financial need; average aid package $19,000

Fayetteville State University

Fayetteville NC
(910) 672-1371
U.S. News ranking: Reg. U. (S), second tier
Website: www.uncfsu.edu
Admissions email: admissions@uncfsu.edu
Public; founded 1867
Freshman admissions: less selective; 2016-2017: 4,611 applied, 2,733 accepted. Either SAT or ACT required. SAT 25/75 percentile: 790-950. High school rank: 7% in top tenth, 27% in top quarter, 66% in top half
Early decision deadline: N/A, notification date: N/A
Early action deadline: N/A, notification date: N/A
Application deadline (fall): 6/30
Undergraduate student body: 4,141 full time, 1,399 part time; 32% male, 68% female; 3% American Indian, 1% Asian, 64% black, 6% Hispanic, 0% multiracial, 0% Pacific Islander, 19% white, 0% international; 97% from in state; 28% live on campus; 1% of students in fraternities, 1% in sororities
Most popular majors: 18% Criminal Justice/Safety Studies, 16% Registered Nursing/Registered Nurse, 14% Business Administration and Management, General, 13% Psychology, General, 6% Liberal Arts and Sciences/Liberal Studies
Expenses: 2017-2018: $7,830 in state, $19,438 out of state; room/board: $9,167
Financial aid: (910) 672-1325; 85% of undergrads determined to have financial need; average aid package $10,283

Gardner-Webb University

Boiling Springs NC
(800) 253-6472
U.S. News ranking: Nat. U., No. 223
Website: www.gardner-webb.edu
Admissions email: admissions@gardner-webb.edu
Private; founded 1905
Freshman admissions: selective; 2016-2017: 4,316 applied, 2,239 accepted. Either SAT or ACT required. SAT 25/75 percentile: 870-1110. High school rank: 16% in top tenth, 43% in top quarter, 77% in top half
Early decision deadline: N/A, notification date: N/A
Early action deadline: N/A, notification date: N/A
Application deadline (fall): rolling

Undergraduate student body: 1,908 full time, 454 part time; 36% male, 64% female; 1% American Indian, 1% Asian, 15% black, 3% Hispanic, 0% multiracial, 0% Pacific Islander, 66% white, 1% international
Most popular majors: 27% Health Professions and Related Programs, 20% Business, Management, Marketing, and Related Support Services, 17% Psychology, 6% Homeland Security, Law Enforcement, Firefighting and Related Protective Services, 5% Biological and Biomedical Sciences
Expenses: 2017-2018: $30,740; room/board: $10,080
Financial aid: (704) 406-4247; 77% of undergrads determined to have financial need; average aid package $24,191

Greensboro College

Greensboro NC
U.S. News ranking: Reg. Coll. (S), No. 44
Website: www.gborocollege.edu
Admissions email: admissions@gborocollege.edu
Private
Affiliation: United Methodist
Freshman admissions: less selective; 2016-2017: 2,687 applied, 974 accepted. Either SAT or ACT required. SAT 25/75 percentile: N/A. High school rank: N/A
Early decision deadline: N/A, notification date: N/A
Early action deadline: N/A, notification date: N/A
Application deadline (fall): N/A
Undergraduate student body: 768 full time, 192 part time; 49% male, 51% female; 0% American Indian, 1% Asian, 30% black, 3% Hispanic, 6% multiracial, 0% Pacific Islander, 56% white, 0% international
Most popular majors: Information not available
Expenses: 2016-2017: $28,000; room/board: $10,400
Financial aid: N/A

Guilford College

Greensboro NC
(800) 992-7759
U.S. News ranking: Nat. Lib. Arts, No. 160
Website: www.guilford.edu
Admissions email: admission@guilford.edu
Private; founded 1837
Affiliation: Friends
Freshman admissions: selective; 2016-2017: 3,321 applied, 2,010 accepted. Neither SAT nor ACT required. SAT 25/75 percentile: 870-1160. High school rank: 10% in top tenth, 29% in top quarter, 67% in top half
Early decision deadline: N/A, notification date: N/A
Early action deadline: 12/1, notification date: 12/15
Application deadline (fall): 8/10
Undergraduate student body: 1,560 full time, 249 part time; 48% male, 52% female; 1% American Indian, 3% Asian, 25% black, 7% Hispanic, 4% multiracial, 0% Pacific Islander, 58% white,

2% international; 67% from in state; 53% live on campus; 0% of students in fraternities, 0% in sororities
Most popular majors: 16% Business, Management, Marketing, and Related Support Services, 14% Psychology, 9% Parks, Recreation, Leisure, and Fitness Studies, 8% Biological and Biomedical Sciences, 8% Homeland Security, Law Enforcement, Firefighting and Related Protective Services
Expenses: 2017-2018: $35,563; room/board: $10,800
Financial aid: (336) 316-2354; 76% of undergrads determined to have financial need; average aid package $25,525

High Point University
High Point NC
(800) 345-6993
U.S. News ranking: Reg. Coll. (S), No. 1
Website: www.highpoint.edu
Admissions email: admiss@ highpoint.edu
Private; founded 1924
Affiliation: United Methodist
Freshman admissions: selective; 2016-2017: 9,683 applied, 7,657 accepted. Either SAT or ACT required. SAT 25/75 percentile: 995-1200. High school rank: 17% in top tenth, 46% in top quarter, 81% in top half
Early decision deadline: 11/1, notification date: 11/27
Early action deadline: 11/15, notification date: 12/15
Application deadline (fall): 7/1
Undergraduate student body: 4,508 full time, 38 part time; 40% male, 60% female; 0% American Indian, 2% Asian, 5% black, 5% Hispanic, 6% multiracial, 0% Pacific Islander, 78% white, 2% international; 21% from in state; 94% live on campus; 19% of students in fraternities, 35% in sororities
Most popular majors: 37% Business, Management, Marketing, and Related Support Services, 14% Communication, Journalism, and Related Programs, 9% Visual and Performing Arts, 7% Biological and Biomedical Sciences, 6% Parks, Recreation, Leisure, and Fitness Studies
Expenses: 2017-2018: $34,005; room/board: $13,350
Financial aid: (336) 841-9128; 41% of undergrads determined to have financial need; average aid package $15,757

Johnson C. Smith University
Charlotte NC
(704) 378-1010
U.S. News ranking: Nat. Lib. Arts, second tier
Website: www.jcsu.edu
Admissions email: admissions@jcsu.edu
Private; founded 1867
Freshman admissions: least selective; 2016-2017: 5,841 applied, 2,646 accepted. Either SAT or ACT required. SAT 25/75 percentile: 740-915. High school rank: 5% in top tenth, 20% in top quarter, 51% in top half

Early decision deadline: N/A, notification date: N/A
Early action deadline: N/A, notification date: N/A
Application deadline (fall): rolling
Undergraduate student body: 1,284 full time, 42 part time; 39% male, 61% female; 0% American Indian, 0% Asian, 84% black, 4% Hispanic, 2% multiracial, 0% Pacific Islander, 1% white, 2% international; 59% from in state; 66% live on campus; 8% of students in fraternities, 8% in sororities
Most popular majors: 22% Social Work, 14% Business Administration and Management, General, 10% Criminology, 8% Mass Communication/Media Studies, 7% Sport and Fitness Administration/Management
Expenses: 2017-2018: $18,236; room/board: $7,100
Financial aid: (704) 378-1035; 92% of undergrads determined to have financial need; average aid package $15,853

Lees-McRae College
Banner Elk NC
(828) 898-8723
U.S. News ranking: Reg. Coll. (S), No. 19
Website: www.lmc.edu
Admissions email: admissions@lmc.edu
Private; founded 1900
Affiliation: Presbyterian Church (USA)
Freshman admissions: selective; 2016-2017: 1,531 applied, 965 accepted. Neither SAT nor ACT required. ACT 25/75 percentile: 18-23. High school rank: 11% in top tenth, 27% in top quarter, 55% in top half
Early decision deadline: N/A, notification date: N/A
Early action deadline: N/A, notification date: N/A
Application deadline (fall): rolling
Undergraduate student body: 978 full time, 13 part time; 34% male, 66% female; 1% American Indian, 1% Asian, 6% black, 4% Hispanic, 1% multiracial, 0% Pacific Islander, 72% white, 2% international; 77% from in state; 58% live on campus; 3% of students in fraternities, 4% in sororities
Most popular majors: 28% Health Professions and Related Programs, 15% Biological and Biomedical Sciences, 15% Education, 12% Homeland Security, Law Enforcement, Firefighting and Related Protective Services, 10% Business, Management, Marketing, and Related Support Services
Expenses: 2017-2018: $26,198; room/board: $10,758
Financial aid: (828) 898-8740; 80% of undergrads determined to have financial need; average aid package $24,611

Lenoir-Rhyne University
Hickory NC
(828) 328-7300
U.S. News ranking: Reg. U. (S), No. 61
Website: www.lr.edu
Admissions email: admission@lr.edu

Private; founded 1891
Affiliation: Evangelical Lutheran Church
Freshman admissions: less selective; 2016-2017: 6,300 applied, 4,417 accepted. Either SAT or ACT required. SAT 25/75 percentile: 870-1090. High school rank: N/A
Early decision deadline: N/A, notification date: N/A
Early action deadline: 11/7, notification date: 11/21
Application deadline (fall): rolling
Undergraduate student body: 1,453 full time, 257 part time; 40% male, 60% female; 1% American Indian, 2% Asian, 13% black, 7% Hispanic, 4% multiracial, 0% Pacific Islander, 68% white, 2% international; 83% from in state; 55% live on campus; 3% of students in fraternities, 13% in sororities
Most popular majors: 20% Health Professions and Related Programs, 20% Parks, Recreation, Leisure, and Fitness Studies, 10% Business, Management, Marketing, and Related Support Services, 7% Psychology, 6% Biological and Biomedical Sciences
Expenses: 2017-2018: $35,350; room/board: $12,150
Financial aid: (828) 328-7304; 86% of undergrads determined to have financial need; average aid package $28,880

Livingstone College
Salisbury NC
(704) 216-6001
U.S. News ranking: Reg. Coll. (S), second tier
Website: www.livingstone.edu/
Admissions email: admissions@ livingstone.edu
Private; founded 1879
Affiliation: African Methodist Episcopal Zion Church
Freshman admissions: least selective; 2016-2017: 6,565 applied, 3,137 accepted. Either SAT or ACT required. ACT 25/75 percentile: 13-17. High school rank: 0% in top tenth, 6% in top quarter, 24% in top half
Early decision deadline: N/A, notification date: N/A
Early action deadline: N/A, notification date: N/A
Application deadline (fall): rolling
Undergraduate student body: 1,188 full time, 16 part time; 49% male, 51% female; 0% American Indian, 0% Asian, 75% black, 0% Hispanic, 2% multiracial, 0% Pacific Islander, 1% white, 0% international; 64% from in state; 80% live on campus; 30% of students in fraternities, 40% in sororities
Most popular majors: 28% Criminal Justice/Safety Studies, 20% Junior High/Intermediate/Middle School Education and Teaching, 17% Business Administration and Management, General, 15% Sport and Fitness Administration/Management, 7% Liberal Arts and Sciences/Liberal Studies
Expenses: 2017-2018: $17,763; room/board: $6,596

Financial aid: (704) 216-6069; 97% of undergrads determined to have financial need; average aid package $13,606

Mars Hill University
Mars Hill NC
(866) 642-4968
U.S. News ranking: Reg. Coll. (S), No. 24
Website: www.mhu.edu
Admissions email: admissions@mhu.edu
Private; founded 1856
Freshman admissions: less selective; 2016-2017: 3,153 applied, 1,789 accepted. Either SAT or ACT required. ACT 25/75 percentile: 17-22. High school rank: 6% in top tenth, 25% in top quarter, 64% in top half
Early decision deadline: N/A, notification date: N/A
Early action deadline: N/A, notification date: N/A
Application deadline (fall): rolling
Undergraduate student body: 1,264 full time, 107 part time; 47% male, 53% female; 1% American Indian, 2% Asian, 20% black, 6% Hispanic, 2% multiracial, 0% Pacific Islander, 66% white, 0% international
Most popular majors: 12% Business, Management, Marketing, and Related Support Services, 9% Public Administration and Social Service Professions, 8% Biological and Biomedical Sciences, 8% Homeland Security, Law Enforcement, Firefighting and Related Protective Services, 7% Psychology
Expenses: 2017-2018: $31,804; room/board: $9,300
Financial aid: (828) 689-1103; 75% of undergrads determined to have financial need; average aid package $21,994

Meredith College
Raleigh NC
(919) 760-8581
U.S. News ranking: Nat. Lib. Arts, No. 163
Website: www.meredith.edu
Admissions email: admissions@ meredith.edu
Private; founded 1891
Freshman admissions: selective; 2016-2017: 1,923 applied, 1,169 accepted. Either SAT or ACT required. SAT 25/75 percentile: 920-1123. High school rank: 23% in top tenth, 48% in top quarter, 83% in top half
Early decision deadline: 10/30, notification date: 11/1
Early action deadline: N/A, notification date: N/A
Application deadline (fall): rolling
Undergraduate student body: 1,616 full time, 69 part time; 0% male, 100% female; 1% American Indian, 3% Asian, 8% black, 6% Hispanic, 4% multiracial, 0% Pacific Islander, 71% white, 2% international; 93% from in state; 54% live on campus; N/A of students in fraternities, N/A in sororities
Most popular majors: 12% Psychology, General, 9% Biology/ Biological Sciences, General, 8% Business Administration and Management, General,

5% Child Development, 5% Mass Communication/Media Studies
Expenses: 2017-2018: $35,916; room/board: $10,718
Financial aid: (919) 760-8565; 75% of undergrads determined to have financial need; average aid package $24,977

Methodist University
Fayetteville NC
(910) 630-7027
U.S. News ranking: Reg. U. (S), No. 85
Website: www.methodist.edu
Admissions email: admissions@ methodist.edu
Private; founded 1956
Affiliation: United Methodist
Freshman admissions: selective; 2016-2017: 4,652 applied, 2,549 accepted. Either SAT or ACT required. ACT 25/75 percentile: 18-23. High school rank: 13% in top tenth, 37% in top quarter, 70% in top half
Early decision deadline: N/A, notification date: N/A
Early action deadline: N/A, notification date: N/A
Application deadline (fall): rolling
Undergraduate student body: 1,949 full time, 220 part time; 54% male, 46% female; 1% American Indian, 1% Asian, 19% black, 7% Hispanic, 4% multiracial, 0% Pacific Islander, 45% white, 9% international; 58% from in state; 52% live on campus; 6% of students in fraternities, 7% in sororities
Most popular majors: 32% Business, Management, Marketing, and Related Support Services, 11% Health Professions and Related Programs, 10% Biological and Biomedical Sciences, 8% Homeland Security, Law Enforcement, Firefighting and Related Protective Services, 6% Parks, Recreation, Leisure, and Fitness Studies
Expenses: 2017-2018: $32,860; room/board: $12,300
Financial aid: (910) 630-7000; 76% of undergrads determined to have financial need; average aid package $22,375

Montreat College
Montreat NC
(800) 622-6968
U.S. News ranking: Reg. U. (S), No. 101
Website: www.montreat.edu
Admissions email: admissions@ montreat.edu
Private; founded 1916
Freshman admissions: less selective; 2016-2017: 849 applied, 521 accepted. Either SAT or ACT required. SAT 25/75 percentile: 850-1060. High school rank: 8% in top tenth, 28% in top quarter, 63% in top half
Early decision deadline: N/A, notification date: N/A
Early action deadline: N/A, notification date: N/A
Application deadline (fall): rolling
Undergraduate student body: 523 full time, 243 part time; 47% male, 53% female; 1% American Indian, 1% Asian, 15% black, 3% Hispanic, 2% multiracial, 0% Pacific Islander, 64% white,

4% international; 71% from in state; 80% live on campus; 0% of students in fraternities, 0% in sororities
Most popular majors: 36% Business Administration and Management, General, 19% Psychology, Other, 9% Business Administration, Management and Operations, Other, 8% Biology/Biological Sciences, General, 6% English Language and Literature, General
Expenses: 2017-2018: $25,755; room/board: $8,600
Financial aid: (828) 669-8012; 81% of undergrads determined to have financial need; average aid package $20,397

North Carolina A&T State University
Greensboro NC
(336) 334-7946
U.S. News ranking: Nat. U., second tier
Website: www.ncat.edu
Admissions email: uadmit@ncat.edu
Public; founded 1891
Freshman admissions: less selective; 2016-2017: 10,367 applied, 5,561 accepted. Either SAT or ACT required. SAT 25/75 percentile: 850-1010. High school rank: 11% in top tenth, 25% in top quarter, 74% in top half
Early decision deadline: N/A, notification date: N/A
Early action deadline: N/A, notification date: N/A
Application deadline (fall): 6/30
Undergraduate student body: 8,747 full time, 921 part time; 45% male, 55% female; 0% American Indian, 1% Asian, 82% black, 3% Hispanic, 4% multiracial, 0% Pacific Islander, 5% white, 1% international; 80% from in state; 41% live on campus; 1% of students in fraternities, 1% in sororities
Most popular majors: 15% Engineering, 9% Business, Management, Marketing, and Related Support Services, 9% Communication, Journalism, and Related Programs, 8% Psychology, 7% Liberal Arts and Sciences, General Studies and Humanities
Expenses: 2017-2018: $6,526 in state, $19,416 out of state; room/board: $7,260
Financial aid: (336) 334-7973; 86% of undergrads determined to have financial need; average aid package $10,989

North Carolina Central University
Durham NC
(919) 530-6298
U.S. News ranking: Reg. U. (S), No. 80
Website: www.nccu.edu
Admissions email: admissions@nccu.edu
Public; founded 1910
Freshman admissions: less selective; 2016-2017: 8,614 applied, 5,745 accepted. Either SAT or ACT required. SAT 25/75 percentile: 810-940. High school rank: 6% in top tenth, 22% in top quarter, 63% in top half

Early decision deadline: N/A, notification date: N/A
Early action deadline: N/A, notification date: N/A
Application deadline (fall): rolling
Undergraduate student body: 5,343 full time, 942 part time; 34% male, 66% female; 0% American Indian, 1% Asian, 80% black, 4% Hispanic, 5% multiracial, 0% Pacific Islander, 7% white, 2% international; 91% from in state; 48% live on campus; N/A of students in fraternities, N/A in sororities
Most popular majors: 16% Law, 13% Criminal Justice/Safety Studies, 11% Psychology, General, 10% Business Administration and Management, General, 10% Family and Consumer Sciences/Human Sciences, General
Expenses: 2016-2017: $5,882 in state, $18,340 out of state; room/board: $8,270
Financial aid: (919) 530-6180

North Carolina State University–Raleigh
Raleigh NC
(919) 515-2434
U.S. News ranking: Nat. U., No. 81
Website: admissions.ncsu.edu
Admissions email: undergrad-admissions@ncsu.edu
Public; founded 1887
Freshman admissions: more selective; 2016-2017: 25,929 applied, 12,034 accepted. Either SAT or ACT required. ACT 25/75 percentile: 27-31. High school rank: 50% in top tenth, 87% in top quarter, 100% in top half
Early decision deadline: N/A, notification date: N/A
Early action deadline: 10/15, notification date: 1/30
Application deadline (fall): 1/15
Undergraduate student body: 20,934 full time, 2,913 part time; 55% male, 45% female; 0% American Indian, 6% Asian, 6% black, 5% Hispanic, 4% multiracial, 0% Pacific Islander, 73% white, 4% international; 90% from in state; 41% live on campus; 12% of students in fraternities, 19% in sororities
Most popular majors: 27% Engineering, 14% Business, Management, Marketing, and Related Support Services, 10% Biological and Biomedical Sciences, 6% Agriculture, Agriculture Operations, and Related Sciences, 5% Social Sciences
Expenses: 2017-2018: $9,058 in state, $27,406 out of state; room/board: $10,854
Financial aid: (919) 515-2421; 49% of undergrads determined to have financial need; average aid package $13,434

North Carolina Wesleyan College
Rocky Mount NC
(800) 488-6292
U.S. News ranking: Reg. Coll. (S), No. 46
Website: www.ncwc.edu
Admissions email: adm@ncwc.edu
Private; founded 1956
Affiliation: United Methodist

Freshman admissions: less selective; 2016-2017: 4,038 applied, 2,486 accepted. Neither SAT nor ACT required. ACT 25/75 percentile: 16-23. High school rank: 12% in top tenth, 30% in top quarter, 55% in top half
Early decision deadline: N/A, notification date: N/A
Early action deadline: N/A, notification date: N/A
Application deadline (fall): rolling
Undergraduate student body: 1,787 full time, 305 part time; 41% male, 59% female; 1% American Indian, 1% Asian, 44% black, 2% Hispanic, 2% multiracial, 0% Pacific Islander, 32% white, 4% international; 72% from in state; 59% live on campus; N/A of students in fraternities, N/A in sororities
Most popular majors: 47% Business Administration and Management, General, 20% Criminal Justice/Law Enforcement Administration, 13% Psychology, General, 6% Computer and Information Sciences, General, 5% Biology/Biological Sciences, General
Expenses: 2017-2018: $30,150; room/board: $10,050
Financial aid: (252) 985-5200; 92% of undergrads determined to have financial need; average aid package $18,258

Pfeiffer University[1]
Misenheimer NC
(800) 338-2060
U.S. News ranking: Reg. U. (S), No. 87
Website: www.pfeiffer.edu
Admissions email: admissions@pfeiffer.edu
Private; founded 1885
Affiliation: United Methodist
Application deadline (fall): rolling
Undergraduate student body: N/A full time, N/A part time
Expenses: 2017-2018: $29,574; room/board: $10,958
Financial aid: (704) 463-3060; 96% of undergrads determined to have financial need; average aid package $23,850

Queens University of Charlotte
Charlotte NC
(800) 849-0202
U.S. News ranking: Reg. U. (S), No. 20
Website: www.queens.edu
Admissions email: admissions@queens.edu
Private; founded 1857
Affiliation: Presbyterian
Freshman admissions: selective; 2016-2017: 1,641 applied, 1,358 accepted. Either SAT or ACT required. SAT 25/75 percentile: 940-1140. High school rank: 16% in top tenth, 43% in top quarter, 78% in top half
Early decision deadline: N/A, notification date: N/A
Early action deadline: 12/1, notification date: 12/15
Application deadline (fall): rolling
Undergraduate student body: 1,307 full time, 310 part time; 30% male, 70% female; 1% American Indian, 2% Asian, 16% black, 9% Hispanic, 2% multiracial, 0% Pacific Islander, 57% white,

7% international; 58% from in state; 70% live on campus; 9% of students in fraternities, 22% in sororities
Most popular majors: 31% Health Professions and Related Programs, 16% Business, Management, Marketing, and Related Support Services, 11% Communication, Journalism, and Related Programs, 8% Biological and Biomedical Sciences, 6% Visual and Performing Arts
Expenses: 2017-2018: $33,532; room/board: $10,804
Financial aid: (704) 337-2225; 67% of undergrads determined to have financial need; average aid package $23,305

Salem College
Winston-Salem NC
(336) 721-2621
U.S. News ranking: Nat. Lib. Arts, No. 117
Website: www.salem.edu
Admissions email: admissions@salem.edu
Private; founded 1772
Affiliation: Moravian Church
Freshman admissions: more selective; 2016-2017: 1,045 applied, 594 accepted. Either SAT or ACT required. SAT 25/75 percentile: 21-27. High school rank: 40% in top tenth, 78% in top quarter, 97% in top half
Early decision deadline: N/A, notification date: N/A
Early action deadline: N/A, notification date: N/A
Application deadline (fall): rolling
Undergraduate student body: 719 full time, 214 part time; 3% male, 97% female; 0% American Indian, 2% Asian, 21% black, 14% Hispanic, 3% multiracial, 0% Pacific Islander, 56% white, 1% international; 72% from in state; 62% live on campus; 0% of students in fraternities, 0% in sororities
Most popular majors: 10% Business Administration and Management, General, 9% Sociology, 8% Biology/Biological Sciences, General, 8% Psychology, General, 8% Speech Communication and Rhetoric
Expenses: 2017-2018: $28,566; room/board: $11,640
Financial aid: N/A; 85% of undergrads determined to have financial need; average aid package $32,459

Shaw University
Raleigh NC
(800) 214-6683
U.S. News ranking: Reg. Coll. (S), second tier
Website: www.shawu.edu
Admissions email: admissions@shawu.edu
Private; founded 1865
Affiliation: Baptist
Freshman admissions: least selective; 2016-2017: 9,608 applied, 4,695 accepted. Either SAT or ACT required. SAT 25/75 percentile: 640-820. High school rank: 1% in top tenth, 4% in top quarter, 24% in top half
Early decision deadline: N/A, notification date: N/A
Early action deadline: N/A, notification date: N/A

Application deadline (fall): 7/30
Undergraduate student body: 1,604 full time, 109 part time; 43% male, 57% female; 0% American Indian, 0% Asian, 66% black, 0% Hispanic, 2% multiracial, 0% Pacific Islander, 1% white, 2% international; 68% from in state; 58% live on campus; N/A of students in fraternities, N/A in sororities
Most popular majors: 23% Business, Management, Marketing, and Related Support Services, 16% Public Administration and Social Service Professions, 10% Communication, Journalism, and Related Programs, 9% Parks, Recreation, Leisure, and Fitness Studies, 8% Social Sciences
Expenses: 2017-2018: $16,480; room/board: $8,158
Financial aid: (919) 546-8565

Southeastern Baptist Theological Seminary
Wake Forest NC
(919) 761-2246
U.S. News ranking: Reg. U. (S), unranked
Website: www.sebts.edu/
Admissions email: admissions@sebts.edu
Private; founded 1950
Affiliation: Southern Baptist
Freshman admissions: least selective; 2016-2017: 156 applied, 156 accepted. Neither SAT nor ACT required. SAT 25/75 percentile: N/A. High school rank: N/A
Early decision deadline: N/A, notification date: N/A
Early action deadline: N/A, notification date: N/A
Application deadline (fall): 8/1
Undergraduate student body: 236 full time, 178 part time; 67% male, 33% female; 0% American Indian, 3% Asian, 5% black, 3% Hispanic, 0% multiracial, 0% Pacific Islander, 86% white, 0% international; 77% from in state; 65% live on campus; 0% of students in fraternities, 0% in sororities
Most popular majors: Information not available
Expenses: 2016-2017: $10,500; room/board: $4,190
Financial aid: N/A

St. Augustine's University
Raleigh NC
(919) 516-4012
U.S. News ranking: Reg. Coll. (S), No. 50
Website: www.st-aug.edu
Admissions email: admissions@st-aug.edu
Private; founded 1867
Freshman admissions: least selective; 2016-2017: 3,789 applied, 2,755 accepted. Either SAT or ACT required. SAT 25/75 percentile: 630-830. High school rank: N/A
Early decision deadline: N/A, notification date: N/A
Early action deadline: N/A, notification date: N/A

Application deadline (fall): rolling
Undergraduate student body: 921 full time, 23 part time; 50% male, 50% female; 1% American Indian, 0% Asian, 89% black, 1% Hispanic, 0% multiracial, 0% Pacific Islander, 1% white, 1% international
Most popular majors: 14% Criminalistics and Criminal Science, 11% Business Administration and Management, General, 9% Sport and Fitness Administration/Management, 8% Communications Technology/Technician, 8% Psychology, General
Expenses: 2016-2017: $17,890; room/board: $7,692
Financial aid: (919) 516-4131

University of Mount Olive

Mount Olive NC
(919) 658-2502
U.S. News ranking: Reg. Coll. (S), No. 19
Website: www.umo.edu/
Admissions email: admissions@umo.edu
Private; founded 1951
Affiliation: Original Free Will Baptist
Freshman admissions: selective; 2016-2017: 2,652 applied, 1,264 accepted. Neither SAT nor ACT required. ACT 25/75 percentile: 17-22. High school rank: N/A
Early decision deadline: N/A, notification date: N/A
Early action deadline: N/A, notification date: N/A
Application deadline (fall): rolling
Undergraduate student body: 1,447 full time, 1,803 part time; 33% male, 67% female; 1% American Indian, 0% Asian, 29% black, 3% Hispanic, 7% multiracial, 0% Pacific Islander, 51% white, 3% international
Most popular majors: 33% Business, Management, Marketing, and Related Support Services, 17% Health Professions and Related Programs, 15% Education, 15% Homeland Security, Law Enforcement, Firefighting and Related Protective Services
Expenses: 2016-2017: $19,000; room/board: $7,600
Financial aid: N/A

University of North Carolina School of the Arts[1]

Winston-Salem NC
(336) 770-3291
U.S. News ranking: Arts, unranked
Website: www.uncsa.edu
Admissions email: admissions@uncsa.edu
Public; founded 1963
Application deadline (fall): 3/15
Undergraduate student body: N/A full time, N/A part time
Expenses: 2017-2018: $9,338 in state, $25,081 out of state; room/board: $8,977
Financial aid: (336) 770-3297; 62% of undergrads determined to have financial need; average aid package $13,596

University of North Carolina–Asheville

Asheville NC
(828) 251-6481
U.S. News ranking: Nat. Lib. Arts, No. 141
Website: www.unca.edu
Admissions email: admissions@unca.edu
Public; founded 1927
Freshman admissions: more selective; 2016-2017: 3,433 applied, 2,676 accepted. Either SAT or ACT required. ACT 25/75 percentile: 23-28. High school rank: 20% in top tenth, 54% in top quarter, 92% in top half
Early decision deadline: N/A, notification date: N/A
Early action deadline: 11/15, notification date: 12/15
Application deadline (fall): 2/15
Undergraduate student body: 3,227 full time, 579 part time; 42% male, 58% female; 0% American Indian, 2% Asian, 4% black, 6% Hispanic, 4% multiracial, 0% Pacific Islander, 78% white, 1% international; 89% from in state; 38% live on campus; 3% of students in fraternities, 3% in sororities
Most popular majors: 12% Psychology, General, 7% Environmental Studies, 6% English Language and Literature, General, 6% Mass Communication/Media Studies, 6% Public Health Education and Promotion
Expenses: 2017-2018: $7,145 in state, $23,868 out of state; room/board: $9,106
Financial aid: (828) 251-6535; 57% of undergrads determined to have financial need; average aid package $12,183

University of North Carolina–Chapel Hill

Chapel Hill NC
(919) 966-3621
U.S. News ranking: Nat. U., No. 30
Website: www.unc.edu
Admissions email: unchelp@admissions.unc.edu
Public; founded 1789
Freshman admissions: most selective; 2016-2017: 34,889 applied, 9,400 accepted. Either SAT or ACT required. ACT 25/75 percentile: 27-32. High school rank: 73% in top tenth, 91% in top quarter, 94% in top half
Early decision deadline: N/A, notification date: N/A
Early action deadline: 10/15, notification date: 1/31
Application deadline (fall): 1/15
Undergraduate student body: 17,869 full time, 654 part time; 42% male, 58% female; 1% American Indian, 10% Asian, 8% black, 8% Hispanic, 4% multiracial, 0% Pacific Islander, 63% white, 2% international; 83% from in state; 51% live on campus; 20% of students in fraternities, 20% in sororities
Most popular majors: 10% Communication and Media Studies, 9% Biology, General, 8% Economics, 8% Psychology, General, 6% Political Science and Government

Expenses: 2017-2018: $9,005 in state, $34,588 out of state; room/board: $11,556
Financial aid: (919) 962-8396; 42% of undergrads determined to have financial need; average aid package $19,946

University of North Carolina–Charlotte

Charlotte NC
(704) 687-5507
U.S. News ranking: Nat. U., No. 198
Website: www.uncc.edu/
Admissions email: admissions@uncc.edu
Public; founded 1946
Freshman admissions: selective; 2016-2017: 17,475 applied, 10,868 accepted. Either SAT or ACT required. ACT 25/75 percentile: 22-26. High school rank: 22% in top tenth, 59% in top quarter, 90% in top half
Early decision deadline: N/A, notification date: N/A
Early action deadline: 11/1, notification date: 1/30
Application deadline (fall): 6/1
Undergraduate student body: 20,263 full time, 3,141 part time; 53% male, 47% female; 0% American Indian, 6% Asian, 16% black, 9% Hispanic, 4% multiracial, 0% Pacific Islander, 59% white, 2% international; 95% from in state; 23% live on campus; 8% of students in fraternities, 11% in sororities
Most popular majors: 20% Business, Management, Marketing, and Related Support Services, 8% Engineering, 8% Health Professions and Related Programs, 8% Psychology, 8% Social Sciences
Expenses: 2017-2018: $6,834 in state, $20,268 out of state; room/board: $12,406
Financial aid: (704) 687-5504; 62% of undergrads determined to have financial need; average aid package $10,277

University of North Carolina–Greensboro

Greensboro NC
(336) 334-5243
U.S. News ranking: Nat. U., second tier
Website: www.uncg.edu/
Admissions email: admissions@uncg.edu
Public; founded 1891
Freshman admissions: selective; 2016-2017: 9,035 applied, 6,680 accepted. Either SAT or ACT required. SAT 25/75 percentile: 910-1100. High school rank: 14% in top tenth, 41% in top quarter, 78% in top half
Early decision deadline: N/A, notification date: N/A
Early action deadline: N/A, notification date: N/A
Application deadline (fall): 3/1
Undergraduate student body: 14,116 full time, 2,165 part time; 34% male, 66% female; 0% American Indian, 5% Asian, 28% black, 8% Hispanic, 5% multiracial, 0% Pacific Islander,

51% white, 2% international; 94% from in state; 33% live on campus; N/A of students in fraternities, N/A in sororities
Most popular majors: 12% Business Administration and Management, General, 7% Registered Nursing/Registered Nurse, 6% Psychology, General, 4% Human Development and Family Studies, General, 4% Kinesiology and Exercise Science
Expenses: 2017-2018: $7,164 in state, $22,410 out of state; room/board: $8,834
Financial aid: (336) 334-5702; 83% of undergrads determined to have financial need; average aid package $11,315

University of North Carolina–Pembroke

Pembroke NC
(910) 521-6262
U.S. News ranking: Reg. U. (S), No. 102
Website: www.uncp.edu
Admissions email: admissions@uncp.edu
Public; founded 1887
Freshman admissions: less selective; 2016-2017: 4,544 applied, 3,345 accepted. Either SAT or ACT required. ACT 25/75 percentile: 18-21. High school rank: 11% in top tenth, 32% in top quarter, 70% in top half
Early decision deadline: N/A, notification date: N/A
Early action deadline: N/A, notification date: N/A
Application deadline (fall): 7/31
Undergraduate student body: 4,510 full time, 1,004 part time; 39% male, 61% female; 15% American Indian, 2% Asian, 36% black, 5% Hispanic, 3% multiracial, 0% Pacific Islander, 37% white, 1% international; 97% from in state; 37% live on campus; N/A of students in fraternities, N/A in sororities
Most popular majors: 13% Criminal Justice/Safety Studies, 11% Business Administration and Management, General, 11% Parks, Recreation, Leisure, and Fitness Studies, Other, 10% Sociology, 9% Biology/Biological Sciences, General
Expenses: 2017-2018: $5,956 in state, $17,547 out of state; room/board: $8,782
Financial aid: (910) 521-6255; 81% of undergrads determined to have financial need; average aid package $10,204

University of North Carolina–Wilmington

Wilmington NC
(910) 962-3243
U.S. News ranking: Reg. U. (S), No. 14
Website: www.uncw.edu
Admissions email: admissions@uncw.edu
Public; founded 1947
Freshman admissions: more selective; 2016-2017: 11,555 applied, 7,487 accepted. Either SAT or ACT required. ACT 25/75

percentile: 22-26. High school rank: 20% in top tenth, 61% in top quarter, 94% in top half
Early decision deadline: N/A, notification date: N/A
Early action deadline: 11/1, notification date: 1/20
Application deadline (fall): 2/1
Undergraduate student body: 12,023 full time, 1,891 part time; 38% male, 62% female; 0% American Indian, 2% Asian, 5% black, 7% Hispanic, 4% multiracial, 0% Pacific Islander, 78% white, 1% international; 87% from in state; 30% live on campus; 5% of students in fraternities, 8% in sororities
Most popular majors: 19% Business Administration and Management, General, 9% Registered Nursing/Registered Nurse, 7% Psychology, General, 6% Biology/Biological Sciences, General, 6% Speech Communication and Rhetoric
Expenses: 2017-2018: $7,048 in state, $21,064 out of state; room/board: $10,490
Financial aid: (910) 962-3177; 56% of undergrads determined to have financial need; average aid package $8,932

Wake Forest University

Winston-Salem NC
(336) 758-4324
U.S. News ranking: Nat. U., No. 27
Website: www.wfu.edu
Admissions email: admissions@wfu.edu
Private; founded 1834
Freshman admissions: most selective; 2016-2017: 14,006 applied, 4,249 accepted. Neither SAT nor ACT required. ACT 25/75 percentile: 28-32. High school rank: 78% in top tenth, 92% in top quarter, 97% in top half
Early decision deadline: 11/15, notification date: N/A
Early action deadline: N/A, notification date: N/A
Application deadline (fall): 1/1
Undergraduate student body: 4,900 full time, 55 part time; 47% male, 53% female; 0% American Indian, 4% Asian, 7% black, 7% Hispanic, 3% multiracial, 0% Pacific Islander, 71% white, 9% international; 23% from in state; 76% live on campus; 35% of students in fraternities, 60% in sororities
Most popular majors: 21% Social Sciences, 20% Business, Management, Marketing, and Related Support Services, 9% Communication, Journalism, and Related Programs, 8% Biological and Biomedical Sciences, 8% Psychology
Expenses: 2017-2018: $51,400; room/board: $15,354
Financial aid: (336) 758-5154; 31% of undergrads determined to have financial need; average aid package $47,288

Warren Wilson College

Asheville NC
(800) 934-3536
U.S. News ranking: Nat. Lib. Arts, No. 160
Website: www.warren-wilson.edu
Admissions email: admit@warren-wilson.edu
Private; founded 1894
Freshman admissions: selective; 2016-2017: 948 applied, 777 accepted. Neither SAT nor ACT required. ACT 25/75 percentile: 23-28. High school rank: 14% in top tenth, 37% in top quarter, 69% in top half
Early decision deadline: 11/15, notification date: 12/1
Early action deadline: 11/1, notification date: 12/1
Application deadline (fall): rolling
Undergraduate student body: 644 full time, 6 part time; 38% male, 62% female; 2% American Indian, 1% Asian, 6% black, 8% Hispanic, 2% multiracial, 0% Pacific Islander, 74% white, 2% international; 26% from in state; 88% live on campus; 0% of students in fraternities, 0% in sororities
Most popular majors: 20% Environmental Studies, 9% History, General, 9% Psychology, General, 8% English Language and Literature, General, 8% Visual and Performing Arts, General
Expenses: 2017-2018: $35,244; room/board: $10,660
Financial aid: (828) 771-2082; 72% of undergrads determined to have financial need; average aid package $30,450

Western Carolina University

Cullowhee NC
(828) 227-7317
U.S. News ranking: Reg. U. (S), No. 38
Website: www.wcu.edu
Admissions email: admiss@email.wcu.edu
Public; founded 1889
Freshman admissions: selective; 2016-2017: 18,297 applied, 7,444 accepted. Either SAT or ACT required. ACT 25/75 percentile: 20-25. High school rank: 14% in top tenth, 38% in top quarter, 76% in top half
Early decision deadline: N/A, notification date: N/A
Early action deadline: 11/15, notification date: 12/15
Application deadline (fall): 3/1
Undergraduate student body: 7,871 full time, 1,300 part time; 45% male, 55% female; 1% American Indian, 1% Asian, 6% black, 6% Hispanic, 4% multiracial, 0% Pacific Islander, 79% white, 1% international; 92% from in state; N/A live on campus; N/A of students in fraternities, N/A in sororities
Most popular majors: 18% Business, Management, Marketing, and Related Support Services, 17% Health Professions and Related Programs, 13% Education, 7% Homeland Security, Law Enforcement, Firefighting and Related Protective Services, 6% Public Administration and Social Service Professions

William Peace University[1]

Raleigh NC
(919) 508-2214
U.S. News ranking: Nat. Lib. Arts, second tier
Website: www.peace.edu
Admissions email: admissions@peace.edu
Private; founded 1857
Application deadline (fall): rolling
Undergraduate student body: N/A full time, N/A part time
Expenses: 2016-2017: $27,080; room/board: $10,350
Financial aid: N/A

Wingate University

Wingate NC
(800) 755-5550
U.S. News ranking: Reg. U. (S), No. 32
Website: www.wingate.edu
Admissions email: info@wingate.edu
Private; founded 1896
Freshman admissions: selective; 2016-2017: 7,581 applied, 5,273 accepted. Either SAT or ACT required. SAT 25/75 percentile: 940-1130. High school rank: 24% in top tenth, 53% in top quarter, 85% in top half
Early decision deadline: N/A, notification date: N/A
Early action deadline: N/A, notification date: N/A
Application deadline (fall): rolling
Undergraduate student body: 2,044 full time, 40 part time; 40% male, 60% female; 1% American Indian, 2% Asian, 15% black, 4% Hispanic, 7% multiracial, 0% Pacific Islander, 63% white, 4% international; 76% from in state; 75% live on campus; 6% of students in fraternities, 19% in sororities
Most popular majors: 13% Biological and Biomedical Sciences, 13% Education, 12% Business, Management, Marketing, and Related Support Services, 12% Public Administration and Social Service Professions, 10% Psychology
Expenses: 2017-2018: $31,120; room/board: $10,780
Financial aid: (704) 233-8010; 78% of undergrads determined to have financial need; average aid package $24,280

Winston-Salem State University[1]

Winston-Salem NC
(336) 750-2070
U.S. News ranking: Reg. U. (S), No. 106
Website: www.wssu.edu
Admissions email: admissions@wssu.edu
Public; founded 1892
Application deadline (fall): 3/15
Undergraduate student body: N/A full time, N/A part time

Expenses: 2016-2017: $5,804 in state, $15,915 out of state; room/board: $9,593
Financial aid: N/A

Bismarck State College

Bismarck ND
(701) 224-2459
U.S. News ranking: Reg. Coll. (Mid. W), second tier
Website: bismarckstate.edu/
Admissions email: bsc.admissions@bismarckstate.edu
Public; founded 1939
Freshman admissions: less selective; 2016-2017: 1,068 applied, 1,068 accepted. Neither SAT nor ACT required. ACT 25/75 percentile: 17-22. High school rank: 4% in top tenth, 15% in top quarter, 43% in top half
Early decision deadline: N/A, notification date: N/A
Early action deadline: N/A, notification date: N/A
Application deadline (fall): rolling
Undergraduate student body: 2,241 full time, 1,735 part time; 57% male, 43% female; 2% American Indian, 1% Asian, 3% black, 3% Hispanic, 3% multiracial, 0% Pacific Islander, 86% white, 0% international; 78% from in state; 14% live on campus; 0% of students in fraternities, 0% in sororities
Most popular majors: 100% Operations Management and Supervision
Expenses: 2017-2018: $4,591 in state, $10,921 out of state; room/board: $6,992
Financial aid: (701) 224-5441; 42% of undergrads determined to have financial need; average aid package $8,814

Dickinson State University

Dickinson ND
(701) 483-2175
U.S. News ranking: Reg. Coll. (Mid. W), No. 51
Website: www.dickinsonstate.edu/
Admissions email: dsu.hawks@dsu.nodak.edu
Public; founded 1918
Freshman admissions: less selective; 2016-2017: 697 applied, 505 accepted. Neither SAT nor ACT required. ACT 25/75 percentile: 17-24. High school rank: N/A
Early decision deadline: N/A, notification date: N/A
Early action deadline: 4/15, notification date: N/A
Application deadline (fall): 8/15
Undergraduate student body: 912 full time, 469 part time; 41% male, 59% female; 5% American Indian, 1% Asian, 1% black, 6% Hispanic, 3% multiracial, 76% Pacific Islander, 1% white, 6% international
Most popular majors: 39% Business, Management, Marketing, and Related Support Services, 15% Education, 8% Parks, Recreation, Leisure, and Fitness Studies, 6% Computer

and Information Sciences and Support Services, 6% Multi/Interdisciplinary Studies
Expenses: 2017-2018: $6,502 in state, $9,150 out of state; room/board: $6,724
Financial aid: (701) 483-2371; 52% of undergrads determined to have financial need; average aid package $11,349

Mayville State University

Mayville ND
(701) 788-4667
U.S. News ranking: Reg. Coll. (Mid. W), No. 45
Website: www.mayvillestate.edu
Admissions email: masuadmissions@mayvillestate.edu
Public; founded 1889
Freshman admissions: selective; 2016-2017: 396 applied, 150 accepted. Either SAT or ACT required. ACT 25/75 percentile: 18-23. High school rank: N/A
Early decision deadline: N/A, notification date: N/A
Early action deadline: N/A, notification date: N/A
Application deadline (fall): rolling
Undergraduate student body: 609 full time, 499 part time; 42% male, 58% female; 3% American Indian, 1% Asian, 11% black, 7% Hispanic, 3% multiracial, 1% Pacific Islander, 74% white, 0% international; 58% from in state; 29% live on campus; N/A of students in fraternities, N/A in sororities
Most popular majors: Adult and Continuing Education and Teaching, Business Administration and Management, General, Early Childhood Education and Teaching, General Studies, Physical Education Teaching and Coaching
Expenses: 2017-2018: $6,456 in state, $9,084 out of state; room/board: $7,624
Financial aid: (701) 788-4767; 66% of undergrads determined to have financial need; average aid package $11,355

Minot State University

Minot ND
(701) 858-3350
U.S. News ranking: Reg. U. (Mid. W), second tier
Website: www.minotstateu.edu
Admissions email: askmsu@minotstateu.edu
Public; founded 1913
Freshman admissions: selective; 2016-2017: 846 applied, 506 accepted. Either SAT or ACT required. ACT 25/75 percentile: 18-23. High school rank: 6% in top tenth, 22% in top quarter, 60% in top half
Early decision deadline: N/A, notification date: N/A
Early action deadline: N/A, notification date: N/A
Application deadline (fall): rolling
Undergraduate student body: 2,021 full time, 1,115 part time; 40% male, 60% female; 2% American Indian, 2% Asian, 6% black, 6% Hispanic, 4% multiracial, 0% Pacific Islander, 66% white, 12% international; 81% from in state; 15% live on campus; N/A

of students in fraternities, N/A in sororities
Most popular majors: Information not available
Expenses: 2017-2018: $6,810 in state, $6,810 out of state; room/board: $6,344
Financial aid: (701) 858-3375; 45% of undergrads determined to have financial need; average aid package $10,508

North Dakota State University

Fargo ND
(701) 231-8643
U.S. News ranking: Nat. U., No. 198
Website: www.ndsu.edu
Admissions email: NDSU.Admission@ndsu.edu
Public; founded 1890
Freshman admissions: selective; 2016-2017: 5,128 applied, 4,759 accepted. Either SAT or ACT required. ACT 25/75 percentile: 21-26. High school rank: 16% in top tenth, 40% in top quarter, 74% in top half
Early decision deadline: N/A, notification date: N/A
Early action deadline: N/A, notification date: N/A
Application deadline (fall): rolling
Undergraduate student body: 10,680 full time, 1,330 part time; 54% male, 46% female; 1% American Indian, 1% Asian, 3% black, 2% Hispanic, 3% multiracial, 0% Pacific Islander, 86% white, 2% international; 43% from in state; 32% live on campus; 7% of students in fraternities, 7% in sororities
Most popular majors: 15% Business, Management, Marketing, and Related Support Services, 13% Engineering, 11% Health Professions and Related Programs, 9% Agriculture, Agriculture Operations, and Related Sciences, 8% Family and Consumer Sciences/Human Sciences
Expenses: 2017-2018: $9,409 in state, $20,571 out of state; room/board: $8,357
Financial aid: (701) 231-6221; 50% of undergrads determined to have financial need; average aid package $11,540

University of Jamestown

Jamestown ND
(701) 252-3467
U.S. News ranking: Reg. Coll. (Mid. W), No. 27
Website: www.uj.edu
Admissions email: admissions@uj.edu
Private; founded 1883
Affiliation: Presbyterian Church (USA)
Freshman admissions: selective; 2016-2017: 1,560 applied, 894 accepted. Either SAT or ACT required. ACT 25/75 percentile: 20-25. High school rank: 13% in top tenth, 39% in top quarter, 73% in top half
Early decision deadline: N/A, notification date: N/A
Early action deadline: N/A, notification date: N/A

Application deadline (fall): 9/10
Undergraduate student body: 914 full time, 41 part time; 50% male, 50% female; 1% American Indian, 1% Asian, 5% black, 7% Hispanic, 0% multiracial, 1% Pacific Islander, 74% white, 10% international; 40% from in state; 76% live on campus; N/A of students in fraternities, N/A in sororities
Most popular majors: 21% Registered Nursing/Registered Nurse, 12% Business Administration and Management, General, 9% Elementary Education and Teaching, 9% Kinesiology and Exercise Science, 7% Criminal Justice/Safety Studies
Expenses: 2017-2018: $21,158; room/board: $7,656
Financial aid: (701) 252-3467; 62% of undergrads determined to have financial need; average aid package $15,820

University of Mary
Bismarck ND
(701) 355-8030
U.S. News ranking: Reg. U. (Mid. W), No. 109
Website: www.umary.edu
Admissions email: marauder@umary.edu
Private; founded 1959
Affiliation: Roman Catholic
Freshman admissions: selective; 2016-2017: 922 applied, 773 accepted. Either SAT or ACT required. ACT 25/75 percentile: 20-26. High school rank: 25% in top tenth, 51% in top quarter, 80% in top half
Early decision deadline: N/A, notification date: N/A
Early action deadline: N/A, notification date: N/A
Application deadline (fall): rolling
Undergraduate student body: 1,734 full time, 484 part time; 36% male, 64% female; 1% American Indian, 1% Asian, 2% black, 4% Hispanic, 3% multiracial, 0% Pacific Islander, 82% white, 1% international
Most popular majors: Information not available
Expenses: 2017-2018: $18,150; room/board: $6,970
Financial aid: (701) 355-8226; 66% of undergrads determined to have financial need; average aid package $13,771

University of North Dakota
Grand Forks ND
(800) 225-5863
U.S. News ranking: Nat. U., No. 192
Website: und.edu
Admissions email: admissions@und.edu
Public; founded 1883
Freshman admissions: selective; 2016-2017: 5,144 applied, 4,305 accepted. Either SAT or ACT required. ACT 25/75 percentile: 21-26. High school rank: 18% in top tenth, 43% in top quarter, 78% in top half
Early decision deadline: N/A, notification date: N/A
Early action deadline: N/A, notification date: N/A

Application deadline (fall): rolling
Undergraduate student body: 8,827 full time, 2,428 part time; 57% male, 43% female; 1% American Indian, 2% Asian, 2% black, 3% Hispanic, 3% multiracial, 0% Pacific Islander, 81% white, 5% international; 40% from in state; 27% live on campus; 11% of students in fraternities, 12% in sororities
Most popular majors: 6% Psychology, General, 6% Registered Nursing/Registered Nurse, 5% Airline/Commercial/Professional Pilot and Flight Crew, 4% Accounting, 4% Mechanical Engineering
Expenses: 2017-2018: $9,862 in state, $21,462 out of state; room/board: $8,548
Financial aid: (701) 777-3121; 47% of undergrads determined to have financial need; average aid package $13,705

Valley City State University
Valley City ND
(701) 845-7101
U.S. News ranking: Reg. Coll. (Mid. W), No. 33
Website: www.vcsu.edu
Admissions email: enrollment.services@vcsu.edu
Public; founded 1890
Freshman admissions: selective; 2016-2017: 372 applied, 365 accepted. Either SAT or ACT required. ACT 25/75 percentile: 18-24. High school rank: N/A
Early decision deadline: N/A, notification date: N/A
Early action deadline: N/A, notification date: N/A
Application deadline (fall): rolling
Undergraduate student body: 798 full time, 497 part time; 42% male, 58% female; 1% American Indian, 1% Asian, 4% black, 6% Hispanic, 3% multiracial, 0% Pacific Islander, 82% white, 3% international; 64% from in state; 35% live on campus; 1% of students in fraternities, 1% in sororities
Most popular majors: 37% Elementary Education and Teaching, 8% Business Administration and Management, General, 5% Wildlife, Fish and Wildlands Science and Management, 4% English/Language Arts Teacher Education, 3% Psychology, General
Expenses: 2017-2018: $7,328 in state, $16,368 out of state; room/board: $6,542
Financial aid: (701) 845-7412; 58% of undergrads determined to have financial need; average aid package $12,489

OHIO

Antioch University
Yellow Springs OH
(937) 769-1818
U.S. News ranking: Reg. U. (Mid. W), unranked
Website: midwest.antioch.edu
Admissions email: admission.aum@antioch.edu
Private; founded 1852
Freshman admissions: least selective; 2016-2017: N/A applied, N/A accepted. Neither

SAT nor ACT required. SAT 25/75 percentile: N/A. High school rank: N/A
Early decision deadline: N/A, notification date: N/A
Early action deadline: N/A, notification date: N/A
Application deadline (fall): rolling
Undergraduate student body: 18 full time, 19 part time; 27% male, 73% female; 0% American Indian, 0% Asian, 14% black, 0% Hispanic, 0% multiracial, 0% Pacific Islander, 51% white, 0% international
Most popular majors: Information not available
Expenses: 2016-2017: $19,572; room/board: N/A
Financial aid: N/A

Art Academy of Cincinnati[1]
Cincinnati OH
U.S. News ranking: Arts, unranked
Website: www.artacademy.edu
Admissions email: admissions@artacademy.edu
Private; founded 1869
Application deadline (fall): N/A
Undergraduate student body: N/A full time, N/A part time
Expenses: 2016-2017: $29,752; room/board: $9,200
Financial aid: N/A

Ashland University
Ashland OH
(419) 289-5052
U.S. News ranking: Nat. U., No. 223
Website: www.ashland.edu/admissions
Admissions email: enrollme@ashland.edu
Private; founded 1878
Freshman admissions: selective; 2016-2017: 3,443 applied, 2,495 accepted. Either SAT or ACT required. ACT 25/75 percentile: 20-25. High school rank: 15% in top tenth, 41% in top quarter, 75% in top half
Early decision deadline: N/A, notification date: N/A
Early action deadline: N/A, notification date: N/A
Application deadline (fall): rolling
Undergraduate student body: 3,414 full time, 1,122 part time; 53% male, 47% female; 0% American Indian, 1% Asian, 13% black, 3% Hispanic, 2% multiracial, 0% Pacific Islander, 76% white, 2% international; 80% from in state; 44% live on campus; 12% of students in fraternities, 11% in sororities
Most popular majors: 23% Education, 19% Business, Management, Marketing, and Related Support Services, 16% Health Professions and Related Programs, 9% Biological and Biomedical Sciences, 7% Homeland Security, Law Enforcement, Firefighting and Related Protective Services
Expenses: 2017-2018: $20,700; room/board: $9,746
Financial aid: (419) 289-5944; 69% of undergrads determined to have financial need; average aid package $15,299

Baldwin Wallace University
Berea OH
(440) 826-2222
U.S. News ranking: Reg. U. (Mid. W), No. 18
Website: www.bw.edu
Admissions email: admission@bw.edu
Private; founded 1845
Affiliation: United Methodist
Freshman admissions: selective; 2016-2017: 4,515 applied, 2,697 accepted. Neither SAT nor ACT required. ACT 25/75 percentile: 21-27. High school rank: 21% in top tenth, 47% in top quarter, 81% in top half
Early decision deadline: N/A, notification date: N/A
Early action deadline: N/A, notification date: N/A
Application deadline (fall): rolling
Undergraduate student body: 3,058 full time, 247 part time; 45% male, 55% female; 0% American Indian, 2% Asian, 10% black, 5% Hispanic, 5% multiracial, 0% Pacific Islander, 78% white, 1% international; 78% from in state; 62% live on campus; 13% of students in fraternities, 24% in sororities
Most popular majors: 25% Business, Management, Marketing, and Related Support Services, 11% Biological and Biomedical Sciences, 11% Health Professions and Related Programs, 10% Visual and Performing Arts, 7% Education
Expenses: 2017-2018: $31,668; room/board: $9,142
Financial aid: (440) 826-2108; 73% of undergrads determined to have financial need; average aid package $23,841

Bluffton University
Bluffton OH
(800) 488-3257
U.S. News ranking: Reg. Coll. (Mid. W), No. 27
Website: www.bluffton.edu
Admissions email: admissions@bluffton.edu
Private; founded 1899
Affiliation: Mennonite Church
Freshman admissions: selective; 2016-2017: 1,480 applied, 733 accepted. Either SAT or ACT required. ACT 25/75 percentile: 19-24. High school rank: 9% in top tenth, 32% in top quarter, 59% in top half
Early decision deadline: N/A, notification date: N/A
Early action deadline: N/A, notification date: N/A
Application deadline (fall): rolling
Undergraduate student body: 728 full time, 137 part time; 50% male, 50% female; 0% American Indian, 1% Asian, 6% black, 4% Hispanic, 4% multiracial, 0% Pacific Islander, 82% white, 1% international; 88% from in state; 87% live on campus; 0% of students in fraternities, 0% in sororities
Most popular majors: 15% Business Administration and Management, General, 13% Organizational Behavior Studies, 12% Social Work, 10% Early Childhood Education and Teaching, 7% Accounting

Expenses: 2017-2018: $31,672; room/board: $10,484
Financial aid: (419) 358-3409; 86% of undergrads determined to have financial need; average aid package $26,316

Bowling Green State University
Bowling Green OH
(419) 372-2478
U.S. News ranking: Nat. U., No. 202
Website: www.bgsu.edu
Admissions email: choosebgsu@bgsu.edu
Public; founded 1910
Freshman admissions: selective; 2016-2017: 14,891 applied, 11,157 accepted. Either SAT or ACT required. ACT 25/75 percentile: 20-25. High school rank: 12% in top tenth, 36% in top quarter, 72% in top half
Early decision deadline: N/A, notification date: N/A
Early action deadline: N/A, notification date: N/A
Application deadline (fall): 7/15
Undergraduate student body: 13,184 full time, 1,668 part time; 44% male, 56% female; 0% American Indian, 1% Asian, 10% black, 4% Hispanic, 4% multiracial, 0% Pacific Islander, 77% white, 2% international; 88% from in state; 44% live on campus; 4% of students in fraternities, 4% in sororities
Most popular majors: 4% Biology/Biological Sciences, General, 4% Education, Other, 4% Education/Teaching of Individuals in Early Childhood Special Education Programs, 4% Psychology, General, 3% Special Education and Teaching, General
Expenses: 2017-2018: $11,057 in state, $18,593 out of state; room/board: $8,918
Financial aid: (419) 372-2651; 65% of undergrads determined to have financial need; average aid package $14,013

Capital University
Columbus OH
(866) 544-6175
U.S. News ranking: Reg. U. (Mid. W), No. 34
Website: www.capital.edu
Admissions email: admission@capital.edu
Private; founded 1830
Affiliation: Evangelical Lutheran Church
Freshman admissions: selective; 2016-2017: 4,287 applied, 2,968 accepted. Either SAT or ACT required. ACT 25/75 percentile: 22-28. High school rank: 20% in top tenth, 46% in top quarter, 83% in top half
Early decision deadline: N/A, notification date: N/A
Early action deadline: N/A, notification date: N/A
Application deadline (fall): 5/1
Undergraduate student body: 2,511 full time, 207 part time; 39% male, 61% female; 0% American Indian, 1% Asian, 10% black, 4% Hispanic, 5% multiracial, 0% Pacific Islander, 75% white, 2% international; 90% from in

state; 59% live on campus; 2% of students in fraternities, 3% in sororities
Most popular majors: 16% Business, Management, Marketing, and Related Support Services, 15% Health Professions and Related Programs, 13% Education, 9% Visual and Performing Arts, 8% Public Administration and Social Service Professions
Expenses: 2017-2018: $34,600; room/board: $10,423
Financial aid: (614) 236-6511; 80% of undergrads determined to have financial need; average aid package $28,446

Case Western Reserve University
Cleveland OH
(216) 368-4450
U.S. News ranking: Nat. U., No. 37
Website: www.case.edu
Admissions email: admission@case.edu
Private; founded 1826
Freshman admissions: most selective; 2016-2017: 23,115 applied, 8,192 accepted. Either SAT or ACT required. ACT 25/75 percentile: 30-34. High school rank: 71% in top tenth, 94% in top quarter, 100% in top half
Early decision deadline: 11/1, notification date: 12/15
Early action deadline: 11/1, notification date: 12/15
Application deadline (fall): 1/15
Undergraduate student body: 4,990 full time, 162 part time; 55% male, 45% female; 0% American Indian, 20% Asian, 4% black, 6% Hispanic, 5% multiracial, 0% Pacific Islander, 50% white, 12% international; 32% from in state; 78% live on campus; 31% of students in fraternities, 39% in sororities
Most popular majors: 9% Bioengineering and Biomedical Engineering, 9% Biology/Biological Sciences, General, 8% Mechanical Engineering, 8% Psychology, General, 6% Registered Nursing/Registered Nurse
Expenses: 2017-2018: $47,500; room/board: $14,784
Financial aid: (216) 368-4530; 49% of undergrads determined to have financial need; average aid package $38,928

Cedarville University
Cedarville OH
(800) 233-2784
U.S. News ranking: Reg. Coll. (Mid. W), No. 13
Website: www.cedarville.edu
Admissions email: admissions@cedarville.edu
Private; founded 1887
Affiliation: Baptist
Freshman admissions: more selective; 2016-2017: 4,092 applied, 2,826 accepted. Either SAT or ACT required. ACT 25/75 percentile: 23-29. High school rank: 36% in top tenth, 68% in top quarter, 90% in top half
Early decision deadline: N/A, notification date: N/A
Early action deadline: N/A, notification date: N/A
Application deadline (fall): 8/1

Undergraduate student body: 3,024 full time, 356 part time; 48% male, 52% female; 0% American Indian, 2% Asian, 1% black, 3% Hispanic, 3% multiracial, 0% Pacific Islander, 87% white, 2% international; 37% from in state; 83% live on campus; 0% of students in fraternities, 0% in sororities
Most popular majors: 19% Health Professions and Related Programs, 11% Business, Management, Marketing, and Related Support Services, 9% Engineering, 9% Visual and Performing Arts, 8% Education
Expenses: 2017-2018: $29,156; room/board: $7,088
Financial aid: (937) 766-7866; 68% of undergrads determined to have financial need; average aid package $20,654

Central State University
Wilberforce OH
(937) 376-6348
U.S. News ranking: Reg. Coll. (Mid. W), second tier
Website: www.centralstate.edu
Admissions email: admissions@centralstate.edu
Public; founded 1887
Freshman admissions: less selective; 2016-2017: 7,669 applied, 3,222 accepted. Either SAT or ACT required. ACT 25/75 percentile: 15-18. High school rank: 5% in top tenth, 20% in top quarter, 49% in top half
Early decision deadline: N/A, notification date: N/A
Early action deadline: N/A, notification date: N/A
Application deadline (fall): rolling
Undergraduate student body: 1,601 full time, 128 part time; 45% male, 55% female; 0% American Indian, 0% Asian, 94% black, 1% Hispanic, 1% multiracial, 0% Pacific Islander, 1% white, 1% international; 55% from in state; 40% live on campus; 1% of students in fraternities, 1% in sororities
Most popular majors: 23% Business, Management, Marketing, and Related Support Services, 13% Psychology, 12% Homeland Security, Law Enforcement, Firefighting and Related Protective Services, 10% Communication, Journalism, and Related Programs, 8% Education
Expenses: 2017-2018: $6,246 in state, $8,096 out of state; room/board: $9,934
Financial aid: (937) 376-6579

Cleveland Institute of Art
Cleveland OH
(216) 421-7418
U.S. News ranking: Arts, unranked
Website: www.cia.edu
Admissions email: admissions@cia.edu
Private; founded 1882
Freshman admissions: selective; 2016-2017: 864 applied, 523 accepted. Either SAT or ACT required. ACT 25/75 percentile: 20-26. High school rank: 19% in top tenth, 38% in top quarter, 67% in top half

Early decision deadline: N/A, notification date: N/A
Early action deadline: 12/1, notification date: 12/15
Application deadline (fall): rolling
Undergraduate student body: 611 full time, 14 part time; 42% male, 58% female; 0% American Indian, 4% Asian, 9% black, 5% Hispanic, 3% multiracial, 0% Pacific Islander, 69% white, 9% international; 64% from in state; 30% live on campus; 1% of students in fraternities, 1% in sororities
Most popular majors: 12% Industrial and Product Design, 11% Illustration, 10% Painting, 8% Game and Interactive Media Design, 8% Medical Illustration/Medical Illustrator
Expenses: 2017-2018: $40,655; room/board: $10,800
Financial aid: (937) 421-7425; 81% of undergrads determined to have financial need; average aid package $27,536

Cleveland Institute of Music
Cleveland OH
(216) 795-3107
U.S. News ranking: Arts, unranked
Website: www.cim.edu/
Admissions email: admission@cim.edu
Private; founded 1920
Freshman admissions: least selective; 2016-2017: 483 applied, 234 accepted. Neither SAT nor ACT required. SAT 25/75 percentile: N/A. High school rank: N/A
Early decision deadline: N/A, notification date: N/A
Early action deadline: N/A, notification date: N/A
Application deadline (fall): 12/1
Undergraduate student body: 233 full time, 0 part time; 51% male, 49% female; 0% American Indian, 4% Asian, 1% black, 0% Hispanic, 0% multiracial, 0% Pacific Islander, 21% white, 25% international
Most popular majors: Information not available
Expenses: 2017-2018: $48,671; room/board: $14,870
Financial aid: (216) 795-3192; 50% of undergrads determined to have financial need; average aid package $34,835

Cleveland State University
Cleveland OH
(216) 687-2100
U.S. News ranking: Nat. U., second tier
Website: www.csuohio.edu
Admissions email: admissions@csuohio.edu
Public; founded 1964
Freshman admissions: selective; 2016-2017: 8,351 applied, 7,359 accepted. Either SAT or ACT required. ACT 25/75 percentile: 19-25. High school rank: 14% in top tenth, 36% in top quarter, 69% in top half
Early decision deadline: N/A, notification date: N/A
Early action deadline: 5/1, notification date: N/A

Application deadline (fall): 8/16
Undergraduate student body: 9,219 full time, 3,214 part time; 47% male, 53% female; 1% American Indian, 4% Asian, 19% black, 5% Hispanic, 0% multiracial, 0% Pacific Islander, 63% white, 5% international; 95% from in state; 6% live on campus; 1% of students in fraternities, 1% in sororities
Most popular majors: 8% Psychology, General, 6% Health Professions and Related Clinical Sciences, Other, 4% Accounting, 4% Business Administration and Management, General, 4% Social Work
Expenses: 2017-2018: $9,796 in state, $13,848 out of state; room/board: $10,914
Financial aid: (216) 687-5594; 73% of undergrads determined to have financial need; average aid package $8,777

College of Wooster
Wooster OH
(330) 263-2322
U.S. News ranking: Nat. Lib. Arts, No. 63
Website: www.wooster.edu/
Admissions email: admissions@wooster.edu
Private; founded 1866
Freshman admissions: more selective; 2016-2017: 5,667 applied, 3,296 accepted. Either SAT or ACT required. ACT 25/75 percentile: 24-30. High school rank: 45% in top tenth, 69% in top quarter, 93% in top half
Early decision deadline: N/A, notification date: N/A
Early action deadline: N/A, notification date: N/A
Application deadline (fall): N/A
Undergraduate student body: 1,983 full time, 20 part time; 45% male, 55% female; 1% American Indian, 5% Asian, 8% black, 5% Hispanic, 0% multiracial, 0% Pacific Islander, 67% white, 11% international; 38% from in state; 99% live on campus; 14% of students in fraternities, 17% in sororities
Most popular majors: 26% Social Sciences, 10% Biological and Biomedical Sciences, 10% History, 10% Physical Sciences, 7% Psychology
Expenses: 2017-2018: $48,600; room/board: $11,400
Financial aid: (330) 263-2317; 55% of undergrads determined to have financial need; average aid package $41,286

Columbus College of Art and Design
Columbus OH
(614) 222-3261
U.S. News ranking: Arts, unranked
Website: www.ccad.edu
Admissions email: admissions@ccad.edu
Private; founded 1879
Freshman admissions: selective; 2016-2017: 612 applied, 485 accepted. Neither SAT nor ACT required. ACT 25/75 percentile: 19-26. High school rank: N/A
Early decision deadline: N/A, notification date: N/A

Early action deadline: N/A, notification date: N/A
Application deadline (fall): 8/15
Undergraduate student body: 999 full time, 61 part time; 32% male, 68% female; 0% American Indian, 4% Asian, 10% black, 6% Hispanic, 5% multiracial, 0% Pacific Islander, 65% white, 7% international
Most popular majors: 25% Illustration, 21% Commercial and Advertising Art, 15% Fine Arts and Art Studies, Other, 11% Animation, Interactive Technology, Video Graphics and Special Effects, 8% Photography
Expenses: 2017-2018: $35,040; room/board: $9,370
Financial aid: (614) 222-3274; 80% of undergrads determined to have financial need; average aid package $21,664

Defiance College
Defiance OH
(419) 783-2359
U.S. News ranking: Reg. Coll. (Mid. W), No. 35
Website: www.defiance.edu
Admissions email: admissions@defiance.edu
Private; founded 1850
Affiliation: United Church of Christ
Freshman admissions: selective; 2016-2017: 1,196 applied, 689 accepted. Either SAT or ACT required. ACT 25/75 percentile: 18-22. High school rank: 10% in top tenth, 22% in top quarter, 69% in top half
Early decision deadline: N/A, notification date: N/A
Early action deadline: N/A, notification date: N/A
Application deadline (fall): rolling
Undergraduate student body: 508 full time, 100 part time; 54% male, 46% female; 0% American Indian, 1% Asian, 10% black, 7% Hispanic, 3% multiracial, 0% Pacific Islander, 78% white, 2% international; N/A from in state; 52% live on campus; 4% of students in fraternities, 1% in sororities
Most popular majors: 14% Education, General, 12% Criminal Justice/Police Science, 10% Business Administration and Management, General, 8% Accounting, 7% Sport and Fitness Administration/Management
Expenses: 2017-2018: $32,190; room/board: $10,050
Financial aid: (419) 783-2376; 91% of undergrads determined to have financial need; average aid package $24,038

Denison University
Granville OH
(740) 587-6276
U.S. News ranking: Nat. Lib. Arts, No. 46
Website: www.denison.edu
Admissions email: admission@denison.edu
Private; founded 1831
Freshman admissions: more selective; 2016-2017: 6,881 applied, 3,001 accepted. Neither SAT nor ACT required. ACT 25/75 percentile: 28-32. High school rank: 56% in top tenth, 82% in top quarter, 100% in top half

Early decision deadline: 11/15, notification date: 12/15
Early action deadline: N/A, notification date: N/A
Application deadline (fall): 1/15
Undergraduate student body: 2,259 full time, 18 part time; 45% male, 55% female; 0% American Indian, 4% Asian, 7% black, 9% Hispanic, 4% multiracial, 0% Pacific Islander, 66% white, 9% international; 26% from in state; 99% live on campus; 22% of students in fraternities, 35% in sororities
Most popular majors: 25% Social Sciences, 16% Biological and Biomedical Sciences, 10% Communication, Journalism, and Related Programs, 8% Psychology, 7% English Language and Literature/Letters
Expenses: 2017-2018: $50,440; room/board: $12,330
Financial aid: (740) 587-6279; 53% of undergrads determined to have financial need; average aid package $41,891

Franciscan University of Steubenville
Steubenville OH
(740) 283-6226
U.S. News ranking: Reg. U. (Mid. W), No. 19
Website: www.franciscan.edu
Admissions email: admissions@franciscan.edu
Private; founded 1946
Affiliation: Roman Catholic
Freshman admissions: more selective; 2016-2017: 1,760 applied, 1,386 accepted. Either SAT or ACT required. ACT 25/75 percentile: 22-28. High school rank: 25% in top tenth, 50% in top quarter, 81% in top half
Early decision deadline: N/A, notification date: N/A
Early action deadline: N/A, notification date: N/A
Application deadline (fall): rolling
Undergraduate student body: 1,995 full time, 95 part time; 40% male, 60% female; 0% American Indian, 2% Asian, 1% black, 11% Hispanic, 2% multiracial, 0% Pacific Islander, 82% white, 1% international; 20% from in state; 80% live on campus; 0% of students in fraternities, 0% in sororities
Most popular majors: 20% Theology/Theological Studies, 9% Business Administration and Management, General, 8% Multicultural Education, 8% Registered Nursing/Registered Nurse, 7% Psychology, General
Expenses: 2017-2018: $26,430; room/board: $8,400
Financial aid: (740) 284-5216; 63% of undergrads determined to have financial need; average aid package $15,628

Franklin University[1]
Columbus OH
U.S. News ranking: Business, unranked
Website: www.franklin.edu
Admissions email: info@franklin.edu
Private; founded 1902
Application deadline (fall): N/A

Undergraduate student body: N/A full time, N/A part time
Expenses: 2016-2017: $11,881; room/board: N/A
Financial aid: N/A

Heidelberg University
Tiffin OH
(419) 448-2330
U.S. News ranking: Reg. U. (Mid. W), No. 60
Website: www.heidelberg.edu
Admissions email: adminfo@heidelberg.edu
Private; founded 1850
Affiliation: United Church of Christ
Freshman admissions: selective; 2016-2017: 1,659 applied, 1,315 accepted. Either SAT or ACT required. ACT 25/75 percentile: 19-25. High school rank: N/A
Early decision deadline: N/A, notification date: N/A
Early action deadline: N/A, notification date: N/A
Application deadline (fall): 8/1
Undergraduate student body: 1,099 full time, 26 part time; 53% male, 47% female; 0% American Indian, 1% Asian, 9% black, 2% Hispanic, 3% multiracial, 0% Pacific Islander, 78% white, 0% international; 84% from in state; 80% live on campus; 11% of students in fraternities, 21% in sororities
Most popular majors: 21% Business, Management, Marketing, and Related Support Services, 10% Education, 9% Health Professions and Related Programs, 9% Psychology, 8% Homeland Security, Law Enforcement, Firefighting and Related Protective Services
Expenses: 2017-2018: $30,200; room/board: $10,200
Financial aid: (419) 448-2293; 89% of undergrads determined to have financial need; average aid package $22,421

Hiram College
Hiram OH
(800) 362-5280
U.S. News ranking: Nat. Lib. Arts, No. 141
Website: www.hiram.edu
Admissions email: admission@hiram.edu
Private; founded 1850
Freshman admissions: selective; 2016-2017: 2,521 applied, 1,366 accepted. Neither SAT nor ACT required. ACT 25/75 percentile: 19-25. High school rank: 16% in top tenth, 33% in top quarter, 61% in top half
Early decision deadline: N/A, notification date: N/A
Early action deadline: N/A, notification date: N/A
Application deadline (fall): rolling
Undergraduate student body: 856 full time, 234 part time; 49% male, 51% female; 0% American Indian, 1% Asian, 17% black, 4% Hispanic, 3% multiracial, 0% Pacific Islander, 65% white, 2% international; 81% from in state; 80% live on campus; 1% of students in fraternities, 6% in sororities
Most popular majors: 31% Business, Management, Marketing, and Related Support Services, 14% Biological and

Biomedical Sciences, 10% Health Professions and Related Programs, 9% Social Sciences, 7% Education
Expenses: 2016-2017: $33,040; room/board: $10,190
Financial aid: (330) 569-5441

John Carroll University
University Heights OH
(216) 397-4294
U.S. News ranking: Reg. U. (Mid. W), No. 6
Website: www.jcu.edu
Admissions email: admission@jcu.edu
Private; founded 1886
Affiliation: Roman Catholic
Freshman admissions: more selective; 2016-2017: 3,857 applied, 3,201 accepted. Either SAT or ACT required. ACT 25/75 percentile: 22-27. High school rank: 27% in top tenth, 56% in top quarter, 86% in top half
Early decision deadline: N/A, notification date: N/A
Early action deadline: 12/1, notification date: 12/15
Application deadline (fall): rolling
Undergraduate student body: 2,937 full time, 91 part time; 51% male, 49% female; 0% American Indian, 2% Asian, 4% black, 4% Hispanic, 2% multiracial, 0% Pacific Islander, 84% white, 2% international; 68% from in state; 54% live on campus; 13% of students in fraternities, 28% in sororities
Most popular majors: 33% Business, Management, Marketing, and Related Support Services, 11% Communication, Journalism, and Related Programs, 10% Biological and Biomedical Sciences, 10% Social Sciences, 8% Psychology
Expenses: 2017-2018: $39,990; room/board: $11,580
Financial aid: (216) 397-4248; 71% of undergrads determined to have financial need; average aid package $30,799

Kent State University
Kent OH
(330) 672-2444
U.S. News ranking: Nat. U., No. 176
Website: www.kent.edu
Admissions email: kentadm@kent.edu
Public; founded 1910
Freshman admissions: selective; 2016-2017: 16,145 applied, 13,782 accepted. Either SAT or ACT required. ACT 25/75 percentile: 21-25. High school rank: 15% in top tenth, 41% in top quarter, 77% in top half
Early decision deadline: N/A, notification date: N/A
Early action deadline: N/A, notification date: N/A
Application deadline (fall): 5/1
Undergraduate student body: 20,687 full time, 2,997 part time; 39% male, 61% female; 0% American Indian, 2% Asian, 9% black, 3% Hispanic, 4% multiracial, 0% Pacific Islander, 75% white, 5% international; 86% from in state; 28% live on campus; N/A of students in fraternities, N/A in sororities

Most popular majors: 21% Business, Management, Marketing, and Related Support Services, 18% Health Professions and Related Programs, 8% Communication, Journalism, and Related Programs, 8% Education, 7% Psychology
Expenses: 2017-2018: $10,012 in state, $18,376 out of state; room/board: $10,916
Financial aid: (330) 672-2972; 64% of undergrads determined to have financial need; average aid package $10,292

Kenyon College
Gambier OH
(740) 427-5776
U.S. News ranking: Nat. Lib. Arts, No. 26
Website: www.kenyon.edu
Admissions email: admissions@kenyon.edu
Private; founded 1824
Freshman admissions: most selective; 2016-2017: 6,403 applied, 1,702 accepted. Either SAT or ACT required. SAT 25/75 percentile: 1230-1440. High school rank: 63% in top tenth, 90% in top quarter, 99% in top half
Early decision deadline: 11/15, notification date: 12/18
Early action deadline: N/A, notification date: N/A
Application deadline (fall): 1/15
Undergraduate student body: 1,688 full time, 20 part time; 45% male, 55% female; 0% American Indian, 4% Asian, 3% black, 5% Hispanic, 8% multiracial, 0% Pacific Islander, 73% white, 5% international; 15% from in state; 100% live on campus; 18% of students in fraternities, 20% in sororities
Most popular majors: 13% English Language and Literature, General, 10% Economics, General, 8% Political Science and Government, General, 7% Psychology, General, 6% International/Global Studies
Expenses: 2017-2018: $53,560; room/board: $12,280
Financial aid: (740) 427-5430; 41% of undergrads determined to have financial need; average aid package $47,203

Lake Erie College
Painesville OH
(855) 467-8676
U.S. News ranking: Reg. U. (Mid. W), second tier
Website: www.lec.edu
Admissions email: admissions@lec.edu
Private; founded 1856
Freshman admissions: selective; 2016-2017: 1,485 applied, 937 accepted. Neither SAT nor ACT required. ACT 25/75 percentile: 18-22. High school rank: 7% in top tenth, 24% in top quarter, 57% in top half
Early decision deadline: N/A, notification date: N/A
Early action deadline: 12/1, notification date: 12/14
Application deadline (fall): 8/1
Undergraduate student body: 745 full time, 210 part time; 48% male, 52% female; 1% American Indian, 1% Asian, 14% black, 2% Hispanic, 3% multiracial, 0% Pacific Islander, 73% white,

3% international; 74% from in state; 66% live on campus; N/A of students in fraternities, N/A in sororities
Most popular majors: 30% Business, Management, Marketing, and Related Support Services, 13% Biological and Biomedical Sciences, 10% Agriculture, Agriculture Operations, and Related Sciences, 9% Education, 8% Homeland Security, Law Enforcement, Firefighting and Related Protective Services
Expenses: 2017-2018: $30,862; room/board: $9,132
Financial aid: (440) 375-7100; 82% of undergrads determined to have financial need; average aid package $23,822

Lourdes University
Sylvania OH
(419) 885-5291
U.S. News ranking: Reg. U. (Mid. W), second tier
Website: www.lourdes.edu
Admissions email: luadmits@lourdes.edu
Private; founded 1958
Freshman admissions: selective; 2016-2017: 919 applied, 821 accepted. Either SAT or ACT required. ACT 25/75 percentile: 18-24. High school rank: 10% in top tenth, 29% in top quarter, 65% in top half
Early decision deadline: N/A, notification date: N/A
Early action deadline: N/A, notification date: N/A
Application deadline (fall): rolling
Undergraduate student body: 842 full time, 286 part time; 36% male, 64% female; 0% American Indian, 0% Asian, 11% black, 9% Hispanic, 4% multiracial, 0% Pacific Islander, 70% white, 1% international; 73% from in state; 36% live on campus; N/A of students in fraternities, N/A in sororities
Most popular majors: 30% Health Professions and Related Programs, 21% Business, Management, Marketing, and Related Support Services, 11% Multi/Interdisciplinary Studies, 7% Education, 5% Biological and Biomedical Sciences
Expenses: 2017-2018: $21,540; room/board: $9,700
Financial aid: (419) 824-3733

Malone University
Canton OH
(330) 471-8145
U.S. News ranking: Reg. U. (Mid. W), No. 75
Website: www.malone.edu
Admissions email: admissions@malone.edu
Private; founded 1892
Affiliation: Friends
Freshman admissions: selective; 2016-2017: 1,762 applied, 1,283 accepted. Either SAT or ACT required. ACT 25/75 percentile: 19-25. High school rank: 16% in top tenth, 37% in top quarter, 72% in top half
Early decision deadline: N/A, notification date: N/A
Early action deadline: N/A, notification date: N/A

Application deadline (fall): rolling **Undergraduate student body:** 1,145 full time, 166 part time; 41% male, 59% female; 0% American Indian, 1% Asian, 12% black, 3% Hispanic, 3% multiracial, 0% Pacific Islander, 80% white, 1% international; 86% from in-state; 63% live on campus; 0% of students in fraternities, 0% in sororities **Most popular majors:** 16% Business Administration, Management and Operations, Other, 13% Registered Nursing/Registered Nurse, 10% Business Administration and Management, General, 8% Communication, Journalism, and Related Programs, Other, 6% Education/Teaching of Individuals with Specific Learning Disabilities **Expenses:** 2017-2018: $29,900; room/board: $9,300 **Financial aid:** (330) 471-8161; 85% of undergrads determined to have financial need; average aid package $22,939

Marietta College
Marietta OH
(800) 331-7896
U.S. News ranking: Reg. Coll. (Mid. W), No. 8
Website: www.marietta.edu
Admissions email: admit@marietta.edu
Private; founded 1797
Freshman admissions: selective; 2016-2017: 2,700 applied, 1,658 accepted. Either SAT or ACT required. ACT 25/75 percentile: 21-26. High school rank: 27% in top tenth, 53% in top quarter, 82% in top half
Early decision deadline: N/A, notification date: N/A
Early action deadline: N/A, notification date: N/A
Application deadline (fall): 4/15
Undergraduate student body: 1,053 full time, 91 part time; 61% male, 39% female; 0% American Indian, 1% Asian, 5% black, 2% Hispanic, 3% multiracial, 0% Pacific Islander, 67% white, 17% international; 67% from in-state; 78% live on campus; 15% of students in fraternities, 30% in sororities
Most popular majors: 29% Petroleum Engineering, 6% Marketing/Marketing Management, General, 5% Advertising, 4% Finance, General, 4% Psychology, General
Expenses: 2017-2018: $36,040; room/board: $11,320
Financial aid: (740) 376-4712; 69% of undergrads determined to have financial need; average aid package $29,627

Miami University–Oxford
Oxford OH
(513) 529-2531
U.S. News ranking: Nat. U., No. 78
Website: www.MiamiOH.edu
Admissions email: admission@MiamiOH.edu
Public; founded 1809
Freshman admissions: more selective; 2016-2017: 29,771 applied, 19,463 accepted. Either

SAT or ACT required. ACT 25/75 percentile: 26-31. High school rank: 39% in top tenth, 71% in top quarter, 95% in top half
Early decision deadline: 11/15, notification date: 12/15
Early action deadline: 12/1, notification date: 2/1
Application deadline (fall): 2/1
Undergraduate student body: 16,434 full time, 547 part time; 49% male, 51% female; 0% American Indian, 2% Asian, 3% black, 4% Hispanic, 3% multiracial, 0% Pacific Islander, 75% white, 12% international; 64% from in state; 46% live on campus; 19% of students in fraternities, 34% in sororities
Most popular majors: 26% Business, Management, Marketing, and Related Support Services, 10% Social Sciences, 9% Communication, Journalism, and Related Programs, 8% Education, 8% Parks, Recreation, Leisure, and Fitness Studies
Expenses: 2017-2018: $14,578 in state, $32,768 out of state; room/board: $12,725
Financial aid: (513) 529-8734; 34% of undergrads determined to have financial need; average aid package $13,606

Mount St. Joseph University
Cincinnati OH
(513) 244-4531
U.S. News ranking: Reg. U. (Mid. W), No. 87
Website: www.msj.edu
Admissions email: admission@mail.msj.edu
Private; founded 1920
Freshman admissions: selective; 2016-2017: 1,029 applied, 906 accepted. Either SAT or ACT required. ACT 25/75 percentile: 19-24. High school rank: 9% in top tenth, 30% in top quarter, 63% in top half
Early decision deadline: N/A, notification date: N/A
Early action deadline: N/A, notification date: N/A
Application deadline (fall): 8/18
Undergraduate student body: 996 full time, 340 part time; 41% male, 59% female; 0% American Indian, 0% Asian, 11% black, 1% Hispanic, 4% multiracial, 0% Pacific Islander, 79% white, 0% international; 83% from in state; 27% live on campus; N/A of students in fraternities, N/A in sororities
Most popular majors: 39% Health Professions and Related Programs, 15% Business, Management, Marketing, and Related Support Services, 7% Education, 7% Liberal Arts and Sciences, General Studies and Humanities, 6% Biological and Biomedical Sciences
Expenses: 2017-2018: $29,100; room/board: $9,266
Financial aid: (513) 244-4418; 80% of undergrads determined to have financial need; average aid package $18,827

Mount Vernon Nazarene University
Mount Vernon OH
(866) 462-6868
U.S. News ranking: Reg. U. (Mid. W), No. 93
Website: www.gotomvnu.com
Admissions email: admissions@mvnu.edu
Private; founded 1968
Affiliation: Church of the Nazarene
Freshman admissions: selective; 2016-2017: 1,276 applied, 947 accepted. Either SAT or ACT required. ACT 25/75 percentile: 20-25. High school rank: 21% in top tenth, 51% in top quarter, 76% in top half
Early decision deadline: N/A, notification date: N/A
Early action deadline: N/A, notification date: N/A
Application deadline (fall): 7/15
Undergraduate student body: 1,748 full time, 83 part time; 38% male, 62% female; 0% American Indian, 1% Asian, 4% black, 3% Hispanic, 2% multiracial, 0% Pacific Islander, 85% white, 1% international; 90% from in state; 78% live on campus; 0% of students in fraternities, 0% in sororities
Most popular majors: 32% Business, Management, Marketing, and Related Support Services, 18% Public Administration and Social Service Professions, 8% Health Professions and Related Programs, 7% Education, 6% Communication, Journalism, and Related Programs
Expenses: 2017-2018: $28,090; room/board: $7,854
Financial aid: (740) 397-9000; 75% of undergrads determined to have financial need; average aid package $18,251

Muskingum University
New Concord OH
(740) 826-8137
U.S. News ranking: Reg. U. (Mid. W), No. 61
Website: www.muskingum.edu
Admissions email: adminfo@muskingum.edu
Private; founded 1837
Affiliation: Presbyterian Church (USA)
Freshman admissions: selective; 2016-2017: 1,819 applied, 1,408 accepted. Either SAT or ACT required. ACT 25/75 percentile: 19-24. High school rank: 20% in top tenth, 37% in top quarter, 70% in top half
Early decision deadline: N/A, notification date: N/A
Early action deadline: N/A, notification date: N/A
Application deadline (fall): 8/1
Undergraduate student body: 1,312 full time, 263 part time; 45% male, 55% female; 0% American Indian, 1% Asian, 5% black, 2% Hispanic, 4% multiracial, 0% Pacific Islander, 79% white, 4% international; 92% from in state; 70% live on campus; 27% of students in fraternities, 42% in sororities
Most popular majors: 24% Health Professions and Related Programs, 17% Business, Management, Marketing, and Related Support

Services, 15% Education, 8% Homeland Security, Law Enforcement, Firefighting and Related Protective Services, 7% Psychology
Expenses: 2017-2018: $27,812; room/board: $11,040
Financial aid: (740) 826-8139; 85% of undergrads determined to have financial need; average aid package $24,239

Notre Dame College of Ohio[1]
Cleveland OH
(216) 373-5355
U.S. News ranking: Reg. U. (Mid. W), second tier
Website: www.notredamecollege.edu
Admissions email: admissions@ndc.edu
Private; founded 1922
Application deadline (fall): rolling
Undergraduate student body: N/A full time, N/A part time
Expenses: 2016-2017: $28,300; room/board: $10,308
Financial aid: (216) 373-5263

Oberlin College
Oberlin OH
(440) 775-8411
U.S. News ranking: Nat. Lib. Arts, No. 26
Website: www.oberlin.edu
Admissions email: college.admissions@oberlin.edu
Private; founded 1833
Freshman admissions: most selective; 2016-2017: 8,518 applied, 2,388 accepted. Either SAT or ACT required. SAT 25/75 percentile: 1250-1450. High school rank: 61% in top tenth, 84% in top quarter, 98% in top half
Early decision deadline: 11/15, notification date: 12/10
Early action deadline: N/A, notification date: N/A
Application deadline (fall): 1/15
Undergraduate student body: 2,869 full time, 26 part time; 43% male, 57% female; 0% American Indian, 4% Asian, 5% black, 8% Hispanic, 7% multiracial, 0% Pacific Islander, 66% white, 9% international; 6% from in state; N/A live on campus; 0% of students in fraternities, 0% in sororities
Most popular majors: 18% Music, 9% Economics, 8% English Language and Literature, General, 8% Environmental Studies, 7% Biology, General
Expenses: 2017-2018: $53,460; room/board: $15,212
Financial aid: (440) 775-8142; 47% of undergrads determined to have financial need; average aid package $41,386

Ohio Christian University
Circleville OH
(877) 762-8669
U.S. News ranking: Reg. Coll. (Mid. W), second tier
Website: www.ohiochristian.edu/
Admissions email: enroll@ohiochristian.edu
Private; founded 1948
Affiliation: Churches of Christ

Freshman admissions: less selective; 2016-2017: N/A applied, N/A accepted. Neither SAT nor ACT required. SAT 25/75 percentile: N/A. High school rank: N/A
Early decision deadline: N/A, notification date: N/A
Early action deadline: N/A, notification date: N/A
Application deadline (fall): N/A
Undergraduate student body: 2,481 full time, 1,732 part time; 36% male, 64% female; N/A American Indian, N/A Asian, N/A black, N/A Hispanic, N/A multiracial, N/A Pacific Islander, N/A white, N/A international
Most popular majors: Information not available
Expenses: 2016-2017: $19,540; room/board: $7,898
Financial aid: N/A

Ohio Dominican University
Columbus OH
(614) 251-4500
U.S. News ranking: Reg. U. (Mid. W), No. 106
Website: www.ohiodominican.edu
Admissions email: admissions@ohiodominican.edu
Private; founded 1911
Affiliation: Roman Catholic
Freshman admissions: selective, 2016-2017: 1,969 applied, 1,027 accepted. Either SAT or ACT required. ACT 25/75 percentile: 19-24. High school rank: 10% in top tenth, 31% in top quarter, 79% in top half
Early decision deadline: N/A, notification date: N/A
Early action deadline: N/A, notification date: N/A
Application deadline (fall): rolling
Undergraduate student body: 1,040 full time, 756 part time; 44% male, 56% female; 0% American Indian, 1% Asian, 21% black, 3% Hispanic, 5% multiracial, 0% Pacific Islander, 58% white, 2% international; 95% from in state; 42% live on campus; 0% of students in fraternities, 0% in sororities
Most popular majors: 29% Business Administration and Management, General, 9% Accounting, 7% Biology/Biological Sciences, General, 7% Sport and Fitness Administration/Management, 6% Kinesiology and Exercise Science
Expenses: 2017-2018: $31,080; room/board: $10,928
Financial aid: (614) 251-4778; 82% of undergrads determined to have financial need; average aid package $22,104

Ohio Northern University
Ada OH
(888) 408-4668
U.S. News ranking: Reg. Coll. (Mid. W), No. 4
Website: www.onu.edu
Admissions email: admissions-ug@onu.edu
Private; founded 1871
Affiliation: United Methodist
Freshman admissions: more selective; 2016-2017: 3,934 applied, 2,522 accepted. Either SAT or ACT required. ACT 25/75

percentile: 23-28. High school rank: 27% in top tenth, 57% in top quarter, 87% in top half **Early decision deadline:** N/A, notification date: N/A **Early action deadline:** N/A, notification date: N/A **Application deadline (fall):** 8/15 **Undergraduate student body:** 2,065 full time, 209 part time; 56% male, 44% female; 0% American Indian, 1% Asian, 4% black, 1% Hispanic, 3% multiracial, 0% Pacific Islander, 80% white, 3% international; 81% from in state; 78% live on campus; 16% of students in fraternities, 26% in sororities **Most popular majors:** 20% Engineering, 16% Business, Management, Marketing, and Related Support Services, 11% Health Professions and Related Programs, 8% Visual and Performing Arts, 7% Biological and Biomedical Sciences **Expenses:** 2017-2018: $30,990; room/board: $11,270 **Financial aid:** (419) 772-2271; 80% of undergrads determined to have financial need; average aid package $26,452

Ohio State University–Columbus

Columbus OH
(614) 292-3980
U.S. News ranking: Nat. U., No. 54
Website: www.osu.edu
Admissions email: askabuckeye@osu.edu
Public; founded 1870
Freshman admissions: more selective; 2016-2017: 44,845 applied, 24,265 accepted. Either SAT or ACT required. ACT 25/75 percentile: 27-31. High school rank: 63% in top tenth, 95% in top quarter, 99% in top half **Early decision deadline:** N/A, notification date: N/A **Early action deadline:** 11/1, notification date: 1/15 **Application deadline (fall):** 2/1 **Undergraduate student body:** 41,862 full time, 3,969 part time; 52% male, 48% female; 0% American Indian, 6% Asian, 5% black, 4% Hispanic, 3% multiracial, 0% Pacific Islander, 69% white, 8% international; 81% from in state; 34% live on campus; 10% of students in fraternities, 17% in sororities **Most popular majors:** 6% Psychology, General, 5% Speech Communication and Rhetoric, 4% Biology/Biological Sciences, General, 4% Finance, General, 3% Marketing/Marketing Management, General **Expenses:** 2017-2018: $10,591 in state, $29,659 out of state; room/board: $12,252 **Financial aid:** (614) 292-8595; 47% of undergrads determined to have financial need; average aid package $13,354

Ohio University

Athens OH
(740) 593-4100
U.S. News ranking: Nat. U., No. 151
Website: www.ohio.edu
Admissions email: admissions@ohio.edu

Public; founded 1804
Freshman admissions: selective; 2016-2017: 20,623 applied, 15,437 accepted. Either SAT or ACT required. ACT 25/75 percentile: 21-26. High school rank: 15% in top tenth, 42% in top quarter, 80% in top half **Early decision deadline:** N/A, notification date: N/A **Early action deadline:** 12/1, notification date: N/A **Application deadline (fall):** 2/1 **Undergraduate student body:** 18,012 full time, 5,776 part time; 40% male, 60% female; 0% American Indian, 1% Asian, 5% black, 3% Hispanic, 3% multiracial, 0% Pacific Islander, 84% white, 2% international; 85% from in state; 45% live on campus; 11% of students in fraternities, 11% in sororities **Most popular majors:** 37% Registered Nursing/Registered Nurse, 4% Liberal Arts and Sciences, General Studies and Humanities, Other, 3% Business Administration and Management, General, 3% Journalism, 3% Speech Communication and Rhetoric **Expenses:** 2017-2018: $11,896 in state, $21,360 out of state; room/board: $12,612 **Financial aid:** (740) 593-4141; 58% of undergrads determined to have financial need; average aid package $9,240

Ohio Wesleyan University

Delaware OH
(740) 368-3020
U.S. News ranking: Nat. Lib. Arts, No. 101
Website: www.owu.edu
Admissions email: owuadmit@owu.edu
Private; founded 1842
Freshman admissions: more selective; 2016-2017: 4,123 applied, 2,950 accepted. Neither SAT nor ACT required. ACT 25/75 percentile: 22-28. High school rank: 22% in top tenth, 45% in top quarter, 76% in top half **Early decision deadline:** 11/15, notification date: 11/30 **Early action deadline:** 1/15, notification date: 1/30 **Application deadline (fall):** 3/1 **Undergraduate student body:** 1,624 full time, 15 part time; 48% male, 52% female; 0% American Indian, 3% Asian, 9% black, 5% Hispanic, 5% multiracial, 0% Pacific Islander, 70% white, 6% international; 53% from in state; 90% live on campus; 39% of students in fraternities, 32% in sororities **Most popular majors:** 14% Biological and Biomedical Sciences, 14% Business, Management, Marketing, and Related Support Services, 12% Social Sciences, 10% Psychology, 7% Visual and Performing Arts **Expenses:** 2017-2018: $44,690; room/board: $11,950 **Financial aid:** (740) 368-3052; 71% of undergrads determined to have financial need; average aid package $36,291

Otterbein University

Westerville OH
(614) 823-1500
U.S. News ranking: Reg. U. (Mid. W), No. 19
Website: www.otterbein.edu
Admissions email: UOtterB@Otterbein.edu
Private; founded 1847
Affiliation: United Methodist
Freshman admissions: more selective; 2016-2017: 3,222 applied, 2,348 accepted. Either SAT or ACT required. ACT 25/75 percentile: 21-26. High school rank: 24% in top tenth, 57% in top quarter, 84% in top half **Early decision deadline:** N/A, notification date: N/A **Early action deadline:** N/A, notification date: N/A **Application deadline (fall):** rolling **Undergraduate student body:** 2,282 full time, 203 part time; 39% male, 61% female; 0% American Indian, 2% Asian, 6% black, 2% Hispanic, 4% multiracial, 0% Pacific Islander, 77% white, 2% international; 87% from in state; 64% live on campus; 10% of students in fraternities, 10% in sororities **Most popular majors:** 21% Health Professions and Related Programs, 14% Business, Management, Marketing, and Related Support Services, 12% Education, 11% Visual and Performing Arts, 9% Parks, Recreation, Leisure, and Fitness Studies **Expenses:** 2017-2018: $31,874; room/board: $10,528 **Financial aid:** (614) 823-1502; 76% of undergrads determined to have financial need; average aid package $23,544

Shawnee State University

Portsmouth OH
(800) 959-2778
U.S. News ranking: Reg. Coll. (Mid. W), second tier
Website: www.shawnee.edu
Admissions email: To_SSU@shawnee.edu
Public; founded 1986
Freshman admissions: selective; 2016-2017: 3,614 applied, 2,659 accepted. Neither SAT nor ACT required. ACT 25/75 percentile: 18-24. High school rank: 3% in top tenth, 12% in top quarter, 33% in top half **Early decision deadline:** N/A, notification date: N/A **Early action deadline:** N/A, notification date: N/A **Application deadline (fall):** rolling **Undergraduate student body:** 3,036 full time, 567 part time; 46% male, 54% female; 1% American Indian, 1% Asian, 6% black, 1% Hispanic, 2% multiracial, 0% Pacific Islander, 86% white, 1% international; 88% from in state; 26% live on campus; 1% of students in fraternities, 1% in sororities **Most popular majors:** 17% Business Administration and Management, General, 10% Psychology, General, 7% Art/Art Studies, General, 5% Biology/Biological Sciences, General, 5% Sociology

Expenses: 2017-2018: $7,365 in state, $14,145 out of state; room/board: $9,922 **Financial aid:** (740) 351-4243; 62% of undergrads determined to have financial need; average aid package $8,972

Tiffin University

Tiffin OH
(419) 448-3423
U.S. News ranking: Reg. U. (Mid. W), No. 93
Website: www.tiffin.edu
Admissions email: admiss@tiffin.edu
Private; founded 1888
Freshman admissions: selective; 2016-2017: 3,653 applied, 2,204 accepted. Neither SAT nor ACT required. ACT 25/75 percentile: 17-22. High school rank: 9% in top tenth, 26% in top quarter, 62% in top half **Early decision deadline:** N/A, notification date: N/A **Early action deadline:** N/A, notification date: N/A **Application deadline (fall):** rolling **Undergraduate student body:** 1,762 full time, 591 part time; 53% male, 47% female; 0% American Indian, 0% Asian, 13% black, 4% Hispanic, 1% multiracial, 0% Pacific Islander, 43% white, 13% international; 74% from in state; 42% live on campus; 5% of students in fraternities, 5% in sororities **Most popular majors:** 40% Business, Management, Marketing, and Related Support Services, 31% Homeland Security, Law Enforcement, Firefighting and Related Protective Services, 10% Psychology, 4% Health Professions and Related Programs, 4% Parks, Recreation, Leisure, and Fitness Studies **Expenses:** 2017-2018: $23,850; room/board: $10,900 **Financial aid:** (419) 448-3375; 73% of undergrads determined to have financial need; average aid package $17,797

Union Institute and University[1]

Cincinnati OH
(800) 861-6400
U.S. News ranking: Nat. U., unranked
Website: www.myunion.edu
Admissions email: admissions@myunion.edu
Private; founded 1964
Affiliation: Other
Application deadline (fall): rolling **Undergraduate student body:** N/A full time, N/A part time **Expenses:** 2016-2017: $12,416; room/board: N/A **Financial aid:** N/A

University of Akron

Akron OH
(330) 972-7077
U.S. News ranking: Nat. U., second tier
Website: www.uakron.edu
Admissions email: admissions@uakron.edu
Public; founded 1870

Freshman admissions: selective; 2016-2017: 13,911 applied, 13,343 accepted. Either SAT or ACT required. ACT 25/75 percentile: 19-26. High school rank: 16% in top tenth, 37% in top quarter, 67% in top half **Early decision deadline:** N/A, notification date: N/A **Early action deadline:** 11/1, notification date: 12/15 **Application deadline (fall):** 8/1 **Undergraduate student body:** 13,827 full time, 3,589 part time; 54% male, 46% female; 0% American Indian, 2% Asian, 12% black, 3% Hispanic, 4% multiracial, 0% Pacific Islander, 75% white, 2% international; 94% from in state; 16% live on campus; N/A of students in fraternities, N/A in sororities **Most popular majors:** 20% Marketing, Other, 15% Chiropractic, 10% Engineering, General, 9% Education, General, 5% Social Sciences, General **Expenses:** 2017-2018: $13,332 in state, $21,863 out of state; room/board: $11,470 **Financial aid:** (330) 972-5860; 69% of undergrads determined to have financial need; average aid package $7,830

University of Cincinnati

Cincinnati OH
(513) 556-1100
U.S. News ranking: Nat. U., No. 133
Website: www.uc.edu
Admissions email: admissions@uc.edu
Public; founded 1819
Freshman admissions: more selective; 2016-2017: 19,370 applied, 14,803 accepted. Either SAT or ACT required. ACT 25/75 percentile: 23-28. High school rank: 19% in top tenth, 48% in top quarter, 83% in top half **Early decision deadline:** N/A, notification date: N/A **Early action deadline:** 12/1, notification date: N/A **Application deadline (fall):** 3/1 **Undergraduate student body:** 21,598 full time, 4,262 part time; 50% male, 50% female; 0% American Indian, 3% Asian, 7% black, 3% Hispanic, 3% multiracial, 0% Pacific Islander, 75% white, 4% international; 85% from in state; 22% live on campus; N/A of students in fraternities, N/A in sororities **Most popular majors:** 17% Business, Management, Marketing, and Related Support Services, 15% Health Professions and Related Programs, 12% Engineering, 10% Visual and Performing Arts, 6% Education **Expenses:** 2017-2018: $11,000 in state, $26,334 out of state; room/board: $11,118 **Financial aid:** (513) 556-6982; 52% of undergrads determined to have financial need; average aid package $8,489

University of Cincinnati–UC Blue Ash College[1]
Cincinnati OH
U.S. News ranking: Reg. Coll. (Mid. W), unranked
Website: www.rwc.uc.edu/
Admissions email: N/A
Public
Application deadline (fall): N/A
Undergraduate student body: N/A full time, N/A part time
Expenses: 2016-2017: $6,010 in state, $14,808 out of state; room/board: N/A
Financial aid: N/A

University of Dayton
Dayton OH
(937) 229-4411
U.S. News ranking: Nat. U., No. 124
Website: www.udayton.edu
Admissions email: admission@udayton.edu
Private; founded 1850
Freshman admissions: selective; 2016-2017: 17,477 applied, 10,547 accepted. Either SAT or ACT required. ACT 25/75 percentile: 24-29. High school rank: 27% in top tenth, 56% in top quarter, 87% in top half
Early decision deadline: N/A, notification date: N/A
Early action deadline: 12/15, notification date: 2/1
Application deadline (fall): 3/1
Undergraduate student body: 7,873 full time, 457 part time; 53% male, 47% female; 0% American Indian, 1% Asian, 3% black, 4% Hispanic, 2% multiracial, 0% Pacific Islander, 79% white, 9% international; 49% from in state; 72% live on campus; 12% of students in fraternities, 21% in sororities
Most popular majors: 30% Business, Management, Marketing, and Related Support Services, 15% Engineering, 8% Education, 7% Communication, Journalism, and Related Programs, 7% Health Professions and Related Programs
Expenses: 2017-2018: $41,750; room/board: $13,180
Financial aid: (800) 427-5029; 46% of undergrads determined to have financial need; average aid package $26,045

University of Findlay
Findlay OH
(800) 548-0932
U.S. News ranking: Reg. U. (Mid. W), No. 38
Website: www.findlay.edu
Admissions email: admissions@findlay.edu
Private; founded 1882
Affiliation: Church of God
Freshman admissions: more selective; 2016-2017: 2,976 applied, 2,172 accepted. Either SAT or ACT required. ACT 25/75 percentile: 20-25. High school rank: 43% in top tenth, 45% in top quarter, 90% in top half
Early decision deadline: N/A, notification date: N/A
Early action deadline: N/A, notification date: N/A
Application deadline (fall): rolling

Undergraduate student body: 2,570 full time, 1,091 part time; 36% male, 64% female; 0% American Indian, 1% Asian, 4% black, 2% Hispanic, 3% multiracial, 0% Pacific Islander, 81% white, 9% international; 81% from in state; 40% live on campus; 2% of students in fraternities, 2% in sororities
Most popular majors: 31% Health Professions and Related Programs, 20% Business, Management, Marketing, and Related Support Services, 10% Agriculture, Agriculture Operations, and Related Sciences, 8% Education, 7% Parks, Recreation, Leisure, and Fitness Studies
Expenses: 2017-2018: $33,320; room/board: $9,720
Financial aid: (419) 434-5678; 64% of undergrads determined to have financial need; average aid package $20,500

University of Mount Union
Alliance OH
(330) 823-2590
U.S. News ranking: Reg. Coll. (Mid. W), No. 11
Website: www.mountunion.edu/
Admissions email: admission@mountunion.edu
Private; founded 1846
Affiliation: United Methodist
Freshman admissions: selective; 2016-2017: 2,525 applied, 1,944 accepted. Neither SAT nor ACT required. ACT 25/75 percentile: 20-26. High school rank: 20% in top tenth, 50% in top quarter, 81% in top half
Early decision deadline: N/A, notification date: N/A
Early action deadline: N/A, notification date: N/A
Application deadline (fall): rolling
Undergraduate student body: 2,113 full time, 27 part time; 52% male, 48% female; 1% American Indian, 1% Asian, 7% black, 3% Hispanic, 3% multiracial, 0% Pacific Islander, 79% white, 0% international; 81% from in state; 71% live on campus; 15% of students in fraternities, 32% in sororities
Most popular majors: 22% Business, Management, Marketing, and Related Support Services, 16% Parks, Recreation, Leisure, and Fitness Studies, 12% Education, 8% Biological and Biomedical Sciences, 8% Psychology
Expenses: 2017-2018: $29,890; room/board: $10,100
Financial aid: N/A; 79% of undergrads determined to have financial need; average aid package $22,637

University of Northwestern Ohio[1]
Lima OH
U.S. News ranking: Reg. Coll. (Mid. W), unranked
Website: www.unoh.edu/
Admissions email: info@unoh.edu
Private
Application deadline (fall): N/A
Undergraduate student body: N/A full time, N/A part time

Expenses: 2016-2017: $10,440; room/board: $6,750
Financial aid: N/A

University of Rio Grande[1]
Rio Grande OH
(740) 245-7208
U.S. News ranking: Reg. Coll. (Mid. W), unranked
Website: www.rio.edu
Admissions email: admissions@rio.edu
Private; founded 1876
Application deadline (fall): rolling
Undergraduate student body: N/A full time, N/A part time
Expenses: 2016-2017: $23,860; room/board: $10,120
Financial aid: (740) 245-7285

University of Toledo
Toledo OH
(419) 530-8888
U.S. News ranking: Nat. U., second tier
Website: www.utoledo.edu
Admissions email: enroll@utnet.utoledo.edu
Public; founded 1872
Freshman admissions: selective; 2016-2017: 10,842 applied, 10,226 accepted. Either SAT or ACT required. ACT 25/75 percentile: 20-26. High school rank: 18% in top tenth, 43% in top quarter, 73% in top half
Early decision deadline: N/A, notification date: N/A
Early action deadline: N/A, notification date: N/A
Application deadline (fall): rolling
Undergraduate student body: 12,955 full time, 3,292 part time; 51% male, 49% female; 0% American Indian, 2% Asian, 12% black, 5% Hispanic, 3% multiracial, 0% Pacific Islander, 69% white, 7% international; 80% from in state; 19% live on campus; N/A of students in fraternities, N/A in sororities
Most popular majors: 21% Business, Management, Marketing, and Related Support Services, 18% Health Professions and Related Programs, 13% Engineering, 6% Education, 6% Multi/Interdisciplinary Studies
Expenses: 2017-2018: $9,240 in state, $18,578 out of state; room/board: $10,236
Financial aid: (419) 530-5833; 63% of undergrads determined to have financial need; average aid package $10,993

Urbana University[1]
Urbana OH
U.S. News ranking: Reg. Coll. (Mid. W), second tier
Website: www.urbana.edu
Admissions email: admiss@urbana.edu
Private
Application deadline (fall): N/A
Undergraduate student body: N/A full time, N/A part time
Expenses: 2016-2017: $22,452; room/board: $9,146
Financial aid: N/A

Ursuline College
Pepper Pike OH
(440) 449-4203
U.S. News ranking: Reg. U. (Mid. W), No. 54
Website: www.ursuline.edu
Admissions email: admission@ursuline.edu
Private; founded 1871
Affiliation: Roman Catholic
Freshman admissions: selective; 2016-2017: 645 applied, 578 accepted. Either SAT or ACT required. ACT 25/75 percentile: 19-24. High school rank: 14% in top tenth, 47% in top quarter, 75% in top half
Early decision deadline: N/A, notification date: N/A
Early action deadline: N/A, notification date: N/A
Application deadline (fall): 2/1
Undergraduate student body: 463 full time, 182 part time; 7% male, 93% female; 0% American Indian, 2% Asian, 25% black, 3% Hispanic, 5% multiracial, 0% Pacific Islander, 58% white, 2% international; 91% from in state; 28% live on campus; N/A of students in fraternities, N/A in sororities
Most popular majors: 53% Health Professions and Related Programs, 15% Business, Management, Marketing, and Related Support Services, 9% Psychology, 5% Communication, Journalism, and Related Programs, 4% Legal Professions and Studies
Expenses: 2017-2018: $31,150; room/board: $10,362
Financial aid: (440) 646-8309; 83% of undergrads determined to have financial need; average aid package $22,926

Walsh University
North Canton OH
(800) 362-9846
U.S. News ranking: Reg. U. (Mid. W), No. 64
Website: www.walsh.edu
Admissions email: admissions@walsh.edu
Private; founded 1958
Affiliation: Roman Catholic
Freshman admissions: selective; 2016-2017: 1,693 applied, 1,315 accepted. Neither SAT nor ACT required. ACT 25/75 percentile: 19-25. High school rank: 20% in top tenth, 40% in top quarter, 73% in top half
Early decision deadline: N/A, notification date: N/A
Early action deadline: N/A, notification date: N/A
Application deadline (fall): rolling
Undergraduate student body: 1,778 full time, 334 part time; 40% male, 60% female; 0% American Indian, 1% Asian, 7% black, 3% Hispanic, 2% multiracial, 0% Pacific Islander, 76% white, 4% international; N/A from in state; N/A live on campus; 0% of students in fraternities, 0% in sororities
Most popular majors: Information not available
Expenses: 2017-2018: $30,650; room/board: $10,530
Financial aid: (330) 490-7146; 84% of undergrads determined to have financial need; average aid package $23,540

Wilberforce University[1]
Wilberforce OH
(800) 367-8568
U.S. News ranking: Reg. Coll. (Mid. W), second tier
Website: www.wilberforce.edu
Admissions email: admissions@wilberforce.edu
Private
Application deadline (fall): N/A
Undergraduate student body: N/A full time, N/A part time
Expenses: 2016-2017: $13,250; room/board: $6,650
Financial aid: N/A

Wilmington College[1]
Wilmington OH
(937) 382-6661
U.S. News ranking: Reg. Coll. (Mid. W), No. 45
Website: www.wilmington.edu
Admissions email: admission@wilmington.edu
Private; founded 1870
Undergraduate student body: N/A full time, N/A part time
Expenses: 2016-2017: $25,000; room/board: $9,600
Financial aid: N/A

Wittenberg University
Springfield OH
(937) 327-6314
U.S. News ranking: Nat. Lib. Arts, No. 168
Website: www.wittenberg.edu/
Admissions email: admission@wittenberg.edu
Private; founded 1845
Affiliation: Lutheran Church–Missouri Synod
Freshman admissions: selective; 2016-2017: 6,906 applied, 5,409 accepted. Neither SAT nor ACT required. ACT 25/75 percentile: 22-28. High school rank: 16% in top tenth, 40% in top quarter, 74% in top half
Early decision deadline: 11/15, notification date: 12/1
Early action deadline: 12/1, notification date: 1/1
Application deadline (fall): rolling
Undergraduate student body: 1,866 full time, 94 part time; 44% male, 56% female; 0% American Indian, 1% Asian, 9% black, 4% Hispanic, 6% multiracial, 0% Pacific Islander, 78% white, 1% international; 75% from in state; 82% live on campus; 38% of students in fraternities, 47% in sororities
Most popular majors: 16% Business, Management, Marketing, and Related Support Services, 13% Biological and Biomedical Sciences, 13% Social Sciences, 8% Education, 8% Psychology
Expenses: 2017-2018: $38,730; room/board: $10,126
Financial aid: (937) 327-7321; 80% of undergrads determined to have financial need; average aid package $27,498

Wright State University

Dayton OH
(937) 775-5700
U.S. News ranking: Nat. U., second tier
Website: www.wright.edu
Admissions email: admissions@wright.edu
Public; founded 1967
Freshman admissions: selective; 2016-2017: 5,897 applied, 5,616 accepted. Either SAT or ACT required. ACT 25/75 percentile: 18-25. High school rank: 18% in top tenth, 38% in top quarter, 68% in top half
Early decision deadline: N/A, notification date: N/A
Early action deadline: N/A, notification date: N/A
Application deadline (fall): rolling
Undergraduate student body: 9,675 full time, 2,829 part time; 48% male, 52% female; 0% American Indian, 3% Asian, 12% black, 4% Hispanic, 4% multiracial, 0% Pacific Islander, 73% white, 4% international; 98% from in state; 20% live on campus; 4% of students in fraternities, 7% in sororities
Most popular majors: 10% Registered Nursing/Registered Nurse, 9% General Studies, 6% Biology/Biological Sciences, General, 6% Mechanical Engineering, 5% Psychology, General
Expenses: 2017-2018: $8,730 in state, $17,350 out of state; room/board: $11,376
Financial aid: (937) 775-4000; 64% of undergrads determined to have financial need; average aid package $10,500

Xavier University

Cincinnati OH
(877) 982-3648
U.S. News ranking: Reg. U. (Mid. W), No. 5
Website: www.xavier.edu
Admissions email: xuadmit@xavier.edu
Private; founded 1831
Affiliation: Roman Catholic
Freshman admissions: selective; 2016-2017: 13,213 applied, 9,061 accepted. Either SAT or ACT required. ACT 25/75 percentile: 23-28. High school rank: 19% in top tenth, 54% in top quarter, 82% in top half
Early decision deadline: N/A, notification date: N/A
Early action deadline: N/A, notification date: N/A
Application deadline (fall): rolling
Undergraduate student body: 4,299 full time, 264 part time; 46% male, 54% female; 0% American Indian, 3% Asian, 9% black, 5% Hispanic, 4% multiracial, 0% Pacific Islander, 72% white, 2% international; 48% from in state; 50% live on campus; N/A of students in fraternities, N/A in sororities
Most popular majors: 31% Business, Management, Marketing, and Related Support Services, 11% Health Professions and Related Programs, 11% Liberal Arts and Sciences, General Studies and Humanities, 6% Social Sciences, 5% Biological and Biomedical Sciences

Expenses: 2017-2018: $37,230; room/board: $12,150
Financial aid: (513) 745-3142; 58% of undergrads determined to have financial need; average aid package $24,513

Youngstown State University

Youngstown OH
(877) 468-6978
U.S. News ranking: Reg. U. (Mid. W), second tier
Website: www.ysu.edu
Admissions email: enroll@ysu.edu
Public; founded 1908
Freshman admissions: selective; 2016-2017: 9,010 applied, 6,071 accepted. Either SAT or ACT required. ACT 25/75 percentile: 18-25. High school rank: 13% in top tenth, 34% in top quarter, 65% in top half
Early decision deadline: N/A, notification date: N/A
Early action deadline: N/A, notification date: N/A
Application deadline (fall): 8/1
Undergraduate student body: 8,786 full time, 2,605 part time; 47% male, 53% female; 0% American Indian, 1% Asian, 10% black, 4% Hispanic, 3% multiracial, 0% Pacific Islander, 76% white, 2% international; 86% from in state; 12% live on campus; 2% of students in fraternities, 3% in sororities
Most popular majors: 7% Criminal Justice/Safety Studies, 6% General Studies, 6% Registered Nursing/Registered Nurse, 5% Social Work, 4% Biology/Biological Sciences, General
Expenses: 2017-2018: $8,757 in state, $14,397 out of state; room/board: $9,090
Financial aid: (330) 941-3505; 73% of undergrads determined to have financial need; average aid package $9,177

OKLAHOMA

Bacone College[1]

Muskogee OK
(888) 682-5514
U.S. News ranking: Reg. Coll. (W), second tier
Website: www.bacone.edu/
Admissions email: admissions@bacone.edu
Private
Application deadline (fall): rolling
Undergraduate student body: N/A full time, N/A part time
Expenses: 2016-2017: $14,850; room/board: $10,100
Financial aid: N/A

Cameron University

Lawton OK
(580) 581-2289
U.S. News ranking: Reg. U. (W), second tier
Website: www.cameron.edu
Admissions email: admissions@cameron.edu
Public; founded 1908
Freshman admissions: less selective; 2016-2017: 1,101 applied, 1,100 accepted. Neither SAT nor ACT required. ACT 25/75 percentile: 17-22. High school rank: 4% in top tenth, 14% in top quarter, 42% in top half

Early decision deadline: N/A, notification date: N/A
Early action deadline: N/A, notification date: N/A
Application deadline (fall): rolling
Undergraduate student body: 3,049 full time, 1,395 part time; 40% male, 60% female; 5% American Indian, 1% Asian, 13% black, 13% Hispanic, 9% multiracial, 1% Pacific Islander, 50% white, 4% international; 86% from in state; 8% live on campus; 2% of students in fraternities, 2% in sororities
Most popular majors: 11% Corrections and Criminal Justice, Other, 10% Business Administration and Management, General, 8% Elementary Education and Teaching, 8% Psychology, General, 6% Communication and Media Studies, Other
Expenses: 2017-2018: $6,180 in state, $15,510 out of state; room/board: $5,452
Financial aid: (580) 581-2293; 68% of undergrads determined to have financial need; average aid package $8,754

East Central University[1]

Ada OK
(580) 559-5239
U.S. News ranking: Reg. U. (W), second tier
Website: www.ecok.edu
Admissions email: admissions@ecok.edu
Public
Application deadline (fall): N/A
Undergraduate student body: N/A full time, N/A part time
Expenses: 2016-2017: $6,279 in state, $15,399 out of state; room/board: $5,350
Financial aid: N/A

Langston University

Langston OK
(405) 466-3231
U.S. News ranking: Reg. U. (W), second tier
Website: www.langston.edu
Admissions email: admissions@langston.edu
Public; founded 1897
Freshman admissions: less selective; 2016-2017: 10,071 applied, 5,203 accepted. Either SAT or ACT required. SAT 25/75 percentile: N/A. High school rank: N/A
Early decision deadline: N/A, notification date: N/A
Early action deadline: N/A, notification date: N/A
Application deadline (fall): rolling
Undergraduate student body: 1,835 full time, 215 part time; 37% male, 63% female; 0% American Indian, 0% Asian, 79% black, 2% Hispanic, 6% multiracial, 0% Pacific Islander, 4% white, 2% international; 55% from in state; 56% live on campus; N/A of students in fraternities, N/A in sororities
Most popular majors: Information not available
Expenses: 2016-2017: $5,734 in state, $13,073 out of state; room/board: $10,050
Financial aid: (405) 466-3357

Mid-America Christian University[1]

Oklahoma City OK
U.S. News ranking: Reg. U. (W), unranked
Website: www.macu.edu
Admissions email: info@macu.edu
Private
Application deadline (fall): N/A
Undergraduate student body: N/A full time, N/A part time
Expenses: 2016-2017: $17,132; room/board: $7,439
Financial aid: N/A

Northeastern State University

Tahlequah OK
(918) 444-2200
U.S. News ranking: Reg. U. (W), second tier
Website: www.nsuok.edu
Admissions email: nsuinfo@nsuok.edu
Public; founded 1846
Freshman admissions: selective; 2016-2017: 1,658 applied, 1,559 accepted. ACT required. ACT 25/75 percentile: 19-24. High school rank: 21% in top tenth, 48% in top quarter, 84% in top half
Early decision deadline: N/A, notification date: N/A
Early action deadline: N/A, notification date: N/A
Application deadline (fall): rolling
Undergraduate student body: 4,894 full time, 2,029 part time; 40% male, 60% female; 18% American Indian, 2% Asian, 4% black, 6% Hispanic, 9% multiracial, 0% Pacific Islander, 48% white, 2% international; 94% from in state; 18% live on campus; 3% of students in fraternities, 2% in sororities
Most popular majors: 9% Psychology, General, 8% Criminal Justice/Law Enforcement Administration, 8% Elementary Education and Teaching, 7% Biology/Biological Sciences, General, 6% Accounting
Expenses: 2017-2018: $6,207 in state, $13,707 out of state; room/board: $6,650
Financial aid: (918) 444-3410; 67% of undergrads determined to have financial need; average aid package $12,453

Northwestern Oklahoma State University

Alva OK
(580) 327-8545
U.S. News ranking: Reg. U. (W), second tier
Website: www.nwosu.edu
Admissions email: recruit@nwosu.edu
Public; founded 1897
Freshman admissions: selective; 2016-2017: 1,066 applied, 467 accepted. Either SAT or ACT required. ACT 25/75 percentile: 18-23. High school rank: 12% in top tenth, 31% in top quarter, 61% in top half
Early decision deadline: N/A, notification date: N/A
Early action deadline: N/A, notification date: N/A

Application deadline (fall): rolling
Undergraduate student body: 1,424 full time, 571 part time; 43% male, 57% female; 7% American Indian, 1% Asian, 7% black, 8% Hispanic, 1% multiracial, 0% Pacific Islander, 61% white, 8% international; 77% from in state; 21% live on campus; N/A of students in fraternities, N/A in sororities
Most popular majors: 12% Registered Nursing/Registered Nurse, 10% Business Administration and Management, General, 9% Psychology, General, 7% Parks, Recreation, Leisure, and Fitness Studies, Other, 6% Agriculture, Agriculture Operations, and Related Sciences
Expenses: 2016-2017: $6,690 in state, $13,538 out of state; room/board: $4,480
Financial aid: N/A

Oklahoma Baptist University

Shawnee OK
(405) 585-5000
U.S. News ranking: Reg. Coll. (W), No. 3
Website: www.okbu.edu
Admissions email: admissions@okbu.edu
Private; founded 1910
Affiliation: Southern Baptist
Freshman admissions: selective; 2016-2017: 4,955 applied, 2,990 accepted. Either SAT or ACT required. ACT 25/75 percentile: 21-26. High school rank: 30% in top tenth, 58% in top quarter, 88% in top half
Early decision deadline: N/A, notification date: N/A
Early action deadline: N/A, notification date: N/A
Application deadline (fall): 8/1
Undergraduate student body: 1,818 full time, 86 part time; 39% male, 61% female; 5% American Indian, 1% Asian, 6% black, 2% Hispanic, 11% multiracial, 0% Pacific Islander, 69% white, 3% international; 51% from in state; 67% live on campus; 3% of students in fraternities, 11% in sororities
Most popular majors: 15% Philosophy and Religious Studies, 13% Health Professions and Related Programs, 12% Education, 9% Psychology, 7% Business, Management, Marketing, and Related Support Services
Expenses: 2017-2018: $26,840; room/board: $7,360
Financial aid: (405) 585-5020; 74% of undergrads determined to have financial need; average aid package $23,506

Oklahoma Christian University

Oklahoma City OK
(405) 425-5050
U.S. News ranking: Reg. U. (W), No. 47
Website: www.oc.edu/
Admissions email: admissions@oc.edu
Private; founded 1950
Affiliation: Churches of Christ
Freshman admissions: selective; 2016-2017: 2,256 applied, 1,372 accepted. Either SAT

or ACT required. ACT 25/75 percentile: 21-28. High school rank: 25% in top tenth, 55% in top quarter, 80% in top half
Early decision deadline: N/A, notification date: N/A
Early action deadline: N/A, notification date: N/A
Application deadline (fall): rolling
Undergraduate student body: 1,844 full time, 130 part time; 51% male, 49% female; 2% American Indian, 1% Asian, 5% black, 6% Hispanic, 7% multiracial, 0% Pacific Islander, 72% white, 7% international; 43% from in state; 81% live on campus; 32% of students in fraternities, 39% in sororities
Most popular majors: 17% Business, Management, Marketing, and Related Support Services, 14% Engineering, 12% Visual and Performing Arts, 9% Health Professions and Related Programs, 7% Liberal Arts and Sciences, General Studies and Humanities
Expenses: 2017-2018: $21,670; room/board: $7,590
Financial aid: (405) 425-5190; 64% of undergrads determined to have financial need; average aid package $23,026

Oklahoma City University
Oklahoma City OK
(405) 208-5050
U.S. News ranking: Reg. U. (W), No. 27
Website: www.okcu.edu
Admissions email: uadmissions@okcu.edu
Private; founded 1904
Affiliation: United Methodist
Freshman admissions: selective; 2016-2017: 1,631 applied, 1,177 accepted. Either SAT or ACT required. ACT 25/75 percentile: 23-30. High school rank: 27% in top tenth, 64% in top quarter, 85% in top half
Early decision deadline: N/A, notification date: N/A
Early action deadline: N/A, notification date: N/A
Application deadline (fall): rolling
Undergraduate student body: 1,590 full time, 174 part time; 34% male, 66% female; 2% American Indian, 3% Asian, 5% black, 9% Hispanic, 8% multiracial, 0% Pacific Islander, 60% white, 11% international; 49% from in state; 52% live on campus; 25% of students in fraternities, 36% in sororities
Most popular majors: 33% Adult Health Nurse/Nursing, 14% General Studies, 6% Music Performance, General, 4% Acting, 4% Dance, General
Expenses: 2017-2018: $30,726; room/board: $10,274
Financial aid: (405) 208-5211; 61% of undergrads determined to have financial need; average aid package $21,048

Oklahoma Panhandle State University
Goodwell OK
(800) 664-6778
U.S. News ranking: Reg. Coll. (W), second tier
Website: www.opsu.edu
Admissions email: opsu. admissions@opsu.edu
Public; founded 1909
Freshman admissions: less selective; 2016-2017: N/A applied, N/A accepted. Neither SAT nor ACT required. SAT 25/75 percentile: N/A. High school rank: N/A
Early decision deadline: N/A, notification date: N/A
Early action deadline: N/A, notification date: N/A
Application deadline (fall): rolling
Undergraduate student body: 885 full time, 322 part time; 49% male, 51% female; 3% American Indian, 1% Asian, 10% black, 25% Hispanic, 4% multiracial, 0% Pacific Islander, 51% white, 3% international
Most popular majors: 14% Registered Nursing/Registered Nurse, 9% Biology/Biological Sciences, General, 7% Business Administration and Management, General, 6% Agribusiness/ Agricultural Business Operations, 6% Psychology, General
Expenses: 2016-2017: $7,294 in state, $8,233 out of state, room/ board: $5,344
Financial aid: N/A

Oklahoma State University
Stillwater OK
(405) 744-5358
U.S. News ranking: Nat. U., No. 156
Website: go.okstate.edu
Admissions email: admissions@ okstate.edu
Public; founded 1890
Freshman admissions: more selective; 2016-2017: 13,055 applied, 9,729 accepted. Either SAT or ACT required. ACT 25/75 percentile: 21-27. High school rank: 25% in top tenth, 54% in top quarter, 84% in top half
Early decision deadline: N/A, notification date: N/A
Early action deadline: N/A, notification date: N/A
Application deadline (fall): rolling
Undergraduate student body: 18,369 full time, 2,724 part time; 51% male, 49% female; 5% American Indian, 2% Asian, 5% black, 7% Hispanic, 9% multiracial, 0% Pacific Islander, 69% white, 4% international; 73% from in state; 45% live on campus; 18% of students in fraternities, 25% in sororities
Most popular majors: 28% Business, Management, Marketing, and Related Support Services, 9% Agriculture, Agriculture Operations, and Related Sciences, 9% Engineering, 7% Family and Consumer Sciences/Human Sciences, 6% Biological and Biomedical Sciences
Expenses: 2017-2018: $8,738 in state, $23,776 out of state; room/ board: $8,558

Financial aid: (405) 744-6604; 51% of undergrads determined to have financial need; average aid package $14,155

Oklahoma State University Institute of Technology– Okmulgee
Okmulgee OK
(918) 293-4680
U.S. News ranking: Reg. Coll. (W), second tier
Website: www.osuit.edu/admissions
Admissions email: osuit.admissions@okstate.edu
Public; founded 1946
Freshman admissions: less selective; 2016-2017: 2,567 applied, 1,039 accepted. Either SAT or ACT required. ACT 25/75 percentile: 16-21. High school rank: 6% in top tenth, 23% in top quarter, 54% in top half
Early decision deadline: N/A, notification date: N/A
Early action deadline: N/A, notification date: N/A
Application deadline (fall): rolling
Undergraduate student body: 1,713 full time, 684 part time; 64% male, 36% female; 12% American Indian, 1% Asian, 4% black, 6% Hispanic, 9% multiracial, 0% Pacific Islander, 51% white, 2% international; 90% from in state; 30% live on campus; N/A of students in fraternities, N/A in sororities
Most popular majors: 60% Computer and Information Systems Security/Information Assurance, 27% Instrumentation Technology/Technician, 13% Civil Engineering Technology/ Technician
Expenses: 2016-2017: $5,100 in state, $10,710 out of state; room/ board: $6,554
Financial aid: (918) 293-5222

Oklahoma State University– Oklahoma City
Oklahoma City OK
(405) 945-3224
U.S. News ranking: Reg. Coll. (W), unranked
Website: www.osuokc.edu/
Admissions email: admissions@ osuokc.edu
Public; founded 1961
Application deadline (fall): rolling
Undergraduate student body: N/A full time, N/A part time
Expenses: 2016-2017: $3,634 in state, $9,922 out of state; room/ board: N/A
Financial aid: (405) 945-3211

Oklahoma Wesleyan University
Bartlesville OK
(866) 222-8226
U.S. News ranking: Reg. U. (W), No. 81
Website: www.okwu.edu
Admissions email: admissions@okwu.edu
Private; founded 1972
Affiliation: Wesleyan

Freshman admissions: less selective; 2016-2017: 2,879 applied, 2,096 accepted. Either SAT or ACT required. ACT 25/75 percentile: 16-22. High school rank: 2% in top tenth, 4% in top quarter, 34% in top half
Early decision deadline: N/A, notification date: N/A
Early action deadline: N/A, notification date: N/A
Application deadline (fall): rolling
Undergraduate student body: 634 full time, 558 part time; 40% male, 60% female; 9% American Indian, 1% Asian, 9% black, 5% Hispanic, 0% multiracial, 0% Pacific Islander, 63% white, 5% international
Most popular majors: 31% Nursing Science, 17% Business, Management, Marketing, and Related Support Services, Other, 7% General Studies, 4% Theological and Ministerial Studies, Other, 2% Business, Management, Marketing, and Related Support Services, Other
Expenses: 2017-2018: $26,090; room/board: $8,344
Financial aid: (918) 335-6282; 78% of undergrads determined to have financial need; average aid package $17,022

Oral Roberts University
Tulsa OK
(800) 678-8876
U.S. News ranking: Reg. U. (W), No. 47
Website: www.oru.edu
Admissions email: admissions@oru.edu
Private; founded 1963
Affiliation: Interdenominational
Freshman admissions: selective; 2016-2017: 2,635 applied, 1,517 accepted. Either SAT or ACT required. ACT 25/75 percentile: 19-24. High school rank: 13% in top tenth, 36% in top quarter, 64% in top half
Early decision deadline: N/A, notification date: N/A
Early action deadline: N/A, notification date: N/A
Application deadline (fall): rolling
Undergraduate student body: 2,603 full time, 685 part time; 40% male, 60% female; 3% American Indian, 2% Asian, 15% black, 10% Hispanic, 7% multiracial, 0% Pacific Islander, 49% white, 8% international; 42% from in state; 59% live on campus; 0% of students in fraternities, 0% in sororities
Most popular majors: 22% Business, Management, Marketing, and Related Support Services, 13% Theology and Religious Vocations, 11% Communication, Journalism, and Related Programs, 9% Education, 7% Health Professions and Related Programs
Expenses: 2017-2018: $26,792; room/board: $8,750
Financial aid: (918) 495-7088; 72% of undergrads determined to have financial need; average aid package $24,085

Rogers State University
Claremore OK
(918) 343-7545
U.S. News ranking: Reg. Coll. (W), second tier
Website: www.rsu.edu/
Admissions email: admissions@rsu.edu
Public; founded 1909
Freshman admissions: selective; 2016-2017: 1,169 applied, 924 accepted. Either SAT or ACT required. ACT 25/75 percentile: 19-21. High school rank: 13% in top tenth, 33% in top quarter, 64% in top half
Early decision deadline: N/A, notification date: N/A
Early action deadline: N/A, notification date: N/A
Application deadline (fall): rolling
Undergraduate student body: 2,372 full time, 1,517 part time; 39% male, 61% female; 11% American Indian, 2% Asian, 4% black, 3% Hispanic, 21% multiracial, 0% Pacific Islander, 59% white, 0% international; 95% from in state; 20% live on campus; 0% of students in fraternities, 2% in sororities
Most popular majors: 30% Business Administration and Management, General, 10% Multi-/Interdisciplinary Studies, Other, 9% Biology/Biological Sciences, General, 9% Social Sciences, General, 7% Registered Nursing/Registered Nurse
Expenses: 2016-2017: $6,430 in state, $14,080 out of state; room/ board: $8,357
Financial aid: (918) 343-7553

Southeastern Oklahoma State University
Durant OK
(580) 745-2060
U.S. News ranking: Reg. U. (W), second tier
Website: www.se.edu
Admissions email: admissions@se.edu
Public; founded 1909
Affiliation: Other
Freshman admissions: selective; 2016-2017: 1,107 applied, 854 accepted. Either SAT or ACT required. ACT 25/75 percentile: 18-23. High school rank: 17% in top tenth, 45% in top quarter, 76% in top half
Early decision deadline: N/A, notification date: N/A
Early action deadline: N/A, notification date: N/A
Application deadline (fall): rolling
Undergraduate student body: 2,411 full time, 721 part time; 46% male, 54% female; 30% American Indian, 1% Asian, 6% black, 6% Hispanic, 0% multiracial, 0% Pacific Islander, 54% white, 0% international
Most popular majors: 19% Engineering Technologies and Engineering-Related Fields, 13% Education, 12% Liberal Arts, and Sciences, General Studies and Humanities, 11% Business, Management, Marketing, and Related Support Services, 8% Psychology

Expenses: 2017-2018: $9,149 in state, $18,929 out of state; room/board: $6,973
Financial aid: (580) 745-2186; 71% of undergrads determined to have financial need; average aid package $11,195

Southern Nazarene University[1]
Bethany OK
(405) 491-6324
U.S. News ranking: Reg. U. (W), second tier
Website: www.snu.edu
Admissions email: admissions@snu.edu
Private; founded 1899
Application deadline (fall): 8/6
Undergraduate student body: N/A full time, N/A part time
Expenses: 2016-2017: $24,468; room/board: $8,970
Financial aid: (405) 491-6310

Southwestern Christian University[1]
Bethany OK
(405) 789-7661
U.S. News ranking: Reg. Coll. (W), No. 21
Website: www.swcu.edu/
Admissions email: admissions@swcu.edu
Private; founded 1946
Application deadline (fall): rolling
Undergraduate student body: N/A full time, N/A part time
Expenses: 2016-2017: $13,080; room/board: $7,233
Financial aid: N/A

Southwestern Oklahoma State University
Weatherford OK
(580) 774-3782
U.S. News ranking: Reg. U. (W), second tier
Website: www.swosu.edu
Admissions email: admissions@swosu.edu
Public; founded 1901
Freshman admissions: selective; 2016-2017: 3,131 applied, 2,844 accepted. Neither SAT nor ACT required. ACT 25/75 percentile: 18-24. High school rank: 24% in top tenth, 48% in top quarter, 76% in top half
Early decision deadline: N/A, notification date: N/A
Early action deadline: N/A, notification date: N/A
Application deadline (fall): rolling
Undergraduate student body: 3,659 full time, 851 part time; 42% male, 58% female; 4% American Indian, 2% Asian, 4% black, 9% Hispanic, 8% multiracial, 0% Pacific Islander, 64% white, 6% international; 90% from in state; 22% live on campus; 3% of students in fraternities, 4% in sororities
Most popular majors: 26% Registered Nursing/Registered Nurse, 14% Business Administration and Management, General, 8% Health Professions and Related Clinical Sciences, Other, 4% Biology/Biological Sciences, General, 3% Kinesiology and Exercise Science

Expenses: 2017-2018: $6,690 in state, $13,440 out of state; room/board: $5,400
Financial aid: (580) 774-3786; 41% of undergrads determined to have financial need; average aid package $5,622

St. Gregory's University
Shawnee OK
(405) 878-5444
U.S. News ranking: Reg. Coll. (W), No. 19
Website: www.stgregorys.edu
Admissions email: admissions@stgregorys.edu
Private; founded 1915
Affiliation: Roman Catholic
Freshman admissions: selective; 2016-2017: 611 applied, 254 accepted. Either SAT or ACT required. ACT 25/75 percentile: 17-23. High school rank: 0% in top tenth, 17% in top quarter, 67% in top half
Early decision deadline: N/A, notification date: N/A
Early action deadline: N/A, notification date: N/A
Application deadline (fall): N/A
Undergraduate student body: 460 full time, 176 part time; 42% male, 58% female; 14% American Indian, 1% Asian, 6% black, 12% Hispanic, 9% multiracial, 0% Pacific Islander, 53% white, 3% international; 71% from in state; N/A live on campus; N/A of students in fraternities, N/A in sororities
Most popular majors: 41% Business, Management, Marketing, and Related Support Services, 9% Education, 9% Health Professions and Related Programs, 9% Psychology
Expenses: 2016-2017: $21,300; room/board: $8,578
Financial aid: (405) 878-5412

University of Central Oklahoma
Edmond OK
(405) 974-2727
U.S. News ranking: Reg. U. (W), No. 76
Website: www.uco.edu/em/become-a-broncho/index.asp
Admissions email: onestop@uco.edu
Public; founded 1890
Freshman admissions: selective; 2016-2017: 5,509 applied, 5,173 accepted. Either SAT or ACT required. ACT 25/75 percentile: 19-24. High school rank: 13% in top tenth, 35% in top quarter, 71% in top half
Early decision deadline: N/A, notification date: N/A
Early action deadline: N/A, notification date: N/A
Application deadline (fall): rolling
Undergraduate student body: 10,565 full time, 4,188 part time; 41% male, 59% female; 4% American Indian, 3% Asian, 9% black, 10% Hispanic, 10% multiracial, 0% Pacific Islander, 57% white, 6% international; 97% from in state; 9% live on campus; 2% of students in fraternities, 3% in sororities

Most popular majors: 12% General Studies, 7% Business Administration and Management, General, 4% Occupational Health and Industrial Hygiene, 4% Psychology, General, 4% Registered Nursing/Registered Nurse
Expenses: 2017-2018: $6,699 in state, $16,460 out of state; room/board: $7,740
Financial aid: (405) 974-2727; 60% of undergrads determined to have financial need; average aid package $6,840

University of Oklahoma
Norman OK
(405) 325-2252
U.S. News ranking: Nat. U., No. 97
Website: www.ou.edu
Admissions email: admrec@ou.edu
Public; founded 1890
Freshman admissions: more selective; 2016-2017: 14,395 applied, 10,196 accepted. Either SAT or ACT required. ACT 25/75 percentile: 23-29. High school rank: 36% in top tenth, 66% in top quarter, 92% in top half
Early decision deadline: N/A, notification date: N/A
Early action deadline: N/A, notification date: N/A
Application deadline (fall): 2/1
Undergraduate student body: 19,200 full time, 3,236 part time; 50% male, 50% female; 4% American Indian, 6% Asian, 5% black, 9% Hispanic, 7% multiracial, 0% Pacific Islander, 61% white, 4% international; 67% from in state; 30% live on campus; 24% of students in fraternities, 32% in sororities
Most popular majors: 22% Business, Management, Marketing, and Related Support Services, 11% Engineering, 9% Health Professions and Related Programs, 8% Communication, Journalism, and Related Programs, 8% Liberal Arts and Sciences, General Studies and Humanities
Expenses: 2017-2018: $9,062 in state, $24,443 out of state; room/board: $10,588
Financial aid: (405) 325-4521; 46% of undergrads determined to have financial need; average aid package $12,709

University of Science and Arts of Oklahoma
Chickasha OK
(405) 574-1357
U.S. News ranking: Nat. Lib. Arts, second tier
Website: www.usao.edu
Admissions email: usao-admissions@usao.edu
Public; founded 1908
Freshman admissions: selective; 2016-2017: 1,085 applied, 544 accepted. Either SAT or ACT required. ACT 25/75 percentile: 20-24. High school rank: 19% in top tenth, 53% in top quarter, 100% in top half
Early decision deadline: N/A, notification date: N/A
Early action deadline: N/A, notification date: N/A

Application deadline (fall): 8/30
Undergraduate student body: 787 full time, 63 part time; 34% male, 66% female; 7% American Indian, 1% Asian, 4% black, 10% Hispanic, 10% multiracial, 0% Pacific Islander, 58% white, 9% international
Most popular majors: 21% Education, 16% Business, Management, Marketing, and Related Support Services, 14% Visual and Performing Arts, 10% Psychology, 9% Health Professions and Related Programs
Expenses: 2017-2018: $7,200 in state, $17,550 out of state; room/board: $5,860
Financial aid: (405) 574-1350; 65% of undergrads determined to have financial need; average aid package $11,157

University of Tulsa
Tulsa OK
(918) 631-2307
U.S. News ranking: Nat. U., No. 87
Website: utulsa.edu
Admissions email: admission@utulsa.edu
Private; founded 1894
Affiliation: Presbyterian Church (USA)
Freshman admissions: most selective; 2016-2017: 8,089 applied, 2,990 accepted. Either SAT or ACT required. ACT 25/75 percentile: 26-33. High school rank: 76% in top tenth, 93% in top quarter, 99% in top half
Early decision deadline: N/A, notification date: N/A
Early action deadline: 11/1, notification date: 12/15
Application deadline (fall): rolling
Undergraduate student body: 3,259 full time, 147 part time; 57% male, 43% female; 3% American Indian, 4% Asian, 5% black, 5% Hispanic, 1% multiracial, 0% Pacific Islander, 57% white, 24% international; 58% from in state; 69% live on campus; 19% of students in fraternities, 21% in sororities
Most popular majors: 24% Engineering, 22% Business, Management, Marketing, and Related Support Services, 7% Biological and Biomedical Sciences, 5% Health Professions and Related Programs, 5% Psychology
Expenses: 2017-2018: $39,502; room/board: $11,116
Financial aid: (918) 631-2526; 42% of undergrads determined to have financial need; average aid package $29,644

OREGON

Art Institute of Portland[1]
Portland OR
U.S. News ranking: Arts, unranked
Website: www.artinstitutes.edu/portland/
Admissions email: N/A
For-profit
Application deadline (fall): N/A
Undergraduate student body: N/A full time, N/A part time
Expenses: 2016-2017: $17,412; room/board: N/A
Financial aid: N/A

Corban University
Salem OR
(800) 845-3005
U.S. News ranking: Reg. U. (W), No. 66
Website: www.corban.edu
Admissions email: admissions@corban.edu
Private; founded 1935
Affiliation: General Baptist
Freshman admissions: selective; 2016-2017: 2,474 applied, 855 accepted. Either SAT or ACT required. SAT 25/75 percentile: 950-1170. High school rank: 23% in top tenth, 33% in top quarter, 85% in top half
Early decision deadline: N/A, notification date: N/A
Early action deadline: N/A, notification date: N/A
Application deadline (fall): 8/1
Undergraduate student body: 973 full time, 49 part time; 40% male, 60% female; 1% American Indian, 2% Asian, 1% black, 3% Hispanic, 8% multiracial, 0% Pacific Islander, 78% white, 3% international; 46% from in state; 63% live on campus; N/A of students in fraternities, N/A in sororities
Most popular majors: 29% Business, Management, Marketing, and Related Support Services, 16% Psychology, 13% Education, 8% English Language and Literature/Letters, 8% Multi/Interdisciplinary Studies
Expenses: 2017-2018: $31,640; room/board: $10,360
Financial aid: (503) 375-7006; 81% of undergrads determined to have financial need; average aid package $21,751

Eastern Oregon University
La Grande OR
(541) 962-3393
U.S. News ranking: Reg. U. (W), second tier
Website: www.eou.edu
Admissions email: admissions@eou.edu
Public; founded 1929
Freshman admissions: less selective; 2016-2017: 1,043 applied, 1,012 accepted. Either SAT or ACT required. SAT 25/75 percentile: 830-1040. High school rank: 9% in top tenth, 35% in top quarter, 68% in top half
Early decision deadline: N/A, notification date: N/A
Early action deadline: 2/1, notification date: N/A
Application deadline (fall): 9/1
Undergraduate student body: 1,691 full time, 1,182 part time; 39% male, 61% female; 2% American Indian, 2% Asian, 3% black, 7% Hispanic, 4% multiracial, 1% Pacific Islander, 75% white, 1% international; 69% from in state; 14% live on campus; 0% of students in fraternities, 0% in sororities
Most popular majors: 33% Business, Management, Marketing, and Related Support Services, 18% Liberal Arts and Sciences, General Studies and Humanities, 9% Education, 6% Homeland Security, Law Enforcement, Firefighting and Related Protective Services, 5% Psychology

Expenses: 2017-2018: $8,362 in state, $19,682 out of state; room/board: $9,250
Financial aid: (800) 452-8639; 75% of undergrads determined to have financial need; average aid package $9,781

George Fox University
Newberg OR
(800) 765-4369
U.S. News ranking: Reg. U. (W), No. 23
Website: www.georgefox.edu
Admissions email: admissions@georgefox.edu
Private; founded 1891
Affiliation: Friends
Freshman admissions: selective; 2016-2017: 3,146 applied, 2,491 accepted. Either SAT or ACT required. SAT 25/75 percentile: 980-1220. High school rank: 24% in top tenth, 59% in top quarter, 89% in top half
Early decision deadline: N/A, notification date: N/A
Early action deadline: 11/1, notification date: 12/9
Application deadline (fall): rolling
Undergraduate student body: 2,474 full time, 233 part time; 44% male, 56% female; 1% American Indian, 4% Asian, 1% black, 12% Hispanic, 7% multiracial, 1% Pacific Islander, 69% white, 0% international; 61% from in state; 40% live on campus; N/A of students in fraternities, N/A in sororities
Most popular majors: 33% Business, Management, Marketing, and Related Support Services, Other, 11% Multi/Interdisciplinary Studies, 9% Fine/Studio Arts, General, 8% Peace Studies and Conflict Resolution, 5% Engineering, General
Expenses: 2017-2018: $35,016; room/board: $10,886
Financial aid: (503) 554-2302; 75% of undergrads determined to have financial need; average aid package $22,722

Lewis & Clark College
Portland OR
(800) 444-4111
U.S. News ranking: Nat. Lib. Arts, No. 76
Website: www.lclark.edu
Admissions email: admissions@lclark.edu
Private; founded 1867
Freshman admissions: more selective; 2016-2017: 7,796 applied, 4,284 accepted. Neither SAT nor ACT required. ACT 25/75 percentile: 27-31. High school rank: 51% in top tenth, 87% in top quarter, 98% in top half
Early decision deadline: 11/1, notification date: 12/15
Early action deadline: 11/1, notification date: 12/31
Application deadline (fall): 3/1
Undergraduate student body: 2,102 full time, 32 part time; 39% male, 61% female; 1% American Indian, 6% Asian, 2% black, 11% Hispanic, 3% multiracial, 0% Pacific Islander, 66% white, 5% international; 11% from in state; 69% live on campus; 0% of students in fraternities, 0% in sororities

Most popular majors: 24% Social Sciences, 13% Psychology, 11% Biological and Biomedical Sciences, 9% Visual and Performing Arts, 8% Communication, Journalism, and Related Programs
Expenses: 2017-2018: $48,988; room/board: $11,996
Financial aid: (503) 768-7090; 57% of undergrads determined to have financial need; average aid package $42,109

Linfield College
McMinnville OR
(800) 640-2287
U.S. News ranking: Nat. Lib. Arts, No. 117
Website: www.linfield.edu
Admissions email: admission@linfield.edu
Private; founded 1858
Affiliation: American Baptist
Freshman admissions: selective; 2016-2017: 2,296 applied, 1,854 accepted. Either SAT or ACT required. SAT 25/75 percentile: 920-1150. High school rank: 27% in top tenth, 64% in top quarter, 94% in top half
Early decision deadline: N/A, notification date: N/A
Early action deadline: 11/1, notification date: 1/15
Application deadline (fall): rolling
Undergraduate student body: 1,602 full time, 30 part time; 38% male, 62% female; 1% American Indian, 5% Asian, 2% black, 14% Hispanic, 12% multiracial, 1% Pacific Islander, 60% white, 3% international; 55% from in state; 77% live on campus; 24% of students in fraternities, 25% in sororities
Most popular majors: 22% Health Professions and Related Programs, 10% Education, 8% Library Science, 7% Biological and Biomedical Sciences, 7% Communication, Journalism, and Related Programs
Expenses: 2017-2018: $41,612; room/board: $12,380
Financial aid: (503) 883-2225; 76% of undergrads determined to have financial need; average aid package $32,663

Marylhurst University
Marylhurst OR
(503) 699-6268
U.S. News ranking: Reg. U. (W), unranked
Website: www.marylhurst.edu
Admissions email: admissions@marylhurst.edu
Private
Freshman admissions: least selective; 2016-2017: 2 applied, 2 accepted. Neither SAT nor ACT required. SAT 25/75 percentile: N/A. High school rank: N/A
Early decision deadline: N/A, notification date: N/A
Early action deadline: N/A, notification date: N/A
Application deadline (fall): rolling
Undergraduate student body: 135 full time, 263 part time; 29% male, 71% female; 1% American Indian, 3% Asian, 3% black, 7% Hispanic, 4% multiracial, 0% Pacific Islander, 71% white,

2% international; 80% from in state; 0% live on campus; 0% of students in fraternities, 0% in sororities
Most popular majors: 33% Business, Management, Marketing, and Related Support Services, 17% Multi/Interdisciplinary Studies, 12% Psychology, 11% Basic Skills and Developmental/Remedial Education, 8% Visual and Performing Arts
Expenses: 2016-2017: $20,835; room/board: N/A
Financial aid: N/A

Northwest Christian University
Eugene OR
(541) 684-7201
U.S. News ranking: Reg. U. (W), No. 91
Website: www.nwcu.edu
Admissions email: admissions@nwcu.edu
Private; founded 1895
Affiliation: Christian Church (Disciples of Christ)
Freshman admissions: less selective; 2016-2017: 427 applied, 285 accepted. Either SAT or ACT required. SAT 25/75 percentile: 863-1080. High school rank: N/A
Early decision deadline: N/A, notification date: N/A
Early action deadline: N/A, notification date: N/A
Application deadline (fall): rolling
Undergraduate student body: 421 full time, 145 part time; 38% male, 62% female; 4% American Indian, 3% Asian, 5% black, 7% Hispanic, 3% multiracial, 1% Pacific Islander, 75% white, 0% international; 76% from in state; 34% live on campus; N/A of students in fraternities, N/A in sororities
Most popular majors: 34% Business, Management, Marketing, and Related Support Services, 27% Education, 17% Psychology, 6% Biological and Biomedical Sciences, 6% Multi/Interdisciplinary Studies
Expenses: 2017-2018: $28,680; room/board: $8,800
Financial aid: (541) 684-7291; 80% of undergrads determined to have financial need; average aid package $21,401

Oregon College of Art and Craft
Portland OR
(971) 255-4192
U.S. News ranking: Arts, unranked
Website: www.ocac.edu/
Admissions email: admissions@ocac.edu
Private; founded 1907
Freshman admissions: selective; 2016-2017: 142 applied, 83 accepted. Neither SAT nor ACT required. ACT 25/75 percentile: 20-27. High school rank: 20% in top tenth, 40% in top quarter, 40% in top half
Early decision deadline: N/A, notification date: N/A
Early action deadline: N/A, notification date: N/A
Application deadline (fall): rolling

Undergraduate student body: 107 full time, 16 part time; 20% male, 80% female; 2% American Indian, 2% Asian, 2% black, 7% Hispanic, 11% multiracial, 1% Pacific Islander, 73% white, 1% international; 36% from in state; 16% live on campus; N/A of students in fraternities, N/A in sororities
Most popular majors: 100% Crafts/Craft Design, Folk Art and Artisanry
Expenses: 2017-2018: $33,160; room/board: $9,900
Financial aid: N/A

Oregon Institute of Technology
Klamath Falls OR
(541) 885-1155
U.S. News ranking: Reg. Coll. (W), No. 6
Website: www.oit.edu
Admissions email: oit@oit.edu
Public; founded 1947
Freshman admissions: selective; 2016-2017: 1,239 applied, 905 accepted. Either SAT or ACT required. SAT 25/75 percentile: 920-1160. High school rank: 23% in top tenth, 56% in top quarter, 87% in top half
Early decision deadline: N/A, notification date: N/A
Early action deadline: N/A, notification date: N/A
Application deadline (fall): 9/4
Undergraduate student body: 2,385 full time, 2,769 part time; 51% male, 49% female; 1% American Indian, 7% Asian, 2% black, 9% Hispanic, 5% multiracial, 1% Pacific Islander, 71% white, 2% international; 71% from in state; 14% live on campus; 0% of students in fraternities, 0% in sororities
Most popular majors: 44% Health Professions and Related Programs, 19% Engineering, 16% Engineering Technologies and Engineering-Related Fields, 7% Business, Management, Marketing and Related Support Services, 5% Psychology
Expenses: 2017-2018: $9,982 in state, $28,367 out of state; room/board: $9,206
Financial aid: (541) 885-1280; 66% of undergrads determined to have financial need; average aid package $10,598

Oregon State University
Corvallis OR
(541) 737-4411
U.S. News ranking: Nat. U., No. 145
Website: oregonstate.edu
Admissions email: osuadmit@oregonstate.edu
Public; founded 1868
Freshman admissions: selective; 2016-2017: 14,595 applied, 11,308 accepted. Either SAT or ACT required. SAT 25/75 percentile: 990-1240. High school rank: 28% in top tenth, 60% in top quarter, 91% in top half
Early decision deadline: N/A, notification date: N/A
Early action deadline: 11/1, notification date: 12/16
Application deadline (fall): 9/1

Undergraduate student body: 18,852 full time, 6,475 part time; 54% male, 46% female; 1% American Indian, 7% Asian, 1% black, 9% Hispanic, 7% multiracial, 0% Pacific Islander, 65% white, 7% international; 70% from in state; 17% live on campus; 11% of students in fraternities, 16% in sororities
Most popular majors: 15% Engineering, 12% Business, Management, Marketing, and Related Support Services, 10% Family and Consumer Sciences/Human Sciences, 7% Agriculture, Agriculture Operations, and Related Sciences, 7% Social Sciences
Expenses: 2017-2018: $10,797 in state, $29,457 out of state; room/board: $12,540
Financial aid: (541) 737-2241; 53% of undergrads determined to have financial need; average aid package $13,265

Pacific Northwest College of Art[1]
Portland OR
U.S. News ranking: Arts, unranked
Website: www.pnca.edu
Admissions email: admissions@pnca.edu
Private
Application deadline (fall): N/A
Undergraduate student body: N/A full time, N/A part time
Expenses: 2016-2017: $34,500; room/board: $12,230
Financial aid: N/A

Pacific University
Forest Grove OR
(800) 677-6712
U.S. News ranking: Reg. U. (W), No. 22
Website: www.pacificu.edu
Admissions email: admissions@pacificu.edu
Private; founded 1849
Freshman admissions: selective; 2016-2017: 2,845 applied, 2,242 accepted. Either SAT or ACT required. SAT 25/75 percentile: 1010-1230. High school rank: N/A
Early decision deadline: N/A, notification date: N/A
Early action deadline: N/A, notification date: N/A
Application deadline (fall): 8/15
Undergraduate student body: 1,857 full time, 73 part time; 41% male, 59% female; 1% American Indian, 12% Asian, 2% black, 14% Hispanic, 11% multiracial, 2% Pacific Islander, 52% white, 1% international; 45% from in state; 59% live on campus; 2% of students in fraternities, 7% in sororities
Most popular majors: 17% Health Professions and Related Programs, 12% Business, Management, Marketing, and Related Support Services, 11% Biological and Biomedical Sciences, 11% Parks, Recreation, Leisure, and Fitness Studies, 7% Social Sciences
Expenses: 2017-2018: $43,594; room/board: $12,162
Financial aid: (503) 352-2222; 82% of undergrads determined to have financial need; average aid package $30,945

Portland State University
Portland OR
U.S. News ranking: Nat. U., second tier
Website: www.pdx.edu
Admissions email: admissions@pdx.edu
Public; founded 1946
Freshman admissions: selective; 2016-2017: 6,373 applied, 5,699 accepted. Neither SAT nor ACT required. ACT 25/75 percentile: 19-25. High school rank: 11% in top tenth, 39% in top quarter, 83% in top half
Early decision deadline: N/A, notification date: N/A
Early action deadline: N/A, notification date: N/A
Application deadline (fall): rolling
Undergraduate student body: 14,208 full time, 7,425 part time; 47% male, 53% female; 1% American Indian, 9% Asian, 4% black, 13% Hispanic, 6% multiracial, 1% Pacific Islander, 57% white, 5% international
Most popular majors: Information not available
Expenses: 2017-2018: $7,302 in state, $21,180 out of state; room/board: $10,043
Financial aid: (503) 725-5442; 66% of undergrads determined to have financial need; average aid package $9,293

Reed College[1]
Portland OR
(503) 777-7511
U.S. News ranking: Nat. Lib. Arts, No. 82
Website: www.reed.edu/
Admissions email: admission@reed.edu
Private
Application deadline (fall): N/A
Undergraduate student body: N/A full time, N/A part time
Expenses: 2016-2017: $52,150; room/board: $13,150
Financial aid: N/A

Southern Oregon University
Ashland OR
(541) 552-6411
U.S. News ranking: Reg. U. (W), No. 76
Website: www.sou.edu
Admissions email: admissions@sou.edu
Public; founded 1926
Freshman admissions: selective; 2016-2017: 2,766 applied, 2,163 accepted. Either SAT or ACT required. SAT 25/75 percentile: 900-1130. High school rank: N/A
Early decision deadline: N/A, notification date: N/A
Early action deadline: N/A, notification date: N/A
Application deadline (fall): rolling
Undergraduate student body: 3,598 full time, 1,716 part time; 41% male, 59% female; 1% American Indian, 2% Asian, 2% black, 12% Hispanic, 10% multiracial, 1% Pacific Islander, 59% white, 3% international; 60% from in state; 17% live on campus; N/A of students in fraternities, N/A in sororities

Most popular majors: 20% Business, Management, Marketing, and Related Support Services, 14% Visual and Performing Arts, 10% Education, 9% Psychology, 7% Parks, Recreation, Leisure, and Fitness Studies
Expenses: 2016-2017: $8,523 in state, $23,170 out of state; room/board: $12,756
Financial aid: N/A; 63% of undergrads determined to have financial need; average aid package $11,131

University of Oregon
Eugene OR
(800) 232-3825
U.S. News ranking: Nat. U., No. 103
Website: www.uoregon.edu
Admissions email: uoadmit@uoregon.edu
Public; founded 1876
Freshman admissions: selective; 2016-2017: 21,821 applied, 16,992 accepted. Either SAT or ACT required. SAT 25/75 percentile: 980-1220. High school rank: 25% in top tenth, 60% in top quarter, 91% in top half
Early decision deadline: N/A, notification date: N/A
Early action deadline: 11/1, notification date: 12/15
Application deadline (fall): 1/15
Undergraduate student body: 18,330 full time, 1,719 part time; 47% male, 53% female; 1% American Indian, 6% Asian, 2% black, 11% Hispanic, 7% multiracial, 0% Pacific Islander, 59% white, 13% international; 58% from in state; 19% live on campus; 14% of students in fraternities, 22% in sororities
Most popular majors: 12% Business/Commerce, General, 9% Social Sciences, General, 7% Economics, General, 7% Psychology, General, 6% Physiology, General
Expenses: 2017-2018: $11,571 in state, $34,611 out of state; room/board: $12,450
Financial aid: (800) 760-6953; 44% of undergrads determined to have financial need; average aid package $10,879

University of Portland
Portland OR
(888) 627-5601
U.S. News ranking: Reg. U. (W), No. 6
Website: www.up.edu
Admissions email: admissions@up.edu
Private; founded 1901
Affiliation: Roman Catholic
Freshman admissions: more selective; 2016-2017: 11,911 applied, 7,267 accepted. Either SAT or ACT required. SAT 25/75 percentile: 1080-1320. High school rank: 44% in top tenth, 75% in top quarter, 97% in top half
Early decision deadline: N/A, notification date: N/A
Early action deadline: N/A, notification date: N/A
Application deadline (fall): 2/1
Undergraduate student body: 3,708 full time, 90 part time; 41% male, 59% female; 0% American Indian, 12% Asian, 1% black,

12% Hispanic, 9% multiracial, 2% Pacific Islander, 59% white, 3% international; 27% from in state; 56% live on campus; 0% of students in fraternities, 0% in sororities
Most popular majors: 21% Health Professions and Related Programs, 18% Business, Management, Marketing, and Related Support Services, 11% Engineering, 9% Biological and Biomedical Sciences, 5% Communication, Journalism, and Related Programs
Expenses: 2017-2018: $44,026; room/board: $12,658
Financial aid: (503) 943-7311; 59% of undergrads determined to have financial need; average aid package $30,450

Warner Pacific College[1]
Portland OR
(503) 517-1020
U.S. News ranking: Reg. Coll. (W), No. 9
Website: www.warnerpacific.edu
Admissions email: admissions@warnerpacific.edu
Private; founded 1937
Application deadline (fall): rolling
Undergraduate student body: N/A full time, N/A part time
Expenses: 2017-2018: $24,500; room/board: $9,300
Financial aid: (503) 517-1091; 80% of undergrads determined to have financial need; average aid package $18,736

Western Oregon University
Monmouth OR
(503) 838-8211
U.S. News ranking: Reg. U. (W), No. 73
Website: www.wou.edu
Admissions email: wolfgram@wou.edu
Public; founded 1856
Freshman admissions: less selective; 2016-2017: 2,901 applied, 2,546 accepted. Neither SAT nor ACT required. SAT 25/75 percentile: 840-1070. High school rank: 12% in top tenth, 35% in top quarter, 73% in top half
Early decision deadline: N/A, notification date: N/A
Early action deadline: N/A, notification date: N/A
Application deadline (fall): rolling
Undergraduate student body: 4,081 full time, 752 part time; 39% male, 61% female; 2% American Indian, 4% Asian, 4% black, 14% Hispanic, 0% multiracial, 3% Pacific Islander, 63% white, 6% international; 81% from in state; 26% live on campus; 1% of students in fraternities, 1% in sororities
Most popular majors: 16% Multi/Interdisciplinary Studies, 13% Business, Management, Marketing, and Related Support Services, 13% Health Professions and Related Programs, 11% Homeland Security, Law Enforcement, Firefighting and Related Protective Services, 7% Psychology
Expenses: 2017-2018: $9,468 in state, $25,653 out of state; room/board: $10,203

Financial aid: (503) 838-8475; 80% of undergrads determined to have financial need; average aid package $9,924

Willamette University
Salem OR
(877) 542-2787
U.S. News ranking: Nat. Lib. Arts, No. 82
Website: www.willamette.edu
Admissions email: bearcat@willamette.edu
Private; founded 1842
Freshman admissions: more selective; 2016-2017: 6,181 applied, 4,825 accepted. Either SAT or ACT required. SAT 25/75 percentile: 1100-1330. High school rank: 41% in top tenth, 74% in top quarter, 96% in top half
Early decision deadline: N/A, notification date: N/A
Early action deadline: 11/15, notification date: 12/31
Application deadline (fall): 2/1
Undergraduate student body: 1,862 full time, 140 part time; 43% male, 57% female; 1% American Indian, 9% Asian, 3% black, 13% Hispanic, 9% multiracial, 0% Pacific Islander, 62% white, 1% international; 21% from in state; 65% live on campus; 27% of students in fraternities, 24% in sororities
Most popular majors: 28% Social Sciences, 8% English Language and Literature/Letters, 8% Physical Sciences, 8% Psychology, 7% Biological and Biomedical Sciences
Expenses: 2017-2018: $48,164; room/board: $11,830
Financial aid: (503) 370-6273; 63% of undergrads determined to have financial need; average aid package $35,895

PENNSYLVANIA

Albright College
Reading PA
(800) 252-1856
U.S. News ranking: Nat. Lib. Arts, second tier
Website: www.albright.edu
Admissions email: admission@albright.edu
Private; founded 1856
Affiliation: United Methodist
Freshman admissions: selective; 2016-2017: 8,832 applied, 4,514 accepted. Neither SAT nor ACT required. SAT 25/75 percentile: 950-1143. High school rank: 19% in top tenth, 44% in top quarter, 76% in top half
Early decision deadline: N/A, notification date: N/A
Early action deadline: N/A, notification date: N/A
Application deadline (fall): rolling
Undergraduate student body: 2,284 full time, 20 part time; 40% male, 60% female; 1% American Indian, 2% Asian, 20% black, 10% Hispanic, 1% multiracial, 0% Pacific Islander, 49% white, 2% international; 59% from in state; 67% live on campus; 15% of students in fraternities, 22% in sororities

Most popular majors: 20% Visual and Performing Arts, 16% Business, Management, Marketing, and Related Support Services, 15% Social Sciences, 7% Biological and Biomedical Sciences, 6% History
Expenses: 2017-2018: $43,454; room/board: $11,606
Financial aid: (610) 921-7515; 90% of undergrads determined to have financial need; average aid package $36,812

Allegheny College
Meadville PA
(800) 521-5293
U.S. News ranking: Nat. Lib. Arts, No. 82
Website: www.allegheny.edu
Admissions email: admissions@allegheny.edu
Private; founded 1815
Affiliation: United Methodist
Freshman admissions: more selective; 2016-2017: 4,724 applied, 3,201 accepted. Neither SAT nor ACT required. SAT 25/75 percentile: 1070-1290. High school rank: 37% in top tenth, 66% in top quarter, 89% in top half
Early decision deadline: 11/1, notification date: 11/15
Early action deadline: 12/1, notification date: 1/1
Application deadline (fall): 2/15
Undergraduate student body: 1,869 full time, 51 part time; 47% male, 53% female; 0% American Indian, 2% Asian, 7% black, 8% Hispanic, 4% multiracial, 0% Pacific Islander, 73% white, 3% international; 51% from in state; 96% live on campus; 25% of students in fraternities, 27% in sororities
Most popular majors: 14% Biology/Biological Sciences, General, 14% Psychology, General, 12% Economics, General, 9% Speech Communication and Rhetoric, 7% Neuroscience
Expenses: 2017-2018: $45,970; room/board: $11,650
Financial aid: (800) 835-7780; 74% of undergrads determined to have financial need; average aid package $39,415

Alvernia University
Reading PA
(610) 796-8220
U.S. News ranking: Reg. U. (N), No. 111
Website: www.alvernia.edu
Admissions email: admissions@alvernia.edu
Private; founded 1958
Affiliation: Roman Catholic
Freshman admissions: selective; 2016-2017: 1,788 applied, 1,332 accepted. Either SAT or ACT required. SAT 25/75 percentile: 880-1090. High school rank: 11% in top tenth, 32% in top quarter, 72% in top half
Early decision deadline: N/A, notification date: N/A
Early action deadline: N/A, notification date: N/A
Application deadline (fall): rolling
Undergraduate student body: 1,719 full time, 604 part time; 26% male, 74% female; 0% American Indian, 2% Asian, 11% black,

More @ usnews.com/bestcolleges

9% Hispanic, 2% multiracial, 0% Pacific Islander, 67% white, 0% international

Most popular majors: 45% Health Professions and Related Programs, 15% Business, Management, Marketing, and Related Support Services, 11% Homeland Security, Law Enforcement, Firefighting and Related Protective Services, 6% Education, 5% Public Administration and Social Service Professions

Expenses: 2017-2018: $33,640; room/board: $11,690

Financial aid: (610) 796-8356; 85% of undergrads determined to have financial need; average aid package $20,349

Arcadia University

Glenside PA
(215) 572-2910
U.S. News ranking: Reg. U. (N), No. 48
Website: www.arcadia.edu
Admissions email: admiss@arcadia.edu
Private; founded 1853
Freshman admissions: selective; 2016-2017: 8,984 applied, 5,684 accepted. Either SAT or ACT required. SAT 25/75 percentile: 1000-1210. High school rank: 28% in top tenth, 59% in top quarter, 86% in top half
Early decision deadline: N/A, notification date: N/A
Early action deadline: N/A, notification date: N/A
Application deadline (fall): rolling
Undergraduate student body: 2,266 full time, 207 part time; 31% male, 69% female; 0% American Indian, 4% Asian, 9% black, 9% Hispanic, 4% multiracial, 0% Pacific Islander, 67% white, 4% international; 59% from in state; 51% live on campus; 0% of students in fraternities, 0% in sororities
Most popular majors: 16% Biology/Biological Sciences, General, 10% Psychology, General, 5% International Business/Trade/Commerce, 4% Criminology, 4% Health/Health Care Administration/Management
Expenses: 2017-2018: $42,330; room/board: $13,660
Financial aid: (215) 572-2980; 80% of undergrads determined to have financial need; average aid package $30,072

The Art Institute of Philadelphia[1]

Philadelphia PA
U.S. News ranking: Arts, unranked
Private
Application deadline (fall): N/A
Undergraduate student body: N/A full time, N/A part time
Expenses: 2016-2017: $17,916; room/board: $11,373
Financial aid: N/A

Art Institute of Pittsburgh[1]

Pittsburgh PA
U.S. News ranking: Arts, unranked
Website: www.artinstitutes.edu/pittsburgh/Admissions
Admissions email: aip@aii.edu
For-profit
Application deadline (fall): N/A
Undergraduate student body: N/A full time, N/A part time
Expenses: 2016-2017: $17,628; room/board: $10,656
Financial aid: N/A

Bloomsburg University of Pennsylvania

Bloomsburg PA
(570) 389-4316
U.S. News ranking: Reg. U. (N), No. 102
Website: www.bloomu.edu
Admissions email: buadmiss@bloomu.edu
Public; founded 1839
Freshman admissions: less selective; 2016-2017: 9,330 applied, 7,236 accepted. Either SAT or ACT required. SAT 25/75 percentile: 870-1070. High school rank: 7% in top tenth, 27% in top quarter, 61% in top half
Early decision deadline: N/A, notification date: N/A
Early action deadline: N/A, notification date: 5/1
Application deadline (fall): rolling
Undergraduate student body: 8,274 full time, 721 part time; 43% male, 57% female; 0% American Indian, 1% Asian, 9% black, 7% Hispanic, 3% multiracial, 0% Pacific Islander, 79% white, 0% international; 91% from in state; 41% live on campus; 0% of students in fraternities, N/A in sororities
Most popular majors: 20% Business Administration and Management, General, 6% Organizational Communication, General, 6% Psychology, General, 5% Health and Physical Education/Fitness, Other, 5% Special Education and Teaching, General
Expenses: 2017-2018: $37,500 in state, $48,738 out of state; room/board: $9,430
Financial aid: (570) 389-4297; 65% of undergrads determined to have financial need; average aid package $9,232

Bryn Athyn College of the New Church

Bryn Athyn PA
(267) 502-6000
U.S. News ranking: Nat. Lib. Arts, second tier
Website: www.brynathyn.edu
Admissions email: admissions@brynathyn.edu
Private; founded 1877
Affiliation: Other
Freshman admissions: less selective; 2016-2017: 215 applied, 176 accepted. Either SAT or ACT required. SAT 25/75 percentile: 785-1105. High school rank: N/A
Early decision deadline: N/A, notification date: N/A
Early action deadline: N/A, notification date: N/A

Application deadline (fall): rolling
Undergraduate student body: 289 full time, 6 part time; 50% male, 50% female; 1% American Indian, 2% Asian, 19% black, 9% Hispanic, 0% multiracial, 0% Pacific Islander, 67% white, 2% international
Most popular majors: Information not available
Expenses: 2017-2018: $21,071; room/board: $11,538
Financial aid: (267) 502-6034; 68% of undergrads determined to have financial need; average aid package $17,254

Bryn Mawr College

Bryn Mawr PA
(610) 526-5152
U.S. News ranking: Nat. Lib. Arts, No. 32
Website: www.brynmawr.edu
Admissions email: admissions@brynmawr.edu
Private; founded 1885
Freshman admissions: more selective; 2016-2017: 3,012 applied, 1,203 accepted. Neither SAT nor ACT required. SAT 25/75 percentile: 1220-1450. High school rank: 66% in top tenth, 90% in top quarter, 96% in top half
Early decision deadline: 11/15, notification date: 12/15
Early action deadline: N/A, notification date: N/A
Application deadline (fall): 1/15
Undergraduate student body: 1,361 full time, 20 part time; 0% male, 100% female; 0% American Indian, 12% Asian, 6% black, 9% Hispanic, 6% multiracial, 0% Pacific Islander, 36% white, 23% international; 16% from in state; 92% live on campus; N/A of students in fraternities. N/A in sororities
Most popular majors: 26% Social Sciences, 11% Biological and Biomedical Sciences, 11% Foreign Languages, Literatures, and Linguistics, 11% Psychology, 9% English Language and Literature/Letters
Expenses: 2017-2018: $50,500; room/board: $15,910
Financial aid: (610) 526-5245; 54% of undergrads determined to have financial need; average aid package $45,900

Bucknell University

Lewisburg PA
(570) 577-3000
U.S. News ranking: Nat. Lib. Arts, No. 33
Website: www.bucknell.edu
Admissions email: admissions@bucknell.edu
Private; founded 1846
Freshman admissions: more selective; 2016-2017: 10,487 applied, 3,138 accepted. Either SAT or ACT required. SAT 25/75 percentile: 1200-1380. High school rank: 59% in top tenth, 84% in top quarter, 98% in top half
Early decision deadline: 11/15, notification date: 12/15
Early action deadline: N/A, notification date: N/A
Application deadline (fall): 1/15

Undergraduate student body: 3,530 full time, 41 part time; 49% male, 51% female; 0% American Indian, 5% Asian, 3% black, 6% Hispanic, 4% multiracial, 0% Pacific Islander, 75% white, 6% international; 22% from in state; 92% live on campus; 39% of students in fraternities, 46% in sororities
Most popular majors: 9% Economics, General, 7% Accounting and Finance, 7% Biology/Biological Sciences, General, 7% Psychology, General, 5% Political Science and Government, General
Expenses: 2017-2018: $53,986; room/board: $13,150
Financial aid: (570) 577-1331; 37% of undergrads determined to have financial need; average aid package $32,500

Cabrini University

Radnor PA
(610) 902-8552
U.S. News ranking: Reg. U. (N), No. 120
Website: www.cabrini.edu
Admissions email: admit@cabrini.edu
Private; founded 1957
Freshman admissions: less selective; 2016-2017: 2,420 applied, 2,268 accepted. Neither SAT nor ACT required. SAT 25/75 percentile: N/A. High school rank: N/A
Early decision deadline: N/A, notification date: N/A
Early action deadline: N/A, notification date: N/A
Application deadline (fall): rolling
Undergraduate student body: 1,384 full time, 266 part time; 39% male, 61% female; 0% American Indian, 2% Asian, 20% black, 10% Hispanic, 4% multiracial, 0% Pacific Islander, 59% white, 0% international
Most popular majors: Information not available
Expenses: 2017-2018: $31,350; room/board: $12,340
Financial aid: (610) 902-8424; 77% of undergrads determined to have financial need; average aid package $16,988

Cairn University[1]

Langhorne PA
(215) 702-4235
U.S. News ranking: Reg. U. (N), second tier
Website: cairn.edu/
Admissions email: admissions@cairn.edu
Private; founded 1913
Application deadline (fall): rolling
Undergraduate student body: N/A full time, N/A part time
Expenses: 2017-2018: $26,493; room/board: $9,803
Financial aid: (215) 702-4243; 81% of undergrads determined to have financial need; average aid package $20,983

California University of Pennsylvania

California PA
(724) 938-4404
U.S. News ranking: Reg. U. (N), second tier
Website: www.calu.edu/
Admissions email: inquiry@calu.edu

Public; founded 1852
Freshman admissions: least selective; 2016-2017: 3,202 applied, 2,994 accepted. Either SAT or ACT required. SAT 25/75 percentile: 810-1030. High school rank: 8% in top tenth, 23% in top quarter, 53% in top half
Early decision deadline: N/A, notification date: N/A
Early action deadline: N/A, notification date: N/A
Application deadline (fall): 8/22
Undergraduate student body: 4,606 full time, 916 part time; 46% male, 54% female; 0% American Indian, 1% Asian, 13% black, 3% Hispanic, 4% multiracial, 0% Pacific Islander, 77% white, 1% international; 89% from in state; 34% live on campus; 5% of students in fraternities, 5% in sororities
Most popular majors: 17% Health Professions and Related Programs, 12% Parks, Recreation, Leisure, and Fitness Studies, 11% Business, Management, Marketing, and Related Support Services, 7% Homeland Security, Law Enforcement, Firefighting and Related Protective Services, 6% Education
Expenses: 2017-2018: $10,844 in state, $14,590 out of state; room/board: $10,186
Financial aid: (724) 938-4415; 77% of undergrads determined to have financial need; average aid package $12,540

Carlow University

Pittsburgh PA
(412) 578-6059
U.S. News ranking: Reg. U. (N), No. 111
Website: www.carlow.edu
Admissions email: admissions@carlow.edu
Private; founded 1929
Affiliation: Roman Catholic
Freshman admissions: selective, 2016-2017: 806 applied, 696 accepted. Either SAT or ACT required. SAT 25/75 percentile: 870-1070. High school rank: 16% in top tenth, 40% in top quarter, 68% in top half
Early decision deadline: N/A, notification date: N/A
Early action deadline: N/A, notification date: N/A
Application deadline (fall): rolling
Undergraduate student body: 1,099 full time, 308 part time; 14% male, 86% female; 0% American Indian, 2% Asian, 19% black, 3% Hispanic, 5% multiracial, 0% Pacific Islander, 64% white, 0% international; 95% from in state; 32% live on campus; 0% of students in fraternities, 5% in sororities
Most popular majors: 26% Registered Nursing/Registered Nurse, 10% Psychology, General, 7% Biology/Biological Sciences, General, 7% Business Administration and Management, General, 6% Early Childhood Education and Teaching
Expenses: 2017-2018: $28,596; room/board: $11,108
Financial aid: (412) 578-6171; 90% of undergrads determined to have financial need; average aid package $19,395

Carnegie Mellon University

Pittsburgh PA
(412) 268-2082
U.S. News ranking: Nat. U., No. 25
Website: www.cmu.edu
Admissions email: undergraduate-admissions@andrew.cmu.edu
Private; founded 1900
Freshman admissions: most selective; 2016-2017: 21,189 applied, 4,601 accepted. Either SAT or ACT required. SAT 25/75 percentile: 1380-1550. High school rank: 75% in top tenth, 95% in top quarter, 99% in top half
Early decision deadline: 11/1, notification date: 12/15
Early action deadline: N/A, notification date: N/A
Application deadline (fall): 1/1
Undergraduate student body: 6,439 full time, 234 part time; 53% male, 47% female; 0% American Indian, 28% Asian, 4% black, 8% Hispanic, 4% multiracial, 0% Pacific Islander, 28% white, 23% international; 15% from in state; 60% live on campus; 17% in sororities
Most popular majors: 12% Information Technology, 10% Electrical and Electronics Engineering, 8% Business Administration and Management, General, 5% Computer Science, 5% Mechanical Engineering
Expenses: 2017-2018: $53,910; room/board: $13,784
Financial aid: (412) 268-8981; 42% of undergrads determined to have financial need; average aid package $40,347

Cedar Crest College

Allentown PA
(800) 360-1222
U.S. News ranking: Reg. Coll. (N), No. 6
Website: www.cedarcrest.edu
Admissions email: cccadmis@cedarcrest.edu
Private; founded 1867
Freshman admissions: selective; 2016-2017: 1,193 applied, 793 accepted. Either SAT or ACT required. SAT 25/75 percentile: 880-1090. High school rank: 18% in top tenth, 55% in top quarter, 77% in top half
Early decision deadline: N/A, notification date: N/A
Early action deadline: N/A, notification date: N/A
Application deadline (fall): rolling
Undergraduate student body: 884 full time, 544 part time; 13% male, 87% female; 0% American Indian, 3% Asian, 9% black, 14% Hispanic, 1% multiracial, 0% Pacific Islander, 58% white, 10% international; 82% from in state; 28% live on campus; N/A of students in fraternities, N/A in sororities
Most popular majors: 44% Health Professions and Related Programs, 11% Psychology, 10% Public Administration and Social Service Professions, 7% Business, Management, Marketing, and Related Support Services, 6% Biological and Biomedical Sciences
Expenses: 2017-2018: $38,092; room/board: $11,208

Financial aid: (610) 606-4666; 91% of undergrads determined to have financial need; average aid package $29,244

Central Penn College

Summerdale PA
(717) 728-2401
U.S. News ranking: Reg. Coll. (N), second tier
Website: www.centralpenn.edu
Admissions email: admissions@centralpenn.edu
For-profit; founded 1881
Freshman admissions: least selective; 2016-2017: 812 applied, 542 accepted. Neither SAT nor ACT required. SAT 25/75 percentile: 660-910. High school rank: N/A
Early decision deadline: N/A, notification date: N/A
Early action deadline: N/A, notification date: N/A
Application deadline (fall): rolling
Undergraduate student body: 326 full time, 1,011 part time; 36% male, 64% female; 2% American Indian, 2% Asian, 26% black, 6% Hispanic, 0% multiracial, 0% Pacific Islander, 59% white, 0% international; 97% from in state; 20% live on campus; 0% of students in fraternities, 0% in sororities
Most popular majors: 46% Business Administration and Management, General, 16% Criminal Justice/Safety Studies, 11% Accounting, 8% Computer Science, 6% Legal Professions and Studies, Other
Expenses: 2017-2018: $18,174; room/board: $7,416
Financial aid: (717) 728-2261; 83% of undergrads determined to have financial need

Chatham University

Pittsburgh PA
(800) 837-1290
U.S. News ranking: Reg. U. (N), No. 75
Website: www.chatham.edu
Admissions email: admissions@chatham.edu
Private; founded 1869
Freshman admissions: selective; 2016-2017: 1,916 applied, 1,015 accepted. Neither SAT nor ACT required. SAT 25/75 percentile: 950-1170. High school rank: 26% in top tenth, 55% in top quarter, 88% in top half
Early decision deadline: N/A, notification date: N/A
Early action deadline: N/A, notification date: N/A
Application deadline (fall): 8/1
Undergraduate student body: 745 full time, 257 part time; 19% male, 81% female; 1% American Indian, 3% Asian, 10% black, 4% Hispanic, 2% multiracial, 0% Pacific Islander, 74% white, 3% international; 81% from in state; 57% live on campus; N/A of students in fraternities, N/A in sororities
Most popular majors: 31% Health Professions and Related Programs, 10% Biological and Biomedical Sciences, 7% Business, Management, Marketing, and Related Support Services, 7% Psychology, 7% Public Administration and Social Service Professions

Expenses: 2017-2018: $36,510; room/board: $11,373
Financial aid: (412) 365-1849; 79% of undergrads determined to have financial need; average aid package $25,627

Chestnut Hill College

Philadelphia PA
(215) 248-7001
U.S. News ranking: Reg. U. (N), No. 137
Website: www.chc.edu
Admissions email: admissions@chc.edu
Private; founded 1924
Affiliation: Roman Catholic
Freshman admissions: less selective; 2016-2017: 1,242 applied, 1,165 accepted. Either SAT or ACT required. SAT 25/75 percentile: 840-1070. High school rank: 6% in top tenth, 26% in top quarter, 62% in top half
Early decision deadline: N/A, notification date: N/A
Early action deadline: N/A, notification date: N/A
Application deadline (fall): rolling
Undergraduate student body: 1,103 full time, 266 part time; 35% male, 65% female; 0% American Indian, 2% Asian, 35% black, 9% Hispanic, 4% multiracial, 0% Pacific Islander, 39% white, 2% international; 63% from in state; 52% live on campus; 0% of students in fraternities, 0% in sororities
Most popular majors: 21% Public Administration and Social Service Professions, 17% Business, Management, Marketing, and Related Support Services, 14% Homeland Security, Law Enforcement, and Related Protective Services, 13% Education, 8% Psychology
Expenses: 2017-2018: $35,180; room/board: $10,400
Financial aid: (215) 248-7182; 86% of undergrads determined to have financial need; average aid package $23,919

Cheyney University of Pennsylvania

Cheyney PA
(610) 399-2275
U.S. News ranking: Nat. Lib. Arts, second tier
Website: www.cheyney.edu
Admissions email: admissions@cheyney.edu
Public; founded 1837
Freshman admissions: least selective; 2016-2017: 2,306 applied, 1,060 accepted. Either SAT or ACT required. SAT 25/75 percentile: 650-860. High school rank: N/A
Early decision deadline: N/A, notification date: N/A
Early action deadline: N/A, notification date: N/A
Application deadline (fall): N/A
Undergraduate student body: 657 full time, 52 part time; 52% male, 48% female; 0% American Indian, 0% Asian, 80% black, 6% Hispanic, 6% multiracial, 0% Pacific Islander, 1% white, 0% international
Most popular majors: 25% Social Sciences, 15% Business, Management, Marketing, and

Related Support Services, 13% Liberal Arts and Sciences, General Studies and Humanities, 10% Parks, Recreation, Leisure, and Fitness Studies, 10% Psychology
Expenses: 2016-2017: $11,356 in state, $17,452 out of state; room/board: $11,852
Financial aid: N/A

Clarion University of Pennsylvania

Clarion PA
(814) 393-2306
U.S. News ranking: Reg. U. (N), No. 137
Website: www.clarion.edu
Admissions email: admissions@clarion.edu
Public; founded 1867
Freshman admissions: less selective; 2016-2017: 2,984 applied, 2,889 accepted. Either SAT or ACT required. SAT 25/75 percentile: 840-1040. High school rank: 8% in top tenth, 26% in top quarter, 61% in top half
Early decision deadline: N/A, notification date: N/A
Early action deadline: N/A, notification date: N/A
Application deadline (fall): rolling
Undergraduate student body: 3,567 full time, 763 part time; 36% male, 64% female; 0% American Indian, 1% Asian, 7% black, 3% Hispanic, 3% multiracial, 0% Pacific Islander, 84% white, 0% international; 92% from in state; 38% live on campus; 6% of students in fraternities, 9% in sororities
Most popular majors: 26% Health Professions and Related Programs, 21% Business, Management, Marketing, and Related Support Services, 11% Liberal Arts and Sciences, General Studies and Humanities, 8% Education, 5% Communication, Journalism, and Related Programs
Expenses: 2017-2018: $10,890 in state, $14,636 out of state; room/board: $11,058
Financial aid: (814) 393-2315; 80% of undergrads determined to have financial need; average aid package $9,580

Curtis Institute of Music[1]

Philadelphia PA
U.S. News ranking: Arts, unranked
Website: www.curtis.edu
Admissions email: admissions@curtis.edu
Private; founded 1924
Application deadline (fall): N/A
Undergraduate student body: N/A full time, N/A part time
Expenses: 2016-2017: $2,525; room/board: $13,234
Financial aid: (215) 717-3188

DeSales University

Center Valley PA
(610) 282-4443
U.S. News ranking: Reg. U. (N), No. 64
Website: www.desales.edu
Admissions email: admiss@desales.edu
Private; founded 1964
Affiliation: Roman Catholic
Freshman admissions: selective; 2016-2017: 2,861 applied,

2,181 accepted. Either SAT or ACT required. SAT 25/75 percentile: 940-1180. High school rank: 25% in top tenth, 45% in top quarter, 75% in top half
Early decision deadline: N/A, notification date: N/A
Early action deadline: N/A, notification date: N/A
Application deadline (fall): 8/1
Undergraduate student body: 1,854 full time, 534 part time; 40% male, 60% female; 0% American Indian, 2% Asian, 4% black, 12% Hispanic, 3% multiracial, 0% Pacific Islander, 73% white, 1% international; 76% from in state; 46% live on campus; N/A of students in fraternities, N/A in sororities
Most popular majors: 31% Business, Management, Marketing, and Related Support Services, 18% Health Professions and Related Programs, 10% Visual and Performing Arts, 8% Psychology, 7% Homeland Security, Law Enforcement, Firefighting and Related Protective Services
Expenses: 2017-2018: $35,900; room/board: $12,800
Financial aid: (610) 282-1100; 77% of undergrads determined to have financial need; average aid package $24,563

Delaware Valley University

Doylestown PA
(215) 489-2211
U.S. News ranking: Reg. U. (N), No. 126
Website: www.delval.edu
Admissions email: admitme@delval.edu
Private; founded 1896
Freshman admissions: selective; 2016-2017: 2,233 applied, 1,527 accepted. Either SAT or ACT required. SAT 25/75 percentile: 870-1090. High school rank: 8% in top tenth, 27% in top quarter, 65% in top half
Early decision deadline: N/A, notification date: N/A
Early action deadline: N/A, notification date: N/A
Application deadline (fall): rolling
Undergraduate student body: 1,767 full time, 199 part time; 41% male, 59% female; 1% American Indian, 1% Asian, 8% black, 8% Hispanic, 0% multiracial, 0% Pacific Islander, 75% white, 0% international; 59% from in state; 53% live on campus; 0% of students in fraternities, 0% in sororities
Most popular majors: 46% Agriculture, Agriculture Operations, and Related Sciences, 20% Biological and Biomedical Sciences, 15% Business, Management, Marketing, and Related Support Services, 11% Natural Resources and Conservation, 4% Homeland Security, Law Enforcement, Firefighting and Related Protective Services
Expenses: 2017-2018: $38,000; room/board: $13,950
Financial aid: (215) 489-2975; 79% of undergrads determined to have financial need; average aid package $24,129

Dickinson College

Carlisle PA
(800) 644-1773
U.S. News ranking: Nat. Lib. Arts,
No. 51
Website: www.dickinson.edu
Admissions email: admissions@
dickinson.edu
Private; founded 1783
Freshman admissions: more
selective; 2016-2017: 6,172
applied, 2,667 accepted. Neither
SAT nor ACT required. SAT
25/75 percentile: 1200-1385.
High school rank: 48% in top
tenth, 82% in top quarter, 99%
in top half
Early decision deadline: 11/15,
notification date: 12/15
Early action deadline: 12/1,
notification date: 2/15
Application deadline (fall): 1/15
Undergraduate student body: 2,376
full time, 44 part time; 41%
male, 59% female; 0% American
Indian, 3% Asian, 5% black, 7%
Hispanic, 4% multiracial, 0%
Pacific Islander, 69% white, 10%
international; 22% from in state;
94% live on campus; 17% of
students in fraternities, 27% in
sororities
Most popular majors: 11%
International Business/Trade/
Commerce, 8% Psychology,
General, 7% Economics, General,
6% Biology/Biological Sciences,
General, 6% Political Science and
Government, General
Expenses: 2017-2018: $52,930;
room/board: $13,236
Financial aid: (717) 245-1308;
55% of undergrads determined to
have financial need; average aid
package $43,737

Drexel University

Philadelphia PA
(800) 237-3935
U.S. News ranking: Nat. U., No. 94
Website: www.drexel.edu
Admissions email:
enroll@drexel.edu
Private; founded 1891
Freshman admissions: more
selective; 2016-2017: 28,535
applied, 21,298 accepted. Either
SAT or ACT required. SAT 25/75
percentile: 1080-1300. High
school rank: 40% in top tenth,
69% in top quarter, 92% in
top half
Early decision deadline: 11/1,
notification date: N/A
Early action deadline: 11/1,
notification date: 12/15
Application deadline (fall): 1/15
Undergraduate student body:
11,068 full time, 2,183 part
time; 51% male, 49% female;
0% American Indian, 14% Asian,
7% black, 6% Hispanic, 4%
multiracial, 1% Pacific Islander,
53% white, 13% international;
53% from in state; 20% live
on campus; 12% of students in
fraternities, 11% in sororities
Most popular majors: 23% Health
Professions and Related Programs,
22% Engineering, 19% Business,
Management, Marketing, and
Related Support Services, 8%
Visual and Performing Arts,
6% Biological and Biomedical
Sciences
Expenses: 2017-2018: $52,002;
room/board: $14,367

Financial aid: (215) 895-1600;
57% of undergrads determined to
have financial need; average aid
package $36,266

Duquesne University

Pittsburgh PA
(412) 396-6222
U.S. News ranking: Nat. U.,
No. 120
Website: www.duq.edu
Admissions email:
admissions@duq.edu
Private; founded 1878
Freshman admissions: more
selective; 2016-2017: 7,655
applied, 5,660 accepted. Neither
SAT nor ACT required. SAT
25/75 percentile: 1055-1230.
High school rank: 25% in top
tenth, 56% in top quarter, 87%
in top half
Early decision deadline: 11/1,
notification date: 11/15
Early action deadline: 12/1,
notification date: 1/15
Application deadline (fall): 7/1
Undergraduate student body: 5,851
full time, 188 part time; 37%
male, 63% female; 0% American
Indian, 3% Asian, 5% black, 3%
Hispanic, 3% multiracial, 0%
Pacific Islander, 80% white, 4%
international; 71% from in state;
57% live on campus; 14% of
students in fraternities, 22% in
sororities
Most popular majors: 30% Health
Professions and Related Programs,
26% Business, Management,
Marketing, and Related Support
Services, 10% Biological and
Biomedical Sciences, 8%
Education, 5% Communication,
Journalism, and Related Programs
Expenses: 2017-2018: $36,394;
room/board: $12,114
Financial aid: (412) 396-6607;
67% of undergrads determined to
have financial need; average aid
package $25,181

East Stroudsburg University of Pennsylvania

East Stroudsburg PA
(570) 422-3542
U.S. News ranking: Reg. U. (N),
second tier
Website: www.esu.edu
Admissions email:
admission@esu.edu
Public; founded 1893
Freshman admissions: less
selective; 2016-2017: 7,449
applied, 5,420 accepted. Neither
SAT nor ACT required. SAT 25/75
percentile: 840-1040. High
school rank: 6% in top tenth, 12%
in top quarter, 58% in top half
Early decision deadline: N/A,
notification date: N/A
Early action deadline: N/A,
notification date: N/A
Application deadline (fall): 5/1
Undergraduate student body: 5,642
full time, 517 part time; 43%
male, 57% female; 0% American
Indian, 2% Asian, 16% black,
11% Hispanic, 5% multiracial,
0% Pacific Islander, 64% white,
0% international; 78% from in
state; 46% live on campus; 5%
of students in fraternities, 4% in
sororities

Most popular majors: 17%
Business Administration and
Management, General, 15%
Public Health, General, 11%
Parks, Recreation and Leisure
Facilities Management, General,
10% Biology/Biological Sciences,
General, 10% Early Childhood
Education and Teaching
Expenses: 2017-2018: $9,968 in
state, $20,876 out of state; room/
board: $9,868
Financial aid: (570) 422-2800

Eastern University

St. Davids PA
(800) 452-0996
U.S. News ranking: Reg. U. (N),
No. 78
Website: www.eastern.edu
Admissions email:
ugadm@eastern.edu
Private; founded 1952
Affiliation: American Baptist
Freshman admissions: selective;
2016-2017: 1,992 applied,
1,219 accepted. Either SAT
or ACT required. SAT 25/75
percentile: 930-1140. High
school rank: N/A
Early decision deadline: N/A,
notification date: N/A
Early action deadline: N/A,
notification date: N/A
Application deadline (fall): rolling
Undergraduate student body: 1,760
full time, 322 part time; 30%
male, 70% female; 0% American
Indian, 2% Asian, 21% black,
20% Hispanic, 1% multiracial,
0% Pacific Islander, 49% white,
2% international; 58% from in
state; 79% live on campus; N/A
of students in fraternities, N/A in
sororities
Most popular majors: 17%
Early Childhood Education
and Teaching, 15% Business
Administration and Management,
General, 6% Registered Nursing/
Registered Nurse, 6% Social
Work, 5% Psychology, General
Expenses: 2017-2018: $32,080;
room/board: $10,980
Financial aid: (610) 225-5102;
92% of undergrads determined to
have financial need; average aid
package $20,823

Edinboro University of Pennsylvania[1]

Edinboro PA
(888) 846-2676
U.S. News ranking: Reg. U. (N),
second tier
Website: www.edinboro.edu
Admissions email:
eup_admissions@edinboro.edu
Public; founded 1857
Application deadline (fall): rolling
Undergraduate student body: N/A
full time, N/A part time
Expenses: 2016-2017: $9,535 in
state, $13,065 out of state; room/
board: $11,154
Financial aid: (814) 732-3500

Elizabethtown College

Elizabethtown PA
(717) 361-1400
U.S. News ranking: Nat. Lib. Arts,
No. 117
Website: www.etown.edu
Admissions email:
admissions@etown.edu
Private; founded 1899

Freshman admissions: selective;
2016-2017: 2,904 applied,
2,134 accepted. Either SAT
or ACT required. SAT 25/75
percentile: 990-1160. High school
rank: 30% in top tenth, 62% in
top quarter, 86% in top half
Early decision deadline: N/A,
notification date: N/A
Early action deadline: N/A,
notification date: N/A
Application deadline (fall): rolling
Undergraduate student body: 1,707
full time, 30 part time; 39%
male, 61% female; 0% American
Indian, 3% Asian, 3% black,
4% Hispanic, 2% multiracial,
0% Pacific Islander, 85% white,
3% international; 66% from in
state; 85% live on campus; N/A
of students in fraternities, N/A in
sororities
Most popular majors: 16%
Business, Management,
Marketing, and Related Support
Services, 11% Biological and
Biomedical Sciences, 11% Health
Professions and Related Programs,
8% Education, 7% Social
Sciences
Expenses: N/A
Financial aid: (717) 361-1404

Franklin and Marshall College

Lancaster PA
(717) 358-3953
U.S. News ranking: Nat. Lib. Arts,
No. 39
Website: www.fandm.edu
Admissions email:
admission@fandm.edu
Private; founded 1787
Freshman admissions: more
selective; 2016-2017: 6,953
applied, 2,529 accepted. Neither
SAT nor ACT required. SAT
25/75 percentile: 1200-1410.
High school rank: 67% in top
tenth, 88% in top quarter, 96%
in top half
Early decision deadline: 11/15,
notification date: 12/15
Early action deadline: N/A,
notification date: N/A
Application deadline (fall): 1/15
Undergraduate student body: 2,225
full time, 30 part time; 47%
male, 53% female; 0% American
Indian, 5% Asian, 6% black, 9%
Hispanic, 2% multiracial, 0%
Pacific Islander, 57% white, 15%
international; 27% from in state;
99% live on campus; 22% of
students in fraternities, 27% in
sororities
Most popular majors: Information
not available
Expenses: 2017-2018: $54,380;
room/board: $13,580
Financial aid: (717) 358-3991;
54% of undergrads determined to
have financial need; average aid
package $47,144

Gannon University

Erie PA
(814) 871-7240
U.S. News ranking: Reg. U. (N),
No. 48
Website: www.gannon.edu
Admissions email: admissions@
gannon.edu
Private; founded 1925
Affiliation: Roman Catholic

Freshman admissions: selective;
2016-2017: 4,710 applied,
3,662 accepted. Either SAT
or ACT required. SAT 25/75
percentile: 920-1130. High
school rank: 22% in top tenth, 49% in
top quarter, 83% in top half
Early decision deadline: N/A,
notification date: N/A
Early action deadline: N/A,
notification date: N/A
Application deadline (fall): rolling
Undergraduate student body: 2,481
full time, 617 part time; 44%
male, 56% female; 0% American
Indian, 2% Asian, 5% black, 3%
Hispanic, 2% multiracial, 0%
Pacific Islander, 74% white, 9%
international; 71% from in state;
44% live on campus; 15% of
students in fraternities, 12% in
sororities
Most popular majors: 31%
Health Professions and Related
Programs, 12% Parks, Recreation,
Leisure, and Fitness Studies,
11% Business, Management,
Marketing, and Related Support
Services, 10% Biological and
Biomedical Sciences, 9%
Engineering
Expenses: 2017-2018: $30,932;
room/board: $12,320
Financial aid: (814) 871-7337;
78% of undergrads determined to
have financial need; average aid
package $24,832

Geneva College

Beaver Falls PA
(724) 847-6500
U.S. News ranking: Reg. U. (N),
No. 75
Website: www.geneva.edu
Admissions email:
admissions@geneva.edu
Private; founded 1848
Freshman admissions: selective;
2016-2017: 1,587 applied,
1,120 accepted. Either SAT
or ACT required. SAT 25/75
percentile: 950-1190. High school
rank: 18% in top tenth, 48% in
top quarter, 80% in top half
Early decision deadline: N/A,
notification date: N/A
Early action deadline: N/A,
notification date: N/A
Application deadline (fall): rolling
Undergraduate student body: 1,308
full time, 155 part time; 49%
male, 51% female; 0% American
Indian, 1% Asian, 9% black,
1% Hispanic, 3% multiracial,
0% Pacific Islander, 83% white,
1% international; 70% from in
state; 70% live on campus; 0%
of students in fraternities, 0% in
sororities
Most popular majors: 14%
Engineering, General, 10%
Business Administration and
Management, General, 10%
Public Administration and Social
Service Professions, 7% Human
Resources Management/Personnel
Administration, General, 4% Multi/
Interdisciplinary Studies
Expenses: 2017-2018: $26,070;
room/board: $9,920
Financial aid: (724) 847-6532;
81% of undergrads determined to
have financial need; average aid
package $21,573

Gettysburg College
Gettysburg PA
(800) 431-0803
U.S. News ranking: Nat. Lib. Arts, No. 46
Website: www.gettysburg.edu
Admissions email: admiss@gettysburg.edu
Private; founded 1832
Freshman admissions: more selective; 2016-2017: 6,816 applied, 2,906 accepted. Either SAT or ACT required. SAT 25/75 percentile: 1210-1360. High school rank: 64% in top tenth, 82% in top quarter, 99% in top half
Early decision deadline: 11/15, notification date: 12/15
Early action deadline: N/A, notification date: N/A
Application deadline (fall): 1/15
Undergraduate student body: 2,371 full time, 13 part time; 47% male, 53% female; 0% American Indian, 2% Asian, 3% black, 6% Hispanic, 3% multiracial, 0% Pacific Islander, 76% white, 7% international; 25% from in state; 94% live on campus; 32% of students in fraternities, 36% in sororities
Most popular majors: 19% Social Sciences, General, 15% Biology/Biological Sciences, General, 12% Business/Commerce, General, 8% English Language and Literature, General, 8% Psychology, General
Expenses: 2017-2018: $52,640; room/board: $12,570
Financial aid: (717) 337-6620; 56% of undergrads determined to have financial need; average aid package $41,554

Grove City College
Grove City PA
(724) 458-2100
U.S. News ranking: Nat. Lib. Arts, No. 126
Website: www.gcc.edu
Admissions email: admissions@gcc.edu
Private; founded 1876
Affiliation: Undenominational
Freshman admissions: more selective; 2016-2017: 1,517 applied, 1,251 accepted. Either SAT or ACT required. SAT 25/75 percentile: 1060-1325. High school rank: 39% in top tenth, 67% in top quarter, 89% in top half
Early decision deadline: 11/15, notification date: 12/15
Early action deadline: N/A, notification date: N/A
Application deadline (fall): 2/1
Undergraduate student body: 2,334 full time, 58 part time; 50% male, 50% female; 0% American Indian, 2% Asian, 0% black, 1% Hispanic, 3% multiracial, 0% Pacific Islander, 92% white, 1% international; 54% from in state; 96% live on campus; 17% of students in fraternities, 21% in sororities
Most popular majors: 8% Biology/Biological Sciences, General, 7% Mechanical Engineering, 6% General Literature, 6% Speech Communication and Rhetoric, 5% Political Science and Government, General
Expenses: 2017-2018: $17,254; room/board: $9,400

Financial aid: (724) 458-2163; 45% of undergrads determined to have financial need; average aid package $7,206

Gwynedd Mercy University
Gwynedd Valley PA
(215) 681-5510
U.S. News ranking: Reg. U. (N), second tier
Website: www.gmercyu.edu/
Admissions email: admissions@gmercyu.edu
Private; founded 1948
Affiliation: Roman Catholic
Freshman admissions: less selective; 2016-2017: 904 applied, 821 accepted. Either SAT or ACT required. SAT 25/75 percentile: 840-1032. High school rank: 7% in top tenth, 20% in top quarter, 57% in top half
Early decision deadline: N/A, notification date: N/A
Early action deadline: N/A, notification date: N/A
Application deadline (fall): 8/20
Undergraduate student body: 1,886 full time, 149 part time; 24% male, 76% female; 0% American Indian, 5% Asian, 20% black, 4% Hispanic, 0% multiracial, 0% Pacific Islander, 50% white, 0% international; 87% from in state; 19% live on campus; 0% of students in fraternities, 0% in sororities
Most popular majors: 40% Health Professions and Related Programs, 34% Business, Management, Marketing, and Related Support Services, 7% Homeland Security, Law Enforcement, Firefighting and Related Protective Services, 6% Education, 5% Psychology
Expenses: 2017-2018: $33,520; room/board: $11,630
Financial aid: (215) 646-7300; 82% of undergrads determined to have financial need; average aid package $20,302

Harrisburg University of Science and Technology
Harrisburg PA
(717) 901-5150
U.S. News ranking: Reg. U. (N), second tier
Website: www.harrisburgu.edu
Admissions email: admissions@harrisburgu.edu
Private; founded 2001
Freshman admissions: less selective; 2016-2017: N/A applied, N/A accepted. Neither SAT nor ACT required. SAT 25/75 percentile: N/A. High school rank: N/A
Early decision deadline: N/A, notification date: N/A
Early action deadline: N/A, notification date: N/A
Application deadline (fall): rolling
Undergraduate student body: 339 full time, 48 part time; 53% male, 47% female; N/A American Indian, N/A Asian, N/A black, N/A Hispanic, N/A multiracial, N/A Pacific Islander, N/A white, N/A international
Most popular majors: 57% Computer and Information Sciences, General, 35% Natural Sciences

Expenses: 2017-2018: $23,900; room/board: $0
Financial aid: (717) 901-5115; 93% of undergrads determined to have financial need; average aid package $20,304

Haverford College
Haverford PA
(610) 896-1350
U.S. News ranking: Nat. Lib. Arts, No. 18
Website: www.haverford.edu
Admissions email: admission@haverford.edu
Private; founded 1833
Freshman admissions: most selective; 2016-2017: 4,066 applied, 870 accepted. Either SAT or ACT required. SAT 25/75 percentile: 1320-1520. High school rank: 94% in top tenth, 99% in top quarter, 100% in top half
Early decision deadline: 11/15, notification date: 12/15
Early action deadline: N/A, notification date: N/A
Application deadline (fall): 1/15
Undergraduate student body: 1,268 full time, 0 part time; 48% male, 52% female; 0% American Indian, 5% Asian, 7% black, 8% Hispanic, 4% multiracial, 0% Pacific Islander, 59% white, 9% international; 12% from in state; 99% live on campus; 0% of students in fraternities, 0% in sororities
Most popular majors: 23% Social Sciences, General, 16% Physical Sciences, 12% Biology/Biological Sciences, General, 9% Psychology, General, 7% English Language and Literature, General
Expenses: 2017-2018: $52,754; room/board: $15,958
Financial aid: (610) 896-1350; 50% of undergrads determined to have financial need; average aid package $49,186

Holy Family University
Philadelphia PA
(215) 637-3050
U.S. News ranking: Reg. U. (N), second tier
Website: www.holyfamily.edu
Admissions email: admissions@holyfamily.edu
Private; founded 1954
Affiliation: Roman Catholic
Freshman admissions: less selective; 2016-2017: 1,441 applied, 987 accepted. Either SAT or ACT required. SAT 25/75 percentile: 830-1040. High school rank: 7% in top tenth, 30% in top quarter, 67% in top half
Early decision deadline: N/A, notification date: N/A
Early action deadline: N/A, notification date: N/A
Application deadline (fall): rolling
Undergraduate student body: 1,424 full time, 526 part time; 26% male, 74% female; 0% American Indian, 5% Asian, 12% black, 6% Hispanic, 0% multiracial, 0% Pacific Islander, 62% white, 0% international; 86% from in state; 17% live on campus; 0% of students in fraternities, 0% in sororities

Most popular majors: 43% Health Professions and Related Programs, 19% Business, Management, Marketing, and Related Support Services, 11% Education, 9% Psychology, 7% Homeland Security, Law Enforcement, Firefighting and Related Protective Services
Expenses: 2017-2018: $30,346; room/board: $13,576
Financial aid: (267) 341-3234; 86% of undergrads determined to have financial need; average aid package $22,642

Immaculata University
Immaculata PA
(610) 647-4400
U.S. News ranking: Nat. U., No. 165
Website: www.immaculata.edu
Admissions email: admiss@immaculata.edu
Private; founded 1920
Affiliation: Roman Catholic
Freshman admissions: selective; 2016-2017: 1,582 applied, 1,304 accepted. Neither SAT nor ACT required. SAT 25/75 percentile: 860-1080. High school rank: 15% in top tenth, 34% in top quarter, 61% in top half
Early decision deadline: N/A, notification date: N/A
Early action deadline: N/A, notification date: N/A
Application deadline (fall): rolling
Undergraduate student body: 943 full time, 612 part time; 25% male, 75% female; 0% American Indian, 2% Asian, 15% black, 6% Hispanic, 2% multiracial, 0% Pacific Islander, 73% white, 1% international; 72% from in state; 33% live on campus; 1% of students in fraternities, 8% in sororities
Most popular majors: 57% Health Professions and Related Programs, 16% Business, Management, Marketing, and Related Support Services, 6% Parks, Recreation, Leisure, and Fitness Studies, 5% Education, 4% Psychology
Expenses: 2017-2018: $27,350; room/board: $12,620
Financial aid: (610) 647-4400

Indiana University of Pennsylvania
Indiana PA
(724) 357-2230
U.S. News ranking: Nat. U., second tier
Website: www.iup.edu
Admissions email: admissions-inquiry@iup.edu
Public; founded 1875
Freshman admissions: less selective; 2016-2017: 8,943 applied, 8,186 accepted. Either SAT or ACT required. SAT 25/75 percentile: 840-1050. High school rank: 8% in top tenth, 27% in top quarter, 60% in top half
Early decision deadline: N/A, notification date: N/A
Early action deadline: N/A, notification date: N/A
Application deadline (fall): rolling
Undergraduate student body: 9,819 full time, 799 part time; 44% male, 56% female; 0% American Indian, 1% Asian, 12% black,

4% Hispanic, 4% multiracial, 0% Pacific Islander, 74% white, 4% international; 95% from in state; 32% live on campus; 9% of students in fraternities, 9% in sororities
Most popular majors: 26% Business, Management, Marketing, and Related Support Services, 17% Social Sciences, 9% Health Professions and Related Programs, 6% Communication, Journalism, and Related Programs, 6% Family and Consumer Sciences/Human Sciences
Expenses: 2017-2018: $12,146 in state, $15,882 out of state; room/board: $12,488
Financial aid: (724) 357-2218; 72% of undergrads determined to have financial need; average aid package $10,336

Juniata College
Huntingdon PA
(877) 586-4282
U.S. News ranking: Nat. Lib. Arts, No. 106
Website: www.juniata.edu
Admissions email: admissions@juniata.edu
Private; founded 1876
Freshman admissions: selective; 2016-2017: 2,386 applied, 1,780 accepted. Neither SAT nor ACT required. SAT 25/75 percentile: 1040-1240. High school rank: 39% in top tenth, 75% in top quarter, 97% in top half
Early decision deadline: 11/15, notification date: 12/23
Early action deadline: N/A, notification date: N/A
Application deadline (fall): 2/15
Undergraduate student body: 1,498 full time, 70 part time; 44% male, 56% female; 0% American Indian, 4% Asian, 3% black, 4% Hispanic, 3% multiracial, 0% Pacific Islander, 73% white, 7% international; 66% from in state; 82% live on campus; 0% of students in fraternities, 0% in sororities
Most popular majors: 19% Biological and Biomedical Sciences, 16% Business, Management, Marketing, and Related Support Services, 11% Natural Resources and Conservation, 7% Physical Sciences, 6% Social Sciences
Expenses: 2017-2018: $43,875; room/board: $12,040
Financial aid: (814) 641-3144; 74% of undergrads determined to have financial need; average aid package $35,585

Keystone College
La Plume PA
(570) 945-8000
U.S. News ranking: Reg. Coll. (N), No. 26
Website: www.keystone.edu
Admissions email: admissions@keystone.edu
Private; founded 1868
Freshman admissions: least selective; 2016-2017: 1,141 applied, 1,114 accepted. Neither SAT nor ACT required. SAT 25/75 percentile: 780-970. High school rank: N/A

Early decision deadline: N/A, notification date: N/A
Early action deadline: N/A, notification date: N/A
Application deadline (fall): 7/1
Undergraduate student body: 1,088 full time, 322 part time; 37% male, 63% female; 0% American Indian, 1% Asian, 8% black, 8% Hispanic, 1% multiracial, 0% Pacific Islander, 73% white, 0% international; 83% from in state; 30% live on campus; 0% of students in fraternities, 0% in sororities
Most popular majors: 19% Business, Management, Marketing, and Related Support Services, 14% Homeland Security, Law Enforcement, Firefighting and Related Protective Services, 14% Psychology, 9% Biological and Biomedical Sciences, 8% Education
Expenses: 2016-2017: $25,798; room/board: $10,352
Financial aid: N/A

King's College
Wilkes-Barre PA
(888) 546-4772
U.S. News ranking: Reg. U. (N), No. 62
Website: www.kings.edu
Admissions email: admissions@kings.edu
Private; founded 1946
Affiliation: Roman Catholic
Freshman admissions: selective; 2016-2017: 3,852 applied, 2,731 accepted. Neither SAT nor ACT required. SAT 25/75 percentile: 940-1160. High school rank: 18% in top tenth, 43% in top quarter, 72% in top half
Early decision deadline: N/A, notification date: N/A
Early action deadline: 12/1, notification date: 12/15
Application deadline (fall): rolling
Undergraduate student body: 1,907 full time, 175 part time; 52% male, 48% female; 0% American Indian, 2% Asian, 3% black, 7% Hispanic, 2% multiracial, 0% Pacific Islander, 74% white, 6% international; 70% from in state; 50% live on campus; 0% of students in fraternities, 0% in sororities
Most popular majors: 11% Criminal Justice/Safety Studies, 9% Accounting, 9% Health Professions and Related Clinical Sciences, Other, 9% Psychology, General, 7% Elementary Education and Teaching
Expenses: 2017-2018: $35,830; room/board: $12,410
Financial aid: (570) 208-5900; 79% of undergrads determined to have financial need; average aid package $24,694

Kutztown University of Pennsylvania
Kutztown PA
(610) 683-4060
U.S. News ranking: Reg. U. (N), No. 126
Website: www.kutztown.edu
Admissions email: admissions@kutztown.edu
Public; founded 1866
Freshman admissions: less selective; 2016-2017: 7,668 applied, 6,117 accepted. Either

SAT or ACT required. SAT 25/75 percentile: 880-1070. High school rank: 6% in top tenth, 22% in top quarter, 57% in top half
Early decision deadline: N/A, notification date: N/A
Early action deadline: N/A, notification date: N/A
Application deadline (fall): rolling
Undergraduate student body: 7,288 full time, 430 part time; 46% male, 54% female; 0% American Indian, 1% Asian, 8% black, 8% Hispanic, 3% multiracial, 0% Pacific Islander, 78% white, 1% international; 88% from in state; 45% live on campus; 5% of students in fraternities, 12% in sororities
Most popular majors: 21% Business Administration and Management, General, 10% Psychology, General, 9% English Language and Literature, General, 7% Criminal Justice/Safety Studies, 6% Parks, Recreation and Leisure Studies
Expenses: 2017-2018: $9,987 in state, $13,733 out of state; room/board: $10,282
Financial aid: (610) 683-4077; 71% of undergrads determined to have financial need; average aid package $8,699

La Roche College
Pittsburgh PA
(800) 838-4572
U.S. News ranking: Reg. Coll. (N), No. 19
Website: www.laroche.edu
Admissions email: admissions@laroche.edu
Private; founded 1963
Affiliation: Roman Catholic
Freshman admissions: less selective; 2016-2017: 1,320 applied, 1,218 accepted. Either SAT or ACT required. SAT 25/75 percentile: 810-1020. High school rank: 15% in top tenth, 30% in top quarter, 68% in top half
Early decision deadline: N/A, notification date: N/A
Early action deadline: N/A, notification date: N/A
Application deadline (fall): rolling
Undergraduate student body: 1,151 full time, 255 part time; 45% male, 55% female; 0% American Indian, 2% Asian, 10% black, 3% Hispanic, 2% multiracial, 0% Pacific Islander, 61% white, 16% international; 91% from in state; 45% live on campus; N/A of students in fraternities, N/A in sororities
Most popular majors: 9% Accounting, 8% Criminal Justice/Safety Studies, 8% Registered Nursing/Registered Nurse, 7% Medical Radiologic Technology/Science-Radiation Therapist, 7% Psychology, General
Expenses: 2017-2018: $27,720; room/board: $11,220
Financial aid: (412) 536-1120; 67% of undergrads determined to have financial need; average aid package $29,356

La Salle University
Philadelphia PA
(215) 951-1500
U.S. News ranking: Reg. U. (N), No. 34
Website: www.lasalle.edu
Admissions email: admiss@lasalle.edu
Private; founded 1863
Affiliation: Roman Catholic
Freshman admissions: selective; 2016-2017: 5,682 applied, 4,367 accepted. Either SAT or ACT required. SAT 25/75 percentile: 870-1080. High school rank: 15% in top tenth, 36% in top quarter, 68% in top half
Early decision deadline: N/A, notification date: N/A
Early action deadline: 11/15, notification date: 12/15
Application deadline (fall): rolling
Undergraduate student body: 3,181 full time, 471 part time; 38% male, 62% female; 0% American Indian, 5% Asian, 19% black, 14% Hispanic, 3% multiracial, 0% Pacific Islander, 51% white, 2% international; 67% from in state; 44% live on campus; 12% of students in fraternities, 12% in sororities
Most popular majors: 21% Registered Nursing/Registered Nurse, 8% Accounting, 8% Marketing/Marketing Management, General, 8% Psychology, General, 7% Communication and Media Studies, Other
Expenses: 2017-2018: $29,500; room/board: $14,636
Financial aid: (215) 951-1070; 82% of undergrads determined to have financial need; average aid package $32,062

Lafayette College
Easton PA
(610) 330-5100
U.S. News ranking: Nat. Lib. Arts, No. 36
Website: www.lafayette.edu
Admissions email: admissions@lafayette.edu
Private; founded 1826
Freshman admissions: more selective; 2016-2017: 8,123 applied, 2,298 accepted. Either SAT or ACT required. SAT 25/75 percentile: 1200-1390. High school rank: 60% in top tenth, 91% in top quarter, 99% in top half
Early decision deadline: 11/15, notification date: 12/15
Early action deadline: N/A, notification date: N/A
Application deadline (fall): 1/15
Undergraduate student body: 2,505 full time, 45 part time; 49% male, 51% female; 0% American Indian, 4% Asian, 5% black, 7% Hispanic, 2% multiracial, 0% Pacific Islander, 66% white, 10% international; 18% from in state; 93% live on campus; 23% of students in fraternities, 34% in sororities
Most popular majors: 35% Social Sciences, 18% Engineering, 9% Biological and Biomedical Sciences, 7% Psychology, 7% Visual and Performing Arts
Expenses: 2017-2018: $50,850; room/board: $15,040

Financial aid: (610) 330-5055; 30% of undergrads determined to have financial need; average aid package $45,615

Lebanon Valley College
Annville PA
(717) 867-6181
U.S. News ranking: Reg. U. (N), No. 24
Website: www.lvc.edu
Admissions email: admission@lvc.edu
Private; founded 1866
Affiliation: United Methodist
Freshman admissions: selective; 2016-2017: 2,561 applied, 1,948 accepted. Neither SAT nor ACT required. SAT 25/75 percentile: 970-1220. High school rank: 30% in top tenth, 59% in top quarter, 86% in top half
Early decision deadline: 11/1, notification date: 12/1
Early action deadline: N/A, notification date: N/A
Application deadline (fall): rolling
Undergraduate student body: 1,602 full time, 110 part time; 46% male, 54% female; 0% American Indian, 2% Asian, 3% black, 5% Hispanic, 3% multiracial, 0% Pacific Islander, 83% white, 0% international; 80% from in state; 78% live on campus; 3% of students in fraternities, 11% in sororities
Most popular majors: 17% Education, 16% Business, Management, Marketing, and Related Support Services, 10% Health Professions and Related Programs, 10% Social Sciences, 9% Biological and Biomedical Sciences
Expenses: 2017-2018: $42,180; room/board: $11,410
Financial aid: (717) 867-6126; 85% of undergrads determined to have financial need; average aid package $31,829

Lehigh University
Bethlehem PA
(610) 758-3100
U.S. News ranking: Nat. U., No. 46
Website: www.lehigh.edu
Admissions email: admissions@lehigh.edu
Private; founded 1865
Freshman admissions: most selective; 2016-2017: 13,403 applied, 3,499 accepted. Either SAT or ACT required. SAT 25/75 percentile: 1230-1420. High school rank: 64% in top tenth, 89% in top quarter, 98% in top half
Early decision deadline: 11/15, notification date: 12/15
Early action deadline: N/A, notification date: N/A
Application deadline (fall): 1/1
Undergraduate student body: 5,003 full time, 77 part time; 56% male, 44% female; 0% American Indian, 8% Asian, 4% black, 9% Hispanic, 3% multiracial, 0% Pacific Islander, 65% white, 8% international; 26% from in state; 66% live on campus; 40% of students in fraternities, 45% in sororities

Most popular majors: 10% Finance, General, 9% Mechanical Engineering, 6% Accounting, 5% Psychology, General, 4% Marketing/Marketing Management, General
Expenses: 2017-2018: $50,740; room/board: $13,120
Financial aid: (610) 758-3181; 39% of undergrads determined to have financial need; average aid package $43,376

Lincoln University
Lincoln University PA
(800) 790-0191
U.S. News ranking: Reg. U. (N), second tier
Website: www.lincoln.edu
Admissions email: admissions@lincoln.edu
Public; founded 1854
Freshman admissions: least selective; 2016-2017: 3,685 applied, 3,211 accepted. Either SAT or ACT required. SAT 25/75 percentile: 750-925. High school rank: 9% in top tenth, 25% in top quarter, 51% in top half
Early decision deadline: N/A, notification date: N/A
Early action deadline: N/A, notification date: N/A
Application deadline (fall): rolling
Undergraduate student body: 1,668 full time, 156 part time; 37% male, 63% female; 0% American Indian, 0% Asian, 84% black, 2% Hispanic, 1% multiracial, 0% Pacific Islander, 1% white, 4% international; 45% from in state; 84% live on campus; 4% of students in fraternities, 3% in sororities
Most popular majors: 16% Public Administration and Social Service Professions, 14% Business, Management, Marketing, and Related Support Services, 11% Health Professions and Related Programs, 10% Social Sciences, 9% Biological and Biomedical Sciences
Expenses: 2017-2018: $11,379 in state, $16,389 out of state; room/board: $9,499
Financial aid: (484) 365-7565; 90% of undergrads determined to have financial need; average aid package $12,445

Lock Haven University of Pennsylvania
Lock Haven PA
(570) 484-2011
U.S. News ranking: Reg. U. (N), No. 137
Website: www.lockhaven.edu
Admissions email: admissions@lockhaven.edu
Public; founded 1870
Freshman admissions: less selective; 2016-2017: 3,750 applied, 3,294 accepted. Either SAT or ACT required. SAT 25/75 percentile: 850-1040. High school rank: 8% in top tenth, 29% in top quarter, 61% in top half
Early decision deadline: N/A, notification date: N/A
Early action deadline: N/A, notification date: N/A
Application deadline (fall): rolling

Undergraduate student body: 3,538 full time, 307 part time; 43% male, 57% female; 0% American Indian, 1% Asian, 9% black, 2% Hispanic, 1% multiracial, 0% Pacific Islander, 84% white, 1% international; 95% from in state; 46% live on campus; 3% of students in fraternities, 4% in sororities
Most popular majors: 14% Health Professions and Related Clinical Sciences, Other, 11% Criminal Justice/Law Enforcement Administration, 8% Sport and Fitness Administration/ Management, 6% Business Administration and Management, General, 5% Parks, Recreation and Leisure Facilities Management, General
Expenses: 2017-2018: $10,576 in state, $19,814 out of state; room/board: $9,968
Financial aid: (570) 484-2452; 75% of undergrads determined to have financial need; average aid package $8,046

Lycoming College
Williamsport PA
(800) 345-3920
U.S. News ranking: Nat. Lib. Arts, No. 147
Website: www.lycoming.edu
Admissions email: admissions@ lycoming.edu
Private; founded 1812
Freshman admissions: selective; 2016-2017: 1,876 applied, 1,305 accepted. Neither SAT nor ACT required. SAT 25/75 percentile: 940-1120. High school rank: 18% in top tenth, 42% in top quarter, 73% in top half
Early decision deadline: 11/1, notification date: 11/15
Early action deadline: 11/15, notification date: 12/1
Application deadline (fall): rolling
Undergraduate student body: 1,245 full time, 27 part time; 48% male, 52% female; 0% American Indian, 1% Asian, 10% black, 9% Hispanic, 3% multiracial, 0% Pacific Islander, 67% white, 5% international; 61% from in state; 88% live on campus; 11% of students in fraternities, 19% in sororities
Most popular majors: 21% Business, Management, Marketing, and Related Support Services, 15% Social Sciences, 12% Psychology, 9% Biological and Biomedical Sciences, 8% Visual and Performing Arts
Expenses: 2017-2018: $38,618; room/board: $11,980
Financial aid: (570) 321-4140; 84% of undergrads determined to have financial need; average aid package $35,046

Mansfield University of Pennsylvania
Mansfield PA
(800) 577-6826
U.S. News ranking: Reg. U. (N), No. 116
Website: www.mansfield.edu
Admissions email: admissns@ mansfield.edu
Public; founded 1857
Freshman admissions: less selective; 2016-2017: 2,997 applied, 1,969 accepted. Neither

SAT nor ACT required. SAT 25/75 percentile: 860-1060. High school rank: 8% in top tenth, 31% in top quarter, 67% in top half
Early decision deadline: N/A, notification date: N/A
Early action deadline: N/A, notification date: N/A
Application deadline (fall): rolling
Undergraduate student body: 1,924 full time, 188 part time; 40% male, 60% female; 0% American Indian, 1% Asian, 10% black, 3% Hispanic, 2% multiracial, 0% Pacific Islander, 81% white, 1% international; 82% from in state; 49% live on campus; 16% of students in fraternities, 10% in sororities
Most popular majors: Information not available
Expenses: 2017-2018: $12,316 in state, $21,766 out of state; room/board: $11,928
Financial aid: (570) 662-4823; 82% of undergrads determined to have financial need; average aid package $10,187

Marywood University
Scranton PA
(866) 279-9663
U.S. News ranking: Reg. U. (N), No. 56
Website: www.marywood.edu
Admissions email: YourFuture@ marywood.edu
Private; founded 1915
Affiliation: Roman Catholic
Freshman admissions: selective; 2016-2017: 2,202 applied, 1,518 accepted. Either SAT or ACT required. SAT 25/75 percentile: 940-1120. High school rank: 11% in top tenth, 40% in top quarter, 82% in top half
Early decision deadline: N/A, notification date: N/A
Early action deadline: N/A, notification date: N/A
Application deadline (fall): rolling
Undergraduate student body: 1,753 full time, 178 part time; 31% male, 69% female; 0% American Indian, 2% Asian, 3% black, 6% Hispanic, 2% multiracial, 0% Pacific Islander, 78% white, 1% international; 69% from in state; 37% live on campus; N/A in sororities
Most popular majors: 27% Health Professions and Related Programs, 14% Business, Management, Marketing, and Related Support Services, 9% Visual and Performing Arts, 7% Education, 7% Psychology
Expenses: 2017-2018: $33,940; room/board: $13,900
Financial aid: (570) 348-6225; 83% of undergrads determined to have financial need; average aid package $24,643

Mercyhurst University
Erie PA
(814) 824-2202
U.S. News ranking: Reg. U. (N), No. 48
Website: www.mercyhurst.edu
Admissions email: admug@mercyhurst.edu
Private; founded 1926
Affiliation: Roman Catholic
Freshman admissions: selective; 2016-2017: 3,254 applied, 2,448 accepted. Neither SAT

nor ACT required. SAT 25/75 percentile: 920-1160. High school rank: 11% in top tenth, 29% in top quarter, 75% in top half
Early decision deadline: N/A, notification date: N/A
Early action deadline: N/A, notification date: N/A
Application deadline (fall): rolling
Undergraduate student body: 2,424 full time, 70 part time; 44% male, 56% female; 1% American Indian, 1% Asian, 5% black, 4% Hispanic, 19% multiracial, 0% Pacific Islander, 58% white, 10% international; 42% from in state; N/A live on campus; 0% of students in fraternities, 0% in sororities
Most popular majors: 23% Business, Management, Marketing, and Related Support Services, 12% Health Professions and Related Programs, 9% Homeland Security, Law Enforcement, Firefighting and Related Protective Services, 9% Military Technologies and Applied Sciences, 8% Visual and Performing Arts
Expenses: 2017-2018: $36,320; room/board: $12,210
Financial aid: (814) 824-2288; 71% of undergrads determined to have financial need; average aid package $29,678

Messiah College
Mechanicsburg PA
(717) 691-6000
U.S. News ranking: Reg. Coll. (N), No. 4
Website: www.messiah.edu
Admissions email: admiss@ messiah.edu
Private; founded 1909
Affiliation: Interdenominational
Freshman admissions: more selective; 2016-2017: 2,596 applied, 2,064 accepted. Either SAT or ACT required. SAT 25/75 percentile: 1020-1260. High school rank: 33% in top tenth, 62% in top quarter, 91% in top half
Early decision deadline: N/A, notification date: N/A
Early action deadline: N/A, notification date: N/A
Application deadline (fall): rolling
Undergraduate student body: 2,648 full time, 140 part time; 39% male, 61% female; 0% American Indian, 2% Asian, 2% black, 4% Hispanic, 4% multiracial, 0% Pacific Islander, 81% white, 5% international; 64% from in state; 85% live on campus; N/A of students in fraternities, N/A in sororities
Most popular majors: 7% Engineering, General, 7% Registered Nursing/Registered Nurse, 6% Psychology, General, 5% Business Administration and Management, General, 5% Health Professions and Related Programs
Expenses: 2017-2018: $34,160; room/board: $10,220
Financial aid: (717) 691-6007; 73% of undergrads determined to have financial need; average aid package $23,627

Millersville University of Pennsylvania
Millersville PA
(717) 871-4625
U.S. News ranking: Reg. U. (N), No. 94
Website: www.millersville.edu
Admissions email: Admissions@ millersville.edu
Public; founded 1855
Freshman admissions: selective; 2016-2017: 6,943 applied, 4,794 accepted. Either SAT or ACT required. SAT 25/75 percentile: 930-1120. High school rank: 9% in top tenth, 30% in top quarter, 64% in top half
Early decision deadline: N/A, notification date: N/A
Early action deadline: N/A, notification date: N/A
Application deadline (fall): rolling
Undergraduate student body: 5,941 full time, 1,039 part time; 44% male, 56% female; 0% American Indian, 3% Asian, 9% black, 9% Hispanic, 2% multiracial, 0% Pacific Islander, 76% white, 1% international; 94% from in state; 31% live on campus; 4% of students in fraternities, 5% in sororities
Most popular majors: 13% Business, Management, Marketing, and Related Support Services, 10% Education, 10% Social Sciences, 9% Communication, Journalism, and Related Programs, 8% Psychology
Expenses: 2017-2018: $11,858 in state, $21,318 out of state; room/board: $13,440
Financial aid: (717) 871-5100; 69% of undergrads determined to have financial need; average aid package $8,437

Misericordia University
Dallas PA
(570) 674-6264
U.S. News ranking: Reg. U. (N), No. 41
Website: www.misericordia.edu/
Admissions email: admiss@ misericordia.edu
Private; founded 1924
Freshman admissions: selective; 2016-2017: 1,823 applied, 1,357 accepted. Either SAT or ACT required. SAT 25/75 percentile: 950-1140. High school rank: 18% in top tenth, 40% in top quarter, 77% in top half
Early decision deadline: N/A, notification date: N/A
Early action deadline: N/A, notification date: N/A
Application deadline (fall): rolling
Undergraduate student body: 1,641 full time, 554 part time; 33% male, 67% female; 0% American Indian, 1% Asian, 3% black, 3% Hispanic, 2% multiracial, 0% Pacific Islander, 89% white, 0% international; 75% from in state; 43% live on campus; 0% of students in fraternities, 0% in sororities
Most popular majors: 15% Health Professions and Related Programs, 14% Business Administration and Management, General, 12% Registered Nursing/Registered Nurse, 6% General Studies, 6% Psychology, General

Expenses: 2017-2018: $31,660; room/board: $13,550
Financial aid: (570) 674-6222; 81% of undergrads determined to have financial need; average aid package $22,829

Moore College of Art & Design[1]
Philadelphia PA
(215) 965-4015
U.S. News ranking: Arts, unranked
Website: www.moore.edu
Admissions email: admiss@moore.edu
Private; founded 1848
Application deadline (fall): rolling
Undergraduate student body: N/A full time, N/A part time
Expenses: 2017-2018: $38,301; room/board: $14,389
Financial aid: N/A

Moravian College
Bethlehem PA
(610) 861-1320
U.S. News ranking: Nat. Lib. Arts, No. 165
Website: www.moravian.edu
Admissions email: admission@ moravian.edu
Private; founded 1742
Affiliation: Moravian Church
Freshman admissions: selective; 2016-2017: 2,512 applied, 2,005 accepted. Either SAT or ACT required. SAT 25/75 percentile: 900-1120. High school rank: 20% in top tenth, 43% in top quarter, 77% in top half
Early decision deadline: N/A, notification date: N/A
Early action deadline: N/A, notification date: N/A
Application deadline (fall): 3/1
Undergraduate student body: 1,794 full time, 212 part time; 41% male, 59% female; 0% American Indian, 2% Asian, 5% black, 10% Hispanic, 2% multiracial, 0% Pacific Islander, 68% white, 7% international; 69% from in state; 67% live on campus; 13% of students in fraternities, 16% in sororities
Most popular majors: 21% Health Professions and Related Programs, 15% Business, Management, Marketing, and Related Support Services, 12% Social Sciences, 10% Biological and Biomedical Sciences, 9% Visual and Performing Arts
Expenses: 2017-2018: $42,024; room/board: $12,694
Financial aid: (610) 861-1330; 80% of undergrads determined to have financial need; average aid package $29,554

Mount Aloysius College
Cresson PA
(814) 886-6383
U.S. News ranking: Reg. Coll. (N), No. 26
Website: www.mtaloy.edu
Admissions email: admissions@ mtaloy.edu
Private; founded 1853
Freshman admissions: less selective; 2016-2017: N/A applied, N/A accepted. Either SAT or ACT required. SAT 25/75 percentile: 870-1030. High school rank: N/A

Early decision deadline: N/A, notification date: N/A
Early action deadline: N/A, notification date: N/A
Application deadline (fall): rolling
Undergraduate student body: 1,085 full time, 635 part time; 31% male, 69% female; 0% American Indian, 0% Asian, 2% black, 1% Hispanic, 0% multiracial, 0% Pacific Islander, 76% white, 5% international; 93% from in state; 29% live on campus; N/A of students in fraternities, N/A in sororities
Most popular majors: 41% Health Professions and Related Programs, 13% Biological and Biomedical Sciences, 12% Business, Management, Marketing, and Related Support Services, 8% Liberal Arts and Sciences, General Studies and Humanities, 6% Psychology
Expenses: 2017-2018: $22,430; room/board: $11,378
Financial aid: (814) 886-6357; 83% of undergrads determined to have financial need; average aid package $14,140

Muhlenberg College
Allentown PA
(484) 664-3200
U.S. News ranking: Nat. Lib. Arts, No. 71
Website: www.muhlenberg.edu
Admissions email: admissions@muhlenberg.edu
Private; founded 1848
Affiliation: Lutheran Church in America
Freshman admissions: more selective; 2016-2017: 4,862 applied, 2,346 accepted. Neither SAT nor ACT required. SAT 25/75 percentile: 1130-1320. High school rank: 36% in top tenth, 71% in top quarter, 93% in top half
Early decision deadline: 2/15, notification date: 12/1
Early action deadline: N/A, notification date: N/A
Application deadline (fall): 2/15
Undergraduate student body: 2,318 full time, 90 part time; 40% male, 60% female; 0% American Indian, 3% Asian, 3% black, 7% Hispanic, 1% multiracial, 0% Pacific Islander, 75% white, 3% international; 24% from in state; 92% live on campus; 17% of students in fraternities, 25% in sororities
Most popular majors: 20% Drama and Dramatics/Theatre Arts, General, 12% Biology/Biological Sciences, General, 9% Social Sciences, 8% Psychology, General, 4% English Language and Literature/Letters
Expenses: 2017-2018: $50,830; room/board: $11,420
Financial aid: (484) 664-3175; 55% of undergrads determined to have financial need; average aid package $33,371

Neumann University
Aston PA
(610) 558-5616
U.S. News ranking: Reg. U. (N), second tier
Website: www.neumann.edu
Admissions email: neumann@neumann.edu
Private; founded 1965

Affiliation: Roman Catholic
Freshman admissions: least selective; 2016-2017: 1,486 applied, 1,393 accepted. Either SAT or ACT required. SAT 25/75 percentile: 800-980. High school rank: N/A
Early decision deadline: N/A, notification date: N/A
Early action deadline: N/A, notification date: N/A
Application deadline (fall): rolling
Undergraduate student body: 1,608 full time, 670 part time; 35% male, 65% female; 0% American Indian, 1% Asian, 23% black, 5% Hispanic, 2% multiracial, 0% Pacific Islander, 53% white, 1% international; 69% from in state; 31% live on campus; N/A of students in fraternities, N/A in sororities
Most popular majors: 18% Liberal Arts and Sciences/Liberal Studies, 12% Psychology, General, 12% Registered Nursing, Nursing Administration, Nursing Research and Clinical Nursing, Other, 9% Criminal Justice/Safety Studies, 8% Education/Teaching of Individuals in Elementary Special Education Programs
Expenses: 2017-2018: $30,050; room/board: $12,520
Financial aid: (610) 558-5521; 83% of undergrads determined to have financial need; average aid package $16,971

Peirce College
Philadelphia PA
(888) 467-3472
U.S. News ranking: Reg. Coll. (N), unranked
Website: www.peirce.edu
Admissions email: info@peirce.edu
Private; founded 1865
Freshman admissions: least selective; 2016-2017: N/A applied, N/A accepted. Neither SAT nor ACT required. SAT 25/75 percentile: N/A. High school rank: N/A
Early decision deadline: N/A, notification date: N/A
Early action deadline: N/A, notification date: N/A
Application deadline (fall): rolling
Undergraduate student body: 318 full time, 1,173 part time; 29% male, 71% female; 0% American Indian, 2% Asian, 69% black, 8% Hispanic, 1% multiracial, 0% Pacific Islander, 19% white, 0% international; 92% from in state; N/A live on campus; N/A of students in fraternities, N/A in sororities
Most popular majors: 58% Business, Management, Marketing, and Related Support Services, 15% Computer and Information Sciences and Support Services, 15% Legal Professions and Studies, 9% Health Professions and Related Programs, 2% Homeland Security, Law Enforcement, Firefighting and Related Protective Services
Expenses: 2016-2017: $14,472; room/board: N/A
Financial aid: N/A

Pennsylvania Academy of the Fine Arts[1]
Philadelphia PA
U.S. News ranking: Arts, unranked
Admissions email: N/A
Private
Application deadline (fall): N/A
Undergraduate student body: N/A full time, N/A part time
Expenses: 2017-2018: $37,096; room/board: $16,720
Financial aid: (215) 972-2019; 93% of undergrads determined to have financial need

Pennsylvania College of Art and Design[1]
Lancaster PA
U.S. News ranking: Arts, unranked
Website: www.pcad.edu
Admissions email: N/A
Private; founded 1982
Application deadline (fall): N/A
Undergraduate student body: N/A full time, N/A part time
Expenses: 2016-2017: $23,800; room/board: $9,653
Financial aid: N/A

Pennsylvania College of Technology
Williamsport PA
(570) 327-4761
U.S. News ranking: Reg. Coll. (N), No. 13
Website: www.pct.edu
Admissions email: admissions@pct.edu
Public; founded 1941
Freshman admissions: less selective; 2016-2017: 6,367 applied, 4,239 accepted. Neither SAT nor ACT required. SAT 25/75 percentile: 840-1050. High school rank: 7% in top tenth, 22% in top quarter, 56% in top half
Early decision deadline: N/A, notification date: N/A
Early action deadline: N/A, notification date: N/A
Application deadline (fall): 7/1
Undergraduate student body: 4,561 full time, 844 part time; 64% male, 36% female; 0% American Indian, 1% Asian, 3% black, 4% Hispanic, 2% multiracial, 0% Pacific Islander, 88% white, 1% international
Most popular majors: 27% Engineering Technologies and Engineering-Related Fields, 18% Health Professions and Related Programs, 16% Mechanic and Repair Technologies/Technicians, 7% Business, Management, Marketing, and Related Support Services, 7% Construction Trades
Expenses: 2017-2018: $16,380 in state, $23,340 out of state; room/board: $10,530
Financial aid: (570) 327-4766; 77% of undergrads determined to have financial need

Pennsylvania State University– University Park
University Park PA
(814) 865-5471
U.S. News ranking: Nat. U., No. 52
Website: www.psu.edu
Admissions email: admissions@psu.edu
Public; founded 1855
Freshman admissions: more selective; 2016-2017: 52,974 applied, 29,878 accepted. Either SAT or ACT required. SAT 25/75 percentile: 1090-1300. High school rank: 36% in top tenth, 77% in top quarter, 97% in top half
Early decision deadline: N/A, notification date: N/A
Early action deadline: N/A, notification date: N/A
Application deadline (fall): rolling
Undergraduate student body: 40,139 full time, 1,220 part time; 54% male, 46% female; 0% American Indian, 6% Asian, 4% black, 6% Hispanic, 3% multiracial, 0% Pacific Islander, 67% white, 12% international; 67% from in state; 35% live on campus; 17% of students in fraternities, 20% in sororities
Most popular majors: 17% Business, Management, Marketing, and Related Support Services, 17% Engineering, 8% Communication, Journalism, and Related Programs, 8% Social Sciences, 6% Computer and Information Sciences and Support Services
Expenses: 2017-2018: $18,436 in state, $33,664 out of state; room/board: $11,280
Financial aid: (814) 865-6301; 49% of undergrads determined to have financial need; average aid package $10,206

Philadelphia University
Philadelphia PA
(215) 951-2800
U.S. News ranking: Reg. U. (N), No. 64
Website: www.philau.edu
Admissions email: admissions@philau.edu
Private; founded 1884
Freshman admissions: selective; 2016-2017: 3,904 applied, 2,369 accepted. Either SAT or ACT required. SAT 25/75 percentile: 960-1130. High school rank: 14% in top tenth, 39% in top quarter, 75% in top half
Early decision deadline: N/A, notification date: N/A
Early action deadline: N/A, notification date: N/A
Application deadline (fall): rolling
Undergraduate student body: 2,321 full time, 360 part time; 33% male, 67% female; 0% American Indian, 5% Asian, 17% black, 9% Hispanic, 2% multiracial, 0% Pacific Islander, 55% white, 4% international; 61% from in state; 47% live on campus; 1% of students in fraternities, 1% in sororities
Most popular majors: 36% Business, Management, Marketing, and Related Support Services, 18% Visual and Performing Arts, 14% Architecture

and Related Services, 14% Health Professions and Related Programs, 6% Psychology
Expenses: 2017-2018: $39,130; room/board: $13,005
Financial aid: (215) 951-2940; 80% of undergrads determined to have financial need; average aid package $27,325

Point Park University
Pittsburgh PA
(800) 321-0129
U.S. News ranking: Reg. U. (N), No. 102
Website: www.pointpark.edu
Admissions email: enroll@pointpark.edu
Private; founded 1960
Freshman admissions: selective; 2016-2017: 4,073 applied, 2,886 accepted. Either SAT or ACT required. SAT 25/75 percentile: 890-1110. High school rank: 12% in top tenth, 36% in top quarter, 71% in top half
Early decision deadline: N/A, notification date: N/A
Early action deadline: N/A, notification date: N/A
Application deadline (fall): rolling
Undergraduate student body: 2,710 full time, 566 part time; 42% male, 58% female; 0% American Indian, 2% Asian, 14% black, 3% Hispanic, 4% multiracial, 0% Pacific Islander, 72% white, 5% international; 75% from in state; 32% live on campus; N/A of students in fraternities, N/A in sororities
Most popular majors: 11% Business Administration and Management, General, 11% Business, Management, Marketing, and Related Support Services, Other, 10% Dance, General, 10% Drama and Dramatics/Theatre Arts, General, 6% Cinematography and Film/Video Production
Expenses: 2017-2018: $30,130; room/board: $11,960
Financial aid: (412) 392-3930; 93% of undergrads determined to have financial need; average aid package $23,782

Robert Morris University
Moon Township PA
(412) 397-5200
U.S. News ranking: Nat. U., No. 176
Website: www.rmu.edu
Admissions email: admissions@rmu.edu
Private; founded 1921
Freshman admissions: selective; 2016-2017: 7,164 applied, 5,720 accepted. Either SAT or ACT required. SAT 25/75 percentile: 940-1140. High school rank: 14% in top tenth, 41% in top quarter, 75% in top half
Early decision deadline: N/A, notification date: N/A
Early action deadline: N/A, notification date: N/A
Application deadline (fall): rolling
Undergraduate student body: 3,940 full time, 444 part time; 58% male, 42% female; 0% American Indian, 1% Asian, 6% black, 2% Hispanic, 3% multiracial, 0% Pacific Islander, 73% white, 12% international; 86% from in state;

46% live on campus; 10% of students in fraternities, 16% in sororities

Most popular majors: 22% Registered Nursing/Registered Nurse, 17% Accounting, 16% Engineering, Other, 14% Business/Commerce, General, 12% Medical Scientist

Expenses: 2017-2018: $29,420; room/board: $11,180

Financial aid: (412) 397-6250; 70% of undergrads determined to have financial need; average aid package $21,873

Rosemont College

Rosemont PA
(800) 331-0708
U.S. News ranking: Reg. U. (N), second tier
Website: www.rosemont.edu
Admissions email: admissions@rosemont.edu
Private; founded 1921
Affiliation: Roman Catholic
Freshman admissions: less selective; 2016-2017: 1,403 applied, 970 accepted. Either SAT or ACT required. SAT 25/75 percentile: 810-1010. High school rank: N/A
Early decision deadline: N/A, notification date: N/A
Early action deadline: N/A, notification date: N/A
Application deadline (fall): 8/11
Undergraduate student body: 523 full time, 123 part time; 38% male, 62% female; 0% American Indian, 3% Asian, 39% black, 7% Hispanic, 5% multiracial, 0% Pacific Islander, 38% white, 0% international; 74% from in state; 77% live on campus; 0% of students in fraternities, 0% in sororities
Most popular majors: 18% Biology/Biological Sciences, General, 15% Business Administration and Management, 15% Elementary Education and Teaching, 10% Psychology, General, 8% Sociology
Expenses: 2017-2018: $19,486; room/board: $11,960
Financial aid: (610) 527-0200

Saint Vincent College

Latrobe PA
(800) 782-5549
U.S. News ranking: Nat. Lib. Arts, No. 147
Website: www.stvincent.edu
Admissions email: admission@stvincent.edu
Private; founded 1846
Freshman admissions: selective; 2016-2017: 2,256 applied, 1,486 accepted. Either SAT or ACT required. SAT 25/75 percentile: 940-1160. High school rank: 20% in top tenth, 51% in top quarter, 82% in top half
Early decision deadline: N/A, notification date: N/A
Early action deadline: N/A, notification date: N/A
Application deadline (fall): 5/1
Undergraduate student body: 1,586 full time, 60 part time; 52% male, 48% female; 0% American Indian, 2% Asian, 5% black, 3% Hispanic, 1% multiracial, 0% Pacific Islander, 85% white,

1% international; 81% from in state; 74% live on campus; 0% of students in fraternities, 0% in sororities
Most popular majors: 26% Business, Management, Marketing, and Related Support Services, 15% Biological and Biomedical Sciences, 11% Communication, Journalism, and Related Programs, 11% Social Sciences, 8% Psychology
Expenses: 2017-2018: $34,830; room/board: $11,399
Financial aid: (724) 805-2627; 78% of undergrads determined to have financial need; average aid package $29,677

Seton Hill University

Greensburg PA
(724) 838-4255
U.S. News ranking: Reg. U. (N), No. 56
Website: www.setonhill.edu
Admissions email: admit@setonhill.edu
Private; founded 1883
Affiliation: Roman Catholic
Freshman admissions: selective; 2016-2017: 2,206 applied, 1,612 accepted. Neither SAT nor ACT required. SAT 25/75 percentile: 930-1170. High school rank: 24% in top tenth, 56% in top quarter, 81% in top half
Early decision deadline: N/A, notification date: N/A
Early action deadline: N/A, notification date: N/A
Application deadline (fall): 8/15
Undergraduate student body: 1,400 full time, 68 part time; 35% male, 65% female; 0% American Indian, 1% Asian, 8% black, 4% Hispanic, 3% multiracial, 0% Pacific Islander, 80% white, 3% international; 76% from in state; 46% live on campus; 0% of students in fraternities, 0% in sororities
Most popular majors: 20% Business, Management, Marketing, and Related Support Services, 11% Visual and Performing Arts, 10% Education, 10% Health Professions and Related Programs, 8% Biological and Biomedical Sciences
Expenses: 2017-2018: $34,910; room/board: $13,954
Financial aid: (724) 838-4293; 84% of undergrads determined to have financial need; average aid package $24,766

Shippensburg University of Pennsylvania

Shippensburg PA
(717) 477-1231
U.S. News ranking: Reg. U. (N), No. 101
Website: www.ship.edu
Admissions email: admiss@ship.edu
Public; founded 1871
Freshman admissions: less selective; 2016-2017: 5,799 applied, 5,121 accepted. Either SAT or ACT required. SAT 25/75 percentile: 870-1070. High school rank: 7% in top tenth, 25% in top quarter, 58% in top half
Early decision deadline: N/A, notification date: N/A

Early action deadline: N/A, notification date: N/A
Application deadline (fall): rolling
Undergraduate student body: 5,545 full time, 367 part time; 50% male, 50% female; 0% American Indian, 2% Asian, 11% black, 5% Hispanic, 3% multiracial, 0% Pacific Islander, 77% white, 1% international; 92% from in state; 33% live on campus; 8% of students in fraternities, 9% in sororities
Most popular majors: 10% Business Administration and Management, General, 9% Psychology, General, 7% Criminal Justice/Safety Studies, 7% Social Work, 6% Marketing/Marketing Management, General
Expenses: 2017-2018: $12,086 in state, $19,944 out of state; room/board: $12,010
Financial aid: (717) 477-1131; 69% of undergrads determined to have financial need; average aid package $8,971

Slippery Rock University of Pennsylvania

Slippery Rock PA
(800) 929-4778
U.S. News ranking: Reg. U. (N), No. 78
Website: www.sru.edu/admissions
Admissions email: asktherock@sru.edu
Public; founded 1889
Freshman admissions: selective; 2016-2017: 5,889 applied, 4,092 accepted. Either SAT or ACT required. SAT 25/75 percentile: 910-1090. High school rank: 13% in top tenth, 37% in top quarter, 73% in top half
Early decision deadline: N/A, notification date: N/A
Early action deadline: N/A, notification date: N/A
Application deadline (fall): rolling
Undergraduate student body: 7,161 full time, 503 part time; 43% male, 57% female; 0% American Indian, 1% Asian, 5% black, 2% Hispanic, 4% multiracial, 0% Pacific Islander, 86% white, 1% international; 90% from in state; 36% live on campus; 2% of students in fraternities, 2% in sororities
Most popular majors: 25% Health Professions and Related Programs, 12% Business, Management, and Related Support Services, 9% Education, 8% Engineering Technologies and Engineering-Related Fields, 6% Parks, Recreation, Leisure, and Fitness Studies
Expenses: 2017-2018: $10,205 in state, $13,951 out of state; room/board: $10,312
Financial aid: (724) 738-2044; 68% of undergrads determined to have financial need; average aid package $9,251

St. Francis University

Loretto PA
(814) 472-3100
U.S. News ranking: Reg. U. (N), No. 18
Website: www.francis.edu/undergraduate_admissions
Admissions email: admissions@francis.edu
Private; founded 1847
Affiliation: Roman Catholic
Freshman admissions: selective; 2016-2017: 1,838 applied, 1,238 accepted. Either SAT or ACT required. SAT 25/75 percentile: 950-1170. High school rank: 22% in top tenth, 50% in top quarter, 74% in top half
Early decision deadline: N/A, notification date: N/A
Early action deadline: N/A, notification date: N/A
Application deadline (fall): 7/30
Undergraduate student body: 1,540 full time, 580 part time; 37% male, 63% female; 0% American Indian, 2% Asian, 6% black, 1% Hispanic, 2% multiracial, 0% Pacific Islander, 83% white, 1% international
Most popular majors: 12% Physician Assistant, 8% Occupational Therapy/Therapist, 7% Business Administration and Management, General, 7% Physical Therapy/Therapist, 6% Registered Nursing/Registered Nurse
Expenses: 2016-2017: $33,344; room/board: $11,000
Financial aid: (814) 472-3010

St. Joseph's University

Philadelphia PA
(610) 660-1300
U.S. News ranking: Reg. U. (N), No. 11
Website: www.sju.edu
Admissions email: admit@sju.edu
Private; founded 1851
Affiliation: Roman Catholic
Freshman admissions: selective; 2016-2017: 8,914 applied, 6,947 accepted. Neither SAT nor ACT required. SAT 25/75 percentile: 1050-1230. High school rank: 20% in top tenth, 50% in top quarter, 84% in top half
Early decision deadline: 11/1, notification date: 12/20
Early action deadline: 11/1, notification date: 12/20
Application deadline (fall): rolling
Undergraduate student body: 4,654 full time, 723 part time; 45% male, 55% female; 0% American Indian, 3% Asian, 6% black, 6% Hispanic, 2% multiracial, 0% Pacific Islander, 79% white, 2% international; 48% from in state; 55% live on campus; 15% in sororities
Most popular majors: 49% Business, Management, Marketing, and Related Support Services, 8% Social Sciences, 7% Communication, Journalism, and Related Programs, 6% Biological and Biomedical Sciences, 6% Psychology
Expenses: 2017-2018: $43,880; room/board: $14,840
Financial aid: (610) 660-2000; 54% of undergrads determined to have financial need; average aid package $27,253

Susquehanna University

Selinsgrove PA
(800) 326-9672
U.S. News ranking: Nat. Lib. Arts, No. 141
Website: www.susqu.edu
Admissions email: suadmiss@susqu.edu
Private; founded 1858
Affiliation: Evangelical Lutheran Church
Freshman admissions: selective; 2016-2017: 6,629 applied, 4,488 accepted. Neither SAT nor ACT required. SAT 25/75 percentile: 1010-1210. High school rank: 23% in top tenth, 51% in top quarter, 86% in top half
Early decision deadline: 11/15, notification date: 12/1
Early action deadline: 11/1, notification date: 12/1
Application deadline (fall): rolling
Undergraduate student body: 2,129 full time, 66 part time; 44% male, 56% female; 0% American Indian, 2% Asian, 7% black, 6% Hispanic, 3% multiracial, 0% Pacific Islander, 80% white, 2% international; 49% from in state; 91% live on campus; 20% of students in fraternities, 15% in sororities
Most popular majors: 16% Speech Communication and Rhetoric, 15% Business Administration and Management, General, 7% Biology/Biological Sciences, General, 7% Creative Writing, 6% Psychology, General
Expenses: 2017-2018: $45,470; room/board: $12,090
Financial aid: (570) 372-4260; 84% of undergrads determined to have financial need; average aid package $34,622

Swarthmore College

Swarthmore PA
(610) 328-8300
U.S. News ranking: Nat. Lib. Arts, No. 3
Website: www.swarthmore.edu
Admissions email: admissions@swarthmore.edu
Private; founded 1864
Freshman admissions: most selective; 2016-2017: 7,717 applied, 988 accepted. Either SAT or ACT required. SAT 25/75 percentile: 1305-1530. High school rank: 91% in top tenth, 96% in top quarter, 100% in top half
Early decision deadline: 11/15, notification date: 12/15
Early action deadline: N/A, notification date: N/A
Application deadline (fall): 1/1
Undergraduate student body: 1,542 full time, 1 part time; 50% male, 50% female; 0% American Indian, 16% Asian, 7% black, 13% Hispanic, 8% multiracial, 0% Pacific Islander, 42% white, 12% international; 12% from in state; 95% live on campus; 11% of students in fraternities, 5% in sororities
Most popular majors: 25% Social Sciences, 12% Biological and Biomedical Sciences, 8% Computer and Information

Sciences and Support Services, 7% Foreign Languages, Literatures, and Linguistics, 6% Education
Expenses: 2017-2018: $50,822; room/board: $14,952
Financial aid: (610) 328-8358; 54% of undergrads determined to have financial need; average aid package $47,255

Temple University
Philadelphia PA
(215) 204-7200
U.S. News ranking: Nat. U., No. 115
Website: www.temple.edu
Admissions email: askanowl@temple.edu
Public; founded 1884
Freshman admissions: more selective; 2016-2017: 33,139 applied, 17,295 accepted. Neither SAT nor ACT required. SAT 25/75 percentile: 1050-1280. High school rank: 24% in top tenth, 58% in top quarter, 92% in top half
Early decision deadline: N/A, notification date: N/A
Early action deadline: 11/1, notification date: 1/10
Application deadline (fall): 3/1
Undergraduate student body: 26,277 full time, 2,998 part time; 48% male, 52% female; 0% American Indian, 11% Asian, 13% black, 6% Hispanic, 3% multiracial, 0% Pacific Islander, 56% white, 6% international; 80% from in state; 19% live on campus; 3% of students in fraternities, 6% in sororities
Most popular majors: 24% Business, Management, Marketing, and Related Support Services, 13% Communication, Journalism, and Related Programs, 7% Parks, Recreation, Leisure, and Fitness Studies, 7% Visual and Performing Arts, 6% Health Professions and Related Programs
Expenses: 2017-2018: $16,274 in state, $27,266 out of state; room/board: $11,478
Financial aid: (215) 204-2244; 68% of undergrads determined to have financial need; average aid package $18,353

Thiel College
Greenville PA
(800) 248-4435
U.S. News ranking: Nat. Lib. Arts, second tier
Website: www.thiel.edu
Admissions email: admission@thiel.edu
Private; founded 1866
Affiliation: Evangelical Lutheran Church
Freshman admissions: selective; 2016-2017: N/A applied, N/A accepted. Either SAT or ACT required. SAT 25/75 percentile: 800-1050. High school rank: 8% in top tenth, 23% in top quarter, 50% in top half
Early decision deadline: N/A, notification date: N/A
Early action deadline: 12/15, notification date: 12/23

Application deadline (fall): rolling
Undergraduate student body: 862 full time, 26 part time; 59% male, 41% female; N/A American Indian, N/A Asian, N/A black, N/A Hispanic, N/A multiracial, N/A Pacific Islander, N/A white, N/A international
Most popular majors: 28% Business, Management, Marketing, and Related Support Services, 15% Public Administration and Social Service Professions, 14% Biological and Biomedical Sciences, 10% Psychology, 6% Education
Expenses: 2016-2017: $29,740; room/board: $11,700
Financial aid: (724) 589-2178

University of Pennsylvania
Philadelphia PA
(215) 898-7507
U.S. News ranking: Nat. U., No. 8
Website: www.upenn.edu
Admissions email: info@admissions.upenn.edu
Private; founded 1740
Freshman admissions: most selective; 2016-2017: 38,918 applied, 3,674 accepted. Either SAT or ACT required. SAT 25/75 percentile: 1380-1570. High school rank: 95% in top tenth, 100% in top quarter, 100% in top half
Early decision deadline: 11/1, notification date: 12/15
Early action deadline: N/A, notification date: N/A
Application deadline (fall): 1/5
Undergraduate student body: 9,706 full time, 313 part time; 50% male, 50% female; 0% American Indian, 21% Asian, 7% black, 10% Hispanic, 4% multiracial, 0% Pacific Islander, 44% white, 12% international; 19% from in state; 54% live on campus; 30% of students in fraternities, 27% in sororities
Most popular majors: 11% Finance, General, 6% Economics, General, 6% Registered Nursing/Registered Nurse, 5% Biology/Biological Sciences, General, 4% Political Science and Government, General
Expenses: 2017-2018: $53,534; room/board: $15,066
Financial aid: (215) 898-1988; 48% of undergrads determined to have financial need; average aid package $46,707

University of Pittsburgh
Pittsburgh PA
(412) 624-7488
U.S. News ranking: Nat. U., No. 68
Website: www.oafa.pitt.edu/
Admissions email: oafa@pitt.edu
Public; founded 1787
Freshman admissions: more selective; 2016-2017: 29,175 applied, 16,165 accepted. Either SAT or ACT required. SAT 25/75 percentile: 1190-1380. High school rank: 52% in top tenth, 86% in top quarter, 99% in top half

Early decision deadline: N/A, notification date: N/A
Early action deadline: N/A, notification date: N/A
Application deadline (fall): rolling
Undergraduate student body: 18,163 full time, 960 part time; 48% male, 52% female; 0% American Indian, 10% Asian, 5% black, 3% Hispanic, 4% multiracial, 0% Pacific Islander, 73% white, 4% international; 72% from in state; 43% live on campus; 10% of students in fraternities, 9% in sororities
Most popular majors: 20% Business, Management, Marketing, and Related Support Services, 13% Health Professions and Related Programs, 11% Engineering, 10% Social Sciences, 8% Biological and Biomedical Sciences
Expenses: 2017-2018: $19,080 in state, $30,642 out of state; room/board: $10,950
Financial aid: (412) 624-7180; 52% of undergrads determined to have financial need; average aid package $12,180

University of Scranton
Scranton PA
(570) 941-7540
U.S. News ranking: Reg. U. (N), No. 6
Website: www.scranton.edu
Admissions email: admissions@scranton.edu
Private; founded 1888
Affiliation: Roman Catholic
Freshman admissions: more selective; 2016-2017: 10,114 applied, 7,540 accepted. Either SAT or ACT required. SAT 25/75 percentile: 1030-1220. High school rank: 30% in top tenth, 62% in top quarter, 90% in top half
Early decision deadline: N/A, notification date: N/A
Early action deadline: 11/15, notification date: 12/15
Application deadline (fall): 3/1
Undergraduate student body: 3,678 full time, 189 part time; 41% male, 59% female; 0% American Indian, 3% Asian, 2% black, 9% Hispanic, 2% multiracial, 0% Pacific Islander, 81% white, 1% international; 40% from in state; 64% live on campus; N/A of students in fraternities, N/A in sororities
Most popular majors: 9% Biology/Biological Sciences, General, 7% Kinesiology and Exercise Science, 7% Registered Nursing/Registered Nurse, 6% Accounting, 4% Business Administration and Management, General
Expenses: 2017-2018: $43,310; room/board: $14,618
Financial aid: (570) 941-7701; 70% of undergrads determined to have financial need; average aid package $26,579

University of Valley Forge
Phoenixville PA
(800) 432-8322
U.S. News ranking: Reg. Coll. (N), No. 35
Website: www.valleyforge.edu/
Admissions email: admissions@valleyforge.edu
Private; founded 1939
Affiliation: Assemblies of God Church
Freshman admissions: less selective; 2016-2017: 465 applied, 366 accepted. Neither SAT nor ACT required. SAT 25/75 percentile: N/A. High school rank: N/A
Early decision deadline: N/A, notification date: N/A
Early action deadline: N/A, notification date: N/A
Application deadline (fall): 8/11
Undergraduate student body: 623 full time, 187 part time; 48% male, 52% female; 0% American Indian, 1% Asian, 17% black, 18% Hispanic, 5% multiracial, 0% Pacific Islander, 54% white, 0% international; 44% from in state; 89% live on campus; 0% of students in fraternities, 0% in sororities
Most popular majors: 15% Youth Ministry, 10% Divinity/Ministry, 10% Theology and Religious Vocations, Other, 7% Business/Commerce, General, 7% Psychology, General
Expenses: 2016-2017: $20,694; room/board: $8,360
Financial aid: N/A

University of the Arts
Philadelphia PA
(215) 717-6049
U.S. News ranking: Arts, unranked
Website: www.uarts.edu
Admissions email: admissions@uarts.edu
Private; founded 1876
Freshman admissions: selective; 2016-2017: 1,616 applied, 1,241 accepted. Neither SAT nor ACT required. SAT 25/75 percentile: 920-1170. High school rank: N/A
Early decision deadline: N/A, notification date: N/A
Early action deadline: N/A, notification date: N/A
Application deadline (fall): rolling
Undergraduate student body: 1,679 full time, 44 part time; 40% male, 60% female; 0% American Indian, 3% Asian, 15% black, 9% Hispanic, 5% multiracial, 0% Pacific Islander, 61% white, 5% international; 41% from in state; 32% live on campus; N/A of students in fraternities, N/A in sororities
Most popular majors: 20% Dance, General, 11% Film/Video and Photographic Arts, Other, 9% Illustration, 8% Music Performance, General, 8% Musical Theatre
Expenses: 2017-2018: $43,100; room/board: $15,710
Financial aid: (215) 717-6170

Ursinus College
Collegeville PA
(610) 409-3200
U.S. News ranking: Nat. Lib. Arts, No. 93
Website: www.ursinus.edu
Admissions email: admission@ursinus.edu
Private; founded 1869
Freshman admissions: more selective; 2016-2017: 2,491 applied, 2,053 accepted. Neither SAT nor ACT required. SAT 25/75 percentile: 1033-1290. High school rank: 24% in top tenth, 51% in top quarter, 82% in top half
Early decision deadline: 12/1, notification date: 12/15
Early action deadline: 11/1, notification date: 12/15
Application deadline (fall): rolling
Undergraduate student body: 1,542 full time, 14 part time; 47% male, 53% female; 0% American Indian, 4% Asian, 6% black, 7% Hispanic, 4% multiracial, 0% Pacific Islander, 74% white, 2% international; 56% from in state; 96% live on campus; 16% of students in fraternities, 25% in sororities
Most popular majors: 16% Biology/Biological Sciences, General, 14% Applied Economics, 10% Psychology, General, 8% Neuroscience, 6% Exercise Physiology
Expenses: 2017-2018: $50,360; room/board: $12,560
Financial aid: (610) 409-3600; 77% of undergrads determined to have financial need; average aid package $36,770

Villanova University
Villanova PA
(610) 519-4000
U.S. News ranking: Nat. U., No. 46
Website: www.villanova.edu
Admissions email: gotovu@villanova.edu
Private; founded 1842
Affiliation: Roman Catholic
Freshman admissions: more selective; 2016-2017: 17,272 applied, 7,514 accepted. Either SAT or ACT required. ACT 25/75 percentile: 30-32. High school rank: 62% in top tenth, 90% in top quarter, 97% in top half
Early decision deadline: N/A, notification date: N/A
Early action deadline: 11/1, notification date: 12/20
Application deadline (fall): 1/15
Undergraduate student body: 6,490 full time, 509 part time; 47% male, 53% female; 0% American Indian, 7% Asian, 5% black, 7% Hispanic, 2% multiracial, 0% Pacific Islander, 75% white, 2% international; 22% from in state; 66% live on campus; 21% of students in fraternities, 37% in sororities
Most popular majors: 31% Business, Management, Marketing, and Related Support Services, 12% Social Sciences, 11% Engineering, 11% Health Professions and Related Programs, 8% Communication, Journalism, and Related Programs
Expenses: 2017-2018: $51,434; room/board: $13,520

Financial aid: (610) 519-4010; 48% of undergrads determined to have financial need; average aid package $36,074

Washington and Jefferson College

Washington PA
(724) 223-6025
U.S. News ranking: Nat. Lib. Arts, No. 106
Website: www.washjeff.edu
Admissions email: admission@washjeff.edu
Private; founded 1781
Freshman admissions: selective; 2016-2017: 7,155 applied, 3,258 accepted. Neither SAT nor ACT required. SAT 25/75 percentile: 1070-1250. High school rank: 24% in top tenth, 59% in top quarter, 90% in top half
Early decision deadline: 12/1, notification date: 12/15
Early action deadline: 1/15, notification date: 2/15
Application deadline (fall): 3/1
Undergraduate student body: 1,386 full time, 10 part time; 51% male, 49% female; 0% American Indian, 2% Asian, 5% black, 3% Hispanic, 4% multiracial, 0% Pacific Islander, 78% white, 4% international; 78% from in state; 95% live on campus; 28% of students in fraternities, 29% in sororities
Most popular majors: 17% Business/Commerce, General, 11% Accounting, 10% Psychology, General, 5% Economics, General, 5% History, General
Expenses: 2017-2018: $46,628; room/board: $12,318
Financial aid: (724) 223-6019; 79% of undergrads determined to have financial need; average aid package $34,948

Waynesburg University

Waynesburg PA
(800) 225-7393
U.S. News ranking: Reg. U. (N), No. 97
Website: www.waynesburg.edu/
Admissions email: admissions@waynesburg.edu
Private; founded 1849
Affiliation: Presbyterian Church (USA)
Freshman admissions: selective; 2016-2017: 1,478 applied, 1,385 accepted. Either SAT or ACT required. SAT 25/75 percentile: 860-1070. High school rank: 12% in top tenth, 37% in top quarter, 74% in top half
Early decision deadline: N/A, notification date: N/A
Early action deadline: N/A, notification date: N/A
Application deadline (fall): rolling
Undergraduate student body: 1,332 full time, 68 part time; 41% male, 59% female; 0% American Indian, 1% Asian, 4% black, 2% Hispanic, 3% multiracial, 0% Pacific Islander, 91% white, 0% international; 83% from in state; 74% live on campus; N/A of students in fraternities, N/A in sororities

Most popular majors: 25% Registered Nursing/Registered Nurse, 11% Criminal Justice/Law Enforcement Administration, 9% Speech Communication and Rhetoric, 7% Psychology, General, 6% Elementary Education and Teaching
Expenses: 2017-2018: $24,010; room/board: $9,820
Financial aid: (724) 852-3208; 82% of undergrads determined to have financial need; average aid package $18,741

West Chester University of Pennsylvania

West Chester PA
(610) 436-3414
U.S. News ranking: Reg. U. (N), No. 64
Website: www.wcupa.edu/
Admissions email: ugadmiss@wcupa.edu
Public; founded 1871
Freshman admissions: selective; 2016-2017: 12,609 applied, 8,127 accepted. Either SAT or ACT required. SAT 25/75 percentile: 970-1150. High school rank: 10% in top tenth, 34% in top quarter, 72% in top half
Early decision deadline: N/A, notification date: N/A
Early action deadline: N/A, notification date: N/A
Application deadline (fall): rolling
Undergraduate student body: 12,824 full time, 1,574 part time; 41% male, 59% female; 0% American Indian, 2% Asian, 11% black, 6% Hispanic, 3% multiracial, 0% Pacific Islander, 76% white, 0% international; 88% from in state; 40% live on campus; 14% of students in fraternities, 19% in sororities
Most popular majors: 21% Business, Management, Marketing, and Related Support Services, 16% Health Professions and Related Programs, 10% Education, 8% English Language and Literature/Letters, 7% Psychology
Expenses: 2017-2018: $10,064 in state, $21,302 out of state; room/board: $8,350
Financial aid: (610) 436-2627; 59% of undergrads determined to have financial need; average aid package $8,137

Westminster College

New Wilmington PA
(724) 946-7100
U.S. News ranking: Nat. Lib. Arts, No. 128
Website: www.westminster.edu
Admissions email: admis@westminster.edu
Private; founded 1852
Affiliation: Presbyterian Church (USA)
Freshman admissions: selective; 2016-2017: 2,622 applied, 1,937 accepted. Either SAT or ACT required. SAT 25/75 percentile: 920-1140. High school rank: 22% in top tenth, 42% in top quarter, 75% in top half
Early decision deadline: N/A, notification date: N/A
Early action deadline: 11/15, notification date: 12/1

Application deadline (fall): 5/1
Undergraduate student body: 1,150 full time, 24 part time; 45% male, 55% female; 0% American Indian, 1% Asian, 5% black, 1% Hispanic, 2% multiracial, 0% Pacific Islander, 72% white, 1% international; 72% from in state; 75% live on campus; 33% of students in fraternities, 49% in sororities
Most popular majors: 19% Business, Management, Marketing, and Related Support Services, 13% Biological and Biomedical Sciences, 13% Education, 11% Social Sciences, 10% Psychology
Expenses: 2017-2018: $36,230; room/board: $11,020
Financial aid: (724) 946-7102

Widener University

Chester PA
(610) 499-4126
U.S. News ranking: Nat. U., No. 192
Website: www.widener.edu
Admissions email: admissions.office@widener.edu
Private; founded 1821
Freshman admissions: selective; 2016-2017: 5,175 applied, 3,608 accepted. Either SAT or ACT required. SAT 25/75 percentile: 930-1130. High school rank: 9% in top tenth, 31% in top quarter, 77% in top half
Early decision deadline: N/A, notification date: N/A
Early action deadline: N/A, notification date: N/A
Application deadline (fall): rolling
Undergraduate student body: 2,978 full time, 613 part time; 44% male, 56% female; 0% American Indian, 4% Asian, 12% black, 5% Hispanic, 3% multiracial, 0% Pacific Islander, 70% white, 4% international; 57% from in state; 42% live on campus; 10% of students in fraternities, 9% in sororities
Most popular majors: 28% Health Professions and Related Programs, 19% Business, Management, Marketing, and Related Support Services, 14% Engineering, 9% Psychology, 5% Communications Technologies/Technicians and Support Services
Expenses: 2017-2018: $44,166; room/board: $14,024
Financial aid: (610) 499-4161; 79% of undergrads determined to have financial need; average aid package $32,580

Wilkes University

Wilkes-Barre PA
(570) 408-4400
U.S. News ranking: Reg. U. (N), No. 78
Website: www.wilkes.edu
Admissions email: admissions@wilkes.edu
Private; founded 1933
Freshman admissions: selective; 2016-2017: 4,245 applied, 3,223 accepted. Either SAT or ACT required. SAT 25/75 percentile: 895-1130. High school rank: 20% in top tenth, 51% in top quarter, 83% in top half
Early decision deadline: N/A, notification date: N/A

Early action deadline: N/A, notification date: N/A
Application deadline (fall): rolling
Undergraduate student body: 2,303 full time, 258 part time; 52% male, 48% female; 0% American Indian, 3% Asian, 5% black, 7% Hispanic, 3% multiracial, 0% Pacific Islander, 72% white, 8% international; 81% from in state; 39% live on campus; 0% of students in fraternities, 0% in sororities
Most popular majors: 21% Business, Management, Marketing, and Related Support Services, 16% Engineering, 12% Health Professions and Related Programs, 8% Psychology, 6% Biological and Biomedical Sciences
Expenses: 2017-2018: $34,896; room/board: $14,270
Financial aid: (570) 408-3845; 80% of undergrads determined to have financial need; average aid package $24,604

Wilson College

Chambersburg PA
(800) 421-8402
U.S. News ranking: Reg. Coll. (N), No. 11
Website: www.wilson.edu
Admissions email: admissions@wilson.edu
Private; founded 1869
Affiliation: Presbyterian Church (USA)
Freshman admissions: less selective; 2016-2017: 1,024 applied, 591 accepted. Neither SAT nor ACT required. SAT 25/75 percentile: 810-1030. High school rank: 18% in top tenth, 49% in top quarter, 85% in top half
Early decision deadline: N/A, notification date: N/A
Early action deadline: N/A, notification date: N/A
Application deadline (fall): rolling
Undergraduate student body: 495 full time, 246 part time; 18% male, 82% female; 0% American Indian, 3% Asian, 7% black, 0% Hispanic, 0% multiracial, 0% Pacific Islander, 54% white, 4% international; 80% from in state; 43% live on campus; N/A of students in fraternities, N/A in sororities
Most popular majors: 28% Veterinary/Animal Health Technology/Technician and Veterinary Assistant, 8% Equestrian/Equine Studies, 6% Elementary Education and Teaching, 6% Kinesiology and Exercise Science, 6% Psychology, General
Expenses: 2017-2018: $24,452; room/board: $11,364
Financial aid: (717) 262-2016; 96% of undergrads determined to have financial need; average aid package $21,525

York College of Pennsylvania

York PA
(717) 849-1600
U.S. News ranking: Reg. U. (N), No. 78
Website: www.ycp.edu
Admissions email: admissions@ycp.edu
Private; founded 1787

Freshman admissions: selective; 2016-2017: 5,747 applied, 3,539 accepted. Either SAT or ACT required. SAT 25/75 percentile: 940-1140. High school rank: 13% in top tenth, 38% in top quarter, 76% in top half
Early decision deadline: N/A, notification date: N/A
Early action deadline: N/A, notification date: N/A
Application deadline (fall): rolling
Undergraduate student body: 3,846 full time, 442 part time; 45% male, 55% female; 0% American Indian, 2% Asian, 5% black, 6% Hispanic, 4% multiracial, 0% Pacific Islander, 82% white, 1% international; 60% from in state; 59% live on campus; 4% of students in fraternities, 7% in sororities
Most popular majors: 20% Business, Management, Marketing, and Related Support Services, 14% Health Professions and Related Programs, 9% Education, 9% Homeland Security, Law Enforcement, Firefighting and Related Protective Services, 7% Communication, Journalism, and Related Programs
Expenses: 2017-2018: $19,430; room/board: $10,830
Financial aid: (717) 849-1682; 67% of undergrads determined to have financial need; average aid package $12,251

RHODE ISLAND

Brown University

Providence RI
(401) 863-2378
U.S. News ranking: Nat. U., No. 14
Website: www.brown.edu/admission/undergraduate/
Admissions email: admission@brown.edu
Private; founded 1764
Freshman admissions: most selective; 2016-2017: 32,390 applied, 3,014 accepted. Either SAT or ACT required. SAT 25/75 percentile: 1370-1570. High school rank: 92% in top tenth, 99% in top quarter, 100% in top half
Early decision deadline: 11/1, notification date: 12/15
Early action deadline: N/A, notification date: N/A
Application deadline (fall): 1/1
Undergraduate student body: 6,565 full time, 361 part time; 47% male, 53% female; 0% American Indian, 14% Asian, 7% black, 12% Hispanic, 6% multiracial, 0% Pacific Islander, 43% white, 11% international; 5% from in state; 76% live on campus; 9% of students in fraternities, 13% in sororities
Most popular majors: 9% Economics, General, 8% Computer Science, 7% Biology/Biological Sciences, General, 6% Entrepreneurship/Entrepreneurial Studies, 5% Political Science and Government, General
Expenses: 2017-2018: $53,419; room/board: $14,020
Financial aid: (401) 863-2721; 44% of undergrads determined to have financial need; average aid package $48,420

Bryant University
Smithfield RI
(800) 622-7001
U.S. News ranking: Reg. U. (N),
No. 10
Website: www.bryant.edu
Admissions email:
admission@bryant.edu
Private; founded 1863
Freshman admissions: more
selective; 2016-2017: 7,314
applied, 5,024 accepted. Neither
SAT nor ACT required. SAT
25/75 percentile: 1085-1255.
High school rank: 19% in top
tenth, 49% in top quarter, 92%
in top half
Early decision deadline: 11/1,
notification date: 12/15
Early action deadline: 12/1,
notification date: 1/15
Application deadline (fall): 2/1
Undergraduate student body: 3,401
full time, 61 part time; 60%
male, 40% female; 0% American
Indian, 4% Asian, 4% black,
7% Hispanic, 1% multiracial,
0% Pacific Islander, 75% white,
7% international; 14% from in
state; 80% live on campus; 3%
of students in fraternities, 6% in
sororities
Most popular majors: 77%
Business, Management,
Marketing, and Related Support
Services, 6% Mathematics and
Statistics, 4% Social Sciences,
3% Communication, Journalism,
and Related Programs, 2%
Computer and Information
Sciences and Support Services
Expenses: 2017-2018: $42,109;
room/board: $15,095
Financial aid: (401) 232-6020;
61% of undergrads determined to
have financial need; average aid
package $24,422

Johnson & Wales University
Providence RI
(800) 342-5598
U.S. News ranking: Reg. U. (N),
No. 64
Website: www.jwu.edu
Admissions email:
pvd@admissions.jwu.edu
Private; founded 1914
Freshman admissions: less
selective; 2016-2017: 16,525
applied, 14,608 accepted. Neither
SAT nor ACT required. SAT 25/75
percentile: 860-1080. High
school rank: N/A
Early decision deadline: N/A,
notification date: N/A
Early action deadline: N/A,
notification date: N/A
Application deadline (fall): rolling
Undergraduate student body: 7,899
full time, 560 part time; 53%
male, 47% female; 0% American
Indian, 1% Asian, 13% black,
12% Hispanic, 7% multiracial,
0% Pacific Islander, 55% white,
8% international; 19% from in
state; 45% live on campus; N/A
of students in fraternities, N/A in
sororities
Most popular majors: 38%
Business, Management,
Marketing, and Related Support
Services, 24% Family and
Consumer Sciences/Human
Sciences, 10% Parks, Recreation,
Leisure, and Fitness Studies, 10%
Personal and Culinary Services,
5% Homeland Security, Law

Enforcement, Firefighting and
Related Protective Services
Expenses: 2017-2018: $31,508;
room/board: $11,970
Financial aid: (401) 598-1857;
76% of undergrads determined to
have financial need; average aid
package $22,031

New England Institute of Technology
East Greenwich RI
(800) 736-7744
U.S. News ranking: Reg. Coll. (N),
second tier
Website: www.neit.edu/
Admissions email:
NEITAdmissions@neit.edu
Private; founded 1940
Affiliation: Other
Freshman admissions: less
selective; 2016-2017: N/A
applied, N/A accepted. Neither
SAT nor ACT required. SAT 25/75
percentile: N/A. High school
rank: N/A
Early decision deadline: N/A,
notification date: N/A
Early action deadline: N/A,
notification date: N/A
Application deadline (fall): rolling
Undergraduate student body: 2,377
full time, 476 part time; 67%
male, 33% female; 1% American
Indian, 2% Asian, 5% black, 12%
Hispanic, 2% multiracial, 0%
Pacific Islander, 63% white, 3%
international
Most popular majors: Business
Administration and Management,
General, Computer/Information
Technology Administration and
Management, Construction
Engineering Technologies,
Recording Arts Technology/
Technician, Web Page, Digital/
Multimedia and Information
Resources Design
Expenses: 2017-2018: $28,740;
room/board: $11,640
Financial aid: (401) 739-5000

Providence College
Providence RI
(401) 865-2535
U.S. News ranking: Reg. U. (N),
No. 1
Website: www.providence.edu
Admissions email: pcadmiss@
providence.edu
Private; founded 1917
Affiliation: Roman Catholic
Freshman admissions: more
selective; 2016-2017: 10,820
applied, 5,954 accepted. Neither
SAT nor ACT required. SAT
25/75 percentile: 1030-1240.
High school rank: 39% in top
tenth, 69% in top quarter, 92%
in top half
Early decision deadline: 11/15,
notification date: 1/1
Early action deadline: 11/1,
notification date: 1/1
Application deadline (fall): 1/15
Undergraduate student body: 4,008
full time, 262 part time; 44%
male, 56% female; 0% American
Indian, 1% Asian, 4% black,
9% Hispanic, 2% multiracial,
0% Pacific Islander, 77% white,
2% international; 10% from in
state; 74% live on campus; 0%
of students in fraternities, 0% in
sororities

Most popular majors: 36%
Business, Management,
Marketing, and Related Support
Services, 11% Social Sciences,
9% Biological and Biomedical
Sciences, 7% Psychology, 6%
Education
Expenses: 2017-2018: $48,760;
room/board: $14,240
Financial aid: (401) 865-2286;
48% of undergrads determined to
have financial need; average aid
package $32,024

Rhode Island College
Providence RI
(800) 669-5760
U.S. News ranking: Reg. U. (N),
second tier
Website: www.ric.edu
Admissions email:
admissions@ric.edu
Public; founded 1854
Freshman admissions: least
selective; 2016-2017: 5,148
applied, 3,845 accepted. Either
SAT or ACT required. SAT 25/75
percentile: 790-1020. High school
rank: 12% in top tenth, 36% in
top quarter, 73% in top half
Early decision deadline: N/A,
notification date: N/A
Early action deadline: N/A,
notification date: N/A
Application deadline (fall): 3/15
Undergraduate student body: 5,598
full time, 1,800 part time; 32%
male, 68% female; 0% American
Indian, 3% Asian, 9% black,
17% Hispanic, 2% multiracial,
0% Pacific Islander, 61% white,
0% international; 85% from in
state; 15% live on campus; N/A
of students in fraternities, N/A in
sororities
Most popular majors: 20% Health
Professions and Related Programs,
14% Education, 14% Psychology,
13% Business, Management,
Marketing, and Related
Support Services, 11% Public
Administration and Social Service
Professions
Expenses: 2017-2018: $8,776 in
state, $21,289 out of state; room/
board: $11,335
Financial aid: (401) 456-8033;
69% of undergrads determined to
have financial need; average aid
package $9,027

Rhode Island School of Design
Providence RI
(401) 454-6300
U.S. News ranking: Arts, unranked
Website: www.risd.edu
Admissions email:
admissions@risd.edu
Private; founded 1877
Freshman admissions: more
selective; 2016-2017: 2,762
applied, 950 accepted. Either
SAT or ACT required. SAT 25/75
percentile: 1080-1340. High
school rank: N/A
Early decision deadline: 11/1,
notification date: 12/7
Early action deadline: N/A,
notification date: N/A
Application deadline (fall): 2/1
Undergraduate student body:
1,999 full time, 0 part time; 31%
male, 69% female; 0% American
Indian, 20% Asian, 3% black,
8% Hispanic, 5% multiracial,
0% Pacific Islander, 32% white,

27% international; 6% from in
state; 60% live on campus; N/A
of students in fraternities, N/A in
sororities
Most popular majors: 16%
Illustration, 16% Industrial and
Product Design, 12% Graphic
Design, 8% Film/Video and
Photographic Arts, Other, 8%
Painting
Expenses: 2017-2018: $48,470;
room/board: $13,050
Financial aid: (401) 454-6661;
39% of undergrads determined to
have financial need; average aid
package $29,371

Roger Williams University
Bristol RI
(401) 254-3500
U.S. News ranking: Reg. U. (N),
No. 37
Website: www.rwu.edu
Admissions email: admit@rwu.edu
Private; founded 1956
Freshman admissions: selective;
2016-2017: 9,829 applied,
7,790 accepted. Neither SAT
nor ACT required. SAT 25/75
percentile: 990-1180. High
school rank: N/A
Early decision deadline: N/A,
notification date: N/A
Early action deadline: 11/1,
notification date: 12/1
Application deadline (fall): 2/1
Undergraduate student body: 4,124
full time, 778 part time; 46%
male, 54% female; 0% American
Indian, 1% Asian, 3% black,
6% Hispanic, 2% multiracial,
0% Pacific Islander, 77% white,
4% international; 23% from in
state; 75% live on campus; N/A
of students in fraternities, N/A in
sororities
Most popular majors: 27%
Business, Management,
Marketing, and Related Support
Services, 9% Homeland Security,
Law Enforcement, Firefighting and
Related Protective Services, 8%
Architecture and Related Services,
7% Biological and Biomedical
Sciences, 7% Psychology
Expenses: 2017-2018: $33,336;
room/board: $15,234
Financial aid: (401) 254-3100,
62% of undergrads determined to
have financial need; average aid
package $20,505

Salve Regina University
Newport RI
(888) 467-2583
U.S. News ranking: Reg. U. (N),
No. 37
Website: www.salve.edu
Admissions email:
admissions@salve.edu
Private; founded 1934
Affiliation: Roman Catholic
Freshman admissions: selective;
2016-2017: 5,158 applied,
3,526 accepted. Neither SAT
nor ACT required. SAT 25/75
percentile: 1020-1180. High
school rank: 17% in top tenth,
45% in top quarter, 81% in
top half
Early decision deadline: N/A,
notification date: N/A
Early action deadline: 11/1,
notification date: 1/1

Application deadline (fall): rolling
Undergraduate student body: 1,975
full time, 149 part time; 30%
male, 70% female; 0% American
Indian, 1% Asian, 2% black,
6% Hispanic, 2% multiracial,
0% Pacific Islander, 82% white,
1% international; 22% from in
state; 56% live on campus; N/A
of students in fraternities, N/A in
sororities
Most popular majors: 17%
Registered Nursing/Registered
Nurse, 10% Criminal Justice/
Law Enforcement Administration,
9% Business Administration
and Management, General, 9%
Psychology, General, 8% Biology/
Biological Sciences, General
Expenses: 2017-2018: $38,986;
room/board: $14,060
Financial aid: (401) 341-2901;
77% of undergrads determined to
have financial need; average aid
package $26,402

University of Rhode Island
Kingston RI
(401) 874-7100
U.S. News ranking: Nat. U.,
No. 156
Website: www.uri.edu
Admissions email:
admission@uri.edu
Public; founded 1892
Freshman admissions: selective;
2016-2017: 21,797 applied,
15,485 accepted. Either SAT
or ACT required. SAT 25/75
percentile: 990-1190. High school
rank: 18% in top tenth, 47% in
top quarter, 85% in top half
Early decision deadline: N/A,
notification date: N/A
Early action deadline: 12/1,
notification date: 1/31
Application deadline (fall): 2/1
Undergraduate student body:
12,176 full time, 2,326 part
time; 44% male, 56% female;
0% American Indian, 3% Asian,
5% black, 10% Hispanic, 2%
multiracial, 0% Pacific Islander,
72% white, 1% international;
54% from in state; 42% live
on campus; 15% of students in
fraternities, 22% in sororities
Most popular majors: 7%
Registered Nursing/Registered
Nurse, 6% Psychology, General,
6% Speech Communication and
Rhetoric, 5% Kinesiology and
Exercise Science, 4% Human
Development and Family Studies,
General
Expenses: 2017-2018: $12,884
in state, $28,874 out of state;
room/board: $12,022
Financial aid: (401) 874-9500;
85% of undergrads determined to
have financial need; average aid
package $15,768

SOUTH CAROLINA

Allen University[1]
Columbia SC
(803) 376-5735
U.S. News ranking: Nat. Lib. Arts,
second tier
Website: www.allenuniversity.edu
Admissions email: admissions@
allenuniversity.edu
Private; founded 1870
Application deadline (fall): rolling

Undergraduate student body: N/A full time, N/A part time
Expenses: 2016-2017: $13,140; room/board: $6,560
Financial aid: (803) 376-5930

Anderson University
Anderson SC
(864) 231-5607
U.S. News ranking: Reg. U. (S), No. 73
Website: www.andersonuniversity.edu
Admissions email: admission@andersonuniversity.edu
Private; founded 1911
Freshman admissions: selective; 2016-2017: 3,316 applied, 1,788 accepted. Either SAT or ACT required. ACT 25/75 percentile: 21-26. High school rank: 37% in top tenth, 55% in top quarter, 84% in top half
Early decision deadline: N/A, notification date: N/A
Early action deadline: N/A, notification date: N/A
Application deadline (fall): rolling
Undergraduate student body: 2,480 full time, 460 part time; 31% male, 69% female; 1% American Indian, 1% Asian, 8% black, 3% Hispanic, 0% multiracial, 0% Pacific Islander, 82% white, 1% international; 81% from in state; 46% live on campus; 0% of students in fraternities, 0% in sororities
Most popular majors: 19% Business, Management, Marketing, and Related Support Services, 19% Education, 15% Health Professions and Related Programs, 10% Visual and Performing Arts, 6% Homeland Security, Law Enforcement, Firefighting and Related Protective Services
Expenses: 2017-2018: $26,920; room/board: $9,680
Financial aid: (864) 231-2181; 72% of undergrads determined to have financial need; average aid package $18,070

Benedict College[1]
Columbia SC
(803) 253-5143
U.S. News ranking: Reg. Coll. (S), second tier
Website: www.benedict.edu
Admissions email: admissions@benedict.edu
Private; founded 1870
Application deadline (fall): rolling
Undergraduate student body: N/A full time, N/A part time
Expenses: 2016-2017: $19,566; room/board: $8,672
Financial aid: N/A

Bob Jones University
Greenville SC
(800) 252-6363
U.S. News ranking: Reg. U. (S), No. 61
Website: www.bju.edu/admission
Admissions email: admission@bju.edu
Private; founded 1927
Affiliation: Evangelical Christian
Freshman admissions: selective; 2016-2017: 1,594 applied, 920 accepted. ACT required. ACT 25/75 percentile: 23-26. High school rank: 13% in top

tenth, 36% in top quarter, 62% in top half
Early decision deadline: N/A, notification date: N/A
Early action deadline: N/A, notification date: N/A
Application deadline (fall): rolling
Undergraduate student body: 2,314 full time, 101 part time; 45% male, 55% female; 0% American Indian, 2% Asian, 2% black, 6% Hispanic, 3% multiracial, 1% Pacific Islander, 78% white, 6% international; 36% from in state; 71% live on campus; N/A of students in fraternities, N/A in sororities
Most popular majors: 7% Business Administration and Management, General, 7% Registered Nursing/Registered Nurse, 5% Accounting, 5% Counseling Psychology, 4% Theological and Ministerial Studies, Other
Expenses: 2017-2018: $16,500; room/board: $111,590
Financial aid: (864) 242-5100; 71% of undergrads determined to have financial need; average aid package $11,412

Charleston Southern University
Charleston SC
(843) 863-7050
U.S. News ranking: Reg. U. (S), No. 89
Website: www.csuniv.edu
Admissions email: enroll@csuniv.edu
Private; founded 1964
Affiliation: Baptist
Freshman admissions: selective; 2016-2017: 4,399 applied, 2,666 accepted. Either SAT or ACT required. ACT 25/75 percentile: 20-24. High school rank: 19% in top tenth, 48% in top quarter, 80% in top half
Early decision deadline: N/A, notification date: N/A
Early action deadline: N/A, notification date: N/A
Application deadline (fall): rolling
Undergraduate student body: 2,896 full time, 308 part time; 38% male, 62% female; 1% American Indian, 2% Asian, 26% black, 4% Hispanic, 3% multiracial, 0% Pacific Islander, 62% white, 1% international
Most popular majors: Information not available
Expenses: 2017-2018: $24,840; room/board: $9,900
Financial aid: (843) 863-7050

The Citadel
Charleston SC
(843) 953-5230
U.S. News ranking: Reg. U. (S), No. 4
Website: www.citadel.edu
Admissions email: admissions@citadel.edu
Public; founded 1842
Affiliation: Other
Freshman admissions: selective; 2016-2017: 2,620 applied, 2,156 accepted. Either SAT or ACT required. ACT 25/75 percentile: 20-25. High school rank: 9% in top tenth, 30% in top quarter, 65% in top half
Early decision deadline: N/A, notification date: N/A

Early action deadline: N/A, notification date: N/A
Application deadline (fall): rolling
Undergraduate student body: 2,504 full time, 269 part time; 89% male, 11% female; 1% American Indian, 2% Asian, 9% black, 7% Hispanic, 4% multiracial, 0% Pacific Islander, 76% white, 1% international; 65% from in state; 100% live on campus; 0% of students in fraternities, 0% in sororities
Most popular majors: 29% Business Administration and Management, General, 19% Engineering, General, 17% Criminal Justice/Law Enforcement Administration, 10% Social Sciences, General, 6% Kinesiology and Exercise Science
Expenses: 2017-2018: $12,056 in state, $33,819 out of state; room/board: $6,600
Financial aid: (843) 953-5187; 57% of undergrads determined to have financial need; average aid package $16,428

Claflin University
Orangeburg SC
(803) 535-5340
U.S. News ranking: Nat. Lib. Arts, second tier
Website: www.claflin.edu
Admissions email: admissions@claflin.edu
Private; founded 1869
Freshman admissions: less selective; 2016-2017: 9,387 applied, 3,926 accepted. Either SAT or ACT required. SAT 25/75 percentile: 830-950. High school rank: 17% in top tenth, 30% in top quarter, 51% in top half
Early decision deadline: N/A, notification date: N/A
Early action deadline: N/A, notification date: N/A
Application deadline (fall): 8/1
Undergraduate student body: 1,873 full time, 32 part time; 35% male, 65% female; 1% American Indian, 1% Asian, 91% black, 2% Hispanic, 0% multiracial, 0% Pacific Islander, 2% white, 2% international
Most popular majors: 20% Criminal Justice/Law Enforcement Administration, 12% Business Administration and Management, General, 8% Mass Communication/Media Studies, 7% Biology/Biological Sciences, General, 6% Psychology, General
Expenses: 2016-2017: $16,098; room/board: $11,116
Financial aid: (803) 535-5720

Clemson University
Clemson SC
(864) 656-2287
U.S. News ranking: Nat. U., No. 67
Website: www.clemson.edu
Admissions email: cuadmissions@clemson.edu
Public; founded 1889
Freshman admissions: more selective; 2016-2017: 23,506 applied, 11,881 accepted. Either SAT or ACT required. ACT 25/75 percentile: 26-31. High school rank: 57% in top tenth, 88% in top quarter, 98% in top half
Early decision deadline: N/A, notification date: N/A

Early action deadline: N/A, notification date: N/A
Application deadline (fall): 5/1
Undergraduate student body: 17,883 full time, 716 part time; 52% male, 48% female; 0% American Indian, 2% Asian, 7% black, 4% Hispanic, 3% multiracial, 0% Pacific Islander, 83% white, 1% international
Most popular majors: 20% Business, Management, Marketing, and Related Support Services, 18% Engineering, 9% Biological and Biomedical Sciences, 7% Agriculture, Agriculture Operations, and Related Sciences, 7% Health Professions and Related Programs
Expenses: 2017-2018: $14,712 in state, $35,654 out of state; room/board: $9,592
Financial aid: (864) 656-2280; 46% of undergrads determined to have financial need; average aid package $11,511

Coastal Carolina University
Conway SC
(843) 349-2170
U.S. News ranking: Reg. U. (S), No. 52
Website: www.coastal.edu
Admissions email: admissions@coastal.edu
Public; founded 1954
Freshman admissions: selective; 2016-2017: 17,768 applied, 10,871 accepted. Either SAT or ACT required. ACT 25/75 percentile: 20-25. High school rank: 9% in top tenth, 33% in top quarter, 69% in top half
Early decision deadline: N/A, notification date: N/A
Early action deadline: N/A, notification date: N/A
Application deadline (fall): 8/1
Undergraduate student body: 8,864 full time, 883 part time; 47% male, 53% female; 0% American Indian, 1% Asian, 20% black, 4% Hispanic, 5% multiracial, 0% Pacific Islander, 67% white, 1% international; 50% from in state; 42% live on campus; 3% of students in fraternities, 5% in sororities
Most popular majors: 8% Business Administration and Management, General, 8% Kinesiology and Exercise Science, 8% Marine Biology and Biological Oceanography, 8% Speech Communication and Rhetoric, 6% Psychology, General
Expenses: 2017-2018: $11,200 in state, $25,872 out of state; room/board: $9,140
Financial aid: (843) 349-2313; 70% of undergrads determined to have financial need; average aid package $10,225

Coker College
Hartsville SC
(843) 383-8050
U.S. News ranking: Reg. Coll. (S), No. 8
Website: www.coker.edu
Admissions email: admissions@coker.edu
Private; founded 1908
Freshman admissions: less selective; 2016-2017: 1,495 applied, 877 accepted. Either SAT or ACT required. ACT 25/75

percentile: 18-22. High school rank: 8% in top tenth, 30% in top quarter, 60% in top half
Early decision deadline: N/A, notification date: N/A
Early action deadline: N/A, notification date: N/A
Application deadline (fall): 8/1
Undergraduate student body: 953 full time, 196 part time; 40% male, 60% female; 1% American Indian, 0% Asian, 30% black, 3% Hispanic, 5% multiracial, 0% Pacific Islander, 56% white, 3% international
Most popular majors: 25% Business/Commerce, General, 10% Health and Physical Education/Fitness, General, 10% Psychology, General, 9% Sociology, 5% Criminology
Expenses: 2016-2017: $27,624; room/board: $8,568
Financial aid: (843) 383-8050

College of Charleston
Charleston SC
(843) 953-5670
U.S. News ranking: Reg. U. (S), No. 12
Website: www.cofc.edu
Admissions email: admissions@cofc.edu
Public; founded 1770
Freshman admissions: selective; 2016-2017: 10,828 applied, 9,110 accepted. Either SAT or ACT required. ACT 25/75 percentile: 22-27. High school rank: 20% in top tenth, 52% in top quarter, 87% in top half
Early decision deadline: N/A, notification date: N/A
Early action deadline: 11/1, notification date: 1/1
Application deadline (fall): 4/1
Undergraduate student body: 9,524 full time, 851 part time; 37% male, 63% female; 0% American Indian, 2% Asian, 8% black, 3% Hispanic, 4% multiracial, 0% Pacific Islander, 79% white, 1% international; 67% from in state; 32% live on campus; 18% of students in fraternities, 32% in sororities
Most popular majors: 25% Business, Management, Marketing, and Related Support Services, 12% Biological and Biomedical Sciences, 10% Visual and Performing Arts, 9% Social Sciences, 6% Education
Expenses: 2017-2018: $12,318 in state, $30,706 out of state; room/board: $12,048
Financial aid: (843) 953-5540; 51% of undergrads determined to have financial need; average aid package $13,505

Columbia College
Columbia SC
(800) 277-1301
U.S. News ranking: Reg. U. (S), No. 57
Website: www.columbiasc.edu
Admissions email: admissions@columbiasc.edu
Private; founded 1854
Affiliation: United Methodist
Freshman admissions: selective; 2016-2017: 526 applied, 458 accepted. Either SAT or ACT required. ACT 25/75 percentile: 18-24. High school rank: 23%

in top tenth, 48% in top quarter, 85% in top half
Early decision deadline: N/A, notification date: N/A
Early action deadline: N/A, notification date: N/A
Application deadline (fall): rolling
Undergraduate student body: 1,032 full time, 424 part time; 27% male, 73% female; 1% American Indian, 1% Asian, 33% black, 4% Hispanic, 3% multiracial, 0% Pacific Islander, 55% white, 2% international; 91% from in state; 26% live on campus; 0% of students in fraternities, 0% in sororities
Most popular majors: 14% Social Work, 10% Speech Communication and Rhetoric, 9% Psychology, General, 8% Behavioral Sciences, 7% Computer and Information Sciences and Support Services, Other
Expenses: 2016-2017: $28,900; room/board: $7,650
Financial aid: (803) 786-3612

Columbia International University
Columbia SC
(800) 777-2227
U.S. News ranking: Reg. U. (S), No. 32
Website: www.ciu.edu
Admissions email: yesciu@ciu.edu
Private; founded 1923
Affiliation: Multiple Protestant Denomination
Freshman admissions: selective; 2016-2017: 518 applied, 185 accepted. Either SAT or ACT required. SAT 25/75 percentile: 930-1190. High school rank: 17% in top tenth, 34% in top quarter, 62% in top half
Early decision deadline: N/A, notification date: N/A
Early action deadline: N/A, notification date: N/A
Application deadline (fall): 8/1
Undergraduate student body: 454 full time, 43 part time; 52% male, 48% female; 0% American Indian, 2% Asian, 11% black, 4% Hispanic, 2% multiracial, 0% Pacific Islander, 73% white, 5% international; 54% from in state; 74% live on campus; N/A of students in fraternities, N/A in sororities
Most popular majors: 61% Theology and Religious Vocations, 17% Liberal Arts and Sciences, General Studies and Humanities, 6% Multi/Interdisciplinary Studies, 6% Psychology, 4% Communication, Journalism, and Related Programs
Expenses: 2016-2017: $21,490; room/board: $7,760
Financial aid: (803) 807-5036

Converse College
Spartanburg SC
(864) 596-9040
U.S. News ranking: Reg. U. (S), No. 27
Website: www.converse.edu
Admissions email: admissions@converse.edu
Private; founded 1889
Freshman admissions: selective; 2016-2017: 1,359 applied, 821 accepted. Either SAT or ACT

required. ACT 25/75 percentile: 20-26. High school rank: 18% in top tenth, 50% in top quarter, 88% in top half
Early decision deadline: N/A, notification date: N/A
Early action deadline: N/A, notification date: N/A
Application deadline (fall): 8/1
Undergraduate student body: 815 full time, 55 part time; 0% male, 100% female; 0% American Indian, 1% Asian, 9% black, 4% Hispanic, 4% multiracial, 0% Pacific Islander, 67% white, 2% international; 76% from in state; 73% live on campus; N/A of students in fraternities, N/A in sororities
Most popular majors: 24% Psychology, 18% Visual and Performing Arts, 12% Business, Management, Marketing, and Related Support Services, 12% Education, 8% Biological and Biomedical Sciences
Expenses: 2017-2018: $18,030; room/board: $10,610
Financial aid: N/A; 82% of undergrads determined to have financial need; average aid package $14,727

Erskine College
Due West SC
(864) 379-8838
U.S. News ranking: Nat. Lib. Arts, second tier
Website: www.erskine.edu
Admissions email: admissions@erskine.edu
Private; founded 1839
Affiliation: Presbyterian
Freshman admissions: selective; 2016-2017: 982 applied, 670 accepted. Either SAT or ACT required. SAT 25/75 percentile: 890-1115. High school rank: 18% in top tenth, 30% in top quarter, 73% in top half
Early decision deadline: N/A, notification date: N/A
Early action deadline: N/A, notification date: N/A
Application deadline (fall): rolling
Undergraduate student body: 602 full time, 12 part time; 50% male, 50% female; 1% American Indian, 1% Asian, 11% black, 3% Hispanic, 0% multiracial, 1% Pacific Islander, 83% white, 0% international; 79% from in state; 97% live on campus; 0% of students in fraternities, 0% in sororities
Most popular majors: 19% Business, Management, Marketing, and Related Support Services, 18% Biological and Biomedical Sciences, 10% English Language and Literature/Letters, 8% Parks, Recreation, Leisure, and Fitness Studies, 8% Physical Sciences
Expenses: 2017-2018: $35,245; room/board: $11,350
Financial aid: (864) 379-8832; 100% of undergrads determined to have financial need; average aid package $23,800

Francis Marion University
Florence SC
(843) 661-1231
U.S. News ranking: Reg. U. (S), No. 89
Website: www.fmarion.edu

Admissions email: admissions@fmarion.edu
Public; founded 1970
Freshman admissions: less selective; 2016-2017: 3,738 applied, 2,301 accepted. Either SAT or ACT required. ACT 25/75 percentile: 17-22. High school rank: 15% in top tenth, 46% in top quarter, 82% in top half
Early decision deadline: N/A, notification date: N/A
Early action deadline: N/A, notification date: N/A
Application deadline (fall): 8/15
Undergraduate student body: 3,133 full time, 426 part time; 31% male, 69% female; 0% American Indian, 1% Asian, 44% black, 2% Hispanic, 3% multiracial, 0% Pacific Islander, 48% white, 1% international
Most popular majors: Information not available
Expenses: 2016-2017: $10,428 in state, $20,308 out of state; room/board: $7,716
Financial aid: (843) 661-1190

Furman University
Greenville SC
(864) 294-2034
U.S. News ranking: Nat. Lib. Arts, No. 53
Website: www.furman.edu/
Admissions email: admissions@furman.edu
Private; founded 1826
Freshman admissions: more selective; 2016-2017: 5,232 applied, 3,545 accepted. Neither SAT nor ACT required. SAT 25/75 percentile: 1120-1320. High school rank: 45% in top tenth, 77% in top quarter, 96% in top half
Early decision deadline: 11/1, notification date: 11/15
Early action deadline: 11/1, notification date: 12/20
Application deadline (fall): 1/15
Undergraduate student body: 2,898 full time, 101 part time; 42% male, 58% female; 0% American Indian, 2% Asian, 5% black, 5% Hispanic, 3% multiracial, 0% Pacific Islander, 78% white, 5% international; 28% from in state; 96% live on campus, 32% of students in fraternities, 62% in sororities
Most popular majors: 11% Health Professions and Related Clinical Sciences, Other, 10% Business Administration, Management and Operations, 10% Political Science and Government, 6% Communication and Media Studies, 5% Biology, General
Expenses: 2017-2018: $48,348; room/board: $12,158
Financial aid: (864) 294-2204; 47% of undergrads determined to have financial need; average aid package $39,063

Lander University
Greenwood SC
(864) 388-8307
U.S. News ranking: Reg. Coll. (S), No. 16
Website: www.lander.edu
Admissions email: admissions@lander.edu
Public; founded 1872
Freshman admissions: selective; 2016-2017: 2,884 applied, 1,781 accepted. Either SAT

or ACT required. ACT 25/75 percentile: 17-23. High school rank: 11% in top tenth, 38% in top quarter, 77% in top half
Early decision deadline: N/A, notification date: N/A
Early action deadline: N/A, notification date: N/A
Application deadline (fall): rolling
Undergraduate student body: 2,550 full time, 184 part time; 31% male, 69% female; 0% American Indian, 0% Asian, 29% black, 2% Hispanic, 2% multiracial, 0% Pacific Islander, 59% white, 4% international
Most popular majors: 23% Business Administration and Management, General, 11% Registered Nursing/Registered Nurse, 10% Kinesiology and Exercise Science, 6% Sociology, 5% Early Childhood Education and Teaching
Expenses: 2017-2018: $11,700 in state, $21,300 out of state; room/board: $8,900
Financial aid: (864) 388-8340; 79% of undergrads determined to have financial need; average aid package $11,261

Limestone College
Gaffney SC
(864) 488-4554
U.S. News ranking: Reg. Coll. (S), No. 39
Website: www.limestone.edu
Admissions email: admiss@limestone.edu
Private; founded 1845
Affiliation: Other
Freshman admissions: selective; 2016-2017: 2,699 applied, 1,412 accepted. Either SAT or ACT required. ACT 25/75 percentile: 19-23. High school rank: 4% in top tenth, 19% in top quarter, 50% in top half
Early decision deadline: N/A, notification date: N/A
Early action deadline: N/A, notification date: N/A
Application deadline (fall): 8/22
Undergraduate student body: 1,173 full time, 22 part time; 62% male, 38% female; 0% American Indian, 0% Asian, 32% black, 6% Hispanic, 4% multiracial, 0% Pacific Islander, 50% white, 8% international; 64% from in state; 71% live on campus; 2% of students in fraternities, 3% in sororities
Most popular majors: 63% Business, Management, Marketing, and Related Support Services, Biological and Biomedical Sciences, Liberal Arts and Sciences, General Studies and Humanities, Public Administration and Social Service Professions
Expenses: 2017-2018: $25,150; room/board: N/A
Financial aid: (864) 488-8251; 80% of undergrads determined to have financial need; average aid package $18,909

Morris College[1]
Sumter SC
U.S. News ranking: Reg. Coll. (S), unranked
Website: www.morris.edu
Admissions email: dcalhoun@morris.edu
Private

Application deadline (fall): N/A
Undergraduate student body: N/A full time, N/A part time
Expenses: 2016-2017: $13,045; room/board: $5,455
Financial aid: N/A

Newberry College
Newberry SC
(800) 845-4955
U.S. News ranking: Reg. Coll. (S), No. 17
Website: www.newberry.edu/
Admissions email: admissions@newberry.edu
Private; founded 1856
Affiliation: Lutheran Church in America
Freshman admissions: less selective; 2016-2017: 1,445 applied, 862 accepted. Either SAT or ACT required. ACT 25/75 percentile: 17-23. High school rank: 10% in top tenth, 36% in top quarter, 63% in top half
Early decision deadline: N/A, notification date: N/A
Early action deadline: N/A, notification date: N/A
Application deadline (fall): rolling
Undergraduate student body: 1,052 full time, 18 part time; 54% male, 46% female; 0% American Indian, 1% Asian, 26% black, 4% Hispanic, 3% multiracial, 0% Pacific Islander, 56% white, 4% international; 79% from in state; 82% live on campus; 13% of students in fraternities, 31% in sororities
Most popular majors: 19% Business Administration and Management, General, 19% Education, General, 11% Parks, Recreation and Leisure Studies, 11% Registered Nursing/Registered Nurse, 7% Biology/Biological Sciences, General
Expenses: 2017-2018: $25,900; room/board: $10,142
Financial aid: (803) 321-5127; 87% of undergrads determined to have financial need; average aid package $21,976

North Greenville University
Tigerville SC
(864) 977-7001
U.S. News ranking: Reg. U. (S), No. 80
Website: www.ngu.edu
Admissions email: admissions@ngu.edu
Private; founded 1892
Affiliation: Southern Baptist
Freshman admissions: selective; 2016-2017: 1,617 applied, 956 accepted. Either SAT or ACT required. ACT 25/75 percentile: 20-29. High school rank: 23% in top tenth, 40% in top quarter, 74% in top half
Early decision deadline: N/A, notification date: N/A
Early action deadline: N/A, notification date: N/A
Application deadline (fall): rolling
Undergraduate student body: 2,102 full time, 243 part time; 50% male, 50% female; 0% American Indian, 1% Asian, 8% black, 3% Hispanic, 2% multiracial, 0% Pacific Islander, 79% white, 0% international; 70% from in state; 66% live on campus; 0% of students in fraternities, 0% in sororities

Most popular majors: 18% Business Administration and Management, General, 15% Sport and Fitness Administration/Management, 14% Liberal Arts and Sciences/Liberal Studies, 12% Bible/Biblical Studies, 10% Elementary Education and Teaching
Expenses: 2017-2018: $18,750; room/board: $10,240
Financial aid: (864) 977-7057; 57% of undergrads determined to have financial need; average aid package $7,494

Presbyterian College
Clinton SC
(864) 833-8230
U.S. News ranking: Nat. Lib. Arts, No. 123
Website: www.presby.edu
Admissions email: admissions@presby.edu
Private; founded 1880
Affiliation: Presbyterian Church (USA)
Freshman admissions: selective; 2016-2017: 2,636 applied, 1,577 accepted. Neither SAT nor ACT required. ACT 25/75 percentile: 20-27. High school rank: 31% in top tenth, 62% in top quarter, 89% in top half
Early decision deadline: 11/1, notification date: 12/1
Early action deadline: 11/15, notification date: 12/15
Application deadline (fall): 6/30
Undergraduate student body: 997 full time, 66 part time; 46% male, 54% female; 0% American Indian, 1% Asian, 13% black, 3% Hispanic, 3% multiracial, 0% Pacific Islander, 76% white, 3% international; 66% from in state; 99% live on campus; 36% of students in fraternities, 50% in sororities
Most popular majors: 22% Business, Management, Marketing, and Related Support Services, 15% Psychology, 12% Biological and Biomedical Sciences, 11% Social Sciences, 7% English Language and Literature/Letters
Expenses: 2017-2018: $37,842; room/board: $10,298
Financial aid: (864) 833-8287; 74% of undergrads determined to have financial need; average aid package $33,431

South Carolina State University
Orangeburg SC
(803) 536-7185
U.S. News ranking: Reg. U. (S), second tier
Website: www.scsu.edu
Admissions email: admissions@scsu.edu
Public; founded 1896
Freshman admissions: least selective; 2016-2017: 2,847 applied, 2,455 accepted. Either SAT or ACT required. ACT 25/75 percentile: 14-17. High school rank: 8% in top tenth, 25% in top quarter, 36% in top half
Early decision deadline: N/A, notification date: N/A
Early action deadline: N/A, notification date: N/A
Application deadline (fall): 7/31

Undergraduate student body: 2,282 full time, 247 part time; 50% male, 50% female; 0% American Indian, 0% Asian, 96% black, 0% Hispanic, 0% multiracial, 0% Pacific Islander, 3% white, 0% international; 84% from in state; 68% live on campus; 9% of students in fraternities, 14% in sororities
Most popular majors: 10% Biology/Biological Sciences, General, 9% Family and Consumer Sciences/Human Sciences, General, 8% Physical Education Teaching and Coaching, 7% Criminal Justice/Law Enforcement Administration, 7% Mass Communication/Media Studies
Expenses: 2016-2017: $10,420 in state, $20,500 out of state; room/board: $9,000
Financial aid: (803) 536-7067

Southern Wesleyan University[1]
Central SC
(864) 644-5550
U.S. News ranking: Reg. U. (S), second tier
Website: www.swu.edu
Admissions email: admissions@swu.edu
Private
Application deadline (fall): N/A
Undergraduate student body: N/A full time, N/A part time
Expenses: 2016-2017: $24,110; room/board: $8,820
Financial aid: N/A

University of South Carolina
Columbia SC
(803) 777-7700
U.S. News ranking: Nat. U., No. 103
Website: www.sc.edu
Admissions email: admissions-ugrad@sc.edu
Public; founded 1801
Freshman admissions: more selective; 2016-2017: 25,057 applied, 17,073 accepted. Either SAT or ACT required. ACT 25/75 percentile: 25-30. High school rank: 28% in top tenth, 63% in top quarter, 93% in top half
Early decision deadline: N/A, notification date: N/A
Early action deadline: 10/15, notification date: 12/20
Application deadline (fall): 12/1
Undergraduate student body: 23,926 full time, 1,630 part time; 47% male, 53% female; 0% American Indian, 3% Asian, 9% black, 4% Hispanic, 4% multiracial, 0% Pacific Islander, 77% white, 2% international; 52% from in state; 29% live on campus; 20% of students in fraternities, 35% in sororities
Most popular majors: 5% Biology, General, 5% Finance and Financial Management Services, 5% Physiology, Pathology and Related Sciences, 5% Research and Experimental Psychology, 4% Public Relations, Advertising, and Applied Communication
Expenses: 2017-2018: $12,262 in state, $32,362 out of state; room/board: $10,008

Financial aid: (803) 777-8134; 51% of undergrads determined to have financial need; average aid package $9,400

University of South Carolina–Aiken
Aiken SC
(803) 641-3366
U.S. News ranking: Reg. Coll. (S), No. 6
Website: web.usca.edu/
Admissions email: admit@sc.edu
Public; founded 1961
Freshman admissions: selective; 2016-2017: 2,177 applied, 1,447 accepted. Either SAT or ACT required. ACT 25/75 percentile: 18-23. High school rank: 15% in top tenth, 40% in top quarter, 80% in top half
Early decision deadline: N/A, notification date: N/A
Early action deadline: N/A, notification date: N/A
Application deadline (fall): 8/1
Undergraduate student body: 2,834 full time, 540 part time; 36% male, 64% female; 1% American Indian, 1% Asian, 27% black, 4% Hispanic, 4% multiracial, 0% Pacific Islander, 58% white, 4% international; 89% from in state; 27% live on campus; 7% of students in fraternities, 9% in sororities
Most popular majors: 23% Business, Management, Marketing, and Related Support Services, 17% Health Professions and Related Programs, 13% Parks, Recreation, Leisure, and Fitness Studies, 10% Education, 6% Biological and Biomedical Sciences
Expenses: 2017-2018: $10,502 in state, $20,702 out of state; room/board: $7,592
Financial aid: (803) 641-3476; 72% of undergrads determined to have financial need; average aid package $10,964

University of South Carolina–Beaufort
Bluffton SC
(843) 208-8000
U.S. News ranking: Reg. Coll. (S), No. 37
Website: www.uscb.edu
Admissions email: admissions@uscb.edu
Public; founded 1959
Freshman admissions: selective; 2016-2017: 2,148 applied, 1,399 accepted. Either SAT or ACT required. ACT 25/75 percentile: 18-24. High school rank: 9% in top tenth, 31% in top quarter, 67% in top half
Early decision deadline: N/A, notification date: N/A
Early action deadline: N/A, notification date: N/A
Application deadline (fall): 7/1
Undergraduate student body: 1,746 full time, 259 part time; 34% male, 66% female; 0% American Indian, 1% Asian, 22% black, 7% Hispanic, 4% multiracial, 0% Pacific Islander, 58% white, 1% international; 18% from in state; N/A live on campus; N/A of students in fraternities, N/A in sororities

Most popular majors: 23% Business Administration and Management, General, 14% Hospitality Administration/Management, General, 13% Registered Nursing/Registered Nurse, 9% Psychology, General, 9% Social Sciences, General
Expenses: 2016-2017: $10,130 in state, $20,570 out of state; room/board: $8,527
Financial aid: (843) 521-4117

University of South Carolina–Upstate
Spartanburg SC
(864) 503-5246
U.S. News ranking: Reg. Coll. (S), No. 14
Website: www.uscupstate.edu/
Admissions email: admissions@uscupstate.edu
Public; founded 1967
Freshman admissions: selective; 2016-2017: 3,633 applied, 2,027 accepted. Either SAT or ACT required. ACT 25/75 percentile: 18-22. High school rank: 10% in top tenth, 37% in top quarter, 74% in top half
Early decision deadline: N/A, notification date: N/A
Early action deadline: N/A, notification date: N/A
Application deadline (fall): rolling
Undergraduate student body: 4,197 full time, 1,397 part time; 35% male, 65% female; 0% American Indian, 3% Asian, 30% black, 5% Hispanic, 3% multiracial, 0% Pacific Islander, 55% white, 1% international; 96% from in state; 16% live on campus; 2% of students in fraternities, 4% in sororities
Most popular majors: 26% Registered Nursing/Registered Nurse, 14% Business Administration and Management, General, 8% Criminal Justice/Law Enforcement Administration, 8% Liberal Arts and Sciences/Liberal Studies, 6% Psychology, General
Expenses: 2016-2017: $10,818 in state, $21,468 out of state; room/board: $7,848
Financial aid: (864) 503-5340; 74% of undergrads determined to have financial need; average aid package $9,598

Voorhees College[1]
Denmark SC
(803) 780-1030
U.S. News ranking: Reg. Coll. (S), second tier
Website: www.voorhees.edu
Admissions email: admissions@voorhees.edu
Private
Application deadline (fall): N/A
Undergraduate student body: N/A full time, N/A part time
Expenses: 2016-2017: $12,630; room/board: $7,346
Financial aid: N/A

Winthrop University
Rock Hill SC
(803) 323-2191
U.S. News ranking: Reg. U. (S), No. 25
Website: www.winthrop.edu
Admissions email: admissions@winthrop.edu
Public; founded 1886
Affiliation: Other
Freshman admissions: selective; 2016-2017: 4,940 applied, 3,384 accepted. Either SAT or ACT required. ACT 25/75 percentile: 20-25. High school rank: 22% in top tenth, 51% in top quarter, 83% in top half
Early decision deadline: N/A, notification date: N/A
Early action deadline: N/A, notification date: N/A
Application deadline (fall): rolling
Undergraduate student body: 4,545 full time, 546 part time; 31% male, 69% female; 0% American Indian, 1% Asian, 30% black, 5% Hispanic, 4% multiracial, 0% Pacific Islander, 58% white, 2% international; 91% from in state; 47% live on campus; 1% of students in fraternities, 2% in sororities
Most popular majors: 21% Business, Management, Marketing, and Related Support Services, 13% Education, 10% Psychology, 10% Visual and Performing Arts, 7% Biological and Biomedical Sciences
Expenses: 2017-2018: $15,220 in state, $29,136 out of state; room/board: $8,740
Financial aid: (803) 323-2189; 75% of undergrads determined to have financial need; average aid package $13,080

Wofford College
Spartanburg SC
(864) 597-4130
U.S. News ranking: Nat. Lib. Arts, No. 71
Website: www.wofford.edu
Admissions email: admissions@wofford.edu
Private; founded 1854
Freshman admissions: more selective; 2016-2017: 2,937 applied, 2,059 accepted. Either SAT or ACT required. ACT 25/75 percentile: 24-29. High school rank: 43% in top tenth, 74% in top quarter, 94% in top half
Early decision deadline: 11/1, notification date: 12/1
Early action deadline: 11/15, notification date: 12/1
Application deadline (fall): 1/15
Undergraduate student body: 1,582 full time, 40 part time; 49% male, 51% female; 0% American Indian, 2% Asian, 8% black, 4% Hispanic, 3% multiracial, 0% Pacific Islander, 81% white, 2% international; 55% from in state; 93% live on campus; 50% of students in fraternities, 55% in sororities
Most popular majors: 14% Biology/Biological Sciences, General, 10% Finance, General, 8% Business/Managerial Economics, 6% Accounting, 6% English Language and Literature, General
Expenses: 2017-2018: $41,955; room/board: $12,140

Financial aid: (864) 597-4160; 64% of undergrads determined to have financial need; average aid package $34,662

SOUTH DAKOTA

Augustana University
Sioux Falls SD
(605) 274-5516
U.S. News ranking: Reg. Coll. (Mid. W), No. 3
Website: www.augie.edu
Admissions email: admission@augie.edu
Private; founded 1860
Affiliation: Evangelical Lutheran Church
Freshman admissions: more selective; 2016-2017: 1,464 applied, 1,012 accepted. Either SAT or ACT required. ACT 25/75 percentile: 23-29. High school rank: 30% in top tenth, 53% in top quarter, 73% in top half
Early decision deadline: N/A, notification date: N/A
Early action deadline: N/A, notification date: N/A
Application deadline (fall): rolling
Undergraduate student body: 1,574 full time, 91 part time; 41% male, 59% female; 0% American Indian, 1% Asian, 2% black, 3% Hispanic, 2% multiracial, 0% Pacific Islander, 84% white, 8% international; 50% from in state; 71% live on campus; N/A of students in fraternities, N/A in sororities
Most popular majors: 16% Business, Management, Marketing, and Related Support Services, 16% Education, General, 15% Health Professions and Related Programs, 7% Foreign Languages, Literatures, and Linguistics, 6% Parks, Recreation, Leisure, and Fitness Studies
Expenses: 2017-2018: $31,960; room/board: $8,008
Financial aid: (605) 274-5216; 59% of undergrads determined to have financial need; average aid package $25,553

Black Hills State University
Spearfish SD
(800) 255-2478
U.S. News ranking: Reg. U. (Mid. W), second tier
Website: www.bhsu.edu
Admissions email: admissions@bhsu.edu
Public; founded 1883
Freshman admissions: selective; 2016-2017: 1,662 applied, 775 accepted. Either SAT or ACT required. ACT 25/75 percentile: 19-24. High school rank: 2% in top tenth, 9% in top quarter, 34% in top half
Early decision deadline: N/A, notification date: N/A
Early action deadline: N/A, notification date: N/A
Application deadline (fall): N/A
Undergraduate student body: 2,221 full time, 1,591 part time; 37% male, 63% female; 4% American Indian, 1% Asian, 1% black, 5% Hispanic, 5% multiracial, 0% Pacific Islander, 82% white, 1% international

of students in fraternities, N/A in sororities
Most popular majors: 39% Registered Nursing/Registered Nurse, 8% Biology/Biological Sciences, General, 7% Athletic Training/Trainer, 4% Business Administration and Management, General, 4% Criminal Justice/Safety Studies
Expenses: 2017-2018: $27,030; room/board: $6,950
Financial aid: (605) 995-2663; 71% of undergrads determined to have financial need; average aid package $23,293

Mount Marty College
Yankton SD
(800) 658-4552
U.S. News ranking: Reg. U. (Mid. W), No. 115
Website: www.mtmc.edu
Admissions email: mmcadmit@mtmc.edu
Private; founded 1936
Freshman admissions: selective; 2016-2017: 473 applied, 306 accepted. Either SAT or ACT required. ACT 25/75 percentile: 19-23. High school rank: N/A
Early decision deadline: N/A, notification date: N/A
Early action deadline: N/A, notification date: N/A
Application deadline (fall): 8/30
Undergraduate student body: 468 full time, 538 part time; 41% male, 59% female; 3% American Indian, 1% Asian, 5% black, 7% Hispanic, 1% multiracial, 1% Pacific Islander, 81% white, 0% international; 59% from in state; 64% live on campus; 0% of students in fraternities, 0% in sororities
Most popular majors: 28% Registered Nursing/Registered Nurse, 23% Education, General, 8% Business Administration and Management, General, 6% Criminal Justice/Safety Studies
Expenses: 2017-2018: $26,310; room/board: $7,846
Financial aid: (605) 668-1589; 79% of undergrads determined to have financial need; average aid package $24,755

National American University[1]
Rapid City SD
U.S. News ranking: Reg. Coll. (Mid. W), unranked
Website: www.national.edu/rc
Admissions email: N/A
For-profit
Application deadline (fall): N/A
Undergraduate student body: N/A full time, N/A part time
Expenses: 2016-2017: $13,989; room/board: N/A
Financial aid: N/A

Northern State University
Aberdeen SD
(800) 678-5330
U.S. News ranking: Reg. U. (Mid. W), No. 99
Website: www.northern.edu
Admissions email: admissions@northern.edu
Public; founded 1901

Freshman admissions: selective; 2016-2017: 959 applied, 854 accepted. Either SAT or ACT required. ACT 25/75 percentile: 19-24. High school rank: 9% in top tenth, 28% in top quarter, 56% in top half
Early decision deadline: N/A, notification date: N/A
Early action deadline: N/A, notification date: N/A
Application deadline (fall): rolling
Undergraduate student body: 1,402 full time, 1,673 part time; 43% male, 57% female; 3% American Indian, 1% Asian, 2% black, 3% Hispanic, 3% multiracial, 0% Pacific Islander, 81% white, 7% international; 71% from in state; 32% live on campus; 0% of students in fraternities, 0% in sororities
Most popular majors: 24% Business, Management, Marketing, and Related Support Services, 21% Education, 11% Biological and Biomedical Sciences, 8% Psychology, 8% Social Sciences
Expenses: 2017-2018: $8,280 in state, $11,209 out of state; room/board: $7,844
Financial aid: (605) 626-2640; 61% of undergrads determined to have financial need; average aid package $10,672

South Dakota School of Mines and Technology
Rapid City SD
(605) 394-2414
U.S. News ranking: Engineering, unranked
Website: www.sdsmt.edu
Admissions email: admissions@sdsmt.edu
Public; founded 1885
Freshman admissions: more selective; 2016-2017: 1,368 applied, 1,166 accepted. Either SAT or ACT required. ACT 25/75 percentile: 24-29. High school rank: 24% in top tenth, 56% in top quarter, 86% in top half
Early decision deadline: N/A, notification date: N/A
Early action deadline: N/A, notification date: N/A
Application deadline (fall): rolling
Undergraduate student body: 2,018 full time, 467 part time; 78% male, 22% female; 2% American Indian, 1% Asian, 2% black, 5% Hispanic, 3% multiracial, 0% Pacific Islander, 84% white, 3% international; 47% from in state; 40% live on campus; 12% of students in fraternities, 22% in sororities
Most popular majors: 25% Mechanical Engineering, 10% Civil Engineering, 9% Chemical Engineering, 9% Computer and Information Sciences, General, 8% Mining and Mineral Engineering
Expenses: 2017-2018: $10,400 in state, $14,580 out of state; room/board: $8,170
Financial aid: (605) 394-2274; 54% of undergrads determined to have financial need; average aid package $14,262

South Dakota State University
Brookings SD
(800) 952-3541
U.S. News ranking: Nat. U., No. 216
Website: www.sdstate.edu
Admissions email: SDSU_Admissions@sdstate.edu
Public; founded 1881
Freshman admissions: selective; 2016-2017: 5,173 applied, 4,695 accepted. Either SAT or ACT required. ACT 25/75 percentile: 20-26. High school rank: 14% in top tenth, 37% in top quarter, 69% in top half
Early decision deadline: N/A, notification date: N/A
Early action deadline: N/A, notification date: N/A
Application deadline (fall): rolling
Undergraduate student body: 8,474 full time, 2,485 part time; 47% male, 53% female; 1% American Indian, 1% Asian, 2% black, 2% Hispanic, 2% multiracial, 0% Pacific Islander, 87% white, 4% international; 56% from in state; 42% live on campus; N/A of students in fraternities, N/A in sororities
Most popular majors: Information not available
Expenses: 2016-2017: $8,172 in state, $11,403 out of state; room/board: $7,744
Financial aid: (605) 688-4695

University of Sioux Falls
Sioux Falls SD
(605) 331-6600
U.S. News ranking: Reg. U. (Mid. W), No. 75
Website: www.usiouxfalls.edu
Admissions email: admissions@usiouxfalls.edu
Private; founded 1883
Freshman admissions: selective; 2016-2017: 1,740 applied, 1,592 accepted. Either SAT or ACT required. ACT 25/75 percentile: 15% in top tenth, 43% in top quarter, 72% in top half
Early decision deadline: N/A, notification date: N/A
Early action deadline: N/A, notification date: N/A
Application deadline (fall): rolling
Undergraduate student body: 1,033 full time, 224 part time; 40% male, 60% female; 1% American Indian, 1% Asian, 5% black, 0% Hispanic, 3% multiracial, 0% Pacific Islander, 87% white, 1% international; 62% from in state; 54% live on campus; N/A of students in fraternities, N/A in sororities
Most popular majors: 29% Business, Management, Marketing, and Related Support Services, 28% Health Professions and Related Programs, 8% Parks, Recreation, Leisure, and Fitness Studies, 6% Education, 6% Psychology
Expenses: 2017-2018: $27,980; room/board: $7,350
Financial aid: (605) 331-6623; 72% of undergrads determined to have financial need; average aid package $20,557

Most popular majors: Information not available
Expenses: 2017-2018: $8,004 in state, $10,920 out of state; room/board: $6,695
Financial aid: (605) 642-6145

Dakota State University
Madison SD
(888) 378-9988
U.S. News ranking: Reg. U. (Mid. W), No. 118
Website: www.dsu.edu
Admissions email: admissions@dsu.edu
Public; founded 1881
Freshman admissions: selective; 2016-2017: 920 applied, 761 accepted. Either SAT or ACT required. ACT 25/75 percentile: 19-25. High school rank: 7% in top tenth, 25% in top quarter, 55% in top half
Early decision deadline: N/A, notification date: N/A
Early action deadline: N/A, notification date: N/A
Application deadline (fall): rolling
Undergraduate student body: 1,293 full time, 1,551 part time; 56% male, 44% female; 1% American Indian, 2% Asian, 4% black, 4% Hispanic, 4% multiracial, 0% Pacific Islander, 83% white, 1% international; 68% from in state; 31% live on campus; 0% of students in fraternities, 0% in sororities
Most popular majors: 42% Computer and Information Sciences and Support Services, 18% Education, 12% Business, Management, Marketing, and Related Support Services, 7% Health Professions and Related Programs, 5% Biological and Biomedical Sciences
Expenses: 2017-2018: $9,147 in state, $12,077 out of state; room/board: $6,720
Financial aid: (605) 256-5152; 70% of undergrads determined to have financial need; average aid package $7,954

Dakota Wesleyan University
Mitchell SD
(800) 333-8506
U.S. News ranking: Reg. Coll. (Mid. W), No. 30
Website: www.dwu.edu
Admissions email: admissions@dwu.edu
Private; founded 1885
Affiliation: United Methodist
Freshman admissions: selective; 2016-2017: 655 applied, 476 accepted. Either SAT or ACT required. ACT 25/75 percentile: 19-24. High school rank: 12% in top tenth, 30% in top quarter, 68% in top half
Early decision deadline: N/A, notification date: N/A
Early action deadline: N/A, notification date: N/A
Application deadline (fall): rolling
Undergraduate student body: 669 full time, 210 part time; 42% male, 58% female; 1% American Indian, 1% Asian, 1% black, 3% Hispanic, 4% multiracial, 0% Pacific Islander, 89% white, 2% international; 74% from in state; N/A live on campus; N/A

University of South Dakota

Vermillion SD
(605) 658-6200
U.S. News ranking: Nat. U.,
No. 223
Website: www.usd.edu
Admissions email:
admissions@usd.edu
Public; founded 1862
Freshman admissions: selective;
2016-2017: 3,607 applied,
3,179 accepted. Either SAT
or ACT required. ACT 25/75
percentile: 19-25. High school
rank: 1% in top tenth, 5% in top
quarter, 25% in top half
Early decision deadline: N/A,
notification date: N/A
Early action deadline: N/A,
notification date: N/A
Application deadline (fall): rolling
Undergraduate student body: 4,943
full time, 2,557 part time; 38%
male, 62% female; 2% American
Indian, 1% Asian, 3% black, 4%
Hispanic, 3% multiracial, 0%
Pacific Islander, 84% white, 2%
international; 66% from in state;
27% live on campus; 11% of
students in fraternities, 10% in
sororities
Most popular majors: 37% Health
Professions and Related Programs,
12% Business, Management,
Marketing, and Related Support
Services, 9% Education, 6%
Biological and Biomedical
Sciences, 6% Psychology
Expenses: 2016-2017: $8,457 in
state, $11,688 out of state; room/
board: $7,535
Financial aid: (605) 677-5446

TENNESSEE

Austin Peay State University

Clarksville TN
(931) 221-7661
U.S. News ranking: Reg. U. (S),
No. 73
Website: www.apsu.edu
Admissions email:
admissions@apsu.edu
Public; founded 1927
Freshman admissions: selective;
2016-2017: 6,272 applied,
5,569 accepted. Neither SAT
nor ACT required. ACT 25/75
percentile: 19-24. High school
rank: 14% in top tenth, 37% in
top quarter, 71% in top half
Early decision deadline: N/A,
notification date: N/A
Early action deadline: N/A,
notification date: N/A
Application deadline (fall): 8/9
Undergraduate student body: 6,956
full time, 2,557 part time; 42%
male, 58% female; 0% American
Indian, 2% Asian, 21% black,
7% Hispanic, 6% multiracial,
0% Pacific Islander, 61% white,
0% international; 90% from in
state; 17% live on campus; 7%
of students in fraternities, 8% in
sororities
Most popular majors: 13%
Business, Management,
Marketing, and Related Support
Services, 13% Health Professions
and Related Programs, 13%
Parks, Recreation, Leisure, and
Fitness Studies, 7% Homeland
Security, Law Enforcement,
Firefighting and Related Protective

Services, 6% Computer and
Information Sciences and Support
Services
Expenses: 2017-2018: $8,225 in
state, $25,750 out of state; room/
board: $9,170
Financial aid: (931) 221-7907;
82% of undergrads determined to
have financial need; average aid
package $10,840

Belmont University

Nashville TN
(615) 460-6785
U.S. News ranking: Reg. U. (S),
No. 5
Website: www.Belmont.edu
Admissions email: buadmission@
belmont.edu
Private; founded 1890
Affiliation: Interdenominational
Freshman admissions: more
selective; 2016-2017: 7,263
applied, 5,886 accepted. Either
SAT or ACT required. ACT 25/75
percentile: 24-29. High school
rank: 29% in top tenth, 60% in
top quarter, 88% in top half
Early decision deadline: N/A,
notification date: N/A
Early action deadline: N/A,
notification date: N/A
Application deadline (fall): 8/1
Undergraduate student body: 5,951
full time, 342 part time; 37%
male, 63% female; 0% American
Indian, 2% Asian, 5% black,
5% Hispanic, 4% multiracial,
0% Pacific Islander, 80% white,
1% international; 30% from in
state; 56% live on campus; 8%
of students in fraternities, 15%
in sororities
Most popular majors: 41%
Visual and Performing Arts,
14% Business, Management,
Marketing, and Related Support
Services, 10% Health Professions
and Related Programs, 6%
Communications Technologies/
Technicians and Support Services,
5% Communication, Journalism,
and Related Programs
Expenses: 2017-2018: $32,820;
room/board: $11,680
Financial aid: (615) 460-5721;
51% of undergrads determined to
have financial need; average aid
package $18,276

Bethel University

McKenzie TN
(731) 352-4030
U.S. News ranking: Reg. U. (S),
second tier
Website: www.bethelu.edu
Private; founded 1842
Affiliation: Cumberland
Presbyterian
Freshman admissions: selective;
2016-2017: 1,353 applied, 900
accepted. Neither SAT nor ACT
required. ACT 25/75 percentile:
17-22. High school rank: 7% in
top tenth, 23% in top quarter,
51% in top half
Early decision deadline: N/A,
notification date: N/A
Early action deadline: N/A,
notification date: N/A
Application deadline (fall): rolling
Undergraduate student body: 3,474
full time, 1,355 part time; 42%
male, 58% female; 0% American
Indian, 0% Asian, 40% black,
2% Hispanic, 1% multiracial,

0% Pacific Islander, 52% white,
1% international; 85% from in
state; 19% live on campus; 2%
of students in fraternities, 1% in
sororities
Most popular majors: 46%
Business, Management,
Marketing, and Related Support
Services, 34% Homeland Security,
Law Enforcement, Firefighting and
Related Protective Services, 6%
Health Professions and Related
Programs, 4% Education, 2%
Visual and Performing Arts
Expenses: 2017-2018: $16,552;
room/board: $9,198
Financial aid: (731) 352-6418;
94% of undergrads determined to
have financial need; average aid
package $11,590

Bryan College

Dayton TN
(800) 277-9522
U.S. News ranking: Reg. U. (S),
No. 68
Website: www.bryan.edu
Admissions email:
admissions@bryan.edu
Private; founded 1930
Freshman admissions: selective;
2016-2017: 1,041 applied, 435
accepted. Either SAT or ACT
required. ACT 25/75 percentile:
21-26. High school rank: 21%
in top tenth, 52% in top quarter,
81% in top half
Early decision deadline: N/A,
notification date: N/A
Early action deadline: N/A,
notification date: N/A
Application deadline (fall): rolling
Undergraduate student body: 852
full time, 570 part time; 46%
male, 54% female; 0% American
Indian, 1% Asian, 3% black,
3% Hispanic, 3% multiracial,
0% Pacific Islander, 54% white,
3% international; 35% from in
state; 73% live on campus; 0%
of students in fraternities, 0% in
sororities
Most popular majors: 55%
Business, Management,
Marketing, and Related Support
Services, 9% Education, 9%
Psychology, 7% Theology and
Religious Vocations, 5% Parks,
Recreation, Leisure, and Fitness
Studies
Expenses: 2017-2018: $25,600;
room/board: $7,300
Financial aid: (423) 775-7339;
80% of undergrads determined to
have financial need; average aid
package $23,175

Carson-Newman University

Jefferson City TN
(800) 678-9061
U.S. News ranking: Reg. U. (S),
No. 66
Website: www.cn.edu
Admissions email:
admitme@cn.edu
Private; founded 1851
Freshman admissions: selective;
2016-2017: 6,496 applied,
4,111 accepted. Either SAT
or ACT required. ACT 25/75
percentile: 20-26. High school
rank: N/A
Early decision deadline: N/A,
notification date: N/A

Early action deadline: N/A,
notification date: N/A
Application deadline (fall): rolling
Undergraduate student body: 1,734
full time, 78 part time; 42%
male, 58% female; 1% American
Indian, 1% Asian, 8% black,
3% Hispanic, 2% multiracial,
0% Pacific Islander, 82% white,
3% international; 80% from in
state; 55% live on campus; N/A
of students in fraternities, N/A in
sororities
Most popular majors: 19%
Business, Management,
Marketing, and Related Support
Services, 17% Health Professions
and Related Programs, 14%
Education, 10% Psychology, 6%
Visual and Performing Arts
Expenses: 2017-2018: $27,400;
room/board: $8,630
Financial aid: (865) 471-3247;
84% of undergrads determined to
have financial need; average aid
package $23,872

Christian Brothers University

Memphis TN
(901) 321-3205
U.S. News ranking: Reg. U. (S),
No. 32
Website: www.cbu.edu
Admissions email:
admissions@cbu.edu
Private; founded 1871
Affiliation: Roman Catholic
Freshman admissions: more
selective; 2016-2017: 2,387
applied, 1,247 accepted. Either
SAT or ACT required. ACT 25/75
percentile: 22-27. High school
rank: 32% in top tenth, 63% in
top quarter, 89% in top half
Early decision deadline: N/A,
notification date: N/A
Early action deadline: N/A,
notification date: N/A
Application deadline (fall): rolling
Undergraduate student body: 1,331
full time, 113 part time; 47%
male, 53% female; 0% American
Indian, 6% Asian, 28% black,
8% Hispanic, 3% multiracial,
0% Pacific Islander, 41% white,
5% international; 80% from in
state; 60% live on campus; N/A
of students in fraternities, N/A in
sororities
Most popular majors: 16%
Business Administration
and Management, General,
14% Nursing Practice, 8%
Natural Sciences, 5% Biology/
Biological Sciences, General, 5%
Psychology, General
Expenses: 2017-2018: $31,790;
room/board: $7,200
Financial aid: (901) 321-4415;
70% of undergrads determined to
have financial need; average aid
package $24,503

Cumberland University

Lebanon TN
(615) 444-2562
U.S. News ranking: Reg. U. (S),
No. 106
Website: www.cumberland.edu
Admissions email: admissions@
cumberland.edu
Private; founded 1842

Early action deadline: N/A,
notification date: N/A
Application deadline (fall): rolling
Undergraduate student body: 1,265
full time, 393 part time; 42%
male, 58% female; 1% American
Indian, 1% Asian, 13% black,
3% Hispanic, 0% multiracial, 0%
Pacific Islander, 60% white, 3%
international
Most popular majors: 43%
Registered Nursing/Registered
Nurse, 7% Physical Education
Teaching and Coaching, 4%
Criminal Justice/Law Enforcement
Administration, 3% Psychology,
General
Expenses: 2017-2018: $21,810;
room/board: $8,950
Financial aid: (615) 547-1244;
81% of undergrads determined to
have financial need; average aid
package $16,174

East Tennessee State University

Johnson City TN
(423) 439-4213
U.S. News ranking: Nat. U.,
second tier
Website: www.etsu.edu
Admissions email:
go2etsu@etsu.edu
Public; founded 1911
Freshman admissions: selective;
2016-2017: 6,835 applied,
5,467 accepted. Either SAT
or ACT required. ACT 25/75
percentile: 20-26. High school
rank: 20% in top tenth, 47% in
top quarter, 75% in top half
Early decision deadline: N/A,
notification date: N/A
Early action deadline: N/A,
notification date: N/A
Application deadline (fall): 8/15
Undergraduate student body: 9,371
full time, 1,694 part time; 44%
male, 56% female; 0% American
Indian, 1% Asian, 6% black, 2%
Hispanic, 3% multiracial, 0%
Pacific Islander, 82% white, 4%
international
Most popular majors: 24% Health
Professions and Related Programs,
13% Business, Management,
Marketing, and Related Support
Services, 7% Liberal Arts and
Sciences, General Studies
and Humanities, 7% Parks,
Recreation, Leisure, and Fitness
Studies, 6% Psychology
Expenses: 2017-2018: $8,679 in
state, $26,463 out of state; room/
board: $12,640
Financial aid: (423) 439-4300;
78% of undergrads determined to
have financial need; average aid
package $10,920

Fisk University
Nashville TN
(888) 702-0022
U.S. News ranking: Nat. Lib. Arts, second tier
Website: www.fisk.edu
Admissions email: admissions@fisk.edu
Private; founded 1866
Freshman admissions: selective; 2016-2017: 3,793 applied, 2,976 accepted. Either SAT or ACT required. ACT 25/75 percentile: 17-22. High school rank: 16% in top tenth, 39% in top quarter, 75% in top half
Early decision deadline: N/A, notification date: N/A
Early action deadline: 11/1, notification date: 12/31
Application deadline (fall): rolling
Undergraduate student body: 707 full time, 16 part time; 34% male, 66% female; 0% American Indian, 0% Asian, 83% black, 1% Hispanic, 2% multiracial, 0% Pacific Islander, 1% white, 3% international
Most popular majors: Information not available
Expenses: 2016-2017: $21,480; room/board: $10,790
Financial aid: (615) 329-8585

Freed-Hardeman University
Henderson TN
(731) 348-3481
U.S. News ranking: Reg. U. (S), No. 46
Website: www.fhu.edu
Admissions email: admissions@fhu.edu
Private; founded 1869
Affiliation: Churches of Christ
Freshman admissions: selective; 2016-2017: 791 applied, 762 accepted. Either SAT or ACT required. ACT 25/75 percentile: 21-27. High school rank: 25% in top tenth, 59% in top quarter, 87% in top half
Early decision deadline: N/A, notification date: N/A
Early action deadline: N/A, notification date: N/A
Application deadline (fall): rolling
Undergraduate student body: 1,228 full time, 174 part time; 42% male, 58% female; 0% American Indian, 1% Asian, 4% black, 2% Hispanic, 2% multiracial, 0% Pacific Islander, 80% white, 1% international; 59% from in state; 89% live on campus; 0% of students in fraternities, 0% in sororities
Most popular majors: 14% Business, Management, Marketing, and Related Support Services, 13% Education, 9% Multi/Interdisciplinary Studies, 9% Theology and Religious Vocations, 7% Psychology
Expenses: 2017-2018: $21,950; room/board: $7,950
Financial aid: (731) 989-6662; 78% of undergrads determined to have financial need; average aid package $18,818

King University
Bristol TN
(423) 652-4861
U.S. News ranking: Reg. U. (S), No. 89
Website: www.king.edu
Admissions email: admissions@king.edu
Private; founded 1867
Affiliation: Presbyterian
Freshman admissions: selective; 2016-2017: 1,601 applied, 823 accepted. Neither SAT nor ACT required. ACT 25/75 percentile: 19-24. High school rank: 14% in top tenth, 43% in top quarter, 85% in top half
Early decision deadline: N/A, notification date: N/A
Early action deadline: N/A, notification date: N/A
Application deadline (fall): rolling
Undergraduate student body: 2,120 full time, 223 part time; 37% male, 63% female; 0% American Indian, 1% Asian, 6% black, 3% Hispanic, 2% multiracial, 0% Pacific Islander, 83% white, 3% international; 65% from in state; 44% live on campus; N/A of students in fraternities, N/A in sororities
Most popular majors: 44% Adult Health Nurse/Nursing, 27% Business Administration and Management, General, 7% Psychology, General, 6% Information Technology, 3% Criminal Justice/Law Enforcement Administration
Expenses: 2017-2018: $28,572, room/board: $8,424
Financial aid: (423) 652-4725; 85% of undergrads determined to have financial need; average aid package $14,306

Lane College[1]
Jackson TN
(731) 426 7533
U.S. News ranking: Reg. Coll. (S), second tier
Website: www.lanecollege.edu
Admissions email: admissions@lanecollege.edu
Private; founded 1882
Application deadline (fall): 7/1
Undergraduate student body: N/A full time, N/A part time
Expenses: 2016-2017: $10,280; room/board: $6,770
Financial aid: N/A

LeMoyne-Owen College
Memphis TN
(901) 435-1500
U.S. News ranking: Reg. Coll. (S), second tier
Website: www.loc.edu/
Admissions email: admission@loc.edu
Private; founded 1862
Affiliation: United Church of Christ
Freshman admissions: least selective; 2016-2017: N/A applied, N/A accepted. Either SAT or ACT required. ACT 25/75 percentile: 13-17. High school rank: N/A
Early decision deadline: N/A, notification date: N/A
Early action deadline: N/A, notification date: N/A
Application deadline (fall): 7/1

Undergraduate student body: 847 full time, 112 part time; 33% male, 67% female; 0% American Indian, 0% Asian, 99% black, 0% Hispanic, 0% multiracial, 0% Pacific Islander, 0% white, 1% international
Most popular majors: 23% Business Administration and Management, General, 12% Criminal Justice/Law Enforcement Administration, 10% Biology/Biological Sciences, General, 6% Education, General, 6% Social Work
Expenses: 2016-2017: $10,900; room/board: N/A
Financial aid: (901) 435-1550

Lee University
Cleveland TN
(423) 614-8500
U.S. News ranking: Reg. U. (S), No. 48
Website: www.leeuniversity.edu
Admissions email: admissions@leeuniversity.edu
Private; founded 1918
Affiliation: Church of God
Freshman admissions: selective; 2016-2017: 2,277 applied, 1,986 accepted. Either SAT or ACT required. ACT 25/75 percentile: 21-28. High school rank: 25% in top tenth, 51% in top quarter, 76% in top half
Early decision deadline: N/A, notification date: N/A
Early action deadline: N/A, notification date: N/A
Application deadline (fall): rolling
Undergraduate student body: 3,828 full time, 993 part time; 39% male, 61% female; 0% American Indian, 1% Asian, 6% black, 3% Hispanic, 2% multiracial, 0% Pacific Islander, 80% white, 4% international; 44% from in state; 47% live on campus; 8% of students in fraternities, 8% in sororities
Most popular majors: 20% Theology and Religious Vocations, 15% Education, 11% Business, Management, Marketing, and Related Support Services, 10% Communication, Journalism, and Related Programs, 10% Psychology
Expenses: 2017-2018: $16,730; room/board: $7,210
Financial aid: (423) 614-8300; 68% of undergrads determined to have financial need; average aid package $11,437

Lincoln Memorial University[1]
Harrogate TN
(423) 869-6280
U.S. News ranking: Reg. U. (S), No. 80
Website: www.lmunet.edu
Admissions email: admissions@lmunet.edu
Private; founded 1897
Application deadline (fall): rolling
Undergraduate student body: N/A full time, N/A part time
Expenses: 2016-2017: $21,050; room/board: $7,550
Financial aid: (423) 869-6336

Lipscomb University
Nashville TN
(615) 966-1776
U.S. News ranking: Nat. U., No. 181
Website: www.lipscomb.edu
Admissions email: admissions@lipscomb.edu
Private; founded 1891
Freshman admissions: more selective; 2016-2017: 3,464 applied, 2,108 accepted. Either SAT or ACT required. ACT 25/75 percentile: 22-28. High school rank: 30% in top tenth, 57% in top quarter, 83% in top half
Early decision deadline: N/A, notification date: N/A
Early action deadline: N/A, notification date: N/A
Application deadline (fall): rolling
Undergraduate student body: 2,656 full time, 330 part time; 38% male, 62% female; 0% American Indian, 3% Asian, 7% black, 6% Hispanic, 3% multiracial, 0% Pacific Islander, 76% white, 3% international; 65% from in state; 50% live on campus; 23% of students in fraternities, 24% in sororities
Most popular majors: 23% Business, Management, Marketing, and Related Support Services, 10% Health Professions and Related Programs, 9% Biological and Biomedical Sciences, 8% Education, 7% Psychology
Expenses: 2017-2018: $30,932; room/board: $12,034
Financial aid: (615) 966-6205; 63% of undergrads determined to have financial need; average aid package $24,556

Martin Methodist College[1]
Pulaski TN
U.S. News ranking: Reg. Coll. (S), unranked
Website: www.martinmethodist.edu
Admissions email: admit@martinmethodist.edu
Private
Application deadline (fall): N/A
Undergraduate student body: N/A full time, N/A part time
Expenses: 2016-2017: $23,708; room/board: $8,100
Financial aid: (931) 424-7366

Maryville College
Maryville TN
(865) 981-8092
U.S. News ranking: Nat. Lib. Arts, second tier
Website: www.maryvillecollege.edu
Admissions email: admissions@maryvillecollege.edu
Private; founded 1819
Affiliation: Presbyterian Church (USA)
Freshman admissions: selective; 2016-2017: 2,613 applied, 1,510 accepted. Either SAT or ACT required. ACT 25/75 percentile: 21-27. High school rank: 20% in top tenth, 42% in top quarter, 71% in top half
Early decision deadline: N/A, notification date: N/A
Early action deadline: N/A, notification date: N/A
Application deadline (fall): 5/1

Undergraduate student body: 1,177 full time, 19 part time; 44% male, 56% female; 0% American Indian, 1% Asian, 13% black, 4% Hispanic, 5% multiracial, 0% Pacific Islander, 75% white, 2% international; 68% from in state; 73% live on campus; 0% of students in fraternities, 0% in sororities
Most popular majors: 17% Business, Management, Marketing, and Related Support Services, 12% Psychology, 10% Biological and Biomedical Sciences, 9% Education, 8% Visual and Performing Arts
Expenses: 2017-2018: $34,196; room/board: $11,144
Financial aid: (865) 981-8100; 84% of undergrads determined to have financial need; average aid package $33,152

Memphis College of Art
Memphis TN
(800) 727-1088
U.S. News ranking: Arts, unranked
Website: www.mca.edu
Admissions email: info@mca.edu
Private; founded 1936
Freshman admissions: less selective; 2016-2017: 390 applied, 159 accepted. Either SAT or ACT required. ACT 25/75 percentile: 18-22. High school rank: N/A
Early decision deadline: N/A, notification date: N/A
Early action deadline: N/A, notification date: N/A
Application deadline (fall): rolling
Undergraduate student body: 298 full time, 40 part time; 34% male, 66% female; 1% American Indian, 1% Asian, 33% black, 7% Hispanic, 3% multiracial, 0% Pacific Islander, 54% white, 0% international; 40% from in state; 42% live on campus; 0% of students in fraternities, 0% in sororities
Most popular majors: Design and Visual Communications, General, Fine/Studio Arts, General
Expenses: 2016-2017: $30,980; room/board: $8,600
Financial aid: (901) 272-5138

Middle Tennessee State University
Murfreesboro TN
(615) 898-2233
U.S. News ranking: Nat. U., second tier
Website: www.mtsu.edu
Admissions email: admissions@mtsu.edu
Public; founded 1911
Freshman admissions: selective; 2016-2017: 8,538 applied, 5,858 accepted. Either SAT or ACT required. ACT 25/75 percentile: 19-25. High school rank: N/A
Early decision deadline: N/A, notification date: N/A
Early action deadline: N/A, notification date: N/A
Application deadline (fall): rolling
Undergraduate student body: 16,019 full time, 3,674 part time; 46% male, 54% female; 0% American Indian, 3% Asian,

21% black, 5% Hispanic, 3% multiracial, 0% Pacific Islander, 64% white, 3% international; 92% from in state; 16% live on campus; 5% of students in fraternities, 8% in sororities
Most popular majors: 17% Business, Management, Marketing, and Related Support Services, 12% Liberal Arts and Sciences, General Studies and Humanities, 8% Visual and Performing Arts, 7% Communication, Journalism, and Related Programs, 6% Multi/Interdisciplinary Studies
Expenses: 2017-2018: $8,948 in state, $27,578 out of state; room/board: $9,154
Financial aid: (615) 898-2422; 69% of undergrads determined to have financial need; average aid package $9,576

Milligan College
Milligan College TN
(423) 461-8730
U.S. News ranking: Reg. U. (S), No. 23
Website: www.milligan.edu
Admissions email: admissions@milligan.edu
Private; founded 1866
Affiliation: Christian Churches and Churches of Christ
Freshman admissions: more selective; 2016-2017: 596 applied, 430 accepted. Either SAT or ACT required. ACT 25/75 percentile: 22-27. High school rank: 37% in top tenth, 65% in top quarter, 89% in top half
Early decision deadline: N/A, notification date: N/A
Early action deadline: N/A, notification date: N/A
Application deadline (fall): 8/16
Undergraduate student body: 762 full time, 118 part time; 40% male, 60% female; 0% American Indian, 2% Asian, 3% black, 6% Hispanic, 3% multiracial, 0% Pacific Islander, 82% white, 4% international; 63% from in state; 72% live on campus; N/A of students in fraternities, N/A in sororities
Most popular majors: 21% Business Administration and Management, General, 13% Registered Nursing/Registered Nurse, 9% Health and Physical Education/Fitness, General, 7% Child Development, 6% Psychology, General
Expenses: 2017-2018: $32,500; room/board: $6,950
Financial aid: (423) 461-8968; 83% of undergrads determined to have financial need; average aid package $23,410

Rhodes College
Memphis TN
(800) 844-5969
U.S. News ranking: Nat. Lib. Arts, No. 51
Website: www.rhodes.edu
Admissions email: adminfo@rhodes.edu
Private; founded 1848
Affiliation: Presbyterian
Freshman admissions: more selective; 2016-2017: 4,481 applied, 2,434 accepted. Either

SAT or ACT required. ACT 25/75 percentile: 27-31. High school rank: 48% in top tenth, 79% in top quarter, 94% in top half
Early decision deadline: 11/1, notification date: N/A
Early action deadline: 11/15, notification date: 1/15
Application deadline (fall): 1/15
Undergraduate student body: 1,984 full time, 15 part time; 44% male, 56% female; 0% American Indian, 6% Asian, 8% black, 5% Hispanic, 4% multiracial, 0% Pacific Islander, 72% white, 3% international; 27% from in state; 70% live on campus; 32% of students in fraternities, 45% in sororities
Most popular majors: 25% Social Sciences, 18% Biological and Biomedical Sciences, 15% Business, Management, Marketing, and Related Support Services, 6% English Language and Literature/Letters, 5% Physical Sciences
Expenses: 2017-2018: $46,504; room/board: $11,358
Financial aid: (901) 843-3810; 36% of undergrads determined to have financial need; average aid package $37,616

Sewanee–University of the South
Sewanee TN
(800) 522-2234
U.S. News ranking: Nat. Lib. Arts, No. 41
Website: www.sewanee.edu
Admissions email: admiss@sewanee.edu
Private; founded 1857
Affiliation: Protestant Episcopal
Freshman admissions: more selective; 2016-2017: 4,423 applied, 1,930 accepted. Neither SAT nor ACT required. ACT 25/75 percentile: 27-31. High school rank: 33% in top tenth, 63% in top quarter, 91% in top half
Early decision deadline: 11/15, notification date: 12/15
Early action deadline: 12/1, notification date: 2/15
Application deadline (fall): 2/1
Undergraduate student body: 1,718 full time, 13 part time; 47% male, 53% female; 0% American Indian, 2% Asian, 4% black, 6% Hispanic, 3% multiracial, 0% Pacific Islander, 82% white, 3% international; 21% from in state; 98% live on campus; 70% of students in fraternities, 80% in sororities
Most popular majors: 18% Economics, General, 12% English Language and Literature, General, 11% Psychology, General, 10% International/Global Studies, 8% History, General
Expenses: 2017-2018: $45,120; room/board: $12,880
Financial aid: (931) 598-1312; 47% of undergrads determined to have financial need; average aid package $33,055

South College[1]
Knoxville TN
U.S. News ranking: Reg. U. (S), unranked
Website: www.southcollegetn.edu/
Admissions email: N/A
For-profit
Application deadline (fall): N/A
Undergraduate student body: N/A full time, N/A part time
Expenses: 2016-2017: $18,375; room/board: N/A
Financial aid: N/A

Southern Adventist University
Collegedale TN
(423) 236-2835
U.S. News ranking: Reg. U. (S), No. 68
Website: www.southern.edu
Admissions email: admissions@southern.edu
Private; founded 1892
Affiliation: Seventh Day Adventist
Freshman admissions: selective; 2016-2017: 2,801 applied, 1,686 accepted. Either SAT or ACT required. ACT 25/75 percentile: 20-26. High school rank: N/A
Early decision deadline: N/A, notification date: N/A
Early action deadline: N/A, notification date: N/A
Application deadline (fall): rolling
Undergraduate student body: 2,113 full time, 431 part time; 42% male, 58% female; 0% American Indian, 10% Asian, 11% black, 22% Hispanic, 5% multiracial, 1% Pacific Islander, 46% white, 4% international
Most popular majors: 20% Registered Nursing/Registered Nurse, 11% Theology/Theological Studies, 8% Biology/Biological Sciences, General, 5% Psychology, General, 4% Elementary Education and Teaching
Expenses: 2017-2018: $21,550; room/board: $6,750
Financial aid: (423) 236-2535; 68% of undergrads determined to have financial need; average aid package $16,232

Tennessee State University
Nashville TN
(615) 963-5101
U.S. News ranking: Nat. U., second tier
Website: www.tnstate.edu
Admissions email: jcade@tnstate.edu
Public; founded 1912
Freshman admissions: less selective; 2016-2017: 8,857 applied, 4,710 accepted. Either SAT or ACT required. ACT 25/75 percentile: 16-20. High school rank: N/A
Early decision deadline: N/A, notification date: N/A
Early action deadline: N/A, notification date: N/A
Application deadline (fall): 7/1
Undergraduate student body: 5,692 full time, 1,315 part time; 41% male, 59% female; 0% American Indian, 1% Asian, 72% black, 1% Hispanic, 2% multiracial, 0% Pacific Islander, 12% white, 11% international

Most popular majors: Information not available
Expenses: 2017-2018: $7,458 in state, $20,178 out of state; room/board: $5,580
Financial aid: (615) 963-5701; 83% of undergrads determined to have financial need; average aid package $11,243

Tennessee Technological University
Cookeville TN
(800) 255-8881
U.S. News ranking: Nat. U., second tier
Website: www.tntech.edu
Admissions email: admissions@tntech.edu
Public; founded 1915
Freshman admissions: more selective; 2016-2017: 5,940 applied, 3,992 accepted. Either SAT or ACT required. ACT 25/75 percentile: 21-27. High school rank: 32% in top tenth, 63% in top quarter, 86% in top half
Early decision deadline: N/A, notification date: N/A
Early action deadline: N/A, notification date: N/A
Application deadline (fall): rolling
Undergraduate student body: 8,440 full time, 997 part time; 55% male, 45% female; 0% American Indian, 2% Asian, 4% black, 3% Hispanic, 3% multiracial, 0% Pacific Islander, 82% white, 5% international; 97% from in state; 24% live on campus; 10% of students in fraternities, 13% in sororities
Most popular majors: 10% Teacher Education, Multiple Levels, 7% Liberal Arts and Sciences/Liberal Studies, 7% Mechanical Engineering, 6% Health and Physical Education/Fitness, General, 6% Registered Nursing/Registered Nurse
Expenses: 2017-2018: $8,700 in state, $26,190 out of state; room/board: $9,400
Financial aid: (931) 372-3073; 70% of undergrads determined to have financial need; average aid package $9,915

Tennessee Wesleyan University
Athens TN
(423) 746-5286
U.S. News ranking: Reg. Coll. (S), No. 15
Website: www.tnwesleyan.edu
Admissions email: admissions@tnwesleyan.edu
Private; founded 1857
Affiliation: United Methodist
Freshman admissions: selective; 2016-2017: 988 applied, 570 accepted. Either SAT or ACT required. ACT 25/75 percentile: 19-25. High school rank: 16% in top tenth, 48% in top quarter, 77% in top half
Early decision deadline: N/A, notification date: N/A
Early action deadline: N/A, notification date: N/A
Application deadline (fall): rolling
Undergraduate student body: 911 full time, 104 part time; 37% male, 63% female; 0% American Indian, 0% Asian, 4% black,

1% Hispanic, 2% multiracial, 0% Pacific Islander, 50% white, 0% international; 87% from in state; 35% live on campus; 6% of students in fraternities, 9% in sororities
Most popular majors: 37% Business, Management, Marketing, and Related Support Services, 32% Health Professions and Related Programs, 7% Parks, Recreation, Leisure, and Fitness Studies, 6% Multi/Interdisciplinary Studies, 4% Homeland Security, Law Enforcement, Firefighting and Related Protective Services
Expenses: 2017-2018: $23,800; room/board: $7,750
Financial aid: (423) 746-5209; 85% of undergrads determined to have financial need; average aid package $18,069

Trevecca Nazarene University
Nashville TN
(615) 248-1320
U.S. News ranking: Nat. U., second tier
Website: www.trevecca.edu
Admissions email: admissions_und@trevecca.edu
Private; founded 1901
Affiliation: Church of the Nazarene
Freshman admissions: selective; 2016-2017: 1,417 applied, 1,024 accepted. Either SAT or ACT required. ACT 25/75 percentile: 19-25. High school rank: N/A
Early decision deadline: N/A, notification date: N/A
Early action deadline: N/A, notification date: N/A
Application deadline (fall): 8/1
Undergraduate student body: 1,251 full time, 841 part time; 40% male, 60% female; 0% American Indian, 1% Asian, 13% black, 13% Hispanic, 2% multiracial, 0% Pacific Islander, 67% white, 2% international; 67% from in state; 41% live on campus; N/A of students in fraternities, N/A in sororities
Most popular majors: 44% Business, Management, Marketing, and Related Support Services, 9% Health Professions and Related Programs, 8% Theology and Religious Vocations, 7% Visual and Performing Arts, 5% Psychology
Expenses: 2017-2018: $25,100; room/board: $8,808
Financial aid: (615) 248-1242

Tusculum College
Greeneville TN
(800) 729-0256
U.S. News ranking: Reg. U. (S), No. 95
Website: www.tusculum.edu
Admissions email: admissions@tusculum.edu
Private; founded 1794
Affiliation: Presbyterian
Freshman admissions: selective; 2016-2017: 2,238 applied, 1,665 accepted. Either SAT or ACT required. ACT 25/75 percentile: 18-23. High school rank: N/A
Early decision deadline: N/A, notification date: N/A

Early action deadline: N/A, notification date: N/A
Application deadline (fall): rolling
Undergraduate student body: 1,417 full time, 168 part time; 47% male, 53% female; 0% American Indian, 0% Asian, 15% black, 3% Hispanic, 2% multiracial, 0% Pacific Islander, 72% white, 4% international; 73% from in state; 50% live on campus; N/A of students in fraternities, N/A in sororities
Most popular majors: 47% Business Administration and Management, General, 12% Psychology, General, 11% Education, General, 7% Registered Nursing/Registered Nurse, 5% Sport and Fitness Administration/Management
Expenses: 2017-2018: $23,700; room/board: $8,700
Financial aid: (423) 636-5377; 84% of undergrads determined to have financial need; average aid package $17,079

Union University
Jackson TN
(800) 338-6466
U.S. News ranking: Nat. U., No. 176
Website: www.uu.edu
Admissions email: admissions@uu.edu
Private; founded 1823
Affiliation: Southern Baptist
Freshman admissions: more selective; 2016-2017: 2,012 applied, 1,259 accepted. Either SAT or ACT required. ACT 25/75 percentile: 23-30. High school rank: 32% in top tenth, 64% in top quarter, 89% in top half
Early decision deadline: N/A, notification date: N/A
Early action deadline: N/A, notification date: N/A
Application deadline (fall): rolling
Undergraduate student body: 1,774 full time, 435 part time; 35% male, 65% female; 0% American Indian, 1% Asian, 19% black, 2% Hispanic, 2% multiracial, 0% Pacific Islander, 71% white, 1% international; 58% from in state; 57% live on campus; 24% of students in fraternities, 20% in sororities
Most popular majors: 24% Health Professions and Related Programs, 21% Business, Management, Marketing, and Related Support Services, 6% Education, 5% Philosophy and Religious Studies, 5% Public Administration and Social Service Professions
Expenses: 2017-2018: $31,580; room/board: $11,200
Financial aid: (731) 661-5015; 76% of undergrads determined to have financial need; average aid package $26,410

University of Memphis
Memphis TN
(901) 678-2111
U.S. News ranking: Nat. U., second tier
Website: www.memphis.edu
Admissions email: recruitment@memphis.edu
Public; founded 1912
Freshman admissions: selective; 2016-2017: 13,216 applied,

12,388 accepted. Either SAT or ACT required. ACT 25/75 percentile: 19-25. High school rank: 13% in top tenth, 36% in top quarter, 69% in top half
Early decision deadline: N/A, notification date: N/A
Early action deadline: N/A, notification date: N/A
Application deadline (fall): 7/1
Undergraduate student body: 12,410 full time, 4,766 part time; 42% male, 58% female; 0% American Indian, 3% Asian, 37% black, 5% Hispanic, 4% multiracial, 0% Pacific Islander, 49% white, 1% international; 93% from in state; 15% live on campus; 1% of students in fraternities, 2% in sororities
Most popular majors: 20% Business, Management, Marketing, and Related Support Services, 11% Multi/Interdisciplinary Studies, 9% Health Professions and Related Programs, 7% Education, 6% Psychology
Expenses: 2017-2018: $18,250 In state, $29,962 out of state; room/board: $9,366
Financial aid: (901) 678-4825; 84% of undergrads determined to have financial need; average aid package $9,985

University of Tennessee
Knoxville TN
(865) 974-1111
U.S. News ranking: Nat. U., No. 103
Website: utk.edu
Admissions email: admissions@utk.edu
Public; founded 1794
Freshman admissions: more selective; 2016-2017: 17,583 applied, 13,578 accepted. Either SAT or ACT required. ACT 25/75 percentile: 24-30. High school rank: N/A
Early decision deadline: N/A, notification date: N/A
Early action deadline: N/A, notification date: N/A
Application deadline (fall): 12/1
Undergraduate student body: 20,778 full time, 1,361 part time; 51% male, 49% female; 0% American Indian, 4% Asian, 7% black, 4% Hispanic, 3% multiracial, 0% Pacific Islander, 79% white, 2% international; 89% from in state; 33% live on campus; 14% of students in fraternities, 24% in sororities
Most popular majors: 22% Business, Management, Marketing, and Related Support Services, 10% Engineering, 8% Social Sciences, 7% Parks, Recreation, Leisure, and Fitness Studies, 7% Psychology
Expenses: 2017-2018: $12,970 In state, $31,160 out of state; room/board: $10,696
Financial aid: (865) 974-1111; 58% of undergrads determined to have financial need; average aid package $13,012

University of Tennessee–Chattanooga
Chattanooga TN
(423) 425-4662
U.S. News ranking: Reg. U. (S), No. 57
Website: www.utc.edu
Admissions email: utcmocs@utc.edu
Public; founded 1886
Freshman admissions: selective; 2016-2017: 7,628 applied, 5,970 accepted. Either SAT or ACT required. ACT 25/75 percentile: 21-26. High school rank: N/A
Early decision deadline: N/A, notification date: N/A
Early action deadline: N/A, notification date: N/A
Application deadline (fall): 5/1
Undergraduate student body: 8,875 full time, 1,295 part time; 44% male, 56% female; 0% American Indian, 2% Asian, 11% black, 4% Hispanic, 5% multiracial, 0% Pacific Islander, 77% white, 1% international; 95% from in state; 31% live on campus; 10% of students in fraternities, 19% in sororities
Most popular majors: 21% Business, Management, Marketing, and Related Support Services, 10% Parks, Recreation, Leisure, and Fitness Studies, 9% Education, 7% Biological and Biomedical Sciences, 7% Health Professions and Related Programs
Expenses: 2016-2017: $8,544 in state, $24,662 out of state; room/board: $8,676
Financial aid: (423) 425-4677; 62% of undergrads determined to have financial need; average aid package $9,747

University of Tennessee–Martin
Martin TN
(800) 829-8861
U.S. News ranking: Reg. U. (S), No. 46
Website: www.utm.edu
Admissions email: admitme@utm.edu
Public; founded 1900
Freshman admissions: selective, 2016-2017: 3,547 applied, 2,366 accepted. Either SAT or ACT required. ACT 25/75 percentile: 20-25. High school rank: 17% in top tenth, 48% in top quarter, 84% in top half
Early decision deadline: N/A, notification date: N/A
Early action deadline: N/A, notification date: N/A
Application deadline (fall): rolling
Undergraduate student body: 4,955 full time, 1,324 part time; 42% male, 58% female; 0% American Indian, 1% Asian, 14% black, 2% Hispanic, 2% multiracial, 0% Pacific Islander, 77% white, 3% international; 93% from in state; 29% live on campus; 12% of students in fraternities, 14% in sororities
Most popular majors: 16% Business, Management, Marketing, and Related Support Services, 13% Agriculture, Agriculture Operations, and Related Sciences, 10% Multi/Interdisciplinary Studies, 9%

Parks, Recreation, Leisure, and Fitness Studies, 8% Education
Expenses: 2016-2017: $9,074 in state, $14,834 out of state; room/board: $7,764
Financial aid: (731) 881-7040; 75% of undergrads determined to have financial need; average aid package $11,218

Vanderbilt University
Nashville TN
(800) 288-0432
U.S. News ranking: Nat. U., No. 14
Website: www.vanderbilt.edu
Admissions email: admissions@vanderbilt.edu
Private; founded 1873
Freshman admissions: most selective; 2016-2017: 32,442 applied, 3,487 accepted. Either SAT or ACT required. ACT 25/75 percentile: 32-35. High school rank: 87% in top tenth, 97% in top quarter, 99% in top half
Early decision deadline: 11/1, notification date: 12/15
Early action deadline: N/A, notification date: N/A
Application deadline (fall): 1/1
Undergraduate student body: 6,817 full time, 54 part time; 49% male, 51% female; 0% American Indian, 12% Asian, 9% black, 9% Hispanic, 5% multiracial, 0% Pacific Islander, 52% white, 7% international; 10% from in state; 90% live on campus; 37% of students in fraternities, 51% in sororities
Most popular majors: 12% Economics, General, 12% Multi/Interdisciplinary Studies, Other, 9% Social Sciences, General, 5% Mathematics, General, 5% Political Science and Government, General
Expenses: 2017-2018: $47,664; room/board: $15,584
Financial aid: (615) 322-3591; 50% of undergrads determined to have financial need; average aid package $46,938

Watkins College of Art, Design & Film[1]
Nashville TN
U.S. News ranking: Arts, unranked
Website: www.watkins.edu
Admissions email: admission@watkins.edu
Private
Application deadline (fall): N/A
Undergraduate student body: N/A full time, N/A part time
Expenses: 2016-2017: $23,700; room/board: $10,000
Financial aid: N/A

Welch College
Gallatin TN
(615) 675-5255
U.S. News ranking: Reg. Coll. (S), No. 26
Website: www.welch.edu
Admissions email: Recruit@welch.edu
Private; founded 1942
Affiliation: Free Will Baptist Church
Freshman admissions: selective; 2016-2017: 155 applied, 99 accepted. Either SAT or ACT required. ACT 25/75 percentile: 17-25. High school rank: 39% in top tenth, 52% in top quarter, 70% in top half

Early decision deadline: N/A, notification date: N/A
Early action deadline: N/A, notification date: N/A
Application deadline (fall): rolling
Undergraduate student body: 209 full time, 111 part time; 53% male, 48% female; 0% American Indian, 2% Asian, 3% black, 4% Hispanic, 0% multiracial, 6% Pacific Islander, 84% white, 0% international; 42% from in state; 52% live on campus; 52% of students in fraternities, 60% in sororities
Most popular majors: 37% Theology and Religious Vocations, 29% Education, 11% Business, Management, Marketing, and Related Support Services, 4% Psychology, 2% Biological and Biomedical Sciences
Expenses: 2017-2018: $18,458; room/board: $7,478
Financial aid: (615) 675-5278; 83% of undergrads determined to have financial need; average aid package $14,398

TEXAS

Abilene Christian University
Abilene TX
(800) 460-6228
U.S. News ranking: Reg. U. (W), No. 18
Website: www.acu.edu
Admissions email: info@admissions.acu.edu
Private; founded 1906
Affiliation: Churches of Christ
Freshman admissions: selective; 2016-2017: 6,172 applied, 5,217 accepted. Either SAT or ACT required. ACT 25/75 percentile: 21-27. High school rank: 21% in top tenth, 56% in top quarter, 84% in top half
Early decision deadline: N/A, notification date: N/A
Early action deadline: 11/1, notification date: 11/15
Application deadline (fall): 2/15
Undergraduate student body: 3,562 full time, 196 part time; 41% male, 59% female; 0% American Indian, 1% Asian, 9% black, 16% Hispanic, 5% multiracial, 0% Pacific Islander, 64% white, 4% international; 87% from in state; 49% live on campus; 28% of students in fraternities, 34% in sororities
Most popular majors: 6% Accounting, 6% Marketing/Marketing Management, General, 6% Psychology, General, 6% Registered Nursing/Registered Nurse, 5% Business Administration and Management, General
Expenses: 2017-2018: $33,330; room/board: $10,378
Financial aid: (325) 674-2300; 67% of undergrads determined to have financial need; average aid package $22,694

Amberton University[1]
Garland TX
(972) 279-6511
U.S. News ranking: Reg. U. (W), unranked
Website: www.amberton.edu
Admissions email: advisor@amberton.edu
Private; founded 1981
Application deadline (fall): rolling
Undergraduate student body: N/A full time, N/A part time
Expenses: 2016-2017: $7,500; room/board: N/A
Financial aid: N/A

Angelo State University[1]
San Angelo TX
(325) 942-2041
U.S. News ranking: Reg. U. (W), second tier
Website: www.angelo.edu
Admissions email: admissions@angelo.edu
Public; founded 1928
Application deadline (fall): 8/29
Undergraduate student body: N/A full time, N/A part time
Expenses: 2016-2017: $8,038 in state, $20,278 out of state; room/board: $7,666
Financial aid: (325) 942-2246

Art Institute of Houston[1]
Houston TX
U.S. News ranking: Arts, unranked
Website: www.artinstitute.edu/houston/
Admissions email: N/A
For-profit
Application deadline (fall): N/A
Undergraduate student body: N/A full time, N/A part time
Expenses: 2016-2017: $17,664; room/board: N/A
Financial aid: N/A

Austin College
Sherman TX
(800) 526-4276
U.S. News ranking: Nat. Lib. Arts, No. 93
Website: www.austincollege.edu
Admissions email: admission@austincollege.edu
Private; founded 1849
Affiliation: Presbyterian
Freshman admissions: more selective; 2016-2017: 3,352 applied, 1,791 accepted. Either SAT or ACT required. ACT 25/75 percentile: 23-29. High school rank: 37% in top tenth, 75% in top quarter, 89% in top half
Early decision deadline: 11/1, notification date: 12/4
Early action deadline: 1/5, notification date: 1/15
Application deadline (fall): 3/1
Undergraduate student body: 1,273 full time, 5 part time; 48% male, 52% female; 1% American Indian, 14% Asian, 8% black, 19% Hispanic, 3% multiracial, 0% Pacific Islander, 52% white, 3% international; 91% from in state; 82% live on campus; 18% of students in fraternities, 10% in sororities
Most popular majors: 19% Social Sciences, 13% Business, Management, Marketing, and Related Support Services, 11%

Psychology, 9% Biological and Biomedical Sciences, 6% Foreign Languages, Literatures, and Linguistics
Expenses: 2017-2018: $38,825; room/board: $12,334
Financial aid: (903) 813-2900; 65% of undergrads determined to have financial need; average aid package $34,859

Baylor University
Waco TX
(800) 229-5678
U.S. News ranking: Nat. U., No. 75
Website: www.baylor.edu
Admissions email: Admissions@Baylor.edu
Private; founded 1845
Freshman admissions: more selective; 2016-2017: 34,636 applied, 13,758 accepted. Either SAT or ACT required. ACT 25/75 percentile: 26-30. High school rank: 41% in top tenth, 75% in top quarter, 97% in top half
Early decision deadline: N/A, notification date: N/A
Early action deadline: 11/1, notification date: 1/15
Application deadline (fall): 2/1
Undergraduate student body: 14,109 full time, 239 part time; 42% male, 58% female; 0% American Indian, 6% Asian, 7% black, 15% Hispanic, 5% multiracial, 0% Pacific Islander, 64% white, 3% international; 71% from in state; 35% live on campus; 16% of students in fraternities, 31% in sororities
Most popular majors: 7% Biology/Biological Sciences, General, 6% Registered Nursing/Registered Nurse, 5% Accounting, 4% Marketing/Marketing Management, General, 4% Psychology, General
Expenses: 2017-2018: $43,790; room/board: $12,588
Financial aid: (254) 710-2611; 54% of undergrads determined to have financial need; average aid package $28,278

Brazosport College[1]
Lake Jackson TX
U.S. News ranking: Reg. Coll. (W), unranked
Website: www.brazosport.edu
Admissions email: N/A
Public
Application deadline (fall): N/A
Undergraduate student body: N/A full time, N/A part time
Expenses: 2016-2017: $3,405 in state, $5,025 out of state; room/board: N/A
Financial aid: N/A

Concordia University Texas[1]
Austin TX
(800) 865-4282
U.S. News ranking: Reg. U. (W), second tier
Website: www.concordia.edu
Admissions email: admissions@concordia.edu
Private; founded 1926
Application deadline (fall): 8/1
Undergraduate student body: N/A full time, N/A part time
Expenses: 2016-2017: $29,260; room/board: $9,836
Financial aid: (512) 313-4672

Dallas Baptist University
Dallas TX
(214) 333-5360
U.S. News ranking: Nat. U., No. 202
Website: www.dbu.edu
Admissions email: admiss@dbu.edu
Private; founded 1898
Affiliation: Baptist
Freshman admissions: selective; 2016-2017: 3,259 applied, 1,405 accepted. Either SAT or ACT required. ACT 25/75 percentile: 19-25. High school rank: 19% in top tenth, 46% in top quarter, 75% in top half
Early decision deadline: N/A, notification date: N/A
Early action deadline: N/A, notification date: N/A
Application deadline (fall): rolling
Undergraduate student body: 2,408 full time, 815 part time; 41% male, 59% female; 1% American Indian, 2% Asian, 14% black, 16% Hispanic, 0% multiracial, 0% Pacific Islander, 60% white, 6% international; 92% from in state; 60% live on campus; 13% of students in fraternities, 21% in sororities
Most popular majors: 13% Business Administration and Management, General, 13% Multi-/Interdisciplinary Studies, Other, 10% Psychology, General, 7% Religious Education, 7% Speech Communication and Rhetoric
Expenses: 2017-2018: $27,480; room/board: $7,740
Financial aid: (214) 333-5363; 66% of undergrads determined to have financial need; average aid package $15,416

East Texas Baptist University
Marshall TX
(800) 804-3828
U.S. News ranking: Reg. Coll. (W), No. 16
Website: www.etbu.edu
Admissions email: admissions@etbu.edu
Private; founded 1912
Affiliation: Baptist
Freshman admissions: selective; 2016-2017: 1,397 applied, 709 accepted. Either SAT or ACT required. ACT 25/75 percentile: 18-22. High school rank: 14% in top tenth, 36% in top quarter, 74% in top half
Early decision deadline: N/A, notification date: N/A
Early action deadline: N/A, notification date: N/A
Application deadline (fall): 8/29
Undergraduate student body: 1,177 full time, 162 part time; 47% male, 53% female; 0% American Indian, 0% Asian, 19% black, 8% Hispanic, 4% multiracial, 0% Pacific Islander, 67% white, 1% international; 90% from in state; 83% live on campus; 1% of students in fraternities, 1% in sororities
Most popular majors: 14% Multi/Interdisciplinary Studies, 13% Health Professions and Related Programs, 12% Education,

11% Business, Management, Marketing, and Related Support Services, 9% Parks, Recreation, Leisure, and Fitness Studies
Expenses: 2017-2018: $25,470; room/board: $8,915
Financial aid: (903) 923-2137; 85% of undergrads determined to have financial need; average aid package $20,132

Hardin-Simmons University
Abilene TX
(325) 670-1206
U.S. News ranking: Reg. U. (W), No. 33
Website: www.hsutx.edu/
Admissions email: enroll@hsutx.edu
Private; founded 1891
Affiliation: Baptist
Freshman admissions: selective; 2016-2017: 1,149 applied, 1,011 accepted. Either SAT or ACT required. ACT 25/75 percentile: 19-24. High school rank: 19% in top tenth, 53% in top quarter, 84% in top half
Early decision deadline: N/A, notification date: N/A
Early action deadline: N/A, notification date: N/A
Application deadline (fall): rolling
Undergraduate student body: 1,523 full time, 198 part time; 45% male, 55% female; 0% American Indian, 1% Asian, 7% black, 17% Hispanic, 4% multiracial, 0% Pacific Islander, 69% white, 1% international; 96% from in state; 47% live on campus; 11% of students in fraternities, 15% in sororities
Most popular majors: 14% Parks, Recreation, Leisure, and Fitness Studies, 13% Health Professions and Related Programs, 12% Business, Management, Marketing, and Related Support Services, 11% Education, 7% Homeland Security, Law Enforcement, Firefighting and Related Protective Services
Expenses: 2017-2018: $27,440; room/board: $8,420
Financial aid: (325) 670-1482; 72% of undergrads determined to have financial need; average aid package $25,683

Houston Baptist University
Houston TX
(281) 649-3211
U.S. News ranking: Reg. U. (W), No. 70
Website: www.hbu.edu
Admissions email: admissions@hbu.edu
Private; founded 1960
Affiliation: Baptist
Freshman admissions: selective; 2016-2017: 15,256 applied, 5,273 accepted. Either SAT or ACT required. SAT 25/75 percentile: 940-1140. High school rank: 22% in top tenth, 56% in top quarter, 85% in top half
Early decision deadline: N/A, notification date: N/A
Early action deadline: N/A, notification date: N/A
Application deadline (fall): rolling

Undergraduate student body: 2,161 full time, 171 part time; 38% male, 62% female; 0% American Indian, 10% Asian, 18% black, 33% Hispanic, 4% multiracial, 0% Pacific Islander, 26% white, 3% international; 96% from in state; 39% live on campus; 5% of students in fraternities, 12% in sororities
Most popular majors: 21% Business, Management, Marketing, and Related Support Services, 20% Health Professions and Related Programs, 10% Biological and Biomedical Sciences, 9% Parks, Recreation, Leisure, and Fitness Studies, 8% Psychology
Expenses: 2017-2018: $31,730; room/board: $8,814
Financial aid: (281) 649-3747; 74% of undergrads determined to have financial need; average aid package $30,060

Howard Payne University
Brownwood TX
(325) 649-8020
U.S. News ranking: Reg. Coll. (W), No. 13
Website: www.hputx.edu
Admissions email: enroll@hputx.edu
Private; founded 1889
Affiliation: Baptist
Freshman admissions: less selective; 2016-2017: 953 applied, 836 accepted. Either SAT or ACT required. SAT 25/75 percentile: 830-1030. High school rank: 11% in top tenth, 32% in top quarter, 62% in top half
Early decision deadline: N/A, notification date: N/A
Early action deadline: N/A, notification date: N/A
Application deadline (fall): rolling
Undergraduate student body: 959 full time, 139 part time; 53% male, 47% female; 1% American Indian, 1% Asian, 10% black, 21% Hispanic, 0% multiracial, 0% Pacific Islander, 57% white, 0% international; 98% from in state; 59% live on campus; 14% of students in fraternities, 17% in sororities
Most popular majors: 20% Business, Management, Marketing, and Related Support Services, 19% Education, 9% Theology and Religious Vocations, 8% Social Sciences, 7% Psychology
Expenses: 2017-2018: $27,690; room/board: $8,304
Financial aid: (325) 649-8014; 85% of undergrads determined to have financial need; average aid package $20,372

Huston-Tillotson University
Austin TX
(512) 505-3029
U.S. News ranking: Reg. Coll. (W), second tier
Website: htu.edu/
Admissions email: admission@htu.edu
Private
Freshman admissions: least selective; 2016-2017: 2,423 applied, 884 accepted. Either SAT or ACT required. SAT 25/75

percentile: 690-920. High school rank: N/A
Early decision deadline: N/A, notification date: N/A
Early action deadline: N/A, notification date: N/A
Application deadline (fall): 5/1
Undergraduate student body: 917 full time, 48 part time; 41% male, 59% female; 0% American Indian, 0% Asian, 65% black, 26% Hispanic, 0% multiracial, 0% Pacific Islander, 5% white, 3% international
Most popular majors: 32% Business, Management, Marketing, and Related Support Services, 13% Parks, Recreation, Leisure, and Fitness Studies, 12% Psychology, 9% Education, 9% Homeland Security, Law Enforcement, Firefighting and Related Protective Services
Expenses: 2016-2017: $14,346; room/board: $7,568
Financial aid: N/A

Jarvis Christian College
Hawkins TX
(903) 730-4890
U.S. News ranking: Reg. Coll. (W), second tier
Website: www.jarvis.edu
Admissions email: Recruitment@jarvis.edu
Private; founded 1912
Affiliation: Christian Church (Disciples of Christ)
Freshman admissions: least selective; 2016-2017: 3,678 applied, 300 accepted. Either SAT or ACT required. SAT 25/75 percentile: 650-843. High school rank: 0% in top tenth, 10% in top quarter, 50% in top half
Early decision deadline: N/A, notification date: N/A
Early action deadline: N/A, notification date: N/A
Application deadline (fall): 8/1
Undergraduate student body: 829 full time, 71 part time; 49% male, 51% female; 0% American Indian, 0% Asian, 82% black, 10% Hispanic, 0% multiracial, 0% Pacific Islander, 5% white, 1% international; 81% from in state; 70% live on campus; 3% of students in fraternities, 3% in sororities
Most popular majors: 24% Business Administration and Management, General, 19% Kinesiology and Exercise Science, 15% Criminal Justice/Safety Studies, 9% Education, General, 8% Business Administration and Management, General
Expenses: 2017-2018: $11,720; room/board: $8,440
Financial aid: (903) 730-4890; 98% of undergrads determined to have financial need; average aid package $12,783

Lamar University
Beaumont TX
(409) 880-8888
U.S. News ranking: Nat. U., second tier
Website: www.lamar.edu
Admissions email: admissions@lamar.edu
Public; founded 1923
Freshman admissions: selective; 2016-2017: 5,613 applied,

4,276 accepted. Either SAT or ACT required. SAT 25/75 percentile: 860-1050. High school rank: 14% in top tenth, 24% in top quarter, 72% in top half
Early decision deadline: N/A, notification date: N/A
Early action deadline: N/A, notification date: N/A
Application deadline (fall): 8/10
Undergraduate student body: 6,193 full time, 3,133 part time; 42% male, 58% female; 0% American Indian, 5% Asian, 27% black, 15% Hispanic, 2% multiracial, 0% Pacific Islander, 48% white, 1% international; 97% from in state; 24% live on campus; N/A of students in fraternities, N/A in sororities
Most popular majors: 20% Health Professions and Related Programs, 15% Business, Management, Marketing, and Related Support Services, 14% Multi-/Interdisciplinary Studies, Other, 9% Engineering, 6% Homeland Security, Law Enforcement, Firefighting and Related Protective Services
Expenses: 2017-2018: $10,111 in state, $22,561 out of state; room/board: $8,740
Financial aid: (409) 880-7011; 62% of undergrads determined to have financial need; average aid package $5,009

LeTourneau University
Longview TX
(903) 233-4300
U.S. News ranking: Reg. U. (W), No. 23
Website: www.letu.edu
Admissions email: admissions@letu.edu
Private; founded 1946
Freshman admissions: more selective; 2016-2017: 1,842 applied, 814 accepted. Neither SAT nor ACT required. SAT 25/75 percentile: 1030-1280. High school rank: 27% in top tenth, 55% in top quarter, 86% in top half
Early decision deadline: N/A, notification date: N/A
Early action deadline: N/A, notification date: N/A
Application deadline (fall): rolling
Undergraduate student body: 1,262 full time, 991 part time; 53% male, 47% female; 0% American Indian, 1% Asian, 9% black, 10% Hispanic, 4% multiracial, 0% Pacific Islander, 62% white, 3% international; 69% from in state; 70% live on campus; N/A of students in fraternities, N/A in sororities
Most popular majors: 25% Business, Management, Marketing, and Related Support Services, 24% Engineering, 10% Education, 7% Transportation and Materials Moving, 6% Psychology
Expenses: 2017-2018: $29,320; room/board: $9,870
Financial aid: (903) 233-4356; 73% of undergrads determined to have financial need; average aid package $22,747

Lubbock Christian University
Lubbock TX
(806) 720-7151
U.S. News ranking: Reg. U. (W), No. 81
Website: www.lcu.edu
Admissions email: admissions@lcu.edu
Private; founded 1957
Affiliation: Churches of Christ
Freshman admissions: selective; 2016-2017: 815 applied, 812 accepted. Either SAT or ACT required. ACT 25/75 percentile: 19-25. High school rank: 20% in top tenth, 43% in top quarter, 74% in top half
Early decision deadline: 10/31, notification date: 12/15
Early action deadline: 6/15, notification date: 7/15
Application deadline (fall): 6/1
Undergraduate student body: 1,267 full time, 204 part time; 40% male, 60% female; 1% American Indian, 1% Asian, 5% black, 22% Hispanic, 0% multiracial, 0% Pacific Islander, 69% white, 2% international; 90% from in state; 37% live on campus; 19% of students in fraternities, 17% in sororities
Most popular majors: 26% Health Professions and Related Programs, 16% Education, 11% Business, Management, Marketing, and Related Support Services, 7% Parks, Recreation, Leisure, and Fitness Studies, 5% Biological and Biomedical Sciences
Expenses: 2017-2018: $21,794; room/board: $6,460
Financial aid: (806) 720-7176; 75% of undergrads determined to have financial need; average aid package $15,407

McMurry University
Abilene TX
(325) 793-4700
U.S. News ranking: Reg. Coll. (W), No. 12
Website: ww2.mcm.edu/
Admissions email: admissions@mcm.edu
Private; founded 1923
Affiliation: United Methodist
Freshman admissions: selective; 2016-2017: 1,884 applied, 905 accepted. Either SAT or ACT required. ACT 25/75 percentile: 18-22. High school rank: 12% in top tenth, 39% in top quarter, 73% in top half
Early decision deadline: N/A, notification date: N/A
Early action deadline: N/A, notification date: N/A
Application deadline (fall): 8/15
Undergraduate student body: 932 full time, 141 part time; 56% male, 44% female; 1% American Indian, 1% Asian, 17% black, 25% Hispanic, 2% multiracial, 0% Pacific Islander, 47% white, 7% international; 95% from in state; 53% live on campus; 15% of students in fraternities, 18% in sororities
Most popular majors: 20% Business, Management, Marketing, and Related Support Services, 17% Education, 11% Social Sciences, 8% Parks, Recreation, Leisure, and Fitness Studies, 8% Psychology

Expenses: 2017-2018: $26,712; room/board: $8,324
Financial aid: (325) 793-4978; 83% of undergrads determined to have financial need; average aid package $21,766

Midland College[1]
Midland TX
U.S. News ranking: Reg. Coll. (W), unranked
Website: www.midland.edu/
Admissions email: pebensberger@midland.edu
Public
Application deadline (fall): N/A
Undergraduate student body: N/A full time, N/A part time
Expenses: 2016-2017: $4,080 in state, $5,280 out of state; room/board: $4,800
Financial aid: N/A

Midwestern State University
Wichita Falls TX
(800) 842-1922
U.S. News ranking: Reg. U. (W), No. 91
Website: www.mwsu.edu
Admissions email: admissions@mwsu.edu
Public; founded 1922
Freshman admissions: selective; 2016-2017: 3,461 applied, 2,577 accepted. Either SAT or ACT required. SAT 25/75 percentile: 870-1080. High school rank: 13% in top tenth, 36% in top quarter, 74% in top half
Early decision deadline: N/A, notification date: N/A
Early action deadline: 8/7, notification date: N/A
Application deadline (fall): 8/1
Undergraduate student body: 4,122 full time, 1,197 part time; 42% male, 58% female; 1% American Indian, 3% Asian, 14% black, 18% Hispanic, 4% multiracial, 0% Pacific Islander, 51% white, 9% international; 92% from in state; 28% live on campus; 8% of students in fraternities, 10% in sororities
Most popular majors: 40% Health Professions and Related Programs, 15% Business, Management, Marketing, and Related Support Services, 12% Education
Expenses: 2017-2018: $8,484 in state, $10,435 out of state; room/board: $8,534
Financial aid: (940) 397-4214; 62% of undergrads determined to have financial need; average aid package $10,027

Our Lady of the Lake University
San Antonio TX
(800) 436-6558
U.S. News ranking: Reg. U. (W), No. 86
Website: www.ollusa.edu
Admissions email: admission@lake.ollusa.edu
Private; founded 1895
Affiliation: Roman Catholic
Freshman admissions: less selective; 2016-2017: 3,111 applied, 1,703 accepted. Either SAT or ACT required. SAT 25/75

percentile: 830-1010. High school rank: 13% in top tenth, 33% in top quarter, 66% in top half
Early decision deadline: N/A, notification date: N/A
Early action deadline: 11/14, notification date: 12/31
Application deadline (fall): 8/1
Undergraduate student body: 1,180 full time, 167 part time; 31% male, 69% female; 0% American Indian, 0% Asian, 8% black, 75% Hispanic, 2% multiracial, 0% Pacific Islander, 10% white, 2% international; 97% from in state; 37% live on campus; 4% of students in fraternities, 3% in sororities
Most popular majors: 15% Communication Sciences and Disorders, General, 13% Psychology, General, 12% Business Administration and Management, General, 12% Social Work, 6% Kinesiology and Exercise Science
Expenses: 2017-2018: $28,192; room/board: $8,288
Financial aid: (210) 431-2558; 85% of undergrads determined to have financial need; average aid package $22,224

Prairie View A&M University
Prairie View TX
(877) 782-6830
U.S. News ranking: Nat. U., second tier
Website: www.pvamu.edu
Admissions email: admission@pvamu.edu
Public; founded 1876
Freshman admissions: least selective; 2016-2017: 5,660 applied, 4,838 accepted. Either SAT or ACT required. SAT 25/75 percentile: 750-940. High school rank: 5% in top tenth, 13% in top quarter, 57% in top half
Early decision deadline: N/A, notification date: N/A
Early action deadline: N/A, notification date: N/A
Application deadline (fall): 6/1
Undergraduate student body: 6,820 full time, 635 part time; 40% male, 60% female; 0% American Indian, 3% Asian, 85% black, 7% Hispanic, 1% multiracial, 0% Pacific Islander, 2% white, 2% international; 93% from in state; 51% live on campus; 1% of students in fraternities, 2% in sororities
Most popular majors: 14% Registered Nursing/Registered Nurse, 9% Criminal Justice/Safety Studies, 7% Chemical Engineering, 6% Kinesiology and Exercise Science, 6% Psychology, General
Expenses: 2016-2017: $10,059 in state, $10,059 out of state; room/board: $8,754
Financial aid: (936) 261-1000; 88% of undergrads determined to have financial need; average aid package $15,280

Rice University

Houston TX
(713) 348-7423
U.S. News ranking: Nat. U., No. 14
Website: www.rice.edu
Admissions email:
admission@rice.edu
Private; founded 1912
Freshman admissions: most
selective; 2016-2017: 18,236
applied, 2,785 accepted. Either
SAT or ACT required. SAT 25/75
percentile: 1410-1570. High
school rank: 88% in top tenth,
97% in top quarter, 99% in
top half
Early decision deadline: 11/1,
notification date: 12/15
Early action deadline: N/A,
notification date: N/A
Application deadline (fall): 1/1
Undergraduate student body: 3,836
full time, 57 part time; 52%
male, 48% female; 0% American
Indian, 24% Asian, 7% black,
14% Hispanic, 4% multiracial,
0% Pacific Islander, 37% white,
12% international; 50% from in
state; 72% live on campus; 0%
of students in fraternities, 0% in
sororities
Most popular majors: 8%
Biochemistry, 7% Chemical
Engineering, 7% Economics,
General, 6% Computer and
Information Sciences, General,
6% Mechanical Engineering
Expenses: 2017-2018: $45,608;
room/board: $13,850
Financial aid: (713) 348-8025;
38% of undergrads determined to
have financial need; average aid
package $41,888

Sam Houston State University

Huntsville TX
(936) 294-1828
U.S. News ranking: Nat. U.,
second tier
Website: www.shsu.edu
Admissions email:
admissions@shsu.edu
Public; founded 1879
Freshman admissions: selective;
2016-2017: 12,540 applied,
9,034 accepted. Either SAT
or ACT required. SAT 25/75
percentile: 870-1070. High school
rank: 14% in top tenth, 55% in
top quarter, 87% in top half
Early decision deadline: N/A,
notification date: N/A
Early action deadline: N/A,
notification date: N/A
Application deadline (fall): 8/1
Undergraduate student body:
14,497 full time, 3,405 part
time; 38% male, 62% female;
1% American Indian, 2% Asian,
18% black, 22% Hispanic, 3%
multiracial, 0% Pacific Islander,
51% white, 1% international;
98% from in state; 19% live
on campus; 1% of students in
fraternities, 1% in sororities
Most popular majors: 23%
Business, Management,
Marketing, and Related Support
Services, 21% Homeland Security,
Law Enforcement, Firefighting and
Related Protective Services, 10%
Multi/Interdisciplinary Studies, 6%
Psychology, 5% Parks, Recreation,
Leisure, and Fitness Studies

Expenses: 2017-2018: $9,890 in
state, $22,340 out of state; room/
board: $9,180
Financial aid: (936) 294-1774;
64% of undergrads determined to
have financial need; average aid
package $10,976

Schreiner University

Kerrville TX
(800) 343-4919
U.S. News ranking: Nat. Lib. Arts,
second tier
Website: www.schreiner.edu
Admissions email: admissions@
schreiner.edu
Private; founded 1923
Affiliation: Presbyterian Church
(USA)
Freshman admissions: selective;
2016-2017: 998 applied, 906
accepted. Either SAT or ACT
required. SAT 25/75 percentile:
900-1080. High school rank:
20% in top tenth, 41% in top
quarter, 77% in top half
Early decision deadline: N/A,
notification date: N/A
Early action deadline: N/A,
notification date: N/A
Application deadline (fall): 8/1
Undergraduate student body: 1,075
full time, 162 part time; 42%
male, 58% female; 0% American
Indian, 1% Asian, 3% black,
37% Hispanic, 2% multiracial,
0% Pacific Islander, 48% white,
1% international; 97% from in
state; 61% live on campus; 4%
of students in fraternities, 6% in
sororities
Most popular majors: 32%
Health Professions and Related
Programs, 12% Parks, Recreation,
Leisure, and Fitness Studies,
10% Biological and Biomedical
Sciences, 8% Business,
Management, Marketing, and
Related Support Services, 5%
Education
Expenses: 2017-2018: $26,750;
room/board: $10,152
Financial aid: (830) 792-7229;
77% of undergrads determined to
have financial need; average aid
package $19,712

South Texas College[1]

McAllen TX
U.S. News ranking: Reg. Coll. (W),
unranked
Website:
www.southtexascollege.edu/
Admissions email: N/A
Public
Application deadline (fall): N/A
Undergraduate student body: N/A
full time, N/A part time
Expenses: 2016-2017: $3,890 in
state, $4,560 out of state; room/
board: N/A
Financial aid: N/A

Southern Methodist University

Dallas TX
(800) 323-0672
U.S. News ranking: Nat. U., No. 61
Website: www.smu.edu
Admissions email:
ugadmission@smu.edu
Private; founded 1911
Freshman admissions: more
selective; 2016-2017: 13,250
applied, 6,482 accepted. Either
SAT or ACT required. ACT 25/75

percentile: 28-32. High school
rank: 49% in top tenth, 77% in
top quarter, 93% in top half
Early decision deadline: 11/1,
notification date: 12/31
Early action deadline: 11/1,
notification date: 12/31
Application deadline (fall): 1/15
Undergraduate student body: 6,296
full time, 225 part time; 50%
male, 50% female; 0% American
Indian, 6% Asian, 5% black,
11% Hispanic, 4% multiracial,
0% Pacific Islander, 65% white,
8% international; 46% from in
state; 54% live on campus; 28%
of students in fraternities, 36%
in sororities
Most popular majors: 23%
Business, Management,
Marketing, and Related Support
Services, 15% Social Sciences,
12% Communication, Journalism,
and Related Programs, 8%
Engineering, 7% Visual and
Performing Arts
Expenses: 2017-2018: $52,498;
room/board: $16,910
Financial aid: (214) 768-3417;
33% of undergrads determined to
have financial need; average aid
package $41,761

Southwestern Adventist University

Keene TX
(817) 645-6749
U.S. News ranking: Reg. Coll. (W),
No. 20
Website: www.swau.edu
Admissions email:
admissions@swau.edu
Private; founded 1893
Affiliation: Seventh Day Adventist
Freshman admissions: less
selective; 2016-2017: 1,551
applied, 775 accepted. Either
SAT or ACT required. SAT 25/75
percentile: 830-1030. High
school rank: 8% in top tenth, 26%
in top quarter, 55% in top half
Early decision deadline: N/A,
notification date: N/A
Early action deadline: N/A,
notification date: N/A
Application deadline (fall): rolling
Undergraduate student body: 671
full time, 118 part time; 42%
male, 58% female; 0% American
Indian, 4% Asian, 16% black,
46% Hispanic, 4% multiracial,
2% Pacific Islander, 21% white,
7% international; 74% from in
state; 48% live on campus; 0%
of students in fraternities, 0% in
sororities
Most popular majors: 17%
Registered Nursing/Registered
Nurse, 7% Business
Administration and Management,
General, 6% Elementary
Education and Teaching,
6% Psychology, General, 5%
Educational Evaluation and
Research
Expenses: 2017-2018: $20,732;
room/board: $7,500
Financial aid: (817) 202-6262;
79% of undergrads determined to
have financial need; average aid
package $17,433

Southwestern Assemblies of God University[1]

Waxahachie TX
(888) 937-7248
U.S. News ranking: Reg. U. (W),
second tier
Website: www.sagu.edu/
Admissions email:
admissions@sagu.edu
Private; founded 1927
Application deadline (fall): rolling
Undergraduate student body: N/A
full time, N/A part time
Expenses: 2016-2017: $19,560;
room/board: $7,144
Financial aid: (972) 825-4730

Southwestern Christian College[1]

Terrell TX
U.S. News ranking: Reg. Coll. (W),
unranked
Website: www.swcc.edu
Admissions email: N/A
Private
Application deadline (fall): N/A
Undergraduate student body: N/A
full time, N/A part time
Expenses: 2016-2017: $8,074;
room/board: $5,600
Financial aid: N/A

Southwestern University

Georgetown TX
(512) 863-1200
U.S. News ranking: Nat. Lib. Arts,
No. 96
Website: www.southwestern.edu
Admissions email: admission@
southwestern.edu
Private; founded 1840
Affiliation: United Methodist
Freshman admissions: more
selective; 2016-2017: 3,773
applied, 1,699 accepted. Either
SAT or ACT required. SAT 25/75
percentile: 1050-1280. High
school rank: 36% in top tenth,
73% in top quarter, 93% in
top half
Early decision deadline: 11/1,
notification date: 12/1
Early action deadline: 12/1,
notification date: 3/1
Application deadline (fall): 6/1
Undergraduate student body: 1,464
full time, 22 part time; 43%
male, 57% female; 0% American
Indian, 4% Asian, 6% black,
21% Hispanic, 4% multiracial,
0% Pacific Islander, 62% white,
2% international; 90% from in
state; 72% live on campus; 22%
of students in fraternities, 21%
in sororities
Most popular majors: 12%
Business, Management,
Marketing, and Related Support
Services, 12% Social Sciences,
11% Psychology, 10% Visual and
Performing Arts, 9% Biological
and Biomedical Sciences
Expenses: 2017-2018: $40,560;
room/board: $11,810
Financial aid: (512) 863-1259;
63% of undergrads determined to
have financial need; average aid
package $34,758

St. Edward's University

Austin TX
(512) 448-8500
U.S. News ranking: Reg. U. (W),
No. 15
Website: www.stedwards.edu
Admissions email: admit@
stedwards.edu
Private; founded 1885
Affiliation: Roman Catholic
Freshman admissions: selective;
2016-2017: 6,046 applied,
4,468 accepted. Either SAT
or ACT required. SAT 25/75
percentile: 1010-1200. High
school rank: 24% in top tenth,
60% in top quarter, 88% in
top half
Early decision deadline: N/A,
notification date: N/A
Early action deadline: N/A,
notification date: N/A
Application deadline (fall): 5/1
Undergraduate student body: 3,610
full time, 446 part time; 39%
male, 61% female; 0% American
Indian, 3% Asian, 4% black,
41% Hispanic, 3% multiracial,
0% Pacific Islander, 37% white,
8% international; 86% from in
state; 37% live on campus; N/A
of students in fraternities, N/A in
sororities
Most popular majors: 9%
Psychology, General, 8%
Communication and Media
Studies, 7% Business
Administration and Management,
General, 5% International/Global
Studies, 5% Kinesiology and
Exercise Science
Expenses: 2017-2018: $43,050;
room/board: $12,940
Financial aid: (512) 448-8516;
69% of undergrads determined to
have financial need; average aid
package $32,523

St. Mary's University of San Antonio

San Antonio TX
(210) 436-3126
U.S. News ranking: Reg. U. (W),
No. 21
Website: www.stmarytx.edu
Admissions email:
uadm@stmarytx.edu
Private; founded 1852
Affiliation: Roman Catholic
Freshman admissions: selective;
2016-2017: 4,346 applied,
3,375 accepted. Either SAT
or ACT required. SAT 25/75
percentile: 950-1130. High school
rank: 27% in top tenth, 55% in
top quarter, 81% in top half
Early decision deadline: N/A,
notification date: N/A
Early action deadline: N/A,
notification date: N/A
Application deadline (fall): rolling
Undergraduate student body: 2,189
full time, 109 part time; 47%
male, 53% female; 0% American
Indian, 2% Asian, 3% black,
68% Hispanic, 1% multiracial,
0% Pacific Islander, 14% white,
9% international; 91% from in
state; 56% live on campus; 6%
of students in fraternities, 6% in
sororities
Most popular majors: 20%
Business, Management,
Marketing, and Related Support
Services, 16% Social Sciences,
15% Biological and Biomedical
Sciences, 8% Parks, Recreation,

Leisure, and Fitness Studies, 7% Homeland Security, Law Enforcement, Firefighting and Related Protective Services
Expenses: 2017-2018: $29,300; room/board: $9,820
Financial aid: (210) 436-3141; 72% of undergrads determined to have financial need; average aid package $24,534

Stephen F. Austin State University
Nacogdoches TX
(936) 468-2504
U.S. News ranking: Reg. U. (W), No. 73
Website: www.sfasu.edu
Admissions email: admissions@sfasu.edu
Public; founded 1923
Freshman admissions: selective; 2016-2017: 11,382 applied, 7,108 accepted. Either SAT or ACT required. SAT 25/75 percentile: 870-1090. High school rank: 13% in top tenth, 41% in top quarter, 76% in top half
Early decision deadline: N/A, notification date: N/A
Early action deadline: N/A, notification date: N/A
Application deadline (fall): rolling
Undergraduate student body: 9,637 full time, 1,503 part time; 36% male, 64% female; 1% American Indian, 1% Asian, 19% black, 17% Hispanic, 3% multiracial, 0% Pacific Islander, 57% white, 1% international; 98% from in state; 44% live on campus; 15% of students in fraternities, 10% in sororities
Most popular majors: 20% Business, Management, Marketing, and Related Support Services, 16% Health Professions and Related Programs, 10% Multi/Interdisciplinary Studies, 8% Parks, Recreation, Leisure, and Fitness Studies, 8% Visual and Performing Arts
Expenses: 2016-2017: $9,537 in state, $21,777 out of state; room/board: $8,868
Financial aid: (936) 468-2230

Sul Ross State University[1]
Alpine TX
(432) 837-8050
U.S. News ranking: Reg. U. (W), second tier
Website: www.sulross.edu
Admissions email: admissions@sulross.edu
Public; founded 1917
Application deadline (fall): rolling
Undergraduate student body: N/A full time, N/A part time
Expenses: 2016-2017: $6,419 in state, $16,211 out of state; room/board: $7,988
Financial aid: (432) 837-8059

Tarleton State University
Stephenville TX
(800) 687-8236
U.S. News ranking: Reg. U. (W), second tier
Website: www.tarleton.edu
Admissions email: uadm@tarleton.edu
Public; founded 1899

Freshman admissions: less selective; 2016-2017: 6,433 applied, 4,740 accepted. Either SAT or ACT required. SAT 25/75 percentile: 850-1060. High school rank: 7% in top tenth, 23% in top quarter, 77% in top half
Early decision deadline: N/A, notification date: N/A
Early action deadline: 3/1, notification date: N/A
Application deadline (fall): 6/1
Undergraduate student body: 8,059 full time, 3,404 part time; 45% male, 55% female; 1% American Indian, 1% Asian, 8% black, 19% Hispanic, 3% multiracial, 0% Pacific Islander, 67% white, 0% international; 98% from in state; 28% live on campus; 11% of students in fraternities, 18% in sororities
Most popular majors: 21% Business, Management, Marketing, and Related Support Services, 15% Multi/Interdisciplinary Studies, 10% Agriculture, Agriculture Operations, and Related Sciences, 8% Health Professions and Related Programs, 7% Parks, Recreation, Leisure, and Fitness Studies
Expenses: 2017-2018: $8,903 in state, $20,886 out of state; room/board: $9,970
Financial aid: (254) 968-9070; 64% of undergrads determined to have financial need; average aid package $9,221

Texas A&M International University
Laredo TX
(956) 326-2200
U.S. News ranking: Reg. U. (W), No. 70
Website: www.tamiu.edu
Admissions email: enroll@tamiu.edu
Public; founded 1970
Freshman admissions: less selective; 2016-2017: 6,309 applied, 3,379 accepted. Either SAT or ACT required. SAT 25/75 percentile: 820-1020. High school rank: 24% in top tenth, 54% in top quarter, 85% in top half
Early decision deadline: N/A, notification date: N/A
Early action deadline: N/A, notification date: N/A
Application deadline (fall): 7/1
Undergraduate student body: 4,860 full time, 1,731 part time; 40% male, 60% female; 0% American Indian, 0% Asian, 0% black, 95% Hispanic, 0% multiracial, 0% Pacific Islander, 2% white, 2% international; 99% from in state; N/A live on campus; N/A of students in fraternities, 1% in sororities
Most popular majors: 20% Business, Management, Marketing, and Related Support Services, 14% Homeland Security, Law Enforcement, Firefighting and Related Protective Services, 13% Psychology, 12% Health Professions and Related Programs, 8% Multi/Interdisciplinary Studies
Expenses: 2017-2018: $8,320 in state, $20,770 out of state; room/board: $8,160

Financial aid: (956) 326-2225; 88% of undergrads determined to have financial need; average aid package $10,737

Texas A&M University– College Station
College Station TX
(979) 845-3741
U.S. News ranking: Nat. U., No. 69
Website: www.tamu.edu
Admissions email: admissions@tamu.edu
Public; founded 1876
Freshman admissions: more selective; 2016-2017: 35,494 applied, 23,594 accepted. Either SAT or ACT required. SAT 25/75 percentile: 1070-1310. High school rank: 66% in top tenth, 90% in top quarter, 99% in top half
Early decision deadline: N/A, notification date: N/A
Early action deadline: N/A, notification date: N/A
Application deadline (fall): 12/1
Undergraduate student body: 45,063 full time, 5,672 part time; 52% male, 48% female; 0% American Indian, 6% Asian, 3% black, 23% Hispanic, 3% multiracial, 0% Pacific Islander, 63% white, 1% international; 96% from in state; 24% live on campus; 4% of students in fraternities, 8% in sororities
Most popular majors: 17% Business, Management, Marketing, and Related Support Services, 14% Engineering, 10% Agriculture, Agriculture Operations, and Related Sciences, 9% Multi/Interdisciplinary Studies, 8% Biological and Biomedical Sciences
Expenses: 2017-2018: $10,030 in state, $30,208 out of state; room/board: $10,368
Financial aid: (979) 846-3236; 45% of undergrads determined to have financial need; average aid package $16,491

Texas A&M University–Commerce
Commerce TX
(903) 886-5000
U.S. News ranking: Nat. U., second tier
Website: www.tamuc.edu/
Admissions email: Admissions@tamuc.edu
Public; founded 1889
Freshman admissions: selective; 2016-2017: 7,986 applied, 3,623 accepted. Either SAT or ACT required. SAT 25/75 percentile: 850-1060. High school rank: 15% in top tenth, 45% in top quarter, 75% in top half
Early decision deadline: N/A, notification date: N/A
Early action deadline: N/A, notification date: N/A
Application deadline (fall): 8/15
Undergraduate student body: 5,510 full time, 2,095 part time; 40% male, 60% female; 1% American Indian, 2% Asian, 22% black, 20% Hispanic, 6% multiracial, 0% Pacific Islander, 46% white, 2% international; 96% from in state; 30% live on campus; 4%

of students in fraternities, 5% in sororities
Most popular majors: 32% Multi/Interdisciplinary Studies, 14% Business, Management, Marketing, and Related Support Services, 9% Liberal Arts and Sciences, General Studies and Humanities, 5% Psychology, 5% Visual and Performing Arts
Expenses: 2017-2018: $8,434 in state, $20,884 out of state; room/board: $8,635
Financial aid: (903) 886-5091; 74% of undergrads determined to have financial need; average aid package $9,652

Texas A&M University– Corpus Christi
Corpus Christi TX
(361) 825-2624
U.S. News ranking: Nat. U., second tier
Website: www.tamucc.edu
Admissions email: admiss@tamucc.edu
Public; founded 1947
Freshman admissions: less selective; 2016-2017: 9,002 applied, 7,773 accepted. Either SAT or ACT required. SAT 25/75 percentile: 850-1060. High school rank: 8% in top tenth, 27% in top quarter, 75% in top half
Early decision deadline: N/A, notification date: N/A
Early action deadline: N/A, notification date: N/A
Application deadline (fall): 7/1
Undergraduate student body: 8,363 full time, 1,849 part time; 41% male, 59% female; 0% American Indian, 3% Asian, 7% black, 49% Hispanic, 1% multiracial, 0% Pacific Islander, 36% white, 2% international; 98% from in state; 22% live on campus; N/A of students in fraternities, N/A in sororities
Most popular majors: 21% Business, Management, Marketing, and Related Support Services, 12% Health Professions and Related Programs, 8% Biological and Biomedical Sciences, 8% Parks, Recreation, Leisure, and Fitness Studies, 6% Engineering
Expenses: 2017-2018: $12,944 in state, $26,061 out of state; room/board: $10,410
Financial aid: (361) 825-2332; 66% of undergrads determined to have financial need; average aid package $9,554

Texas A&M University–Kingsville
Kingsville TX
(361) 593-2315
U.S. News ranking: Nat. U., second tier
Website: www.tamuk.edu
Admissions email: admissions@tamuk.edu
Public; founded 1925
Freshman admissions: selective; 2016-2017: 7,373 applied, 6,071 accepted. Neither SAT nor ACT required. ACT 25/75 percentile: 17-23. High school rank: 16% in top tenth, 42% in top quarter, 77% in top half

Early decision deadline: N/A, notification date: N/A
Early action deadline: N/A, notification date: N/A
Application deadline (fall): N/A
Undergraduate student body: 5,124 full time, 1,687 part time; 52% male, 48% female; 0% American Indian, 1% Asian, 7% black, 71% Hispanic, 1% multiracial, 0% Pacific Islander, 17% white, 3% international; 99% from in state; 28% live on campus; N/A of students in fraternities, N/A in sororities
Most popular majors: 18% Engineering, 10% Multi/Interdisciplinary Studies, 9% Health Professions and Related Programs, 8% Biological and Biomedical Sciences, 8% Business, Management, Marketing, and Related Support Services
Expenses: 2017-2018: $8,462 in state, $20,912 out of state; room/board: $8,760
Financial aid: (361) 593-3911; 77% of undergrads determined to have financial need; average aid package $10,369

Texas A&M University– Texarkana[1]
Texarkana TX
(903) 223-3069
U.S. News ranking: Reg. U. (W), second tier
Website: www.tamut.edu
Admissions email: admissions@tamut.edu
Public; founded 1971
Application deadline (fall): rolling
Undergraduate student body: N/A full time, N/A part time
Expenses: 2017-2018: $8,666 in state, $9,708 out of state; room/board: $9,600
Financial aid: (903) 334 6601; 71% of undergrads determined to have financial need; average aid package $10,067

Texas Christian University
Fort Worth TX
(800) 828-3764
U.S. News ranking: Nat. U., No. 78
Website: www.tcu.edu
Admissions email: frogmail@tcu.edu
Private; founded 1873
Affiliation: Christian Church (Disciples of Christ)
Freshman admissions: more selective; 2016-2017: 19,972 applied, 7,506 accepted. Either SAT or ACT required. ACT 25/75 percentile: 25-30. High school rank: 44% in top tenth, 74% in top quarter, 93% in top half
Early decision deadline: 11/1, notification date: 12/5
Early action deadline: 11/1, notification date: 12/15
Application deadline (fall): 2/15
Undergraduate student body: 8,608 full time, 283 part time; 40% male, 60% female; 1% American Indian, 3% Asian, 5% black, 12% Hispanic, 0% multiracial, 0% Pacific Islander, 72% white, 5% international; 54% from in

state; 49% live on campus; 41% of students in fraternities, 58% in sororities
Most popular majors: 22% Business, Management, Marketing, and Related Support Services, 16% Communication, Journalism, and Related Programs, 14% Health Professions and Related Programs, 11% Social Sciences, 6% Visual and Performing Arts
Expenses: 2017-2018: $44,760; room/board: $12,360
Financial aid: (817) 257-7858; 38% of undergrads determined to have financial need; average aid package $29,456

Texas College[1]
Tyler TX
U.S. News ranking: Reg. Coll. (W), unranked
Website: www.texascollege.edu
Admissions email: cmarshall-biggins@texascollege.edu
Private
Application deadline (fall): N/A
Undergraduate student body: N/A full time, N/A part time
Expenses: 2016-2017: $17,208; room/board: N/A
Financial aid: N/A

Texas Lutheran University
Seguin TX
(800) 771-8521
U.S. News ranking: Reg. Coll. (W), No. 2
Website: www.tlu.edu
Admissions email: admissions@tlu.edu
Private; founded 1891
Affiliation: Evangelical Lutheran Church
Freshman admissions: selective; 2016-2017: 2,131 applied, 908 accepted. Either SAT or ACT required. SAT 25/75 percentile: 880-1070. High school rank: 20% in top tenth, 51% in top quarter, 85% in top half
Early decision deadline: 11/1, notification date: 12/15
Early action deadline: 12/15, notification date: 2/15
Application deadline (fall): 2/1
Undergraduate student body: 1,213 full time, 70 part time; 49% male, 51% female; 0% American Indian, 1% Asian, 10% black, 32% Hispanic, 1% multiracial, 0% Pacific Islander, 54% white, 0% international; 98% from in state; 62% live on campus; 7% of students in fraternities, 11% in sororities
Most popular majors: 21% Health Professions and Related Programs, 13% Education, 13% Personal and Culinary Services, 8% Biological and Biomedical Sciences, 8% Social Sciences
Expenses: 2017-2018: $29,960; room/board: $9,590
Financial aid: (830) 372-8078; 78% of undergrads determined to have financial need; average aid package $24,260

Texas Southern University
Houston TX
(713) 313-7071
U.S. News ranking: Nat. U., second tier
Website: www.tsu.edu
Admissions email: admissions@tsu.edu
Public; founded 1947
Freshman admissions: least selective; 2016-2017: 10,878 applied, 5,601 accepted. Either SAT or ACT required. SAT 25/75 percentile: 715-900. High school rank: 6% in top tenth, 21% in top quarter, 58% in top half
Early decision deadline: 12/1, notification date: N/A
Early action deadline: N/A, notification date: N/A
Application deadline (fall): 8/1
Undergraduate student body: 5,776 full time, 786 part time; 44% male, 56% female; 1% American Indian, 2% Asian, 78% black, 6% Hispanic, 0% multiracial, 0% Pacific Islander, 3% white, 10% international; 91% from in state; 23% live on campus; 2% of students in fraternities, 3% in sororities
Most popular majors: 8% Biology/Biological Sciences, General, 6% Accounting, 6% Banking and Financial Support Services, 6% General Studies, 6% Health/Health Care Administration/Management
Expenses: 2016-2017: $9,000 in state, $21,240 out of state; room/board: $9,664
Financial aid: (713) 313-7071

Texas State University
San Marcos TX
(512) 245-2364
U.S. News ranking: Nat. U., second tier
Website: www.txstate.edu
Admissions email: admissions@txstate.edu
Public; founded 1899
Freshman admissions: selective; 2016-2017: 21,524 applied, 15,239 accepted. Either SAT or ACT required. SAT 25/75 percentile: 930-1120. High school rank: 14% in top tenth, 52% in top quarter, 93% in top half
Early decision deadline: N/A, notification date: N/A
Early action deadline: N/A, notification date: N/A
Application deadline (fall): 5/1
Undergraduate student body: 28,180 full time, 6,064 part time; 43% male, 57% female; 0% American Indian, 2% Asian, 10% black, 36% Hispanic, 3% multiracial, 0% Pacific Islander, 47% white, 1% international; 98% from in state; 19% live on campus; 5% of students in fraternities, 5% in sororities
Most popular majors: 7% Kinesiology and Exercise Science, 7% Multi-/Interdisciplinary Studies, Other, 7% Psychology, General, 6% Business Administration and Management, General, 4% Computer and Information Sciences, General
Expenses: 2017-2018: $10,621 in state, $23,071 out of state; room/board: $8,804

Texas Tech University
Lubbock TX
(806) 742-1480
U.S. News ranking: Nat. U., No. 176
Website: www.ttu.edu
Admissions email: admissions@ttu.edu
Public; founded 1923
Freshman admissions: more selective; 2016-2017: 23,311 applied, 14,592 accepted. Either SAT or ACT required. SAT 25/75 percentile: 1020-1200. High school rank: 21% in top tenth, 53% in top quarter, 87% in top half
Early decision deadline: N/A, notification date: N/A
Early action deadline: N/A, notification date: N/A
Application deadline (fall): 8/1
Undergraduate student body: 26,627 full time, 3,336 part time; 55% male, 45% female; 0% American Indian, 3% Asian, 6% black, 24% Hispanic, 2% multiracial, 0% Pacific Islander, 59% white, 5% international; 94% from in state; 24% live on campus; 6% of students in fraternities, 13% in sororities
Most popular majors: 21% Business, Management, Marketing, and Related Support Services, 13% Engineering, 9% Multi/Interdisciplinary Studies, 8% Family and Consumer Sciences/Human Sciences, 6% Parks, Recreation, Leisure, and Fitness Studies
Expenses: 2017-2018: $10,771 in state, $23,011 out of state; room/board: $9,384
Financial aid: (806) 834-5509; 49% of undergrads determined to have financial need; average aid package $10,249

Texas Wesleyan University
Fort Worth TX
(817) 531-4422
U.S. News ranking: Reg. U. (W), No. 59
Website: www.txwes.edu
Admissions email: admission@txwes.edu
Private; founded 1890
Affiliation: United Methodist
Freshman admissions: selective; 2016-2017: 2,959 applied, 1,218 accepted. Either SAT or ACT required. SAT 25/75 percentile: 925-1070. High school rank: 12% in top tenth, 38% in top quarter, 74% in top half
Early decision deadline: N/A, notification date: N/A
Early action deadline: N/A, notification date: N/A
Application deadline (fall): rolling
Undergraduate student body: 1,487 full time, 418 part time; 49% male, 51% female; 1% American Indian, 2% Asian, 15% black, 29% Hispanic, 6% multiracial, 0% Pacific Islander, 31% white, 16% international; 94% from in state; 30% live on campus; 5% of students in fraternities, 4% in sororities

Financial aid: (512) 245-2315; 59% of undergrads determined to have financial need; average aid package $10,311

Texas Woman's University
Denton TX
(940) 898-3188
U.S. News ranking: Nat. U., second tier
Website: www.twu.edu
Admissions email: admissions@twu.edu
Public; founded 1901
Freshman admissions: less selective; 2016-2017: 5,414 applied, 4,648 accepted. Neither SAT nor ACT required. SAT 25/75 percentile: 820-1050. High school rank: 14% in top tenth, 43% in top quarter, 80% in top half
Early decision deadline: N/A, notification date: N/A
Early action deadline: N/A, notification date: N/A
Application deadline (fall): 7/15
Undergraduate student body: 7,014 full time, 3,394 part time; 13% male, 87% female; 0% American Indian, 8% Asian, 19% black, 29% Hispanic, 4% multiracial, 0% Pacific Islander, 38% white, 1% international; 99% from in state; 21% live on campus; 12% of students in fraternities, 88% in sororities
Most popular majors: 28% Health Professions and Related Programs, 14% Liberal Arts and Sciences, General Studies and Humanities, 11% Multi/Interdisciplinary Studies, 10% Business, Management, Marketing, and Related Support Services, 7% Family and Consumer Sciences/Human Sciences
Expenses: 2017-2018: $9,366 in state, $21,816 out of state; room/board: $7,910
Financial aid: (940) 898-3050; 69% of undergrads determined to have financial need; average aid package $14,764

Trinity University
San Antonio TX
(800) 874-6489
U.S. News ranking: Reg. U. (W), No. 1
Website: www.trinity.edu
Admissions email: admissions@trinity.edu
Private; founded 1869
Affiliation: Presbyterian
Freshman admissions: more selective; 2016-2017: 7,255 applied, 2,950 accepted. Either SAT or ACT required. SAT 25/75 percentile: 1160-1370. High school rank: 41% in top tenth, 75% in top quarter, 93% in top half
Early decision deadline: 11/1, notification date: 12/15

Most popular majors: 13% Multi-/Interdisciplinary Studies, Other, 11% Psychology, General, 8% Business Administration and Management, General, 7% Criminal Justice/Safety Studies, 7% Political Science and Government, General
Expenses: 2017-2018: $27,392; room/board: $9,538
Financial aid: (817) 531-4420; 74% of undergrads determined to have financial need; average aid package $23,340

Early action deadline: 11/1, notification date: 12/15
Application deadline (fall): 2/1
Undergraduate student body: 2,283 full time, 51 part time; 47% male, 53% female; 0% American Indian, 6% Asian, 4% black, 20% Hispanic, 5% multiracial, 0% Pacific Islander, 56% white, 7% international; 77% from in state; 77% live on campus; 19% of students in fraternities, 31% in sororities
Most popular majors: 25% Business, Management, Marketing, and Related Support Services, 17% Social Sciences, 9% Biological and Biomedical Sciences, 6% Communication, Journalism, and Related Programs, 6% English Language and Literature/Letters
Expenses: 2017-2018: $41,344; room/board: $13,136
Financial aid: (210) 999-8005; 46% of undergrads determined to have financial need; average aid package $36,123

University of Dallas
Irving TX
(800) 628-6999
U.S. News ranking: Reg. U. (W), No. 13
Website: www.udallas.edu
Admissions email: ugadmis@udallas.edu
Private; founded 1956
Affiliation: Roman Catholic
Freshman admissions: selective; 2016-2017: 2,135 applied, 1,718 accepted. Either SAT or ACT required. SAT 25/75 percentile: 1040-1290. High school rank: 34% in top tenth, 61% in top quarter, 90% in top half
Early decision deadline: N/A, notification date: N/A
Early action deadline: 12/1, notification date: 1/15
Application deadline (fall): 8/1
Undergraduate student body: 1,374 full time, 33 part time; 45% male, 55% female; 1% American Indian, 6% Asian, 2% black, 22% Hispanic, 3% multiracial, 0% Pacific Islander, 63% white, 3% international
Most popular majors: 15% Business, Management, Marketing, and Related Support Services, 11% English Language and Literature/Letters, 11% Theology and Religious Vocations, 10% Biological and Biomedical Sciences, 10% Social Sciences
Expenses: 2017-2018: $38,716; room/board: $11,960
Financial aid: (972) 721-5266; 62% of undergrads determined to have financial need; average aid package $30,907

University of Houston
Houston TX
(713) 743-1010
U.S. News ranking: Nat. U., No. 192
Website: www.uh.edu
Admissions email: admissions@uh.edu
Public; founded 1927
Freshman admissions: more selective; 2016-2017: 19,860 applied, 11,627 accepted. Either SAT or ACT required. SAT 25/75 percentile: 1040-1250. High

More @ usnews.com/bestcolleges

school rank: 32% in top tenth, 66% in top quarter, 89% in top half
Early decision deadline: N/A, notification date: N/A
Early action deadline: N/A, notification date: N/A
Application deadline (fall): 6/15
Undergraduate student body: 25,794 full time, 10,077 part time; 51% male, 49% female; 0% American Indian, 22% Asian, 10% black, 33% Hispanic, 3% multiracial, 0% Pacific Islander, 25% white, 4% international; 98% from in state; 19% live on campus; 4% of students in fraternities, 3% in sororities
Most popular majors: 28% Business, Management, Marketing, and Related Support Services, 7% Engineering, 6% Communication, Journalism, and Related Programs, 6% Psychology, 5% Biological and Biomedical Sciences
Expenses: 2017-2018: $11,887 in state, $27,337 out of state; room/board: $9,984
Financial aid: (713) 743-1010; 62% of undergrads determined to have financial need; average aid package $12,167

University of Houston–Clear Lake
Houston TX
(281) 283-2500
U.S. News ranking: Reg. U. (W), No. 63
Website: www.uhcl.edu
Admissions email: admissions@uhcl.edu
Public; founded 1974
Freshman admissions: selective; 2016-2017: 1,056 applied, 685 accepted. Either SAT or ACT required. SAT 25/75 percentile: 930-1110. High school rank: 19% in top tenth, 44% in top quarter, 79% in top half
Early decision deadline: N/A, notification date: N/A
Early action deadline: N/A, notification date: N/A
Application deadline (fall): 6/1
Undergraduate student body: 2,693 full time, 2,877 part time; 36% male, 64% female; 0% American Indian, 6% Asian, 8% black, 38% Hispanic, 3% multiracial, 0% Pacific Islander, 42% white, 2% international; N/A from in state; 3% live on campus; N/A of students in fraternities, N/A in sororities
Most popular majors: 25% Business, Management, Marketing, and Related Support Services, 23% Multi/Interdisciplinary Studies, 10% Psychology, 5% Health Professions and Related Programs, 5% Social Sciences
Expenses: 2017-2018: $8,188 in state, $23,668 out of state; room/board: $9,732
Financial aid: (281) 283-2480; 66% of undergrads determined to have financial need; average aid package $9,024

University of Houston–Downtown
Houston TX
(713) 221-8522
U.S. News ranking: Reg. U. (W), second tier
Website: www.uhd.edu
Admissions email: uhdadmit@uhd.edu
Public; founded 1974
Freshman admissions: less selective; 2016-2017: 4,187 applied, 3,470 accepted. Either SAT or ACT required. SAT 25/75 percentile: 820-990. High school rank: 6% in top tenth, 32% in top quarter, 74% in top half
Early decision deadline: N/A, notification date: N/A
Early action deadline: N/A, notification date: N/A
Application deadline (fall): 7/1
Undergraduate student body: 6,329 full time, 6,536 part time; 40% male, 60% female; 0% American Indian, 9% Asian, 21% black, 46% Hispanic, 1% multiracial, 0% Pacific Islander, 16% white, 5% international; 100% from in state; 0% live on campus; 1% of students in fraternities, 1% in sororities
Most popular majors: 34% Business, Management, Marketing, and Related Support Services, 26% Multi/Interdisciplinary Studies, 9% Homeland Security, Law Enforcement, Firefighting and Related Protective Services, 9% Psychology, 4% Communication, Journalism, and Related Programs
Expenses: 2017-2018: $7,241 in state, $19,481 out of state; room/board: N/A
Financial aid: (713) 221-8041; 72% of undergrads determined to have financial need; average aid package $9,191

University of Houston–Victoria
Victoria TX
(877) 970-4848
U.S. News ranking: Reg. U. (W), second tier
Website: www.uhv.edu/
Admissions email: admissions@uhv.edu
Public; founded 1973
Freshman admissions: least selective; 2016-2017: 5,074 applied, 2,678 accepted. Neither SAT nor ACT required. SAT 25/75 percentile: 780-1000. High school rank: 6% in top tenth, 18% in top quarter, 62% in top half
Early decision deadline: N/A, notification date: N/A
Early action deadline: N/A, notification date: N/A
Application deadline (fall): 8/1
Undergraduate student body: 1,586 full time, 1,371 part time; 36% male, 64% female; 0% American Indian, 6% Asian, 17% black, 38% Hispanic, 2% multiracial, 0% Pacific Islander, 34% white, 1% international; 100% from in state; 27% live on campus; 0% of students in fraternities, 0% in sororities
Most popular majors: 40% Business, Management, Marketing, and Related Support Services, 22% Multi/Interdisciplinary Studies, 12% Psychology, 8% Computer and Information

Sciences and Support Services, 5% Homeland Security, Law Enforcement, Firefighting and Related Protective Services
Expenses: 2017-2018: $7,468 in state, $21,075 out of state; room/board: $7,663
Financial aid: N/A

University of Mary Hardin-Baylor
Belton TX
(254) 295-4520
U.S. News ranking: Reg. U. (W), No. 54
Website: www.umhb.edu
Admissions email: admission@umhb.edu
Private; founded 1845
Affiliation: Baptist
Freshman admissions: selective; 2016-2017: 8,954 applied, 7,056 accepted. Either SAT or ACT required. SAT 25/75 percentile: 920-1120. High school rank: 20% in top tenth, 47% in top quarter, 76% in top half
Early decision deadline: N/A, notification date: N/A
Early action deadline: N/A, notification date: N/A
Application deadline (fall): rolling
Undergraduate student body: 2,996 full time, 282 part time; 37% male, 63% female; 1% American Indian, 2% Asian, 15% black, 21% Hispanic, 3% multiracial, 0% Pacific Islander, 57% white, 1% international; 98% from in state; 57% live on campus; N/A of students in fraternities, N/A in sororities
Most popular majors: 25% Health Professions and Related Programs, 17% Business, Management, Marketing, and Related Support Services, 10% Education, 7% Parks, Recreation, Leisure, and Fitness Studies, 6% Biological and Biomedical Sciences
Expenses: 2017-2018: $27,700; room/board: $7,894
Financial aid: (254) 295-4517; 79% of undergrads determined to have financial need; average aid package $17,510

University of North Texas
Denton TX
(940) 565-2681
U.S. News ranking: Nat. U., second tier
Website: www.unt.edu
Admissions email: unt.freshmen@unt.edu
Public; founded 1890
Freshman admissions: selective; 2016-2017: 16,826 applied, 12,046 accepted. Either SAT or ACT required. SAT 25/75 percentile: 980-1200. High school rank: 20% in top tenth, 54% in top quarter, 91% in top half
Early decision deadline: N/A, notification date: N/A
Early action deadline: N/A, notification date: N/A
Application deadline (fall): 8/1
Undergraduate student body: 25,513 full time, 5,696 part time; 48% male, 52% female; 0% American Indian, 6% Asian, 14% black, 24% Hispanic, 4% multiracial, 0% Pacific Islander, 48% white, 3% international; 97% from in state; 20% live

on campus; 2% of students in fraternities, 2% in sororities
Most popular majors: 20% Business, Management, Marketing, and Related Support Services, 12% Multi/Interdisciplinary Studies, 9% Liberal Arts and Sciences, General Studies and Humanities, 9% Visual and Performing Arts, 7% Communication, Journalism, and Related Programs
Expenses: 2017-2018: $10,906 in state, $23,716 out of state; room/board: $9,268
Financial aid: (940) 565-3901; 62% of undergrads determined to have financial need; average aid package $11,134

University of North Texas–Dallas
Dallas TX
U.S. News ranking: Reg. U. (W), No. 95
Public; founded 2010
Freshman admissions: less selective; 2016-2017: 1,863 applied, 1,270 accepted. Either SAT or ACT required. SAT 25/75 percentile: 820-985. High school rank: 21% in top tenth, 45% in top quarter, 75% in top half
Early decision deadline: N/A, notification date: N/A
Early action deadline: N/A, notification date: N/A
Application deadline (fall): 8/10
Undergraduate student body: 1,375 full time, 920 part time; 32% male, 68% female; 0% American Indian, 2% Asian, 33% black, 50% Hispanic, 2% multiracial, 0% Pacific Islander, 11% white, 1% international; 98% from in state; N/A live on campus; N/A of students in fraternities, N/A in sororities
Most popular majors: Information not available
Expenses: 2016-2017: $7,848 in state, $20,088 out of state; room/board: N/A
Financial aid: N/A

University of St. Thomas
Houston TX
(713) 525-3500
U.S. News ranking: Reg. U. (W), No. 26
Website: www.stthom.edu
Admissions email: admissions@stthom.edu
Private; founded 1947
Affiliation: Roman Catholic
Freshman admissions: selective; 2016-2017: 942 applied, 729 accepted. Either SAT or ACT required. SAT 25/75 percentile: 990-1175. High school rank: 31% in top tenth, 57% in top quarter, 85% in top half
Early decision deadline: N/A, notification date: N/A
Early action deadline: 12/1, notification date: 12/15
Application deadline (fall): 5/1
Undergraduate student body: 1,391 full time, 423 part time; 40% male, 60% female; 0% American Indian, 12% Asian, 7% black, 44% Hispanic, 3% multiracial, 0% Pacific Islander, 24% white,

9% international; 97% from in state; 22% live on campus; N/A of students in fraternities, N/A in sororities
Most popular majors: 24% Business, Management, Marketing, and Related Support Services, 13% Biological and Biomedical Sciences, 13% Liberal Arts and Sciences, General Studies and Humanities, 9% Health Professions and Related Programs, 8% Psychology
Expenses: 2017-2018: $32,660; room/board: $8,850
Financial aid: (713) 525-2151; 64% of undergrads determined to have financial need; average aid package $24,458

University of Texas of the Permian Basin
Odessa TX
(432) 552-2605
U.S. News ranking: Reg. U. (W), No. 91
Website: www.utpb.edu
Admissions email: admissions@utpb.edu
Public; founded 1973
Freshman admissions: selective; 2016-2017: 1,307 applied, 1,065 accepted. Either SAT or ACT required. SAT 25/75 percentile: 850-1060. High school rank: 17% in top tenth, 50% in top quarter, 87% in top half
Early decision deadline: N/A, notification date: N/A
Early action deadline: N/A, notification date: N/A
Application deadline (fall): 8/24
Undergraduate student body: 2,168 full time, 3,495 part time; 43% male, 57% female; 1% American Indian, 2% Asian, 6% black, 53% Hispanic, 1% multiracial, 0% Pacific Islander, 34% white, 3% international; 96% from in state; 21% live on campus; 0% of students in fraternities, 0% in sororities
Most popular majors: 22% Business Administration and Management, General, 14% Psychology, General, 8% Petroleum Engineering, 8% Sociology, 6% Multi-/Interdisciplinary Studies, Other
Expenses: 2017-2018: $7,124 in state, $8,274 out of state; room/board: $10,970
Financial aid: (432) 552-2620; 76% of undergrads determined to have financial need; average aid package $10,560

University of Texas–Arlington
Arlington TX
(817) 272-6287
U.S. News ranking: Nat. U., second tier
Website: www.uta.edu
Admissions email: admissions@uta.edu
Public; founded 1895
Freshman admissions: selective; 2016-2017: 12,558 applied, 8,768 accepted. Either SAT or ACT required. SAT 25/75 percentile: 950-1190. High school rank: 31% in top tenth, 74% in top quarter, 96% in top half
Early decision deadline: N/A, notification date: N/A

Early action deadline: N/A, notification date: N/A
Application deadline (fall): rolling
Undergraduate student body: 16,679 full time, 16,096 part time; 38% male, 62% female; 0% American Indian, 11% Asian, 15% black, 26% Hispanic, 3% multiracial, 0% Pacific Islander, 38% white, 3% international; 87% from in state; 10% live on campus; 5% of students in fraternities, 3% in sororities
Most popular majors: 43% Health Professions and Related Programs, 11% Business, Management, Marketing, and Related Support Services, 6% Engineering, 5% Biological and Biomedical Sciences, 5% Liberal Arts and Sciences, General Studies and Humanities
Expenses: 2017-2018: $9,952 in state, $25,152 out of state; room/board: $8,924
Financial aid: (817) 272-3568; 81% of undergrads determined to have financial need; average aid package $11,076

University of Texas–Austin
Austin TX
(512) 475-7399
U.S. News ranking: Nat. U., No. 56
Website: www.utexas.edu
Public; founded 1883
Freshman admissions: more selective; 2016-2017: 47,511 applied, 19,182 accepted. Either SAT or ACT required. SAT 25/75 percentile: 1140-1410. High school rank: 70% in top tenth, 92% in top quarter, 98% in top half
Early decision deadline: N/A, notification date: N/A
Early action deadline: N/A, notification date: N/A
Application deadline (fall): 12/1
Undergraduate student body: 37,234 full time, 2,934 part time; 47% male, 53% female; 0% American Indian, 21% Asian, 4% black, 23% Hispanic, 4% multiracial, 0% Pacific Islander, 42% white, 5% international; 95% from in state; 18% live on campus; 15% of students in fraternities, 18% in sororities
Most popular majors: 12% Engineering, 11% Biological and Biomedical Sciences, 11% Business, Management, Marketing, and Related Support Services, 11% Communication, Journalism, and Related Programs, 11% Social Sciences
Expenses: 2017-2018: $10,136 in state, $35,766 out of state; room/board: $10,070
Financial aid: (512) 475-6282; 40% of undergrads determined to have financial need; average aid package $12,283

University of Texas–Dallas
Richardson TX
(972) 883-2270
U.S. News ranking: Nat. U., No. 145
Website: www.utdallas.edu
Admissions email: interest@utdallas.edu
Public; founded 1969

Freshman admissions: more selective; 2016-2017: 12,686 applied, 8,625 accepted. Either SAT or ACT required. SAT 25/75 percentile: 1140-1380. High school rank: 32% in top tenth, 61% in top quarter, 88% in top half
Early decision deadline: N/A, notification date: N/A
Early action deadline: N/A, notification date: N/A
Application deadline (fall): 5/1
Undergraduate student body: 14,323 full time, 3,027 part time; 57% male, 43% female; 0% American Indian, 30% Asian, 6% black, 18% Hispanic, 4% multiracial, 0% Pacific Islander, 36% white, 4% international; 96% from in state; 25% live on campus; 2% of students in fraternities, 3% in sororities
Most popular majors: 26% Business, Management, Marketing, and Related Support Services, 15% Biological and Biomedical Sciences, 11% Engineering, 9% Computer and Information Sciences and Support Services, 7% Psychology
Expenses: 2017-2018: N/A in state, N/A out of state; room/board: $11,112
Financial aid: (972) 883-4020; 52% of undergrads determined to have financial need; average aid package $13,241

University of Texas–El Paso
El Paso TX
(915) 747-5890
U.S. News ranking: Nat. U., second tier
Website: www.utep.edu
Admissions email: futureminer@utep.edu
Public; founded 1914
Freshman admissions: less selective; 2016-2017: 8,684 applied, 8,682 accepted. Either SAT or ACT required. SAT 25/75 percentile: 810-1030. High school rank: 17% in top tenth, 40% in top quarter, 67% in top half
Early decision deadline: N/A, notification date: N/A
Early action deadline: N/A, notification date: N/A
Application deadline (fall): rolling
Undergraduate student body: 13,341 full time, 7,180 part time; 47% male, 53% female; 0% American Indian, 1% Asian, 2% black, 84% Hispanic, 1% multiracial, 0% Pacific Islander, 6% white, 5% international
Most popular majors: 17% Business, Management, and Related Support Services, 12% Health Professions and Related Programs, 10% Engineering, 9% Biological and Biomedical Sciences, 9% Multi/Interdisciplinary Studies
Expenses: 2017-2018: $7,651 in state, $21,396 out of state; room/board: $9,495
Financial aid: (915) 747-5204; 78% of undergrads determined to have financial need; average aid package $13,801

University of Texas–Rio Grande Valley
Edinburg TX
(888) 882-4026
U.S. News ranking: Nat. U., second tier
Website: www.utrgv.edu/en-us/index.htm
Admissions email: admissions@utrgv.edu
Public; founded 2013
Freshman admissions: selective; 2016-2017: 9,174 applied, 5,763 accepted. Either SAT or ACT required. ACT 25/75 percentile: 18-22. High school rank: 24% in top tenth, 58% in top quarter, 86% in top half
Early decision deadline: N/A, notification date: N/A
Early action deadline: N/A, notification date: N/A
Application deadline (fall): 7/1
Undergraduate student body: 17,959 full time, 6,474 part time; 44% male, 56% female; 0% American Indian, 1% Asian, 0% black, 91% Hispanic, 0% multiracial, 0% Pacific Islander, 3% white, 2% international
Most popular majors: Information not available
Expenses: 2016-2017: $7,438 in state, $17,230 out of state; room/board: $7,950
Financial aid: N/A

University of Texas–San Antonio
San Antonio TX
(210) 458-4599
U.S. News ranking: Nat. U., second tier
Website: www.utsa.edu
Admissions email: prospects@utsa.edu
Public; founded 1969
Freshman admissions: selective; 2016-2017: 15,500 applied, 11,843 accepted. Either SAT or ACT required. SAT 25/75 percentile: 920-1130. High school rank: 18% in top tenth, 60% in top quarter, 91% in top half
Early decision deadline: N/A, notification date: N/A
Early action deadline: N/A, notification date: N/A
Application deadline (fall): 6/1
Undergraduate student body: 20,222 full time, 4,502 part time; 50% male, 50% female; 0% American Indian, 5% Asian, 9% black, 54% Hispanic, 3% multiracial, 0% Pacific Islander, 24% white, 2% international; 98% from in state; 17% live on campus; 3% of students in fraternities, 5% in sororities
Most popular majors: 24% Business, Management, Marketing, and Related Support Services, 8% Engineering, 8% Psychology, 7% Homeland Security, Law Enforcement, Firefighting and Related Protective Services, 6% Biological and Biomedical Sciences
Expenses: 2017-2018: $9,380 in state, $23,379 out of state; room/board: $7,190
Financial aid: (210) 458-7172; 66% of undergrads determined to have financial need; average aid package $9,836

University of Texas–Tyler
Tyler TX
(903) 566-7203
U.S. News ranking: Reg. U. (W), No. 90
Website: www.uttyler.edu
Admissions email: admissions@uttyler.edu
Public; founded 1971
Freshman admissions: selective; 2016-2017: 2,636 applied, 1,828 accepted. Either SAT or ACT required. SAT 25/75 percentile: 950-1150. High school rank: 12% in top tenth, 39% in top quarter, 69% in top half
Early decision deadline: N/A, notification date: N/A
Early action deadline: N/A, notification date: N/A
Application deadline (fall): 8/28
Undergraduate student body: 4,808 full time, 2,235 part time; 45% male, 55% female; 0% American Indian, 4% Asian, 10% black, 18% Hispanic, 6% multiracial, 0% Pacific Islander, 59% white, 2% international; 99% from in state; 19% live on campus; 2% of students in fraternities, 4% in sororities
Most popular majors: Information not available
Expenses: 2016-2017: $7,602 in state, $20,082 out of state; room/board: $9,970
Financial aid: N/A

University of the Incarnate Word
San Antonio TX
(210) 829-6005
U.S. News ranking: Reg. U. (W), No. 47
Website: www.uiw.edu
Admissions email: admis@uiwtx.edu
Private; founded 1881
Affiliation: Roman Catholic
Freshman admissions: less selective; 2016-2017: 3,934 applied, 3,614 accepted. Either SAT or ACT required. SAT 25/75 percentile: 850-940. High school rank: 14% in top tenth, 36% in top quarter, 71% in top half
Early decision deadline: N/A, notification date: N/A
Early action deadline: N/A, notification date: N/A
Application deadline (fall): rolling
Undergraduate student body: 4,532 full time, 1,891 part time; 40% male, 60% female; 0% American Indian, 2% Asian, 8% black, 58% Hispanic, 2% multiracial, 0% Pacific Islander, 19% white, 6% international; 90% from in state; 17% live on campus; N/A of students in fraternities, N/A in sororities
Most popular majors: 12% Business Administration and Management, General, 8% Biology/Biological Sciences, General, 6% Psychology, General, 4% Elementary Education and Teaching, 3% Marketing/Marketing Management, General
Expenses: 2017-2018: $29,990; room/board: $12,436
Financial aid: (210) 829-6008; 77% of undergrads determined to have financial need; average aid package $21,039

Wade College[1]
Dallas TX
U.S. News ranking: Reg. Coll. (W), unranked
For-profit
Application deadline (fall): N/A
Undergraduate student body: N/A full time, N/A part time
Expenses: 2016-2017: $13,675; room/board: N/A
Financial aid: N/A

Wayland Baptist University
Plainview TX
(806) 291-3500
U.S. News ranking: Reg. U. (W), second tier
Website: www.wbu.edu
Admissions email: admitme@wbu.edu
Private; founded 1908
Affiliation: Baptist
Freshman admissions: less selective; 2016-2017: 651 applied, 648 accepted. Either SAT or ACT required. ACT 25/75 percentile: 17-22. High school rank: 8% in top tenth, 30% in top quarter, 59% in top half
Early decision deadline: N/A, notification date: N/A
Early action deadline: N/A, notification date: N/A
Application deadline (fall): rolling
Undergraduate student body: 1,070 full time, 2,706 part time; 51% male, 49% female; 1% American Indian, 2% Asian, 17% black, 30% Hispanic, 4% multiracial, 1% Pacific Islander, 40% white, 2% international; 68% from in state; 19% live on campus; 1% of students in fraternities, 2% in sororities
Most popular majors: 35% Business Administration and Management, General, 25% Liberal Arts and Sciences, General Studies and Humanities, Other, 8% Criminal Justice/Law Enforcement Administration, 8% Public Administration and Social Service Professions, 5% Christian Studies
Expenses: 2017-2018: $19,430; room/board: $7,296
Financial aid: (806) 291-3520; 76% of undergrads determined to have financial need; average aid package $13,894

West Texas A&M University
Canyon TX
(806) 651-2020
U.S. News ranking: Reg. U. (W), No. 81
Website: www.wtamu.edu
Admissions email: admissions@mail.wtamu.edu
Public; founded 1910
Freshman admissions: selective; 2016-2017: 6,163 applied, 3,686 accepted. Either SAT or ACT required. ACT 25/75 percentile: 18-24. High school rank: 14% in top tenth, 43% in top quarter, 77% in top half
Early decision deadline: N/A, notification date: N/A
Early action deadline: N/A, notification date: N/A
Application deadline (fall): rolling

Undergraduate student body: 5,650 full time, 1,739 part time; 44% male, 56% female; 0% American Indian, 1% Asian, 5% black, 27% Hispanic, 2% multiracial, 0% Pacific Islander, 60% white, 2% international
Most popular majors: 14% Business, Management, Marketing, and Related Support Services, 12% Health Professions and Related Programs, 12% Multi/Interdisciplinary Studies, 9% Agriculture, Agriculture Operations, and Related Sciences, 9% Liberal Arts and Sciences, General Studies and Humanities
Expenses: 2017-2018: $7,557 in state, $9,418 out of state; room/board: $7,196
Financial aid: (806) 651-2055; 61% of undergrads determined to have financial need; average aid package $8,537

Wiley College[1]
Marshall TX
(800) 658-6889
U.S. News ranking: Reg. Coll. (W), second tier
Website: www.wileyc.edu
Admissions email: admissions@wileyc.edu
Private; founded 1873
Application deadline (fall): rolling
Undergraduate student body: N/A full time, N/A part time
Expenses: 2016-2017: $12,064; room/board: $6,974
Financial aid: (903) 927-3216

UTAH

Brigham Young University–Provo
Provo UT
(801) 422-2507
U.S. News ranking: Nat. U., No. 61
Website: www.byu.edu
Admissions email: admissions@byu.edu
Private; founded 1875
Affiliation: Latter Day Saints (Mormon Church)
Freshman admissions: more selective; 2016-2017: 12,739 applied, 6,520 accepted. Either SAT or ACT required. ACT 25/75 percentile: 27-31. High school rank: 55% in top tenth, 86% in top quarter, 98% in top half
Early decision deadline: N/A, notification date: N/A
Early action deadline: N/A, notification date: N/A
Application deadline (fall): 2/1
Undergraduate student body: 28,012 full time, 2,967 part time; 52% male, 48% female; 0% American Indian, 2% Asian, 1% black, 6% Hispanic, 4% multiracial, 1% Pacific Islander, 83% white, 3% international; 34% from in state; 19% live on campus; N/A of students in fraternities, N/A in sororities
Most popular majors: 17% Business, Management, Marketing, and Related Support Services, 11% Biological and Biomedical Sciences, 8% Education, 8% Engineering, 8% Health Professions and Related Programs
Expenses: 2017-2018: $5,460; room/board: $7,530

Financial aid: (801) 422-4104; 48% of undergrads determined to have financial need; average aid package $7,436

Dixie State University
Saint George UT
(435) 652-7702
U.S. News ranking: Reg. Coll. (W), unranked
Website: www.dixie.edu
Admissions email: admissions@dixie.edu
Public; founded 1911
Freshman admissions: less selective; 2016-2017: 15,486 applied, 15,486 accepted. Neither SAT nor ACT required. ACT 25/75 percentile: 17-23. High school rank: 9% in top tenth, 26% in top quarter, 59% in top half
Early decision deadline: N/A, notification date: N/A
Early action deadline: N/A, notification date: N/A
Application deadline (fall): 8/15
Undergraduate student body: 5,673 full time, 3,320 part time; 45% male, 55% female; 1% American Indian, 1% Asian, 3% black, 12% Hispanic, 3% multiracial, 2% Pacific Islander, 75% white, 2% international
Most popular majors: 22% Business, Management, Marketing, and Related Support Services, 15% Communication, Journalism, and Related Programs, 12% Health Professions and Related Programs, 10% Education, 9% Multi/Interdisciplinary Studies
Expenses: 2016-2017: $4,840 in state, $13,855 out of state; room/board: $5,615
Financial aid: (435) 652-7575; 66% of undergrads determined to have financial need; average aid package $10,256

Snow College
Ephraim UT
(435) 283-7159
U.S. News ranking: Reg. Coll. (W), unranked
Website: www.snow.edu/admissions/
Admissions email: admissions@snow.edu
Public; founded 1888
Freshman admissions: selective; 2016-2017: 8,626 applied, 8,626 accepted. Either SAT or ACT required. ACT 25/75 percentile: 17-23. High school rank: N/A
Early decision deadline: N/A, notification date: N/A
Early action deadline: N/A, notification date: N/A
Application deadline (fall): rolling
Undergraduate student body: 3,323 full time, 2,027 part time; 46% male, 54% female; 1% American Indian, 1% Asian, 1% black, 5% Hispanic, 1% multiracial, 3% Pacific Islander, 84% white, 3% international; 88% from in state; N/A live on campus; N/A of students in fraternities, N/A in sororities
Most popular majors: 44% General Studies, 11% Registered Nursing/Registered Nurse, 5% Music, General, 3% Business/Commerce, General, 3% Engineering, General

Expenses: 2016-2017: $3,592 in state, $12,070 out of state; room/board: $5,200
Financial aid: N/A

Southern Utah University
Cedar City UT
(435) 586-7740
U.S. News ranking: Reg. U. (W), No. 76
Website: www.suu.edu
Admissions email: admissionsinfo@suu.edu
Public; founded 1897
Freshman admissions: selective; 2016-2017: 10,573 applied, 7,642 accepted. Either SAT or ACT required. ACT 25/75 percentile: 20-26. High school rank: 19% in top tenth, 48% in top quarter, 77% in top half
Early decision deadline: N/A, notification date: N/A
Early action deadline: N/A, notification date: N/A
Application deadline (fall): 5/1
Undergraduate student body: 5,879 full time, 2,528 part time; 43% male, 57% female; 1% American Indian, 1% Asian, 2% black, 6% Hispanic, 1% multiracial, 2% Pacific Islander, 76% white, 4% international; 85% from in state; 8% live on campus; N/A of students in fraternities, N/A in sororities
Most popular majors: 13% Business, Management, Marketing, and Related Support Services, 12% Education, 8% Family and Consumer Sciences/Human Sciences, 8% Health Professions and Related Programs, 8% Psychology
Expenses: 2017-2018: $6,676 in state, $20,288 out of state; room/board: $7,067
Financial aid: (435) 586-7735; 63% of undergrads determined to have financial need; average aid package $9,027

University of Utah
Salt Lake City UT
(801) 581-8761
U.S. News ranking: Nat. U., No. 110
Website: www.utah.edu
Admissions email: admissions@utah.edu
Public; founded 1850
Freshman admissions: more selective; 2016-2017: 14,308 applied, 10,934 accepted. Either SAT or ACT required. ACT 25/75 percentile: 21-27. High school rank: 35% in top tenth, 62% in top quarter, 85% in top half
Early decision deadline: N/A, notification date: N/A
Early action deadline: 12/1, notification date: 1/15
Application deadline (fall): 4/1
Undergraduate student body: 17,197 full time, 6,592 part time; 54% male, 46% female; 0% American Indian, 6% Asian, 1% black, 12% Hispanic, 5% multiracial, 0% Pacific Islander, 70% white, 5% international; 80% from in state; 15% live on campus; 6% of students in fraternities, 8% in sororities
Most popular majors: 7% Communication and Media Studies, 7% Psychology,

General, 5% Economics, General, 4% Biology/Biological Sciences, General, 4% Business Administration and Management, General
Expenses: 2017-2018: $9,166 in state, $26,408 out of state; room/board: $9,936
Financial aid: (801) 581-6211; 48% of undergrads determined to have financial need; average aid package $18,758

Utah State University
Logan UT
(435) 797-1079
U.S. News ranking: Nat. U., No. 216
Website: www.usu.edu
Admissions email: admit@usu.edu
Public; founded 1888
Freshman admissions: selective; 2016-2017: 15,401 applied, 13,899 accepted. Either SAT or ACT required. ACT 25/75 percentile: 20-27. High school rank: 19% in top tenth, 44% in top quarter, 74% in top half
Early decision deadline: N/A, notification date: N/A
Early action deadline: N/A, notification date: N/A
Application deadline (fall): rolling
Undergraduate student body: 16,991 full time, 7,847 part time; 47% male, 53% female; 2% American Indian, 1% Asian, 1% black, 6% Hispanic, 2% multiracial, 0% Pacific Islander, 82% white, 1% international; 74% from in state; N/A live on campus; 4% of students in fraternities, 4% in sororities
Most popular majors: 10% Communication Sciences and Disorders, General, 8% Economics, General, 4% Business Administration and Management, General, 4% Physical Education Teaching and Coaching, 3% Psychology, General
Expenses: 2017-2018: $7,174 in state, $20,726 out of state; room/board: $6,060
Financial aid: (435) 797-0173; 55% of undergrads determined to have financial need; average aid package $9,705

Utah Valley University
Orem UT
(801) 863-8706
U.S. News ranking: Reg. U. (W), unranked
Website: www.uvu.edu/
Admissions email: admissions@uvu.edu
Public; founded 1941
Freshman admissions: selective; 2016-2017: 10,341 applied, 10,336 accepted. Neither SAT nor ACT required. ACT 25/75 percentile: 18-25. High school rank: 9% in top tenth, 28% in top quarter, 59% in top half
Early decision deadline: N/A, notification date: N/A
Early action deadline: N/A, notification date: N/A
Application deadline (fall): 8/1
Undergraduate student body: 17,804 full time, 16,902 part time; 54% male, 46% female; 1% American Indian, 1% Asian, 1% black, 11% Hispanic, 3% multiracial, 1% Pacific Islander, 78% white, 2% international; 85% from in state; N/A live

on campus; N/A of students in fraternities, N/A in sororities
Most popular majors: 20% Business, Management, Marketing, and Related Support Services, 10% Education, 10% Psychology, 7% Computer and Information Sciences and Support Services, 7% Homeland Security, Law Enforcement, Firefighting and Related Protective Services
Expenses: 2017-2018: $5,652 in state, $16,066 out of state; room/board: $6,118
Financial aid: (801) 863-6746; 59% of undergrads determined to have financial need; average aid package $7,730

Weber State University
Ogden UT
(801) 626-6744
U.S. News ranking: Reg. U. (W), No. 86
Website: weber.edu
Admissions email: admissions@weber.edu
Public; founded 1889
Freshman admissions: selective; 2016-2017: 6,199 applied, 6,199 accepted. Neither SAT nor ACT required. ACT 25/75 percentile: 18-24. High school rank: 10% in top tenth, 29% in top quarter, 61% in top half
Early decision deadline: N/A, notification date: N/A
Early action deadline: N/A, notification date: N/A
Application deadline (fall): 8/28
Undergraduate student body: 10,980 full time, 15,132 part time; 46% male, 54% female; 1% American Indian, 2% Asian, 2% black, 11% Hispanic, 3% multiracial, 1% Pacific Islander, 75% white, 2% international; 89% from in state; 4% live on campus; 1% of students in fraternities, 1% in sororities
Most popular majors: 15% Registered Nursing/Registered Nurse, 6% Selling Skills and Sales Operations, 4% Computer Science, 4% Criminal Justice/Safety Studies, 3% Accounting
Expenses: 2017-2018: $5,712 in state, $15,260 out of state; room/board: $8,400
Financial aid: (801) 626-7569; 58% of undergrads determined to have financial need; average aid package $5,920

Western Governors University[1]
Salt Lake City UT
U.S. News ranking: Reg. U. (W), unranked
Website: www.wgu.edu/
Admissions email: info@wgu.edu
Private; founded 1996
Application deadline (fall): N/A
Undergraduate student body: N/A full time, N/A part time
Expenses: 2016-2017: $6,070; room/board: N/A
Financial aid: (877) 435-7948

Westminster College

Salt Lake City UT
(801) 832-2200
U.S. News ranking: Reg. U. (W),
No. 19
Website:
www.westminstercollege.edu
Admissions email: admission@
westminstercollege.edu
Private; founded 1875
Affiliation: Undenominational
Freshman admissions: selective;
2016-2017: 1,938 applied,
1,820 accepted. Either SAT
or ACT required. ACT 25/75
percentile: 22-27. High school
rank: 19% in top tenth, 52% in
top quarter, 84% in top half
Early decision deadline: N/A,
notification date: N/A
Early action deadline: N/A,
notification date: N/A
Application deadline (fall): 8/16
Undergraduate student body: 2,013
full time, 114 part time; 44%
male, 56% female; 1% American
Indian, 3% Asian, 2% black,
10% Hispanic, 4% multiracial,
0% Pacific Islander, 71% white,
5% international; 60% from in
state; 32% live on campus; 0%
of students in fraternities, 0% in
sororities
Most popular majors: 29% Health
Professions and Related Programs,
28% Business, Management,
Marketing, and Related Support
Services, 7% Biological and
Biomedical Sciences, 6%
Communication, Journalism, and
Related Programs, 6% Psychology
Expenses: 2017-2018: $33,040;
room/board: $9,244
Financial aid: (801) 832-2500;
60% of undergrads determined to
have financial need; average aid
package $26,199

VERMONT

Bennington College

Bennington VT
(800) 833-6845
U.S. News ranking: Nat. Lib. Arts,
No. 87
Website: www.bennington.edu
Admissions email: admissions@
bennington.edu
Private; founded 1932
Freshman admissions: selective;
2016-2017: 1,236 applied, 741
accepted. Neither SAT nor ACT
required. SAT 25/75 percentile:
1190-1378. High school rank:
N/A
Early decision deadline: 11/15,
notification date: 12/20
Early action deadline: 12/1,
notification date: 2/1
Application deadline (fall): 1/3
Undergraduate student body: 682
full time, 29 part time; 36%
male, 64% female; 1% American
Indian, 2% Asian, 3% black, 9%
Hispanic, 5% multiracial, 0%
Pacific Islander, 60% white, 15%
international
Most popular majors: 48% Visual
and Performing Arts, 10%
English Language and Literature/
Letters, 6% Social Sciences,
5% Biological and Biomedical
Sciences, 5% Foreign Languages,
Literatures, and Linguistics
Expenses: 2017-2018: $52,420;
room/board: $15,040

Financial aid: (802) 440-4325;
70% of undergrads determined to
have financial need; average aid
package $37,844

Castleton University[1]

Castleton VT
(800) 639-8521
U.S. News ranking: Reg. Coll. (N),
No. 24
Website: www.castleton.edu
Admissions email:
info@castleton.edu
Public; founded 1787
Application deadline (fall): rolling
Undergraduate student body: N/A
full time, N/A part time
Expenses: 2016-2017: $11,314
in state, $26,722 out of state;
room/board: $9,988
Financial aid: N/A

Champlain College

Burlington VT
(800) 570-5858
U.S. News ranking: Reg. U. (N),
No. 91
Website: www.champlain.edu
Admissions email: admission@
champlain.edu
Private; founded 1878
Freshman admissions: selective;
2016-2017: 4,576 applied,
3,201 accepted. Either SAT
or ACT required. SAT 25/75
percentile: 1020-1240. High
school rank: 15% in top tenth,
40% in top quarter, 72% in
top half
Early decision deadline: 11/1,
notification date: N/A
Early action deadline: N/A,
notification date: N/A
Application deadline (fall): 1/15
Undergraduate student body: 2,225
full time, 42 part time; 62%
male, 38% female; 0% American
Indian, 2% Asian, 2% black,
5% Hispanic, 3% multiracial,
0% Pacific Islander, 72% white,
1% international; 21% from in
state; 69% live on campus; N/A
of students in fraternities, N/A in
sororities
Most popular majors: 9% Business
Administration and Management,
General, 7% Applied Psychology,
7% Graphic Design, 6% Speech
Communication and Rhetoric, 6%
Writing, General
Expenses: 2017-2018: $39,818;
room/board: $14,906
Financial aid: (802) 860-2777;
71% of undergrads determined to
have financial need; average aid
package $27,169

College of St. Joseph[1]

Rutland VT
(802) 773-5286
U.S. News ranking: Reg. Coll. (N),
second tier
Website: www.csj.edu
Admissions email:
admissions@csj.edu
Private; founded 1956
Application deadline (fall): 8/15
Undergraduate student body: N/A
full time, N/A part time
Expenses: 2016-2017: $22,550;
room/board: $11,250
Financial aid: (802) 776-5262

Goddard College

Plainfield VT
(800) 906-8312
U.S. News ranking: Reg. U. (N),
unranked
Website: www.goddard.edu
Admissions email: admissions@
goddard.edu
Private; founded 1863
Freshman admissions: least
selective; 2016-2017: 16 applied,
9 accepted. Neither SAT nor ACT
required. SAT 25/75 percentile:
N/A. High school rank: N/A
Early decision deadline: N/A,
notification date: N/A
Early action deadline: N/A,
notification date: N/A
Application deadline (fall): N/A
Undergraduate student body: 182
full time, 12 part time; 28%
male, 72% female; 4% American
Indian, 3% Asian, 1% black, 2%
Hispanic, 5% multiracial, 0%
Pacific Islander, 68% white, 0%
international
Most popular majors: Information
not available
Expenses: 2017-2018: $16,260;
room/board: $1,648
Financial aid: (800) 468-4888;
78% of undergrads determined to
have financial need; average aid
package $8,679

Green Mountain College

Poultney VT
(802) 287-8207
U.S. News ranking: Reg. U. (N),
second tier
Website: www.greenmtn.edu
Admissions email: admiss@
greenmtn.edu
Private; founded 1834
Affiliation: United Methodist
Freshman admissions: selective;
2016-2017: 881 applied, 692
accepted. Neither SAT nor ACT
required. SAT 25/75 percentile:
900-1170. High school rank: N/A
Early decision deadline: N/A,
notification date: N/A
Early action deadline: 11/1,
notification date: 12/14
Application deadline (fall): rolling
Undergraduate student body: 479
full time, 36 part time; 45%
male, 55% female; 1% American
Indian, 1% Asian, 5% black,
3% Hispanic, 2% multiracial,
0% Pacific Islander, 57% white,
2% international; 17% from in
state; 79% live on campus; 0%
of students in fraternities, 0% in
sororities
Most popular majors: 17% Resort
Management, 14% Environmental
Studies, 8% Parks, Recreation and
Leisure Studies, 6% Elementary
Education and Teaching, 6%
Environmental Design/Architecture
Expenses: 2016-2017: $37,002;
room/board: $11,722
Financial aid: (802) 287-8285

Johnson State College[1]

Johnson VT
(800) 635-2356
U.S. News ranking: Reg. U. (N),
second tier
Website: www.jsc.edu
Admissions email:
JSCAdmissions@jsc.edu
Public; founded 1828

Application deadline (fall): rolling
Undergraduate student body: N/A
full time, N/A part time
Expenses: 2016-2017: $11,290
in state, $23,746 out of state;
room/board: $9,988
Financial aid: N/A

Landmark College[1]

Putney VT
U.S. News ranking: Reg. Coll. (N),
unranked
Private
Application deadline (fall): N/A
Undergraduate student body: N/A
full time, N/A part time
Expenses: 2016-2017: $52,650;
room/board: $10,970
Financial aid: N/A

Lyndon State College[1]

Lyndonville VT
(802) 626-6413
U.S. News ranking: Reg. Coll. (N),
No. 33
Website: www.lyndonstate.edu
Admissions email: admissions@
lyndonstate.edu
Public; founded 1911
Application deadline (fall): rolling
Undergraduate student body: N/A
full time, N/A part time
Expenses: 2016-2017: $11,290
in state, $22,978 out of state;
room/board: $9,988
Financial aid: N/A

Marlboro College

Marlboro VT
(800) 343-0049
U.S. News ranking: Nat. Lib. Arts,
No. 117
Website: www.marlboro.edu
Admissions email: admissions@
marlboro.edu
Private; founded 1946
Freshman admissions: selective;
2016-2017: 161 applied, 154
accepted. Neither SAT nor ACT
required. ACT 25/75 percentile:
24-30. High school rank: N/A
Early decision deadline: 11/15,
notification date: 12/1
Early action deadline: 1/15,
notification date: 2/1
Application deadline (fall): rolling
Undergraduate student body:
194 full time, 2 part time; 46%
male, 54% female; 2% American
Indian, 1% Asian, 3% black,
3% Hispanic, 5% multiracial,
0% Pacific Islander, 77% white,
2% international; 12% from in
state; 82% live on campus; 0%
of students in fraternities, 0% in
sororities
Most popular majors: 31% Visual
and Performing Arts, 13% English
Language and Literature/Letters,
11% Social Sciences, 8% History
Expenses: 2017-2018: $40,425;
room/board: $11,930
Financial aid: (802) 258-9237;
85% of undergrads determined to
have financial need; average aid
package $36,348

Middlebury College

Middlebury VT
(802) 443-3000
U.S. News ranking: Nat. Lib. Arts,
No. 6
Website: www.middlebury.edu
Admissions email: admissions@
middlebury.edu

Private; founded 1800
Freshman admissions: most
selective; 2016-2017: 8,819
applied, 1,423 accepted. Either
SAT or ACT required. ACT 25/75
percentile: 30-33. High school
rank: 85% in top tenth, 95% in
top quarter, 99% in top half
Early decision deadline: 11/1,
notification date: 12/15
Early action deadline: N/A,
notification date: N/A
Application deadline (fall): 1/1
Undergraduate student body: 2,506
full time, 26 part time; 48%
male, 52% female; 0% American
Indian, 7% Asian, 3% black,
9% Hispanic, 5% multiracial,
0% Pacific Islander, 64% white,
9% international; 7% from in
state; 95% live on campus; 0%
of students in fraternities, 0% in
sororities
Most popular majors: 20%
Economics, General, 7%
Neuroscience, 7% Political
Science and Government, General,
6% Environmental Studies, 5%
English Language and Literature/
Letters, Other
Expenses: 2017-2018: $52,496;
room/board: $14,968
Financial aid: (802) 443-5228;
44% of undergrads determined to
have financial need; average aid
package $48,000

Norwich University

Northfield VT
(800) 468-6679
U.S. News ranking: Reg. U. (N),
No. 86
Website: www.norwich.edu
Admissions email:
nuadm@norwich.edu
Private; founded 1819
Freshman admissions: selective;
2016-2017: 3,604 applied,
2,522 accepted. Neither SAT
nor ACT required. SAT 25/75
percentile: 930-1140. High
school rank: 9% in top tenth, 28%
in top quarter, 64% in top half
Early decision deadline: N/A,
notification date: N/A
Early action deadline: N/A,
notification date: N/A
Application deadline (fall): rolling
Undergraduate student body: 2,479
full time, 671 part time; 78%
male, 22% female; 1% American
Indian, 3% Asian, 5% black, 5%
Hispanic, 6% multiracial, 0%
Pacific Islander, 75% white, 1%
international
Most popular majors: 28%
Homeland Security, Law
Enforcement, Firefighting and
Related Protective Services, 14%
Military Science, Leadership and
Operational Art, 9% Engineering,
8% Business, Management,
Marketing, and Related Support
Services, 8% Health Professions
and Related Programs
Expenses: 2017-2018: $38,662;
room/board: $13,372
Financial aid: (802) 485-2001;
74% of undergrads determined to
have financial need; average aid
package $33,486

Southern Vermont College

Bennington VT
(802) 447-6300
U.S. News ranking: Reg. Coll. (N), second tier
Website: svc.edu/
Admissions email: admissions@svc.edu
Private; founded 1974
Freshman admissions: least selective; 2016-2017: 476 applied, 298 accepted. Either SAT or ACT required. SAT 25/75 percentile: 770-990. High school rank: 4% in top tenth, 12% in top quarter, 47% in top half
Early decision deadline: N/A, notification date: N/A
Early action deadline: N/A, notification date: N/A
Application deadline (fall): rolling
Undergraduate student body: 351 full time, 7 part time; 40% male, 60% female; 1% American Indian, 1% Asian, 11% black, 7% Hispanic, 2% multiracial, 0% Pacific Islander, 50% white, 1% international
Most popular majors: 20% Psychology, General, 14% Radiologic Technology/Science-Radiographer, 13% Criminal Justice/Law Enforcement Administration, 11% Registered Nursing/Registered Nurse, 6% Business Administration and Management, General
Expenses: 2017-2018: $24,620; room/board: $11,000
Financial aid: N/A; 90% of undergrads determined to have financial need; average aid package $17,913

St. Michael's College

Colchester VT
(800) 762-8000
U.S. News ranking: Nat. Lib. Arts, No. 106
Website: www.smcvt.edu
Admissions email: admission@smcvt.edu
Private; founded 1904
Affiliation: Roman Catholic
Freshman admissions: selective; 2016-2017: 5,013 applied, 3,860 accepted. Neither SAT nor ACT required. SAT 25/75 percentile: 1100-1270. High school rank: 26% in top tenth, 49% in top quarter, 75% in top half
Early decision deadline: N/A, notification date: N/A
Early action deadline: 11/1, notification date: 12/21
Application deadline (fall): 2/1
Undergraduate student body: 1,868 full time, 34 part time; 44% male, 56% female; 0% American Indian, 2% Asian, 2% black, 4% Hispanic, 2% multiracial, 0% Pacific Islander, 85% white, 4% international; 16% from in state; 95% live on campus; 0% of students in fraternities, 0% in sororities
Most popular majors: 19% Business, Management, Marketing, and Related Support Services, 14% Social Sciences, 12% Biological and Biomedical Sciences, 10% Psychology, 8% Natural Resources and Conservation

Expenses: 2017-2018: $43,640; room/board: $11,750
Financial aid: (802) 654-3243; 64% of undergrads determined to have financial need; average aid package $30,235

Sterling College[1]

Craftsbury Common VT
U.S. News ranking: Nat. Lib. Arts, unranked
Website: www.sterlingcollege.edu
Admissions email: admissions@sterlingcollege.edu
Private; founded 1958
Application deadline (fall): N/A
Undergraduate student body: N/A full time, N/A part time
Expenses: 2016-2017: $36,495; room/board: $9,560
Financial aid: N/A

University of Vermont

Burlington VT
(802) 656-3370
U.S. News ranking: Nat. U., No. 97
Website: www.uvm.edu
Admissions email: admissions@uvm.edu
Public; founded 1791
Freshman admissions: more selective; 2016-2017: 22,476 applied, 15,495 accepted. Either SAT or ACT required. SAT 25/75 percentile: 1100-1300. High school rank: 33% in top tenth, 74% in top quarter, 97% in top half
Early decision deadline: N/A, notification date: N/A
Early action deadline: 11/1, notification date: 12/15
Application deadline (fall): 1/15
Undergraduate student body: 10,183 full time, 976 part time; 43% male, 57% female; 0% American Indian, 3% Asian, 1% black, 4% Hispanic, 3% multiracial, 0% Pacific Islander, 82% white, 5% international; 28% from in state; 49% live on campus; 7% of students in fraternities, 8% in sororities
Most popular majors: 10% Business Administration and Management, General, 6% Psychology, General, 5% Environmental Studies, 4% Biology/Biological Sciences, General, 4% Political Science and Government, General
Expenses: 2017-2018: $17,740 in state, $41,356 out of state; room/board: $12,022
Financial aid: (802) 656-5700; 54% of undergrads determined to have financial need; average aid package $25,251

Vermont Technical College

Randolph Center VT
(802) 728-1244
U.S. News ranking: Reg. Coll. (N), No. 19
Website: www.vtc.edu
Admissions email: admissions@vtc.edu
Public; founded 1866
Freshman admissions: less selective; 2016-2017: 584 applied, 406 accepted. Neither SAT nor ACT required. SAT 25/75 percentile: 820-1050. High school rank: 15% in top tenth, 26% in top quarter, 54% in top half

Early decision deadline: N/A, notification date: N/A
Early action deadline: N/A, notification date: N/A
Application deadline (fall): rolling
Undergraduate student body: 1,104 full time, 521 part time; 52% male, 48% female; 1% American Indian, 2% Asian, 2% black, 2% Hispanic, 3% multiracial, 0% Pacific Islander, 86% white, 2% international; 86% from in state; 23% live on campus; N/A of students in fraternities, N/A in sororities
Most popular majors: Information not available
Expenses: 2017-2018: $15,000 in state, $27,312 out of state; room/board: $10,290
Financial aid: (802) 728-1248; 74% of undergrads determined to have financial need; average aid package $14,736

VIRGINIA

Averett University

Danville VA
(800) 283-7388
U.S. News ranking: Reg. Coll. (S), No. 17
Website: www.averett.edu
Admissions email: admit@averett.edu
Private; founded 1859
Freshman admissions: less selective; 2016-2017: 2,247 applied, 1,275 accepted. Either SAT or ACT required. SAT 25/75 percentile: 810-1010. High school rank: 6% in top tenth, 23% in top quarter, 56% in top half
Early decision deadline: N/A, notification date: N/A
Early action deadline: N/A, notification date: N/A
Application deadline (fall): rolling
Undergraduate student body: 831 full time, 28 part time; 51% male, 49% female; 1% American Indian, 1% Asian, 32% black, 3% Hispanic, 0% multiracial, 0% Pacific Islander, 58% white, 5% international; 64% from in state; 58% live on campus; 4% of students in fraternities, 3% in sororities
Most popular majors: 21% Health Professions and Related Programs, 14% Business, Management, Marketing, and Related Support Services, 9% Homeland Security, Law Enforcement, Firefighting and Related Protective Services, 9% Parks, Recreation, Leisure, and Fitness Studies, 7% Education
Expenses: 2016-2017: $31,980; room/board: $8,990
Financial aid: (434) 791-5646; 86% of undergrads determined to have financial need; average aid package $25,270

Bluefield College

Bluefield VA
(276) 326-4231
U.S. News ranking: Reg. Coll. (S), No. 41
Website: www.bluefield.edu
Admissions email: admissions@bluefield.edu
Private; founded 1922
Affiliation: Baptist
Freshman admissions: less selective; 2016-2017: 836 applied, 709 accepted. Either

SAT or ACT required. SAT 25/75 percentile: 790-1010. High school rank: 7% in top tenth, 25% in top quarter, 59% in top half
Early decision deadline: N/A, notification date: N/A
Early action deadline: N/A, notification date: N/A
Application deadline (fall): rolling
Undergraduate student body: 805 full time, 164 part time; 47% male, 53% female; 0% American Indian, 0% Asian, 24% black, 4% Hispanic, 3% multiracial, 0% Pacific Islander, 63% white, 4% international; 76% from in state; 59% live on campus; 6% of students in fraternities, 6% in sororities
Most popular majors: 23% Public Health/Community Nurse/Nursing, 20% Organizational Leadership, 17% Public Administration and Social Service Professions, 8% Criminal Justice/Safety Studies, 7% Kinesiology and Exercise Science
Expenses: 2017-2018: $24,800; room/board: $8,843
Financial aid: (276) 326-4604; 87% of undergrads determined to have financial need; average aid package $16,128

Bridgewater College

Bridgewater VA
(800) 759-8328
U.S. News ranking: Nat. Lib. Arts, second tier
Website: www.bridgewater.edu
Admissions email: admissions@bridgewater.edu
Private; founded 1880
Affiliation: Church of Brethren
Freshman admissions: selective; 2016-2017: 7,485 applied, 3,949 accepted. Either SAT or ACT required. SAT 25/75 percentile: 910-1110. High school rank: 15% in top tenth, 42% in top quarter, 78% in top half
Early decision deadline: N/A, notification date: N/A
Early action deadline: N/A, notification date: N/A
Application deadline (fall): 5/1
Undergraduate student body: 1,876 full time, 6 part time; 47% male, 53% female; 0% American Indian, 1% Asian, 13% black, 6% Hispanic, 6% multiracial, 0% Pacific Islander, 68% white, 1% international; 73% from in state; 82% live on campus; N/A of students in fraternities, N/A in sororities
Most popular majors: 19% Business, Management, Marketing, and Related Support Services, 14% Parks, Recreation, Leisure, and Fitness Studies, 11% Biological and Biomedical Sciences, 7% Psychology, 6% Family and Consumer Sciences/Human Sciences
Expenses: 2017-2018: $33,820; room/board: $12,440
Financial aid: (540) 828-5376; 81% of undergrads determined to have financial need; average aid package $29,897

Christopher Newport University

Newport News VA
(757) 594-7015
U.S. News ranking: Reg. U. (S), No. 11
Website: www.cnu.edu
Admissions email: admit@cnu.edu
Public; founded 1960
Freshman admissions: more selective; 2016-2017: 7,532 applied, 4,682 accepted. Neither SAT nor ACT required. SAT 25/75 percentile: 1060-1250. High school rank: 19% in top tenth, 54% in top quarter, 87% in top half
Early decision deadline: 11/15, notification date: 12/15
Early action deadline: 12/1, notification date: 1/15
Application deadline (fall): 5/1
Undergraduate student body: 4,856 full time, 74 part time; 43% male, 57% female; 0% American Indian, 3% Asian, 8% black, 5% Hispanic, 5% multiracial, 0% Pacific Islander, 75% white, 0% international; 92% from in state; 78% live on campus; 24% of students in fraternities, 34% in sororities
Most popular majors: 13% Biology/Biological Sciences, General, 13% Business Administration and Management, General, 13% Speech Communication and Rhetoric, 12% Psychology, General, 7% Political Science and Government, General
Expenses: 2017-2018: $13,654 in state, $25,450 out of state; room/board: $11,224
Financial aid: (757) 594-7170; 45% of undergrads determined to have financial need; average aid package $9,346

College of William & Mary

Williamsburg VA
(757) 221-4223
U.S. News ranking: Nat. U., No. 32
Website: www.wm.edu
Admissions email: admission@wm.edu
Public; founded 1693
Freshman admissions: most selective; 2016-2017: 14,382 applied, 5,253 accepted. Either SAT or ACT required. SAT 25/75 percentile: 1250-1470. High school rank: 78% in top tenth, 96% in top quarter, 99% in top half
Early decision deadline: 11/1, notification date: 12/1
Early action deadline: N/A, notification date: N/A
Application deadline (fall): 1/1
Undergraduate student body: 6,209 full time, 67 part time; 42% male, 58% female; 0% American Indian, 8% Asian, 7% black, 9% Hispanic, 5% multiracial, 0% Pacific Islander, 59% white, 6% international; 70% from in state; 73% live on campus; 26% of students in fraternities, 36% in sororities
Most popular majors: 24% Social Sciences, 11% Business, Management, Marketing, and Related Support Services, 10% Biological and Biomedical Sciences, 8% Psychology, 7% Multi/Interdisciplinary Studies

Expenses: 2017-2018: $20,287 in state, $43,099 out of state; room/board: $11,799
Financial aid: (757) 221-2420; 35% of undergrads determined to have financial need; average aid package $22,315

ECPI University

Virginia Beach VA
(866) 499-0336
U.S. News ranking: Reg. Coll. (S), unranked
Website: www.ecpi.edu/
Admissions email: request@ecpi.edu
For-profit; founded 1966
Freshman admissions: least selective; 2016-2017: 4,812 applied, 3,422 accepted. Neither SAT nor ACT required. SAT 25/75 percentile: N/A. High school rank: N/A
Early decision deadline: N/A, notification date: N/A
Early action deadline: N/A, notification date: N/A
Application deadline (fall): rolling
Undergraduate student body: 11,065 full time, 766 part time; 42% male, 58% female; 1% American Indian, 3% Asian, 42% black, 9% Hispanic, 3% multiracial, 1% Pacific Islander, 40% white, 0% international
Most popular majors: 24% Computer and Information Systems Security/Information Assurance, 13% Criminal Justice/ Safety Studies, 10% Business Administration and Management, General, 10% Computer Technology/Computer Systems Technology, 8% Automation Engineer Technology/Technician
Expenses: 2017-2018: $15,031; room/board: N/A
Financial aid: N/A; 63% of undergrads determined to have financial need; average aid package $14,861

Eastern Mennonite University

Harrisonburg VA
(800) 368-2665
U.S. News ranking: Reg. U. (S), No. 41
Website: www.emu.edu
Admissions email: admiss@emu.edu
Private; founded 1917
Affiliation: Mennonite Church
Freshman admissions: selective; 2016-2017: 1,215 applied, 743 accepted. Either SAT or ACT required. SAT 25/75 percentile: 890-1170. High school rank: N/A
Early decision deadline: N/A, notification date: N/A
Early action deadline: N/A, notification date: N/A
Application deadline (fall): rolling
Undergraduate student body: 1,081 full time, 178 part time; 35% male, 65% female; 0% American Indian, 2% Asian, 9% black, 8% Hispanic, 3% multiracial, 0% Pacific Islander, 72% white, 4% international
Most popular majors: 45% Health Professions and Related Programs, 9% Business, Management, Marketing, and Related Support Services, 9% Liberal Arts and Sciences, General Studies and Humanities, 5% Public

Administration and Social Service Professions, 5% Visual and Performing Arts
Expenses: 2017-2018: $35,800; room/board: $11,000
Financial aid: N/A

Emory and Henry College

Emory VA
(800) 848-5493
U.S. News ranking: Nat. Lib. Arts, No. 168
Website: www.ehc.edu
Admissions email: ehadmiss@ehc.edu
Private; founded 1836
Affiliation: United Methodist
Freshman admissions: selective; 2016-2017: 1,455 applied, 1,017 accepted. Either SAT or ACT required. SAT 25/75 percentile: 890-1120. High school rank: 14% in top tenth, 45% in top quarter, 75% in top half
Early decision deadline: 11/15, notification date: 12/15
Early action deadline: N/A, notification date: N/A
Application deadline (fall): rolling
Undergraduate student body: 1,001 full time, 23 part time; 49% male, 51% female; 0% American Indian, 1% Asian, 9% black, 5% Hispanic, 2% multiracial, 0% Pacific Islander, 76% white, 1% international; 42% from in state; 78% live on campus; N/A of students in fraternities, N/A in sororities
Most popular majors: 16% Social Sciences, 13% Business, Management, Marketing, and Related Support Services, 9% Education, 7% Biological and Biomedical Sciences, 6% History
Expenses: 2017-2018: $35,050; room/board: $11,820
Financial aid: (276) 944-6105; 84% of undergrads determined to have financial need; average aid package $29,365

Ferrum College

Ferrum VA
(800) 868-9797
U.S. News ranking: Reg. Coll. (S), No. 46
Website: www.ferrum.edu
Admissions email: admissions@ferrum.edu
Private; founded 1913
Freshman admissions: least selective; 2016-2017: 3,327 applied, 2,396 accepted. Neither SAT nor ACT required. SAT 25/75 percentile: 770-960. High school rank: 3% in top tenth, 12% in top quarter, 43% in top half
Early decision deadline: N/A, notification date: N/A
Early action deadline: N/A, notification date: N/A
Application deadline (fall): rolling
Undergraduate student body: 1,274 full time, 22 part time; 55% male, 45% female; 1% American Indian, 0% Asian, 35% black, 6% Hispanic, 6% multiracial, 0% Pacific Islander, 49% white, 1% international
Most popular majors: 17% Criminal Justice/Safety Studies, 11% Business Administration

and Management, General, 11% Chiropractic, 11% Physical Education Teaching and Coaching, 5% Social Sciences, General
Expenses: 2016-2017: $31,915; room/board: $11,090
Financial aid: N/A

George Mason University

Fairfax VA
(703) 993-2400
U.S. News ranking: Nat. U., No. 140
Website: www2.gmu.edu
Admissions email: admissions@gmu.edu
Public; founded 1972
Freshman admissions: selective; 2016-2017: 15,548 applied, 12,592 accepted. Neither SAT nor ACT required. SAT 25/75 percentile: 1060-1250. High school rank: 21% in top tenth, 52% in top quarter, 88% in top half
Early decision deadline: N/A, notification date: N/A
Early action deadline: 11/1, notification date: 12/15
Application deadline (fall): 1/15
Undergraduate student body: 19,262 full time, 4,550 part time; 49% male, 51% female; 0% American Indian, 19% Asian, 11% black, 14% Hispanic, 5% multiracial, 0% Pacific Islander, 43% white, 5% international; 90% from in state; 25% live on campus; 7% of students in fraternities, 8% in sororities
Most popular majors: 7% Criminal Justice/Police Science, 6% Biology/Biological Sciences, General, 6% Information Technology, 6% Psychology, General, 5% Accounting
Expenses: 2017-2018: $11,924 in state, $34,370 out of state; room/board: $11,090
Financial aid: (703) 993-2353; 57% of undergrads determined to have financial need; average aid package $13,174

Hampden-Sydney College

Hampden-Sydney VA
(800) 755-0733
U.S. News ranking: Nat. Lib. Arts, No. 96
Website: www.hsc.edu
Admissions email: hsapp@hsc.edu
Private; founded 1775
Affiliation: Presbyterian
Freshman admissions: selective; 2016-2017: 3,403 applied, 1,892 accepted. Either SAT or ACT required. SAT 25/75 percentile: 1010-1230. High school rank: 10% in top tenth, 40% in top quarter, 77% in top half
Early decision deadline: 11/1, notification date: 12/1
Early action deadline: 1/15, notification date: 2/15
Application deadline (fall): 3/1
Undergraduate student body: 1,027 full time, 0 part time; 100% male, 0% female; 0% American Indian, 1% Asian, 5% black,

4% Hispanic, 4% multiracial, 0% Pacific Islander, 84% white, 1% international; 70% from in state; 95% live on campus; 34% of students in fraternities, N/A in sororities
Most popular majors: 22% Business/Managerial Economics, 15% Economics, General, 11% Biology/Biological Sciences, General, 11% History, General, 7% International Relations and Affairs
Expenses: 2017-2018: $43,940; room/board: $14,420
Financial aid: (434) 223-6265; 64% of undergrads determined to have financial need; average aid package $32,430

Hampton University

Hampton VA
(757) 727-5328
U.S. News ranking: Reg. U. (S), No. 21
Website: www.hamptonu.edu
Admissions email: admissions@ hamptonu.edu
Private; founded 1868
Freshman admissions: selective; 2016-2017: 11,165 applied, 7,237 accepted. Neither SAT nor ACT required. SAT 25/75 percentile: 860-1040. High school rank: 24% in top tenth, 51% in top quarter, 93% in top half
Early decision deadline: N/A, notification date: N/A
Early action deadline: 11/1, notification date: 12/31
Application deadline (fall): 3/1
Undergraduate student body: 3,652 full time, 184 part time; 33% male, 67% female; 0% American Indian, 0% Asian, 96% black, 1% Hispanic, 0% multiracial, 0% Pacific Islander, 2% white, 1% international; 29% from in state; 65% live on campus; 5% of students in fraternities, 4% in sororities
Most popular majors: 10% Biology/ Biological Sciences, General, 10% Psychology, General, 8% Business Administration and Management, General, 8% Organizational Communication, General, 7% Business Administration, Management and Operations, Other
Expenses: 2017-2018: $25,442; room/board: $11,218
Financial aid: (757) 727-5332; 60% of undergrads determined to have financial need; average aid package $5,946

Hollins University

Roanoke VA
(800) 456-9595
U.S. News ranking: Nat. Lib. Arts, No. 112
Website: www.hollins.edu
Admissions email: huadm@hollins.edu
Private; founded 1842
Freshman admissions: selective; 2016-2017: 2,901 applied, 1,737 accepted. Either SAT or ACT required. SAT 25/75 percentile: 1020-1233. High school rank: 23% in top tenth, 40% in top quarter, 91% in top half
Early decision deadline: 11/1, notification date: 11/15

Early action deadline: 11/15, notification date: 12/1
Application deadline (fall): N/A
Undergraduate student body: 644 full time, 10 part time; 0% male, 100% female; 1% American Indian, 2% Asian, 12% black, 6% Hispanic, 5% multiracial, 0% Pacific Islander, 65% white, 5% international; 53% from in state; 87% live on campus; N/A of students in fraternities, 0% in sororities
Most popular majors: 18% English Language and Literature/Letters, 14% Multi/Interdisciplinary Studies, 12% Visual and Performing Arts, 10% Biological and Biomedical Sciences, 8% Psychology
Expenses: 2017-2018: $38,285; room/board: $13,120
Financial aid: (540) 362-6332; 82% of undergrads determined to have financial need; average aid package $35,508

James Madison University

Harrisonburg VA
(540) 568-5681
U.S. News ranking: Reg. U. (S), No. 7
Website: www.jmu.edu
Admissions email: admissions@jmu.edu
Public; founded 1908
Freshman admissions: selective; 2016-2017: 21,304 applied, 15,366 accepted. Either SAT or ACT required. SAT 25/75 percentile: 1030-1220. High school rank: 19% in top tenth, 38% in top quarter, 94% in top half
Early decision deadline: N/A, notification date: N/A
Early action deadline: 11/1, notification date: 1/15
Application deadline (fall): 1/15
Undergraduate student body: 18,554 full time, 994 part time; 41% male, 59% female; 0% American Indian, 5% Asian, 5% black, 6% Hispanic, 4% multiracial, 0% Pacific Islander, 75% white, 2% international; 77% from in state; 12% live on campus; 2% of students in fraternities, 5% in sororities
Most popular majors: 17% Health Professions and Related Programs, 16% Business, Management, Marketing, and Related Support Services, 8% Communication, Journalism, and Related Programs, 8% Education, 6% Social Sciences
Expenses: 2017-2018: $10,830 in state, $27,194 out of state; room/board: $9,822
Financial aid: (540) 568-7820; 40% of undergrads determined to have financial need; average aid package $8,528

Liberty University

Lynchburg VA
(800) 543-5317
U.S. News ranking: Nat. U., second tier
Website: www.liberty.edu
Admissions email: admissions@ liberty.edu
Private; founded 1971
Affiliation: Evangelical Christian

Freshman admissions: selective; 2016-2017: 22,984 applied, 6,369 accepted. Either SAT or ACT required. SAT 25/75 percentile: 950-1190. High school rank: 26% in top tenth, 50% in top quarter, 78% in top half
Early decision deadline: N/A, notification date: N/A
Early action deadline: N/A, notification date: N/A
Application deadline (fall): rolling
Undergraduate student body: 27,112 full time, 19,938 part time; 42% male, 58% female; 0% American Indian, 1% Asian, 11% black, 5% Hispanic, 2% multiracial, 0% Pacific Islander, 48% white, 2% international; 40% from in state; 59% live on campus; N/A of students in fraternities, N/A in sororities
Most popular majors: 14% Business, Management, Marketing, and Related Support Services, 13% Health Professions and Related Programs, 8% Psychology, 7% Communication, Journalism, and Related Programs, 7% Parks, Recreation, Leisure, and Fitness Studies
Expenses: 2017-2018: $24,304; room/board: $9,850
Financial aid: (434) 582-2270; 72% of undergrads determined to have financial need; average aid package $15,118

Longwood University
Farmville VA
(434) 395-2060
U.S. News ranking: Reg. U. (S), No. 27
Website: www.longwood.edu/
Admissions email: admissions@longwood.edu
Public; founded 1839
Freshman admissions: less selective; 2016-2017: 5,282 applied, 3,906 accepted. Either SAT or ACT required. SAT 25/75 percentile: 870-1070. High school rank: 9% in top tenth, 31% in top quarter, 76% in top half
Early decision deadline: N/A, notification date: N/A
Early action deadline: 12/1, notification date: 1/15
Application deadline (fall): rolling
Undergraduate student body: 3,952 full time, 434 part time; 33% male, 67% female; 0% American Indian, 1% Asian, 9% black, 5% Hispanic, 4% multiracial, 0% Pacific Islander, 75% white, 2% international; 95% from in state; 78% live on campus; 4% of students in fraternities, 11% in sororities
Most popular majors: 18% Liberal Arts and Sciences, General Studies and Humanities, 12% Business, Management, Marketing, and Related Support Services, 8% Health Professions and Related Programs, 7% Homeland Security, Law Enforcement, Firefighting and Related Protective Services, 7% Parks, Recreation, Leisure, and Fitness Studies
Expenses: 2016-2017: $12,240 in state, $26,670 out of state; room/board: $10,685
Financial aid: (434) 395-2077

Lynchburg College
Lynchburg VA
(434) 544-8300
U.S. News ranking: Reg. U. (S), No. 38
Website: www.lynchburg.edu
Admissions email: admissions@lynchburg.edu
Private; founded 1903
Affiliation: Christian Church (Disciples of Christ)
Freshman admissions: selective; 2016-2017: 5,223 applied, 3,331 accepted. Either SAT or ACT required. SAT 25/75 percentile: 920-1120. High school rank: N/A
Early decision deadline: 11/15, notification date: 12/15
Early action deadline: N/A, notification date: N/A
Application deadline (fall): rolling
Undergraduate student body: 1,938 full time, 141 part time; 39% male, 61% female; 0% American Indian, 1% Asian, 12% black, 5% Hispanic, 5% multiracial, 0% Pacific Islander, 73% white, 3% international; 69% from in state; 75% live on campus; 10% of students in fraternities, 14% in sororities
Most popular majors: 17% Health Professions and Related Programs, 16% Social Sciences, 12% Biological and Biomedical Sciences, 12% Business, Management, Marketing, and Related Support Services, 8% Communication, Journalism, and Related Programs
Expenses: 2017-2018: $37,690; room/board: $10,680
Financial aid: N/A; 76% of undergrads determined to have financial need; average aid package $27,341

Mary Baldwin University
Staunton VA
(800) 468-2262
U.S. News ranking: Reg. U. (S), No. 43
Website: www.marybaldwin.edu
Admissions email: admit@marybaldwin.edu
Private; founded 1842
Freshman admissions: selective; 2016-2017: 2,706 applied, 2,692 accepted. Either SAT or ACT required. SAT 25/75 percentile: 860-1080. High school rank: 9% in top tenth, 27% in top quarter, 48% in top half
Early decision deadline: N/A, notification date: N/A
Early action deadline: N/A, notification date: N/A
Application deadline (fall): rolling
Undergraduate student body: 866 full time, 444 part time; 8% male, 92% female; 1% American Indian, 2% Asian, 24% black, 7% Hispanic, 4% multiracial, 0% Pacific Islander, 55% white, 1% international; 81% from in state; 84% live on campus; N/A of students in fraternities, N/A in sororities
Most popular majors: 16% Business, Management, Marketing, and Related Support Services, 14% Social Sciences, 13% Psychology, 8% Public

Administration and Social Service Professions, 7% Liberal Arts and Sciences, General Studies and Humanities
Expenses: 2017-2018: $31,050; room/board: $9,410
Financial aid: (540) 887-7025; 87% of undergrads determined to have financial need; average aid package $24,347

Marymount University
Arlington VA
(703) 284-1500
U.S. News ranking: Reg. U. (S), No. 52
Website: www.marymount.edu
Admissions email: admissions@marymount.edu
Private; founded 1950
Affiliation: Roman Catholic
Freshman admissions: less selective; 2016-2017: 2,476 applied, 2,242 accepted. Neither SAT nor ACT required. SAT 25/75 percentile: 860-1085. High school rank: 13% in top tenth, 31% in top quarter, 70% in top half
Early decision deadline: N/A, notification date: N/A
Early action deadline: N/A, notification date: N/A
Application deadline (fall): rolling
Undergraduate student body: 2,124 full time, 199 part time; 36% male, 64% female; 0% American Indian, 7% Asian, 15% black, 18% Hispanic, 3% multiracial, 0% Pacific Islander, 30% white, 14% international; 61% from in state; 34% live on campus; N/A of students in fraternities, N/A in sororities
Most popular majors: 26% Registered Nursing/Registered Nurse, 16% Business Administration and Management, General, 9% Information Technology, 8% Public Health Education and Promotion, 5% Psychology, General
Expenses: 2017-2018: $30,426; room/board: $12,805
Financial aid: (703) 284-1530; 62% of undergrads determined to have financial need; average aid package $19,015

Norfolk State University
Norfolk VA
(757) 823-8396
U.S. News ranking: Reg. U. (S), second tier
Website: www.nsu.edu
Admissions email: admissions@nsu.edu
Public; founded 1935
Freshman admissions: least selective; 2016-2017: 4,430 applied, 3,786 accepted. Either SAT or ACT required. SAT 25/75 percentile: 620-860. High school rank: 4% in top tenth, 17% in top quarter, 47% in top half
Early decision deadline: N/A, notification date: N/A
Early action deadline: N/A, notification date: N/A
Undergraduate student body: 4,002 full time, 737 part time; 36% male, 64% female; 0% American Indian, 1% Asian, 85% black, 3% Hispanic, 4% multiracial, 0% Pacific Islander, 4% white,

0% international; 81% from in state; 49% live on campus; N/A of students in fraternities, N/A in sororities
Most popular majors: 11% Social Work, 10% Psychology, General, 9% Business/Commerce, General, 8% Registered Nursing/Registered Nurse, 8% Sociology
Expenses: 2017-2018: $9,036 in state, $20,478 out of state; room/board: $9,866
Financial aid: (757) 823-8381

Old Dominion University
Norfolk VA
(757) 683-3685
U.S. News ranking: Nat. U., second tier
Website: www.odu.edu
Admissions email: admissions@odu.edu
Public; founded 1930
Freshman admissions: selective; 2016-2017: 11,352 applied, 9,608 accepted. Neither SAT nor ACT required. SAT 25/75 percentile: 890-1140. High school rank: 9% in top tenth, 31% in top quarter, 69% in top half
Early decision deadline: N/A, notification date: N/A
Early action deadline: 12/1, notification date: 1/15
Application deadline (fall): 2/1
Undergraduate student body: 15,203 full time, 4,590 part time; 46% male, 54% female; 0% American Indian, 4% Asian, 29% black, 8% Hispanic, 7% multiracial, 0% Pacific Islander, 46% white, 1% international; 93% from in state; 23% live on campus; 9% of students in fraternities, 7% in sororities
Most popular majors: 18% Health Professions and Related Programs, 15% Business, Management, Marketing, and Related Support Services, 12% Social Sciences, 9% Engineering, 9% Psychology
Expenses: 2017-2018: $10,350 in state, $10,350 out of state; room/board: $11,268
Financial aid: (757) 683-3683; 68% of undergrads determined to have financial need; average aid package $10,584

Radford University
Radford VA
(540) 831-5371
U.S. News ranking: Reg. U. (S), No. 43
Website: www.radford.edu
Admissions email: admissions@radford.edu
Public; founded 1910
Freshman admissions: less selective; 2016-2017: 7,447 applied, 6,047 accepted. Neither SAT nor ACT required. SAT 25/75 percentile: 860-1050. High school rank: 6% in top tenth, 22% in top quarter, 56% in top half
Early decision deadline: N/A, notification date: N/A
Early action deadline: 12/1, notification date: 1/15
Application deadline (fall): rolling
Undergraduate student body: 8,104 full time, 349 part time; 43% male, 57% female; 0% American Indian, 1% Asian, 15% black, 7% Hispanic, 5% multiracial, 0% Pacific Islander, 69% white,

1% international; 95% from in state; 35% live on campus; 9% of students in fraternities, 9% in sororities
Most popular majors: 9% Multi-/Interdisciplinary Studies, Other, 8% Physical Education Teaching and Coaching, 7% Business Administration and Management, General, 7% Criminal Justice/Safety Studies, 7% Psychology, General
Expenses: 2017-2018: $10,627 in state, $22,262 out of state; room/board: $9,131
Financial aid: (540) 831-5408; 60% of undergrads determined to have financial need; average aid package $10,116

Randolph College
Lynchburg VA
(800) 745-7692
U.S. News ranking: Nat. Lib. Arts, No. 138
Website: www.randolphcollege.edu/
Admissions email: admissions@randolphcollege.edu
Private; founded 1891
Freshman admissions: selective; 2016-2017: 1,214 applied, 1,010 accepted. Either SAT or ACT required. SAT 25/75 percentile: 900-1150. High school rank: 16% in top tenth, 45% in top quarter, 82% in top half
Early decision deadline: N/A, notification date: N/A
Early action deadline: 11/15, notification date: 1/1
Application deadline (fall): rolling
Undergraduate student body: 645 full time, 18 part time; 34% male, 66% female; 0% American Indian, 2% Asian, 13% black, 6% Hispanic, 4% multiracial, 0% Pacific Islander, 69% white, 6% international, 65% from in state; 85% live on campus; 0% of students in fraternities, 0% in sororities
Most popular majors: 20% Social Sciences, 11% Biological and Biomedical Sciences, 9% English Language and Literature/Letters, 8% Physical Sciences, 8% Visual and Performing Arts
Expenses: 2017-2018: $38,155; room/board: $13,070
Financial aid: (434) 947-8000; 74% of undergrads determined to have financial need; average aid package $30,377

Randolph-Macon College
Ashland VA
(800) 888-1762
U.S. News ranking: Nat. Lib. Arts, No. 126
Website: www.rmc.edu
Admissions email: admissions@rmc.edu
Private; founded 1830
Freshman admissions: selective; 2016-2017: 2,842 applied, 1,745 accepted. Either SAT or ACT required. SAT 25/75 percentile: 975-1190. High school rank: 24% in top tenth, 46% in top quarter, 84% in top half
Early decision deadline: N/A, notification date: N/A
Early action deadline: 11/15, notification date: 1/1

Application deadline (fall): 3/1
Undergraduate student body: 1,415 full time, 31 part time; 47% male, 53% female; 0% American Indian, 2% Asian, 8% black, 4% Hispanic, 0% multiracial, 0% Pacific Islander, 78% white, 2% international; 74% from in state; 85% live on campus; 25% of students in fraternities, 23% in sororities
Most popular majors: 16% Biology/Biological Sciences, General, 12% Communication and Media Studies, 11% Economics, Other, 10% Psychology, General, 6% Accounting
Expenses: 2017-2018: $40,000; room/board: $11,480
Financial aid: (804) 752-7259; 74% of undergrads determined to have financial need; average aid package $28,588

Regent University
Virginia Beach VA
(888) 718-1222
U.S. News ranking: Nat. U., second tier
Website: www.regent.edu
Admissions email: admissions@regent.edu
Private; founded 1978
Affiliation: Undenominational
Freshman admissions: selective; 2016-2017: 1,953 applied, 1,616 accepted. Either SAT or ACT required. SAT 25/75 percentile: 920-1140. High school rank: 10% in top tenth, 33% in top quarter, 66% in top half
Early decision deadline: N/A, notification date: N/A
Early action deadline: N/A, notification date: N/A
Application deadline (fall): 8/1
Undergraduate student body: 2,206 full time, 1,600 part time; 38% male, 62% female; 1% American Indian, 2% Asian, 28% black, 7% Hispanic, 5% multiracial, 0% Pacific Islander, 54% white, 1% international; 46% from in state; 17% live on campus; N/A of students in fraternities, N/A in sororities
Most popular majors: 23% Business Administration and Management, General, 21% Speech Communication and Rhetoric, 14% Psychology, General, 13% Divinity/Ministry, 7% English Language and Literature, General
Expenses: 2017-2018: $17,450; room/board: $8,480
Financial aid: (757) 352-4125; 81% of undergrads determined to have financial need; average aid package $10,870

Roanoke College
Salem VA
(540) 375-2270
U.S. News ranking: Nat. Lib. Arts, No. 138
Website: www.roanoke.edu
Admissions email: admissions@roanoke.edu
Private; founded 1842
Affiliation: Evangelical Lutheran Church
Freshman admissions: selective; 2016-2017: 4,459 applied, 3,257 accepted. Either SAT or ACT required. SAT 25/75

percentile: 970-1200. High school rank: 21% in top tenth, 47% in top quarter, 79% in top half
Early decision deadline: 11/15, notification date: 12/15
Early action deadline: N/A, notification date: N/A
Application deadline (fall): 3/15
Undergraduate student body: 1,933 full time, 59 part time; 41% male, 59% female; 0% American Indian, 1% Asian, 6% black, 4% Hispanic, 4% multiracial, 0% Pacific Islander, 82% white, 3% international; 54% from in state; 76% live on campus; 23% of students in fraternities, 21% in sororities
Most popular majors: 20% Business Administration and Management, General, 10% Biology/Biological Sciences, General, 8% History, General, 8% Psychology, General, 7% Communication and Media Studies
Expenses: 2017-2018: $42,444; room/board: $13,258
Financial aid: (540) 375-2235; 74% of undergrads determined to have financial need; average aid package $32,685

Shenandoah University
Winchester VA
(540) 665-4581
U.S. News ranking: Nat. U., No. 223
Website: www.su.edu
Admissions email: admit@su.edu
Private; founded 1875
Affiliation: United Methodist
Freshman admissions: selective; 2016-2017: 1,911 applied, 1,682 accepted. Either SAT or ACT required. SAT 25/75 percentile: 880-1120. High school rank: N/A
Early decision deadline: N/A, notification date: N/A
Early action deadline: N/A, notification date: N/A
Application deadline (fall): rolling
Undergraduate student body: 2,024 full time, 75 part time; 40% male, 60% female; 1% American Indian, 3% Asian, 12% black, 7% Hispanic, 3% multiracial, 0% Pacific Islander, 57% white, 4% international; 61% from in state; 49% live on campus; N/A of students in fraternities, N/A in sororities
Most popular majors: 25% Registered Nursing/Registered Nurse, 11% Business Administration and Management, General, 7% Psychology, General, 6% Biology/Biological Sciences, General, 6% Criminal Justice/Law Enforcement Administration
Expenses: 2017-2018: $31,920; room/board: $10,180
Financial aid: (540) 665-4538; 74% of undergrads determined to have financial need; average aid package $19,949

Southern Virginia University[1]
Buena Vista VA
U.S. News ranking: Nat. Lib. Arts, second tier
Private
Application deadline (fall): N/A

Undergraduate student body: N/A full time, N/A part time
Expenses: 2016-2017: $14,900; room/board: $7,500
Financial aid: N/A

Sweet Briar College
Sweet Briar VA
(800) 381-6142
U.S. News ranking: Nat. Lib. Arts, No. 134
Website: www.sbc.edu
Admissions email: admissions@sbc.edu
Private; founded 1901
Freshman admissions: selective; 2016-2017: 950 applied, 884 accepted. Either SAT or ACT required. SAT 25/75 percentile: 880-1180. High school rank: 15% in top tenth, 38% in top quarter, 68% in top half
Early decision deadline: N/A, notification date: N/A
Early action deadline: N/A, notification date: N/A
Application deadline (fall): rolling
Undergraduate student body: 356 full time, 9 part time; 2% male, 98% female; 0% American Indian, 2% Asian, 10% black, 10% Hispanic, 4% multiracial, 0% Pacific Islander, 71% white, 2% international; 51% from in state; 93% live on campus; N/A of students in fraternities, N/A in sororities
Most popular majors: 18% Biological and Biomedical Sciences, 18% Social Sciences, 13% Business, Management, Marketing, and Related Support Services, 10% Psychology, 8% Visual and Performing Arts
Expenses: 2017-2018: $37,155; room/board: $12,900
Financial aid: (434) 381-6156; 78% of undergrads determined to have financial need; average aid package $34,421

University of Mary Washington
Fredericksburg VA
(540) 654-2000
U.S. News ranking: Reg. U. (S), No. 17
Website: www.umw.edu
Admissions email: admit@umw.edu
Public; founded 1908
Freshman admissions: selective; 2016-2017: 6,270 applied, 4,668 accepted. Neither SAT nor ACT required. SAT 25/75 percentile: 1010-1210. High school rank: 15% in top tenth, 46% in top quarter, 85% in top half
Early decision deadline: 11/1, notification date: 12/15
Early action deadline: 11/15, notification date: 1/31
Application deadline (fall): 2/1
Undergraduate student body: 3,859 full time, 498 part time; 36% male, 64% female; 0% American Indian, 4% Asian, 7% black, 8% Hispanic, 5% multiracial, 0% Pacific Islander, 70% white, 1% international; 90% from in state; 57% live on campus; 0% of students in fraternities, 0% in sororities
Most popular majors: 17% Social Sciences, 14% Business, Management, Marketing, and Related Support Services,

10% English Language and Literature/Letters, 9% Biological and Biomedical Sciences, 9% Psychology
Expenses: 2017-2018: $12,128 in state, $27,374 out of state; room/board: $10,911
Financial aid: (540) 654-2468; 44% of undergrads determined to have financial need; average aid package $9,747

University of Richmond
Univ. of Richmond VA
(804) 289-8640
U.S. News ranking: Nat. Lib. Arts, No. 23
Website: www.richmond.edu
Admissions email: admission@richmond.edu
Private; founded 1830
Freshman admissions: more selective; 2016-2017: 10,422 applied, 3,385 accepted. Either SAT or ACT required. SAT 25/75 percentile: 1220-1420. High school rank: 61% in top tenth, 85% in top quarter, 98% in top half
Early decision deadline: 11/15, notification date: 12/15
Early action deadline: 11/1, notification date: 1/15
Application deadline (fall): 1/15
Undergraduate student body: 3,000 full time, 36 part time; 48% male, 52% female; 0% American Indian, 8% Asian, 6% black, 8% Hispanic, 4% multiracial, 0% Pacific Islander, 59% white, 9% international; 19% from in state; 91% live on campus; 21% of students in fraternities, 29% in sororities
Most popular majors: 37% Business, Management, Marketing, and Related Support Services, 15% Social Sciences, 10% Biological and Biomedical Sciences, 6% Multi/Interdisciplinary Studies, 5% Psychology
Expenses: 2017-2018: $50,910; room/board: $11,820
Financial aid: (804) 289-8438; 42% of undergrads determined to have financial need; average aid package $45,784

University of Virginia
Charlottesville VA
(434) 982-3200
U.S. News ranking: Nat. U., No. 25
Website: www.virginia.edu
Admissions email: undergradadmission@virginia.edu
Public; founded 1819
Freshman admissions: most selective; 2016-2017: 32,377 applied, 9,668 accepted. Either SAT or ACT required. SAT 25/75 percentile: 1240-1460. High school rank: 89% in top tenth, 98% in top quarter, 99% in top half
Early decision deadline: N/A, notification date: N/A
Early action deadline: 11/1, notification date: 1/31
Application deadline (fall): 1/1
Undergraduate student body: 15,484 full time, 847 part time; 45% male, 55% female; 0% American Indian, 13% Asian, 7% black, 6% Hispanic, 4% multiracial, 0% Pacific Islander,

59% white, 5% international; 73% from in state; 39% live on campus; 24% of students in fraternities, 27% in sororities
Most popular majors: 11% Economics, General, 9% Business/Commerce, General, 7% Biology/Biological Sciences, General, 7% International Relations and Affairs, 6% Psychology, General
Expenses: 2017-2018: $16,146 in state, $46,975 out of state; room/board: $11,220
Financial aid: (434) 982-6000; 32% of undergrads determined to have financial need; average aid package $26,422

University of Virginia–Wise
Wise VA
(888) 282-9324
U.S. News ranking: Nat. Lib. Arts, second tier
Website: www.uvawise.edu
Admissions email: admissions@uvawise.edu
Public; founded 1954
Freshman admissions: selective; 2016-2017: 1,050 applied, 816 accepted. Either SAT or ACT required. SAT 25/75 percentile: 850-1070. High school rank: 15% in top tenth, 41% in top quarter, 71% in top half
Early decision deadline: N/A, notification date: N/A
Early action deadline: 12/1, notification date: 12/15
Application deadline (fall): 8/15
Undergraduate student body: 1,300 full time, 921 part time; 41% male, 59% female; 0% American Indian, 1% Asian, 11% black, 2% Hispanic, 0% multiracial, 0% Pacific Islander, 77% white, 0% international; 96% from in state; 36% live on campus; 5% of students in fraternities, 7% in sororities
Most popular majors: 16% Business, Management, Marketing, and Related Support Services, 15% Education, 10% Social Sciences, 9% Biological and Biomedical Sciences, 8% Psychology
Expenses: 2017-2018: $9,759 in state, $26,385 out of state; room/board: $10,314
Financial aid: (276) 376-7130; 81% of undergrads determined to have financial need; average aid package $12,601

Virginia Commonwealth University
Richmond VA
(800) 841-3638
U.S. News ranking: Nat. U., No. 171
Website: www.vcu.edu
Admissions email: ugrad@vcu.edu
Public; founded 1838
Freshman admissions: selective; 2016-2017: 17,176 applied, 12,805 accepted. Neither SAT nor ACT required. SAT 25/75 percentile: 980-1200. High school rank: 19% in top tenth, 47% in top quarter, 85% in top half
Early decision deadline: N/A, notification date: N/A
Early action deadline: N/A, notification date: N/A

Application deadline (fall): 1/17
Undergraduate student body: 20,554 full time, 3,658 part time; 41% male, 59% female; 0% American Indian, 13% Asian, 19% black, 9% Hispanic, 6% multiracial, 0% Pacific Islander, 48% white, 3% international; 93% from in state; 21% live on campus; N/A of students in fraternities, N/A in sororities
Most popular majors: 13% Business, Management, Marketing, and Related Support Services, 11% Visual and Performing Arts, 9% Psychology, 8% Biological and Biomedical Sciences, 8% Homeland Security, Law Enforcement, Firefighting and Related Protective Services
Expenses: 2017-2018: $13,570 in state, $32,942 out of state; room/board: $10,187
Financial aid: (804) 828-6181; 57% of undergrads determined to have financial need; average aid package $11,118

Virginia Military Institute
Lexington VA
(800) 767-4207
U.S. News ranking: Nat. Lib. Arts, No. 65
Website: www.vmi.edu
Admissions email: admissions@vmi.edu
Public; founded 1839
Freshman admissions: more selective; 2016-2017: 1,843 applied, 939 accepted. Either SAT or ACT required. SAT 25/75 percentile: 1060-1240. High school rank: 16% in top tenth, 46% in top quarter, 86% in top half
Early decision deadline: 11/15, notification date: 12/15
Early action deadline: N/A, notification date: N/A
Application deadline (fall): 2/1
Undergraduate student body: 1,713 full time, 0 part time; 89% male, 11% female; 1% American Indian, 4% Asian, 6% black, 6% Hispanic, 1% multiracial, 0% Pacific Islander, 80% white, 2% international; 61% from in state; 100% live on campus; N/A of students in fraternities, N/A in sororities
Most popular majors: 19% Civil Engineering, General, 17% International Relations and Affairs, 16% Economics, General, 10% History, General, 8% Mechanical Engineering
Expenses: 2017-2018: $18,214 in state, $43,902 out of state; room/board: $9,236
Financial aid: (540) 464-7208; 50% of undergrads determined to have financial need; average aid package $24,611

Virginia State University
Petersburg VA
(804) 524-5902
U.S. News ranking: Reg. U. (S), No. 102
Website: www.vsu.edu
Admissions email: admiss@vsu.edu
Public; founded 1882
Freshman admissions: least selective; 2016-2017: 5,722 applied, 5,406 accepted. Either

SAT or ACT required. SAT 25/75 percentile: 730-900. High school rank: 5% in top tenth, 22% in top quarter, 57% in top half
Early decision deadline: N/A, notification date: N/A
Early action deadline: N/A, notification date: N/A
Application deadline (fall): 5/1
Undergraduate student body: 4,023 full time, 142 part time; 43% male, 57% female; 0% American Indian, 1% Asian, 61% black, 1% Hispanic, 0% multiracial, 0% Pacific Islander, 2% white, 0% international
Most popular majors: 13% Criminal Justice/Safety Studies, 13% Physical Education Teaching and Coaching, 11% Mass Communication/Media Studies, 7% Psychology, General, 5% Social Work
Expenses: 2017-2018: $8,726 in state, $18,841 out of state; room/board: $10,880
Financial aid: (800) 823-7214; 100% of undergrads determined to have financial need; average aid package $11,225

Virginia Tech
Blacksburg VA
(540) 231-6267
U.S. News ranking: Nat. U., No. 69
Website: www.vt.edu
Admissions email: vtadmiss@vt.edu
Public; founded 1872
Freshman admissions: more selective; 2016-2017: 25,000 applied, 17,718 accepted. Either SAT or ACT required. SAT 25/75 percentile: 1100-1320. High school rank: 40% in top tenth, 78% in top quarter, 97% in top half
Early decision deadline: 11/1, notification date: 12/15
Early action deadline: N/A, notification date: N/A
Application deadline (fall): 12/1
Undergraduate student body: 25,213 full time, 578 part time; 57% male, 43% female; 0% American Indian, 10% Asian, 4% black, 6% Hispanic, 4% multiracial, 0% Pacific Islander, 67% white, 6% international
Most popular majors: 24% Engineering, 18% Business, Management, Marketing, and Related Support Services, 9% Family and Consumer Sciences/Human Sciences, 8% Social Sciences, 7% Biological and Biomedical Sciences
Expenses: 2016-2017: $12,852 in state, $29,371 out of state; room/board: $8,424
Financial aid: (540) 231-5179; 42% of undergrads determined to have financial need; average aid package $17,594

Virginia Union University
Richmond VA
(804) 257-5600
U.S. News ranking: Nat. Lib. Arts, second tier
Website: www.vuu.edu/
Admissions email: admissions@vuu.edu
Private; founded 1865
Affiliation: Baptist
Freshman admissions: least selective; 2016-2017: 6,026

applied, 2,470 accepted. Either SAT or ACT required. SAT 25/75 percentile: 700-890. High school rank: 9% in top tenth, 22% in top quarter, 53% in top half
Early decision deadline: N/A, notification date: N/A
Early action deadline: N/A, notification date: N/A
Application deadline (fall): 6/30
Undergraduate student body: 1,338 full time, 50 part time; 43% male, 57% female; 0% American Indian, 0% Asian, 94% black, 1% Hispanic, 0% multiracial, 0% Pacific Islander, 1% white, 0% international
Most popular majors: 23% Criminology, 14% Psychology, General, 9% Business Administration and Management, General, 9% Teacher Education, Multiple Levels, 8% Biology/Biological Sciences, General
Expenses: 2017-2018: $16,534; room/board: $8,412
Financial aid: (804) 257-5854; 93% of undergrads determined to have financial need; average aid package $12,908

Virginia Wesleyan University
Norfolk VA
(800) 737-8684
U.S. News ranking: Nat. Lib. Arts, second tier
Website: www.vwc.edu
Admissions email: admissions@vwc.edu
Private; founded 1961
Affiliation: United Methodist
Freshman admissions: less selective; 2016-2017: 1,654 applied, 1,488 accepted. Either SAT or ACT required. SAT 25/75 percentile: 850-1060. High school rank: 9% in top tenth, 26% in top quarter, 63% in top half
Early decision deadline: N/A, notification date: N/A
Early action deadline: N/A, notification date: N/A
Application deadline (fall): rolling
Undergraduate student body: 1,319 full time, 55 part time; 38% male, 62% female; 1% American Indian, 1% Asian, 25% black, 8% Hispanic, 6% multiracial, 0% Pacific Islander, 51% white, 1% international; 74% from in state; N/A live on campus; N/A of students in fraternities, N/A in sororities
Most popular majors: 14% Business, Management, Marketing, and Related Support Services, 12% Social Sciences, 11% Homeland Security, Law Enforcement, Firefighting and Related Protective Services, 9% Multi/Interdisciplinary Studies, 9% Psychology
Expenses: 2017-2018: $36,660; room/board: $8,944
Financial aid: (757) 455-3345; 81% of undergrads determined to have financial need; average aid package $24,802

Washington and Lee University
Lexington VA
(540) 463-8710
U.S. News ranking: Nat. Lib. Arts, No. 10
Website: www.wlu.edu
Admissions email: admissions@wlu.edu
Private; founded 1749
Affiliation: Other
Freshman admissions: most selective; 2016-2017: 5,101 applied, 1,203 accepted. Either SAT or ACT required. ACT 25/75 percentile: 30-33. High school rank: 83% in top tenth, 99% in top quarter, 100% in top half
Early decision deadline: 11/1, notification date: 12/22
Early action deadline: N/A, notification date: N/A
Application deadline (fall): 1/1
Undergraduate student body: 1,824 full time, 6 part time; 52% male, 48% female; 0% American Indian, 3% Asian, 2% black, 4% Hispanic, 3% multiracial, 0% Pacific Islander, 83% white, 4% international; 15% from in state; 74% live on campus; 73% of students in fraternities, 75% in sororities
Most popular majors: 10% Business Administration and Management, General, 9% Accounting and Business/Management, 9% Economics, General, 8% Political Science and Government, General, 6% Journalism
Expenses: 2017-2018: $50,170; room/board: $11,730
Financial aid: (540) 458-8720; 42% of undergrads determined to have financial need; average aid package $48,392

WASHINGTON

Art Institute of Seattle[1]
Seattle WA
U.S. News ranking: Arts, unranked
Website: www.ais.edu
Admissions email: N/A
For-profit
Application deadline (fall): N/A
Undergraduate student body: N/A full time, N/A part time
Expenses: 2016-2017: $17,556; room/board: $12,456
Financial aid: N/A

Bellevue College[1]
Bellevue WA
U.S. News ranking: Reg. Coll. (W), unranked
Website: www.bellevuecollege.edu
Admissions email: N/A
Public
Application deadline (fall): N/A
Undergraduate student body: N/A full time, N/A part time
Expenses: 2016-2017: $3,624 in state, $8,968 out of state; room/board: N/A
Financial aid: N/A

Central Washington University
Ellensburg WA
(509) 963-1211
U.S. News ranking: Reg. U. (W), No. 44
Website: www.cwu.edu
Admissions email: admissions@cwu.edu
Public; founded 1891
Freshman admissions: less selective; 2016-2017: 7,340 applied, 5,823 accepted. Either SAT or ACT required. SAT 25/75 percentile: 960-1150. High school rank: N/A
Early decision deadline: N/A, notification date: N/A
Early action deadline: N/A, notification date: N/A
Application deadline (fall): rolling
Undergraduate student body: 9,473 full time, 1,574 part time; 49% male, 51% female; 1% American Indian, 4% Asian, 4% black, 15% Hispanic, 7% multiracial, 1% Pacific Islander, 55% white, 3% international; 95% from in state; 31% live on campus; N/A of students in fraternities, N/A in sororities
Most popular majors: 27% Business, Management, Marketing, and Related Support Services, 12% Education, 10% Social Sciences, 7% Homeland Security, Law Enforcement, Firefighting and Related Protective Services, 6% Biological and Biomedical Sciences
Expenses: 2017-2018: $7,153 in state, $21,260 out of state; room/board: $10,684
Financial aid: (509) 963-2091; 65% of undergrads determined to have financial need; average aid package $11,434

Centralia College[1]
Centralia WA
U.S. News ranking: Reg. Coll. (W), unranked
Public
Application deadline (fall): N/A
Undergraduate student body: N/A full time, N/A part time
Expenses: 2016-2017: $4,188 in state, $4,600 out of state; room/board: $10,140
Financial aid: N/A

City University of Seattle[1]
Seattle WA
U.S. News ranking: Reg. U. (W), unranked
Website: www.cityu.edu
Admissions email: info@cityu.edu
Private; founded 1973
Application deadline (fall): N/A
Undergraduate student body: N/A full time, N/A part time
Expenses: 2016-2017: $16,748; room/board: $9,648
Financial aid: N/A

Columbia Basin College[1]
Pasco WA
U.S. News ranking: Reg. Coll. (W), unranked
Public
Application deadline (fall): N/A

Undergraduate student body: N/A full time, N/A part time
Expenses: 2016-2017: $4,163 in state, $6,436 out of state; room/board: N/A
Financial aid: N/A

Cornish College of the Arts[1]
Seattle WA
U.S. News ranking: Arts, unranked
Website: www.cornish.edu
Admissions email: admission@cornish.edu
Private; founded 1914
Application deadline (fall): N/A
Undergraduate student body: N/A full time, N/A part time
Expenses: 2016-2017: $38,820; room/board: $10,950
Financial aid: (206) 726-5013

Eastern Washington University
Cheney WA
(509) 359-2397
U.S. News ranking: Reg. U. (W), No. 86
Website: www.ewu.edu
Admissions email: admissions@ewu.edu
Public; founded 1882
Freshman admissions: less selective; 2016-2017: 4,224 applied, 4,033 accepted. Either SAT or ACT required. SAT 25/75 percentile: 850-1080. High school rank: N/A
Early decision deadline: N/A, notification date: N/A
Early action deadline: N/A, notification date: N/A
Application deadline (fall): 5/15
Undergraduate student body: 10,032 full time, 1,185 part time; 46% male, 54% female; 1% American Indian, 3% Asian, 4% black, 15% Hispanic, 6% multiracial, 0% Pacific Islander, 64% white, 5% international; 94% from in state; 17% live on campus; 4% of students in fraternities, 5% in sororities
Most popular majors: 20% Business, Management, Marketing, and Related Support Services, 9% Biological and Biomedical Sciences, 9% Health Professions and Related Programs, 8% Education, 8% Psychology
Expenses: 2017-2018: $7,098 in state, $24,444 out of state; room/board: $11,638
Financial aid: (509) 359-2314; 64% of undergrads determined to have financial need; average aid package $13,877

Evergreen State College
Olympia WA
(360) 867-6170
U.S. News ranking: Reg. U. (W), No. 33
Website: www.evergreen.edu
Admissions email: admissions@evergreen.edu
Public; founded 1967
Freshman admissions: selective; 2016-2017: 1,901 applied, 1,853 accepted. Either SAT or ACT required. SAT 25/75 percentile: 920-1180. High school rank: 5% in top tenth, 26% in top quarter, 54% in top half

---

Early decision deadline: N/A, notification date: N/A
Early action deadline: N/A, notification date: N/A
Application deadline (fall): rolling
Undergraduate student body: 3,458 full time, 329 part time; 44% male, 56% female; 2% American Indian, 3% Asian, 5% black, 11% Hispanic, 8% multiracial, 0% Pacific Islander, 66% white, 1% international; 75% from in state; 23% live on campus; N/A of students in fraternities, N/A in sororities
Most popular majors: 83% Liberal Arts and Sciences/Liberal Studies, 17% Biological and Physical Sciences
Expenses: 2017-2018: $7,416 in state, $25,008 out of state; room/board: $9,681
Financial aid: (360) 867-6205; 67% of undergrads determined to have financial need; average aid package $12,646

Gonzaga University
Spokane WA
(800) 322-2584
U.S. News ranking: Reg. U. (W), No. 4
Website: www.gonzaga.edu
Admissions email: admissions@gonzaga.edu
Private; founded 1887
Affiliation: Roman Catholic
Freshman admissions: more selective; 2016-2017: 7,324 applied, 4,928 accepted. Either SAT or ACT required. SAT 25/75 percentile: 1110-1300. High school rank: 36% in top tenth, 69% in top quarter, 93% in top half
Early decision deadline: N/A, notification date: N/A
Early action deadline: 11/15, notification date: 1/15
Application deadline (fall): 2/1
Undergraduate student body: 5,073 full time, 87 part time; 47% male, 53% female; 1% American Indian, 5% Asian, 1% black, 10% Hispanic, 6% multiracial, 0% Pacific Islander, 72% white, 1% international; 49% from in state; 59% live on campus; N/A of students in fraternities, N/A in sororities
Most popular majors: 22% Business, Management, Marketing, and Related Support Services, 14% Social Sciences, 11% Engineering, 10% Biological and Biomedical Sciences, 8% Psychology
Expenses: 2017-2018: $41,330; room/board: $11,550
Financial aid: (509) 313-6562; 54% of undergrads determined to have financial need; average aid package $29,634

Heritage University[1]
Toppenish WA
U.S. News ranking: Reg. U. (W), unranked
Website: www.heritage.edu
Admissions email: admissions@heritage.edu
Private
Application deadline (fall): N/A
Undergraduate student body: N/A full time, N/A part time
Expenses: 2016-2017: $19,122; room/board: N/A
Financial aid: N/A

Lake Washington Institute of Technology
Kirkland WA
(425) 739-8104
U.S. News ranking: Reg. Coll. (W), unranked
Website: www.lwtech.edu/
Admissions email: admissions@lwtech.edu
Public; founded 1949
Freshman admissions: least selective; 2016-2017: 359 applied, 359 accepted. Neither SAT nor ACT required. SAT 25/75 percentile: N/A. High school rank: N/A
Early decision deadline: N/A, notification date: N/A
Early action deadline: N/A, notification date: N/A
Application deadline (fall): N/A
Undergraduate student body: 2,183 full time, 2,168 part time; 40% male, 60% female; 0% American Indian, 10% Asian, 4% black, 8% Hispanic, 6% multiracial, 0% Pacific Islander, 65% white, 1% international
Most popular majors: Information not available
Expenses: 2016-2017: $4,059 in state, $9,403 out of state; room/board: N/A
Financial aid: N/A

North Seattle College[1]
Seattle WA
U.S. News ranking: Reg. Coll. (W), unranked
Public
Application deadline (fall): N/A
Undergraduate student body: N/A full time, N/A part time
Expenses: 2016-2017: $3,819 in state, $4,226 out of state; room/board: N/A
Financial aid: N/A

Northwest University
Kirkland WA
(425) 889-5231
U.S. News ranking: Reg. U. (W), No. 63
Website: www.northwestu.edu
Admissions email: admissions@northwestu.edu
Private; founded 1934
Affiliation: Assemblies of God Church
Freshman admissions: selective; 2016-2017: 560 applied, 523 accepted. Either SAT or ACT required. SAT 25/75 percentile: 940-1190. High school rank: N/A
Early decision deadline: N/A, notification date: N/A
Early action deadline: 11/15, notification date: 12/15
Application deadline (fall): rolling
Undergraduate student body: 922 full time, 16 part time; 35% male, 65% female; 2% American Indian, 4% Asian, 5% black, 9% Hispanic, 5% multiracial, 1% Pacific Islander, 69% white, 4% international
Most popular majors: 15% Registered Nursing/Registered Nurse, 12% Psychology, General, 10% Organizational Communication, General, 9% Theological and Ministerial Studies, Other, 7% Business Administration and Management, General

---

Expenses: 2017-2018: $30,320; room/board: $8,400
Financial aid: (425) 889-5210; 80% of undergrads determined to have financial need; average aid package $17,684

Olympic College[1]
Bremerton WA
U.S. News ranking: Reg. Coll. (W), unranked
Website: www.olympic.edu
Admissions email: N/A
Public
Application deadline (fall): N/A
Undergraduate student body: N/A full time, N/A part time
Expenses: 2016-2017: $3,618 in state, $4,064 out of state; room/board: $9,588
Financial aid: N/A

Pacific Lutheran University
Tacoma WA
(800) 274-6758
U.S. News ranking: Reg. U. (W), No. 16
Website: www.plu.edu
Admissions email: admission@plu.edu
Private; founded 1890
Affiliation: Lutheran Church in America
Freshman admissions: selective; 2016-2017: 3,769 applied, 2,896 accepted. Either SAT or ACT required. SAT 25/75 percentile: 980-1230. High school rank: 50% in top tenth, 85% in top quarter, 96% in top half
Early decision deadline: N/A, notification date: N/A
Early action deadline: N/A, notification date: N/A
Application deadline (fall): N/A
Undergraduate student body: 2,702 full time, 80 part time; 37% male, 63% female; 1% American Indian, 9% Asian, 3% black, 8% Hispanic, 8% multiracial, 1% Pacific Islander, 66% white, 3% international; 76% from in state; 48% live on campus; 0% of students in fraternities, 0% in sororities
Most popular majors: 15% Business, Management, Marketing, and Related Support Services, 11% Health Professions and Related Programs, 9% Social Sciences, 7% Biological and Biomedical Sciences, 7% Physical Sciences
Expenses: 2017-2018: $40,722; room/board: $10,520
Financial aid: (253) 535-8491; 74% of undergrads determined to have financial need; average aid package $36,609

Peninsula College[1]
Port Angeles WA
U.S. News ranking: Reg. Coll. (W), unranked
Website: www.pencol.edu
Admissions email: N/A
Public
Application deadline (fall): N/A
Undergraduate student body: N/A full time, N/A part time
Expenses: 2016-2017: $4,344 in state, $4,751 out of state; room/board: N/A
Financial aid: N/A

Saint Martin's University
Lacey WA
(800) 368-8803
U.S. News ranking: Reg. U. (W), No. 44
Website: www.stmartin.edu
Admissions email: admissions@stmartin.edu
Private; founded 1895
Affiliation: Roman Catholic
Freshman admissions: selective; 2016-2017: 1,344 applied, 1,281 accepted. Either SAT or ACT required. SAT 25/75 percentile: 895-1150. High school rank: 23% in top tenth, 51% in top quarter, 85% in top half
Early decision deadline: N/A, notification date: N/A
Early action deadline: N/A, notification date: N/A
Application deadline (fall): 7/31
Undergraduate student body: 1,072 full time, 210 part time; 50% male, 50% female; 1% American Indian, 6% Asian, 6% black, 16% Hispanic, 6% multiracial, 3% Pacific Islander, 55% white, 4% international; 72% from in state; 37% live on campus; 0% of students in fraternities, 0% in sororities
Most popular majors: 20% Business, Management, Marketing, and Related Support Services, 16% Engineering, 12% Psychology, 8% Biological and Biomedical Sciences, 5% Health Professions and Related Programs
Expenses: 2017-2018: $35,656; room/board: $11,030
Financial aid: (360) 486-8868; 82% of undergrads determined to have financial need; average aid package $25,969

Seattle Central College[1]
Seattle WA
U.S. News ranking: Reg. Coll. (W), unranked
Public
Application deadline (fall): N/A
Undergraduate student body: N/A full time, N/A part time
Expenses: 2016-2017: $3,925 in state, $4,332 out of state; room/board: N/A
Financial aid: N/A

Seattle Pacific University
Seattle WA
(800) 366-3344
U.S. News ranking: Nat. U., No. 151
Website: www.spu.edu
Admissions email: admissions@spu.edu
Private; founded 1891
Freshman admissions: selective; 2016-2017: 4,034 applied, 3,521 accepted. Either SAT or ACT required. SAT 25/75 percentile: 990-1230. High school rank: N/A
Early decision deadline: N/A, notification date: N/A
Early action deadline: 11/15, notification date: 1/5
Application deadline (fall): 2/1
Undergraduate student body: 2,998 full time, 97 part time; 33% male, 67% female; 0% American Indian, 11% Asian, 4% black,

10% Hispanic, 9% multiracial, 1% Pacific Islander, 59% white, 4% international; 64% from in state; 53% live on campus; 0% of students in fraternities, 0% in sororities
Most popular majors: Information not available
Expenses: 2017-2018: $40,893; room/board: $11,232
Financial aid: (206) 281-2061; 70% of undergrads determined to have financial need; average aid package $34,030

Seattle University
Seattle WA
(206) 296-2000
U.S. News ranking: Reg. U. (W), No. 7
Website: www.seattleu.edu
Admissions email: admissions@ seattleu.edu
Private; founded 1891
Freshman admissions: more selective; 2016-2017: 8,149 applied, 5,001 accepted. Either SAT or ACT required. SAT 25/75 percentile: 1070-1290. High school rank: 31% in top tenth, 64% in top quarter, 94% in top half
Early decision deadline: N/A, notification date: N/A
Early action deadline: 11/15, notification date: 12/23
Application deadline (fall): rolling
Undergraduate student body: 4,532 full time, 248 part time; 39% male, 61% female; 0% American Indian, 16% Asian, 3% black, 10% Hispanic, 8% multiracial, 1% Pacific Islander, 44% white, 11% international; 41% from in state; 45% live on campus; 0% of students in fraternities, 0% in sororities
Most popular majors: 24% Business, Management, Marketing, and Related Support Services, 14% Health Professions and Related Programs, 9% Visual and Performing Arts, 7% Engineering, 7% Social Sciences
Expenses: 2017-2018: $42,885; room/board: $12,072
Financial aid: (206) 296-5852; 55% of undergrads determined to have financial need; average aid package $33,772

South Seattle College[1]
Seattle WA
U.S. News ranking: Reg. Coll. (W), unranked
Website: www.southseattle.edu
Admissions email: N/A
Public
Application deadline (fall): N/A
Undergraduate student body: N/A full time, N/A part time
Expenses: 2016-2017: $3,854 in state, $4,261 out of state; room/board: N/A
Financial aid: N/A

University of Puget Sound
Tacoma WA
(253) 879-3211
U.S. News ranking: Nat. Lib. Arts, No. 68
Website: www.pugetsound.edu
Admissions email: admission@ pugetsound.edu

Private; founded 1888
Freshman admissions: more selective; 2016-2017: 6,398 applied, 5,048 accepted. Neither SAT nor ACT required. SAT 25/75 percentile: 1100-1330. High school rank: 34% in top tenth, 66% in top quarter, 91% in top half
Early decision deadline: 11/15, notification date: 12/15
Early action deadline: 12/1, notification date: 2/15
Application deadline (fall): 1/15
Undergraduate student body: 2,487 full time, 21 part time; 40% male, 60% female; 0% American Indian, 6% Asian, 1% black, 8% Hispanic, 9% multiracial, 0% Pacific Islander, 73% white, 0% international; 20% from in state; 66% live on campus; 29% of students in fraternities, 30% in sororities
Most popular majors: 19% Social Sciences, 12% Biological and Biomedical Sciences, 11% Business, Management, Marketing, and Related Support Services, 9% Psychology, 7% Visual and Performing Arts
Expenses: 2017-2018: $48,090; room/board: $12,120
Financial aid: (253) 879-3214; 49% of undergrads determined to have financial need; average aid package $31,725

University of Washington
Seattle WA
(206) 543-9686
U.S. News ranking: Nat. U., No. 56
Website: www.washington.edu
Admissions email: pseegert@uw.edu
Public; founded 1861
Freshman admissions: more selective; 2016-2017: 43,517 applied, 19,733 accepted. Either SAT or ACT required. SAT 25/75 percentile: 1120-1370. High school rank: 62% in top tenth, 91% in top quarter, 100% in top half
Early decision deadline: N/A, notification date: N/A
Early action deadline: N/A, notification date: N/A
Application deadline (fall): 12/1
Undergraduate student body: 28,380 full time, 2,553 part time; 48% male, 52% female; 0% American Indian, 25% Asian, 3% black, 8% Hispanic, 7% multiracial, 0% Pacific Islander, 41% white, 15% international; 83% from in state; 27% live on campus; 16% of students in fraternities, 15% in sororities
Most popular majors: 15% Social Sciences, 12% Biological and Biomedical Sciences, 11% Business, Management, Marketing, and Related Support Services, 9% Engineering, 6% Communication, Journalism, and Related Programs
Expenses: 2017-2018: $10,974 in state, $35,538 out of state; room/board: $12,117
Financial aid: (206) 543-6101; 41% of undergrads determined to have financial need; average aid package $19,100

Walla Walla University
College Place WA
(509) 527-2327
U.S. News ranking: Reg. U. (W), No. 47
Website: www.wallawalla.edu
Admissions email: info@wallawalla.edu
Private; founded 1892
Freshman admissions: selective; 2016-2017: 1,963 applied, 1,219 accepted. Either SAT or ACT required. SAT 25/75 percentile: 920-1210. High school rank: N/A
Early decision deadline: N/A, notification date: N/A
Early action deadline: N/A, notification date: N/A
Application deadline (fall): rolling
Undergraduate student body: 1,585 full time, 115 part time; 50% male, 50% female; 1% American Indian, 6% Asian, 3% black, 15% Hispanic, 1% multiracial, 1% Pacific Islander, 65% white, 3% international; 38% from in state; 72% live on campus; N/A of students in fraternities, N/A in sororities
Most popular majors: 24% Health Professions and Related Programs, 13% Business, Management, Marketing, and Related Support Services, 13% Engineering, 8% Biological and Biomedical Sciences, 7% Visual and Performing Arts
Expenses: 2017-2018: $27,495; room/board: $7,155
Financial aid: (509) 527-2815; 65% of undergrads determined to have financial need; average aid package $22,193

Washington State University
Pullman WA
(888) 468-6978
U.S. News ranking: Nat. U., No. 140
Website: www.wsu.edu
Admissions email: admissions@wsu.edu
Public; founded 1890
Freshman admissions: selective; 2016-2017: 23,223 applied, 16,731 accepted. Either SAT or ACT required. SAT 25/75 percentile: 930-1165. High school rank: 36% in top tenth, 54% in top quarter, 85% in top half
Early decision deadline: N/A, notification date: N/A
Early action deadline: N/A, notification date: N/A
Application deadline (fall): rolling
Undergraduate student body: 21,652 full time, 3,252 part time; 48% male, 52% female; 1% American Indian, 6% Asian, 3% black, 14% Hispanic, 7% multiracial, 0% Pacific Islander, 61% white, 5% international; 89% from in state; 24% live on campus; 21% of students in fraternities, 25% in sororities
Most popular majors: 20% Business, Management, Marketing, and Related Support Services, 12% Social Sciences, 11% Engineering, 8% Health Professions and Related Programs, 7% Communication, Journalism, and Related Programs

Expenses: 2017-2018: $11,391 in state, $25,817 out of state; room/board: $11,356
Financial aid: (509) 335-9711; 59% of undergrads determined to have financial need; average aid package $12,491

Western Washington University
Bellingham WA
(360) 650-3440
U.S. News ranking: Reg. U. (W), No. 19
Website: www.wwu.edu
Admissions email: admit@wwu.edu
Public; founded 1893
Freshman admissions: selective; 2016-2017: 10,519 applied, 8,743 accepted. Either SAT or ACT required. SAT 25/75 percentile: 990-1220. High school rank: 22% in top tenth, 56% in top quarter, 89% in top half
Early decision deadline: N/A, notification date: N/A
Early action deadline: N/A, notification date: N/A
Application deadline (fall): 1/31
Undergraduate student body: 13,413 full time, 1,179 part time; 44% male, 56% female; 0% American Indian, 7% Asian, 2% black, 9% Hispanic, 9% multiracial, 0% Pacific Islander, 72% white, 1% international; 90% from in state; 27% live on campus; N/A of students in fraternities, N/A in sororities
Most popular majors: 13% Business, Management, Marketing, and Related Support Services, 11% Social Sciences, 7% Multi/Interdisciplinary Studies, 7% Visual and Performing Arts, 6% Health Professions and Related Programs
Expenses: 2017-2018: $7,653 in state, $21,597 out of state; room/board: $10,971
Financial aid: (360) 650-2422; 48% of undergrads determined to have financial need; average aid package $14,074

Whitman College
Walla Walla WA
(509) 527-5176
U.S. News ranking: Nat. Lib. Arts, No. 41
Website: www.whitman.edu
Admissions email: admission@ whitman.edu
Private; founded 1883
Freshman admissions: more selective; 2016-2017: 3,749 applied, 1,915 accepted. Neither SAT nor ACT required. SAT 25/75 percentile: 1200-1420. High school rank: 55% in top tenth, 82% in top quarter, 96% in top half
Early decision deadline: 11/15, notification date: 12/20
Early action deadline: N/A, notification date: N/A
Application deadline (fall): 1/15
Undergraduate student body: 1,453 full time, 40 part time; 43% male, 57% female; 0% American Indian, 5% Asian, 1% black, 7% Hispanic, 7% multiracial, 0% Pacific Islander, 71% white, 6% international; 35% from in state; 64% live on campus; 39% of students in fraternities, 43% in sororities

Most popular majors: 10% Biology/Biological Sciences, General, 10% Psychology, General, 9% Biochemistry and Molecular Biology, 8% Economics, General, 7% Political Science and Government, General
Expenses: 2017-2018: $49,780; room/board: $12,524
Financial aid: (509) 527-5178; 45% of undergrads determined to have financial need; average aid package $33,008

Whitworth University
Spokane WA
(800) 533-4668
U.S. News ranking: Reg. U. (W), No. 8
Website: www.whitworth.edu
Admissions email: admissions@ whitworth.edu
Private; founded 1890
Affiliation: Presbyterian Church (USA)
Freshman admissions: selective; 2016-2017: 3,262 applied, 2,889 accepted. Neither SAT nor ACT required. SAT 25/75 percentile: 1000-1260. High school rank: 28% in top tenth, 60% in top quarter, 90% in top half
Early decision deadline: N/A, notification date: N/A
Early action deadline: 11/15, notification date: 12/1
Application deadline (fall): 8/1
Undergraduate student body: 2,258 full time, 50 part time; 40% male, 60% female; 1% American Indian, 5% Asian, 2% black, 9% Hispanic, 7% multiracial, 0% Pacific Islander, 72% white, 3% international; 71% from in state; 54% live on campus; 0% of students in fraternities, 0% in sororities
Most popular majors: 14% Business, Management, Marketing, and Related Support Services, 10% Social Sciences, 8% Multi/Interdisciplinary Studies, 8% Physical Sciences, 7% Psychology
Expenses: 2017-2018: $42,186; room/board: $11,496
Financial aid: (509) 777-4335; 69% of undergrads determined to have financial need; average aid package $34,546

WEST VIRGINIA

Alderson Broaddus University
Philippi WV
(800) 263-1549
U.S. News ranking: Reg. Coll. (S), No. 26
Website: www.ab.edu
Admissions email: admissions@ab.edu
Private; founded 1871
Affiliation: American Baptist
Freshman admissions: selective; 2016-2017: 4,103 applied, 1,698 accepted. Either SAT or ACT required. ACT 25/75 percentile: 18-23. High school rank: 9% in top tenth, 27% in top quarter, 59% in top half
Early decision deadline: N/A, notification date: N/A
Early action deadline: N/A, notification date: N/A

Application deadline (fall): 8/25
Undergraduate student body: 934 full time, 47 part time; 54% male, 46% female; 1% American Indian, 1% Asian, 18% black, 4% Hispanic, 1% multiracial, 0% Pacific Islander, 70% white, 5% international; 37% from in state; 84% live on campus; 4% of students in fraternities, 5% in sororities
Most popular majors: 14% Registered Nursing/Registered Nurse, 12% Biology/Biological Sciences, General, 9% Business Administration and Management, General, 6% Sport and Fitness Administration/Management, 5% Athletic Training/Trainer
Expenses: 2017-2018: $26,610; room/board: $8,390
Financial aid: (304) 457-6354; 84% of undergrads determined to have financial need; average aid package $22,284

American Public University System
Charles Town WV
(877) 777-9081
U.S. News ranking: Reg. U. (S), unranked
Website: www.apus.edu
For-profit; founded 1991
Freshman admissions: least selective; 2016-2017: N/A applied, N/A accepted. Neither SAT nor ACT required. SAT 25/75 percentile: N/A. High school rank: N/A
Early decision deadline: N/A, notification date: N/A
Early action deadline: N/A, notification date: N/A
Application deadline (fall): rolling
Undergraduate student body: 2,451 full time, 37,211 part time; 64% male, 36% female; 1% American Indian, 2% Asian, 17% black, 11% Hispanic, 4% multiracial, 1% Pacific Islander, 57% white, 1% international
Most popular majors: 17% Business Administration and Management, General, 8% Criminal Justice/Safety Studies, 8% International/Global Studies, 6% Kinesiology and Exercise Science, 5% Psychology, General
Expenses: 2017-2018: $8,100; room/board: N/A
Financial aid: (877) 755-2787

Bethany College
Bethany WV
(304) 829-7611
U.S. News ranking: Nat. Lib. Arts, second tier
Website: www.bethanywv.edu
Admissions email: enrollment@bethanywv.edu
Private; founded 1840
Affiliation: Churches of Christ
Freshman admissions: less selective; 2016-2017: 1,126 applied, 727 accepted. Either SAT or ACT required. ACT 25/75 percentile: 17-23. High school rank: 7% in top tenth, 21% in top quarter, 54% in top half
Early decision deadline: N/A, notification date: N/A
Early action deadline: N/A, notification date: N/A
Application deadline (fall): rolling

Undergraduate student body: 627 full time, 5 part time; 61% male, 39% female; 0% American Indian, 1% Asian, 20% black, 6% Hispanic, 3% multiracial, 0% Pacific Islander, 49% white, 2% international
Most popular majors: Information not available
Expenses: 2017-2018: $28,444; room/board: $10,270
Financial aid: (304) 829-7601; 88% of undergrads determined to have financial need; average aid package $33,740

Bluefield State College
Bluefield WV
(304) 327-4065
U.S. News ranking: Reg. Coll. (S), No. 50
Website: www.bluefieldstate.edu
Admissions email: bscadmit@bluefieldstate.edu
Public; founded 1895
Freshman admissions: selective; 2016-2017: 653 applied, 544 accepted. Either SAT or ACT required. ACT 25/75 percentile: 17-22. High school rank: 13% in top tenth, 42% in top quarter, 74% in top half
Early decision deadline: N/A, notification date: N/A
Early action deadline: N/A, notification date: N/A
Application deadline (fall): rolling
Undergraduate student body: 1,117 full time, 245 part time; 38% male, 62% female; 0% American Indian, 1% Asian, 8% black, 1% Hispanic, 2% multiracial, 0% Pacific Islander, 86% white, 2% international; 98% from in state; 0% live on campus; 4% of students in fraternities, 4% in sororities
Most popular majors: 18% Engineering Technologies and Engineering-Related Fields, 18% Health Professions and Related Programs, 15% Liberal Arts and Sciences, General Studies and Humanities, 14% Business, Management, Marketing, and Related Support Services, 12% Homeland Security, Law Enforcement, Firefighting and Related Protective Services
Expenses: 2017-2018: $9,560 in state, $13,032 out of state; room/board: N/A
Financial aid: (304) 327-4022; 84% of undergrads determined to have financial need; average aid package $3,009

Concord University
Athens WV
(888) 384-5249
U.S. News ranking: Reg. U. (S), second tier
Website: www.concord.edu
Admissions email: admissions@concord.edu
Public; founded 1872
Freshman admissions: selective; 2016-2017: 2,960 applied, 2,402 accepted. Either SAT or ACT required. ACT 25/75 percentile: 19-24. High school rank: 22% in top tenth, 47% in top quarter, 80% in top half
Early decision deadline: N/A, notification date: N/A

Early action deadline: N/A, notification date: N/A
Application deadline (fall): rolling
Undergraduate student body: 1,878 full time, 224 part time; 41% male, 59% female; 0% American Indian, 1% Asian, 6% black, 1% Hispanic, 2% multiracial, 0% Pacific Islander, 85% white, 4% international; 87% from in state; 38% live on campus; 2% of students in fraternities, 5% in sororities
Most popular majors: 20% Liberal Arts and Sciences, General Studies and Humanities, 18% Business, Management, Marketing, and Related Support Services, 17% Education, 7% Social Sciences, 6% Biological and Biomedical Sciences
Expenses: 2017-2018: $7,584 in state, $16,492 out of state; room/board: $8,642
Financial aid: (304) 384-5338; 75% of undergrads determined to have financial need; average aid package $8,425

Davis and Elkins College[1]
Elkins WV
(304) 637-1230
U.S. News ranking: Nat. Lib. Arts, second tier
Website: www.davisandelkins.edu
Admissions email: admiss@davisandelkins.edu
Private
Application deadline (fall): N/A
Undergraduate student body: N/A full time, N/A part time
Expenses: 2016-2017: $28,842; room/board: $9,800
Financial aid: N/A

Fairmont State University
Fairmont WV
(304) 367-4010
U.S. News ranking: Reg. U. (S), second tier
Website: www.fairmontstate.edu
Admissions email: admit@fairmontstate.edu
Public; founded 1865
Freshman admissions: selective; 2016-2017: 3,431 applied, 2,227 accepted. Either SAT or ACT required. ACT 25/75 percentile: 18-23. High school rank: 14% in top tenth, 35% in top quarter, 70% in top half
Early decision deadline: N/A, notification date: N/A
Early action deadline: N/A, notification date: N/A
Application deadline (fall): 8/15
Undergraduate student body: 3,279 full time, 472 part time; 45% male, 55% female; 0% American Indian, 1% Asian, 6% black, 2% Hispanic, 4% multiracial, 0% Pacific Islander, 85% white, 3% international
Most popular majors: Information not available
Expenses: 2017-2018: $7,296 in state, $15,398 out of state; room/board: $9,184
Financial aid: (304) 367-4826; 71% of undergrads determined to have financial need; average aid package $8,761

Glenville State College
Glenville WV
(304) 462-4128
U.S. News ranking: Reg. Coll. (S), No. 57
Website: www.glenville.edu
Admissions email: admissions@glenville.edu
Public; founded 1872
Freshman admissions: less selective; 2016-2017: 1,316 applied, 914 accepted. Either SAT or ACT required. ACT 25/75 percentile: 16-22. High school rank: 5% in top tenth, 24% in top quarter, 58% in top half
Early decision deadline: N/A, notification date: N/A
Early action deadline: N/A, notification date: N/A
Application deadline (fall): rolling
Undergraduate student body: 1,059 full time, 582 part time; 58% male, 42% female; 1% American Indian, 0% Asian, 17% black, 2% Hispanic, 1% multiracial, 0% Pacific Islander, 71% white, 0% international; 86% from in state; 58% live on campus; 5% of students in fraternities, 7% in sororities
Most popular majors: Information not available
Expenses: 2017-2018: $7,342 in state, $16,598 out of state; room/board: $9,942
Financial aid: (304) 426-6171; 84% of undergrads determined to have financial need; average aid package $14,500

Marshall University
Huntington WV
(800) 642-3499
U.S. News ranking: Reg. U. (S), No. 43
Website: www.marshall.edu
Admissions email: admissions@marshall.edu
Public; founded 1837
Freshman admissions: selective; 2016-2017: 4,891 applied, 4,374 accepted. Either SAT or ACT required. ACT 25/75 percentile: 19-24. High school rank: N/A
Early decision deadline: N/A, notification date: N/A
Early action deadline: N/A, notification date: N/A
Undergraduate student body: 7,997 full time, 1,618 part time; 43% male, 57% female; 0% American Indian, 1% Asian, 7% black, 2% Hispanic, 3% multiracial, 0% Pacific Islander, 84% white, 1% international; 80% from in state; N/A live on campus; N/A of students in fraternities, N/A in sororities
Most popular majors: 18% Health Professions and Related Programs, 16% Business, Management, Marketing, and Related Support Services, 13% Education, 13% Liberal Arts and Sciences, General Studies and Humanities, 6% Psychology
Expenses: 2017-2018: $7,798 in state, $17,856 out of state; room/board: $9,254
Financial aid: (304) 696-3162; 71% of undergrads determined to have financial need; average aid package $10,625

Ohio Valley University
Vienna WV
(877) 446-8668
U.S. News ranking: Reg. Coll. (S), No. 40
Website: www.ovu.edu
Admissions email: admissions@ovu.edu
Private; founded 1958
Affiliation: Churches of Christ
Freshman admissions: selective; 2016-2017: 845 applied, 537 accepted. Neither SAT nor ACT required. ACT 25/75 percentile: 18-23. High school rank: 14% in top tenth, 29% in top quarter, 68% in top half
Early decision deadline: N/A, notification date: N/A
Early action deadline: N/A, notification date: N/A
Application deadline (fall): 8/15
Undergraduate student body: 390 full time, 14 part time; 52% male, 48% female; 0% American Indian, 1% Asian, 11% black, 5% Hispanic, 3% multiracial, 0% Pacific Islander, 58% white, 12% international; 32% from in state; 51% live on campus; 45% of students in fraternities, 57% in sororities
Most popular majors: 29% Business, Management, Marketing, and Related Support Services, 16% Education, 15% Psychology, 10% Multi/Interdisciplinary Studies, 10% Theology and Religious Vocations
Expenses: 2017-2018: $21,100; room/board: $7,700
Financial aid: (304) 865-6077; 76% of undergrads determined to have financial need; average aid package $15,975

Salem International University[1]
Salem WV
U.S. News ranking: Reg. U. (S), unranked
Website: www.salemu.edu
Admissions email: admissions@salemu.edu
For-profit
Application deadline (fall): N/A
Undergraduate student body: N/A full time, N/A part time
Expenses: 2016-2017: $14,600; room/board: $7,480
Financial aid: N/A

Shepherd University
Shepherdstown WV
(304) 876-5212
U.S. News ranking: Nat. Lib. Arts, second tier
Website: www.shepherd.edu
Admissions email: admission@shepherd.edu
Public; founded 1871
Freshman admissions: less selective; 2016-2017: 1,546 applied, 1,421 accepted. Either SAT or ACT required. ACT 25/75 percentile: 19-24. High school rank: N/A
Early decision deadline: N/A, notification date: N/A
Early action deadline: N/A, notification date: N/A
Application deadline (fall): rolling
Undergraduate student body: 2,700 full time, 736 part time; 42% male, 58% female; 0% American Indian, 2% Asian, 9% black, 4% Hispanic, 2% multiracial,

0% Pacific Islander, 81% white, 0% international; 65% from in state; 33% live on campus; 3% of students in fraternities, 4% in sororities
Most popular majors: 12% Business, Management, Marketing, and Related Support Services, 12% Liberal Arts and Sciences, General Studies and Humanities, 11% Health Professions and Related Programs, 10% Education, 8% Social Sciences
Expenses: 2017-2018: $7,328 in state, $17,873 out of state; room/board: $10,054
Financial aid: (304) 876-5470; 65% of undergrads determined to have financial need; average aid package $12,399

University of Charleston
Charleston WV
(800) 995-4682
U.S. News ranking: Reg. U. (S), No. 78
Website: www.ucwv.edu
Admissions email: admissions@ucwv.edu
Private; founded 1888
Freshman admissions: selective; 2016-2017: 1,801 applied, 934 accepted. Either SAT or ACT required. ACT 25/75 percentile: 18-24. High school rank. N/A
Early decision deadline: N/A, notification date: N/A
Early action deadline: N/A, notification date: N/A
Application deadline (fall): rolling
Undergraduate student body: 1,218 full time, 543 part time; 55% male, 45% female; 0% American Indian, 1% Asian, 8% black, 2% Hispanic, 2% multiracial, 0% Pacific Islander, 52% white, 9% international
Most popular majors: Information not available
Expenses: 2017-2018: $29,600, room/board: $9,100
Financial aid: (304) 357-4944; 75% of undergrads determined to have financial need; average aid package $21,500

West Liberty University
West Liberty WV
(304) 336-8076
U.S. News ranking: Reg. Coll. (S), No. 37
Website: www.westliberty.edu
Admissions email: admissions@westliberty.edu
Public; founded 1837
Freshman admissions: selective; 2016-2017: 1,781 applied, 1,277 accepted. Either SAT or ACT required. ACT 25/75 percentile: 18-23. High school rank: 11% in top tenth, 33% in top quarter, 72% in top half
Early decision deadline: N/A, notification date: N/A
Early action deadline: N/A, notification date: N/A
Application deadline (fall): rolling
Undergraduate student body: 1,808 full time, 301 part time; 37% male, 63% female; 0% American Indian, 0% Asian, 3% black, 1% Hispanic, 1% multiracial, 0% Pacific Islander, 73% white, 2% international; 68% from in

state; 44% live on campus; 3% of students in fraternities, 4% in sororities
Most popular majors: 18% Information Resources Management, 14% General Studies, 7% Biology/Biological Sciences, General, 7% Dental Hygiene/Hygienist, 6% Elementary Education and Teaching
Expenses: 2017-2018: $7,038 in state, $14,394 out of state; room/board: $9,120
Financial aid: (304) 336-8016

West Virginia State University
Institute WV
(304) 766-4345
U.S. News ranking: Nat. Lib. Arts, second tier
Website: www.wvstateu.edu
Admissions email: admissions@wvstateu.edu
Public; founded 1891
Freshman admissions: less selective; 2016-2017: 3,462 applied, 3,333 accepted. Either SAT or ACT required. ACT 25/75 percentile: 17-22. High school rank: N/A
Early decision deadline: N/A, notification date: N/A
Early action deadline: N/A, notification date: N/A
Application deadline (fall): 8/15
Undergraduate student body: 1,797 full time, 1,636 part time; 43% male, 57% female; 6% American Indian, 0% Asian, 15% black, 2% Hispanic, 10% multiracial, 0% Pacific Islander, 59% white, 1% international; 86% from in state; N/A live on campus; 5% of students in fraternities, 2% in sororities
Most popular majors: 18% General Studies, 16% Elementary Education and Teaching, 11% Criminal Justice/Safety Studies, 10% Business Administration and Management, General, 7% Social Work
Expenses: 2017-2018: $7,546 in state, $16,550 out of state; room/board: $11,866
Financial aid: (304) 204-4361; 79% of undergrads determined to have financial need; average aid package $12,222

West Virginia University
Morgantown WV
(304) 442-3146
U.S. News ranking: Nat. U., No. 187
Website: www.wvu.edu
Admissions email: go2wvu@mail.wvu.edu
Public; founded 1867
Freshman admissions: selective; 2016-2017: 21,558 applied, 16,411 accepted. Either SAT or ACT required. ACT 25/75 percentile: 20% in top tenth, 44% in top quarter, 76% in top half
Early decision deadline: N/A, notification date: N/A
Early action deadline: N/A, notification date: N/A
Application deadline (fall): 8/1
Undergraduate student body: 20,524 full time, 1,826 part time; 54% male, 46% female; 0% American Indian, 2% Asian,

5% black, 4% Hispanic, 4% multiracial, 0% Pacific Islander, 79% white, 6% international; 52% from in state; 15% live on campus; 7% of students in fraternities, 6% in sororities
Most popular majors: 14% Engineering, 12% Business, Management, Marketing, and Related Support Services, 8% Multi/Interdisciplinary Studies, 7% Communication, Journalism, and Related Programs, 7% Social Sciences
Expenses: 2017-2018: $8,376 in state, $23,616 out of state; room/board: $10,576
Financial aid: (304) 293-8571; 56% of undergrads determined to have financial need; average aid package $6,839

West Virginia University– Parkersburg[1]
Parkersburg WV
U.S. News ranking: Reg. Coll. (S), unranked
Website: www.wvup.edu
Admissions email: info@mail.wvup.edu
Public
Application deadline (fall): N/A
Undergraduate student body: N/A full time, N/A part time
Expenses: 2016-2017: $3,384 in state, $7,920 out of state; room/board: N/A
Financial aid: N/A

West Virginia Wesleyan College
Buckhannon WV
(800) 722-9933
U.S. News ranking: Reg. U. (S), No. 48
Website: www.wvwc.edu
Admissions email: admissions@wvwc.edu
Private; founded 1890
Affiliation: United Methodist
Freshman admissions: selective; 2016-2017: 1,730 applied, 1,337 accepted. Either SAT or ACT required. ACT 25/75 percentile: 22% in top tenth, 54% in top quarter, 85% in top half
Early decision deadline: N/A, notification date: N/A
Early action deadline: N/A, notification date: N/A
Application deadline (fall): 8/15
Undergraduate student body: 1,367 full time, 29 part time; 45% male, 55% female; 0% American Indian, 0% Asian, 8% black, 3% Hispanic, 4% multiracial, 0% Pacific Islander, 79% white, 6% international; 63% from in state; 79% live on campus; 25% of students in fraternities, 25% in sororities
Most popular majors: 14% Physical Sciences, 12% Business, Management, Marketing, and Related Support Services, 10% Psychology, 9% Education, 9% Parks, Recreation, Leisure, and Fitness Studies
Expenses: 2017-2018: $30,752; room/board: $8,436
Financial aid: (304) 473-8080; 79% of undergrads determined to have financial need; average aid package $27,645

Wheeling Jesuit University
Wheeling WV
(800) 624-6992
U.S. News ranking: Reg. U. (S), No. 41
Website: www.wju.edu
Admissions email: admiss@wju.edu
Private; founded 1954
Affiliation: Roman Catholic
Freshman admissions: selective; 2016-2017: 1,020 applied, 951 accepted. Either SAT or ACT required. ACT 25/75 percentile: 18-23. High school rank: 17% in top tenth, 36% in top quarter, 69% in top half
Early decision deadline: N/A, notification date: N/A
Early action deadline: N/A, notification date: N/A
Application deadline (fall): rolling
Undergraduate student body: 790 full time, 155 part time; 49% male, 51% female; 1% American Indian, 1% Asian, 8% black, 3% Hispanic, 2% multiracial, 1% Pacific Islander, 75% white, 5% international; 34% from in state; 68% live on campus; N/A of students in fraternities, N/A in sororities
Most popular majors: 31% Health Professions and Related Programs, 24% Business, Management, Marketing, and Related Support Services, 8% Psychology, 6% Biological and Biomedical Sciences, 6% Physical Sciences
Expenses: 2017-2018: $28,110; room/board: $8,996
Financial aid: (304) 243-2304; 77% of undergrads determined to have financial need; average aid package $25,276

WISCONSIN

Alverno College
Milwaukee WI
(414) 382-6100
U.S. News ranking: Reg. U. (Mid. W), No. 54
Website: www.alverno.edu
Admissions email: admissions@alverno.edu
Private; founded 1887
Affiliation: Roman Catholic
Freshman admissions: selective; 2016-2017: 698 applied, 516 accepted. Either SAT or ACT required. ACT 25/75 percentile: 18-22. High school rank: 14% in top tenth, 38% in top quarter, 73% in top half
Early decision deadline: N/A, notification date: N/A
Early action deadline: N/A, notification date: N/A
Application deadline (fall): rolling
Undergraduate student body: 1,080 full time, 333 part time; 0% male, 100% female; 1% American Indian, 5% Asian, 13% black, 23% Hispanic, 4% multiracial, 0% Pacific Islander, 53% white, 0% international; 94% from in state; 16% live on campus; 0% of students in fraternities, 1% in sororities
Most popular majors: 36% Health Professions and Related Programs, 18% Business, Management, Marketing, and Related Support Services, 12% Liberal Arts and

Sciences, General Studies and Humanities, 7% Psychology, 6% Biological and Biomedical Sciences
Expenses: 2017-2018: $28,277; room/board: $8,296
Financial aid: (414) 382-6040; 91% of undergrads determined to have financial need; average aid package $23,988

Beloit College
Beloit WI
(608) 363-2500
U.S. News ranking: Nat. Lib. Arts, No. 76
Website: www.beloit.edu
Admissions email: admiss@beloit.edu
Private; founded 1846
Freshman admissions: more selective; 2016-2017: 3,855 applied, 2,693 accepted. Neither SAT nor ACT required. ACT 25/75 percentile: 24-30. High school rank: 31% in top tenth, 62% in top quarter, 86% in top half
Early decision deadline: 11/1, notification date: 11/30
Early action deadline: 12/1, notification date: 12/15
Application deadline (fall): rolling
Undergraduate student body: 1,337 full time, 57 part time; 46% male, 54% female; 0% American Indian, 3% Asian, 5% black, 9% Hispanic, 3% multiracial, 0% Pacific Islander, 62% white, 13% international; 17% from in state; 89% live on campus; 19% of students in fraternities, 20% in sororities
Most popular majors: 6% Anthropology, 6% Business/Managerial Economics, 6% Creative Writing, 6% Education, General, 6% Psychology, General
Expenses: 2017-2018: $48,706; room/board: $8,436
Financial aid: (608) 363-2696; 63% of undergrads determined to have financial need; average aid package $39,076

Cardinal Stritch University
Milwaukee WI
(414) 410-4040
U.S. News ranking: Nat. U., second tier
Website: www.stritch.edu
Admissions email: admissions@stritch.edu
Private; founded 1937
Affiliation: Roman Catholic
Freshman admissions: selective; 2016-2017: 774 applied, 631 accepted. Neither SAT nor ACT required. ACT 25/75 percentile: 18-22. High school rank: N/A
Early decision deadline: N/A, notification date: N/A
Early action deadline: N/A, notification date: N/A
Application deadline (fall): rolling
Undergraduate student body: 1,205 full time, 329 part time; 34% male, 66% female; 0% American Indian, 3% Asian, 20% black, 14% Hispanic, 3% multiracial, 0% Pacific Islander, 48% white, 11% international; 87% from in state; 19% live on campus; 6% of students in fraternities, 1% in sororities

Most popular majors: 31% Organizational Leadership, 16% Business Administration and Management, General, 7% Registered Nursing, Nursing Administration, Nursing Research and Clinical Nursing, Other, 6% Business/Commerce, General, 4% Elementary Education and Teaching
Expenses: 2017-2018: $28,844; room/board: $8,118
Financial aid: (414) 410-4016; 69% of undergrads determined to have financial need; average aid package $20,277

Carroll University
Waukesha WI
(262) 524-7220
U.S. News ranking: Reg. U. (Mid. W), No. 38
Website: www.carrollu.edu/
Admissions email: info@carrollu.edu
Private; founded 1846
Affiliation: Presbyterian
Freshman admissions: more selective; 2016-2017: 3,463 applied, 2,478 accepted. Either SAT or ACT required. ACT 25/75 percentile: 21-26. High school rank: 20% in top tenth, 53% in top quarter, 88% in top half
Early decision deadline: N/A, notification date: N/A
Early action deadline: N/A, notification date: N/A
Application deadline (fall): rolling
Undergraduate student body: 2,734 full time, 267 part time; 35% male, 65% female; 0% American Indian, 4% Asian, 2% black, 7% Hispanic, 3% multiracial, 0% Pacific Islander, 81% white, 3% international
Most popular majors: Information not available
Expenses: 2017-2018: $31,144; room/board: $9,230
Financial aid: (262) 524-7296; 78% of undergrads determined to have financial need; average aid package $22,332

Carthage College
Kenosha WI
(262) 551-6000
U.S. News ranking: Nat. Lib. Arts, No. 163
Website: www.carthage.edu
Admissions email: admissions@carthage.edu
Private; founded 1847
Freshman admissions: more selective; 2016-2017: 6,640 applied, 4,630 accepted. Neither SAT nor ACT required. ACT 25/75 percentile: 21-27. High school rank: 26% in top tenth, 51% in top quarter, 81% in top half
Early decision deadline: N/A, notification date: N/A
Early action deadline: N/A, notification date: N/A
Application deadline (fall): rolling

Undergraduate student body: 2,644 full time, 174 part time; 45% male, 55% female; 0% American Indian, 2% Asian, 5% black, 6% Hispanic, 3% multiracial, 0% Pacific Islander, 70% white, 1% international; 35% from in state; 65% live on campus; 7% of students in fraternities, 10% in sororities
Most popular majors: 28% Business, Management, Marketing, and Related Support Services, 10% Education, 9% Biological and Biomedical Sciences, 8% Visual and Performing Arts, 6% Communication, Journalism, and Related Programs
Expenses: 2016-2017: $40,265; room/board: $10,974
Financial aid: (262) 551-6001

Concordia University Wisconsin
Mequon WI
(262) 243-4300
U.S. News ranking: Reg. U. (Mid. W), No. 51
Website: www.cuw.edu
Admissions email: admissions@cuw.edu
Private; founded 1881
Affiliation: Lutheran Church–Missouri Synod
Freshman admissions: selective; 2016-2017: 2,633 applied, 1,668 accepted. Either SAT or ACT required. ACT 25/75 percentile: 21-27. High school rank: 20% in top tenth, 46% in top quarter, 80% in top half
Early decision deadline: N/A, notification date: N/A
Early action deadline: N/A, notification date: N/A
Application deadline (fall): 8/15
Undergraduate student body: 2,698 full time, 1,132 part time; 35% male, 65% female; 1% American Indian, 2% Asian, 13% black, 2% Hispanic, 3% multiracial, 0% Pacific Islander, 74% white, 2% international; 77% from in state; 49% live on campus; 0% of students in fraternities, 0% in sororities
Most popular majors: 28% Business, Management, Marketing, and Related Support Services, 28% Health Professions and Related Programs, 8% Biological and Biomedical Sciences, 8% Homeland Security, Law Enforcement, Firefighting and Related Protective Services, 7% Education
Expenses: 2017-2018: $28,600; room/board: $10,530
Financial aid: (262) 243-2025; 80% of undergrads determined to have financial need; average aid package $21,208

Edgewood College
Madison WI
(608) 663-2294
U.S. News ranking: Nat. U., No. 181
Website: www.edgewood.edu
Admissions email: admissions@edgewood.edu
Private; founded 1927
Affiliation: Roman Catholic

Freshman admissions: selective; 2016-2017: 1,035 applied, 808 accepted. Either SAT or ACT required. ACT 25/75 percentile: 21-25. High school rank: 15% in top tenth, 46% in top quarter, 77% in top half
Early decision deadline: N/A, notification date: N/A
Early action deadline: N/A, notification date: N/A
Application deadline (fall): 8/15
Undergraduate student body: 1,450 full time, 211 part time; 28% male, 72% female; 0% American Indian, 3% Asian, 3% black, 6% Hispanic, 3% multiracial, 0% Pacific Islander, 79% white, 4% international; 92% from in state; 34% live on campus; N/A of students in fraternities, N/A in sororities
Most popular majors: 24% Registered Nursing/Registered Nurse, 10% Business/Commerce, General, 10% Psychology, General, 5% Biology/Biological Sciences, General, 5% Business Administration and Management, General
Expenses: 2017-2018: $28,500; room/board: $10,494
Financial aid: (608) 663-2305; 76% of undergrads determined to have financial need; average aid package $21,457

Herzing University[1]
Madison WI
(800) 596-0724
U.S. News ranking: Reg. U. (Mid. W), unranked
Website: www.herzing.edu/
Admissions email: info@msn.herzing.edu
For-profit; founded 1965
Application deadline (fall): N/A
Undergraduate student body: N/A full time, N/A part timel
Expenses: 2017-2018: $13,850; room/board: N/A
Financial aid: N/A

Lakeland University[1]
Plymouth WI
(920) 565-1226
U.S. News ranking: Reg. U. (Mid. W), second tier
Website: www.lakeland.edu
Admissions email: admissions@lakeland.edu
Private; founded 1862
Application deadline (fall): rolling
Undergraduate student body: N/A full time, N/A part time
Expenses: 2016-2017: $26,560; room/board: $8,530
Financial aid: N/A

Lawrence University
Appleton WI
(800) 227-0982
U.S. News ranking: Nat. Lib. Arts, No. 58
Website: www.lawrence.edu
Admissions email: admissions@lawrence.edu
Private; founded 1847
Freshman admissions: more selective; 2016-2017: 3,579 applied, 2,254 accepted. Neither SAT nor ACT required. ACT 25/75 percentile: 26-31. High school rank: 43% in top tenth, 73% in top quarter, 95% in top half

Early decision deadline: N/A, notification date: N/A
Early action deadline: 11/1, notification date: 12/15
Application deadline (fall): 1/15
Undergraduate student body: 1,503 full time, 29 part time; 46% male, 54% female; 0% American Indian, 5% Asian, 4% black, 8% Hispanic, 3% multiracial, 0% Pacific Islander, 68% white, 11% international; 29% from in state; 96% live on campus; 15% of students in fraternities, 15% in sororities
Most popular majors: 20% Visual and Performing Arts, 16% Social Sciences, 13% Biological and Biomedical Sciences, 11% Foreign Languages, Literatures, and Linguistics, 9% Psychology
Expenses: 2017-2018: $46,101; room/board: $10,032
Financial aid: (920) 832-6583; 59% of undergrads determined to have financial need; average aid package $38,487

Maranatha Baptist University
Watertown WI
(920) 206-2327
U.S. News ranking: Reg. Coll. (Mid. W), No. 56
Website: www.mbu.edu
Admissions email: admissions@mbu.edu
Private; founded 1968
Freshman admissions: selective; 2016-2017: 398 applied, 271 accepted. Either SAT or ACT required. ACT 25/75 percentile: 19-26. High school rank: 11% in top tenth, 24% in top quarter, 58% in top half
Early decision deadline: N/A, notification date: N/A
Early action deadline: N/A, notification date: N/A
Application deadline (fall): rolling
Undergraduate student body: 681 full time, 272 part time; 45% male, 55% female; 0% American Indian, 1% Asian, 2% black, 4% Hispanic, 4% multiracial, 0% Pacific Islander, 86% white, 1% international
Most popular majors: 22% Education, 15% Multi/Interdisciplinary Studies, 14% Theology and Religious Vocations, 13% Health Professions and Related Programs, 13% Liberal Arts and Sciences, General Studies and Humanities
Expenses: 2017-2018: $14,910; room/board: $7,000
Financial aid: (920) 206-2318; 84% of undergrads determined to have financial need; average aid package $10,154

Marian University
Fond du Lac WI
(920) 923-7650
U.S. News ranking: Reg. U. (Mid. W), No. 122
Website: www.marianuniversity.edu/

Admissions email: admissions@marianuniversity.edu
Private; founded 1936
Affiliation: Roman Catholic
Freshman admissions: selective; 2016-2017: 1,245 applied, 961 accepted. Either SAT or ACT required. ACT 25/75 percentile: 17-23. High school rank: 6% in top tenth, 26% in top quarter, 58% in top half
Early decision deadline: N/A, notification date: N/A
Early action deadline: N/A, notification date: N/A
Application deadline (fall): rolling
Undergraduate student body: 1,184 full time, 303 part time; 30% male, 70% female; 0% American Indian, 1% Asian, 6% black, 6% Hispanic, 1% multiracial, 0% Pacific Islander, 81% white, 2% international; 84% from in state; 24% live on campus; 0% of students in fraternities, 4% in sororities
Most popular majors: 34% Health Professions and Related Programs, 18% Business, Management, Marketing, and Related Support Services, 10% Homeland Security, Law Enforcement, Firefighting and Related Protective Services, 8% Public Administration and Social Service Professions, 7% Parks, Recreation, Leisure, and Fitness Studies
Expenses: 2017-2018: $27,370; room/board: $6,750
Financial aid: (920) 923-8737; 91% of undergrads determined to have financial need; average aid package $16,769

Marquette University
Milwaukee WI
(800) 222-6544
U.S. News ranking: Nat. U., No. 90
Website: www.marquette.edu
Admissions email: admissions@marquette.edu
Private; founded 1881
Affiliation: Roman Catholic
Freshman admissions: more selective; 2016-2017: N/A applied, N/A accepted. Either SAT or ACT required. ACT 25/75 percentile: 24-29. High school rank: 31% in top tenth, 65% in top quarter, 94% in top half
Early decision deadline: N/A, notification date: N/A
Early action deadline: N/A, notification date: N/A
Application deadline (fall): 12/1
Undergraduate student body: 7,974 full time, 264 part time; 46% male, 54% female; 0% American Indian, 6% Asian, 4% black, 11% Hispanic, 4% multiracial, 0% Pacific Islander, 72% white, 3% international; 32% from in state; 53% live on campus; 5% of students in fraternities, 11% in sororities
Most popular majors: 25% Business, Management, Marketing, and Related Support Services, 11% Biological and

Biomedical Sciences, 11% Communication, Journalism, and Related Programs, 11% Engineering, 8% Social Sciences
Expenses: 2017-2018: $39,900; room/board: $11,890
Financial aid: (414) 288-4000; 57% of undergrads determined to have financial need; average aid package $27,906

Milwaukee Institute of Art and Design
Milwaukee WI
(414) 291-8070
U.S. News ranking: Arts, unranked
Website: www.miad.edu
Admissions email: admissions@miad.edu
Private; founded 1974
Freshman admissions: least selective; 2016-2017: 921 applied, 492 accepted. Neither SAT nor ACT required. SAT 25/75 percentile: N/A. High school rank: 7% in top tenth, 26% in top quarter, 62% in top half
Early decision deadline: N/A, notification date: N/A
Early action deadline: 12/1, notification date: 12/15
Application deadline (fall): 8/15
Undergraduate student body: 617 full time, 13 part time; 35% male, 65% female; 0% American Indian, 3% Asian, 7% black, 14% Hispanic, 6% multiracial, 0% Pacific Islander, 66% white, 1% international; 58% from in state; 46% live on campus; 0% of students in fraternities, 0% in sororities
Most popular majors: 23% Graphic Design, 20% Industrial and Product Design, 17% Illustration, 12% Fine/Studio Arts, General, 6% Animation, Interactive Technology, Video Graphics and Special Effects
Expenses: 2017-2018: $36,230; room/board: $9,180
Financial aid: (414) 847-3270; 83% of undergrads determined to have financial need; average aid package $23,779

Milwaukee School of Engineering
Milwaukee WI
(800) 332-6763
U.S. News ranking: Reg. U. (Mid. W), No. 11
Website: www.msoe.edu
Admissions email: explore@msoe.edu
Private; founded 1903
Freshman admissions: more selective; 2016-2017: 2,686 applied, 1,781 accepted. Either SAT or ACT required. ACT 25/75 percentile: 25-30. High school rank: N/A
Early decision deadline: N/A, notification date: N/A
Early action deadline: N/A, notification date: N/A
Application deadline (fall): rolling
Undergraduate student body: 2,561 full time, 114 part time; 74% male, 26% female; 0% American Indian, 4% Asian, 2% black, 5% Hispanic, 2% multiracial, 0% Pacific Islander, 67% white, 11% international; 67% from in state; 40% live on campus; 5% of students in fraternities, 12% in sororities

Most popular majors: 30% Mechanical Engineering, 20% Electrical and Electronics Engineering, 10% Computer Software Engineering, 7% Computer Engineering, General, 6% Chemical and Biomolecular Engineering
Expenses: 2017-2018: $39,429; room/board: $9,102
Financial aid: (414) 277-7224; 75% of undergrads determined to have financial need; average aid package $27,296

Mount Mary University
Milwaukee WI
(414) 930-3024
U.S. News ranking: Reg. U. (Mid. W), No. 99
Website: www.mtmary.edu
Admissions email: mmu-admiss@mtmary.edu
Private; founded 1913
Affiliation: Roman Catholic
Freshman admissions: selective; 2016-2017: 689 applied, 388 accepted. Either SAT or ACT required. ACT 25/75 percentile: 18-23. High school rank: 23% in top tenth, 51% in top quarter, 84% in top half
Early decision deadline: N/A, notification date: N/A
Early action deadline: N/A, notification date: N/A
Application deadline (fall): rolling
Undergraduate student body: 714 full time, 93 part time; 1% male, 99% female; N/A American Indian, N/A Asian, N/A black, N/A Hispanic, N/A multiracial, N/A Pacific Islander, N/A white, N/A international; 93% from in state; 30% live on campus; N/A of students in fraternities, N/A in sororities
Most popular majors: 20% Business, Management, and Related Support Services, 18% Health Professions and Related Programs, 12% Multi/Interdisciplinary Studies, 12% Psychology, 8% Public Administration and Social Service Professions
Expenses: 2017-2018: $28,940; room/board: $8,530
Financial aid: (414) 930-3163; 93% of undergrads determined to have financial need; average aid package $23,843

Northland College
Ashland WI
(715) 682-1224
U.S. News ranking: Nat. Lib. Arts, second tier
Website: www.northland.edu
Admissions email: admit@northland.edu
Private; founded 1892
Affiliation: United Church of Christ
Freshman admissions: selective; 2016-2017: 1,335 applied, 721 accepted. Neither SAT nor ACT required. ACT 25/75 percentile: 21-26. High school rank: 17% in top tenth, 48% in top quarter, 79% in top half
Early decision deadline: N/A, notification date: N/A
Early action deadline: N/A, notification date: N/A
Application deadline (fall): rolling

Undergraduate student body: 560 full time, 22 part time; 49% male, 51% female; 3% American Indian, 0% Asian, 1% black, 5% Hispanic, 1% multiracial, 0% Pacific Islander, 83% white, 3% international; 50% from in state; 75% live on campus; 0% of students in fraternities, 0% in sororities
Most popular majors: 26% Natural Resources and Conservation, 13% Physical Sciences, 12% Biological and Biomedical Sciences, 9% Business, Management, Marketing, and Related Support Services, 8% Social Sciences
Expenses: 2017-2018: $35,157; room/board: $8,886
Financial aid: (715) 682-1255; 84% of undergrads determined to have financial need; average aid package $37,720

Ripon College
Ripon WI
(800) 947-4766
U.S. News ranking: Nat. Lib. Arts, No. 117
Website: www.ripon.edu
Admissions email: adminfo@ripon.edu
Private; founded 1851
Freshman admissions: selective; 2016-2017: 2,552 applied, 1,666 accepted. Either SAT or ACT required. ACT 25/75 percentile: 21-26. High school rank: 21% in top tenth, 47% in top quarter, 82% in top half
Early decision deadline: N/A, notification date: N/A
Early action deadline: N/A, notification date: N/A
Application deadline (fall): rolling
Undergraduate student body: 783 full time, 10 part time; 48% male, 52% female; 0% American Indian, 1% Asian, 2% black, 6% Hispanic, 2% multiracial, 0% Pacific Islander, 83% white, 4% international; 75% from in state; 90% live on campus; 41% of students in fraternities, 27% in sororities
Most popular majors: 15% Biology/ Biological Sciences, General, 15% Business/Commerce, General, 12% Health and Physical Education/Fitness, General, 10% History, General, 10% Psychology, General
Expenses: 2017-2018: $41,835; room/board: $8,156
Financial aid: (920) 748-8101; 83% of undergrads determined to have financial need; average aid package $31,115

Silver Lake College
Manitowoc WI
(920) 686-6175
U.S. News ranking: Reg. U. (Mid. W), second tier
Website: www.sl.edu
Admissions email: admissions@sl.edu
Private; founded 1935
Affiliation: Roman Catholic
Freshman admissions: less selective; 2016-2017: 481 applied, 264 accepted. Neither SAT nor ACT required. ACT 25/75 percentile: 14-22. High school rank: N/A
Early decision deadline: N/A, notification date: N/A

Early action deadline: N/A, notification date: N/A
Application deadline (fall): rolling
Undergraduate student body: 214 full time, 143 part time; 34% male, 66% female; 0% American Indian, 3% Asian, 13% black, 8% Hispanic, 1% multiracial, 0% Pacific Islander, 63% white, 5% international; 91% from in state; 46% live on campus; 0% of students in fraternities, 0% in sororities
Most popular majors: 19% Business Administration and Management, General, 18% Psychology, General, 14% Elementary Education and Teaching, 7% Biology/Biological Sciences, General, 7% Registered Nursing/Registered Nurse
Expenses: 2017-2018: $27,360; room/board: $7,200
Financial aid: (920) 686-6175; 83% of undergrads determined to have financial need

St. Norbert College
De Pere WI
(800) 236-4878
U.S. News ranking: Nat. Lib. Arts, No. 134
Website: www.snc.edu
Admissions email: admit@snc.edu
Private; founded 1898
Affiliation: Roman Catholic
Freshman admissions: more selective; 2016-2017: 3,605 applied, 2,934 accepted. Either SAT or ACT required. ACT 25/75 percentile: 22-27. High school rank: 24% in top tenth, 54% in top quarter, 85% in top half
Early decision deadline: N/A, notification date: N/A
Early action deadline: N/A, notification date: N/A
Application deadline (fall): rolling
Undergraduate student body: 2,054 full time, 48 part time; 43% male, 57% female; 1% American Indian, 1% Asian, 1% black, 4% Hispanic, 2% multiracial, 0% Pacific Islander, 88% white, 3% international; 79% from in state; 84% live on campus; 10% of students in fraternities, 10% in sororities
Most popular majors: 17% Business/Commerce, General, 13% Elementary Education and Teaching, 12% Speech Communication and Rhetoric, 9% Biology/Biological Sciences, General, 6% Psychology, General
Expenses: 2017-2018: $36,593; room/board: $9,467
Financial aid: (920) 403-3071; 74% of undergrads determined to have financial need; average aid package $26,079

University of Wisconsin–Eau Claire
Eau Claire WI
(715) 836-5415
U.S. News ranking: Reg. U. (Mid. W), No. 37
Website: www.uwec.edu
Admissions email: admissions@uwec.edu
Public; founded 1916
Freshman admissions: selective; 2016-2017: 5,706 applied, 5,079 accepted. Either SAT or ACT required. ACT 25/75 percentile: 22-26. High school

rank: 17% in top tenth, 47% in top quarter, 90% in top half
Early decision deadline: N/A, notification date: N/A
Early action deadline: N/A, notification date: N/A
Application deadline (fall): 8/20
Undergraduate student body: 9,311 full time, 670 part time; 38% male, 62% female; 0% American Indian, 4% Asian, 1% black, 3% Hispanic, 2% multiracial, 0% Pacific Islander, 89% white, 2% international; 71% from in state; 41% live on campus; N/A of students in fraternities, N/A in sororities
Most popular majors: 22% Business, Management, Marketing, and Related Support Services, 14% Health Professions and Related Programs, 7% Parks, Recreation, Leisure, and Fitness Studies, 6% Communication, Journalism, and Related Programs, 6% Education
Expenses: 2017-2018: $8,816 in state, $16,736 out of state; room/board: $7,538
Financial aid: (715) 836-3000; 52% of undergrads determined to have financial need; average aid package $9,479

University of Wisconsin–Green Bay
Green Bay WI
(920) 465-2111
U.S. News ranking: Reg. U. (Mid. W), No. 99
Website: www.uwgb.edu
Admissions email: uwgb@uwgb.edu
Public; founded 1965
Freshman admissions: selective; 2016-2017: 2,126 applied, 1,966 accepted. Either SAT or ACT required. ACT 25/75 percentile: 20-25. High school rank: N/A
Early decision deadline: N/A, notification date: N/A
Early action deadline: N/A, notification date: N/A
Application deadline (fall): rolling
Undergraduate student body: 4,009 full time, 2,749 part time; 33% male, 67% female; 1% American Indian, 3% Asian, 2% black, 4% Hispanic, 3% multiracial, 0% Pacific Islander, 85% white, 1% international; 92% from in state; 34% live on campus; 1% of students in fraternities, 1% in sororities
Most popular majors: 15% Business Administration and Management, General, 10% Liberal Arts and Sciences/ Liberal Studies, 9% Psychology, General, 7% Human Biology, 7% Registered Nursing, Nursing Administration, Nursing Research and Clinical Nursing, Other
Expenses: 2017-2018: $7,878 in state, $15,728 out of state; room/board: $7,306
Financial aid: (920) 465-2075; 67% of undergrads determined to have financial need; average aid package $10,328

University of Wisconsin–La Crosse

La Crosse WI
(608) 785-8939
U.S. News ranking: Reg. U. (Mid. W), No. 33
Website: www.uwlax.edu
Admissions email: admissions@uwlax.edu
Public; founded 1909
Freshman admissions: more selective; 2016-2017: 5,801 applied, 4,782 accepted. Either SAT or ACT required. ACT 25/75 percentile: 23-27. High school rank: 22% in top tenth, 59% in top quarter, 95% in top half
Early decision deadline: N/A, notification date: N/A
Early action deadline: N/A, notification date: N/A
Application deadline (fall): rolling
Undergraduate student body: 9,175 full time, 524 part time; 44% male, 56% female; 0% American Indian, 2% Asian, 1% black, 4% Hispanic, 3% multiracial, 0% Pacific Islander, 89% white, 1% international; 78% from in state; 36% live on campus; 1% of students in fraternities, 1% in sororities
Most popular majors: 21% Business, Management, Marketing, and Related Support Services, 14% Biological and Biomedical Sciences, 12% Health Professions and Related Programs, 9% Parks, Recreation, Leisure, and Fitness Studies, 9% Psychology
Expenses: 2016-2017: $9,091 in state, $17,612 out of state; room/board: $6,156
Financial aid: (608) 785-8604; 47% of undergrads determined to have financial need; average aid package $7,701

University of Wisconsin–Madison

Madison WI
(608) 262-3961
U.S. News ranking: Nat. U., No. 46
Website: www.wisc.edu
Admissions email: onwisconsin@admissions.wisc.edu
Public; founded 1848
Freshman admissions: more selective; 2016-2017: 32,887 applied, 17,304 accepted. Either SAT or ACT required. ACT 25/75 percentile: 27-31. High school rank: 54% in top tenth, 89% in top quarter, 99% in top half
Early decision deadline: N/A, notification date: N/A
Early action deadline: 11/1, notification date: 1/31
Application deadline (fall): 2/1
Undergraduate student body: 28,608 full time, 3,102 part time; 49% male, 51% female; 0% American Indian, 6% Asian, 2% black, 5% Hispanic, 3% multiracial, 0% Pacific Islander, 75% white, 8% international; 67% from in state; 26% live on campus; 9% of students in fraternities, 8% in sororities
Most popular majors: 8% Biology/Biological Sciences, General, 8% Economics, General, 5% Political Science and Government, General, 5% Psychology, General, 4% Speech Communication and Rhetoric

Expenses: 2017-2018: $10,533 in state, $34,782 out of state; room/board: $10,842
Financial aid: (608) 262-3060; 37% of undergrads determined to have financial need; average aid package $14,921

University of Wisconsin–Milwaukee

Milwaukee WI
(414) 229-2222
U.S. News ranking: Nat. U., second tier
Website: www.uwm.edu
Admissions email: uwmlook@uwm.edu
Public; founded 1956
Freshman admissions: selective; 2016-2017: 9,834 applied, 7,124 accepted. Neither SAT nor ACT required. ACT 25/75 percentile: 20-25. High school rank: 9% in top tenth, 19% in top quarter, 67% in top half
Early decision deadline: N/A, notification date: N/A
Early action deadline: N/A, notification date: N/A
Application deadline (fall): 8/11
Undergraduate student body: 17,578 full time, 3,797 part time; 48% male, 52% female; 0% American Indian, 7% Asian, 8% black, 10% Hispanic, 4% multiracial, 0% Pacific Islander, 67% white, 4% international; 89% from in state; 18% live on campus; N/A of students in fraternities, N/A in sororities
Most popular majors: 24% Business, Management, Marketing, and Related Support Services, 10% Health Professions and Related Programs, 7% Engineering, 7% Visual and Performing Arts, 6% Education
Expenses: 2016-2017: $9,493 in state, $19,851 out of state; room/board: $10,030
Financial aid: N/A

University of Wisconsin–Oshkosh

Oshkosh WI
(920) 424-0202
U.S. News ranking: Reg. U. (Mid. W), No. 73
Website: www.uwosh.edu
Admissions email: admissions@uwosh.edu
Public; founded 1871
Freshman admissions: selective; 2016-2017: 5,635 applied, 3,688 accepted. Either SAT or ACT required. ACT 25/75 percentile: 20-24. High school rank: 9% in top tenth, 35% in top quarter, 75% in top half
Early decision deadline: N/A, notification date: N/A
Early action deadline: N/A, notification date: N/A
Application deadline (fall): rolling
Undergraduate student body: 8,341 full time, 3,719 part time; 40% male, 60% female; 0% American Indian, 4% Asian, 3% black, 4% Hispanic, 2% multiracial, 0% Pacific Islander, 86% white, 1% international; 93% from in state; 29% live on campus; 3% of students in fraternities, 3% in sororities

Most popular majors: 18% Business, Management, Marketing, and Related Support Services, 14% Health Professions and Related Programs, 10% Education, 7% Communication, Journalism, and Related Programs, 7% Public Administration and Social Service Professions
Expenses: 2017-2018: $7,600 in state, $15,174 out of state; room/board: $7,792
Financial aid: (920) 424-3377; 65% of undergrads determined to have financial need; average aid package $8,558

University of Wisconsin–Parkside

Kenosha WI
(262) 595-2355
U.S. News ranking: Nat. Lib. Arts, second tier
Website: www.uwp.edu
Admissions email: admissions@uwp.edu
Public; founded 1968
Freshman admissions: selective; 2016-2017: 1,629 applied, 1,328 accepted. Neither SAT nor ACT required. ACT 25/75 percentile: 18-23. High school rank: 10% in top tenth, 33% in top quarter, 72% in top half
Early decision deadline: N/A, notification date: N/A
Early action deadline: N/A, notification date: N/A
Application deadline (fall): rolling
Undergraduate student body: 3,247 full time, 1,029 part time; 47% male, 53% female; 0% American Indian, 3% Asian, 9% black, 14% Hispanic, 4% multiracial, 0% Pacific Islander, 67% white, 1% international; 83% from in state; 17% live on campus; 1% of students in fraternities, 1% in sororities
Most popular majors: 28% Business, Management, Marketing, and Related Support Services, 11% Psychology, 10% Homeland Security, Law Enforcement, Firefighting and Related Protective Services, 9% Social Sciences, 6% Biological and Biomedical Sciences
Expenses: 2017-2018: $7,389 in state, $15,378 out of state; room/board: $7,924
Financial aid: (262) 595-2004; 64% of undergrads determined to have financial need; average aid package $9,498

University of Wisconsin–Platteville

Platteville WI
(608) 342-1125
U.S. News ranking: Reg. U. (Mid. W), No. 99
Website: www.uwplatt.edu
Admissions email: admit@uwplatt.edu
Public; founded 1866
Freshman admissions: selective; 2016-2017: 4,115 applied, 3,266 accepted. Either SAT or ACT required. ACT 25/75 percentile: 20-25. High school rank: 13% in top tenth, 40% in top quarter, 76% in top half
Early decision deadline: N/A, notification date: N/A

Early action deadline: N/A, notification date: N/A
Application deadline (fall): rolling
Undergraduate student body: 7,001 full time, 792 part time; 66% male, 34% female; 0% American Indian, 1% Asian, 1% black, 3% Hispanic, 3% multiracial, 0% Pacific Islander, 90% white, 1% international; 76% from in state; 41% live on campus; 5% of students in fraternities, 7% in sororities
Most popular majors: 24% Engineering, 13% Business, Management, Marketing, and Related Support Services, 11% Agriculture, Agriculture Operations, and Related Sciences, 11% Homeland Security, Law Enforcement, Firefighting and Related Protective Services, 8% Education
Expenses: 2016-2017: $7,488 in state, $15,339 out of state; room/board: $7,160
Financial aid: (608) 342-1836

University of Wisconsin–River Falls

River Falls WI
(715) 425-3500
U.S. News ranking: Reg. U. (Mid. W), No. 93
Website: www.uwrf.edu
Admissions email: admit@uwrf.edu
Public; founded 1874
Freshman admissions: selective; 2016-2017: 3,236 applied, 2,330 accepted. Either SAT or ACT required. ACT 25/75 percentile: 20-25. High school rank: 12% in top tenth, 36% in top quarter, 72% in top half
Early decision deadline: N/A, notification date: N/A
Early action deadline: N/A, notification date: N/A
Application deadline (fall): rolling
Undergraduate student body: 4,946 full time, 558 part time; 39% male, 61% female; 1% American Indian, 3% Asian, 2% black, 3% Hispanic, 0% multiracial, 0% Pacific Islander, 88% white, 3% international
Most popular majors: 18% Agriculture, Agriculture Operations, and Related Sciences, 14% Business, Management, Marketing, and Related Support Services, 12% Education, 10% Communication, Journalism, and Related Programs, 9% Biological and Biomedical Sciences
Expenses: 2017-2018: $8,013 in state, $15,586 out of state; room/board: $7,760
Financial aid: (715) 425-3141; 66% of undergrads determined to have financial need; average aid package $6,735

University of Wisconsin–Stevens Point

Stevens Point WI
(715) 346-2441
U.S. News ranking: Reg. U. (Mid. W), No. 54
Website: www.uwsp.edu
Admissions email: admiss@uwsp.edu
Public; founded 1894
Freshman admissions: selective; 2016-2017: 4,005 applied,

3,068 accepted. Neither SAT nor ACT required. ACT 25/75 percentile: 20-25. High school rank: 12% in top tenth, 38% in top quarter, 73% in top half
Early decision deadline: N/A, notification date: N/A
Early action deadline: N/A, notification date: N/A
Application deadline (fall): rolling
Undergraduate student body: 7,644 full time, 652 part time; 47% male, 53% female; 0% American Indian, 3% Asian, 2% black, 4% Hispanic, 2% multiracial, 0% Pacific Islander, 86% white, 2% international; 88% from in state; 37% live on campus; 3% of students in fraternities, 4% in sororities
Most popular majors: 16% Wildlife, Fish and Wildlands Science and Management, 12% Business Administration and Management, General, 10% Communication Sciences and Disorders, General, 10% Elementary Education and Teaching, 9% Biology/Biological Sciences, General
Expenses: 2017-2018: $8,309 in state, $16,576 out of state; room/board: $7,291
Financial aid: (715) 346-4771; 58% of undergrads determined to have financial need; average aid package $9,474

University of Wisconsin–Stout

Menomonie WI
(715) 232-1411
U.S. News ranking: Reg. U. (Mid. W), No. 70
Website: www.uwstout.edu
Admissions email: admissions@uwstout.edu
Public; founded 1891
Freshman admissions: selective; 2016-2017: 3,445 applied, 3,023 accepted. Either SAT or ACT required. ACT 25/75 percentile: 19-25. High school rank: 8% in top tenth, 28% in top quarter, 64% in top half
Early decision deadline: N/A, notification date: N/A
Early action deadline: N/A, notification date: N/A
Application deadline (fall): 4/26
Undergraduate student body: 6,831 full time, 1,567 part time; 55% male, 45% female; 0% American Indian, 3% Asian, 2% black, 1% Hispanic, 4% multiracial, 0% Pacific Islander, 87% white, 2% international; 67% from in state; 40% live on campus; 2% of students in fraternities, 3% in sororities
Most popular majors: 36% Business, Management, Marketing, and Related Support Services, 9% Engineering Technologies and Engineering-Related Fields, 9% Visual and Performing Arts, 8% Family and Consumer Sciences/Human Sciences, 7% Education
Expenses: 2017-2018: $9,456 in state, $17,423 out of state; room/board: $6,744
Financial aid: (715) 232-1363; 56% of undergrads determined to have financial need; average aid package $11,000

University of Wisconsin–Superior

Superior WI
(715) 394-8230
U.S. News ranking: Reg. Coll. (Mid. W), No. 36
Website: www.uwsuper.edu
Admissions email: admissions@uwsuper.edu
Public; founded 1893
Freshman admissions: selective; 2016-2017: 1,148 applied, 797 accepted. Either SAT or ACT required. ACT 25/75 percentile: 19-24. High school rank: 6% in top tenth, 23% in top quarter, 59% in top half
Early decision deadline: N/A, notification date: N/A
Early action deadline: N/A, notification date: N/A
Application deadline (fall): 8/1
Undergraduate student body: 1,806 full time, 559 part time; 39% male, 61% female; 2% American Indian, 1% Asian, 2% black, 2% Hispanic, 4% multiracial, 0% Pacific Islander, 80% white, 9% international; 59% from in state; 33% live on campus; N/A of students in fraternities, N/A in sororities
Most popular majors: 18% Business, Management, Marketing, and Related Support Services, 12% Multi/Interdisciplinary Studies, 10% Biological and Biomedical Sciences, 10% Communication, Journalism, and Related Programs, 8% Education
Expenses: 2017-2018: $15,716 in state, $15,716 out of state; room/board: $6,730

Financial aid: (715) 394-8200; 63% of undergrads determined to have financial need; average aid package $11,428

University of Wisconsin–Whitewater

Whitewater WI
(262) 472-1440
U.S. News ranking: Reg. U. (Mid. W), No. 61
Website: www.uww.edu
Admissions email: uwwadmit@mail.uww.edu
Public; founded 1868
Freshman admissions: selective; 2016-2017: 6,228 applied, 5,056 accepted. Either SAT or ACT required. ACT 25/75 percentile: 20-25. High school rank: 9% in top tenth, 28% in top quarter, 72% in top half
Early decision deadline: N/A, notification date: N/A
Early action deadline: N/A, notification date: N/A
Application deadline (fall): 5/1
Undergraduate student body: 10,088 full time, 1,292 part time; 51% male, 49% female; 0% American Indian, 2% Asian, 4% black, 6% Hispanic, 5% multiracial, 0% Pacific Islander, 82% white, 1% international; 80% from in state; 39% live on campus, 5% of students in fraternities, 7% in sororities
Most popular majors: 8% Finance, General, 7% Accounting, 6% Social Work, 5% Physical Education Teaching and Coaching, 5% Speech Communication and Rhetoric

Expenses: 2017-2018: $7,662 in state, $16,235 out of state; room/board: $6,442
Financial aid: (262) 472-1130; 57% of undergrads determined to have financial need; average aid package $8,347

Viterbo University[1]

La Crosse WI
(608) 796-3010
U.S. News ranking: Reg. U. (Mid. W), No. 115
Website: www.viterbo.edu
Admissions email: admission@viterbo.edu
Private
Application deadline (fall): N/A
Undergraduate student body: N/A full time, N/A part time
Expenses: 2016-2017: $26,150; room/board: $8,510
Financial aid: N/A

Wisconsin Lutheran College

Milwaukee WI
(414) 443-8811
U.S. News ranking: Reg. Coll. (Mid. W), No. 17
Website: www.wlc.edu
Admissions email: admissions@wlc.edu
Private; founded 1973
Affiliation: Wisconsin Evangelical Lutheran Synod
Freshman admissions: selective; 2016-2017: 658 applied, 594 accepted. Either SAT or ACT required. ACT 25/75 percentile: 21-27. High school rank: 18% in top tenth, 46% in top quarter, 75% in top half

Early decision deadline: N/A, notification date: N/A
Early action deadline: N/A, notification date: N/A
Application deadline (fall): rolling
Undergraduate student body: 915 full time, 85 part time; 43% male, 57% female; 0% American Indian, 1% Asian, 5% black, 6% Hispanic, 3% multiracial, 0% Pacific Islander, 82% white, 1% international; 75% from in state; 59% live on campus; N/A of students in fraternities, N/A in sororities
Most popular majors: 19% Business Administration, Management and Operations, Other, 13% Business Administration and Management, General, 8% Psychology, General, 7% Registered Nursing/Registered Nurse, 6% Biology/Biological Sciences, General
Expenses: 2017-2018: $29,140; room/board: $9,910
Financial aid: (414) 443-8856; 82% of undergrads determined to have financial need; average aid package $20,867

WYOMING

University of Wyoming

Laramie WY
(307) 766-5160
U.S. News ranking: Nat. U., No. 181
Website: www.uwyo.edu
Admissions email: admissions@uwyo.edu
Public; founded 1886

Freshman admissions: selective; 2016-2017: 4,882 applied, 4,642 accepted. Either SAT or ACT required. ACT 25/75 percentile: 21-27. High school rank: 22% in top tenth, 48% in top quarter, 79% in top half
Early decision deadline: N/A, notification date: N/A
Early action deadline: N/A, notification date: N/A
Application deadline (fall): 8/10
Undergraduate student body: 8,102 full time, 1,686 part time; 49% male, 51% female; 1% American Indian, 1% Asian, 1% black, 7% Hispanic, 3% multiracial, 0% Pacific Islander, 73% white, 4% international; 62% from in state; 23% live on campus; 6% of students in fraternities, 6% in sororities
Most popular majors: 9% Registered Nursing/Registered Nurse, 5% Criminal Justice/Safety Studies, 5% Elementary Education and Teaching, 5% Psychology, General, 4% Business Administration and Management, General
Expenses: 2017-2018: $5,217 in state, $16,827 out of state; room/board: $10,320
Financial aid: (307) 766-2116; 46% of undergrads determined to have financial need; average aid package $9,742